Teacher Wraparound Edition

Mary Bronson Merki, Ph.D.

Don Merki, Ph.D.

Contributing Authors
Michael J. Cleary, Ed.D.
Kathleen Middleton, M.S.

New York, New York   Columbus, Ohio   Chicago, Illinois   Peoria, Illinois   Woodland Hills, California

Glencoe

The *McGraw·Hill* Companies

Send all inquiries to:
Glencoe/McGraw-Hill
21600 Oxnard Street, Suite 500
Woodland Hills, California 91367

ISBN: 0-07-826326-3 (Student Edition)
ISBN: 0-07-826327-1 (Teacher Wraparound Edition)

1 2 3 4 5 6 7 8 9 0   071   08 07 06 05 04 03

Consultants

Pamela R. Connolly

Curriculum Coordinator for Health
and Physical Education

Diocese of Pittsburgh

North Catholic High School

Pittsburgh, Pennsylvania

Tinker D. Murray, Ph.D.

Professor and Coordinator of Exercise and Sports
Science Program

Southwest Texas State University

San Marcos, Texas

Don Rainey, M.S.

Instructor, Coordinator of Physical Fitness
and Wellness Program

Southwest Texas State University

San Marcos, Texas

Michael Rulon

Health/Physical Education Teacher

Johnson Junior High School

Adjunct Faculty

Laramie County Community College

Cheyenne, Wyoming

Teacher Reviewers

Jill English, Ph.D., C.H.E.S.

Assistant Professor

California State University, Fullerton

Fullerton, California

Randi Frank

Health Educator

Williams High School

Plano, Texas

Debra C. Harris, Ph.D.

Department Chair

Health and Physical Education

West Linn High School

West Linn, Oregon

Cheryl Miller-Page, C.H.E.S.

Health Education Specialist

Salem Keizer Public Schools

Salem, Oregon

Linda B. Salzman

Health Education Consultant and Trainer

Wilmington, North Carolina

Joan Stear

Health and Dance Educator

West Clermont Institute of Performing Arts

Glen Este High School

Cincinnati, Ohio

Contents

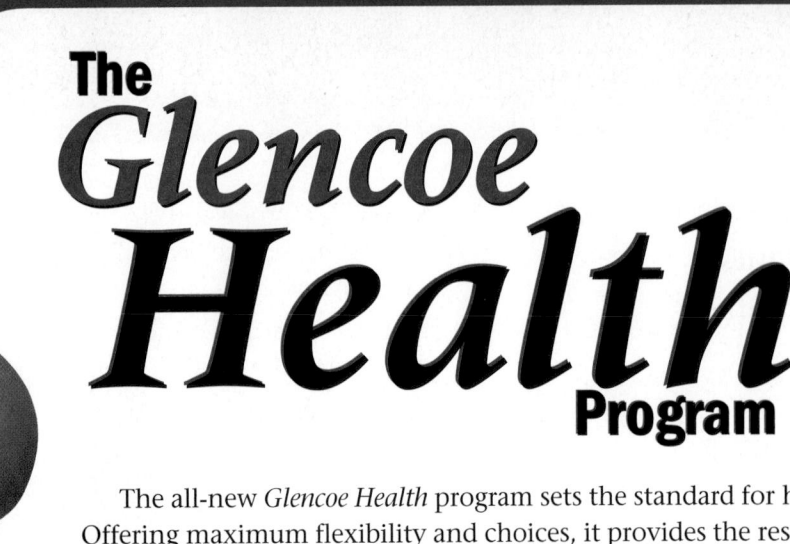

The *Glencoe Health* Program

The all-new *Glencoe Health* program sets the standard for health education. Offering maximum flexibility and choices, it provides the resources and state-of-the-art technology that today's health educators want. Its comprehensive content, outstanding design, and real-life applications will interest and motivate your students. Loaded with activities, *Glencoe Health* provides a wide variety of opportunities for your students to build important health skills. Most importantly, this total teaching program will empower your students to make choices that promote health and wellness for themselves and others.

▶ Provides Research-Based Content

Glencoe Health has achieved the highest degree of accuracy through rigorous scientifically-based research. This all-new edition is the product of the most recent research studies, teacher feedback, and detailed editorial development. The result is an up-to-date, solid foundation for an engaging, stimulating, and high-quality health education course for your students.

▶ Meets the Challenge of Health Education for Teens

The transitions experienced by teens during adolescence can be demanding and challenging. *Glencoe Health* helps your students recognize the consequences of risky behavior and develop the skills to make healthy choices. It demonstrates the importance of protective factors in students' lives that build resiliency during adolescence. These include the presence of supportive parents, dedicated teachers, positive peer relationships, and role models. The goal is to empower teens to make responsible decisions to protect their health and the health of others.

▶ Designed for All Learning Styles and Ability Levels

Glencoe Health offers engaging, relevant, and appropriate content for the widest range of learners – from young scholars and athletes to visual learners and low achievers. The research-based content is presented in a visually dynamic style that will engage and motivate your students. The program has been designed to offer a variety of lesson plan options and embedded assessment that develop the knowledge, health skills, behaviors, and problem-solving skills of all your students – regardless of their learning styles and ability levels.

▶ Meets the National Health Education Standards

Throughout the program, health content is correlated to the National Health Education Standards. The comprehensive chart on each Planning Guide shows how each lesson meets those standards. In addition, the integrated activities in every chapter help students practice and apply the important health skills—addressing the National Health Education Standards, lesson by lesson.

Promotes Health Skills and Provides Assessment

Glencoe Health is loaded with classroom activities that provide application, reinforcement, and enrichment with embedded assessments. These skills-based activities support the National Health Education Standards, building accountability toward academic achievement:

Health Skills Activity These activities offer realistic scenarios for students to practice skills in communication, decision making, refusal, conflict resolution, and goal setting.

Hands-On Health This feature presents engaging activities, often with partners, which strengthen your students' understanding of health content and build their health skills.

Real-Life Application These activities give students experience in analyzing information, evaluating facts, and forming conclusions about health using primary source material as a platform.

Exploring Issues This feature promotes critical thinking by offering pro and con views on contemporary health topics and challenges students to define their own views.

Promotes Positive Healthy Behaviors

Glencoe Health informs, guides, and encourages teens to adopt a healthy lifestyle and practice behaviors that enhance their well-being and safety by:

- Developing effective health skills that can be applied to real-life situations
- Fostering critical thinking and encouraging responsible decision making
- Delivering a strong and consistent abstinence message to promote positive health behaviors and character development
- Highlighting positive and negative influences of peer pressure and the media
- Encouraging a positive attitude about health information and related issues

Offers a Wealth of Resources

The program provides outstanding resources that give teachers unlimited choices. These comprehensive resources include:

- **Complete Teacher Support.** The Teacher Wraparound Edition (TWE) offers a wide selection of print, audio, and technology resources. The Teacher Classroom Resources (TCR) box has over 20 blackline master booklets with health labs, performance assessment activities, lesson quizzes, chapter and unit tests, transparencies, and much more.
- **Integrated Technology Options.** Directly correlated to points of use in the text, videos, CD-ROMs, audio CDs, puzzlemakers, computerized testbanks, and the Internet are integrated into the program for maximum utility and ease of use.

"Health is directly linked to educational achievement, quality of life, and economic productivity."

World Health Organization

The Student Edition—An Overview

Presented in a visually dynamic, highly readable format, *Glencoe Health* employs self-contained lessons and a variety of activities, along with colorful graphics, informative charts, and tables. The student edition provides the foundations of knowledge and health skills that will have enduring value for a lifetime. Reinforcing a strong and consistent abstinence message, the text offers a bounty of positive modeling influences based on the latest research in health science. Included are decision-making, goal-setting, and stress-management skills development, promoting and reinforcing healthy communication and conflict resolution.

Chapter Opener

Each chapter begins with elements designed to quickly launch a student's focus and interest on the chapter's topic. A vibrant two-page photo carries an engaging topical theme directly relevant to the chapter's content, while the chapter opener activities immediately entice the student to relate to the subject on a deeper, more meaningful level.

Chapter Activities

Students are quickly engaged in chapter content through one of the following opener activities.

- **Personal Health Inventory** provides a process for students to evaluate their personal habits and attitudes about topics within the chapter, and upon completion of chapter study, the opportunity to see how those perspectives and behaviors may have changed.

- **Myth or Fact?** checks student knowledge about common misconceptions and factual information on the chapter topic.

- **Case Study features** present a scenario or situation from an individual teen's perspective that explores the message of the chapter content.

Quick Write directs students to engage in a reflective process to express previous knowledge and personal perspectives on a chapter topic, reinforcing writing skills through the structuring and use of critical, evaluative language.

Chapter 7

Achieving Good Mental Health

Lesson 1 Your Mental and Emotional Health

Lesson 2 Developing a Positive Identity

Lesson 3 Understanding Emotions

Lesson 4 Managing Emotions

What's Your Health Status?

Read each statement below and respond by writing yes, no, or sometimes for each item. Write yes only for items that you practice regularly.

1. I take responsibility for and consider the consequences of my personal behavior.
2. I express emotions in positive ways.
3. I recognize my personal strengths and weaknesses.
4. I accept and learn from constructive criticism.
5. I have values that benefit me and the people around me in healthful ways.
6. I accept new challenges and face problems rather than avoid them.
7. I think that I am important to other people.
8. I resist negative peer pressure.
9. I am proud of who I am.
10. I have a generally positive outlook on life.

When you complete the chapter, review your personal inventory again, and identify two or three behavior changes you can make to improve your mental and emotional health.

Quick Write

Using Visuals. Being mentally and emotionally healthy means building a healthy identity and learning to express your emotions in appropriate ways. How do family and friends influence your mental and emotional health?

168

Chapter Features and Health Skills Practice

In order to establish a solid foundation in health skills, the chapter features in *Glencoe Health* provide practice, application, and reinforcement of the following health skills to enhance healthful behaviors and reinforce avoidance of risk behaviors.

In addition, chapter features broaden a student's strengths in academic areas such as language arts and science. They also help the student become familiar with professional health-related career opportunities.

Health-Skills Activity presents realistic situations in the form of scenarios that foster development of skills in communication, decision making, refusal, conflict resolution and goal setting.

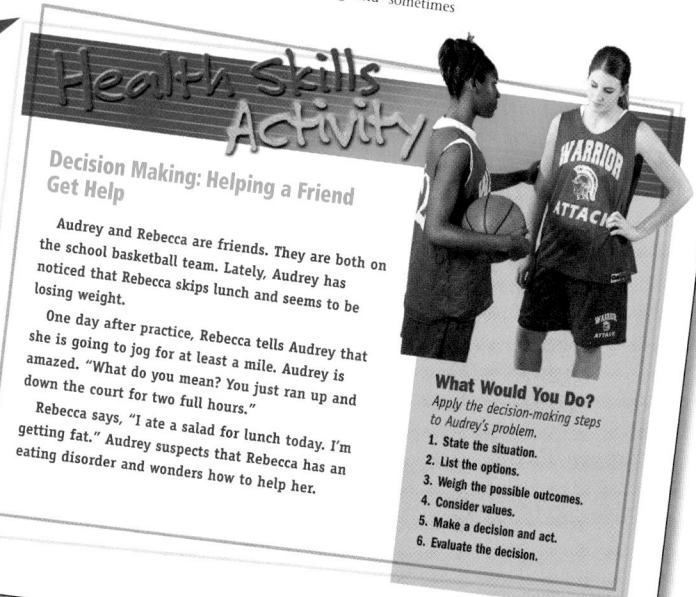

HEALTH CONSEQUENCES OF BULIMIA NERVOSA

Repeated binging, purging, and fasting can cause serious health problems or even death. Frequent vomiting and diarrhea can lead to dehydration, kidney damage, and irregular heartbeat. Vomiting also destroys tooth enamel; causes tooth decay; and damages the tissues of the stomach, esophagus, and mouth. Frequent use of laxatives disrupts digestion and absorption and may cause nutrient deficiencies. Laxative abuse can also change the composition of the blood. Treatment of bulimia nervosa usually includes both medication and psychological counseling.

Binge Eating Disorder

People with **binge eating disorder**, *a disorder characterized by compulsive overeating*, consume huge amounts of food at one time but do not try to purge. This disorder may signal the use of food as a coping mechanism for strong emotions or depression. Treatment involves professional psychological counseling and sometimes medication.

Health Skills Activity

Decision Making: Helping a Friend Get Help

Audrey and Rebecca are friends. They are both on the school basketball team. Lately, Audrey has noticed that Rebecca skips lunch and seems to be losing weight.

One day after practice, Rebecca tells Audrey that she is going to jog for at least a mile. Audrey is amazed. "What do you mean? You just ran up and down the court for two full hours."

Rebecca says, "I ate a salad for lunch today. I'm getting fat." Audrey suspects that Rebecca has an eating disorder and wonders how to help her.

What Would You Do?
Apply the decision-making steps to Audrey's problem.
1. State the situation.
2. List the options.
3. Weigh the possible outcomes.
4. Consider values.
5. Make a decision and act.
6. Evaluate the decision.

Student Edition

Additional Features in the Student Text

Hands-On Health Activity presents students, often with partners, the chance to create a product or demonstration that applies the health skill to content they are learning. The activities strengthen understanding and develop skills that emphasize health strategies and reinforce healthy behavior.

Hands-On Health ACTIVITY

Saying No to a Driver Who Has Been Drinking

You've heard the statement "Don't drink and drive." It's also dangerous to ride in a car if you suspect the driver has been drinking. Here are some ways to refuse that ride.

- Make a firm commitment to yourself not to ride with someone who has been drinking. If you know that alcohol will be available at a party, don't go.
- When you suspect a driver has been drinking, be prepared to make the right choice for your health and safety. Be strong. Find another way home.

Direct Statements: "I am not riding with you. You have been drinking."
Excuses: "I forgot to tell you—my dad is picking me up."
Insults: "You are really crazy to drive after drinking."
Humor: "I'm not getting in that car with you; I value my life."
Alternate suggestion: "Give me the keys; I'll drive."

What You'll Need
- 1 index card per student
- colored pencils or markers
- hole punch
- scissors

What You'll Do
1. Working with a small group, brainstorm a list of refusal strategies a teen can use to avoid riding in a car with a driver who has been drinking.
2. Write and present a skit that has dialogue showing one or more successful refusal skills. Be sure that every group member has a part.
3. Act out your skit for the class. Analyze each skit for the dialogue you think is most effective. Remember

and practice these statements so that you'll be prepared if a drinking driver offers you a ride.

Apply and Conclude
On your own, cut a 3″ × 5″ index card in half so that you have a 3″ × 2½″ card. Punch a hole in one corner. Write "Don't Ride with a Drunk Driver" on the card. Then write at least two statements you can use to refuse such a ride. Use markers to make the card eye-catching. After your teacher laminates the card, place it on your key ring.

NO THANKS, MY PARENTS ARE PICKING ME UP.

Don't ride with a driver who has been DRINKING!

Type 2 diabetes is nearing epidemic propor[tion] States because of an increased number of older population and a greater prevalence of obes[ity] lifestyles. A diet high in fat, calories, and cholest[erol] risk of diabetes. Thus, choosing lower-fat, lower-ca[lorie] can help reduce the risk of this disease. Increased [physical activity] also reduces risk because it helps control weight an[d] cholesterol levels.

Treatment of type 2 diabetes includes weight management and regular physical activity. Individuals with this disease must

Real-Life Application

Raising Teen Awareness of Diabetes

Over the last decade, diabetes and obesity have increased dramatically in both adults and teens. Examine the graph and answer the questions. Then use this information to create an advocacy message to encourage others to practice healthful behaviors to control their weight and reduce their risk of diabetes.

Obesity and Diabetes in U.S. Adults

Diabetes
Obese

1990: 4.9%, 12.0%
1998: 6.5%, 17.9%
2000: 7.3%, 19.8%

Prevalence of Overweight Among U.S. Adolescents

1963-70: 4
1971-74: 4
1988-94: 5
1976-80: 11
1999: 13

Source: CDC, Behavioral Risk Factor Surveillance System (1991-2000)

1. What do you observe about the relationship between the rates of diabetes and obesity in Graph 1?
2. What do you think would happen to the rate of diabetes if the rate of obesity began to decrease?
3. Look at Graph 2. What can you infer about the rate of diabetes in teens?
4. Why are healthful eating habits and physical activity lifestyle behaviors that reduce the risk of diabetes?

ACTIVITY
In small groups, generate a list of lifestyle behaviors that people can practice to maintain a healthful weight and reduce their risk of diabetes. Create a 60-second public service announcement (PSA) to persuade teens to start good health habits early in life. Include at least one fact about diabetes and one lifestyle behavior that can reduce the risk of diabetes.

Real-Life Application uses primary source material to give students applications in analyzing, evaluating, and making informed personal decisions about health.

Exploring Issues

Should Random Drug Testing of Athletes Be Performed?

A number of high schools in the United States have adopted a policy of random drug testing of student athletes even if there is no indication that the athletes are using drugs. What's your position on the subject of random drug testing of school athletes? Here are two points of view.

Viewpoint 1: Maya D., age 17
Random drug testing of school athletes is unfair and an invasion of privacy, especially if there's no evidence that the person has been using drugs. Students who want to participate in school sports shouldn't have to give up their privacy just to be on an athletic team. Besides, why should athletes be singled out—isn't that discrimination?

Viewpoint 2: Graham H., age 16
I understand Maya's argument, but I think that schools have a right to know whether students are using drugs. They aren't out to catch us doing something wrong. They're concerned about our health and the environment in which we live and learn. People may not like the rules, but schools must follow the policy. We don't want our school to be represented by athletes who use drugs and get away with it. That's dangerous *and* embarrassing.

ACTIVITIES

1. Take the pro or con position, and expand upon it. Use online or print resources to back up your views. Be sure to investigate each supporting point raised in an argument.

2. Some school districts are advocating drug testing of all students who want to be involved in any extra-curricular activities. What might be the pros and cons of such an approach?

A health care provider can advise you about whether you need this type of supplement. It's important to take the recommended dosage of any supplement. High doses, or *megadoses*, of a nutritional supplement can be harmful.

Safety First!

Safety should be a major concern when you participate in sports and other physical activities. You can reduce your risk of injury by

▶ visiting a health care professional for a health screening before beginning a new activity. A **health screening** is *a search or*

Lesson 4 Training and Sa...

Exploring Issues promotes critical thinking by offering pro and con perspectives on pressing contemporary health topics and challenges the student to define their own attitudes and beliefs from an informed point of view.

Eye on the Media

Internet Etiquette and Relationships

Technology such as e-mail has made it easy to keep in touch with family and friends who are far away. Like strong speaking and listening skills, strategies for effective online communication can strengthen relationships. In this activity, you will develop a list of Internet etiquette strategies that promote healthy, respectful communication.

Problems with Online Communication	Possible Solutions
Privacy Issues	• Avoid sending e-mails dealing with private or sensitive issues. They can be forwarded to anyone.
Chain e-mails	• Do not send or forward such e-mails to others. • Politely ask friends and relatives not to send or forward them to you.
Viruses in attachments	• Make sure antivirus software is installed. • Do not open attachments from unknown or unreliable sources.

ACTIVITY

In a group, brainstorm potential problems with online communication and ways to resolve those problems. Use the chart above as a model, and try to come up with as many issues and solutions as possible. You might consider how traditional communication strategies (such as specific speaking and listening skills) can apply to online activities like e-mail and instant messaging. After completing your chart, use it to develop a list of Internet Etiquette Rules.

Make copies of your list, and share it with family and friends.

EXPRESS YOUR VIEWS

Write a one-page essay explaining the importance of online etiquette. Discuss how its use impacts relationships with family, friends, and peers. Your essay should promote communication strategies that maintain and strengthen healthy relationships.

Eye on the Media provides students with a forum to critically evaluate the media messages that impact them every day. The activities help students use media literacy skills to analyze, identify, and interpret how the media influences one's attitudes and behaviors.

Student Edition

Health Minute offers strategies and tips for responsible and healthy behavior in context with the chapter's topic.

▶ **Vectors.** An *organism, usually an arthropod, such as a tick, that carries and transmits pathogens to humans or other animals* is known as a **vector**. For example, a mosquito may take in pathogens when it feeds on an infected person. The mosquito then injects some of those pathogens into the next person it bites, thus spreading the disease. Common vectors include flies, mosquitoes, and ticks. Lyme disease and malaria are spread by vectors.

▶ **Water and food.** Careless handling and storage of food are major sources of contamination and illness. For example, salmonella (sal-muh-NE-luh) bacteria in undercooked poultry can cause food poisoning. Water supplies that become contaminated with human or animal feces can cause illnesses such as hepatitis A.

Airborne Transmission

Pathogens from a sneeze or a cough may float in the air for a long time and travel long distances. Airborne transmission is different from direct contact because the pathogens don't settle quickly on surfaces. You don't have to be close to an infected person to inhale the pathogens. Diseases that are transmitted this way include chicken pox, tuberculosis, and influenza. A person can get inhalation anthrax by inhaling soil containing the bacteria.

Preventing the Spread of Disease

Reducing your risk of communicable diseases isn't complicated. Practicing healthful behaviors based on good hygiene and common sense will help you avoid infection.

Washing Hands

Handwashing is the single most effective way to prevent the spread of disease. Wash your hands before you prepare food, before you eat, and after you use the bathroom. Clean hands carefully before inserting contact lenses or putting on makeup. After handling animals, especially reptiles, or animal wastes, make it a habit to wash your hands. When someone in your home is ill, keep hands clean to prevent the spread of pathogens.

Handling Food Properly

Foodborne illness occurs in places where food is h improperly. Always wash your hands before you handle foo paper towels, not dishcloths or sponges, to keep surfaces and ment clean. Separate raw meat from other foods. Cook its proper temperature. Chill cold and leftover foods quick proper temperature.

Health Minute

Strategies for Avoiding Diseases Transmitted by Vectors

Use these strategies where mosquitoes or ticks are common:

▶ Wear long-sleeved shirts, long pants, socks, and hats.

▶ Tuck shirts in at the waist, and tuck pants into socks.

▶ Wear boots, not sandals.

▶ Apply repellents to clothing, boots, socks, and all exposed skin.

▶ Check yourself and your clothing frequently. Wearing light-colored clothing can help you spot ticks and mosquitoes.

Lesson 4

12. What are some challenges a person with disabilities might face?

13. What kind of disability would someone with Down syndrome have?

14. What are two of the provisions of the Americans with Disabilities Act?

▶ THINKING CRITICALLY

1. **Evaluating.** What effect does physical activity have on the cardiovascular system? How does this information affect the goals you set for maintaining health? *(LESSON 1)*

2. **Synthesizing.** Suppose a friend tells you that she wants to get a tan because people with tans look healthier. What would you tell her? *(LESSON 2)*

3. **Summarizing.** Type 2 diabetes is becoming more common among children and teens. Write a letter directed to parents of young children that explains how parents can help their children avoid developing the disease. *(LESSON 3)*

4. **Analyzing.** In the past many people have had misconceptions about individuals with physical and mental challenges. What factors do you think contributed to negative attitudes toward people with disabilities? *(LESSON 4)*

▶ HEALTH SKILLS APPLICATION

1. **Practicing Healthful Behaviors.** Ask your parents about the history of cardiovascular disease in their families. Use this information to identify any potential risks you might have for developing cardiovascular disease. What steps can you take to reduce your risk? *(LESSON 1)*

2. **Analyzing Influences.** Look at product ads in a variety of magazines. Identify pictures that show people involved in behaviors that increase the risk of developing cancer. Describe how each of these behaviors puts a person at risk of developing cancer. Summarize your findings and report them to the class. *(LESSON 2)*

3. **Accessing Information.** Find out about the most common pollen allergens in your community. Gather information about when they are most prevalent and where you can get information about daily pollen counts. Display the information in the classroom. *(LESSON 3)*

4. **Advocacy.** Survey a local business to see how it might be made more accessible for individuals who have disabilities. Write a letter to the owner of the business making suggestions for improvement. *(LESSON 4)*

⁕ BEYOND the Classroom

Parent Involvement

Advocacy. Find out about health fairs or other events in your community that support cancer education. Contact local chapters of the American Cancer Society for information. See how you and your parents can become involved.

School and Community

CPR Classes. Locate agencies in your community that teach CPR. Arrange for someone from the agency to teach CPR at your school. Help organize the event and prepare posters or flyers to let people know about it.

Beyond the Classroom extends the student's perspectives into topical relevance emphasizing parent involvement with a focus on the student's local community and other areas.

CROSS-CURRICULUM CONNECTIONS

Language Arts connection

Conduct an Interview. A good way to gather accurate information is to interview knowledgeable people. As a class, brainstorm a list of experts on injury prevention, weather emergencies, and natural disasters, such as health care professionals, driver education teachers, and meteorologists. Your teacher will divide the class into teams and assign each team an expert to interview. Report your findings to the class.

Social Studies connection

Write a Report. Firefighters, including volunteer firefighters, not only put out fires, they also teach the community how to prevent them. Research the development of the volunteer fire department in American history. Write a brief report that discusses how the demands on volunteer fire departments have changed throughout the years, as well as how fire departments teach fire safety.

Math connection

Calculate the Magnitude. Earthquakes are measured using the Richter Scale, which was developed in 1935 by Charles Richter at the California Institute of Technology. It is a logarithmic scale, which means that each number represents a power of 10. Therefore a magnitude 4.3 quake can also be written as $10^{4.3}$. How many times more powerful is a magnitude 3 earthquake than a magnitude 1 earthquake?

Science connection

Research a Topic. Certain activities, such as typing on a computer keyboard, require that specific muscles and tendons perform repetitive motions. This can lead to carpal tunnel syndrome, a condition characterized by varying degrees of numbness, pain, and tingling in the hands and forearms. Research carpal tunnel syndrome and write a report on your findings.

▯ CAREER Corner

Paramedic

Are you interested in helping other people in emergency situations? Paramedics are trained to give immediate and skilled care to people in all types of medical emergencies. These emergencies range from car crashes, heart attacks, and drownings to helping with childbirth. Lives depend upon the quick and competent care of paramedics as they provide assistance to and transport sick or injured people.

Would you like to study to be a paramedic? To enter this profession, you'll need emergency medical training. Find out more about this and other health careers by clicking on Career Corner at **health.glencoe.com**.

Career Corner supplies insights into skills and steps required to build a career in a variety of health professions. Additional careers and information on requirements for education, training, and professional qualifications, and other considerations are referenced on Glencoe's Health Web site: **health.glencoe.com**

Also Includes:

Health Online directs students to point-of-use activities provided on Glencoe's Health Web site to enhance lesson content.

Quick Start supplies the student with immediate activity involvement at the beginning of each lesson that reinforces reading and writing skills in the health area being presented.

Hotlink appears throughout the text to cross-reference highlighted terms and subjects to important material in other chapters of the text.

Character Check presents activities that incorporate character education, encouraging students to build traits of good character and to model character traits by participating in service learning throughout their community.

Did You Know? offers crucial and detailed insights into particular aspects of the topic covered within the chapter.

Q&A raises important questions on subjects relating to the chapter material, and supplies informative and useful answers.

Technology Option appears with each lesson review and presents chapter- and lesson-related activities on Glencoe's Health Web site.

- **Glossary/Glosario** defines each vocabulary term in English, then separately in the Spanish Glosario.

- **Index** provides a fundamental reference aid that assists students find all topics and terms throughout the text.

- **Appendix** is a special reference section that provides additional resources, including *Healthy People 2010* objectives and information from the President's Council on Physical Fitness and Sports.

Teacher Wraparound Edition

Complete Support for the Health Teacher

The Teacher Wraparound Edition provides comprehensive lesson plans, teaching suggestions, supplemental information, cross-references, and more—all conveniently "wrapped" around every page of the reduced student text. The format of concise and easy-to-follow lesson plans gives a wide variety of teaching strategies to motivate students and to introduce, teach, and reinforce concepts. Alternative teaching strategies that allow teachers to customize the program to accommodate a broad range of different teaching and learning styles is a key aspect of the TWE's design.

Teacher Planning Guide

National Health Education Standards

Block Scheduling

TeacherWorks™: All-In-One Planner and Resource Center

Glencoe's new and exclusive TeacherWorks™ allows you to customize your lesson plans, access all teacher resources, and organize your daily teaching plan.

- **Interactive Teacher Edition**—Access the complete Teacher Wraparound Edition electronically.

- **Interactive Lesson Planner with Calendar**—Planning made easy! Organize your week, month, semester, or year with all the lesson resources you need to make teaching creative, timely, and relevant.

- **Point-and-Click Access to Teaching Resources**—Find all your classroom resources with just a few easy clicks. Review or print blackline masters right from your computer.

- **Correlates to National Health Education Standards**—Access National Standards correlations or insert your own state standards and match them directly to the electronic Teacher Wraparound Edition.

- **Hotlinks to the Internet**—Connect directly to Glencoe's customized Health Web site for access to activities and prescreened Web links.

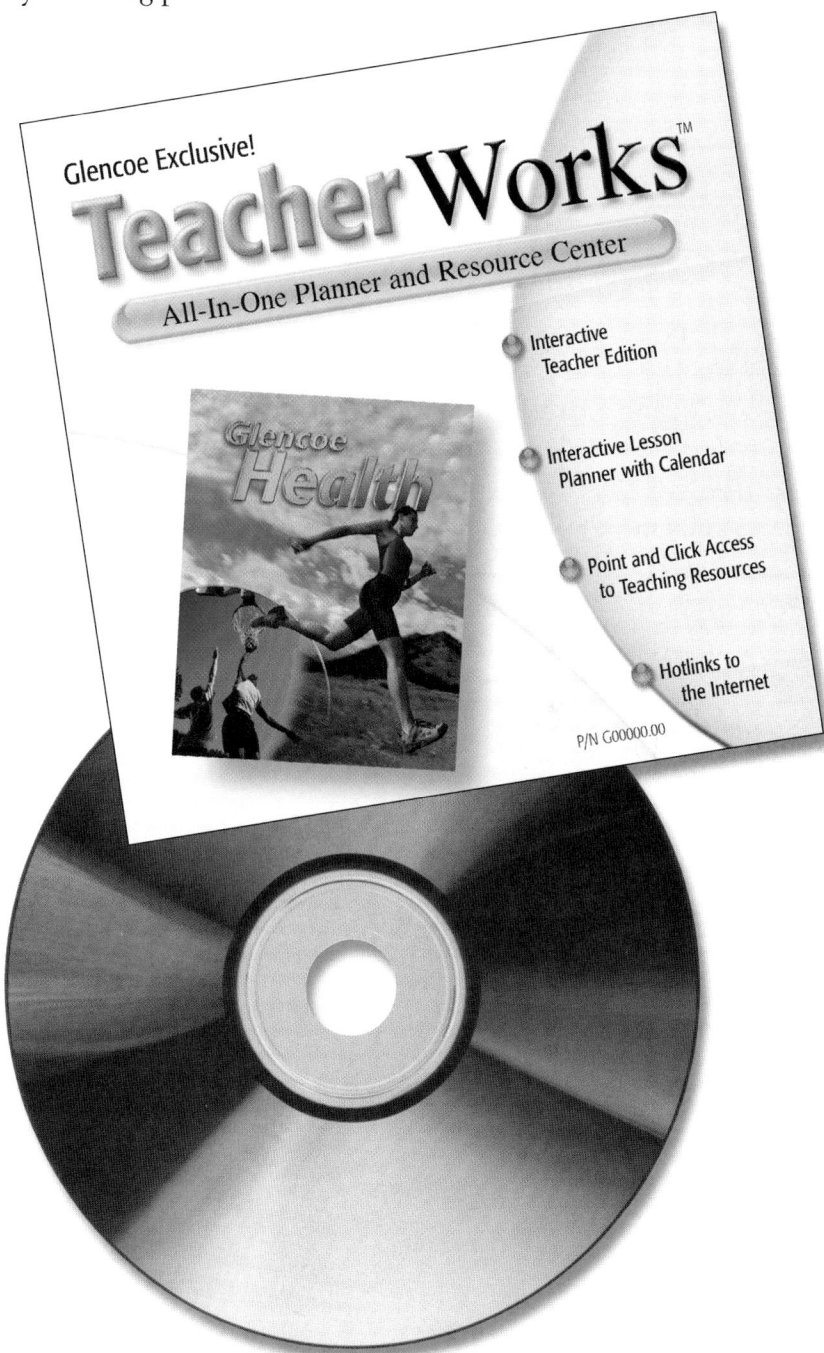

Glencoe Exclusive!
TeacherWorks™
All-In-One Planner and Resource Center

Glencoe Health

- Interactive Teacher Edition
- Interactive Lesson Planner with Calendar
- Point and Click Access to Teaching Resources
- Hotlinks to the Internet

P/N G00000.00

Teacher Wraparound Edition

Organized with the Teacher's Needs in Mind

Lesson Plans

The teaching material follows a consistent, easy-to-use pattern. The complete lesson cycle—Focus, Teach, Assess, and Close—make it easy to plan a lesson. The lesson plan includes:

① FOCUS

Quick Start motivator activity immediately engages students

Tying to Prior Knowledge connects to what students already know

Introducing Vocabulary activity helps students build health vocabulary skills

② TEACH

Activities related to the lesson's content are identified by one of four codes. These codes give teachers insights into the activity's suitability for students of varying learning styles and abilities.

Lesson 4

Being a Resilient Teen

① FOCUS

QUICK START Have students work together to name difficult events that a teen might experience. Record their ideas on the board. Then let partners share ideas about factors that could help a teen bounce back.

TYING TO PRIOR KNOWLEDGE
Let students share what they already understand about being resilient. Encourage them to give examples. Then explain that they will learn more about resiliency in this lesson.

Health Skills Features
"The Power of Assets," p. 217

INTRODUCING VOCABULARY
- Have volunteers look up the vocabulary terms in the Glossary and then, in their own words, explain the terms to the rest of the class.
- Ask students to complete the Chapter 8 Study Guide in the *Student Activity Workbook.*

Lesson 4

Being a Resilient Teen

VOCABULARY
resiliency
protective factors

YOU'LL LEARN TO
- Explain what it means to be resilient.
- Develop strategies to promote resiliency throughout the life span.
- Explore methods for developing protective factors.
- Evaluate how having protective factors helps people avoid risk behaviors.

QUICK START List five difficult events that a teen may experience. Then, brainstorm factors that might help the teen bounce back from such events. Write a few sentences explaining how these factors would help someone get through difficult times.

Everyone goes through times of stress, disappointments, and difficulty. Sometimes, people have no control over events that can change their lives. A natural disaster may strike, or a loved one may die. When hardships and tragedies happen, it can be hard for people to cope with the situation and with their feelings.

What Is Resiliency?

Some people find it easier than others to bounce back from events that have hurt them in some way. The event may be a personal disappointment, such as failing a test or breaking up with a boyfriend or girlfriend. In some cases, a large number of people may be involved in or affected by an event, such as a big earthquake or a war. Being able to overcome disappointments and survive traumatic events is a sign of resiliency. **Resiliency** *(ri-ZIL-yuhn-see) is the ability to adapt effectively and recover from disappointment, difficulty, or crisis.* Resilient people are able to handle adversity in healthful ways and achieve long-term success in spite of negative circumstances.

When difficult events occur, seeking and giving support is one way to cope. What else can help a person bounce back from disappointments or crises?

214 Chapter 8 Mental/...

Lesson 4 Resources

Teacher Classroom Resources
- Concept Mapping Activity 30
- Lesson Plan 30
- Lesson Quiz 30
- Reteaching Activity 30

Student Activity Workbook
- Applying Health Skills 30
- Chapter 8 Study Guide

Factors That Affect Resiliency

Many factors can influence a person's level of resiliency. Having some of the **developmental assets** discussed in Chapter 7 will very likely strengthen a person's resiliency. For example, having a supportive family and a strong sense of self-worth can help an individual bounce back from setbacks or other difficulties. The factors that affect a person's resiliency can be divided into two categories: external and internal.

External Factors

These factors include your family, your school or community, and your peers. They may also include elements that are less concrete, for example, opportunities to participate in school projects or community events. Although you may have little control over these factors, you can work to strengthen some of them. In order to example, you could join a community youth program in order to have access to more opportunities and to form healthy peer relationships.

Internal Factors

Internal factors are the ones you have control over. Making a conscious effort to strengthen these factors will increase your resiliency and improve your mental/emotional health. Your attitudes, perceptions, and behaviors make up your internal factors, which also include:

► **Commitment to learning.** Being actively engaged in your education increases your self-esteem and gives you a sense of belonging in the school community.

► **Positive values.** You demonstrate positive values through your words and actions. For example, you show caring when you help a younger sibling study for a test. By avoiding risk behaviors, you show that you take responsibility for your health. When your behavior reflects positive values, you will feel good about yourself and the decisions you make.

developmental assets For a list of developmental assets, see Chapter 7, page 179.

By contributing to the community, these teens are also building their protective factors. How might helping others strengthen a teen's resiliency?

Lesson 4 Being a Resilient Teen **215**

Dealing with Sensitive Issues

Coping with Crisis During periods of local or national crisis, students may exhibit a variety of reactions, depending on their level of involvement and their personal sense of loss. Emotional responses vary in intensity; students may need guidance from teachers, parents, and counselors to understand how to deal with these emotions. Various expressions of fear, anxiety, and loss should be expected; but teachers and other school staff members should keep a watchful eye for severe stress and grief reactions in students. For resources to help identify students who exhibit extreme reactions and who may need additional support, visit the link to the National Association of School Psychologists at health.glencoe.com.

Chapter 8 • Lesson 4

② TEACH

Reinforcing Concepts
Have students identify natural disasters and tragedies that have been covered in local, national, or world news reports. Ask: How does resiliency help people directly affected by these events? Why do some people who are indirectly affected also need the coping skills of resiliency?

hotlink
Have students work with partners to review the developmental assets discussed in Chapter 7. Ask: Which assets are especially likely to strengthen resiliency? Why?

ACTIVE READING

Word Forms
Help students recognize that they can use different forms of a word to help identify a word's meaning. For example, with the word *resilient* or *resilience,* students might be familiar with the word *resiliency,* which will help them understand *resiliency.* Working with other words on this page, you might have students name other forms of words such as supportive (support), perception (perceive), commitment (commit), responsibility (responsible, responsibly). For more strategies, see the Guided Reading Activities booklet.

Discussing
Help students discuss the relationship between developmental assets and protective factors.

215

Special Feature Boxes

Each activity in the Student Text has a corresponding box in the Teacher Wraparound Edition that provides alternative ways for students to address the activity and offers additional health skills practice.

3 ASSESS

Assessment techniques help determine the level of mastery and include strategies for reteaching students who might have difficulty with important lesson concepts. Enrichment activities are designed for students who are motivated to explore the content on deeper and more enriched levels.

4 CLOSE

Bringing closure to a lesson, these activities reinforce important concepts from the lesson.

Providing Guidance and Support

Strategies presented in the Dealing with Sensitive Issues box suggest ways of approaching some of the sensitive health topics that often directly affect the lives of students and their ability to learn. Such issues as self esteem, drug problems, and many others are addressed in ways that offer teachers solutions for guiding and supporting students. Health Literacy brings background on relevant information to increase student's knowledge of up-to-date health information.

Chapter 7 • Lesson 1

Exploring Issues

SHOULD LEARNING STYLES BE TAKEN INTO ACCOUNT IN THE CLASSROOM?

Have students think about their own strongest learning style. Ask: Do you remember information better if you write it down (visual), listen to it (auditory), or see something done then do it yourself (kinesthetic)? Have students read the feature and investigate different learning styles. Discuss the types of assessments that would best reflect each type of learning style. For the second activity, review what they know about self-esteem. Ask: What factors help build self-esteem? Point out that building a sense of competence—a belief that a person can meet goals and achieve success—leads to high self-esteem.

Critical Thinking

Have students work with partners or in small groups to explore their ideas about behavior and personality:

- How do you think your personality affects your behavior?
- How do you think your behavior influences the development of your personality?

Reinforcing Concepts

Have students draw flow charts, graphs, patterns, or pictures to depict the influences on personality. Let them share their finished work with the rest of the class. **ELL** Visual/Spatial

176

Exploring Issues

Should Learning Styles Be Taken Into Account in the Classroom?

Academic performance affects many teens' view of themselves. Being a good student is one way teens can meet the need to be valued and recognized. Because students learn and demonstrate their knowledge in different ways, some teachers use different testing methods. For instance, teachers may test students according to the way each one learns best—through seeing, through hearing, or through doing. Do you think teachers should use multiple methods to accommodate different learning styles? Here are two points of view.

Viewpoint 1: Melissa J., age 15

I'm proud of my grades. I study every night and always work extra hard before exams. It's not fair to apply different standards just because some students can't handle a written test. Why should I have to write an essay while someone else in class has fun drawing a picture or building a diorama? How can the teacher possibly grade these different projects fairly? It's like comparing apples and oranges. Students should be given real tests, not whatever makes them feel good. That's not the way the real world works after graduation. Those students just need to work harder.

Viewpoint 2: Gary D., age 16

I do study hard for tests, but even when I know the content, I still do lousy on multiple-choice tests. If that's the only way I can demonstrate my knowledge, I end up looking stupid. Students have different strengths and weaknesses—and so do people in the real world. Look at athletes or dancers. They demonstrate their knowledge and talent by performing, not by taking a written test. I'm not saying you should get rid of all pencil-and-paper tests or forget about writing papers. I just think teachers should offer students a variety of approaches to accommodate different ways of learning. It's only fair.

ACTIVITIES

1. Research one of the different learning styles mentioned above, including visual (seeing), auditory (hearing), and tactile/kinesthetic (touching, doing). Describe the style and how students in that category learn best.

2. Write a paragraph explaining which viewpoint you favor and why. Be sure to link your discussion to the issue of school performance and self-esteem.

176 Chapter 7 Achieving Good Mental Health

Dealing with Sensitive Issues

Self-Esteem Students sometimes feel concerned when issues of self-esteem are raised in class. Many feel that their self-esteem cannot be changed. This is particularly discouraging for students who perceive their self-esteem as low or negative.

To help these students—and, indeed, all the students—emphasize the fact that self-esteem can be improved. Suggest these tips:

- Focus on your strengths.
- Set realistic goals for yourself.
- Ask for help when you need it.
- View your mistakes as opportunities for learning.

Dealing with Sensitive Issues

Giving Support Statistics on alcohol and illegal drug use suggest that many of the students in today's health classrooms have experimented with or have tried these substances. Your role as a teacher is to identify students in trouble, give the students support, and refer them to other sources of help.

The first step in helping a student you suspect has a drug problem is showing the student you care. If you broach the problem with the student, be sure to do it in private. Also, take care to avoid conveying value judgments about the issue. Refer to Glencoe's professional booklet, *Dealing with Sensitive Issues*, for more information.

⩘ HEALTH LITERACY

Health Influences Ask whether students are familiar with the expression "Look on the bright side." The expression suggests that having a positive outlook protects and promotes health on all three sides of the health triangle. Laughter, in particular, can influence positive physiological changes as well as improve mental outlook or mood. One scientific study found that laughter stimulates the production of endorphins, which help control pain. Another study demonstrated that stress-related hormones decreased during bouts of laughter. Humor and a positive outlook can help one cope with life pressures such as getting homework done on time, taking tests, and getting along with friends.

Bottom Column Annotations

Boxes at the bottom of the page present additional information related to the content of the Student Text. These boxes supplement the core lesson plan by focusing on various areas of interest. Categories include:

- Technology Options
- More About. . .
- School to Work
- Home and Community
- Health Literacy

- Promoting Coordinated School Health
- Curriculum Connections
- Meeting Individual Needs
- Meeting Student Diversity
- Answers to Lesson Review

- Cooperative Learning Activities
- What Teens Want to Know
- Myths & Reality
- Dealing with Sensitive Issues
- Portfolio Assessment

Myths & Reality

MYTH. Drugs affect all people the same way

FACT. Specific hazards of drug abuse differ from

MYTH.
"Drug over doses ca... happen to me. I'm

School to Work

Amphetamine Abuse Sometimes drugs are abus... effort to accomplis... something worthwhile... Assign stu... dents to

are abused not for a high, but in a misguided

Portfolio Assessment

Self-Evaluation Direct students to review the Health Skills Activities and other activities comple... studen... to sele... one fin... ished

explain what they learned and how the examples they selected show their progress.

...acher Classroom Resources. Assign

What Teens Want to Know

Why is marijuana sometimes used to treat illness, but is still an illegal drug?
Some patients who suffer from debilitating and life threatening diseases such as cancer and HIV/AIDS, benefit from marijuana use because it relieves pain, and helps them take in food when their bodies are fighting the disease. However, it remains

illegal because it contains 421 different chemicals and the carcinogens in marijuana smoke are more abundant than those in tobacco smoke. Marijuana is considered addictive, with a three- to six-month withdrawal period. When smoked, over 150 chemicals are combusted and turn into more than 2,000 chemicals.

Internet Activities

Each Health Online box offers teachers a quick reference to relevant, engaging Internet resources available at Glencoe's expanded Web site for students. Teachers may present Web links, activities, health-related articles, and Web-based projects created especially to enhance the health content and referenced at point of use within the chapters.

HEALTH Online

Ask students to further explore the subject of club drugs using the Web Links to view the National Institute on Drug Abuse Web site. You may wish to set aside class time for a Q & A on the topic.

Human Sexuality

This is a full-color text that may be used as a primary text for a human sexuality course or as an extension of *Glencoe Health*. A Teacher Annotated Edition is available.

This program explores issues that deal with self-esteem and healthy decision making. Topics include understanding emotions, communication skills, understanding sexuality, dealing with peer pressure, developing refusal skills, and recognizing how and where to get help.

Human Sexuality addresses the complex issues adolescents face in coping with sexuality. Segments highlight what teens can do to be sexually responsible, such as practicing abstinence, resisting peer pressure, and talking to parents and other responsible adults.

This program also explores facts and dispels myths surrounding one of the world's most serious health issues. The model explains what HIV/AIDS is and how it affects the immune system, how the virus is spread and how it is not, and the importance of abstinence.

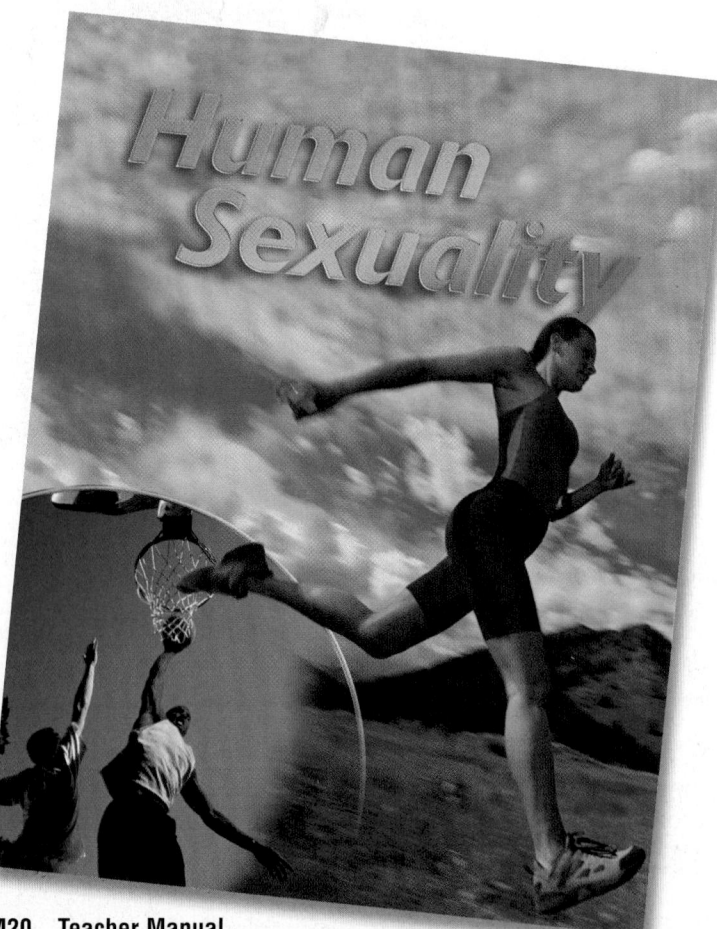

Table of Contents

Glencoe Health Video Program

Featuring New Health Video Segments

This new *Glencoe Health* video program features engaging video segments that include scenarios and updates on health topics to enhance student learning. The video is categorized into the following units for ease of use:

- A Healthy Foundation
- Physical Activity and Nutrition
- Mental and Emotional Health
- Promoting Safe and Healthy Relationships
- Personal Care and Body Systems
- Growth and Development
- Tobacco, Alcohol, and Other Drugs
- Diseases and Disorders
- Injury Prevention and Environmental Health

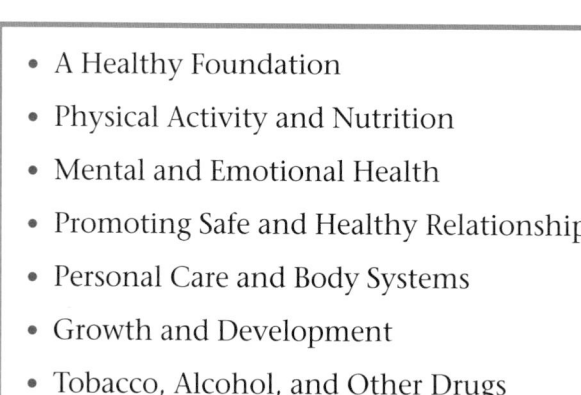

Media and Technology Resources

MINDJOGGER
VIDEOQUIZ

Glencoe Health MindJogger Videoquiz presents chapter quizzes in a fun, video-gameshow format. Available on videocassettes, the videoquizzes may be used for self-assessment or as an opportunity to review chapter content.

Glencoe Health Video

Enliven classroom discussions with this engaging health video. A variety of health and fitness topics are featured with a lively format geared toward the health classroom.

TECHNOLOGY OPTIONS

MINDJOGGER
VIDEOQUIZ

To preview or review chapter content, you may wish to use the MindJogger Videoquiz that accompanies Chapter 26.

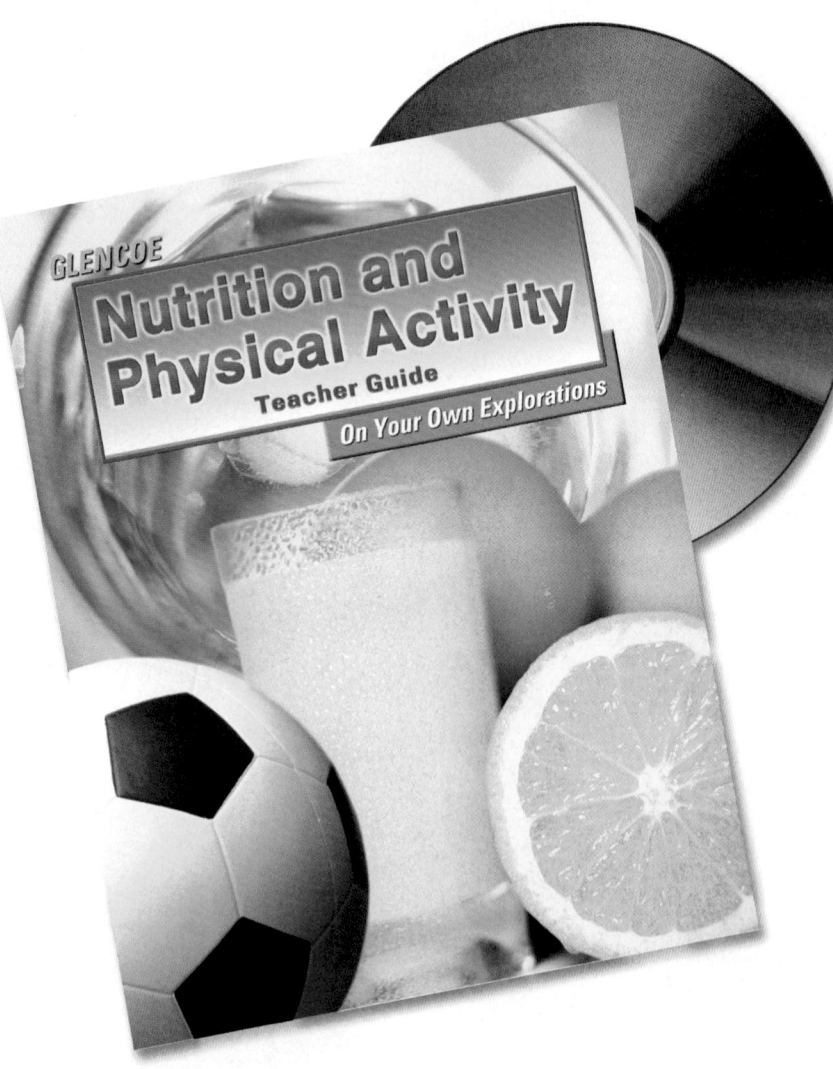

Nutrition and Physical Activity: On Your Own Explorations

Take students on an interactive journey through a typical Friday and Saturday in a teen's life with this new multimedia CD-ROM program. Students will make critical decisions about food intake and physical activity and evaluate these choices to make sure that they are the most healthful ones.

Vocabulary PuzzleMaker

Build vocabulary skills with custom-designed puzzles. Create word searches and crossword puzzles using vocabulary words from each lesson in the text.

TeacherWorks™

🔘 Custom design your lesson plan with this easy-to-use CD-ROM. The electronic format allows teachers to select a pre-set plan or to create their own—either way, it offers access to electronic files of all reproducible resources at the click of a button.

ExamView® Pro Testmaker

🔘 This computer software test bank for Macintosh and IBM-compatible computers provides questions in various formats and the capability to add your own questions.

Audio CD Program (English, Spanish)

🎧 The audio CDs contain summaries of chapter content for review, for reteaching, or for use when you do not have time to teach a particular chapter. Each summary is accompanied by a chapter activity and test based on the content of the audio CD. Spanish summaries are also provided.

Teaching Transparencies Binder

This convenient three-ring binder contains 88 full-color transparencies and a Teaching Strategies and Activities Instructor Guide.

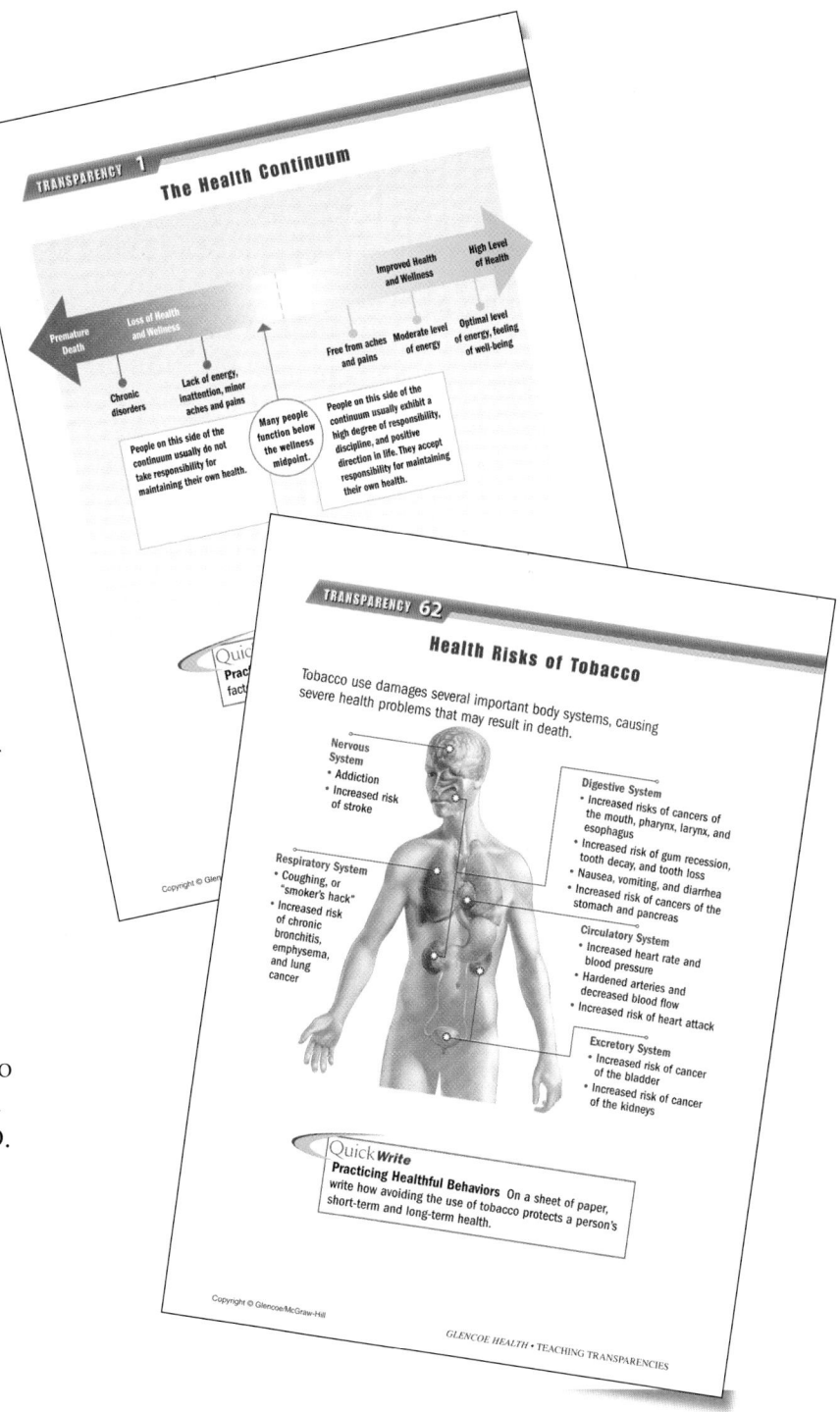

Glencoe Health Online

Visit *Glencoe Health* online at: health.glencoe.com

The *Glencoe Health* Online homepage on the Internet provides up-to-date resources and activities to complement Glencoe's comprehensive health program.

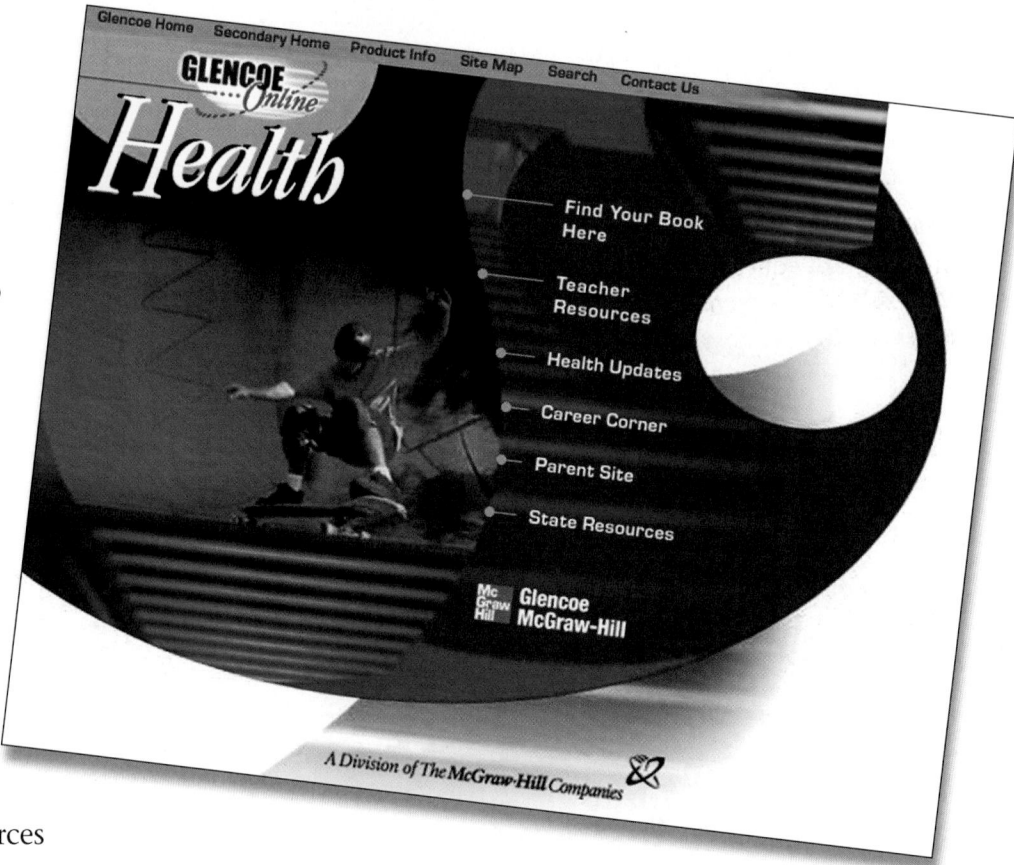

For Teachers

- **Textbook Resources**—more activities to enhance the student text
- **Block Schedule Lesson Plans**—cross-curriculum, reading skills, and media lessons designed for longer block schedule lesson plans
- **Technology Projects**—help students integrate the use of technology for classroom assignments
- **Professional Articles**—current issues and trends in health education
- **Correlation to Standards**—organized by lesson and by National Health Education Standards
- **National Organizations**—health resources presented here for your convenience

For Students

- **Web Links**—preselected Internet links extend lesson content
- **Health Updates**—health in the news to keep students informed
- **Career Corner**—resources to plan for a career in health
- **Student Activities**—educational projects that make use of Internet resources

For Parents

- Guidelines and tips for using the Internet
- Parent letters in English and Spanish

Teacher Support for Students Using the Internet

As you encourage students to explore the extensive health resources available, Glencoe provides you with tools to make the Internet an effective educational tool.

Teaching Today

Timesaving teaching tips, articles on important educational topics, Web-based teaching resources, and downloadable classroom materials provided every day.

Guide to Using the Internet

This booklet, prepared especially for the health teacher, includes basic information about using Glencoe's Health Web site, guidelines for evaluating Web sites, and special notes on ways to protect students from potential hazards.

Meeting Individual Needs

Each student brings his or her unique set of abilities, perceptions, and needs into the classroom. The *Glencoe Health* Teacher Wraparound Edition offers you a variety of strategies so that your students can learn health concepts and skills through many different methods.

Teaching strategies that appear throughout the chapter have been identified and coded by ability level to give teachers an idea of their suitability for students of varying learning styles and abilities.

Making Health Accessible for All Students

Teaching strategies in the Meeting Individual Needs and Meeting Student Diversity boxes incorporate cultural perspectives, strategies for the physically and mentally challenged, and effective approaches for addressing different learning styles.

MEETING STUDENT DIVERSITY

Language Diversity Use the following suggestions to help students who have difficulty with English:

- Pair those learners with native speakers of English wh... mary in lan... guage that... helps stu-

dents with language diversity to the Glencoe Health Audiocassette Program. Available in English and Spanish, this component provides an audio and written summary of the

---

Meeting Individual Needs

Attitudes and Mental Habits In general, a student's success will depend as much on his or her attitudes and mental habits as on the use of information and appropriate thinking skills. Performance tasks allow both students and teachers to observe what attitudes and habits are operating as work progresses. Examples include the following:

- showing individual responsibility
- valuing team work
- having initiative and being diligent
- being an intellectual risk-taker
- planning actions rather than being impulsive
- showing concern for the global community

Chapter 6 • Lesson 1

② TEACH

Community Involvement

Have students examine the contents of any vending machine at school or in the community and make a list of the foods and beverages offered. Tell them to analyze the nutrients in the foods and beverages, noting especially the amounts of sugars in each. Ask them to report their findings to the class. L2

Explaining

Provide food-related magazines for students to collect pictures of high-calorie foods and drinks that total about 3,500 calories. Explain that this is the number of calories that would have to be cut out of an individual's eating plan each week to result in the loss of 1 pound of body fat. ELL
Visual/Spatial Intelligence

Cooperative Learning

Have students work in small groups. Have them apply their understanding of sound nutritional principles to create menus for a restaurant for health conscious people. The menus might include symbols for low-sugar, low-sodium, and low-fat foods. Have each group present their menu to the class for feedback. L3

145

Key to Ability Levels

L1 **Level 1** strategies should be within the ability range of all students. Full class participation is often required. Teacher direction is usually needed.

L2 **Level 2** strategies for average to above-average students or for small groups. Some teacher direction is needed.

L3 **Level 3** strategies are designed for students able and willing to work independently. Minimal teacher direction is needed.

ELL **English Language Learners** strategies should be within the ability range of students learning the English language.

Block Scheduling strategies are useful in a block scheduling format.

Reading and Writing in the Content Area

The *Glencoe Health* program is designed to increase health literacy by improving reading comprehension and deepening students' understanding of ideas and concepts. The reading strategies are active, constructive, and engaging.

In the Student Edition

Quick Write and Quick Start activities are lesson openers that give students an opportunity to demonstrate their abilities with quick, motivating writing challenges. The activities also act as pre-assessments for teachers.

Caption Questions throughout each chapter help students to comprehend what they have read through interpreting the visual. This is especially useful for less proficient readers.

In the Teacher Wraparound Edition

Active Reading strategies throughout the teacher edition include reading exercises that link directly to the lesson content, giving students additional opportunities to build proficiency in reading and writing. These exercises aid students in mastering language skills. For additional strategies, refer to the *Guided Reading Activities* booklet.

ACTIVE READING

Metacognition Journal
In this strategy, each student analyzes his or her own thought processes while reading. Have students record what they have learned about each of the ways HIV is transmitted, and write why this knowledge is important. For more activities, see the *Guided Reading Activities* booklet in the TCR. 📁

Teacher Classroom Resources

Ancillaries

- Cross-Curriculum Activities
- Concept Mapping Activities
- Guided Reading Activities
- Reteaching Activities

Technology

- Audio CD Program (English and Spanish)
- MindJogger Videoquizzes
- Vocabulary PuzzleMaker
- Glencoe Health Online

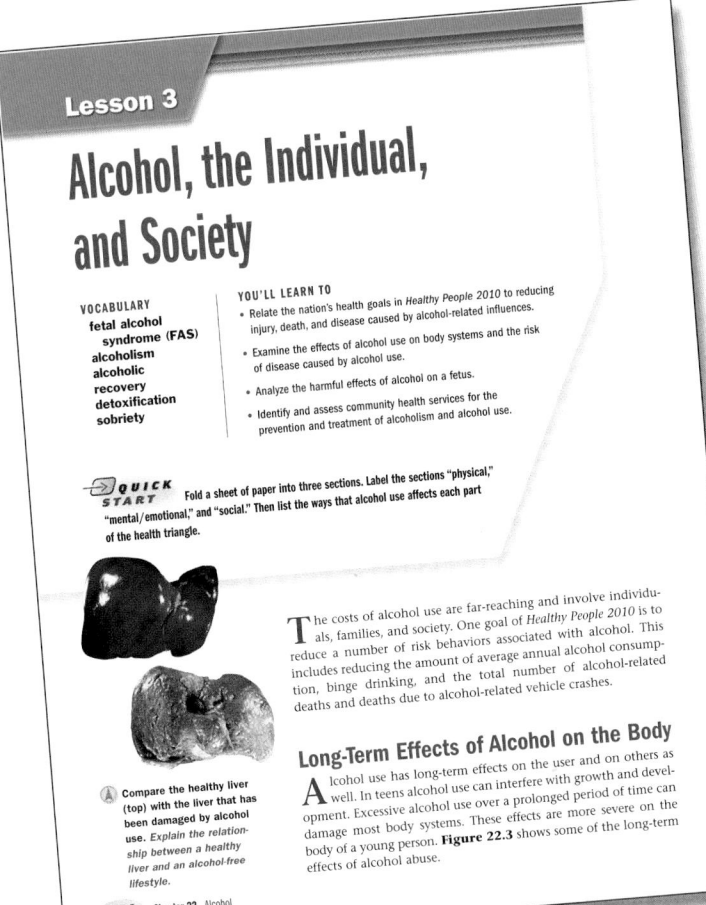

Lesson 3

Alcohol, the Individual, and Society

VOCABULARY
fetal alcohol syndrome (FAS)
alcoholism
alcoholic
recovery
detoxification
sobriety

YOU'LL LEARN TO
- Relate the nation's health goals in *Healthy People 2010* to reducing injury, death, and disease caused by alcohol-related influences.
- Examine the effects of alcohol use on body systems and the risk of disease caused by alcohol use.
- Analyze the harmful effects of alcohol on a fetus.
- Identify and assess community health services for the prevention and treatment of alcoholism and alcohol use.

QUICK START Fold a sheet of paper into three sections. Label the sections "physical," "mental/emotional," and "social." Then list the ways that alcohol use affects each part of the health triangle.

The costs of alcohol use are far-reaching and involve individuals, families, and society. One goal of *Healthy People 2010* is to reduce a number of risk behaviors associated with alcohol. This includes reducing the amount of average annual alcohol consumption, binge drinking, and the total number of alcohol-related deaths and deaths due to alcohol-related vehicle crashes.

Compare the healthy liver (top) with the liver that has been damaged by alcohol use. *Explain* the relationship between a healthy liver and an alcohol-free lifestyle.

Long-Term Effects of Alcohol on the Body

Alcohol use has long-term effects on the user and on others as well. In teens alcohol use can interfere with growth and development. Excessive alcohol use over a prolonged period of time can damage most body systems. These effects are more severe on the body of a young person. **Figure 22.3** shows some of the long-term effects of alcohol abuse.

574 Chapter 22 Alcohol

Media Literacy In the Health Classroom

Eye on the Media

Arm students with the critical skills they need to evaluate the daily bombardment of messages they receive!

Following the four-step model developed by the Center for Media Literacy, *Glencoe Health* has provided a wealth of activities and scenarios to aid students in analyzing media messages. These steps include:

- **Awareness:** the understanding and interpreting of messages
- **Analysis:** analyzing the message
- **Reflection:** considering the impact of the message
- **Action:** evaluating the impact of the message and taking action for change

Eye on the Media activities empower teachers to help students frame context around the multitude of mass media messages that they encounter daily. The features encourage students to investigate the techniques used by the media industry, revealing how the media constructs and influences many of our perceptions of different cultures and of our own lives. Allowing students to pull from their personal experiences and value systems, Eye on the Media scenarios help students transform media constructs into informative knowledge bases of understanding.

Eye ON THE Media

Which Antismoking Ads Are More Effective with Teens?

NHES Standard 4 Students will analyze the influence of culture, media, technology, and other factors on health.

Objective

Students will identify different techniques in antismoking advertisements and analyze the effectiveness of these advertisements on teen audiences.

Motivator

Ask students to recall a specific antismoking advertisement they have seen.

Teaching Strategies

Awareness Ask students to read the opening paragraph and identify techniques used in antismoking ads.

Analysis Students should recognize that the image in the text focuses on the health risks of tobacco use.

Reflection Encourage students to be specific when describing why certain techniques might be more effective than others.

Take Action Have students write to their congressman or senator advocating for funding antismoking advertisements.

✓ Assessment

Students' one-page analyses should compare the two ads discussed and give supporting evidence for their viewpoint on which is more effective.

556

Eye ON THE Media

Which Antismoking Ads Are Most Effective with Teens?

Studies show that antismoking ads aimed at teen audiences are effective in helping teens make the healthful decision to avoid tobacco use. Antismoking advertisements may be sponsored by health organizations, by nonprofit companies, or by tobacco companies. Some ads use satire or humor while others give hard facts about the health risks of tobacco use. Use the activity below to help you identify different techniques in antismoking ads and analyze the effectiveness of these ads on teens.

ACTIVITY

Read the script of the television ad. Using the Internet and your library as resources, find an antismoking advertisement created by a tobacco company. Compare the tobacco company ad with the ad pictured above.

1. How do the messages of each ad differ?

2. What techniques are used in each ad? Does either ad use satire or humor? Does either ad use dramatic visuals to convey its message?

3. Does each ad contain credible information? How do you know it is credible?

4. How does each ad explain or show the harmful effects of smoking?

EXPRESS YOUR VIEWS

Write a letter to the editor of your local newspaper advocating for citizens to take action to promote a tobacco-free society. Include your views on which antismoking ads you find most effective for teens and why.

More About...

Legacy Foundation The language within the Master Settlement Agreement reached between the tobacco companies and 46 states in 1998 set aside money to form The Legacy Foundation, a national organization formed to combat tobacco use, sponsored the ad in the activity. It was created by a panel of teens working with an advertising firm. The 46 states that entered into the settlement agreement with the tobacco companies also receive money earmarked for smoking cessation and prevention programs. Have students research what their state is doing with the tobacco settlement money. Have groups create a proposal to send to a state representative or state senator, detailing a plan on how to spend the tobacco settlement money in their state.

Eye on the Media activities improve students' ability to interpret "media language." By understanding the media's use of language, students work with a diversity of grammar, syntax, and metaphor systems. The exercises ultimately encourage students to construct their own persuasive arguments through the study and use of critical language skills.

Students develop media literacy skills through:

- **Explaining** the effects and impact of social, technical, and various cultural movements portrayed in the media.
- **Differentiating** between primary and secondary sources of information.
- **Identifying** bias in written, oral, and visual material.
- **Analyzing** the relationships between ideas, culture, and industries as they are represented in various media.
- **Recognizing** fallacious, deceptive, or faulty modes of persuasion.
- **Comparing and Contrasting** various media coverage of the same topic.

Students gain practice in:

- **Organizing** information acquired from a variety of media.
- **Deconstructing** media constructs to get to the main message.

Students develop critical thinking by:

- **Evaluating** the validity of a source.
- **Examining** the credibility of information.
- **Recognizing** techniques used to convey messages.
- **Critiquing** media messages.
- **Identifying** and describing motive.

Teaching Health Skills

The National Health Education Standards focus on concepts and knowledge (NHES 1) and on health skills (NHES 2–7). As education moves to become standards-based, *Glencoe Health* utilizes the National Health Education Standards to provide a foundation for health skills development.

The *Glencoe Health* program incorporates performance assessment tasks in the skills features with specific assessment criteria. Students have the opportunity to learn about a health skill in the context of a lifelike situation. Then they practice the skill and engage in an activity. This provides the teacher with a demonstration of student work that can be assessed. Each skill feature includes a performance task that is assessed using specific scoring criteria. The scoring criteria ask students to provide evidence of proficiency in one of the health skills.

Situation

Students are presented with a potential real-life situation that requires the use of a health skill to reduce risk and enhance health. In this case, the necessary skill is refusal strategies

Skills Described

Students are provided with important components of the skill within the context of the situation. In this case, examples of skill application are also provided.

Skills Practice and Application

Students are presented with an activity that provides critical practice in using the skill. Student practice takes place during the skits. The product developed for assessment is the key ring reminder card.

Teaching Strategies

Clear, concise teaching strategies explain how the feature specifically links the standards, objectives, process, and assessment.

Skills Assessed

Student products are used as the evidence of skill development. Scoring assessments directly relate to the Health Standards. They are used to judge the quality of student work on this performance task.

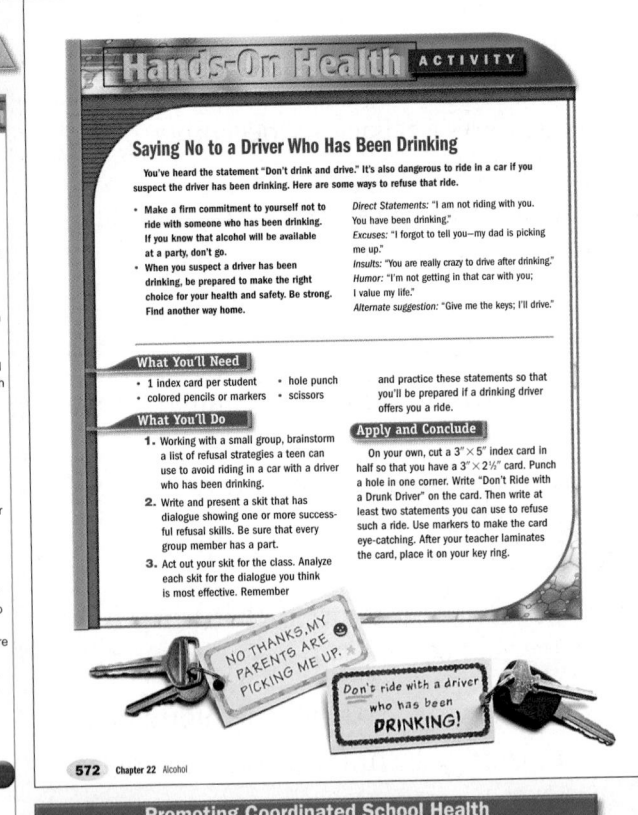

Connecting Skills to Real Life

Great care has been taken to make the connections among standards, curriculum instruction, and assessment. Therefore, you will see that the standards addressed are linked to the features in the text. The teaching strategies in the Teacher Wraparound provide appropriate practice as a part of the instruction. Finally, the assessment is a natural extension of the instruction and the criteria point directly back to the standard.

Research shows that students who practice health skills in lifelike situations are more likely to apply those skills in their own life. The Health Skills Activity feature employs dialogue as a starting point for students to apply essential health skills that require communication, such as refusal skills, conflict resolution, decision making and goal setting.

Situation

Students are presented with a scenario that challenges them to use a health skill to reduce risk and enhance health. In this case, the necessary skill is decision making.

Skills Described

Students are provided with direction to apply the skill to this situation. In this case, students are reminded of the six steps of the decision-making process.

Skills Practice and Application

The activity and student written response provides critical practice in the use of the skill, resulting in a student product that can be used for assessment purposes.

Teaching Strategies

Teachers are given the methodology for effectively using the feature with strategies that specifically link the standards, objectives, process, and assessment.

Skills Assessed

Student products are used as the evidence of skill development. Scoring criteria directly relate to the Health Standards. They are used to judge the quality of student work on this performance task.

Promoting Health Skills and Assessment

Health Skills Overview

The following are health skills that students develop and practice throughout life. Research has shown that the cultivation of these skills helps teens and adults promote health and contribute to overall wellness. These are skills that can be modeled and used daily to promote individual, family, and community health.

 ## Accessing Information

This skill addresses the important steps to take for accessing valid health information and appropriate health services. Key components of this skill include:

✔ citation of specific sources

✔ evaluation of the validity of the source

✔ rationale for the appropriateness of the source

✔ ability to access appropriate community resources to meet specific needs

✔ type of help available from the sources

 ## Practicing Healthful Behaviors

This skill is the actual practice of healthful behavior. It includes the steps and procedures used to promote wellness. Key components of this skill are:

✔ demonstration of healthful behaviors, habits, and/or techniques

✔ identification of protective behaviors, e.g., first-aid techniques, safety steps, strategies to avoid/manage unhealthy or dangerous situations

✔ listing steps in correct order

 ## Stress Management

This skill involves specific techniques for reducing and managing stress. The key components of this skill are:

✔ ability to identify situations that cause stress

✔ demonstration of techniques that help manage and reduce stress, e.g., deep breathing, exercise, relaxation strategies

 ## Analyzing Influences

This skill involves analysis of the dynamic factors of families, media, peers, personal interests, and pressures that affect health decisions. Key components of this skill are:

✔ identification and analysis of external and internal factors

✔ attention to interrelationships and complexity of influences

✔ variety of influences as appropriate

 ## Communication

This skill is an interactive process between and among individuals to clarify ideas, thoughts, needs, and feelings. Key components for this skill are:

✔ interactions among individuals

✔ clear, organized message

✔ listening skills

✔ use of "I" messages

✔ respectful tone

✔ appropriate body language

✔ reason(s) for their request

Conflict Resolution

This skill gives students practice in a variety of effective communication techniques to resolve conflicts. Key components of this skill are:

✔ Take turns explaining each side of the conflict without interruption
✔ Use "I" messages
✔ Listen carefully, and ask appropriate questions
✔ Brainstorm solutions
✔ Agree on a solution that benefits both sides

Goal Setting

This skill is an interactive process for individuals. It requires planning and revision throughout the application of the process. Key components of this skill are:

✔ clear progression through a goal-setting process
✔ inclusion of a clear goal statement
✔ identification of a realistic goal
✔ plan for reaching the goal
✔ evaluation or reflection on the action

Refusal Skills

This skill involves specific strategies for refusing to engage in risky behaviors. Key components of this skill are:

✔ inclusion of the word no in their response
✔ an explanation of why they are refusing
✔ alternatives to the proposed activity
✔ body language they would use to back up their words
✔ a description of walking away from the situation if necessary

Advocacy

This skill calls for the use of persuasion to promote positive health choices personally and for others. The key components of this skill are:

✔ clear, health-enhancing stand
✔ support for the position with relevant information
✔ awareness of the audience
✔ encouragement of others to make healthful choices
✔ passion/conviction

Decision Making

This skill requires speculation into the future based on a particular action. Students speculate that if this action is taken, certain results can be expected. The evaluation of potential results determines what decision is most health-enhancing. The key components of this skill are:

✔ clear description of the situation
✔ several options with possible outcomes of each
✔ influence of values on possible decisions
✔ health-enhancing decision and an evaluation of it

Activities

Concept Mapping Activities provide a developmental approach for students to practice concept mapping. They can be used to preview or review a lesson's content by visually reinforcing main ideas and clarifying relationships.

Cross-Curriculum Activities give students an opportunity to relate health information to the content of other subject areas, including math, social studies, language arts, and fine arts.

Current Health Issues uses two formats that allow students to explore new health technologies and to develop viewpoints on pertinent or controversial health issues by presenting opposing or divergent views.

Decision-Making Activities give students an opportunity to practice the decision-making process as they consider a variety of hypothetical situations.

Enrichment Activities allow students the opportunity to explore lesson concepts further. Answers for the teacher are provided at the back of the booklet.

Guided Reading Activities are designed to assess students' comprehension of the lesson content. The format of the activities varies.

Guide to Using the Internet provides strategies for incorporating Internet activities into the health classroom.

Health Labs give students experience with making observations and hypotheses, collecting and recording data, and forming conclusions based on analysis and interpretations of experimental results. Teacher pages provide help and answers to questions.

Reteaching Activities allow students who are having difficulty with mastering the major concepts of a lesson to review the concepts from a different perspective.

The Student Activity Workbook contains a Study Guide and Health Inventory for each chapter and an Applying Health Skills activity for each lesson. A Teacher Annotated Edition is available.

Assessment

Lesson Quizzes provide a one-page quiz for each lesson in *Glencoe Health.* Answers for the teacher are provided at the back of the booklet.

Chapter and Unit Tests provide two forms of chapter tests, A and B. Either or both forms may be used as alternative or makeup tests. Also included are unit tests that cover all the chapters within each unit.

Performance Assessment Activities assess learning in ways that require a student to demonstrate how they can apply health knowledge and skills. They provide teachers with flexible and creative ways to judge student progress.

Teaching Resources

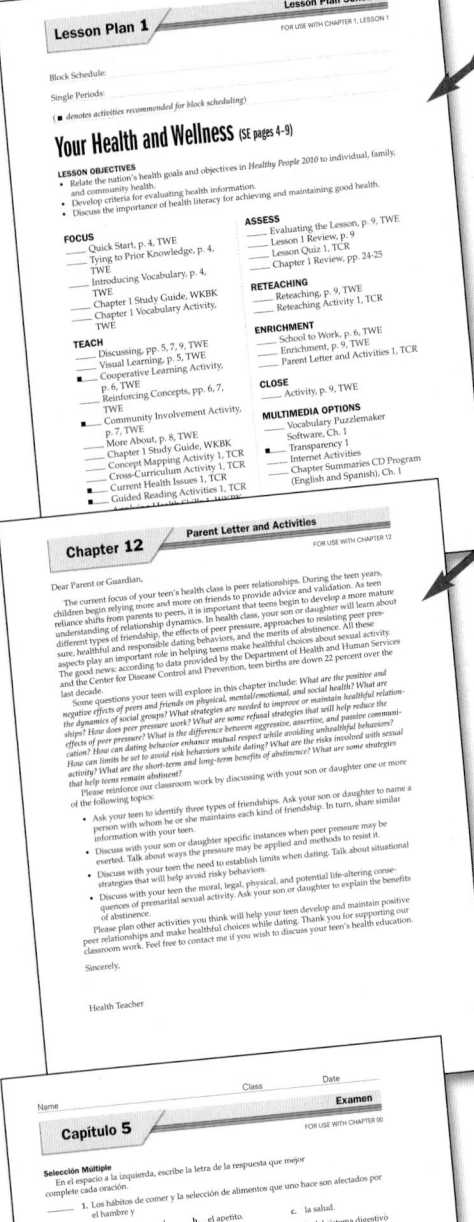

Lesson Plans with Block Scheduling

are provided for each lesson in *Glencoe Health*. The lesson plans include references to all resources available in *Glencoe Health*.

Transparency Teaching Strategies and Activities

includes 88 transparencies plus an activity booklet complete with teaching strategies for use with the transparencies.

Parent Letters and Activities

include introductory teacher material about how to use theses letters and how to inform parents or guardians of the instructional program and assessment techniques to be employed. This material appears in English and Spanish.

English Summaries, Quizzes, and Activities

include brief summaries of each of the 29 chapters of *Glencoe Health*. The summaries are followed by quizzes and activities that help students grasp the chapter content and assess their knowledge. Answers for the teachers are provided at the back of the booklet. (Accompanied by audio CDs)

Spanish Summaries, Quizzes, and Activities

include brief summaries of each of the 29 chapters of *Glencoe Health*. The summaries are followed by quizzes and activities that help students grasp the chapter content and assess their knowledge. Answers for the teachers are provided at the back of the booklet. (Accompanied by audio CDs)

Building Home, School, and Community Involvement

Education involves much more than classroom activities and homework assignments. In order to gain real knowledge, skills, and understanding, students will need to apply what they learn to their own lives, the lives of their families, and the life of their community.

The activities in *Home, School, and Community Involvement* help students to achieve that goal. These activities guide students in communicating effectively with family members, extending their education into their daily home life. The activities present specific guidelines for family and community projects that students can undertake independently, in groups, or as a class.

As students undertake these activities, they will learn important lessons about health, their families, their community, and—most significantly—about themselves. When teens apply their knowledge and skills to real life, they become more engaged in the learning process and are better able to retain the information that they have acquired.

Glencoe Professional Health Series

Planning a Coordinated School Health Program

What is coordinated school health? This booklet has been designed to answer that question and to increase awareness of the need for coordinated school health programs throughout the United States.

Dealing with Sensitive Issues

Health educators often need to discuss many sensitive issues with their students. To guide educators, this booklet provides background information and teaching strategies.

Promoting Character Education

This booklet outlines the principles of character education and strategies for developing a caring school community. It includes background information for teachers and activity ideas designed to help students build good character.

Home, School, and Community Involvement

This guide has been designed to enable students to involve family and community members in their health education. Reproducible activities are provided, including great ideas for service learning projects.

Course Presentation

Glencoe Health is a comprehensive health text with 29 chapters and 109 lessons. The study of this text may extend over the course of one semester or one year. Consider the following possible outlines as course outlines.

OUTLINE 1 Full Course

One-year (36-week) course, 29 chapters

Unit 1	A Healthy Foundation	
	Chapters 1, 2, 3	[3 weeks]
Unit 2	Physical Activity and Nutrition	
	Chapters 4, 5, 6	[4 weeks]
Unit 3	Mental and Emotional Health	
	Chapters 7, 8, 9	[4 weeks]
Unit 4	Promoting Safe and Healthy Relationships	
	Chapters 10, 11, 12, 13	[5 weeks]
Unit 5	Personal Care and Body Systems	
	Chapters 14, 15, 16, 17, 18	[6 weeks]
Unit 6	Growth and Development	
	Chapters 19, 20	[2 weeks]
Unit 7	Tobacco, Alcohol, and Other Drugs	
	Chapters 21, 22, 23	[5 weeks]
Unit 8	Diseases and Disorders	
	Chapters 24, 25, 26	[4 weeks]
Unit 9	Injury Prevention and Environmental Health	
	Chapters 27, 28, 29	[3 weeks]

OUTLINE 2 Health Survey Course

One-semester (18-week) course, 29 chapters

Unit 1	A Healthy Foundation	
	Chapters 1, 2, 3	[1 week]
Unit 2	Physical Activity and Nutrition	
	Chapters 4, 5, 6	[3 weeks]
Unit 3	Mental and Emotional Health	
	Chapters 7, 8, 9	[2 weeks]
Unit 4	Promoting Safe and Healthy Relationships	
	Chapters 10, 11, 12, 13	[2 weeks]
Unit 5	Personal Care and Body Systems	
	Chapters 14, 15, 16, 17, 18	[3 weeks]
Unit 6	Growth and Development	
	Chapters 19, 20	[1 week]
Unit 7	Tobacco, Alcohol, and Other Drugs	
	Chapters 21, 22, 23	[2 weeks]
Unit 8	Diseases and Disorders	
	Chapters 24, 25, 26	[2 weeks]
Unit 9	Injury Prevention and Environmental Health	
	Chapters 27, 28, 29	[2 weeks]

OUTLINE 3 Physical Fitness and Nutrition

One-semester (18-week) course, 20 chapters

Unit 1	A Healthy Foundation	
	Chapters 1, 2, 3	[1 week]
Unit 2	Physical Activity and Nutrition	
	Chapters 4, 5, 6	[5 weeks]
Unit 5	Personal Care and Body Systems	
	Chapters 14, 15, 16, 17, 18	[5 weeks]
Unit 7	Tobacco, Alcohol, and Other Drugs	
	Chapters 21, 22, 23	[3 weeks]
Unit 8	Diseases and Disorders	
	Chapters 24, 25, 26	[3 weeks]
Unit 9	Injury Prevention and Environmental Health	
	Chapters 27, 28, 29	[1 week]

OUTLINE 4
Mental, Emotional and Social Health

One-semester (18-week) course, 23 chapters

Unit 1	A Healthy Foundation	
	Chapters 1, 2, 3	[1 week]
Unit 3	Mental and Emotional Health	
	Chapters 7, 8, 9	[4 weeks]
Unit 4	Promoting Safe and Healthy Relationships	
	Chapters 10, 11, 12, 13	[5 weeks]
Unit 5	Personal Care and Body Systems	
	Chapters 14, 15, 16, 17, 18	[3 weeks]
Unit 6	Growth and Development	
	Chapters 19, 20	[1 week]
Unit 7	Tobacco, Alcohol, and Other Drugs	
	Chapters 21, 22, 23	[2 weeks]
Unit 8	Diseases and Disorders	
	Chapters 24, 25, 26	[2 weeks]

Glencoe Health Meets the National Health Education Standards

The National Health Education Standards were created with the goal of improving educational achievement for students and improving health in the United States through the promotion of health literacy. The Health Standards detail the knowledge and skills essential to the development of health literacy in the form of performance indicators.

Health Education Standard 1:

Students will comprehend concepts related to health promotion and disease prevention.

Performance Indicators:

As a result of health instruction in Grades 9–11, students will:

1.1 Analyze how behavior can impact health maintenance and disease prevention.

1.2 Describe the interrelationships of mental, emotional, social, and physical health throughout adulthood.

1.3 Explain the impact of personal health behaviors on the functioning of body systems.

1.4 Analyze how the family, peers, and community influence the health of individuals.

1.5 Analyze how the environment influences the health of the community.

1.6 Describe how to delay onset and reduce risks of potential health problems during adulthood.

1.7 Analyze how public health policies and government regulations influence health promotion and disease prevention.

1.8 Analyze how the prevention and control of health problems are influenced by research and medical advances.

Health Education Standard 2:

Students will demonstrate the ability to access valid health information and health-promoting products and services.

Performance Indicators:

As a result of health instruction in Grades 9–11, students will:

2.1 Evaluate the validity of health information, products, and services.

2.2 Demonstrate the ability to evaluate resources from home, school, and community that provide valid health information.

2.3 Evaluate factors that influence personal selection of health products and services.

2.4 Demonstrate the ability to access school and community health services for self and others.

2.5 Analyze the cost and accessibility of health care services.

2.6 Analyze situations requiring professional health services.

Health Education Standard 3:

Students will demonstrate the ability to practice health-enhancing behaviors and reduce health risks.

Performance Indicators:

As a result of health instruction in Grades 9–11, students will:

3.1 Analyze the role of individual responsibility for enhancing health.

3.2 Evaluate a personal health assessment to determine strategies for health enhancement and risk reduction.

3.3 Analyze the short-term and long-term consequences of safe, risky and harmful behaviors.

3.4 Develop strategies to improve or maintain personal, family and community health.

3.5 Develop injury prevention and management strategies for personal, family, and community health.

3.6 Demonstrate ways to avoid and reduce threatening situations.

3.7 Evaluate strategies to manage stress.

Health Education Standard 4:

Students will analyze the influence of culture, media, technology, and other factors on health.

Performance Indicators:

As a result of health instruction in Grades 9–11, students will:

4.1 Analyze how cultural diversity enriches and challenges health behaviors.

4.2 Evaluate the effect of media and other factors on personal, family, and community health.

4.3 Evaluate the impact of technology on personal, family, and community health.

4.4 Analyze how information from the community influences health.

Health Education Standard 5:

Students will demonstrate the ability to use interpersonal communication skills to enhance health.

Performance Indicators:

As a result of health instruction in Grades 9–11, students will:

5.1 Demonstrate skills for communicating effectively with family, peers, and others.

5.2 Analyze how interpersonal communication affects relationships.

5.3 Demonstrate healthy ways to express needs, wants, and feelings.

5.4 Demonstrate ways to communicate care, consideration, and respect of self and others.

5.5 Demonstrate strategies for solving interpersonal conflicts without harming self or others.

5.6 Demonstrate refusal, negotiation, and collaboration skills to avoid potentially harmful situations.

5.7 Analyze the possible causes of conflict in schools, families, and communities.

5.8 Demonstrate strategies used to prevent conflict.

Health Education Standard 6:

Students will demonstrate the ability to use goal-setting and decision-making skills to enhance health.

Performance Indicators:

As a result of health instruction in Grades 9–11, students will:

6.1 Demonstrate the ability to utilize various strategies when making decisions related to health needs and risks of young adults.

6.2 Analyze health concerns that require collaborative decision making.

6.3 Predict immediate and long-term impact of health decisions on the individual, family, and community.

6.4 Implement a plan for attaining a personal health goal.

6.5 Evaluate progress toward achieving personal health goals.

6.6 Formulate an effective plan for lifelong health.

Health Education Standard 7:

Students will demonstrate the ability to advocate for personal, family, and community health.

Performance Indicators:

As a result of health instruction in Grades 9–11, students will:

7.1 Evaluate the effectiveness of communication methods for accurately expressing health information and ideas.

7.2 Express information and opinions about health issues.

7.3 Utilize strategies to overcome barriers when communicating information, ideas, feelings, and opinions about health issues.

7.4 Demonstrate the ability to influence and support others in making positive health choices.

7.5 Demonstrate the ability to work cooperatively when advocating for healthy communities.

7.6 Demonstrate the ability to adapt health messages and communication techniques to the characteristics of a particular audience.

Glencoe Health Meets the National Health Education Standards

The Chapter Planning Guide provides a correlation to the National Health Education Standards for material covered in each lesson.

Chapter 26 *Noncommunicable Diseases and Disab*

Lessons	Standards		Featur
	National	State/Local	
1 Drug Use, Misuse, and Abuse	National Health Education Standard 1.2, 1.7, 3.1, 3.3		Real-Life Ap • Health Information (Accessing Inform 577
2 Marijuana, Inhalants, and Anabolic Steroids	National Health Education Standard 1.2, 1.3, 3.1, 3.3		Exploring Iss • Should Schools Tests?, page 58
3 Psychoactive Drugs	National Health Education Standard 3.3, 5.6, 6.1, 6.3		Health Sk • Decision Makir Pressure, page

TM41

Scope & Sequence

Content Strands	Chapter 1 Living a Healthy Life	Chapter 2 Building Health Skills and Character
Personal Health	• Role of lifestyle factors in overall health (1-1) • Health as combination of physical, mental/emotional, and social well-being (1-2) • Influences on health (1-2) • Accepting responsibility for your health (1-3) • Prevention and risk behaviors (1-3) • Importance of abstinence from risk behaviors (1-3)	• Demonstrating interpersonal communication skills, including refusal and conflict resolution skills (2-1) • Learning self-management skills (2-1) • Analyzing influences on health (2-1) • Accessing reliable health information (2-1) • Advocating for health (2-1) • Learning decision-making and goal-setting steps (2-2)
Consumer and Community Health	• Importance of health education (1-1) • Goals of *Healthy People 2010* (1-1) • Being health literate (1-1) • Health messages delivered through media and technology (1-2)	• Developing criteria for evaluating health information (2-1) • Service learning in communities (2-3)
Injury Prevention and Safety	• Examining risks to your physical health (1-3)	• Using refusal skills to avoid unsafe behaviors (2-1)
Alcohol, Tobacco, and Other Drugs	• The avoidance of tobacco, alcohol, and other drugs as a health-promoting lifestyle factor (1-1) • Use of tobacco, alcohol, and other drugs as high-risk behaviors (1-3)	
Physical Activity and Nutrition	• Eating nutritious foods as a health-promoting lifestyle factor (1-1) • Engaging in regular physical activity as a health-promoting lifestyle factor (1-1)	• Character and health behaviors, including proper nutrition and regular physical activity (2-3)
Environmental Health	• How environment influences your health (1-2)	
Family Living	• How heredity and culture influence your health (1-2) • Family support and encouragement as protective factors (1-2)	• Importance of character for self, others, and community (2-3) • Demonstrating consideration and respect for self, family, and others (2-3) • Positive role modeling (2-3)
Individual Growth and Development	• Lifelong commitment to wellness (1-1) • How personal attitudes and behaviors affect health (1-2) • Choosing abstinence (1-3)	• Character and core ethical values (2-3) • Traits of good character (2-3)
Communicable and Chronic Disease	• Chronic disorders and the health continuum (1-1)	

Chapter 3 Being a Health-Literate Consumer	Chapter 4 Physical Activity for Life	Chapter 5 Nutrition and Your Health
• Selecting health care providers and services (3-2) • Medical history (3-2) • Advocating for public health (3-4)	• Benefits of physical activity to health (4-1) • Health risks of physical inactivity (4-1) • Physical activity and weight control (4-1) • Basic components of physical fitness (4-2) • Target heart range (4-2) • Planning a physical activity program (4-3) • Principles of an effective workout (4-3) • Treating physical activity injuries (4-5)	• The functions of the six basic nutrients in maintaining health (5-2) • Selecting healthful meals and snacks using the *Dietary Guidelines for Americans* and the Food Guide Pyramid (5-3)
• Choosing health care products (3-1) • Reading product labels (3-1) • Consumer rights and responsibilities (3-1) • Choosing and paying for health care services (3-2) • Types of health services (3-2) • Resolving consumer problems (3-3)	• Importance of receiving a health screening before beginning a physical activity program (4-4)	• Influences on food choices (5-1) • *Dietary Guidelines for Americans* (5-3) • The Food Guide Pyramid (5-3) • Nutrition labeling (5-4)
• Protection against unsafe products (3-1) • Product labels and safety concerns (3-1) • Avoiding health fraud (3-3) • National health agencies (3-4)	• Warming up and cooling down (4-3) • Considering personal safety during physical activity (4-4) • Proper use of sports equipment to prevent injury (4-4) • Preventing weather-related injuries (4-5)	• Food safety and prevention of foodborne illness (5-4)
	• Avoiding harmful substances as part of maintaining a training program (4-4) • Health risks of taking anabolic steroids (4-4)	
• Evaluating sports safety equipment (3-1)	• Measuring and improving cardiorespiratory endurance, muscular strength and endurance, and flexibility (4-2) • Aerobic versus anaerobic exercise (4-2) • Nutrition and hydration as part of a physical activity program (4-4) • Nutritional supplements (4-4)	• Understanding calories and nutrients (5-1) • Carbohydrates as fuel food (5-2) • Understanding complete and incomplete proteins (5-2) • Saturated versus unsaturated fatty acids (5-2) • Role of fats in health (5-2) • Water- and fat-soluble vitamins and minerals (5-2) • Vital role of water in body processes (5-2) • Understanding serving sizes (5-3)
• Public health services and the environment (3-4)	• Considering your environment when choosing physical activities (4-3) • Cold and hot weather health risks (4-3)	• Influence of environment on food choices (5-1)
• Family's role in choosing health services (3-1)	• Participating in physical activity with family members (4-1)	• Influence of family on food choices (5-1)
• Developing skills to communicate effectively with health care providers (3-2)	• Managing stress through physical activity (4-1) • Importance of lifestyle activities (4-1)	• Understanding how emotions affect eating habits (5-1) • Importance of good nutrition throughout the life span (5-1)
• Immunizations as part of a medical history (3-2)	• Physical inactivity and increased risk for diabetes, osteoporosis, and heart disease (4-1)	• Proper nutrition and disease prevention (5-1) • Role of dietary fiber in the prevention of digestive disorders and heart disease (5-2) • Saturated fats and the risk of heart disease (5-2) • Food allergies, intolerances, and foodborne illness (5-4)

Scope & Sequence

Content Strands	Chapter 6 Managing Weight and Body Composition	Chapter 7 Achieving Good Mental Health
Personal Health	• Using body mass index to determine a healthy weight range (6-1) • Health risks of overweight and underweight (6-1) • Healthful weight-management strategies (6-1)	• Signs of good mental health (7-1) • Recognizing physical, emotional, and self-fulfilling needs (7-1) • Understanding mental and emotional benefits of abstinence (7-1) • Analyzing learning styles (7-1) • Developing a positive identity (7-2) • Recognizing personal strengths and weaknesses (7-2) • Role of emotions on personal health (7-3)
Consumer and Community Health	• Recognizing fad diets (6-2) • Recognizing that people with eating disorders need help from professional health services (6-2) • Benefits and risks of dietary supplements (6-3)	• Mental health and the world's homeless population (7-1) • Importance of empathy toward others (7-2) • Contributing to the community (7-2)
Injury Prevention and Safety	• Risky weight-loss strategies (6-2) • Causes, symptoms, and treatment of eating disorders (6-2)	• Importance of safety to good mental health (7-1)
Alcohol, Tobacco, and Other Drugs	• Avoiding alcohol, tobacco, and other drugs during pregnancy (6-3)	• Avoiding risk behaviors (7-2)
Physical Activity and Nutrition	• Understanding calories and the energy equation (6-1) • The relationship among body composition, diet, and fitness (6-1) • The role of physical activity in weight management (6-1) • Essentials of nutrition for peak athletic performance (6-3) • Health benefits of vegetarianism (6-3)	• Engaging in physical activities to relieve negative feelings (7-4)
Environmental Health		• Influence of environment on personality (7-1)
Family Living	• The role of proper nutrition in promoting optimal health for both the baby and the mother (6-3) • Nutrition and prevention of birth defects (6-3) • Nutrition for infants and young children (6-3) • Nutrition and the aging process (6-3)	• Role of positive and negative feedback from your family and others (7-1) • Link between heredity and personality (7-1) • Forming meaningful relationships (7-2)
Individual Growth and Development	• Helping someone with an eating disorder (6-2)	• Maslow's hierarchy of human needs (7-1) • Personality and behavior (7-1) • Promoting positive self-esteem (7-2) • Positive self-talk and constructive criticism (7-2) • Identifying and expressing emotions (7-3) • Suggestions for managing anger (7-4)
Communicable and Chronic Disease	• Excess weight and the increased risk of cardiovascular disease, type 2 diabetes, cancer, and osteoarthritis (6-1) • Underweight and decreased immunity (6-1) • Vegetarianism and prevention of lifestyle diseases (6-3)	• Understanding how promoting mental/emotional health helps prevent disease (7-1)

Chapter 8 Managing Stress and Anxiety	Chapter 9 Mental and Emotional Problems	Chapter 10 Skills for Healthy Relationships
• Effects of stress on body systems (8-1) • Types of stressors (8-1) • Understanding the stages of the body's stress response (8-1) • Techniques for stress management (8-2) • Time management techniques (8-2) • Symptoms of anxiety and depression (8-3) • Being a resilient teen (8-4)	• Understanding mental disorders (9-1) • Types of mental disorders and their characteristics (9-1) • Recognizing warning signs of suicide (9-2) • Coping with emotional loss (9-4) • Coping with death (9-4) • Coping with disasters and crises (9-4)	• Building and maintaining healthy relationships (10-1) • Recognizing characteristics of healthy relationships (10-1) • Demonstrating character in relationships (10-1) • Effective communication skills (10-2) • Demonstrating empathy (10-2) • Demonstrating healthful strategies for resolving conflicts (10-3)
• Seeking help and support from community health resources (8-3)	• Evaluating self-help resources (9-3) • Types of mental health professionals (9-3) • Community and mental health services to cope with grief (9-4)	• Community relationships (10-1)
• Injuries as a physical stressor (8-2)	• Strategies for suicide prevention (9-2)	• Disapproval of bullying (10-2) • Avoiding unsafe situations (10-3) • Using peer mediation processes (10-3)
• Risks of substance abuse to relieve stress (8-1)	• Substance abuse and clinical depression (9-1)	
• Physical activity as an outlet for stress (8-2) • Benefits of nutritious foods to reduce stress (8-2)	• Eating disorders (9-1) • Importance of good nutrition and regular physical activity in coping with crises (9-4)	
• Environmental stressors (8-1)		
• Seeking support from your family during stressful times (8-2) • Life events that cause stress (8-2) • Being a supportive friend (8-3) • Getting help for anxiety and depression (8-3) • Factors that affect resiliency (8-4)	• Clinical depression and heredity (9-1) • Family history and suicide risk (9-2) • Helping others seek help (9-2)	• Understanding family relationships (10-1) • Using constructive feedback with family and friends (10-2)
• Recognizing signs of stress (8-1) • Time management and stress reduction (8-2) • Importance of relaxation and laughter (8-2) • Resiliency and protective factors (8-4)	• Understanding personality disorders (9-1) • Recognizing the warning signs of suicide (9-2) • Understanding when to seek professional help (9-3) • The grieving process (9-4)	• Understanding relationships (10-1) • Essentials of effective communication (10-2) • Developing good listening skills (10-2) • Understanding non-verbal communication (10-2) • Avoiding obstacles to effective communication (10-2)
• Stress as an asthma trigger (8-1) • Stress and the immune system (8-1)	• Post-traumatic stress syndrome (9-1) • Mood disorders (9-1)	

Scope & Sequence

Content Strands	Chapter 11 Family Relationships	Chapter 12 Peer Relationships
Personal Health	• Strengthening Family Relationships (11-1) • Coping with family changes (11-2) • Recognizing changes in family structures (11-2) • Resiliency and the family (11-2)	• Evaluate the influence of peers on health (12-1) • Forming healthy friendships (12-1) • Demonstrating refusal skills (12-2) • Understanding passive, aggressive, and assertive communication techniques (12-2) • Practicing healthful dating behaviors (12-3) • Setting dating guidelines (12-3) • Choosing abstinence as a responsible decision (12-4)
Consumer and Community Health	• Impact of families on society (11-1) • Community services for families in crisis (11-4) • Counseling and mediation options available (11-4)	• Negative aspects of cliques (12-1) • Positive peer pressure and contributing to the community (12-2)
Injury Prevention and Safety	• Applying strategies for avoiding violence within the family (11-3)	• Resisting peer pressure to take part in unsafe activities (12-2) • Avoiding risk situations on a date (12-3)
Alcohol, Tobacco, and Other Drugs	• Substance abuse and family stress (11-2) • AA and other support groups (11-3)	• Avoiding alcohol and other drugs (12-3)
Physical Activity and Nutrition		• Athletic activities as a dating option (12-3)
Environmental Health		
Family Living	• Importance of the family as a protective factor (11-1) • Primary functions of the family to meet physical, mental/emotional, and social needs (11-1) • Sharing culture and family traditions (11-1) • Dynamics of family roles and responsibilities (11-2) • Understanding separation and divorce (11-2) • Facts about child and spousal abuse (11-3) • Support groups for families (11-4)	• Consequences of sexual activity before marriage (12-4)
Individual Growth and Development	• Responsibilities of the children in the family (11-1) • Ways to cope with family stress (11-2) • Breaking the cycle of family violence (11-3)	• Kinds of peer relationships (12-1) • Using refusal skills (12-2) • Dating and learning interpersonal skills (12-3)
Communicable and Chronic Disease	• Serious illness and family stress (11-2)	• Consequences of sexually transmitted diseases and AIDS as a result of sexual activity (12-3)

Chapter 13 **Violence Prevention**	Chapter 14 **Personal Care and Healthy Behaviors**	Chapter 15 **Skeletal, Muscular, and Nervous System**
• Using self-defense strategies (13-1) • Recognizing threats to personal safety (13-3) • Preventing rape and date rape (13-4)	• Structure and function of the skin (14-1) • Acne and other skin problems (14-1) • Caring for teeth (14-2) • Caring for eyes (14-3) • Practicing health behaviors to care for eyes (14-3) • Practicing health behaviors to care for ears (14-4)	• Structure and function of the skeletal system (15-1) • Caring for the skeletal system (15-2) • Structure and function of the muscular system (15-3) • Care of the muscular system (15-3) • Functions and structure of the nervous system (15-4) • Practicing health behaviors to care for the nervous system (15-5)
• Safety in neighborhoods (13-1) • Safety in schools (13-2) • Peer mediation programs (13-2) • The problem of violence in society (13-3) • Violence in the media (13-3) • Help for abuse victims and abusers (13-4)	• Importance of early detection of skin problems (14-1) • Examining product claims (14-2) • Importance of dental examination (14-2) • Importance of eye examinations (14-3) • Controlling noise levels at public events (14-4)	• Screening for scoliosis (15-2)
• Taking precautions to protect safety (13-1) • Learning self-defense strategies (13-1) • Walking away from bullying (13-2) • Reducing risks of violence (13-2) • Influence of weapon availability on violence (13-3) • Influence of media on violence (13-3) • Escaping a sexual attack (13-3) • Avoiding gang-related violence (13-3)	• Using sunscreen and sun protection (14-1) • Wearing eye protection (14-2) • Controlling volume levels to prevent ear damage (14-4)	• Practicing behaviors to prevent osteoporosis (15-2) • Preventing repetitive motion injury (15-2) • Strengthening muscle tone to prevent injuries (15-3) • Preventing spinal cord injuries (15-5)
• Alcohol and drug abuse and increased violence (13-3) • Alcohol and drug abuse and date rape (13-4)		• Alcohol and drug use and effects on the nervous system (15-5)
• Martial arts and other self-defense classes (13-1)	• Physical activity and health (14-1) • Importance of nutrition and healthy skin (14-1)	• Importance of weight-bearing exercise throughout the life span (15-3) • Calcium intake and building bone mass (15-2)
	• Sun and environmental conditions on the skin (14-1)	
• Keeping homes safe (13-1) • Parental involvement and safety (13-2)	• Positive effects of good hygiene (14-1, 14-2)	
• Taking responsibility for personal safety (13-1) • Contributing to a safe school environment (13-2) • How to avoid abuse (13-4)	• Daily routine and personal health behaviors (14-1)	
	• Risks of hepatitis B, hepatitis C, and HIV through body piercing and tattooing (14-1) • Identifying early stages of melanoma (14-1)	• Understanding osteoporosis and scoliosis (15-2)

Scope & Sequence

Content Strands	Chapter 16 Cardiovascular and Respiratory System	Chapter 17 Digestive and Urinary Systems
Personal Health	• Functions and structure of the cardiovascular system (16-1) • Understanding the functions of the heart and blood (16-1) • Functions of the lymphatic system (16-1) • Understanding blood pressure (16-2) • Functions and structure of the respiratory system (16-3) • Problems of the respiratory system (16-3)	• Function and structure of the digestive system (17-1) • The organs that aid digestion (17-1) • Identify health behaviors on the digestive system (17-2) • Symptoms of gallstones, appendicitis and other digestive disorders (17-2) • Functions and structure of the urinary system (17-3) • Urinary tract and bladder infections (17-3) • Recognizing kidney problems (17-3)
Consumer and Community Health	• Evaluating health information sources (16-1) • Blood donation (16-2) • Warning signs that prompt individuals to seek care for respiratory problems (16-4)	• Community services available for chronic kidney disorders (17-3)
Injury Prevention and Safety		
Alcohol, Tobacco, and Other Drugs	• Avoiding tobacco and illegal drugs (16-2) • Smoking and the respiratory system (16-3) • Emphysema and tobacco smoke (16-3)	• Alcohol effects on the liver (17-2)
Physical Activity and Nutrition	• Good nutrition and care of your cardiovascular and lymphatic systems (16-1) • Iron deficiency and anemia (16-2)	• Good nutrition for a healthy digestive system (17-2) • Adding fiber to your diet (17-2) • Lactose intolerance (17-2)
Environmental Health	• Air pollution and effects on the respiratory system (16-3)	
Family Living	• Family history and cardiovascular health (16-1)	• Avoiding stress for healthy digestion (17-2) • Parental consent for organ and tissue donation (17-3)
Individual Growth and Development	• Congenital heart defects (16-2)	• Water intake and a healthy urinary system (17-3)
Communicable and Chronic Disease	• Heart disease and being overweight (16-2) • Understanding leukemia (16-2) • Immune deficiency, Hodgkin's disease, and tonsillitis (16-2) • Understanding asthma (16-4)	• Overcoming chronic kidney disease (17-3) • Organ donation (17-3)

Chapter 18
Endocrine and Reproductive Systems

- Structure and function of the endocrine system (18-1)
- Structure and function of the male reproductive system (18-2)
- Care for the male reproductive system (18-2)
- Understanding hernias and sterility (18-2)
- Functions and structure of the female reproductive system (18-3)
- Infertility and its causes (18-3)

- Testicular self-exam (18-2)
- Visiting a gynecologist for a pelvic exam (18-3)
- Breast self-exam (18-3)

- Wearing protective equipment (18-2)

- Drug use and risk of sterility (18-2)

- Balanced diet for healthy endocrine system (18-1)
- Physical activity to relieve stress (18-1)

- Advocating for self-exams for early detection (18-1, 18-2)
- Communicating with family about reproductive system concerns (18-3)

- Performing a testicular exam (18-2)
- Character and responsibilities of reproductive health (18-2)
- Process of menstruation (18-3)
- Performing breast self-examination (18-3)
- Physical and emotional problems relating to menstruation (18-3)

- Prostate and testicular cancer (18-2)
- Risks of ovarian cysts and cancers of the female reproductive system (18-3)
- Damaging effects of STDs on reproductive systems (18-2, 18-3)

Chapter 19
Prenatal Development and Birth

- Having a healthy pregnancy (19-1)
- Effects of medicines and drugs on pregnancy (19-1)
- Miscarriages and still births (19-1)
- Understanding and identifying genetic disorders (19-2)

- Choosing a health professional for prenatal care (19-1)
- Analyzing viewpoints on genetic testing (19-2)
- Health screenings and immunizations in childhood (19-4)

- Understanding fetal alcohol syndrome (19-1)
- Risk of tobacco and alcohol on fetal development (19-2)

- Role of nutrients on prenatal development (19-1)
- Importance of proper nutrition in promoting health of mother and baby (19-2)

- Influence of environmental hazards on prenatal development (19-2)

- Role of chromosomes and genes in heredity (19-3)
- Family counseling for genetic disorders (19-3)

- The process of prenatal development (19-1)
- How twins are formed (19-1)
- Stages of the birth process (19-1)
- Difference between dominant and recessive genes (19-2)
- Four stages of development from infancy to late childhood (19-4)
- Being a positive role model to children (19-4)

- Genetic and congenital disorders (19-3)

Chapter 20
Adolescence and the Life Cycle

- Developing personal identity (20-1)
- Using refusal skills/ abstinence from sexual activity (20-2)

- Peer influence on attitudes about sex (20-2)
- Role of culture, society and media in developing attitudes towards sex (20-2)
- Public health and programs for older adults (20-4)

- Choosing abstinence from tobacco, alcohol, and drugs (20-2)

- Maintaining health through physical activity for life (20-4)
- Importance of good nutrition throughout the life cycle (20-4)

- Family values as a protective factor against sexual activity (20-2)
- Role of parents, grandparents, and other family members in promoting healthy families (20-3)
- Marriage and parenthood (20-3)
- Responsibilities of parenthood (20-3)

- Physical change during puberty (20-1)
- Mental, emotional, and social maturation during puberty (20-1)
- Developmental tasks of adolescence (20-1)
- Forming a personal identity (20-1)
- Sexual activity and adolescence (20-2)
- Lifestyle behaviors that contribute to health throughout the lifespan (20-4)

- Avoiding STDs through abstinence (20-2)
- Understanding HIV/AIDS and other STDs (20-2)
- Research for disease prevention (20-4)

Scope & Sequence

Content Strands	Chapter 21 Tobacco	Chapter 22 Alcohol
Personal Health	• Harmful effects of using tobacco on body systems (21-2) • Strategies for preventing tobacco use (21-2) • Health benefits of quitting smoking (21-2)	• Recognizing factors that influence alcohol use (22-1) • Understanding alcohol tolerance and withdrawal (22-2) • Recognizing binge drinking and traits of the alcoholic (22-3)
Consumer and Community Health	• Tobacco warning labels (21-1) • Toward a smoke free-society (21-3) • Healthy People 2010 Goals (21-3)	• Teens and alcohol (22-1) • Analyzing alcohol advertising (22-1) • Drunk driving organizations MADD and SADD (22-2) • National health goals to reduce injury, death caused by alcohol-related influences (22-1)
Injury Prevention and Safety		• Danger of driving under the influence (22-2) • Avoiding mixing alcohol with other drugs (22-2)
Alcohol, Tobacco, and Other Drugs	• Understanding tobacco addiction (21-1) • Chemicals and other harmful substances in cigarettes (21-1) • Health risks of smokeless tobacco, pipes, and cigars (21-2) • Techniques for quitting smoking (21-2)	• Understanding the components and effects of alcohol (22-1) • Alcohol consumption and consequences (22-1) • Link between sexual activity and alcohol consumption (22-1) • Short term and long term effects of drinking (22-2) • The three stages of alcoholism (22-3)
Physical Activity and Nutrition	• Relationship between smoking and physical activity (21-1)	• Alcohol slows motor skills (22-1) • Participation in sports and zero tolerance (22-1)
Environmental Health	• Effects of smoking on nonsmokers (21-2) • Promoting a Smoke-free Environment (21-3)	
Family Living		• Fetal alcohol syndrome (22-3) • Alcohol and the family (22-3)
Individual Growth and Development	• Awareness of advertising and peer pressure to smoke (21-1) • Health risks from smoking during pregnancy (21-2) • Stress management and quitting smoking (21-2) • Health risks from smoking on children (21-3)	• Decision making skills and choosing not to drink (22-1) • Using refusal skills to turn down alcohol (22-2)
Communicable and Chronic Disease	• Cancer causing chemicals in cigarettes (21-1) • Link between smoking and chronic bronchitis, emphysema, and lung cancer (21-2) • Smoking and cardiovascular system diseases (21-2)	• Heavy alcohol use and liver conditions (22-2)

Chapter 23 Medicines and Drugs	Chapter 24 Communicable Diseases	Chapter 25 Sexually Transmitted Infections and HIV/AIDS
• Understanding the classification of medicines (23-1) • Medicines for pain relief and cardiovascular problems (23-1) • Physical dangers of substance abuse (23-2) • Medicinal uses of psychoactive drugs (23-4) • Committing to a drug-free life (23-4)	• Pathogens that cause communicable diseases (24-1) • Practice healthful behaviors that prevent communicable diseases (24-1) • Importance of lymphocytes in fighting pathogens (24-1) • Caring for the immune system (24-2) • The common cold and other respiratory infections (24-2) • Immunization and vaccines for disease prevention (24-3)	• Understanding the facts and myths about STDs (25-1) • Practicing abstinence from sexual activity before marriage (25-1) • Long-term and short-term effects of STDs (25-1)
• Medicine safety (23-1) • FDA testing process for new medicines (23-2) • Facts about teen drug use (23-2) • Drug testing debate (23-1) • Dangers of new designer drugs (23-3) • Illegal transport of drugs (23-3) • Drug-free school zones (23-4) • Community programs for drug dependency (26-4)	• Community immunizations (24-2)	• The current STD epidemic (25-1) • Rise in STDs among teens (25-1) • Social responsibilities of a person infected with an STD (25-2) • Seeking treatment for STDs (25-2) • Global HIV/AIDS statistics (25-4) • AIDS-related research and medications (25-4)
• Tips for safe use of medicines (23-1) • Drug use and risky behaviors (23-1) • Driving under the influence of drugs (23-3)	• Reducing risk of communicable disease (24-1)	
• Physiological dependence on medicines (23-1) • The costs of substance abuse to the individual, their family, and others (23-2) • The use of anabolic steroids and inhalants (23-3) • Marijuana and cannabis derivatives (23-3) • Types of psychoactive drugs (23-4) • Psychological and physiological effects of stimulants, depressants, narcotics and hallucinogens (23-4)	• Injection drug use and communicable diseases (24-1)	• Sharing needles from injection drug use and the risk of HIV infection (25-3)
• Drug use affects coordination (23-1) • Athletes and drug testing (23-3)	• Strengthening your immune system with proper nutrition (24-1) • Food safety procedures (24-1)	
	• Toxic dumping and the spread of pathogens (24-1) • Foodborne illness and the spread of pathogens into the environment (24-1)	• HIV as a retrovirus and the obstacles to finding a cure (25-3)
• Medicine safety at home (23-1)		• HIV transmission through pregnancy (25-3)
• Recognizing medicine misuse (23-1) • Understanding medicine labels (23-1) • Substance abuse and the developing fetus (23-2) • Physical and psychological effects of marijuana (23-3) • Resisting peer pressure to use drugs (23-4)	• Immunity and your body's barriers against disease (24-1) • Your body's passive and active immunity (24-2) • Daily measures to protect against disease (24-2)	• Practicing abstinence to avoid STDs (25-1) • Understanding the myths about HIV transmission (25-3) • Sexual intercourse as a high risk behavior (25-3) • Abstinence as protection against HIV infection (25-4)
• Vaccines, antitoxins, and disease prevention (23-1) • Cancer causing chemicals in marijuana (23-3) • Injection drug use and HIV/AIDS (23-4)	• Transmission of communicable disease (24-1) • Communicable diseases of the respiratory and nervous systems (24-2) • Symptoms and treatment of measles, mononucleosis, and hepatitis A, B and C (24-3) • Emerging infections (24-3)	• Symptoms and treatment for common STDs—human papillomavirus, chlamydia, gonorrhea, genital warts, herpes, trichomoniasis, and syphilis, (25-2) • Difference between HIV and AIDS (25-3) • Symptoms and stages of HIV infection (25-3)

Scope & Sequence

Content Strands	Chapter 26 Noncommunicable Diseases	Chapter 27 Injury Prevention and Safe Behaviors
Personal Health	• Making healthful choices to prevent cardiovascular disease (26-1) • Understanding types of cardiovascular diseases (26-1) • Warning signs of heart attack (26-1) • Differences between benign and malignant tumors (26-2)	• Understanding the accident chain (27-1) • Treatment for a muscle cramp while swimming (27-2) • Protecting yourself from heat exhaustion (27-2) • Protecting yourself from hypothermia (27-2) • Importance of wearing a safety belt (27-3)
Consumer and Community Health	• New diagnostic tools, surgical procedures, and treatments for cardiovascular disease (26-1) • Cancer treatments—surgery, radiation, and chemotherapy (26-2) • Role of society in providing equal rights for people with disabilities (26-4)	• Smoke alarms and fire extinguishers—consumer products for fire safety (27-1) • OSHA and workplace safety (27-1) • National services for weather emergencies and natural disasters (27-4)
Injury Prevention and Safety	• Sunscreen as protection from harmful ultraviolet rays (26-2) • Preventing injury to protect against developing osteoarthritis (26-3)	• Strategies for preventing fires, falls and electrical shock (27-1) • Strategies for preventing poisoning (27-1) • Firearm safety (27-1) • Vehicular and bicycle safety guidelines (27-3) • Preparing an emergency survival kit (27-4)
Alcohol, Tobacco, and Other Drugs	• Tobacco use and the risk of heart disease (26-1) • Smoking, a risk factor for cancer (26-2)	• Dangers of operating a vehicle under the influence of alcohol or other drugs (27-3)
Physical Activity and Nutrition	• Proper nutrition to prevent the risk of cardiovascular disease (26-1) • Cholesterol and atherosclerosis (26-1) • Cancer and dietary risk factors (26-2) • Sugar intake and diabetes (26-3)	• Safety for recreational activities and water sports (27-2) • Skating safety guidelines (27-3)
Environmental Health	• Environmental risk factors for cardiovascular disease (26-1) • Carcinogens and cancer (26-2) • Allergies as a result of environmental factors (26-3)	• Safety in weather emergencies and natural disasters (27-4)
Family Living	• Heredity as a risk factor for cardiovascular disease (26-1) • Genetic disorders that induce mental retardation (26-4)	• Family fire safety guidelines (27-1)
Individual Growth and Development	• Reducing the risk of cancer with a healthy lifestyle (26-2) • Managing asthma (26-3) • Physical and mental challenges of living with disabilities (26-4)	• Influence of emotional state on driving (27-3) • Protecting yourself from road rage (27-3)
Communicable and Chronic Disease	• Understanding types of cardiovascular disease (26-1) • Types of cancers (26-2) • STDs and cancer risks (26-2) • Types of diabetes (26-3) • Understanding arthritis (26-3)	• Techniques for preventing chronic conditions related to computer tasks (27-1) • Disease causing pathogens in natural bodies of water (27-2)

Chapter 28
First Aid and Emergencies

- Treatment strategies for bleeding and burns (28-1)
- First aid for shock (28-2)
- Treating muscle, joint, and bone injuries (28-3)
- First aid for fainting and concussion (28-3)
- How to care for animal bites (28-3)
- First aid for nosebleeds (28-3)
- First aid for poisoning (28-4)
- First aid for snakebites and insect stings (28-4)

- Contacting a poison control center (28-4)

- Steps to take in an emergency situation (28-1)
- Understanding the chain of survival (28-2)

- First aid for injuries sustained during physical activity (28-3)

- Learning CPR for adults, children, and infants (28-2)
- How to help an adult, child, or infant who is choking (28-2)

- The importance of using universal precautions to prevent the spread of disease when providing first aid (28-1)

Chapter 29
Environmental Health

- Health concerns associated with air pollution (29-1)

- Potential dangers of hazardous wastes (29-2)
- Impact of population growth and urban development (29-2)
- Contamination of drinking water supplies (29-2)
- Social responsibility of conservation (29-3)
- Guidelines for community recycling (29-3)

- Safe disposal of hazardous wastes (29-2)
- Increased safety as a result of community planning (29-2)

- Cigarette smoke as a source of air pollution (29-1)

- Increase in level of physical activity as a result of community planning (29-2)

- Strategies for reducing air pollution (29-1)
- Disposal of solid wastes (29-2)
- Strategies for reducing land and water pollution (29-2)
- Strategies for precycling (29-3)
- Environmental benefits of recycling (29-3)

- Guidelines for conserving natural resources in the home (29-3)

- Becoming involved in protecting the environment (29-3)

- Relationship between air pollution and chronic respiratory disorders (29-1)
- Relationship between nuclear wastes and the development of cancer and genetic abnormalities (29-2)

Health Resources

Action on Smoking and Health
2013 H Street NW
Washington, DC 20006

Administration on Aging
330 Independence Avenue SW
Washington, DC 20201

**Al-Anon/Alateen Family
Group Headquarters**
1600 Corporate Landing Parkway
Virginia Beach, VA 23454-5617

**Alcoholics Anonymous
Central Office**
475 Riverside Drive 11th floor
New York, NY 10010-1501

**American Academy of Pediatrics
National Headquarters**
141 Northwest Point Road
Elk Grove Village, IL 60007-1098

**American Automobile Association
Foundation for Traffic Safety
Administrative Office**
1440 New York Avenue NW
Suite 201
Washington, DC 20005

**American Cancer Society
National Headquarters**
1599 Clifton Road NE
Atlanta, GA 30329

American Counseling Association
5999 Stevenson Avenue
Alexandria, VA 22304

American Dental Association
211 East Chicago Avenue
Chicago, IL 60611

**American Heart Association
National Center**
7272 Greenville Avenue
Dallas, TX 75231-4596

**American Society of
Nutritional Sciences**
9650 Rockville Pike
Suite 4500
Bethesda, MD 20814

American Lung Association
61 Broadway, Gth floor
New York, NY 10006

American Medical Association
515 North State Street
Chicago, IL 60610

American Optometric Association
243 North Lindbergh Boulevard
St. Louis, MO 63141

American Society of Safety Engineers
1800 East Oakton Street
Des Plaines, IL 60018-2187

**Asthma and Allergy Foundation of
America (AAFA)**
1233 20th Street, NW
Suite 402
Washington, DC 20036

**Centers for Disease Control and
Prevention (CDC)**
1600 Clifton Road
Atlanta, GA 30333

Council on Environmental Quality
722 Jackson Place NW
Washington, DC 20503

**Department of Health and Human
Services**
**SAMHSA's National Clearinghouse for
Alcohol and Drug Information**
Information Specialist
P.O. Box 2345
Rockville, MD 20847-2345

**ERIC—Clearinghouse on Teacher
Education—Health Education**
1307 New York Avenue, NW Suite 300
Washington, DC 20005-4701

**Juvenile Diabetes Research Foundation
International**
120 Wall Street
New York, NY 10005-4001

**March of Dimes Birth Defects
Foundation**
1275 Mamaroneck Avenue
White Plains, NY 10605

**Mothers Against Drunk Driving
Headquarters**
511 East John Carpenter Freeway
Suite 700
Irving, TX 75062

National Disability Sports Alliance
25 West Independence Way
Kingston, RI 02881

**National Cancer Institute (NCI)—
Public Inquiries Office**
6116 Executive Boulevard, MSCP322
Suite 3036A
Bethesda, MD 20892-8322

National Center for Health Statistics
Centers for Disease Control and
Prevention
6525 Belcrest Road
Hyattsville, MD 20782

**National Council on Alcoholism and
Drug Dependence**
20 Exchange Place
Suite 2902
New York, NY 10005

National Dairy Council
10255 West Higgins Road
Suite 900
Rosemont, IL 60018-5606

**National Fire Protection Association
(NFPA)**
1 Batterymarch Park
Quincy, MA 02269-9101

**National Health Information Center
(NHIC)**
Referral Specialist
P.O. Box 1133
Washington, DC 20013-1133

**National Institute of Arthritis and
Musculoskeletal and Skin Diseases
(NIAMS) Information Clearinghouse**
National Institutes of Health
1 AMS Circle
Bethesda, MD 20892-3675

**The National Institute of Allergy and
Infectious Diseases**
NIAID Office of Communications and
Public Liaison
Building 31, Room 7A-50
31 Center Drive MSC 2520
Bethesda, MD 20892-2520

**National Institute of Mental Health
(NIMH)**
Public Inquiries
6001 Executive Boulevard
Room 8184, MSC 9663
Bethesda, MD 20892-9663

National Mental Health Association
1021 Prince Street
Alexandria, VA 22314-2971

National Parents-Teachers Association
Drug and Alcohol Abuse Prevention
Project
330 North Wabash Ave., Suite 2100
Chicago, IL 60611-3690

National Safety Council
1121 Spring Lake Drive
Itasca, IL 60143-3201

**National Society for Crippled Children
and Adults**
230 West Monroe Street
Suite1800
Chicago, IL 60606

National Wildlife Federation
8925 Leesburg Pike
Vienna, VA 22180

Office on Smoking and Health
Centers for Disease Control and
Prevention
Publications
Mail Stop K-50
4770 Buford Highway, NE
Atlanta, GA 30341-3717

Sierra Club
85 Second Street
Second Floor
San Francisco, CA 94105-3441

Students Against Destructive Decisions
255 Main Street
P.O. Box 800
Marlboro, MA 01752

United Cerebral Palsy, Inc.
1660 L Street, NW
Suite 700
Washington, DC 20036

U.S. Food and Drug Administration
Office of Consumer Affairs
5600 Fishers Lane
Rockville, MD 20857-001

**USDA Food and Nutrition Information
and Education Resources Center**
National Agricultural Library,
U.S. Department of Agriculture
10301 Baltimore Avenue,
Room 304
Beltsville, MD 20705

Wheelchair Sports USA
3595 East Fountain Blvd., Suite L-1
Colorado Springs, CO 80910-1740

Glencoe Health

NINTH EDITION

Mary Bronson Merki, Ph.D.

Don Merki, Ph.D.

Contributing Authors

Michael J. Cleary, Ed.D.

Kathleen Middleton, M.S.

New York, New York   Columbus, Ohio   Chicago, Illinois   Peoria, Illinois   Woodland Hills, California

About the Authors

Mary Bronson Merki, Ph.D., has taught health education in grades K–12, as well as health education methods classes at the undergraduate and graduate levels. As Health Education Specialist for the Dallas School District, Dr. Bronson Merki developed and implemented a district-wide health education program, *Skills for Living,* which was used as a model by the state education agency. She has assisted school districts throughout the country in developing local health education programs. She is also the author of Glencoe's *Teen Health* textbook series.

Michael J. Cleary, Ed.D., C.H.E.S., is Professor and School Health Education Coordinator at Slippery Rock University. Dr. Cleary taught at Evanston Township High School in Evanston, Illinois, and later became the Lead Teacher Specialist at the McMillen Center for Health Education in Fort Wayne, Indiana. Dr. Cleary has published and presented widely on curriculum development and portfolio assessment in K–12 health education. Dr. Cleary is the co-author of *Managing Your Health: Assessment for Action.*

Don Merki, Ph.D., has taught health education for 35 years. He teaches at the University of New Mexico, featuring classes in substance abuse, mental health, adopting a healthy lifestyle, HIV/AIDS and sexually transmitted diseases, and stress and life management skills. He has taught students from broad cultural and ethnic backgrounds from elementary to graduate school. Dr. Merki recently served as a consultant to the School of Family Medicine's Alcohol and Substance Abuse Prevention Program at the University of New Mexico, Albuquerque.

Kathleen Middleton, M.S., C.H.E.S., is a nationally recognized expert in health education, curriculum development, and assessment. Kathleen serves as the health education consultant for the CCSSO-SCASS Health Education Assessment Project. She has more than 25 years experience in health education, including teaching at the middle school, high school, and college levels. Ms. Middleton is the author of *Comprehensive School Health Challenge.* She has served as administrator for Health and Physical Education for the Monterey County Office of Education.

Glencoe

The McGraw-Hill Companies

Printed in the United States of America.

Send all inquiries to:
Glencoe/McGraw-Hill
21600 Oxnard Street, Suite 500
Woodland Hills, California 91367

ISBN: 0-07-826326-3 (Student Edition)
ISBN: 0-07-826327-1 (Teacher Wraparound Edition)

1 2 3 4 5 6 7 8 9 0   071   08 07 06 05 04 03

Health Consultants

UNIT 1: A Healthy Foundation

Kristen D. Fink, M.A.,
Executive Director, Community of Caring
Arlington, Virginia

Betty M. Hubbard, Ed.D., C.H.E.S.
Professor of Health Education
Department of Health Sciences
University of Central Arkansas
Conway, Arkansas

UNIT 2: Physical Activity and Nutrition

Roberta L. Duyff, R.D., C.F.C.S.
Food and Nutrition Education Consultant
St. Louis, Missouri

Tinker D. Murray, Ph.D.
Professor and Coordinator of Exercise and Sports
    Science Program
Southwest Texas State University
San Marcos, Texas

Don Rainey, M.S.
Instructor, Coordinator of Physical Fitness
    and Wellness Program
Southwest Texas State University
San Marcos, Texas

UNIT 3: Mental and Emotional Health

Lee C. Ancona, Ph.D.
Health Educator
Lamar High School
Arlington, Texas

Betty M. Hubbard, Ed.D., C.H.E.S.
Professor of Health Education
Department of Health Sciences
University of Central Arkansas
Conway, Arkansas

Peter T. Whelley
Adjunct Faculty
University System of New Hampshire
Moultonsborough, New Hampshire

Gordon D. Wrobel, Ph.D.
Consultant, National Association of School
    Psychologists
Bethesda, Maryland

UNIT 4: Promoting Safe and Healthy Relationships

Cheryl Page, C.H.E.S.
Health Education Specialist
Salem Keizer Public Schools
Salem, Oregon

Jeanne Title
Coordinator, Prevention Education
Napa County Office of Education and
    Napa Valley Unified School District
Napa, California

UNIT 5: Personal Care and Body Systems

Patrick M. Forese, M.S.
Allied Health Educator
Slippery Rock University
Grove City High School
Grove City, Pennsylvania

UNIT 6: Growth and Development

Stephanie S. Allen, M.S., R.N.
Senior Lecturer, Baylor University
Louise Herrington School of Nursing
Dallas, Texas

Marilyn Hightower, M.S.N.
Lecturer, Baylor University
Louise Herrington School of Nursing
Dallas, Texas

Alice B. Pappas, Ph.D., R.N.
Associate Dean/Associate Professor
Baylor University
Louise Herrington School of Nursing
Dallas, Texas

Health Consultants (continued)

UNIT 7: Tobacco, Alcohol, and Other Drugs

Nancy S. Maylath, M.P.H., H.S.D.
Director, Student Wellness Office
Purdue University
West Lafayette, Indiana

Jeanne Title
Coordinator, Prevention Education
Napa County Office of Education and
     Napa Valley Unified School District
Napa, California

UNIT 8: Diseases and Disorders

Beverly J. Bradley, Ph.D., R.N., C.H.E.S
Assistant Clinical Professor
University of California, San Diego
San Diego, California

Michael T. Brady, M.D.
Professor and Vice-Chair
Department of Pediatrics
Children's Hospital, Columbus
The Ohio State University
Columbus, Ohio

UNIT 9: Injury Prevention and Environmental Health

David A. Sleet, Ph.D.
Associate Director for Science
Division of Unintentional Injury Prevention
Centers for Disease Control and Prevention
     (CDC)
Atlanta, Georgia

Teacher Reviewers

Pamela R. Connolly
Curriculum Coordinator for Health and
     Physical Education
Diocese of Pittsburgh
North Catholic High School
Pittsburgh, Pennsylvania

Jill English, Ph.D., C.H.E.S.
Assistant Professor
California State University, Fullerton
Fullerton, California

Debra C. Harris, Ph.D.
Department Chair, Health and Physical
     Education
West Linn High School
West Linn, Oregon

Pamela Hoalt, Ph.D.
Professor of Health Education
Malone College
Canton, Ohio

Michael Rulon
Health/Physical Education Teacher
Johnson Junior High School
Adjunct Faculty, Laramie County
     Community College
Cheyenne, Wyoming

Linda B. Salzman
Health Education Consultant and Trainer
Wilmington, North Carolina

Joan Stear
Health and Dance Educator
West Clermont Institute of Performing Arts
Glen Este High School
Cincinnati, Ohio

Contents

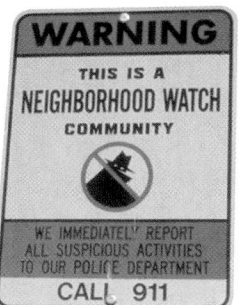

UNIT 5 Personal Care and Body Systems

UNIT 6   Growth and Development

Health Skills Activity

Hands-On Health ACTIVITY

Real-Life Application

Exploring Issues

1

Lessons	Standards		Features
	National	**State/Local**	
1 **Your Health and Wellness** *pages 4–9*	National Health Education Standards **1.1, 1.4, 2.1, 3.4, 6.4**		**Health Skills Activity** • Health for All *(Goal Setting)*, page 8
2 **Promoting a Healthy Lifestyle** *pages 10–16*	National Health Education Standards **1.1, 1.2, 3.1, 4.2, 4.3**		**Hands-On Health** • Health Influences *(Analyzing Influences)*, page 15
3 **Your Behavior and Reducing Health Risks** *pages 17–21*	National Health Education Standards **3.3, 7.4**		**Real-Life Application** • Analyzing Risk Behaviors *(Advocacy)*, page 19

Reproducible Resources	Assessment	Technology
Student Activity Workbook for use with each chapter 📁 Concept Mapping Activity 1 📁 Cross-Curriculum 1 📁 Current Health Issues 1 📁 Guided Reading Activities 1 📁 Lesson Plan 1 📁 Parent Letter and Activities 1 📁 Reteaching Activity 1	📁 Lesson Quiz 1	🕹 Transparency 1 💿 TeacherWorks® 🖥 Internet Activities
📁 Concept Mapping Activity 2 📁 Decision-Making Activity 1 📁 Guided Reading Activities 2 📁 Lesson Plan 2 📁 Reteaching Activity 2	📁 Lesson Quiz 2	🕹 Transparency 2 💿 TeacherWorks®
📁 Enrichment Activity 1 📁 Concept Mapping Activity 3 📁 Guided Reading Activities 3 📁 Health Lab 1 📁 Lesson Plan 3 📁 Reteaching Activity 3	📁 Lesson Quiz 3	🕹 Transparency 3 💿 TeacherWorks®

OUT OF TIME

If time does not permit teaching the entire chapter, use:
- Figure 1.1, p. 5
- Health Skills Activity, p. 8
- Hands-On Health, p. 15
- Real-Life Application, p. 19

Language Diversity

- 🎧 English Audio CD Program
- 🎧 Spanish Audio CD Program
- 📁 English Summaries, Quizzes, and Activities
- 📁 Spanish Summaries, Quizzes, and Activities
- 📁 Spanish Parent Letters and Activities

End of Chapter Assessment

Blackline Masters

- 📁 Chapter 1 Test
- 📁 Performance Assessment Activity 1

Technology

- 💿 Vocabulary PuzzleMaker
- 📼 MindJogger Videoquiz
- 💿 **Exam***View*® Pro Testmaker

Professional Health Series

Dealing with Sensitive Issues
Planning a Coordinated School Health Program
Promoting Character Education
Home, School, and Community Involvement

Key to Ability Levels

Teaching strategies that appear throughout the chapter have been identified by one of the following codes to give teachers an idea of their suitability for students of varying learning styles and abilities.

L1 Strategies should be within the ability range of all students. Full class participation is often required. Teacher direction is usually needed.

L2 Strategies are designed for average to above-average students or for small groups. Some teacher direction is needed.

L3 Strategies are designed for students able and willing to work independently. Minimal teacher direction is needed.

ELL Strategies should be within the ability range of students learning the English language.

▭ Block scheduling strategies are useful in a block scheduling format.

Living a Healthy Life

CHAPTER OVERVIEW

Chapter 1 defines *health* and discusses major influences on an individual's health. Personal responsibility is stressed as a primary means of promoting health.

Lesson 1 Health is a combination of physical, mental/emotional, and social well-being. Individuals make daily choices that affect their health, positively or negatively. People who are health literate are able to understand their options and make wise choices.

Lesson 2 The three elements of health—physical, mental/emotional, and social—are interconnected and should be kept in balance. Influences on health include heredity, environment, attitude, behavior, media, and technology.

Lesson 3 To take responsibility for their own health, teens can become aware of risk behaviors in their lives and then make any necessary changes.

Health Skills Features

- Health Skills Activity (*Goal Setting*), p. 8
- Hands-On Health (*Analyzing Influences*), p. 15
- Real-Life Application (*Advocacy*), p. 19

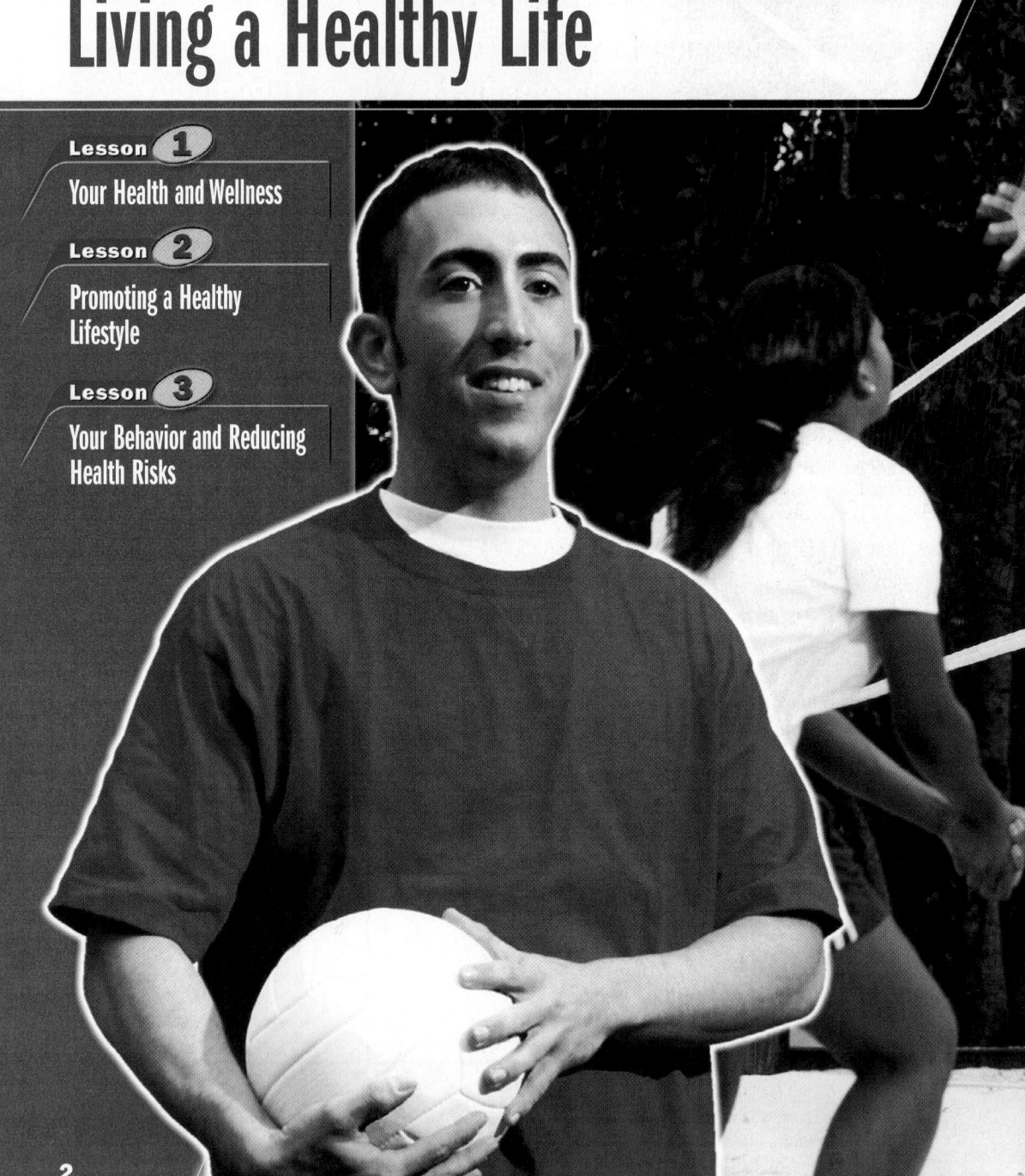

Chapter 1

Living a Healthy Life

Lesson 1
Your Health and Wellness

Lesson 2
Promoting a Healthy Lifestyle

Lesson 3
Your Behavior and Reducing Health Risks

2

MEETING STUDENT DIVERSITY

Language Diversity Use the following suggestions to help students who have difficulty with English:

- Pair English language learners with native speakers of English who can restate the Chapter Summary in language that helps students comprehend important concepts.

- 🎧 Direct auditory learners or those students with language diversity to the *Glencoe Health Audio CD Program*. Available in English and Spanish, this component provides an audio and written summary of the chapter.

- Use photographs, drawings, or magazine clippings to help students visualize the important concepts of the chapter.

Myth or Fact?

How Much Do You Know About Health and Healthy Behaviors?

Health information—and misinformation—is everywhere. Which of these statements do you think is a fact? A myth? Read the statements below and record your opinion, *Myth* or *Fact,* for each.

1. Teens need more sleep than adults do.

2. Being an effective communicator can improve your overall health.

3. The health decisions you make as a teen have little impact on your health as an adult.

4. Two 10-minute walks provide nearly the same health benefits as a continuous 20-minute walk.

5. Water is a nutrient.

6. Setting goals can only help you achieve long-term accomplishments, such as establishing a career.

7. Acne flare-ups are a result of eating chocolate and greasy foods.

8. Tanning beds are safe because they use UVA light, which doesn't cause burns.

9. All stress is negative and should be avoided.

10. The relationships you have with family, friends, and peers do not affect your physical health.

Keep your responses for review later in the chapter and throughout the course. Periodically review your answers, and change or modify them on the basis of what you have learned.

Quick *Write*

Using Visuals. Each day you make decisions that affect your health. What you choose to eat, your level of physical activity, how you manage stress, and the types of relationships you have all influence your overall feeling of well-being. Make a list of five decisions you've made this week that have had a positive effect on your health.

3

Chapter 1

INTRODUCING THE CHAPTER

Myth or Fact?

1. Fact

2. Fact

3. Myth: Teens who practice healthful behaviors (choosing nutritious foods and getting regular physical activity, for example) lower the risk of many diseases, both now and in the future.

4. Fact

5. Fact

6. Myth: Goal setting can help people achieve both short- and long-term goals.

7. Myth: Food plays no role in triggering acne or making it worse.

8. Myth: UVA damages skin and increases the risk of cancer.

9. Myth: Some stress energizes people and helps them strive to reach goals.

10. Myth: Relationships do affect physical health.

Quick *write*

Using Visuals Have volunteers describe the teens in the picture and discuss what makes them look healthy. Ask: What decisions do you think they have made that had positive effects on their health?

Your Health and Wellness

①FOCUS

 QUICK START Give students two minutes to complete the Quick Start sentence. Then have students meet in groups to compare and discuss their responses. Ask each group to compose one ending that best completes the sentence, and let the groups share their sentences with the rest of the class.

TYING TO PRIOR KNOWLEDGE

Refer to the Quick Start assignment, and point out that students already have some clear ideas about good health. Tell them they will explore that topic more thoroughly as they study Chapter 1.

Health Skills Features

"Health for All," p. 8

GOAL SETTING

INTRODUCING VOCABULARY

- Write these words on the board: *heal, well, prevent, educate, literate*. Ask how the words on the board relate to the vocabulary terms. Then have students use the Glossary to check the definition of each term.

- Ask students to complete the Chapter 1 Study Guide in the *Student Activity Workbook*.

Lesson 1

Your Health and Wellness

VOCABULARY
health
wellness
prevention
health education
Healthy People 2010
health literacy

YOU'LL LEARN TO
- Relate the nation's health goals and objectives in *Healthy People 2010* to individual, family, and community health.
- Develop criteria for evaluating health information.
- Discuss the importance of health literacy for achieving and maintaining good health.

 QUICK START On a sheet of paper, complete the following statement:
When you have good health, you . . .

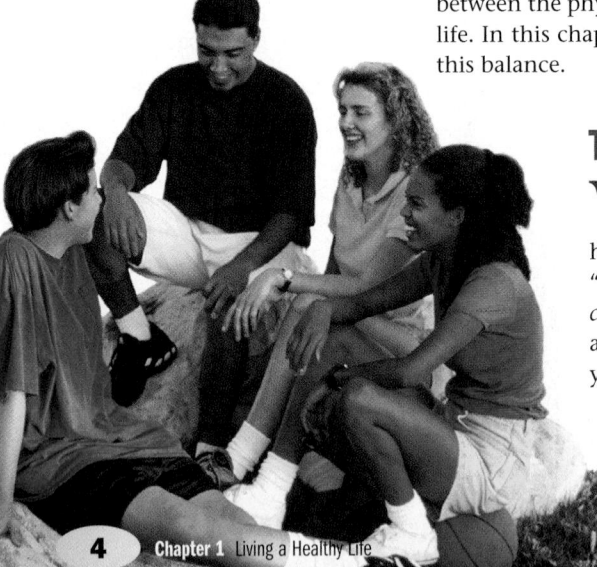

Spending time with friends is an important part of health. *Give an example of how relationships can have a positive impact on health.*

4 Chapter 1 Living a Healthy Life

Suppose someone asks whether you are healthy. How would you answer? Would you consider only your physical health? For example, would you think of how often you are sick? Throughout this course, you will see that health is much more than just the absence of disease. A state of well-being comes from a balance between the physical, mental/emotional, and social aspects of your life. In this chapter you will look at ways to achieve and maintain this balance.

The Importance of Good Health

What is your usual response to the question, "How are you?" A true description of your health would require much more than a simple "fine" or "okay." **Health** is *the combination of physical, mental/emotional, and social well-being*. It is not an absolute state. Being healthy doesn't mean that you will never be sick or that you will be guaranteed a position on the basketball team. Instead, being healthy means striving to be the best *you* can be at any given time.

Lesson 1 Resources

Teacher Classroom Resources

📁 Concept Mapping Activity 1
📁 Cross-Curriculum 1
📁 Current Health Issues 1
📁 Guided Reading Activities 1
📁 Lesson Plan 1
📁 Lesson Quiz 1

📁 Parent Letter and Activities 1
📁 Reteaching Activity 1
Student Activity Workbook
📁 Applying Health Skills 1
📁 Chapter 1 Study Guide
Multimedia
🖐 Transparency 1

The Health Continuum

Health is dynamic, or subject to constant change. For example, you might be the top performer for your basketball team on Tuesday and sick in bed with the flu on Wednesday. Think of your health at any moment as a point along a *continuum*. This continuum spans the complete spectrum of health from chronic disease and premature death to a high level of health. Along the continuum are many points where your health could be located at any given time. This point changes from day to day and year to year.

Changes along the continuum may occur suddenly, such as when you get injured playing a sport. At this time of your life, it's even common for your emotions to shift suddenly from moment to moment. Knowing that these emotional shifts are normal can help you maintain a healthful balance as you move along the continuum.

Changes may also be so gradual that you're not even aware that you're moving from one side of the continuum to the other. Take a look at **Figure 1.1.** Where do you fit on the health continuum right now? Where would you like to be in a month? A year?

A person with a balanced life is said to have a high degree of **wellness**, *an overall state of well-being, or total health*. It comes from a way of living each day that includes making decisions and practicing behaviors that are based on sound health knowledge and healthful attitudes. Achieving wellness requires an ongoing, lifelong commitment to physical, mental/emotional, and social health.

When you feel your best, you will perform at your best. *How might maintaining a high level of wellness help you reach your goals?*

Chapter 1 • Lesson 1

② TEACH

Discussing

Let students discuss how they usually respond when someone asks, "How are you?" Ask: How much does your response tell about your health? **L1**

VISUAL LEARNING

Figure 1.1 Guide students in studying and discussing Figure 1.1. Begin by explaining that a continuum depicts opposites at each end. In this continuum, the opposite ends represent premature death and a high level of health. Graduated states of health between those two extremes are represented in the center of the continuum. Ask:

- What would you conclude about the health of a person who ranks at the midpoint of this continuum?
- What advice would you give to a person who ranks to the left of the midpoint? Near the right end of the continuum?
- Does a person ever reach the right of the continuum (high level of health) and stay there? Explain your answer.

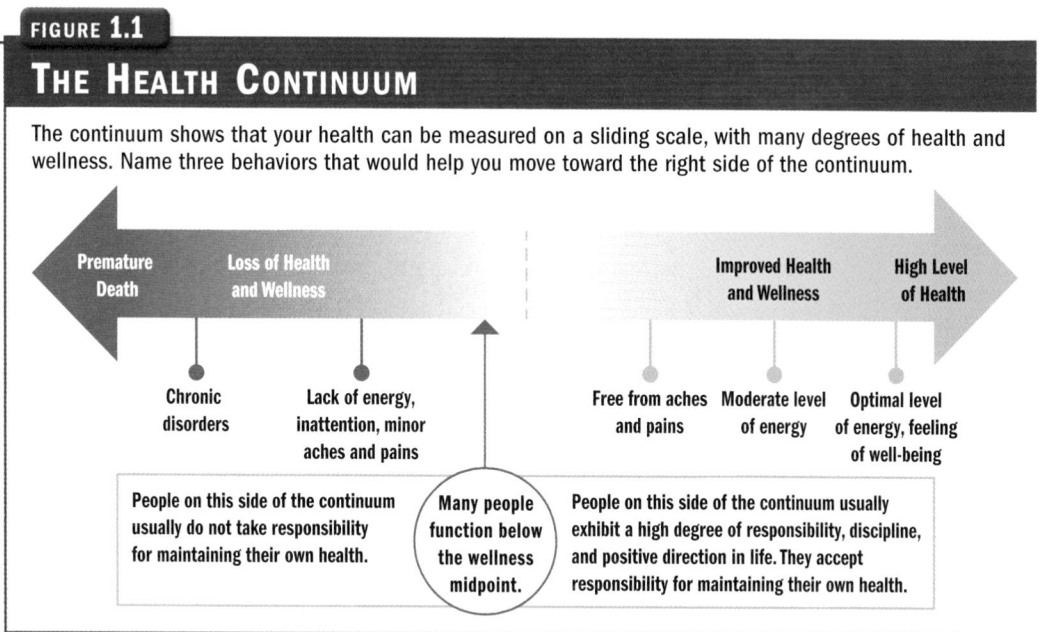

FIGURE 1.1

THE HEALTH CONTINUUM

The continuum shows that your health can be measured on a sliding scale, with many degrees of health and wellness. Name three behaviors that would help you move toward the right side of the continuum.

| Premature Death | Loss of Health and Wellness | | | Improved Health and Wellness | High Level of Health |

| Chronic disorders | Lack of energy, inattention, minor aches and pains | | Free from aches and pains | Moderate level of energy | Optimal level of energy, feeling of well-being |

People on this side of the continuum usually do not take responsibility for maintaining their own health.

Many people function below the wellness midpoint.

People on this side of the continuum usually exhibit a high degree of responsibility, discipline, and positive direction in life. They accept responsibility for maintaining their own health.

Promoting Coordinated School Health

The Purpose The primary purpose of a coordinated school health program is to help your community's school tap into a system of health programming already in place. Most schools have health instruction and physical education classes, counselors, nurses, substance-abuse prevention programs, and programs linked with state and local health agencies. Where is your school or school system in terms of developing a coordinated school health program? For help in developing such a program or in strengthening an existing program, consult *Planning a Coordinated School Health Program.*

Cooperative Learning

Divide students into cooperative groups, and have the members of each group discuss the lifestyle factors that promote good health. Ask: How does each behavior improve physical, mental/emotional, and social well-being?

ACTIVE READING

Study Skills

Explain that previewing a lesson is one part of reading carefully and thoughtfully. One part of previewing is glancing through the lesson, reading the main headings and subheadings as well as the captions for pictures and graphs. Another part of previewing is reading the review questions before reading the chapter. Tell students that review questions provide clues to the most important facts and ideas; students should keep these questions in mind as they read and take notes about the lesson. When they finish reading a lesson, students can use the questions to see how fully they recall the most important concepts presented. For more strategies, see the Guided Reading Activities booklet in the TCR.

Reinforcing Concepts

Guide students in discussing the preventive measures identified in the text. Then have volunteers suggest other specific actions teens can take to help prevent illness and injury.

Research has shown that teens need more sleep than adults do. Establishing a regular sleep schedule can help you get enough sleep each night. *What are two other actions you can take to ensure that you get an adequate amount of sleep?*

Promoting Your Health

The decisions you make each day have an impact on your health. What you choose to wear, eat, and do can have personal health consequences that you may or may not have considered. For example, not wearing the proper safety gear when participating in a physical activity increases the chances of serious injury in the event of an accident. Eating high-calorie snacks can result in unhealthful weight gain. Making responsible decisions about health and developing health-promoting habits is crucial to achieving and maintaining wellness.

Lifestyle Factors

Experts have identified habits that affect people's overall health, happiness, and *longevity*—or how long they live. These habits, or *lifestyle factors,* are personal behaviors related to the way a person lives. They help determine his or her level of health. Certain lifestyle factors are linked to specific diseases—for example, smoking and lung cancer. Other lifestyle factors promote good health. These include:

▶ getting 8 to 10 hours of sleep each night.

▶ starting each day with a healthy breakfast.

▶ eating a variety of nutritious foods each day.

▶ being physically active for at least 20 minutes a day, three or more days a week.

▶ maintaining a healthy weight.

▶ avoiding tobacco, alcohol, and other drugs.

▶ abstaining from sexual activity before marriage.

▶ managing stress.

▶ maintaining positive relationships.

▶ practicing safe behaviors to prevent injuries.

Fitting these health-promoting lifestyle factors into your life will help ensure a high level of wellness.

Wellness and Prevention

A key to your wellness is **prevention**—*practicing health and safety habits to remain free of disease and injury*. Wearing safety belts, applying sunscreen, and avoiding unsafe areas are just a few examples of preventive measures. What other actions could you take to prevent illness and injury?

6 **Chapter 1** Living a Healthy Life

School to Work

Performance on the Job Have students work individually or in pairs to brainstorm the possible effects of health and wellness choices on an employee's performance. For example, how might job performance be affected by high energy or low energy, by an optimistic outlook or a pessimistic outlook, by comfort or discomfort in social settings?

What personal choices affect these factors? Ask students to list their examples under one of these three heads: *Physical Health, Mental/Emotional Health, Social Health.* Then let students meet in groups to discuss how each factor on their lists might relate to specific occupations such as postal worker, construction worker, teacher, and sales clerk.

The Importance of Health Education

Health is critical to quality of life. Learning how to become and stay healthy should be a top priority. That's why **health education**—*the providing of accurate health information to help people make healthy choices*—is important. The goal of health education is to give people the tools they need to help them live long, energetic, and productive lives.

The Nation's Health Goals

Health education affects more than just students. *Healthy People 2010* is *a nationwide health promotion and disease prevention plan designed to serve as a guide for improving the health of all people in the United States.* The plan, which is revised every 10 years, aims to promote health and prevent illness, disability, and early death.

GOALS OF *HEALTHY PEOPLE 2010*

Healthy People 2010 has established two main goals for the future: increase quality and years of healthy life for all Americans and remove health differences that result from factors such as gender, race, education, disability, and location. To reach these goals, individuals, families, and communities must work together.

A nation's health depends on the health of the individuals in that nation. Studies have shown, for example, that as people become more educated, the general health of a population improves. Therefore, to benefit the health of the larger community, it is up to each individual to be the best he or she can be. Achieving wellness empowers each individual to improve the community in which he or she lives. This, of course, can be extended to global health issues. As more individuals take charge of their own wellness, the more global health will improve. Individuals, families, and communities each have a role to play:

▶ **Individuals** can take an active role in their own health. You can learn to make informed decisions, master skills that enable you to apply your decisions, access reliable health care information and services, and promote the health of others. The information in this book will help you put many of these strategies into action.

▶ **Families** can shape the attitudes and beliefs that result in healthful behaviors. Parents and guardians play an important role in meeting the nation's health goals when they teach their children the values and skills necessary to maintain good health.

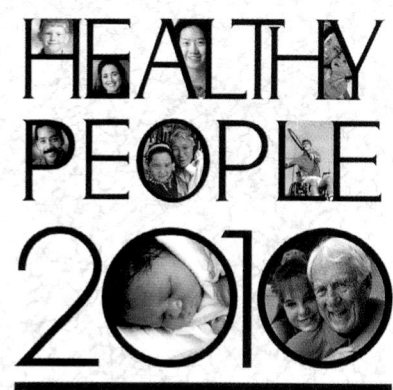

HEALTHY PEOPLE 2010

Understanding and Improving Health

▲ *Healthy People 2010* **is a plan designed to promote the health of all Americans. What are the nation's health goals as stated in** Healthy People 2010?

HEALTH *Online*

To access reliable information about the nation's health goals, link to the site map for *Healthy People 2010* from **health.glencoe.com**.

Reinforcing Concepts

Guide students in considering the definition of *health education*. Be sure they recognize that it is not limited to classrooms. Ask: Where else do you think health education takes place? Do you ever educate others in health? Explain. ▣

Discussing

Ask students what they would say to a teen who insists, "It doesn't matter what I do—I'm not going to change the health of anyone across town, much less around the world." ▣

Community Involvement

Explain that one way for an individual to have a direct and positive effect on community health is to become involved in a community project. Information about community projects in your area can be obtained by calling or checking the Web sites of local hospitals and county health departments. Have students individually make a list of projects they would be interested in working on and to investigate one or more. After collecting information, ask students to work together to make a class list of local community projects with brief descriptions, including contact information. Have a pair of volunteers record the list of projects on a class poster. Post the list in the classroom, outside the library, or in the front hall of the school to build student awareness. ▣

⟩ *More About...*

Healthy People 2010 This comprehensive plan for improving the nation's wellness expands upon the health goals in *Healthy People* (the Surgeon General's 1979 report) and *Healthy People 2000: National Health Promotion and Disease Prevention Objectives.* In addition to its two main goals for improving health, *Healthy People 2010* focuses on 28 areas of health, each containing a specific goal. Refer students to the Appendix for a list of these areas, and encourage them to conduct additional research on *Healthy People 2010*.

Health Skills Activity

HEALTH FOR ALL

NHES Standard 6 Students will demonstrate the ability to use goal-setting and decision-making skills to enhance health.

Objectives

- Relate the nation's health goals and objectives in *Healthy People 2010* to individual, family, and community health.
- Develop and implement a plan for attaining a personal health goal.

Motivator

Give students one minute to list specific healthful habits they think they should be practicing but are not.

Teaching Strategies

1. Advise students to use their lists to help them identify a goal.
2. Have students with similar goals work in small groups.

✓Assessment

Using a rubric, student work should provide comprehensive evidence of the following criteria to achieve the highest score:

- ✔ clear progression through a goal-setting process
- ✔ inclusion of a clear goal statement
- ✔ identification of a realistic goal
- ✔ plan for reaching the goal
- ✔ evaluation or reflection on action

Goal Setting: Health for All

For class James must set a health goal and explain how reaching his goal will help him, his family, and his community. He has asked his sister to help him.

"Becky, how could a person's health affect anyone else?"

"I can think of lots of ways," Becky says.

"Like what?" James asks.

"Cigarette smoking," Becky replies. "If someone in the family smokes, others in the family are exposed. The community is affected, too. Tobacco use means more illness and more health care needs."

"Yeah," James agrees, "and more fires and litter."

"Do you understand the assignment better now?" Becky asks.

James nods. He wonders what goal to set.

What Would You Do?

Put yourself in James's shoes. Choose a goal that will enhance your health and the health of others. Apply the goal-setting steps to help you reach your goal.

1. Identify a specific goal and write it down.
2. List the steps you will take to reach your goal.
3. Identify potential problems and ways to get help and support from others.
4. Set up checkpoints to evaluate your progress.
5. Reward yourself once you have achieved your goal.

▶ **Communities** can offer behavior-changing classes such as tobacco-cessation programs and provide health services. They can also take steps to ensure a safe environment.

The best chances for success occur when individuals, families, and communities work together. For example, a health care professional can provide information to his or her patients and encourage them to practice healthy behaviors. Individuals then have the personal responsibility to put that information into practice.

Becoming Health Literate

Health literacy refers to *a person's capacity to learn about and understand basic health information and services and use these resources to promote his or her health and wellness.* This text will give you the information and tools you need to become health literate.

More About...

The National Health Education Standards One of the main goals of the National Health Education Standards is to move toward "health literacy." Health literacy is the capacity of individuals to obtain, interpret, and understand basic health information and services and the competence to use such information and services in ways that promote health. The health standards were developed by applying the characteristics of a well-educated, literate person within the context of health. For more information about the National Health Education Standards, contact:

American Association for Health Education
1950 Association Drive
Reston, VA 20191

A health-literate individual needs to be

▶ **a critical thinker and problem solver**—a person who can evaluate health information before making a decision and who knows how to make responsible, healthy choices.

▶ **a responsible, productive citizen**—someone who acts in a way that promotes the health of the community and who chooses safe, healthful, and legal behaviors that are consistent with family guidelines and that show respect for the individual and others.

▶ **a self-directed learner**—a person who has developed evaluation criteria for health information. These criteria include whether the information is reliable, accurate, and current. Such information is available through various media, through technology such as the Internet, and from health care professionals.

▶ **an effective communicator**— someone who is able to express his or her health knowledge in a variety of ways.

Helping others make healthy choices is part of being a responsible, productive citizen. *List three ways to help others make healthy decisions.*

 Lesson 1 *Review*

Reviewing Facts and Vocabulary

1. Write a paragraph using the terms *health, wellness,* and *health education.*

2. Relate the nation's health goals and objectives to individual, family, and community health: What can an individual do to address the goals of *Healthy People 2010?*

3. What three criteria can help you evaluate health information?

Thinking Critically

4. **Analyzing.** How can promoting healthy behaviors such as avoiding tobacco help prevent disease?

5. **Evaluating.** Explain how being health literate helps you achieve and maintain good health.

Applying Health Skills

Practicing Healthful Behaviors. Review the health-promoting lifestyle factors discussed in this lesson. For one week, keep track of how many of them you participate in. Then identify three healthy behaviors that you took part in each day. Also identify one or two factors that you could improve.

TECHNOLOGY *OPTION*

SPREADSHEETS You can use spreadsheet software to make a chart for tracking your performance of healthy lifestyle factors. See **health.glencoe.com** for tips on how to use a spreadsheet.

Lesson 1 Your Health and Wellness **9**

Discussing

Guide students in discussing health literacy. Ask:

• What are some characteristics of a health-literate individual?

• Do you think you are health literate? What do you think you need to learn to become more health literate? 🔟

③ ASSESS

EVALUATING THE LESSON

Assign and discuss the Lesson 1 Review; then administer, grade, and discuss Lesson Quiz 1 in the TCR. 📁

RETEACHING

• Have students work with partners to write informal outlines of the lesson.

• Ask students to complete Reteaching Activity 1 in the TCR. 📁

ENRICHMENT

Have students use online sources to learn more about *Healthy People 2010:* What organization created it? What are its focus areas? What has it identified as the leading health indicators? Have students choose one of the objectives and explain how they can meet that objective or help others to do so.

 Lesson 1 *Review*

Answers to Reviewing Facts and Vocabulary

1. Paragraphs will vary.
2. Take an active role, learn to make informed decisions, practice skills that enable you to apply your decisions, use reliable health care services, promote the health of others.
3. It should be reliable, accurate, and current.

Answers to Thinking Critically

4. Promoting healthy behaviors, such as avoiding tobacco, helps prevent diseases like lung cancer.
5. Possible answer: Being health literate gives you the tools and information to make healthful decisions about personal behaviors.

④ CLOSE

Ask students how they would revise the sentences they wrote for the Quick Start assignment at the beginning of this lesson.

Lesson 2

Promoting a Healthy Lifestyle

1 FOCUS

QUICK START Have a volunteer read the Quick Start assignment aloud, and remind students that health involves physical, mental/ emotional, and social well-being. Have students write their own lists and then share and discuss their responses.

TYING TO PRIOR KNOWLEDGE

Ask students to recall the definitions of *health* and *wellness*. Explain that they will learn more about promoting health and wellness as they study Lesson 2.

Health Skills Features

"Health Influences," p. 15

ANALYZING INFLUENCES

INTRODUCING VOCABULARY

Ask students to complete the Chapter 1 Study Guide in the *Student Activity Workbook*.

Promoting a Healthy Lifestyle

VOCABULARY
heredity
environment
peers
culture
media

YOU'LL LEARN TO
- Describe the importance of taking responsibility for establishing and implementing health maintenance for individuals of all ages.
- Explain how influences such as heredity, environment, culture, media, and technology have impacted the health status of individuals, families, communities, and the world.
- Analyze the health messages delivered through media and technology.

QUICK START List three of your favorite activities or hobbies. Then briefly describe the positive effect each has on your health.

Participating in fun activities with family members enhances your health.

How does staying up late affect you in the morning? How do you feel after engaging in physical activity? The actions you take regarding one aspect of your health have an effect on the other aspects as well.

Your Health Triangle

The three elements of health—physical, mental/emotional, and social—are interconnected, like the sides of a triangle. When one side receives too much or too little attention, the whole triangle can become lopsided and unbalanced. To be truly healthy, you need to keep all three sides of your health triangle in balance.

Physical Health

Your physical health has to do with how well your body functions. When you are in good physical health, you have enough energy to perform the activities of daily life and to cope with everyday challenges and stresses. You are also able to resist diseases and protect yourself from injury.

Being physically healthy involves getting adequate sleep and rest, eating nutritious meals, drinking enough water, and being

10 Chapter 1 Living a Healthy Life

Lesson 2 Resources

Teacher Classroom Resources
- Concept Mapping Activity 2
- Decision-Making Activity 1
- Guided Reading Activities 2
- Lesson Plan 2
- Lesson Quiz 2
- Reteaching Activity 2

Student Activity Workbook
- Applying Health Skills 2
- Chapter 1 Study Guide

Multimedia
- Transparency 2

physically active on a regular basis. It also includes practicing good hygiene and getting regular medical and dental checkups and treatments when you need them. Good physical health also involves paying attention to what you put into your body. It means avoiding harmful substances, such as tobacco, alcohol, and other drugs.

Mental/Emotional Health

Your feelings about yourself, how well you meet the demands of daily life, and your ability to process information are all important parts of your mental/emotional health. People with good mental/emotional health enjoy challenges, like learning new things, and see mistakes as opportunities to grow and change. They also accept responsibility for their actions and stand up for their beliefs and values.

People with good mental/emotional health are in touch with their feelings and can express them in appropriate ways. They can usually deal with the frustrations of life without being overwhelmed by them. They avoid dwelling on negative thoughts. Instead, they consider their situation and then use positive thoughts and actions to move forward.

Social Health

Your social health involves the way you get along with others. It includes your ability to make and keep friends and to work and play in cooperative ways, seeking and lending support when necessary. It involves communicating well and showing respect and care for yourself and others.

The health triangle is made up of three elements—physical, mental/emotional, and social health. *How might something affecting the physical side of your health triangle—an injury, for example—affect the other two sides?*

SOCIAL

PHYSICAL

MENTAL/EMOTIONAL

What Teens Want to Know

I'm young. Why should I care about my health? Good health allows you to feel good and enjoy life. The choices and decisions you make today will affect your health both now and in the future. It is difficult to break bad habits, such as overeating or physical inactivity, once they are established. Learn to make healthful decisions about the food you eat, the amount of physical activity you engage in, and the amount of sleep you get. Maintain a healthful lifestyle during the teen years to prevent illnesses when you are an adult. Resist pressure to smoke cigarettes, experiment with alcohol or illegal drugs, or use violence to resolve conflicts. These actions will safeguard your health now and lead to a healthy future.

2 TEACH

Quick Demo

Use a double-pan balance to help students consider the concept of balance. Place several pennies or pebbles in one pan. Point out the imbalance that exists. Now, add pennies or pebbles to the other pan so that the two pans are in balance. Discuss the analogy between balancing the pans and balancing each aspect of the health triangle.
L2 **Visual/Spatial**

Discussing

Guide students in describing and discussing the health triangle.

- What activity is shown on each side of the triangle?
- How does each activity represent good health?
- Why is it important that all three sides of the triangle are equal?
- Have volunteers give examples of how they are practicing good health in each side of the triangle. L1

Reinforcing Concepts

As students discuss the attitudes and actions that indicate good mental/emotional health, ask volunteers to give specific examples of using positive thinking to move forward despite difficult situations. Explain how dwelling on negative thoughts can impact health. L1

Critical Thinking

Ask students: How do you think your social health is affected by your physical health? By your mental/emotional health? L1

Cooperative Learning

Divide the class into small cooperative groups, and provide groups with poster board, old magazines, scissors, markers, and glue. Have each group draw a large health triangle on their poster board and label each side. Assign half the groups to illustrate each side of their triangles with pictures of healthful behaviors, and the other half to illustrate all three sides with pictures of unhealthful behaviors. Let the members of each group present their finished poster to the rest of the class. Have each group tell how the behaviors they have illustrated impact overall health. **ELL**

 Visual/Spatial

Activity

Have interested volunteers research the experiments and writing of Gregor Mendel, who published the first description of how traits are inherited. Ask these students to summarize their findings in a brief oral report. **L3**

Discussing

Encourage students to discuss how inherited physical traits might affect all three aspects of health—physical, mental/emotional, and social. **L1**

▲ **People from the same family often share many of the same physical traits.** *What physical similarities do the people in this family share? What are some health factors that can be inherited?*

hotlink

heredity For more information on heredity, see Chapter 19, page 498.

Keeping a Balance

Each side of your health triangle is equally important to your health. You might think of the three areas of health as the legs of a tripod on which a camera is mounted. If one leg is shorter than the other two, the tripod will tilt or fall. It's much the same with your health. An unbalanced health triangle is likely to cause you problems at some point. When you work to keep your physical, mental/emotional, and social health in balance, you are much more likely to function at your highest level.

Influences on Your Health

Imagine that the story of your health were made into a movie. The movie would portray your health from your birth until today. The movie might also focus on the following questions:

▶ What situations and people affected your health at each stage of your life?

▶ How have influences on your health changed through the years?

▶ How do early influences still affect you today?

There are several important influences on your health. They include heredity; environment; media and technology; and, most importantly, your values, attitude, and behavior.

Heredity

Your **heredity** refers to *all the traits that were biologically passed on to you from your parents.* You probably are familiar with heredity in terms of your physical traits such as eye color, hair color, and height. Heredity also influences your general level of health. Inheriting specific genes may put you at risk for certain illnesses, such as diabetes, requiring you to take steps to reduce your risk or manage the illness. Other genes may strengthen your resistance to disease. Beyond your physical health, heredity can also influence personality and basic intellectual abilities and talents.

Cooperative Learning Activity

Heredity Scientists around the world have participated in an extensive exploration of the genetic factors that contribute to human development. The U.S. Human Genome Project is a 13-year effort to identify and map all the genes on every chromosome in the human body. This project is part of a worldwide investigation; more than 1,000 scientists representing more than 50 countries are members of the Human Genome Organization (HUGO).

Ask students to work in groups to research the recent findings of HUGO. Have students brainstorm ways scientists may use this information, both the pros and cons. Organize a debate encouraging some students to speak in favor of the genome project and some to argue against it.

Environment

Your **environment** is *the sum of your surroundings*, including your family, your neighborhood, your school, your job, and your life experiences. Environment includes all the places you go in a given day and the physical conditions in which you live. It also includes all the people in your life, and your culture.

PHYSICAL ENVIRONMENT

Your physical environment influences every aspect of your health. A person who lives in a safe environment is likely to enjoy good physical and mental/emotional health. In contrast, someone who lives in an area with a high crime rate may experience stress or feel concern for personal safety.

Environmental factors such as air pollution also affect health. Pollen, dust, or smog in the air can cause allergies. Living with a smoker can increase the risk of respiratory problems.

SOCIAL ENVIRONMENT

Your social environment includes your family and other people with whom you come into contact each day. A supportive social environment made up of family and other adult role models can help a person develop positive values, a commitment to learning, and confidence in future success.

As a teen an important part of your social environment is your peers. **Peers** are *people of the same age who share similar interests*. Your peers include your friends and classmates. Loyal and supportive friends who care about their health can have a positive effect on your own health. Peers who take part in dangerous, unhealthy, and illegal behaviors like using tobacco, alcohol, or other drugs could create pressure for you to be "part of the group." Standing up to peer pressure can be challenging. Choosing friends who care about their health and yours supports a positive peer environment.

hot link

environment For more information on environmental influences on health, see Chapter 29, page 764.

Climate is one factor that can influence health. *What other aspects of a person's physical environment can affect his or her health?*

Activity

Ask students to write a short paragraph describing the physical environment in which they would most like to live. Have students exchange papers and review them for spelling and grammar, as well as content. Then have the pairs compare and discuss their finished works. **Visual/Spatial**

Activity

Have students draw a circle to represent their social environment. In the center of their circle, have them represent themselves. Then have them place the names of people or groups that make up the rest of their social environment. Have them place important relationships closer to the center and less important relationships near the perimeter. Then have students meet in small groups to discuss what they have learned from their diagrams. Ask: How do the people and groups in each part of your social environment affect your physical, mental/emotional, and social health?

Service Learning

Ask: What could be done to create a more supportive environment at school? Record students' responses on the board. As a class, choose one idea and adopt it as a class project. Have students develop a timeline for implementing the project.

More About...

Humor and Positive Outlook Remind students of the expression: *Look on the bright side.* Ask them to explain what they think it means. Help them recognize that the expression suggests that a positive outlook can promote health on all three sides of the health triangle. Laughter, in particular, can influence positive physiological changes as well as improving mental outlook or mood.

One scientific study found that laughter stimulated the production of endorphins, chemicals that help control pain. Another study demonstrated that stress-related hormones decreased during bouts of laughter. Humor and a positive outlook can help one cope with life pressures such as getting homework done on time, taking tests, and getting along with others.

Discussing

Encourage students to share their responses to these questions:

- Why is it important to understand the culture (or cultures) of your own family?

- Why is it important to understand the cultures of other families in your community? Of families with whom you don't have direct contact? **L1**

Activity

Ask interested students to plan and draw cartoons that illustrate the benefits of a positive attitude. Post these cartoons on a class bulletin board, and allow time for students to examine and discuss them. **L1** **Visual/Spatial**

Discussing

Ask students: What are the health benefits of laughing and of having a sense of humor? As students consider the importance of using a sense of humor to handle difficulties, help them distinguish between laughing *with* others and laughing *at* them. **L1**

Cooperative Learning

Have students meet in groups to brainstorm lists of behaviors that can have positive effects on their well-being in the school environment. How does each listed behavior affect physical health? Mental/emotional health? Social health? **L2**

CULTURE

Culture refers to *the collective beliefs, customs, and behaviors of a group*. This group may be an ethnic group, a community, a nation, or a specific part of the world. The language your family speaks, the foods you enjoy, the traditions you have, and the religion you practice are all part of your cultural environment. Your culture gives you a sense of identity. Understanding culture can help you know yourself better and be tolerant of others.

Attitude

The way you view situations—your attitude—greatly affects the choices you make. For example, in order to practice good health habits, you must believe that there is some benefit to you and that problems may result if you don't develop these habits.

Attitude can play a major role in health and wellness. Studies have shown that people who tend to see the positive in situations are more likely to have better health than those who see only the negative. Try to view challenging situations positively and think in realistic terms. Doing so will help you make healthful decisions, reach your goals, and successfully manage your life.

Behavior

Although you have no control over your heredity and only limited control over your environment, you have a great deal of control over your behavior. Suppose your family has a history of heart disease. This doesn't mean that you will "follow in their footsteps." You can lower your risk of developing the disease by practicing healthy habits, such as reducing your intake of high-fat foods and engaging in regular physical activity.

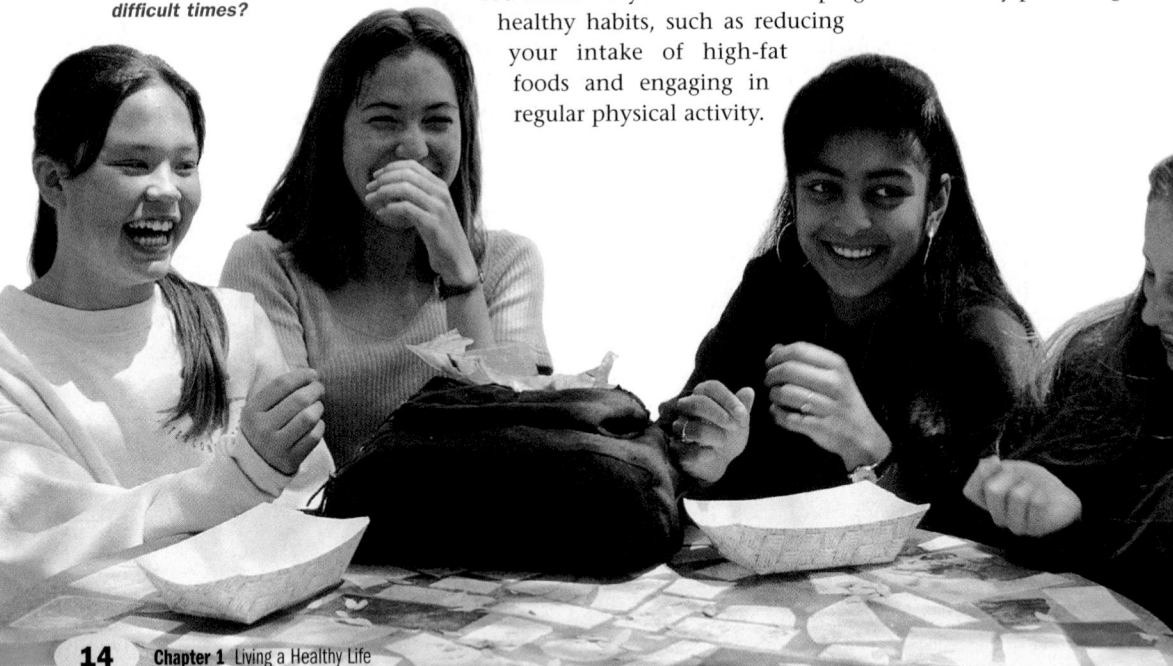

▼ Maintaining a sense of humor can help you handle the difficulties that inevitably occur in life. *How can humor be used to ease tension during difficult times?*

⌐⋀⋁⋀⌐ HEALTH LITERACY ⌐

Responsible Citizen Have students research the major environmental health hazards in their area. If students need direction, refer them to the Web sites of state and county agencies such as the Department of Public Works, a local water or waste management district, or an air quality board.

Have students list steps they can take, as an individual and as part of their community, to protect their health from the environmental dangers they have identified. Then have them list steps they can take to help reduce pollution or avoid contributing to it.

Hands-On Health ACTIVITY

Health Influences

There are many influences on your health each day. In this activity you will record the influences that affect your health for one day.

What You'll Need

- pencil and paper

What You'll Do

1. Divide a sheet of paper into a grid of 12 rows and 3 columns. Label the columns "Activity," "Element of Health" (physical, mental/emotional, social), and "Influence."

2. Throughout the day, record activities that influence your physical, mental/emotional, or social health. Identify the element of health being affected and whether the influence is positive or negative. For example: *Activity:* Worked hard on my science project. *Element:*

Mental. *Influence:* Positive because I am learning new information and developing my thinking skills. *Activity:* Watched TV and ate cookies. *Elements:* Physical and mental/emotional. *Influence:* Negative because an ad for cookies made me hungry, and I should be physically active instead of sitting on the couch.

3. Compare your grid with that of a classmate. How are your influences the same, and how are they different? Did you respond to similar influences in different ways? If so, why?

Apply and Conclude

In your private health journal, write a paragraph on what you have learned about health influences. What are the major influences in your life?

Your behavior affects not only your physical health but also your mental/emotional and social health. For example, mastering a new skill can give you a sense of accomplishment and enhance your self-esteem. Learning how to resolve conflicts peacefully can have a positive influence on your relationships with others.

Media

The media is a major influence on health. **Media**, or *the various methods of communicating information*, includes radio, television, film, newspapers, magazines, books, and the Internet. Although the media's main purpose has been to provide information and entertainment, it also plays a powerful role in shaping public opinion.

Advances in information delivery systems, such as the Internet, have put access to information from thousands of sources at your fingertips. Unfortunately, not all sources are reliable or accurate.

More About...

Analyzing Media Messages Students may wonder how to analyze media messages. Share the following tips with them.

- Recognize that people create messages with a purpose, often to sell something.
- Each form of media uses specialized language and images to attract attention or create an emotional response.

- No two people respond to the same media message in exactly the same way. Age, values, memories, and education make each person's response somewhat different.
- Media messages have their own points of view. You have a choice as to whether or not to accept the viewpoints being promoted.

Source: American Academy of Pediatrics

Hands-On Health

HEALTH INFLUENCES

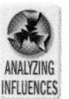
ANALYZING INFLUENCES

NHES Standard 4 Students will analyze the influence of culture, media, technology, and other factors on health.

Objectives

- Examine influences on physical, mental/emotional, and social health.
- Explain how influences—such as heredity, environment, culture, media, and technology—impact one's health status.

Motivator

Ask students to list some of their daily activities and how these activities influence their health. Write responses on the board.

Teaching Strategies

1. Using the list developed for the Motivator, model for students how to start their grid.
2. Encourage students to ask their parents or guardians for help in identifying influences and their impact.

✓Assessment

Using a rubric, student work should provide comprehensive evidence of the following criteria to achieve the highest score:

✔ identify or cite specific sources
✔ evaluate validity of source
✔ provide rationale for appropriateness of source
✔ demonstrate ability to access appropriate community resources to meet specific needs
✔ identify the type of help available from source

③ ASSESS

EVALUATING THE LESSON

Assign and discuss the Lesson 2 Review; then administer, grade, and discuss Lesson Quiz 2 in the TCR. 📁

RETEACHING

- Have students work with partners to draw and label a health triangle. Then have them list six factors that influence health.

- Ask students to complete Reteaching Activity 2 in the TCR. 📁

ENRICHMENT

Have students form cooperative groups and then choose a specific TV show. Encourage all the group members to watch that show and then work together to list the ways in which the TV show—and the commercials broadcasted during the show—attempted to influence viewers' opinions, both positively and negatively, on health-related issues.

④ CLOSE

Ask each student in the class to name a specific factor that influences health.

For example, some advertisers may make exaggerated claims to try to persuade you to buy a product. For reliable information, stick to publications from professional health organizations, such as the American Medical Association, the American Heart Association, and the Centers for Disease Control and Prevention. Generally, Web sites and publications from accredited universities and government agencies are also reliable sources of information.

HEALTH Online

To learn more about advances in medical technology, click on Interactive Projects at **health.glencoe.com.**

Technology

Technological advances also influence health. Advances in medical screenings and treatment for diseases such as heart disease, cancer, and AIDS have helped large numbers of people live longer, healthier lives. Other technological advances help keep our air, land, and water clean. However, advances in technology can have a downside. Technology has replaced many of the physical activities that once were part of daily life. People drive or ride instead of walk. They may watch TV, play video games, or work on the computer instead of being physically active. Recognizing the impact of these influences can help you live a more active, healthy life.

▶ Lesson 2 Review

Reviewing Facts and Vocabulary

1. Describe the importance of taking responsibility for health maintenance by keeping the three areas of health in balance.

2. Define the terms *culture* and *media*, and explain how each influences health.

3. Explain how technology has impacted health.

Thinking Critically

4. **Applying.** Select the side of your health triangle that you think is most affected by personal behavior. Explain your choice.

5. **Analyzing.** If you were looking for facts about weight lifting, how might you analyze the health messages delivered through a Web site for a company that sells weight equipment versus information provided by the American Academy of Pediatrics (AAP)?

Applying Health Skills

Analyzing Influences. The United States has many cultures within its population. Investigate which cultures are represented in or near your community. Select one and prepare a presentation on traditions and other factors that might influence the health of people growing up in that particular culture.

TECHNOLOGY *O P T I O N*

PRESENTATION SOFTWARE Presentation software can help you emphasize important points about traditions and culture. Find help in using presentation software at **health.glencoe.com.**

▶ Lesson 2 Review

Answers to Reviewing Facts and Vocabulary

1. Keeping your health triangle in balance will help you function at your highest level.

2. Culture—the collective beliefs, customs, and behaviors of a group—can influence behavior; media—methods of communicating information—can influence behavior and provide health information.

3. Technology has improved many aspects of health, but has reduced the amount of physical activity people get.

Answers to Thinking Critically

4. Answers will vary.

5. The AAP's Web site would be more reliable because they are not selling anything.

Your Behavior and Reducing Health Risks

VOCABULARY

risk behaviors
cumulative risks
abstinence

YOU'LL LEARN TO

- Describe ways to promote health and reduce risks.

- Associate risk-taking with consequences.

- Analyze the importance of abstinence from risk behaviors, including sexual activity before marriage.

- Communicate the importance of practicing abstinence.

⇒ *QUICK* *START*   Draw and label a health triangle on a sheet of paper. For each side of the triangle, identify two decisions you have made during the past few days that could affect your health. Place a " + " by those decisions that were healthful and a " — " by those that could have been or were harmful.

P art of becoming an adult is learning how to make responsible decisions. You may already be responsible for buying your own clothes, making your own breakfast or lunch, and managing your schedule. As you move toward adulthood, you become increasingly responsible for decisions regarding your health. It's important to remember that the choices you make during adolescence can have an effect on your health for the rest of your life.

Understanding Health Risks

T he first step in becoming responsible for your health is to increase your awareness of risk behaviors in your life. **Risk behaviors** are *actions that can potentially threaten your health or the health of others.* A second step is to examine your current behaviors and make any necessary changes.

Wearing protective gear is one way to reduce health risks. *What are other ways to reduce health risks when engaging in physical activity?*

1 FOCUS

⇒ *QUICK START*   On the board, draw and label a health triangle. Have a volunteer read the Quick Start assignment aloud, and let other volunteers suggest decisions—healthful or unhealthful; write these examples on the appropriate side of the health triangle on the board. Then have students complete the assignment independently.

TYING TO PRIOR KNOWLEDGE

Have students briefly explain some steps they can take to reduce their health risks. Explain that they will learn about more of these behaviors as they study this lesson.

Health Skills Features

"Analyzing Risk Behaviors," p. 19.

ADVOCACY

INTRODUCING VOCABULARY

Ask students to complete the Chapter 1 Study Guide in the *Student Activity Workbook.* ☞

Lesson 3 Resources

Teacher Classroom Resources

☞ Concept Mapping Activity 3

☞ Enrichment Activity 1

☞ Guided Reading Activities 3

☞ Health Lab 1

☞ Lesson Plan 3

☞ Lesson Quiz 3

☞ Reteaching Activity 3

Student Activity Workbook

☞ Applying Health Skills 3

☞ Chapter 1 Study Guide

Multimedia

🖱 Transparency 3

② TEACH

Critical Thinking

Ask: In what ways is taking responsibility for your health the same as taking responsibility for your life?

Reinforcing Concepts

Ask volunteers to describe the teen in the photograph on page 17. What protective gear is the teen wearing? How does it reduce the teen's health risks?

Then have students brainstorm a list of other ways to reduce health risks when participating in sports and other physical activities. **L1**

VISUAL LEARNING

Figure 1.2 Have students meet in pairs to read the bar graph and discuss its meaning. Ask each group to write one sentence explaining what they can conclude from the graph.

Health Skills Practice

Peer Influences Ask: How do your friends influence your willingness to take risks? Do they encourage certain risk behaviors, or do they encourage you to avoid such behaviors? Explain that students should be aware of the influence their friends have on their attitudes and actions. Have them write private health journal entries analyzing the influence of their friends and describing what changes (if any) they feel they could make to improve their health.

ANALYZING INFLUENCES

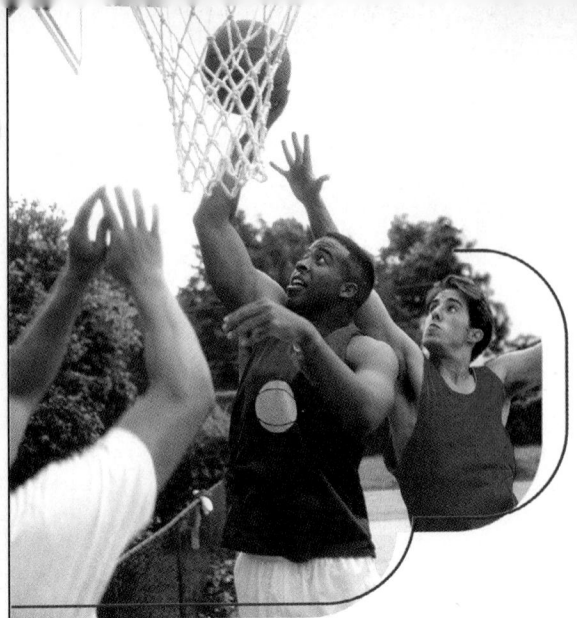

△ **Regular physical activity reduces health risks.**

Recognizing Risk Behaviors

The Centers for Disease Control and Prevention (CDC) and other public health agencies routinely survey teens nationwide to monitor their risk behaviors. In the most recent youth risk behavior survey, questionnaires on personal risk factors were gathered from teens in grades 9 through 12 in 33 states. The six categories of personal health risk factors and some of the results are shown in **Figure 1.2.**

When you analyze this data, you'll see that there is encouraging news. Most teens are *not* drinking alcohol or using tobacco. Over two thirds of teens wear safety belts when riding in cars. Where do you fit in? Are you making responsible decisions about your own health and well-being? Throughout this course, you will learn strategies for minimizing many types of risks.

FIGURE 1.2

TEEN RISK BEHAVIORS

The majority of teens are avoiding many risk behaviors or are taking preventive measures to improve their health.

The Youth Risk Behaviors Survey (YRBS) gathers data on the following:

- Behaviors that contribute to unintentional and intentional injuries
- Tobacco use
- Alcohol and other drug use
- Sexual behaviors that contribute to unplanned pregnancy and sexually transmitted infections (STIs) (including HIV infection)
- Unhealthy dietary behaviors
- Physical inactivity

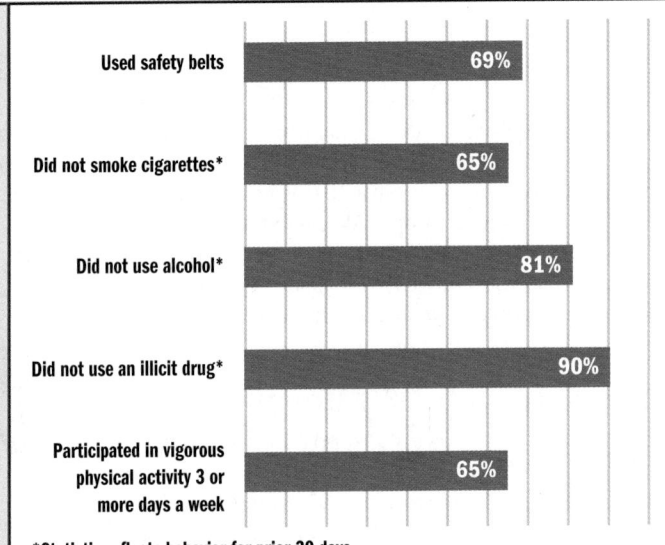

Behavior	Percent
Used safety belts	69%
Did not smoke cigarettes*	65%
Did not use alcohol*	81%
Did not use an illicit drug*	90%
Participated in vigorous physical activity 3 or more days a week	65%

*Statistic reflects behavior for prior 30 days.

Source: Based on data from the Centers for Disease Control and Prevention (CDC) and the National Household Survey on Drug Abuse (NHSDA)

Promoting Coordinated School Health

The Cost of Prevention Many people believe that a person's lifestyle cannot be influenced by schools and social agencies. Others believe that schools cannot afford the costs of problems stemming from low self-esteem, dropout rate from school, participation in high-risk behaviors, sexually transmitted diseases and teen pregnancy, health costs associated with poor prenatal care, ineffective parenting practices, malnutrition, and poor mental health. One mechanism for schools to improve the health of their students, faculty, and staff is through a coordinated school health program. For help in developing such a program or in strengthening an existing program, consult *Planning a Coordinated School Health Program.*

Real-Life Application

Analyzing Risk Behaviors

Review Figure 1.2 on page 18. Your teacher will provide you with additional information on youth risk behaviors or instruct you on how to access this information.

> **Choose one category of personal health risk factors:**
>
> - Behaviors that may contribute to intentional and unintentional injuries
> - Tobacco use
> - Alcohol and other drug use
> - Sexual behaviors that contribute to unplanned pregnancy, STIs, and HIV
> - Unhealthy dietary behaviors
> - Physical inactivity

ACTIVITY

Using the statistics in Figure 1.2 and the additional information you obtained, create a convincing poem, poster, song lyric, or cartoon advocating for risk-reducing behavior among your peers. Share your advocacy message with other students in your class or school.

Cumulative Risks and Consequences

The consequences of risk behaviors may add up over time. These **cumulative risks** are *related risks that increase in effect with each added risk*. Smoking one cigarette, for example, is not likely to result in death. Neither is eating one high-fat meal or getting one sunburn. If these behaviors are repeated over time, however, the negative effects accumulate and lead to serious health consequences.

Cumulative risks may also result from combinations of risk factors. For example, driving faster than the posted speed limit is a risk factor that can have deadly results. Another is not wearing a safety belt when you drive or ride in a car. Driving in bad weather is a third risk factor. The combination of these three factors greatly magnifies the potential for harm to yourself and to others. The more risk behaviors you participate in, the more likely you are to experience negative consequences at some point. Cumulative risks can and do occur in all areas of health and safety.

Did You Know ?

Scientists have discovered that the brain undergoes structural changes during the teen years. Some of those changes may mean that it's natural for teens to want to take on new challenges. *Healthy* challenges include running for class president, trying out for a play, and introducing yourself to a new student.

More About...

Health Risk Appraisal To monitor behaviors that place adolescents most at risk for premature mortality, the Centers for Disease Control and Prevention (CDC) developed the Youth Risk Behavior Surveillance System (YRBSS). The YRBSS measures six categories of behaviors: behaviors that may contribute to unintentional and intentional injuries; tobacco use; alcohol and other drug use; sexual behaviors that contribute to unplanned pregnancy and STDs, including HIV infection; unhealthy dietary behaviors; and physical inactivity. You may wish to visit the CDC Web site for more information about the YRBSS.

Real-Life Application

ANALYZING RISK BEHAVIORS

 ADVOCACY

NHES Standard 7 Students will demonstrate the ability to advocate for personal, family, and community health.

Objectives

- Analyze strategies to promote health and reduce risks.

- Demonstrate the ability to promote risk-reducing behavior in peers.

Motivator

Ask students for examples of how friends influence one another to practice health-promoting behaviors.

Teaching Strategies

1. Divide the class into small groups, and assign each group a category of risk factors.
2. Remind students to make their messages persuasive and appealing to teens. Have them include positive actions teens can take to reduce health risks.

✓ Assessment

Using a rubric, student work should provide comprehensive evidence of the following criteria to achieve the highest score:

✓ clear, health-enhancing stand
✓ support for the position with relevant information
✓ awareness of the audience
✓ encouragement of others to make healthful choices
✓ passion/conviction

Critical Thinking

As students discuss the examples of cumulative risks they have just read about, ask:

- In what sense is smoking one cigarette, eating one high-fat meal, or getting one sunburn actually the beginning of cumulative risks?

- How can you distinguish between one unwise choice and the number of unwise choices that may result in a cumulative risk?

- Why is good health about choices? **L1**

Reinforcing Concepts

Have volunteers describe what might happen in a situation where all three driving-related risk behaviors listed on page 19 were present? How could eliminating one risk behavior improve the possible consequences? **L1**

Explaining

Point out that people often think of abstinence as involving only the avoidance of sexual activity before marriage. Explain that abstinence also involves avoiding the use of tobacco, alcohol, and other drugs, as well as avoiding other risk behaviors. **L1**

Reinforcing Concepts

Be sure students understand that even teens who have been sexually active can choose abstinence from sexual activity. Ask: What are the benefits of choosing abstinence after being sexually active? **L1**

Abstaining from Risk Behaviors

The only way to avoid the consequences of some of the most serious risk behaviors is to practice abstinence. **Abstinence** is *avoiding harmful behaviors,* including the use of tobacco, alcohol, and other drugs and sexual activity before marriage. Choosing to abstain from high-risk behaviors is one of the most important health decisions you can make as a teen.

Abstaining from Tobacco, Alcohol, and Other Drugs

When you abstain from using tobacco, alcohol, and other drugs, you avoid many negative consequences. Using these substances harms all aspects of your health. The physical and psychological effects are well documented—these substances can cause addiction and can seriously harm the body. They can even cause death. Substance use often isolates a person from family and friends, a negative effect on social health. There are legal consequences as well—it is illegal for people under 21 to purchase, possess, or consume alcohol. People under 18 cannot purchase tobacco, and many states restrict purchasing to people over 21. The purchase and use of other drugs are illegal for all people, no matter what their age.

How you behave affects not only yourself but others around you. What positive effects on others might result from your participation in a campaign that promotes abstinence from substance use?

Abstaining from Sexual Activity

Abstinence from sexual activity is the preferred choice of behavior for unmarried persons of high-school age. Why? Abstinence from sexual activity protects teens against many negative consequences. Even teens who have been sexually active in the past can choose abstinence. Teens who abstain from sexual activity

▶ never have to worry about unplanned pregnancy.

▶ will not be faced with the difficult decisions associated with unplanned pregnancy, such as being a single parent.

▶ will not have to take on the many responsibilities of caring for a child.

▶ don't have to worry about sexually transmitted infections (including HIV infection).

▶ are free of the emotional problems that usually accompany sexual activity, such as guilt, regret, and rejection.

▶ are making a choice that is always legal.

Cooperative Learning Activity

Good Health Habits *SURGEON GENERAL'S WARNING: Smoking causes lung cancer, heart disease, emphysema, and may complicate pregnancy.* Point out to students that this and similar warning labels appear on all cigarette packages and advertisements. Ask: Why, in light of such warnings, do people continue to smoke? Why do some teens start smoking even though they

know tobacco products are dangerous?

Then have students meet in groups to discuss risk behaviors and health. Encourage students to broaden their group discussions to include alcohol, illegal drugs, and sexual activity before marriage. Ask each group to decide on the most effective strategy for encouraging teens to abstain from risk behaviors.

With the worry of having a sexual relationship eliminated, you are free to establish nonsexual closeness with members of the opposite gender. Through these relationships you can develop genuine feelings of love, trust, and friendship. When you choose to abstain from sexual activity, you can focus on the real priorities of your life: setting and achieving your goals and following your dreams.

Responsible teens abstain from high-risk behaviors. Choosing abstinence will benefit your lifelong health.

 Avoiding high-risk behaviors and choosing friends who do so is one of the best ways to achieve and maintain wellness.

Lesson 3 Review

Reviewing Facts and Vocabulary

1. How are risk behaviors associated with consequences?
2. What are *cumulative risks*? Use this term in a complete sentence.
3. Analyze the importance of abstinence from sexual activity before marriage.

Thinking Critically

4. **Analyzing.** Why is it important to learn about risk behaviors in the teen years?
5. **Synthesizing.** How can you communicate the importance of practicing abstinence to other teens?

Applying Health Skills

Accessing Information. Choose one of the health-risk behaviors from Figure 1.2 that is of personal concern to you. Research how student trends in this behavior have changed over the last five years. Present your data in a line graph.

SPREADSHEETS You can use spreadsheet software to make your graph. Click on **health.glencoe.com** to access information on how to use a spreadsheet to represent data graphically.

Lesson 3 Your Behavior and Reducing Health Risks **21**

Critical Thinking

Have students share their responses to this question: What are the benefits of developing feelings of love, trust, and friendship while practicing abstinence from sexual activity? **L1**

③ ASSESS

EVALUATING THE LESSON

Assign and discuss the Lesson 3 Review; then administer, grade, and discuss Lesson Quiz 3 in the TCR. 📁

RETEACHING

- Have students sketch two stick figures or symbols showing two different kinds of cumulative risks.
- Ask students to complete Reteaching Activity 3 in the TCR. 📁

ENRICHMENT

Have students work in small groups to plan, create, and present slide shows, videos, or computer-generated presentations encouraging teens to practice abstinence from risk behaviors.

④ CLOSE

Have each student share what he or she considers the most important benefit of practicing abstinence.

Lesson 3 Review

Answers to Reviewing Facts and Vocabulary

1. Possible answer: Risk behaviors are associated with negative effects on your own health or the health of others.
2. Related risks that increase in effect with each added risk. Sentences will vary.
3. To avoid the many negative consequences of sexual activity.

Answers to Thinking Critically

4. Many risks are cumulative. Knowing about risks and consequences now can improve health both now and in adulthood.
5. Possible answer: Emphasize the many benefits of abstaining from risk behaviors.

Teens in the Media

NHES Standard 4 Students will analyze the influence of culture, media, technology, and other factors on health.

Objective

Reflect on how making healthful media choices has a positive effect on health.

Motivator

Ask students to think about all the forms of media that they come in contact with each day.

Teaching Strategies

Awareness Encourage students to keep comprehensive lists in their journals of the media they encounter daily.

Analysis As students encounter various forms of media, ask them to think about the image of teens being portrayed. Ask: Do the teens featured avoid risk behaviors? Do the teens make healthful choices? Are they health literate?

Reflection Have volunteers read excerpts from their journals to the class. Ask students whether it has been easy or difficult to find media images of youth who are making healthful choices.

Take Action Write to a media organization—such as a magazine, Internet site, or television network—indicating why it's important to show images of teens engaged in healthful behaviors.

✓Assessment

Students should keep their journal for at least one week. Student journals should have comprehensive lists of media and should answer all the questions listed in the activity.

22

Eye ON THE Media

Teens in the Media

Every day, you make decisions about the media—you choose what television shows to watch, what music to listen to, and what books and magazines to read. These choices can have a significant influence on your overall health.

Think about the TV shows you watch, the music you listen to, and the magazines and books you read. To get an idea of how teens are portrayed in the different forms of media, answer these questions:

Are the teens eating nutritious foods and engaging in regular physical activity?

Do the teens have a positive outlook on life?

Do the teens have healthful family relationships?

Do the teens avoid violence and try to resolve conflicts peacefully?

Do the teens avoid tobacco, alcohol, and other drugs?

Do the teens practice abstinence from sexual activity?

ACTIVITY

Begin a daily journal of your interaction with various forms of media. Record in your journal the names of the programs you watch, the titles of songs you listen to, the titles of books and magazines you read, and the names of Web sites you visit. Ask yourself whether or not the teens depicted in a particular form of media are modeling healthful behaviors and making responsible choices, and write answers to the questions above. Keep the journal for a week.

On the basis of the data in your journal, would you say that there are plenty of healthful images of teens in the media, or do you believe that there is a lack of images of teens making healthful choices and leading healthy lives? Write a paper discussing your view.

EXPRESS YOUR VIEWS

Write a paragraph on how watching TV shows, reading books and magazines, listening to music, or visiting Web sites that promote a healthy lifestyle might positively influence your own health.

More About...

Teen Images Some studies of media images of teens show that teen stereotypes are still the rule rather than the exception. TV shows about teens often portray teens as troublemakers rather than as responsible citizens and contributing members of a community. News stories may also show teens in a negative light. Help students to recognize these stereotypes as they share their journal entries. Ask them to watch the national and local news for images of teens. Encourage students to try to find nonstereotypical images.

CROSS-CURRICULUM CONNECTIONS

Write a Play. Dreaming about the future and setting goals to succeed are part of living a healthy life. Take a few minutes to imagine what lies ahead for you. Write a one-person play about how your life will be if you choose a particular path. Then look at your present reality. Consider what steps you need to take to fulfill your dream. What obstacles or risks might you face? Who will support you on this path?

Write an Analysis. Many technological advances have had a positive impact on health. For example, the development of a medical test known as the computerized tomography (CT) scan has made it possible for certain diseases to be diagnosed earlier and more accurately than before. Use online and print resources to research a technological advance such as the CT scan, and write a short analytical essay on your findings.

Calculate the Amount. Figure 1.2 on page 18 indicates that, according to the Youth Risk Behaviors Survey, in a given 30-day period 65 percent of high-school students did not smoke. Town Center High School has 420 seniors. How many of the seniors at this high school smoked within a given 30-day period?

Present Research Findings. Getting an adequate amount of sleep each night is essential for optimum health and wellness, especially for teens. During sleep, the body passes through several distinct stages, each characterized by specific types of brain activity. Conduct research to find out more about the different stages of sleep. Write up your findings in the form of a report and present it to the class.

Health Educator

Do you have an interest in improving the health of young people? Do you enjoy working with individuals and groups? If so, it might be worth your time to look into health education as a career.

To be a public school health teacher, you must be credentialed. This would include having a four-year college degree and completing an approved teacher-training program. To find out more about this and other health careers, click on Career Corner at **health.glencoe.com**.

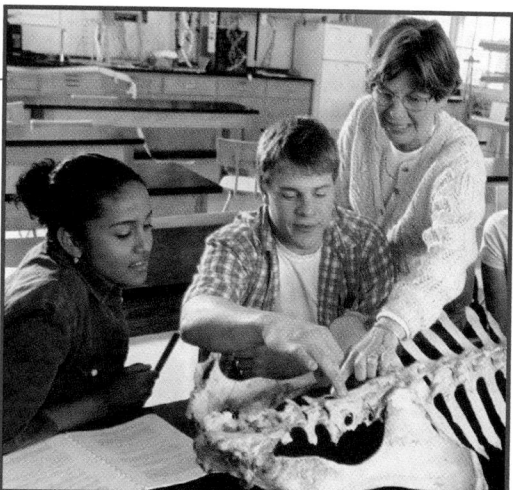

CROSS-CURRICULUM CONNECTIONS

Enrich student learning by connecting the topic of living a healthy life to one of the four subject areas presented on this page. The activity may be completed individually or with a partner.

Language Arts Discuss how to write in the first person. Focus on the importance of character development.

Social Studies Explain that an analytical essay is a way to gather and sort information about a subject. First, you break the topic into its parts and then think about how the parts are connected.

Math Answer: $(100-65)/100 \times 420 = 147$

Science Direct students to reliable sources of information on sleep.

Have students read and discuss the Career Corner information on becoming a health educator. Ask interested students to explore the Glencoe Health Web site at **health.glencoe.com** for more information on this career.

Portfolio Assessment

Self-Evaluation Direct students to review the Health Skills Activities and other activities completed in the chapter. Encourage each student to select one finished product or activity that demonstrates his or her best work for the chapter and that represents the student's learning goals. Have students explain what they have learned and how the examples they have selected show their progress.

Teacher Classroom Resources Assign Performance Assessment 1, "Good Health—Let's All Catch It!," in the TCR.

Chapter 1 Review

CHECKING COMPREHENSION

- Assign and discuss the chapter review.
- Use the Chapter 1 MindJogger Videoquiz to review the chapter. ▣

CHAPTER 1 REVIEW ANSWERS

Exploring Health Terms

1. health
2. wellness
3. health education
4. *Healthy People 2010*
5. health literacy
6. prevention
7. environment
8. media
9. culture
10. Heredity
11. peers
12. False—abstinence
13. False—Risk behaviors
14. True

Recalling the Facts

1. To promote health and prevent illness; disability, and early death.
2. Any five: Get adequate sleep each night; eat a healthy breakfast daily; eat a nutritious, balanced diet; get adequate physical activity three or more days a week; maintain a healthy weight; avoid the use of tobacco, alcohol, and other drugs; abstain from sexual activity before marriage; manage stress; maintain positive relationships; practice safe behaviors.
3. Communities can offer behavior-changing classes, provide health services, and take steps to ensure a safe environment.

> **EXPLORING HEALTH TERMS** *Answer the following questions on a sheet of paper.*

Lesson 1 *Match each definition with the correct term.*

health	health literacy
Healthy People 2010	health education
wellness	prevention

1. The combination of physical, mental/emotional, and social well-being.
2. An overall state of well-being, or total health.
3. The providing of accurate health information to help people make healthy choices.
4. A nationwide health promotion and disease prevention plan designed to serve as a guide for improving the health of all people in the United States.
5. A person's capacity to learn about and understand basic health information and services and use these resources to promote his or her health and wellness.
6. Practicing health and safety habits to remain free of disease and injury.

Lesson 2 *Replace the underlined words with the correct term.*

heredity	media	peers
culture	environment	

7. One part of your <u>culture</u> is where you live.
8. Radio and television are examples of <u>environment</u>.
9. Your <u>heredity</u> influences such things as your language and what you eat.
10. <u>Media</u> is the sum of an individual's traits that were biologically passed along by both parents.
11. People of the same age who share similar interests are your <u>culture</u>.

Lesson 3 *Identify each statement as True or False. If false, replace the underlined term with the correct term.*

risk behaviors	cumulative risks
abstinence	

12. Avoiding harmful behaviors, including sexual activity before marriage and the use of tobacco, alcohol, and other drugs, is known as <u>risk behaviors</u>.
13. <u>Abstinence</u> can potentially threaten your health or the health of others.
14. <u>Cumulative risks</u> are related risks that increase in effect with each added risk.

> **RECALLING THE FACTS** *Use complete sentences to answer the following questions.*

Lesson 1

1. What is the purpose of *Healthy People 2010*?
2. List five lifestyle factors that promote good health.
3. What can communities do to address the goals of *Healthy People 2010*?

Lesson 2

4. Which aspect of health reflects your ability to enjoy challenges and handle frustrations?
5. Identify six categories of influences on health.
6. Over which influences on health do you have the most control?

Lesson 3

7. What is the first step toward becoming responsible for your health?
8. Describe the two ways that cumulative risks occur.
9. List three benefits of abstinence from sexual activity before marriage.

4. Mental and emotional health.
5. Any six: heredity, environment (physical or social), culture, media, technology, attitude, behavior.
6. Attitude and behavior.
7. Increase awareness of risk behaviors.
8. Cumulative risks occur when a risk behavior is repeated over time or when several risk behaviors take place at the same time.
9. Any three: Teens will not have to worry about unplanned pregnancy and the difficult decisions associated with it; will not have the responsibility of caring for a child; will not have to worry about STDs (including HIV); are free of the mental and emotional problems that accompany sexual activity.

➤ THINKING CRITICALLY

1. **Analyzing.** Review the health continuum shown on page 5. What behaviors would contribute to the loss of health and wellness? What behaviors would move a person toward a high level of health? *(LESSON 1)*

2. **Synthesizing.** John is a good student, has lots of friends, and spends much of his free time practicing the guitar with his band. He eats a lot of fast-food burgers and is 10 pounds overweight. Draw his health triangle. *(LESSON 2)*

3. **Summarizing.** Explain why abstinence from risk behaviors is the most responsible behavior for teens, and provide an example of its application. *(LESSON 3)*

➤ HEALTH SKILLS APPLICATION

1. **Advocacy.** Write a letter to parents informing them of the nation's health goals and the role of *Healthy People 2010.* Highlight things that they can do individually and as a family to impact the health of all people in the United States. *(LESSON 1)*

2. **Analyzing Influences.** Consider how each of the influences on health affects your own wellness. On a sheet of paper, make two columns—one titled *Positive* and the other titled *Negative.* Identify the positive and negative aspects of each influence and record them in the appropriate column. *(LESSON 2)*

3. **Goal Setting.** What would be possible consequences of using an illegal drug? Provide an example of how a goal would be negatively affected by these consequences. *(LESSON 3)*

 BEYOND *the* Classroom

Parent Involvement

Analyzing Influences. With a parent, analyze the influence of laws, policies, and practices on a health-related issue. Topics may include regulations for smoking in public buildings, policies and practices for fire and safety in your school, and traffic laws. Write a brief report that summarizes your findings.

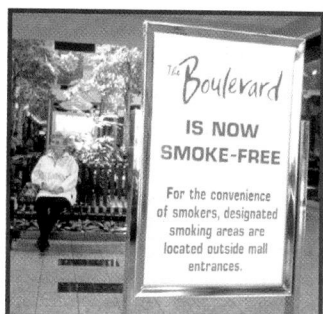

The **Boulevard**
IS NOW SMOKE-FREE

For the convenience of smokers, designated smoking areas are located outside mall entrances.

School and Community

Restaurant Inspection. Talk with a health inspector about food-handling requirements and other health codes for restaurant workers. Find out whether you or a small group of students could observe the inspection of a restaurant. Share what you have learned with your class.

Thinking Critically

1. Answers will vary.

2. His social and mental/emotional health seem excellent although his physical health could be improved; therefore, his health triangle should be drawn so that it's slightly out of balance.

3. Abstinence is the only way to avoid the consequences that come with certain risk behaviors. Examples will vary. Possible answer: Abstaining from sexual activity will protect against STDs and unplanned pregnancy.

Health Skills Application

1. Answers will vary although they should reflect much of the information provided in the text.

2. Answers will vary.

3. Answers may include: health problems, loss of respect, getting arrested. Possible negative effects on goals: not being able to play on team if caught, poor performance in school.

EVALUATE

- Use the reproducible Chapter 1 Test in the TCR, or construct your own using the Testmaker software. 📁 💿

- Use Performance Assessment 1 in the TCR. 📁

ENRICHMENT

Ask students to complete Enrichment Activity 1 in the TCR. 📁

 BEYOND *the* Classroom

Keep students involved in the community, and encourage parent participation by assigning the activities on this page for students to work on outside of class.

Lessons	Standards		Features
	National	**State/Local**	
1 **Building Health Skills** *pages 28–32*	National Health Education Standards **1.4, 2.2, 3.7, 5.1, 5.5**		**Health Skills Activity** • The Ball's In Your Court *(Communication)*, page 29
2 **Making Responsible Decisions and Setting Goals** *pages 33–36*	National Health Education Standards **6.1, 6.4, 6.5**		**Hands-On Health** • Setting Your Personal Health Goal *(Goal Setting)*, page 35
3 **Building Character** *pages 37–41*	National Health Education Standards **5.4, 7.2, 7.6**		**Real-Life Application** • Character in Action *(Accessing Information)*, page 39 **Exploring Issues** • Should Service Learning Be Required? page 40

Reproducible Resources	Assessment	Technology
Student Activity Workbook for use with each chapter 📁 Concept Mapping Activity 4 📁 Current Health Issues 2 📁 Guided Reading Activities 4 📁 Lesson Plan 4 📁 Parent Letter and Activities 2 📁 Reteaching Activity 4	📁 Lesson Quiz 4	🖐 Transparency 4 💿 TeacherWorks® 💻 Internet Activities
📁 Concept Mapping Activity 5 📁 Enrichment Activity 2 📁 Guided Reading Activities 5 📁 Lesson Plan 5 📁 Reteaching Activity 5	📁 Lesson Quiz 5	🖐 Transparency 5 💿 TeacherWorks®
📁 Concept Mapping Activity 6 📁 Cross-Curriculum Activity 2 📁 Decision-Making Activity 2 📁 Guided Reading Activities 6 📁 Health Lab 2 📁 Lesson Plan 6 📁 Reteaching Activity 6	📁 Lesson Quiz 6	🖐 Transparency 6 💿 TeacherWorks®

0:00 OUT OF TIME

If time does not permit teaching the entire chapter, use:
- Health Skills Activity, p. 29
- Figure 2.2, p. 30
- Figure 2.3, p. 34
- Hands-On Health, p. 35

Language Diversity

🎧 English Audio CD Program
🎧 Spanish Audio CD Program
📁 English Summaries, Quizzes, and Activities
📁 Spanish Summaries, Quizzes, and Activities
📁 Spanish Parent Letters and Activities

End of Chapter Assessment

Blackline Masters

📁 Chapter 2 Test
📁 Performance Assessment Activity 2

Technology

💿 Vocabulary PuzzleMaker
📼 MindJogger Videoquiz
💿 Exam*View*® Pro Testmaker

Professional Health Series

Dealing with Sensitive Issues
Planning a Coordinated School Health Program
Promoting Character Education
Home, School, and Community Involvement

Key to Ability Levels

Teaching strategies that appear throughout the chapter have been identified by one of the following codes to give teachers an idea of their suitability for students of varying learning styles and abilities.

L1 Strategies should be within the ability range of all students. Full class participation is often required. Teacher direction is usually needed.

L2 Strategies are designed for average to above-average students or for small groups. Some teacher direction is needed.

L3 Strategies are designed for students able and willing to work independently. Minimal teacher direction is needed.

ELL Strategies should be within the ability range of students learning the English language.

🔲 Block scheduling strategies are useful in a block scheduling format.

Building Health Skills and Character

CHAPTER OVERVIEW

Chapter 2 discusses basic health skills. Teens who develop these skills are prepared to promote their own health, as well as the health of others, throughout their lives. The chapter also helps students understand how they can develop and demonstrate good character.

Lesson 1 Communication skills help people develop and maintain positive relationships. Refusal skills help people say no to risk behaviors. Conflict resolution skills help people use cooperation to end disagreements. Self-management skills, including practicing healthful behaviors and managing stress, and the skills of analyzing influences and accessing valid information help people take responsibility for their own health. Health advocacy skills allow people to promote the health of others and the community.

Lesson 2 Knowing and using the steps of the decision-making process helps individuals make healthful choices. People can set and reach goals by using action plans.

Lesson 3 By considering and acting on positive values, individuals can build and demonstrate good character.

Health Skills Features

- Health Skills Activity (*Communication*), p. 29
- Hands-On Health (*Goal Setting*), p. 35
- Real-Life Application (*Accessing Information*), p. 39
- Exploring Issues, p. 40

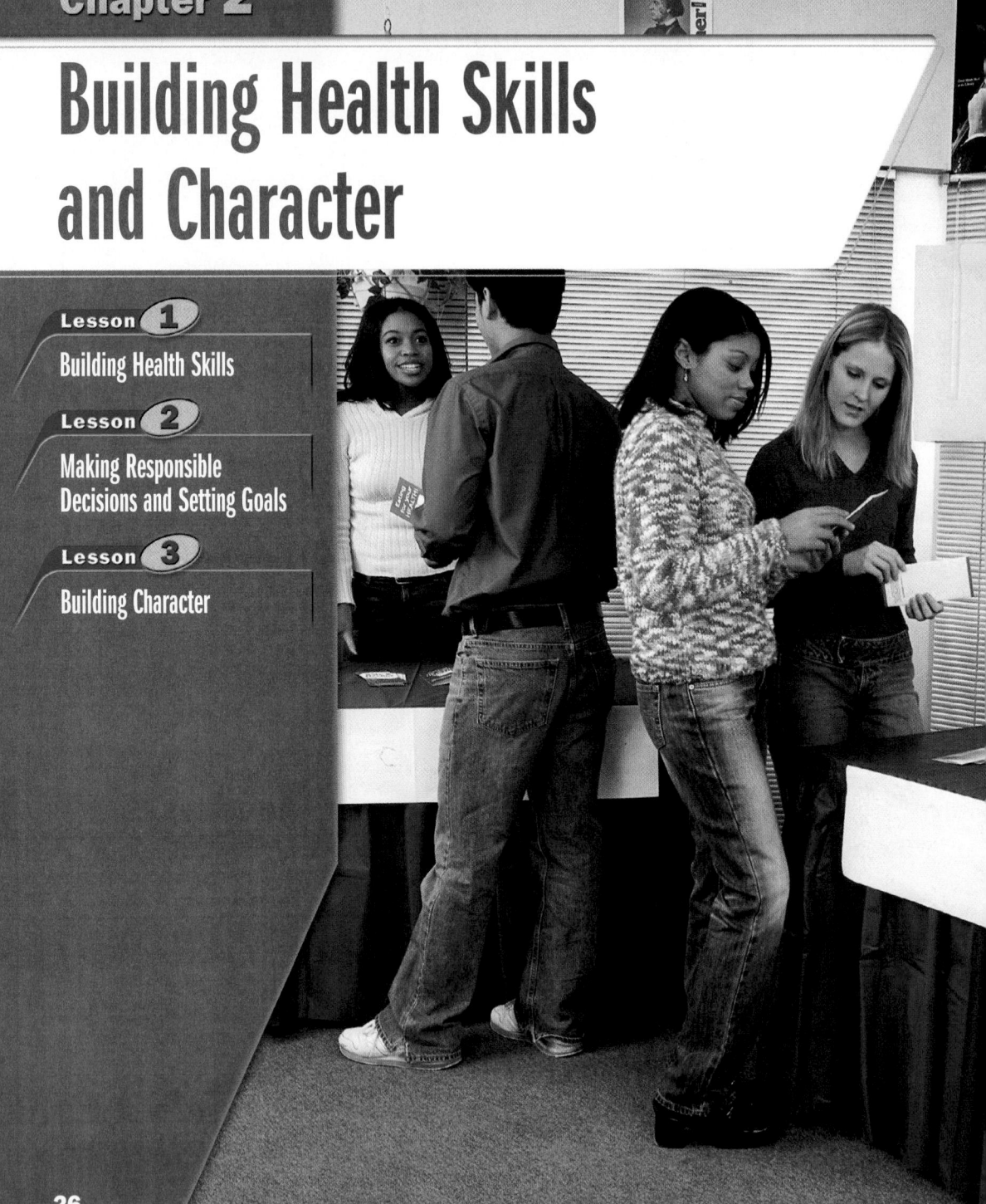

Chapter 2

Building Health Skills and Character

Lesson 1
Building Health Skills

Lesson 2
Making Responsible Decisions and Setting Goals

Lesson 3
Building Character

26

MEETING STUDENT DIVERSITY

Language Diversity Use the following suggestions to help students who have difficulty with English:

- Pair English language learners with native speakers of English who can restate the Chapter Summary in language that helps students comprehend important concepts.

- Direct auditory learners or those students with language diversity to the *Glencoe Health Audio CD Program*. Available in English and Spanish, this component provides an audio and written summary of the chapter.

- Use photographs, drawings, or magazine clippings to help students visualize the important concepts of the chapter.

Personal Health Inventory ✓

Do You Practice Effective Health Skills?

Read each statement below, and respond by writing *yes*, *no*, or *sometimes* for each item. Write *yes* only for items that you practice regularly or are sure about.

1. I know how to access reliable health information and services.
2. I care about the well-being of others and encourage them to make healthy choices.
3. I am aware of what influences my actions and decisions.
4. I communicate my thoughts and feelings clearly.
5. I am comfortable saying no to friends and peers who want to engage in risky or unhealthy activities.
6. I use problem-solving skills to resolve conflicts in a peaceful, respectful manner.
7. I engage in regular physical activity and eat nutritious foods.
8. I am aware of sources of stress in my life and know how to reduce or manage them.
9. When making decisions, I consider how the consequences might affect my health and the health of others.
10. I set personal health goals.

When you complete the chapter, review your personal inventory and identify two or three behavior changes you could make to improve your health.

27

Quick*Write*

Using Visuals. List skills that you think would help teens lead healthy lives. What skills are the teens in this photo demonstrating? Which skills do you practice on a regular basis to maintain or improve your health?

INTRODUCING THE CHAPTER

Personal Health Inventory ✓

Have students meet in groups to read and discuss the statements in the Personal Health Inventory. Have students consider:

- How does each statement affect my health?
- With which aspect of health—physical, mental/emotional, or social—is the statement most directly related?

After group discussions, have students work independently to respond to the inventory. Explain that the inventory is a private tool students can use periodically to check their health status. Remind students to keep their inventories. When they have completed the chapter, they can review their responses and plan improvements.

Quick*Write*

Using Visuals Have students describe and discuss the photograph on these pages. Then give students about three minutes to write their responses to the Quick Write assignment. When everyone has finished writing, ask volunteers to share their ideas with the rest of the class.

TECHNOLOGY OPTIONS

MINDJOGGER
VIDEOQUIZ

To preview or review chapter content, you may wish to use the Chapter 2 MindJogger Videoquiz. ◗◖

HEALTH *Online*

Online Resources for the Teacher For a fresh approach to health topics and an in-depth look at health issues, use these online resources found under Teacher Resources at **health.glencoe.com**:

- Block Schedule Lesson Plans
- Technology Projects
- Health Updates

Building Health Skills

Lesson 1

1 FOCUS

QUICK START Give students two minutes to jot down their ideas. Then ask volunteers to talk about some of the skills and qualities on their list.

TYING TO PRIOR KNOWLEDGE

Ask students to recall the definition of health. Explain that they will learn more about developing health-related skills as they read this lesson.

Health Skills Features

"The Ball's in Your Court," p. 29

INTRODUCING VOCABULARY

- Divide the class into groups of six. Assign each student in the group a vocabulary term. Have students look up the terms in the Glossary and discuss their meanings.

- Ask students to complete the Chapter 2 Study Guide in the *Student Activity Workbook.*

VISUAL LEARNING

Figure 2.1 Have volunteers read aloud the listed health skills. Encourage students to share what they think each involves and to give examples of how these skills can be used. Explain that students will learn more about these skills as they study the lessons in this chapter.

28

Building Health Skills

VOCABULARY

health skills
interpersonal communication
refusal skills
conflict resolution
stress management
advocacy

YOU'LL LEARN TO

- Demonstrate communication skills in building and maintaining healthy relationships.
- Develop refusal strategies and conflict resolution skills.
- Apply self-management strategies.
- Analyze influences on behavior.
- Develop criteria for evaluating health information.

QUICK START On a sheet of paper, list the skills and qualities necessary for effective communication. Then, explain how having strong communication skills can impact your health in positive ways.

FIGURE 2.1

THE HEALTH SKILLS

Developing and practicing these health skills will provide a lifetime of benefits.

Interpersonal Communication
- Communication Skills
- Refusal Skills
- Conflict Resolution

Self Management
- Practicing Healthful Behaviors
- Stress Management

Analyzing Influences

Accessing Information

Decision Making/Goal Setting

Advocacy

The choices you make and the actions you take—including the foods you eat, the friends you choose, and the activities you participate in—can affect your health. Taking responsibility for your health begins with a commitment to take charge of your actions and behaviors in a way that reduces risks and promotes wellness. The first step is to develop *health skills*. **Health skills**, or life skills, are *specific tools and strategies that help you maintain, protect, and improve all aspects of your health.* **Figure 2.1** presents a basic overview of the health skills.

Interpersonal Skills

One of the traits of a health-literate individual is having effective communication skills. Effective communication involves not only making yourself heard but also being a good listener. **Interpersonal communication** is *the exchange of thoughts, feelings, and beliefs between two or more people.*

28 **Chapter 2** Building Health Skills and Character

Lesson 1 *Resources*

Teacher Classroom Resources
- Concept Mapping Activity 4
- Current Health Issues 2
- Guided Reading Activities 4
- Lesson Plan 4
- Lesson Quiz 4
- Parent Letter and Activities 2
- Reteaching Activity 4

Student Activity Workbook
- Applying Health Skills 4
- Chapter 2 Study Guide

Multimedia
- Transparency 4

Strategies for effective **communication** include:

▶ **Clearly say what you mean.** Use *"I" messages* to state your position, for example, "I feel frustrated when our plans change." This helps you avoid placing blame on others.

▶ **Pay attention to *how* you say something.** Use a respectful tone. Make sure your facial expressions and gestures reflect your verbal message.

▶ **Be a good listener.** Avoid interrupting the speaker, and show that you are listening by nodding or asking appropriate questions.

ho⬛link

communication For more information on communication skills, see Chapter 10, page 254.

Health Skills Activity

Communication: The Ball's in Your Court

When Mark arrives late at the basketball court, his friend Phillipe throws the ball at him, shouting, "You're a half hour late!"

"Well, excuse me, Mr. Punctual," Mark laughs.

"You're never on time. It's like you assume I have nothing better to do than wait around for you," Phillipe says.

"Sorry, bud, but some things came up," Mark answers.

"Yeah? Well, I'm outta here." Phillipe throws up his hands and turns to walk away.

"Wait, let me explain," Mark says calmly.

Phillipe hesitates, wondering how to respond.

What Would You Do?

How can Mark and Phillipe use effective communication skills to continue their discussion more effectively? Write an ending to this scenario, using the guidelines below.

1. Use "I" messages.
2. Speak calmly and clearly, using a respectful tone.
3. Listen carefully, and ask appropriate questions.
4. Show appropriate body language.

② TEACH

Health Skills Activity

THE BALL'S IN YOUR COURT

COMMUNICATION SKILLS

NHES Standard 5 Students will demonstrate the ability to use interpersonal communication skills to enhance health.

Objectives

• Demonstrate communication skills in building and maintaining healthy relationships.

• Demonstrate healthy ways to express needs, wants, and feelings.

Motivator

Ask students to recall a disagreement with a friend.

Teaching Strategies

1. Remind students to avoid "you" statements that blame or accuse the other person.
2. Ask students to consider each character's point of view.

✓Assessment

Using a rubric, student work should provide comprehensive evidence of the following criteria to achieve the highest score:

✔ use of "I" statements
✔ respectful tone of voice
✔ listening skills and clarification by asking appropriate questions
✔ appropriate body language

⌇⌇⌇ HEALTH LITERACY

Interpersonal Skills Communication skills are vital to success in many areas. In fact, a lack of communication skills has been reported by employers to be the primary deficiency of today's workers. Also, communication breakdown is said to be a major factor in marriage and family problems. On the positive side, effective communication enhances human interactions in most circumstances. Developing a strong foundation of these skills will provide many benefits. Have students consider how effective communication skills can enhance the student-teacher relationship. Ask students to identify communication skills they do well and those they can improve. Have students write three ways to improve one of their skills.

29

Discussing

Guide students in discussing the significance of the fact that health skills are also called life skills. **L1**

Activity

Write the following sentence on the board: *So what happened next?* Let students take turns reading the sentence aloud, varying its meaning by changing the tone of voice, the words emphasized, and their body language. Help students discuss the various messages that can be communicated by this short sentence. **L1**

VISUAL LEARNING

Figure 2.2 Have students meet in groups to read and discuss the refusal strategies. Then have students take turns demonstrating these strategies for the other members of their group.

CHARACTER ✓ CHECK

Respect Help students discuss how teens who avoid risky situations demonstrate respect for themselves and their values. Then let volunteers share their responses to the Character Check questions.

FIGURE 2.2

REFUSAL STRATEGIES

Sometimes you must reinforce your decision to say no.

SAY NO IN A FIRM VOICE.
Do this calmly and clearly. Use expressions such as "I'd rather not."

EXPLAIN WHY.
State your feelings. Tell the other person that the suggested activity or behavior goes against your values or beliefs.

SUGGEST ALTERNATIVES.
Propose a safe, healthful activity to do instead.

USE APPROPRIATE BODY LANGUAGE.
Make it clear that you don't intend to back down from your position. Look directly into the other person's eyes.

LEAVE IF NECESSARY.
If the other person continues to pressure you, or simply won't take no for an answer, just walk away.

CHARACTER ✓ CHECK

Respect. When you apply refusal skills to avoid risky situations, you demonstrate respect for yourself and your values. **How can using refusal skills help you uphold your values and the values of your family?**

Refusal Skills

Think about how you handle situations in which you are asked to do something that you know is harmful or wrong. In such circumstances, you need to use refusal skills. **Refusal skills** are *strategies that can help you say no when you are urged to take part in behaviors that are unsafe or unhealthful, or that go against your values.* Practicing these strategies, including the ones shown in **Figure 2.2,** will help you resist risky behaviors.

Conflict Resolution Skills

In addition to practicing effective refusal skills, it is important to develop strategies for dealing with conflicts or disagreements. **Conflict resolution** is *the process of ending a conflict through cooperation and problem solving.* The key to conflict resolution is respecting the other person's rights as well as your own. Willingness to compromise will also help achieve a resolution that satisfies everyone. Follow these steps when dealing with a conflict:

► Take time to calm down and think through the situation.

► When discussing the conflict, speak calmly and listen attentively, asking questions when appropriate.

► Use a polite tone and try to brainstorm solutions where no one loses respect. Work to resolve the conflict peacefully.

30 **Chapter 2** Building Health Skills and Character

Cooperative Learning Activity

Refusal Skills Divide students into groups of three or four to role-play situations in which teens use effective communication and refusal skills. Within each group, one student should suggest a situation in which such skills are needed. Two other group members should role-play the situation. In groups with a fourth member, have that student evaluate the use of communication and refusal skills.

Have group members switch roles and repeat the process until every member has performed every task. Observers can give a positive critique by completing the sentence: *What I liked most about your refusal was . . .*

Self-Management Skills

When you practice self management, you take responsibility for your health and act in specific ways that promote your wellness. Two self-management skills, practicing healthful behaviors and managing stress, help provide a foundation of good health.

Practicing Healthful Behaviors

Choices you make today will affect your health in the future. Healthful behaviors are more than just actions that can protect you from illness or injury. These behaviors support every aspect of your health. Eating nutritious foods and getting regular medical and dental checkups as well as avoiding the use of tobacco, alcohol, and other drugs, are all behaviors that help you maintain and strengthen your overall health. Practicing healthful behaviors also involves expressing your feelings in healthful ways, building your self-esteem, and maintaining healthy relationships.

Managing Stress

Stress, the body's and mind's reactions to everyday demands, is a natural part of life. Being late to class, balancing many activities, and winning an award can all cause stress. Learning **stress management**, or *ways to deal with or overcome the negative effects of stress*, will become increasingly important as you assume more responsibility for your health and take on additional roles as an adult. Some strategies for managing stress include engaging in physical activity, listening to soothing music, managing time effectively, taking a warm bath, and laughing.

Analyzing Influences

How do you determine what health choices are right for you? Many factors influence your health. *Internal influences,* which include your knowledge, values, likes, dislikes, and desires, are based on your experiences and your perspective on life. You have a great deal of control over your internal influences. *External influences,* which come from outside sources, include your family, your friends and peers, your environment, your culture, laws, and the media. As you become aware of these influences, you will be better able to make healthful choices about everything from your personal behavior to which health products you buy.

Practicing healthful behaviors includes making everyday activities safe for you and those around you. *What healthful behaviors do you practice on a regular basis?*

Discussing

Ask students to explain what the term *self management* suggests to them. Ask: Are there any limits on teens' capacities for self management? If so, what are they? If not, why not? **L1**

Health Skills **Practice**

Healthy Relationships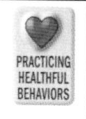
Have students meet in small groups to discuss their responses to these questions:

- What can teens do to maintain healthy relationships with adult family members?
- How can they maintain healthy relationships with siblings? With peers?

Discuss the groups' responses as a class. Then have students write their own plans in their private health journal for improving their relationships or for maintaining healthy relationships.

Discussing

Ask students to identify a healthful choice many teens make every day. (The decision not to smoke a cigarette is an example.) Then have students discuss specific internal and external influences that might help a teen make that healthful decision. **L1**

⌁⌁ *HEALTH LITERACY*

Medical Self-Care The growing medical self-care movement encourages people to take an active role in disease prevention and treatment. With access to health care providers, medical books, journals, and information from online services, many people who practice medical self-care also obtain the kits necessary to perform diagnostic laboratory tests.

Tests that may be performed at home include the confirmation of pregnancy, the detection of blood in stool samples, and measurement of blood glucose and cholesterol. When used as directed, home tests approved by the FDA are accurate and reliable. Emphasize that an individual should see a health care professional if a home test is positive for a problem.

Discussing

Lead students in a discussion about the importance of health advocacy. Ask: What effect does positively influencing others have on your own health?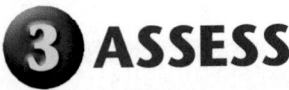

③ ASSESS

EVALUATING THE LESSON

Assign and discuss the Lesson 1 Review; then administer, grade, and discuss Lesson Quiz 4 in the TCR. 📁

RETEACHING

- Have students work with partners to write one sentence about each of the health skills discussed in this lesson.
- Ask students to complete Reteaching Activity 4 in the TCR. 📁

ENRICHMENT

Have interested students research, using print and online sources, the physical symptoms of stress. Have them summarize their findings in written reports. Remind them to proofread their writing for errors. They may need to develop several drafts before handing in their final error-free drafts.

④ CLOSE

Invite several volunteers to the front of the room and suggest a risky behavior to each. Have students demonstrate effective use of refusal skills.

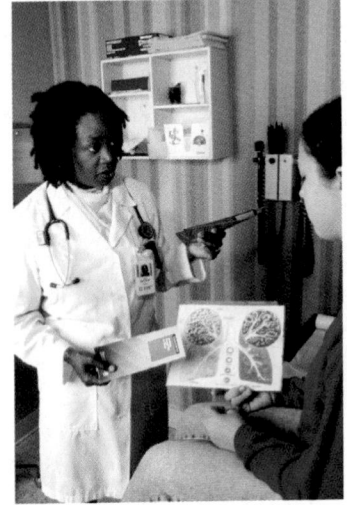

▼ **Talking to a health professional can help you obtain accurate, reliable information.** *Where else can you find valid health information?*

Accessing Information

Learning how to find and recognize trustworthy information will help you be better prepared to make healthful choices. When evaluating health information, check the validity of the source. Keep in mind that reliable sources of health information include:

▶ parents, guardians, and other trusted adults.

▶ library resources, such as encyclopedias and nonfiction books on science, medicine, nutrition, and fitness.

▶ reliable Internet sites, such as those posted by government and educational institutions.

▶ newspaper and magazine articles by health professionals or experts.

▶ government agencies, health care providers, and health organizations.

Advocacy

Advocacy is *taking action to influence others to address a health-related concern or to support a health-related belief.* This skill enables you to positively influence the health of those around you. In this responsible role, you can help others become informed and publicly support health causes that concern and interest you. Encouraging family, friends, peers, and community members to practice healthful behaviors is one way to practice health advocacy.

▶ Lesson 1 *Review*

Reviewing Facts and Vocabulary

1. Define the term *interpersonal communication*, and identify the role of "I" messages.

2. List five refusal strategies.

3. What is *stress management*? Identify three ways to reduce the effects of stress.

Thinking Critically

4. **Analyzing.** What are the advantages of peacefully resolving conflicts?

5. **Applying.** What are two ways you could show support for a health cause or organization?

Applying Health Skills

Stress Management. List all the healthful strategies you used this past week to relieve stress. Which ones helped the most?

SPREADSHEETS You can keep track of events and organize your thoughts by using a spreadsheet. For help in using spreadsheet software, go to **health.glencoe.com.**

32 **Chapter 2** Building Character and Health Skills

▶ Lesson 1 *Review*

Answers to Reviewing Facts and Vocabulary

1. The exchange of thoughts, feelings, and beliefs between two or more people. They help speakers avoid placing blame.

2. See Figure 2.2 for a list of refusal skills.

3. Ways to deal with or overcome the negative effects of stress; possible answers: running, relaxing, and laughing.

Answers to Thinking Critically

4. Possible answer: There will be no bad feelings; the resolution is likely to be fair and accepted by everyone involved.

5. Answers will vary but could include: handing out literature; participating in a walkathon; or wearing a pin or ribbon to symbolize the cause.

Making Responsible Decisions and Setting Goals

VOCABULARY

decision-making skills
values
goal
short-term goal
long-term goal
action plan

YOU'LL LEARN TO

• Identify decision-making skills that promote individual, family, and community health.

• Summarize the advantages of seeking advice and feedback regarding decision-making skills.

• Identify the processes involved in choosing and achieving goals.

 QUICK START What goals have you set for yourself in the past year? What steps did you take to reach your goals?

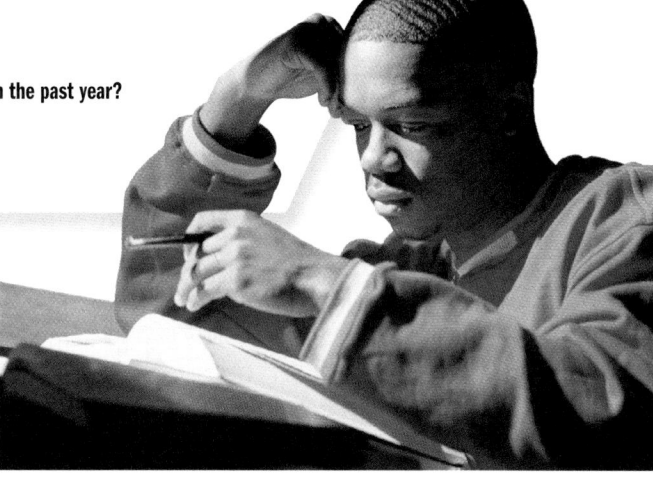

When you make decisions or set goals, you are exercising power over how healthy, happy, and productive you can be. Making responsible decisions and setting meaningful goals are important skills that can have a great impact on your life.

This teen made the decision to study for his exam instead of going out with friends. *What responsible decisions have you made in the past week?*

The Decision-Making Process

Decision-making skills are *steps that enable you to make a healthful decision.* The steps are designed to help you make decisions that protect your rights and health while respecting the rights and health of others. The six basic steps for making a decision are described in **Figure 2.3** on page 34. Often, you will find it helpful to seek advice from those with more experience, such as parents and guardians. Doing so can provide valuable feedback and strengthen family bonds and values.

Making Responsible Decisions and Setting Goals

1 FOCUS

 QUICK START Have a volunteer read the Quick Start assignment aloud. Suggest that each student think of a few personal goals they have set in the last year. Encourage students to keep that goal in mind as they write their responses to the Quick Start questions.

TYING TO PRIOR KNOWLEDGE

Ask: What are your goals? Let several volunteers respond. Point out that students are already familiar with making decisions and setting goals. They will learn more about these processes as they read the lesson.

Health Skills Features

"Setting Your Personal Health Goal," p. 35

GOAL SETTING

INTRODUCING VOCABULARY

• Have students meet in small groups to discuss possible relationships between vocabulary terms.

• Ask students to complete the Chapter 2 Study Guide in the *Student Activity Workbook*.

 Lesson 2 Resources

Teacher Classroom Resources

📁 Concept Mapping Activity 5
📁 Enrichment Activity 2
📁 Guided Reading Activities 5
📁 Lesson Plan 5
📁 Lesson Quiz 5
📁 Reteaching Activity 5

Student Activity Workbook

📁 Applying Health Skills 5
📁 Chapter 2 Study Guide

Multimedia

 Transparency 5

2 TEACH

Reinforcing Concepts

Ask students to cite examples of decisions that would require teens to seek the advice of adult family members. Have students summarize the advantages of seeking advice and feedback regarding such decisions. **L1**

Discussing

Ask students to identify some values that they think are commonly held. Ask:

• Does everyone hold these values? Why or why not?

• What kinds of conflicts can result from differences in values? **L1**

VISUAL LEARNING

Figure 2.3 Have students meet in groups to read and discuss the steps of the decision-making process. Ask group members to choose a major decision that many teens face and discuss how they might apply this process in that case.

Reinforcing Concepts

Ask students to suggest further examples of both short-term and long-term goals. Ask: How could an action plan help you reach goals such as these? Help students realize that short-term goals are frequently steps to accomplish long-term goals. **L1**

FIGURE 2.3

STEPS OF THE DECISION-MAKING PROCESS

Step 1: STATE THE SITUATION
Examine the situation and ask yourself: What decisions need to be made? Consider all the facts and who else is involved.

Step 2: LIST THE OPTIONS
What are the possible choices you could make? Remember that sometimes it is appropriate not to take action. Share your options with parents or guardians, siblings, teachers, or friends. Ask for their advice.

Step 3: WEIGH THE POSSIBLE OUTCOMES
Weigh the consequence of each option. Use the word *HELP* to guide your choice.
  • **H** *(Healthful)* What health risks, if any, will this option present?
  • **E** *(Ethical)* Does this choice reflect what you and your family believe is right?
  • **L** *(Legal)* Does this option violate any local, state, or federal laws?
  • **P** *(Parent Approval)* Would your parents or guardians approve of this choice?

Step 4: CONSIDER VALUES
Values are *the ideas, beliefs, and attitudes about what is important that help guide the way you live.* A responsible decision will reflect your values.

Step 5: MAKE A DECISION AND ACT ON IT
Use everything you know at this point to make a responsible decision. You can feel good that you have carefully prepared and thought about the situation and your options.

Step 6: EVALUATE THE DECISION
After you have made the decision and taken action, reflect on what happened. What was the outcome? How did your decision affect your health and the health of those around you? What did you learn? Would you take the same action again? If not, how would your choice differ?

Setting Personal Health Goals

Consider your plans for the future. What do you want to do with your life? Do your plans include further education and a family? What kind of career are you interested in pursuing? Setting goals can help you shape your life in positive ways by focusing your energy on behaviors that you want to develop or change. A **goal** is *something you aim for that takes planning and work.* Goal setting is also an effective way to build self-confidence, increase your self-esteem, and improve your overall health.

Cooperative Learning Activity

Analyzing Characters In small discussion groups, encourage students to talk about the decisions made by characters in novels or short stories they are currently reading or have recently read. Ask group members to discuss their responses to questions such as these:

• What decision did the character make?

• Did the character follow the steps of the decision-making process? How?
• What were the outcomes of the decision?
• How did the character feel about the outcomes?
• If you had been in that character's situation, what would you have done?

Types of Goals

Every goal involves planning. When you set a goal and plan strategies to reach it, you will need to consider how much time it will take to accomplish the goal. A **short-term goal**, such as finishing a project by Friday or cleaning your room before dinner, is *a goal that you can reach in a short period of time*. A **long-term goal** is *a goal that you plan to reach over an extended period of time*. Examples include improving your grades for the semester or making the cross country team next season. A long-term goal may take months or even years to accomplish. Often, short-term goals are steps in a plan to achieve a long-term goal. What kinds of short-term goals might help a person become a physician or a computer technician?

Health Minute

Setting Goals

Some guidelines to remember:

► Make sure that your goals are your own, not someone else's.
► Set a goal because it will help you grow, not because you want to outdo someone.
► If you do not achieve your goal, use what you've learned to set a new goal.

Hands-On Health ACTIVITY

Setting Your Personal Health Goal

In this activity, you will set a personal health goal and work to achieve it.

What You'll Need

• notebook
• pencil

What You'll Do

For the next week, use your notebook as a personal health goal journal. Record your efforts to reach your goal. At the end of the week, write a reflective summary of what you learned in the process.

1. **Set a goal.** Do you want to get along better with family members? Eat more nutritiously? Be more active? Set a realistic health goal, and write it down. Explain why you have chosen this goal and what changes you hope to accomplish.

2. **List steps to meet the goal.** Examine a variety of options to achieve the goal you have set. List the steps you will take to reach your goal.

3. **Identify sources of help.** List the names of people who can help and support you as you work toward your goal.

4. **Evaluate your progress, and adjust plans if necessary.** If there have been obstacles, give yourself more time, and work to overcome them. If you are moving ahead of schedule, you may want to set a more challenging goal.

Apply and Conclude

After a week, examine your progress. Has your plan been effective? How can it be strengthened? Extend your one-week plan to four weeks. Make it a habit to continue to set and work toward new health goals.

Lesson 2 Making Responsible Decisions and Setting Goals **35**

Hands-On Health

SETTING YOUR PERSONAL HEALTH GOAL

GOAL SETTING

NHES Standard 6 Students will demonstrate the ability to use goal-setting and decision-making skills to enhance health.

Objectives

• Identify the processes involved in choosing and achieving goals.
• Develop and implement a plan for a personal health goal.

Motivator

Give the class three minutes to brainstorm personal health goals as you list them on the board.

Teaching Strategies

1. Inform students that substituting healthy habits for those that are less healthy can make it easier to reach a goal (for example, taking a walk after school instead of eating a high-fat snack).
2. Tell students to include a regular reward system to reinforce their efforts.

✓ Assessment

Using a rubric, student work should provide comprehensive evidence of the following criteria to achieve the highest score:

✔ clear progression through a goal-setting process
✔ inclusion of a clear goal statement
✔ identification of a realistic goal
✔ plan for reaching the goal
✔ evaluation or reflection on action

More About...

Setting Goals Having goals is important for one's mental health because setting and reaching goals can improve one's self-esteem. Some people avoid setting goals because they see their lives as a series of events that just happen to them. Such people feel that they have little control over their futures, and that perception can lead to low self-esteem. Other people have a more optimistic attitude. These people have a sense of being in charge of their futures—that perception results in high self-esteem. Remind students that achieving goals is not a matter of luck. Things don't *just work out*. However, anyone who learns to set goals and follow action plans can make positive events happen.

Health Minute

Have students meet in groups to read and discuss the guidelines for setting goals. Ask: How can each of these guidelines make your goals more meaningful?

③ ASSESS

EVALUATING THE LESSON

Assign and discuss the Lesson 2 Review; then administer, grade, and discuss Lesson Quiz 5 in the TCR. 📁

RETEACHING

- Have students work in pairs. Have one student write, in his or her own words, the steps in the decision-making process. Ask the other student to do the same for the steps in an action plan for achieving goals.

- Ask students to complete Reteaching Activity 5 in the TCR. 📁

④ CLOSE

Have each student write one or two sentences identifying the most important new insight gained from studying this lesson.

▼ Reaching your goals through hard work brings personal satisfaction.

Achieving Your Goals

To establish and reach your goals, create an **action plan**, or *a multistep strategy to identify and achieve your goals.* Follow these steps:

- ▶ **Set a specific, realistic goal, and write it down.** State your goal as something positive. This will help motivate you.

- ▶ **List the steps you will take to reach your goal.** Look for ways to break your goal into smaller, short-term goals.

- ▶ **Identify sources of help and support.** Such sources might include friends, family members, peers, teachers, or neighbors.

- ▶ **Set a reasonable time frame for reaching your goal.** After deciding on a reasonable time, put it in writing.

- ▶ **Evaluate your progress by establishing checkpoints.** Periodically check how you are progressing, and make any necessary adjustments that will help you reach your goal.

- ▶ **Reward yourself for achieving your goal.** Enjoy the personal satisfaction reaching a goal brings. You might celebrate your achievement with your family or friends.

▶ Lesson 2 Review

Reviewing Facts and Vocabulary

1. What are the six steps of the decision-making process?
2. Summarize the advantages of seeking advice regarding decision-making skills.
3. Explain the difference between short-term and long-term goals, and provide an example of each.

Thinking Critically

4. **Applying.** Identify a major health-related decision that teens might have to make. How can teens access information and use decision-making skills to make an informed choice?
5. **Synthesizing.** Explain and defend this statement: *Decision making and goal setting are interrelated.*

36 **Chapter 2** Building Health Skills and Character

Applying Health Skills

Decision Making. Cari's friends want her to skip school to go to the beach with them. Apply the six steps of decision making to Cari's situation, and help her make a responsible choice.

WORD PROCESSING Use word-processing software to present your application of the decision-making steps. See **health.glencoe.com** for tips on using word-processing programs.

▶ Lesson 2 Review

Answers to Reviewing Facts and Vocabulary

1. See Figure 2.3.
2. By seeking advice and feedback, one can get a better sense of how a decision might play out. Advice and feedback can also help reinforce personal and family values.
3. Short-term goals can be reached in a short length of time. Long-term goals can be reached over an extended length of time. Short-term goals are often steps in a plan to achieve a long-term goal. Examples will vary.

Answers to Thinking Critically

4. Answers will vary.
5. Decision-making supports goal setting and vice versa. Explanations will vary.

Building Character

VOCABULARY

character
role model

YOU'LL LEARN TO

• Discuss the importance of good character for self, others, and community.

• Apply communication skills and practice behaviors that demonstrate consideration and respect for self, family, and others.

• Identify ways to demonstrate good character.

QUICK START On a sheet of paper, complete this sentence: *I am taking responsibility when I* . . . Then, write a paragraph explaining your statement.

As you have learned, it is important to consider and act on your most important beliefs and values when making a decision. Values shape your priorities, and they help you distinguish right from wrong. The values that help you make healthful, well-informed decisions are also traits of good character. **Character** can be defined as *those distinctive qualities that describe how a person thinks, feels, and behaves.*

What Is Good Character?

Good character is an outward expression of inner values. A person with good character demonstrates *core ethical values,* such as responsibility, honesty, integrity, and respect. These values are held in high regard across all cultures and age groups. Core ethical values are the highest of all human values, and they guide you toward healthy, responsible choices. When your behavior reflects such standards, you can feel confident that you are demonstrating the traits of a person with good character.

Character helps shape behavior. *What values might prompt the teen in the photo to return the found wallet?*

Lesson 3 Building Character **37**

①FOCUS

QUICK START Ask several volunteers to suggest completions for the Quick Start statement. Then let students work independently to write their own sentences and paragraphs. Have volunteers share their paragraphs.

TYING TO PRIOR KNOWLEDGE

Ask: What do you think is involved in having good character? After a brief discussion, tell students they will learn more about building character as they study this lesson.

Health Skills Features

"Character in Action," p. 39

ACCESSING INFORMATION

"Should Service Learning Be Required?" p. 40

INTRODUCING VOCABULARY

• Have volunteers use dictionaries to look up the definitions of the terms.

• Ask students to complete the Chapter 2 Study Guide in the *Student Activity Workbook.*

Lesson 3 *Resources*

Teacher Classroom Resources

📁 Concept Mapping Activity 6

📁 Cross-Curriculum Activity 2

📁 Decision Making Activity 2

📁 Guided Reading Activities 6

📁 Health Lab 2

📁 Lesson Plan 6

📁 Lesson Quiz 6

📁 Reteaching Activity 6

Student Activity Workbook

📁 Applying Health Skills 6

📁 Chapter 2 Study Guide

Multimedia

🖱 Transparency 6

② TEACH

Discussing

Encourage students to share their responses to these questions:

- Do you think character remains the same throughout your life, or do you think character can and does change? Give examples to support your opinion.

- What are some ways to demonstrate good character? **L1**

VISUAL LEARNING

Figure 2.4 Guide students in reading and discussing the traits of good character. Ask volunteers to explain each in their own words and to give specific examples.

Critical Thinking

Ask students to share their responses to these questions:

- Are the traits listed in Figure 2.4 the only traits of good character?

- Which other traits would you add to the list? Why?

- Are there some traits that are important to you but might not be important to others? If so, what are they? **L1**

HEALTH Online

Ask students to use the Web Links to learn more about how other teens have demonstrated positive character traits. Then have students discuss what they have learned. How can you apply these ideas in your own life?

FIGURE 2.4

TRAITS OF GOOD CHARACTER

A person of good character demonstrates these traits in his or her actions and behaviors.

Trustworthiness: If you are trustworthy, you are honest, loyal, and reliable—you do what you say you'll do. You have the courage to do the right thing, and you don't deceive, cheat, or steal.

Respect: Showing respect means being considerate of others and tolerant of differences. It also means using good manners. You make decisions that show you respect your health and the health of others. You treat people and property with care.

Responsibility: Being responsible means using self-control—you think before you act and consider the consequences. You are accountable for your choices and decisions—you don't blame others for your actions. Responsible people try to do their best, and they persevere even when things don't go as planned.

Fairness: If you are fair, you play by the rules, take turns, and share. You are open-minded, and you listen to others. You don't take advantage of others, and you don't assign blame to others.

Caring: A caring person is kind and compassionate. When you care about others, you express gratitude, you are forgiving, and you help people in need.

Citizenship: If you advocate for a safe and healthy school and community, you are demonstrating good citizenship. A good citizen obeys laws and rules and respects authority. Being a good neighbor and cooperating with others are also parts of good citizenship.

Character and Health

Because your character plays a significant role in your decisions, actions, and behavior, it impacts all aspects of your health. Developing good character enhances each side of your health triangle. For example, if you view yourself with respect and value your physical health, you are more likely to take care of your body by eating nutritious foods and keeping physically active. When you act with responsibility and fairness, both your mental/emotional and social health will improve. When you feel good about yourself, your relationships with others are strengthened.

HEALTH Online

Learn more about putting good character into action by clicking on Web Links at **health.glencoe.com**.

Traits of Good Character

There are several different traits that contribute to good character. **Figure 2.4** identifies six primary traits of good character. Developing and strengthening these traits will assist you in becoming the best person you can be.

38 Chapter 2 Building Health Skills and Character

— School to Work —

Core Ethical Values Ask how students think core ethical values might be applied in the workplace. Then explain that some businesses have adopted their own guidelines of ethical conduct based on core ethical values. Have a group of interested volunteers use online resources to learn about some of these guidelines. Ask these students to

share with the rest of the class the guidelines established by these businesses. Ask:

- How are the lists from various businesses similar? How are they different?

- How do you think these guidelines would affect people associated with the business?

Developing Your Character

Character and core ethical values are learned when you're young and developed throughout your life. To take a more active role in your character development:

► Stand up for your beliefs.

► Learn from people who demonstrate good character traits. Ask family members for tips on strengthening values.

► Join volunteer groups in your school or community. Form friendships with people who exhibit core ethical values.

Real-Life Application

Character in Action

A person with good character can inspire people to make a difference in the world. The teen showcased here began a pen-pal program that links young people suffering from life-threatening illness with other teens around the country.

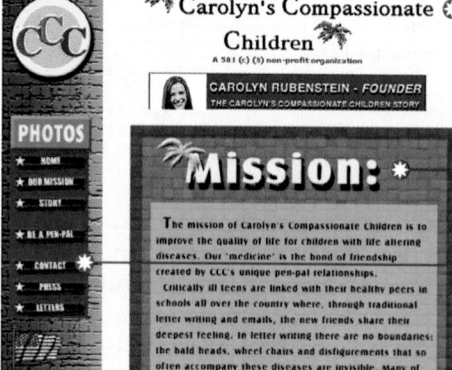

Carolyn's Compassionate Children
A 501 (c) (3) non-profit organization

CAROLYN RUBENSTEIN - FOUNDER
THE CAROLYN'S COMPASSIONATE CHILDREN STORY

Mission:

The mission of Carolyn's Compassionate Children is to improve the quality of life for children with life altering diseases. Our 'medicine' is the bond of friendship created by CCC's unique pen-pal relationships.

Critically ill teens are linked with their healthy peers in schools all over the country where, through traditional letter writing and emails, the new friends share their deepest feeling. In letter writing there are no boundaries: the bald heads, wheel chairs and disfigurements that so often accompany these diseases are invisible. Many of the participants experience, for the first time through the letters, the normal teen-age activities they are isolated from.

• **Character Traits:** Compassion, caring, and courage.

• **Mission:** Create a support network among teens with life-threatening diseases.

• **Taking Action:** Contact hospitals and other organizations to establish a network.

ACTIVITY

Choose an organization with volunteer opportunities. Research information on the organization's mission and programs. Which character traits do members of the organization display? Why are these traits necessary to meet the organization's goals? Write a paragraph summarizing your findings.

CHARACTER IN ACTION

ACCESSING INFORMATION

NHES Standard 2 Students will demonstrate the ability to access valid health information and health-promoting products and services.

Objectives

• Discuss the importance of good character for self, others, and community.

• Demonstrate the ability to evaluate community health organizations that provide health information or services.

Motivator

Ask students to explain how volunteering demonstrates good character.

Teaching Strategies

1. Bring in newspapers, phone books, and brochures on charitable organizations.

2. Encourage students to contact organizations in which they are interested and inquire about volunteer opportunities.

Assessment

Using a rubric, student work should provide comprehensive evidence of the following criteria to achieve the highest score:

✔ citation of specific source
✔ evaluation of the source
✔ ability to access appropriate community resources to meet specific needs
✔ explanation of how information from the source relates to character

Home and Community

Mentoring Programs Many communities offer mentoring programs for students in elementary, middle, and even high schools. In such programs, adults usually spend time with individual students, offering support and encouragement and serving as positive role models. Ask a group of interested volunteers to learn about mentoring programs in their community. Ask:

• What programs are available?
• What group or agency sponsors each program?
• Who are the mentors in these programs?
• Whom do the programs serve?
• Do any of the programs accept teen mentors? What are the requirements?

Ask these volunteers to discuss their findings with the rest of the class.

Exploring Issues

SHOULD SERVICE LEARNING BE REQUIRED?

Ask students to describe service learning. Service learning combines learning with community service without pay. Ask students who have volunteered either independently or as part of a school program to share their experiences. Have students read the feature and discuss the viewpoints in small groups. Then discuss the issues as a class.

Discussing

Help students discuss their responses to these questions: Can teens be role models? How? For whom? L1

Critical Thinking

Have students identify several athletes or performers whom young people sometimes look to as role models. Ask:

- What kinds of character traits do these celebrities demonstrate?

- Who is responsible for the status they have as role models?

- Do you think it is fair to expect a person with unusual athletic or performing ability to serve as a role model? Why or why not?

- What are the risks when an athlete or performer demonstrates inappropriate character traits? L1

Exploring Issues

Should Service Learning Be Required?

Since volunteering is a valuable experience, do you think schools should require service learning?

Viewpoint 1: Chad D., age 16
My experience of volunteering at a senior center through a school service learning program was very positive and taught me a lot of things that can't be learned in a classroom. I wouldn't have known about this opportunity if my school didn't require it. I think it's a great idea to require service learning in schools; it'll open people's eyes to volunteer and career opportunities.

Viewpoint 2: Lisa H., age 15
Isn't the whole point of volunteering that it's done by choice? I'm afraid that forcing it on students may turn them away from the idea. Some teens already have jobs, family commitments, or roles in their faith community that help them demonstrate good character. Service learning should be an *option* in the curriculum. That way, students can make their own decisions about how, when, and where they want to give back to the community.

ACTIVITY

What do you think? Do you agree with Chad that service learning offers benefits not available in the classroom? What do you think of Lisa's argument that mandatory service learning is a contradiction in terms? Present your views in a one-page essay.

Teens can be important role models for younger students.

Positive Role Models

Having positive role models is important in developing and strengthening good character traits. A **role model** is *someone whose success or behavior serves as an example for others.* Many people look to their families for role models. Parents, grandparents, and siblings are often the people who best support your goals and promote your health. They can inspire and encourage basic values such as working hard, staying focused, planning ahead, being honest, and engaging in safe and healthful behaviors. Other role models may include teachers, coaches, religious leaders, and volunteers.

Think about the character traits that your role models demonstrate. Do you show the same traits in your daily actions? When your behaviors reflect good character, you may inspire others to act in kind, responsible ways, too. In return, you will experience increased feelings of self-worth, satisfaction, and a sense of purpose.

40 Chapter 2 Building Health Skills and Character

Curriculum Connections

Social Studies Have volunteers research how other cultures define good character and compare the traits to those listed in the text.

Language Arts Ask students to consider the kind of character they are intent on building. Have them imagine themselves at the age of 35. Have students write fictional journal entries about their attitudes and behaviors. They may want to reflect on their fictional high school years and discuss their strengths and weaknesses. Have students develop several drafts of their writing. Remind them to proofread for errors, before handing in a final draft.

Demonstrating Character

By demonstrating good character, you practice behaviors that have a positive effect on both yourself and others at home, at school, and in your community.

▶ **Make a difference at home.** You demonstrate trustworthiness and reliability at home when you carry out your responsibilities. By showing respect and caring in daily actions, you will also strengthen your family relationships.

▶ **Make a difference at school.** At this stage in life, you are probably beginning to evaluate the rules that others have set for you. By observing school rules, you show respect for teachers and fellow students.

▶ **Make a difference in your community.** Good citizenship means obeying laws, respecting the needs of others, and being tolerant of differences. Take advantage of the opportunity you have to model good character and be a positive influence on those around you.

Helping out with household tasks is a way to demonstrate good character at home. *How do you contribute to your home, school, and community?*

Lesson 3 *Review*

Reviewing Facts and Vocabulary

1. What is *character*? How is good character related to values?

2. Name the six primary traits of good character.

3. List three ways of demonstrating good character in your home, your school, and your community.

Thinking Critically

4. **Synthesizing.** Why do you think that caring, responsibility, and respect are values that exist across cultures?

5. **Applying.** In what ways can you use communication skills to demonstrate consideration and respect for self, family, and others?

Applying Health Skills

Advocacy. Prepare a message about an important health cause or organization. The message should be appropriate for a specific audience, such as children, teens, parents, or individuals with a disability.

PRESENTATION SOFTWARE You can use presentation software to include images in your advocacy message. Find help in using presentation software at **health.glencoe.com.**

Lesson 3 Building Character **41**

Activity

Have students draw a three-column chart with these column headings: *Home, School, Community.* In each column, have students list at least three specific things they can do to make a positive difference in each of these areas.

3 ASSESS

EVALUATING THE LESSON

Assign and discuss the Lesson 3 Review; then administer, grade, and discuss Lesson Quiz 6 in the TCR.

RETEACHING

• Have students write three short paragraphs, each describing how to demonstrate good character. Remind them to proofread their writing for spelling and grammar.

• Ask students to complete Reteaching Activity 6 in the TCR.

4 CLOSE

Have students complete the following sentence: *A person with good character…*

Lesson 3 *Review*

Answers to Reviewing Facts and Vocabulary

1. It is the distinctive qualities that describe how a person thinks, feels, and behaves. It is an outward expression of inner values.

2. Trustworthiness, respect, responsibility, fairness, caring, citizenship.

3. See page 41.

Answers to Thinking Critically

4. Possible answer: These traits enable people to have strong and lasting relationships, which are important to all communities.

5. Examples may include listening to others and communicating wants and needs in a nonthreatening way.

41

Health Advocacy in the Media

NHES Standard 4 Students will analyze the influence of culture, media, technology, and other factors on health.

Objective

Examine how good citizenship and media attention can impact various public health issues.

Motivator

Have students brainstorm a list of the ways in which they can demonstrate good citizenship in their school or community.

Teaching Strategies

Awareness Remind students that the media plays a crucial role in the success of advocacy campaigns by making people aware of the situation and showing how to become involved.

Analysis Ask students to pay close attention to how the celebrity draws media focus to the cause. Does the celebrity host large fund-raisers or talk about the cause in interviews? Has the celebrity testified before Congress regarding the issue?

Reflection Conduct a brief discussion on how the involvement of these celebrities reflects their character.

Take Action Discuss the importance of involvement in their local community. Encourage students to follow through with their proposals by implementing the plans they have suggested.

✓Assessment

Student outlines should explain what the organization does, what sort of media attention they receive, and what the celebrity has done to further the cause.

42

Eye ON THE Media

Health Advocacy in the Media

Advocacy organizations are usually nonprofit companies that raise awareness about and raise money for different social, political, or health causes. A high-profile media personality can benefit the cause of an advocacy organization by bringing attention to the cause. In this activity, you will examine how good citizenship and media attention can have a positive impact on various public health issues.

```
┌──────────────────────────────────────────┐
│   Name of organization and its purpose    │
└──────────────────────────────────────────┘
              │
      ┌────────────────┐
      │ Media Campaigns │
      └────────────────┘
```

Type of media: charity golf tournament	Type of media: TV game show	Type of media:	Type of media:
Purpose: to raise funds for research	**Purpose:** to raise money and raise public awareness	**Purpose:**	**Purpose:**
Celebrity involvement: [Name of celebrity] sponsors the event and encourages media to attend.	**Celebrity involvement:** [Name of celebrity] enters game show as a contestant to win money for the cause.	**Celebrity involvement:**	**Celebrity involvement:**

ACTIVITY

Identify a high-profile media personality who is involved in a health advocacy organization or cause. Research the purpose of the organization and the role the celebrity plays in advocating for its cause. Review the media attention the organization gets and by what means. Organize the information you collect into a chart like the one above.

EXPRESS YOUR VIEWS

Write a proposal that suggests how you can help bring local attention to the cause of the health advocacy organization you have researched. Include strategies on how to use local media to help raise awareness or to help raise money for the issue or cause.

More About...

Elizabeth Taylor raises money for AIDS research and treatment, and Christopher Reeve works to raise awareness of spinal cord research. There are many examples of how celebrity and media attention can raise awareness and help further the cause of public health issues worldwide. The United Nations has used celebrities to help promote its causes for years. Celebrities who have volunteered their time for the UN and various UN agencies include Audrey Hepburn, Muhammad Ali, Magic Johnson, Michael Douglas, and many more. The UN screens possible celebrity advocates not only for their ability to bring media attention to the cause but also for their good character traits and their dedication to humanitarian issues.

CROSS-CURRICULUM CONNECTIONS

Campaign for Character. Demonstrating good character can promote your health and bring you personal satisfaction. Create a poster for younger students that stresses the importance of developing good character. Present and explain the six primary traits of good character, and encourage your audience to take an active role in strengthening these traits. To back up your message, you might include anecdotes from your own experiences as well as examples of people you admire.

Write a Report. Louis Pasteur, Clara Barton, and Jonas Salk are all individuals who have made significant contributions to community health. Choose one of these historical figures or another individual who has striven to improve the health of others. Research that person's life and accomplishments, focusing on his or her contributions to the field of health. What qualities and actions helped this individual achieve his or her goals?

Add Up Your Goal. Laurie has set a long-term goal to make the swim team next year. To help her reach that goal, she has decided she will swim three days a week for the next thirty weeks. For each session, she plans to swim five laps. How many laps will Laurie swim by the end of the thirty weeks?

Research a Topic. Managing stress is an important aspect of developing good health skills. In recent years, the old adage "laughter is the best medicine" has been proven by scientists and medical researchers to be more fact than myth. Research laughter, how it affects the body, and particularly, how it affects brain chemistry. Write a brief report explaining how laughter works and why laughter might be an important part of developing your personal health skills.

Family Counselor

Do you have a keen understanding of how values direct behavior within a family? Are you able to deal with people from varied backgrounds? If so, a career as a family counselor might be for you. These professionals work with entire families or with individual family members to solve problems and improve relationships.

To enter this profession, you'll need a four-year college degree and a master's degree in counseling. Find out more about this and other health careers by clicking on Career Corner at **health.glencoe.com**.

Chapter 2 Review **43**

CROSS-CURRICULUM CONNECTIONS

Enrich student learning by connecting the topic of building health skills and character to one of the four subject areas presented on this page. The activity may be completed individually or with a partner.

Language Arts Discuss strategies for developing an engaging poster. Remind students that the language should appeal to younger students.

Social Studies Suggest students look at several different sources for research, including biographies and autobiographies.

Math Answer: 3 days/week $\times$ 30 weeks $\times$ 5 laps/day = 450 laps.

Science Direct students to appropriate resources in the library on current scientific research regarding laughter and its effects on the brain and the body. Students should explain that stress hormones could be reduced by laughter.

Have students read and discuss the Career Corner information on family counseling. Ask interested students to explore the Glencoe Health Web site at **health.glencoe.com** for more information on this career.

Portfolio Assessment

Self-Evaluation Direct students to review the Health Skills Activities and other activities completed in the chapter. Encourage each student to select one finished product or activity that demonstrates his or her best work for the chapter and that represents the student's learning goals. Have students explain what they have learned and how the examples they have selected demonstrate their growth in health literacy, knowledge, and skills.

Teacher Classroom Resources Assign Performance Assessment 2, "Effective Communication Skills," in the TCR.

Chapter 2 *Review*

CHECKING COMPREHENSION

- Assign and discuss the chapter review.
- Use the Chapter 2 MindJogger Videoquiz to review the chapter. ▶◀

CHAPTER 2 REVIEW ANSWERS

Exploring Health Terms

1. interpersonal communication
2. Conflict resolution
3. stress management
4. Advocacy
5. goal
6. long-term goal
7. action plan
8. values
9. character
10. role model

Recalling the Facts

1. Clearly say what you mean; pay attention to how you say something; be a good listener; be aware of your body language.

2. Strategies that can help you say no when you are urged to take part in behaviors that are unsafe, unhealthful, or that go against your values.

3. Take time to calm down and think over the situation; speak calmly and listen attentively, asking questions when appropriate; use a polite tone, and try to brainstorm solutions in which no one loses respect.

4. Self-management skills provide practice in behaviors that benefit both short- and long-term health. Examples include practicing healthful behaviors and stress management.

5. Steps that enable you to make a healthful decision.

▶ EXPLORING HEALTH TERMS *Answer the following questions on a sheet of paper.*

Lesson 1 *Replace the underlined words with the correct term.*

conflict resolution	advocacy
refusal skills	stress management
interpersonal communication	
health skills	

1. "I" messages are a form of <u>refusal skills</u>.
2. <u>Advocacy</u> is a process to help you resolve conflict through cooperation and problem solving.
3. People use <u>conflict resolution</u> to manage the body's reactions to everyday demands.
4. <u>Stress management</u> is a responsible role in which you influence others' health behaviors.

Lesson 2 *Match each definition with the correct term.*

action plan	goal
decision-making skills	values
long-term goal	short-term goal

5. Something you aim for that takes planning and work.
6. A goal that you can plan to reach over an extended period of time.
7. A multistep strategy for identifying and achieving your goals.
8. The ideas, beliefs, and attitudes about what is important that help guide the way you live.

Lesson 3 *Fill in the blanks with the correct term.*

character	role model

A person with high standards usually exhibits good (_9_). This person often makes a positive (_10_).

▶ RECALLING THE FACTS *Use complete sentences to answer the following questions.*

Lesson 1

1. List the strategies for effective communication.
2. What are refusal skills?
3. What steps should you follow to resolve a conflict?
4. Why are self-management skills important? Give an example of two of these skills.

Lesson 2

5. What are decision-making skills?
6. Define the term *value*.
7. Explain how the word *HELP* can assist you in weighing the possible consequences of a decision and making the right choice.
8. What are the six steps of a goal-setting action plan?

Lesson 3

9. Describe what it means to demonstrate the character trait of trustworthiness.
10. How does character impact your health?
11. How can you take an active role in your character development?
12. What are some benefits of being a positive role model?

---

6. The ideas, beliefs, and attitudes about what is important that help guide the way you live.

7. The letters that make up the word HELP assist you in recalling questions to ask regarding each possible choice. H is for healthful; E is for ethical; L is for legal; and P is for parent approval. Take these factors into account during the decision-making process.

8. Set a specific, realistic goal, and write it down; list the steps to reach the goal; identify sources of help and support; set a reasonable time frame for reaching the goal; evaluate your progress by establishing checkpoints; reward yourself for achieving the goal.

9. Trustworthy people are honest, loyal, and reliable. They have the courage to do the right thing, and they don't deceive, cheat, or steal.

► THINKING CRITICALLY

1. **Synthesizing.** Gwen tries her best to fit in with a group that she recognizes takes unnecessary risks. She follows along anyway and usually suffers the consequences of her decisions. What skill does Gwen need to develop? Explain how this skill could improve her overall health. *(LESSON 1)*

2. **Analyzing.** Why is recognizing consequences important when using the decision-making process? How do values enter into the decision-making process? *(LESSON 2)*

3. **Evaluating.** Identify a trait of good character that you possess, and list ways that you demonstrate that trait. *(LESSON 3)*

► HEALTH SKILLS APPLICATION

1. **Communication Skills.** List examples of body language that you or others use when communicating. Pick two examples, and explain how they reinforce verbal messages. *(LESSON 1)*

2. **Decision Making.** Imagine that you are trying to improve your grades to make the basketball team. Which activity would you attend if they occurred at the same time—an extra basketball practice or a study session? Use the decision-making steps to help you make your choice. *(LESSON 2)*

3. **Analyzing Influences.** Do all individuals who are famous because of their achievements make positive role models? Why or why not? *(LESSON 3)*

BEYOND the Classroom

Parent Involvement

Advocacy. Learn more about a nonprofit organization in your community. With your parents, find out how your family could become involved. By volunteering your time, you can help the organization achieve its mission, get firsthand knowledge of how it operates, and help individuals with special needs in your community.

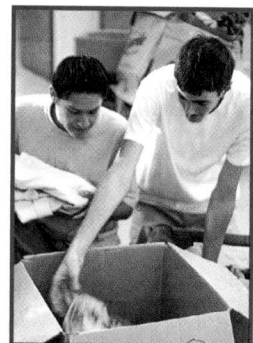

School and Community

Conduct an Interview. In certain professions—teaching and law, for example—effective communication is especially critical. Interview an individual from one of these professions, and learn about the guidelines he or she uses to ensure good communication.

10. Good character enhances each side of the health triangle. If you view yourself with respect, you are more likely to take care of your physical health. When you act with responsibility and fairness, both mental/emotional and social health are improved. When you feel good about yourself, relationships with others are strengthened.

11. Possible answers: By being aware of how your thoughts, words, and actions are perceived by others; by learning from people who demonstrate good character traits; by joining volunteer groups; by forming friendships with people who exhibit core ethical values.

12. A positive role model experiences increased feelings of self-worth, increased personal contentment, and sense of purpose and community.

Thinking Critically

1. Learning to use refusal skills would benefit Gwen most. She can use this skill to say no to activities that she knows are risky. Doing so could better protect her health.

2. Considering consequences helps you identify whether a course of action is in line with personal and family values, is healthful, and is legal. Weighing the consequences helps you achieve the best possible outcome for your decision.

3. Answers will vary.

Health Skills Application

1. Possible answers: A frown could reflect confusion, concern, or anger. A smile usually reflects happiness.

2. Answers will vary but should show thoughtful application of the decision-making steps.

3. Although they are famous, their behavior may not reflect the highest values.

EVALUATE

• Use the reproducible Chapter 2 Test in the TCR, or construct your own using the Testmaker software.

• Use Performance Assessment 2 in the TCR.

ENRICHMENT

Ask students to complete Enrichment Activity 2 in the TCR.

BEYOND the Classroom

Keep students involved in the community, and encourage parent participation by assigning the activities on this page for students to work on outside of class.

45

Lessons	Standards		Features
	National	**State/Local**	
1 **Making Consumer Choices** *pages 48–53*	National Health Education Standards 2.1, 2.2, 2.3		*Real-Life* **Application** • Reading Product Labels *(Accessing Information)*, page 51
2 **Choosing Community Health Services** *pages 54–59*	National Health Education Standards 2.4, 2.5, 2.6, 6.1		Health Skills **Activity** • Getting a Sports Physical *(Decision Making)*, page 56
3 **Managing Consumer Problems** *pages 60–63*	National Health Education Standards 5.1, 5.3		*Real-Life* **Application** • Writing a Letter of Complaint *(Accessing Information)*, page 62
4 **Understanding Public Health Services** *pages 64–67*	National Health Education Standards 1.7, 7.5		Hands-On Health • Raising Awareness of Public Health Programs *(Advocacy)*, page 66

Reproducible Resources	Assessment	Technology
Student Activity Workbook for use with each chapter 📁 Concept Mapping Activity 7 📁 Guided Reading Activities 7 📁 Health Lab 3 📁 Lesson Plan 7 📁 Parent Letter and Activities 3 📁 Reteaching Activity 7	📁 Lesson Quiz 7	💿 TeacherWorks® 💻 Internet Activities
📁 Concept Mapping Activity 8 📁 Current Health Issues 3 📁 Decision-Making Activity 3 📁 Guided Reading Activities 8 📁 Lesson Plan 8 📁 Reteaching Activity 8	📁 Lesson Quiz 8	🖎 Transparency 7 💿 TeacherWorks®
📁 Concept Mapping Activity 9 📁 Guided Reading Activities 9 📁 Lesson Plan 9 📁 Reteaching Activity 9	📁 Lesson Quiz 9	🖎 Transparency 8 💿 TeacherWorks®
📁 Concept Mapping Activity 10 📁 Cross-Curriculum Activity 3 📁 Enrichment Activity 3 📁 Guided Reading Activities 10 📁 Lesson Plan 10 📁 Reteaching Activity 10	📁 Lesson Quiz 10	🖎 Transparency 9 💿 TeacherWorks®

0:00 OUT OF TIME

If time does not permit teaching the entire chapter, use:
- Figure 3.1, p. 49
- Real-Life Application, p. 51
- Figure 3.3, p. 55
- Health Minute, p. 61
- Figure 3.4, p. 67

Language Diversity

🎧 English Audio CD Program
🎧 Spanish Audio CD Program
📁 English Summaries, Quizzes, and Activities
📁 Spanish Summaries, Quizzes, and Activities
📁 Spanish Parent Letters and Activities

End of Chapter Assessment

Blackline Masters

📁 Chapter 3 Test
📁 Performance Assessment Activity 3
📁 Unit 1 Test

Technology

💿 Vocabulary PuzzleMaker
📼 MindJogger Videoquiz
💿 *ExamView®* Pro Testmaker

Professional Health Series

Dealing with Sensitive Issues
Planning a Coordinated School Health Program
Promoting Character Education
Home, School, and Community Involvement

Key to Ability Levels

Teaching strategies that appear throughout the chapter have been identified by one of the following codes to give teachers an idea of their suitability for students of varying learning styles and abilities.

L1 Strategies should be within the ability range of all students. Full class participation is often required. Teacher direction is usually needed.

L2 Strategies are designed for average to above-average students or for small groups. Some teacher direction is needed.

L3 Strategies are designed for students able and willing to work independently. Minimal teacher direction is needed.

ELL Strategies should be within the ability range of students learning the English language.

🔲 Block scheduling strategies are useful in a block scheduling format.

CHAPTER OVERVIEW

Chapter 3 discusses the skills and information students need as they become health-literate consumers. Guidelines are provided for selecting health products and services, and agencies that handle complaints and safeguard public health are identified.

Lesson 1 Consumers should be aware of the factors that influence their choices about health products and services. They should also know how to evaluate health products for appropriateness and safety.

Lesson 2 A variety of health care providers and health care facilities meet medical needs. Several forms of health insurance are available to help with medical costs.

Lesson 3 Consumers should be alert to health fraud and malpractice. Several agencies are available to help health consumers with problems.

Lesson 4 Agencies are available to administer public health at the local, national, and international levels.

Health Skills Features

- Real-Life Application (*Accessing Information*), p. 51
- Health Skills Activity (*Decision Making*), p. 56
- Real-Life Application (*Accessing Information*), p. 62
- Hands-On Health (*Advocacy*), p. 66

46

Chapter 3

Being a Health-Literate Consumer

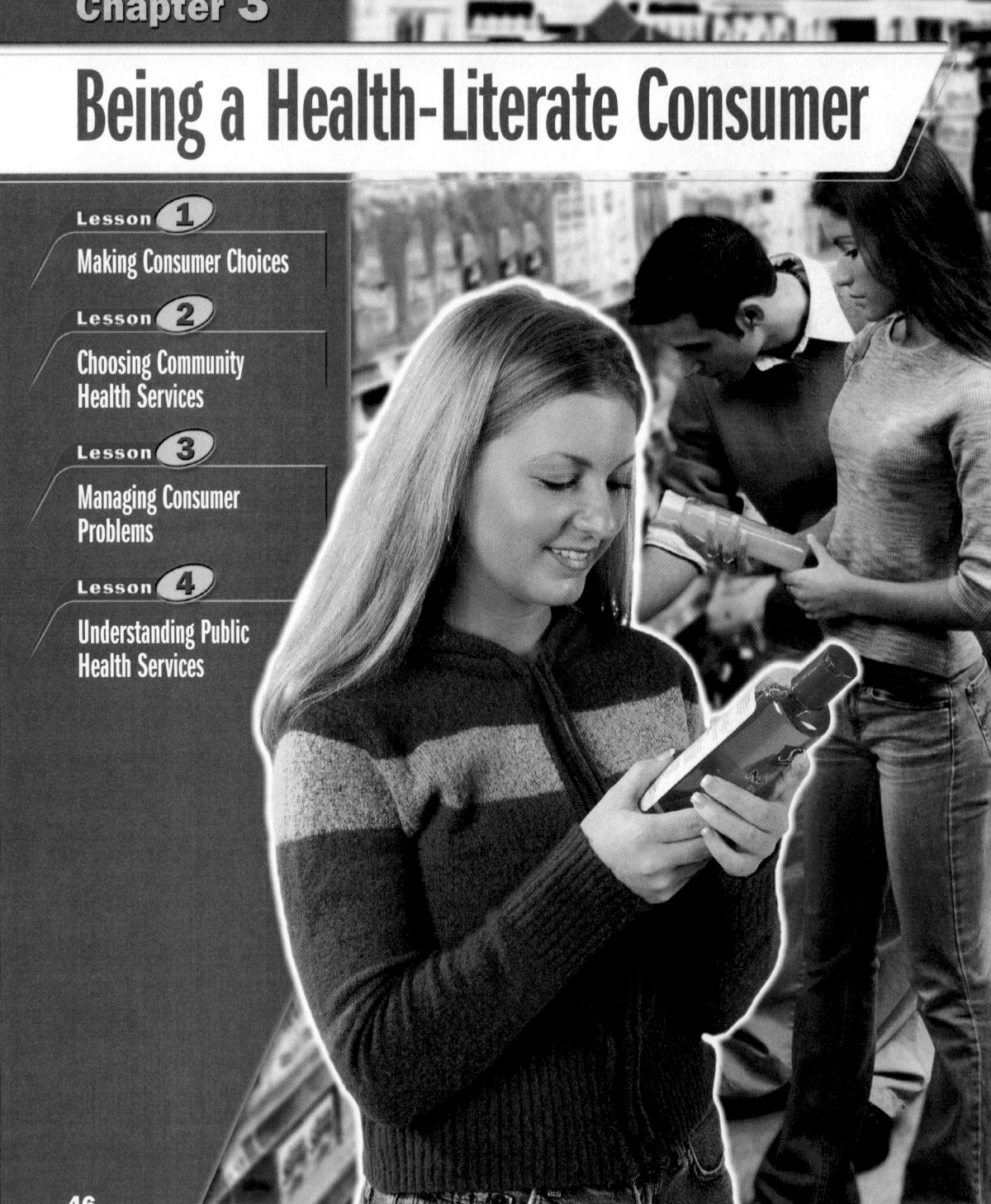

Lesson 1
Making Consumer Choices

Lesson 2
Choosing Community Health Services

Lesson 3
Managing Consumer Problems

Lesson 4
Understanding Public Health Services

46

MEETING STUDENT DIVERSITY

Language Diversity Use the following suggestions to help students who have difficulty with English:

- Pair English language learners with native speakers of English who can restate the Chapter Summary in language that helps students comprehend important concepts.

- Direct auditory learners or those students with language diversity to the *Glencoe Health Audio CD Program.* Available in English and Spanish, this component provides an audio and written summary of the chapter.

- Use photographs, drawings, or magazine clippings to help students visualize the important concepts of the chapter.

Personal Health Inventory ✓

What's Your Health Status?

Read each statement below and respond by writing *yes* or *no* for each item.

1. As a consumer of health care products and services, I understand that choices are influenced by a variety of factors.

2. I know my rights as a consumer.

3. I have regular medical and dental checkups.

4. I am knowledgeable about where to go for specific health concerns.

5. I read directions and warnings carefully before using any health care product.

6. I evaluate advertisements and confirm any health claims before purchasing a product.

7. I pay attention to the effectiveness of the health care products that I use and the medical treatments that I receive.

8. I know where and how to get help with a consumer problem.

9. I know about public health agencies and their functions.

10. I am aware of specific public health agencies in my community.

Keep this personal inventory for review later in the chapter. When you complete the chapter, review your answers and identify two or three areas in which you could improve as a consumer of health care products and services.

Quick **Write**

Using Visuals. What is one way to make sure that you are purchasing the product that best meets your needs? Read the label. Make a list of the different types of information you have seen on product labels. How have you used this information to decide what to purchase?

47

Personal Health Inventory ✓

Have students meet in cooperative groups to read and discuss the statements in the Personal Health Inventory. Encourage group members to expand on each statement. For example, they might identify several factors that influence choices of health products and services, and they might name several rights that consumers have.

After the group discussions, have students complete the inventory independently. Remind students that their responses are for their own use only; they should answer honestly and then keep their inventories. When they have finished reading Chapter 3, students should review their responses and make plans to improve their skills as consumers of health care products and services.

Quick **Write**

Using Visuals Have students look at the photographs. Ask:

- What are the teens doing?
- How do you think the teen will decide which product to buy?

After a brief discussion, have students read and respond to the Quick Write assignment. Let students work independently to write their lists and explanations. Then encourage them to share and discuss their ideas.

TECHNOLOGY OPTIONS

MINDJOGGER

VIDEOQUIZ

To preview or review chapter content, you may wish to use the Chapter 3 MindJogger Videoquiz.

HEALTH **Online**

Online Resources for the Teacher For a fresh approach to health topics and an in-depth look at health issues, use these online resources found under Teacher Resources at **health.glencoe.com:**

- Block Schedule Lesson Plans
- Technology Projects
- Health Updates

Making Consumer Choices

 FOCUS

Lesson 1

Making Consumer Choices

VOCABULARY
health consumer
media
advertising
comparison shopping
warranty
online shopping

YOU'LL LEARN TO
- Identify the factors that influence consumer decisions about health care products and services.
- Analyze the health messages delivered through advertising in the media.
- Demonstrate ways to utilize criteria to evaluate health products for appropriateness.

 QUICK START List five influences on your choice of health care products or services. Circle the two that most often affect your decisions.

QUICK START Have students read the Quick Start assignment, and invite volunteers to name several health care products and services. Then give students five minutes to write their lists. Encourage volunteers to share and discuss their ideas.

TYING TO PRIOR KNOWLEDGE

Let student volunteers describe some of the health care products and services they have recently chosen along with resources they have used to assess these products. Explain that, as they read this lesson, they will learn more about making such choices.

Health Skills Features

"Reading Product Labels," p. 51

ACCESSING INFORMATION

INTRODUCING VOCABULARY

- Allow five minutes for partners to discuss the vocabulary terms, sharing their current understanding of each. Then have the partners work together to find and read the terms' definitions in the Glossary.

- Ask students to complete the Chapter 3 Study Guide in the *Student Activity Workbook.*

 Part of being a wise consumer involves making informed purchasing decisions about health- and fitness-related products.

Many health care products and services are available to the consumer. Supermarket and drug store shelves are lined with dozens of well-known brands of personal care products. Phone books list hundreds of different types of health care professionals, clinics, and other health services. What information do you need before you make a decision regarding health care products and services?

Being an Informed Health Consumer

In the years to come, you will become more responsible for decisions regarding your health. Although most decisions about health services are still in the hands of your parents or guardians, you are probably already making choices about such products as shampoo, skin cleansers, or deodorant. Learning about available health products and services and understanding how to judge their effectiveness and reliability will help you become an informed health consumer. A **health consumer** is *anyone who purchases or uses health products or services.*

Lesson 1 Resources

Teacher Classroom Resources
- Concept Mapping Activity 7
- Guided Reading Activities 7
- Health Lab 3
- Lesson Plan 7
- Lesson Quiz 7
- Parent Letter and Activities 3
- Reteaching Activity 7

Student Activity Workbook
- Applying Health Skills 7
- Chapter 3 Study Guide

Influences on Your Decisions

Many factors influence your decision to buy specific products and services. Internal factors, such as habit and personal taste, can play a role, as can such external factors as the opinions of family members and friends, and cost. One important external factor that influences purchasing decisions is the **media**, or *the various methods of communicating information*. Television, radio, newspapers, magazines, and the Internet are all forms of media.

Media and Advertising

Many health products and services are promoted through advertising. **Advertising** is *a written or spoken media message designed to interest consumers in purchasing a product or service*. Advertisements provide information that can help you make purchasing decisions. Remember, however, that the primary purpose of advertising is to get your attention so that you will want to buy the product featured in the ad. **Figure 3.1** lists some of the techniques that advertisers use to convey a certain message to the consumer and persuade him or her to buy a product. These hidden messages are often designed to appeal to the emotions of potential buyers.

FIGURE 3.1

HIDDEN MESSAGES IN ADVERTISING

Advertisers use several techniques to persuade consumers to purchase their products.

Technique	Example	Hidden Message
Bandwagon	Group of people using a product or service	Everyone is using it—you should too.
Rich and famous	Product displayed in expensive home	It will make you feel rich and famous.
Free gifts	Redeemable coupons for merchandise	It's too good a deal to pass up.
Great outdoors	Scenes of nature	If it's associated with nature, it must be healthy.
Good times	People smiling and laughing	The product will add fun to your life.
Testimonial	People for whom a product has worked	It worked for them, so it will work for you, too.

② TEACH

Discussing

Ask students to raise their hands if they believe they are knowledgeable health consumers. Then have some of those who raised their hands explain what specific actions they take when purchasing health care products. **L1**

Reinforcing Concepts

Have students discuss what factors they consider when buying athletic shoes. Ask: What questions might you want to ask to ensure that you are buying the best shoes for your feet and your needs? **L1**

VISUAL LEARNING

Figure 3.1 Read about and discuss the advertising techniques in Figure 3.1 as a class. Divide students into six groups and assign each group an advertising technique. Then have students describe one current TV ad that uses each assigned technique.

FYI

In one recent year, 161 million dollars was spent in advertising a single prescription drug.

Promoting Coordinated School Health

Developing a Vision Are students encouraged to make responsible decisions at school? Do they face consequences for their actions, both positive and negative? Are they encouraged to evaluate possible outcomes, weigh options, and consider the impact their actions will have on themselves and others? These are questions that relate to everyday classroom conduct, to administrative policies, and to the input parents and community groups may have on the school and the students. These are also questions that are essential as groups work together to develop their shared vision of a coordinated school health program. For more information, consult *Planning a Coordinated School Health Program*.

Cooperative Learning

Have students bring magazine ads to class and meet in groups to discuss the ads. Ask:

- What advertising technique is used in the ad?
- What hidden message does the ad communicate?
- How might the hidden message impact you as a consumer? **L2**

Discussing

Encourage students to discuss their own experiences with comparison shopping. Ask:

- What did you plan to buy?
- How many different products did you compare? At how many stores?
- Which product did you finally choose to buy? Why? **L1**

Cooperative Learning

Have students work in cooperative groups to explore aspects of comparison shopping. Let the members of each group agree on a specific kind of health product and then gather information about cost, features, quality, warranty, safety, and recommendations for at least two different brands of that product. If possible, have students cut out magazine ads for those brands as well. Then have group members choose which item they would purchase and present their decision, along with the reasons, to the rest of the class. **L2**

Comparing Choices

Advertising is one source of information about products and services. However, keep in mind that this information may be misleading, since advertising is designed to inform and persuade you to purchase a product. As a consumer, how do you make wise purchasing decisions? One way is to comparison shop. **Comparison shopping** is *a method of judging the benefits of different products by comparing several factors, such as quality, features, and cost.* Here are some criteria to consider as you evaluate products and services.

▶ **Cost.** Decide on a price range for your purchase. Then compare prices of the same brand or similar brands at different stores.

▶ **Features.** Decide which product features are important to you. This will allow you to avoid paying for features that you don't need and will help ensure that you purchase products with features that you find especially useful or desirable.

▶ **Quality.** Well-made products offer superior performance. An inexpensive product is no bargain if it falls apart or doesn't work.

▶ **Warranty.** Before you purchase a product, especially one that is costly, ask about the warranty. A **warranty** is *a company's or a store's written agreement to repair a product or refund your money should the product not function properly.* Always read a warranty in its entirety—including the fine print—and make sure that you understand its terms. Some warranties cover only certain aspects of a product or its use.

▶ **Safety.** Safety considerations should be foremost in your mind when choosing sports, recreation, or home-safety products.

- The **Underwriters Laboratory (UL)** is a product-safety testing and certification organization. The UL logo on electrical appliances, fire extinguishers, and other products indicates that the product has passed strict safety standards.

- **Snell**, a nonprofit foundation, and the **American National Standards Institute (ANSI)** monitor safety standards for helmets and other protective equipment. Look for their logos on any equipment you are thinking of buying.

▶ **Recommendations.** Talk to people who have used the product that you are considering purchasing. Parents or other trusted adults are good sources of information. Independent testing organizations such as the Consumers Union rate products.

Ⓥ **Accessing product information before you go to the store makes comparison shopping easier.** *Where can you find information on the safety and effectiveness of protective equipment?*

50 Chapter 3

More About...

Advertising and Health Popular media and advertising can affect consumer choices. For example, advertising may encourage consumption of high-fat convenience foods. Much of this advertising is directed at children and teens. Balancing the messages in these ads with pro-nutrition messages could have a powerful impact on health. In recent years, widespread public education programs that include antismoking messages in the media have reduced cigarette smoking. Another example of the positive effect of advertising is the popular campaign to encourage milk consumption. Ads featuring celebrity endorsements are credited with a 30 percent increase in milk consumption.

Real-Life Application

Reading Product Labels

You can use the information on a product label to make an informed decision about whether to purchase the product. Study the label below, and then complete the activity for practice in evaluating products.

SPF 35 SUNBUSTER LOTION

ACTIVE INGREDIENTS: Avobenzone, Octocrylene, Octyl Salicylate, Oxybenzone

PRODUCT'S INTENDED USE: Provides protection against both UVA and UVB rays to help prevent sunburn, premature aging, and skin cancer.

PRECAUTIONS: Discontinue use if signs of irritation or rash appear. Avoid contact with eyes.

DIRECTIONS FOR USE: Apply liberally to all exposed areas before sun exposure. Waterproof for up to 80 minutes of swimming. Reapply after swimming, excessive perspiration, or vigorous activity.

MANUFACTURER'S CONTACT INFORMATION: Call **800-555-1234** Weekdays 9 a.m. to 9 p.m. Eastern Time.

- If two different brands have the same ingredients, which would be the wiser purchase?
- Why should a consumer read this section carefully?
- How can ignoring this section pose a risk to one's health?
- Why might a consumer need this information?

ACTIVITY

Bring in the container or label of a personal care product that you use. Draw the label on a large sheet of construction paper. Using the above sample as a guide, draw arrows and label the different types of information. Use online Internet or library resources to find out more about the product. Write this additional information on the back of the paper. Tell the class about your product. Discuss whether you will continue using this product, and explain why or why not.

PRODUCT LABELS

One way to compare two similar products is to read their labels. Important information on product labels includes the product's name and intended use, directions for use, precautions and warnings, manufacturer's information, and the amount in the container. On most labels you'll also find the ingredients listed by weight in descending order. The label will also identify the active ingredients— the ones that make the product effective. This means that when you are comparing two acne medications, for example, you can compare labels to determine which contains more of the active ingredient.

Lesson 1 Making Consumer Choices **51**

Cooperative Learning Activity

Comparison Shopping Have students work in groups to plan and create informational flyers about comparison shopping. Groups should begin by discussing the information they want to include, such as reasons for comparison shopping or questions to ask while shopping. Then they should plan the pictures, designs, and words that will best communicate that information. Remind them to think about who might read their flyers. Inspire them to use language appropriate for that group and purpose. Ask groups to present their flyers to the class. You may wish to display flyers in the classroom.

Real-Life Application

READING PRODUCTS LABELS

ACCESSING INFORMATION

NHES Standard 2 Students will demonstrate the ability to access valid health information and health-promoting products and services.

Objectives

- Evaluate the validity of personal care products.
- Demonstrate ways to utilize criteria to evaluate health products for appropriateness.

Motivator

Hold up several sunscreen products. Ask: How do you choose a sunscreen?

Teaching Strategies

1. Point out that price should not be the only factor to consider when purchasing a product.
2. Emphasize that people should look at the ingredients when comparing products. This is especially important if an individual might be allergic to any of the ingredients.

✓ Assessment

Using a rubric, student work should provide comprehensive evidence of the following criteria to achieve the highest score:

✔ citation of specific sources
✔ evaluation of the validity of the source
✔ rationale for the appropriateness of the source

Discussing

Encourage students to compare their experiences shopping in stores, from catalogs, and online. Ask: What are the advantages and disadvantages of each kind of shopping? L1

Your Rights as a Consumer

As a consumer you have certain rights, both before and after you purchase a product or service. **Figure 3.2** summarizes these rights. Usually, consumer rights are recognized and respected. Most stores and service providers strive to keep their customers satisfied. Sometimes, however, consumers need help resolving a complaint. You will learn more about how to handle consumer problems in Lesson 3.

Today's Consumer Choices

Consumers today have more choices than ever before when it comes to product selection and ways to shop. **Online shopping** involves *using the Internet to buy products and services.* Below are some points to consider when shopping online.

▶ **Price.** Online sources sometimes offer lower prices. However, some of these savings may be lost by the added cost of shipping.

▶ **Convenience.** Items are delivered directly to the home. For many people this convenience outweighs the potential problem of repackaging and mailing items that may need to be returned.

FIGURE 3.2

YOUR CONSUMER RIGHTS

- **The right to safety.** You have the right to purchase products and services that will not harm you or others.
- **The right to choose.** You have the right to select from many products at competitive prices.
- **The right to be informed.** You have the right to truthful information about products and services.
- **The right to be heard.** You have the right to join in the making of laws that govern buying and selling.
- **The right to have problems corrected.** You have the right to seek compensation when you have been treated unfairly.
- **The right to consumer education.** You have the right to learn the skills necessary to help you make wise choices.

52   **Chapter 3** Being a Health-Literate Consumer

▶ **Product information.** Online descriptions provide only limited information about a product, and you can only view a picture of an item—you can't actually examine it or try it on before you buy.

If you decide to purchase products online, there are some safeguards you should consider. First, get permission from your parents or guardians. Next, make sure that the site is secure. This means that information such as credit card numbers will not be accessible to others. Check the organization's return policy, and make sure that you understand it completely. Finally, write down any confirmation numbers or other information related to your purchase. You will need these numbers if a problem arises.

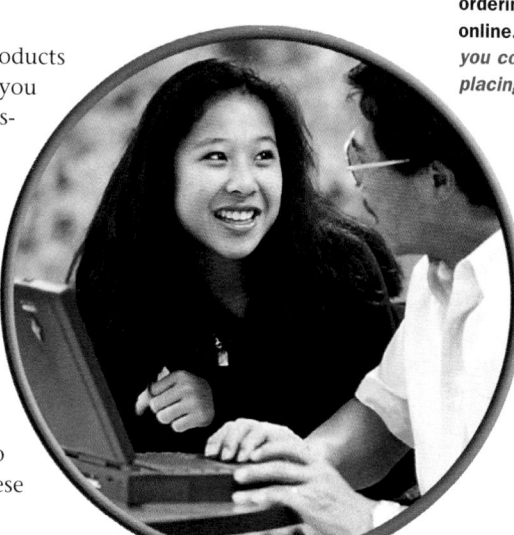

Ⓨ Be sure to get your parents' or guardians' permission before ordering merchandise online. *What else should you consider before placing an online order?*

 Lesson 1 *Review*

Reviewing Facts and Vocabulary

1. Why might some health messages delivered through advertising in the media be misleading?

2. What is a *warranty*? Why it is important to read a warranty in its entirety?

3. List three safeguards you should consider when shopping online.

Thinking Critically

4. **Synthesizing.** Demonstrate ways to utilize criteria to evaluate health products for appropriateness: What factors would you consider when deciding which of two bicycle helmets to buy? List the factors in order of importance.

5. **Analyzing.** Explain the advantages and disadvantages of seeking information about a product from someone who uses the product.

Applying Health Skills

Analyzing Influences. Recall a purchase you have made recently. List all the factors that influenced your decision. Include any advertising you have seen for the product, recommendations of family and friends, safety considerations (if any), and incentives such as coupons or sales. Review your list, circle the most influential factor, and explain why that factor was most important in your purchasing decision.

SPREADSHEETS Making a list is easy when you use a spreadsheet. See **health.glencoe.com** for help in using spreadsheet software.

Lesson 1 Making Consumer Choices **53**

Discussing

Guide students in discussing the safeguards for shopping online. Ask:

• With whom should you check before buying anything online? Why?

• How can you make sure a site is secure?

• How can you find out about an organization's return policy?

• How can you find a confirmation number for your purchase? Where should you record that information?

• How can you find a site's customer service contact information? ▪

 ③ ASSESS

EVALUATING THE LESSON

Assign and discuss the Lesson 1 Review; then administer, grade, and discuss Lesson Quiz 7 in the TCR. 🗁

RETEACHING

• Have students work in groups to list the main ideas presented in this lesson.

• Ask students to complete Reteaching Activity 7 in the TCR. 🗁

④ CLOSE

Have each student complete this sentence: *As a health consumer, I . . .*

▶ **Lesson 1** *Review*

Answers to Reviewing Facts and Vocabulary

1. Some ads might be misleading because their purpose is to sell a product.

2. A company's or a store's written agreement to repair a product or refund your money should the product not function properly.

3. Any 3 from page 53.

Answers to Thinking Critically

4. Possible answers: safety (should be first), comfort, price, appearance.

5. Advantages: insight about how well it was made, how well it worked, and so on. Disadvantages: the person might be biased or have a different need.

Choosing Community Health Services

① FOCUS

QUICK START
Ask a volunteer to read the Quick Start assignment aloud, and give students three minutes to write their lists. Then have students share and compare their responses. Point out the variety of different situations and health care professionals that students named.

TYING TO PRIOR KNOWLEDGE

Referring to the Quick Start assignment, point out that students are already familiar with several types of health services. Explain that Lesson 2 presents more information about choosing and using these services.

Health Skills Features

"Getting a Sports Physical," p. 56

DECISION MAKING

INTRODUCING VOCABULARY

Ask students to complete the Chapter 3 Study Guide in the *Student Activity Workbook.*

Choosing Community Health Services

VOCABULARY
- health care system
- primary care physician
- specialist
- preventive care
- health insurance
- medical history

YOU'LL LEARN TO
- Identify situations requiring professional health services, such as primary and preventive care, for people of all ages.
- Identify, describe, and assess available health-related services in the community that relate to disease prevention and health promotion.
- Compare and analyze the cost, availability, and accessibility of health services for people of all ages.

QUICK START Identify three situations for which you might require professional health services, as well as the type of health care professional that would provide that service.

 Most schools require that a student get a physical exam before participating in a sports program.

B eing a health-literate consumer means more than just being informed about products. It also involves understanding your options in health care services.

Types of Health Services

Y ou have probably received immunizations and had your ears and eyes checked during health screenings. The health care professionals you have seen are part of a **health care system**, which includes *all the medical care available to a nation's people, the way they receive care, and the method of payment.* Health care can be divided into general care and specialized care. General care includes **primary care physicians**, or *medical doctors who provide physical checkups and general care,* as well as school nurses and dentists. Specialized care includes **specialists**, or *medical doctors trained to handle particular kinds of patients or medical conditions.* **Figure 3.3** lists a variety of health care specialists.

Lesson 2 Resources

Teacher Classroom Resources
- Concept Mapping Activity 8
- Current Health Issues 3
- Decision-Making Activity 3
- Guided Reading Activities 8
- Lesson Plan 8
- Lesson Quiz 8
- Reteaching Activity 8

Student Activity Workbook
- Applying Health Skills 8
- Chapter 3 Study Guide

Multimedia
- Transparency 7

FIGURE 3.3

SOME HEALTH CARE SPECIALISTS

Specialist	Specializes In
Allergist	allergies
Dermatologist	skin diseases
Gynecologist	care of female reproductive system
Neurologist	nervous system problems
Oncologist	cancer
Ophthalmologist	care of eyes
Orthodontist	adjustments of teeth to improve bite and jaw alignment
Orthopedist	skeletal deformities or injuries
Pediatrician	primary care for children
Psychiatrist	mental health
Urologist	urinary tract problems

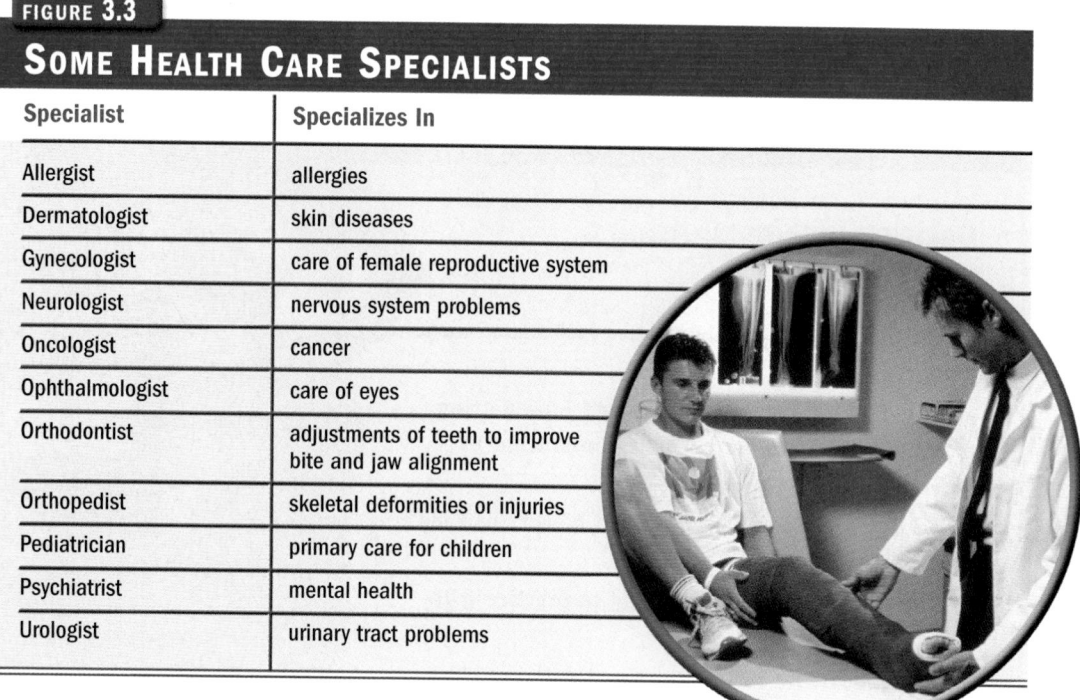

An orthopedist is a specialist who treats injuries of the skeletal system. *Describe the difference between a primary care physician and a specialist.*

Whenever you've seen a doctor for a checkup or a dentist for an oral exam, you've used preventive care. **Preventive care** involves *actions that prevent the onset of disease or injury.* Many teens have had preventive care in the form of vision and hearing screenings, sports physicals, and testing for scoliosis (a spinal disorder).

Facilities for Health Care Services

Communities may have more than one type of health care facility. The services provided by these facilities may be offered as inpatient care or outpatient care. *Inpatient care* requires the patient to stay at the facility overnight and is provided for patients with a serious injury or illness. *Outpatient care* allows the patient to be treated and then return home. Health care facilities include:

▶ **Private practices.** Physicians in private practice work for themselves. Most of their patients are seen at an office on an outpatient basis, although the physicians are usually associated with a hospital in case inpatient care is required.

▶ **Clinics.** Physicians may provide outpatient care in a community clinic rather than an office.

Lesson 2 Choosing Community Health Services **55**

2 TEACH

VISUAL LEARNING

Figure 3.3 Guide students in reading and discussing the health care specialists named in Figure 3.3. Ask: Why do you think a patient might consult each kind of specialist?

Activity

Have each student select one of the health care specialists listed in Figure 3.3 as the topic of a short research report. Ask students to learn about the required education and training, the range of health services offered, and the career prospects for that specialty. Let students summarize their findings in brief written reports. ▣2

Cooperative Learning

Divide the class into six groups, and assign each group one of the listed facilities for health care services. Ask group members to read about their assigned facility and to discuss any experiences they may have had. For instance, were they treated there? Is this type of facility located or available in your community? Have one member of the group act as a note taker. Then have each group present the information on their facility to the rest of the class. ▣1

More About...

Scoliosis Scoliosis is a sideways curvature of the spine. It is usually noticed between the ages of 10 and 14. The cause of most cases is unknown. A scoliosis screening involves checking whether the patient's shoulders look level, the head is centered, and opposite sides of the body look level. While the patient bends over, the health care professional checks whether one side of the rib cage is higher than the other. X rays are sometimes taken. Many children have mild curves and need only periodic checkups to make sure the curvature is not worsening. Braces or surgery may be required for more severe cases.

Health Skills Activity

GETTING A SPORTS PHYSICAL

DECISION MAKING

NHES Standard 6 Students will demonstrate the ability to use goal-setting and decision-making skills to enhance health.

Objectives

- Identify situations requiring preventive care.
- Identify decision-making skills that promote individual health.

Motivator

Ask volunteers to describe what a physician checks for during a physical exam. How does this relate to participating in sports?

Teaching Strategies

1. Have the class discuss reasons for getting a physical exam before participating in a sports program.
2. Let students work in small groups to arrive at one health-promoting decision and develop a dialogue for Dan to defend his decision based on health information.

✓ Assessment

Using a rubric, student work should provide comprehensive evidence of the following criteria to achieve the highest score:

- ✔ clear description of the situation
- ✔ several options with possible outcomes of each
- ✔ influence of values on possible decisions
- ✔ health-enhancing decision and an evaluation of it

Health Skills Activity

Decision Making: Getting a Sports Physical

Dan and two of his friends have just signed up for cross-country.

"Hey, Dan," Brent says. "Mike and I are getting together to practice before the tryouts. Want to join us?"

"I'd like to," Dan answers, "but I haven't had my sports physical yet."

Mike says, "You don't need that to practice with Brent and me."

Dan replies, "I'll feel better about running if I have my physical first."

"Look, Dan," Brent says, "There's only a few days left before tryouts. You'd better get in some practice time, or you might not make the team."

Dan wonders what he should do.

What Would You Do?

Apply the steps to help Dan make a health-enhancing decision.

1. State the situation.
2. List the options.
3. Weigh the possible outcomes.
4. Consider values.
5. Make a decision and act.
6. Evaluate the decision.

▶ **Group practices.** Doctors in a group practice share office space, equipment, and support staff. Otherwise, they function in the same manner as those in private practice.

▶ **Hospitals.** Hospitals generally offer both inpatient and outpatient care. Some physicians work at the hospital. Those in private or group practice are there only when needed.

▶ **Emergency rooms.** Located within most hospitals, emergency rooms provide care for potentially life-threatening illnesses or injuries.

▶ **Urgent care centers.** These centers, staffed by primary care physicians, usually handle emergencies that are not life threatening. Patients may go to these centers if their primary care physician is unavailable or if they don't have one.

56 Chapter 3 Being a Health-Literate Consumer

Home and Community

Medical Specialists Find out if any students have relatives or family friends who are medical specialists. Then ask these students to conduct informal interviews with the specialists. Encourage students to find out about the doctor's medical training and current practice, as well as the interests and goals that led to the choice of his or her particular field of medicine. How is the specialty different from the practice of general medicine? From other specialties? What does the doctor consider to be the particular advantages and disadvantages of his or her specialty? After the interviews, have students write short reports and discuss their findings with the rest of the class.

How People Pay for Health Services

Health care can be a major expense. Many families have some form of **health insurance**, *a plan in which private companies or government programs pay for part or all of a person's medical costs*. To maintain membership in such a plan, the insured person pays a periodic *premium*, or fee, for coverage. In conventional insurance plans, the insured person pays for doctor visits and other forms of treatment out of pocket. An *out-of-pocket expense* is one that the patient must pay for. The patient is then reimbursed by the insurance company for a fixed portion, often 80 percent of the cost of the visit. Hospital care is covered in much the same way. In most insurance plans, members must also pay a *deductible*. This is an amount a member must pay in out-of-pocket expenses before the plan will start reimbursing for health care services.

Managed Care

Some insurance plans are called *managed care plans*. These plans emphasize preventive care and offer reduced physician charges for their members in an attempt to control costs. There are several types of managed care plans:

▶ **Health Maintenance Organizations (HMOs).** Members of an HMO pay a monthly premium but receive most or all medical services with few or no out-of-pocket expenses. Some HMOs require a small co-payment for an office visit. Usually HMO members can see only those physicians who have signed an agreement with the HMO.

▶ **Preferred Provider Organizations (PPOs).** Medical providers connected with PPOs agree to charge the organization less than their regular fee for member usage. Members pay a monthly premium to use providers in the plan but can choose a provider outside the plan. Using outside providers, however, results in higher out-of-pocket expenses.

▶ **Point of Service (POS) plans.** Members of this type of plan can choose providers inside or outside the plan. Choosing an outside provider often results in higher premiums and higher out-of-pocket expenses.

How do people get health insurance? There are several ways for people to obtain health insurance. Many people who work are insured through their employers. Often employees can choose from several plans to find the one that best meets their needs. Self-employed people often purchase their own insurance. People who cannot afford insurance may be covered by Medicaid, the federal government's medical insurance program.

Most managed care plans offer preventive health services to their members. *Why is preventive care important?*

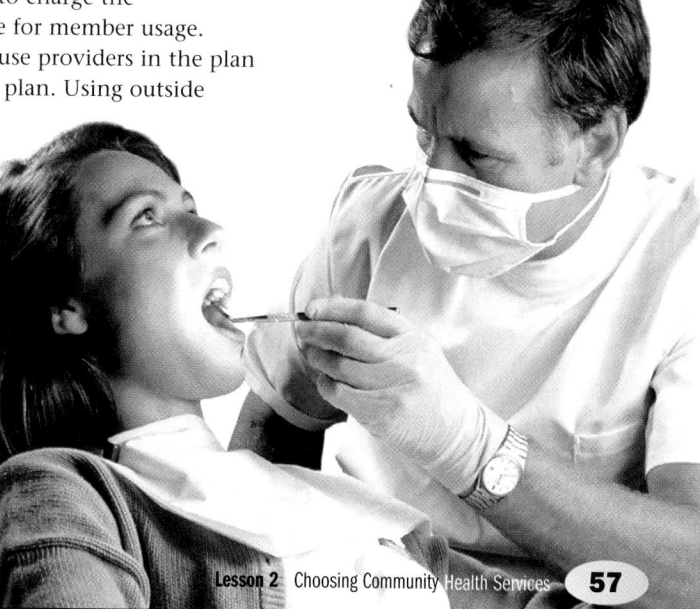

Activity

Have half the class research government-sponsored health insurance programs and the other half research several well-known private health insurance companies in their community or state. Have students learn how and why each program was developed, and how the programs are used by the population.

Discussing

Ask students to explain why more and more health consumers are joining health maintenance organizations. Why do students think more doctors are also be coming part of these organiza-tions? Ask students to find out what a PPO is. Have them compare HMO to PPO plans and discuss the pros and cons.

Let a volunteer read the question aloud, and encourage students to share their own ideas about the answer. Then have students read and discuss the information about health insurance.

Home and Community

Managed Care Providers One factor that may concern health insurance consumers is the choice of physicians in a particular health insurance plan. Students may benefit from examining a list of HMO and PPO providers in the community. You may want to share with students a handbook from one or more managed care plans in your area. Allow students time to see if their physicians are listed in the book. Discuss some of the basic coverages as well as special incentives each plan may offer, such as weight loss programs, gym membership reimbursement, and physical therapy. Then have them decide which plan they would be most interested in joining.

Discussing

Guide students in reading about and discussing the current trends in health care. Ask: What special needs do these facilities and practices meet? **L1**

Health Skills Practice

Communicating Clearly

Have students meet in groups to discuss the importance of communicating clearly and comfortably with a health care professional:

- Why is it important to be prepared for a visit with your health care professional?

- In what circumstances might it be useful to write down the questions you plan to ask?

- What should you do if your health care professional does not have time to answer all your questions?

- What should you do if you are not comfortable with the health care service you receive?

After the group discussions, have each student write a private journal entry explaining how he or she plans to improve communication with a health care professional.

Activity

Have groups of students imagine that they are looking for a new health care professional. Where would they look for potential candidates? How would they determine whether he or she will meet their needs? What questions might they ask this professional? Discuss the results of the activity as a class. **L2**

Most health care providers request a medical history from their first-time patients.

Did You Know ?

➤ You have the right to access your medical records by contacting your doctor. Copies can be made for another health care professional of your choosing and, in some states, for your personal use. Insurance companies and government agencies typically are able to access your records as well. Laws protect your confidentiality by limiting access by other individuals or organizations.

Trends in Health Care

To help reduce expenses and improve the quality of care, the health community continually updates the types of care offered and the procedures used to implement care. Current trends include the following:

▶ **Birthing centers** are homelike settings that involve family members in the delivery of a baby. Birthing centers are usually less expensive than hospitals. However, they are appropriate only for women with low-risk pregnancies.

▶ **Drug treatment centers** specialize in treating people with drug and alcohol problems, usually outside of a hospital setting.

▶ **Continuing care and assisted living facilities** provide short- and long-term care for people who need help with daily tasks but who do not require professional medical care. Many older adults benefit from this kind of care.

▶ **Hospices** provide care for people who are terminally ill. Hospice workers are experts at managing pain and providing emotional support for the patient and his or her family.

▶ **Telemedicine** is the practice of medicine over distance through the use of telecommunications equipment. A medical specialist located hundreds of miles away can be brought into an examination room through a live interactive electronic system.

You and Your Health Care

A good doctor-patient relationship is critical to quality health care. This relationship requires open communication and a sense of trust. A health care professional can treat you and make recommendations for your health, but you need to take an active role in your medical care. Your relationship with your health care provider is a partnership—each of you must apply skills to effectively maintain your health. A good place to start is with an awareness of your own **medical history**, *complete and comprehensive information about your immunizations and any health problems you have had to date.* Most doctors' offices will ask you to fill out a medical history during your first visit. This form usually requires you to provide information about your own health habits, as well as the health of close family members. Ask your parents to help you obtain this information. The information in your medical history gives a health care provider an idea of your overall level of wellness.

School to Work

Actuaries Actuaries determine risk, make price decisions, and formulate investment strategies for large companies. Many actuaries work for health insurance companies. Actuaries must calculate or estimate the probabilities of an event taking place, such as death, injury, or disability. Most applicants for beginning actuarial jobs hold a bachelor's degree in mathematics, actuarial science, statistics, or a business-related discipline, such as economics, finance, or accounting.

Patient Skills

These tips can help you make the most out of your next medical appointment:

▶ Before you go, write down your reasons for seeing the doctor.

▶ While you are at the office, ask questions about any diagnoses, medications, or procedures that you do not understand or are unsure about.

▶ Inform the staff of any allergies you have or any medications you are taking. If a prescription is needed, this information can help the physician determine the right medication for you.

MEDICINE USE

If the physician prescribes a medicine for you, ask the pharmacist any questions you have about the medication. If the doctor recommends an over-the-counter medication, compare products by reading labels and make sure that you understand what symptoms each medicine is intended to treat.

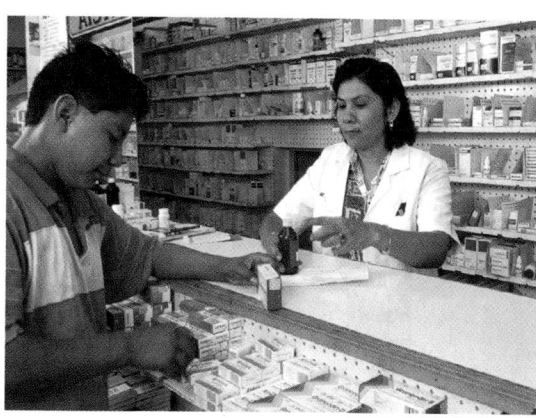

A pharmacist is a reliable source of information about both prescription and over-the-counter medications. *What types of questions might you ask a pharmacist?*

Lesson 2 Review

Reviewing Facts and Vocabulary

1. Distinguish between *primary care physicians* and medical *specialists*.

2. Identify situations requiring primary and preventive care.

3. List three actions that can help you make the most of your next medical appointment.

Thinking Critically

4. **Analyzing.** Compare and analyze the cost, availability, and accessibility of health services for people who don't have health insurance.

5. **Applying.** The incidence of type 2 diabetes is increasing in teens in the United States. Some of the factors that lead to this disease are being overweight and inactive. How might information in a teen's medical history aid a health care professional in diagnosing this disease?

Applying Health Skills

Accessing Information. Use your local telephone book and other sources to identify available health-related services in your community that relate to disease prevention and health promotion. Make a table that describes and assesses each of these services.

SPREADSHEETS You can create a table by using spreadsheet software. For help in using spreadsheet software, see **health.glencoe.com**.

Discussing

Help students discuss the importance of developing and practicing patient skills.

3 ASSESS

EVALUATING THE LESSON

Assign and discuss the Lesson 2 Review; then administer, grade, and discuss Lesson Quiz 8 in the TCR. 📁

RETEACHING

• Have students work with partners to write an informal outline of this lesson.

• Ask students to complete Reteaching Activity 8 in the TCR. 📁

ENRICHMENT

Encourage students to compare the health care system in the United States with that of Canada. Have them identify the advantages and disadvantages of each system. Can they think of ways to combine the advantages of each into one improved health care system? Let students share and discuss their ideas.

4 CLOSE

Ask students to recall the most important facts they have learned in this lesson.

Lesson 2 Review

Answers to Reviewing Facts and Vocabulary

1. Primary care physicians provide checkups and general care. Specialists are trained to handle particular patients or medical conditions.

2. Checkups and general care as well as vision and hearing screenings, sports physicals, and testing for scoliosis.

3. Answers will vary, but should include some of the tips on page 59.

Answers to Thinking Critically

4. Answers will vary.

5. Possible answer: It might alert the physician to check for type 2 diabetes if other symptoms of the disease were present.

Managing Consumer Problems

Lesson 3

① FOCUS

QUICK START Have a volunteer read the Quick Start assignment aloud, and give students a few minutes to jot down their ideas. Then have students share and discuss their responses. Encourage a few volunteers to role-play responses to the situation.

TYING TO PRIOR KNOWLEDGE

Have students recall the Quick Start situation and then identify other kinds of consumer problems they may have faced. How did they handle those problems? Explain that students will learn more about managing consumer problems as they study this lesson.

Health Skills Features

"Writing a Letter of Complaint," p. 62

ACCESSING INFORMATION

INTRODUCING VOCABULARY

- Have students find and read the definitions of *fraud, malpractice,* and *advocate.* Then have them determine synonyms for each term.

- Ask students to complete the Chapter 3 Study Guide in the *Student Activity Workbook.*

Managing Consumer Problems

VOCABULARY
fraud
health fraud
malpractice
consumer advocates

YOU'LL LEARN TO

- Identify potential problems with health care products and services.

- Understand how to resolve problems related to health care products and services.

- Explore methods for addressing critical health issues that result from fraud.

QUICK START Suppose that you purchased a new hair dryer that broke the first time you used it. Explain how you would deal with the problem.

M ost health care products and services you purchase will live up to their claims. However, some products and services may be faulty, useless, or even potentially harmful. Thus, it's important to learn how to handle consumer problems.

Problems with Products

S ometimes products are defective. Find out about a seller's return policy before purchasing a product. Many items can be returned to the store from which they were purchased. Others may need to be sent back to the manufacturer. Information in the product warranty will help you determine which course of action to follow. Before you attempt to return a product, reread the instructions to make sure that you are using the product correctly. If the product is truly defective, you must then decide whether you want a replacement or your money back. Put your reasons for returning the item in a letter, and keep a copy for future reference. Return the item in its original packaging. If you are mailing the item, be sure to get a shipping receipt to prove that you sent it.

 Always keep your sales receipt. Some stores require receipts as part of their return policy, and many manufacturers require receipts to validate a product's warranty.

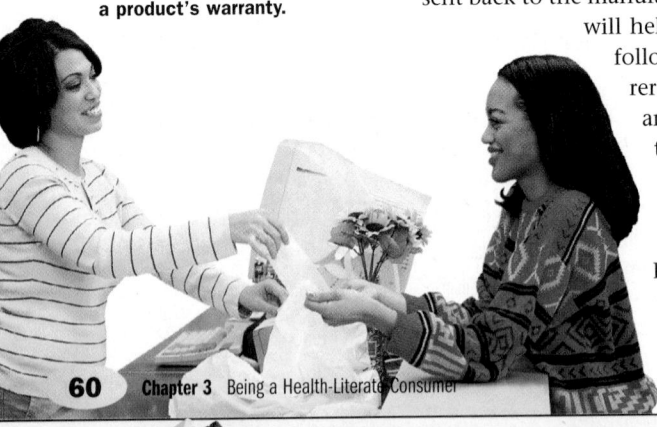

60 Chapter 3 Being a Health-Literate Consumer

Lesson 3 *Resources*

Teacher Classroom Resources

📁 Concept Mapping Activity 9

📁 Guided Reading Activities 9

📁 Lesson Plan 9

📁 Lesson Quiz 9

📁 Reteaching Activity 9

Student Activity Workbook

📁 Applying Health Skills 9

📁 Chapter 3 Study Guide

Multimedia

 Transparency 8

Health Fraud

Fraud is *deliberate deceit or trickery.* Some individuals and businesses employ fraud to sell defective products or ineffective services. These people often go out of business as soon as consumer complaints expose them. **Health fraud**, also known as quackery, is the *sale of worthless products or services that claim to prevent diseases or cure other health problems.*

Fraudulent Products

Several types of products are particularly susceptible to health fraud:

▶ **Weight-loss products.** Ads for some diet pills, fad diets, and exercise equipment claim that a person can lose weight virtually overnight. Weight loss is effectively achieved only through healthful eating habits and regular physical activity.

▶ **Beauty and anti-aging products.** Many tooth whiteners, hair enhancers, and wrinkle creams may work temporarily, but none offer permanent results. Products that aren't approved by the Food and Drug Administration (FDA) may harm you.

Fraudulent Treatments

Another type of health fraud is clinics that specialize in "miracle" cures for ailments such as arthritis or that feature a remarkable and unusual treatment, such as consuming substances extracted from peach pits to cure cancer. These methods are ineffective and may even be dangerous. Of course, not all clinics offering specialized treatments are fraudulent. Check with a health care professional before seeking treatment at such a clinic.

OTHER PROBLEMS WITH HEALTH SERVICES

Some people experience problems with their regular health care providers. Sometimes these problems can be solved by changing health care professionals. Other concerns are more complicated. Health care professionals can sometimes be negligent or guilty of **malpractice**—*failure by a health professional to meet accepted standards.* To make sure that you are getting the best medical treatment possible, always get a second opinion from another health care professional for any major health concern, such as those involving surgery or other extensive treatment. If you have a serious problem with a health care professional, you may be able to get help from a regulatory organization such as the American Medical Association or from a state licensing board.

Health Minute
Red Flags of Fraud

Look for the phrases below in ads for health care products and services—they may indicate health fraud.

Possible signs of health fraud:

▶ "secret formula"
▶ "miracle cure"
▶ "overnight results"
▶ "all natural"
▶ "available only through mail-order"
▶ "hurry, this offer expires soon"
▶ "one-time offer"

Having an open, trusting relationship with your health care provider can help resolve many concerns about a diagnosis or treatment. *Why should you get a second opinion for any serious health concern?*

② TEACH

Activity

Have students ask their parents, grandparents, or other adult relatives about types of product fraud that they have observed over the years. Alternatively, you may wish to provide a list of fraudulent products for students to ask family members about. Suggest that students ask questions such as these:

• Did you, or anyone you know, use any of the products?

• What were some of the claims made about these products?

• What, if any, adverse effects came from the use of these products?

Let students compare and discuss their interview findings. **L2**

Reinforcing Concepts

Let volunteers explain the difference between fraudulent treatments and malpractice. **L1**

Health Minute

Guide students in reading and discussing Red Flags of Fraud. Ask volunteers to recall ads they have seen or heard that include these possible signs of fraud.

∿∿ HEALTH LITERACY

Responsible/Productive Citizen In some cases, certain health care products may seriously harm consumers' health. After exhausting other avenues, consumers may resort to class-action lawsuits or boycotts. Encourage students to research some instances of consumers harmed by health care products. Have them find out how the consumers filed a complaint. Did they boycott or file a class-action lawsuit? What was the outcome? How did the manufacturer compensate those affected? Do you think this compensation was adequate or fair? Why or why not?

Real-Life Application

WRITING A LETTER OF COMPLAINT

ACCESSING INFORMATION

NHES Standard 2 Students will demonstrate the ability to access valid health information and health-promoting products and services.

Objectives

- Identify potential problems with health care products and services.
- Demonstrate how to resolve problems related to health care products and services.

Motivator

Display a pair of athletic shoes. Ask students what they would do if the shoes fell apart after only two weeks of use.

Teaching Strategies

1. Ask students to brainstrom specific health products they might use as well as what could go wrong with each product. List these on the board.

2. Remind students to maintain a respectful, assertive tone in their letters. Most companies are eager to resolve consumer complaints in a satisfactory manner.

✓ Assessment

Using a rubric, student work should provide comprehensive evidence of the following criteria to achieve the highest score:

✔ ability to access appropriate community resources to meet specific needs

✔ type of help available from the sources

Real-Life Application

Writing a Letter of Complaint

A carefully written letter of complaint can help secure fair treatment for yourself if a product or service does not meet your expectations. Study the letter and answer the questions. Then compose your own letter of complaint.

> Name of Company
> Street Address
> City, State, ZIP code
>
> Dear (contact person):
>
> On (date), I (bought, had repaired) a (name of product) at (location). Unfortunately, your product has not performed well. (state the problem).
>
> To resolve the problem, I would appreciate (state what you want—money back, exchange, repair). Enclosed are copies (do not send originals) of my records (include receipts and other documents).
>
> I look forward to your reply and a resolution to the problem and will wait until (set a time limit) before seeking help from a consumer protection agency or the Better Business Bureau. Please contact me at (phone number and address).
>
> Sincerely,
>
> Your name (signed)

○ Why is it important to provide this information early in the letter?

○ Why do you need to be specific here? Why should you not send the original documents?

○ Why might mentioning a consumer protection agency or the Better Business Bureau make the company more likely to act on your letter?

Source: Federal Consumer Information Center, U.S. General Services Administration.

ACTIVITY

With a partner, identify a health care product with which you might not be or have not been satisfied. Develop a three-part complaint letter about the product, using the sample above as a guide. Read your completed letter to the class. Have your classmates evaluate the letter, and adjust it on the basis of their feedback.

Help for Consumer Problems

If you try to resolve a problem with a product and are dissatisfied with the result, seek help from one of these groups:

▶ **Business organizations** such as the Better Business Bureau (BBB) deal with complaints against local merchants. The core services of the BBB include dispute resolution and truth-in-advertising complaints.

62 **Chapter 3** Being a Health-Literate Consumer

Myths & Reality

MYTH. Because of government regulations, all advertising must be accurate.

FACT. Ads may use exaggerations and inflated opinions to sell products. This practice is called puffery. Puffery statements are not illegal. The Federal Trade Commission cannot prove that they are false. They cannot be proven true either—and can be very misleading to consumers. An example of puffery: "Three out of four doctors recommend . . ." (How many were surveyed? What kind of doctors were surveyed?)

▶ **Consumer advocates** are *people or groups whose sole purpose is to take on regional, national, and even international consumer issues.* Some groups, like the Consumers Union, test products, inform the public, and play a role in protecting consumers when problems arise. Others work to expose fraud and teach consumers about their rights and responsibilities.

▶ **Local, state, and federal government agencies** ensure that consumers' rights are protected. The federal government, for example, has established a number of specialized agencies that deal with health-related products and services. The Federal Trade Commission works to prevent false or deceptive advertising. The Food and Drug Administration ensures that medicines are safe, effective, and properly labeled. The Consumer Product Safety Commission protects consumers against harmful products and can recall dangerous ones. Small claims courts are state courts that handle legal disputes involving amounts of money below a certain limit. The consumer and the merchant present their case to a judge, who then makes a decision.

HEALTH Online
Go to **health.glencoe.com** to learn more about the U.S. Consumer Product Safety Commission.

 Lesson 3 *Review*

Reviewing Facts and Vocabulary

1. Define the term *fraud*.
2. Under what circumstances might you want to seek a second medical opinion?
3. When might a person file suit in small claims court?

Thinking Critically

4. **Analyzing.** Why is health fraud considered one of the worst types of fraud?
5. **Evaluating.** List several criteria you would use to distinguish between an effective complaint against a health care product that didn't fulfill its claim and an ineffective complaint.

Applying Health Skills

Communication Skills. Imagine that your aunt sent away for a wrinkle cream that was "guaranteed to make you look ten years younger in only three weeks." After using the product for a month, she finds that not only does she not look younger, but her skin is red and irritated. Write a dialogue in which you explain to your aunt the likelihood that she is a victim of health fraud and explore methods for addressing this critical health issue.

WORD PROCESSING Use word-processing software to write and edit your dialogue. For help in using word-processing software, see **health.glencoe.com**.

Lesson 3 Managing Consumer Problems **63**

EVALUATING THE LESSON

Assign and discuss the Lesson 3 Review; then administer, grade, and discuss Lesson Quiz 9 in the TCR. ☞

RETEACHING

• Have students work with partners to revise their responses to the Quick Start assignment.
• Ask students to complete Reteaching Activity 9 in the TCR. ☞

ENRICHMENT

Have students identify and research a local or state agency that protects consumers' rights. Let them summarize their findings in written reports. Remind them to proofread their reports before handing in a final draft.

4 CLOSE

Have students take turns identifying specific consumer problems and how to manage them.

 Lesson 3 *Review*

Answers to Reviewing Facts and Vocabulary

1. Fraud is deliberate deceit or trickery.
2. For major health concerns, such as those involving surgery or other extensive treatment.
3. When there is a legal dispute involving money below a certain dollar amount.

Answers to Thinking Critically

4. Possible answer: People who purchase fraudulent health products have had their hopes falsely raised. Products and treatments may be more than ineffective; they may be life-threatening.
5. Answers will vary.

Understanding Public Health Services

1 FOCUS

QUICK START Give students a few minutes to list public health agencies with which they are familiar. Then let volunteers read their lists aloud, and lead a class discussion on the services that each agency provides.

TYING TO PRIOR KNOWLEDGE

Remind students that they are already familiar with some public health services. Explain that, as they read this lesson, students will learn more about these services and the impact of various health services, both locally and worldwide.

Health Skills Features

"Raising Awareness of Public Health Programs," p. 66

ADVOCACY

INTRODUCING VOCABULARY

- Ask volunteers to read aloud the Glossary definitions of the vocabulary terms. Then encourage students to discuss their understanding of the terms.

- Ask students to complete the Chapter 3 Study Guide in the *Student Activity Workbook*.

Understanding Public Health Services

VOCABULARY
public health
epidemiology

YOU'LL LEARN TO
- Analyze the impact of the availability of health services in the community and the world.

- Explain the benefits of positive relationships among community health professionals in promoting a healthy community.

QUICK START On a sheet of paper, list a few public health agencies with which you are familiar. What service does each provide to the public?

Materials provided by these organizations are reliable sources of health information.

T hanks to advances in **public health**, *a community-wide effort to monitor and promote the welfare of the population,* Americans are living longer, healthier lives.

Public Health Agencies

P ublic health issues are addressed at the local, national, and global level.

Health at the Local Level

State, county, and city health departments focus on disease prevention. Their functions include overseeing standards for water and sewage systems, waste disposal, and the sanitation of restaurants. A local health inspector, for example, may close a restaurant for failing a routine inspection. Nonprofit agencies have local chapters that are devoted to particular health concerns. The March of Dimes, for example, works to reduce birth defects.

Lesson 4 *Resources*

Teacher Classroom Resources
- Concept Mapping Activity 10
- Cross-Curriculum Activity 3
- Enrichment Activity 3
- Guided Reading Activities 10
- Lesson Plan 10
- Lesson Quiz 10
- Reteaching Activity 10

Student Activity Workbook
- Applying Health Skills 10
- Chapter 3 Study Guide

Multimedia
 Transparency 9

Health at the National Level

Several agencies also work at the national level to protect health.

▶ **The National Cancer Institute (NCI)** is the federal government's principal agency for **cancer** research.

▶ **The Environmental Protection Agency (EPA)** is responsible for protecting the country's air, water, and land.

▶ The U.S. Department of Labor's **Occupational Safety and Health Administration (OSHA)** works to prevent injuries and safeguard the health of workers across the country.

▶ **The United States Department of Agriculture (USDA)** leads the federal anti-hunger effort with food stamp, school lunch, and school breakfast programs. One agency of the USDA, the **Food Safety and Inspection Service (FSIS)**, is responsible for the safety of meat, poultry, and egg products.

▶ **The Department of Health and Human Services (DHHS)** oversees more than 300 health-related programs. These programs are administered by 13 agencies, which include the following:

- **The Centers for Medicare and Medicaid Services (CMS)** administer federal insurance programs, which help provide health care to low-income and elderly Americans.

- **The Food and Drug Administration (FDA)** ensures the safety of food, drugs, and cosmetics.

- **The National Institutes of Health (NIH)** conduct medical research and provide funding for medical research carried out at other institutions.

- **The Substance Abuse and Mental Health Service Administration (SAMHSA)** provides programs that aid substance abusers and people with mental/emotional disorders.

- **The Centers for Disease Control and Prevention (CDC)** conduct research and collect data that help control the spread of diseases. Part of the CDC's job involves **epidemiology**, or *the scientific study of patterns of disease in a population.*

- **The Federal Trade Commission (FTC)** was established to enforce antitrust and consumer protection laws. The FTC works to promote fair competition in the nation's markets and to ensure that consumers are given the right to make informed choices.

hotlink

cancer To learn more about cancer, see Chapter 26, page 681.

OSHA inspectors work to prevent injuries and protect the health of workers in the United States. *How might periodic inspections of a workplace help ensure workers' safety?*

Lesson 4 Understanding Public Health Services **65**

Chapter 3 • Lesson 4

② TEACH

Discussing

Have students read through the list of organizations. Ask them to share any information they may know about these organizations. You may want to bring to class articles from newspapers or magazines that feature any of the organizations, or ask students to share current news events that may involve them. Ask: What have you heard or what do you know about these organizations? Why do you think they may have been created? What purposes do they serve?

Activity

Have students work with partners or in small groups to learn more about each of the listed agencies that work at the national level to protect health. Suggest that students use online and library resources to research the history and responsibilities of their agency. Then have each pair or group discuss its findings with the rest of the class. **L2**

hotlink

Ask a few volunteers to read more about cancer in Chapter 26, Lesson 2. Have these volunteers share the information with the rest of the class; help students discuss which federal agencies might deal with issues related to cancer.

Curriculum Connections

Social Studies Ask students to research the history of the Department of Health and Human Services. Have students draw timelines showing how the department evolved and which responsibilities the department undertook at various stages.

Math Have students use online sources to learn about the budget for one of the national health agencies. Ask them to gather statistics on spending in various categories for a given year. Then have students plan and draw a pie graph showing how the agency's money was spent.

65

Hands-On Health

RAISING AWARENESS OF PUBLIC HEALTH PROGRAMS

ADVOCACY

NHES Standard 7 Students will demonstrate the ability to advocate for personal, family, and community health.

Objectives

- Identify and describe a public health agency, and advocate for increased awareness of how this organization promotes public health.
- Present information about community public health services.

Motivator

Ask students where they might access information in the community about a specific disease.

Teaching Strategies

1. Provide printouts of information from the Web sites of various agencies.
2. Suggest that students investigate specific agencies, such as those related to agriculture (e.g., food inspection) or the environment.

✓ Assessment

Using a rubric, student work should provide comprehensive evidence of the following criteria to achieve the highest score:

- ✔ clear, health-enhancing stand
- ✔ support for the position with relevant information
- ✔ awareness of the audience
- ✔ encouragement of others to make healthful choices
- ✔ passion/conviction

Hands-On Health ACTIVITY

Raising Awareness of Public Health Programs

In this activity your group will create a public service announcement (PSA) to highlight the mission of a public health agency or program.

What You'll Need

- paper and pen
- telephone directory (one per group)
- Internet access (optional)

What You'll Do

1. In your group, examine the list of agencies in the "Government" section of the phone directory. Agencies will often list specific offices that indicate what they do, such as "Lead Poisoning Program" or "Food Safety."
2. Find out the mission and history of one agency or office. What health problems does this agency seek to address? What services does it provide? If possible, research this information online.
3. Write a PSA script that promotes the agency or office. Make sure that you convey how this agency promotes public health. Target the message to high-school students.
4. Arrange with your teacher and school administrators to present your PSA to your school.

Apply and Conclude

As a class, brainstorm a list of other ways of highlighting the contributions of public-health agencies or programs. Then write a paragraph describing the importance of raising people's awareness of these organizations and programs.

Public Health on a Global Scale

Some countries don't have the medical technologies or services that are available in the United States and other developed nations. War, drought, floods, or other crises can lead to starvation, unsanitary living conditions, and uncontrolled disease. Government agencies and private organizations from around the world extend aid to developing countries in times of crisis. One key organization is the World Health Organization (WHO). An agency of the United Nations with a membership of nearly 200 countries and territories, WHO has programs to eradicate diseases such as polio and cholera and to address pollution. Another organization, the International Committee of the Red Cross, provides emergency aid to victims of armed conflict, disease outbreaks, and natural disasters.

More About...

The Red Cross The Red Cross is an international agency that helps people worldwide during times of war or disaster. Started in Switzerland during the 19th century, The Red Cross now has societies in 160 nations.

The agency provides medical treatment, food, clothing, and shelter; facilitates communication; and offers counseling and financial assistance following any disaster regardless of cause. In addition, The Red Cross sponsors classes in areas such as first aid, water safety, cardiopulmonary resuscitation (CPR), home nursing, and preparation for parenthood. The agency is also known for its blood donation work.

FIGURE 3.4

ADVOCATING FOR PUBLIC HEALTH

There are many ways that teens can advocate for public health
Here are just a few:

- Follow all health and safety laws and ordinances; for example, keep your immunizations up to date.
- Set an example by practicing healthful behaviors, such as always wearing a helmet when biking or skating.
- Avoid actions that could endanger the health or safety of others, such as reckless driving.
- Get involved in events that promote public health. Participating in events such as community walks or 10K runs for charity improves your own health as well as the health of others.
- Find out which community groups deal with public health issues. Identify their goals and support them.
- Inform the proper authorities if you notice a condition or activity that threatens public health.

Advocacy—Taking Action for Public Health

Individuals can play a critical role in promoting public health. **Figure 3.4** lists some of the ways you can help promote public health in your own community.

 Lesson 4 *Review*

Reviewing Facts and Vocabulary

1. Define the term *public health*.
2. Identify the public health agency that provides insurance programs for low-income and older Americans.
3. List two organizations that work to maintain world health.

Thinking Critically

4. **Applying.** Why might restaurant inspections be handled by government agencies rather than the restaurants themselves?
5. **Analyzing.** Analyze the impact of the availability of health services in the community and the world.

Applying Health Skills

Accessing Information. Research public-health agencies in your community. Make a four-column chart in which you list the name of each agency, describe what each one does, tell whether each is a government or private agency, and describe opportunities for volunteering to advocate for public health. Share this information with your class.

SPREADSHEETS Making a table is easy when you use a spreadsheet. Find help in using spreadsheets at **health.glencoe.com.**

Lesson 4 Understanding Public Health Services **67**

Figure 3.4 Let students meet in groups to read and discuss the information about advocating for public health. Have group members work together to list specific steps teens can take to be effective public health advocates.

❸ ASSESS

EVALUATING THE LESSON

Assign and discuss the Lesson 4 Review; then administer, grade, and discuss Lesson Quiz 10 in the TCR. 🗀

RETEACHING

- Ask students to use the main headings to review the contents of this lesson. Let volunteers summarize the information presented in the section following each main heading.

- Ask students to complete Reteaching Activity 10 in the TCR. 🗀

❹ CLOSE

Have student write the following sentence, adding their own sentence endings: *I plan to advocate for public health by . . .*

▶ Lesson 4 *Review*

Answers to Reviewing Facts and Vocabulary

1. A community-wide effort to monitor and promote the welfare of the population.
2. The Centers for Medicare and Medicaid Services.
3. World Health Organization and International Committee of the Red Cross.

Answers to Thinking Critically

4. Possible answer: Representatives of a government agency would likely to be more objective and apply public health laws more fairly than employees of the restaurant itself.
5. Answers will vary.

Eye ON THE Media

Today's "Health Beat"

NHES Standard 4 students will analyze the influence of culture, media, technology, and other factors on health.

Objective

Examine newspapers' coverage of health topics and consider the potential impact of increased coverage of health topics on a community, state, or the nation.

Motivator

Ask students to recall news items they have recently heard regarding a specific health topic.

Teaching Strategies

Awareness Inform students that studies have shown that the percentage of people who follow health topics in the media varies depending upon the health issue.

Analysis Ask students to note what types of health topics are featured most frequently.

Reflection Have students review any articles on health public policy or legislation and determine whether they think there is any bias in the reporting.

Take Action Encourage students to write a letter to the editor of the newspaper, advocating for increased coverage of youth-related health topics.

✓Assessment

Each student should complete a survey of health articles in two different editions of the chosen newspaper. Each survey should contain complete information, including a brief summary of the article's contents. Students' opinion papers should address the questions posed.

Eye ON THE Media

Today's "Health Beat"

Many newspapers have a health beat or a health section. What kinds of health topics do newspapers cover? How does your local newspaper compare with newspapers in other locations? In this activity, you will examine the health coverage in various newspapers and consider the impact that increased coverage of health topics may have on a community or state or on the nation as a whole.

- **Name of newspaper:**
- **Date:**
- **Title of health article:**
- **Type of article:** (preventive health, nutrition, fitness, disease outbreaks, federal or state legislative health issues, and so on)
- **Length of article:**
- **Intended audience:** (youths, seniors, males/females, registered voters, legislators or government officials, African Americans, Hispanic Americans, other minority groups, and so on)
- **Brief summary:**

ACTIVITY

Choose a specific newspaper, and look through it for health articles or the health section. Examine articles in two different editions of the newspaper you've selected, recording information about each article in a chart like the one above. Compare the information you have collected with others. In a class discussion, consider the following questions: How does the health coverage in the newspaper you examined compare with that in other papers? Do the papers cover the same kinds of topics? Do they devote similar amounts of space to health topics?

EXPRESS YOUR VIEWS

Use the questions as a starting point for a one-page opinion paper: Why do you think media coverage of health topics has increased in recent years? What impact might increased coverage of health topics have on your community or state or on the nation as a whole?

More About...

Health in the News The Kaiser/Harvard School of Public Health regularly surveys a cross-section of Americans to discover how they follow coverage of health topics in the media. Recent findings include the following: Women were more likely to follow health news stories than men. Americans over the age of 65 were more likely to follow health stories than those under the age of 65. In contrast, those under the age of 30 were the least likely to follow health stories in the media. Students interested in taking this lesson further can write a creative proposal suggesting how their local newspaper might engage younger readers in health-related stories. What kinds of health topics might interest Americans under the age of 30? Under the age of 18?

CROSS-CURRICULUM CONNECTIONS

Publish a Newspaper. As a class, create a newspaper that includes news stories and feature articles on health products and services as well as editorials on consumer health concerns that are relevant to teens. Your teacher will organize the class into teams and assign each team a news beat. Create a final product, and obtain permission to distribute your publication to the entire school.

Give an Oral Report. Consumer and health advocacy groups safeguard citizens from unreliable or hazardous products and services. Select and research an independent testing source such as the Consumers Union, a government agency such as the Federal Trade Commission, or a consumer activist such as Ralph Nader. Determine what led to the development of the organization or what motivated the individual to become a consumer activist. Give a short oral report to your class.

Calculate the Better Value. You are trying to decide which brand of energy drink to buy. One ounce equals 0.029574 liters. Zippy is $1.50 for 32 ounces; Get-Going is $1.35 for a liter. Assuming that both products have the same ingredients in the same proportions, which is the better deal?

Conduct Research. Chlorofluorocarbons (CFCs) were once used as aerosol propellants in health care products such as deodorant. In the 1970s it was determined that CFCs were significantly depleting the ozone layer, and their use has been progressively banned throughout the world. Research the history of the use of CFCs and the legislation enacted to eliminate the use of these and other ozone-depleting substances.

Public Health Specialist

Are you interested in a career in health education and wellness? Do you have a real concern for the welfare of your community? If so, then a career as a public health specialist might be a good choice for you.

To enter this profession, you need a bachelor's degree with a specialization in a biological, medical, or physical science; food science or technology; chemistry; nutrition; engineering; epidemiology; or another related scientific field. For more information on this and other health careers, click on Career Corner at **health.glencoe.com**.

Portfolio Assessment

Self-Evaluation Direct students to review the Health Skills Activities and other activities completed in the chapter. Encourage each student to select one finished product or activity that demonstrates his or her best work for the chapter and that represents the student's learning goals. Have students explain what they have learned and how the examples they have selected show their progress.

Teacher Classroom Resources Assign Performance Assessment 3, "Volun-teen," in the TCR.

CROSS-CURRICULUM CONNECTION

Enrich student learning by connecting the topic of being a health-literate consumer to one of the four subject areas presented on the page. The activity may be completed individually or with a partner.

Language Arts Explain to students that news writing involves objective reporting of facts, but feature writing uses more colorful language, appealing to our human interest. Editorials are opinion pieces.

Social Studies Explain to students that an oral report requires thorough research with multiple sources as well as organization and rehearsal of the presentation.

Math Answer: Get-Going $1/0.029574 = 33.813485$ oz., $\$1.35/33.813485$ oz. = $\$0.0399249$/oz. for Get-Going compared to $\$1.50/32$oz. = $\$0.046875$/oz. for Zippy.

Science Students' timelines should indicate the history of the use of CFCs and government regulation of these substances, including the Clean Air Act, its amendment in 1990, and the Montreal Protocol on Ozone Depletion.

Have students read and discuss the Career Corner information on public health specialists. Ask interested students to explore the Glencoe Health Web site at **health.glencoe.com** for more information on this career.

CHECKING COMPREHENSION

- Assign and discuss the chapter review.
- Use the Chapter 3 MindJogger Videoquiz to review the chapter. ▣

CHAPTER 3 REVIEW ANSWERS

Exploring Health Terms

1. health consumer
2. online shopping
3. comparison shopping
4. media
5. health care system
6. preventive care
7. Health insurance
8. medical history
9. fraud
10. malpractice
11. consumer advocate
12. public health
13. epidemiology

Recalling the Facts

1. Habit, personal taste.
2. Any three: bandwagon, rich and famous, free gifts, great outdoors, good times, testimonial.
3. By weight in descending order with the ingredients in greatest amount listed first.
4. Emergency rooms provide care for potentially life-threatening illnesses or injuries. Urgent care centers handle emergencies that are not life threatening and patients who do not have primary care physicans.
5. An amount an insurance plan member must pay in out-of-pocket expenses before the plan will start reimbursing for health care services.

> **EXPLORING HEALTH TERMS** *Answer the following questions on a sheet of paper.*

Lesson 1 *Match each definition with the correct term.*

advertising   media
comparison shopping   online shopping
health consumer   warranty

1. Anyone who purchases or uses health products or services.
2. Using the Internet to buy products and services.
3. A method of judging the benefits of different products by comparing several similar factors for each one.
4. The various methods of communicating information.

Lesson 2 *Fill in the blanks with the correct term.*

health care system   preventive care
health insurance   primary care physician
medical history   specialist

5. The _____ includes all the medical care available to a nation's people, the way they receive care, and the method of payment.
6. Actions that prevent the onset of disease or injury are known as _____.
7. _____ is a plan in which private companies or government programs pay for part or all of a person's medical costs.
8. Complete and comprehensive information about your immunizations and any health problems you have had to date is your _____.

Lesson 3 *Replace the underlined words with the correct term.*

consumer advocate   health fraud
fraud   malpractice

9. Deliberate deceit or trickery is <u>malpractice</u>.
10. When a health care professional fails to meet accepted medical standards, he or she is guilty of <u>consumer advocacy</u>.
11. A person or group whose sole purpose is to take on regional, national, and even international consumer issues is a <u>health fraud</u>.

70   Chapter 3   Review

Lesson 4 *Answer each question with the correct term.*

epidemiology   public health

12. What is a community-wide effort to monitor and promote the welfare of the population?
13. What is the scientific study of patterns of disease in a population?

> **RECALLING THE FACTS** *Use complete sentences to answer the following questions.*

Lesson 1

1. List two internal factors that can influence your buying decisions.
2. List three techniques advertisers use to persuade consumers to buy their products.
3. How are ingredients listed on a product label?

Lesson 2

4. Describe the health care that is provided by emergency rooms and urgent care centers.
5. What is a deductible?
6. Why do health care professionals have new patients fill out a medical history?

Lesson 3

7. List the steps to follow before you try to return a product.
8. What should you do if you have an unresolved problem with a health care provider?
9. Which government office can recall a dangerous product from the marketplace?

Lesson 4

10. What is the focus of state, county, and city health departments?
11. Identify the federal government's principal agency for cancer research.
12. List three ways you can advocate for public health.

---

6. To help assess the patient's past and current level of wellness and to alert the health care professional to possible hereditary factors that may influence the development of certain diseases.

7. Reread the instructions to make sure you are using the product correctly. If the product is truly defective; decide whether you want a replacement or your money back; put your reasons for returning the item in a letter, and keep a copy for future reference; return the item in its original packaging; if mailing the item, get a shipping receipt to prove that you sent it.

8. Change health care providers; for a more serious problem, seek help from a regulatory agency such as the American Medical Association or from a state licensing board.

9. Consumer Product Safety Commission.

10. Disease prevention.

➤ THINKING CRITICALLY

1. **Synthesizing.** Think of a health-related product or service that you recently purchased. What factors influenced your decision to buy the product or service? Distinguish between the internal and external factors. *(LESSON 1)*

2. **Evaluating.** What advantages over a private practice would a group practice provide a physician who is just starting out? *(LESSON 2)*

3. **Applying.** Jerome bought an exercise machine that promised to produce "rock-hard abs" in only three weeks. He used the machine according to the instructions, but after a month he was dissatisfied with the results. What conclusion might he draw from this experience? *(LESSON 3)*

4. **Analyzing.** What benefits are gained from positive relationships among community health professionals in promoting a healthy community? Explain your answer. *(LESSON 4)*

➤ HEALTH SKILLS APPLICATION

1. **Accessing Information.** Investigate a type of health-related product, such as a piece of sports equipment or a sports drink. Choose three products in that category and compare costs, quality, and any other appropriate factors. After you have done your research, decide which item you would purchase and explain why. *(LESSON 1)*

2. **Practicing Healthful Behaviors.** Identify those actions you presently take that could be considered preventive care. What additional actions could you take to protect yourself from disease? *(LESSON 2)*

3. **Advocacy.** Create an awareness campaign to help educate older adults in your community about the problem of health fraud. You may wish to create a poster, newsletter, or videotape to present your health message. *(LESSON 3)*

4. **Accessing Information.** Interview the manager of a local restaurant. Find out what state and local health laws the restaurant must follow. Share the information with your class. *(LESSON 4)*

BEYOND *the* Classroom

Parent Involvement

Interpersonal Communication. Sit down with your parents, and discuss their choice in health insurance plans. Talk about the plan's coverage, costs of premiums, choices in physicians, and any out-of-pocket expenses your parents might incur. If your parents have no insurance, discuss with them what you have found out about health insurance plans in class.

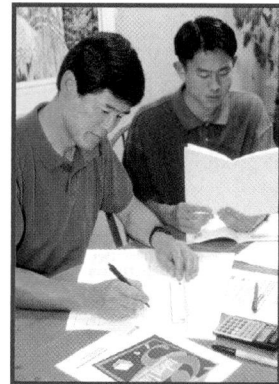

School and Community

Community Health Services. Research a health service for people of all ages that is available in your community. Identify its purpose, funding, and programs. Find out what volunteer opportunities, if any, are available at the organization. Summarize your findings in a one-page report that you present to the class.

Chapter 3 Review **71**

11. The National Cancer Institute.

12. Any three: Follow all health and safety laws and ordinances; set an example by following healthful behaviors; avoid actions that could endanger the health or safety of others; get involved in events that promote public health; identify and support community groups that deal with public health issues; inform the proper authorities if you notice a condition or activity that threatens public health.

Thinking Critically

1. Answers will vary.

2. Possible answer: A group practice would allow the physician to share office space, equipment, and support staff. This would save on costs.

3. Answers should show an awareness that changes in body shape require a commitment to physical activity including a comprehensive fitness routine.

4. Possible answer: Community resources can be better spent if agencies work together; emerging community health problems can be identified more readily if agencies share information.

Health Skills Application

1.–4. Answers will vary.

EVALUATE

- Use the reproducible Chapter 3 Test in the TCR, or construct your own using the Testmaker software. 📁 💿

- Use Performance Assessment 3 in the TCR. 📁

ENRICHMENT

Ask students to complete Enrichment Activity 3 in the TCR. 📁

BEYOND *the* Classroom

Keep students involved in the community, and encourage parent participation by assigning the activities on this page for students to work on outside of class.

Lessons	Standards		Features
	National	**State/Local**	
1 Physical Activity and Your Health *pages 74–79*	National Health Education Standards 1.1, 1.3, 1.6, 3.2		**Hands-On Health** • Promote the Benefits of Physical Activity *(Advocacy)*, page 76
2 Fitness and You *pages 80–86*	National Health Education Standards 1.1, 1.3, 3.2, 3.4		**Real-Life Application** • Targeting Cardiovascular Fitness *(Goal Setting)*, page 84
3 Planning a Personal Activity Program *pages 87–92*	National Health Education Standards 3.2, 3.4, 6.5, 6.6		**Health Skills Activity** • Starting a Physical Activity Program *(Goal Setting)*, page 89
4 Training and Safety for Physical Activities *pages 93–97*	National Health Education Standards 2.6, 3.2, 3.4, 7.2		**Exploring Issues** • Should Random Drug Testing of Athletes Be Performed? page 95
5 Physical Activity Injuries *pages 98–103*	National Health Education Standards 3.5, 7.4, 7.6		**Real-Life Application** • Being Safe While Physically Active *(Advocacy)*, page 100

Reproducible Resources	Assessment	Technology
Student Activity Workbook for use with each chapter 📁 Concept Mapping Activity 11 📁 Guided Reading Activities 11 📁 Health Lab 4 📁 Lesson Plan 11 📁 Parent Letter and Activities 4 📁 Reteaching Activity 11	📁 Lesson Quiz 11	🕹 Transparency 10 💿 TeacherWorks® 💻 Internet Activities
📁 Concept Mapping Activity 12 📁 Cross-Curriculum Activity 4 📁 Current Health Issues 4 📁 Guided Reading Activities 12 📁 Lesson Plan 12 📁 Reteaching Activity 12	📁 Lesson Quiz 12	🕹 Transparency 11 💿 TeacherWorks®
📁 Concept Mapping Activity 13 📁 Guided Reading Activities 13 📁 Lesson Plan 13 📁 Reteaching Activity 13	📁 Lesson Quiz 13	🕹 Transparency 12 💿 TeacherWorks®
📁 Concept Mapping Activity 14 📁 Decision-Making Activity 4 📁 Guided Reading Activities 14 📁 Lesson Plan 14 📁 Reteaching Activity 14	📁 Lesson Quiz 14	💿 TeacherWorks®
📁 Concept Mapping Activity 15 📁 Enrichment Activity 4 📁 Guided Reading Activities 15 📁 Lesson Plan 15 📁 Reteaching Activity 15	📁 Lesson Quiz 15	🕹 Transparency 13 💿 TeacherWorks®

0:00 OUT OF TIME

- Hands-On Health, p. 76
- Real-Life Application, p. 84
- Figure 4.3, p. 88
- Figure 4.4, p. 91
- Figure 4.5, p. 102

Language Diversity

- 🎧 English Audio CD Program
- 🎧 Spanish Audio CD Program
- 📁 English Summaries, Quizzes, and Activities
- 📁 Spanish Summaries, Quizzes, and Activities
- 📁 Spanish Parent Letters and Activities

End of Chapter Assessment

Blackline Masters

- 📁 Chapter 4 Test
- 📁 Performance Assessment Activity 4

Technology

- 💿 Vocabulary PuzzleMaker
- 📼 MindJogger Videoquiz
- 💿 **Exam*View*®** Pro Testmaker

Professional Health Series

Dealing with Sensitive Issues
Planning a Coordinated School Health Program
Promoting Character Education
Home, School, and Community Involvement

CHAPTER OVERVIEW

Chapter 4 identifies the benefits of regular physical activity and presents the basics of a fitness program.

Lesson 1 Regular physical activity benefits all three aspects of health. It can also lower the risk of many diseases.

Lesson 2 The five areas of health-related fitness are cardiorespiratory endurance, muscular strength, muscular endurance, flexibility, and body composition. All areas contribute to total fitness.

Lesson 3 Before planning an activity program, set realistic goals. A program should be based on the principles of overload, progression, and specificity.

Lesson 4 Becoming physically fit involves beginning a training program and following safety procedures.

Lesson 5 With any physical activity, there is a risk of injury. Most minor injuries can be prevented or treated, but major injuries require medical treatment.

Health Skills Features

- Hands-On Health (*Advocacy*), p. 76
- Real-Life Application (*Practicing Healthful Behaviors*), p. 84
- Health Skills Activity (*Goal Setting*), p. 89
- Exploring Issues, p. 95
- Real-Life Application (*Advocacy*), p. 100

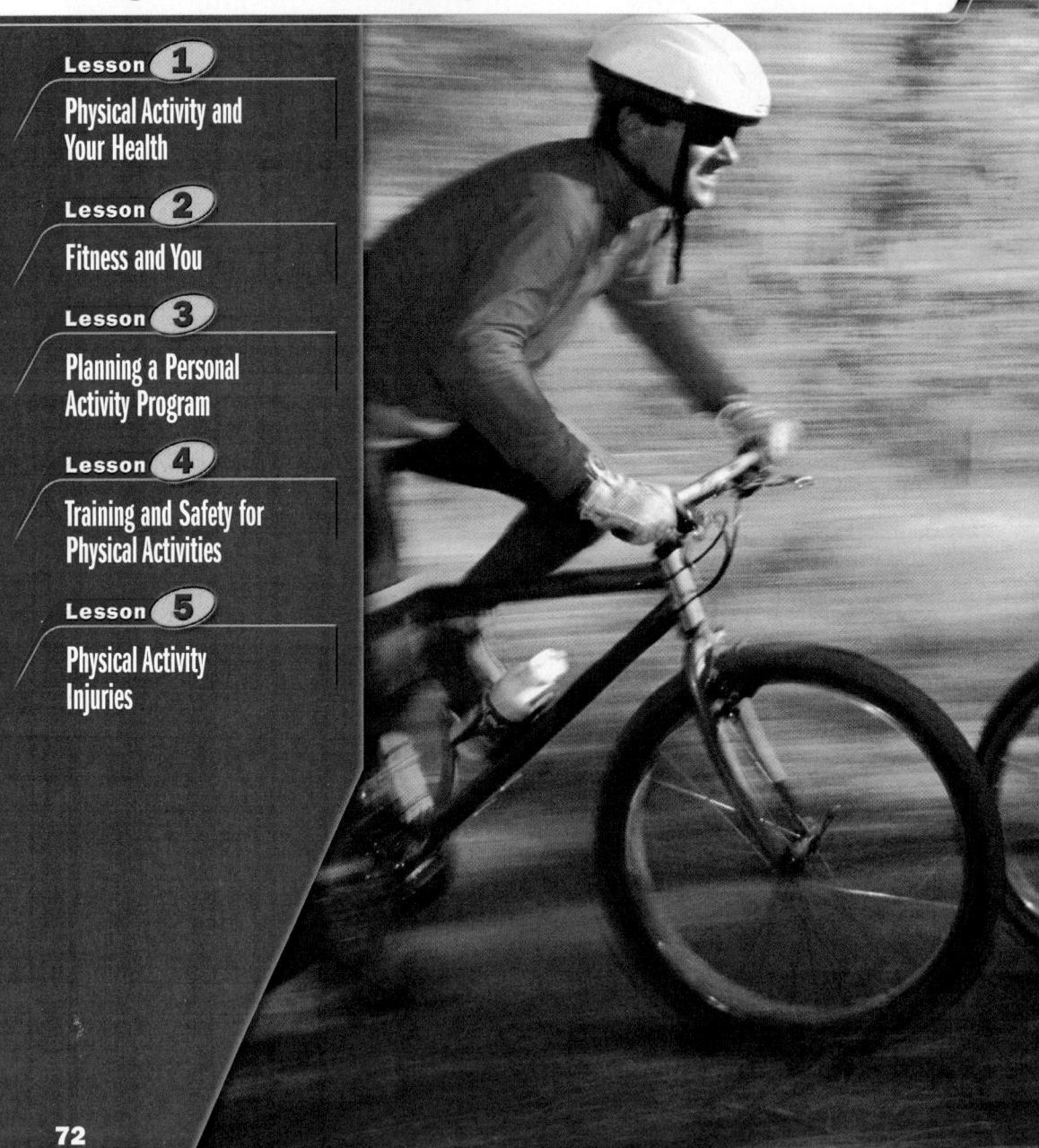

Chapter 4

Physical Activity for Life

Lesson 1
Physical Activity and Your Health

Lesson 2
Fitness and You

Lesson 3
Planning a Personal Activity Program

Lesson 4
Training and Safety for Physical Activities

Lesson 5
Physical Activity Injuries

72

MEETING STUDENT DIVERSITY

Language Diversity Use the following suggestions to help students who have difficulty with English:

- Pair English language learners with native speakers of English who can restate the Chapter Summary in language that helps students comprehend important concepts.

- Direct auditory learners or those students with language diversity to the *Glencoe Health Audio CD Program*. Available in English and Spanish, this component provides an audio and written summary of the chapter.

- Use photographs, drawings, or magazine clippings to help students visualize the important concepts of the chapter.

Personal Health Inventory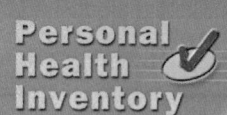

What's Your Health Status?

Read each statement below and respond by writing *yes, no,* or *sometimes* for each item. Write *yes* only for items that you practice regularly.

1. I participate in some form of physical activity every day.

2. Whenever possible, I walk rather than drive or get a ride.

3. My level of physical activity helps me maintain my weight within a healthy range.

4. I enjoy a wide variety of physical activities and sports.

5. I participate in aerobic activities such as cycling, swimming, or in-line skating.

6. I follow a nutritious diet; avoid harmful substances such as tobacco, alcohol, and other drugs; and get adequate rest.

7. I do at least 20 minutes of nonstop vigorous exercise a minimum of three times a week.

8. When I buy athletic equipment, safety is a primary consideration.

9. I take proper precautions to minimize the risk of injury while engaging in physical activities.

10. I know and follow safety rules for the activities in which I participate.

Keep this personal inventory for review later in the chapter. After you complete the chapter, review your answers and identify two or three behavior changes you can make to improve your health.

Quick *Write*

Using Visuals. You know that being active is important to your physical health, but do you realize how it affects your mental/emotional and social health? Give two examples of how the physical activity pictured here helps these teens keep their health triangles in balance.

73

INTRODUCING THE CHAPTER

Personal Health Inventory

Introduce the Personal Health Inventory, and point out that the statements relate to physical activity. Have students read the statements and record their responses privately. Remind students to keep their answers for review after they have completed the chapter.

Discuss with students how good performance in sports and other physical activities is dependent upon the development of specific skills and the preparation of the body and mind. Explain to students that this chapter will focus on these aspects of fitness. It will also discuss injuries that are associated with physical activity.

Quick *write*

Using Visuals Ask students to jot down two benefits of the physical activity featured in the photo. As they share their answers, write them on the board.

TECHNOLOGY OPTIONS

MINDJOGGER
VIDEOQUIZ

To preview or review chapter content, you may wish to use the Chapter 4 MindJogger Videoquiz.

HEALTH *Online*

Online Resources for the Teacher For a fresh approach to health topics and an in-depth look at health issues, use these online resources found under Teacher Resources at **health.glencoe.com:**

- Block Schedule Lesson Plans
- Technology Projects
- Health Updates

Physical Activity and Your Health

 FOCUS

QUICK START

Have students create a list of physical activities they enjoy and participate in regularly. Then have them add three new activities they would like to try. Ask volunteers to share their lists.

TYING TO PRIOR KNOWLEDGE

Ask students to list some benefits of physical activity. Point out that regular physical activity can improve overall well-being and that this lesson will focus on the role that physical activity plays in physical, mental/emotional, and social health.

Health Skills Features

"Promote the Benefits of Physical Activity," p. 76

 ADVOCACY

INTRODUCING VOCABULARY

- Ask students to complete the Chapter 4 Study Guide in the *Student Activity Workbook.*

Physical Activity and Your Health

VOCABULARY
- physical activity
- physical fitness
- sedentary lifestyle
- osteoporosis
- metabolism

YOU'LL LEARN TO
- Understand the importance of regular physical activity for enhancing and maintaining personal health throughout the life span.
- Examine the effects of regular physical activity on body systems.
- Analyze the relationship between regular physical activity and disease prevention.
- Discover ways to incorporate physical activity into daily life.

QUICK START

On a sheet of paper, make a list of the physical activities in which you participate on a regular basis. Then add to your list three others you would like to try. Briefly describe why each of these activities appeals to you.

What kinds of physical activities do you enjoy? Do you like to play basketball? Maybe you prefer skiing, riding mountain bikes, or playing volleyball. Whatever your preference, regular physical activity enhances your health.

Tasks such as vacuuming, raking leaves, or washing the car can help you fit more physical activity into your life. *What physical activities do you include in your daily routine?*

What Is Physical Activity?

P**hysical activity** is *any form of movement that causes your body to use energy.* It may be purposeful, such as when you exercise or play sports. It may also occur as part of your regular routine—for example, when you wash the car or take the dog for a walk. Many forms of physical activity can improve your level of **physical fitness**, *the ability to carry out daily tasks easily and have enough reserve energy to respond to unexpected demands.* Maintaining a high level of physical fitness gives you a sense of total well-being and is an important lifelong health goal.

74 Chapter 4 Physical Activity for Life

Lesson 1 *Resources*

Teacher Classroom Resources
- Concept Mapping Activity 11
- Guided Reading Activities 11
- Health Lab 4
- Lesson Plan 11
- Lesson Quiz 11
- Parent Letter and Activities 4
- Reteaching Activity 11

Student Activity Workbook
- Applying Health Skills 11
- Chapter 4 Study Guide

Multimedia
 Transparency 10

What Are the Benefits of Physical Activity?

Physical activity provides health benefits that last a lifetime. It helps strengthen not only the physical but also the mental/emotional and social sides of your health triangle.

Benefits to Physical Health

Physical activity makes your body stronger, increases your energy, and improves your posture. It can reduce chronic fatigue and stiffness and can improve motor responses. It strengthens your muscles and bones and helps reduce the risk of many serious diseases.

Regular physical activity also contributes to the functioning of many body systems, including the following:

▶ **Cardiovascular System.** Regular physical activity strengthens the heart muscle, allowing it to pump blood more efficiently.

▶ **Respiratory System.** When you engage in regular physical activity, your respiratory system begins to work more efficiently—you can breathe larger amounts of air, and the muscles used in respiration don't tire as quickly. This helps you perform such activities as running farther without getting out of breath.

▶ **Nervous System.** By helping you respond more quickly to stimuli, physical activity can improve your reaction time. This is especially helpful when driving or cycling.

Benefits to Mental/Emotional Health

Being physically active has many positive effects on your mental/emotional health. It can help reduce stress. Doing some stretching exercises before bed, for example, can help you relax tense muscles and sleep better after a difficult day at school. Physical activity also allows you to manage anger or frustration in a healthy way. By stimulating the release of certain chemicals that affect the brain, physical activity can improve your

hot link

cardiovascular and respiratory systems To learn more about the cardiovascular and respiratory systems, see Chapter 16, page 414.

nervous system For more information on the nervous system, see Chapter 15, page 399.

Ⓥ **Participating in a community event such as the one shown here is a good way to be physically active, to help others, and to engage in positive social interaction.**

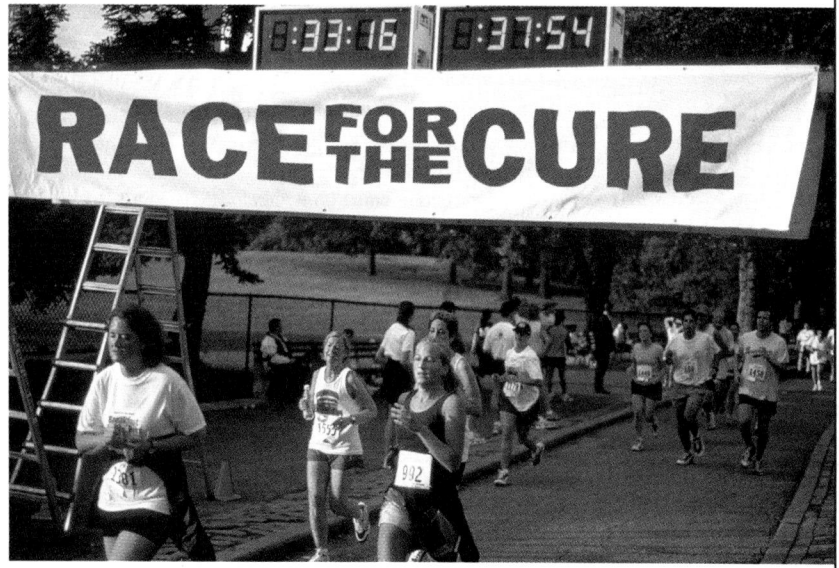

② TEACH

Discussing

Describe in detail one individual, perhaps a weight lifter, who works out at a gym five times a week. Ask the class whether this individual is fit. Encourage volunteers to explain their answers. Point out that being physically fit means being able to carry out daily tasks easily and have enough reserve energy to respond to unexpected demands. Stress that fitness is more than muscle development. Ask students to explain how fitness is related to self-esteem. L1 **Verbal/Linguistic**

Explaining

Talk about the benefits of physical activity to bone formation. Explain that among many other benefits, regular weight-bearing activities put stress on bones, which, in turn, stimulates bone formation. Physical activity protects against bone loss. L1

Guest Speaker

Invite an aerobic dance instructor to demonstrate dance movements and speak to the students about his or her classes. Ask him or her to lead the class in some simple routines. L1

⟩ School to Work

Active Commuting Have volunteers conduct a poll in your school to find out how many students walk, bike, ride in a car, or take public transit to school. Tell them to record the results in a SCHOOL category. Suggest that they establish a WORK category as well. For the WORK category, have them find out how many students and/or adult members of their household walk, bike, ride in a car or take public transit to work. Ask students to tabulate the results, and post them in the classroom. Allow time to discuss the findings as well as ways to encourage use of physical activity as a means of transportation. To promote walking and biking, have students establish a "walk or bike to school" day each week and create posters to gain support for the initiative.

Hands-On Health

ADVOCACY

PROMOTE THE BENEFITS OF PHYSICAL ACTIVITY

NHES Standard 7 Students will demonstrate the ability to advocate for personal, family, and community health.

Objectives

- Examine the benefits of physical activity on physical, mental/emotional, and social health.

- Design and analyze health messages delivered through media.

Motivator

Give students two minutes to list as many benefits of physical activity on health as they can.

Teaching Strategies

1. Advise students to use their lists for the activity.
2. Encourage each student to choose a different activity and provide a variety of benefits.
3. Tell students that ads should appeal to teens.

✓ Assessment

Using a rubric, student work should provide comprehensive evidence of the following criteria to achieve the highest score:

✔ clear, health-enhancing stand
✔ support for the position with relevant information
✔ awareness of the audience
✔ encouragement of others to make healthful choices
✔ passion/conviction

---

mood and decrease your risk of depression. Other ways that physical activity benefits your mental/emotional health include

▶ helping you look and feel better, which can increase your self-confidence.

▶ contributing to a positive self-concept by giving you a sense of pride and accomplishment in taking care of yourself.

▶ reducing mental fatigue by bringing more oxygen to the brain. This improves your concentration, allowing you to think more clearly and work more productively.

▶ giving you a "can-do" spirit when faced with new challenges.

Hands-On Health ACTIVITY

Promote the Benefits of Physical Activity

In this activity you will think of ways that different activities benefit all three parts of the health triangle. Then you'll choose an activity and create a plan to try it out.

What You'll Need

- paper and pencil
- markers or colored pencils

What You'll Do

1. Make a four-column chart on a sheet of paper. Label the columns "Activity," "Physical," "Mental/Emotional," and "Social."
2. Work in a group of three. Take turns identifying and recording a physical activity that you enjoy. Then work together to think of a physical, mental/emotional, and social benefit of each activity listed. Record these in the appropriate columns.
3. Choose one of the activities on your chart. Using markers or colored pencils, create an ad that illustrates the physical, mental/emotional, and social benefits of that activity. Present your finished ad to the class.

Apply and Conclude

Based on class presentations, choose an activity that you're interested in but have never tried. Write a plan to try the activity to see if you like it.

∿∿ HEALTH LITERACY

Responsible Citizen Have students work in groups to discuss how technology reduces the physical activity necessary to perform daily tasks. Encourage them to brainstorm a list of inventions or services that provide fitness benefits to the people using or delivering them and environmental benefits to global or local ecosystems. Examples might include a shopping or errand-running service on foot or by bicycle, or a gardening service that doesn't use power mowers, leaf blowers, or weed pullers. A sample invention might harness energy generated by people using non-electric treadmills and stationary bicycles to power appliances at a gym. Tell each student to create an ad for the service or product and display them in the classroom.

Benefits to Social Health

Are you a member of a recreational or school team? Do you swim laps at a neighborhood pool? Do you like hiking or exploring trails in your community? If so, you have probably met—and possibly formed friendships with—others who share your interests. Participating in a fitness regimen with friends can be fun and may motivate you to stick with your fitness program; in turn, you can help motivate your friends. Physical activity can also benefit social health by

▶ building self-confidence, which helps you cope better in social situations, such as when you meet new people.

▶ giving you the opportunity to interact and cooperate with others.

▶ helping you manage stress, which can enhance your relationships with others.

Risks of Physical Inactivity

According to the Centers for Disease Control and Prevention (CDC), some teens do not make physical activity a part of their lives. The CDC's findings, compiled in its *CDC Fact Book 2000/2001*, include these troubling facts about the level of physical activity among U.S. high school students.

▶ More than one in three teens (35 percent) do *not* participate regularly in vigorous physical activity (that is, for at least 20 minutes three times a week).

▶ Regular participation in vigorous physical activity declines significantly during the teen years, from 73 percent of ninth graders to 61 percent of twelfth graders.

▶ Only 29 percent of teens attend a daily physical education class—a serious decline from 42 percent in 1991.

Clearly, many teens have a **sedentary lifestyle**, or *a way of life that involves little physical activity*. They may spend much of their time watching TV, playing video games, or working on the computer rather than being physically active. The negative effects of a sedentary lifestyle may include

▶ unhealthful weight gain, which is linked to several potentially life-threatening conditions, including cardiovascular disease, type 2 diabetes, and cancer. Cardiovascular disease is the leading cause of death among Americans. **Diabetes** is a serious disorder that prevents the body from converting food into energy.

CHARACTER CHECK

Responsibility. When you participate in regular physical activity, you take responsibility for your health. By taking care of yourself, you are saying that you are worth investing in. Be positive about the benefits these activities bring you, and don't forget to compliment yourself: "I like how I feel, and I like how I look!" **Write three other positive statements that reflect the benefits you receive from regular physical activity.**

hot link

diabetes For more information on reducing your risk of developing diabetes, see Chapter 26, page 691.

Chapter 4 • Lesson 1

CHARACTER CHECK

Responsibility Direct students to write down three positive statements about the benefits of regular physical activity. Have volunteers share their statements with the class. Then ask students which side of the health triangle is represented by each of the statements.

Discussing

Ask students to keep a daily log that calculates the amount of time they spend watching TV, playing video games, or sitting at the computer. Were students surprised at the number of hours? Encourage students to cut down on the amount of time they spend engaging in sedentary activities. Discuss ways students can replace sedentary activity with physical activity. L2

hot link

Review with students the two types of diabetes. Type 1 diabetes develops most often in children and is not associated with any lifestyle behaviors. Type 2 diabetes, which is increasing in children and teens, is linked to a sedentary lifestyle and unhealthful weight gain. Tell students that they will learn more about both types of diabetes and cardiovascular disease in Chapter 26.

More About...

Sedentary Lifestyles Before the development of modern technology, physical activity was a part of everyday life and necessary for survival. Then came the age of labor-saving devices—inventions that ranged from indoor plumbing and the automobile to dishwashers and computers. These advancements made life easier, but they also contributed to more sedentary lifestyles. Sedentary living has been shown to be harmful to one's health, leading to unhealthful weight gain in the short term and a variety of serious diseases in the long term. What suggestions might teens have to regain an active lifestyle?

VISUAL LEARNING

Figure 4.1 Have a volunteer read aloud the information in Figure 4.1. Ask: Which of these healthful alternatives have you tried? Have students brainstorm additional ways to include more physical activity in their lives. Then ask for suggestions on how they could encourage family members and friends to be more physically active.

hotlink

Emphasize that metabolic rate depends on factors such as age, gender (males have a slightly higher metabolism than females), weight, body fat, and surrounding temperature.

Critical Thinking

Present the following scenario: Two teens decide to include more physical activity in their lives. Kayla begins walking to school, in-line skating, and swimming. Kyle decides to lift weights for an hour every night. After a week, Kyle gives up weight lifting. Kayla, however, continues to be physically active. Ask students: Why did Kayla's plan work better than Kyle's? **L1**

Did You Know ?

The number of obese adult Americans doubled between 1980 and 1999. During the same period, the number of overweight teens tripled. In children and teens, these weight increases correspond to higher occurrences of asthma and type 2 diabetes. Eating a well-balanced diet and increasing the amount of physical activity can help reverse these trends.

▶ an increased risk of **osteoporosis**, *a condition characterized by a decrease in bone density, producing porous and fragile bones.* Porous and fragile bones fracture more easily than healthy bones.

▶ a reduced ability to manage stress.

▶ decreased opportunities to meet and form friendships with active people who value and live a healthy lifestyle.

You can lower your risk of these and many other health problems by including more physical activity in your daily life. For example, when you go shopping, walk to the store or, if you have to drive, park farther away from the entrance. **Figure 4.1** suggests other healthful alternatives to sedentary activities.

FIGURE 4.1

APPROACHES TO EVERYDAY ACTIVITIES

Instead of . . .	Try . . .
• Taking an elevator or escalator	• Taking the stairs
• Playing video or computer games	• Playing soccer, basketball, or tennis
• Getting a ride to a friend's house	• Walking, skating, or riding your bike there
• Using a shopping cart	• Carrying groceries to the car
• Watching TV or taking a nap	• Gardening or mowing the lawn
• Taking the car through a car wash	• Washing the car yourself

Physical Activity and Weight Control

The CDC reports that more than one-half of American adults and 14 percent of teens are overweight. This situation can be traced to a sedentary lifestyle and overeating. To stay within a weight range that is healthy for you, it's important to develop good eating habits and be physically active on a regular basis.

Understanding how the food you eat gets converted into energy can help you maintain a healthy weight. **Metabolism** is *the process by which your body gets energy from food.* Food's energy value is measured in units of heat called calories. Your body needs a sufficient number of calories each day to function properly. Additional calories must be burned through physical activity or they will be stored in the body as fat. When you are physically active, your metabolic rate rises and your body burns more calories than when it is at rest. The number of calories burned depends in part on the nature of the

What Teens Want to Know

What does the expression "burning calories" mean? The process of burning, or combustion, is one form of a reaction called *oxidation.* This means the uniting of oxygen with other substances. Food that is used by your body for fuel combines with oxygen and releases energy. Your body uses this energy for body heat, for automatic processes, and for physical activities. So when you run down the basketball court, dance, climb the stairs, or pound a nail with a hammer, you really are "burning" calories.

activity. When you stop being active, your metabolic rate slowly returns to normal. For several hours afterward, however, you continue to burn more calories than you did before you began the activity.

Hiking is a physical activity that you can enjoy throughout your life. *Name two safety considerations to keep in mind while hiking.*

Fitting Physical Activity into Your Life

Health professionals recommend that teens incorporate 60 minutes of moderate physical activity into their daily lives. This may sound difficult, but it doesn't have to be. Any activities that get you moving count toward your daily total. For example, walk or bike to school instead of getting a ride. Suggest to your family that you go for a hike or a swim on the weekend. Organize a basketball game with friends. Be sure to include some activities that you can participate in throughout your life. Hiking, swimming, golfing, biking, racquetball, tennis, and bowling are just a few examples of lifelong activities.

 Lesson 1 *Review*

Reviewing Facts and Vocabulary

1. What is the difference between *physical activity* and *physical fitness*?
2. Examine and briefly describe the effects of regular physical activity on three body systems.
3. Analyze the relationship between regular physical activity and disease prevention.

Thinking Critically

4. **Analyzing.** Explain why watching television and walking affect metabolism differently.
5. **Synthesizing.** Why does it take longer to get the maximum health benefit from a leisurely walk than from swimming laps?

Applying Health Skills

Advocacy. Design a pamphlet with eye-catching headlines and graphics to educate younger students about the importance of physical activity. Your pamphlet should encourage and guide them to determine and then participate in the types of physical activity best suited to their interests and abilities.

WORD PROCESSING Word processing can give your pamphlet a professional look. See **health.glencoe.com** for tips on how to get the most from your word-processing program.

Lesson 1 Physical Activity and Your Health **79**

③ ASSESS

EVALUATING THE LESSON

Assign and discuss the Lesson 1 Review; then administer, grade, and discuss Lesson Quiz 11 in the TCR.

RETEACHING

- To prepare, divide the lesson into three parts. Then divide the class into groups and assign each group a different section of the lesson. Allow 10 minutes for students to discuss the main ideas and any experiences they may have had with the concepts. Then have volunteers summarize the information in their sections for the class, providing examples presented by the group. You may want to allow a few additional minutes for questions.
- Ask students to complete Reteaching Activity 11 in the TCR.

ENRICHMENT

Choose students to investigate the use of new high-tech methods for evaluating athletic performance, such as computer-based products.

④ CLOSE

Ask students to discuss any personal goals they established as a result of reading the information in this lesson.

 Lesson 1 *Review*

Answers to Reviewing Facts and Vocabulary

1. See definitions on page 74.
2. Answers will vary but should include effects on the cardiovascular, respiratory, and nervous systems.
3. Possible answer: Regular physical activity can help prevent unhealthful weight gain, which is linked to several diseases.

Answers to Thinking Critically

4. Walking burns more calories than watching TV, allowing less food energy to be stored as fat.
5. Possible answer: The more vigorous an activity, the more quickly the maximum health benefits are achieved.

Fitness and You

1 FOCUS

 QUICK START Write the phrase *Physical Fitness* on the board. As students identify statements that describe physical fitness, write them under the phrase. Then have students complete their own lists with additional ideas.

TYING TO PRIOR KNOWLEDGE

Tell students the five areas of health-related fitness are cardiorespiratory endurance, muscular strength, muscular endurance, flexibility, and body composition. Have students write down the area they think is most important and the reason for their choice. Tell them that they will learn more about each of these elements as they study this lesson.

Health Skills Features

"Targeting Cardiovascular Fitness," p. 84

PRACTICING HEALTHFUL BEHAVIORS

INTRODUCING VOCABULARY

- Ask students to write their own definitions of the five elements of fitness. Have them check the accuracy of their definitions in the Glossary.

- Ask students to complete the Chapter 4 Study Guide in the *Student Activity Workbook.*

Lesson 2

Fitness and You

VOCABULARY

- **cardiorespiratory endurance**
- **muscular strength**
- **muscular endurance**
- **flexibility**
- **body composition**
- **exercise**
- **aerobic exercise**
- **anaerobic exercise**

YOU'LL LEARN TO

- Identify and describe the five areas of health-related fitness.
- Examine the relationship among body composition, diet, and fitness.
- Understand how to improve each of the five areas of health-related fitness.
- Examine the effects of fitness on body systems.

 QUICK START What does it mean to be physically fit? Write "Physical Fitness" at the top of a sheet of paper. Then write all the ways you can think of to describe a person's level of physical fitness.

 These teens are improving their fitness levels. *Explain how this activity improves cardiorespiratory endurance.*

Do you have trouble running a mile even though you work out three times a week? Does your best friend excel at track but have a hard time doing push-ups? As you can see from these examples, every person's level of physical fitness is different.

Elements of Fitness

To have total fitness, you need to take into account the five areas of health-related fitness. These are the areas that affect your overall health and well-being.

▶ **Cardiorespiratory endurance**—*the ability of the heart, lungs, and blood vessels to utilize and send fuel and oxygen to the body's tissues during long periods of moderate-to-vigorous activity.*

▶ **Muscular strength**—*the amount of force a muscle can exert.*

▶ **Muscular endurance**—*the ability of the muscles to perform physical tasks over a period of time without becoming fatigued.*

80 Chapter 4 Physical Activity for Life

 ## Lesson 2 *Resources*

Teacher Classroom Resources

- 📁 Concept Mapping Activity 12
- 📁 Cross-Curriculum Activity 4
- 📁 Current Health Issues 4
- 📁 Guided Reading Activities 12
- 📁 Lesson Plan 12
- 📁 Lesson Quiz 12
- 📁 Reteaching Activity 12

Student Activity Workbook

- 📁 Applying Health Skills 12
- 📁 Chapter 4 Study Guide

Multimedia

- 🖳 Transparency 11

▶ **Flexibility**—*the ability to move a body part through a full range of motion.*

▶ **Body composition**—*the ratio of body fat to lean body tissue, including muscle, bone, water, and connective tissue such as ligaments, cartilage, and tendons.*

Various activities and tests can help you evaluate each area of fitness. When you know your strengths and weaknesses, you can take steps to improve your physical fitness through exercise. **Exercise** is *purposeful physical activity that is planned, structured, and repetitive and that improves or maintains personal fitness.*

Measuring Cardiorespiratory Endurance

Cardiovascular disease is the leading cause of death in the United States. Keeping your cardiovascular system healthy is the most effective way of reducing your risk of developing this life-threatening disease. Cardiovascular health depends on maintaining good cardiorespiratory endurance. Can you run a mile without stopping or hike for most of the day without getting tired? If so, you have good cardiorespiratory endurance.

CARDIORESPIRATORY ENDURANCE—STEP TEST

The three-minute step test can be used to measure your cardiorespiratory endurance. This test enables you to determine the rate at which your heart beats following a period of physical activity.

1. Use a sturdy bench about 12 inches high. Fully extending each leg as you step, step up with your right foot and then with your left. Then step down with your right foot first.

2. Repeat at the rate of 24 steps per minute for three minutes.

3. Take your pulse. To do this, find a pulse point on your wrist using the first two fingers of your other hand. *Do not use the thumb, which has its own pulse.* If you have trouble finding the pulse in your wrist, try finding the pulse point in your neck just below your jaw. Count the number of beats you feel for one minute.

4. Find your pulse rate on the chart to evaluate your cardiorespiratory endurance.

Measuring Muscular Strength and Endurance

You need muscular strength for activities that involve lifting, pushing, or jumping and muscular endurance to perform such activities repeatedly. Having good muscular strength and endurance gives you the necessary power to carry out your daily tasks without becoming fatigued. People with good muscular strength and endurance often have better posture and fewer back problems.

▼ As you do the step test, your heart rate increases. **Explain why physical activity causes your heart to beat faster.**

STEP TEST SCORING CHART

Beats/ Minute	Rating
85–95	Excellent
96–105	Good
106–125	Fair
126 or more	Needs Improvement

Lesson 2 Fitness and You **81**

2 TEACH

Cooperative Learning

Divide students into pairs. Have them assess cardiorespiratory (heart and lung) endurance using the three-minute step test on this page. (You will need a sturdy bench and a stopwatch.) L2

Discussing

Ask students to identify sports and other physical activities that require muscular strength. Which focus on upper body strength? Lower body strength? Both? L1

Community Involvement

Ask volunteers to interview an older adult in their family, extended family, or neighborhood. Have them ask questions such as: What kinds of exercise did you do as a teenager? As a young adult? During middle age? Do you still exercise? If so, what kinds of exercise or other physical activity do you engage in now? What kinds of obstacles to exercising do you encounter? How do you deal with these obstacles? What would you do differently in the area of physical fitness if you could? Request that students share the results of the interview with the class. L3
Interpersonal

Cooperative Learning Activity

Active Calendar Finding time for exercise can be a challenge. Even so, most teens manage to budget time for recreation and socializing. Group students for a discussion of typical teen social activities. These may include not only inactive events, such as parties, meals, movies, and concerts, but also a variety of sports and other active pastimes. Have students plan a calendar of social events for one weekend in which they get some form of physical activity, such as dancing or playing tennis. The activity may also serve as a means of transportation, such as walking to a movie.

Cooperative Learning

As a homework assignment, have students work with a partner to research the specific benefits of abdominal strength and endurance. Have them write their findings in a paragraph. ⬛▬ L1

Discussing

Find an appropriate place, such as a gym, to assess students' upper body strength and endurance as discussed on this page. Record and save each student's score. Discuss exercises or activities that will help build upper body strength and endurance. Later in the year, repeat the exercise, and compare each student's past and present scores. L1

Community Involvement

Have several volunteers visit a community center or other local facility that offers exercise or stretching classes for older adults. Ask: Which aspects of fitness are emphasized in these classes? How are they emphasized? Why? Let the volunteers discuss what they have learned with the rest of the class. Suggest that some students might volunteer to help in these classes. L3

Critical Thinking

Have students compare the scoring charts for curl-ups, the arm hang, and the sit-and-reach. Ask: How do the scoring goals vary for males and females? What do you think accounts for this difference? What do these scores indicate about the strength and flexibility of an individual male compared to the strength and flexibility of an individual female? L1

Curl-ups measure abdominal strength. *How might abdominal strength improve your posture?*

CURL-UPS HEALTHY RANGE SCORING CHART		
Age	Male	Female
13	21 or more	18 or more
14+	24 or more	18 or more

The arm hang is used to measure upper body strength and endurance. *What are the benefits of having good upper body strength and endurance?*

ARM HANG HEALTHY RANGE SCORING CHART		
Age	Male (Time in Seconds)	Female (Time in Seconds)
12	7–14	7–14
13–15	12–20	7–14

ABDOMINAL MUSCLE STRENGTH AND ENDURANCE—CURL-UPS

The body has different muscle groups, so there are different ways to measure muscular strength and endurance. Curl-ups often are used to measure abdominal strength.

1. Lie on your back with your knees bent at about a 45-degree angle and your feet slightly apart. Position your arms at your sides.

2. With your heels flat on the floor, curl your shoulders slowly off the ground, moving your arms forward toward your feet as you rise.

3. Slowly return to the original position. Do one curl-up every three seconds; continue until you can't do any more at the specified pace.

4. Find your score on the chart to rate your abdominal strength.

UPPER BODY STRENGTH AND ENDURANCE—ARM HANG

The arm hang is one test that is used to measure upper body strength and endurance. For this test, work with two other people.

1. Grasp the horizontal bar with your palms facing away from you.

2. Raise your body so that your chin is above the bar and your elbows are flexed to hold your chest near the bar. One person should act as a spotter to make sure that you are not swinging as you hang from the bar.

3. Hold the position described in Step 2 for as long as possible. The third person will time you with a stopwatch and will stop the watch if your chin touches the bar, your head tilts backward, or your chin falls below the bar.

4. Compare your score with those in the chart to rate your upper body strength and endurance.

Measuring Flexibility

When sitting on the floor with your legs outstretched, can you reach forward and touch your toes? If so, you have good flexibility. Being flexible can increase your athletic performance, help you feel more comfortable, and reduce the risk of muscle strains and other injuries. It can also help prevent lower back problems. Some track and field events, gymnastics, ballet and other forms of dance, figure skating, and the martial arts require a great deal of flexibility.

BODY FLEXIBILITY—SIT-AND-REACH

You can use the back saver sit-and-reach test, developed by the Cooper Institute of Aerobics Research in Dallas, Texas, to assess the flexibility of your lower back and the backs of your thighs. Before taking the test, do some light stretching to warm up your muscles.

82 **Chapter 4** Physical Activity for Life

Meeting Individual Needs

The Physically and Mentally Challenged Many individuals who are physically or mentally challenged participate in and enjoy physical activities. Have students research the Special Olympics. Ask volunteers to interview young people who participate in the Special Olympics and those who volunteer during the events.

Also, ask students to find articles in newspapers and magazines about athletic accomplishments of individuals who are physically challenged. Survey the community for such individuals, and ask whether they would be willing to be interviewed by one or two classmates.

1. Tape a yardstick on top of a 12-inch-high box so that it protrudes 9 inches toward you. The "zero" end should be nearest you. Put the back of the box against a wall.

2. Sit on the floor. Remove your shoes, and fully extend one leg so that the sole of your foot is flat against the side of the box beneath the yardstick. Bend your other knee so that your foot is flat on the floor two to three inches from the side of the extended leg.

3. Place the palm of one hand over the back of the other hand. Extend your arms over the yardstick, reaching forward as far as you can.

4. Repeat Step 3 four times. On the fourth try, hold the position for at least one second and notice where your fingertips are on the yardstick. Record your score to the nearest inch.

5. Switch the position of your legs and repeat the test.

6. Find your scores on the chart to determine your flexibility.

SIT-AND-REACH HEALTHY RANGE SCORING CHART

Gender	Number of Inches
Male	8
Female	10 (ages 13–14) 12 (ages 15+)

Measuring Body Composition

Being physically active and eating a balanced diet can improve the way you look. These healthful practices can also help you avoid the health problems associated with being overweight. To look and feel your best, it is helpful to have some idea of your body composition—that is, how much of your body is composed of fat and how much is composed of everything else. In general, males with 25 percent or more body fat and females with 30 percent or more body fat are at risk of developing cardiovascular problems. Carrying too much weight also places added stress on the skeletal system. To maintain a healthy body composition, eat a nutritious, balanced diet and participate in regular physical activity.

The "pinch test" is a common method of determining body composition. It is conducted with a tool called a *skinfold caliper*, a gauge that measures the thickness of the fat beneath a fold of skin. The tester measures folds of skin on three to seven different parts of the body, usually including the back of a shoulder, the back of an arm, the abdomen, hip, and thigh. The average of the measurements is then calculated to estimate the total proportion of body fat.

Improving Your Fitness

You can choose from many different physical activities and exercises to improve your fitness level, but most fall into one of two categories: aerobic exercise or anaerobic exercise. **Aerobic exercise** is *any activity that uses large muscle groups, is rhythmic in nature, and can be maintained continuously for at least 10 minutes three times a day or for 20 to 30 minutes at one time.* Examples of aerobic exercise include running, cycling, swimming, and dancing.

The pinch test is often used to determine how much of a person's body is composed of fat.

Cooperative Learning

Divide the class into pairs. Allow 10 minutes for each partner to determine the other's flexibility as discussed on this page. **L1**

Service Learning

Challenge students to write articles about the importance of the five aspects of health-related fitness to submit to the school newspaper. The articles should feature classroom activities involving assessment of cardiorespiratory endurance, abdominal muscle strength and endurance, upper body strength and endurance, and flexibility. Provide a camera and film for taking photographs of the activities to submit with the articles. **L3** **Verbal/Linguistic**

FYI

For you to get the maximum health benefits, your workout should include both aerobic and anaerobic exercises. Devote 75–80 percent of your workout time to aerobic activity and 20–25 percent to anaerobic activity.

What Teens Want to Know

How can I make sure that my workout is safe? The American Academy of Pediatrics recommends the following guidelines for resistance training for teens:

- Use low-resistance exercises (little or no weight and few repetitions) until you learn proper techniques.
- Add weight only after 8 to 15 repetitions can be performed.

- Include all muscle groups in your routine, and perform each exercise through the full range of motion at each joint.
- Perform workouts for 20 to 30 minutes, three times a week.

Including both aerobic and resistance exercises in your physical activity program can help you improve body composition by reducing body fat and building lean muscle.

Real-Life Application

TARGETING CARDIOVASCULAR FITNESS

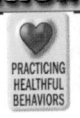

PRACTICING HEALTHFUL BEHAVIORS

NHES Standard 3 Students will demonstrate the ability to practice health-enhancing behaviors and reduce health risks.

Objectives

- Examine the effects of heart rate on the cardiovascular system.
- Assess and apply strategies to improve and maintain cardio-vascular fitness.

Motivator

Have students estimate their target heart range (THR).

Teaching Strategies

1. With a volunteer, go through the steps for finding THR. How did this result compare with the student's estimate?

2. Demonstrate how to take a radial pulse: Turn one hand so that the palm faces up. Position the index and middle fingers of the other hand across the wrist so that fingertips are resting on the thumb side. Carotid pulse: Feel for the pulse on either side of the neck just below the jaw. Tell students not to press when using this method.

✓ Assessment

Using a rubric, student work should provide comprehensive evidence of the following criteria to achieve the highest score:

✔ demonstration of healthful techniques

✔ correct calculation of their target heart range

✔ identification of aerobic activities

✔ actions to slow down or increase the heart rate during each activity

---

Real-Life Application

Targeting Cardiovascular Fitness

Use these steps to find your target heart range—the ideal range for your heart rate during aerobic activity. Then do the activity to help you apply this information.

Target Heart Range

○ **Maximum target heart rate.** Exercising above this rate can result in injury.

Target heart range. To safely build cardiorespiratory endur-ance, keep your heart rate within this range. Take your pulse for 6 seconds and multiply this number by 10 to determine the number of beats per minute.

○ **Minimum target heart rate.** Exercising below this rate will not build cardiorespiratory endurance.

ACTIVITY

Prepare a written plan describing how you will apply this information. Include your target heart range (with your calculations), two aerobic activities, how you will check your heart rate while you are doing each activity, and how you will keep your heart rate within the target range.

Finding Your Target Heart Range

1. Sit quietly for five minutes, and then take your pulse. This is your resting heart rate. Suppose that it is 66 beats per minute.

2. Subtract your age from 220 to find your maximum heart rate. For example, if you are 16, your maximum heart rate will be 204.

3. Subtract your resting heart rate from your maximum heart rate. (Example: $204 - 66 = 138$)

4. Multiply the number you arrived at in Step 3 by 60 percent and again by 85 percent. Round to the nearest whole numbers. (Example: $138 \times 0.60 = 83$; $138 \times 0.85 = 117$)

5. Add your resting heart rate to the numbers you arrived at in Step 4. (Example: $83 + 66 = 149$; $117 + 66 = 183$) The resulting totals represent your target heart range (between 149 and 183).

Anaerobic exercise involves *intense short bursts of activity in which the muscles work so hard that they produce energy without using oxygen.* Running a 100-meter dash and lifting weights are examples of anaerobic exercises.

Improving Cardiorespiratory Endurance

When you do aerobic exercises, your heart rate increases and your heart sends more oxygen to your muscles to use as energy. Over time, this strengthens the heart muscle, allowing it to pump blood more efficiently. Aerobic exercise also affects your respiratory system by increasing the lungs' capacity to hold air. **Caution:** Don't force

---

Home and Community

Community Fitness Have students explore free or low-cost physical activity options in their community. Do schools, parks, or community centers offer workout facilities? Do large apartment buildings or recreational centers provide swimming pools or gyms? Do safe bike and jogging paths or lanes exist? Is a body of water appropriate for water sports

accessible? Does the climate encourage out-door activity year round? Does it snow in the winter? If so, what inexpensive winter sports are available? Encourage students to create a fitness directory based on their findings. They could also design or "invent" new kinds of inexpensive physical activities to include in their directory.

yourself to continue an aerobic activity if you become exhausted. Before beginning a fitness program that includes aerobic activities, consult a health care professional. This is especially important if you have asthma or another respiratory disorder. It is also recommended for people with heart disease.

Improving Muscular Strength and Endurance

Anaerobic exercises improve muscular strength and endurance. The more work the muscles do, the stronger they become. Sprinting is an example of an anaerobic activity. Resistance or strength training, which builds muscles by requiring them to move in opposition to a force, is also a form of anaerobic exercise. Free weights, exercise machines, or your own body weight can provide resistance. In addition to building and strengthening muscle, resistance exercises help the body keep blood sugar levels normal and help maintain healthy **cholesterol** levels.

As indicated in **Figure 4.2,** there are three types of resistance training exercise. Exercises such as these tone muscles, improve muscular strength, and increase muscular endurance.

Improving Flexibility

When you have good flexibility, you can easily bend, turn, and stretch your body. You can improve your flexibility through regular

hot link

cholesterol See Chapter 5, page 118 for information on cholesterol.

FIGURE **4.2**

TYPES OF RESISTANCE EXERCISE

Isometric Exercise	Isotonic Exercise	Isokinetic Exercise
An activity that uses muscle tension to improve muscular strength with little or no movement of the body part	An activity that combines muscle contraction and repeated movement	An activity in which a resistance is moved through an entire range of motion at a controlled rate of speed
Other Examples: pushing against a wall or any other immovable object	**Other Examples:** doing calisthenics, push-ups, pull-ups, sit-ups; using a rowing machine	**Other Examples:** using a stationary bike or treadmill designed to control resistance and speed

Lesson 2 Fitness and You **85**

Discussing

Have volunteers tell the class about their own workout routines. Then ask the class: Which activities in your routine are aerobic and which are anaerobic? Remind students that to get the maximum benefits, their workouts should include both aerobic and anaerobic exercise.

Cooperative Learning

Provide basic art supplies, and have students work in small groups to design logos for T-shirts promoting their favorite kind of aerobic exercise. Choose some of the designs to feature in a display titled "These Aerobic Exercises Rate an A+!" **L1** **Visual/Spatial**

VISUAL LEARNING

Figure 4.2 Read aloud the definitions of isometric, isotonic, and isokinetic exercises featured in Figure 4.2. Then have volunteers demonstrate an isometric exercise and an isotonic exercise. Ask students: Why do you think exercise machines are used for isokinetic exercises?

HEALTH LITERACY

Group or Individual Activities Some people prefer to exercise on their own schedule and at their own convenience. Others prefer classes or group activities that provide the structure of a regular schedule and group interaction. Ask students to list various types of physical activities, including solitary scheduled and unscheduled activities as well as group scheduled and unscheduled activities. Have them rank the activities in order of preference. Then have them list the advantages and disadvantages of each type from their point of view. Finally, students should choose three activities best suited to their personal needs.

❸ ASSESS

EVALUATING THE LESSON

Assign and discuss the Lesson 2 Review; then administer, grade, and discuss Lesson Quiz 12 in the TCR. 📁

RETEACHING

- Have students list the physical activities they do in a typical week. Then ask them to decide which characteristics each type of activity has. Does it increase cardiorespiratory endurance? Improve muscular strength and endurance? Improve flexibility?

- Ask students to complete Reteaching Activity 12 in the TCR. 📁

ENRICHMENT

Have volunteers create a short puppet show involving two puppets named A. Robic and Anna Robic. Direct them to write a short script in which the puppets define, describe, and demonstrate the basics of aerobic and anaerobic exercise. Arrange for the puppet show to be presented to an elementary school class.

❹ CLOSE

Write the five elements of fitness—cardiorespiratory endurance, muscular strength, muscular endurance, flexibility, and body composition—on slips of paper. Divide the class into five groups, and have one student from each group draw a slip. Ask each group to create a list of key concepts about their fitness element. Then have each group read the list aloud.

 Regular, gentle stretching of muscles and joints helps increase flexibility. *What exercises do you include in your routine to increase your flexibility?*

stretching exercises. Just be sure to move slowly and gently. For example, to stretch the muscles of your upper body, stand with your arms extended behind your back, hands clasped; raise your arms until you feel tightness in your shoulders and chest; and hold for 20 seconds.

Improving and Maintaining Bone Strength

The decisions you make concerning physical activity and nutrition can affect the health of your skeletal system now and later in life. You probably already know that calcium—found in dairy products and certain green vegetables—is essential for building strong bones. Resistance training and weight-bearing aerobic activities—those that force you to work against gravity, such as walking and stair climbing—can also help increase bone mass, strengthening your skeletal system.

It's very important to build strong bones during your teen years because this time period is your last opportunity to significantly increase bone mass. During a person's late twenties and early thirties, bone mass and density begin to decline. This can lead to osteoporosis.

▶ Lesson 2 *Review*

Reviewing Facts and Vocabulary

1. Identify and describe the five areas of health-related fitness.

2. Examine and briefly describe the relationship among body composition, diet, and fitness.

3. Examine and briefly describe the effects of resistance training on the muscular and skeletal systems.

Thinking Critically

4. **Analyzing.** Sam has been doing 50 curl-ups each day. Explain what area of health-related fitness this exercise benefits. What other types of physical activities or exercises should Sam add to his routine to improve his total health-related fitness?

5. **Evaluating.** Keesha, who has asthma, wants to begin an exercise program. She is thinking of signing up for a high-impact aerobic class. Is this a good strategy for Keesha? Explain your answer.

Applying Health Skills

Practicing Healthful Behaviors. Help family members determine their target heart ranges. Then make a list of aerobic activities you could do together. Determine how you all could use this information to improve your cardiorespiratory endurance. Remember: get a health screening before beginning an exercise program.

SPREADSHEETS Using spreadsheet software, design a table that lists target heart ranges for people of various ages and with different resting heart rates. See **health.glencoe.com** for information on how to use a spreadsheet.

▶ Lesson 2 *Review*

Answers to Reviewing Facts and Vocabulary

1. See pages 80–81 for definitions.
2. A nutritious, balanced diet and regular physical activity will help maintain a healthy body composition.
3. It improves muscular strength and endurance and strengthens bones.

Answers to Thinking Critically

4. Curl-ups improve abdominal strength and endurance; aerobic activities, activities that build other muscle groups, and stretching activities should be added.
5. No. She has a respiratory disease and should consult her doctor first.

Planning a Personal Activity Program

VOCABULARY
overload
progression
specificity
warm-up
workout
F.I.T.T.
cool-down
resting heart rate

YOU'LL LEARN TO

• Set realistic fitness goals.

• Synthesize information and apply critical-thinking, decision-making, and problem-solving skills to develop a personal physical activity program.

• Identify the basic principles of a physical activity program.

 QUICK START List the physical activities in which you have participated during the past week. Classify each activity as *aerobic, anaerobic,* or *other,* and explain your choice.

K nowing the many health benefits of physical activity may inspire you to begin a personal activity program—but having a reason or goal for being physically active is even more inspiring. Setting fitness goals can help you get started by providing you with a plan of action.

Setting Physical Activity Goals

H ow can you be sure to include physical activity in your daily routine? The first step is to set realistic fitness goals. Then you can develop a plan to meet your goals. To meet the USDA recommendations, teens should get 60 minutes of physical activity every day. This may include all sorts of activities, from participating in physical education classes and playing sports to doing household tasks such as mowing the lawn and cleaning your room.

Participating in a school sports program may inspire you to set fitness goals and begin a physical activity program.

Lesson 3 *Resources*

Teacher Classroom Resources

📁 Concept Mapping Activity 13

📁 Guided Reading Activities 13

📁 Lesson Plan 13

📁 Lesson Quiz 13

📁 Reteaching Activity 13

Student Activity Workbook

📁 Applying Health Skills 13

📁 Chapter 4 Study Guide

Multimedia

🕹 Transparency 12

Planning a Personal Activity Program

 FOCUS

QUICK START At the top of the board, write the headings *Aerobic, Anaerobic,* and *Other.* As students identify activities they have participated in during the past week, write their responses in the appropriate column on the board. Ask students to explain why each activity is classified in a particular column.

TYING TO PRIOR KNOWLEDGE

Ask students to think about what physical activity goals they might want to pursue. Have them jot down three or four goals for this year.

Health Skills Features

"Starting a Physical Activity Program," p. 89

 GOAL SETTING

INTRODUCING VOCABULARY

• Write the terms *warm-up* and *cool-down* on the board. Ask volunteers to describe a safe warm-up or cool-down activity.

• Ask students to complete the Chapter 4 Study Guide in the *Student Activity Workbook.* 📖

② TEACH

Discussing

Ask students to raise their hands if they engage in physical activity on a regular basis. Then call on those students to describe how they feel after a workout. Students will probably say they feel refreshed, exhilarated, and invigorated after a workout. Tell students that these are natural responses due to the release of mood-enhancing chemicals called endorphins in the brain. Next, lead students in a discussion of the advantages of a physical activity program, such as the ability to cope more effectively with the challenges of daily life, having more energy, reducing body fat, looking and feeling better, and so on. **ELL**

Discussing

Have each student create a personal and private contract that states specific fitness goals he or she wishes to achieve by the end of the course. Discuss how achieving a fitness goal might positively affect a person's self-esteem. **L1**

VISUAL LEARNING

Figure 4.3 Have students examine the pyramid. Tell them that it is a guide for helping people find ways to increase physical activity in their lives. The activities at the base of the pyramid should be done every day. As you go up the pyramid, the activities can be done several times per week. At the tip are activities best done infrequently. Have students give other examples of activities for each level.

Your school or community may offer programs that provide a variety of fun and healthful physical activities.

Getting Started

Figure 4.3 provides suggestions about how to divide your time when doing various types of physical activity.

FIGURE 4.3

PHYSICAL ACTIVITY PYRAMID

Sedentary Activities
Do infrequently
Examples: watching television, talking on the phone, playing computer games, surfing the Internet

Anaerobic Activities
2–3 days *per week* (all major muscle groups)
Examples: biceps curl, push-ups, abdominal curl, bench press, calf raise, shoulder press

Flexibility Activities
2 or more days *per week* (all major joints)
Examples: side lunge, step stretch, hurdler stretch, calf stretch, yoga stretches

Aerobic Activities
3–5 days *per week* (20–60 minutes *per session*)
Examples: cycling, brisk walking, running, dancing, in-line skating, playing basketball, cross-country skiing

Moderate-Intensity Physical Activities
About 30 minutes *per day*
Examples: walking, climbing stairs, gardening or yard work, walking a dog, housecleaning

Choosing Activities

Including different types of physical activities in your fitness program can help make it more enjoyable. As your fitness level increases and your interests change, you can alter your program. Other factors that may affect your activity choices include:

▶ **Cost.** Some activities require specialized—and possibly expensive—equipment. Think about what you can afford, and keep in mind that you may discover after a time that an activity just doesn't suit you.

88 **Chapter 4** Physical Activity for Life

Curriculum Connections

Language Arts Have students write a short essay that addresses the following questions: What activity would you enjoy doing as a regular part of your life, now and in the future? How might your ability to perform this activity change as you grow older? How might your ability to continue this activity change as your responsibilities in life change? Would it become more difficult to continue this activity as time goes by? Ask volunteers to read their responses to the class. Have students look through newspapers and magazines to find examples of older adults who are physically active.

▶ **Where you live.** For convenience you'll want to choose activities that you can do locally, without spending a lot of time traveling. Think about the features of your local area. Is the land flat or hilly? What type of climate do you live in? To what activities does the region best lend itself?

▶ **Your level of health.** Some health conditions have risks that need to be considered when planning physical activities. For example, some types of physical activity can aggravate **asthma,** a disease of the respiratory system.

▶ **Time and place.** Build your program into your daily routine. Do not schedule jogging at 6:00 a.m. if you are not a morning person. Design your schedule to help you achieve your goals.

▶ **Personal safety.** Think about your **personal safety** as you develop a fitness program. If you plan to run long distances, avoid going through unsafe areas or running after dark.

▶ **Comprehensive planning.** Select activities that address all five areas of health-related fitness.

hot link

asthma To learn more about asthma, see Chapter 26, page 690.
personal safety For more information on issues related to personal safety, see Chapter 13, page 330.

Health Skills Activity

Goal Setting: Starting a Physical Activity Program

William wants to start a physical activity program, but he's not sure where to begin. He really wants to improve his cardiorespiratory and muscle endurance, and he knows that his flexibility and muscle strength need work, too. He's also thinking about signing up for soccer; tryouts are in three months. What can William do to improve his fitness level and make the soccer team?

What Would You Do?
Apply the five goal-setting steps to William's situation.

1. Identify a specific goal and write it down.
2. List the steps you will take to reach your goal.
3. Identify potential problems and ways to get help and support from others.
4. Set up checkpoints to evaluate your progress.
5. Reward yourself once you have achieved your goal.

STARTING A PHYSICAL ACTIVITY PROGRAM

NHES Standard 6 Students will demonstrate the ability to use goal-setting and decision-making skills to enhance health.

Objectives
- Examine the relationship between fitness and physical activity.
- Develop and implement a plan for a physical activity program.

Motivator
Ask students to think of physical activities that William could participate in. List them on the board.

Teaching Strategies
1. Suggest that students use the list on the board to develop a detailed plan for William.
2. Remind students to choose a variety of activities to improve all areas of fitness.

✓ Assessment

Using a rubric, student work should provide comprehensive evidence of the following criteria to achieve the highest score:
- ✔ clear progression through a goal-setting process
- ✔ inclusion of a clear goal statement
- ✔ identification of a realistic goal
- ✔ plan for reaching the goal
- ✔ evaluation or reflection on the action

Curriculum Connections

Social Studies The popularity of some types of physical activity differs in various parts of the United States. This is due in part to differences in climate, terrain, natural resources, local customs, economic resources, and so on. Have students use reliable library and online resources to identify types of physical activity commonly enjoyed in various geographical areas of the country (such as snowboarding in the mountains and surfing in coastal regions). For additional information, direct students to the phone listings for each state's office of tourism.

To expand this activity to global areas, have students determine what physical activities are popular in other countries and explain why.

Health Minute

Ask a volunteer to read aloud the tips for avoiding boredom in a workout routine. Have students suggest other ideas to add to the list.

Reinforcing Concepts

Have students list a number of fitness activities that they think they will participate in throughout their lives. Then ask them to develop a second list of activities that they would like to try and to determine what resources would be needed to try them. Challenge students to try several of the new activities throughout the course and to share their reactions with the class. **L2**

ACTIVE READING

Organizing Information

Have students create their own personal activity programs. Tell them to make a five-column chart and title each column with one of the following headings: *who, what, when, where,* and *why.* Have students think of several activities to include in their plan. Have them write the activities in the *what* column. Then have students complete the remaining columns. In the *who* column students may want to indicate whether they would perform the activity alone, with a partner, or on a team. Remind students to include a variety of activities for the most healthful plan. For more strategies, see the *Guided Reading Activities* booklet in the TCR.

Health Minute

Avoiding Boredom in Your Workout Routine

If your workout becomes boring:

▶ Vary your routine by cross training. For example, skate one day and swim the next.

▶ Work out with a friend. This can be more fun than working out alone and can help you both stay motivated.

▶ Try listening to music while working out. When you have something else to focus on, the workout session may seem to pass more quickly. (**Note:** Listen to music only when participating in indoor activities. When exercising outdoors, you need to be alert to possible dangers.)

▶ Take a break to give your body time to recharge.

Cross Training

Engaging in a variety of physical activities to strengthen different muscle groups is known as cross training. Jumping rope, swimming, jogging, and cycling are good cross-training activities for athletes.

Basics of a Physical Activity Program

Because it focuses on *your* goals and interests, your fitness program is unique. However, all effective fitness programs are based on these three principles:

▶ **Overload**, *working the body harder than it is normally worked*, builds muscular strength and contributes to overall fitness. It is achieved by increasing repetitions or by doing more sets (groups of 6 to 12 repetitions) of an exercise.

▶ **Progression** is *the gradual increase in overload necessary to achieve higher levels of fitness*. As an activity becomes easier to do, increase the number of repetitions or sets or increase the amount of time spent doing the activity.

▶ **Specificity** indicates that *particular exercises and activities improve particular areas of health-related fitness*. For example, resistance training builds muscular strength and endurance, while aerobic activity improves cardiorespiratory endurance.

To gain the most benefit from an exercise program, you'll want to include three basic stages for each activity. These are the *warm-up*, the *workout*, and the *cool-down*. Include each stage in every session even when you're in a hurry.

The Warm-Up

The **warm-up**, *an activity that prepares the muscles for work*, is the first stage in any physical activity routine. Begin the warm-up by taking a brisk walk to raise your body temperature. Then, slowly stretch large muscles to increase their elasticity and reduce the risk of injury. After stretching individual muscles, perform the physical activity slowly for about five minutes. For example, if you are running, jog slowly for about five minutes and then increase your pace to a run. Warming up allows your pulse rate to increase gradually. A sudden increase in pulse rate places unnecessary strain on the heart and blood vessels.

The Workout

The part of an exercise program when the activity is performed at its highest peak is called the **workout**. To be effective, the activity needs to follow the *F.I.T.T.* formula—*frequency, intensity, time/ duration,* and *type of activity*—outlined in **Figure 4.4.**

HEALTH LITERACY

Cross Training Cross training is when one practices several different types of exercise in a fitness program. Someone who cross trains might do an intense aerobic dance workout one day, bike the next day, swim the third day, and lift weights the fourth day. As an alternative, he or she might combine within one workout session swimming for the upper body and aerobic dance for the lower body. This variation can not only combat boredom, but it also prevents overuse of muscles and joints. Cross training can help people achieve a higher level of health-related fitness.

FREQUENCY

You should schedule workouts three to four times each week, with only one or two days between sessions. The frequency of your workouts depends partly on your fitness goals and the type of activity you do—as well as on your schedule and possibly even the weather. Exercising more than three times each week for six months should help *get* you physically fit. To *maintain* your fitness level, continue your program at least three times each week.

INTENSITY

Working your muscles and cardiorespiratory system at an intensity that allows you to reach overload will help you improve your fitness level. Begin slowly to build endurance. Doing too much too soon is harmful and can cause chronically sore muscles.

When weight training, start with a light weight and build to heavier weights. For aerobics, work toward your target heart range. If you are out of shape, it may take about six months before you can work out for 20 to 30 minutes within your target heart range.

TIME/DURATION

Slowly build up the amount of time you spend doing aerobic exercises. The goal in aerobics is to work within your target heart range for 20 to 30 minutes. When weight training, do the exercises slowly, taking at least two seconds to lower a weight. Rest for one or two minutes between sets. Also, vary the exercises to strengthen your muscles in the full range of motion.

TYPE

To get the maximum health benefits from your workout routine, devote 75–80 percent of your workout time to aerobic activity and 20–25 percent to anaerobic activity. Choose activities that you enjoy, or you may find it difficult to complete your workouts.

The Cool-Down

Ending a workout abruptly can cause your muscles to tighten and may make you feel dizzy. To avoid these effects, you need to cool down after a workout. The **cool-down** is *an activity that prepares the muscles to return to a resting state.*

FIGURE 4.4

THE *F.I.T.T.* FORMULA

Include each of these elements in your workout.

 F **requency**
how often you do the activity each week

 I **ntensity**
how hard you work at the activity per session

 T **ime/duration**
how much time you devote to a session

 T **ype**
which activities you select

◁ **The warm-up is an important part of any physical activity routine.** *Explain how stretching prepares muscles for exercise and prevents injuries.*

Lesson 3 Planning a Personal Activity Program **91**

VISUAL LEARNING

Figure 4.4 Ask a volunteer to read aloud the *F.I.T.T.* formula shown in Figure 4.4. Tell students to write each element on a sheet of paper, and next to each one, describe that aspect of their own workout. Have volunteers share their responses with the class. Ask: Is this workout effective? Why or why not?

Explaining

Discuss with students any professional athletic events they have attended. Ask whether the athletes began competing without advance preparation. No. They never start a practice or game without a warm-up. Explain that the same applies to anyone starting a workout. The body needs time to adjust to increased physical activity. Have volunteers explain the difference between warming up and cooling down. 🔳

Activity

Ask the class to sketch examples of activities that would be appropriate for warm-up and cool-down exercises. Have them insert their illustrations in their fitness journals to serve as reminders. **ELL**

— *School to Work* —

Physical Activity and the Job Many of today's employers recognize the benefits of physically fit employees. Accordingly, some companies have taken steps to promote physical activity among staff, such as providing on-site exercise equipment or offering memberships for nearby health clubs. Have students research several major employers in their community and find out what they do to encourage physical activity among employees. Suggest that students summarize their findings in a brief oral report. You may wish to give students the alternative of researching an occupation that requires a high level of physical activity. ▭▭

Building Heart and Lung Endurance Have students set a goal to increase their aerobic activity level in order to improve their level of cardiorespiratory endurance. Encourage them to keep a diary of their activities and assess their resting heart rate each week. After six weeks, have students graph their resting heart rates. If the number has decreased, they have achieved their goal.

ASSESS

EVALUATING THE LESSON

Assign and discuss the Lesson 3 Review; then administer, grade, and discuss Lesson Quiz 13 in the TCR.

RETEACHING

- Have students develop an outline of the lesson using the headings as a guide.
- Ask students to complete Reteaching Activity 13 in the TCR.

ENRICHMENT

Have students investigate exercise routines on videotapes or TV programs. Ask them to discuss their favorites with the class and explain their reasons.

CLOSE

Have students work in pairs to quiz each other on the most important concepts learned in the lesson.

 Using a calendar or journal can help you keep track of your fitness program.

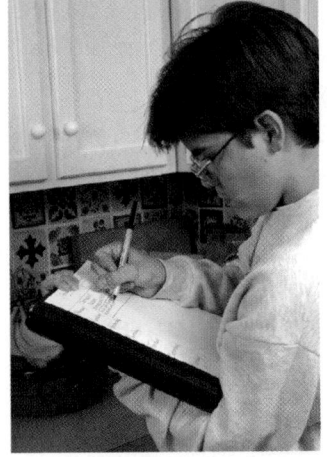

Begin the cool-down by slowing down the activity. Continue the activity at this slower pace for about five minutes, then stretch for five minutes.

Monitoring Your Progress

To monitor your progress, keep a fitness journal. In your journal, list your goals and note the frequency, intensity, duration, and type of each activity in which you participate. At the end of 12 weeks, and every 6 weeks after that, compare the figures to evaluate your progress.

Resting Heart Rate

Your **resting heart rate** is *the number of times your heart beats in one minute when you are not active.* Your resting heart rate can also be used to evaluate your progress. A person of average fitness has a resting heart rate of about 72 to 84 beats per minute. Just four weeks of a fitness program can decrease that rate by 5 to 10 beats per minute. A resting heart rate below 72 indicates a good fitness level.

Lesson 3 Review

Reviewing Facts and Vocabulary

1. How can using the Physical Activity Pyramid help you meet your fitness goals?
2. Identify and define the three principles upon which all effective fitness programs are based.
3. What do the letters in the *F.I.T.T.* formula stand for?

Thinking Critically

4. **Analyzing.** How is your resting heart rate an indication of your level of fitness?
5. **Synthesizing.** Maria is a runner. Describe how she could include the three stages of an effective exercise program in her fitness routine.

Applying Health Skills

Goal Setting. Use the goal-setting steps to develop a personal fitness program. Synthesize information from this lesson and apply critical-thinking and decision-making skills to determine what activities to include and how you will incorporate them into a formal plan. Think of obstacles that could prevent you from following your plan, and apply problem-solving skills to figure out how to overcome these obstacles.

SPREADSHEETS Use spreadsheet software to design a table that can help you organize your physical activity schedule and track your progress. See **health.glencoe.com** for information on how to use a spreadsheet.

Lesson 3 Review

Answers to Reviewing Facts and Vocabulary

1. It provides suggestions on how to divide your time when exercising, which can help you meet your goals for improving various aspects of fitness.
2. See page 90 for descriptions of overload, progression, and specificity.
3. Frequency, intensity, time/duration, and type of activity

Answers to Thinking Critically

4. Resting heart rate decreases when one is physically fit, so it's an indicator of fitness.
5. Answers should include descriptions of the warm-up, the workout, and the cool-down.

Training and Safety for Physical Activities

VOCABULARY
training program
hydration
anabolic steroids
health screening

YOU'LL LEARN TO
- Recognize health-promoting strategies that can enhance a training program.
- Understand the importance of preventive health screenings before beginning a physical activity program.
- Identify safety concerns related to various physical activities.

QUICK START Divide a sheet of paper into two columns. In the first column, list five physical activities you enjoy doing. In the second column, list any special equipment, including safety gear, needed for each activity.

Beginning a new physical activity can be exciting. It also requires some preparation to make sure that you stay safe and get the most out of the activity.

Training and Peak Performance

The first step in becoming fit is to take good care of your body. Eat nutritious foods and drink plenty of fluids, especially water. Getting adequate rest is also essential. To keep your body in top form, it is also important that you avoid harmful substances such as tobacco, alcohol, and other drugs.

The next step in improving fitness often involves beginning a training program for your chosen activity. A **training program** is *a program of formalized physical preparation for involvement in a sport or another physical activity*. Consult your physical education teacher, coach, or another trusted adult to help you set your training goals.

 A physical education teacher or coach can help you establish your goals for a training program.

Training and Safety for Physical Activities

① FOCUS

QUICK START Write the headings *Physical Activities* and *Special Equipment* on the board. Ask volunteers to share some of the physical activities they enjoy doing and the equipment needed for each activity. Write their responses on the board. Then discuss why the equipment listed is necessary and how it can provide protection.

TYING TO PRIOR KNOWLEDGE

Ask volunteers to describe ways they have prepared for an athletic event. Tell students that they will learn about the elements of a training program in this lesson.

Health Skills Features

"Should Random Drug Testing of Athletes Be Performed?" p. 95

INTRODUCING VOCABULARY
- Ask students to complete the Chapter 4 Study Guide in the *Student Activity Workbook*.

Lesson 4 Resources

Teacher Classroom Resources
📁 Concept Mapping Activity 14
📁 Decision-Making Activity 4
📁 Guided Reading Activities 14
📁 Lesson Plan 14
📁 Lesson Quiz 14
📁 Reteaching Activity 14

Student Activity Workbook
📁 Applying Health Skills 14
📁 Chapter 4 Study Guide

2 TEACH

Activity

Suggest that volunteers read current articles about the specialized sports drinks now on the market. Ask: What benefits do advertisements for these drinks emphasize? What actual benefits—if any—do the drinks offer? Under what circumstances should teens choose sports drinks over water? Have the volunteers share their findings with the rest of the class. **L2**

Quick Demo

Bring a variety of sports drinks to class. Have students compare ingredient labels. Ask: What is the primary ingredient in each? Of what benefit are the ingredients to an athlete? What are some alternate sources of those ingredients? **L1**

Activity

Assign a group of volunteers to review current research on the sleep needs of teens, focusing on both the number of hours and the timing of those hours. Have the group summarize their findings for the class. Then have students discuss how they might adjust their schedules to get the sleep they need. **L2**

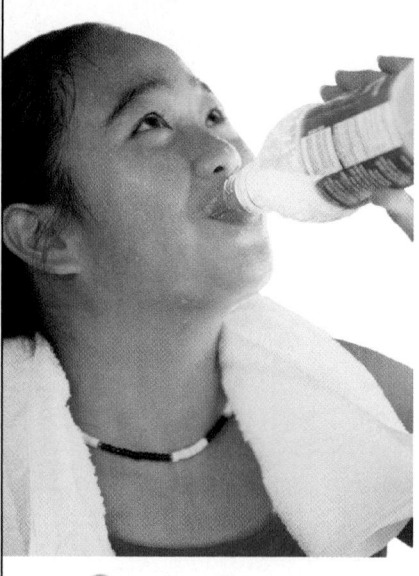

Ⓐ **Drinking water is important before, during, and after vigorous physical activity.** *Explain why hydration is so important during any physical activity.*

hot link

anabolic steroids For more information on the harmful effects of anabolic steroids, see Chapter 23, page 601.

Nutrition and Hydration

What you eat and drink is an important part of any training program. Food provides the energy necessary for peak performance. You will learn more about nutrition and healthy food choices in Chapter 5. Equally important is hydration, especially when you are engaged in vigorous physical activity. **Hydration** is *taking in fluids so that the body functions properly.* When you are adequately hydrated, you are more alert and focused, your reaction time is faster because your muscles respond more quickly and are less likely to cramp, and your endurance is greater. To stay hydrated, drink plenty of water before, during, and after vigorous physical activity.

Adequate Rest

Sleep, which helps your body rest and reenergize, is also essential for any training program. Getting too little sleep can disrupt the nervous system, causing slowed reaction time, lack of concentration (increasing the possibility of errors and accidents), forgetfulness, irritability, and even depression. On average, teens need 8 to 10 hours of sleep every night to function at their best.

Avoiding Harmful Substances

Avoiding harmful substances such as tobacco, alcohol, anabolic steroids, and other drugs is another part of maintaining an athletic training program.

ANABOLIC STEROIDS

Anabolic steroids are *synthetic substances that are similar to the male hormone testosterone.* Because these substances cause the body to make muscle tissue, some athletes take them to increase muscle mass and enhance performance. However, anabolic steroids have very harmful effects, including increased risk of cancer and heart disease; sterility, or the inability to produce children; skin problems such as acne and hair loss; unusual weight gain or loss; sexual underdevelopment and dysfunction; and violent, suicidal, or depressive tendencies.

It is illegal to use anabolic steroids without a prescription, and those who test positive for steroid use are disqualified from competitions. Thus, abstinence is the best choice when it comes to the use of steroids.

NUTRITIONAL SUPPLEMENTS

Nutritional supplements are nonfood substances that contain one or more nutrients that the body needs, such as vitamins or minerals. The best way to get nutrients is from food, but sometimes a multiple vitamin and mineral supplement may be appropriate.

94 **Chapter 4** Physical Activity for Life

Home and Community

Community Training Facilities Have students research training and recreational opportunities in their community. They should look for facilities such as recreation centers, parks, swimming pools, tennis courts, skating rinks, and ski slopes. They should also include organized activity programs such as sports teams, classes, and activity clubs. Instruct students to use this information to create a brochure for people who have recently moved to the community. Students may wish to illustrate their brochures with photographs or sketches. Display the finished brochures in the classroom.

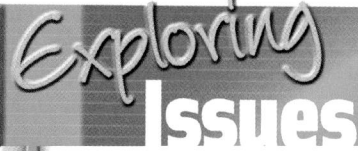

Should Random Drug Testing of Athletes Be Performed?

A number of high schools in the United States have adopted a policy of random drug testing of student athletes even if there is no indication that the athletes are using drugs. What's your position on the subject of random drug testing of school athletes? Here are two points of view.

Viewpoint 1: Maya D., age 17

Random drug testing of school athletes is unfair and an invasion of privacy, especially if there's no evidence that the person has been using drugs. Students who want to participate in school sports shouldn't have to give up their privacy just to be on an athletic team. Besides, why should athletes be singled out—isn't that discrimination?

Viewpoint 2: Graham H., age 16

I understand Maya's argument, but I think that schools have a right to know whether students are using drugs. They aren't out to catch us doing something wrong. They're concerned about our health and the environment in which we live and learn. People may not like the rules, but schools must follow the policy. We don't want our school to be represented by athletes who use drugs and get away with it. That's dangerous *and* embarrassing.

ACTIVITIES

1. **Take the pro or con position, and expand upon it. Use online or print resources to back up your views. Be sure to investigate each supporting point raised in an argument.**

2. **Some school districts are advocating drug testing of all students who want to be involved in any extra-curricular activities. What might be the pros and cons of such an approach?**

A health care provider can advise you about whether you need this type of supplement. It's important to take the recommended dosage of any supplement. High doses, or *megadoses*, of a nutritional supplement can be harmful.

Safety First!

Safety should be a major concern when you participate in sports and other physical activities. You can reduce your risk of injury by

▶ visiting a health care professional for a health screening before beginning a new activity. A **health screening** is *a search or*

Discussing

Ask students to suggest specific reasons for avoiding tobacco, alcohol, and other drugs. Ask: What effect can substance use have on a training program? How can the use of these substances harm a person's physical health? Mental/emotional health? Social health? **L1**

Activity

Have each student select and read the biography of a successful athlete. Then have students write essays discussing the attitudes that contributed to the athlete's success. **L3**

Exploring Issues

SHOULD RANDOM DRUG TESTING OF ATHLETES BE PERFORMED?

Ask volunteers to share what they know about drug testing. Then have students read the feature to learn more about drug testing of school athletes and to explore the two viewpoints. Divide the class into groups and assign each group the pro or con position. Encourage groups to find facts to defend their point of view. Students should find evidence of whether random drug testing influences school athletes not to use drugs. They also should state whether athletes should be singled out from other groups of students and explain why or why not. Allow students to debate the issues.

More About...

Steroid Abuse Since the late 1950s both athletes and nonathletes have used anabolic steroids illegally to improve athletic ability and physical appearance. The serious side effects of steroid use have been well documented, including risk of cancer, heart disease, and sterility. According to recent studies, adolescent steroid users are also more likely to use other drugs and to share needles, thereby increasing the risk of HIV infection. Since the largest group known to use anabolic steroids is under the age of 15, preventive measures should start by the beginning of middle school. Examples include peer counseling and presentations by physicians, coaches, athletes, school principals, and school health care officials.

Discussing

Ask students to compose a list of any ten sports and/or physical activities. Have them rank each according to its potential for injury, with number one representing the activity that has the greatest risk of causing injury and number ten representing the one with the least risk. Lead a class discussion of the lists and reasons for the rankings. **L1**

Activity

Have several volunteers talk with coaches or physical education teachers at school about the ways that sporting equipment can decrease injuries. Have students present a report on this topic and demonstrate the use of equipment that can help prevent injuries. **L3**

Quick Demo

Ask volunteers to bring to class a picture or illustration of a piece of sporting gear that they think offers good value, comfort, and protection from injury during physical activity. Have them present the item to the class and discuss the reasons for their choice. **L1**

What Are Herbal Supplements?

Herbal supplements are chemical substances derived from plants that may be sold as dietary supplements. Little research has been conducted on their effects or safety, and not much is known about how they work. Nutritionists recommend eating a variety of fruits, vegetables, and whole grains to get the plant chemicals your body needs.

To avoid sports injuries, choose the proper athletic gear. *Match each piece of equipment with an appropriate sport or other physical activity.*

check for diseases or disorders that an individual would otherwise not have knowledge of or seek help for. This screening helps ensure that you do not have a health condition that could make the activity dangerous for you and that you're fit enough to begin the activity you've chosen.

▶ using the proper safety equipment for your chosen activity.

▶ being alert to the surrounding environment, including other players and spectators.

▶ playing at your skill level and knowing your physical limits.

▶ warming up before and cooling down after every activity.

▶ staying within areas that have been designated for physical activities, such as skateboarding parks and bicycle paths.

▶ obeying all rules and restrictions—for example, those that restrict swimming to certain areas or that prohibit skateboarding on sidewalks.

▶ practicing good sportsmanship.

If you should become injured or ill during physical activity, tell a physical education teacher, coach, or another adult immediately.

Personal Safety

You can reduce risks to your personal safety by selecting the right time and place for your activity. This is especially true if you work out alone. If you run or jog, choose a well-used park during daylight hours, when other people are there. If you can't avoid night-time physical activity, wear reflective clothing so that others can see you. Wearing a whistle that you can blow to attract attention if you are in danger is also a good idea. Also, be aware of the effects of weather: bicycling or running—and even walking—can be a health risk when it's wet and slippery outside.

Using Proper Equipment

Before you begin any new physical activity, learn to use the equipment involved. Check the equipment to make sure that it fits and is in good condition. Always wear the safety gear recommended for that particular activity. Many sports have strict requirements for protective equipment. These tips may also help.

▶ Wear a helmet when bicycling, skateboarding, or skating. Also, when skateboarding or skating, wear knee and elbow pads, gloves, and wrist guards.

96 **Chapter 4** Physical Activity for Life

HEALTH LITERACY

Safety Handbook Suggest that students consider physical activities that require them to use the large muscles of the body. Examples might include both activities related to daily life, such as lifting heavy objects at work, cycling to school, or gardening at home, and sports activities, such as tennis, baseball, or track. Assign each student one of the activities. Direct students to research the most common injuries associated with their assigned activity and to write a one-page explanation of the precautions a person might take while participating in the activity. Compile the precautions to form a safety handbook.

- Avoid riding at night, if possible. If you must, make sure your bike has reflective tape, a rear reflector, and a headlight. Skateboards and skates also should be outlined with reflective tape. When participating in any outdoor activity at night, wear light-colored clothing with reflective patches on the front and back so that drivers and pedestrians can see you more easily.

- Males participating in contact sports—such as football and hockey—should wear athletic supporters or cups to protect the groin area. Females should wear sports bras to prevent stretching of the ligaments that support the breasts.

Whatever activity you choose, it's essential to use the proper safety equipment. *What safety equipment are the teens pictured here using?*

Proper footwear and clothing also are important. Athletic shoes should be comfortable and should have a cushioned heel, good arch support, and ample toe room. Laced shoes are best for proper control of your foot in the shoe. Wear socks to cushion your feet and keep them dry. In general, choose comfortable, nonrestrictive clothing. When it's warm outside, dress lightly. In cool weather, wear several loose-fitting layers that you can easily remove as you warm up.

Lesson 4 Review

Reviewing Facts and Vocabulary

1. Define the term *hydration*.
2. What are *anabolic steroids*? Name three ways they can harm health.
3. Why is it important to get a preventive health screening before beginning a physical activity program?

Thinking Critically

4. **Evaluating.** How can practicing good sportsmanship help you stay safe when participating in a sport?
5. **Analyzing.** Enrique wants to play on the school football team in the fall. To prepare, he plans to participate in a training program in the spring and summer. List five things Enrique should do before and during his training program.

Applying Health Skills

Accessing Information. Working with a classmate, search the Web for three schools that have adopted the policy of random drug testing of school athletes. Compare your school's policy with theirs, noting both similarities and differences.

TECHNOLOGY *OPTION*

WEB SITES Use the information you find to develop a Web page explaining your school's approach to random drug testing of school athletes. See **health.glencoe.com** for help in planning and building a Web site.

3 ASSESS

EVALUATING THE LESSON

Assign and discuss the Lesson 4 Review; then administer, grade, and discuss Lesson Quiz 14 in the TCR.

RETEACHING

- Ask students to create a list of the steps to take to become physically fit. Have them include the parts of a training program.
- Ask students to complete Reteaching Activity 14 in the TCR.

ENRICHMENT

Ask students to research an extreme sport—such as bicycle stunt riding, skysurfing, or kiteskiing—in which safety is a major concern. Have them find out what special safety equipment is used and why it is important.

4 CLOSE

Ask students to write a summary of the most important concepts learned in the lesson.

Lesson 4 Review

Answers to Reviewing Facts and Vocabulary

1. *Hydration* is taking in fluids so that the body functions properly.
2. Substances similar to testosterone. See page 94 for harmful effects.
3. It helps ensure that one does not have a health condition that could make physical activity dangerous and confirms that a person is fit enough to begin an activity.

Answers to Thinking Critically

4. It leads to cooperation and fairness in sports and helps prevent team members from becoming violent or acting out inappropriately.
5. Answers will vary.

Physical Activity Injuries

Lesson 5

1 FOCUS

QUICK START   Draw three columns on the board, and list the four seasons in the left column. In the middle column, list activities students participate in only during that season. Then ask students how they prepare for weather conditions specific to that season, and write their responses in the right column.

TYING TO PRIOR KNOWLEDGE

Ask volunteers to submit in writing a recent injury that they or someone they know suffered as a result of participating in a sport or physical activity. As a class, discuss ways in which each of the injuries might have been prevented. To protect privacy, apply a "no name" rule when discussing the injuries.

Health Skills Features

"Being Safe While Physically Active," p. 100

ADVOCACY

INTRODUCING VOCABULARY

- Have students write a definition of one of the vocabulary terms and give an example of how this injury or condition might occur.

- Ask students to complete the Chapter 4 Study Guide in the *Student Activity Workbook.*

Physical Activity Injuries

VOCABULARY
- overexertion
- heat cramps
- heatstroke
- frostbite
- hypothermia
- muscle cramp
- strain
- sprain

YOU'LL LEARN TO
- Identify weather-related risks associated with various physical activities.
- Analyze strategies for preventing and responding to accidental injuries related to physical activity.
- Identify physical activity injuries requiring professional health services for people of all ages.

QUICK START   List activities you do only during specific seasons of the year. Next to each activity, describe how you prepare for the weather conditions of that season.

 These teens are taking specific precautions to prevent sports injuries. *What safety precautions did you take in your most recent outdoor activity?*

With any activity that involves movement, there is always a risk of accident or injury. The risk of injury during physical activity increases when a person is not in good physical condition or has not sufficiently warmed up or cooled down. Attempting physical activities that are beyond your level of ability also increases the risk of injury.

Weather-Related Risks

Taking your physical activity routine outdoors can be a great change of pace, but some weather-related health problems need to be taken into consideration. These problems can be avoided by not participating in outdoor physical activity when temperatures are extremely high or extremely low. Factors such as wind, humidity, and air pollution can increase your risk of injury or illness. Be aware of wind chill factors, ultraviolet (UV) indexes, and air quality alerts. You also should pay attention to weather warnings. Stay inside if there is a threat of tornadoes, thunderstorms, flash floods, or blizzards.

98   Chapter 4   Physical Activity for Life

Lesson 5 Resources

Teacher Classroom Resources
- 📁 Concept Mapping Activity 15
- 📁 Enrichment Activity 4
- 📁 Guided Reading Activities 15
- 📁 Lesson Plan 15
- 📁 Lesson Quiz 15
- 📁 Reteaching Activity 15

Student Activity Workbook
- 📁 Applying Health Skills 15
- 📁 Chapter 4 Study Guide

Multimedia
- Transparency 13

Hot-Weather Health Risks

Two concerns during hot weather are dehydration, or excessive loss of water from the body, and poor air quality. Smog can damage the lungs, so avoid outdoor physical activities during smog alerts. To avoid dehydration, drink plenty of water before, during, and after physical activity.

Many hot-weather health problems are related to **overexertion**, or *overworking the body*. For example, heat exhaustion—an overheating of the body that results in cold, clammy skin and symptoms of shock—is caused by overexertion in a hot, humid atmosphere. Other symptoms include dizziness, headache, shortness of breath, and nausea. Heat exhaustion may be preceded or accompanied by **heat cramps**, *muscle spasms that result from a loss of large amounts of salt and water through perspiration*. If you experience any of these symptoms, move to a cool place and lie down with your feet elevated. Take small sips of water as you start to recover. If symptoms are severe, or if vomiting occurs, get medical help immediately.

Continuing to exercise with the symptoms of heat exhaustion and dehydration can lead to **heatstroke**, *a condition in which the body loses the ability to rid itself of excessive heat through perspiration*. This causes hyperthermia, a sudden increase in body temperature, which can be life-threatening. A person suffering from heatstroke may have difficulty breathing and may collapse suddenly. If heatstroke occurs, immediately call for medical help. Then move the person to a cool place, and sponge him or her with cold water until help arrives.

Cold-Weather Health Risks

When participating in cold-weather activities, dress in three layers to keep warm. The first layer should pull moisture and perspiration away from your body. Many synthetic fabrics have been specifically developed to help keep the skin dry. The middle layer should provide insulation. Wool or synthetic fleece fabrics can help keep you warm even if they get wet. A coated nylon windshell as the top layer will help keep warmth in and water and wind out. A hat is also a must—70 percent of the body's heat is lost through the head. Removing layers as you warm up or adding them as the temperature drops can help you adjust to changes in the weather.

When you begin any cold-weather activity, start slowly and be sure to warm up your muscles. Staying hydrated is as important in

🔺 **Staying hydrated is essential when working out in hot or cold weather.** *What other steps can this player take to protect himself from health problems associated with working out in hot weather?*

Did You Know ❓

Altitude sickness is a risk in some mountain sports. It usually occurs at altitudes of 7,000 feet or higher, where there are lower levels of oxygen. Symptoms include severe headache, nausea, and weakness. The best ways of preventing altitude sickness are to give yourself time to adjust to activity at high altitudes, to drink plenty of water, and to avoid alcohol and caffeine.

② TEACH

Reinforcing Concepts

Discuss how the risks of heatstroke can be greatly reduced by being prepared for hot-weather conditions. Ask students to name some ways to prepare for high temperatures or hot weather when exercising.

Discussing

Lead a class discussion about the short-term and possible long-term effects of heat exhaustion, heat cramps, and heatstroke. Conclude by addressing prevention and treatment methods. L1

Discussing

Ask students to identify and evaluate common myths related to the treatment of each injury discussed in the lesson. Myths might include treating frostbite with hot water, applying heat to sprains, working through the pain, and so on. L1

⟩ *More About...*

Hot-Weather Health Risks Engaging in physical activity on hot, humid days can be dangerous. Scientists have developed a heat index that combines heat and humidity values so that the risks of prolonged activity in various conditions can be assessed. For example, 90° + 60% humidity = a heat index of 100, the apparent temperature; 100° + 60% humidity = a heat index of 132. A heat index of 80 to 90 means fatigue is possible; 90 to 105 indicates that heat cramps and heat exhaustion are possible; 105 to 130 signifies that heat cramps and heat exhaustion are likely and heatstroke possible; 130 or above indicates that heatstroke is likely.

Real-Life Application

BEING SAFE WHILE PHYSICALLY ACTIVE

ADVOCACY

NHES Standard 7 Students will demonstrate the ability to advocate for personal, family, and community health.

Objectives

- Analyze strategies for preventing accidental injuries.
- Demonstrate the ability to influence others in using proper equipment when participating in physical activity.

Motivator

Ask a volunteer to tell about a time when he or she was injured while participating in a sport. As a class, discuss how this injury could have been prevented.

Teaching Strategies

1. Ensure that a variety of sports are being researched.
2. Suggest that students include in their posters precautions to take in hot or cold weather.
3. Access **health.glencoe.com** for links to sites that provide reliable information on sports injuries.

✓ Assessment

Using a rubric, student work should provide comprehensive evidence of the following criteria to achieve the highest score:

✔ clear, health-enhancing stand
✔ support for the position with relevant information
✔ awareness of the audience
✔ encouragement of others to make healthful choices
✔ passion/conviction

cold weather as it is in hot weather. Two specific health risks from cold weather are particularly important to keep in mind: frostbite and hypothermia.

▶ **Frostbite** is *a condition that results when body tissues become frozen*, and it requires professional medical treatment. You can avoid frostbite by dressing warmly and covering all exposed skin—especially the ears, face, feet, and fingers, where frostbite most often occurs. An early warning sign of frostbite, called frostnip, is a whitening of the skin of the toes, fingers, nose, or ears. If this happens or if you notice a lack of feeling in any exposed area, get indoors right away and warm the area with warm water.

Helmets, goggles, and gloves are proper equipment when snowboarding.

Real-Life Application

Being Safe While Physically Active

Sports and recreational activities are the second most frequent cause of injury for teens. Many such injuries can be prevented by being cautious and by wearing proper equipment. Examine the graph, and choose a sport or recreational activity in which you or your friends participate. Using reliable online and print resources, research your sport to find injury statistics. For example, what injuries are most common for this sport? How many teens are injured each year in this sport? How many of these injuries are treated in emergency rooms? What protective equipment and precautions can reduce injury in this sport?

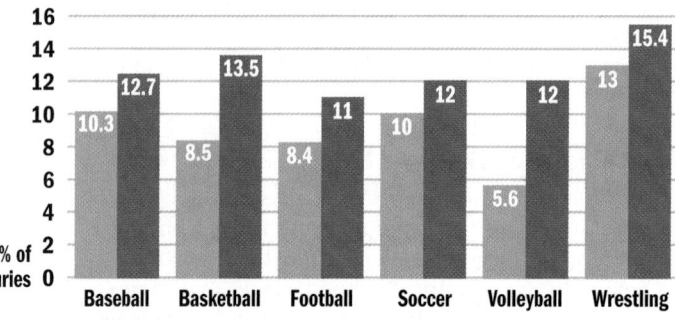

Frequency (%) of High School Sport Injuries

Major   Moderate

% of injuries

	Baseball	Basketball	Football	Soccer	Volleyball	Wrestling
Major	10.3	8.5	8.4	10	5.6	13
Moderate	12.7	13.5	11	12	12	15.4

Source: Based on data from the National Athletic Trainers' Association

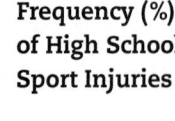

ACTIVITY

Using the activity you have researched, create a poster that explains how teens can get injured while participating in the activity and presents ways of staying safe. Make your poster colorful and attention-getting to appeal to a teen audience. Be sure to give it a catchy title.

∿∿ HEALTH LITERACY

Self-Directed Learner Even in temperate climates, prolonged exposure to moderately cool temperatures can cause hypothermia. Similarly, prolonged immersion in water can result in hypothermia even if the water is not very cold. Have students research hypothermia, the various conditions that can cause it, and its prevention and treatment. How, for example, can people guard against hypothermia when lost in the wilderness with insufficient clothing? How can one conserve body heat after a boating accident far from shore? Instruct students to write up their findings in a format that might appear in an outdoor survival handbook.

▶ **Hypothermia** is *a condition in which body temperature becomes dangerously low*. It is usually associated with cold weather, but it also can result from lengthy exposure to wind or rain or from submersion in cold water. When hypothermia occurs, the body loses the ability to warm itself. As body temperature drops, the brain cannot function and body systems begin to shut down. A person with this condition may become disoriented and lose motor control. Because hypothermia can lead to death, it requires immediate medical attention.

When participating in cold-weather activities, pay attention to your body. Shivering is a sign that your body is losing heat. If you begin to feel cold or to shiver, go to a warm, dry place; wrap yourself in a blanket; and drink warm liquids to slowly raise your body temperature.

Protecting Yourself from Sun and Wind

Prolonged exposure to sun and wind is another weather-related risk of outdoor physical activity. Windburn occurs when skin is exposed to freezing wind, causing it to become red, tight, and sore to the touch. Reduce the risk of windburn by wearing protective clothing and using lip balm. The sun's UV rays cause *sunburn*, a burning of the outer layers of the skin. Mild sunburn makes your skin red and slightly sore. Severe sunburn causes blistering of the skin, swelling, and pain. In addition to increasing the risk of sunburn, repeated or prolonged exposure to the sun speeds the skin's aging process and increases your risk of developing **skin cancer.** The most dangerous hours for UV exposure are from 10:00 a.m. to 4:00 p.m. To protect yourself against sunburn:

▶ Cover as much of the body with clothing as possible when outdoors and wear broad-brimmed hats on sunny days.

▶ Use sunscreen and lip balm with a sun protection factor (SPF) of *at least* 15. The SPF number indicates the sunscreen's ability to screen out the sun's harmful UV rays. Because UV rays penetrate clouds, you need to wear sunscreen on cloudy days, too.

▶ Apply sunscreen 30 minutes before you go outside, spreading it liberally and evenly over all areas of your skin that will be exposed. Reapply it at least every two hours.

UV rays can also damage your eyes. A *cataract*, a cloudy covering over the lens of the eye, is caused in part by sun exposure. Wear a visor or a hat with a brim, and use sunglasses, even during the winter months. Because sunlight is reflected off snow, those participating in winter sports need to wear goggles to protect their eyes from both UV exposure and glare.

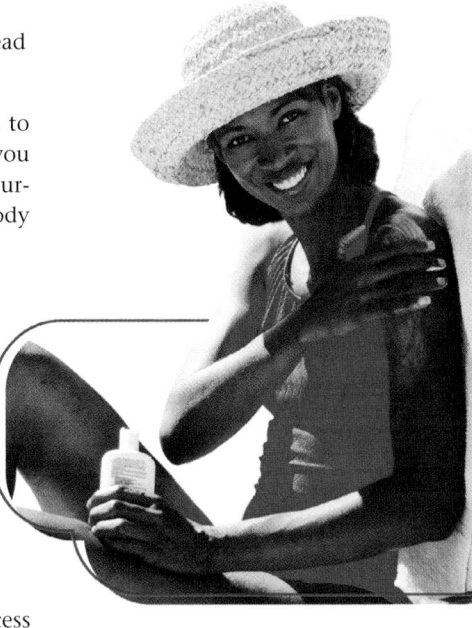

Ⓥ **Apply sunscreen frequently when you participate in outdoor activities.** *Why is it important to use sunscreen in both hot and cold weather?*

hot link

skin cancer For more information about skin cancer, see Chapter 26, page 683.

hot link

Tell students that recent studies have shown that just one or two severe sunburns during childhood or adolescence greatly increases a person's chances of developing skin cancer in adulthood. Have students do research to learn about the UV Index and how they can use it to help prevent sunburn.

Explaining

Explain that for adequate sun protection, a sunblock with an SPF of 15 or greater is recommended. SPF, which is rated from 2 to 15 or greater, indicates how long a person can stay in the sun without getting sunburned. Explain that if you normally burn after 15 minutes in the sun, an SPF of 8 will allow you to stay out for 8 times 15, or 120 minutes (2 hours). It is important to note that an SPF of 15 will increase the time you can remain in the sun to no more than 3 hours and 45 minutes.

Promoting Coordinated School Health

Identifying Major Problems Once a committee has been founded to serve the school health program, members will need to consider specific problems to address. One method of receiving input regarding areas for action is through a survey. For more information about drafting such a survey, consult *Planning a Coordinated School*

Health Program. After the surveys have been collected and the information processed, the committee should brainstorm a priority list of concerns. The priority ratings are (1) critical problems, (2) moderate problems, and (3) minor problems. The top two or three issues can become candidates for priority action.

Activity

Ask interested students to find articles from sports and fitness magazines that describe athletic injuries. Have students write short summaries of the articles. Then discuss the consequences of the injuries and ways they might have been prevented. Close with a discussion comparing the information in the magazines with that in the lesson. **L2**

VISUAL LEARNING

Figure 4.5 Have volunteers read aloud the description for one step in the *R.I.C.E.* procedure, as outlined in Figure 4.5. Ask: Have you or anyone you know ever used this procedure? What effect did it have on the injury? Have students design a logo or bumper sticker to remind people of the four steps in the *R.I.C.E.* procedure. Display student artwork in the classroom.

Community Involvement

Choose several students to develop a list of interview questions to ask a physical therapist. Assist them in making arrangements to visit a physical therapist to find answers to the questions. Have the students report their findings to the class. **L2**

Guest Speaker

Invite an athletic trainer or emergency room physician to class to discuss common sports injuries and how to prevent and treat them. Have students prepare a list of questions to ask the speaker. **L2**

 Ligaments are strong bands of tissue that connect the bones to one another at a moveable joint. Sprains result if these bands are stretched or torn.

 Many minor sports injuries can be treated by following the *R.I.C.E.* procedure. *Which part of the R.I.C.E. procedure is pictured here?*

Minor Injuries

Have you ever had sore muscles after a physical activity or experienced the pain of a twisted ankle? Muscles are often sore 24 to 48 hours after a strenuous workout. Warming up, cooling down, and stretching can prevent or reduce muscle soreness. Other minor injuries that affect the skeletal or muscular systems include muscle cramps, strains, and sprains. A **muscle cramp** is *a spasm or sudden tightening of a muscle*. It happens when a muscle is tired, overworked, or dehydrated. Drinking cool water may ease muscle cramping. A **strain** is *a condition resulting from damaging a muscle or tendon*. A **sprain** is *an injury to the ligament surrounding a joint*. Symptoms of a sprain include pain, swelling, and difficulty moving. Severe sprains require medical treatment. Warming up can help prevent muscle strains and sprains.

Treatment for Minor Injuries

Minor injuries such as muscle cramps, strains, and some sprains are easily treated. Muscle cramps can be relieved through light massage. Minor strains and sprains can be treated using the *R.I.C.E.* procedure described in **Figure 4.5.**

Major Injuries

Pain—especially extreme pain—may signal that you have a major injury. If you experience extreme pain, numbness, or disorientation or hear a "cracking" sound during a fall, get appropriate medical treatment immediately.

FIGURE 4.5

THE *R.I.C.E.* PROCEDURE

R est Avoid using the affected muscle or joint. This may mean not using the affected area for several days.

I ce Ice helps reduce pain and swelling. Place ice cubes in a plastic bag, and wrap the bag in a towel. Hold the towel-wrapped bag on the affected area for 20 minutes. Remove the bag for 20 minutes, and then reapply the bag for another 20 minutes. Repeat this process every three waking hours over the course of 72 hours.

C ompression Light pressure through the use of an elastic bandage can help reduce swelling. The bandage should not be so tight that it cuts off the blood supply to the area, and it should be loosened at night.

E levation Raising the affected limb above the level of the heart helps reduce pain and swelling, especially at night.

Curriculum Connections

History Ask students to research historical events, such as mountain-climbing expeditions, in which individuals experienced weather-related risks and injuries. Have them present an oral report on their findings.

Physical Education If your school has a swimming program, have students practice how to safely manage a severe cramp that occurs in deep water.

Language Arts Have students research an athlete who overcame an injury and write a brief paper summarizing the athlete's experience.

Major injuries include:

▶ **Fractures and Dislocations.** Fractures are any break in a bone. A fracture causes swelling and often extreme pain, and it usually requires immobilization to heal properly. Dislocations result when a bone is forced from its normal position at a joint. A dislocation sometimes causes a "popping" sound when it occurs. A physician must put the bone back into place and immobilize the joint so that the tissue can heal.

▶ **Tendonitis.** This is a condition in which the tendons, bands of fiber that connect muscles to bones, are stretched or torn from overuse. Treatment includes rest, medication, and physical therapy.

▶ **Concussions.** Concussions result from blows to the head and can cause swelling of the brain, resulting in unconsciousness or even death. Concussions can lead to serious neurological problems. If you receive any blow to the head and experience headache, dizziness, or loss of memory or consciousness, see a health care professional immediately.

This teen's safety gear helps protect him from serious injury. *What type of serious injury might the face mask prevent?*

 Lesson 5 *Review*

Reviewing Facts and Vocabulary

1. What is *hypothermia*? With which types of weather is this condition often associated?

2. Analyze and describe strategies for preventing muscle soreness after a workout.

3. Identify which injuries described in this lesson require the attention of professional health services.

Thinking Critically

4. **Evaluating.** Explain why muscle cramps might be more dangerous for a swimmer than for a jogger.

5. **Analyzing.** On a hot day, a runner begins to have trouble breathing and also becomes pale, dizzy, and nauseous. From what condition is this runner likely to be suffering? How might the condition have been prevented? Analyze and describe strategies for responding to this condition.

Applying Health Skills

Communication Skills. Imagine that your friend has suffered a minor sprain to her ankle while in-line skating. Analyze and describe how she could use the *R.I.C.E.* procedure to respond to this accidental injury.

WORD PROCESSING Use a word-processing program to create your own chart outlining the *R.I.C.E.* procedure. See health.glencoe.com for tips on how to get the most from your word-processing program.

Lesson 5 Physical Activity Injuries **103**

③ ASSESS

EVALUATING THE LESSON

Assign and discuss the Lesson 5 Review; then administer, grade, and discuss Lesson Quiz 15 in the TCR. 📁

RETEACHING

- Divide students into pairs. Ask each student to develop a quiz about common sports injuries and how they can be prevented. Then have students exchange quizzes with their partners as a form of review.

- Ask students to complete Reteaching Activity 15 in the TCR. 📁

ENRICHMENT

Ask volunteers to interview an athlete they know who has had a broken arm or leg in a cast for several weeks. Have them find out how the inactivity caused by wearing the cast affected the muscles and previous degree of conditioning. Let students share what they have learned with the class.

④ CLOSE

Remind students that injuries are a risk with any physical activity. It is important to keep in mind, however, that many problems can be prevented by being prepared and knowing your limits. It is equally important to know how to treat injuries if they do occur.

 Lesson 5 *Review*

Answers to Reviewing Facts and Vocabulary

1. A condition in which body temperature becomes dangerously low; it is associated with cold, wet, and windy weather and submersion in cold water.

2. Answers should include warming up, cooling down, and stretching.

3. Severe heat exhaustion, heatstroke, frostbite, hypothermia, severe sprain, bone fractures and dislocations, tendonitis, and concussions.

Answers to Thinking Critically

4. They can increase the risk of drowning.

5. Heat exhaustion; drinking water, not exercising in the heat; see page 99 for treatment.

Truth in Fitness Advertising?

NHES Standard 4 Students will analyze the influence of culture, media, technology, and other factors on health.

Objective

Analyze and evaluate how ads for fitness products portray the concept of fitness, or "being fit."

Motivator

Ask students to think about what is required to maintain a fit, healthy body.

Teaching Strategies

Awareness After students have watched an infomercial, have them share the information and discuss their findings.

Analysis Have students think of the kinds of activities that constitute a fit life and compare these to the advertising claims they viewed.

Reflection Pose this question to the class: Does physical appearance always represent an example of health and fitness? Explain why or why not.

Take Action Ask students to consider how commercials for exercise equipment can portray truthful fitness strategies.

✓Assessment

Students should turn in their notes along with their reviews. Reviews should include supporting evidence from their notes and the class discussion. They also should contain an opinion on the benefits of the product advertised and make suggestions for a more truthful or realistic product ad.

Eye ON THE Media

Truth in Fitness Advertising?

TV infomercials for fitness products usually feature in-shape spokespeople with "rock-hard abs" or bulging biceps. Are these typical results from using the advertised product? In this activity you will explore advertising techniques and evaluate the effectiveness of a fitness product.

Before

ACTIVITY

Watch a TV infomercial for a particular fitness product, and answer the following questions.

1. What product is being advertised? What are the claims being made in the infomercial? Note any key statements describing the product's advantages.

2. What specific information does the advertiser provide about using the product? For instance, how often must a person use the product in order to get the desired results?

3. Who is the spokesperson? Does this person lend any credibility to the advertiser's claims?

Compare your notes with those of your classmates. Discuss the claims made in these infomercials in light of what you have learned in your text about improving various aspects of health-related fitness.

EXPRESS YOUR VIEWS

Write a paragraph expressing your overall impressions of the infomercial you watched. How much of what is being advertised is based on accurate statements? Explain whether you think the product might provide any fitness benefits, and compare that with the advertiser's claims. If you thought that the product claims were exaggerated, include suggestions on how the advertiser could present a more realistic advertisement about the product's capabilities.

) More About...

Advertising and Teens In the book titled *Social Communication in Advertising: Persons, Products and Images of Well-Being*:

". . . the ways in which messages are presented in advertising reach deeply into our most serious concerns: interpersonal and family relations, the sense of happiness and contentment, sex roles and stereotyping, the uses of affluence . . . influences on younger generations . . . and many others."

This argument suggests that classroom instruction on media literacy should include a critical look at the impact commercials can have on teens and how they see themselves and others.

CROSS-CURRICULUM CONNECTIONS

Compose an Essay. "Ripping through the water while swimming laps" or "straining and puffing while on a daily jog" are examples of phrases that illustrate the sensory details of physical activity. Capture the sights, sounds, feel, taste, and smell of your favorite physical activity in a brief descriptive essay. Focus on using adjectives, adverbs, and action verbs. Use metaphors to create an even more vivid picture.

Create a Visual Aid. One of the earliest examples of organized exercise is the Olympic Games in 776 B.C.E. At these first Games, the Greeks hosted just one event—the *stade*, a 180-meter distance race. Research a historical aspect of physical exercise and design a visual aid, like a poster, to present your findings to the class.

Compute the Calories. A foot-pound (ft-lb) is the amount of energy required to lift a 1-pound object one foot. Kilocalories are units of heat that measure food energy as well as the energy used by the body. Kilocalories can be converted to foot-pounds as follows: 1 kcal = 3088.025 ft-lb. Walking up one flight of stairs is equal to lifting yourself 10 feet. How many calories would a 180-pound man use walking up one flight of stairs?

Conduct Research. There are three different types of muscles in the human body: skeletal, smooth, and cardiac. Skeletal muscles are used for voluntary motion and are the ones we think of when playing sports or lifting weights. Cardiac and smooth muscles produce the involuntary activities of the body, controlling movement in the heart (cardiac), arterial, and digestive systems. Research the different muscle tissue types, and discuss what kind of exercise is best for each.

CAREER
Corner

Sports Medicine

Would you like to work with athletes and others who lead physically active lives? If so, you may enjoy a career in sports medicine. Physicians specializing in sports medicine treat injuries related to sports and other physical activities.

To enter this profession, you will need to complete a four-year college program, four years of medical school, and from one to seven years of residency training. Learn more about this and other related health careers by clicking on Career Corner at **health.glencoe.com**.

Chapter 4 Review **105**

CROSS-CURRICULUM CONNECTIONS

Enrich student learning by connecting the topic of physical activity to one of the four subject areas presented on this page. The activity may be completed individually or with a partner.

Language Arts Review with students the definitions of adjectives, adverbs, action verbs, and metaphors.

Social Studies Explain that effective visual aids, like posters and timelines, need to include clear photographs and drawings as well as pertinent information. Show examples. Direct students toward reliable online and library resources.

Math Answer: 180 lb × 10 ft/3088.025 ft-lb = 0.583 or approximately ½ calorie

Science Cardiac muscle responds to sustained aerobic activity. Smooth muscle benefits from the increased respiratory and circulatory capacity induced by aerobic activity. Skeletal muscle increases in size and strength from resistance training with incremental increase in the weights used.

CAREER
Corner

Have students read the Career Corner feature. Direct interested students to explore the Glencoe Health Web site at **health.glencoe.com** for more information on this topic.

Portfolio Assessment

Self-Evaluation Direct students to review the Health Skills Activities and other activities completed in the chapter. Encourage each student to select one finished product that demonstrates his or her best work for the chapter and that represents the student's learning goals. Have students explain what they have learned and how the examples they have selected demonstrate their growth in health literacy, knowledge, and skills.

Teacher Classroom Resources Assign Performance Assessment 4, "Promoting Physical Fitness," in the TCR.

Chapter 4 *Review*

CHAPTER 4 REVIEW ANSWERS

Exploring Health Terms

1. Metabolism
2. sedentary lifestyle
3. osteoporosis
4. exercise
5. Aerobic exercise
6. Anaerobic exercise
7. workout
8. warm-up
9. cool-down
10. training program
11. hydration
12. health screening
13. false: overexertion
14. true
15. false: sprain

Recalling the Facts

1. Physical activity improves reaction time by helping you respond more quickly to stimuli.
2. Regular physical activity can reduce the risk of unhealthful weight gain, which can lead to cardiovascular disease, type 2 diabetes, and cancer.
3. Answers will vary. Students may suggest joining a team, being active with friends (shooting hoops, riding bikes to the store instead of riding in a car), or replacing sedentary activities (playing computer games, watching TV) with more active ones (household chores, taking a walk, washing the car).
4. Muscular strength, one of the five areas of health-related fitness, is the amount of force a

106

► EXPLORING HEALTH TERMS
Answer the following questions on a sheet of paper.

Lesson 1 *Replace the underlined words with the correct term.*

physical activity   osteoporosis
physical fitness   sedentary lifestyle
metabolism

1. <u>Osteoporosis</u> refers to the process by which your body gets energy from food.
2. Watching television and taking naps are characteristic of a <u>physical activity</u>.
3. <u>Physical fitness</u> is a condition characterized by a decrease in bone density, producing porous and fragile bones.

Lesson 2 *Fill in the blanks with the correct term.*

body composition   muscular strength
exercise   aerobic exercise
flexibility   anaerobic exercise
muscular endurance
cardiorespiratory endurance

Purposeful physical activity that is planned, structured, and repetitive and that improves or maintains fitness is (_4_). (_5_) is any rhythmic activity that uses large muscle groups and can be maintained continuously for 20 to 30 minutes at one time. (_6_) involves short bursts of activity in which the muscles work so hard that they produce energy without using oxygen.

Lesson 3 *Replace the underlined words with the correct term.*

overload   workout
progression   cool-down
specificity   *F.I.T.T.*
warm-up   resting heart rate

7. The part of an exercise program when the activity is performed at its highest peak is called the <u>overload</u>.
8. A <u>workout</u> is an activity that prepares the muscles for work.
9. An activity that prepares the muscles to return to a resting state is a <u>progression</u>.

Lesson 4 *Match each definition with the correct term.*

health screening   hydration
training program   anabolic steroids

10. A program of formalized physical preparation for involvement in a sport or another physical activity.
11. Taking in fluids so that the body functions properly.
12. A search or check for diseases or disorders that an individual would otherwise not have knowledge of or seek help for.

Lesson 5 *Identify each statement as True or False. If false, replace the underlined term with the correct term.*

overexertion   hypothermia
heatstroke   muscle cramp
heat cramps   strain
frostbite   sprain

13. Many hot-weather health problems, such as heat exhaustion and heat cramps, are related to <u>hypothermia</u>.
14. <u>Frostbite</u> is a condition that results when body tissues become frozen.
15. A <u>muscle cramp</u> is an injury to the ligament surrounding a joint.

► RECALLING THE FACTS
Use complete sentences to answer the following questions.

Lesson 1

1. Examine and briefly describe the effects of regular physical activity on the nervous system.
2. Analyze the relationship between regular physical activity and disease prevention: How can engaging in regular physical activity now and in adulthood reduce your risks of cardiovascular disease, type 2 diabetes, and cancer?
3. What are three ways to incorporate physical activity into your daily life?

muscle can exert. Curl-ups are often used to measure abdominal strength; the arm hang is one test that is used to measure upper body strength.

5. Aerobic exercise increases heart rate, allowing the heart to send more oxygen to the muscles to use as energy. This strengthens the heart and the entire cardiovascular system. Aerobic exercise also benefits the respiratory system by increasing the lungs' capacity to hold air.

6. The three types of resistance training are isometric exercise, isotonic exercise, and isokinetic exercise.

7. Progression is the gradual increase in the overload necessary to achieve higher levels of fitness.

8. Every physical activity session should include a warm-up, a workout, and a cool-down.

9. Using the *F.I.T.T.* formula can help you target the number of times you will work out each week (F), how hard or intensely you will work out (I), how long each session will

Lesson 2

4. What is muscular strength, and how is it measured?

5. Examine and briefly describe how aerobic exercise benefits the cardiovascular and respiratory systems.

6. What are the three types of resistance training exercises?

Lesson 3

7. In the context of physical activity, what is meant by the term *progression*?

8. What three elements should be part of every physical activity session?

9. How can the *F.I.T.T.* formula help you meet your fitness goals?

Lesson 4

10. Why are proper nutrition and adequate rest important factors in a physical activity training program?

11. Why is starting a fitness program a situation that requires a preventive health screening?

12. List three ways to stay safe when exercising alone outdoors.

Lesson 5

13. What are two advantages to dressing in layers when outside in cold weather?

14. Analyze and describe a strategy for responding to minor strains and sprains.

15. What symptoms signal a major injury that requires treatment by professional health services?

➤ THINKING CRITICALLY

1. **Analyzing.** Why do you think many teens lead a sedentary lifestyle? *(LESSON 1)*

2. **Evaluating.** Samantha does not enjoy participating in formal group exercise programs such as those at a health club. What physical activities might she include in her daily life to obtain the benefits of both aerobic exercise and anaerobic exercise? *(LESSON 2)*

3. **Synthesizing.** Develop a physical activity program that includes all areas shown in the Physical Activity Pyramid in Figure 4.3. *(LESSON 3)*

4. **Explaining.** Why is it important to be alert to the surrounding environment when playing a sport? Give two specific examples. *(LESSON 4)*

5. **Applying.** Brianna is an enthusiastic but inexperienced skier. She accepts an invitation to go skiing even though it is 10°F below zero. What strategies would you give her for preventing illness and injury while participating in this activity? *(LESSON 5)*

➤ HEALTH SKILLS APPLICATION

1. **Practicing Healthful Behaviors.** Identify three sedentary activities from your daily life and suggest a physical activity you could do in place of each. *(LESSON 1)*

2. **Goal Setting.** Identify two areas of your health-related fitness that need improvement. Use the goal-setting steps to develop a plan for improving these areas. *(LESSON 2)*

3. **Advocacy.** Prepare a short presentation in which you encourage teens to develop their own fitness programs based on the principles of overload, progression, and specificity. *(LESSON 3)*

4. **Refusal Skills.** With a classmate, role-play a scenario in which you refuse a friend's offer of an herbal supplement that claims to enhance athletic performance. *(LESSON 4)*

5. **Accessing Information.** Locate three sources in your community from whom you can request information about sports injuries. Summarize the information you receive from each source, and share your findings with the class. *(LESSON 5)*

be (T), and the type of activity you will include in your workout (T). Each of these elements should be a part of fitness goals.

10. Proper nutrition provides the body with the energy needed for physical activities. Rest recharges the body.

11. A health care screening can confirm that a fitness program can be safely undertaken.

12. Any three: select the right time and place for the activity; exercise during daylight hours; if exercising at night, wear reflective clothing and carry a whistle; be aware of the effects of weather conditions.

13. Layers help keep the body warm; they also can be added or removed as the temperature or weather conditions change.

14. *R.I.C.E:* rest, ice, compression, elevation.

15. Extreme pain, numbness, disorientation, cracking sound during a fall.

Thinking Critically

1. Responses will vary but may include the development of time- and energy-saving devices.

2. Possible responses include running, bicycling, jogging, and swimming (aerobic exercise); calisthenics, weight training, and resistance training (anaerobic exercise).

3. Responses should include all areas of the Physical Activity Pyramid.

4. Responses should include the concept that paying attention to your surroundings can help you be alert to situations that can lead to injury. Examples will vary.

5. Strategies will vary but should include wearing the proper clothing for cold-weather activity; having a good breakfast; staying hydrated; avoiding overexertion, and observing all relevant safety rules and procedures. If Brianna does these things, she will reduce the risk of (a) strain or overexertion and injury, and (b) hypothermia and possibly frostbite.

Health Skills Application

1.–5. Answers will vary.

EVALUATE

- Use the reproducible Chapter 4 Test in the TCR, or construct your own using the Testmaker software. 📁 💿

- Use Performance Assessment 4 in the TCR. 📁

ENRICHMENT

Ask students to complete Enrichment Activity 4 in the TCR. 📁

Lessons	Standards		Features
	National	**State/Local**	
1 Nutrition During the Teen Years *pages 110–113*	National Health Education Standards 1.1, 1.6, 4.1, 4.2, 7.2		**Exploring Issues** • Should Soft Drinks and Snacks Be Taxed to Fund Health Education Programs? page 112
2 Nutrients *pages 114–121*	National Health Education Standards 1.6, 6.4		**Hands-On Health** • Reducing Your Intake of Fats *(Goal Setting)*, page 118
3 Guidelines for Healthful Eating *pages 122–129*	National Health Education Standards 1.3, 3.4		**Real-Life Application** • Smart Snacking *(Practicing Healthful Behaviors)*, page 127
4 Food and Healthy Living *pages 130–137*	National Health Education Standards 1.1, 3.4		

Reproducible Resources	Assessment	Technology
Student Activity Workbook for use with each chapter	📁 Lesson Quiz 16	💿 TeacherWorks® 🖥 Internet Activities
📁 Concept Mapping Activity 16 📁 Decision-Making Activity 5 📁 Guided Reading Activities 16 📁 Lesson Plan 16 📁 Parent Letter and Activities 5 📁 Reteaching Activity 16		
📁 Concept Mapping Activity 17 📁 Enrichment Activity 5 📁 Guided Reading Activities 17 📁 Lesson Plan 17 📁 Reteaching Activity 17	📁 Lesson Quiz 17	🕹 Transparency 14 💿 TeacherWorks®
📁 Concept Mapping Activity 18 📁 Cross-Curriculum Activity 5 📁 Current Health Issues 5 📁 Guided Reading Activities 18 📁 Lesson Plan 18 📁 Reteaching Activity 18	📁 Lesson Quiz 18	🕹 Transparency 15 💿 TeacherWorks®
📁 Concept Mapping Activity 19 📁 Guided Reading Activities 19 📁 Health Lab 5 📁 Lesson Plan 19 📁 Reteaching Activity 19	📁 Lesson Quiz 19	🕹 Transparency 16 💿 TeacherWorks®

Key to Ability Levels

Teaching strategies that appear throughout the chapter have been identified by one of the following codes to give teachers an idea of their suitability for students of varying learning styles and abilities.

L1 Strategies should be within the ability range of all students. Full class participation is often required. Teacher direction is usually needed.

L2 Strategies are designed for average to above-average students or for small groups. Some teacher direction is needed.

L3 Strategies are designed for students able and willing to work independently. Minimal teacher direction is needed.

ELL Strategies should be within the ability range of students learning the English language.

💊 Block scheduling strategies are useful in a block scheduling format.

0:00 OUT OF TIME

If time does not permit teaching the entire chapter use:
- Exploring Issues, p. 112
- Figure 5.1, p. 119
- Figure 5.2, p. 120
- Figure 5.3, p. 121
- Health Minute, p. 126
- Figure 5.7, p. 131

Language Diversity

- 🎧 English Audio CD Program
- 🎧 Spanish Audio CD Program
- 📁 English Summaries, Quizzes, and Activities
- 📁 Spanish Summaries, Quizzes, and Activities
- 📁 Spanish Parent Letters and Activities

End of Chapter Assessment

Blackline Masters

- 📁 Chapter 5 Test
- 📁 Performance Assessment Activity 5

Technology

- 💿 Vocabulary PuzzleMaker
- 📼 MindJogger Videoquiz
- 💿 **Exam***View*® Pro Testmaker

Professional Health Series

Dealing with Sensitive Issues
Planning a Coordinated School Health Program
Promoting Character Education
Home, School, and Community Involvement

Nutrition and Your Health

CHAPTER OVERVIEW

Chapter 5 identifies the elements necessary for proper nutrition and explains how students can make healthful food choices.

Lesson 1 Good nutrition supplies the body with the calories and nutrients needed for maximum energy and wellness. Food choices are influenced by a number of factors.

Lesson 2 To function properly, the human body needs the nutrients found in food. These nutrients are classified into six groups—carbohydrates, proteins, fats, vitamins, minerals, and water.

Lesson 3 *The Dietary Guidelines for Americans* and the Food Guide Pyramid are tools that can help individuals develop healthy eating habits.

Lesson 4 Information on food labels can help people make wise food choices. To keep food safe and reduce the risk of foodborne illness, follow these four steps: clean, separate, cook, and chill.

Health Skills Features

- Exploring Issues, p. 112
- Hands-On Health (*Goal Setting*), p. 118
- Real-Life Application (*Practicing Healthful Behaviors*), p. 127

Nutrition and Your Health

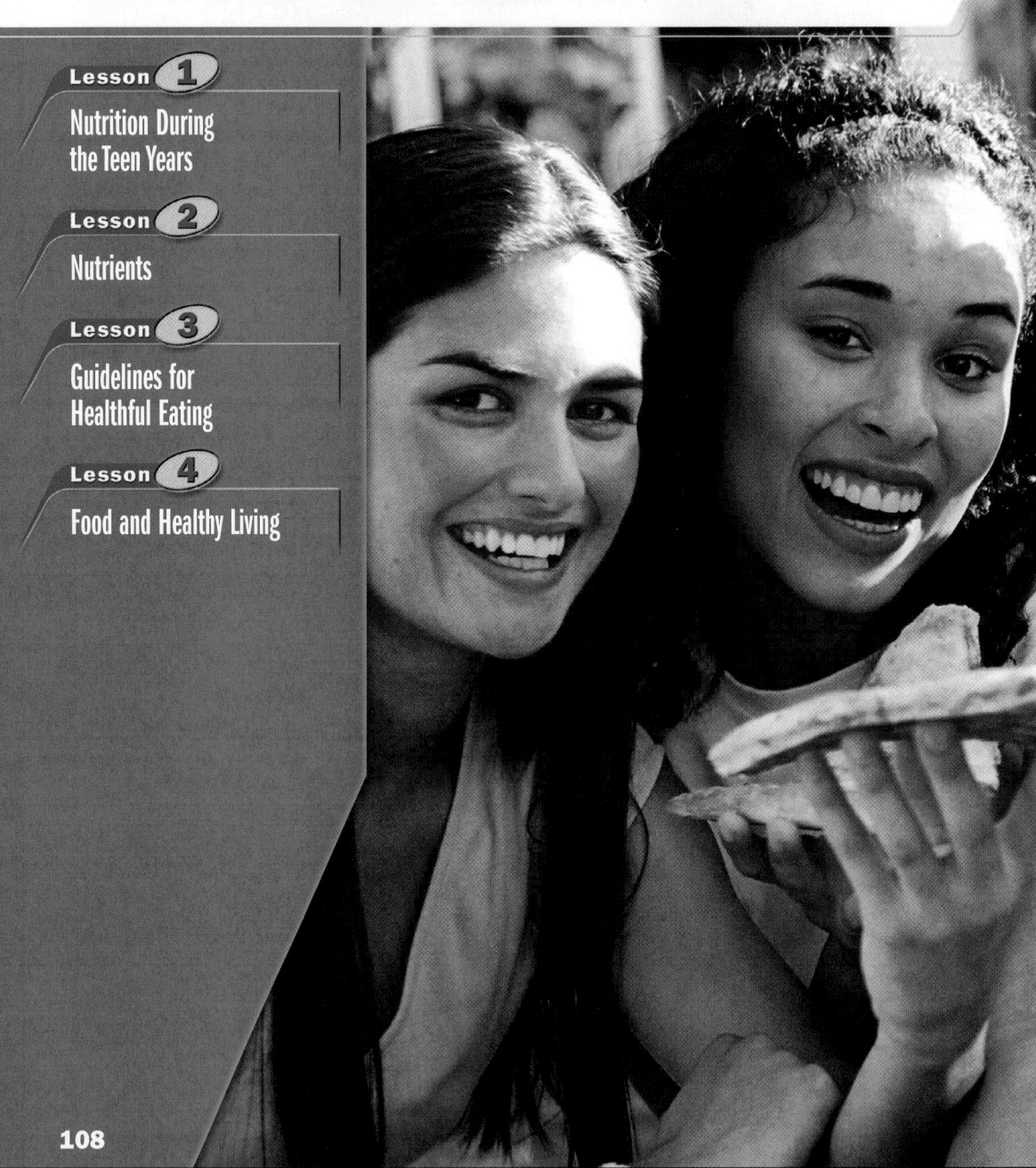

Lesson 1
Nutrition During the Teen Years

Lesson 2
Nutrients

Lesson 3
Guidelines for Healthful Eating

Lesson 4
Food and Healthy Living

108

MEETING STUDENT DIVERSITY

Language Diversity Use the following suggestions to help students who have difficulty with English:

- Pair English language learners with native speakers of English who can restate the Chapter Summary in language that helps students comprehend important concepts.

- 🎧 Direct auditory learners or those students with language diversity to the *Glencoe Health Audio CD Program.* Available in English and Spanish, this component provides an audio and written summary of the chapter.

- Use photographs, drawings, or magazine clippings to help students visualize the important concepts of the chapter.

Myth or Fact? ✓

What Do You Know About Healthful Eating?

Read the statements below and respond by writing *Myth* or *Fact* for each item. You may want to jot down reasons for each of your choices.

1. Meat should make up the largest part of my daily food intake.

2. The foods I eat now can affect my health later in life.

3. It's *what* I eat that really counts, not how much I eat.

4. To help maintain a healthy weight, I must balance the energy in the foods I eat with the energy I use in physical activity.

5. The calories in a doughnut are more likely to be converted to fat in my body than the calories in a piece of fruit.

6. The Food Guide Pyramid provides a good guideline for my daily food intake.

7. Eating a healthy breakfast each day can help me perform better in school.

8. The best way for me to get the nutrients I need is to take a daily vitamin and mineral supplement.

Keep your responses for review later in the chapter. After you complete the chapter, review your answers and change or modify them on the basis of what you have learned.

109

Quick*Write*

Using Visuals. Food and social activities often go together. Describe how friends and family members influence your eating habits and food choices.

INTRODUCING THE CHAPTER

Myth or Fact? ✓

For each statement, have students write *Myth* or *Fact* and a reason for their response. Then share the correct answers with students.

1. Myth: Most of the foods you eat daily should be grain products.

2. Fact: Eating healthfully now can reduce your risk of disease later in life.

3. Myth: Both what you eat and how much you eat count. For example, eating large quantities of low-fat foods can still lead to weight gain.

4. Fact

5. Myth: Any calories not used by the body will be stored as fat.

6. Fact: The Food Guide Pyramid can help you eat healthfully—for variety, balance, and moderation.

7. Fact: Eating a nutritious breakfast improves mental and physical performance and helps prevent fatigue.

8. Myth: Following the recommendations of the Food Guide Pyramid should provide the average person with the nutrients he or she needs.

Quick*write*

Using Visuals Direct students to look at the photograph and discuss how friends influence eating habits and food choices.

Nutrition During the Teen Years

❶ FOCUS

QUICK START Review various reasons for eating, such as hunger, boredom, and so on. After students have completed the activity, ask volunteers to share their responses and discuss as a class.

TYING TO PRIOR KNOWLEDGE

Ask volunteers to name favorite foods and explain why they like them. Ask: What foods do you dislike? Why? Explain that sometimes we eat the same foods out of habit and that this lesson will explore influences on food choices.

Health Skills Features

"Should Soft Drinks and Snacks Be Taxed to Fund Health Education Programs?" p. 112

INTRODUCING VOCABULARY

- Point out that *nutrition* and *nutrients* come from the same word: *nutrire*, meaning "to feed, nourish." Have students suggest other words that sound similar. (*nutritious, nutritionist*) Ask students to use both vocabulary terms in a paragraph.

- Ask students to complete the Chapter 5 Study Guide in the *Student Activity Workbook.* 📁

Nutrition During the Teen Years

VOCABULARY
nutrition
calories
nutrients
hunger
appetite

YOU'LL LEARN TO
- Explain the relationship between nutrition, quality of life, and disease.
- Evaluate various influences on food choices.
- Explain the immediate and long-term benefits of nutrition on body systems.

QUICK START On a sheet of paper, list six of the foods you eat most often for meals or snacks. Then describe why you eat each of these foods. Do you base your choice on their health benefits? Their taste or appearance? Their convenience?

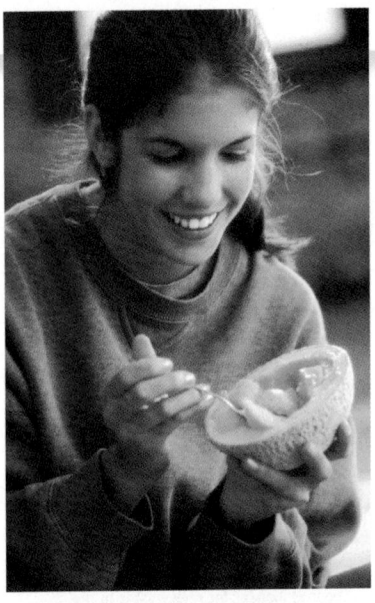

Choosing fresh fruit as a snack is a good way to supply your body with the nutrients it needs. *What's your favorite healthful snack?*

Picture yourself biting into a crisp, juicy apple or a slice of cheese pizza with zesty tomato sauce. Do these foods appeal to you? What other foods do you like? Enjoying a wide variety of healthful foods is an important part of good **nutrition—** *the process by which the body takes in and uses food.* Because not all foods offer the same benefits, making healthful food choices is important to your overall level of health.

The Importance of Good Nutrition

Good nutrition enhances your quality of life and helps prevent disease. It provides you with the calories and nutrients your body needs for maximum energy and wellness. **Calories**, or more correctly, kilocalories, are the *units of heat that measure the energy used by the body and the energy that foods supply to the body.* This energy fuels everything you do, from exercising and playing sports to doing your homework and talking with friends. **Nutrients** are the *substances in food that your body needs to grow, to repair itself, and to supply you with energy.* Making healthy food choices will provide your body with the nutrients it needs to help you look your best and perform at your peak.

110 Chapter 5 Nutrition and Your Health

Lesson 1 *Resources*

Teacher Classroom Resources
📁 Concept Mapping Activity 16
📁 Decision-Making Activity 5
📁 Guided Reading Activities 16
📁 Lesson Plan 16
📁 Lesson Quiz 16

📁 Parent Letter and Activities 5
📁 Reteaching Activity 16
Student Activity Workbook
📁 Applying Health Skills 16
📁 Chapter 5 Study Guide

What Influences Your Food Choices?

Have you ever wondered why you choose the foods you do? Taste, of course, plays an important part in your choice of foods. You probably won't eat a food—even if you know it's healthful—if you don't like its taste. To gain insight into your eating habits, it's important to understand the difference between your physical *need* for food and your psychological *desire* for food—between hunger and appetite. Distinguishing between the two can help you make more healthful food choices.

Hunger and Appetite

Hunger, an unlearned, inborn response, is *a natural physical drive that protects you from starvation*. When your stomach is empty, its walls contract, stimulating nerve endings. The nerves signal your brain that your body needs food. When you eat, the walls of the stomach are stretched and the nerve endings are no longer stimulated. You have satisfied your physical need for food.

The physical need for food isn't the only reason people eat. Have you ever eaten something "just to be sociable" or in response to a familiar sensation—for example, the aroma of freshly baked bread? In such cases you are eating in response to appetite rather than to hunger. **Appetite** is *a desire, rather than a need, to eat*. Whether you are responding to hunger or to appetite when you eat, many factors influence your food choices and eating habits, including your emotions and a number of factors in your environment.

Food and Emotions

Food is sometimes used to meet emotional needs. For example, do you tend to eat more—or less—when you feel stressed, frustrated, or depressed? Do you sometimes snack just because you're bored? Do you reward yourself with a food treat when you've achieved a goal? Using food to relieve tension or boredom or to reward yourself can result in overeating and unhealthful weight gain. On the other hand, if you lose interest in eating whenever you're upset, you may miss getting enough of the nutrients your body needs. Recognizing when emotions are guiding your food choices can help you break such patterns and improve your eating habits.

Food and Your Environment

A number of environmental factors influence food choices:

▶ **Family, friends, and peers.** Many of your eating habits were shaped as you were growing up, when adults planned your meals. Now you may prefer certain foods because you've grown up eating them. Friends and peers can influence you to try new foods.

Health Minute
Managing Your Eating Habits

To manage your eating habits:

▶ **Try not to be overly influenced by others in making food choices.** Make choices with your health in mind—not just your appetite.

▶ **Pay attention to quantity.** Start off with reasonably sized servings, and, if possible, use a smaller plate. Listen to your body's "hunger clock" rather than to your appetite. When you feel full, stop eating. It takes 20 minutes for your stomach to signal your brain that it is satisfied.

▶ **Make something other than food the focus of social occasions.** If you are getting together with friends, for example, consider a setting other than a restaurant, such as a park or community center.

② TEACH

Discussing

Ask students who have lived in other regions of the United States to describe some of the differences in food customs they have experienced among the various regions. **Verbal/Linguistic Intelligence**

Community Involvement

Invite students to form small groups to visit ethnic restaurants and try a variety of menu selections. Allow time for students to share their experiences.

Discussing

Encourage students to describe one of their family's favorite foods and explain why it is special. Examples might include an old family recipe, a food that is served on special occasions, or a food that is part of a cultural tradition.

Health Minute

Ask a volunteer to read aloud the tips for managing eating habits. Then lead a class discussion on these strategies and have students brainstorm additional ideas.

Curriculum Connections

Science Hunger and appetite are complex physiological processes that are regulated by various structures in the brain, in particular, the hypothalamus and the pituitary gland. Have students use reliable online and library resources to learn more about the role that the hypothalamus and the pituitary gland play in the regulation of hunger and appetite. Direct students to compose a written report detailing their findings, and ask volunteers to present their reports to the class.

Exploring Issues

SHOULD SOFT DRINKS AND SNACKS BE TAXED TO FUND HEALTH EDUCATION PROGRAMS?

Have students read the feature, write their responses to the questions, and compare their opinions with those of other students. To help them answer the second question, point out that obesity is responsible for $117 billion in health costs. Everyone pays for this with insurance, including government insurance. People who do eat healthfully and maintain an appropriate weight are paying some of those costs.

ACTIVE READING

Survey and Question

SQ3R (an acronym for Survey, Question, Read, Recite, and Review) is an effective study technique to boost comprehension and recall. To apply this strategy, ask students to scan the chapter. Have them read titles, headings, and captions and scan illustrative material to form a general idea about the organization and content of the selection. Then ask students to form questions about what they would like to learn about the topic and what questions they expect to be answered in the selection. Next, instruct students to read the selection to answer their questions. Explain to students that, as they read, they are likely to find the answers to some of their questions. For more strategies, see the *Guided Reading Activities* booklet in the TCR.

Exploring Issues

Should Soft Drinks and Snacks Be Taxed to Fund Health Education Programs?

Some health advocates have recommended that soft drinks and high-calorie snacks be taxed. They believe that these foods are partly to blame for the recent rise in obesity rates. Each item would be taxed one to two cents, and the money would fund programs that promote healthful eating and physical activity. Read what two teens have to say about this issue:

Viewpoint 1: Zack H., age 16

I'd pay an extra penny or two for snacks if the money was being used for a good cause. Cigarettes and alcohol are taxed—why not soft drinks and high-calorie snacks? Every year, obesity causes almost as many deaths as tobacco. Health advocates have shown that antitobacco messages can change behavior. I think nutrition campaigns could do the same thing.

Viewpoint 2: Songhee L., age 16

How can you compare soft drinks and snacks to tobacco and alcohol? People have to eat. There are no good or bad foods, just unhealthful eating patterns. The answer to obesity is making the right food choices. A sedentary lifestyle also contributes to overweight and obesity. Why not tax video games and computer software? Also, why stop at soft drinks and snack foods? Why not tax cheese, butter, and salad dressing?

ACTIVITIES

1. Do you think campaigns or formal programs on nutrition would influence people to make healthful eating choices? Why or why not?

2. Should the government be responsible for individual eating choices? Explain.

▶ **Cultural and ethnic background.** Your food choices may reflect your cultural heritage or ethnic background. For example, corn, beans, and tortillas might be common foods in many Mexican-American households.

▶ **Convenience and cost.** Convenience and cost of foods may be top priorities for some people. For example, busy families may rely on foods that can be prepared quickly, such as microwavable meals.

112 Chapter 5 Nutrition and Your Health

Cooperative Learning Activity

Body Image and the Media Teens may become obsessed with weight or body image by comparing themselves unfavorably to media images of models and celebrities. Explain that the photos in many ads are enhanced using computer technology. Have students collect and share several magazine ads or describe TV commercials that feature unrealistic images against which teens might measure themselves. Direct them to examine the ads. Ask: What unrealistic qualities do the ads project? Overly slender bodies? Bulging muscles? Have the class form a panel to discuss the role of the media in projecting nonrealistic body images for teens.

▶ **Advertising.** Advertisers spend millions of dollars each year to influence your decisions about food. Part of making informed food choices involves carefully analyzing the health messages delivered through food advertisements. Then you, rather than advertisers, will control your food choices.

Nutrition Throughout the Life Span

 Eating nutritious meals as a family can contribute to the health of all family members.

Good nutrition is essential for health throughout life but particularly during adolescence—one of the fastest periods of growth you'll experience. Healthful eating provides you with the nutrients you need for growth and development, gives you energy for sports and other activities, enables you to stay mentally alert, and helps you feel good and look your best. A healthful and balanced eating plan also helps prevent unhealthful weight gain, obesity, and type 2 diabetes—conditions that have become more common among children and teens in recent years. Making healthful food choices now also lowers your risk of developing many life-threatening conditions as you get older. These conditions include heart disease and stroke, certain cancers, and osteoporosis.

▶ Lesson 1 Review

Reviewing Facts and Vocabulary

1. Briefly explain the relationship between nutrition, quality of life, and disease.
2. Define the term *appetite*.
3. Name three influences—other than family—on people's food choices.

Thinking Critically

4. **Evaluating.** Give examples of how your family has influenced your food choices.
5. **Applying.** How does what you eat now affect your health, both now and as you grow older?

Applying Health Skills

Analyzing Influences. Look through magazines and find five food advertisements that contain specific health claims. Analyze the health message that each advertisement delivers about its product. How might it influence your food choice? Present your findings in the form of a table.

SPREADSHEETS Spreadsheet software can be used to create your table. For help in using spreadsheet software, go to **health.glencoe.com**.

Lesson 1 Nutrition During the Teen Years **113**

3 ASSESS

EVALUATING THE LESSON

Assign and discuss the Lesson 1 Review; then administer, grade, and discuss Lesson Quiz 16 in the TCR. 📁

RETEACHING

- Direct students to write a paragraph explaining how healthful food choices made during the teen years will benefit them throughout life. Have them proofread their paragraphs for organization and content.

- Ask students to complete Reteaching Activity 16 in the TCR. 📁

ENRICHMENT

Ask students to interview one person to find out what factors influence his or her food choices. Have students write a paragraph on their findings. Remind them to check their work for spelling and grammar.

4 CLOSE

Ask students why it might be challenging to make healthy food choices as a teen. Who and what influences their choices? How can they be more aware of the impact of their choices?

▶ Lesson 1 Review

Answers to Reviewing Facts and Vocabulary

1. Good nutrition enhances quality of life and helps prevent disease.
2. A desire, rather than a need, to eat.
3. Any three: emotions, friends, peers, cultural and ethnic background, convenience, cost, advertising.

Answers to Thinking Critically

4. Answers will vary.
5. Possible answer: Now—provides the body with the energy it needs to function and grow; helps reduce the risk of overweight, obesity, type 2 diabetes. Future—reduces the risk of heart disease, stroke, cancer, and osteoporosis.

Lesson 2

Nutrients

① FOCUS

QUICK START Have several volunteers share their ideas of a nutritious meal and its health benefits with the class. Ask: What similarities do you see among these meals? How might any meal be made more nutritious?

TYING TO PRIOR KNOWLEDGE

Have students list the following nutrients on a sheet of paper: carbohydrates, proteins, fats, vitamins, minerals, and water. Under each nutrient, have them list as many foods as they can that are good sources of that nutrient. Have students check their answers as they study this lesson.

Health Skills Features

"Reducing Your Intake of Fats," p. 118

GOAL SETTING

INTRODUCING VOCABULARY

- Have students make sets of flash cards to review the definitions of each of the vocabulary terms. Remind them to use a dictionary or glossary as necessary.

- Ask students to complete the Chapter 5 Study Guide in the *Student Activity Workbook*. 📁

Lesson 2

Nutrients

VOCABULARY
- **carbohydrates**
- **fiber**
- **proteins**
- **lipid**
- **vitamins**
- **minerals**

YOU'LL LEARN TO
- Describe the functions of the six basic nutrients in maintaining health.
- Demonstrate knowledge of nutrients in a variety of foods.
- Analyze the relationship between good nutrition and disease prevention.

 QUICK START What's your idea of a healthful meal? On a sheet of paper, describe a nutritious meal that you would enjoy. Then make a list of the health benefits that you think you would get from this meal.

 Each of these foods is rich in one or more nutrients. *Which of these foods do you eat regularly?*

To survive, the human body needs the nutrients found in food. These nutrients are classified into six groups: carbohydrates, proteins, fats, vitamins, minerals, and water. Each plays a unique part in maintaining the normal growth and functioning of your body. Together, they are essential to your overall health and wellness.

Carbohydrates

Do you like potatoes, pasta, and bread? These foods are rich in carbohydrates. **Carbohydrates** are *the starches and sugars present in foods*. Made up of carbon, oxygen, and hydrogen, carbohydrates are the body's preferred source of energy, providing four calories per gram. Your body uses energy from carbohydrates to perform every task, including sitting and reading the words on this page. Depending on their chemical makeup, carbohydrates are classified as either simple or complex. Most nutritionists recommend that 55 to 60 percent of your daily calories come from carbohydrates, mainly complex carbohydrates.

Lesson 2 *Resources*

Teacher Classroom Resources
- 📁 Concept Mapping Activity 17
- 📁 Enrichment Activity 5
- 📁 Guided Reading Activities 17
- 📁 Lesson Plan 17
- 📁 Lesson Quiz 17
- 📁 Reteaching Activity 17

Student Activity Workbook
- 📁 Applying Health Skills 17
- 📁 Chapter 5 Study Guide

Multimedia
- 🖨 Transparency 14

Simple and Complex Carbohydrates

Simple carbohydrates are *sugars,* such as fructose and lactose (found in fruit and milk, respectively). You're probably most familiar with sucrose. It occurs naturally in many plants, such as sugarcane and sugar beets, and is refined to make table sugar. Sugars are added to many manufactured food products.

Complex carbohydrates, or *starches,* are found in whole grains, seeds, nuts, legumes (dried peas and beans), and tubers (root vegetables such as potatoes). The body must break down complex carbohydrates into simple carbohydrates before it can use them for energy.

The Role of Carbohydrates

Your body converts all carbohydrates to glucose, a simple sugar that is the body's main source of energy. Glucose that your body does not use right away is stored in the liver and muscles as a starch-like substance called glycogen (GLI-coh-jen). When more energy is needed, your body converts the glycogen back to glucose. However, it's possible to take in more carbohydrates than your body can use right away or can store as glycogen. When this happens, your body converts and stores the excess carbohydrates as body fat. You can avoid consuming excess carbohydrates by learning to make informed food choices and maintaining healthful eating habits.

Fiber

Fiber is *an indigestible complex carbohydrate* that is found in the tough, stringy parts of vegetables, fruits, and whole grains. Although it can't be digested and used as energy, fiber helps move waste through the digestive system and thereby helps prevent intestinal problems such as constipation. Eating enough fiber throughout your life may reduce your risk of heart disease. Some types of fiber have also been shown to help control diabetes by reducing blood glucose levels.

To stay healthy, eat 20 to 35 grams of fiber each day. Fruits and vegetables with edible skins and whole-grain products such as bran cereals, oatmeal, and brown rice are excellent sources of fiber.

Health Minute

Getting More Fiber into Your Diet

To get 20–35 grams of fiber daily:

▶ Start your day with a whole-grain breakfast cereal, such as oatmeal.

▶ Choose whole fruit instead of fruit juice.

▶ Make sure you eat at least five servings of fruits and vegetables each day.

▶ Select high-fiber snacks (popcorn, raw vegetables, nuts, and fruit with edible skins).

▶ Eat legumes at least two or three times a week.

▶ Substitute whole-grain ingredients (whole-wheat flour, bran) for low-fiber ingredients (white flour) in recipes whenever possible.

⑦ **Each of these foods is a rich source of carbohydrates.**

Lesson 2 Nutrients **115**

② TEACH

Critical Thinking

Tell students to list all the simple and complex carbohydrates they have eaten in the past 24 hours. Ask each student to compare the two lists and write a conclusion statement about his or her intake of carbohydrates. **L1**

Activity

Have the class research the relationship between carbohydrates and tooth decay. **L3**

Quick Demo

Remind students that they need 20–35 grams of fiber each day for good health. Bring a variety of breakfast cereals to class along with a measuring cup and plastic bowls. Tell students to check the nutritional label on each box to calculate how many servings of that cereal they would have to eat to meet the daily fiber requirement. Then have them measure the required number of servings into the bowls. **L1 Visual/Spatial Intelligence**

Health Minute

Divide the class into small groups. Ask for a volunteer to read aloud the tips for getting more fiber into your diet. Have each group compile a list of additional tips, and then have groups compare lists. Ask students: Why is it so important to get enough fiber in your diet?

Activity

Have students find definitions of *whole grains* and give examples. Whole grains consist of the endosperm, germ, and bran. Whole wheat bread contains a whole grain; white bread has only the endosperm. Discuss the health benefits of whole grains. They have more fiber and more nutrients, especially the B vitamins and vitamin E. **L2**

Critical Thinking

Ask students to record their food choices for 24 hours. Then have them discuss how many estimated servings they consumed as complete and incomplete proteins. **L2**

Discussing

Present this case study to the class: Tim, a vegetarian, is coming for a two-day visit. He doesn't eat meat, poultry, or fish. What foods should you offer? Lead students in brainstorming a list of tasty, nutritious foods to offer Tim that stay within the guidelines of his vegetarian diet. **L1**

Proteins

A vital part of every cell in your body, **proteins** are *nutrients that help build and maintain body cells and tissues*. Proteins are made of long chains of substances called amino acids. Your body can manufacture all but 9 of the 20 different amino acids that make up proteins. The 9 that your body can't make are called *essential amino acids*—you must get them from the foods you eat.

Complete and Incomplete Proteins

The proteins in food are classified into two groups, *complete proteins* and *incomplete proteins*.

▶ **Complete proteins** contain adequate amounts of all nine essential amino acids. Animal products—such as fish, meat, poultry, eggs, milk, cheese, and yogurt—and many soybean products are good sources of complete proteins.

▶ **Incomplete proteins** lack one or more of the essential amino acids. Sources include beans, peas, nuts, and whole grains. Consuming a combination of incomplete proteins, for example, rice and beans or peanut butter and bread, is equivalent to consuming a complete protein. You don't have to combine the incomplete proteins in one meal to get this benefit, you just need to eat them both over the course of the day.

The Role of Proteins

Proteins have many functions. During major growth periods, such as infancy, childhood, adolescence, and pregnancy, the body builds new cells and tissues from the amino acids in proteins. Throughout your life your body replaces damaged or worn-out cells by making new ones from protein. The body also uses protein to make enzymes, hormones, and antibodies. Enzymes are substances that control the rate of chemical reactions in your cells. Hormones regulate the activities of different cells, and antibodies help identify and destroy disease-causing organisms. Proteins also supply the body with energy, although they are not the body's main energy source. Like carbohydrates, proteins provide four calories per gram and excess protein is converted to body fat.

Each of these foods is a good source of protein. *Which of these foods contain complete proteins? Which contain incomplete proteins?*

∿∿ HEALTH LITERACY

Vegetarian Diets Consuming enough complete protein may be a challenge for some vegetarians. Lacto-ovo vegetarians avoid only meat, poultry, and fish, so they can get complete proteins from eggs, milk, cheese, and yogurt. (*Lacto* means milk, and *ovo* means eggs.) *Vegans* eliminate all animal products from their diet. Unless they combine foods carefully, their meals will not provide the protein they need. Three equations help create vegetarian meals with complete protein:

- Legumes + Grains = Complete Protein
- Legumes + Nuts or Seeds = Complete Protein
- Any Plant Protein + Eggs or Dairy Products = Complete Protein

Fats

Some fat in the diet is necessary for good health. Fats are a type of **lipid** (LIHP-uhd), *a fatty substance that does not dissolve in water.* Fats provide more than twice the energy of carbohydrates or proteins—nine calories per gram.

The building blocks of fats are called fatty acids, molecules made mostly of long chains of carbon atoms, with pairs of hydrogen atoms and single oxygen atoms attached. Fatty acids that the body needs, but cannot produce, are called *essential fatty acids*. Depending on their chemical composition, fatty acids are classified as either saturated or unsaturated. Most fats are a mixture of these two types.

Saturated and Unsaturated Fatty Acids

A *saturated fatty acid* holds all the hydrogen atoms it can. Fats high in saturated fatty acids are usually solid at room temperature. Animal fats and tropical oils—such as palm oil, palm kernel oil, and coconut oil—have a high proportion of saturated fatty acids. Fats in beef, pork, egg yolks, and dairy foods are higher in saturated fatty acids than are the fats in chicken and fish. A high intake of saturated fats is associated with an increased risk of heart disease.

Most vegetable fats—including olive, canola, soybean, corn, and cottonseed oils—contain a high proportion of unsaturated fatty acids. An *unsaturated fatty acid* has at least one unsaturated bond—a place where hydrogen can be added to the molecule. Unsaturated fats are usually liquids (oils) at room temperature. In contrast to saturated fats, unsaturated fats have been associated with a reduced risk of heart disease.

The Role of Fats

Besides providing a concentrated form of energy, fats are essential for other important health functions. They transport vitamins A, D, E, and K in your blood and serve as sources of *linoleic* (lih-noh-LAY-ihk) *acid,* an essential fatty acid that is needed for growth and healthy skin. Fats also add flavor and texture to food, and, because they take longer to digest than carbohydrates or proteins, they help satisfy hunger longer than other nutrients do. Foods that are high in fats also tend to be high in calories, and consuming excess amounts of fat increases your risk of unhealthful weight gain and obesity. Therefore, most nutritionists recommend eating only moderate amounts of fat—no more that 20 to 30 percent of your total daily calorie intake.

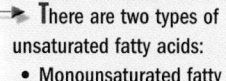
Did You Know ?

There are two types of unsaturated fatty acids:

- Monounsaturated fatty acids have only one unsaturated bond. These fatty acids are liquid at room temperature but start to solidify when refrigerated. They are found in olive oil and canola oil.
- Polyunsaturated fatty acids have more than one unsaturated bond. These fatty acids are liquid both at room temperature and in the refrigerator. They are found in safflower oil and corn oil.

The foods pictured here all contain fat. *Classify each food shown here as a source of saturated fat or unsaturated fat.*

Discussing

Talk about why fats are important in the body. Then ask students to identify the dangers of having too much fat in their diets. Diets high in fat may be high in calories, which can lead to unhealthful weight gain and obesity. For many people, high-fat diets increase the risk of heart disease. **L1**

Critical Thinking

Ask: Is it healthy to cut all fat out of your eating plan? If not, why not? Among other functions, fat transports vitamins in the bloodstream, provides energy, and is needed for healthy skin. **L1**

Cooperative Learning

Divide the class into six groups. Using food composition charts, have students investigate differences in fat content among these foods: (1) whole, 2 percent, and skim milk; (2) cheddar and skim milk mozzarella cheese; (3) ice cream and ice milk; (4) chicken with and without skin; (5) butter, margarine, and lard; and (6) bologna and lean lunch meat. **L2**

Activity

Suggest that students locate and read current consumer health articles on dietary fat in newspapers or magazines or on the Internet. Ask them to share the main ideas of the articles with the class. Lead students in evaluating the reliability of the information. **L1**

More About...

Trans Fatty Acids Hydrogenation, the process of adding missing hydrogen atoms to unsaturated fats, makes these fats more saturated and firmer in texture. Margarine, for example, is a hydrogenated form of vegetable oil. The fats that result from hydrogenation are called *trans fatty acids.* Trans fatty acids are widely used in processed foods. Although many foods containing these fats are advertised as being healthier than foods containing saturated fat, recent studies indicate that trans fatty acids may present as great a health risk as the saturated fats they replace.

Ask interested students to research products containing trans fatty acids. Have students present the information on poster boards to share with the class.

Hands-On Health

REDUCING YOUR INTAKE OF FATS

GOAL SETTING

NHES Standard 6 Students will demonstrate the ability to use goal-setting and decision-making skills to enhance health.

Objectives

- Analyze the amount of fat in fast foods and snacks.
- Set a goal and implement a plan to reduce fat intake.

Motivator

Hold up a picture of a double bacon cheeseburger or other high-fat fast food. Point out that these foods have as much as 60 grams of fat—almost as much as a female teen should get for an entire day.

Teaching Strategies

1. Remind students to pay attention to recommended serving sizes when determining fat grams per serving.
2. Obtain nutritional information from several fast-food restaurants and distribute to the class.

✓Assessment

Using a rubric, student work should provide comprehensive evidence of the following criteria to achieve the highest score:

✔ clear progression through a goal-setting process
✔ inclusion of a clear goal statement
✔ identification of a realistic goal
✔ plan for reaching the goal
✔ evaluation or reflection on the action

Hands-On Health ACTIVITY

Reducing Your Intake of Fats

Consuming too much fat can increase the risk of heart disease and unhealthful weight gain. Most teen boys need no more than 84 grams of fat each day. Most teen girls need no more than 66 grams each day. Analyzing the amount of fat in fast foods and snacks can help you see how to reduce your consumption of fats.

What You'll Need

- paper and pencil

What You'll Do

1. List every fast-food and snack item you eat and the portion size of each over the next three days. Next to each item, record how many grams of fat were in that portion. You can find fat grams in snacks by reading the label on packaged food products or by using a computerized dietary analysis program. Fast-food restaurants can provide a list of nutritional information about their products.

2. Determine the total number of fat grams you consumed over the three-day period. Then divide by three to find your daily average. What did you discover? Were there any surprises?

3. Using your dietary analysis as a guide, set a goal to reduce your fat intake for the next three days. Write a detailed plan describing the steps you will take to reach your goal.

Apply and Conclude

Follow your plan for three days. As a class, share which low-fat substitutions you tried and enjoyed.

The Role of Cholesterol

Cholesterol is a waxy lipidlike substance that circulates in blood. Your body uses the small amount it manufactures to make cell membranes and nerve tissue and to produce many hormones, vitamin D, and bile, which helps digest fats. Excess blood cholesterol is deposited in arteries, including the arteries of the heart. This increases the risk of heart disease.

High cholesterol may be hereditary, and cholesterol levels tend to rise as people age. Although heredity and age are out of your control, you can significantly reduce your risk of heart disease by eating a diet low in saturated fats and cholesterol. A high intake of saturated fats is linked to increased cholesterol production. Dietary cholesterol is found only in animal products such as egg yolks, meats (especially organ meats), and high-fat milk products. Losing excess weight can also lower cholesterol levels.

More About...

Types of Cholesterol Lipoproteins (ly-poh-PROH-teenz) are molecules made by the liver that transport cholesterol in the blood. The cholesterol carried by low-density lipoproteins (LDLs) tends to build up in arteries. The higher the level of LDLs in the blood, the greater the risk of heart disease. High-density lipoproteins (HDLs) carry excess blood cholesterol back to the liver, where it can be eliminated. Thus, HDL cholesterol helps prevent buildup in the blood vessels. A high level of HDLs helps lower the risk of heart disease.

To reduce the risk of heart disease, limit intake of saturated fats and dietary cholesterol, both of which raise LDL levels. Increasing physical activity and losing excess weight can elevate HDL levels.

Vitamins

Vitamins are *compounds that help regulate many vital body processes, including the digestion, absorption, and metabolism of other nutrients.* Vitamins are classified as either water- or fat-soluble.

Water-soluble vitamins, listed in **Figure 5.1,** dissolve in water and pass easily into the blood during digestion. The body doesn't store these vitamins, so you need to replenish them regularly through the foods you eat. Fat-soluble vitamins are absorbed, stored, and transported in fat. Your body stores these vitamins in your fatty tissue, liver, and kidneys. Excess buildup of these vitamins in your body can be toxic. **Figure 5.2** on page 120 provides more information about fat-soluble vitamins.

FIGURE 5.1

WATER-SOLUBLE VITAMINS

Vitamin/Amount Needed Each Day	Role in Body	Food Source
C (ascorbic acid) Teen female: 60 mg Teen male: 60 mg	protects against infection, helps form connective tissue, helps heal wounds, maintains elasticity and strength of blood vessels, promotes healthy teeth and gums	citrus fruits, cantaloupe, tomatoes, cabbage, broccoli, potatoes, peppers
B₁ (thiamine) Teen female: 1.1 mg Teen male: 1.5 mg	converts glucose into energy or fat, contributes to good appetite	whole-grain or enriched cereals, liver, yeast, nuts, legumes, wheat germ
B₂ (riboflavin) Teen female: 1.3 mg Teen male: 1.8 mg	essential for producing energy from carbohydrates, fats, and proteins; helps keep skin healthy	milk, cheese, spinach, eggs, beef liver
Niacin Teen female: 15 mg Teen male: 20 mg	important for maintenance of all body tissues; helps in energy production; needed by body to utilize carbohydrates, to synthesize body fat, and for cell respiration	milk, eggs, poultry, beef, legumes, peanut butter, whole grains, enriched and fortified grain products
B₆ Teen female: 1.5 mg Teen male: 2.0 mg	essential for amino acid and carbohydrate metabolism, helps turn the amino acid *tryptophan* into serotonin (a messenger to the brain) and niacin	wheat bran and wheat germ, liver, meat, whole grains, fish, vegetables
Folic acid Teen female: 180 mcg Teen male: 200 mcg	necessary for production of genetic material and normal red blood cells, reduces risk of birth defects	nuts and other legumes, orange juice, green vegetables, folic acid-enriched breads and rolls, liver
B₁₂ Teen female: 2.0 mcg Teen male: 2.0 mcg	necessary for production of red blood cells and for normal growth	animal products such as meat, fish, poultry, eggs, milk, and other dairy foods; some fortified foods

Lesson 2 Nutrients **119**

Discussing

Have students debate whether vitamin supplements are necessary for healthy individuals. Ask them to collect information to support their position. Hold a class debate, with each student having 30 seconds to present his or her supportive evidence. Establish a rule that students cannot repeat, as part of their debate, what anyone else has said. At the end, have students draw conclusions about vitamin supplements and current consumer information regarding them. **L2**

VISUAL LEARNING

Figure 5.1 Read aloud the title and column headings for Figure 5.1. Have all students follow along as volunteers read aloud the amount needed each day, role in the body, and food sources for each vitamin. Ask students: Do you think most teens get the recommended amounts of these vitamins? Why or why not?

Explaining

Explain to students that foods containing water-soluble vitamins need to be cooked carefully so that the vitamins are not destroyed by heat or lost through steam or in cooking water. To conserve water-soluble vitamins in food:

- Cook fruits and vegetables quickly, or steam them.
- Cover food during cooking.

School to Work

Nutrition in the Cafeteria In most institutional settings, meals are planned to provide a balanced selection of healthy foods. Have students interview the food manager of a hospital, child care center, or other institution. Tell them to ask how the food manager applies the information in this chapter when planning weekly menus. Ask where planners obtain the nutritional information they need to plan balanced meals. Students may then write a menu for an institutional meal and explain the nutritional need met by each item. Have students evaluate the menus.

Reinforcing Concepts

On the board, list the categories of nutrients. Next to each, write one source of the nutrient and, in one simple sentence, describe why the body needs this nutrient. Have ELL students copy this information into their class notes for later review.

VISUAL LEARNING

Figure 5.2 Direct students to review the information presented in Figure 5.2. Have students speculate why the amounts needed each day differ for teen females and males. Then have them discuss which of the listed food sources they consume regularly.

FYI

Antioxidants are chemical compounds, including vitamins C and E, that protect the body from free radicals. Free radicals, which are formed during numerous metabolic processes, trigger destructive chemical reactions and destroy genes and cells. Fruits and vegetables are rich sources of antioxidants.

Service Learning

Have students work in groups to develop a lesson for an elementary class on the importance of nutrients. Groups might write skits, design games, or produce a video. If possible, arrange to have one or more lessons presented to a grade school class or Scout meeting, and so on. L3
Kinesthetic Intelligence

FIGURE 5.2

FAT-SOLUBLE VITAMINS

Vitamin/Amount Needed Each Day	Role in Body	Food Source
A Teen female: 800 mcg Teen male: 1,000 mcg	helps maintain skin tissue, strengthens tooth enamel, promotes use of calcium and phosphorous in bone formation, promotes cell growth, keeps eyes moist, helps eyes adjust to darkness, may aid in cancer prevention	milk and other dairy products, green vegetables, carrots, deep-orange fruits, liver
D Teen female: 5 mcg Teen male: 5 mcg	promotes absorption and use of calcium and phosphorous, essential for normal bone and tooth development	fortified milk, eggs, fortified breakfast cereals, sardines, salmon, beef, margarine; produced in skin exposed to sun's ultraviolet rays
E Teen female: 8 mg Teen male: 10 mg	may help in oxygen transport, may slow the effects of aging, may protect against destruction of red blood cells	present in vegetable oils, apples, peaches, nectarines, legumes, nuts, seeds, wheat germ
K Teen female: 55 mcg Teen male: 65 mcg	essential for blood clotting, assists in regulating blood calcium level	spinach, broccoli, eggs, liver, cabbage, tomatoes

You get many of the minerals your body needs from these types of foods.

Minerals

Minerals are *substances that the body cannot manufacture but that are needed for forming healthy bones and teeth and for regulating many vital body processes.* Several key minerals are described in **Figure 5.3.**

Water

Water is vital to every body function. It transports other nutrients to and carries wastes from your cells. Water also lubricates your joints and mucous membranes. It enables you to swallow and digest foods, absorb other nutrients, and eliminate wastes. Through perspiration, water helps maintain normal body temperature. It's important to drink at least 8 cups of water a day to maintain health. Plain water, milk, and juice are the best sources of this nutrient. Beverages containing caffeine, such as tea, coffee, and some soft drinks, are not good choices—they cause you to lose some water through increased urination. Certain foods, such as fruits and vegetables, also contain some water.

More About...

Fluid Replacement Sports drinks designed to replace salts lost in perspiration are not necessary unless an individual loses more than 3 quarts of water (about 6 pounds of weight) during an activity. People lose proportionately more water than salts when they perspire. Thus, the most pressing need is to replace the lost water. Salt tablets are not recommended, and concentrated salt should not be consumed unless large quantities of water are drunk at the same time.

FIGURE 5.3

SOME IMPORTANT MINERALS

Mineral/Amount Needed Each Day	Role in Body	Food Source
Calcium Teen female: 1,300 mg Teen male: 1,300 mg	building material of bones and teeth (skeleton contains about 99% of body calcium), regulation of body functions (heart muscle contraction, blood clotting)	dairy products; leafy vegetables; canned fish with soft, edible bones; tofu processed with calcium sulfate
Phosphorous Teen female: 1,250 mg Teen male: 1,250 mg	combines with calcium to give rigidity to bones and teeth, essential in cell metabolism, helps maintain proper acid-base balance of blood	milk and most other dairy foods, peas, beans, liver, meat, fish, poultry, eggs, broccoli, whole grains
Magnesium Teen female: 360 mg Teen male: 410 mg	enzyme activator related to carbohydrate metabolism, aids in bone growth and muscle contraction	whole grains, milk, dark green leafy vegetables, legumes, nuts
Iron Teen female: 15 mg Teen male: 12 mg	part of the red blood cells' oxygen and carbon dioxide transport system, important for use of energy in cells and for resistance to infection	meat, shellfish, poultry, legumes, peanuts, dried fruits, egg yolks, liver, fortified breakfast cereal, enriched rice

 Lesson 2 *Review*

Reviewing Facts and Vocabulary

1. Compare the energy provided to the body by carbohydrates, proteins, and fats.

2. Analyze the relationship between good nutrition and disease prevention: How can reducing your saturated fat intake help lower the risk of heart disease?

3. What are *vitamins*?

Thinking Critically

4. **Analyzing.** Your friend Steve wants to cut down on his intake of saturated fats and cholesterol. What advice would you give him?

5. **Synthesizing.** What are the benefits of eating a variety of fruits and vegetables?

Applying Health Skills

Goal Setting. Copy your school's weekly lunch menus, and examine each day's options. Using what you've learned about nutrients in this lesson, list the most healthful food choices available each day. Then set a goal to eat healthful school lunches for the next week. Use the goal-setting steps to help you create a plan.

SPREADSHEETS Use spreadsheet software to keep track of the meals you create from each day's school menu. Find help in using spreadsheet software at **health.glencoe.com**.

Lesson 2 Nutrients **121**

 VISUAL LEARNING

Figure 5.3 Have students examine the information in Figure 5.3. Help them understand the importance of these minerals for good health by asking: What health problems might result if a person did not have enough calcium in his or her diet? Enough iron?

③ ASSESS

EVALUATING THE LESSON

Assign and discuss the Lesson 2 Review; then administer, grade, and discuss Lesson Quiz 17 in the TCR. 📁

RETEACHING

- Have students create an outline of the main ideas covered in this lesson.

- Ask students to complete Reteaching Activity 17 in the TCR. 📁

④ CLOSE

Write the six nutrients—carbohydrates, proteins, fats, vitamins, minerals, and water—on slips of paper. Divide the class into six groups, and have one student from each group draw a slip. Ask each group to create a list of facts about their nutrient. Then have groups read their list aloud.

 Lesson 2 *Review*

Answers to Reviewing Facts and Vocabulary

1. Carbohydrates/proteins: 4 calories per gram; fats: 9 calories per gram.

2. Reducing saturated fat intake can lower blood cholesterol levels, which decreases heart disease risk.

3. Vitamins are compounds that help regulate many vital body processes, including the digestion, absorption, and metabolism of other nutrients.

Answers to Thinking Critically

4. Possible answer: Reduce consumption of animal products.

5. Fruits and vegetables provide vitamins and minerals; many provide fiber.

Guidelines for Healthful Eating

1 FOCUS

QUICK START   Review the five food groups with the class. Then have students brainstorm ideas for healthful eating habits for each food group. After students have completed their word webs, ask for volunteers to share their webs with the class.

TYING TO PRIOR KNOWLEDGE

Ask students to list the five food groups on a sheet of paper, and under each group, write the names of at least three foods that belong in that group. Have students put a checkmark next to the foods they eat most often. Challenge students to discover the importance of eating a variety of foods from each of the food groups as they explore this lesson.

Health Skills Features

"Smart Snacking," p. 127

PRACTICING HEALTHFUL BEHAVIORS

INTRODUCING VOCABULARY

- Divide students into pairs. Have one student write a sentence that uses both vocabulary terms. Have the other write the meaning of both terms based on context.

- Ask students to complete the Chapter 5 Study Guide in the *Student Activity Workbook*.

122

Lesson 3

Guidelines for Healthful Eating

VOCABULARY
Dietary Guidelines for Americans
Food Guide Pyramid

YOU'LL LEARN TO
- Evaluate the concepts of balance, variety, and moderation, using the Food Guide Pyramid and national dietary guidelines.
- Examine the effects of healthful eating behaviors on body systems.
- Select healthful meals and snacks as part of a balanced diet.

QUICK START   Make a word web of healthful eating habits. Write "Healthful Eating" in the middle of a sheet of paper. Then, around the edges of the paper, add phrases such as "Eat five fruits and vegetables a day"—one phrase for each of the major food groups. Connect these to the center phrase with lines.

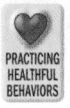 **Choosing nutritious foods from the thousands of products available can be a challenge.** *What are some factors to consider when shopping for food?*

No single food provides all the nutrients your body needs. That's why it is so important to eat a balanced variety of nutrient-rich foods each day. There are tools to help you select the most nutritious foods in the appropriate amounts.

Dietary Guidelines for Americans

The U.S. Department of Agriculture (USDA) and the Department of Health and Human Services (DHHS) have published a booklet titled *Nutrition and Your Health: Dietary Guidelines for Americans.* The **Dietary Guidelines for Americans** is *a set of recommendations for healthful eating and active living.*

The recommendations in the *Dietary Guidelines* are grouped into three broad areas known as the ABCs of good health. Following the ABCs will help you stay fit and will ensure variety, balance, and moderation in your food choices. It can also help lower your risk of developing chronic diseases, such as those of the cardiovascular system.

122   **Chapter 5** Nutrition and Your Health

Lesson 3 *Resources*

Teacher Classroom Resources
- 📁 Concept Mapping Activity 18
- 📁 Cross-Curriculum Activity 5
- 📁 Current Health Issues 5
- 📁 Guided Reading Activities 18
- 📁 Lesson Plan 18
- 📁 Lesson Quiz 18
- 📁 Reteaching Activity 18

Student Activity Workbook
- 📁 Applying Health Skills 18
- 📁 Chapter 5 Study Guide

Multimedia
- 🖨 Transparency 15

A: Aim for Fitness

The "A" in the ABCs of good health deals with fitness goals. In addition to healthful eating, regular physical activity is important to staying well. To improve or maintain fitness, follow these guidelines.

▶ **Aim for a healthy weight.** Maintaining a healthy weight helps you look and feel good. A health care professional can help you determine a healthy weight for your height and age and the best way to achieve or maintain that weight.

▶ **Be physically active each day.** Daily physical activity benefits your overall health and can improve fitness. To maintain fitness, try to include at least 60 minutes of moderate physical activity in your daily routine.

B: Build a Healthy Base

The "B" in the ABCs relates to building a healthful eating plan. The "base" of this food plan is the **Food Guide Pyramid**, *a guide for making healthful daily food choices*. The following guidelines can help you build a healthy base.

▶ **Make your food choices carefully.** Eat the recommended number of daily servings from each of the five major food groups in the Food Guide Pyramid.

▶ **Choose a variety of grain products, especially whole grains.** Most of your daily food choices should be grain products. Whole-grain products are rich in complex carbohydrates and fiber, as well as some vitamins and minerals. Examples of whole-grain products include whole-wheat bread, oatmeal, and brown rice.

▶ **Choose a variety of fruits and vegetables daily.** Fruits and vegetables are rich in vitamins and minerals; some are high in fiber. Eating a variety of these foods will keep you healthy and may help protect you from many chronic diseases.

▶ **Keep food safe to eat.** You can reduce your risk of illness by cooking foods thoroughly, handling food with clean utensils, refrigerating perishable foods, and washing your hands before and after you handle foods. These steps make it less likely that food will cause sickness from harmful organisms and other contaminants.

Ⓨ **Choosing a variety of fruits and vegetables each day is an important part of building a healthy base.** *What fruits and vegetables would you choose as an afternoon snack?*

Lesson 3 Guidelines for Healthful Eating **123**

② TEACH

Activity

Organize a group "scrambler." Divide the class into five groups to compete against one another. Provide a list of foods that belong in the five food groups. Have each student group attempt to place all the listed foods in the correct groups as quickly as possible. Students with the fastest time and accuracy win. ◧

Explaining

Stress the value of selecting low-fat foods in the milk and meat groups, low-fat and low-sugar preparation methods for the fruit and vegetable groups, and high-fiber and whole-grain foods in the bread and cereals group. To confirm that students can identify low-fat, low-sugar, high-fiber, and whole-grain foods on their own, have them give examples of each. ◧

Discussing

Many foods that are naturally low in fat often are prepared with considerable added fat. Fried and creamed dishes, dressings, and condiments often make some of the lowest fat foods into some of the highest fat meals. Ask students to suggest at least one high-fat and one low-fat method of preparing each of the following: chicken, fish, potatoes, corn, and apples. ◧

∿ HEALTH LITERACY

Maintaining a Healthy Weight Here's one way to get a rough idea of your daily calorie needs. If you are extremely inactive, you need about 12 calories per pound to stay at your current weight. If you are involved in light activity, such as doing homework or household tasks, you need 15 calories per pound. When you're moderately active, such as when you are walking briskly or cycling, you need up to 20 calories per pound. So if you are a moderately active person weighing 140 pounds, your needs are 140 × 20, or 2,800 calories a day.

Cooperative Learning

Ask students to name their favorite foods, and record the names of those foods on the board. Then have students form cooperative groups, and divide the listed foods among the groups. Ask the members of each group to evaluate the foods they have been assigned, identify where the foods fit in the Food Guide Pyramid, and decide how frequently the foods should be eaten. Let each group discuss its evaluations with the rest of the class. L1

VISUAL LEARNING

Figure 5.4 Have students review the five food groups and the recommended number of daily servings as shown in the Food Guide Pyramid. Ask students to write down the names of the five food groups, and next to each one, note the average number of servings from that group that they eat each day. Tell students to incorporate this information into a graph or chart that represents their own eating habits. Then have them compare their graphs or charts with the Food Guide Pyramid. Ask students: Is your eating plan balanced? If not, what changes could you make to improve your food choices?

HEALTH Online

For more information on the Food Guide Pyramid, go to **health.glencoe.com.**

The Food Guide Pyramid

The Food Guide Pyramid, shown in **Figure 5.4,** is a useful tool for making healthful food choices each day. Notice that grain products are at the base of the pyramid—this means that most of your daily servings should come from the grain group. By eating the recommended number of daily servings from each food group, you'll achieve a balanced eating plan. The tip of the pyramid (Fats, Oils, and Sweets) is not a food group; these products should be consumed sparingly.

Keep in mind that meals often include foods from more than one group. What groups are represented in a meal of spaghetti with meat sauce?

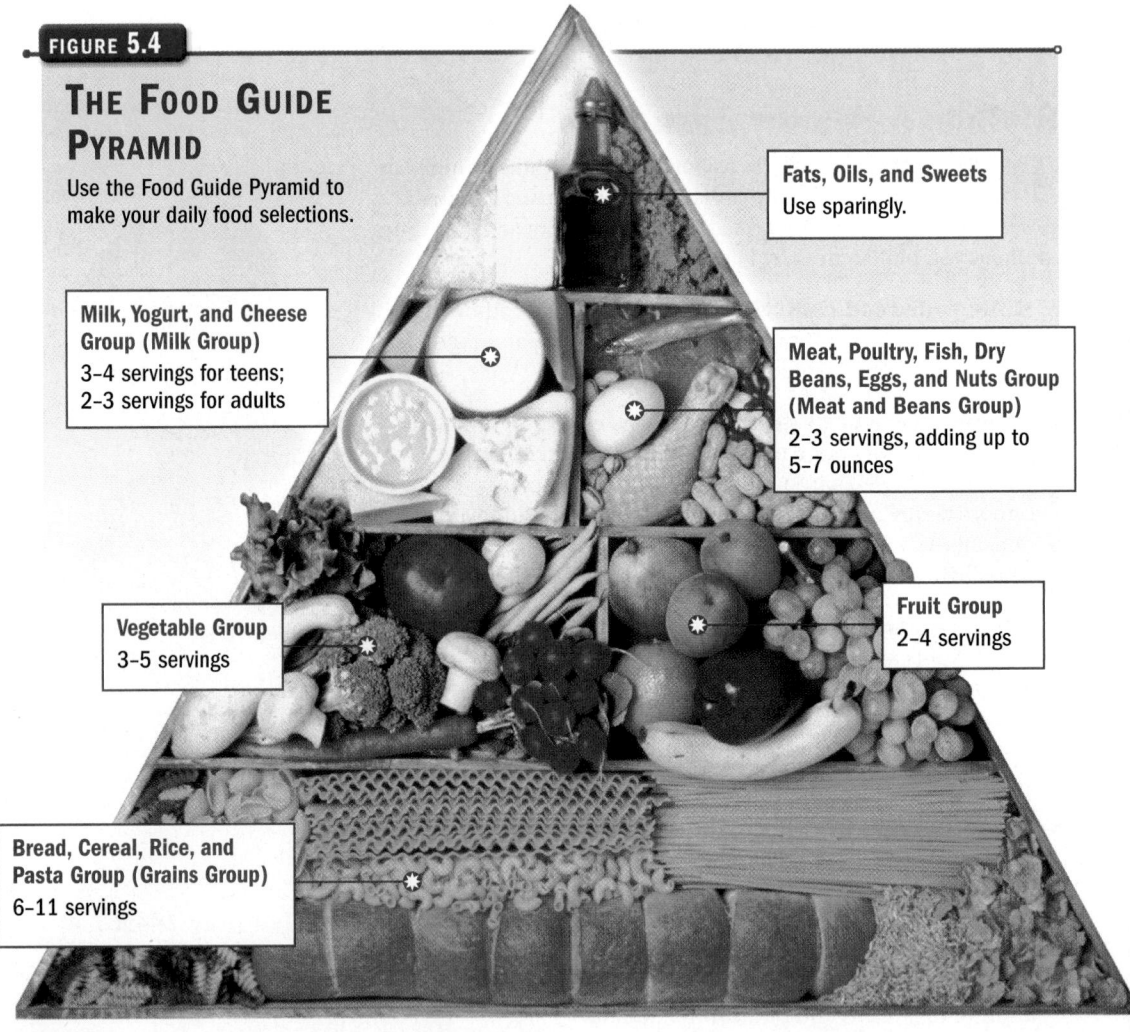

FIGURE 5.4

THE FOOD GUIDE PYRAMID

Use the Food Guide Pyramid to make your daily food selections.

Fats, Oils, and Sweets
Use sparingly.

Milk, Yogurt, and Cheese Group (Milk Group)
3–4 servings for teens;
2–3 servings for adults

Meat, Poultry, Fish, Dry Beans, Eggs, and Nuts Group (Meat and Beans Group)
2–3 servings, adding up to 5–7 ounces

Vegetable Group
3–5 servings

Fruit Group
2–4 servings

Bread, Cereal, Rice, and Pasta Group (Grains Group)
6–11 servings

More About...

The Food Guide Pyramid The Food Guide Pyramid represents a clear, useful depiction of current recommendations for healthful eating. Following these recommendations offers important health benefits to people of all ages, including:

• Increased energy and improved physical and mental performance.

• Achievement or maintenance of a healthful body weight.

• Protection against five of the ten leading causes of death, including stroke, coronary heart disease, certain cancers, diabetes, and atherosclerosis.

FIGURE 5.5

Chapter 5 • Lesson 3

SERVING SIZES

Grains Group	Vegetable Group	Fruit Group	Milk Group	Meat and Beans Group
• 1 slice bread • 1 tortilla • ½ small bagel • 1 cup dry cereal • ½ cup cooked cereal, rice, or pasta	• 1 cup raw leafy vegetables • ½ cup cooked or raw vegetables • ¾ cup vegetable juice	• 1 medium apple, orange, pear, or banana • ½ cup chopped, cooked, or canned fruit • ¾ cup fruit juice	• 1 cup milk or yogurt • 1.5 oz. natural cheese, such as Swiss • 2 oz. processed cheese	• 2–3 oz. cooked lean meat, fish, or poultry **Equivalents of 1 oz. of meat:** • ½ cup cooked dry beans/tofu • 1 egg • 2 tbsp. peanut butter • ⅓ cup nuts

Understanding Serving Sizes

The Food Guide Pyramid's recommended number of daily servings may seem like a lot of food to eat in one day. However, understanding what constitutes a serving will help you see how much food is actually being recommended. **Figure 5.5** lists sample serving sizes for each food group. Understanding serving sizes will help you practice portion control. A portion is how much of a food you eat in one meal. Visualizing some common objects can help you estimate serving sizes and control portions. For example, a medium apple is about the size of a tennis ball. One serving of meat is about the size of a regular computer mouse. A piece of meat twice this size equals two servings. To balance your daily food choices, try to eat enough servings from all five major food groups.

C: Choose Sensibly

The "C" in the ABCs of good health involves making sensible food choices, including

► choosing a diet that is low in saturated fat and cholesterol and moderate in total fat.

► choosing beverages and foods to moderate your intake of sugars.

► choosing and preparing foods with less salt.

CHARACTER CHECK

Citizenship. Citizenship means doing what you can to improve your community. For example, there may be people in your community who go hungry. **Find out how to organize an effort to collect nonperishable food items for a local food bank or homeless shelter. How could this benefit the whole community?**

Figure 5.5 Have volunteers read aloud the sample serving sizes for each food group shown in Figure 5.5. Remind students that a recommended serving may be smaller than they think. Discuss the current trend of restaurants offering extra-large portions. Ask students: What long-term effects might this trend have on public health?

Critical Thinking

Discuss with students the differences in the number of recommended servings for foods from the major groups:

• How do you think age, gender, and activity levels affect the recommended number of servings?

• Do you think all 14-year-old boys should eat more than all 14-year-old girls? Explain.

• Do you think all the members of a soccer team should have the same number of servings from each food group? Why or why not? **L1**

Health Skills Practice

On-The-Go Food Choices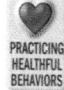
Read aloud the following to students: Skipping a meal may seem easy, but it is hard on your growing body. To get the balanced nutrition you need, plan ahead. Make a list of at least five healthy food choices you can eat "on the run" or carry in your backpack to add to a meal. You're looking for foods that are rich in nutrients and low in saturated fat and cholesterol. Read food labels, and write down three choices.

Cooperative Learning Activity

Healthy Fast-Food Recommendations

Some people rely on fast food when they are away from home at mealtimes and do not have the time or the money to eat at restaurants with the healthiest food choices. However, many fast-food restaurants offer healthy options. Divide students into groups. Have each group member collect menus and nutrition brochures from two fast-food restaurants in your area. Direct groups to choose one of the healthiest items and one of the unhealthiest items from each fast-food establishment. Have them discuss whether they would be willing to choose the healthiest foods. Of the foods they are willing to eat, which is the healthiest at each establishment? Students may wish to provide their recommendations to interested classmates.

Reinforcing Concepts

Provide a variety of food labels, and ask students to determine the percentage of calories from fat in one serving. Have them summarize their findings in a chart, ranking each food from highest to lowest in percentage of fat content. **L3**

Explaining

Point out that sugar comes in many forms. Among the most common are sucrose, lactose, fructose, dextrose, and maltose. Encourage students to look for these sugars on food package labels. Also, remind them to look for words such as sugar, brown sugar, honey, corn syrup, corn sweeteners, and concentrated fruit juice. **L1**

Quick Demo

On colored paper plates, have students shake a salt shaker as if they were salting a serving of French fries. Then have them use measuring spoons to measure the salt. Ask how much salt they would have used in this instance: About how much sodium is that? Less than $\frac{1}{4}$ teaspoon of salt a day is needed to meet the body's sodium needs. Talk about ways to reduce salt intake. **L1**

Health Minute

Ask for volunteers to read aloud the strategies for making healthful food choices. Have students choose one of these strategies and create a catchy slogan that might appear on a T-shirt or bumper sticker. Have volunteers share their slogans with the class.

Health Minute

These strategies can help you make healthful food choices.

To limit dietary fat and cholesterol:

▶ Aim to get most of your calories from whole grains, vegetables, and fruits.

▶ Read labels on prepared foods to determine how much total fat, saturated fat, and cholesterol a serving of the food contains.

▶ Calculate the percentage of fat in one serving: Divide calories from fat by total calories.

▶ Try to choose foods that have 3 grams or less of fat per serving. These foods are considered low in fat.

Moderation in Fats

While some dietary fats are necessary for good health, most Americans eat too many fats. The *Dietary Guidelines* recommends that no more than 30 percent of daily calories come from fats, yet most Americans consume a diet that averages a significantly higher percentage. Eating less fat, especially saturated fat, lowers your risk of cardiovascular disease. You don't have to completely eliminate your favorite high-fat foods to limit your intake to no more than 30 percent of calories from fat. If you eat high-fat foods at one meal, eat foods that are lower in fats at other meals.

Moderation in Sugar

You might think that you don't eat much added sugar, but sugars are hidden everywhere, including in prepared foods. You can moderate your sugar intake by

▶ learning to identify added sugars by their names on food packages. Corn syrup, honey, and molasses are all types of sugar, as are ingredients ending with *-ose*, such as sucrose and maltose.

▶ balancing foods that have added sugars with foods that have less added sugars.

▶ limiting your intake of foods that have added sugars but few other nutrients. For example, choose 100 percent fruit juice or water instead of regular soda.

▶ choosing fresh fruits or canned fruits packed in water or juice.

Moderation in Salt

Sodium is an essential mineral. It helps transport nutrients into your cells and helps move wastes out. It also helps maintain normal blood pressure and nerve function. However, most Americans consume far too much salt, much of it from processed foods. Consuming less salt can reduce your chances of developing high blood pressure and may also benefit your skeletal system by decreasing the loss of calcium from bone. Try these tips to moderate your salt intake.

▶ Read the Nutrition Facts panel on food labels to find out how much sodium a serving contains.

▶ Season foods with herbs and spices instead of with salt.

▶ When eating at restaurants, ask for foods that are prepared without salt or salty flavorings or with reduced amounts of them.

▶ Taste foods before you salt them, and then go easy with the salt shaker.

▶ Choose fruits and vegetables often. They contain very little salt unless it is added in processing.

Curriculum Connections

Social Studies Have students choose a country and research the eating patterns in that country. They may wish to interview a foreign student. Ask them to find answers to questions such as: How many meals are eaten each day? What are some typical meals? Are foods high (or low) in fat, sugar, and salt? Are snacks an important part of the eating plan? What percentage of meals are eaten at home? Are fast foods popular? Then have students imagine they are from that country. Invite them to write a letter describing their typical diet, favorite foods, etc. Remind them to check their work for spelling and grammar. Have students write a final draft for classroom display.

Real-Life Application

Smart Snacking

Eating several small snacks each day can help growing teens get the nutrients they need. You can choose snacks that promote good health without adding too much fat or too many calories.

Nutrition Facts

Serving Size 1 cookie (17g)
Servings Per Container about 27

Amount Per Serving	
Calories 90	Calories from Fat 45
	% Daily Value*
Total Fat 5g	**8%**
Saturated Fat 2.5g	**13%**
Cholesterol 5mg	**2%**
Sodium 80mg	**3%**
Total Carbohydrate 11g	**4%**
Dietary Fiber 0g	**0%**
Sugars 6g	
Protein 1g	

Vitamin A	0% •	Vitamin C	0%
Calcium	0% •	Iron	2%

* Percent Daily Values are based on a 2,000 calorie diet. Your daily values may be higher or lower depending on your calorie needs:

ACTIVITY

In small groups, examine the snack labels that your group or teacher has brought to class. Use the above callouts to help you identify snacks that are low in fat and sugar. In a paragraph, explain other ways the information on labels can help you choose nutritious snacks.

Calories from Fat
Look at this section of the Nutrition Facts panel to find out how much fat is in the snack you are choosing.

Total Fat
This gives you an overview of the fat in the snack. The amount of fat is listed in grams. Remember that fats provide 9 calories per gram, so even small amounts of fats can add a lot of calories.

Saturated Fat
This tells how much of the fat in the snack is saturated. Remember, limiting saturated fats can help reduce the risk of heart disease.

Total Carbohydrate
Under this heading you'll find information about sugars. These, too, are listed in grams. Carbohydrates provide 4 calories per gram.

Healthful Eating Patterns

Whether you eat three meals a day or even more "mini-meals," *variety, moderation,* and *balance* are the foundation of a healthful eating plan. Many people, including teens, find making healthful food choices particularly challenging when having breakfast, snacking, and eating out. Keep in mind that nutrition guidelines apply to all of your daily food choices, not to just a single meal or food. Any food that supplies calories and nutrients can be part of a healthful eating plan. You don't have to deprive yourself of your favorite foods. With a little planning, you can fit them into your diet.

Lesson 3 Guidelines for Healthful Eating **127**

Promoting Coordinated School Health

Role Models Teachers, administrators, and other school staff members can be important role models for students. So can adult family members and other members of the local community. Because eating involves all three components of health—physical, mental/emotional, and social—mealtimes provide a good opportunity for adults to model appropriate choices and behaviors.

Take the time to join students occasionally for lunch (or breakfast, if it is served at your school), and encourage other staff members to do the same. Also, encourage students to invite parents, guardians, or other adult family members or friends to visit the school for a meal. For more information, consult *Planning a Coordinated School Health Program.*

Reinforcing Concepts

Encourage students to plan a breakfast menu that includes at least one nontraditional breakfast food. Stress that the menu should be well balanced and supply about one-third of the day's calories. Discuss the completed menus. Ask volunteers to list nontraditional breakfast foods or breakfast ideas from other cultures that they enjoy eating. **L2**

Discussing

Snacking is a typical teen eating pattern. Have students list snack foods in each food group, including the Fats, Oils, and Sweets group. Ask them to identify which snacks are the most nutritious. **L1**

VISUAL LEARNING

Figure 5.6 Direct students to review the information shown in Figure 5.6. Divide the class into small groups. Direct groups to use classroom resources, including the Internet, to find five additional healthful snacks. Have each group create a new chart using the same headings as Figure 5.6 but including information on the healthful snacks they have found. List one snack from each student group on the board.

⚠ **Many types of foods can be part of a healthy breakfast.** *Name three nontraditional breakfast foods that you might like to try.*

The Importance of Breakfast

You've probably heard the saying, "Breakfast is the most important meal of the day." While you sleep, your body uses energy for functions such as breathing and keeping your heart beating. By the time you wake up, your body needs a fresh supply of energy. Studies show that eating a nutritious breakfast improves mental and physical performance and reduces fatigue later in the day. If you eat breakfast, you tend to perform better in school, get better grades, and miss fewer days of school. Eating breakfast may also help you maintain a healthy weight. Skipping this meal may cause you to overeat later in the day.

Breakfast foods don't have to be "traditional," such as cereal or eggs. Try eating pizza, peanut butter on toast, or a stuffed tomato. To get enough vitamin C, add citrus juice, fruit, or tomato juice to your meal. Breakfast is also a good time to eat a high-fiber cereal and get one calcium-rich serving of milk, cheese, or yogurt.

Nutritious Snacks

A healthful eating plan can include sensible snacks. When you think about snacks, you might think of potato chips, soft drinks, and candy bars. These foods contain a lot of calories but very few nutrients. They may also be high in fat, added sugars, or salt. More healthful snacks include whole-grain products, fruits, and vegetables. Food companies have also started offering healthier snack choices, such as potato chips that are baked instead of fried. **Figure 5.6** lists some healthful snack items.

FIGURE 5.6

SENSIBLE SNACKS

Food	Food Group	Total Calories per Serving	Calories from Fat
Air-popped popcorn, 3 cups (plain)	Grains	23	0
Apple, 1 medium	Fruit	80	0
Bagel, ½ (small, 2 oz.)	Grains	83	10
Bread stick, 1	Grains	42	6
Frozen juice bar, 4 oz.	Fruit	75	0
Skim milk, 1 cup	Milk	90	0
Sugar-free gelatin (½ cup) with ½ cup sliced banana	Fruit	76	0
Graham cracker squares, 3	Grains	80	15
Pretzel sticks, 50 small	Grains	60	9
Fat-free, sugar-free yogurt, 6 oz.	Milk	86	0

〜∿〜 **HEALTH LITERACY** 〜∿〜

Nutritious Snacks Present students with the following tips for healthy snack choices:

- To add protein to the diet, try hard-boiled eggs, pieces of cheese, chunks of tuna, or slices of leftover roast or steak.
- To add vitamin C to the diet, try strawberries, other berries, melon, tomatoes, citrus fruits, raw pineapple, or nectarines.
- To add vitamin A to the diet, eat carrot sticks, raw broccoli, green pepper rings, or dark green vegetables. Also try yellow fruits and vegetables.
- To add calcium to the diet, try any low-fat dairy product, custard, or cottage cheese.
- To add B vitamins and minerals to the diet, eat whole-grain or enriched breads and cereals, dairy products, nuts, or raisins.

Eating Out, Eating Right

Part of healthful eating is making sensible food choices when you eat out. It might help to use the Food Guide Pyramid when ordering restaurant food. Also, be aware that many menu items may be fried or topped with mayonnaise, butter, or high-fat sauces. For less fat, order foods that are grilled, baked, or broiled, and ask that high-fat sauces not be used at all or be served on the side. Many fast-food restaurants list the calorie counts and other nutrition information for the foods they serve. You can ask to see this list before placing your order.

When eating out, don't forget to think about portion control. The portion sizes of most restaurant meals are much larger than the serving sizes in the Food Guide Pyramid. You may want to eat only part of a portion and take the rest home to enjoy later. As an alternative, offset the larger meal with a smaller meal later.

When eating out, don't hesitate to ask how a particular dish is cooked or what ingredients it contains. *Name two other ways to make healthy food choices when eating out.*

Lesson 3 Review

Reviewing Facts and Vocabulary

1. Define the *Dietary Guidelines for Americans*.
2. What is the purpose of the Food Guide Pyramid?
3. Examine the effects of healthful eating behaviors on body systems: How can decreasing salt intake benefit the cardiovascular and skeletal systems?

Thinking Critically

4. **Analyzing.** Why might a person eat fewer servings than recommended by the Food Guide Pyramid and still gain an unhealthful amount of weight?
5. **Evaluating.** For lunch Josh had a cheeseburger, fries, and a nondiet soft drink. What could he choose for his afternoon snack and dinner to balance out his high-fat, high-sugar, high-salt meal?

Applying Health Skills

Advocacy. Work with a partner to create a poster that encourages teens to adopt healthful eating habits. Use pictures cut from magazines, computer graphics, or your own drawings to illustrate your poster.

WEB SITES Use information and drawings from your poster to create a Web page encouraging teens to develop healthful eating habits. See **health.glencoe.com** for help with planning and building your own Web site.

Lesson 3 Guidelines for Healthful Eating **129**

Activity

Have students create their ideal nutritious menu for school lunches, including creative descriptors and icons for low-fat, low-sugar, and low-salt foods. Remind them to check their work for spelling and grammar.

3 ASSESS

EVALUATING THE LESSON

Assign and discuss the Lesson 3 Review; then administer, grade, and discuss Lesson Quiz 18 in the TCR.

RETEACHING

- Direct students to choose partners. Have students test one another on lesson content by having each student create a five-question quiz to exchange with his or her partner. After students have finished taking the quiz, they can check their answers against the book.
- Ask students to complete Reteaching Activity 18 in the TCR.

ENRICHMENT

Have students research current studies on the effects of dietary fat on health. Encourage them to share their findings with the class.

Lesson 3 Review

Answers to Reviewing Facts and Vocabulary

1. A set of recommendations for healthy eating and active living.
2. A guide for making healthful daily food choices.
3. Consuming less salt can reduce the risk of developing high blood pressure and decrease the loss of calcium from bone.

Answers to Thinking Critically

4. Possible answer: If a person does not control portion sizes, he or she may actually be eating more servings than recommended in the Pyramid.
5. Answers will vary. Food choices should include foods that are low in fat, sugar, and salt.

4 CLOSE

Have students work in small groups to write a summary of the main ideas outlined in the *Dietary Guidelines for Americans*. Have them proofread their work for organization and content.

Food and Healthy Living

Lesson 4

Food and Healthy Living

1 FOCUS

 QUICK START Draw a word web on the board by writing *Nutrition Labels* in the center and have students share their written responses to the Quick Start activity.

TYING TO PRIOR KNOWLEDGE

Have students write down the name of a packaged food product they like—perhaps a breakfast cereal, canned soup, or snack item. Then have them write down at least five pieces of information that can be found on the product's packaging. Tell students that they will be learning more about food labels in this lesson.

INTRODUCING VOCABULARY

- Direct students' attention to the vocabulary terms *food allergy, food intolerance,* and *foodborne illness.* Discuss with the class the meaning of each of these terms. Then have students compose a short paragraph using the three terms.

- Ask students to complete the Chapter 5 Study Guide in the *Student Activity Workbook.* 📁

VOCABULARY
- **food additives**
- **food allergy**
- **food intolerance**
- **foodborne illness**
- **pasteurization**
- **cross-contamination**

YOU'LL LEARN TO
- Utilize the information on food labels.
- Develop specific eating plans to meet changing nutritional requirements, such as special dietary needs and food allergies.
- Analyze the influence of policies and practices on the prevention of foodborne illness.
- Develop and analyze strategies related to the prevention of foodborne illness.

→ **QUICK START** The nutrition labels on food products contain information that can help you choose healthy foods. Make a list of the types of information that could assist you in making healthy food choices.

 The labels on packaged food products contain valuable information for the consumer.

Using the Food Guide Pyramid is one good way to assess the nutritional contribution of a particular food to your overall eating pattern. Similarly, the information on packaged and prepared foods can help you determine whether or not a particular product meets your nutritional needs. When you know exactly what you're buying, you'll be able to make sound decisions about what you're eating. Part of health literacy also involves understanding and evaluating food product claims.

Nutrition Labeling

Examine almost any food package, and you'll find a Nutrition Facts panel. The law requires that these information panels be placed on packages of food that are intended for sale. The information provided in a Nutrition Facts panel is shown in **Figure 5.7.**

130 Chapter 5 Nutrition and Your Health

Lesson 4 *Resources*

Teacher Classroom Resources
- 📁 Concept Mapping Activity 19
- 📁 Guided Reading Activities 19
- 📁 Health Lab 5
- 📁 Lesson Plan 19
- 📁 Lesson Quiz 19
- 📁 Reteaching Activity 19

Student Activity Workbook
- 📁 Applying Health Skills 19
- 📁 Chapter 5 Study Guide

Multimedia
- Transparency 16

FIGURE 5.7

Chapter 5 • Lesson 4

NUTRITION FACTS

Nutrition Facts
Serving Size 30g (about 12 pretzels)
Servings Per Container 30

Amount Per Serving	
Calories 110	Calories from Fat 10

	% Daily Value*
Total Fat 1g	**2%**
Saturated Fat 0g	**0%**
Cholesterol 0mg	**0%**
Sodium 300mg	**13%**
Total Carbohydrate 23g	**8%**
Dietary Fiber 1g	**4%**
Sugars Less than 1g	
Protein 3g	

Vitamin A	0% •	Vitamin C	0%
Calcium	0% •	Iron	4%

* Percent Daily Values are based on a 2,000
calorie diet. Your daily values may be higher
or lower depending on your calorie needs:

Total Fat	Less Than	65g	80g
Sat Fat	Less Than	20g	25g
Cholesterol	Less Than	300mg	300mg
Sodium	Less Than	2,400mg	2,400mg
Total Carbohydrate		300g	375g
Dietary Fiber		25g	30g

Calories per gram:
Fat 9 • Carbohydrate 4 • Protein 4

Serving Size and Servings Per Container
- Nutrient and calorie content is calculated according to serving size. The serving size on the label may differ from sizes in the Food Guide Pyramid. The number of servings in the package is also listed.

Calories and Calories from Fat
- The number of calories in one serving and how many of these calories come from fat is given here.

Nutrients (Top section)
- The amounts of total fat, saturated fat, cholesterol, and sodium per serving are listed in either grams (g) or milligrams (mg).
- The amounts of total carbohydrates, dietary fiber, sugars, and protein per serving are given.

Nutrients (Bottom section)
- Major vitamins and minerals are listed with their Percent Daily Values.

Percent Daily Value
- This section tells you how much the nutrients in one serving contribute to your total daily eating plan. The general guideline is that 20% or more of a nutrient is a lot and 5% or less isn't very much. Choose foods that are high in fiber, vitamins, and minerals and low in fat, cholesterol, and sodium.

The Footnote (Lower part of Nutrition Facts Panel)
- This information is the same from product to product. It contains advice about the amounts of certain nutrients that should be eaten each day.

Ingredients List

Most food labels also list the food's ingredients by weight, in descending order, with the ingredient in the greatest amount listed first. However, food labels that list several similar ingredients can be confusing. For example, when three sweeteners—sugar, honey, and corn syrup—are used in the same product, each is listed separately; therefore, they appear lower on the list than they would if they were counted as one ingredient, "sugars." This may give the impression that the product contains less sugar than it really does.

FOOD ADDITIVES

Some ingredients are **food additives**, *substances intentionally added to food to produce a desired effect.* Additives may be used to enhance a food's flavor or color or lengthen its storage life.

Lesson 4 Food and Healthy Living **131**

Food Labels Nutrition labels list ingredients by weight in descending order. This can be deceptive, however, since fat, sodium, or sugar may be added in several forms. For example, on a jar of plum jam with 3 ounces of plums, 2 ¾ ounces of cane sugar, and 2 ¼ ounces of corn syrup, the ingredients read "plums, cane sugar, corn syrup." This suggests that the jam contains more fruit than sugar, when the amounts are almost the same. Have students find five food products that list more than one type of sugar, fat, or sodium; copy the list of ingredients and total grams of fat, sugar, and sodium; and report their findings to the class.

② TEACH

Figure 5.7 Ask for volunteers to read aloud the information shown in Figure 5.7. Have students work in small groups to create a Nutrition Facts panel for a fictional food product. Tell them to include a name and description of the product. Have groups exchange Nutrition Facts panels for evaluation. Ask students: Does the panel include all of the required information? Does the nutrition information seem realistic given the product description? Would the name and description appeal to its target audience?

Critical Thinking

Ask students to bring nutrition information labels from cereal boxes, snack foods, and other processed foods to class. Collect the labels, read aloud the nutrient content from one label, and ask the class to guess the type of food. Discuss why some packaged foods are calorie rich but nutrient poor. **L1**

Cooperative Learning

Divide the class into two teams. Give food labels with nutrient information to each team. Have one team call out a nutrient listed on a package. In 15 seconds, the other team must name a health benefit of the nutrient and one food where the nutrient can be found. If the team answers correctly, they receive a point. The first team to reach 20 points wins. **L2**

Explaining

Explain that some foods are enriched or fortified to improve their nutrient value. Enriched foods contain nutrients that have been replaced after being lost in processing. For example, many breads contain refined grains that are enriched with vitamins B and iron. Fortification is the addition of nutrients not originally present in foods. For example, most milk is fortified with vitamin D because this vitamin helps deposit calcium in bones.

Activity

Point out that food additives—including artificial flavors, dyes, taste enhancers, and preservatives—are very common. Then have students study labels on prepared foods (such as hot dogs, luncheon meats, cereals, ice cream, yogurt, and powdered drinks) to compile lists of chemical additives to foods. Ask students to use library and online resources to research each of the additives. Have them give a brief report to the class about the advantages and disadvantages of each additive, drawing conclusions and making generalizations as necessary.
L3

Did You Know ?

Certified organic foods must meet a set of strict national standards. They must be produced and processed without conventional pesticides and fertilizers, bioengineering, radiation, hormones, or antibiotics. To be labeled "USDA Organic," a food product must be at least 95 percent organic.

Claims on food products must meet strict guidelines. Check the Nutrition Facts panel for more specific information. *What do the labels on each of these food products tell you?*

SUGAR AND FAT SUBSTITUTES

In response to the public's concerns about excess calories in foods, the food industry has developed a number of substitutes for sugar and fat. Many diet drinks, for example, are sweetened with *aspartame*, which is essentially calorie-free. Fructose, the natural sugar in fruit, is sometimes used as a sweetener. Because fructose is sweeter than table sugar, less sweetener is needed and fewer calories are added to the food. Some potato chips are made with fat replacers so that they supply few calories from fat. An example of a fat replacer is *olestra*, which passes through the body undigested. Because olestra is not absorbed, some people find that its consumption can produce gastrointestinal problems such as diarrhea.

Product Labeling

Along with nutrition information, food labels may state the potential health benefits of a food. In some cases the label may also detail the conditions under which the food was produced or grown—for example, whether or not a food is organic or contains organic ingredients.

Nutrient Content Claims

Product labels may advertise a food's nutrient value. Claims such as "100% Fat-Free" or "Light in Sodium" describe the nutrient content of a food. Some specific terms include the following:

▶ **Light or Lite.** The calories have been reduced by at least one third, or the fat or sodium has been reduced by at least 50 percent.

▶ **Less.** The food contains 25 percent less of a nutrient or of calories than a comparable food.

Curriculum Connections

Science Divide the class into three groups. Have each group conduct one of the following demonstrations to explore the functions of food additives. Let each group compare the results and draw conclusions to be discussed in class. (1) *Flavor.* Have students make oatmeal cookies with and without salt and vanilla. (2) *Appearance.*

Have students cut an apple in half and brush one half with citric or ascorbic acid. Let both halves sit for several minutes. (3) *Preservation.* In separate plastic bags, store bakery bread without additives and supermarket bread with additives. Let the bread sit for several days at room temperature.

- **Free.** The food contains no amount, or an insignificant amount, of total fat, saturated fat, cholesterol, sodium, sugars, or calories.

- **More.** The food contains 10 percent more of the Daily Value for a vitamin, a mineral, protein, or fiber.

- **High, Rich In, or Excellent Source Of.** The food contains 20 percent or more of the Daily Value for a vitamin, a mineral, protein, or fiber.

- **Lean.** The food is a meat, poultry, fish, or shellfish product that has less than 10 grams of total fat, less than 4 grams of saturated fat, and less than 95 mg of cholesterol per 3-ounce serving.

Open Dating

Many food products have *open dates* on their labels. The open dates on products such as milk and canned goods reflect their freshness. Canned foods eaten after these dates are safe, but they may not taste as fresh. Open dates on food such as meat can help you make decisions about the food's safety. Below are some common types of open dating you may see on product labels.

- **Expiration date.** The last date you should use the product.

- **Freshness date.** The last date a food is considered to be fresh.

- **Pack date.** The date on which the food was packaged.

- **Sell-by date (or pull date).** The last date the product should be sold. You can store and use a product after its sell-by date.

Food Sensitivities

D o you know anyone who feels ill after eating certain foods? This person may have a special sensitivity to the food or to an additive in the food.

Food Allergies

A **food allergy** is *a condition in which the body's immune system reacts to substances in some foods.* These substances, called **allergens,** are proteins that the body responds to as if they were pathogens, or foreign invaders. Allergies to peanuts, tree nuts, eggs, wheat, soy, fish, and shellfish are most common. Scratch tests, in which tiny amounts of suspected allergens are injected under the skin, are a common test for allergies. A simple blood test can also indicate whether a person is allergic to a specific food.

People with allergies have different types of allergic reactions. These reactions may include rash, hives, or itchiness of the skin;

(A) Milk containers are labeled with a sell-by date. *What does this date indicate?*

hotlink

allergens To learn more about allergens and allergies, see Chapter 26, page 688.

Discussing

Encourage students to share their own experiences with product labels on food packages:

- Do you check these labels in the store before purchasing a product? If so, what do you look for? If not, why not?

- Do you check these labels at home before eating a particular food? Why or why not?

- For whom do you think these labels are designed? How effective do you think they are?

- Do you think there are things missing on labels? What kinds of information may not be included? **L1**

Reinforcing Concepts

Potato chips are a popular snack with many teens. Have small groups of students brainstorm a list of other favorite snack foods. Then have group members rate each snack food on the list according to its appeal and health value. **L2**

Cross-Curriculum Activity

Art Have small groups of students brainstorm ideas for a new nutritious breakfast cereal. Then ask each group to create a full-page magazine advertisement for the new product. Tell students that the advertisement should appeal to teens and should include at least one nutrient content claim such as *lite, less, free,* or *more.* Have students proofread their advertisements and check for errors. Display final drafts in the classroom, and encourage a class discussion about their appeal and effectiveness. **L2 Visual/Spatial Intelligence**

Promoting Coordinated School Health

Identifying Major Problems Once a committee has been formed to serve the school health program, members will need to consider specific problems to address. One method of receiving input regarding areas for action is through a survey. For more information about drafting such a survey, consult *Planning a Coordinated School Health Program.* After the surveys have been collected and the information processed, the committee should brainstorm a priority list of concerns. The priority ratings are (1) critical problems, (2) moderate problems, and (3) minor problems. The top two or three issues can become candidates for priority action.

Community Involvement

Have several students visit a supermarket to survey the ingredient lists of packaged cookies and crackers. Ask them to list specific products (if any) that someone with an allergy to wheat could eat. Request that they share their findings with the class. **L2** ▯

Discussing

Have volunteers discuss allergic reactions they have had to food products. Ask: What type of reaction did you have? Did you know what caused the reaction? How did you find out? How long have you had the allergy? What steps, if any, have you taken to prevent another reaction? **L1**

FYI

In children, the most common food allergens are eggs, milk, and peanuts. Children sometimes become less allergic to substances as they grow older. They are more likely to outgrow allergies to milk and soy than allergies to other foods. Adults, however, generally never lose their allergies.

Activity

Have volunteers do research to learn about the latest developments in the diagnosis, prevention, and treatment of food allergies or intolerances. For example, how are food allergies or intolerances diagnosed? Are medicines available to prevent or counteract an allergic reaction or intolerance? How do doctors treat a severe allergic reaction? Have students present their findings to the class in brief oral reports. **L2** ▯

Did You Know ?

Lactose intolerance, the inability or reduced ability to digest the natural sugar in milk, is a manageable condition. Small amounts of milk consumed more frequently may be easier to digest. Drinking milk with food helps, too. Another option is to get milk's nutrients from yogurt or cheese, which usually don't cause a problem. Health care professionals can provide lactase enzymes and can explain how to use them. Also, lactose-reduced milk and other products containing the same nutrients as milk are offered at many supermarkets.

> Foods that can cause allergic reactions include milk products, soy products, peanuts, wheat, and shellfish. *What should you do if you have a severe reaction to any food?*

vomiting, diarrhea, or abdominal pain; or itchy eyes and sneezing. If you eat something and experience any of these symptoms, consult a health care professional. Serious allergic reactions, such as difficulty breathing, can be deadly. If you or someone else experiences a severe allergic reaction, call for medical help immediately.

Food Intolerances

Food intolerances are more common than food allergies. A **food intolerance** is *a negative reaction to a food or part of food caused by a metabolic problem, such as the inability to digest parts of certain foods or food components.* Food intolerance may be associated with certain foods, such as milk or wheat, or with some food additives. Some types of food intolerance may be hereditary, such as the reduced ability to digest lactose (milk sugar) or gluten, a protein in some grain products.

Foodborne Illness

You've seen the signs in restaurant restrooms: "Employees must wash their hands before returning to work." Restaurants have this policy because handwashing after using the restroom is one way to prevent **foodborne illness**, or *food poisoning.* Foodborne illness may result from eating food contaminated with pathogens (disease-causing organisms), the poisons they produce, or poisonous chemicals. Many times the contaminant can't be seen, smelled, or tasted. The best way to protect yourself is to become knowledgeable about the causes of such illnesses and ways to keep food safe.

Allergic Reaction ○

∿ HEALTH LITERACY

Health Information People who have serious allergies or other potentially life-threatening conditions sometimes wear medical identification tags or bracelets. These can take the form of "dog tags" or pieces of jewelry. Identification tags can be essential in treating people with allergies, especially if there has been an accident or the individual is unconscious.

Suggest that students find out more about this special form of identification:

- Who should have a medical identification tag?
- What information should be included on the tag?
- Where and how can the tags be obtained?

Causes and Symptoms of Foodborne Illness

According to the Centers for Disease Control and Prevention (CDC), bacteria and viruses cause most common foodborne illnesses. Bacteria that contaminate food include *Campylobacter*, *Salmonella*, and *E. coli* O157:H7. Viruses include the Norwalk and Norwalk-like viruses. Foods become contaminated with these pathogens in two main ways:

▶ Food may be contaminated with pathogens spread by an infected person.

▶ Animals raised or caught for food may harbor disease-causing organisms in their tissues. If meat or milk from such an animal is consumed without being thoroughly cooked or pasteurized, the organism may cause illness. These organisms can also contaminate other foods. **Pasteurization** is *the process of treating a substance with heat to destroy or slow the growth of pathogens.*

Common symptoms of foodborne illness include nausea, vomiting, diarrhea, and fever. Most people recover from these symptoms in a few days. However, foodborne illnesses can be very serious for older adults, very young children, people who are malnourished, or those with weakened immune systems. Individuals who have a fever greater than 101.5°F, who experience prolonged vomiting or diarrhea, or who show signs of dehydration—a decrease in urination, a dry mouth and throat, or dizziness when standing up—should consult a doctor.

Minimizing Risks of Foodborne Illness

Most cases of foodborne illness occur in the home, where pathogens can contaminate food products, kitchen surfaces, cooking and serving dishes, and eating utensils. To help keep food safe to eat, follow the four steps recommended by the Partnership for Food Safety Education: clean, separate, cook, and chill.

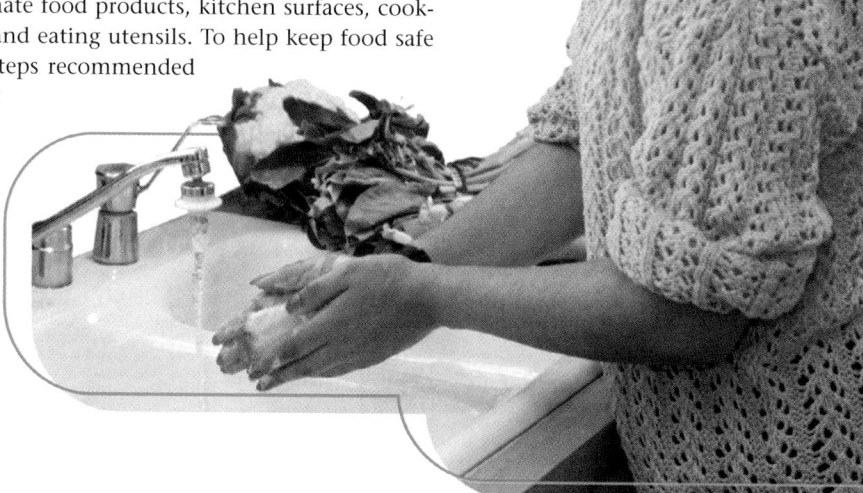

Washing your hands after using the bathroom and before handling or eating foods greatly reduces your risk of foodborne illness and the risk of passing pathogens to others. *What are some of the symptoms of foodborne illness?*

Quick Demo

Allow volunteers to demonstrate correct handwashing and surface-cleaning techniques to avoid cross-contamination of food. Have other students discuss the demonstration. Ask: Do you think that technique will keep food safe? How could it be improved? **ELL**

Community Involvement

Select volunteers to visit several local restaurants. Have them learn what precautions are taken by restaurants to decrease the likelihood of foodborne illness or contamination. Ask them to find answers to questions such as: What local agency is involved in regulating food production and cleanliness? What procedure is used to determine the cleanliness of a restaurant? What state guidelines exist that govern procedures and standards of food cleanliness and safety? (You may wish to contact your local health department to acquire their guidelines for restaurants and introduce this information into your discussion.) **L3**

Activity

Ask for volunteers to do research to learn more about pasteurization. Have them find answers to these questions: When was pasteurization invented? Who is the process named after? Which food products are most commonly pasteurized? Have students write a brief report on their findings. **L3**

Home and Community

Preventing Foodborne Illness Encourage students to evaluate their kitchens at home for precautions against foodborne illness. Are plastic or other nonporous cutting boards used? Are separate cutting boards used for meats and for other foods? Are raw meats kept separate from other foods? Are cleaning cloths washed frequently in the hot water cycle of the washing machine? Do those who cook in the family wash their hands after handling raw meat and before handling other foods? Are hot foods kept hot and cold foods cold? Are leftovers refrigerated promptly?

Reinforcing Concepts

Ask volunteers to check the temperature in their refrigerators and freezers at home. Have them find out whether the temperatures are adequate to prevent foodborne illness and food spoilage. **L1**

Enrichment

Invite the school nurse or other health care professional to speak to the class about food-related health problems such as severe allergic reactions and food-borne illnesses. Ask the speaker to describe the symptoms of these problems, and instruct students on the actions to take if they or someone else shows these symptoms. Remind students to ask questions and take notes.

FYI

About 76 million cases of foodborne illness occur in the United States every year. About 325,000 of these cases are serious enough to require medical treatment in a hospital, and as many as 5,000 people die from these types of illnesses.

▶ **Clean.** Before preparing food and after using the bathroom, handling pets, changing diapers, or touching any other obvious source of pathogens, wash your hands thoroughly in hot, soapy water. To prevent **cross-contamination**, *the spreading of bacteria or other pathogens from one food to another,* wash your hands, cutting boards, utensils, plates, and countertops with hot, soapy water after preparing each food item. It is also recommended that you use cutting boards made of nonporous materials, such as plastic or glass, for preparing foods. When possible, use disposable paper towels instead of dishcloths to clean kitchen surfaces. Also, remember to wash fruits and vegetables before you eat them.

▶ **Separate.** To avoid cross-contamination, separate raw meat, seafood, and poultry from other items in your shopping cart. At home, store these foods separately from other foods. The bottom shelf of the refrigerator is a good place to keep these foods because their juices won't run onto other foods. Use separate cutting boards for raw meats and raw vegetables or foods that are ready to be eaten. Never place cooked food on a plate that previously held raw meat, seafood, or poultry. After contact with raw meats, wash cutting boards and other utensils (as well as your hands) in hot, soapy water.

Ⓨ **Wash cutting boards in hot, soapy water.** *How can using different cutting boards for raw meats and raw vegetables help protect you from foodborne illness?*

▶ **Cook.** Cook foods to a safe temperature: 160°F for ground beef, 170°F for roasts and poultry, and 145°F for fish. Use a meat thermometer to make sure meats and fish are cooked thoroughly. When thoroughly cooked, meat or poultry juices should run clear. Properly cooked fish should be opaque and flake easily with a fork. Don't eat raw ground beef or ground beef that is still pink after being cooked. Avoid dishes that contain partially cooked or raw eggs. Sauces, soups, and gravies should be brought to a boil before serving.

▶ **Chill.** Cold temperatures slow the multiplication of bacteria. Refrigerate or freeze perishable foods as soon as you get home. Foods that need to be kept cold should be refrigerated quickly at temperatures of 40°F or less. Frozen foods should be stored at 0°F. Refrigerate or freeze prepared foods and leftovers within two hours after a meal—even sooner on a hot day. Divide leftovers into small, shallow containers to help them cool more quickly. Remove any stuffing before freezing meats or poultry. Don't over-pack the refrigerator; air needs

More About...

Cross-Contamination Regardless of the season, pathogens can be spread from one area to another or from raw foods that need to be cooked to ready-to-eat foods such as produce and sandwiches. To help prevent cross-contamination, refrigerate raw meats in a pan or on a plate so juices do not drip onto food below. If possible, keep raw meats on the bottom shelf of the refrigerator. Also, throw out wooden cooking utensils that are splitting, because the cracks in the wood may harbor pathogens that can cause food-borne illness. Clean can openers regularly with hot, soapy water, and change dish-cloths frequently.

to circulate around the food to keep it cool. Don't defrost foods on a kitchen counter. Instead, thaw these foods in a refrigerator, under cold running water, or by using a microwave's defrost function. At a picnic, keep hot foods hot and cold foods cold. Thoroughly cook meats at the picnic site. Discard foods that have been sitting out for two hours—one hour if the temperature is above 85°F.

 Proper preparation of picnic foods will help ensure that these foods remain safe to eat. *Why should you discard any picnic food that's been sitting out for two hours?*

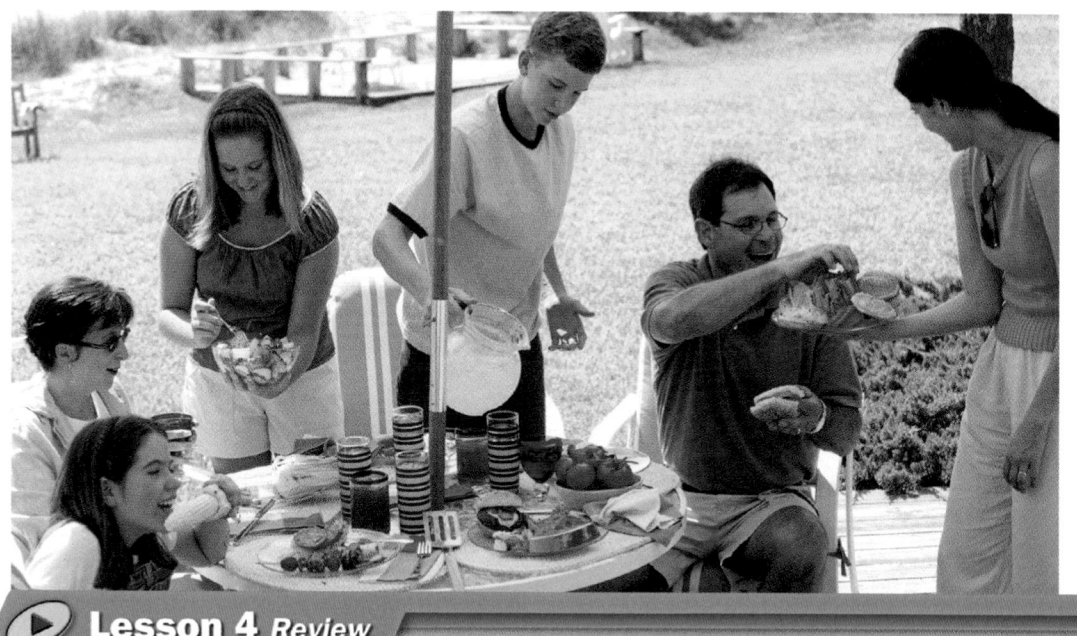

Lesson 4 *Review*

Reviewing Facts and Vocabulary

1. What can the ingredients list of a food product tell you?
2. How does a *food allergy* differ from a *food intolerance*?
3. What is *pasteurization*?

Thinking Critically

4. **Analyzing.** How does the policy that requires food service workers to wash their hands help prevent foodborne illness?
5. **Applying.** Develop a strategy to store food that's left over from dinner.

Applying Health Skills

Accessing Information. Find three to five reliable online sources of information about foodborne illness. Use these resources to create a pamphlet titled "Preventing Foodborne Illness."

WORD PROCESSING   Word processing can give your pamphlet a professional look. See **health.glencoe.com** for tips on how to get the most out of your word-processing program.

Lesson 4   Food and Healthy Living   **137**

3 ASSESS

EVALUATING THE LESSON

Assign and discuss the Lesson 4 Review; then administer, grade, and discuss Lesson Quiz 19 in the TCR. 📁

RETEACHING

- Have students work together in small groups to create a list of information that can be found on food labels.
- Ask students to complete Reteaching Activity 19 in the TCR. 📁

ENRICHMENT

Have students conduct research on a specific pathogen that can cause foodborne illness. Then have them prepare a one-page fact sheet about the pathogen, including ways to reduce the risk of illness caused by this pathogen.

4 CLOSE

Have students work together in small groups to create a public service announcement, to be read on a popular radio station, about ways to reduce the risk of foodborne illness.

Lesson 4 *Review*

Answers to Reviewing Facts and Vocabulary

1. Information about the food's contents, listed in descending order by weight.
2. A food allergy is a condition in which the body's immune system reacts to substances in some foods; a food intolerance is a negative reaction to a food or part of a food caused by a metabolic problem.
3. The process of treating a substance with heat.

Answers to Thinking Critically

4. Handwashing prevents the spread of pathogens that cause foodborne illness.
5. Refrigerate or freeze leftovers within two hours after a meal, sooner on a hot day. Divide leftovers into small containers.

Analyzing Food Ads

NHES Standard 4 Students will analyze the influence of culture, media, technology, and other factors on health.

Objective

Recognize the different techniques that food advertisers use to appeal to children and teens.

Motivator

Have students think of TV ads for fast food and convenience foods. Ask them for specific details on the ads.

Teaching Strategies

Awareness Ask students to explain whether or not the TV ads they came up with in the Motivator are targeted at young people.

Analysis Encourage students to be specific and detailed as they complete their charts.

Reflection As students consider the pros and cons of requiring warning labels on food products, ask them to include in their debate information on the risks of consuming excess quantities of fast food and high-calorie snacks.

Take Action The Ad Council is a nonprofit organization that helps develop public service announcements (PSAs) with socially responsible messages. Have students write a letter to the Ad Council explaining why it is important to counter fast-food and convenience-food advertising with PSAs on healthful foods.

✓Assessment

Student essays should contain an analysis of the TV ad that draws information from the chart they completed in the activity.

Eye ON THE Media

Analyzing Food Ads

Being overweight is associated with many serious health problems, including type 2 diabetes. Ads for fast food and high-calorie snacks may influence young people to consume foods that contribute to unhealthful weight gain. In this activity you will learn to recognize the different techniques food advertisers use to appeal to children and teens.

Language	Color	Music	Types of Characters	Editing Methods

ACTIVITY

One way to critique a TV ad is to consider its style. An ad's style includes its use of language, color, and music; types of characters featured; and methods of film editing. Ads for breakfast cereals, for example, often feature cartoon characters to draw in children. Fast-food ads may have a fast-paced editing style, such as that seen in music videos, to appeal to teens.

Critique a TV ad for a food product that is targeted to children or teens. Use a chart like the one above to describe each element of the ad. Then write an essay indicating how the style of the ad is attempting to draw in its target audience. Explain why the advertised food should not be targeted to children or teens. Include information on why the food is a poor nutritional choice for a healthful eating plan.

EXPRESS YOUR VIEWS

Should fast-food and convenience-food manufacturers be required to put warning labels on their products that describe the health risks of consuming a particular food? Hold a class debate on this issue.

More About...

Diabetes in Children Type 2 diabetes, once found primarily in adults over the age of 40, has been on the rise in children over the past five years. Overweight children are particularly at risk for developing type 2 diabetes, as are children in certain ethnic groups (African Americans, Latinos, and Native Americans), and children with a family history of the disorder. A healthful, moderate eating plan and regular physical activity can help prevent type 2 diabetes. Ask students to consider how the wide availability of fast food and high-calorie snacks might be a factor in the increase of type 2 diabetes in children.

CROSS-CURRICULUM CONNECTIONS

Write a Story. Compose a short story about a family enjoying a traditional feast featuring their native cuisine. You may wish to focus on your own cultural or ethnic background, or choose one that you are interested in. Research that culture's cuisine and dining customs to incorporate into your story, and be sure to use vivid, descriptive language to set the scene.

Give an Oral Report. Early settlers in America had to modify their diets based on the foods available in the area where they settled. Your teacher will divide you into groups and assign you a particular U.S. region to study. Research what groups settled in that area and how they adapted their diets to incorporate the foods available in that region. Create a visual aid, and present an oral report to the class.

Calculate the Calories. The USDA's *Dietary Guidelines for Americans* recommends that no more than 30 percent of daily calories come from fat. Mike is a teen whose recommended daily calorie intake is 2,800 calories. Keeping in mind that a gram of fat yields 9 calories, if the total fat content of Mike's breakfast and lunch totals 38.6 grams, how many more calories from fat can he eat that day and still remain within the recommended limits?

Conduct Research. The French chemist Louis-Camille Maillard noticed that certain chemical compounds appeared in foods during the cooking process that were not present in the raw food. This phenomenon is now called the Maillard Reaction. List some common foods, such as bread, meats, and vegetables, and research the compounds produced in the Maillard Reaction when they are cooked.

Dietetic Technician

Do you enjoy planning meals and cooking? Do you like interacting with others? If so, you may enjoy a career as a dietetic technician. This career allows you to assist dietitians in the planning of healthful meals.

To enter this field, you must first complete a two-year associate's degree program. You'll also need to complete an accredited dietetic technician program and pass a national exam. To maintain certification, you'll need to stay up-to-date on nutrition trends. Find out more about this and other health careers by clicking on Career Corner at **health.glencoe.com**.

Chapter 5 Review **139**

Portfolio Assessment

Self-Evaluation Direct students to review the Health Skills Activities and other activities completed in the chapter. Encourage each student to select one finished product or activity that demonstrates his or her best work for the chapter and that represents the student's learning goals. Have students explain what they have learned and how the examples they have selected demonstrate their growth in health literacy, knowledge, and skills.

Teacher Classroom Resources Assign Performance Assessment 5, "The Importance of Nutrients," in the TCR.

CHECKING COMPREHENSION

- Assign and discuss the chapter review.
- Use the Chapter 5 MindJogger Videoquiz to review the chapter. ▶◀

CHAPTER 5 REVIEW ANSWERS

Exploring Health Terms

1. nutrition
2. Calories
3. nutrients
4. carbohydrates
5. fiber
6. proteins
7. lipid
8. *Dietary Guidelines for Americans*
9. Food Guide Pyramid
10. food additives
11. foodborne illness
12. cross-contamination

Recalling the Facts

1. Hunger is a physical need to eat; appetite is a desire, rather than a need, to eat.

2. Answers should include specific examples of food choices made as a result of the influence of friends and peers.

3. See page 113.

4. Glucose not used by the body to produce energy is stored in the skeletal muscles and liver in the form of the starch known as glycogen.

5. Water transports other nutrients to and carries wastes from cells; lubricates joints and mucous membranes; allows swallowing and digesting of foods, absorption of other nutrients, and elimination of wastes; and helps maintain body temperature.

Chapter 5 *Review*

➤ EXPLORING HEALTH TERMS
Answer the following questions on a sheet of paper.

Lesson 1 *Fill in the blanks with the correct term.*

hunger	nutrition	calories
nutrients	appetite	

The process by which the body takes in and uses food is (**_1_**). (**_2_**) are the units of heat that measure the energy used by the body and the energy that foods supply to the body. The substances in food that your body needs to function properly are (**_3_**).

Lesson 2 *Match each definition with the correct term.*

vitamins	lipid	carbohydrates
proteins	fiber	minerals

4. The starches and sugars present in foods.
5. An indigestible complex carbohydrate.
6. Nutrients that help build and maintain body cells and tissues.
7. A fatty substance that does not dissolve in water.

Lesson 3 *Fill in the blanks with the correct term.*

Food Guide Pyramid
Dietary Guidelines for Americans

8. The _____ is a set of recommendations for healthful eating and active living prepared by the USDA and DHHS.
9. The _____ is a guide for making healthful daily food choices.

Lesson 4 *Match each definition with the correct term.*

food allergy	pasteurization
food additives	cross-contamination
foodborne illness	food intolerance

10. Substances intentionally added to food to produce a desired effect.
11. Another name for food poisoning.
12. The spreading of bacteria or other pathogens from one food to another.

➤ RECALLING THE FACTS
Use complete sentences to answer the following questions.

Lesson 1

1. How does hunger differ from appetite?
2. Give an example of how friends and peers can influence food choices.
3. Why is good nutrition especially important during the teen years?

Lesson 2

4. What is the relationship between glucose and glycogen?
5. How does water benefit the body?
6. List three minerals that are important for health.

Lesson 3

7. What are the ABCs of good health?
8. Most of the foods you eat each day should come from which three parts of the Food Guide Pyramid?
9. How many servings should you eat each day from the Milk Group? From the Meat and Beans Group?

Lesson 4

10. What does the Percent Daily Value column of a food label tell you?
11. What are some symptoms of a food allergy?
12. How can you keep picnic foods safe to eat?

6. Any three: calcium, phosphorus, magnesium, iron.

7. Aim for Fitness; Build a Healthy Base; Choose Sensibly.

8. Most of the foods eaten in a day should come from the Grains group, the Vegetable group, and the Fruit group.

9. For teens, three to four servings from the Milk group; two to three servings (5–7 ounces) from the Meat and Beans group.

10. The percentage of the recommended amount of a nutrient each serving of the food provides for a person eating 2,000 calories per day.

11. Rash, hives, or itchiness of the skin; vomiting, diarrhea, or abdominal pain; and itchy eyes and sneezing. In severe cases, a person also may have difficulty breathing.

12. See pages 136–137.

➤ THINKING CRITICALLY

1. **Synthesizing.** Use specific examples to explain how strong emotions such as anger and fear might affect your eating habits. *(LESSON 1)*

2. **Evaluating.** Explain why it's important to know whether a fat is saturated or unsaturated. *(LESSON 2)*

3. **Applying.** What would you say to someone who always skips breakfast because he or she isn't hungry in the morning? *(LESSON 3)*

4. **Analyzing.** Several hours after eating dinner, you begin to feel nauseous and feverish and you have some abdominal cramps. What type of problem might these symptoms suggest? *(LESSON 4)*

➤ HEALTH SKILLS APPLICATION

1. **Advocacy.** Watch 30 minutes of television and keep a record of the food commercials shown. Analyze the health messages delivered through these food ads. Then write a script for an advertisement that encourages viewers to try a particular healthful food. *(LESSON 1)*

2. **Goal Setting.** Develop a table that summarizes what you have learned about the nutrients your body needs. Include in your table the name of each type of nutrient, why your body needs the nutrient, and what foods you can eat to make sure you include enough of the nutrient in your eating plan. Then set a goal to improve your intake of one or more of these nutrients. Use the goal-setting steps to reach your goal. *(LESSON 2)*

3. **Accessing Information.** Use reliable online resources to do more in-depth research on the relationship between nutrition and heart disease. How can good nutrition prevent this disease and improve quality of life? Summarize your findings in a one-page report. *(LESSON 3)*

4. **Practicing Healthful Behaviors.** Analyze how healthful practices might reduce the risk of foodborne illness, a communicable disease. Then develop a plan that features safe cooking strategies to reduce the spread of foodborne pathogens. *(LESSON 4)*

BEYOND *the* Classroom

Parent Involvement

Accessing Information. Work with your family to make a list of the prepared and fast foods you most enjoy eating. Then look through cookbooks to find recipes for similar treats that contain less fat, sugar, and salt. Make a recipe booklet of these healthful alternatives, and set a goal to try one new recipe each week.

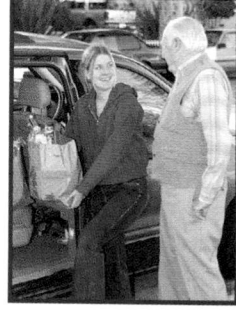

School and Community

Meals on Wheels. Many communities have organizations such as Meals on Wheels or other groups that provide nutritious meals to older adults or physically challenged individuals who are unable to prepare meals for themselves. Find out whether your community has such an organization and how you and your classmates can become involved.

Thinking Critically

1. Examples should indicate an understanding that emotions may affect appetite and cause a person to eat more or less than he or she normally would.

2. A high intake of saturated fats raises the level of cholesterol in the blood. This, in turn, may increase the risk of heart disease. Unsaturated fats have been associated with a reduced risk of heart disease.

3. Repsonses will vary, but should include information on the health benefits of starting each day with a nutritious breakfast.

4. The symptoms may indicate foodborne illness.

Health Skills Application

1.–4. Answers will vary.

EVALUATE

• Use the reproducible Chapter 5 Test in the TCR, or construct your own using the Testmaker software.

• Use Performance Assessment 5 in the TCR.

ENRICHMENT

Ask students to complete Enrichment Activity 5 in the TCR.

BEYOND *the* Classroom

Keep students involved in the community, and encourage parent participation by assigning the activities on this page for students to work on outside of class.

Lessons	Standards		Features
	National	**State/Local**	
1 Maintaining a Healthy Weight *pages 144–150*	National Health Education Standards **1.6, 3.4, 7.2**		**Exploring Issues** • Should Schools Limit the Use of Vending Machines? page 149
2 Fad Diets and Eating Disorders *pages 151–156*	National Health Education Standards **2.6, 7.4, 7.6**		**Hands-On Health** • Fad Diets Harm Health *(Advocacy)*, page 153 **Health Skills Activity** • Helping a Friend Get Help *(Decision Making)*, page 155
3 Nutrition for Individual Needs *pages 157–163*	National Health Education Standards **6.1, 6.3, 7.4**		**Real-Life Application** • Meatless Meals *(Practicing Healthful Behaviors)*, page 160

Reproducible Resources	Assessment	Technology
Student Activity Workbook for use with each chapter 📁 Concept Mapping Activity 20 📁 Cross-Curriculum Activity 6 📁 Decision-Making Activity 6 📁 Enrichment Activity 6 📁 Guided Reading Activities 20 📁 Lesson Plan 20 📁 Parent Letter and Activities 6 📁 Reteaching Activity 20	📁 Lesson Quiz 20	🕹 Transparency 17 💿 TeacherWorks® 🖥 Internet Activities
📁 Concept Mapping Activity 21 📁 Guided Reading Activities 21 📁 Lesson Plan 21 📁 Reteaching Activity 21	📁 Lesson Quiz 21	💿 TeacherWorks®
📁 Concept Mapping Activity 22 📁 Current Health Issues 6 📁 Guided Reading Activities 22 📁 Health Lab 6 📁 Lesson Plan 22 📁 Reteaching Activity 22	📁 Lesson Quiz 22	🕹 Transparency 18 💿 TeacherWorks®

Key to Ability Levels

Teaching strategies that appear throughout the chapter have been identified by one of the following codes to give teachers an idea of their suitability for students of varying learning styles and abilities.

L1 Strategies should be within the ability range of all students. Full class participation is often required. Teacher direction is usually needed.

L2 Strategies are designed for average to above-average students or for small groups. Some teacher direction is needed.

L3 Strategies are designed for students able and willing to work independently. Minimal teacher direction is needed.

ELL Strategies should be within the ability range of students learning the English language.

🔲 Block scheduling strategies are useful in a block scheduling format.

0:00 OUT OF TIME

If time does not permit teaching the entire chapter use:
- Figure 6.2, p. 148
- Hands-On Health, p. 153
- Health Skills Activity, p. 155
- Real-Life Application, p. 160

Language Diversity

🎧 English Audio CD Program
🎧 Spanish Audio CD Program
📁 English Summaries, Quizzes, and Activities
📁 Spanish Summaries, Quizzes, and Activities
📁 Spanish Parent Letters and Activities

End of Chapter Assessment

Blackline Masters

📁 Chapter 6 Test
📁 Performance Assessment Activity 6
📁 Unit 2 Test

Technology

💿 Vocabulary PuzzleMaker
📼 MindJogger Videoquiz
💿 **Exam***View*® ProTestmaker

Professional Health Series

Dealing with Sensitive Issues
Planning a Coordinated School Health Program
Promoting Character Education
Home, School, and Community Involvement

Managing Weight and Body Composition

CHAPTER OVERVIEW

Chapter 6 discusses weight management, fad diets, eating disorders, and the specific nutritional needs of such individuals as athletes and vegetarians.

Lesson 1 Weight management is really an issue of energy intake and expenditure. An effective weight-management plan involves developing healthy eating habits and being physically active throughout life.

Lesson 2 Fad diets and other quick weight-loss strategies carry certain risks. An obsession with thinness, along with psychological pressures, can lead to eating disorders, including anorexia nervosa, bulimia nervosa, and binge eating disorder. These disorders require medical assistance and psychological counseling.

Lesson 3 Many people—including infants, children, older adults, athletes, vegetarians, and pregnant women—have specific nutritional needs. Dietary supplements may be appropriate for some people, but must be used carefully. Nutritional needs change throughout a person's life.

Health Skills Features

- Exploring Issues, p. 149
- Hands-On Health (*Advocacy*), p. 153
- Health Skills Activity (*Decision Making*), p. 155
- Real-Life Application (*Accessing Information*), p. 160

Chapter 6

Managing Weight and Body Composition

Lesson 1
Maintaining a Healthy Weight

Lesson 2
Fad Diets and Eating Disorders

Lesson 3
Nutrition for Individual Needs

142

MEETING STUDENT DIVERSITY

Language Diversity Use the following suggestions to help students who have difficulty with English:

- Pair English language learners with native speakers of English who can restate the Chapter Summary in language that helps students comprehend important concepts.

- Direct auditory learners or those students with language diversity to the *Glencoe Health Audio CD Program*. Available in English and Spanish, this component provides an audio and written summary of the chapter.

- Use photographs, drawings, or magazine clippings to help students visualize the important concepts of the chapter.

Case Study

Kevin's Story

Kevin has always had a weight problem. When he was younger, it didn't seem to matter much that he was a little bigger than the other boys. In fact, the extra weight came in handy when playing his favorite sport—football.

Now Kevin is 15, and things seem very different to him. He's worried about how he looks and feels. "Being overweight is supposed to be a girl's problem," says Kevin. "It's embarrassing that I have to worry about my weight."

Kevin finds it difficult to make healthy food choices. He often eats at fast-food restaurants and snacks on candy bars and potato chips. He also doesn't get much physical activity.

In the past Kevin has tried quick fixes to lose weight. "One time I went on a fad diet, but that didn't really work," says Kevin. "I lost weight at first, but then I started feeling really run down, so I went back to my old way of eating. Before I knew it, I had regained all the weight I lost, plus a few extra pounds."

Kevin knows he has to change his lifestyle in order to lose weight, but he doesn't know what steps to take.

What advice would you give Kevin? Write a short paragraph describing what you think he could do to address his problem more effectively. Reread this story and your response when you complete the chapter. What additional advice would you give Kevin about maintaining a healthy weight?

Quick Write

Using Visuals. Maintaining a healthy weight involves being physically active and making healthful food choices. Write a brief paragraph describing the healthful food choices these teens are making.

INTRODUCING THE CHAPTER

Case Study

Have students read and briefly discuss Kevin's story. Ask: Why have Kevin's previous attempts at weight loss failed? How are his current eating and activity habits hindering his progress? After students have written down their advice to Kevin, have volunteers read their paragraphs aloud. Lead the class in discussing the steps Kevin might take to lose weight healthfully. Remind students that they will reread this story and their responses after completing this chapter.

Display a number of diet books in your classroom. Ask students why they think there are so many books written on this subject. Ask each student to select one book and read about the author's professional training and experience. Discuss the levels of training in nutrition for various professionals. Point out that nutritionists are the most highly trained in this field. Tell students they will learn more about weight management, including healthy ways to lose or gain weight, in this chapter.

Quick write

Using Visuals Direct students to look at the photograph. Ask: What healthful food choices are these teens making? How will these food choices help them maintain a healthy weight?

TECHNOLOGY OPTIONS

MINDJOGGER
VIDEOQUIZ

To preview or review chapter content, you may wish to use the Chapter 6 MindJogger Videoquiz.

Online Resources for the Teacher For a fresh approach to health topics and an in-depth look at health issues, use these online resources found under Teacher Resources at **health.glencoe.com:**

- Block Schedule Lesson Plans
- Technology Projects
- Health Updates

Maintaining a Healthy Weight

1 FOCUS

QUICK START   Ask volunteers to share their lists of feelings about body appearance and write their responses on the board. Then lead a class discussion on the factors that influence these feelings.

TYING TO PRIOR KNOWLEDGE

Have volunteers give examples of weight-loss methods, and write them on the board. Then ask students to share their impressions of how well these weight-loss methods work.

Health Skills Features

"Should Schools Limit the Use of Vending Machines?" p. 149

INTRODUCING VOCABULARY

- Have students work in pairs. Have one student from each pair write a paragraph using three of the vocabulary terms. Then have them exchange paragraphs. Ask the other student to write the definition of the words based on the context. Tell both students to check the paragraph for proper spelling and grammar.

- Ask students to complete the Chapter 6 Study Guide in the *Student Activity Workbook*.

144

Maintaining a Healthy Weight

VOCABULARY
- body image
- body mass index (BMI)
- overweight
- obesity
- underweight
- nutrient-dense foods

YOU'LL LEARN TO
- Examine the relationship among body composition, diet, and fitness.
- Analyze the relationship between maintaining a healthy weight and disease prevention.
- Describe healthful ways to manage weight.

QUICK START   On a sheet of paper, list three feelings a person might have about his or her body's appearance. Then write down three factors that might influence these feelings.

 Media images can have an impact on a person's body image. *How might messages sent by media images negatively affect body image?*

When you look in the mirror, how do you feel about what you see? Are you happy with the way you look, or do you wish some things were different? *The way you see your body* is called your **body image**. Body image is affected by several factors, including media images and the attitudes of family and friends.

For many people body image is tied to perception of weight. Your own healthy weight probably won't be the same as the weight of a fashion model, a bodybuilder, or your best friend. However, you can use some general guidelines to assess your weight and keep it within a healthy range.

The Weight-Calorie Connection

To understand how to manage your weight effectively, it's important to understand calories. As you've learned, calories are units used to measure energy—both the energy in food and the energy your body uses for life processes and physical activities. Maintaining a healthy weight, even while you're growing, is a matter of energy balance: the calories you consume must equal the calories your body burns.

144   **Chapter 6**   Managing Weight and Body Composition

Lesson 1 *Resources*

Teacher Classroom Resources
- 📁 Concept Mapping Activity 20
- 📁 Cross-Curriculum Activity 6
- 📁 Decision-Making Activity 6
- 📁 Enrichment Activity 6
- 📁 Guided Reading Activities 20
- 📁 Lesson Plan 20
- 📁 Lesson Quiz 20

- 📁 Parent Letter and Activities 6
- 📁 Reteaching Activity 20

Student Activity Workbook
- 📁 Applying Health Skills 20
- 📁 Chapter 6 Study Guide

Multimedia
- Transparency 17

Calories: Their Source

Some foods have more calories than others. The specific number of calories depends on portion size as well as the amounts of carbohydrates, proteins, and fats in the food. Both carbohydrates and proteins supply four calories per gram. Fats supply more than twice that number—nine calories per gram. For this reason, even small amounts of fat in a food greatly increase its calorie content. The way a food is prepared or cooked also affects the calorie count.

The Energy Equation

Tipping the balance of the energy equation will result in weight loss or gain. If you take in fewer calories than you burn, you lose weight. If you take in more calories than you burn, you gain weight.

One pound of body fat equals about 3,500 calories. Eating 500 fewer calories per day than you need to maintain your weight will result in the loss of one pound of body fat after one week (500 calories per day × 7 days = 3,500 calories). Burning an additional 500 calories per day through physical activity would result in a similar weight loss.

Determining Your Appropriate Weight Range

Your appropriate weight is influenced by several factors, including gender, age, height, body frame, growth rate, metabolic rate, and activity level. As a teen you are still growing, so you need more calories than an adult does. Tall and large-framed people need more calories than short and small-framed people. Because an active person burns more calories than a sedentary person does, he or she can consume more calories without gaining weight than a sedentary person can.

Body Mass Index

One way to evaluate whether your weight is within a healthy range is to determine body mass index. **Body mass index (BMI)** is *a ratio that allows you to assess your body size in relation to your height and weight.* Because BMI for children and teens takes age and gender into account, different charts are used for males and females. **Figure 6.1** on page 146 explains how to determine your BMI. A different chart is used for adults.

As you calculate your BMI, keep in mind that many different ratios of height to weight can be healthy. Teens grow at different rates and in different ways. There is no single size, shape, or growth pattern that's normal for everyone.

Did You Know

▶ Adding just 100 extra calories to your daily food intake without changing your activity level will add 10 pounds to your weight in one year.

Height and gender are two factors that need to be considered when evaluating a person's weight.

2 TEACH

Community Involvement

Have students examine the contents of any vending machine at school or in the community and make a list of the foods and beverages offered. Tell them to analyze the nutrients in the foods and beverages, noting especially the amounts of sugars in each. Ask them to report their findings to the class. **L2**

Explaining

Provide food-related magazines for students to collect pictures of high-calorie foods and drinks that total about 3,500 calories. Explain that this is the number of calories that would have to be cut out of an individual's eating plan each week to result in the loss of 1 pound of body fat. **ELL**
Visual/Spatial Intelligence

Cooperative Learning

Have students work in small groups. Have them apply their understanding of sound nutritional principles to create menus for a restaurant for health conscious people. The menus might include symbols for low-sugar, low-sodium, and low-fat foods. Have each group present their menu to the class for feedback. **L3**

School to Work

Energy for Work People's daily calorie requirements vary by occupation. Some physically active workers burn more calories than office workers, for example. Instruct students to choose an occupation such as dancer, professional athlete, construction worker, window washer, or farm laborer. Have them find the number of calories burned while engaged in specific movements. In many cases they may need to research movements similar to those used in the work performed. Suggest that they use their research to calculate how much the workday calorie requirement of such a worker exceeds that of a word processor of the same size, age, and gender.

VISUAL LEARNING

Figure 6.1 Guide students in learning how to use the chart in Figure 6.1 for determining BMI. For practice, ask them to determine the BMI of a few sample teens, such as a female teen who is 5'6" and weighs 125 pounds and a male teen who is 5'8" and weighs 180 pounds. When students demonstrate knowledge of how to use the chart, have them determine their own BMI. As always, maintain student privacy.

Discussing

Ask students why males of a certain height and frame size weigh more than females of the same height and frame size. Males' small frames are larger than females' small frames. Males tend to have more muscle tissue, which is dense. Females have more fat tissue, which is less dense. **L2**

Explaining

Tell students that pinching a fold of skin and measuring its thickness is one way of telling if a person has excess body fat. This is because extra fat is stored under the skin. Average male bodies are made up of approximately 12½ percent fat, and average female bodies are on average made up of approximately 20 percent fat. **L1**

FIGURE 6.1

DETERMINING BMI

Use this formula to find your BMI:

BMI = weight (in pounds) × 703/[height (in inches)]^2

Here's how to find the BMI for a 16-year-old male who weighs 145 pounds and is 65 inches tall:

BMI = 145 × 703 / 65^2

BMI = 101,935 / 4,225

BMI = 24.12 or 24

Find this result in the chart. This teen's BMI indicates that he is within an appropriate weight range.

Source: Adapted from CDC information

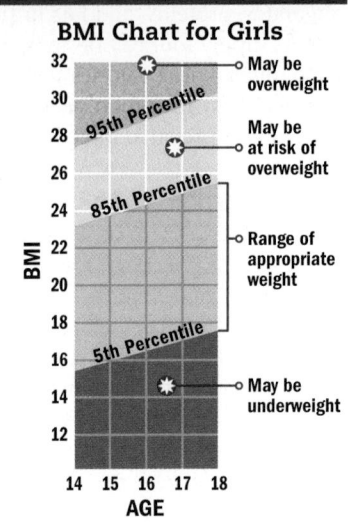

If your BMI falls above the 85th percentile or below the 5th percentile, consult a health care professional for further evaluation. However, keep in mind that this does not necessarily mean that you are over- or underweight.

Body Composition

Body composition, or the ratio of body fat to lean body tissue, needs to be taken into account when assessing weight. Diet and fitness affect a person's body composition. For example, a weight-lifting program will increase muscle mass. A high-calorie diet can increase the amount of stored body fat.

Body Weight versus Body Fat

The terms *overweight* and *obesity* are often used interchangeably, but they are not the same. **Overweight** is *a condition in which a person is heavier than the standard weight range for his or her height.* **Obesity** refers specifically to *having an excess amount of body fat.* Being overweight or obese can endanger health. In certain cases being overweight may not pose health risks. Athletes such as bodybuilders or football players may be overweight because of excess muscle tissue rather than excess body fat.

Weight-Related Health Risks

BMI for adults serves as a general guide to evaluate some health risks. Adults with high BMIs are at increased risk of cardiovascular disease; type 2 diabetes; cancer; high blood pressure; and osteoarthritis, a joint disease. Maintaining a healthy weight can help prevent the development of these diseases.

146 **Chapter 6** Managing Weight and Body Composition

─∿∿─ HEALTH LITERACY ─

Analyzing Food Influences In the United States, many health problems result from dietary excess. People eat for many reasons, only one of which is hunger. The sight or smell of food may be tempting, and numerous social functions involve food. In some parts of the world, people eat whatever is available, and many health problems result from hunger or nutritional deficiencies. Have students list what they ate during the past 24 hours, the time they ate, and their reason for eating. Suggest that they consider the following influences: hunger, temptation, boredom, stress, scheduled meals, social occasions, enjoyment, and comfort. Have them speculate about how their reasons would differ if food were scarce or hard to obtain.

Overweight: A Health Risk

Being overweight is a serious problem in the United States. The latest findings from the CDC indicate that 14 percent of teens are overweight. Excess body fat strains the muscles and the skeletal system. It forces the heart and lungs to work harder and increases the risk of high blood pressure and high blood cholesterol. Being overweight or obese also increases the risk of type 2 diabetes, asthma, and some cancers.

Why are some people overweight? Genetics may play a role, but overweight and obesity usually result from consuming excess calories and from physical inactivity. To maintain a healthy weight and avoid the health risks associated with overweight and obesity, follow the ABCs of good health as described in the **Dietary Guidelines for Americans:**

▶ **Aim for Fitness.** Get 60 minutes of physical activity daily.

▶ **Build a Healthy Base.** Eat the recommended number of daily servings from each of the five major food groups in the **Food Guide Pyramid.**

▶ **Choose Sensibly.** Balance high-fat choices with low-fat foods, and moderate your intake of sugar.

Underweight: A Health Risk

Some teens are very thin while they are growing. Being thin may also be normal because of genetics or a fast metabolism. Other people, however, diet or exercise excessively to stay thin. A person who is too thin has little stored fat to provide the body with an energy reserve and may not be consuming enough calories and nutrients for health and growth. This may lead to fatigue and a decreased ability to fight illness. How do you know whether you are underweight? **Underweight** refers to *a condition in which a person is less than the standard weight range for his or her height.* A health care professional can help you determine whether you are underweight.

hotlink

Dietary Guidelines for Americans For more information on the *Dietary Guidelines*, see Chapter 5, page 122.
Food Guide Pyramid See Chapter 5, page 124, to learn more about using the Food Guide Pyramid to make healthy food choices.

ⓨ **Physical activities such as swimming burn calories and can help you manage your weight.** *What other physical activities can help you manage your weight?*

Curriculum Connections

Math Have students compute how many calories they need to maintain their present weight. Ask them to compare this figure to the total number of calories they consume in a day.

History Ask students to research how society's view of the ideal figure has changed through the years. Have them create a display or time line illustrating their findings.

Family and Consumer Sciences Have students plan a week's worth of menus to meet their individual goals of healthy weight management.

Health Skills Practice

Influences on Body Image Have students think about people they know who feel insecure or embarrassed about their weight. Ask students whether they think these individuals really need to lose (or gain) weight or are reacting to pressure from society, the media, friends, and family. Have students analyze the ways in which these outside pressures influence body image. **L1**

Guest Speaker

Invite a school nurse or dietitian to talk to the class about reaching and maintaining a healthy weight. Encourage students to prepare a list of questions to ask the speaker. **L1**

hotlink

Ask students to provide examples of factors that contribute to sedentary and active lifestyles. You may also want students to look at this issue from a historical point of view. Discuss the impact of sedentary and active lifestyles on weight management.

Critical Thinking

Ask students: Why is there an obsession with being thin? Who do people compare themselves to? Is this comparison fair? **L2**

Discussing

Talk about the value of consulting a doctor, nurse, or dietitian before starting a program to lose or gain weight. **L1**

Community Involvement

Ask volunteers to visit local fast-food restaurants to see how they have responded to people's increasing concerns about healthful food choices. Have students report their findings to the class. Discuss how fast-food alternatives such as salads and baked potatoes may be healthful choices as long as they are not covered with high-fat salad dressings, margarine, butter, or cheese. **L1** ▪

Explaining

Stress that slow, steady weight loss or gain is healthier and more likely to be permanent than rapid, variable weight loss or gain. **L1**

VISUAL LEARNING

Figure 6.2 Have students review the information and photographs shown in Figure 6.2. Ask: What are other examples of nutrient-dense, low-calorie foods? What other physical activities are good ways to burn more calories?

FIGURE 6.2

THE BEST WEIGHT-LOSS STRATEGY

Eat Fewer Calories
Eat more foods that are high in nutrients and low in calories.

Burn More Calories
Burn more calories through physical activity.

Healthful Ways to Manage Weight

The teen years are a period of rapid growth and change, so some fluctuations in your weight are normal during this time. Following the ABCs of good health will help most teens maintain a healthy weight. However, if you want to begin a formal weight-management plan, these strategies can help:

▶ **Target your appropriate weight.** Speak with a health care professional to determine a weight range that is healthy for you.

▶ **Set realistic goals.** Gaining or losing one-half pound to one pound per week is a safe and realistic goal.

▶ **Personalize your plan.** Think about your food preferences and lifestyle when designing your weight management program.

▶ **Put your goal and plan in writing.** You might also find it helpful to keep a journal of what and when you eat to become more aware of your eating habits.

▶ **Evaluate your progress.** Track your progress by weighing yourself weekly at the same time of day. Remember that time periods when your weight does not change are normal.

Healthy Weight-Loss Strategies

A health care provider is your best source of information about your appropriate weight. If he or she recommends that you lose weight, use the best weight-loss strategy, illustrated in **Figure 6.2**. Here are some other tips for losing weight.

▶ **Eat 1,700 to 1,800 calories daily to meet your body's energy needs.** To reach this goal, eat at least the minimum number of servings from each of the five groups in the Food Guide Pyramid. Eating fewer than 1,400 calories a day may cause you to miss out on essential nutrients.

▶ **Include your favorites in moderation.** Eat smaller portions of your favorite high-calorie foods, and eat them less frequently. Instead of giving up ice cream altogether, for example, have a small scoop once a week.

▶ **Eat a variety of low-calorie, nutrient-dense foods.** **Nutrient-dense foods** are *foods that are high in nutrients as compared with their calorie content.* Whole-grain products, vegetables, and fruits are examples of low-calorie, nutrient-dense foods.

▶ **Drink plenty of water.** Eight glasses a day will help keep your body functioning at its best.

More About...

Weight-Loss Strategies Here are some helpful hints for students trying to lose weight: (1) Be patient. Don't try to lose weight in a hurry. Modify your eating habits gradually. (2) Have healthy foods available and be determined to eat them. (3) If you have setbacks, don't panic or give up. Stay calm and analyze the situation. For example, if you find yourself craving a high-calorie snack, take a moment to consider why you want to eat that snack. Instead of giving in to a craving, go for a walk or call a friend. If you do give in to a craving every now and then, don't criticize yourself. Just take steps to get back on track.

Exploring Issues

Should Schools Limit the Use of Vending Machines?

In schools across the country, vending machines offer soda, candy, and other snacks. Some schools limit the types of foods offered in vending machines or restrict student access to the machines. Should schools set rules concerning vending machines? Here are two points of view.

Viewpoint 1: Philip S., age 16

Most of the food in vending machines is high in sugar, fat, or salt—definitely not part of a healthful eating plan. I've seen kids eat only the foods from vending machines for lunch. If access to the vending machines were limited, students would have to eat more healthful meals. I think that schools have every right to put limits on access or to change the foods offered.

Viewpoint 2: Katie T., age 15

I don't think schools need to limit the types of snacks in vending machines or restrict students' access to them. It's up to the individual to make responsible decisions about his or her food choices. Besides, eating snacks high in sugar, fat, or salt is okay once in a while.

ACTIVITIES

1. Are vending machines interfering with students' efforts to eat healthfully? Why or why not?

2. Should schools control the contents of vending machines or restrict access to them? Explain your answer.

Healthy Weight-Gain Strategies

Follow these tips to gain weight healthfully:

▶ **Increase your calorie intake.** Choose foods high in complex carbohydrates, such as breads, pasta, and potatoes. Limit foods high in fat and sugar.

▶ **Eat often and take second helpings.** Choose more than the minimum number of servings from each food group in the Food Guide Pyramid.

▶ **Eat nutritious snacks.** Snack two to three hours before meals to avoid spoiling your appetite.

▶ **Build muscle.** A supervised resistance-training program will help you gain weight by increasing muscle mass.

HEALTH Online

Go to **health.glencoe.com** to learn more about the basics of healthy weight management from Shape Up America.

Lesson 1 Maintaining a Healthy Weight **149**

Myths & Reality

MYTH. A person can lose weight simply by eating fewer calories.

FACT. Most people cannot permanently lose weight just by eating fewer calories. The human body tries to maintain a fixed weight, or set point; when a person eats less, the body thinks it is starving. It has a built-in safeguard to protect it from the famines human beings have had to face throughout history. As soon as an individual reduces the calories he or she consumes, the metabolic rate slows down, and the body begins to use fewer calories for all of its processes. However, a small amount of daily physical activity can help speed up the metabolic rate and thereby lower the person's set point.

Exploring Issues

SHOULD SCHOOLS LIMIT THE USE OF VENDING MACHINES?

If your school permits students access to vending machines, have small groups of students discuss the following: If they don't offer healthful choices, do students balance their intake of unhealthful snacks as part of an overall healthful eating plan? How would their eating plan change if they did not have access? If your school does not have vending machines or limits their access, ask students whether their eating habits might change if they did. If yes, how? Then have students read the feature and answer the questions.

Reinforcing Concepts

Have students use a calorie chart to determine how many calories are burned through their daily activities. **L2 Mathematical Intelligence**

Service Learning

Have students design refrigerator magnets or signs to promote healthful snacking. Choose some of the projects to display in the classroom. **L1**

HEALTH Online

As students plan their own healthful eating program, have them check the Web Links for weight-management tips and safe workout practices.

③ ASSESS

EVALUATING THE LESSON

Assign and discuss the Lesson 1 Review; then administer, grade, and discuss Lesson Quiz 20 in the TCR. 📁

RETEACHING

- Make up some advice-column-type questions that can be answered at least in part with information from the lesson. Have students work individually to compose responses. Remind students to proofread for errors before creating a final draft. Then have students read one another's responses, and comment on the advice given.

- Ask students to complete Reteaching Activity 20 in the TCR. 📁

ENRICHMENT

Ask students to pretend that they are creators of a chain of fast-food restaurants that feature only healthy food choices. Have them work in groups to decide on a restaurant name, a nutritionally balanced menu featuring low-calorie fast foods, and a promotional campaign that is targeted to teens.

④ CLOSE

Have students close their textbooks and write an outline of the lesson's major concepts. Afterward, request that they open their textbooks to check the accuracy of their outlines. Conclude with a brief discussion of the most important concepts learned in the lesson.

▼ **Fruit and vegetable drinks are nutrient-dense snacks that can be part of a healthy weight-management plan.** *What are some other examples of nutrient-dense snacks?*

Physical Activity and Weight Management

Whether you want to lose, gain, or maintain weight, regular physical activity should be part of your plan. Aerobic exercise burns calories and helps you lose fat. Weight lifting or resistance training will increase muscle mass and produce a firm, lean body shape. Also, since muscle is more efficient than fat at burning calories, having more lean muscle tissue increases the number of calories your body burns, even at rest. Here are some added benefits of regular physical activity:

► It helps relieve the stress that often leads to over- or undereating.

► It promotes a normal appetite response, which helps you gain, lose, or maintain weight.

► It increases self-esteem, which helps keep your plan on track.

Research consistently shows that regular physical activity, combined with healthy eating habits, is the most efficient and healthful way to manage your weight and live a healthy life. Choose activities that you enjoy and that fit your personality. You will soon discover your body's capabilities and begin to look and feel your best.

▶ Lesson 1 *Review*

Reviewing Facts and Vocabulary

1. List three factors that influence what an individual's appropriate weight should be.
2. Explain the difference between the terms *overweight* and *obesity*.
3. Examine and briefly describe the relationship among body composition, diet, and fitness.

Thinking Critically

4. **Analyzing.** How can keeping a food journal help a person manage his or her weight?
5. **Hypothesizing.** Why is it important to eat a variety of low-calorie, nutrient-dense foods if you're trying to lose weight?

Applying Health Skills

Practicing Healthful Behaviors. Vicki wants to be sure that she maintains a healthy weight range as she moves through her teen years. What behaviors can Vicki practice to help her meet this goal? Write a short story that shows how Vicki practices these behaviors.

TECHNOLOGY *OPTION*

WORD PROCESSING Word processing can give your short story a professional look. See **health.glencoe.com** for tips on how to get the most out of your word-processing program.

150 **Chapter 6** Managing Weight and Body Composition

▶ Lesson 1 *Review*

Answers to Reviewing Facts and Vocabulary

1. Any three: gender, age, height, body frame, growth rate, metabolism, activity level.
2. See page 146 for definitions.
3. Diet and fitness affect a person's body composition—the ratio of body fat to lean body tissue.

Answers to Thinking Critically

4. Possible answer: It can help a person see exactly what he or she eats and why.
5. When limiting your caloric intake, you want to be sure that calories you take in are providing all the nutrients you need.

Fad Diets and Eating Disorders

VOCABULARY
fad diets
weight cycling
eating disorder
anorexia nervosa
bulimia nervosa
binge eating
  disorder

YOU'LL LEARN TO

- Describe the risks of fad diets and other dangerous weight-loss strategies.

- Describe the causes, symptoms, and treatment of eating disorders.

- Provide help to someone with an eating disorder.

- Identify the presence of an eating disorder as a situation requiring assistance from professional health services.

➡ **QUICK START** Write the term *diet* in the center of a sheet of paper. Around this term, write five to ten words or phrases that come to mind when you hear the word *diet*.

"**M**iracle patch lets you lose weight without dieting!" "One pill helps you burn fat and lose pounds!" Are you familiar with promises like these? They often appear in print ads and TV commercials. You may hear them on the radio. Such ads promise quick and easy weight loss. What do they actually deliver?

Risky Weight-Loss Strategies

A number of weight-loss strategies not only fail to produce long-term results but also can cause serious health problems. Part of being a health-literate consumer involves recognizing the potential health risks associated with some weight-loss plans and products.

Fad Diets

If you see an ad like the one shown here, be wary. Such ads are often for **fad diets**, *weight-loss plans that are popular for only a short time.* These diets often are hard to stick with because they limit food variety. The "grapefruit diet" is an example of a food-limiting fad diet. Some fad diets are costly because they require dieters to buy certain products. Fad diets that severely restrict the foods a dieter eats fail to provide the body with the nutrients it needs for health and growth. Any weight lost on fad diets is usually regained.

> "I Lost 142 Pounds Fast! Eat 5 and 6 Meals a Day of All My Favorite Foods!!"
> "This Is The Easiest Diet That I Had Ever Tried!"
>
> NOW YOU CAN EAT ALL YOU WANT OF THESE GREAT FOODS WHILE EXTRA WEIGHT DISAPPEARS:
>
> "Dietol-7 Users Have Lost Over 5 Million Pounds!"
>
> BACON, EGGS, ROAST PORK, ROAST BEEF, SPARE RIBS, CHICKEN, SHRIMP, LOBSTER DRIPPING IN BUTTER) AND MUCH MORE...
>
> Available at most nutrition centers and other fine stores
>
> SHIPPED CONFIDENTIALLY

🅐 **Fad diets may promise quick and easy weight loss, but any weight lost on these diets is usually regained.** *What features does a healthful weight-loss program have?*

Lesson 2 Resources

Teacher Classroom Resources

📁 Concept Mapping Activity 21

📁 Guided Reading Activities 21

📁 Lesson Plan 21

📁 Lesson Quiz 21

📁 Reteaching Activity 21

Student Activity Workbook

📁 Applying Health Skills 21

📁 Chapter 6 Study Guide

Fad Diets and Eating Disorders

① FOCUS

➡ **QUICK START**   Write the word *diet* on the board. As students create their word webs, ask volunteers to share some of their responses, and write them on the board. Ask students: Are the majority of responses positive or negative? Why do you think this is so?

TYING TO PRIOR KNOWLEDGE

Ask volunteers to share what they know about eating disorders. Lead the class in discussing reasons some teens might develop eating disorders or poor eating patterns.

Health Skills Features

"Fad Diets Harm Health," p. 153

ADVOCACY

"Helping a Friend Get Help," p. 155

DECISION MAKING

INTRODUCING VOCABULARY

- Ask students to create and share a brief public service announcement for a popular teen radio station about eating disorders, using the terms *anorexia nervosa, bulimia nervosa,* and *binge eating disorder.*

- Ask students to complete the Chapter 6 Study Guide in the *Student Activity Workbook.* 📁

2 TEACH

Cross Curriculum Activity

Math Have students find the number of calories in a single serving of their favorite snack foods. (Help students to understand what constitutes a serving size.) Ask volunteers to compile the calorie information into a one-page handout for the class.

Health Skills Practice

Weight-Loss Strategies

ACCESSING INFORMATION

Have students locate examples of diet plans from magazines and newspapers and bring them to class. Lead students in a discussion of the relative merits of the different plans. Ask them if any of the advice seems dangerous (such as an extremely low-calorie diet) and which of the plans seems most sensible. **L2**

Explaining

Tell students that most people regain the weight they've lost on fad diets or other quick weight-loss methods. Often, dieters will gain back more weight than they had lost as soon as they return to their regular eating habits. Stress the importance of eating for health. **L1**

Did You Know?

→ Some weight-loss products contain a substance called *ephedra*. Manufacturers may claim that ephedra can suppress appetite, promote weight loss, and increase energy and physical endurance. However, ephedra can lead to heart attacks, strokes, or even death.

Always read the labels of products before you buy or use them, and never take a product containing ephedra.

⚠ Effective weight management involves making healthy lifestyle choices. *What steps can a person take to successfully manage his or her weight?*

Liquid Diets

A person on a liquid diet replaces all of his or her food intake with a special liquid formula. These very-low-calorie diets generally do not meet the body's energy needs. As a result, they often leave the dieter feeling fatigued. Many liquid diets do not provide the body with fiber and needed nutrients. Relying on high-protein, low-carbohydrate liquids as the only source of nutrients can cause serious health problems and even death. Because of the potential dangers associated with liquid diets, the U.S. Food and Drug Administration (FDA) requires these products to carry warning labels and recommends that they be used only under close medical supervision.

Fasting

To fast is to abstain from eating. Although this may seem like a sure way to lose weight, fasting for more than short periods deprives your body of needed nutrients and energy. Without a fresh supply of nutrients each day, your body begins breaking down protein stored in muscle tissue for energy. If the person who is fasting also avoids liquids, he or she may become dehydrated.

Some religious and cultural rituals involve brief periods of fasting. Such fasting is not dangerous for the average person because the fast is of limited duration. However, fasting may not be advisable for those with diabetes or other health conditions. If you are unsure about how cultural or religious fasting may affect a medical condition, consult a health care professional for advice.

Diet Pills

Many diet pills work by suppressing appetite. They may cause drowsiness, anxiety, a racing heart, or other serious side effects. Diet pills may also be addictive. Some cause the body to lose more water than normal, which can lead to dehydration. Diet pills may claim to "burn," "block," or "flush" fat from the body, but a low-risk pill that meets these claims has not yet been developed.

Weight Cycling

Some diet plans or products may seem to help people lose weight quickly, but the weight loss is usually from water, not body fat. Water weight lost is quickly regained. *The repeated pattern of loss and regain of body weight* is called **weight cycling**. Weight cycling is common in people who follow fad diets. Some reports have suggested that weight cycling is harmful, although other studies do not support this finding. In general, slow and steady weight loss is the best strategy for long-lasting results.

Curriculum Connections

Language Arts Encourage students to become consumer reporters and investigate the following approaches to weight management: diet candies, diet pills, liposuction, liquid meals, weight-loss clubs, gastric bypass surgery, and a currently popular diet. Have them write a "Consumer Update," describing the approach, effectiveness, cost, and safety of each. Remind students to proofread for errors. Then have them write a final draft. Make copies of their reports to distribute to the entire class.

Hands-On Health ACTIVITY

Fad Diets Harm Health

In a society obsessed by weight and appearance, the promise of quick weight loss is hard to resist. However, fad diets are not only ineffective in producing long-term weight loss, they're also potentially harmful. In this activity you will create a poster advocating against fad diets.

What You'll Need

- poster board
- markers

What You'll Do

1. As a class, brainstorm potentially harmful effects of fad diets.
2. In groups of two or three, come up with a simple concept that conveys the message that fad diets can harm health. Your concept should be relevant to high school students.
3. Make a poster illustrating your message. Include supporting information about healthful weight-loss strategies in the poster.
4. Ask permission to display your posters at school.

Apply and Conclude

Is your poster persuasive? What advocacy techniques did you use to persuade others? How will your poster have a positive effect on the health of your audience? Why is this an important health issue for teens?

The Risks of Eating Disorders

Sometimes a person's concerns about weight and efforts to lose weight can get out of control. Becoming obsessed with thinness can lead to eating disorders. An **eating disorder** is an *extreme, harmful eating behavior that can cause serious illness or even death*. The exact cause of eating disorders is unknown. They may be brought on by mental or emotional factors such as poor body image, social and family pressures, and perfectionism. Some scientists think that the cause may be partly genetic. Teens with a family history of weight problems, depression, or substance abuse may be more at risk for developing an eating disorder.

About 90 percent of those with eating disorders are female. It's estimated that about one percent of females ages 16 to 18 have this illness. Eating disorders are a serious health problem, and people who suffer from them need professional help.

Lesson 2 Fad Diets and Eating Disorders **153**

⎍⋀⋁⋀⎍ HEALTH LITERACY

Critical Thinker Assign students to examine articles in general-interest and women's magazines for a period of four weeks. Tell them to pay particular attention to the magazines displayed near supermarket checkout lines. Have students record the number of articles about weight-loss strategies, especially fad diets. Encourage them to compare the number of weight-loss articles with the number of articles on developing a nutritious eating plan. Have them write up their conclusions about the consumer's relationship with food, weight, and dieting. ▭▭

Critical Thinking

Ask students: What are some of the health consequences of bulimia nervosa? Why does treatment include psychological counseling in addition to medication? The health consequences of bulimia nervosa include dehydration, kidney damage, and irregular heartbeat, all of which are associated with frequent vomiting or diarrhea. Vomiting also erodes tooth enamel, causes tooth decay, and damages the tissues of the stomach, esophagus, and mouth. Frequent laxative use may disrupt digestion and interfere with nutrient absorption, resulting in deficiencies. Because the development of bulimia nervosa may be due in part to psychological issues, such as low self-esteem, psychotherapy is usually a component of treatment. **L1**

Discussing

Have students describe the food choices they make when they are angry, sad, or frustrated. Ask them whether the choices are different from the choices they make when they are happy, excited, or content. If so, have them describe how their choices are different and why they think this is so. **L1**

People with anorexia often see themselves as overweight even when they are very thin. *What type of help does an individual with an eating disorder need?*

Anorexia Nervosa

Anorexia nervosa is *a disorder in which the irrational fear of becoming obese results in severe weight loss from self-imposed starvation.* Anorexia nervosa is a psychological disorder with emotional and physical consequences. The disorder relates to an individual's self-concept and coping abilities. Outside pressures, high expectations, a need to be accepted, and a need to achieve are characteristics associated with the development of anorexia. Medical specialists have also found that genetics and other biological factors may play an equally powerful role in the development of this disorder. Hormones and certain brain chemicals have been shown to trigger the illness in some people.

Anorexia develops most often in teenage girls and young women. Symptoms include extremely low caloric intake, an obsession with exercising, emotional problems, an unnatural interest in food, a distorted body image, and denial of an eating problem.

HEALTH CONSEQUENCES OF ANOREXIA NERVOSA

Physical consequences of anorexia are related to malnutrition and starvation. A drastic reduction of body fat may cause females with anorexia to stop menstruating. Other consequences include loss of bone density, low body temperature, low blood pressure, slowed metabolism, and reduction in organ size. People with anorexia may develop serious heart problems, including an irregular heartbeat that can lead to cardiac arrest and sudden death.

Treatment for anorexia nervosa may include a stay at a clinic or hospital where the person can receive nutrients to regain weight and strength. Anorexia nervosa also requires psychological treatment to address the problems that lead to the disorder.

Bulimia Nervosa

Bulimia nervosa is *a disorder in which some form of purging or clearing of the digestive tract follows cycles of overeating.* A person with bulimia often fasts or follows a strict diet and then *binges,* or quickly consumes large amounts of food. After eating, the person may vomit or take laxatives to purge the food from the body. Following a binge, the person may again try dieting to gain a sense of control and avoid putting on weight. The exact cause of bulimia has not been determined, but societal pressures, self-esteem issues, and family problems may be factors.

154 **Chapter 6** Managing Weight and Body Composition

What Teens Want to Know

I think my friend might have anorexia nervosa. How can I tell for sure? The only way to know for sure if someone has anorexia nervosa is for the person to be diagnosed by a health care professional. However, some signs of anorexia nervosa include low calorie intake; extreme interest in food; obsessive involvement in strenuous activity; intense fear of being obese; inaccurate image of one's body; attitude of extreme perfectionism; emotional problems; extreme weight loss; constipation; and, in females, absence of menstrual periods. Early diagnosis and care improve the chance of recovery, so it is important for anyone who may have anorexia nervosa to seek professional help.

HEALTH CONSEQUENCES OF BULIMIA NERVOSA

Repeated binging, purging, and fasting can cause serious health problems or even death. Frequent vomiting and diarrhea can lead to dehydration, kidney damage, and irregular heartbeat. Vomiting also destroys tooth enamel; causes tooth decay; and damages the tissues of the stomach, esophagus, and mouth. Frequent use of laxatives disrupts digestion and absorption and may cause nutrient deficiencies. Laxative abuse can also change the composition of the blood. Treatment of bulimia nervosa usually includes both medication and psychological counseling.

Binge Eating Disorder

People with **binge eating disorder**, *a disorder characterized by compulsive overeating,* consume huge amounts of food at one time but do not try to purge. This disorder may signal the use of food as a coping mechanism for strong emotions or depression. Treatment involves professional psychological counseling and sometimes medication.

Decision Making: Helping a Friend Get Help

Audrey and Rebecca are friends. They are both on the school basketball team. Lately, Audrey has noticed that Rebecca skips lunch and seems to be losing weight.

One day after practice, Rebecca tells Audrey that she is going to jog for at least a mile. Audrey is amazed. "What do you mean? You just ran up and down the court for two full hours."

Rebecca says, "I ate a salad for lunch today. I'm getting fat." Audrey suspects that Rebecca has an eating disorder and wonders how to help her.

What Would You Do?

Apply the decision-making steps to Audrey's problem.

1. State the situation.
2. List the options.
3. Weigh the possible outcomes.
4. Consider values.
5. Make a decision and act.
6. Evaluate the decision.

Health Skills Activity

HELPING A FRIEND GET HELP

DECISION MAKING

NHES Standard 6 Students will demonstrate the ability to use goal-setting and decision-making skills to enhance health.

Objectives

- Describe the symptoms of eating disorders.
- Apply decision-making skills to make a health-promoting decision.

Motivator

As a class, ask students to describe possible signs of an eating disorder.

Teaching Strategies

1. Remind students of the seriousness of eating disorders and that an adult should always be told if a disorder is suspected.
2. Ask volunteers to suggest how Audrey might express her concerns in an empathetic way.

✓Assessment

Using a rubric, student work should provide comprehensive evidence of the following criteria to achieve the highest score:

✔ clear description of the situation
✔ several options with possible outcomes of each
✔ influence of values on possible decisions
✔ health-enhancing decision and an evaluation of it

Home and Community

Help for Eating Disorders Have students research community sources of help for individuals suffering from anorexia nervosa, bulimia nervosa, or binge eating disorder. They could check with local hospitals, mental health facilities, and support groups such as Overeaters Anonymous. Have students prepare a list of survey questions to ask about the types of treatment available, the length of most kinds of treatment, fees, qualifications, and training of personnel. Ask students to share materials from the community programs and their findings with the class.

③ ASSESS

EVALUATING THE LESSON

Assign and discuss the Lesson 2 Review; then administer, grade, and discuss Lesson Quiz 21 in the TCR.

RETEACHING

- Have students identify products that claim quick and easy weight loss. Challenge them to explain why these claims are likely to be false.

- Ask students to complete the Reteaching Activity 21 in the TCR.

ENRICHMENT

Have interested students interview an expert to find out how starvation from anorexia or dehydration from bulimia affects the body. Have them determine why lack of food or water ultimately causes death. Ask them to discuss their findings with the class.

④ CLOSE

Lead a class discussion on ways to deal with peer pressure that is related to food choices.

 Psychologists and clinics that specialize in the treatment of eating disorders may offer support groups for people with these disorders. *Why might support groups be helpful to individuals with eating disorders?*

HEALTH CONSEQUENCES OF BINGE EATING DISORDER

Binge eating disorder often results in unhealthful weight gain, which contributes to health problems such as type 2 diabetes, heart disease, and stroke. Gallbladder problems, high blood pressure, high cholesterol, and increased risk of certain types of cancer have also been associated with this disorder.

Help for Eating Disorders

People with eating disorders need professional medical and psychological help. They may also benefit from support groups and clinics. All eating disorders are serious. If you believe a friend might be developing an eating disorder, you may want to discuss the problem with a trusted adult such as a parent, a counselor, or a school nurse. You can also help by encouraging your friend to seek professional help and by being supportive.

▶ Lesson 2 Review

Reviewing Facts and Vocabulary

1. Define the term *fad diets*.
2. Describe the causes, symptoms, and treatment of the eating disorder anorexia nervosa.
3. What is *bulimia nervosa*?

Thinking Critically

4. **Evaluating.** Describe the similarities and differences between bulimia nervosa and binge eating disorder.
5. **Analyzing.** Why do people with eating disorders require assistance from professional health services?

Applying Health Skills

Advocacy. Think of ways to inform teens about the dangers of fad diets and other risky weight-loss strategies. With a group of classmates, plan and create a video or public service announcement (PSA) that tells teens about these dangers and gives tips for healthy weight loss.

TECHNOLOGY *OPTION*

WEB SITES Use your video or PSA as part of a Web page you develop on healthy weight management. See health.glencoe.com for help in planning and building your own Web site.

▶ Lesson 2 Review

Answers to Reviewing Facts and Vocabulary

1. Weight-loss plans that are popular for only a short time.
2. See Anorexia Nervosa on page 154.
3. A disorder in which some form of purging or clearing of the digestive tract follows cycles of overeating.

Answers to Thinking Critically

4. Like bulimics, people with binge eating disorder eat large amounts of food at one time. Unlike bulimics, they do not purge to rid their bodies of the food.
5. Professional health services are needed to address the physical and psychological aspects of eating disorders.

Nutrition for Individual Needs

VOCABULARY

electrolytes
rehydration
vegetarian
vegan
dietary supplement
megadose
herbal supplement

YOU'LL LEARN TO

- Understand the specific nutritional needs of different groups.

- Explain the importance of proper nutrition in promoting optimal health for pregnant women, infants, and young children.

- Identify good nutrition as a health-promoting behavior that will enhance and maintain personal health throughout life.

 QUICK START An individual's nutritional needs change throughout his or her life. Brainstorm a list of times in a person's life during which nutritional needs may change. Briefly explain each of your choices.

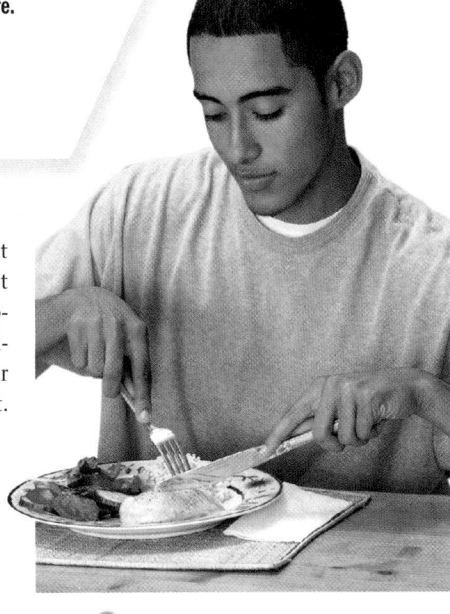

Does it seem to you that everyone has a different idea about proper nutrition? Some friends may tell you that eating meat is unhealthy, and others may insist that eating too many carbohydrates is bad for you. What can you believe? In truth, proper nutrition may depend on the individual. A pregnant woman, for example, has different nutritional needs than those of an older adult.

Performance Nutrition

Do you play on a sports team or take aerobics classes? Good nutrition can help you perform your best in any physical activity.

The Training Diet

No single food will help you build muscle or increase speed. The best eating plan for athletes is one that is balanced, moderate, and varied. Your body's need for protein, vitamins, and minerals does not change greatly when training for sports or competition. However, because physical activity burns calories, athletes and other active individuals need to eat more calories from nutrient-dense foods to maintain their weight and energy levels when training.

Eating well-balanced meals and snacks each day is an important part of any training program. *Why is it important for physically active people to have a well-balanced eating plan?*

Lesson 3 Resources

Teacher Classroom Resources

📁 Concept Mapping Activity 22

📁 Current Health Issues 6

📁 Guided Reading Activities 22

📁 Health Lab 6

📁 Lesson Plan 22

📁 Lesson Quiz 22

📁 Reteaching Activity 22

Student Activity Workbook

📁 Applying Health Skills 22

📁 Chapter 6 Study Guide

Multimedia

💾 Transparency 18

Lesson 3

Nutrition for Individual Needs

1 FOCUS

 QUICK START As a class, brainstorm a list of times in a person's life when nutritional needs may change. Write some of the responses on the board.

TYING TO PRIOR KNOWLEDGE

Write the following statement on the board: *Athletes have different nutritional needs than nonathletes.* Ask: Do you agree with this statement? Why or why not? Tell students that the nutritional needs of athletes and other individuals with specific concerns will be discussed in this lesson.

Health Skills Features

"Meatless Meals," p. 160 ACCESSING INFORMATION

INTRODUCING VOCABULARY

- Direct students to look up the definitions of *vegetarian* and *vegan* in the dictionary. Have them write a brief paragraph that compares and contrasts the terms. Then have them exchange papers with a partner to check for accuracy.

- Ask students to complete the Chapter 6 Study Guide in the *Student Activity Workbook.* 📁

2 TEACH

Critical Thinking

Ask students: Why is there so much misinformation regarding athletes and dieting? People look for quick, easy answers to gain more speed, strength, etc. **L2**

Explaining

Let students explain what being an athlete involves: Is a training diet appropriate only for teens who participate in organized sports? Encourage students to clarify and support their answers. **L1**

hot link

Have students research the specific symptoms and dangers of heatstroke. How can this condition be recognized? How should it be treated? Have students discuss their findings in class.

Cooperative Learning

Have students work in small groups to brainstorm a list of sports or other activities in which weight is considered important. Ask each group to share a few of their ideas, and record them on the board. Then let the groups of students divide the activities into two lists, one in which participants strive to keep their weight down and the other in which participants try to keep their weight up. **L1**

hot link

heatstroke For more information on the physical effects of heatstroke, see Chapter 4, page 99.

⚑ **Resistance training helps build muscle mass.**

hot link

anabolic steroids For more information about the dangers of anabolic steroids, see Chapter 23, page 601.

HYDRATION

Your body naturally loses fluids through perspiration, breathing, and waste elimination. The amount of fluids lost increases during physical activity, especially in hot weather. These fluids must be replaced to avoid dehydration and **heatstroke.** Becoming dehydrated can lead to an imbalance of **electrolytes,** *minerals that help maintain the body's fluid balance.* The minerals sodium, chloride, and potassium are all electrolytes.

To maintain your body's electrolyte balance, you must take in as much water and electrolytes as you lose through perspiration and body wastes. Drink 16 to 24 ounces of fluids two to three hours before a heavy workout and 6 to 12 ounces of fluids every 15 to 20 minutes during heavy workouts. **Rehydration,** or *restoring lost body fluids,* is important after physical activity and competition. Drink 16 ounces of fluid for every pound of body weight lost through sweat. It's best to drink plain water to replenish fluids lost during exercise.

"Making Weight"

In sports such as wrestling and boxing, participants compete in specific weight classes, so maintaining a certain weight is important. Always compete at a weight that's right for you.

LOSING WEIGHT

Competing in a weight class that is below your healthy weight can be dangerous. Fasting, crash dieting, or trying to sweat off extra weight before weigh-in can cause dehydration and harm your performance and your health. Over time, such practices may also lead to a loss of muscle mass. Athletes who need to lose weight should follow a sensible plan and try to lose only one-half pound to one pound each week.

GAINING WEIGHT

A program that combines balanced nutrition and exercise is the healthful way to gain weight. A supervised resistance-training or weight-lifting program can help build muscle mass. The extra calories you need for gaining weight should come from nutrient-dense foods, not from protein supplements. For best results, a slow, steady weight gain of no more than one to two pounds per week is recommended. Using **anabolic steroids** or other bodybuilding drugs to build muscle mass is not healthy. Many of these drugs have dangerous side effects ranging from acne and breast development in men to heart attacks and liver cancer. Use of these substances is illegal; athletes who test positive for steroids and similar drugs often are disqualified from their sport.

158 Chapter 6 Managing Weight and Body Composition

More About...

Athletes and Body Weight Body weight is important in many sports. For example, extra weight is an advantage in football, while sports such as wrestling have weight restrictions. Being lean with good muscle mass is advantageous in many sports.

An athlete's weight should be within a healthy weight range for him or her and remain stable. Crash dieting and taking sweat baths before a weigh-in are unhealthy. They result in fatigue, dehydration, muscle loss, and poor performance. Athletes who need extra weight for contact sports should begin a slow, steady program of weight gain. Building extra muscle mass takes time and exercise.

Eating Before Competition

Eating three to four hours before competition allows the stomach to empty yet gives an athlete the necessary energy and keeps him or her free from hunger pangs while competing.

Before competing, choose a meal that's high in carbohydrates and low in fat and protein, both of which stay in the digestive system for a longer period of time. Pasta, rice, vegetables, breads, and fruits are good sources of carbohydrates. Also, remember to drink plenty of water before, during, and after competing.

Vegetarianism

A **vegetarian** is *a person who eats mostly or only plant foods.* Some people are vegetarians for religious or cultural reasons. Others make this choice because of their concern for the environment or for how food animals are raised or slaughtered. Many people become vegetarians for health reasons. By cutting out the saturated fats and cholesterol found in many or all animal products, vegetarians may reduce their risk of cardiovascular disease and some cancers. Also, vegetarians may consume more fruits, vegetables, and whole grains—foods that are linked to a reduced risk of many health problems. **Figure 6.3** describes four vegetarian eating styles.

FIGURE 6.3

VEGETARIAN EATING PLANS

No matter which plan a person follows, a vegetarian eating style still involves choosing nutritious foods.

Plan Name	Foods Included
Lacto-ovo vegetarianism	• Dairy *(lacto)* foods and eggs *(ovo)* in addition to foods from plant sources.
Lacto vegetarianism	• Dairy foods in addition to foods from plant sources.
Ovo vegetarianism	• Eggs in addition to foods from plant sources. Soy milk and soy cheese are often substituted for dairy products.
Vegan	• Foods from plant sources only. Soy milk and soy cheese are often substituted for dairy products.

Cooperative Learning

Let students form small cooperative groups, and have each group select a competitive sports event, such as a track meet, a volleyball game, or a gymnastics competition. Have group members work together to plan a specific meal for an athlete to eat before the competition. **L1**

Activity

Have students do research to refute these common sports nutrition myths: (1) Honey provides immediate energy. (2) Sucking ice before a workout will prevent dehydration. (3) Taking a salt tablet will help prevent dehydration. **L2**

Discussing

Help students identify and discuss the reasons people give for accepting or rejecting vegetarianism. Encourage students to share their responses to each suggested reason. Ask volunteers to explain their own reasons for following (or for choosing not to follow) a vegetarian eating plan. **L1**

VISUAL LEARNING

Figure 6.3 Guide students in studying the information shown in Figure 6.3. Divide the class into four groups and assign each group a vegetarian eating plan. Have each group create a week's worth of food choices. Encourage students to include a variety of foods that provide a balanced diet and include adequate amounts of iron, zinc, and B vitamins.

Curriculum Connections

Family and Consumer Sciences Team up with a food and nutrition class to discuss nutrient-dense vs. empty-calorie foods.

Science Have students research the ingredients in sports drinks and report their findings to the class.

Language Arts Help students write letters to their favorite athletes, asking about their training diets and pre-competition meals. Students may need to write outlines to help organize their ideas. Instruct students to develop drafts and proofread for errors before completing their final drafts.

Real-Life Application

MEATLESS MEALS

ACCESSING INFORMATION

NHES Standard 2 Students will demonstrate the ability to access valid health information and health-promoting products and services.

Objective

Demonstrate the ability to access and apply health information regarding healthful vegetarian meals.

Motivator

Give students two minutes to write down meatless foods that they enjoy.

Teaching Strategies

1. Suggest that students incorporate items from their lists into their menus.
2. Remind students that some meatless foods, such as cheese, are high in fat. Advise them to limit the inclusion of high-fat foods in their menus.
3. Ask students who are practicing vegetarians to share their meal-planning strategies.

✓ Assessment

Using a rubric, student work should provide comprehensive evidence of the following criteria to achieve the highest score:

✔ citation of specific sources
✔ evaluation of the validity of the source
✔ rationale for the appropriateness of the source
✔ type of help available from the sources

Real-Life Application

Meatless Meals

Some people have chosen to become vegetarians. A little planning can ensure that vegetarian meals contain sufficient amounts of nutrients.

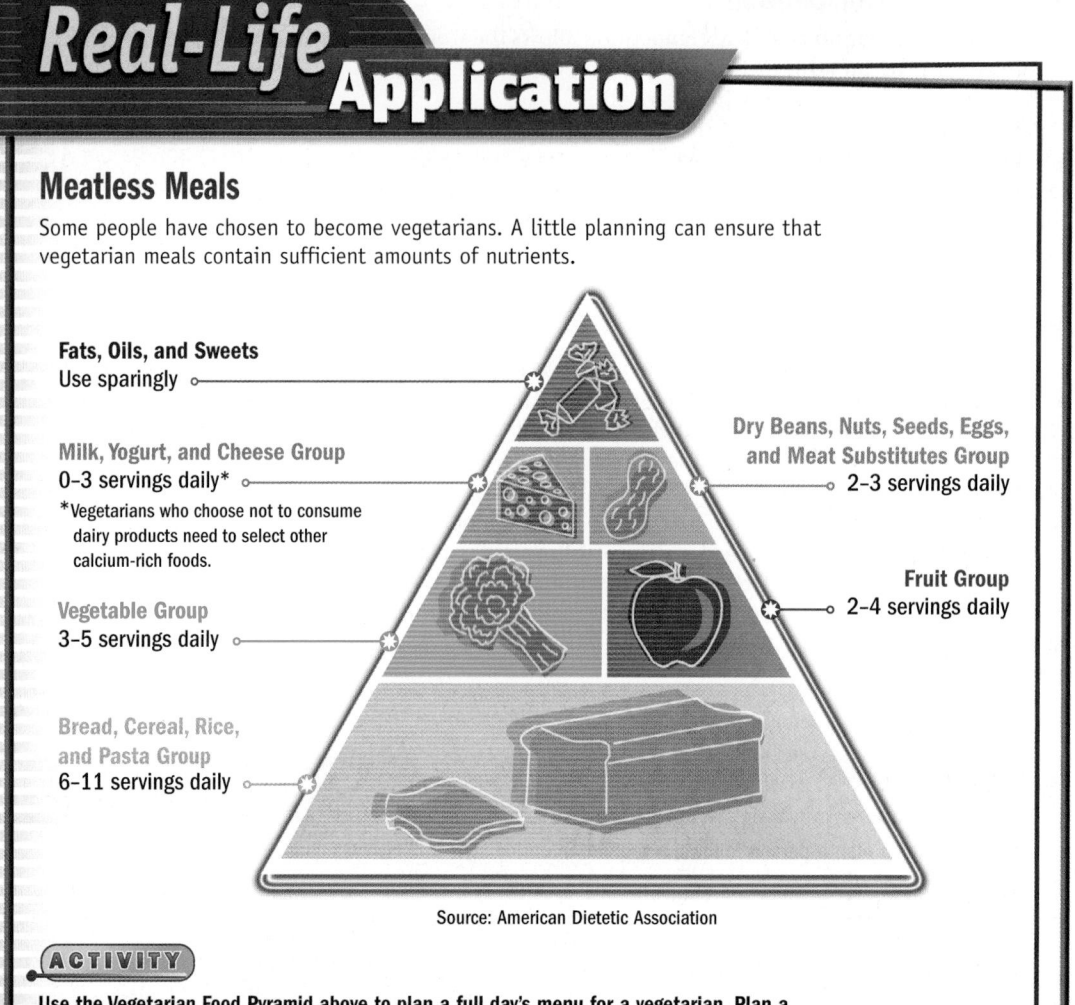

Fats, Oils, and Sweets
Use sparingly

Milk, Yogurt, and Cheese Group
0–3 servings daily*
*Vegetarians who choose not to consume dairy products need to select other calcium-rich foods.

Vegetable Group
3–5 servings daily

Bread, Cereal, Rice, and Pasta Group
6–11 servings daily

Dry Beans, Nuts, Seeds, Eggs, and Meat Substitutes Group
2–3 servings daily

Fruit Group
2–4 servings daily

Source: American Dietetic Association

ACTIVITY

Use the Vegetarian Food Pyramid above to plan a full day's menu for a vegetarian. Plan a breakfast, a mid-morning snack, a lunch, a mid-afternoon snack, and an evening meal.

MEETING NUTRIENT NEEDS

Vegetarians need to eat a variety of incomplete proteins in a way that will yield complete protein over the course of a day. They must also make sure they get enough iron, zinc, and B vitamins, nutrients often found in animal products. For vegetarians the key to getting complete proteins and enough vitamins lies in eating adequate amounts of various nutrient-dense foods, including fruits, vegetables, leafy greens, whole grains, nuts, seeds, and legumes, as well as dairy foods or eggs. **Vegans** are *vegetarians who eat only plant foods.*

160 Chapter 6 Managing Weight and Body Composition

Promoting Coordinated School Health

The Team In a coordinated school health program, each campus would have a site-based decision-making committee made up of teachers, campus staff, parents, community members, and business representatives. In addition to academic performance objectives, students' physical and psychological needs must also be addressed. Schools might already have a dropout-prevention committee working with school/community drug-prevention committees. These committees can also focus on students' academic performance as related to health. For more information about developing such a program, consult *Planning a Coordinated School Health Program.*

Because vegans consume no meat or dairy products, they must obtain vitamin D, vitamin B_{12}, and calcium from other sources.

Dietary Supplements

Do you take a multivitamin and mineral supplement regularly? These tablets are one type of **dietary supplement**, *a non-food form of one or more nutrients*. Dietary supplements may contain vitamins, minerals, fiber, protein, or herbs. Supplements can be in pill, capsule, powder, or liquid form.

Eating healthful meals and snacks based on the Food Guide Pyramid can provide you with all the nutrients your body needs. However, taking a multivitamin and mineral supplement may sometimes be appropriate. A health care provider may recommend these supplements to people with certain lifestyles or medical conditions. For example, a calcium supplement may be recommended for vegans or for people who are lactose intolerant. Iron tablets might be recommended for someone with iron-deficiency anemia.

Vitamin and mineral supplements may also be recommended for older adults, pregnant or nursing women, people receiving certain medical treatments, and those recovering from illness. If you are in doubt about your own requirements, ask a health care provider.

Risks of Dietary Supplements

Dietary supplements must be used carefully. Taking a **megadose**, or *a very large amount of a dietary supplement*, can be dangerous. Vitamins A, D, E, and K, for example, are stored in body fat and may cause toxicity if taken in large amounts.

An **herbal supplement** is a *chemical substance from plants that may be sold as a dietary supplement*. These substances are often sold as "natural" nutrition aids. However, the safety and nutritional claims of many of these products are not based on conclusive scientific evidence. Currently, manufacturers of herbal products are responsible for product safety and label claims unless the product is known to be dangerous. The Center for Food Safety and Applied Nutrition (CFSAN) of the U.S. FDA alerts consumers to potentially dangerous dietary supplements. Some herbal supplements known to have dangerous side effects include ephedra, lobelia, yohimbe, and chaparral.

Q&A

Are herbal products safe because they're natural?

Just because something is natural doesn't mean it's harmless. Certain herbs are poisonous. Others may be harmless on their own, but may interact dangerously with prescription or over-the-counter drugs. Consult a health care provider before taking any herbal supplement.

Labeling laws require manufacturers to include information about a supplement's ingredients. *Where would you go to find reliable information about supplements?*

ACTIVE READING

If/Then Statements

Creating their own statements about nutrition and dietary supplements will introduce students to these subjects. Model writing an If/Then statement such as "If I follow the Food Guide Pyramid, then I will probably not need to take dietary supplements." Tell students to look for more facts to add to their If/Then statements as they continue reading the lesson. For more strategies, see the *Guided Reading Activities* booklet in the TCR.

Discussing

Ask students to indicate whether they have taken vitamins or other dietary supplements. Let volunteers explain why they do—or do not—take such supplements regularly. Lead a class discussion on the potential benefits and risks of dietary supplements. **L2**

Discussing

Ask students to identify specific nutrient-dense foods: Which of these foods do you like? How can you incorporate more of these foods into your daily eating plan? How can eating more nutrient-dense foods help reduce your need for dietary supplements? **L1**

Lesson 3 Nutrition for Individual Needs **161**

Cooperative Learning Activity

Nutrition Time Line Divide students into five groups. Assign each group one of the stages in a person's life: infancy, childhood, adolescence, adulthood, and late adulthood. Ask each group to find out the specific nutritional needs of individuals during that stage of life. Have each group share their findings with the class. Then ask volunteers to compile the information to create an illustrated time line that shows how nutritional needs change throughout life. Remind students to check for errors before completing their final drafts.

Guest Speaker

Invite a local obstetrician or nurse-midwife to speak to the class, explaining the dietary recommendations he or she usually makes to pregnant patients. If the health care provider gives dietary lists or handouts to patients, ask that these be shared with students. Also, ask the health care professional to explain why he or she recommends prenatal vitamins for most patients. **L1**

Service Learning

Have students work in small groups to write a public service announcement for women about the importance of good nutrition during pregnancy. Have a member of each group read the announcement to the class. **L2**

Critical Thinking

Have students share their responses to these questions: Do you think vegan parents should limit the eating plans of their very young children to exclude all non-plant foods? Why or why not? **L1**

Activity

Ask volunteers to read about heart-healthy programs aimed at helping older adults reduce their risk of heart attack and stroke. What are the essential elements of the program? What results has the program documented? What difficulties, if any, are associated with the program? **L2**

Nutrition Throughout the Life Span

People have different nutritional needs at different stages of life. Many children and most teens, for example, need more calories each day than less active adults. While the nutritional needs of these groups vary slightly, most people can get all the calories and nutrients they need each day by following the recommendations from the *Dietary Guidelines* and the Food Guide Pyramid.

Nutrition During Pregnancy

A developing fetus depends on its mother for all its needs, so it's important for pregnant females to eat healthfully and to avoid harmful substances such as tobacco, alcohol, and other drugs. In addition to eating properly, pregnant females are encouraged to increase their intake of foods rich in the nutrients listed below. A health care provider may also recommend that a pregnant female take a multivitamin and mineral supplement to help meet these nutrient needs.

▶ **Folate.** Getting enough folate, or folic acid, early in pregnancy can prevent spinal defects in the developing fetus. Sources of this B vitamin include fruits, dark green leafy vegetables, and fortified grain products.

▶ **Iron.** Increased blood volume during pregnancy produces an increased demand for this mineral. Found in meat, poultry, fish, dark green leafy vegetables, and enriched grain products, iron helps build and renew hemoglobin, the oxygen-carrying compound in blood cells.

▶ **Calcium.** Calcium helps build the bones and teeth of the developing fetus and replaces any calcium taken from the mother's bones. Calcium is found in most dairy products, dark green leafy vegetables, canned fish with edible bones, and calcium-fortified cereals and juices.

Nutrition for Infants and Young Children

Breastfeeding is the best way to feed infants. If breastfeeding isn't possible, fortified formulas provide the nutrients that infants need. As a baby grows through its first year, breast milk or formula is supplemented with a variety of solid foods, usually starting with cereal grains, then vegetables and fruits, and then meat or poultry.

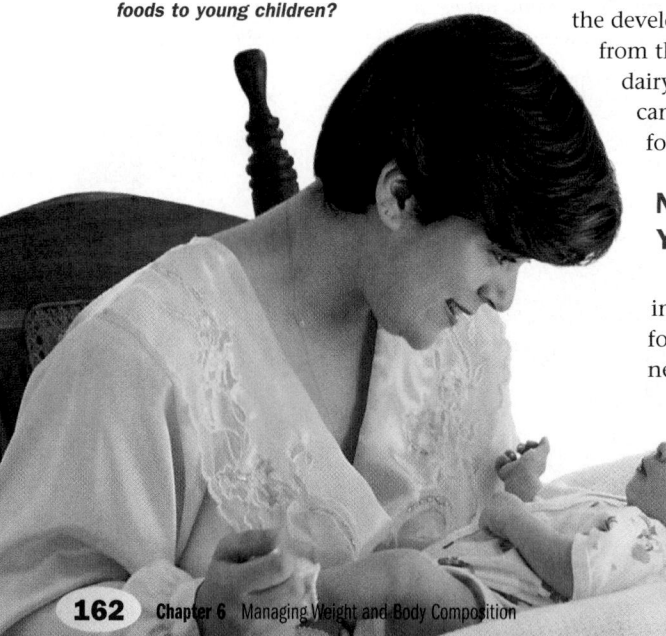

Good nutrition during early childhood is important for the health of the individual throughout his or her life span. *Why is it important to provide a variety of foods to young children?*

More About...

Breastfeeding Most health care professionals agree that breastfeeding is the best choice when it comes to feeding newborns. Breast milk is recommended for a variety of reasons. Because it contains natural immunities from the mother, breast milk helps protect infants from many illnesses, including respiratory problems, diarrhea, and ear infections. Breast milk can also lower a newborn's risk of developing some liver problems. Although some infants are allergic to formula, they do not have the same reaction to breast milk. Breastfeeding also provides long-term benefits for infants, including normal growth and reduced chance of being overweight.

After a child's first birthday, many parents substitute whole milk for formula or breast milk. The fats in whole milk provide essential nutrients for a child's developing nervous system. By this time most children are eating a variety of foods. This variety provides the energy and nutrients needed for growth and encourages the child to enjoy different foods.

Between a child's second and fifth birthdays, parents should gradually replace whole milk with low- or non-fat milk to meet calcium and vitamin D needs while reducing fat intake.

Nutrition and Older Adults

Most older adults can get all the calories and nutrients they need each day by following the recommendations in the *Dietary Guidelines* and the Food Guide Pyramid. Older adults may be advised to follow a special diet if they have a specific health problem.

In certain cases, health care providers might recommend that older adults take a dietary supplement to help meet their nutrient needs. For example, some older adults may take medications that interfere with nutrient absorption.

 Proper nutrition and active lifestyles help many of today's older adults remain in good health.

 Lesson 3 *Review*

Reviewing Facts and Vocabulary

1. What type of meal should an athlete eat before competing?
2. Define the term *vegetarian*.
3. Explain what a *megadose* is and why it may be dangerous.

Thinking Critically

4. **Synthesizing.** Explain why proper nutrition is especially important in promoting optimal health for pregnant women, infants, and young children.
5. **Analyzing.** How does good nutrition enhance and maintain personal health throughout life?

Applying Health Skills

Advocacy. Many people think that taking vitamins, minerals, and herbal supplements will improve their health. Develop a pamphlet to educate others about the best ways of getting the nutrients needed for good health. Include information on the safe use of supplements.

 TECHNOLOGY *OPTION*

PRESENTATION SOFTWARE By using presentation software, you can include art and graphics in a slide show on the importance of good nutrition. Find help in using presentation software at **health.glencoe.com**.

Lesson 3 Nutrition for Individual Needs **163**

 Lesson 3 *Review*

Answers to Reviewing Facts and Vocabulary

1. A precompetition meal should be high in carbohydrates and low in fat and protein, and should include plenty of water.
2. A vegetarian is a person who eats mostly or only plant foods.
3. A megadose is a very large amount of a dietary supplement. Some may be toxic.

Answers to Thinking Critically

4. Answers should include the nutritional requirements of a pregnant female, a developing fetus, an infant, and a young child.
5. Answers will vary, but should address various age groups.

Lesson 3 Review

EVALUATING THE LESSON

Assign and discuss the Lesson 3 Review; then administer, grade, and discuss Lesson Quiz *22* in the TCR.

RETEACHING

- Ask students to identify the specific nutritional needs of athletes and how these needs are best met.
- Ask students to complete Reteaching Activity 22 in the TCR.

ENRICHMENT

Have students plan a day's menu for a pregnant female. Ask them to highlight the foods that are rich in folate, iron, and calcium.

4 CLOSE

Remind students that an eating plan that follows the guidelines provided by the Food Guide Pyramid will meet the majority of their nutritional needs. Point out that taking a multivitamin and mineral supplement may be appropriate in certain situations.

Body Image in Teen Magazines

NHES Standard 4 Students will analyze the influence of culture, media, technology, and other factors on health.

Objective

Examine messages in teen magazines about what constitutes a healthy weight, as well as weight-management techniques.

Motivator

Ask volunteers to name their favorite magazines and give three reasons that they enjoy reading these particular magazines.

Teaching Strategies

Awareness As students review teen magazines, encourage them to look for the general messages on weight management that these magazines send.

Analysis Ask teens whether or not the magazine ads are consistent with articles that tell teens to strive for overall fitness.

Reflection Have the class brainstorm topics for the magazine.

Take Action Invite students to write letters to magazines that do not contain realistic body images of teens and ask them to change their policy.

✓Assessment

Student articles should make use of concepts presented in the chapter, including body mass index, eating disorders, nutrient-dense foods, and other topics. After researching and writing, groups should compile their work into a magazine format.

164

Eye ON THE Media

Body Image in Teen Magazines

Teen magazines often feature images of very thin and fit models. Readers who feel that they don't "measure up" to these models in terms of weight may develop a negative body image. Use the activity below to help you examine messages in teen magazines about weight.

ACTIVITY

Look through a number of teen magazines. What sorts of images of teens do the magazines contain? Are a variety of body types featured? What is the magazine's take on weight management? Do the articles and ads focus on having a moderate, balanced eating plan and increasing physical activity as ways of managing weight healthfully?

As a class, produce a magazine devoted to the topic of healthy weight management for teens. Be sure to include all the elements of a magazine, including feature articles on exercise, nutrition, and body composition; a cover; letters from readers; an advice column; and advertisements. You might also want to include recipes, fictional stories, and a Buyer's Guide/Buyer Beware column.

EXPRESS YOUR VIEWS

Some teen magazines refuse to publish articles and ads on dieting because of the potential these items have for contributing to teens' negative body image. Others continue to feature such articles and ads. As a class, discuss whether magazines should contain information and ads on dieting.

More About...

Images of Teens in Magazines A nonprofit advocacy group called Dads and Daughters, or DADS, has begun to put pressure on the editorial boards of teen and youth magazines to stop them from giving teens diet tips and to include teens of all shapes and sizes in their magazines. The group has been somewhat successful, and one major teen magazine has vowed to stop this practice. DADS has also asked advertisers to keep their ads socially responsible, particularly when it comes to body images of teen girls. The organization is urging companies to adopt a Best Advertising Practices policy that includes featuring images that are age appropriate, promote a healthful lifestyle, avoid perfectionism, and show girls of all shapes and sizes.

CROSS-CURRICULUM CONNECTIONS

Create a Flyer. Many communities are encouraging their members to eat healthfully and be more physically active. Using a persuasive writing style, create a flyer that gives teens tips on how to develop healthy eating habits and include more physical activity into their lives. Obtain permission from the proper school officials to distribute your flyer to the school community.

Write a Report. Eating disorders have been recorded as early as ancient Greek and Roman times. Research the history of eating disorders in the last three decades. Address theories on the possible causes of eating disorders, and determine why it was not until the 1970s that public awareness of these illnesses increased. Write a report based on your research.

Calculate Calorie Ranges. Nutritionists recommend that 55 to 60 percent of daily calories come from complex carbohydrates. What is the range of calories that should come from complex carbohydrates for a teen who consumes 2,200 calories per day? What is the range for a teen who consumes 2,800 calories per day?

Investigate the Topic. Reducing calorie intake can slow down a person's metabolism, a process that is similar to what happens in people who are suffering from starvation. Research this biological process and explain why the body responds to decreased caloric intake in this way. Present your findings in a brief report.

Registered Dietitian

Are you interested in the special nutritional needs of athletes, older adults, or pregnant women? Would you like to inspire others to make healthful food choices? If you answered yes to these questions, you may enjoy a career as a registered dietitian.

Registered dietitians use a variety of skills in their jobs. They must be critical thinkers to analyze an individual's eating habits. They must base their nutritional advice on sound science. Good communication skills are necessary to help people understand how to make food choices. Registered dietitians must show sensitivity to people's needs, cultures, and lifestyles. Find out more about becoming a registered dietitian or working in a related field by clicking on Career Corner at **health.glencoe.com**.

Portfolio Assessment

Self-Evaluation Direct students to review the Health Skills Activities and other activities completed in the chapter. Encourage each student to select one finished product or activity that demonstrates his or her best work for the chapter and that represents the student's learning goals. Have students explain what they have learned and how the examples they have selected demonstrate their growth in health literacy, knowledge, and skills.

Teacher Classroom Resources Assign Performance Assessment 6, "Helping a Friend," in the TCR.

CROSS-CURRICULUM CONNECTIONS

Enrich student learning by connecting the topic of weight management and body composition to one of the four subject areas presented on this page. The activity may be completed individually or with a partner.

Language Arts Provide pointers on persuasive and descriptive writing. Recommend helpful graphic-arts computer programs.

Social Studies Remind students to explore the topic by gathering factual information from several different reliable sources.

Math For a teen with a daily intake of 2,200 calories, 1,210 to 1,320 of those calories should come from complex carbohydrates (.55 × 2,200 = 1,210; .60 × 2,200 = 1,320). For a teen with a daily intake of 2,800 calories, 1,540 to 1,680 of those calories should come from complex carbohydrates (.55 × 2,800 = 1,540; .60 × 2,800 = 1,680).

Science Students' research should provide more details about how reducing calorie intake signals the body to lower its metabolic rate. Reports may also address how physical activity and building muscle mass can counteract this mechanism.

Have students read the Career Corner feature on this page. Ask interested students to explore the Glencoe Health Web site at **health.glencoe.com** for more information on this topic.

Chapter 6 *Review*

CHECKING COMPREHENSION

- Assign and discuss the chapter review.
- Use the Chapter 6 MindJogger Videoquiz to review the chapter. ▷◁

CHAPTER 6 REVIEW ANSWERS

Exploring Health Terms

1. body image
2. body mass index (BMI)
3. nutrient-dense
4. Underweight
5. False: weight cycling
6. True
7. True
8. False: binge eating disorder
9. rehydration
10. vegan
11. dietary supplement
12. herbal supplement

Recalling the Facts

1. Maintaining a healthy weight is a matter of energy balance: The calories you consume must equal the calories your body burns.

2. Any three: cardiovascular disease, type 2 diabetes, cancer, high blood pressure, osteoarthritis.

3. Any three: target your appropriate weight, set realistic goals, personalize your plan, put your goal and plan in writing, evaluate your progress.

4. Aerobic activities burn calories and help with fat loss. Weight lifting or resistance training will increase muscle mass, causing the body to burn more calories, even at rest.

➤ EXPLORING HEALTH TERMS *Answer the following questions on a sheet of paper.*

Lesson 1 *Replace the underlined words with the correct term.*

body mass index (BMI)	underweight
overweight	obesity
nutrient-dense foods	body image

1. The way you see your body is your <u>BMI</u>.
2. The ratio of weight to height used to assess body size is <u>body image</u>.
3. Fruits and vegetables are <u>nutrient-poor foods</u>.
4. <u>Obesity</u> refers to weighing less than the standard weight range for a certain height.

Lesson 2 *Identify each statement as True or False. If false, replace the underlined term with the correct term.*

bulimia nervosa	eating disorder
fad diets	anorexia nervosa
weight cycling	binge eating disorder

5. The repeated pattern of loss and regain of body weight is <u>bulimia nervosa</u>.
6. An extreme, harmful eating behavior that can cause serious illness or even death is an <u>eating disorder</u>.
7. <u>Anorexia nervosa</u> is a condition in which the irrational fear of becoming obese results in severe weight loss from self-imposed starvation.
8. Compulsive overeating is called <u>weight cycling</u>.

Lesson 3 *Match each definition with the correct term.*

dietary supplement	rehydration
electrolytes	vegan
herbal supplement	vegetarian
megadose	

9. Restoring lost body fluids.
10. A person who eats only plant foods.
11. A nonfood form of one or more nutrients.
12. A chemical substance from plants that may be sold as a dietary supplement.

➤ RECALLING THE FACTS *Use complete sentences to answer the following questions.*

Lesson 1

1. Explain the relationship between energy balance and a healthy weight.
2. Analyze the relationship between maintaining a healthy weight and disease prevention: Name three diseases that can be prevented by maintaining a healthy weight.
3. List three weight-management strategies.
4. How does regular physical activity help promote a healthy weight?

Lesson 2

5. What are some risks of long-term fasting?
6. Name three risks associated with diet pills.
7. Describe the causes, symptoms, and treatment of the eating disorder bulimia nervosa.
8. Describe the causes, symptoms, and treatment of binge eating disorder.

Lesson 3

9. Explain how dehydration and electrolyte imbalance are related.
10. How can a vegetarian diet benefit health?
11. Why might taking an herbal supplement be risky?
12. Why might a pregnant woman need to take a dietary supplement?

5. Fasting denies the body of food energy. Without a daily supply of nutrients, the body breaks down protein stored in muscle tissue to supply the energy it needs to function. Those who avoid liquids while fasting also become dehydrated.

6. Any three: diet pills may cause drowsiness, anxiety, or a racing heart; some are addictive; some may cause dehydration.

7. Causes: exact cause is unknown, but genetics, social pressures, self-esteem issues, and family problems may be factors. Symptoms: cycle of fasting or following a very strict diet, bingeing, and vomiting or taking laxatives to force food from the body; Treatment: medication and psychological counseling.

8. Causes: may be genetic, may be used to cope with strong emotions or depression; Symptoms: eating huge amounts of food at one time; Treatment: psychological counseling, and sometimes medication.

➤ THINKING CRITICALLY

1. **Synthesizing.** Why might a person who is on a weight-loss plan become undernourished? How can this condition be avoided? *(LESSON 1)*

2. **Analyzing.** Find two diet plans featured in magazines. Use what you know about good nutrition and the Food Guide Pyramid to identify the strengths and weaknesses of each plan. *(LESSON 2)*

3. **Applying.** Apply what you have learned about nutrition and vegetarian eating by using the Food Guide Pyramid to plan a sample one-day vegan menu. *(LESSON 3)*

➤ HEALTH SKILLS APPLICATION

1. **Analyzing Influences.** Many factors, including media messages, influence body image. Identify the three factors that you think have the greatest effect on a teen's body image. Explain what role you think each factor plays in determining body image and whether the effect is positive or negative. *(LESSON 1)*

2. **Communicating.** Your friend Amy confides that she maintains her weight by alternating periods of fasting with eating large amounts of food. After eating, she vomits to rid her body of the food. Amy says that this practice is not harmful and helps her control her weight. Write a script describing what you would say to Amy. With a partner, role-play your scenario for the class. *(LESSON 2)*

3. **Accessing Information.** Use reliable online and print resources to find information on at least three dietary supplements known to have harmful side effects. Make a two-column chart that lists in the first column the health claims the supplement manufacturers use to promote their products and, in the second column, the potential side effects of using or abusing the product. Ask permission to post your findings in the weight-training room at your school. *(LESSON 3)*

 BEYOND *the* Classroom

Parent Involvement

Goal Setting. Sometimes it's easier to set and achieve goals if you work with others. With family members, draw up a plan for achieving a specific nutritional health goal. Your goal may be to lose weight, eat more fruits and vegetables, or anything else that applies to your own needs. Use the goal-setting steps to help you reach your goal.

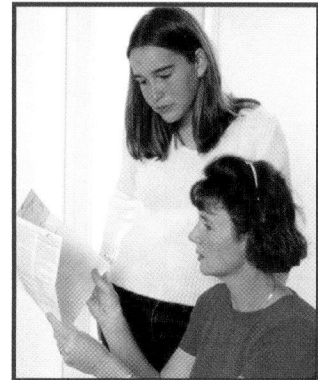

School and Community

Overeaters Anonymous. Overeaters Anonymous (OA) is a group that offers support to those who are trying to overcome eating problems. Contact a branch of this organization in your community. Find out what services OA provides and how "sponsors" are used to help support people in recovery. Share your findings in a brief report.

Chapter 6 Review **167**

Thinking Critically

1. Unless careful food choices are made, reducing calorie intake can also reduce intake of important nutrients. To avoid becoming undernourished, a person who is trying to lose weight should choose a variety of low-calorie, nutrient-dense foods and keep portions to a reasonable size.

2. Responses will vary depending on the diet plans selected. Students should recognize that any diet plan recommending too few (less than 1,400) calories per day or that restricts the dieter to only a few types of food is unhealthful because it does not meet the recommendations of the Food Guide Pyramid. Students should also analyze the plans for physical activity recommendations.

3. Responses will vary.

Health Skills Application

1.–3. Answers will vary.

EVALUATE

- Use the reproducible Chapter 6 Test in the TCR, or construct your own using the Testmaker software.

- Use Performance Assessment 6 in the TCR.

ENRICHMENT

Ask students to complete Enrichment Activity 6 in the TCR.

BEYOND *the* Classroom

Keep students involved in the community, and encourage parent participation by assigning the activities on this page for students to work on outside of class.

9. Electrolytes are minerals that help maintain the body's fluid balance. Dehydration can lead to an imbalance of these minerals.

10. A vegetarian diet can reduce the risk of heart disease, high blood pressure, and some forms of cancer.

11. Because the safety and nutritional claims of many herbal supplements are not based on conclusive scientific evidence, taking these types of supplements can be risky.

12. The nutrients a pregnant female ingests provide nutrition not only for her but also for the developing baby. Some nutrients—such as folate, calcium, and iron—must be ingested during pregnancy to ensure the health of both the mother and the baby. A pregnant female might need to take a dietary supplement to meet these nutrient needs.

Chapter 7 *Achieving Good Mental Health*

Lessons	Standards		Features
	National	**State/Local**	
1 **Your Mental and Emotional Health** *pages 170–177*	National Health Education Standards **1.1, 1.2, 3.1, 5.3**		**Exploring Issues** • Should Learning Styles Be Taken Into Account in the Classroom? page 176
2 **Developing a Positive Identity** *pages 178–183*	National Health Education Standards **1.2, 1.4, 4.2**		**Real-Life Application** • Identify and Strengthen Your Developmental Assets *(Analyzing Influences)*, page 180
3 **Understanding Emotions** *pages 184–187*	National Health Education Standards **1.2, 5.1, 5.3, 5.5**		**Health Skills Activity** • Expressing Your Feelings *(Communication)*, page 186
4 **Managing Emotions** *pages 188–191*	National Health Education Standards **1.4, 3.4, 5.3**		**Hands-On Health** • Managing Anger *(Stress Management)*, page 191

Reproducible Resources	Assessment	Technology
Student Activity Workbook for use with each chapter 📁 Concept Mapping Activity 23 📁 Cross-Curriculum Activity 7 📁 Current Health Issues 7 📁 Guided Reading Actvities 23 📁 Lesson Plan 23 📁 Parent Letter and Activities 7 📁 Reteaching Activity 23	📁 Lesson Quiz 23	🎮 Transparency 19 💿 TeacherWorks® 🖥 Internet Activities
📁 Concept Mapping Activity 24 📁 Guided Reading Activities 24 📁 Lesson Plan 24 📁 Reteaching Activity 24	📁 Lesson Quiz 24	🎮 Transparency 20 💿 TeacherWorks®
📁 Concept Mapping Activity 25 📁 Decision-Making Activity 7 📁 Enrichment Activity 7 📁 Guided Reading Activities 25 📁 Health Lab 7 📁 Lesson Plan 25 📁 Reteaching Activity 25	📁 Lesson Quiz 25	💿 TeacherWorks®
📁 Concept Mapping Activity 26 📁 Guided Reading Activities 26 📁 Lesson Plan 26 📁 Reteaching Activity 26	📁 Lesson Quiz 26	🎮 Transparency 21 💿 TeacherWorks®

0:00 OUT OF TIME

If time does not permit teaching the entire chapter use:
- Figure 7.2, p. 172
- Health Minute, p. 182
- Health Skills Activity, p. 186
- Hands-On Health, p. 191

Language Diversity

🎧 English Audio CD Program
🎧 Spanish Audio CD Program
📁 English Summaries, Quizzes, and Activities
📁 Spanish Summaries, Quizzes, and Activities
📁 Spanish Parent Letters and Activities

End of Chapter Assessment

Blackline Masters

📁 Chapter 7 Test
📁 Performance Assessment Activity 7

Technology

💿 Vocabulary PuzzleMaker
📼 MindJogger Videoquiz
💿 **Exam***View*® Pro Testmaker

Professional Health Series

Dealing with Sensitive Issues
Planning a Coordinated School Health Program
Promoting Character Education
Home, School, and Community Involvement

Achieving Good Mental Health

CHAPTER OVERVIEW

Chapter 7 discusses the characteristics of mental health. Students are introduced to Maslow's hierarchy of needs; the emotions that impact thinking, behavior, and relationships; and strategies for dealing with emotions in healthful ways.

Lesson 1 All individuals have basic needs, presented by Abraham Maslow as a hierarchy. Each individual has a unique personality, influenced by both heredity and environment.

Lesson 2 Developmental assets help young people grow up as healthy, responsible individuals. Teens can strengthen these assets and build healthy identities.

Lesson 3 Emotions affect all three aspects of the health triangle. Learning to identify various emotions is the first step in developing healthy ways to respond to those emotions.

Lesson 4 Learning to cope with emotions in healthful ways is important to positive mental health.

Health Skills Features

- Exploring Issues, p. 176
- Real-Life Application (*Analyzing Influences*), p. 180
- Health Skills Activity (*Communication*), p. 186
- Hands-On Health (*Stress Management*), p. 191

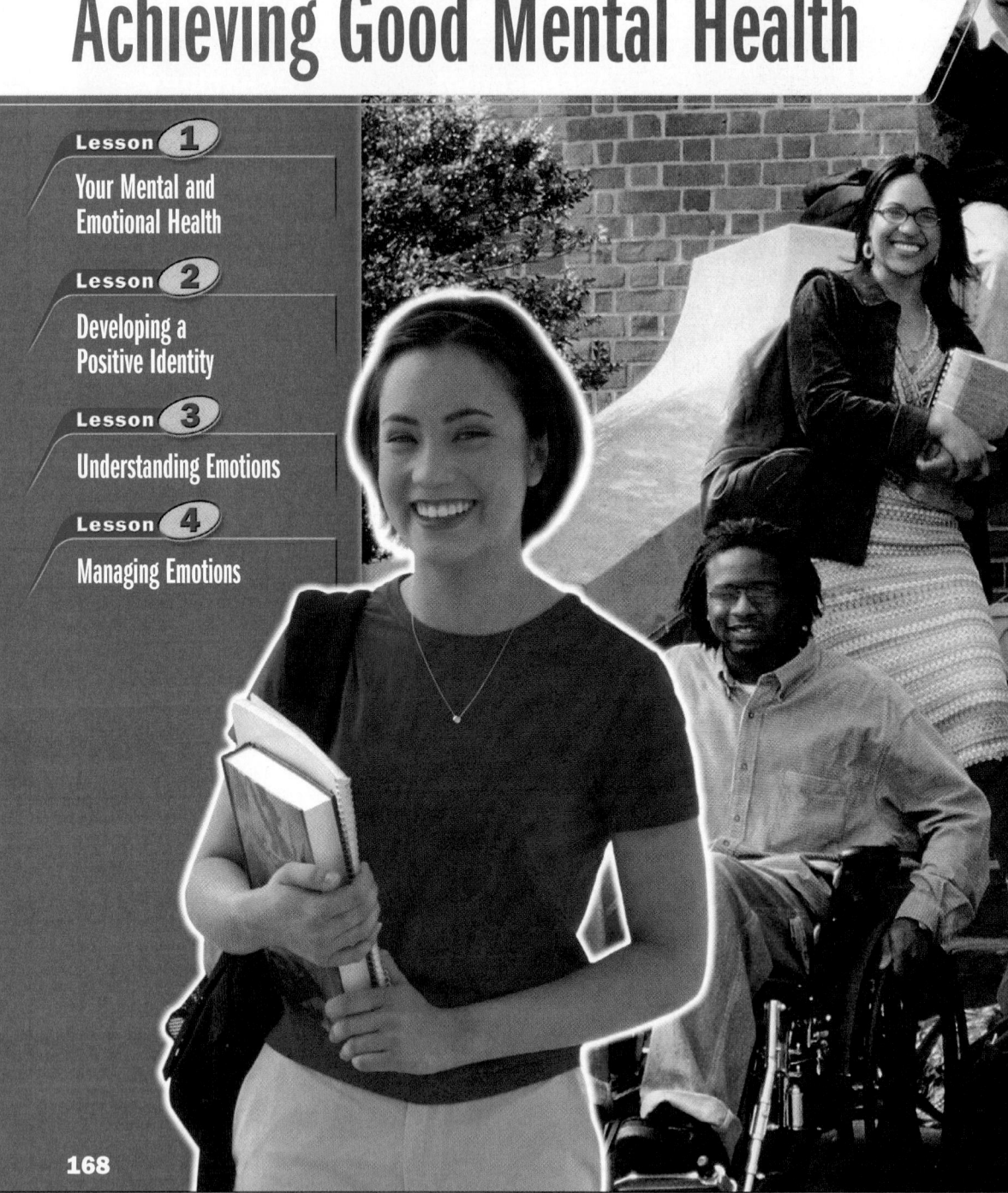

Achieving Good Mental Health

Lesson 1
Your Mental and Emotional Health

Lesson 2
Developing a Positive Identity

Lesson 3
Understanding Emotions

Lesson 4
Managing Emotions

168

MEETING STUDENT DIVERSITY

Language Diversity Use the following suggestions to help students who have difficulty with English:

- Pair English language learners with native speakers of English who can restate the Chapter Summary in language that helps students comprehend important concepts.

- Direct auditory learners or those students with language diversity to the *Glencoe Health Audio CD Program*. Available in English and Spanish, this component provides an audio and written summary of the chapter.
- Use photographs, drawings, or magazine clippings to help students visualize the important concepts of the chapter.

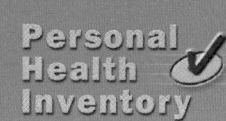

Personal Health Inventory ✓

What's Your Health Status?

Read each statement below and respond by writing *yes, no,* or *sometimes* for each item. Write *yes* only for items that you practice regularly.

1. I take responsibility for and consider the consequences of my personal behavior.

2. I express emotions in positive ways.

3. I recognize my personal strengths and weaknesses.

4. I accept and learn from constructive criticism.

5. I have values that benefit me and the people around me in healthful ways.

6. I accept new challenges and face problems rather than avoid them.

7. I think that I am important to other people.

8. I resist negative peer pressure.

9. I am proud of who I am.

10. I have a generally positive outlook on life.

When you complete the chapter, review your personal inventory again, and identify two or three behavior changes you can make to improve your mental and emotional health.

Quick **Write**

Using Visuals. Being mentally and emotionally healthy means building a healthy identity and learning to express your emotions in appropriate ways. How do family and friends influence your mental and emotional health?

169

INTRODUCING THE CHAPTER

Personal Health Inventory ✓

Have students complete the Personal Health Inventory and record their answers in their private health journals. Remind students that their responses are private; honest responses will be most helpful.

Remind students to keep their inventory responses and to review them when they have finished studying Chapter 7.

Quick **write**

Using Visuals Have students look at the photographs, and invite volunteers to describe the scene. Ask: What signs of mental and emotional health can you see here? How do you think the teens are influencing one another's mental and emotional health? Then have students work independently to write their responses to the Quick Write question.

TECHNOLOGY OPTIONS

MINDJOGGER
VIDEOQUIZ

To preview or review chapter content, you may wish to use the Chapter 7 MindJogger Videoquiz. ▷◁

Online Resources for the Teacher For a fresh approach to health topics and an in-depth look at health issues, use these online resources found under Teacher Resources at **health.glencoe.com:**

• Block Schedule Lesson Plans
• Technology Projects
• Health Updates

Your Mental and Emotional Health

Lesson 1

Your Mental and Emotional Health

 FOCUS

QUICK START Have students read the Quick Start and work with partners to list as many characteristics of good mental health as possible. Then have students review their lists independently, circling the characteristics that apply to themselves and describing how they can strengthen a specific characteristic. In a brief class discussion, let students share and discuss their ideas.

TYING TO PRIOR KNOWLEDGE

Have students recall the three components of health—physical, mental/emotional, and social. Guide them in briefly discussing what they already know about the importance of good mental and emotional health.

Health Skills Features

"Should Learning Styles Be Taken into Account in the Classroom?" p. 176

INTRODUCING VOCABULARY

- As a homework assignment, have students write statements that use the vocabulary words in context.

- Ask students to complete the Chapter 7 Study Guide in the *Student Activity Workbook*. 📁

VOCABULARY

mental/emotional health
hierarchy of needs
self-actualization
personality
modeling

YOU'LL LEARN TO

- Identify the characteristics of good mental and emotional health.
- Explain the importance of meeting needs in healthful ways.
- Analyze the importance and benefits of abstinence as it relates to emotional health.
- Analyze the relationship between mental health promotion and disease prevention.

QUICK START Fold a sheet of paper in half. On one half, write as many characteristics as you can think of that describe a person with good mental health. Circle those characteristics that apply to you. Then select a characteristic that you would like to develop. On the other half of your paper, write what you can do to strengthen that characteristic.

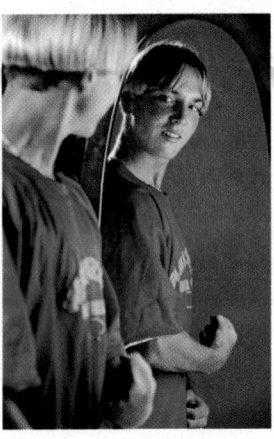

⚓ **A person with good mental/emotional health has positive self-esteem.** *What are some of the positive feelings you have about yourself?*

How do you see yourself? Would you describe yourself as serious, friendly, confident, or shy? Do you think you have a positive outlook? Are you generally a happy person? Do you look forward to facing life's challenges? Your responses to these questions reflect aspects of your mental/emotional health.

The Characteristics of Good Mental/Emotional Health

Mental/emotional health is the *ability to accept yourself and others, adapt to and manage emotions, and deal with the demands and challenges you meet in life.* Someone who is mentally and emotionally healthy can usually handle a wide variety of feelings and situations. He or she can make wise choices that demonstrate both strong values and responsible behavior.

170 Chapter 7 Achieving Good Mental Health

 Lesson 1 Resources

Teacher Classroom Resources
📁 Concept Mapping Activity 23
📁 Cross-Curriculum Acivity 7
📁 Current Health Issues 7
📁 Guided Reading Activities 23
📁 Lesson Plan 23
📁 Lesson Quiz 23

📁 Parent Letter and Activities 7
📁 Reteaching Activity 23
Student Activity Workbook
📁 Applying Health Skills 23
📁 Chapter 7 Study Guide
Multimedia
🖱 Transparency 19

People with good mental/emotional health demonstrate the following characteristics:

▶ **Positive Self-Esteem.** Your feelings of confidence and self-esteem are directly related to your general level of wellness. A person with positive self-esteem is better able to accept challenges and take failure in stride.

▶ **Sense of Belonging.** Having emotional attachment to family members, friends, teachers, and other people around you provides comfort and assurance. It promotes stability and makes you feel a part of your community.

▶ **Sense of Purpose.** Recognizing your own value and importance enables you to set and achieve goals and engage in activities that are personally rewarding, such as working hard in school, participating in sports, or doing community service.

▶ **Positive Outlook.** Seeing the bright side and having hope about life reduces stress and increases your energy level. It also increases the possibility of success.

▶ **Autonomy.** Having the confidence to make responsible and safe decisions promotes self-assurance and a sense of independence.

How would you assess your own mental/emotional health? How many of the attributes of good mental/emotional health listed in **Figure 7.1** apply to you?

FIGURE 7.1

SIGNS OF GOOD MENTAL/ EMOTIONAL HEALTH

In general, teens with good mental/emotional health
- are realistic about their strengths and weaknesses.
- are responsible for their personal behavior.
- avoid high-risk behaviors, such as using tobacco, alcohol, or other drugs.
- are open-minded, flexible, and able to see several sides of an issue.
- are fun-loving and able to relax alone or with others.
- respect both their own needs and the needs of others.
- respect each person's value as a human being—including their own.
- invest time and energy in developing nurturing relationships.
- express their emotions in ways that do not hurt themselves or others.
- put their talents and abilities to good use.
- view change as a challenge and an opportunity.

② TEACH

Explaining

Explain how mental health can affect physical health. Tell students that the mind-body connection is so strong that people have made themselves physically ill through worry. Conversely, people have used laughter and their own positive attitudes to make themselves physically well. **L1**

Discussing

Guide students in discussing the listed characteristics of good mental and emotional health. Ask:

- Which of these characteristics might seem difficult for an individual to control? Why?
- What can teens do to develop those characteristics? **L1**

Critical Thinking

Let students share their responses to these questions:

- How can the actions and attitudes of parents positively affect the self-esteem of children?
- How important are the actions and attitudes of peers to the self-esteem of teens? **L1**

VISUAL LEARNING

Figure 7.1 Have students meet in groups to read and discuss the signs of good mental and emotional health. Ask group members to list at least two specific habits or actions that might reflect each of these signs.

⌁⌁⌁ HEALTH LITERACY

Effective Communicator Sometimes, a single conversation, act, or even glance can have a profound effect—positive or negative—on a person's self-esteem. Pair students to brainstorm a list of situations that hold the potential for one person to affect another's self-esteem. For example: One teen asks another for a date, a player beats another at tennis before an audience, a friend constantly borrows things and does not take care of them. Have students role-play the situations by handling them in ways that protect self-esteem.

171

List, Group, Label

Have students categorize the following words into high and low self-esteem: *motivated, lazy, determined, doubting, confident, positive.* Ask: How do these words relate to mental and emotional health?

This activity encourages students to categorize words in meaningful ways; categorizing can help students understand words more clearly and organize their knowledge. Point out that the words in the group are characteristics of self-esteem. Ask students to add as many other words or phrases to the list as possible, and challenge them to defend their choices. Accept all reasonable responses. Some possible words and phrases are *hardworking, focused, kind, depressed,* and *considerate.* Next, ask students to group the terms as they are related to high or low self-concept. For example, *motivated, confident,* and *positive* are all related to high self-esteem; *lazy* and *doubting* are related to low self-esteem. For more strategies, see the *Guided Reading Activities* booklet. 📂 🔲

VISUAL LEARNING

Figure 7.2 Ask volunteers to describe the shape and the pictures in Figure 7.2. What is each pictured teen doing? What needs are being met for that teen? Who is helping to meet those needs?

Discussing

As students consider the needs identified by Maslow, ask:
- Why are these needs presented as a hierarchy?
- Why are physical needs considered most basic? 🔲

A Pyramid of Needs

Many theories have been developed to explain human development and mental health by examining behavior. One important theory was created by Abraham Maslow, a pioneer in psychology. Maslow organized human needs in the form of a pyramid, as shown in **Figure 7.2**. This **hierarchy of needs** is *a ranked list of those needs essential to human growth and development, presented in ascending order, starting with basic needs and building toward the need for reaching your highest potential.*

FIGURE 7.2

MASLOW'S HIERARCHY OF NEEDS

When people have met their physical needs, they can begin to focus on meeting their emotional needs.

LEVEL 5—REACHING POTENTIAL
Need for self-actualization

LEVEL 4—FEELING RECOGNIZED
Need to achieve, need to be recognized

LEVEL 3—BELONGING
Need to love and be loved, need to belong

LEVEL 2—SAFETY
Need to be secure from danger

LEVEL 1—PHYSICAL
Need to satisfy basic needs of hunger, thirst, sleep, and shelter

172 Chapter 7 Achieving Good Mental Health

More About...

Abraham Maslow Abraham Maslow (1908–1970) is considered one of the founders of humanistic psychology. Rather than focusing on the functioning of disturbed or mentally ill patients, Maslow studied the lives and activities of individuals he considered both successful and productive. For his examples, he looked both to history and to his personal acquaintances and friends. As he studied these individuals, he searched for the components of positive mental health. His conclusions are summarized in his Hierarchy of Needs.

Physical Needs

Survival needs such as food, water, sleep, and shelter from the elements are among the needs at the bottom of the pyramid. People who are denied these basic needs become physically weak and may develop illnesses. Many people in our society take for granted that basic physical needs are easily met. However, there are many people for whom food, clean water, and shelter are not easily obtained. For example, people who are homeless may face many difficulties meeting their basic physical needs.

Need for Safety

Satisfying the need for safety includes more than just safeguarding yourself against physical harm. In fact, the safety needs that are essential to your personality can also be psychological in nature. You need the safety of familiar places and people that help you feel secure, such as your home, your family, or trusted friends.

Need to Be Loved and to Belong

Everyone needs to give love and to know that he or she is loved in return. Babies who are denied emotional attention may be stunted mentally. They may fail to thrive, and they may even develop behavioral problems later.

Humans are social beings. We need to interact with other people and to know that we are valued members of a group that enhances our physical, mental, or social health. Most people generally want to belong to a community, such as a family, a circle of friends, or a social group such as a school club or a sports team. Feeling a sense of belonging can increase your confidence and strengthen your mental/emotional health.

Need to Be Valued and Recognized

Most of us feel a need to be appreciated, to be personally valued by family, friends, and peers. One way you might meet this need is by participating in productive activities, such as studying hard for exams, playing an instrument or sport, volunteering at a hospital, or writing short stories. By being able to do something well, you gain respect and a feeling of self-worth.

CHARACTER CHECK

Compassion is a trait that you can express when you understand the needs of others. People who are compassionate are not just aware of other's distress; they have a desire to ease suffering. Homelessness is a growing problem in all communities, both urban and rural. How can you show compassion for people who are unable to meet their basic need for shelter?

Participating in team sports can give teens a sense of belonging. *What other positive actions can teens take to fulfill this need?*

Lesson 1 Your Mental and Emotional Health **173**

Critical Thinking

Discuss with students the importance of friends in meeting the need to be loved and to belong. Ask students to write paragraphs describing the kind of friend they are. Next, have them write paragraphs describing the type of person they would like to have as a friend. Collect the papers and without revealing any names, read some of the paragraphs to the class. Discuss the similarities and differences between the qualities listed in the paragraphs read. **L2** **Verbal/Linguistic**

CHARACTER CHECK

Compassion Guide students in discussing their understanding of the word *compassion*. Ask: For whom do you feel compassion? Why? Then have students meet in groups to explore their ideas in response to the Character Check question. Encourage groups to follow through on their ideas and participate in an effective project to help community members in need.

Discussing

Guide students in discussing the benefits of volunteering. Ask: Which of your own needs are met when you volunteer to help others? Allow time for students to share their experiences as a volunteer. **L2**

Curriculum Connections

Art Many photographers specialize in capturing emotional moments. Ask an art teacher to talk about photography as an art form of capturing emotion and to share poignant works by famous photographers such as Margaret Bourke-White.

Divide the class into small groups. Using personal photographs, have each group create a book showing the emotions of adolescence. To encourage students to study the photographs, have them write a caption for each. Students who enjoy doing their own photography might work together to record on film the emotions expressed by students in your school.

Discussing

Have students brainstorm a list of actions teens can take to meet their need for belonging and affection such as joining an after-school club. Record all suggestions on the board. Then guide students in discussing their ideas:

- Which behaviors can help teens strengthen and/or establish healthy relationships?

- Which behaviors might pose a risk to mental and emotional health or to other aspects of health? Why? **L1**

hotlink

Have volunteers recall—or look up—the definition of *abstinence* (the conscious decision to avoid harmful behaviors including sexual activity before marriage and the use of tobacco, alcohol, and other drugs). Ask: How can practicing abstinence help you meet your needs? How can abstinence improve your mental and emotional health?

Discussing

Ask students whether they have ever heard—or even made—remarks like these: That person has such a dull personality! Those two have such sparkling personalities—everyone wants to be friends with them.

Encourage students to explain what they think those remarks really mean. **L1**

hotlink

abstinence For more information about the benefits of abstinence, see Chapter 12, page 318.

 Practicing abstinence and meeting needs in healthy ways will strengthen your mental/emotional health. *What other decisions can you make to promote your health?*

Need to Reach Your Potential

At the top of the pyramid is the need to reach your full potential as a person. This quest for **self-actualization**—*the striving to become the best you can be*—includes having goals that motivate and inspire you. Self-actualization means having the courage to make changes in your life in order to reach your goals and grow as a person. During your teen years, you begin to recognize your potential and set goals for your future. You see more clearly what your talents are, what your dreams are, and who it is you want to become. Self-actualization is a lifelong process. Part of the process is learning the self-discipline you need to reach your goals.

Meeting Your Needs

The ways you choose to meet your needs affect your mental/emotional health. For example, meeting the need for affection by building and maintaining respectful, loving relationships with people you care about will strengthen your mental/emotional health. However, sometimes people choose risky ways to fulfill their needs. Some teens may decide to join a gang to feel a sense of belonging or engage in sexual activity in an attempt to feel loved. Such decisions carry dangerous consequences. Gang membership can lead to physical harm and trouble with the law. Sexual activity can result in unplanned pregnancy, sexually transmitted diseases, and the loss of self-respect and the respect of others. Practicing **abstinence** and finding healthful ways to meet emotional needs are critical in developing and maintaining good mental health.

174 Chapter 7 Achieving Good Mental Health

Cooperative Learning Activity

Personality Tests Students may already be familiar with some of the many personality tests available. Some personality tests can be administered only by specially trained counselors; others may be given in the school's career center whereas still others are available on the Internet.

Have interested students work together to research selected personality tests. Ask them to find out when, where, and how the tests can be given and what kinds of results the tests provide. Let these students share their findings with the rest of the class. Follow up with a class discussion in which students share their ideas about the relevance and reliability of personality tests.

Understanding Your Personality

Your **personality** is *a complex set of characteristics that makes you unique.* It's what makes you different from everyone else and determines how you will react in certain situations. Personality is an important factor in how you choose to meet your needs. Thus, it plays a major role in your overall mental health.

Influences on Your Personality

Personality includes an individual's emotional makeup, attitudes, thoughts, and behaviors. It is composed of tendencies that you were born with and characteristics that you have developed in response to life situations and experiences. The two main influences on your personality are heredity and environment.

PERSONALITY AND HEREDITY

Just as you inherit physical traits such as hair and eye color, you inherit some personality traits from your biological parents and ancestors. Heredity plays a role in determining a person's basic intellectual abilities and temperament, or emotional tendencies. There is also evidence that heredity may influence behaviors such as risk-taking and talents such as athletic or artistic abilities. This doesn't mean that you have no control over how smart you become or what you do. Your inherited brain chemistry is only one of the many factors contributing to your personality and behavior.

PERSONALITY AND ENVIRONMENT

Your environment includes everything that surrounds you in your day-to-day life. This means your family, friends, peers, home, neighborhood, school, and every other person, place, object, event, or activity in your life. All of these influences can have an impact on your developing personality.

Among the people in your environment are some who serve as role models for your behavior. Most people naturally engage in **modeling**, or *observing and learning from the behaviors of those around you*, sometimes without even thinking about it. If the behavior of your role model is healthful, the effect on your developing personality will also be healthful. The values you learn from your role models help shape the person you are and the way you live your life.

Many influences can help shape personality traits, such as a sense of self-discipline and the desire to excel. *Who are the role models in your life who have helped shape your personality?*

Health Skills Practice

Self Affirmations Explain to students that affirmations are statements of encouragement. Affirmations can strengthen your confidence and build good feelings about yourself. They are personal, positive statements written in the present tense. Here are examples: *I am confident when taking a test. I eat healthful foods to help me feel my best.*

PRACTICING HEALTHFUL BEHAVIORS

Have students write affirmations in their private health journals that will help them feel better about themselves. Remind students that their affirmations should be "I" or "me" statements. Suggest that students repeat their affirmations several times every day. After a week or two, ask volunteers to share their responses to using affirmations.

Activity

Have interested volunteers use library or online resources to learn about personality research with identical twins raised in different homes. Have these volunteers share their findings with the rest of the class. Encourage students to discuss what the research shows about the effects of heredity and environment on personality. L3

Curriculum Connections

Language Arts Have students write a story about someone they admire greatly. Suggest that students describe the qualities that make this person so admirable. Ask students to answer these questions in their stories or essays: How has this person influenced your life? What contributions has he or she made to your self-esteem?

Social Studies Ask students to do a study of TV, radio, and music messages that repeatedly tell American society to enjoy life and not to worry. Have students draw conclusions about the impact of the positive and negative influence of these messages.

Exploring Issues

SHOULD LEARNING STYLES BE TAKEN INTO ACCOUNT IN THE CLASSROOM?

Have students think about their own strongest learning style. Ask: Do you remember information better if you write it down (visual), listen to it (auditory), or see something done then do it yourself (kinesthetic)? Have students read the feature and investigate different learning styles. Discuss the types of assessments that would best reflect each type of learning style. For the second activity, review what they know about self-esteem. Ask: What factors help build self-esteem? Point out that building a sense of competence—a belief that a person can meet goals and achieve success—leads to high self-esteem.

Critical Thinking

Have students work with partners or in small groups to explore their ideas about behavior and personality:

- How do you think your personality affects your behavior?
- How do you think your behavior influences the development of your personality? **L2**

Reinforcing Concepts

Have students draw flow charts, graphs, patterns, or pictures to depict the influences on personality. Let them share their finished work with the rest of the class. **ELL** **Visual/Spatial**

Should Learning Styles Be Taken Into Account in the Classroom?

Academic performance affects many teens' view of themselves. Being a good student is one way teens can meet the need to be valued and recognized. Because students learn and demonstrate their knowledge in different ways, some teachers use different testing methods. For instance, teachers may test students according to the way each one learns best—through seeing, through hearing, or through doing. Do you think teachers should use multiple methods to accommodate different learning styles? Here are two points of view.

Viewpoint 1: Melissa J., age 15

I'm proud of my grades. I study every night and always work extra hard before exams. It's not fair to apply different standards just because some students can't handle a written test. Why should I have to write an essay while someone else in class has fun drawing a picture or building a diorama? How can the teacher possibly grade these different projects fairly? It's like comparing apples and oranges. Students should be given real tests, not whatever makes them feel good. That's not the way the real world works after graduation. Those students just need to work harder.

Viewpoint 2: Gary D., age 16

I do study hard for tests, but even when I know the content, I still do lousy on multiple-choice tests. If that's the only way I can demonstrate my knowledge, I end up looking stupid. Students have different strengths and weaknesses—and so do people in the real world. Look at athletes or dancers. They demonstrate their knowledge and talent by performing, not by taking a written test. I'm not saying you should get rid of all pencil-and-paper tests or forget about writing papers. I just think teachers should offer students a variety of approaches to accommodate different ways of learning. It's only fair.

ACTIVITIES

1. **Research one of the different learning styles mentioned above, including visual (seeing), auditory (hearing), and tactile/kinesthetic (touching, doing). Describe the style and how students in that category learn best.**

2. **Write a paragraph explaining which viewpoint you favor and why. Be sure to link your discussion to the issue of school performance and self-esteem.**

Dealing with Sensitive Issues

Self-Esteem Students sometimes feel concerned when issues of self-esteem are raised in class. Many feel that their self-esteem cannot be changed. This is particularly discouraging for students who perceive their self-esteem as low or negative.

To help these students—and, indeed, all the students—emphasize the fact that self-esteem can be improved. Suggest these tips:

- Focus on your strengths.
- Set realistic goals for yourself.
- Ask for help when you need it.
- View your mistakes as opportunities for learning.

Personality and Behavior

The one aspect of your personality over which you have the most control is your behavior. How you make decisions, what decisions you make, whether you recognize the consequences of those decisions, and what actions you take can make a great difference in the quality of your life and in your levels of physical and mental/emotional health.

Promoting Mental/Emotional Health

Knowing the factors that affect your mental/emotional health will help you choose behaviors that promote health. Being mentally and emotionally healthy can improve your physical health and help prevent some diseases. For example, meeting needs in healthful ways by abstaining from risk behaviors such as gang involvement and sexual activity will protect you from physical harm. People who are able to cope with their emotions and deal with the stress in their lives are also less susceptible to illnesses such as colds and other upper-respiratory infections. Engaging in behaviors that promote mental/emotional health may help prevent disease, and it will strengthen all three sides of your health triangle.

Showing respect and caring are outward signs of positive aspects of your personality. *In what positive ways do you demonstrate your personality through your daily behaviors?*

 Lesson 1 *Review*

Reviewing Facts and Vocabulary

1. Define the term *mental/emotional health*. Identify three characteristics of a mentally and emotionally healthy person.

2. List the needs included in Maslow's hierarchy of needs.

3. How does heredity influence personality?

Thinking Critically

4. **Evaluating.** Analyze the importance and benefits of abstinence as it relates to emotional health.

5. **Synthesizing.** Analyze the relationship between mental health promotion and disease prevention.

Applying Health Skills

Practicing Healthful Behaviors. The need to belong and to be loved is a basic human need. What are some healthy choices that provide positive ways for meeting this need? What are the consequences of meeting this need in negative ways? Make a two-column table to organize your thoughts.

WORD PROCESSING Sometimes it's easier to organize and display your thoughts if you use a word-processing program. See **health.glencoe.com** for tips on how to use a word processor to create a table.

Lesson 1 Your Mental and Emotional Health **177**

 Lesson 1 *Review*

Answers to Reviewing Facts and Vocabulary

1. See pages 170-171.
2. Physical needs, need for safety, to be loved, to be valued, to reach one's potential.
3. It plays a role in determining intellectual abilities and temperament and can influence certain behaviors and talents.

Answers to Thinking Critically

4. It allows a person to meet emotional needs in healthful ways; it reduces risk of STD infection and unplanned pregnancy, and helps maintain self-respect.
5. Good mental/emotional health makes one more likely to practice healthful behaviors to prevent disease.

3 ASSESS

EVALUATING THE LESSON

Assign and discuss the Lesson 1 Review; then administer, grade, and discuss Lesson Quiz 23 in the TCR.

RETEACHING

- Have students work with partners to list the five needs in Maslow's hierarchy. Then have the partners list at least two specific examples for each kind of need.

- Ask students to complete Reteaching Activity 23 in the TCR.

ENRICHMENT

Ask a group of volunteers to learn about Howard Gardner's theory of multiple intelligences. Suggest that they use both library and online sources and that they explore all intelligences. How do these intelligences differ? How do individuals with each form of intelligence learn best? What could the implications be for students, teachers, and schools? Have these volunteers share their findings with the rest of the class, using presentations that appeal to a variety of intelligences.

4 CLOSE

Ask each student to write a short paragraph describing his or her own personality and file it in his or her private health journal.

Developing a Positive Identity

1 FOCUS

QUICK START Refer students to the Quick Start activity and give them three or four minutes to write their lists. Then have student volunteers share their lists with partners. Conclude by asking student volunteers to tell the rest of the class one interesting fact they have learned about their partners.

TYING TO PRIOR KNOWLEDGE

Help students recall what they have already learned about personality and self-esteem. Explain that they will learn more about these topics as they relate to mental/emotional health.

Health Skills Features

"Identify and Strengthen Your Developmental Assets," p. 180

ANALYZING INFLUENCES

INTRODUCING VOCABULARY

- Have students work with partners to write informal definitions of the vocabulary terms. Then ask them to check their definitions against those in the Glossary, revising if necessary.

- Ask students to complete the Chapter 7 Study Guide in the *Student Activity Workbook.*

Developing a Positive Identity

VOCABULARY
personal identity
developmental assets
constructive criticism

YOU'LL LEARN TO
- Recognize developmental assets.
- Explore strategies for developing a healthy identity.
- Relate how self-esteem and a positive outlook benefit your mental/emotional health.

 QUICK START On a sheet of paper, list your talents and abilities. What are your special qualities? What other traits make you the person you are?

 Your personal identity is made up of many different pieces. *What are some aspects of your identity that make you unique?*

If you were to write an essay describing who you are, you might begin by giving your name and age. Then you might identify your various roles, such as a son or daughter, brother or sister, student, club member, or athlete. You might also describe your talents, interests, hobbies, and accomplishments. All these elements help define the person you are. They contribute to your **personal identity**, *your sense of yourself as a unique individual.*

Your Personal Identity

During the teen years, you begin to develop a stronger sense of who you are. You learn about yourself through your interactions and relationships with other people. The knowledge you gain from your experiences will help you see yourself more clearly. Developing your personal identity is like putting a jigsaw puzzle together. The pieces of this puzzle include

- your interests.
- your likes and dislikes.
- your talents and abilities.
- your values and beliefs.
- your goals.

178 **Chapter 7** Achieving Good Mental Health

Lesson 2 *Resources*

Teacher Classroom Resources
- Concept Mapping Activity 24
- Guided Reading Activities 24
- Lesson Plan 24
- Lesson Quiz 24
- Reteaching Activity 24

Student Activity Workbook
- Applying Health Skills 24
- Chapter 7 Study Guide

Multimedia
- Transparency 20

Your Developmental Assets

As you mature, it is important to recognize the developmental assets that will help you build a healthy, positive identity. **Developmental assets** are the *building blocks of development that help young people grow up as healthy, caring, and responsible individuals.* These assets, listed in **Figure 7.3,** can help you achieve wellness as you mature into a dependable, conscientious adult. Remember that developmental assets can be found in many aspects of your life and that you can always work to strengthen these assets.

② TEACH

Discussing

Guide students in discussing the difference between personality and personal identity. Ask: How does your personality affect your personal identity? **L1**

Critical Thinking

In their private health journals, have students record their own values and beliefs, listing as many as possible. Ask them to check the five most important values or beliefs, and circle the one they consider most important. Then ask: What does this journal entry show about you and your personal identity? **L2**

FIGURE 7.3

DEVELOPMENTAL ASSETS

The Search Institute, a nonprofit organization, compiled this list of 40 assets that can help young people make healthful decisions on the road to adulthood.

Support—family support, positive family communication, relationships with other adults, caring neighborhood, caring school climate, parental involvement in schooling

Empowerment—being valued by adults in the community; serving a purpose by having a role in the community; feeling safe at home, at school, and in the neighborhood

Boundaries and Expectations—family boundaries (clear rules and consequences), school boundaries, neighborhood boundaries, adult role models, positive peer influences, high expectations

Constructive Use of Time—creative activities, youth programs, time at home, sports

Commitment to Learning—being motivated to achieve, being involved at school, doing homework, reading for pleasure

Positive Values—compassion, equality and social justice, integrity, honesty, responsibility, self-control

Social Competencies—planning and decision making, interpersonal communication, having knowledge and tolerance of different cultures, resistance skills, peaceful conflict resolution skills

Positive Identity—personal power, self-esteem, sense of purpose, positive view of personal future

VISUAL LEARNING

Figure 7.3 Guide students in reading and discussing the developmental assets listed in Figure 7.3. Ask questions such as these:

- Do you think many teens have the benefit of all these assets?
- Which of these assets can teens seek out or strengthen on their own? How?
- Do you consider any of these assets especially important? If so, which? Why?

Lesson 2 Developing a Positive Identity **179**

What Teens Want to Know

Are Fame and Fortune the Keys to Personal Satisfaction? For most people, fame and fortune are *not* the keys to personal satisfaction. Researchers have found that the expression *Money does not buy happiness* is as true today as it was years ago. Instead, they found people were happy when they had the opportunity to choose what they did and be successful at what they did.

People also rated having close relationships and high self-esteem as important for happiness and personal satisfaction. In other words, happiness comes from having control of your life and becoming good at whatever you choose to do. Feeling connected to family and friends and feeling good about yourself are also important factors.

Real-Life Application

IDENTIFY AND STRENGTHEN YOUR DEVELOPMENTAL ASSETS

ANALYZING INFLUENCES

NHES Standard 4 Students will analyze the influence of culture, media, technology, and other factors on health.

Objectives

- Identify developmental assets and explain why they are personal strengths.
- Analyze the effect of developmental assets on decision making.

Motivator

Ask students: What developmental assets would a friend or family member see in you?

Teaching Strategies

1. Have students work in pairs to identify assets in each other that each may not have thought of.
2. Remind students to concentrate on assets, not weaknesses.

✓Assessment

Using a rubric, student work should provide comprehensive evidence of the following criteria to achieve the highest score:

✔ identification and analysis of external and internal factors
✔ attention to interrelationships and complexity of influences
✔ variety of influences as appropriate

Real-Life Application

Identify and Strengthen Your Developmental Assets

Developmental assets increase the likelihood that a person will behave in ways that will enhance his or her health. Use the chart and questions to help you analyze the influences in your life and strengthen your developmental assets.

External Assets

- **Support**
- **Empowerment**
- **Boundaries and Expectations**
- **Constructive Use of Time**

External developmental assets are the positive experiences that support and empower you as you grow up. They include the standards set by parents or guardians, the expectations and encouragement of teachers, and the laws and rules established by the community.

Internal Assets

- **Commitment to Learning**
- **Positive Values**
- **Social Competencies**
- **Positive Identity**

Internal developmental assets are the personal strengths, commitments, and values that you use to guide the decisions you make. For example, if you respect yourself, you will not harm your health by using tobacco, alcohol, or other drugs.

ACTIVITIES

1. Identify the external developmental assets in each of the following areas, and describe at least one way that each asset provides a positive influence in your life: family relationships, peer relationships, the school environment, the community environment.

2. Identify your internal developmental assets, and explain why these are personal strengths. Consider the following: accomplishments, strengths, and values.

3. Write a summary about the assets in your life. Reflect on the positive influences these assets have on the decisions you make. Use the following sentence beginnings in your summary:

   I learned that . . . I am proud that . . . I was surprised that . . . I would like to improve . . .

Working Toward a Healthy Identity

Once you recognize your developmental assets as important influences on your personal identity, you can take active steps to strengthen these assets and build a healthy identity. This process requires both self-acceptance and self-improvement.

180 **Chapter 7** Achieving Good Mental Health

More About...

Mental Fitness In France, there is a long history of doing mental exercises to stimulate the brain, memory, and imagination.

Formal workshops, courses, and programs in clubs and clinics are now giving middle-aged and older adults in France challenging new mental puzzles and exercises to keep their minds working in top form. Among the mental aerobics they routinely do is finding synonyms and antonyms for words and memorizing people's names, train schedules, and poems.

Remind students that, to keep their minds in top-notch form both today and long into the future, they should give their brains a workout every day.

Recognize Your Strengths and Weaknesses

An essential step in developing a healthy identity is viewing your strengths and weaknesses in honest, realistic ways. Accept and take pride in your strengths and accomplishments. Whether you are a caring family member, a trustworthy friend, an honor student, a good basketball player, or a talented singer, you should feel proud of the positive aspects of your identity.

At the same time, assess your weaknesses without being overly self-critical, and set goals for improvement. For example, if you tend to put things off, or procrastinate, try to develop new work habits that will lessen the pressure of having to do everything at the last minute. You may be able to use one of your strengths to help you address a weakness. For example, your strength might be that you are a fast learner and will quickly learn new work habits. Using your strengths and addressing your weaknesses helps you develop competence and effectiveness.

Demonstrate Positive Values

Your values, or your beliefs and ideas about what is important in your life, guide your actions and influence the decisions you make. You can demonstrate your values in many ways. For instance, you show honesty and integrity when you don't cheat on tests. When you comfort a sad friend, you demonstrate caring and compassion. Making sure that your behavior reflects your personal values and standards will reinforce your positive identity.

Develop a Purpose in Your Life

Think of having a sense of purpose as a framework for your mental health as you grow toward adulthood and work to build a healthy identity. Having a sense of purpose means establishing goals and working to achieve them. Some of the goals you establish will be short-term, such as studying for and passing an exam. Others will be long-term, such as making plans for higher education and acquiring job skills.

Form Meaningful Relationships

Relationships provide one means of developing a sense of purpose in your life. Family and friends enable you to express yourself and share your experiences, beliefs, and feelings. Positive relationships with family, friends, teachers, and coaches also give you a support system that will help you build confidence and develop a sense of security and belonging.

The relationship between this coach and her team is part of a caring school climate. *Explain how having this asset can help teens build a healthy identity.*

Discussing

Help students discuss the process of working toward a healthy identity:

- How long do you think this process takes?

- How does an individual's identity change in different stages of life?

- In what ways do you think an individual's identity is likely to remain the same through different life stages? **L1**

Activity

Engage the class in a brainstorm session. Have each student write five typical weaknesses teens in general may feel. Then have a student compile a list on the board, placing a checkmark by each repeated weakness. Have students form pairs to address ways to overcome the ten most mentioned weaknesses. Allow students to report their ideas to the class and lead a discussion on each. **L2**

Activity

Ask students to identify adults whom they admire and to interview those adults about their goals and values in life. They might ask questions such as these:

- What values guide your life now?

- Have your values changed over the years? If so, in what ways?

- What life goals have you established based on your values?

Provide class time during which students can share the results of their research and discuss what they have learned from these interviews. **L2**

Cooperative Learning Activity

Advice Column Have pairs of students work together to compose letters to an advice columnist, asking for help. The letter should come from a fictional teen who has trouble recognizing and appreciating his or her own strengths; in fact, this teen seems to focus only on personal weaknesses. Ask students to make their letters interesting and specific.

Then let each pair of students trade letters with another pair. Have partners cooperate in composing a helpful response from the advice columnist. Remind students to help the fictional letter writer understand his or her situation and to make specific suggestions for recognizing and appreciating personal strengths.

181

Activity

Ask a group of volunteers to gather information about local volunteer opportunities that can help teens contribute to the community. Let the volunteers share this information with the rest of the class, either in a bulletin board display or in an oral presentation. **L3**

Have volunteers read aloud the listed behaviors of people with high self-esteem. Guide students in discussing specific actions and attitudes that indicate high self-esteem. Then ask students to write private health journal entries, recording how they plan to improve their own self-esteem.

Reinforcing Learning

Have students plan and draw cartoons that illustrate the advantages of realistic thinking and/or the problems caused by a pattern of negative thinking. **L2** **Visual/Spatial**

Cooperative Learning

Let students meet in small groups to discuss the benefits of giving and receiving constructive criticism. Then have group members plan and present a fictitious skit in which teens use constructive criticism to help one another. **L2**

Working Toward High Self-Esteem

People with high self-esteem:

- take responsibility for their behavior.
- generally have a positive outlook on life.
- like and accept who they are overall.
- try to learn from their successes as well as from their mistakes.
- build and maintain healthy relationships.

To improve self-esteem:

- think of appropriate ways to share your positive attributes.
- engage in behaviors that will promote your health.

Contribute to the Community

Your community is an extended support system for you and your family; it provides services and resources to meet many of your needs. Giving back to the community is part of being a good citizen, and it helps you feel a sense of accomplishment. For example, you might help out a neighbor or participate in a community clean-up campaign. Apply your strengths to improving others' quality of life, and strengthen your sense of belonging in the process.

Avoid Unhealthful Risk Behaviors

Risk-taking is a normal part of growing up—it helps define and develop identity. Healthful risk-taking has a positive effect on development. Engaging in sports, artistic or creative activities, public speaking, travel, and making friends all involve some risk. Such risks challenge you to develop skills and mature in new ways.

Unhealthful risk-taking, such as using tobacco, alcohol, or other drugs; reckless driving; and gang affiliation, can be dangerous. Refuse to participate in such behavior. Keep in mind the aspects of your identity, such as your values, that you are trying to uphold.

Self-Esteem and Positive Outlook

When you have a healthy identity, you will experience increased self-esteem and a higher level of mental/emotional health. Self-esteem comes from the understanding that you are a unique and valuable human being. How you feel mentally and physically and how you take care of yourself are all affected by what you think of yourself. Teens with high self-esteem are in a strong position to meet the challenges of adult life.

Along with self-esteem, having a positive outlook is also directly related to your general level of wellness. Studies have shown that

Teens find many ways to contribute to their community, including building houses for the homeless. *How does helping others contribute to a positive identity?*

people with a positive outlook live longer and are healthier, both mentally and physically. Remind yourself that no matter what happens, there is always hope. Then, when something goes wrong, make a plan to address the problem. Try to see challenges as opportunities for growing and learning.

More About...

Constructive Criticism Share the following guidelines for giving and receiving constructive criticism.

When Giving Constructive Criticism:

- Give constructive criticism in private.
- Focus on what can be done in the future.
- Praise the good points of an idea or behavior before pointing out weaknesses.

- Focus on the specific problem, not the person.
- Offer help whenever possible.

When Receiving Constructive Criticism:

- Consider the reason for the feedback.
- Focus on the message.
- Ask for clarification if you don't understand what someone is trying to tell you.

Realistic Patterns of Thinking

In order to increase your self-esteem and develop a positive outlook on life, it is essential to see events realistically. Some people fall into a pattern of seeing events as worse than they actually are. For example, a teen who has just failed an exam may think that he or she is stupid and will always fail. By looking at the situation realistically, the teen will realize that he or she was simply unprepared for that day's work and will resolve to study harder next time.

Sometimes, to help yourself see events more realistically, you might seek **constructive criticism**, or *nonhostile comments that point out problems and encourage improvement*. Constructive criticism can help you view a situation more objectively, without the emotional influences that can alter your perception and thinking.

ANALYZING YOUR SELF-TALK

Listen to your self-talk. Replace negative messages with constructive criticism. If you make a mistake, tell yourself that all people make mistakes; learn from yours and move on. Also, don't be afraid of telling yourself "Good job!" when you've done something that deserves praise. Such positive self-talk will benefit your self-esteem, your general outlook on life, and your mental/emotional health.

This teen uses constructive criticism from the teacher to improve her skills and thus raise her self-esteem. *Why is self-esteem important to mental and emotional health?*

3 ASSESS

EVALUATING THE LESSON

Assign and discuss the Lesson 2 Review; then administer, grade, and discuss Lesson Quiz 24 in the TCR. 📁

RETEACHING

- Have each student list the five most important ideas presented in the lesson. Then have students meet in groups to share and compare their lists.
- Ask students to complete Reteaching Activity 24 in the TCR. 📁

ENRICHMENT

Let students work with partners or in small groups to plan story lines in which a teen—or a group of teens—learns a difficult lesson from experience. Ask students to prepare and practice a short play depicting their story. Then have each pair or group perform their play for the rest of the class. 📼

4 CLOSE

In a short class discussion, have students identify community service activities they would like to take part in. Ask:

- What contribution do you think you could make?
- How would you benefit from performing that community service?

Encourage students to follow up and take part in community service projects.

▶ Lesson 2 *Review*

Reviewing Facts and Vocabulary

1. Define *personal identity*. List five elements that contribute to one's personal identity.
2. Name three of the positive values listed as developmental assets.
3. List three strategies for building a positive identity.

Thinking Critically

4. **Synthesizing.** Why do you think developmental assets increase the likelihood that a person will not engage in risk behaviors?
5. **Analyzing.** Describe how positive identity and high self-esteem help you with goal setting, developing relationships, and contributing to your community.

Applying Health Skills

Goal Setting. Evaluate aspects of your identity. Is there an area you would like to improve? Make a specific goal to strengthen one aspect of your identity. Using the steps of goal setting, write down plans and strategies to help you achieve your goal.

TECHNOLOGY *OPTION*

SPREADSHEETS Using a spreadsheet can help you organize a list. To learn more about how to use a spreadsheet, see health.glencoe.com.

Lesson 2 Developing a Positive Identity **183**

▶ Lesson 2 *Review*

Answers to Reviewing Facts and Vocabulary

1. See page 178.
2. Any three positive values listed on page 179.
3. Any three: Recognize strengths and weaknesses, demonstrate positive values, develop a purpose, form meaningful relationships, contribute to community, avoid unhealthful risk behaviors.

Answers to Thinking Critically

4. Answers should discuss how having assets increases a person's self-worth and helps prevent unhealthful behaviors.
5. Possible answer: Positive identity can help you set goals. It could influence your relationships, helping you relate to other people and find ways to assist them.

Understanding Emotions

1 FOCUS

QUICK START   Have students write their lists and then share and compare the named emotions. Write a class list on the board, and ask volunteers to answer the Quick Start questions.

TYING TO PRIOR KNOWLEDGE

Point out to students that their Quick Start lists and discussion show they already know quite a bit about emotions. They will learn more about emotions and health as they study this lesson.

Health Skills Features

"Expressing Your Feelings," p. 186

COMMUNICATION SKILLS

INTRODUCING VOCABULARY

- Have students use the Glossary to look up the definitions to the vocabulary words. Then have them write a short story using the four terms.

- Ask students to complete the Chapter 7 Study Guide in the *Student Activity Workbook.*

Understanding Emotions

VOCABULARY
emotions
hormone
empathy
hostility

YOU'LL LEARN TO
- Analyze how emotions influence your overall health.
- Appraise the significance of changes occurring during adolescence.
- Explore ways to demonstrate empathy toward others.
- Demonstrate communication skills in building and maintaining healthy relationships.

QUICK START   In one minute, list as many emotions as you can. Then compare your list with those of your classmates. Which emotions are most common? Why might some emotions, such as empathy, be on fewer lists?

 Actors portray strong emotions by using body language and changes in their voices. *What emotions are these actors trying to express?*

rt imitates life. This familiar phrase is particularly true in regard to drama. Acting requires the performer to express a character's emotions both verbally and physically. How might an actor express joy or sorrow as part of a play?

Understanding Your Emotions

Emotions are *signals that tell your mind and body how to react.* Sometimes referred to as feelings, emotions are your responses to certain thoughts and events. To communicate emotions, you use combinations of words or other sounds, facial expressions, and body language. Emotions affect all sides of your health triangle.

▶ Joy can prompt the release of brain chemicals that cause you to experience warmth and a sense of well-being. Feeling this way promotes mental/emotional health and positively influences your relationships and thus your social health.

▶ Fear can trigger physical changes, including increased perspiration, a rise in heart rate, and a tightening of muscles. This "fight-or-flight" response enables you to defend yourself or flee the scene.

184   **Chapter 7**   Achieving Good Mental Health

Lesson 3 *Resources*

Teacher Classroom Resources
- Concept Mapping Activity 25
- Decision-Making Activity 7
- Enrichment Activity 7
- Guided Reading Activities 25
- Health Lab 7

- Lesson Plan 25
- Lesson Quiz 25
- Reteaching Activity 25

Student Activity Workbook
- Applying Health Skills 25
- Chapter 7 Study Guide

► Strong emotions like anger can cause both physical and mental responses, such as a rise in heart rate and feelings of distress. Inappropriate responses, such as lashing out, can be harmful to you or to people around you.

Identifying Your Emotions

Sometimes you know exactly what you are feeling and why. At other times, you may experience emotions that seem to have no apparent cause. Moreover, the many changes brought on by hormones during puberty can affect your emotions. A **hormone** is *a chemical secreted by your glands that regulates the activities of different body cells.* Hormones may cause you to swing quickly between extreme emotions such as elation and depression. Mixed emotions, such as when you feel both jealous of and happy for a friend, also can be challenging. Accurately identifying what you are feeling is an important first step toward knowing how to respond in a healthy way.

Happiness

Think of other words that might describe how you feel when you are happy. You might say you are pleased or that you feel good or carefree. Happiness can be described as being satisfied or feeling positive. When you are happy, you usually feel energetic, creative, and sociable.

Sadness

Sadness is a normal, healthy reaction to difficult events. Causes of sadness can range from being disappointed or rejected to experiencing the loss of a loved one. Feelings of sadness may be mild and fleeting, or they may be deep and long-lasting. When you are sad, you may feel easily discouraged and have less energy.

Love

Love involves strong affection, deep concern, and respect. It includes supporting the growth and individual needs of another person and respecting that person's boundaries and values. Love can be expressed through words or actions, such as good deeds. It comes in many forms, such as caring about family and friends, loyalty to siblings, and a deep sense of being connected to your community and country.

Sadness may bring feelings of hurt, isolation, or helplessness. *How can you comfort a friend who is feeling down?*

Lesson 3 Understanding Emotions **185**

② TEACH

Reinforcing Concepts

Let volunteers express specific emotions without using words. Have each interested student select a specific emotion (referring to the Quick Start list on the board, if necessary) and demonstrate that emotion using only posture, facial expressions, and movements. Ask the other students to identify the emotion being demonstrated. **L1 Bodily/Kinesthetic**

Explaining

Present the following list of tips for minimizing mood swings:

• Eat well-balanced meals.

• Avoid tobacco, alcohol, and other drugs.

• Get plenty of sleep.

• Develop close relationships with family and friends. **L1**

Cooperative Learning

Have students form cooperative learning groups, and provide each group with a colored sheet of construction paper; each group should have a different color. Have group members decide on a single emotion that their color suggests. Then ask them to cut (or tear) the paper into pieces and arrange those pieces in a pattern, picture, or design that reinforces the emotion they have decided on. Let each group share its project with the rest of the class, and have other students try to guess the emotion suggested. **L2** **Visual/Spatial**

— School to Work —

Emotions on the Job Have students work in groups, and let each group choose a specific occupation such as a server in a restaurant, a computer programmer, a store manager, or a nurse. Ask group members to brainstorm situations that would provoke an emotional response in such a worker. Then have them role-play positive and negative ways to handle the situations and emotions. Ask each group to role-play one of their situations for the rest of the class. Follow with a class discussion about how emotions—and the way they are handled—can affect a worker's job performance and his or her relationships with coworkers and customers.

Health Skills Activity

EXPRESSING YOUR FEELINGS

NHES Standard 5 Students will demonstrate the ability to use interpersonal communication skills to enhance health.

Objectives

- Demonstrate communication skills in maintaining healthy relationships.
- Demonstrate healthy ways to express feelings.

Motivator

Ask: How do you feel when someone is late? What communication skills have you used in that situation?

Teaching Strategies

1. Allow students to work in pairs to adopt the roles of the friends in the feature.
2. Remind students to focus on the problem behavior, not the person.

✔Assessment

Using a rubric, student work should provide comprehensive evidence of the following criteria to achieve the highest score:

✔ use of "I" statements
✔ respectful tone
✔ clear, organized message
✔ listening skills

Explaining

Being or pretending to be happy all the time is not necessarily mentally healthy. An array of emotions is healthy as long as one emotion does not dominate another or is not expressed inappropriately. L1

Empathy

Empathy is *the ability to imagine and understand how someone else feels*. When you feel empathy, you feel connected to another person's emotions. An empathetic person listens attentively and communicates understanding when people express their feelings. Demonstrating empathy can help strengthen your emotional bonds and enhance your relationships.

Fear

When you are startled by someone or something, you probably feel some degree of fear. Feelings of fear can increase your alertness and help you escape from potentially harmful situations. However, fear that results from an imagined threat can prevent people from leading normal lives. For example, an exaggerated fear of being in a crowd can result in a life of solitude. This type of fear is called a **phobia** and requires professional help.

hotlink

phobia To learn more about phobias, see Chapter 9, page 225.

Communication: Expressing Your Feelings

Tara feels a knot in her stomach when she sees her friend Suzanne. The last time she agreed to go to a concert with Tara, Suzanne failed to show up. It hurt Tara's feelings that Suzanne didn't care enough about their friendship to show up.

Suzanne says excitedly, "Tara, did you see who's playing this weekend? Let's get there early, okay?"

Tara feels torn between two choices. She could ignore her feelings by keeping them bottled up. Her other option would be to communicate her hurt and disappointment, but that would risk hurting Suzanne's feelings.

What Would You Do?

Use the following communication skills to write a dialogue in which Tara expresses her hurt and disappointment in a way that spares Suzanne's feelings.

1. Use "I" messages.
2. Keep your tone respectful.
3. Provide a clear, organized message that states the problem.
4. Listen to the other person's side without interrupting.

More About...

Fear Here are some common and not-so-common phobias:

- hematophobia (fear of blood)
- ailurophobia (fear of cats)
- demophobia (fear of crowds)
- nyctophobia (fear of the dark)
- thanatophobia (fear of death)
- mysophobia (fear of dirt)
- batrachophobia (fear of frogs)

- belonephobia (fear of needles)
- agoraphobia (fear of open spaces)
- algophobia (fear of pain)
- ophidiophobia (fear of snakes)
- arachnophobia (fear of spiders)
- xenophobia (fear of strangers)
- phobophobia (fear of phobias)
- panophobia (fear of everything)

Guilt

Guilt often results from acting against one's values or from failing to act when action might have brought about a better outcome. Although guilt can eat at you, it can also act as your conscience and motivate you to make some positive changes in your behavior. Sometimes, people may feel guilty for things they have no control over. For example, some teens blame themselves when parents divorce even though they are not the cause of the separation. Being able to recognize when you are not responsible for a negative outcome will save you from needless guilt.

Anger

Anger is a common reaction to being emotionally hurt or physically harmed. When anger isn't handled in constructive ways, it can result in violence, bringing physical and emotional harm to you and others. **Hostility**, *the intentional use of unfriendly or offensive behavior*, can be particularly damaging, not only to others but also to the hostile person. People who show chronic hostile behavior are four to seven times more likely to die of heart disease than those who are not prone to hostility. Knowing what causes your anger and how you can respond to it healthfully can help you gain control.

HEALTH Online

Explore more about emotions and the role they play in our lives at **health.glencoe.com.**

Lesson 3 Review

Reviewing Facts and Vocabulary

1. How can emotions influence your overall health?
2. Define *empathy*. How can a person demonstrate empathy?
3. How might guilty feelings lead to positive results?

Thinking Critically

4. **Evaluating.** Appraise the significance of changes occurring during adolescence: What effects do changing hormone levels have on emotions?
5. **Synthesizing.** List three situations that may cause a teen to feel anger. Then, explain how each of these situations can be dealt with in healthful ways.

Applying Health Skills

Conflict Resolution. Write a skit in which unpleasant emotions cause a conflict between two friends. Your skit should demonstrate positive communication skills that aid the teens in handling their strong emotions and resolving their differences.

TECHNOLOGY OPTION

WORD PROCESSING Word-processing software can help you write and revise your skit. For more information on using word-processing software, click on **health.glencoe.com.**

Lesson 3 Understanding Emotions **187**

Lesson 3 Review

Answers to Reviewing Facts and Vocabulary

1. Physical health: by causing physiological responses; mental/emotional: by affecting the way a person perceives self, others, and situations; social health: by bringing others closer or driving them away.
2. The ability to imagine and understand how someone else feels; by listening attentively and being understanding.
3. It can motivate positive changes in behavior.

Answers to Thinking Critically

4. Hormones may make emotions seem more intense or cause emotional swings.
5. Answers will vary.

---

3 ASSESS

EVALUATING THE LESSON

Assign and discuss the Lesson 3 Review; then administer, grade, and discuss Lesson Quiz 25 in the TCR. 📁

RETEACHING

- Have students write their own lists of the emotions discussed in Lesson 3. After each emotion name, identify at least one situation that may elicit that emotion.
- Ask students to complete Reteaching Activity 25 in the TCR. 📁

ENRICHMENT

Suggest that interested students write and perform their own musical compositions, each expressing a specific emotion. Possible compositions include hummed tunes, solo instrumental works (as on a piano, violin, or drum), songs, and raps.

4 CLOSE

Have each student write a sentence summarizing the most important concept that he or she has learned in this lesson.

Managing Emotions

Lesson 4

Managing Emotions

VOCABULARY

defense mechanisms
suppression

YOU'LL LEARN TO

* Evaluate the effects of peers, family, and friends on emotional health.

* Demonstrate strategies for communicating emotions and needs in healthful ways.

> **QUICK START** There are many ways to communicate emotions to others. List three emotions, and describe how you usually communicate them.

Healthful expression of feelings increases your ability to enjoy life. *What are some positive ways to express emotions?*

Emotions are neither good nor bad. How you deal with your emotions, however, can strongly influence your overall level of health. Learning to recognize emotions and dealing with them in healthful ways are especially important to good mental health.

Dealing with Emotions in Positive Ways

As you were growing up, you learned various ways of expressing your emotions from others, from your environment, and from your experiences. Perhaps your family members talk openly about their feelings and encourage sharing them. Maybe your friends express themselves indirectly with looks or smiles or with behaviors such as laughing or hugging. Perhaps some of your peers don't talk about or express feelings much, and you've learned from their example that emotions are private. Regardless of what you have learned, it is important to evaluate methods of communicating feelings and practice healthful ways of expression.

Negative ways of dealing with feelings do nothing to solve problems. Exaggerating emotions for effect, pretending that feelings are not there at all, or intentionally hurting another person while expressing feelings can worsen the situation and create new problems.

FOCUS

> **QUICK START** Give students about three minutes to jot down their Quick Start responses. Then give each interested student a chance to read aloud one description of how he or she communicates an emotion, without naming the emotion. Ask the other students to identify each emotion.

TYING TO PRIOR KNOWLEDGE

Help students recall what they have learned about recognizing their own emotions. Explain that, in this lesson, they will learn more about positive ways of dealing with their emotions.

Health Skills Features

"Managing Anger," p. 161

STRESS MANAGEMENT

INTRODUCING VOCABULARY

* Give students five minutes to define the terms in writing.

* Ask students to complete the Chapter 7 Study Guide in the *Student Activity Workbook*.

Lesson 4 *Resources*

Teacher Classroom Resources

📁 Concept Mapping Activity 26

📁 Guided Reading Activies 26

📁 Lesson Plan 26

📁 Lesson Quiz 26

📁 Reteaching Activity 26

Student Activity Workbook

📁 Applying Health Skills 26

📁 Chapter 7 Study Guide

Multimedia

💾 Transparency 21

Responding to Your Emotions

You can use some of the following strategies for interpreting and responding to most emotions.

▶ Look below the surface of your emotion. Ask yourself: What am I really reacting to? Does the intensity of my emotion match the situation?

▶ Consider whether or not the situation to which you are reacting will matter tomorrow, next week, or next year.

▶ Don't take action on a strong feeling until you have thoroughly considered the possible consequences of your action.

▶ Use positive feelings to inspire yourself. Relieve negative or upsetting feelings by engaging in physical activities or by talking to a family member or trusted friend.

▶ If a negative feeling doesn't go away, seek help from a parent, another trusted adult, or a health care professional.

Managing Difficult Emotions

You've probably been overwhelmed by strong emotions at one time or another. Intense emotions can affect your attitude and behavior in ways that are upsetting. However, you can learn to manage strong emotions. When you feel your emotions building, recognize the feeling and manage it by taking slow, deep breaths and relaxing. You might also get away from the situation to compose yourself. Sometimes you can control your feelings by analyzing the situations that cause the feelings. Writing in a private journal, playing music, or talking your feelings over with a parent or trusted friend can help you reflect on both your emotions and the situation that led to them.

Defense Mechanisms

Because of the way emotions affect you, you may try to avoid the ones that cause you discomfort by using **defense mechanisms**. These are *mental processes that protect individuals from strong or stressful emotions and situations*. **Figure 7.4** on page 190 lists some of the most common defense mechanisms. Sometimes, these responses occur unconsciously and may help protect you from feeling too much emotional pain. For instance, the use of **suppression**, *holding back or restraining*, can provide a temporary escape from an unpleasant situation. In the long run, however, defense mechanisms may keep you from facing what is really troubling you. That's why it's important to develop strategies for dealing with difficult emotions in healthful ways.

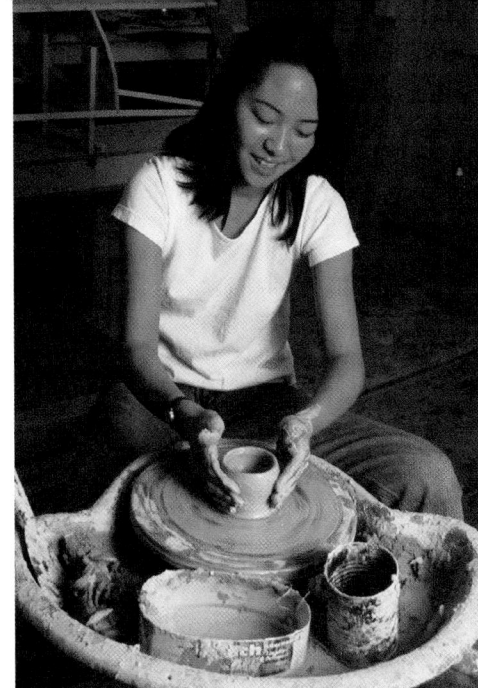

Creating art is a healthful way to handle your emotions. *The next time you feel a strong emotion, try doing something creative.*

② TEACH

Discussing

Guide students in discussing the importance of planning effective ways to manage difficult emotions. Ask: why is it important to plan your strategies ahead of time when you are not feeling strong emotions? **L1**

Critical Thinking

Have students discuss their responses to these questions:

• When can it be considered healthy to use defense mechanisms? Why?

• Under what circumstances is the use of defense mechanisms unhealthy? Why? **L1**

Cooperative Learning

Divide the class into small groups, and assign each group a different defense mechanism. (See Figure 7.4 on page 190 for a list of defense mechanisms.) Have group members work together to plan and perform a skit in which one or more characters uses the assigned mechanism. Ask other students to identify the defense mechanism shown in each skit. **L2** **Bodily/Kinesthetic**

Myths & Reality

MYTH. All defense mechanisms are psychologically unhealthy.

FACT. There are times when defense mechanisms can give people relief from stress and help them cope with problems. Difficulties occur when people depend on defense mechanisms to help them avoid facing daily problems.

MYTH. There are positive and negative emotions.

FACT. Although some emotions may be difficult or unpleasant to experience, emotions themselves are not positive or negative. All emotions are normal. It is how one responds to emotions that is positive or negative. Managing and expressing feelings in healthful ways is an important part of wellness.

Figure 7.4 Have students work together to read about and discuss the Common Defense Mechanisms. Let volunteers describe specific examples of each.

Hands-On Health

MANAGING ANGER

STRESS MANAGEMENT

NHES Standard 3 Students will demonstrate the ability to practice health enhancing behaviors and reduce health risk.

Objectives

- Recognize the importance of coping with anger.

- Identify specific ways to practice anger management skills.

Motivator

Have students brainstorm what they do when they are angry. Write the list on the board.

Teaching Strategies

1. Advise students to identify activities they are likely to try.
2. Allow students to work in groups to share ideas.

✓ Assessment

Using a rubric, student work should provide comprehensive evidence of the following criteria to achieve the highest score:

✔ identification of anger management skills to reduce stress
✔ comparison of anger management techniques
✔ demonstration of at least one technique that helps manage anger and stress

---

FIGURE 7.4

COMMON DEFENSE MECHANISMS

- **Repression.** Involuntary pushing of unpleasant feelings out of conscious thought.
- **Suppression.** Conscious, intentional pushing of unpleasantness from one's mind.
- **Rationalization.** Making excuses to explain a situation or behavior rather than directly taking responsibility for it.
- **Regression.** Reverting to behaviors more characteristic of an earlier stage of development rather than dealing with the conflict in a mature manner.
- **Denial.** Unconscious lack of acknowledgement of something that is obvious to others.
- **Compensation.** Making up for weaknesses and mistakes through gift-giving, hard work, or extreme efforts.
- **Projection.** Attributing your own feelings or faults to another person or group.
- **Idealization.** Seeing someone else as perfect, ideal, or more worthy than everyone else.

Handling Fear

Fear is an emotion many people work to overcome. Overcoming fear requires a strategy. The first step is to identify your fear. Analyzing the situation that causes the fear often helps. Talking about your fear with someone you trust may also give you a fresh outlook. This person may remind you of other fears you have faced successfully or know of resources that can help you. Some fear is healthy and natural; only when fear is irrational or uncontrollable should you consider it a problem.

Dealing with Guilt

Guilt can be a very destructive emotion. When you feel guilty about something, try to get at the underlying source and address that issue. If you have hurt someone, for example, admit your mistake and make amends. Learn from the experience, and resolve to be more careful and responsible in the future. Discussing the situation with family or friends can also help make you feel better. Keep in mind that some situations may not be in your control. Viewing such circumstances realistically and honestly will help you see that you are not responsible and should not feel guilty for them.

Managing Anger

Anger can be one of the most difficult emotions to handle. The first step in constructively dealing with anger is similar to dealing with guilt—you must try to get at the underlying source and address it. Even if there is nothing you can do about the source of your anger, you can find ways to cope with your feelings. Refer to the Hands-On Health Activity for some general anger-management techniques.

More About...

Strategies for Managing Anger Doctors at Duke University Medical Center have developed a 12-step program to help people deal with their angry feelings. These are some of the steps:

- Try seeing an upsetting issue from the other person's perspective.
- Learn to relax.

- Practice trusting other people.
- Develop your listening skills.
- Learn to assert yourself. Using assertiveness—instead of aggression—can improve your relationships and help you achieve your goals.
- Remember that life is short. Ask yourself whether you really have time to get angry.

Hands-On Health **ACTIVITY**

Managing Anger

In this activity you'll identify and develop healthy strategies to handle anger.

What You'll Need

• pencil and paper

What You'll Do

1. Write the following headings on your paper.
   • Do something to relax.
   • Rechannel your energy.
   • Talk to someone you trust.
   • Get some physical activity.

2. Under each heading, list at least two *specific* activities you can try.

3. Compare your list with a partner's. How are your techniques similar or different? What does this tell you about how individuals handle anger?

Apply and Conclude

Working with your partner, create a comic strip that illustrates at least one effective anger management skill.

▶ Lesson 4 *Review*

Reviewing Facts and Vocabulary

1. List three strategies for interpreting, responding to, and communicating an emotion in healthful ways.

2. What are five common defense mechanisms?

3. Give four examples of anger-management techniques.

Thinking Critically

4. **Analyzing.** Evaluate the effects of various relationships on emotional health: In what ways do peers, family, and friends influence how you express and manage emotions?

5. **Explaining.** Describe the results that may occur when you take time to reflect before responding to a strong emotion.

Applying Health Skills

Communication Skills. Write a one-act play. Focus on someone using the strategies listed at the beginning of this lesson to decide how to react to and express a specific feeling.

TECHNOLOGY *OPTION*

WORD PROCESSING You can use word-processing software to help you draft, revise, and edit your play. See **health.glencoe.com** for tips on using a word-processing program.

Lesson 4 Managing Emotions **191**

---

3 ASSESS

EVALUATING THE LESSON

Assign and discuss the Lesson 4 Review; then administer, grade, and discuss Lesson Quiz 26 in the TCR.

RETEACHING

• Have students work with partners to review and discuss healthy ways to handle fear, guilt, and anger.

• Ask students to complete Reteaching Activity 26 in the TCR.

ENRICHMENT

Have interested students use library and/or online resources to learn more about defense mechanisms. Ask these students to share their findings with the rest of the class.

4 CLOSE

Have each student complete the following sentence, either orally or in writing:

The next time I feel really angry, I will . . .

▶ Lesson 4 *Review*

Answers to Reviewing Facts and Vocabulary

1. Any three: Look below the surface; consider whether it will matter later; consider the consequences before acting; be inspired by positive feelings; seek help for persistent negative feelings.

2. Any five listed in Figure 7.4 on page 190.

3. See techniques in Hands-On Health.

Answers to Thinking Critically

4. The ways in which others express and manage emotions can influence how you deal with emotions.

5. Possible answer: Better able to understand and deal with a situation or emotion and less likely to overreact.

Eye ON THE Media

Emotional Health in TV Programs

NHES Standard 4 Students will analyze the influence of culture, media, technology, and other factors on health.

Objective

Examine the ways emotions are expressed on different TV programs.

Motivator

Have students brainstorm healthy ways of dealing with difficult emotions.

Teaching Strategies

Awareness Ask students to think of an instance in which they might have expressed an emotion in an inappropriate or unhealthy way.

Analysis Ask whether the overall message of the program was a positive or negative example of emotional health.

Reflection Ask students which types of programs were more emotionally healthy.

Take Action Students can write a letter to the network that aired the program.

✓ Assessment

Student charts should contain entries that clearly show their analysis of the program's emotional health. Student reviews should contain a synopsis of the plot, an explanation of characters, and specific examples to support their viewpoint about the program's overall message concerning emotional health.

Eye ON THE Media

Emotional Health in TV Programs

There are healthy and unhealthy ways of dealing with your emotions. In this activity, you will examine the ways in which emotions are expressed on different television programs and analyze the messages these programs send on the subject of emotional health.

Emotion	How it was expressed	How other characters reacted
Frustration	The character snapped at a younger sibling.	His mother made him apologize and then asked him to discuss what was wrong.

ACTIVITY

Watch a sitcom, drama, reality show, or talk show. Record the ways in which different emotions are expressed throughout the program. Use a chart like the one above to help organize your notes.

Consider the overall message the program sends regarding emotional health. Do the characters demonstrate healthy ways of dealing with difficult emotions? Do they suffer consequences as a result of inappropriate behavior? Are unhealthful ways of expressing emotions corrected? Rate the emotional health of the program, using a scale of 1 to 5, with 5 being the highest and 1 being the lowest.

EXPRESS YOUR VIEWS

Write a one-page review of the program that includes a synopsis of the plot and characters and a description of the consequences of the characters' behaviors. Indicate whether the program provided a positive or negative example of how to express or deal with emotions. Support your viewpoint with specific examples from the program.

More About...

The Effects of TV The Kaiser Family Foundation recently conducted a scientific study of children and the media. Among their findings was that the average child between ages 2–18 watches nearly three hours of television every day. Researchers assert that "Anything strongly related to the psychological and social adjustment of children deserves attention." Students can research on the Internet how these reviewers rate movies for their health message. Have students create a detailed ratings system for rating the emotional health of television programs. Throughout the year, students can write reviews of television programs they see, rate them according to their system, and publish it in the school newspaper.

CROSS-CURRICULUM CONNECTIONS

Create a Poem. Reaching for the stars means striving to become the best you can be. Working toward this self-actualization is an important aspect of good mental health. Poet Langston Hughes described it this way: "We have tomorrow, bright before us like a flame." Using Hughes's words as a model, choose a symbol that represents you and your quest to fulfill your potential. Write a poem about your self-image and incorporate your symbol.

Research a Biography. Developing a sense of purpose in your life means moving beyond your own needs to contributing to your community. Many successful people, such as Nelson Mandela and Mother Theresa, have chosen paths of self-sacrifice in life. Write a short research report on a well-known figure who has worked to improve the quality of life of others. Determine why helping others was a priority for this person.

Calculate Demographics. According to the U.S. Department of Health and Human Services, the percentage of females reporting significant emotional problems is 22 percent among adolescents aged 14 to 17. Suppose that the study surveyed 3.7 million girls ages 14 to 15 and 3.5 million girls ages 16 to 17. How many girls aged 14 to 17 would have reported significant emotional problems?

Investigate a Body System. Hormones play an important role in influencing mental and emotional health. The endocrine system produces hormones in ductless glands located throughout the body. These hormones transmit chemical signals to which the body responds. Create a chart showing the glands of the endocrine system, their location in the body, the hormones they secrete, and the function of each in the body. Discuss the problems that might arise from imbalances in the system and what conditions can cause them.

CAREER Corner

School Counselor

Do you have empathy, and do you like helping others? Are you interested in teaching and working with students and their families? If so, a career as a school psychologist or counselor might be for you. These professionals assist students with personal, family, educational, and mental health problems.

To enter this profession, you'll need a four-year college degree and at least a two-year graduate degree. Find more information about this and other health careers by clicking on Career Corner at **health.glencoe.com**.

Chapter 7 Review **193**

Portfolio Assessment

CHECKING COMPREHENSION

- Assign and discuss the chapter review.
- Use the Chapter 7 MindJogger Videoquiz to review the chapter. 📼

CHAPTER 7 REVIEW ANSWERS

Exploring Health Terms

1. personality
2. hierarchy of needs
3. self-actualization
4. modeling
5. Personal identity
6. developmental asset
7. constructive criticism
8. emotion
9. hormone
10. hostility
11. true
12. false; suppression

Recalling the Facts

1. See Figure 7.1 on page 171.
2. Strengthens a person's mental and emotional health and protects the individual from harmful consequences.
3. Answers may include family, friends, home, neighborhood, and school.
4. Support, empowerment, boundaries and expectations, constructive use of time, commitment to learning, positive values, social competencies, positive identity.
5. Establishing goals and working to achieve them.
6. Healthful risk-taking helps a person develop skills and mature.

▶ **EXPLORING HEALTH TERMS** *Answer the following questions on a sheet of paper.*

Lesson 1 *Match each definition with the correct term.*

hierarchy of needs   **self-actualization**
mental/emotional health   **modeling**
personality

1. The sum of behavioral and emotional tendencies that affect a person's life.
2. A ranked list of those needs essential to human growth and development.
3. Striving to become the best you can be.
4. Observing and learning from the behavior of others.

Lesson 2 *Replace the underlined words with the correct term.*

constructive criticism   **personal identity**
developmental asset

5. <u>Constructive criticism</u> is made up of elements such as interests, abilities, values, and goals.
6. A <u>personal identity</u> is a building block of development that helps you grow up as a healthy, caring, and responsible individual.
7. Giving thoughtful recommendations on how a friend can improve a skill is an example of <u>developmental asset</u>.

Lesson 3 *Fill in the blanks with the correct term.*

emotion   **hormone**
empathy   **hostility**

A(n) **(8)** _____ tells your mind and body how to react. A change in the level of a(n) **(9)** _____ can affect how you react to situations and thus can affect your emotions. Anger sometimes results in **(10)** _____ , which can damage a relationship.

Lesson 4 *Identify each statement as True or False. If false, replace the underlined term with the correct term.*

suppression   **defense mechanisms**

11. People sometimes use <u>defense mechanisms</u> to avoid dealing with an unpleasant emotion.
12. <u>Projection</u> is the intentional pushing of unpleasantness out of one's mind.

▶ **RECALLING THE FACTS** *Use complete sentences to answer the following questions.*

Lesson 1

1. In general, teens with good mental/emotional health demonstrate what characteristics?
2. Why is it important to meet needs in positive ways?
3. List four environmental influences that can affect the development of someone's personality.

Lesson 2

4. Identify the eight categories of developmental assets.
5. What does it mean to develop a sense of purpose?
6. How can healthful risk-taking have a positive effect on development?
7. How does high self-esteem and a positive outlook affect a person's health?

Lesson 3

8. List seven basic emotions.
9. Why is it harmful to feel hostile often?
10. Identify two causes of guilt.

Lesson 4

11. What are some ways of managing strong emotions?
12. Identify two strategies for dealing with guilt.

7. People with high self-esteem take care of themselves and are ready to meet life's challenges. People with a positive outlook live longer and are healthier.
8. Answers may include happiness, sadness, love, empathy, fear, guilt, and anger.
9. People who show chronic hostile behavior are four to seven times more likely to die of heart disease.

10. Answers may vary. Guilt results from acting against one's values or from failing to act when direct action might have brought about a better outcome. Some people also feel guilty over things they cannot control, such as parents' divorce.
11. Possible answers are identified on page 189.

➤ THINKING CRITICALLY

1. **Evaluating.** Identify a positive role model in your life. Explain the qualities and characteristics that make her or him a positive role model. *(LESSON 1)*

2. **Synthesizing.** Identify three of your strengths and three of your weaknesses. Outline ways that you can use your strengths to address your weaknesses. *(LESSON 2)*

3. **Analyzing.** Why is empathy an important characteristic? Explain actions you can take to demonstrate empathy. *(LESSON 3)*

4. **Evaluating.** List three unhealthful responses to a difficult emotion such as guilt or anger. Explain why these responses are unhealthful, and then provide healthier alternatives for dealing with the emotion. *(LESSON 4)*

➤ HEALTH SKILLS APPLICATION

1. **Analyzing Influences.** Make a list of the factors that you think have the strongest influence on your

personality. Identify which of these are hereditary influences and which are environmental influences. *(LESSON 1)*

2. **Communication Skills.** Think of a person in your life who has given you constructive criticism or positive feedback. Write a thank-you letter to this person. Indicate how this feedback has affected your feelings of self-esteem. *(LESSON 2)*

3. **Advocacy.** Create a small booklet that promotes emotional health by explaining positive ways for teens to deal with difficult emotions or mood swings. *(LESSON 3)*

4. **Practicing Healthful Behaviors.** For one week, maintain an "anger log." After each instance of anger, rate the experience from 1 (mildly irritated) to 10 (hostile). Include the trigger for your anger, what you felt like doing at the time, and how you actually handled the emotion. If necessary, determine ways to improve your anger-management skills. *(LESSON 4)*

 BEYOND *the* Classroom

Parent Involvement

Advocacy. Learn more about local charities and shelters in your community. With your parents or guardians, find out what items and experience are needed and what volunteer positions are available. Use this information to make leaflets or posters that inform others of ways they can help individuals meet their needs.

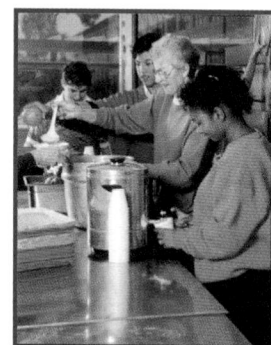

School and Community

Service Learning. Find out whether your school has a service-learning program. If it does, determine what community volunteer opportunities exist. If your school doesn't have such a program, run a Web search for the Corporation for National and Community Service to locate specific opportunities in your community in fields that interest you.

12. Admitting if you made a mistake and discussing the situation with family or friends can help.

Thinking Critically

1. Answers will vary. Role models should demonstrate positive values, be supportive, and provide guidance in making responsible choices.

2. Answers will vary; accept all thoughtful student responses.

3. Answers will vary. Students may explain that empathy improves relationships. Ways to demonstrate empathy include listening attentively, expressing understanding, and making supportive comments.

4. Answers will vary; accept all thoughtful student responses.

Health Skills Application

1.–4. Answers will vary.

EVALUATE

- Use the reproducible Chapter 7 Test in the TCR, or construct your own using the Testmaker software. 📁 💿

- Use Performance Assessment 7 in the TCR. 📁

ENRICHMENT

Ask students to complete Enrichment Activity 7 in the TCR. 📁

 BEYOND *the* Classroom

Keep students involved in the community, and encourage parent participation by assigning the activities on this page for students to work on outside of class.

Lessons	Standards		Features
	National	**State/Local**	
1 **Effects of Stress** *pages 198–204*	National Health Education Standards 1.1, 1.2, 6.1		*Exploring* **Issues** • Change: Positive or Negative? page 203
2 **Managing Stress** *pages 205–209*	National Health Education Standards 1.1, 1.2, 3.4, 3.7		**Hands-On Health** • Managing Your Time *(Stress Management)*, page 207
3 **Anxiety and Teen Depression** *pages 210–213*	National Health Education Standards 2.6, 3.4, 5.4		Health Skills *Activity* • Being a Supportive Friend *(Communication)*, page 212
4 **Being a Resilient Teen** *pages 214–217*	National Health Education Standards 1.1, 1.4, 3.4		*Real-Life* **Application** • The Power of Assets *(Analyzing Influences)*, page 217

Reproducible Resources	Assessment	Technology
Student Activity Workbook for use with each chapter 📁 Concept Mapping Activity 27 📁 Cross-Curriculum Activity 8 📁 Guided Reading Actvities 27 📁 Health Lab 8 📁 Lesson Plan 27 📁 Parent Letter and Activities 8 📁 Reteaching Activity 27	📁 Lesson Quiz 27	🖨 Transparency 22 💿 Teacher Works® 💻 Internet Activities
📁 Concept Mapping Activity 28 📁 Decision-Making Activity 8 📁 Enrichment Activity 8 📁 Guided Reading Actvities 28 📁 Lesson Plan 28 📁 Reteaching Activity 28	📁 Lesson Quiz 28	🖨 Transparency 23 💿 Teacher Works®
📁 Concept Mapping Activity 29 📁 Current Health Issues 8 📁 Guided Reading Activities 29 📁 Lesson Plan 29 📁 Reteaching Activity 29	📁 Lesson Quiz 29	💿 Teacher Works®
📁 Concept Mapping Activity 30 📁 Guided Reading Activities 30 📁 Lesson Plan 30 📁 Reteaching Activity 30	📁 Lesson Quiz 30	💿 Teacher Works®

0:00 OUT OF TIME

If time does not permit teaching the entire chapter use:

- Figure 8.1, p. 200
- Hands-On Health, p. 207
- Health Minute, p. 211
- Real-Life Application, page 217

Language Diversity

- 🎧 English Audio CD Program
- 🎧 Spanish Audio CD Program
- 📁 English Summaries, Quizzes, and Activities
- 📁 Spanish Summaries, Quizzes, and Activities
- 📁 Spanish Parent Letters and Activities

End of Chapter Assessment

Blackline Masters

- 📁 Chapter 8 Test
- 📁 Performance Assessment Activity 8

Technology

- 💿 Vocabulary PuzzleMaker
- 📼 MindJogger Videoquiz
- 💿 **Exam***View*® Pro Testmaker

Professional Health Series

Dealing with Sensitive Issues
Planning a Coordinated School Health Program
Promoting Character Education
Home, School, and Community Involvement

Managing Stress and Anxiety

CHAPTER OVERVIEW

Chapter 8 discusses stress, anxiety, and depression, and helps students understand how they can become resilient individuals.

Lesson 1 Stress, the reaction of the body and mind to everyday challenges and demands, is a natural part of life. It can have positive or negative effects. Excessive or prolonged stress has a detrimental effect on physical, mental/emotional, and social health.

Lesson 2 The ability to identify personal stressors, avoid unnecessary stressors, and manage responses to unavoidable stressors can help individuals protect all aspects of their health.

Lesson 3 Anxiety—feelings of unease and worry—should be managed in healthy ways. Depression is a prolonged feeling of helplessness, hopelessness, and sadness. Teens with persistent anxiety or depression can benefit from professional help.

Lesson 4 Resiliency, the ability to adapt effectively and recover from difficulty, disappointment, or crisis, throughout the lifespan can be identified and developed.

Health Skills Features

- Exploring Issues, p. 203
- Hands-On Health (*Stress Management*), p. 207
- Health Skills Activity (*Communication*), p. 212
- Real-Life Application (*Analyzing Influences*), p. 217

Chapter 8

Managing Stress and Anxiety

Lesson 1
Effects of Stress

Lesson 2
Managing Stress

Lesson 3
Anxiety and Teen Depression

Lesson 4
Being a Resilient Teen

196

MEETING STUDENT DIVERSITY

Language Diversity Use the following suggestions to help students who have difficulty with English:

- Pair English language learners with native speakers of English who can restate the Chapter Summary in language that helps students comprehend important concepts.

- 🎧 Direct auditory learners or those students with language diversity to the *Glencoe Health Audio CD Program*. Available in English and Spanish, this component provides an audio and written summary of the chapter.

- Use photographs, drawings, or magazine clippings to help students visualize the important concepts of the chapter.

Case Study

Zoe's Story

Zoe has always been focused and well organized. She's known since she was a very young girl that she wanted to be a dancer and has done everything she can to ensure that she would achieve this goal.

Lately, however, Zoe feels as though her life is getting out of control. Homework is taking up too much time. Her friends expect her to go out with them when she has dance practice. Her family always seems to have something big planned when she needs to prepare for an exam or finish a project.

These pressures are beginning to take a toll on Zoe's health. She's been having trouble sleeping and gets angry very easily. She often feels overwhelmed, as if she can't cope with the demands of everyday life. Being tired all the time is having a negative effect on her schoolwork and dancing. Zoe knows that she needs to do something about her problem but isn't sure what steps to take.

What advice would you give Zoe? Write a sentence or two describing what you would say to her. Reread this story and your response when you complete the chapter. Identify how stress might be affecting *your* life and what you do to manage it.

Quick Write

Using Visuals. Communicating with friends, family members, and other people you trust can help you handle the stress of the teen years and help you get through the ups and downs of life. What other strategies can help relieve stress?

197

INTRODUCING THE CHAPTER

Case Study

Have students meet in small groups to read and discuss Zoe's story. Encourage group members to share their responses to Zoe's situation: Does it sound familiar, or is it hard to imagine? What could make Zoe—and other high school students—feel so overwhelmed? If you were one of Zoe's classmates, do you think you would notice a change in her? If so, what (if anything) would you say or do?

After the group discussions, have students work independently to write a few sentences of advice to Zoe. Remind students to keep their writing so they can review and revise it when they finish reading Chapter 8.

Quick Write

Using Visuals Have students look at the photograph. Ask: Who is talking? Who is listening? How do you imagine these teens are benefiting from talking and listening?

After a brief class discussion, have students write their own responses to the Quick Write question. Then have several volunteers read their responses aloud.

MINDJOGGER
VIDEOQUIZ

To preview or review chapter content, you may wish to use the Chapter 8 MindJogger Videoquiz.

HEALTH *Online* **Online Resources for the Teacher** For a fresh approach to health topics and an in-depth look at health issues, use these online resources found under Teacher Resources at **health.glencoe.com:**

- Block Schedule Lesson Plans
- Technology Projects
- Health Updates

Effects of Stress

Lesson 1

Effects of Stress

① FOCUS

QUICK START Give students two minutes to list situations that cause them stress. Then let volunteers share situations from their lists and guide students in discussing what causes stress in each situation.

TYING TO PRIOR KNOWLEDGE

Ask students: What thoughts and emotions do you have when you are stressed? What physical symptoms do you sometimes feel when you are stressed? Then point out that students already know quite a bit about stress; they will learn more as they read this lesson.

Health Skills Features

"Change: Positive or Negative?" p. 203

INTRODUCING VOCABULARY

- Write the vocabulary terms on the board. Ask volunteers to give a definition for each term in their own words. Then have students check the definitions in the Glossary.

- Ask students to complete the Chapter 8 Study Guide in the *Student Activity Workbook*. 📁

VOCABULARY

stress
perception
stressor
psychosomatic
    response
chronic stress

YOU'LL LEARN TO

- Examine causes of stress.

- Describe the effects of stress on body systems.

- Analyze how stress can affect physical, mental/emotional, and social health.

- Discuss how substance abuse harms mental and emotional health.

QUICK START List five situations that you think cause teens to feel stressed. Next to each item, write down why you think that particular situation is a source of stress for teens.

🔻 Disagreements with friends can be a source of stress that affects all aspects of your health triangle. *How does your perception change the way an event affects you?*

E veryone experiences stress—it's a natural part of life. **Stress** is *the reaction of the body and mind to everyday challenges and demands.* You might experience stress during your daily routine, such as when you're running late or when you can't find your keys. Taking an important exam, playing in a state championship basketball game, missing the bus, or arguing with a friend can all be sources of stress. No matter what the source, stress can affect your physical, mental/emotional, and social health. Learning how to manage stress is an important part of staying healthy.

Stress in Your Life

H ow much stress you feel depends in part on your perception of events that cause stress. **Perception** is *the act of becoming aware through the senses.* One way to manage stress is to change how you perceive and react to events that cause it. Imagine, for example, that you and your best friend have just had an argument. You believe that this disagreement has destroyed your friendship. Your friend, on the other hand, sees the argument as a simple disagreement that you will eventually work out. Because of your perception of the event, you are more likely to experience a higher level of stress than your friend.

198 **Chapter 8** Managing Stress and Anxiety

Lesson 1 *Resources*

Teacher Classroom Resources

📁 Concept Mapping Activity 27

📁 Cross-Curriculum Activity 8

📁 Guided Reading Activities 27

📁 Health Lab 8

📁 Lesson Plan 27

📁 Lesson Quiz 27

📁 Parent Letter and Activities 8

📁 Reteaching Activity 27

Student Activity Workbook

📁 Applying Health Skills 27

📁 Chapter 8 Study Guide

Multimedia

🖨 Transparency 22

Reacting to Stress

Stress is not necessarily good or bad in and of itself, but it can have positive or negative effects. It can motivate you to do your best and give you the extra energy you need to reach your goals. For example, some people may perform better under the stress of competition. However, sometimes the effects of stress can be unhealthy. Losing sleep after arguing with a friend or being so worried about a test that you don't perform well are examples of the negative effects of stress.

What Causes Stress?

To learn how to manage stress, you need to know what causes it. A **stressor** is *anything that causes stress*. People, objects, places, events, and situations are all potential stressors. Some stressors affect almost everyone in a similar way. The sound of a siren, for example, heightens alertness in most people. Other stressors affect different people in different ways. Going to a new school, for example, can cause anticipation in some people but a sense of anxiety in others. Psychologists have identified five general categories of stressors:

▶ **Biological stressors,** such as illnesses, disabilities, or injuries

▶ **Environmental stressors,** such as poverty, pollution, crowding, noise, or natural disasters

▶ **Cognitive, or thinking stressors,** such as the way you perceive a situation or how it affects you and the world around you

▶ **Personal behavior stressors,** such as negative reactions in the body and mind caused by using tobacco, alcohol, or other drugs or by a lack of physical activity

▶ **Life situation stressors,** such as the death of a pet, the separation or divorce of parents, or having trouble in relationships with peers

Part of how you perceive these stressors has to do with your past experiences. If you had a positive experience the first time you participated in a school play, you'll probably look forward to future performances. On the other hand, if you experienced stage fright, you may feel anxious about being involved in similar events. Your attitudes, values, and beliefs also play a role.

The stress of competition motivates this teen to practice every day. *In what other ways can stress have a positive effect on teens?*

② TEACH

Discussing

Have students complete and discuss the following statements: *When I am at the doctor's office, I feel . . . During a test, I feel . . . Having a disagreement with a friend makes me feel . . .* Explain that understanding situations and events that upset you can help you deal with stress. **L1**

Reinforcing Concepts

Have students create a cartoon strip of a teen meeting a date's parents for the first time. Post the strips in the class. Talk about the kinds of stress involved in the situation. **ELL**

Guest Speaker

Invite the school counselor or a psychologist from the community to speak with the class about stress and ways to deal with stressors. Afterward, have students write papers summarizing the presentation. **L2**

Activity

Have students work in pairs to brainstorm additional examples for each category of stressors: biological, environmental, cognitive, personal behavior, and life situations. Ask: How can understanding stressors help one deal with stress? **L2**

School to Work

Wellness and the Workplace Stress is an important factor in the workplace. Stress-related health disorders cause significant absenteeism at work, thus costing businesses millions of dollars each year. Because of this, many businesses hold seminars to help their employees deal with stress. Some also provide exercise facilities for their employees.

A number of larger businesses offer an entire wellness program. Such programs can include counselors to help employees with diet, drug and alcohol abuse, smoking cessation, and other behaviors of concern to the company and its employees. Companies sometimes offer incentives to boost morale and encourage participation.

hot link

Let volunteers review the information about the nervous system and the endocrine system as they relate to stress. Have these volunteers discuss the information with the rest of the class.

VISUAL LEARNING

Figure 8.1 Have volunteers read aloud each of the steps in the alarm response. Then have students read and discuss the physical symptoms of the alarm response: How does each prepare a person for "fight" or "flight"?

Health Skills Practice

Reducing Stress

Encourage students to discuss the daily stress related to school—class assignments, tests, projects, and so on. Then have students list healthy habits they have (or can develop) to reduce the negative effects of school stress.

STRESS MANAGEMENT

Cooperative Learning

Have students generate a list of common stressors (*car horns, oversleeping, taking a test*) and record their suggestions on the board. Divide the class into two teams. Have the teams debate whether each of the listed items is a "positive" or a "negative" stressor. Note that some may be both. Encourage both teams to present persuasive arguments in support of their positions. L2

The Body's Stress Response

When you perceive a situation or event to be a threat, your body begins a stress response. For example, if a car alarm suddenly goes off as you walk by, you may jump at the sound or feel your heart start to race. The sudden, loud noise is a stressor that makes you respond instantly, without even thinking about it.

Two major body systems, the **nervous system** and the **endocrine system,** are active during the body's response to stressors. This response is largely involuntary, or automatic. It happens in three stages and can occur regardless of the type of stressor.

Alarm

Alarm is the first stage in the stress response. This is when the body and mind go on high alert. This reaction, illustrated and explained in **Figure 8.1,** is sometimes referred to as the "fight-or-flight response" because it prepares the body to either defend itself or flee from a threat.

hot link

nervous system For more information about the nervous system, see Chapter 15, page 399.
endocrine system To learn more about the endocrine system, see Chapter 18, page 464.

FIGURE 8.1

THE ALARM RESPONSE

1. Alarm begins when the hypothalamus, a small area at the base of the brain, receives danger signals from other parts of the brain. The hypothalamus releases a hormone that acts on the pituitary gland.

2. The pituitary then secretes a hormone that stimulates the adrenal glands.

3. The adrenal glands secrete adrenaline. Adrenaline is the "emergency hormone" that prepares the body to respond to a stressor.

Physical Symptoms
- pupil dilation
- increase in perspiration
- faster heart rate and pulse
- rise in blood pressure
- faster respiration rate
- narrowing of arteries to internal organs and skin
- increased blood flow to muscles and brain
- increase in muscle tension
- release of blood sugar, fats, and cholesterol

200 **Chapter 8** Managing Stress and Anxiety

Myths & Reality

MYTH. When you need to avoid stress, turn off the sound; silence is an effective stress-reducer.

FACT. Silence works for some, but not everybody. For many people, music is more relaxing than complete silence. The kind of music depends on the individual and on circumstances. Some people find natural sounds like birds chirping more relaxing than music.

MYTH. Any form of responsibility is an additional stressor.

FACT. Not all forms of responsibility are the same. Some responsibilities, like owning a pet, can be very beneficial. Having a pet as a companion can be a great stress reducer.

Resistance

If exposure to a stressor continues, the next stage of the stress response is *resistance*. During this stage, your body adapts to the rush created by alarm and reacts to the stressor. This is the stage in which you "fight" or take "flight." Your body is briefly able to perform at a higher level of endurance. In the case of "fight," your ability to resist a physical challenge or attack may be enhanced. In the case of "flight," you may be able to run faster and farther than you normally could to escape from danger. The resistance stage is why people in extremely high-stress situations have been known to accomplish incredible feats, such as lifting an automobile to save a child trapped underneath.

Fatigue

When exposure to stress is prolonged, the body loses its ability to adapt to the situation and fatigue may set in. During *fatigue*, the third stage of the stress response, a tired feeling takes over that lowers your level of activity. In this stage, your ability to manage other stressors effectively is very low. Both the mind and body have become exhausted. Fatigue can affect the body in several ways.

▶ **Physical fatigue** results when the muscles work vigorously for long periods, often leading to soreness and pain. Reaction time becomes impaired, and muscles tire very quickly.

▶ **Psychological fatigue** can result from constant worry, overwork, depression, boredom, isolation, or feeling overwhelmed by too many responsibilities.

▶ **Pathological fatigue** is tiredness brought on by overworking the body's defenses in fighting disease. Anemia, the flu, being overweight, and poor nutrition can all bring on pathological fatigue. Use of drugs such as alcohol can intensify the feeling of fatigue.

Prolonged or repeated stress can lead to stress-related illnesses caused by the changes that take place in your body during these three stages. Although a stress-related illness can be minor, such as sleeplessness or upset stomach, it can also be life threatening, such as high blood pressure, heart disease, or stroke. Even the effects of stressors that are often ignored, such as the bothersome hassles in a daily routine, can build up over time and cause problems.

➤ **A** person under stress may experience a variety of symptoms.
- **Physical Signs:** headaches, upset stomach, muscle aches and tightness, ringing in ears
- **Emotional Signs:** edginess, frustration, crying
- **Mental Signs:** trouble reading or thinking clearly, lack of creativity, losing sense of humor and perspective
- **Behavioral Signs:** not eating, overeating, compulsive talking, tapping feet, drumming fingers, changes in sleep patterns

Prolonged illness can overwork the body's immune system and result in pathological fatigue. *What can you do to reduce stress and speed recovery during an illness?*

Discussing

Guide the class in a discussion of the relationship between physical fatigue and psychological fatigue: In what ways do they feel the same? How do you think one might lead to the other? ◼

Activity

Have volunteers use library or online resources to find out about current research on chronic fatigue syndrome: Why is stress being considered as a cause? How might the condition increase stress? Ask the volunteers to discuss their findings with the rest of the class. L3 ◻▬

Discussing

Discuss taking action to handle a stressful situation. Students may wish to talk with a parent, friend, or expert to get ideas on taking control of stress. Then discuss the following strategies.

- Take a deep breath and think it through. Ask: Is the situation serious?
- Redirect the stress response. Suggestion: physical activity.
- Put things into perspective. Stop and think.
- Give yourself breaks. Listen and pay attention to your body.

Encourage volunteers to describe their own experiences with each approach. How effective did they find each strategy? Then ask students to suggest and discuss other strategies for handling stress. ◼

Cooperative Learning Activity

Tension Tamers Have students work in groups to learn, practice, and evaluate these activities designed to relieve tension:

- *Shoulder Lift.* Hunch your shoulders up to your ears for a few seconds and then release. Repeat.
- *Elastic Jaw.* Take a few deep breaths. Open your mouth, and shift your jaw to the right as far as you can without discomfort. Hold for a count of three. Repeat on the left side. Do this exercise ten times.
- *Tense-Relax.* Make a fist, and tense the muscles in your hand and forearm and then release. Repeat with the other hand. You can do the same with your abdomen, thigh, buttocks, and toes.

Explaining

Be sure students understand that many psychosomatic illnesses may be a result of stress, but they are not "all in your head." For example, a psychosomatic skin rash requires both physical treatment (as an ointment) and mental and emotional treatment (as lifestyle changes and relaxation techniques). **L1**

Discussing

Ask students about the physical and emotional signs of stress. Ask:

- How do these signs affect a person's ability to study?
- How do they affect friendships?
- What do they do to family relationships? **L2**

Activity

Assign interested students to locate and read current findings about the relationship between stress and physical illnesses such as heart disease, high blood pressure, asthma, ulcers, colitis, and migraine headaches. Ask them to share their findings with the class. **L3**

Cross-Curriculum Activity

Math Have students work together to plan a survey and gather information about headaches among teens at school. For example, students might find out how many students have headaches every month, every week, or every day; or they might find out what percentage of students who suffer from headache consider their headaches stress-induced. Then have students plan, draw, and label graphs to show their findings. **L2**

---

hotlink

asthma For more information about asthma and other non-communicable diseases, see Chapter 26, page 690.

Some headaches are caused by psychosomatic responses to stress. *What healthful behaviors can help protect you from the negative effects of stress?*

Stress and Your Health

Stress is an unavoidable part of life. Sometimes stress can make life fun, exciting, enjoyable, and challenging. Excessive or prolonged stress, however, can negatively impact all aspects of your health.

Physical Effects

Sometimes stress can lead to a **psychosomatic response**. This is *a physical reaction that results from stress rather than from an injury or illness*. *Psycho* means "of the mind," and *somatic* means "of the body." Psychosomatic responses may include sleep disorders, skin disorders, and stomach and digestive problems. Other health problems that may sometimes be stress-related include:

▶ **Headache.** Headache caused by stress is the most common type of headache. It is estimated that, in any given year, about 70 percent of all people worldwide will have at least one stress headache. Many headaches are related to tension. When stressed, the muscles in the head and neck contract. Migraine headaches, which affect about one in ten people, may also be triggered by stress. During a migraine attack, inflamed blood vessels and nerves around the brain cause severe throbbing, which is often accompanied by nausea and vomiting.

▶ **Asthma.** For some people, stress can trigger an **asthma** attack. During an asthma attack, breathing becomes difficult as the bronchioles, or air-carrying tubes of the lungs, constrict. The person may cough, wheeze, or fight to get air. If untreated, some cases of asthma can be life threatening. If you have asthma, it is important to discover what sets off your attacks and how to avoid or manage these triggers.

▶ **High blood pressure.** Prolonged stress can cause an increase in a person's levels of cholesterol, the fatty substance that can block arteries. High cholesterol levels can result in high blood pressure, a condition that contributes to heart disease and stroke.

▶ **Weakened immune system.** Extended exposure to stress can reduce the body's ability to fight disease by weakening the immune system. When your immune system is weakened, you may be more prone to colds, flu, or more severe infections.

∿ HEALTH LITERACY

Health Information Most illnesses have psychological and physical components. The relationship between the mind and body, or emotions and physical reactions, is described in commonly-used expressions such as *gut wrenching*, and *worried sick*. Anxiety and emotional stress can increase the likelihood of physical health problems. An illness is suspected to be a psychosomatic response when the presence of a disease is eliminated by a thorough medical examination, and there is evidence of a psychological problem. It is confirmed when resolution of the problem causes the physical symptoms to disappear. Headaches, abdominal pain, fatigue, and chest pain are common psychosomatic complaints among teens.

Exploring Issues

Change: Positive or Negative?

Change can be a source of stress for many teens. While some people take change in stride, others have a difficult time dealing with disruptions to their routine. Here are two points of view on change.

Viewpoint 1: Tyrone B., age 16

I don't like it when things change. It seems like whenever I'm perfectly happy with my life, something comes along to ruin it. I've been living with my mom ever since the divorce. Now my parents want me to live with Dad for the summer. I love my dad, but he lives about an hour away. I won't get to hang out with my friends all summer or play in the summer soccer league.

Viewpoint 2: Marshall M., age 16

Hey, life is an adventure, right? If things were always the same, I'd get bored. Change brings new opportunities. For instance, I couldn't get into the music class I wanted last semester, so I took an art class that I'd never considered. It was fun learning new things and meeting new people.

ACTIVITY

Are you more like Tyrone or Marshall? How do you usually deal with the changes in your life? Can you apply the same set of skills to every situation in which change occurs?

Mental/Emotional and Social Effects

Stress can also impact mental/emotional and social health. It can interfere with daily activities and relationships with others.

▶ **Difficulty concentrating.** It can be hard to focus during stressful situations. This can cause negative self-talk and the distorted belief that failure is inevitable.

▶ **Mood swings.** Feeling happy one moment and sad the next is a common reaction to stress. Teens may experience mood swings as a result of the hormonal changes of adolescence as well as social and academic pressures. These emotional shifts may put a strain on relationships with family and friends.

▶ **Risks of substance abuse.** Stress can increase a person's vulnerability to **drug use.** Many people give stress as the reason they started drinking or smoking. However, use of these substances actually increases stress and leads to even bigger problems.

hotlink

drug use For more information about the harmful consequences of drug use, see Chapter 23, page 592.

Exploring Issues

CHANGE: POSITIVE OR NEGATIVE?

Have students discuss the meaning of these sayings: "Make the best of it," and "When life hands you lemons, make lemonade." After students have read the feature, ask: How have the responses of these two teens influenced their levels of stress? How might Tyrone and Marshall have responded differently? Is it possible to not be happy with change but still develop a positive attitude toward it? How? Ask students to write their responses to the activities. Have volunteers share recent changes in their lives and the effective ways they dealt with them. List the changes and the strategies on the board; then ask how the strategies could be applied to other situations that are potentially stressful.

Cross-Curriculum Activity

Art Have students draw a picture, create a design, or make a collage to express their own experiences with stress. Invite students to use colors and patterns to evoke certain moods and feelings. Students may wish to write a brief paragraph on the back describing their work of art and the feelings expressed. **ELL**

Home and Community

Service Workers Discuss with students the particular stressors faced by police officers, firefighters, and emergency medical workers. Invite students to share their own ideas about why people choose these kinds of careers and how individuals learn to react to intense, intermittent work-related stress.

Then ask a few interested volunteers to interview a local police officer, firefighter, or emergency medical worker about the stress that he or she experiences at work. What effects of adrenaline does he or she notice? How does he or she respond to those effects? Let the volunteers discuss their findings with the rest of the class.

Reinforcing Concepts

Ask students to write entries in their private health journals, noting specific ways they can use strategies such as exercising, support, taking part in hobbies, and avoiding additional stressors to control the effects of chronic stress.

 3 ASSESS

EVALUATING THE LESSON

Assign and discuss the Lesson 1 Review; then administer, grade, and discuss Lesson Quiz 27 in the TCR.

RETEACHING

- Have students work with partners to write, in their own words, a definition of *stress* and a list of at least six events or situations that commonly cause stress.
- Ask students to complete Reteaching Activity 27 in the TCR.

ENRICHMENT

Have each student develop and write out a weekly physical activity plan that will help him or her relieve the effects of chronic stress without overloading his or her schedule (thus adding another stressor).

 4 CLOSE

Have each student identify an important new fact or idea he or she has gained from reading this lesson.

204

 Hobbies are a great way to relax and reduce your level of stress. *What do you do to relax?*

Taking Control of Chronic Stress

One type of prolonged stress is **chronic stress**, or *stress associated with long-term problems that are beyond a person's control.* The body's reaction to chronic stress is less intense than a fight-or-flight response, but it lasts longer, sometimes for months. Symptoms can include upset stomach, headache, insomnia, change in appetite, and feeling anxious.

Fortunately, even if you can't eliminate the stress, you *can* do something to reduce its effects. Taking care of yourself and keeping the three sides of your health triangle in balance is a good start. Here are some strategies for controlling the effects of stress:

► **Engage in physical activity.** Physical activities, such as tennis and swimming, improve your body's health, and they also affect your brain chemistry, helping to calm you down.

► **Look for support among your friends and family.** Chances are, they know exactly how you feel. Go to a movie or eat out together. Talk about what's bothering you.

► **Find a hobby or activity that relaxes you.** You might learn something new and make new friends.

► **Avoid using tobacco, alcohol, and other drugs.** These substances can lead to addiction and cause other problems.

Lesson 1 *Review*

Reviewing Facts and Vocabulary

1. List the five general categories of stressors.
2. Describe the three stages of the body's response to stress.
3. Define *psychosomatic response*.

Thinking Critically

4. **Analyzing.** What healthful alternatives would you recommend to a teen who is thinking about using drugs to deal with stress? Explain the importance of alternatives to substance abuse.
5. **Applying.** Why is it important to practice healthful behaviors and protect yourself from prolonged or excessive stress?

Applying Health Skills

Decision Making. Describe a scenario in which a teen feels overwhelmed by a stressor. Then, use the six steps of decision making to demonstrate how the teen can handle the stressful situation in an effective way.

WORD PROCESSING Use word-processing software to present your decision-making steps. For more information about word processing, see **health.glencoe.com.**

Lesson 1 *Review*

Answers to Reviewing Facts and Vocabulary

1. Biological, environmental, cognitive, personal behavior, life situation.
2. Alarm: puts the body on high alert; resistance: adapts body to the alarm stage and reacts to the stressor; fatigue: the body loses its ability to adapt to stress.
3. A physical reaction that results from stress rather than an injury or illness.

Answers to Thinking Critically

4. Possible answers: physical activity, social support, or hobbies. Drug use only increases stress, causing health problems.
5. Excessive stress can cause health problems.

Managing Stress

VOCABULARY

stress-management skills
relaxation response

YOU'LL LEARN TO

- Identify personal causes of stress.
- Demonstrate refusal strategies for avoiding some stressful situations.
- Develop strategies for managing stress.
- Examine how healthful behaviors help reduce stress.

→ **QUICK START** Make a T-chart. In the left column, list three sources of stress in your life. Classify these stressors as life events, physical stressors, or daily hassles. In the right column, briefly describe what you do to help deal with each particular stressor.

Identifying stressors and managing stress can help you stay healthy and prevent disease. Although it is impossible to live completely free of stress, it *is* possible to learn ways to manage it.

Identifying Personal Causes of Stress

The first step in stress management is to identify the source of the stress. To help identify your personal stressors, look at what is happening around you right now. Is any of the following causing you stress?

▶ **Life events.** These can include getting a driver's license; graduation; moving or relocating; addition of family members by marriage, birth, or adoption; major illness; and parents' divorce or separation.

▶ **Physical stressors.** These can include pollution, excessive noise, physical injury, lack of rest, drug use, and excessive dieting or exercise.

▶ **Daily hassles.** These may include time pressures, too many responsibilities, deadlines, and conflicts with fellow students.

(Y) **If you can identify your stressors, you have a better chance of controlling them.** *What positive behaviors would help you control the stress of a particularly busy week?*

Lesson 2 Managing Stress **205**

Lesson 2 Resources

Teacher Classroom Resources

📁 Concept Mapping Activity 28

📁 Decision-Making Activity 8

📁 Enrichment Activity 8

📁 Guided Reading Activities 28

📁 Lesson Plan 28

📁 Lesson Quiz 28

📁 Reteaching Activity 28

Student Activity Workbook

📁 Applying Health Skills 28

📁 Chapter 8 Study Guide

Multimedia

🖱 Transparency 23

Lesson 2

Managing Stress

1 FOCUS

→ **QUICK START** Have volunteers give examples of stressors that are life events, physical stressors, and daily hassles. Then draw a T-chart on the board as an example, and have students work independently to complete the Quick Start assignment.

TYING TO PRIOR KNOWLEDGE

Have volunteers recall the definitions of *stress, stressor,* and *chronic stress.* Explain that, as students read this lesson, they will learn more about stress and how to manage it.

Health Skills Features

"Managing Your Time," p. 207

STRESS MANAGEMENT

INTRODUCING VOCABULARY

- Have students work with partners to discuss the vocabulary terms and compose definitions in their own words. Then have them find and record the definitions from the Glossary.

- Ask students to complete the Chapter 8 Study Guide in the *Student Activity Workbook.* 📁

2 TEACH

Discussing

Ask students to answer the following questions: During an average day, when do you feel the greatest need to relax? Why? What do you do to relax? **L1**

Activity

Assign students to interview someone in each of the following age groups: 13–18, 19–25, 26–35, 36–55, and 56 and older. Ask them to find out what each person's greatest stressors are and what he or she does to manage stress. Have students make a chart and write a report to share with the class. Help them draw conclusions about how stress varies with age. **L3**

VISUAL LEARNING

Figure 8.3 Guide students in reading and discussing the suggestions for overcoming test anxiety. Encourage students to share their own experiences with using these strategies. Then invite a group of volunteers to plan and perform a short skit demonstrating the benefits of using such strategies.

Cooperative Learning

Ask a group of volunteers to develop a list of suggestions for avoiding the stress associated with taking standardized tests such as the SAT and the ACT. The students might gather information from library and online sources, from informal interviews, and from personal experience. Have volunteers share their lists with the rest of the class. **L2**

Avoiding Stress with Refusal Skills

You may be able to avoid certain stressful situations altogether. Sometimes, just walking away from a tense situation will help calm you down. Say no at appropriate times when you see the possibility of stress, conflict, or threat. For example, you can avoid the potentially stressful situation of being at a party where there will be no adult supervision by simply refusing to go.

Ways to Manage Stress

Sometimes, you can manage stress by changing the way you perceive or react to the stressor. You may be able to get a new perspective on a stressful situation by thinking of it as a learning opportunity instead of a threat. Other ways to manage stress include planning ahead, getting enough sleep, getting regular physical activity, eating nutritious food, and avoiding tobacco, alcohol, and other drugs.

Plan Ahead

When you plan ahead, you decide in advance what you want to accomplish and what steps you'll take. Thinking through a situation in advance also helps you recognize where variations to your plan may occur. This better prepares you for unexpected changes. A well-thought-out plan is not a rigid series of steps to follow but rather a flexible map with many ways of reaching your goal. **Figure 8.2** shows ways to reduce stress as you plan for and take your next test.

HEALTH Online

Learn more about stress and ways to manage stress by clicking on Web Links at **health.glencoe.com**.

FIGURE 8.2

OVERCOMING TEST ANXIETY

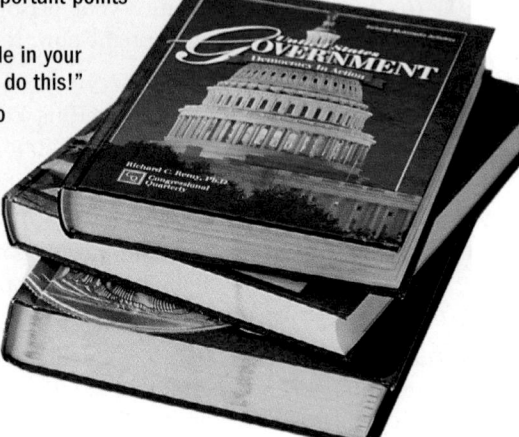

- Plan for tests well in advance, studying a little bit each night.
- Learn to outline material, highlighting and numbering important points so you can spot them quickly.
- During the test, do some deep breathing. Get comfortable in your chair. Give yourself a quick positive message like, "I can do this!"
- Answer all the questions you are sure of; then go back to answer the ones that are more difficult.
- After getting your corrected test back, examine your mistakes and try to understand why you made them. If you don't understand them, ask questions.

206 **Chapter 8** Managing Stress and Anxiety

∿ HEALTH LITERACY

Health Influences Ask whether students are familiar with the expression "Look on the bright side." The expression suggests that having a positive outlook protects and promotes health on all three sides of the health triangle. Laughter, in particular, can influence positive physiological changes as well as improve mental outlook or mood. One scientific study found that laughter stimulates the production of endorphins, which help control pain. Another study demonstrated that stress-related hormones decreased during bouts of laughter. Humor and a positive outlook can help one cope with life pressures such as getting homework done on time, taking tests, and getting along with friends.

Hands-On Health ACTIVITY

Managing Your Time

When you manage your time well, you reduce your stress. In this activity, you'll develop a time-management plan for the coming week.

What You'll Need

- pencil
- large sheet of paper

What You'll Do

1. Divide your paper into seven columns, one for each day of the week. Create and label 24 rows, one for every hour of the day.

2. Pencil in the week's activities, including time for school, work, exercise, sleep, family, and friends. Include specific goals or deadlines, such as "History paper due." Include preparation time, such as "Go to library to research history paper."

3. Analyze your schedule. Are you surprised at how much time you spend on some activities? Where do you see conflicts? Are there things you'd like to do that you are not doing? Do you have adequate time to relax? To eat healthful meals and get plenty of physical activity?

4. Prioritize your tasks. Write "A" next to any task you need to do, "B" next to any you would like to get done, and "C" for any that can wait.

5. Rework your schedule. Be flexible, and remember that you may not be able to do everything. Try to consolidate tasks and delete low-priority activities.

Apply and Conclude

Keep your time-management schedule on hand as you go through the week. At the end of the week, evaluate your schedule and change it if necessary.

Get Adequate Sleep

Not getting enough sleep can affect your ability to concentrate. This in turn becomes a source of stress because it can interfere with schoolwork, athletics, and even relationships with others. To avoid the stress caused by lack of adequate sleep, manage your time wisely so that you get enough rest each night. Getting eight to nine hours of sleep will help you face the challenges and demands of your day. You will be in a better mood, you will think more clearly, you will look and feel better, and you will improve your chances of success.

Lesson 2 Managing Stress **207**

Hands-On Health

MANAGING YOUR TIME

STRESS MANAGEMENT

NHES Standard 3 Students will demonstrate the ability to practice health-enhancing behaviors and reduce health risks.

Objectives

- Relate the importance of managing personal time to managing stress.
- Implement a plan for managing time.

Motivator

Ask students to identify two or three activities they would do if they had more time. (Answers may include: get more physical activity, read, study harder, etc.)

Teaching Strategies

1. Have students complete the time-management activity. Offer them assistance in prioritizing tasks.
2. Suggest students refer to this schedule throughout the week.

✓ Assessment

Using a rubric, student work should provide comprehensive evidence of the following criteria to achieve the highest score:

✔ identification of priorities
✔ effective management of time to reduce stress
✔ application of realistic time-management schedule

Curriculum Connections

Physical Education Have students use library and online resources to learn about lifetime sports and other physical activities that can help teens and their families manage daily stressors. Then have students share and discuss their findings.

Science Have students learn about the uses of biofeedback and meditation in dealing with stress. Let students discuss their findings, comparing and contrasting the two approaches. Encourage students who have tried any form of either practice to share their experiences.

Cooperative Learning

Have students work in pairs or small groups to list specific foods and beverages teens are likely to consume when they feel stressed. Then have them analyze whether these are healthy food choices. If necessary, ask them to identify a healthy alternative to each item on their lists. Note that the alternatives might include a specific form of physical activity, a talk with a friend, or another non-food suggestion. **L1**

FYI

A survey of American adults in a recent year found that 61 percent of respondents consider the threat of terrorism a major source of stress.

Reinforcing Concepts

Have students design, draw, and label posters that show a variety of relaxation techniques. **L2**

Health Minute

Let students discuss what they know or have heard about the positive effects of physical activity on stress. After they have read and discussed the Health Minute information, ask how students' understanding and opinions have changed.

---

hotlink

physical activity For more information about physical activity, see Chapter 4, page 72.
nutrition For more information about nutrition, see Chapter 5, page 108.

Health Minute

Sweat Your Stress Away

When you're feeling stressed:

▶ Go running, bicycling, or skating.
▶ Play soccer, volleyball, or basketball.
▶ Participate in aerobic dance or martial arts.

Physical activity will:

▶ calm you down.
▶ improve your mood.
▶ improve your appearance.
▶ increase your ability to handle physical and emotional stress.
▶ aid digestion and help you sleep better.
▶ help you maintain a healthy weight.
▶ improve immune system function.
▶ remind you that you are in control of your responses to life.

Get Regular Physical Activity

Participating in regular **physical activity** is another helpful technique for managing stress. When you are under stress, your body has an excess of nervous energy. Engaging in physical activities, such as jogging, walking, or even cleaning your room, can release this pent-up energy. As a result, you will feel more relaxed.

Eat Nutritious Food

Balanced **nutrition** is important for overall health, but it's also important in dealing with stress. Poor eating habits can actually be a source of stress by causing fatigue, weakness, and a reduced ability to concentrate. Inappropriate dieting and over- or under-eating can also put the body under additional stress. Too much stress can cause poor absorption of vitamins and minerals, which can lead to deficiencies.

Eating healthfully can help prevent the health problems associated with stress. To help reduce stress and feel more energetic, eat a variety of different foods, drink plenty of water, and eat fresh food whenever possible. Here are a few nutrition tips that will help you when you are dealing with stress.

▶ **Eat regular meals.** Common reactions to stress can be either snacking all day or not wanting to eat at all.

▶ **Limit "comfort" foods.** Although foods such as brownies and cookies may make you feel good or even bring back happy memories, they are loaded with fat and sugar.

▶ **Limit caffeine.** The stimulant effect of caffeine causes a rise in blood pressure. Thus, caffeine will actually increase the physical effects of stress on the body.

Avoid Tobacco, Alcohol, and Other Drugs

Some people make the mistake of turning to tobacco, alcohol, or other drugs to relieve stress. However, using these substances does not relieve stress; it increases one's problems and harms one's health. Substance use makes the body more prone to disease and has dangerous long-term effects.

Stress-Management Techniques

When stressors can't be avoided or minimized, their effects can usually be managed. Developing and practicing **stress-management skills**, or *skills that help an individual handle stress in a healthful, effective way*, is one of the steps to good mental health.

School to Work

Job-Related Stress Stress is a fact of life in many professions. Reasons for the stress may vary. For example, pilots, peace officers, and paramedics may experience stress because they take responsibility for other people's lives. Salespeople may be under pressure to make a certain number of sales. Factory workers may be exposed to high levels of noise. Have students work in groups. Let group members take turns naming specific occupations they consider to have high levels of stress. Then have other group members identify possible sources of stress in each job and suggest strategies for managing job-related stress.

Successful techniques for managing stress include the following:

▶ **Redirect your energy.** You might work on a creative project or go jogging. No matter what you choose to do, the activity will release your nervous energy.

▶ **Relax and laugh.** The **relaxation response** is *a state of calm that can be reached if one or more relaxation techniques are practiced regularly*. Some relaxation techniques include deep breathing, thinking pleasant thoughts, and stretching. Laughing can help, too. Laughing lowers your blood pressure and makes you feel more relaxed.

▶ **Keep a positive outlook.** A positive outlook can help relieve stress because the way you think often determines how you feel.

▶ **Seek out support.** Confide in someone you trust, such as a parent, guardian, sibling, teacher, or close friend. Just talking with someone about your problem may help you feel better about it.

Ⓐ **Spending quality time with a parent or other family member can help relieve stress.** *In what ways can family members help during stressful times?*

Reinforcing Concepts

Have students write journal entries identifying the stress management skills they want to develop.

③ ASSESS

EVALUATING THE LESSON

Assign and discuss the Lesson 2 Review; then administer, grade, and discuss Lesson Quiz 28 in the TCR. 🗀

RETEACHING

• Have small groups of students discuss the pictures in this lesson and the strategies being utilized to manage stress.

• Ask students to complete Reteaching Activity 28 in the TCR. 🗀

ENRICHMENT

Have interested students work together to create original relaxation tapes, including music, natural sounds, and/or words.

④ CLOSE

Let each student identify a specific stressful situation or event. Have volunteers suggest strategies for handling the stress.

▶ Lesson 2 *Review*

Reviewing Facts and Vocabulary

1. List three personal causes of stress.
2. Name three ways to protect yourself from stress.
3. Define the term *relaxation response*, and identify three relaxation techniques.

Thinking Critically

4. **Applying.** To help reduce the effects of stress, Cathy drinks milk, fruit juice, or water instead of cola drinks. Why is this an effective stress-management technique?

5. **Synthesizing.** Jarod has a big biology test on Friday. As he is heading to his room to study, his friend Ben calls and asks him to go bowling. Use the techniques discussed in this lesson to help Jerod balance his activities and manage his stress.

Applying Health Skills

Stress Management. Make a "How to Survive" flyer advising teens on ways to manage the stress of one of the following life events: moving to a new school, not making a team, getting a failing grade, winning a major award, receiving a scholarship.

WORD PROCESSING You can use word-processing software to give your flyer a more professional look. See **health.glencoe.com** for tips on using a word-processing program.

Lesson 2 Managing Stress **209**

▶ Lesson 2 *Review*

Answers to Reviewing Facts and Vocabulary

1. Examples include specific life events, physical stressors, and/or daily hassles.
2. Possible answers: Plan ahead; get regular physical activity; get adequate sleep.
3. A state of calm that can be reached if one or more relaxation techniques are practiced on a regular basis; possible examples include deep breathing, thinking pleasant thoughts, stretching, laughing.

Answers to Thinking Critically

4. These drinks, as opposed to cola, do not contain caffeine.
5. Answers will vary. Jarod could use good planning to balance activities or use refusal skills to stay home and study.

Anxiety and Teen Depression

1 FOCUS

QUICK START Have students brainstorm a list of common stressors that can cause teens to feel anxious. Then let students work independently to write their paragraphs.

TYING TO PRIOR KNOWLEDGE

Ask several volunteers to describe, in their own words, the feelings of anxiety. Explain that, as students read this lesson, they will learn more about recognizing and coping with anxiety.

Health Skills Features

"Being a Supportive Friend," p. 212

COMMUNICATION SKILLS

INTRODUCING VOCABULARY

- Refer to the vocabulary terms for this lesson. Ask students to write a definition for each term and use it in a sentence. Let volunteers share their responses; correct any misconceptions.

- Ask students to complete the Chapter 8 Study Guide in the *Student Activity Workbook.*

Anxiety and Teen Depression

VOCABULARY
anxiety
depression

YOU'LL LEARN TO
- Identify symptoms of anxiety and depression.
- Develop strategies for coping with anxiety and depression.
- Identify warning signs of major depression that should prompt individuals to seek professional help.

QUICK START Make a list of common stressors that can cause teens to feel anxious. Pick one and write a paragraph describing ways to manage this stressor.

▲ **Anxiety can have many sources.** *What are some common sources of anxiety for teens?*

The teen years bring new pressures, challenges, and responsibilities that can sometimes seem overwhelming. School, sports, friends, and other factors can make your life seem hectic and complicated. This is also a time when you are making major decisions that affect your future. It is no mystery that these stressors can cause anxious feelings, sleeping difficulties, or even mild depression.

What Is Anxiety?

Everyone feels anxious from time to time. Brief feelings of worry, insecurity, fear, self-consciousness, or even panic are common stress responses. Occasional anxiety in life is natural. **Anxiety** is *the condition of feeling uneasy or worried about what may happen.* Sometimes anxious feelings can have positive results, such as motivating you to work hard on a school presentation or keeping you alert in risky situations. Other times, anxiety can get in the way of a person's performance. For example, someone giving a speech may feel so nervous that he or she stumbles on a few lines. Some symptoms of anxiety include

▶ feelings of fear or dread.

▶ perspiration, trembling, restlessness, or muscle tension.

▶ rapid heart rate, lightheadedness, or shortness of breath.

210 **Chapter 8** Managing Stress and Anxiety

Lesson 3 *Resources*

Teacher Classroom Resources
📁 Concept Mapping Activity 29
📁 Current Health Issues 8
📁 Guided Reading Activities 29
📁 Lesson Plan 29
📁 Lesson Quiz 29
📁 Reteaching Activity 29

Student Activity Workbook
📁 Applying Health Skills 29
📁 Chapter 8 Study Guide

Some teens experience another form of anxiety when they strive for perfection. They may think that they should get perfect grades or be the best on the team. A perfectionist's anxiety comes from believing that nothing he or she does will be good enough. Placing this type of pressure on oneself can lead to frustration and unhappiness. Having realistic expectations and taking a positive view of your accomplishments can help you avoid the anxiety caused by perfectionism.

Managing Anxiety

Stress-management techniques, such as redirecting your energy or doing relaxation exercises, can be used to reduce the day-to-day anxieties of life. Some people try to escape their anxiety by turning to alcohol or other drugs. They don't realize that such drugs produce only a temporary, false sense of relaxation. These substances cause problems that will make it even harder for the person to function. There are much healthier, more effective ways to manage anxiety, including engaging in physical activity and getting support from family and friends.

What Is Depression?

Nearly everyone experiences the occasional sad mood that lasts for a few days. These are natural feelings that can usually be managed by following these suggestions:

► Write your feelings in a private journal.

► Draw, dance, or engage in some other creative activity.

► Talk about your feelings with your family and friends.

► Do something nice for someone else. It will take the focus away from you and your feelings.

Sometimes, however, these feelings indicate a more serious condition known as depression. **Depression,** *a prolonged feeling of helplessness, hopelessness, and sadness*, is much stronger than the occasional sad mood and is not as easy to manage.

There are two types of depression, depending on the cause of the feeling and length of time it lasts.

► **Reactive depression** is a response to a stressful event, such as the death of a friend. While this type of depression can last longer than a case of the "blues," most times it eventually goes away as the person finds a way to manage the event that caused it.

Health Minute

Overcoming Social Anxiety

Social anxiety is the condition of feeling uneasy or extremely shy in certain social circumstances.

Someone with social anxiety is:

► more likely to avoid others.

► less likely to participate in extracurricular activities.

► less likely to speak up in class.

► more likely to have difficulty initiating casual conversations.

To overcome social anxiety:

► Practice replacing self-critical thoughts with more supportive ideas.

► Start small, such as by smiling, nodding, and greeting people.

► Speak in a louder voice, and use frequent eye contact.

► As a listener, ask open-ended questions in response during conversation.

► Become more knowledgeable about current events or another area of interest so you'll have some conversation starters.

► Practice conversation and positive thinking skills often.

---

2 TEACH

Discussing

Help students discuss the problems associated with perfectionism: How can a teen set more realistic expectations for himself or herself? What can a teen do to help a friend whose perfectionism causes anxiety? L1

Critical Thinking

Ask students to keep a personal journal of their daily experiences with stress, anxiety, fear, and the "blues." Have them write about how they dealt with their feelings. Remind them that their journals are personal and will not be shared with anyone. L1

FYI

The National Institute of Mental Health reports that three to four percent of Americans suffer from general anxiety disorder during the course of a year. Research shows that the condition often coexists with clinical depression and/or substance abuse.

Health Minute

Have a volunteer read aloud the information about symptoms of social anxiety and the strategies for overcoming the condition. Invite students to suggest other strategies to add to the list, and write these on the board.

More About...

Teen Depression Among teens, depressive symptoms, which include sad or hopeless moods, occur about eight times more often than serious depression. The key difference between depressed moods and serious depression is the duration of symptoms. Depressed moods are relatively short-lived and rarely affect performance in school or relationships. Seriously depressed teens are profoundly pessimistic for prolonged periods. Along with acting moody, they may be very self-critical and preoccupied with suicide or death. Depressed teens may also experience physical symptoms including fatigue and changes in appetite and weight.

BEING A SUPPORTIVE FRIEND

COMMUNICATION SKILLS

NHES Standard 5 Students will demonstrate the ability to use interpersonal communication skills to enhance health.

Objectives

• Demonstrate ways to demonstrate empathy toward others.

• Use communication skills that demonstrate support for a person who shows signs of depression.

Motivator

As a class, brainstorm and list strategies to comfort and support a depressed friend.

Teaching Strategies

1. Have students read the scenario and write a response demonstrating effective communication skills.
2. Remind students to demonstrate effective listening techniques in their dialogues.

✓Assessment

Using a rubric, student work should provide comprehensive evidence of the following criteria to achieve the highest score:

✔ use of "I" messages
✔ demonstration of respect and empathy
✔ effective listening skills
✔ message of comfort and support

▶ **Major depression** is a medical condition requiring treatment. It is more severe and lasts much longer than reactive depression. Major depression may develop from reactive depression, or it might be a chemical imbalance in the brain or a genetic tendency. Major depression will be discussed in greater detail in the next chapter.

Symptoms of Teen Depression

Although depression is a common emotional problem among teens, its symptoms can sometimes go unheeded. Many young people who are suffering from depression don't act sad or seem outwardly different to their family or friends. Symptoms of depression can include an irritable or restless mood; withdrawal from friends and activities that were previously important or enjoyable; a change in appetite or weight; feelings of guilt or worthlessness; and a sense of hopelessness.

Health Skills Activity

Communication: Being a Supportive Friend

Sandy and Karen have been friends for a long time. A few days ago, Sandy's boyfriend and his family moved to another state. On a Friday night, Sandy was feeling especially sad because that was the night she and her boyfriend usually went to the movies. Karen knew Sandy would be feeling this way so she dropped by to offer her support. Sandy was crying in her room when Karen arrived.

Karen put her arm around her friend. "I know it's hard. I'm here if you want to talk."

"He hasn't even been gone a week and I'm feeling so lost. We always went out on Friday nights. I don't know how I'm going to get through this," Sandy cried.

What Would You Do?
Write an ending to this scenario in which Karen comforts Sandy and shows her support through strong communication skills.

1. Use "I" messages.
2. Speak calmly and clearly.
3. Listen carefully.
4. Show respect and empathy.

212 **Chapter 8** Managing Stress and Anxiety

Cooperative Learning Activity

Analyzing Advertisements Ask a group of interested students to research advertisements for specific medications designed to treat anxiety and depression. These students should find examples of ads (as on television and in magazines) for medications. They should also use library and online resources to research the effects such ads have had on doctors and patients.

Have these students describe and/or display sample ads and present the findings of their research. Then encourage the entire class to consider whether such ads have a positive or negative influence on the health community. Why?

Many people experience a few of these symptoms once in a while. This is normal. It's *not* normal to experience several of them at the same time for two weeks or more. In addition, if depression causes a person to start using drugs or to have thoughts about suicide, professional help is needed.

Getting Help for Anxiety and Depression

Mild forms of anxiety and depressive feelings can be relieved by talking with supportive people, getting more physical activity, or volunteering. If anxiety or depression persists, however, a person may begin to lose interest in activities that used to be enjoyable. Changes in mood, sleep patterns, or energy levels may result, causing difficulty concentrating in school or inability to perform day-to-day activities. When anxiety or depression begins to interfere with life in such a manner, it's time to seek help.

Both anxiety and depression are very treatable. Talk to a parent or other trusted adult, and seek help from a counselor, school psychologist, or other health care professional.

 Some teens and their parents visit the school counselor for confidential help regarding emotional health. *Who else might you turn to for help with a mental or emotional problem?*

 Lesson 3 *Review*

Reviewing Facts and Vocabulary

1. Define the term *anxiety*. What might be a positive result of anxiety? What might be a negative result?

2. List two strategies for managing day-to-day anxieties.

3. What is *depression*? Under what circumstances should a depressed teen seek professional help?

Thinking Critically

4. **Evaluating.** Why might participating in activities such as volunteering help relieve mild depression?

5. **Analyzing.** Why might a teen experiencing anxiety turn to alcohol or other drugs? Why is this dangerous?

Applying Health Skills

Analyzing Influences. Divide a sheet of paper into three columns. Head one column *Family*, one *Friends*, and one *School*. In each column, list how anxiety could affect your relationships and responsibilities.

SPREADSHEETS Using spreadsheet software will help you organize your table. See **health.glencoe.com** for information on how to use a spreadsheet.

Lesson 3 Anxiety and Teen Depression **213**

 Lesson 3 *Review*

Answers to Reviewing Facts and Vocabulary

1. Condition of feeling uneasy or worried about what may happen; results will vary.

2. Any two: redirect your energy; do relaxation exercises; engage in physical activity; get support from family and friends.

3. A prolonged feeling of helplessness, hopelessness, and sadness; see pages 212–213 for circumstances.

Answers to Thinking Critically

4. Such activities increase energy, self-esteem, and take focus away from problems and feelings of depression.

5. Answers will vary, but should indicate the harmful effects of drug use.

Reinforcing Concepts

Guide students in discussing the difference between sadness and depression. Ask: What should teens do when they are not sure whether they are sad or depressed? Who are some people a teen could talk to for help with depression?

3 ASSESS

EVALUATING THE LESSON

Assign and discuss the Lesson 3 Review; then administer, grade, and discuss Lesson Quiz 29 in the TCR.

RETEACHING

- Have students identify and discuss characters (as from stories, TV programs, or movies) who suffer from anxiety or depression.

- Ask students to complete Reteaching Activity 29 in the TCR.

ENRICHMENT

Ask interested students to write and perform a skit demonstrating healthful ways of dealing with anxiety or depression.

4 CLOSE

Go around the room, inviting each student to contribute a different fact from this lesson about anxiety or depression.

Being a Resilient Teen

Lesson 4

Being a Resilient Teen

❶ FOCUS

 QUICK START Have students work together to name difficult events that a teen might experience. Record their ideas on the board. Then let partners share ideas about factors that could help a teen bounce back.

TYING TO PRIOR KNOWLEDGE

Let students share what they already understand about being resilient. Encourage them to give examples. Then explain that they will learn more about resiliency in this lesson.

Health Skills Features
"The Power of Assets," p. 217   **ANALYZING INFLUENCES**

INTRODUCING VOCABULARY

- Have volunteers look up the vocabulary terms in the Glossary and then, in their own words, explain the terms to the rest of the class.

- Ask students to complete the Chapter 8 Study Guide in the *Student Activity Workbook.* 📁

VOCABULARY
resiliency
protective factors

YOU'LL LEARN TO

- Explain what it means to be resilient.

- Develop strategies to promote resiliency throughout the life span.

- Explore methods for developing protective factors.

- Evaluate how having protective factors helps people avoid risk behaviors.

QUICK START List five difficult events that a teen may experience. Then, brainstorm factors that might help the teen bounce back from such events. Write a few sentences explaining how these factors would help someone get through difficult times.

▼ **When difficult events occur, seeking and giving support is one way to cope.** *What else can help a person bounce back from disappointments or crises?*

Everyone goes through times of stress, disappointments, and difficulty. Sometimes, people have no control over events that can change their lives. A natural disaster may strike, or a loved one may die. When hardships and tragedies happen, it can be hard for people to cope with the situation and with their feelings.

What Is Resiliency?

Some people find it easier than others to bounce back from events that have hurt them in some way. The event may be a personal disappointment, such as failing a test or breaking up with a boyfriend or girlfriend. In some cases, a large number of people may be involved in or affected by an event, such as a big earthquake or a war. Being able to overcome disappointments and survive traumatic events is a sign of resiliency. **Resiliency** (ri-ZIL-yuhn-see) is *the ability to adapt effectively and recover from disappointment, difficulty, or crisis.* Resilient people are able to handle adversity in healthful ways and achieve long-term success in spite of negative circumstances.

214 Chapter 8 Managing Stress and Anxiety

Lesson 4 *Resources*

Teacher Classroom Resources

📁 Concept Mapping Activity 30

📁 Lesson Plan 30

📁 Lesson Quiz 30

📁 Reteaching Activity 30

Student Activity Workbook

📁 Applying Health Skills 30

📁 Chapter 8 Study Guide

Factors That Affect Resiliency

Many factors can influence a person's level of resiliency. Having some of the **developmental assets** discussed in Chapter 7 will very likely strengthen a person's resiliency. For example, having a supportive family and a strong sense of self-worth can help an individual bounce back from setbacks or other difficulties. The factors that affect a person's resiliency can be divided into two categories: external and internal.

External Factors

These factors include your family, your school or community, and your peers. They may also include elements that are less concrete, for example, opportunities to participate in school projects or community events. Although you may have little control over these factors, you can work to strengthen some of them. For example, you could join a community youth program in order to have access to more opportunities and to form healthy peer relationships.

Internal Factors

Internal factors are the ones you have control over. Making a conscious effort to strengthen these factors will increase your resiliency and improve your mental/emotional health. Your attitudes, perceptions, and behaviors make up your internal factors, which also include:

▶ **Commitment to learning.** Being actively engaged in your education increases your self-esteem and gives you a sense of belonging in the school community.

▶ **Positive values.** You demonstrate positive values through your words and actions. For example, you show caring when you help a younger sibling study for a test. By avoiding risk behaviors, you show that you take responsibility for your health. When your behavior reflects positive values, you will feel good about yourself and the decisions you make.

hotlink

developmental assets For a list of developmental assets, see Chapter 7, page 179.

▼ By contributing to the community, these teens are also building their protective factors. *How might helping others strengthen a teen's resiliency?*

Lesson 4 Being a Resilient Teen **215**

Dealing with Sensitive Issues

Coping with Crisis During periods of local or national crisis, students may exhibit a variety of reactions, depending on their level of involvement and their personal sense of loss. Emotional responses vary in intensity; students may need guidance from teachers, parents, and counselors to understand how to deal with these emotions. Various expressions of fear, anxiety, and loss should be expected; but teachers and other school staff members should keep a watchful eye for severe stress and grief reactions in students. For resources to help identify students who exhibit extreme reactions and who may need additional support, visit the link to the National Association of School Psychologists at **health.glencoe.com.**

② TEACH

Reinforcing Concepts

Have students identify natural disasters and tragedies that have been covered in local, national, or world news reports. Ask: How does resiliency help people directly affected by these events? Why do some people who are indirectly affected also need the coping skills of resiliency? **L1**

hotlink

Have students work with partners to review the developmental assets discussed in Chapter 7. Ask: Which assets are especially likely to strengthen resiliency? Why?

ACTIVE READING

Word Forms

Help students recognize that they can use different forms of a word to help identify a word's meaning. For example, students might be familiar with the word *resilient* or *resilience*, which will help them understand *resiliency*. Working with other words on this page, you might have students name other forms of words such as *supportive (support)*, *perception (perceive)*, *commitment (commit)*, *responsibility (responsible, responsibly)*. For more strategies, see the *Guided Reading Activities* booklet. 📁 **L1**

Discussing

Help students discuss the relationship between developmental assets and protective factors. **L1**

216

Real-Life Application

THE POWER OF ASSETS

ANALYZING INFLUENCES

NHES Standard 4 Students will analyze the influence of culture, media, technology, and other factors on health.

Objectives

- Explain the relationship between unsafe behaviors and developmental assets.
- Analyze the influence of assets on personal decisions to avoid risk behavior.

Motivator

Stretch out a large rubber band, and let it snap back. Explain that students who are resilient are able to bounce back from difficulties just as the rubber band did. They are also less likely to engage in high-risk behaviors.

Teaching Strategies

1. Review the developmental assets in Chapter 7 with students.
2. After students have completed their tables, have them share their ideas on how these assets can protect people from risk behaviors.

✓ Assessment

Using a rubric, student work should provide comprehensive evidence of the following criteria to achieve the highest score:

✔ identification and analysis of external and internal assets
✔ attention to interrelationships and complexity of influences
✔ explanation of how assets influence behavior

CHARACTER CHECK

Responsibility. Although you can't control external events, you *can* control how you respond to them. For example, you can choose to adapt to and learn from each situation and challenge. **Think about a recent disappointment or difficulty. How did you bounce back from the situation? How can you apply what you learned about yourself to similar events in the future?**

Teens who respect themselves and care about their futures are better able to resist pressure to engage in high-risk behaviors. *What other protective factors might help a teen say no to risky behaviors?*

216 Chapter 8 Managing Stress and Anxiety

▶ **Social competency.** Being socially competent means that you have empathy and friendship skills. It also means that you can resist negative peer pressure and resolve conflicts nonviolently.

▶ **Positive identity.** Having a positive identity gives you a sense of control over what happens to you. It indicates positive self-esteem and a sense of purpose. You are also likely to have a positive view of your future, an asset that allows you to recover more easily from setbacks.

Resiliency and Your Protective Factors

In addition to strengthening your resiliency, your developmental assets also protect you from risk behaviors such as drug use, sexual activity, and gang involvement. For this reason, developmental assets are often seen as **protective factors**, *conditions that shield individuals from the negative consequences of exposure to risk*. These factors can reduce the possible harmful effect of a difficult event or risky situation. They may also influence a person to respond to a situation in a healthy way.

Building Resiliency by Strengthening Your Protective Factors

Teens who do not have all their external protective factors in place can strengthen the ones they do have. For example, developing a better relationship with the adult members of your family can enhance positive family communication. Teens can also find support from teachers, coaches, clergy, or other caring adults. Internal protective factors can also be improved. Actions you can take include the following.

▶ Become involved in extra-curricular activities at school.

▶ Make a commitment to learning by reading for pleasure at least three hours per week.

▶ Stand up for your beliefs, and refuse to act against your values.

▶ Be honest with yourself and others.

▶ Resist negative peer pressure, and avoid dangerous situations.

▶ Learn about people from other cultures or ethnic backgrounds.

▶ Develop a sense of purpose.

▶ Develop a positive outlook about your future.

What Teens Want to Know

Is it safe to use herbal supplements to relieve stress? It can be dangerous to take herbal supplements to relieve stress because they are not regulated by the Food and Drug Administration (FDA). Manufacturers of these supplements may make claims that are unproven. Some of these products are fat-soluble and can build up to toxic levels in the body. Talk to your health care provider before using any product that claims to relieve stress.

Real-Life Application

The Power of Assets

Developmental assets strengthen your resiliency, and they can protect you from participating in risk behaviors. The more assets you have in place, the more equipped you are to avoid unsafe behaviors. This graph illustrates how teens with more than 30 assets steer clear of activities that will harm their health.

ACTIVITY

Make a two-column table. Next, review the list of developmental assets in Chapter 7 and select five assets. List these in the left column of your table. In the right column, explain how you think each specific asset can protect you from the risk behaviors in the graph shown here.

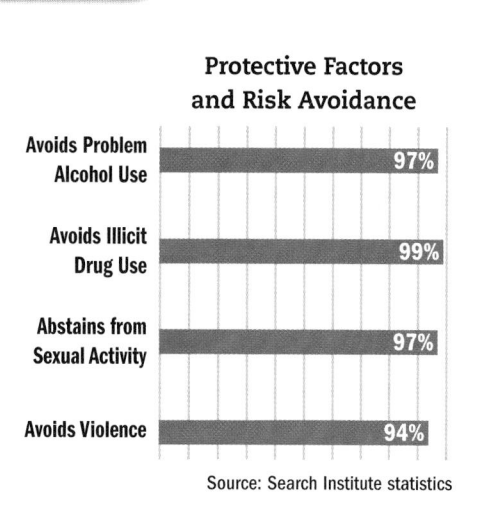

Protective Factors and Risk Avoidance

- Avoids Problem Alcohol Use — 97%
- Avoids Illicit Drug Use — 99%
- Abstains from Sexual Activity — 97%
- Avoids Violence — 94%

Source: Search Institute statistics

③ ASSESS

EVALUATING THE LESSON

Assign and discuss the Lesson 4 Review; then administer, grade, and discuss Lesson Quiz 30 in the TCR.

RETEACHING

- Have students work in groups to define *resiliency* in their own words and to list steps teens can take to strengthen their own resiliency.
- Ask students to complete Reteaching Activity 30 in the TCR.

ENRICHMENT

Have students write a paragraph in their personal journals about a time when they demonstrated resiliency. Invite volunteers share their paragraphs with the class.

④ CLOSE

Have students identify at least one step they plan to take to strengthen their own resiliency.

▶ Lesson 4 Review

Reviewing Facts and Vocabulary

1. Define *resiliency*. Why is it important?
2. List three external factors and three internal factors that can affect a person's resiliency.
3. How do protective factors help a person avoid risk behaviors?

Thinking Critically

4. **Analyzing.** Make a list of at least five of your personal stressors. What protective factors do you have or can you develop to help you deal with each one?
5. **Synthesizing.** How does developing a positive outlook strengthen your resiliency?

Applying Health Skills

Goal Setting. Review your protective factors. Is there an area you would like to strengthen? Using the steps of goal setting, make a plan to develop a specific protective factor. Then, put your plan into action!

TECHNOLOGY OPTION

PRESENTATION   Use presentation software to develop your plan. Visit **health.glencoe.com** for more information about presentation software.

Lesson 4   Being a Resilient Teen   **217**

▶ Lesson 4 Review

Answers to Reviewing Facts and Vocabulary

1. The ability to adapt effectively and recover from disappointment, difficulty, or crisis.
2. External—family, school, community, peers, opportunities. Internal—attitudes, perceptions, behaviors, commitment to learning, positive values, social competency, positive identity.
3. They can reduce harmful effects or influence a person to respond in a healthy way.

Answers to Thinking Critically

4. Answers will vary.
5. Answers will vary.

ADVERTISING STRESS RELIEF

NHES Standard 4 Students will analyze the influence of culture, media, technology, and other factors on health.

Objective

Assess the validity of advertising that claims its products reduce or help manage stress.

Motivator

Tell students that advertisers often use the idea of stress management to sell their products.

Teaching Strategies

Awareness Have students describe the "look and feel" of the ads they analyzed.

Analysis Ask students why these types of ads may be popular.

Reflection Ask students if any of them came upon an ad that made valid claims about promoting stress relief. How is this product different from the products that made exaggerated claims?

Take Action After their analysis, have students write a letter to the makers of a product whose claims were not valid. Students should explain why using the product does not relieve stress and identify effective ways to manage stress.

✓Assessment

Students should use their charts as a vehicle for developing a one-page essay. The essay should contain the essential features of the ad, the claims the ad makes, an analysis as to the validity of the claims, and what the real outcome is of using the product. Students should also discuss effective ways to manage stress and anxiety.

Advertising Stress Relief

Ads on television, billboards, radio, the Internet, and in magazines and newspapers often tell us that use of specific products can help us relieve the stresses of everyday life. Some of these claims can be unrealistic. For example, ads for coffee sometimes imply that drinking coffee helps the consumer relax. However, coffee contains caffeine, which can intensify feelings of stress. To protect your health, it is important to determine the validity of advertising claims regarding stress relief.

Type of product	Claims made	Are claims valid? Why/why not?	Real outcome of use of product	Alternatives that will manage stress
				1.
				2.
				3.

ACTIVITY

Find an ad that claims that the use of the product alleviates stress or anxiety. Using the chart above as a guide, analyze the ad. Ask these questions: What is the product? How does the ad claim the product will alleviate stress? Are the claims valid? Why or why not? What is a possible outcome of using the product? If use of the product will not help manage stress, list three alternatives that will.

Write an essay on your findings. Discuss all the features contained in the ad, including the claims made, whether or not the claims are valid,

and the real consequences of using the product.

EXPRESS YOUR VIEWS

Many ads that claim to relieve stress are playing on the popular notions of what is relaxing. Some ads might tell you that shopping is relaxing, that eating a certain kind of food is soothing, or that washing your hair with a certain shampoo is calming. However, are these claims valid? Hold a class discussion on whether or not the claims made in such ads are valid.

More About...

Targeting Teen Consumers Although ads that claim their products help the consumer relax are abundant, they aren't generally targeted to a youth audience. Ads that are targeted to youth often look very different from ads that are selling stress relief.

Ads for youth focus on the excitement and energy the product will give the youth. Ads for relaxing products are often targeted to stressed-out parents and other adults with high-pressure careers.

CROSS-CURRICULUM CONNECTIONS

Write an Essay or Poem. Children often cling to their favorite stuffed animal when they are scared during the night. As we grow older, we may still turn to certain objects to help us deal with anxieties. Write about your "security blanket." Perhaps it is a special photograph, a touching song, or a good luck charm. Write an essay or a poem that expresses your feelings about how this object helps you manage daily stress.

Write a Report. For centuries, people have been keeping journals as an antidote to life's stresses. Some journals, such as Anne Frank's *Diary of a Young Girl*, have gone beyond their therapeutic value by leaving behind a way for others to explore the anxieties of a particular time or event. Write a report on a well-known journal. Focus on how this writer handled the stress of the time and remained resilient.

Calculate Cost. Stress costs the United States $2.5 billion per year: $1 billion in direct medical payments and another $1.5 billion in insurance premiums, absenteeism, and accidents. The 2000 census shows 281,421,906 people living in the U.S. How much money does stress cost each person per year?

Research a Topic. Stress occurs in all lifeforms. Plants are subject to many forms of environmental stress, including variations in the quality and composition of air, soil, and water. Research plant stressors and the difference between the effects of intermittent stress and continuous stress. How is stress experienced by plants similar to or different from the human experience of psychological stress?

Time Management Consultant

Are you a good organizer? Are you able to handle many tasks efficiently? If so, time management may be the career for you. Many time management consultants have business degrees with an emphasis on project management. In their work, they apply their time management skills to get more done in less time.

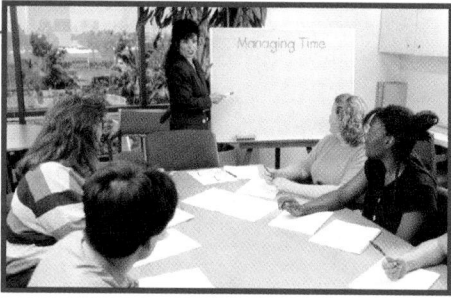

Time management consultants can be found in almost every industry, from construction and information systems to healthcare, financial services, education, and training. To become a time management consultant, you will need an undergraduate degree in business. Some time management consultants get special certification after college in order to develop their skills further. You can find out more about this and other health careers by clicking on Career Corner at **health.glencoe.com**.

Chapter 8 Review **219**

Portfolio Assessment

Self-Evaluation Direct students to review the Health Skills Activities and other activities completed in the chapter. Encourage each student to select one finished product or activity that demonstrates his or her best work for the chapter and that represents the student's learning goals. Have students explain what they have learned and how the examples they have selected demonstrate their growth in health literacy, knowledge, and skills.

Teacher Classroom Resources Assign Performance Assessment 8, "Stressor Assessor," in the TCR.

CROSS-CURRICULUM CONNECTIONS

Enrich student learning by connecting the topic of stress and stress management to one of the four subject areas presented on this page. The activity may be completed individually or with a partner.

Language Arts Remind students that their essay or a poem should be rich in sensory details and impressions.

Social Studies Provide a list of possible authors, such as abolitionist John Woolman or scientist Charles Darwin.

Math Answer: $2,500,000,000/281,421,906 = $8.88

Science The main idea here is that intermittent stress with adequate recovery time will lead to the ability to withstand greater stress in the future. Sports training relies on this principle to some degree. However, continuous overwhelming stress will kill an organism. Students might relate this principle to psychological stress by suggesting that learning to deal with everyday psychological stress prepares us to deal with future stress.

Have students read the Career Corner feature. Ask interested students to explore the Glencoe Health Web site at **health.glencoe.com** for more information on this topic.

CHECKING COMPREHENSION

- Assign and discuss the chapter review.
- Use the Chapter 8 MindJogger Videoquiz to review the chapter. ▣◖

CHAPTER 8 REVIEW ANSWERS

Exploring Health Terms

1. perception
2. stressor
3. psychosomatic response
4. stress-management skills
5. relaxation response
6. True
7. False; anxiety
8. protective factor
9. resiliency

Recalling the Facts

1. The hypothalamus receives signals from other parts of the brain. The hypothalamus releases a hormone that acts on the pituitary gland. This gland secretes a hormone to stimulate the adrenal glands, which in turn secrete adrenaline. Adrenaline causes increased amounts of blood, oxygen, and sources of energy to flow to the brain, heart, and muscles.

2. Pathological

3. Prolonged stress can compromise the immune system, meaning the body cannot fight disease as well. A person will be more prone to colds, flu, or even severe infections or cancers.

4. Planning gives you more control over what is happening to you; a sense of control minimizes feelings of stress.

5. Physical activity uses the excess energy that can result from stress. This helps you relax.

► EXPLORING HEALTH TERMS
Answer the following questions on a sheet of paper.

Lesson 1 *Match each definition with the correct term.*

stress	perception
stressor	psychosomatic response
chronic stress	

1. The act of becoming aware through the senses.
2. An event or situation that causes stress.
3. A physical reaction that results from stress rather than from injury or illness.

Lesson 2 *Fill in the blanks with the correct term.*

relaxation response
stress-management skills

Redirecting your energy, keeping a positive outlook, and seeking out support are examples of (_4_). Using techniques such as laughing and deep breathing exercises can cause a (_5_).

Lesson 3 *Identify each statement as True or False. If false, replace the underlined term with the correct term.*

anxiety   **depression**

6. Depression is a prolonged feeling of helplessness.
7. Some symptoms of depression are rapid heart rate and shortness of breath.

Lesson 4 *Fill the blanks with the correct term.*

resiliency
protective factor

A condition that shields a person from the negative consequences of exposure to risk is a (_8_). If you are able to recover from difficulty, disappointment, and crisis, you are said to have (_9_).

► RECALLING THE FACTS
Use complete sentences to answer the following questions.

Lesson 1

1. What occurs in your body during the alarm stage of the stress response?
2. Which type of fatigue results in illness?
3. What is the effect of prolonged stress on the immune system?

Lesson 2

4. How does planning help you manage stress?
5. How does physical activity help reduce the effects of stress?
6. How is nutrition related to stress?

Lesson 3

7. How might perfectionism lead to anxiety?
8. What are three ways to manage mild depression?
9. What are three symptoms of depression?

Lesson 4

10. Over which category of the factors that affect resiliency does a person have the most control?
11. What does "commitment to learning" mean?
12. List three things you can do to build your protective factors and strengthen your resiliency.

6. Answers may discuss any or all of the following factors: Stress can affect your appetite, causing poor eating habits; stress affects the absorption of vitamins and minerals; good nutrition can help prevent health problems associated with stress.

7. The constant self-imposed pressure of trying to be without flaw and trying to make no mistakes can lead to anxiety.

8. Any three: Write about your feelings in a private journal, engage in creative activity, talk with family or friends, eat healthfully, get enough sleep, get enough physical activity, do something nice for someone else.

9. Any three: irritable or restless mood; withdrawal from friends and activities, change in appetite or weight; sleeping more or less than usual; difficulty thinking or concentrating; loss of energy; feelings of guilt or worthlessness; sense of hopelessness.

➤ THINKING CRITICALLY

1. **Summarizing.** Examine the causes and effects of stress. Write a paragraph describing common stressors and effects of stress. *(LESSON 1)*

2. **Synthesizing.** Describe one potentially stressful situation for which planning might reduce your stress. Make an outline of a plan for that situation. *(LESSON 2)*

3. **Analyzing.** Compare the physical symptoms of anxiety with those of depression. What do anxiety and depression have in common? *(LESSON 3)*

4. **Evaluating.** How might learning about people of other cultures or ethnic backgrounds strengthen your resiliency? *(LESSON 4)*

➤ HEALTH SKILLS APPLICATION

1. **Accessing Information.** Using library resources or the Internet, research the relationship between stress and disease. Write a paragraph explaining what you learned. Identify your sources, and explain why you think they are reliable. *(LESSON 1)*

2. **Refusal Skills.** Describe a scenario in which using refusal skills effectively could help you avoid a potentially stressful situation. Then, write three effective refusal statements you could use to avoid the situation. *(LESSON 2)*

3. **Communication Skills.** Suppose you have a friend who is showing symptoms of depression. For example, he or she has withdrawn from activities you used to share and enjoy. How would you talk with your friend? How could you tell whether he or she needed professional help? *(LESSON 3)*

4. **Analyzing Influences.** Consider the protective factors in your life. Which have the strongest influence on your health behaviors? Why do you think this is so? *(LESSON 4)*

BEYOND *the* Classroom

Parent Involvement

Accessing Information. With a parent, investigate stress-management resources in your community. Your local Yellow Pages may be a good place to start. Make a list of agencies and their services. Discuss which resource your family members would most likely use if daily stress were to become a health concern. Which resource would be most helpful in dealing with a highly stressful event?

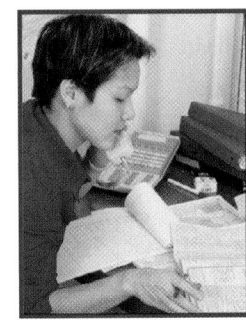

School and Community

Stress Management Classes. Contact a wellness center in a hospital in your area. Ask whether there are stress management seminars or classes that you could observe. Attend a session and report to your class on what you have learned.

10. Internal factors

11. Being motivated to do well in school and being actively engaged in your education.

12. Any three: Become involved in school activities, make a commitment to learning by reading for pleasure, stand up for what you believe and stay true to your values, be honest with yourself and others, resist negative peer pressure, learn about other cultures, develop a sense of purpose, develop a positive outlook.

Thinking Critically

1. Paragraphs should reflect clear understanding of the causes and effects of stress.

2. Possible situations could include studying for exams or learning a skill such as driving.

3. Answers should indicate that depression slows the body and its systems down whereas anxiety tends to excite or speed them up. Both affect health.

4. Possible answer: By learning about people of other background and cultures, you strengthen your social health.

Health Skills Application

1. Answers will vary.

2. Answers will vary.

3. Responses should demonstrate empathy and include questions to gather information about symptoms. See pages 212–213 for signs that professional help is needed.

4. Answers will vary.

EVALUATE

- Use the reproducible Chapter 8 Test in the TCR, or construct your own using the Testmaker software.
- Use Performance Assessment 8 in the TCR.

ENRICHMENT

Ask students to complete Enrichment Activity 8 in the TCR.

BEYOND *the* Classroom

Keep students involved in the community, and encourage parent participation by assigning the activities on this page for students to work on outside of class.

221

Lessons	Standards		Features
	National	State/Local	
1 **Mental Disorders** *pages 224–229*	National Health Education Standards 1.2, 2.6		
2 **Suicide Prevention** *pages 230–233*	National Health Education Standards 2.6, 6.1		**Health Skills Activity** • When a Friend Seems Troubled *(Decision Making)*, page 232
3 **Getting Help** *pages 234–237*	National Health Education Standards 2.1, 2.2, 2.6, 3.4		**Real-Life Application** • Evaluating Sources of Self-Help *(Accessing Information)*, page 235
4 **Understanding Death and Grief** *pages 238–241*	National Health Education Standards 2.6, 5.3, 5.4		**Hands-On Health** • An Encouraging Word *(Communication)*, page 240

Reproducible Resources	Assessment	Technology
Student Activity Workbook for use with each chapter 📁 Concept Mapping Activity 31 📁 Cross-Curriculum Activity 9 📁 Decision-Making Activity 9 📁 Guided Reading Activities 31 📁 Lesson Plan 31 📁 Parent Letter and Activities 9 📁 Reteaching Activity 31	📁 Lesson Quiz 31	🕹 Transparency 24 💿 TeacherWorks® 💻 Internet Activities
📁 Concept Mapping Activity 32 📁 Enrichment Activity 9 📁 Guided Reading Activities 32 📁 Lesson Plan 32 📁 Reteaching Activity 32	📁 Lesson Quiz 32	💿 TeacherWorks®
📁 Concept Mapping Activity 33 📁 Current Health Issues 9 📁 Guided Reading Activities 33 📁 Health Lab 9 📁 Lesson Plan 33 📁 Reteaching Activity 33	📁 Lesson Quiz 33	🕹 Transparency 25 💿 TeacherWorks®
📁 Concept Mapping Activity 34 📁 Guided Reading Activities 34 📁 Lesson Plan 34 📁 Reteaching Activity 34	📁 Lesson Quiz 34	💿 TeacherWorks®

0:00 OUT OF TIME

If time does not permit teaching the entire chapter, use:

- Health Minute, p. 229
- Figure 9.2, p. 231
- Real-Life Application, p. 235
- Hands-On Health, p. 240

Language Diversity

🎧 English Audio CD Program

🎧 Spanish Audio CD Program

📁 English Summaries, Quizzes, and Activities

📁 Spanish Summaries, Quizzes, and Activities

📁 Spanish Parent Letters and Activities

End of Chapter Assessment

Blackline Masters

📁 Chapter 9 Test

📁 Performance Assessment Activity 9

📁 Unit 3 Test

Technology

💿 Vocabulary PuzzleMaker

📼 MindJogger Videoquiz

💿 **Exam**View® Pro Testmaker

Professional Health Series

Dealing with Sensitive Issues
Planning a Coordinated School Health Program
Promoting Character Education
Home, School, and Community Involvement

Key to Ability Levels

Teaching strategies that appear throughout the chapter have been identified by one of the following codes to give teachers an idea of their suitability for students of varying learning styles and abilities.

L1 Strategies should be within the ability range of all students. Full class participation is often required. Teacher direction is usually needed.

L2 Strategies are designed for average to above-average students or for small groups. Some teacher direction is needed.

L3 Strategies are designed for students able and willing to work independently. Minimal teacher direction is needed.

ELL Strategies should be within the ability range of students learning the English language.

Block scheduling strategies are useful in a block scheduling format.

CHAPTER OVERVIEW

Chapter 9 describes common mental disorders and identifies the warning signs of suicide. The chapter also discusses sources of help for mental and emotional problems and describes the process of dealing with grief.

Lesson 1 Mental disorders—which prevent people from living happy, healthful, and productive lives—may be organic or functional. The four main categories of functional disorders are *anxiety disorders*, *mood disorders*, *eating disorders*, and *conduct disorders*.

Lesson 2 Suicide is a serious but preventable problem. Risk factors include depression, alcohol or drug abuse, and a family history of mental disorders. Verbal and behavioral warning signs can alert others to the risk of teen suicide.

Lesson 3 Specific signs of mental illness can help individuals identify problems and seek professional help. Many kinds of mental health professionals can help people with mental disorders, and several different treatment methods are available.

Lesson 4 Many kinds of losses, including loss through death, can cause a grief response. Understanding the stages in the grieving process can help people cope.

Health Skills Features

- Health Skills Activity (*Decision Making*), p. 232
- Real-Life Application (*Accessing Information*), p. 235
- Hands-On Health (*Communication*), p. 240

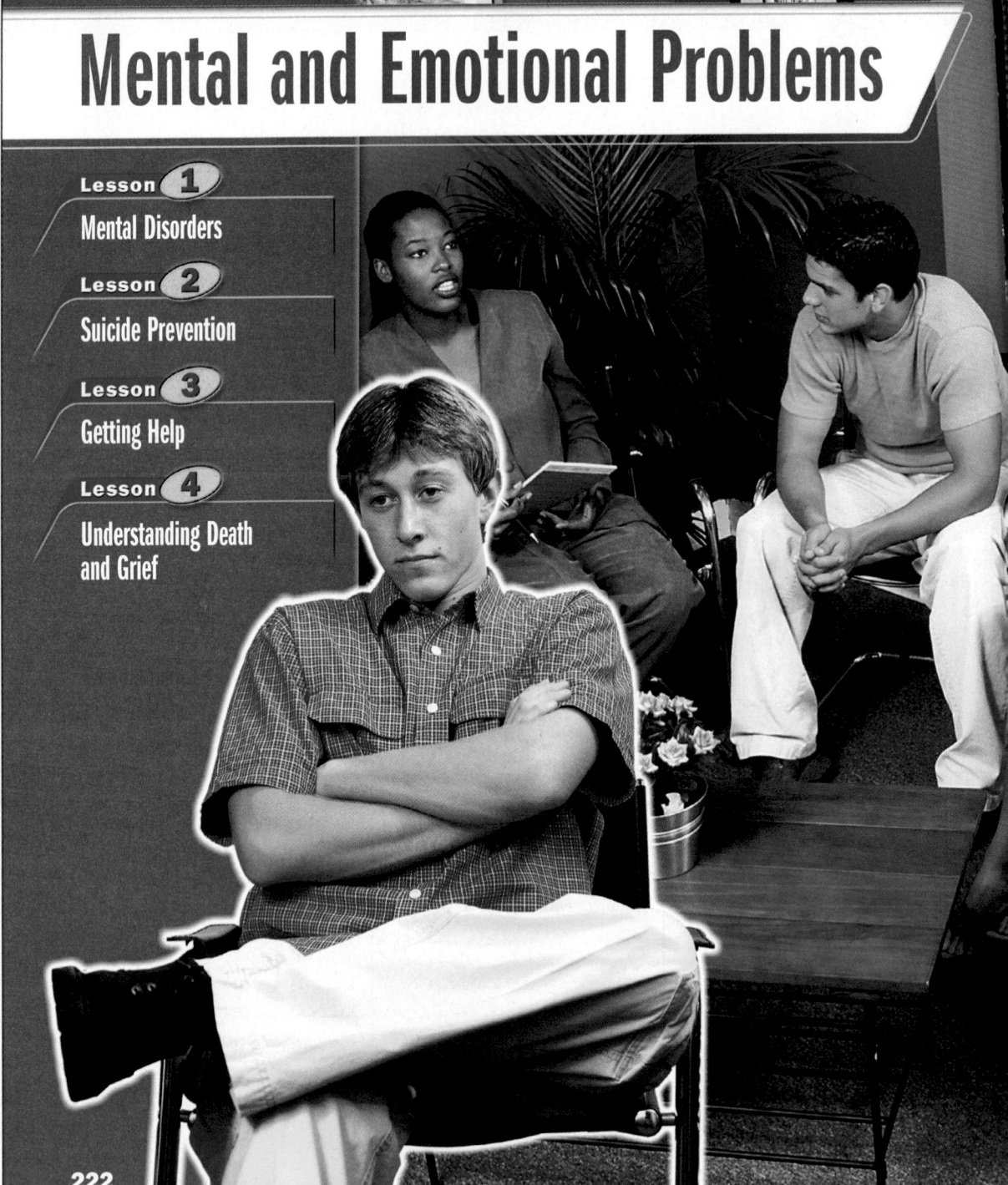

Mental and Emotional Problems

Lesson 1
Mental Disorders

Lesson 2
Suicide Prevention

Lesson 3
Getting Help

Lesson 4
Understanding Death and Grief

222

MEETING STUDENT DIVERSITY

Language Diversity Use the following suggestions to help students who have difficulty with English:

- Pair English language learners with native speakers of English who can restate the Chapter Summary in language that helps students comprehend important concepts.

- 🎧 Direct auditory learners or those students with language diversity to the *Glencoe Health Audio CD Program*. Available in English and Spanish, this component provides an audio and written summary of the chapter.

- Use photographs, drawings, or magazine clippings to help students visualize the important concepts of the chapter.

Chapter 1

Myth or Fact?

What Do You Know About Mental and Emotional Disorders?

Read the statements below and respond by writing *Myth* or *Fact* for each item. You may want to record reasons for each of your choices.

1. People who have mental and emotional disorders are typically violent.

2. Mental and emotional disorders are true medical illnesses like heart disease and diabetes.

3. Most people can "snap out of" their depression if they try hard enough.

4. Depression and other mental or emotional disorders do not affect children or adolescents.

5. People are less likely to seek treatment for mental disorders than for physical disorders.

6. People who talk about suicide should always be taken seriously.

7. Being treated for a mental or an emotional disorder means that an individual has failed in some way or is responsible for the problem.

8. Getting help for a mental problem is difficult and expensive.

Keep your responses for review as you read the chapter. When you complete the chapter, review your answers again and make any necessary changes on the basis of what you have learned.

223

Quick*Write*

Using Visuals. Taking time to be with supportive people and setting aside time to be alone can help keep your emotions in balance. Sometimes, however, feelings such as anger, loneliness, fear, or sadness can seem overwhelming. How do you manage these strong emotions? When should a person seek help in dealing with intense feelings?

INTRODUCING THE CHAPTER

Myth or Fact?

Have students read the statements and their responses.

1. Myth. Violence among people with a mental disorder is not much higher than in the general population.

2. Fact.

3. Myth. Severe depression results from changes in brain chemistry or brain function.

4. Myth. In the United States, 20 percent of children and adolescents have some form of mental disorder.

5. Fact.

6. Fact.

7. Myth. Mental illness cannot be ignored. It takes courage to seek professional help.

8. Myth. A trusted adult, friend, physician, or clergy member can help. Professional help is often low-cost or free.

Quick*write*

Using Visuals Have students read and discuss the Quick Write assignment. Emphasize that everyone feels overwhelmed by troubling emotions sometimes. Let students write their responses independently. Then ask volunteers to share their ideas.

TECHNOLOGY OPTIONS

MINDJOGGER
VIDEOQUIZ

To preview or review chapter content, you may wish to use the Chapter 9 MindJogger Videoquiz.

HEALTH *Online*

Online Resources for the Teacher For a fresh approach to health topics and an in-depth look at health issues, use these online resources found under Teacher Resources at **health.glencoe.com:**

• Block Schedule Lesson Plans
• Technology Projects
• Health Updates

Mental Disorders

Lesson 1

1 FOCUS

QUICK START Give students two or three minutes to jot down their lists. Then invite volunteers to read their lists aloud, and record a class list on the board. Ask: What attitudes do these words communicate? How might learning more about mental disorders affect those attitudes?

TYING TO PRIOR KNOWLEDGE

Have volunteers recall a few facts they may know about anxiety and depression. Explain that students will learn more about these and other disorders as they study Lesson 1.

INTRODUCING VOCABULARY

- Have partners work together to check the definition of each vocabulary term in the Glossary or Glosario. Then let students take turns giving a definition and having their partner identify the defined term.

- Ask students to complete the Chapter 9 Study Guide in the *Student Activity Workbook.* 📁

Mental Disorders

VOCABULARY
mental disorder
anxiety disorder
post-traumatic
  stress disorder
mood disorder
conduct disorder

YOU'LL LEARN TO
- Distinguish types of mental disorders.
- Identify situations requiring professional mental health services.
- Identify and describe the types of mental disorders that affect our society.

QUICK START On a sheet of paper, write as many words as you can think of when you hear the term *mental disorder*. Categorize the words as positive or negative. What might this indicate about attitudes regarding mental disorders?

Almost everyone experiences periods of sadness, anxiety, and anger. For most people, these feelings are short-lived. For millions of others, however, these feelings persist for weeks, months, and even years. If such feelings begin to interfere with an individual's behavior or daily activities, he or she may be suffering from a mental disorder.

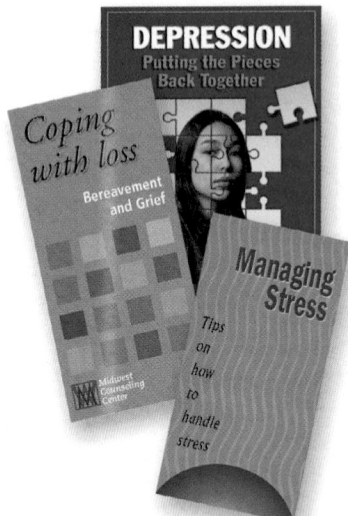

Information about mental disorders is available in most health clinics. *Where else could you find reliable information on a mental disorder?*

What Are Mental Disorders?

A **mental disorder** is *an illness of the mind that can affect the thoughts, feelings, and behaviors of a person, preventing him or her from leading a happy, healthful, and productive life.* People who suffer from some form of mental disorder are often identified by their inability to cope in healthy ways with life's changes, demands, problems, or traumas. Each year, about 20 percent of the U.S. population—54 million people—are affected by some form of mental disorder. Even though professional help is necessary, fewer than 8 million people with mental disorders actually seek treatment. Of the 20 percent of children and adolescents who suffer from mental health problems, only one-third receive the help they need.

224 Chapter 9 Mental and Emotional Problems

Lesson 1 *Resources*

Teacher Classroom Resources
- 📁 Concept Mapping Activity 31
- 📁 Cross-Curriculum Activity 9
- 📁 Decision-Making Activity 9
- 📁 Guided Reading Activities 31
- 📁 Lesson Plan 31
- 📁 Lesson Quiz 31

- 📁 Parent Letter and Activities 9
- 📁 Reteaching Activity 31

Student Activity Workbook
- 📁 Applying Health Skills 31
- 📁 Chapter 9 Study Guide

Multimedia
- 🖥 Transparency 24

Some people are reluctant to seek treatment for mental/emotional problems because they feel embarrassed or ashamed. Another reason is the stigma associated with mental disorders. A *stigma* is a negative label or a mark of shame. Misconceptions and stereotypes may prevent some people from seeing mental disorders as medical conditions. However, mental disorders require medical attention just as physical illnesses do. In fact, many mental and emotional disturbances involve imbalances in brain chemistry. The sooner a person seeks treatment, the sooner he or she will be on the road to recovery.

Types of Mental Disorders

Mental disorders are classified as either organic or functional. An *organic disorder* is caused by a physical illness or an injury that affects the brain. Brain tumors, infections, chemical imbalances, exposure to drugs and toxins, or injuries resulting in brain damage may lead to organic mental disorders.

A *functional disorder* has a psychological cause and does not involve brain damage. These disorders may result from heredity, stress, emotional conflict, fear, ineffective coping skills, or other conditions. Often, functional disorders are tied to disturbing events in childhood, such as abuse, serious illness, or the traumatic death of a close relative. These disorders may also be tied to recent events, such as divorce, economic hardships, or natural disasters.

Anxiety Disorders

About 4 million Americans suffer from **anxiety disorder**, *a condition in which real or imagined fears are difficult to control.* An anxiety disorder is characterized by chronic fear. People with anxiety disorders often arrange their lives to avoid situations that make them feel anxious or fearful. Anxiety disorders can be classified according to four main types: phobias, obsessive-compulsive disorders, panic disorders, and post-traumatic stress disorders.

PHOBIA

A phobia is a strong and irrational fear of something specific, such as high places or dogs. People with phobias do everything they can to avoid the object of their fear. As a result, a person with a phobia may be unable to live a normal life. For example, people with *agoraphobia* have a fear of open or public places. Their phobia may make them prisoners in their own homes. Some mental health professionals believe that certain phobias are caused by childhood experiences. The fear resulting from these experiences lasts far past the actual threat.

Why are mental disorders a critical health issue?
In the United States, half of the people suffering from mental disorders are untreated, 40 percent of the homeless have some form of mental/emotional problem, and about 20 percent of people in prison have a mental disorder. It is a national concern to get professional mental help for those who need it.

Source: National Alliance for the Mentally Ill

 Arachnophobia, a fear of spiders, is a common phobia. People with phobias can seek help from classes, support groups, and mental health professionals.

Lesson 1 Mental Disorders **225**

② TEACH

Critical Thinking

Help students discuss why people with mental disorders are sometimes reluctant to seek treatment or discuss their problems. Then ask: What can a person do to help himself or herself or his or her family members overcome that reluctance? **L1**

Discussing

Have students brainstorm a list of words that stigmatize people experiencing mental illness. Discuss the impact of these words on a person who has a mental disorder and his or her family and friends. **L1**

Reinforcing Concepts

Help students discuss the definitions of organic disorders and functional disorders. Let several volunteers explain the difference in their own words. Students might also give examples of characters (as from books and movies) who have organic or functional disorders. **L1**

Cooperative Learning

Divide the class into four groups, and assign each group one of the four types of anxiety disorder. Have group members work together to read and discuss the information on their assigned disorder. Then have each group present its information to the rest of the class. **L2** **Interpersonal**

ACTIVE READING

Taking Notes

Remind students that taking notes is a valuable study skill. Note-taking can help students understand what they read, prepare for a test, or write a report. To model an example of taking notes from a text, have them read a section of this lesson together and write notes of the content on the board or on an overhead transparency. Read the notes aloud as a class. When students take their own notes, encourage them to use abbreviations, key words, symbols, and short phrases. When they finish reading and taking notes on a lesson, students should review what they have written to be sure their notes make sense. For more strategies, see the *Guided Reading Activities* booklet in the TCR.

CHARACTER CHECK

Caring Guide students in reading and discussing the Character Check information. Ask: What factors motivate people to tease others? How does teasing show a lack of respect for others? How does it show a lack of respect for oneself? Have students brainstorm answers to the Character Check question and record their responses on the board.

Explaining

Help students recall (from Chapter 8) the distinction between *reactive depression* (a response to an especially stressful event) and *major depression* (a medical condition requiring treatment).

Post-traumatic stress disorder may occur in the aftermath of a crisis. *What can members of a community do to support one another during crises?*

CHARACTER CHECK

Caring. People who suffer from mental disorders are sometimes seen as different. Although some people think it's fun to tease someone who is "different," such teasing is cruel and hurtful. When you show your disapproval of such behavior, you demonstrate consideration and caring for the person being teased. **What are some other ways of showing caring and respect for someone who is seen as "different"?**

OBSESSIVE-COMPULSIVE DISORDER

A person with obsessive-compulsive disorder is trapped in a pattern of repeated thoughts or behaviors. The term *obsessive* refers to persistent, recurrent, and unwanted thoughts that prevent people from attending to normal daily activities. *Compulsive* refers to repeated, irresistible behaviors. A person with obsessive-compulsive disorder might, for example, feel the urge to wash his or her hands constantly throughout the day.

PANIC DISORDER

A person with a panic disorder has sudden, unexplained feelings of terror. These "panic attacks" are accompanied by symptoms such as trembling, a pounding heart, shortness of breath, or dizziness. Panic disorder is a condition in which fear and anxiety get in the way of a person's ability to function and enjoy life. Panic attacks may occur at any time or place, but most are triggered by a particular object, condition, or situation.

POST-TRAUMATIC STRESS DISORDER

Post-traumatic stress disorder is *a condition that may develop after exposure to a terrifying event that threatened or caused physical harm.* This disorder is common after a personal assault, such as rape; natural or human-made disasters, such as earthquakes or bombings; accidents, such as plane crashes; or military combat. Symptoms may include flashbacks (sudden recall of a terrifying event), nightmares, emotional numbness, sleeplessness, guilt, and problems with concentration. The disorder may arise weeks or months after the event that caused it.

Mood Disorders

A **mood disorder** is an *illness, often with an organic cause, that involves mood extremes that interfere with everyday living.* These extremes are not the highs and lows that everyone experiences, nor are they the mood swings sometimes experienced during adolescence. The emotional swings of mood disorders are extreme in both intensity and duration.

CLINICAL DEPRESSION

Most people who say they are depressed are suffering from a passing case of the blues. For some people, however, depression doesn't go away. Their feelings of sadness, hopelessness, or despair last for more than a few weeks and interfere with daily interests and activities. This type of depression, known as clinical depression, can affect a person's ability to concentrate, sleep, perform at school or work, or handle everyday decisions and challenges. Clinical depression is a chemical imbalance that a person cannot overcome without professional help.

More About...

Panic Disorder The National Institute of Mental Health (NIMH) reports that the onset of panic disorder usually occurs when individuals are young adults, between the ages of 18 and 24. The illness sometimes runs in families and it is more common among women than men. It may last for a few brief months or continue for many years.

Information from the NIMH stresses that panic disorder is a real illness that can be treated with medicine and/or therapy. Physical symptoms during a panic attack can include chest pains, unusual sweating, and nausea. People with panic disorder often report that they feel like they are dying during an attack.

Approximately 19 million Americans are affected by clinical depression each year. Depression often runs in families and can be biologically based, but it can also be caused by life events. Sometimes it may be a symptom of substance abuse or addiction, because alcohol and other drugs can affect brain chemistry.

BIPOLAR DISORDER

This disorder, also known as manic-depressive disorder, is marked by extreme mood changes, energy levels, and behavior. Characteristics of the manic "highs" and depressive "lows" of this disorder are described in **Figure 9.1.** Although adults with bipolar disorder may behave normally between episodes of extreme emotion, teens with the disorder tend to alternate rapidly between the two extremes with few clear periods of wellness between episodes.

Eating Disorders

Psychological pressures, possible genetic factors, and an obsession with body image and thinness can lead to an **eating disorder.** People with eating disorders such as anorexia and bulimia suffer from life-threatening disturbances in eating behavior. Eating disorders are not a failure of will or behavior; they are real, treatable medical illnesses. A person who suffers from an eating disorder can experience a wide range of physical health complications, including serious heart conditions and kidney failure, which may lead to death. It is therefore critical that a person with an eating disorder get help immediately.

HEALTH Online

Learn more about teens and depression by clicking on Health Updates at health.glencoe.com.

hot link

eating disorders For more information about eating disorders, see Chapter 6, page 153.

VISUAL LEARNING

Figure 9.1 Guide students in reading and discussing the manic and depressive symptoms listed in Figure 9.1. Be sure students recognize that these symptoms occur together and in cycles for a person with bipolar disorder. For example, most people experience pressured speech or are distracted sometimes; these behaviors alone do not indicate any mental disorder. Then ask: What do you think are the most important differences between adolescent mood swings and bipolar disorder?

FYI

The National Institute of Mental Health reports that depressive disorders often co-occur with anxiety disorders.

hot link

Ask students to recall what they have learned about eating disorders in Chapter 6. Encourage them to check facts and extend their understanding by reviewing the information there.

HEALTH Online

Encourage students to read and discuss online resources about teens and depression.

FIGURE 9.1

MANIA AND DEPRESSION—FLIP SIDES OF MOOD DISORDERS FOR TEENS

Manic Symptoms:	Depressive Symptoms:
• **Severe changes in mood**—is either excessively happy or silly, or very irritable, angry, agitated, or aggressive	• **Irritability,** persistent sadness, frequent crying
• **Grandiosity**—unrealistically high self-esteem, feeling all-powerful	• **Preoccupation with death** or suicide
• **Very high energy level**—including the ability to go with little or no sleep for days without feeling tired	• **Loss of enjoyment** in favorite activities
• **Pressured speech**—talks too much, too fast, changes topics too quickly, and does not allow interruption	• **Frequent physical complaints** such as headaches or stomachaches
• **Distractibility**—attention moves constantly from one thing to another	• **Low energy level,** fatigue, poor concentration, boredom
• **Repeated high-risk behavior**—alcohol or drug use, reckless driving, or sexual activity	• **Dramatic change in eating or sleeping patterns,** such as overeating or oversleeping

Source: American Academy of Child and Adolescent Psychiatry

Lesson 1 Mental Disorders **227**

What Teens Want to Know

Am I responsible for taking care of a friend or loved one who seems troubled? Sometimes, it takes all of your time and energy to keep your own stress under control. Yet, what is your obligation to friends, sisters, brothers, or parents? Are you responsible for their health and safety? These are questions you must answer for yourself. Everyone who is mentally and physically capable must take responsibility for his or her own behavior. Even if you help a friend, the final outcome is your friend's responsibility. Another consideration is how you feel when you need help. The golden rule—to treat others as you would have them treat you—still makes a lot of sense.

Discussing

Help students discuss the particular problems that children and adolescents with conduct disorders might face with family members, with friends, and at school. **L1**

Cooperative Learning

Let students meet in groups to read about and discuss schizophrenia. Ask: What makes this mental disorder especially difficult for patients? For patients' family and friends? **L1**

Discussing

Guide students in comparing the three types of personality disorders: What do all three have in common? How is each different from the others? **L1**

Service Learning

Ask: What do you think younger students should know about common mental disorders? How do you think that information could be most effectively communicated? Then invite a group of interested students to work together to plan an educational project (such as a skit, dialogue, or slide show). If possible, arrange for students to present their project to younger students. **L3**

Conduct Disorders

Children and adolescents who act out their impulses toward others in destructive ways may have a **conduct disorder**, *a pattern of behavior in which the rights of others or basic social rules are violated.* Examples include lying, theft, aggression, violence, truancy, arson, and vandalism. The condition is more common among males than females. Although they may project an image of toughness, people with this disorder usually have low self-esteem. They may also have symptoms of other mental disorders including anxiety, depression, and substance abuse. Without treatment, many teens with this disorder will be unable to adapt to the demands of adulthood and will continue to have problems relating to others, holding a job, and behaving in appropriate ways.

Schizophrenia

Schizophrenia (skit-suh-FREE-nee-uh) is a severe mental disorder in which a person loses contact with reality. Symptoms of schizophrenia include delusions, hallucinations, and thought disorders. Causes of this condition may be a combination of genetic factors and chemical and structural changes in the brain. The disease affects about 1 percent of the population. Schizophrenia affects both men and women and usually first appears between the ages of 15 and 35.

People who suffer from schizophrenia have difficulty understanding the difference between real and imaginary events. This inability leads to unpredictable behavior, difficulty functioning, and lack of good health habits. A common misconception about people who suffer from this disorder is that all of them are violent or have multiple or split personalities. However, schizophrenic people are usually not a threat to others. Professional help and medication are necessary to successfully treat schizophrenia.

Personality Disorders

The term *personality* refers to an individual's unique traits and behavior patterns. People with healthy personalities can cope with the day-to-day challenges of life. However, people afflicted with personality disorders think and behave in ways that make it difficult for them to get along with others. Over the course of their lives, usually beginning in adolescence, they are in constant conflict with others—family, friends, teachers, coworkers, or supervisors. About 10 percent of the population has one of the several types of

Teens with a conduct disorder may act with aggression, but they often have low self-esteem. *How might an untreated conduct disorder affect a teen's future?*

Myths & Reality

MYTH. The lives of people with mental disorders are completely different from those of most other people.

FACT. Many people with mental illnesses go to school, get married, work, have families, do laundry, shop for groceries, and so on—like everyone else.

MYTH. Today, people are more knowledgeable and accepting about mental disorders.

FACT. Unfortunately, a stigma still exists. According to a nationwide survey conducted by the National Mental Health Association, 43 percent of the population considers depression to be an emotional or personal weakness.

personality disorder. Counseling, and sometimes medication, are recommended as treatment.

▶ **Antisocial personality disorder.** People with this disorder tend to be irritable, aggressive, impulsive, and violent. In many cases, they are unable to show remorse for their behavior.

▶ **Borderline personality disorder.** People with this disorder frequently experience a series of troubled relationships. They tend to engage in high-risk activities, and many have poor self-esteem. Although they fear abandonment, they frequently lash out violently at the people they need most.

▶ **Passive-aggressive personality disorder.** People with this disorder are often uncooperative. They resent being told what to do, yet they rely on others' direction. Angry over issues of control, they show their anger, but only indirectly. For example, a passive-aggressive person who doesn't want to take part in an activity either may forget to show up or may arrive late and leave early.

As with all mental and emotional problems, it is important to recognize the signs of personality disorders and seek professional help.

Health Minute

Improving Attitudes About Mental Disorders

To help defeat the social stigma of mental disorders:

▶ Use respectful language when referring to a person with a mental disorder.
▶ Emphasize abilities over limitations.
▶ Express disapproval if someone shows disrespect or inconsideration toward people with mental disorders.
▶ Encourage people who have emotional problems to seek help.

Health Minute

Have volunteers read the Health Minute suggestions aloud. Have volunteers act out ways to follow the suggestions for overcoming stigmas.

3 ASSESS

EVALUATING THE LESSON

Assign and discuss the Lesson 1 Review; then administer, grade, and discuss Lesson Quiz 31 in the TCR. 📁

RETEACHING

• Have students work with partners to write an informal outline of the lesson.

• Ask students to complete Reteaching Activity 31 in the TCR. 📁

ENRICHMENT

Suggest that students research the life and work of an individual who had both a mental disorder and the experience of notable achievement. (For example, John Nash, who won a Nobel Prize in spite of schizophrenia.) Have students present written or oral reports of their findings.

▶ Lesson 1 Review

Reviewing Facts and Vocabulary

1. Define the term *mental disorder*, and explain how organic and functional disorders differ.

2. What do clinical depression and bipolar disorder have in common?

3. Compare and contrast the characteristics of schizophrenia and antisocial personality disorder.

Thinking Critically

4. **Synthesizing.** Although scientific evidence shows that mental disorders are medical conditions, the stigma attached to these illnesses persists. Why do you think this is so?

5. **Analyzing.** How do eating disorders differ from the other types of mental disorders?

Applying Health Skills

Advocacy. Teens suffering from mental disorders often feel confused, isolated, scared, or ashamed. Create a Bill of Rights for people with mental disorders; your list should advocate demonstrating empathy. Focus on specific ways for students to be supportive, patient, and understanding.

TECHNOLOGY OPTION

PRESENTATION SOFTWARE Using presentation software, you can highlight certain points that you want to make. Find help in using presentation software at **health.glencoe.com**.

Lesson 1 Mental Disorders **229**

▶ Lesson 1 Review

Answers to Reviewing Facts and Vocabulary

1. See page 224 for definition. Organic: caused by physical illness or injury. Functional: has a psychological cause.

2. Both are mood disorders; people with bipolar disorder sometimes exhibit symptoms of clinical depression.

3. Person with schizophrenia not usually a threat to others; person with antisocial personality disorder frequently at odds with others and may be violent.

Answers to Thinking Critically

4. Fear of and misunderstanding about mental disorders perpetuate this stigma.

5. Eating disorders can result in death from physical complications.

4 CLOSE

Ask students to write brief personal statements in their private health journals explaining how their attitudes toward mental disorders have changed in response to the information in this lesson.

Suicide Prevention

1 FOCUS

 QUICK START Give students one or two minutes to list three warning signs of suicide. Then have volunteers share their lists. Lead the class in discussing why they think these are warning signs and how family members and friends can help someone considering suicide.

TYING TO PRIOR KNOWLEDGE

Ask students which of the conditions described in Lesson 1 may be associated with suicide. Then explain that they will explore this topic as they study Lesson 2.

Health Skills Features

"When a Friend Seems Troubled," p. 232

DECISION MAKING

INTRODUCING VOCABULARY

- Have students check the definitions of all three vocabulary terms in the Glossary.

- Ask students to complete the Chapter 9 Study Guide in the *Student Activity Workbook.*

Lesson 2

Suicide Prevention

VOCABULARY
alienation
suicide
cluster suicides

YOU'LL LEARN TO
- Identify the warning signs of suicide.
- Analyze strategies for preventing suicides.
- Develop strategies for coping with depression.
- Develop strategies for coping with feelings in the aftermath of a tragedy.

QUICK START Write down three danger signs you might detect in someone who is thinking about suicide. Then explain why you think these are warning signs of suicide. What do you think family members and friends can do to help a loved one who is exhibiting these signs?

⚠ **Recognizing signs of depression and seeking help is critical to suicide prevention.**

Life can be difficult for everyone at times. Challenges, responsibilities, and pressures can pile up and seem overwhelming. These feelings can be further complicated by troubling life events, such as the divorce of parents or the death of a friend or family member. For some people, this emotional overload can lead to depression or **alienation**, *feeling isolated and separated from everyone else.* When such painful feelings become unbearable, some people may try drastic, self-destructive measures to escape their pain. **Suicide**, the most drastic of all measures, is *the act of intentionally taking one's own life.* Suicide is a serious problem, but it is preventable.

Suicide Risk Factors

Most suicidal thoughts, behaviors, and actions are expressions of extreme distress, not bids for attention. More than 90 percent of the people who kill themselves are suffering from depression or another mental disorder or are abusing alcohol or drugs. Other suicidal risk factors include a history of physical or sexual abuse, a history of previous suicide attempts, or a family history of emotional disorders or suicides.

230 Chapter 9 Mental and Emotional Problems

Lesson 2 *Resources*

Teacher Classroom Resources
- Concept Mapping Activity 32
- Enrichment Activity 9
- Guided Reading Activities 32
- Lesson Plan 32
- Lesson Quiz 32

- Parent Letter and Activities 9
- Reteaching Activity 32

Student Activity Workbook
- Applying Health Skills 32
- Chapter 9 Study Guide

FIGURE 9.2

TEEN SUICIDE: RECOGNIZING THE WARNING SIGNS

The warning signs of suicide should be taken seriously. The more signs a person exhibits, the more likely he or she is thinking about suicide.

Verbal Signs	Nonverbal or Behavioral Signs
• Direct statements such as these: "I want to die." "I don't want to live anymore." "I wish I were dead." • Indirect statements such as these: "I won't have to put up with this much longer." "I just want to go to sleep and never wake up." "They'll be sorry when I'm gone." "Soon this pain will be over." "I can't take it anymore." "Nothing matters." "I won't be a problem for you much longer." "What's the use?" • Writing poems, song lyrics, or diary entries that deal with death. • Suicide threats or insinuations that are either direct or indirect.	• An unusual obsession with death • Withdrawal from friends • Dramatic changes in personality, hygiene, or appearance • Impulsive, irrational, or bizarre behavior • An overwhelming sense of guilt, shame, or rejection; negative self-evaluation • Significant deterioration in schoolwork or recreational performance • Preoccupation with giving away personal belongings • Substance abuse • Frequent complaints about physical symptoms such as stomachaches, headaches, fatigue • Persistent boredom and indifference • Violent actions, rebellious behavior, or running away • Intolerance for praise or rewards

Sources: National Mental Health Association; American Academy of Child and Adolescent Psychiatry

Preventing Suicide

Although most thoughts about committing suicide are impulsive and temporary, the unfortunate consequence—death or debilitating injury—is permanent. The warning signs of suicide are described in **Figure 9.2.** Your ability to recognize these signs in yourself or others can mean the difference between life and death. When a teen talks about committing suicide—whether it's done in a serious, casual, or even humorous way—*he or she must be taken seriously.* Never bargain with someone who is thinking about suicide. Any discussion or suggestion about suicide requires immediate intervention. Seek adult assistance without delay.

Despite the fact that depression is very treatable, untreated depression is the leading cause of suicide. People who appear to have mental health problems need to be encouraged repeatedly to seek help—especially if they seem suicidal. With adequate help and support, people suffering from depression, extreme stress, or other mental and emotional problems can often find new purpose and happiness.

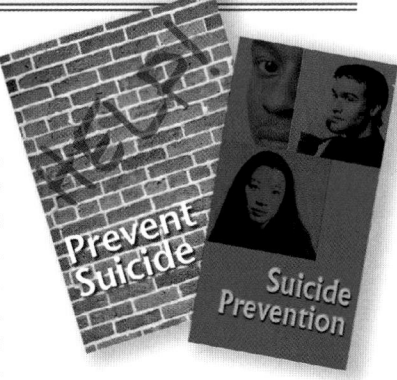

Lesson 2 Suicide Prevention **231**

② TEACH

Discussing

Help students discuss the importance of taking any talk of suicide seriously. Ask: Whom could you ask for help if you thought a friend or family member was considering suicide? **L1**

VISUAL LEARNING

Figure 9.2 Guide students in reading and discussing the verbal and nonverbal warning signs of suicide. Point out specific examples and help students consider the importance of recognizing these remarks and behaviors as indications of serious situations.

Critical Thinking

Remind students that a person suffering from depression feels both helpless and hopeless. Ask: How do those feelings make it difficult for a depressed person to get help? What can be done to overcome those difficulties? **L1**

Critical Thinking

Present the following situation: *A friend says, "I really need to talk. Can you help me? But you have to promise not to tell anyone—I mean anyone! Will you promise?"* Ask: What is the best response to that friend? Why? **L2**

Cooperative Learning Activity

Identifying Sources of Help Every community has resources for helping individuals who feel suicidal. However, they may not be widely publicized or easy to find in a crisis. Discuss with students the importance of knowing about such local resources before one needs them. Ask: What would you consider the best form for publicizing information about these resources? (Examples might include flyers, brochures, business-size information cards, and magnets.) Then ask a group of volunteers to gather information about local resources, including the name and phone number of each agency. Have them work together to present the information in the form students consider most useful.

Health Skills Activity

WHEN A FRIEND SEEMS TROUBLED

DECISION MAKING

NHES Standard 6 Students will demonstrate the ability to use goal setting and decision-making skills to enhance health.

Objectives

- Recognize signs of suicidal behaviors.
- Analyze and apply decision-making skills to help prevent suicides.

Motivator

Give students two minutes to list warning signs of suicide.

Teaching Strategies

1. Emphasize that if a person is unsure whether a friend is seriously troubled, it is better to be safe than sorry and to share concerns with a trusted adult.
2. Reinforce the idea that suicide prevention will require professional help.
3. Allow students to work in small groups to discuss how Jordan might use the model.

✓ Assessment

Using a rubric, student work should provide comprehensive evidence of the following criteria to achieve the highest score:

✔ progression through a decision-making process
✔ identification of the decision to be made
✔ consideration of options and consequences
✔ taking action or making a decision
✔ evaluation or reflection on the decision

Health Skills Activity

Decision Making: When a Friend Seems Troubled

When Ian started exhibiting signs of depression, his friend Jordan tried to persuade him to get help. Ian admitted that he was unhappy. However, he told Jordan, "I appreciate your trying to help me, but it's okay; I'm handling my problems by myself."

Jordan knows that Ian is a private person, but Jordan has never seen his friend this "down" before. Jordan wants to tell someone about his concerns, but he is hesitant about betraying a confidence.

What Would You Do?
Apply the six steps of the decision-making model to Jordan's concerns.

1. State the situation.
2. List the options.
3. Weigh the possible outcomes.
4. Consider values.
5. Make a decision and act.
6. Evaluate the decision.

Did You Know ?

▶ You can use *CLUES* to remember how to communicate effectively with a friend who is suffering emotionally.
Connect (Make contact.)
Listen (Take time and pay attention.)
Understand (Let the person know that you empathize with his or her feelings.)
Express Concern (Say that you care, and stay with the person.)
Seek Help (Encourage the person to talk to an adult, and tell an adult yourself.)

Source: University of Minnesota Extension Service

Helping Others

Suicidal people often believe that their death will not matter to anyone. For this reason, it is critical to show concern and empathy for someone who is talking about suicide. All talk of suicide must be taken seriously. Remember, the suicidal person needs professional help—immediately. When you are with someone who appears to be suicidal, show you care by following these steps.

▶ **Initiate a meaningful conversation.** Showing interest and compassion for a person is an important first step. Listen closely to what that person says; be patient and understanding.

▶ **Show support and ask questions.** Remind the person that most problems have solutions. Make it clear that you understand that the person wants to end his or her pain, but emphasize that suicide is *not* the answer. Share the fact that most suicide survivors later express gratitude that they did not die.

▶ **Try to persuade the person to seek help.** Encourage the person to talk with a parent, counselor, therapist, or other trusted adult. Offer to go with the person to get help.

232 Chapter 9 Mental and Emotional Problems

Curriculum Connections

Language Arts Have interested students read a story in which the protagonist deals with suicide. Ask students to summarize and discuss how the suicide was handled. Ask: How do you think the character's actions were influenced by the time in which he or she lived?

History Ask: How has suicide been regarded in various cultures during specific periods in history? Let interested students choose a culture and a time period and research the attitudes toward and practice of suicide during that time and in that place.

Multiple Suicides

Sometimes within a teen population, **cluster suicides** occur. These are *a series of suicides occurring within a short period of time and involving several people in the same school or community*. Studies have shown that cluster suicides in the United States occur mainly among teens and young adults and may account for as much as 5 percent of all suicides in any given year. Some cluster suicides are the result of pacts or agreements between two or more people to take part in suicide. Others result when individuals commit suicide in response to the suicide of a friend or a suicide that has been sensationalized in the media.

The Centers for Disease Control and Prevention (CDC) has developed guidelines for preventing cluster suicides. Among their recommendations is the evaluation and counseling of close friends and relatives of suicide victims because these people may themselves be at high risk for suicide. The CDC also recommends that the media report on suicide in a way that does not glorify the victim, oversimplify the victim's motivation, or portray the suicide as an understandable response to pressure or emotional pain.

(Y) Suicide can affect people beyond the victim's immediate family and friends.
Why might a teen be affected by the suicide of someone who is a stranger?

 Lesson 2 *Review*

Reviewing Facts and Vocabulary

1. Name five warning signs of suicide.
2. List three risk factors of suicide.
3. Describe some of the strategies for suicide prevention.

Thinking Critically

4. **Analyzing.** How might support from family, friends, or mental health professionals help prevent suicides? What strategies might each of those groups offer to help an individual cope with stress, depression, and anxiety?
5. **Synthesizing.** Why is empathy important when talking with a suicidal person?

Applying Health Skills

Accessing Information. Compile a list of local resources for suicide prevention. This list should include mental health professionals, school counselors, hospital emergency rooms, suicide hotlines, and local authorities (including representatives of the police and fire departments).

WEB SITES Researching valid Web sites can provide additional information on resources for suicide intervention. See **health.glencoe.com** for more information on using Web sites.

Lesson 2 Suicide Prevention **233**

---

(3) ASSESS

EVALUATING THE LESSON

Assign and discuss the Lesson 2 Review; then administer, grade, and discuss Lesson Quiz 32 in the TCR.

RETEACHING

- Invite students to work in small groups to list at least eight warning signs of suicide and three strategies for preventing suicide.
- Ask students to complete Reteaching Activity 32 in the TCR.

ENRICHMENT

Ask a small group of interested students to interview a suicide counselor or a person who answers a suicide hotline. What special training does the person have? What are the main objectives in talking with someone contemplating suicide? What problems are most commonly heard? Have these students share their findings with the rest of the class.

(4) CLOSE

Have each student write a paragraph explaining the strategies for suicide prevention. Remind them to check for spelling and grammar.

 Lesson 2 *Review*

Answers to Reviewing Facts and Vocabulary

1. See Figure 9.2 on page 231 for possible answers.
2. Any three of risk factors of suicide identified on page 230.
3. Possible answers: seek adult assistance; persuade the suicidal person to seek professional help; show concern and empathy.

Answers to Thinking Critically

4. Possible answer: Support and intervention will show that other people are concerned and empathetic; they might convince a suicidal person that his or her life matters. Strategies will vary.
5. Being able to relate to someone's emotional pain helps show that you care.

Getting Help

❶ FOCUS

QUICK START Have a volunteer read the Quick Start assignment aloud. Give students three minutes to jot down their responses. Then have students read aloud their responses while you list each explanation on the board.

TYING TO PRIOR KNOWLEDGE

Remind students that they are already familiar with a number of sources of help for various kinds of problems. Tell them that in this lesson they will learn where and how to get help with mental and emotional problems.

Health Skills Features

"Evaluating Sources of Self-Help," p. 235

ACCESSING INFORMATION

INTRODUCING VOCABULARY

- Ask students: What do the vocabulary terms have in common? How is each different from the other? After a brief discussion, have students use the Glossary to check the definition of each term.

- Ask students to complete the Chapter 9 Study Guide in the *Student Activity Workbook.* 📁

Getting Help

VOCABULARY

psychotherapy
behavior therapy
cognitive therapy
group therapy
biomedical
   therapy

YOU'LL LEARN TO

- Relate the importance of early detection and warning signs that prompt people to seek mental health care.

- Explore the methods for addressing critical mental health issues.

- Identify and describe mental health services.

QUICK START On a sheet of paper, explain why some people may find it difficult to seek help for mental and emotional problems.

 Many sources of help are available to people who have mental health concerns. *How would you evaluate sources of help for appropriateness?*

Recognizing the early symptoms of mental and emotional problems is critically important to getting help for them. Knowing some specific symptoms of mental disorders can help a person determine if he or she should seek help.

Knowing When to Get Help

It can be difficult to ask for help in coping with mental or emotional problems. Our thoughts are private, and we tend to hide those that embarrass us or those we can't control. However, we usually need help most when we feel like asking for it least. Seek help if any of the feelings or behaviors listed below persist over a period of days or weeks and begin to interfere with other aspects of daily living.

▶ You feel trapped with no way out, or you worry all the time.

▶ Your feelings affect your sleep, eating habits, school work, job performance, or relationships.

▶ Your family or friends express concern about your behavior.

▶ You are becoming involved with alcohol or other drugs.

▶ You are becoming increasingly aggressive, violent, or reckless.

Lesson 3 *Resources*

Teacher Classroom Resources

📁 Concept Mapping Activity 33

📁 Current Health Issues 9

📁 Guided Reading Activities 33

📁 Lesson Plan 33

📁 Lesson Quiz 33

📁 Reteaching Activity 33

Student Activity Workbook

📁 Applying Health Skills 33

📁 Chapter 9 Study Guide

Multimedia

🖱 Transparency 25

Signs That Professional Help Is Needed

Some symptoms that are severe enough to require intervention by a mental health professional include: prolonged sadness for no specific reason; frequent outbursts of anger; overwhelming fear, anxiety, or anger at the world; unexplainable change in sleeping or eating habits; and social withdrawal. Of course, if you have any doubt about your mental health, you should always get assistance. Like most forms of sickness, mental disorders may get worse if left untreated.

Did You Know ?

The first source of help for teens with mental health concerns is a parent or guardian. After discussing the issue, parents and their teens can evaluate the available options and seek help together.

Real-Life Application

Evaluating Sources of Self-Help

Thousands of self-help materials are available in print, on tapes and CDs, and online. Many people have benefited from self-help resources, but others have wasted time and money and sometimes risked their health. Use these questions to evaluate self-help materials.

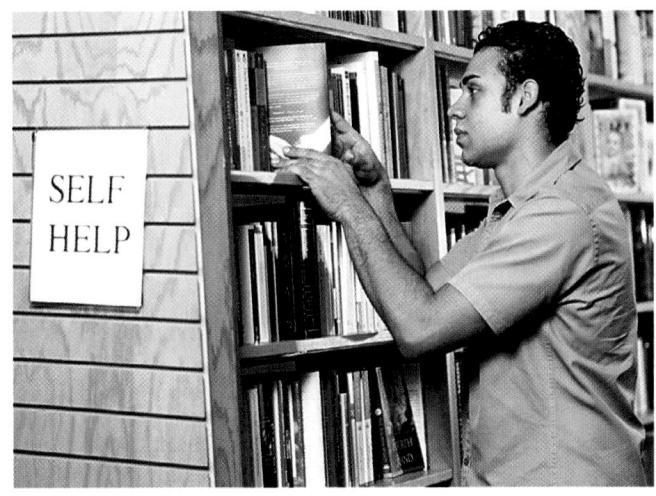

ACTIVITY

Choose a self-help book, magazine article, CD, or Web site and evaluate the information using the criteria listed here. Share your findings with the class, and recommend any useful and appropriate sources to the school librarian.

Are you being advised to try medication or some other remedy?
Check first with a health professional. Certain herbs, for example, can be harmful and even life-threatening.

What are the qualifications of the authors?
Do they have university-based training in mental health? Have they published in professional journals? For books, check the reference section for citations from professional journals.

Is the material backed by a nationally known and respected mental health organization?
Look for recommendations from organizations such as the American Psychological Association or the National Institute of Mental Health.

Is a cost involved?
If you are asked online for a credit card number or personal information, use caution and check with a parent or guardian.

Dealing with Sensitive Issues

Teens and Mental Health Professionals
Help students recognize that people see mental health professionals for many reasons, not just because they have a mental disorder. Explain that people seek help to strengthen family or marital relationships, to cope with sudden loss such as the death of a family member, or to manage stress. Those seeking professional help can also include people who need help adjusting to a new or difficult situation; or those dealing with addiction, alcohol abuse, problems at school or work, or divorce. Tell students that therapy helps people to understand themselves better and thus to live more healthful and productive lives.

You may wish to invite a guest speaker from a school or community clinic to elaborate on some reasons for seeking help.

2 TEACH

Real-Life Application

EVALUATING SOURCES OF SELF-HELP

ACCESSING INFORMATION

NHES Standard 2 Students will demonstrate the ability to access valid health information and health-promoting products and services.

Objectives

- Develop evaluation criteria for health information.

- Demonstrate the ability to evaluate resources from home, school, and community that provide valid health information.

Motivator

Display a variety of self-help books and magazines.

Teaching Strategies

1. Have students work in small groups to apply evaluation criteria.

2. Suggest that students try to find one valid and one questionable resource, then compare them.

Assessment

Using a rubric, student work should provide comprehensive evidence of the following criteria to achieve the highest score:

✔ citation of specific sources
✔ evaluation of the validity of the source
✔ rationale for the appropriateness of the source

Discussing

Help students discuss the importance of recognizing feelings and behaviors that indicate a need for help. Remind students that everyone feels worried sometimes. However, worry that lasts for weeks and interferes with daily living is a sign that help is needed.
L1

Health Skills Practice

Important Listening Skills What makes a good listener? How do listening skills change when a friend seems depressed or possibly suicidal? Invite students meet in groups to discuss their ideas in response to these questions.

COMMUNICATION SKILLS

VISUAL LEARNING

Figure 9.3 Have students read about and discuss each kind of mental health professional. Let volunteers add details to each description and, if possible, name local practitioners.

Cooperative Learning

Have students meet in groups to discuss the stumbling blocks to seeking help. How can each be overcome? **L1**

FIGURE 9.3

MENTAL HEALTH PROFESSIONALS

- **Psychiatrist**—a physician who specializes in diagnosing and treating mental disorders and can prescribe medications
- **Neurologist**—a physician who specializes in organic disorders of the brain and nervous system
- **Clinical Psychologist**—a professional who diagnoses and treats emotional and behavioral disorders by means of counseling but cannot prescribe medications
- **Counselor**—a professional who works to help people with personal and educational matters
- **Psychiatric Social Worker**—a professional who provides guidance and treatment for clients with emotional problems, usually in the setting of a mental hospital, mental health clinic, or family service agency
- **School Psychologist**—a professional who specializes in the assessment of learning, emotional, and behavioral problems of schoolchildren

Seeking Help

Most people tend to wait too long before seeking help even though there are many people in their lives who are willing and eager to assist them. Besides parents and guardians, who are usually the most accessible, there are teachers, school psychologists, counselors, coaches, clergy members, and crisis hotlines. According to the Surgeon General, school is the place where children and teens are most likely to receive treatment. **Figure 9.3** provides a list of mental health professionals to whom a person might be referred for help.

STUMBLING BLOCKS TO SEEKING HELP

Some people are afraid to seek help for mental or emotional problems. They see these problems as a sign of weakness, not as a legitimate illness. If you or someone you know is reluctant to seek help, remember these facts.

▶ Asking for help from a mental health professional does not mean that a person is weak. Rather, asking for needed help is a sign of strength. It shows responsibility for one's own wellness.

▶ People who have mental disorders often cannot get better on their own. Serious disorders, clinical depression, compulsions, and addictions are complex and require professional intervention.

▶ Sharing your deepest thoughts with a "stranger" is not painful or embarrassing. In fact, most people are surprised and happy to find that unloading problems is a great relief.

Home and Community

Counseling Students may seek support and counseling from their peers as their first step in getting help with problems. Often, teens don't know when to provide friendly support and when to refer their friend to a trained adult. Young people may feel that a problem isn't serious enough to bother an adult or that adults would not understand.

It's important to empower students with knowledge about mental illness and to know the difference between just feeling "blue" and being depressed. Let students know who is available to counsel students in the school and in the community, including students' parents and guardians.

Therapy Methods

A mental health professional may use any of several treatment methods, depending on his or her area of expertise and the needs of the patient. The following are the most commonly used therapy methods.

▶ **Psychotherapy** is *an ongoing dialogue between a patient and a mental health professional.* The dialogue is designed to find the root cause of a problem and devise a solution.

▶ **Behavior therapy** is *a treatment process that focuses on changing unwanted behaviors through rewards and reinforcements.*

▶ **Cognitive therapy** is *a treatment method designed to identify and correct distorted thinking patterns that can lead to feelings and behaviors that may be troublesome, self-defeating, or self-destructive.*

▶ **Group therapy** involves *treating a group of people who have similar problems and who meet regularly with a trained counselor.*

▶ **Biomedical therapy** is *the use of certain medications to treat or reduce the symptoms of a mental disorder.* It is sometimes used alone, but is often combined with other treatment methods, such as those listed above.

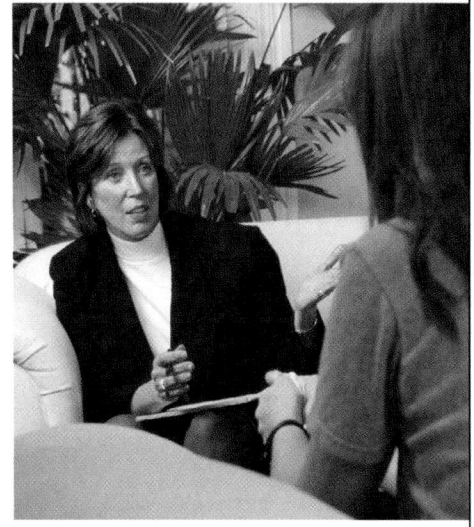

Most forms of therapy involve counseling. *What are some short-term and long-term benefits of receiving help for a mental health problem?*

Lesson 3 Review

Reviewing Facts and Vocabulary

1. Identify three signals that may indicate a person needs help with a mental or an emotional problem.
2. Why do some people delay seeking help for mental or emotional problems?
3. Define *group therapy*, and use the term in a sentence.

Thinking Critically

4. **Synthesizing.** Identify at least three personal qualities one would need to fill a position at a mental health clinic.
5. **Analyzing.** What factors might determine from whom you would seek help for a mental problem?

Applying Health Skills

Decision Making. Imagine that you have a friend who is always making negative comments and seems to be withdrawing from his or her normal activities. Use the six steps of decision making to determine what actions to take.

TECHNOLOGY *OPTION*

WORD PROCESSING Using a word-processing program can help you better organize your thoughts. See **health.glencoe.com** for information on using word-processing software.

Lesson 3 Getting Help **237**

Lesson 3 Review

Answers to Reviewing Facts and Vocabulary

1. Any three of the signals on page 234.
2. Possible answer: They may feel ashamed or embarrassed about their problem.
3. The form of therapy that usually involves groups of people who have similar problems and who meet regularly with a counselor. Sentences will vary.

Answers to Thinking Critically

4. Possible answers: empathy, good communication skills, compassion, and ability to analyze a situation.
5. Possible answers: severity of problem, accessibility, qualifications, level of expertise, and trustworthiness of mental health professional.

---

③ ASSESS

EVALUATING THE LESSON

Assign and discuss the Lesson 3 Review; then administer, grade, and discuss Lesson Quiz 33 in the TCR. ☞

RETEACHING

- Have students write one fact from each heading to review the most important concepts.
- Ask students to complete Reteaching Activity 33 in the TCR. ☞

ENRICHMENT

Have students recall TV shows in which characters deal with mental health problems and/or services. Ask them to write brief summaries to be shared with the rest of the class. Then encourage students to discuss the depiction of mental health problems and services: How were problems handled? Were they solved? If so, how? Which services did the characters access? With what success? Conclude by asking: Does this TV show reinforce positive or negative thinking about mental health and mental disorders? Why? ▭

④ CLOSE

In their private health journals, have students create a diagram comprised of three concentric circles. In the inner circle, have them identify who they could go to for help with *any* problem. In the circle surrounding the inner circle, have them identify who they could go to for help with *most* problems. In the outer circle, have them identify who they could go to for help with *some* problems.

Understanding Death and Grief

1 FOCUS

QUICK START Draw an empty word web on the board as an example. Write *grief* in the center shape. Then have students copy the web and complete it, adding their own words in each surrounding shape.

TYING TO PRIOR KNOWLEDGE

Invite volunteers to share their own definitions of grief. Explain that students will learn more about the grieving process as they study this lesson.

Health Skills Features

"An Encouraging Word," p. 240

COMMUNICATION SKILLS

INTRODUCING VOCABULARY

- Have students look up each vocabulary term in the Glossary.

- Ask students to complete the Chapter 9 Study Guide in the *Student Activity Workbook*. 🗁

Understanding Death and Grief

VOCABULARY
coping
grief response
mourning

YOU'LL LEARN TO
- Describe the different kinds of emotional loss.
- Identify the stages of the grieving process.
- Discuss the ways in which people cope with emotional loss.
- Examine issues related to death and grieving.
- Analyze the importance of using community mental health services to help cope with grief.

QUICK START What words come to mind when you imagine dealing with the loss of someone or something of great value? Write the word *grief* at the center of a sheet of paper. Write words you associate with grieving on your paper, and make a word web by drawing lines from those words to the word *grief*.

Flowers and cards are appropriate expressions of sympathy for someone who has suffered a loss. *In what other ways can you show support?*

L oss is a part of life. Although it is always difficult and painful to lose someone you love or care for, learning to cope with grief is an important part of human development. The strong bonds we form with others can help us deal with loss in appropriate ways and accept it as a part of the entire life experience.

Different Kinds of Loss

Y ou have probably experienced losses that resulted in emotional distress. Perhaps you missed a chance to play in a championship game because of an injury or failed to get the grade you needed on an important exam. You may have experienced rejection; the breakup of a relationship; or the loss of a pet, friend, or family member to death. Maybe you have had to move or change schools and have felt the loss of whatever—or whomever—you left behind. A strong emotional attachment can make loss deeply painful.

238 **Chapter 9** Mental and Emotional Problems

Lesson 4 *Resources*

Teacher Classroom Resources
🗁 Concept Mapping Activity 34
🗁 Guided Reading Activities 34
🗁 Lesson Plan 34
🗁 Lesson Quiz 34
🗁 Reteaching Activity 34

Student Activity Workbook
🗁 Applying Health Skills 34
🗁 Chapter 9 Study Guide

Expressions of Grief

Coping is *dealing successfully with difficult changes in your life.* When a loss occurs, it's common and natural to experience a **grief response,** *an individual's total response to a major loss.* The way a person responds to loss is unique to the situation and to the individual. If a death is sudden or traumatic, for example, the response is likely to be somewhat different from the response to a death that resulted from a long-term illness. A person's perspective on the lost relationship and his or her ability to remain open to interaction in other relationships might also affect the response to loss.

The Grieving Process

Mental health professionals have recognized a common phenomenon, called the *grieving process,* that occurs during the grief response. The purpose of this process is to reach closure, or acceptance of a loss. There is no correct way of experiencing loss, but the stages of grief reflect a variety of reactions that may occur as people work through the process. The reactions, which were identified in part by the noted Swiss American doctor Elisabeth Kübler-Ross, include the following:

▶ **Denial or Numbness.** In this stage, the person cannot believe the loss has occurred. This part of the process protects the person from being overwhelmed by his or her emotions.

▶ **Emotional Releases.** These reactions come with recognition of the loss and often involve periods of crying, which is important to the healing process.

▶ **Anger.** Feeling powerless and unfairly deprived, the person may lash out at whatever is perceived to be responsible for the loss. Sometimes a general resentment toward life sets in.

▶ **Bargaining.** As the reality of the loss becomes clear, the person may promise to change if only what was lost can be returned, even for a little while.

▶ **Depression.** Beyond the natural feelings of sadness, feelings of isolation, alienation, and hopelessness occur as the person recognizes the extent of the loss.

▶ **Remorse.** The person may become preoccupied with thoughts about what he or she could have done to prevent the loss or make things better.

▶ **Acceptance.** This stage can involve a sense of power, allowing the person to face reality in constructive ways and make significant and meaningful gestures surrounding the idea of loss.

▶ **Hope.** Eventually the person reaches a point when remembering becomes less painful and he or she begins to look ahead to the future.

Health Minute

Breaking Up

The breakup of a relationship can cause a person to experience many of the stages of grief. These feelings are a natural part of the healing process.

Overcoming a breakup:

▶ Allow yourself to feel the pain associated with the breakup. Denying your feelings only prolongs the grief process.

▶ Recognize that self-blame and guilt are defenses against feeling out of control. Remember that you can't control another person's decisions or behaviors.

▶ Be thankful for the good times you've had and the contributions the relationship has made to your life.

▶ Give yourself time to heal. Allow yourself to have new experiences and to make new friends, but avoid comparing new relationships with the one that has ended.

---

② TEACH

Discussing

Guide students in discussing the relationship between coping and a grief response. Emphasize that dealing successfully with difficult changes involves experiencing—not ignoring—painful feelings. **L1**

Cooperative Learning

Divide the class into eight small groups. Assign each group one of the stages of loss. Ask each group to identify behaviors they might see in someone at this stage. How can a friend show support to someone in each stage? **L1**

Critical Thinking

The death of a close relative may affect different family members in different ways. Ask students how family members can help each other through this difficult time. Where else can people turn for support and understanding? **L1**

Health Minute

Have students meet in groups to read and discuss the Health Minute introduction and suggestions. Encourage group members to describe some of the feelings involved in a breakup and to relate those feelings to the stages of the grieving process.

Activity

Have a small group of volunteers research grief counseling as a career and, if possible, interview a local grief counselor. Ask these students to share their findings with the rest of the class. **L3**

239

More About...

Coping with Loss Almost all societies express grief through rituals of mourning for the dead. When the mourning period is over, a ritual of reintegrating the mourners back into the group usually takes place. This is important because death is the most socially and emotionally disruptive event the majority of people ever experience.

Worldwide expressions of grief vary. They may include shaving one's head, going unbathed, or smearing the body with clay or ashes. Mourners may tear their clothing, gash themselves, wail, or go into seclusion for varying lengths of time.

Hands-On Health

AN ENCOURAGING WORD

COMMUNICATION SKILLS

NHES Standard 5 Students will demonstrate the ability to use interpersonal communication skills to enhance health.

Objectives

- Examine issues related to death and grieving.
- Demonstrate the ability to support others who experience loss.

Motivator

Display a variety of greeting cards. Ask students how they feel when a friend offers a note or card of encouragement.

Teaching Strategies

1. Have several greeting cards available to use as models.
2. Approve students' draft messages before allowing them access to the card stock paper. Re-direct students if messages are frivolous or inappropriate.
3. Ask volunteer services at local hospitals, extended care facilities, and hospices what types of cards would be most appreciated.

✓ Assessment

Using a rubric, student work should provide comprehensive evidence of the following criteria to achieve the highest score:
- ✔ written message of comfort and support
- ✔ use of appropriate images
- ✔ ability to show empathy

Hands-On Health ACTIVITY

An Encouraging Word

Much of the day-to-day comforting of terminally ill persons is carried out by dedicated volunteers. These volunteers often experience a profound sense of loss when the patient passes away. A word of support in the form of a card will encourage these volunteers to continue their important work.

What You'll Need

- card stock paper
- felt-tip pens in different colors
- computer with clip art software (optional)

What You'll Do

1. On 8½" x 11" notebook paper, compose several versions of a message. Many volunteers report that inspirational messages are helpful.

2. Sketch the artwork you will include in your card. The artwork should emphasize serenity, peace, or hope. You may want to examine clip art options from a computer program for ideas.

3. Decide what "goodies," such as a flower or candy, to include with your card.

4. Create your card, using card stock paper and felt-tip pens or computer clip art.

Apply and Conclude

Send your card to a hospital, hospice, or other facility in which volunteers provide support for terminally ill people. Then compose a reflective essay describing what you have learned about dealing with loss and grieving by empathizing with those who work with terminally ill patients.

Did You Know ❓

➤ Unresolved grief tends to affect the grieving process at the next occurrence of a loss—causing a person to express some emotions and responses that have been held back. The surfacing of unresolved grief reactions can slow and complicate the healing process.

Coping with Death

To help cope with death, allow some time to reflect on who you were before the loss and who you will be after grieving. Focus on what you were able to do in the relationship, not what you could or should have done. Remember the wonderful things about the person and the good times you've shared. Another way to reach closure is by seeking support from others or writing a letter to say good-bye.

Helping Others Through the Grieving Process

Support from family and friends is important during **mourning**, or *the act of showing sorrow or grief*. While it is up to the individual to go through the grieving process, he or she doesn't have to do it alone. You can help by showing empathy or just being there to listen. Share your memories and appreciation of the person who is gone. Talking about experiences and memories can help survivors bridge the transition.

Curriculum Connections

Language Arts Death and grief can be particularly difficult for children. In response to their needs, various books are now available to help children understand the death of a family member or friend and accept their own grief response. Ask a group of interested students to identify, read, and review at least five such books. Have students create written reviews of the books, comparing and contrasting treatment of the theme. It may help students to organize their thoughts beforehand into an outline. Remind students to proofread for errors before writing their final drafts.

Grief Counseling

Seeing a counselor or therapist who specializes in grief can help people through the grieving process. These specialists often can be found through community mental health services, such as hospices.

Coping with Disasters and Crises

Traumatic or sudden events, such as natural disasters, can leave people feeling a range of emotions from numb and helpless to horrified and afraid. Using effective coping mechanisms can ease the process of recovery.

▶ Spend time with other people, and discuss your feelings.

▶ Get back to daily routines as quickly as possible.

▶ Eat nutritious foods, exercise, and get enough rest and sleep.

▶ Do something positive to help your community through the event, such as assisting with cleanup or raising money for aid.

Ⓨ Memorial services are times for remembering and showing respect. *What are some other ways to remember a loved one?*

 Lesson 4 *Review*

Reviewing Facts and Vocabulary

1. Name the stages that may be involved in the grieving process.
2. Define the term *grief response*.
3. List three strategies for coping with disasters and crises.

Thinking Critically

4. **Analyzing.** How might coping with a death resulting from a long-term illness differ from coping with a sudden death caused by an accident?
5. **Applying.** Recall a story of personal loss that you saw in a movie or on a TV show or that you read about in a magazine article or book. Write a paragraph that describes the process the grieving character went through to reach closure.

Applying Health Skills

Communication Skills. How could you express support to a friend who is suffering from a tragic loss? Make a list of things you could say to comfort someone in such a situation. Your statements should show consideration, respect, and empathy.

SPREADSHEETS Spreadsheets offer a quick and easy way to organize and edit a list. See **health.glencoe.com** for tips on using spreadsheets.

Lesson 4 Understanding Death and Grief **241**

---

❸ ASSESS

EVALUATING THE LESSON

Assign and discuss the Lesson 4 Review; then administer, grade, and discuss Lesson Quiz 34 in the TCR. 🗁

RETEACHING

- Have students sketch designs or pictures to represent the stages of the grieving process.

- Ask students to complete Reteaching Activity 34 in the TCR. 🗁

ENRICHMENT

Let students work in groups to gather information from magazines or newspapers about recent traumatic or sudden events. What happened? How did people respond? What support was offered to the victims? What mourning rituals and activities for positive contribution were organized by the community? Who participated? Have each group discuss its findings with the rest of the class.

❹ CLOSE

Have each student identify, either orally or in writing, an important new fact he or she has learned about grief.

 Lesson 4 *Review*

Answers to Reviewing Facts and Vocabulary

1. Denial or numbness, emotional releases, anger, bargaining, depression, remorse, acceptance, hope.
2. An individual's total response to a major loss.
3. Any three strategies identified on page 241.

Answers to Thinking Critically

4. Possible answer: A long-term illness may offer an opportunity to gradually go through some of the stages of the grieving process. It can also provide time for final interactions. A sudden death leaves no time for preparation.
5. Paragraphs will vary.

Creating Positive Media Influences

NHES Standard 4 Students will analyze the influence of culture, media, technology, and other factors on health.

Objective

Help design a media campaign that will promote awareness of mental health issues.

Motivator

Ask students to brainstorm ways in which mass media might convey positive messages about mental health and mental health care.

Teaching Strategies

Awareness Tell students that media attention can increase public awareness about critical health issues and help dispel stereotypes and decrease discrimination.

Analysis Media attention on the Americans with Disabilities Act (ADA) helped bring about President Bush's mental health initiatives.

Reflection As students begin creating their media campaign, ask them to recall positive media images they have seen of people with disabilities.

Take Action Encourage students to write a letters to local newspapers, showing support for the fair and equitable treatment of people with mental illnesses.

✓ Assessment

Each group of students should focus on one particular aspect of the media campaign. The pieces should convey compassionate encouragement for those who suffer from mental illnesses or educate the public about mental illnesses and promote fair treatment for people who suffer from them.

242

Eye ON THE Media

Creating Positive Media Influences

In April 2002, President George W. Bush's New Freedom Commission on Mental Health initiated a comprehensive study to assess the mental health care system in the United States. The commission's efforts brought national media attention to the issue of mental health. In this activity, you will help design a media campaign in your community that will promote awareness of mental health issues.

"Our country must make a commitment: Americans with mental illness deserve our understanding, and they deserve excellent care."

ACTIVITY

Based on what you have learned, you and your class will design a positive media campaign that will accomplish the following: encourage people to seek help when faced with mental or emotional problems; convey empathy for people who suffer from mental or emotional problems; and teach the public that people with mental illnesses should be treated fairly.

Your teacher will divide the class into groups to create the following components of your media campaign: a slogan, a direct mail marketing piece, a billboard, and a print ad for a newspaper or magazine.

EXPRESS YOUR VIEWS

In a class discussion, share your views on the potential impact of media portrayals of mentally ill people. What can television dramas and local news programs do to help educate the public about mental health issues?

242 Chapter 9 Review

More About...

Government Initiatives President George W. Bush's New Freedom Commission on Mental Health was a call to action for government and private sector organizations in the mental health care system. For instance, in recent decades, advocates in the mental health field have struggled to ensure that insurance companies cover treatments for mental illnesses to the same degree that they cover treatments for other illnesses such as diabetes or high blood pressure. Government initiatives such as those outlined by the New Freedom Commission on Mental Health lend credence to the efforts of mental health advocates striving for equitable treatment of people with mental illnesses.

CROSS-CURRICULUM CONNECTIONS

Write a Poem. Knowing that they have the love and support of friends and family can help people through the grieving process. Imagine that a friend has suffered the loss of a loved one. Write a poem expressing sympathy, support, and hope to help the friend through the difficult time.

Research Cultural Rituals. Rituals to help people cope with death go back to ancient times. Study various burial traditions and ceremonies from throughout the ages, and share your findings in a short oral presentation to your class. How are these customs similar to or different from the ways Americans confront death today?

Calculate Percentage. Among children and adolescents, the portion of those who suffer from mental health problems is 20 percent. If a third of these individuals receive treatment, what percentage of all children and adolescents do *not* get help for mental disorders?

Research Neurotransmitters. Abnormal levels of neurotransmitters can contribute to mental illness. Research the following neurotransmitters: dopamine, serotonin, glutamate, phenylethylamine, epinephrine, norepinephrine, acetylcholine, oxytocin. Create a chart that shows their relationship to the forms of mental disorders discussed in the chapter.

CAREER Corner

Psychologist

Are you interested in human behavior and the mental processes related to behavior? Do you enjoy talking with people and helping them with their problems? If so, a career as a psychologist might be for you. Psychologists counsel individuals to help them resolve mental and emotional problems.

If you want to be an advocate for children, you might consider specializing in school psychology. A school psychologist specializes in educational assessment, childhood development, behavioral management, individual and group counseling, and consultation.

To become a psychologist, you will need at least a master's degree. A doctoral degree is required for clinical counseling. Find out more about this and other health careers by clicking on Career Corner at **health.glencoe.com**.

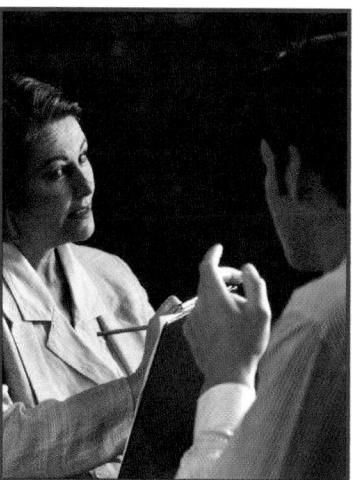

Chapter 9 Review **243**

CROSS-CURRICULUM CONNECTIONS

Enrich student learning by connecting the topic of mental and emotional problems to one of the four subject areas presented on this page. The activity may be completed individually or with a partner.

Language Arts Poems may be in free verse or follow more traditional formats. Messages should be thoughtful and sincere.

Social Studies Ask a local grief counselor to visit your classroom to discuss modern day funeral customs.

Math Answer:
$20\% \times 33.33\% = 6.7\%$

Science Have students access reliable print or online sources to research the neurotransmitters. Appropriate connections between the neurotransmitters and mental disorders should be presented.

CAREER Corner

Have students read and discuss the Career Corner feature. Ask interested students to explore the Glencoe Health Web site at **health.glencoe.com** for more information on career possibilities for psychologists.

Portfolio Assessment

Self-Evaluation Direct students to review the Health Skills Activities and other activities completed in the chapter. Encourage each student to select one finished product or activity that demonstrates his or her best work for the chapter and that represents the student's learning goals. Have students explain what they have learned and how the examples they have selected demonstrate their growth in health literacy, knowledge, and skills.

Teacher Classroom Resources Assign Performance Assessment 9, "Phobias," in the TCR.

CHECKING COMPREHENSION

- Assign and discuss the chapter review.
- Use the Chapter 9 MindJogger Videoquiz to review the chapter. ▶◀

CHAPTER 9 REVIEW ANSWERS

Exploring Health Terms

1. mental disorder
2. mood disorder
3. conduct disorder
4. cluster suicide
5. suicide
6. alienation
7. Group therapy
8. biomedical therapy
9. cognitive therapy
10. behavior therapy
11. Psychotherapy
12. coping
13. grief response
14. mourning

Recalling the Facts

1. Events may include personal assault (rape, muggings), natural or human-caused disasters (fires, earthquakes, floods, bombings), car or plane crashes, and military combat.
2. Anorexia nervosa and bulimia nervosa.
3. People with antisocial personality disorder tend to be irritable, aggressive, impulsive, and violent. In many cases, they are unable to show remorse for their behavior.
4. Seek immediate help from a trusted adult.

▶ **EXPLORING HEALTH TERMS** Answer the following questions on a sheet of paper.

Lesson 1 Match each definition with the correct term.

anxiety disorder conduct disorder
eating disorder mental disorder
post-traumatic stress disorder mood disorder

1. An illness of the mind that can affect the thoughts, feelings, and behaviors of a person, preventing him or her from leading a happy, healthy, productive life.
2. An illness, often with an organic cause, that relates to emotions and may involve mood extremes that interfere with everyday living.
3. A pattern of behavior in which the rights of others or basic social rules are violated.

Lesson 2 Fill in the blanks with the correct term.

suicide cluster suicide alienation

A (_4_) can occur in a community when a local (_5_) is sensationalized in the media. These behaviors often result from feelings of depression and (_6_).

Lesson 3 Replace the underlined words with the correct term.

behavior therapy biomedical therapy
cognitive therapy group therapy
psychotherapy

7. Psychotherapy usually involves several people.
8. A psychiatrist may use behavior therapy if medication is needed in the treatment.
9. A distorted thinking pattern requires group therapy.
10. The therapy that uses rewards and reinforcements is called cognitive therapy.
11. Biomedical therapy involves an ongoing dialogue between a patient and a mental health professional.

Lesson 4 Match each definition with the correct term.

mourning grief response coping

12. Dealing successfully with difficult changes in your life.
13. An individual's total response to a major loss.
14. The act of showing sorrow or grief.

▶ **RECALLING THE FACTS** Use complete sentences to answer the following questions.

Lesson 1

1. What types of events are associated with post-traumatic stress disorder?
2. Name two eating disorders.
3. Describe antisocial personality disorder.

Lesson 2

4. What should you do if you recognize the warning signs of suicide in yourself or others?
5. List three actions a person can take if he or she is with someone who appears to be suicidal.
6. What are the CDC's guidelines for preventing cluster suicides?

Lesson 3

7. Where are teens and children most likely to receive treatment for mental health problems?
8. Name six types of mental health professionals.
9. List three therapy methods for treating mental disorders.

Lesson 4

10. List three examples of loss.
11. What is one means of reaching closure after the death of a loved one?
12. How can you help someone who is mourning?

5. Initiate a meaningful conversation, show support and ask questions, try to persuade the person to seek help.
6. Evaluation and counseling of close friends and relatives of suicide victims; media reports that do not glorify suicide victims, oversimplify the victim's motivation, or portray suicide as an understandable response to pressure or emotional pain.
7. In school.
8. Psychiatrist, neurologist, psychologist, counselor, psychiatric social worker, school psychologist.
9. Any three: psychotherapy, behavior therapy, biomedical therapy, cognitive therapy, group therapy.

► THINKING CRITICALLY

1. **Summarizing.** If a teen with a conduct disorder does not get treatment, he or she may have trouble adapting to adulthood. Explain this statement using examples from the text or from your own observations. *(LESSON 1)*

2. **Synthesizing.** How might you respond to someone who expresses the desire to take his or her life and asks you to promise not to tell anyone? *(LESSON 2)*

3. **Applying.** A friend tells you that she is uncomfortable seeking help from a mental health professional for a mental disorder. What could you say to her? *(LESSON 3)*

4. **Synthesizing.** What are some skills a grief counselor should exhibit? Where might you access the help of such a counselor? *(LESSON 4)*

► HEALTH SKILLS APPLICATION

1. **Analyzing Influences.** Briefly describe some movies or television shows that have portrayed characters with mental disorders. Do you think that these depictions are realistic, accurate, and sensitive? How do you think media representations of mental disorders affect how the public views mental problems? *(LESSON 1)*

2. **Advocacy.** Write a letter to your school newspaper to raise awareness of teen suicide as a serious problem. Include information on what everyone can do to help prevent teen suicide. *(LESSON 2)*

3. **Accessing Information.** Evaluate the availability of mental health professionals in your community. *(LESSON 3)*

4. **Practicing Healthful Behaviors.** Develop a strategy for coping with loss. Think about what would make you feel better if you were grieving a loss. Make a list of actions you could take to cope with the situation and with your feelings. *(LESSON 4)*

 BEYOND *the* Classroom

Parent Involvement

Accessing Information. Learn more about family counseling centers that are available in your community. With your parents, create a pamphlet that highlights the services offered through the centers, the costs of these services, and where financial assistance for counseling can be found. Provide the pamphlet to your school counselor.

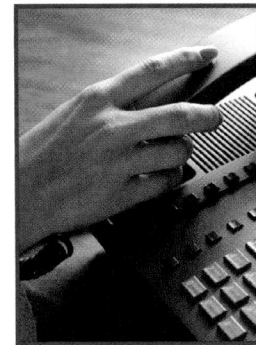

School and Community

Crisis Centers. Identify local crisis centers that help teens deal with mental health problems. Contact the centers to determine how a person could become a volunteer either in the centers or on their associated hotlines.

10. Any three: loss of a friend; death of a pet, friend, or family member; the loss of a position or desired outcome such as a place on a team, a grade, or a scholarship; breaking up with a boyfriend or girlfriend.

11. Possible answer: by seeking support from others or writing a letter to say good-bye.

12. Possible answer: by showing empathy or just listening.

Thinking Critically

1. Answers will vary, but should discuss how the person may develop antisocial behaviors and have problems maintaining relationships and holding a job.

2. Answers will vary but should emphasize that such a promise should not be agreed to or kept.

3. Answers will vary but should explain that getting professional treatment for a mental disorder is no different from getting treatment for a physical illness.

4. Answers will vary but should mention characteristics such as empathy, compassion, and strong communication skills. Grief counselors may be available through community resources including religious institutions, funeral homes, and mental health services.

Health Skills Application

1.–4. Answers will vary.

EVALUATE

- Use the reproducible Chapter 9 Test in the TCR, or construct your own using the Testmaker software.
- Use Performance Assessment 9 in the TCR.

ENRICHMENT

Ask students to complete Enrichment Activity 9 in the TCR.

 BEYOND *the* Classroom

Keep students involved in the community, and encourage parent participation by assigning the activities on this page for students to work on outside of class.

Lessons	Standards		Features
	National	**State/Local**	
1 **Foundations of Healthy Relationships** *pages 248–253*	National Health Education Standards **1.4, 5.1, 5.2, 5.3, 5.4**		**Real-Life Application** • The Importance of Good Character to Friendships *(Communication)*, page 253
2 **Communicating Effectively** *pages 254–261*	National Health Education Standards **5.1, 5.2, 5.3, 5.4**		**Hands-On Health** • Demonstrating Empathy *(Practicing Healthful Behaviors)*, page 258 **Health Skills Activity** • Expressing Disapproval of Bullying *(Communication)*, page 259
3 **Resolving Conflict** *pages 262–267*	National Health Education Standards **5.5, 5.6, 5.7, 5.8**		**Exploring Issues** • What Causes Conflict to Escalate? page 265

Reproducible Resources	Assessment	Technology
Student Activity Workbook for use with each chapter	📁 Lesson Quiz 35	🕹 Transparency 26
📁 Concept Mapping Activity 35		💿 TeacherWorks®
📁 Decision-Making Activity 10		💻 Internet Activities
📁 Guided Reading Activities 35		
📁 Lesson Plan 35		
📁 Parent Letter and Activities 10		
📁 Reteaching Activity 35		
📁 Concept Mapping Activity 36	📁 Lesson Quiz 36	🕹 Transparency 27
📁 Cross-Curriculum Activity 10		💿 TeacherWorks®
📁 Current Health Issues 10		
📁 Enrichment Activity 10		
📁 Guided Reading Activities 36		
📁 Health Lab 10		
📁 Lesson Plan 36		
📁 Reteaching Activity 36		
📁 Concept Mapping Activity 37	📁 Lesson Quiz 37	🕹 Transparency 28
📁 Guided Reading Activities 37		💿 TeacherWorks®
📁 Lesson Plan 37		
📁 Reteaching Activity 37		

0:00 OUT OF TIME

If time does not permit teaching the entire chapter, use:
- Figure 10.1, p. 252
- Real-Life Application, p. 253
- Health Skills Activity, p. 259
- Figure 10.5, p. 264

Language Diversity

- 🎧 English Audio CD Program
- 🎧 Spanish Audio CD Program
- 📁 English Summaries, Quizzes, and Activities
- 📁 Spanish Summaries, Quizzes, and Activities
- 📁 Spanish Parent Letters and Activities

End of Chapter Assessment

Blackline Masters

- 📁 Chapter 10 Test
- 📁 Performance Assessment Activity 10

Technology

- 💿 Vocabulary PuzzleMaker
- 📼 MindJogger Videoquiz
- 💿 **Exam***View* ® Pro Testmaker

Professional Health Series

Dealing with Sensitive Issues
Planning a Coordinated School Health Program
Promoting Character Education
Home, School, and Community Involvement

Key to Ability Levels

Teaching strategies that appear throughout the chapter have been identified by one of the following codes to give teachers an idea of their suitability for students of varying learning styles and abilities.

L1 Strategies should be within the ability range of all students. Full class participation is often required. Teacher direction is usually needed.

L2 Strategies are designed for average to above-average students or for small groups. Some teacher direction is needed.

L3 Strategies are designed for students able and willing to work independently. Minimal teacher direction is needed.

ELL Strategies should be within the ability range of students learning the English language.

🔲 Block scheduling strategies are useful in a block scheduling format.

Skills for Healthy Relationships

CHAPTER OVERVIEW

Chapter 10 discusses the skills needed to build healthy relationships. These skills include communication, cooperation, compromise, and conflict resolution.

Lesson 1 Relationships allow us to meet our needs to be loved, safe, secure, valued, and recognized. The bond between individuals shapes not only social health but also mental/emotional and physical health. Demonstrating good character can help build healthy relationships.

Lesson 2 An essential part of any relationship is the ability to communicate well. The basic communication skills include speaking, listening, and body language. These and other communication techniques can be developed and promote effective communication.

Lesson 3 Conflicts are a normal part of life. Understanding the causes of conflicts in relationships can help keep the conflict from building. When conflict does occur, negotiation and mediation serve well as processes for conflict resolution.

Health Skills Features

- Real-Life Application (*Communication*), p. 253
- Hands-On Health (*Practicing Healthful Behaviors*), p. 258
- Health Skills Activity (*Communication*), p. 259
- Exploring Issues, p. 265

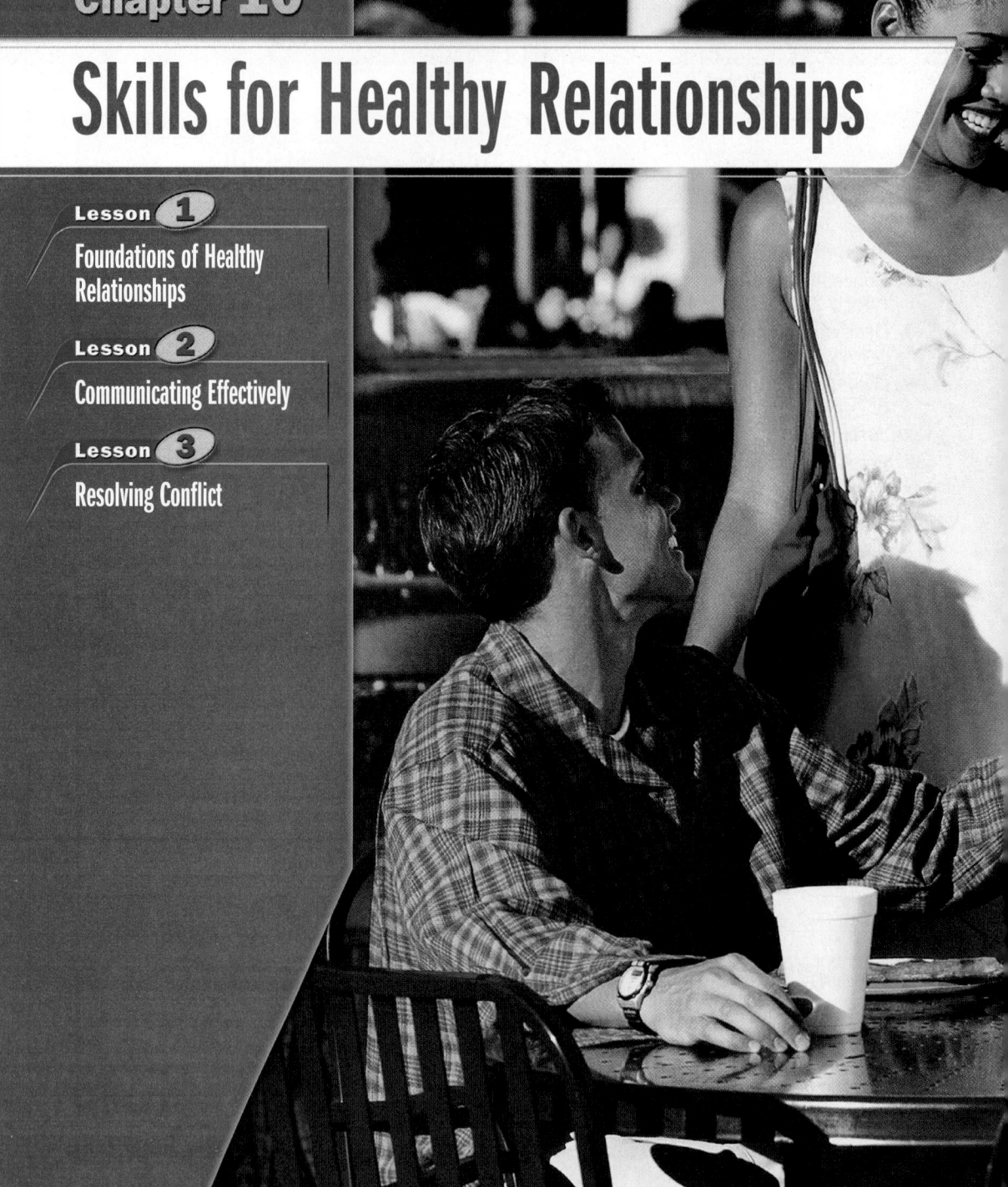

Skills for Healthy Relationships

Lesson 1
Foundations of Healthy Relationships

Lesson 2
Communicating Effectively

Lesson 3
Resolving Conflict

246

MEETING STUDENT DIVERSITY

Language Diversity Use the following suggestions to help students who have difficulty with English:

- Pair English language learners with native speakers of English who can restate the Chapter Summary in language that helps students comprehend important concepts.

- Direct auditory learners or those students with language diversity to the *Glencoe Health Audio CD Program.* Available in English and Spanish, this component provides an audio and written summary of the chapter.

- Use photographs, drawings, or magazine clippings to help students visualize the important concepts of the chapter.

Personal Health Inventory

What's Your Health Status?

Read each statement below and respond by writing *yes*, *no*, or *sometimes* for each item. Write *yes* only for items that you practice regularly.

1. I treat others with respect.
2. I am a good team player.
3. I am trustworthy.
4. I resolve differences through compromise.
5. I am willing to work at my relationships.
6. I am a good listener.
7. I communicate well with others.
8. I ask questions when I am uncertain about what is being said.
9. I make eye contact when communicating with others.
10. I am aware of my body language and the messages it sends to others.

Keep this personal inventory for review later in the chapter. After you complete the chapter, review your answers and identify two or three behavior changes you could make to improve your social health.

Quick Write

Using Visuals. Friendships are an important part of our lives. What kinds of skills do you think help friendships remain healthy and strong?

247

INTRODUCING THE CHAPTER

Personal Health Inventory

Have students read and discuss the Personal Health Inventory statements. Ask: How do the habits identified relate to building and maintaining healthy relationships? After a brief discussion, have students record their responses in their private health journals.

Ask students to brainstorm the qualities they look for in a friend. Have them then consider which of these characteristics they personally display on a consistent basis. Tell students that many attributes of a friend can be learned as well as other skills that contribute to healthy relationships. Finally, explain that as students read the lessons in Chapter 10, they will learn more about developing and maintaining healthy relationships with the different people in their lives.

Quick Write

Using Visuals Direct students to look at the photograph and guide them in discussing the importance of friendships and other relationships in their lives. Encourage volunteers to list the skills that they think are needed to maintain healthy relationships.

TECHNOLOGY OPTIONS

MINDJOGGER
VIDEOQUIZ

To preview or review chapter content, you may wish to use the Chapter 10 MindJogger Videoquiz.

HEALTH *Online*

Online Resources for the Teacher For a fresh approach to health topics and an in-depth look at health issues, use these online resources found under Teacher Resources at **health.glencoe.com:**

- Block Schedule Lesson Plans
- Technology Projects
- Health Updates

Foundations of Healthy Relationships

Lesson 1

Foundations of Healthy Relationships

1 FOCUS

QUICK START Ask volunteers to share their lists of characteristics needed for healthy relationships. Write some of the responses on the board. As a class, discuss the characteristics, and rank each one in order of importance.

TYING TO PRIOR KNOWLEDGE

Have students list the names of people with whom they interact regularly. Explain that this lesson focuses on the characteristics and roles of maintaining these relationships in a healthful way.

Health Skills Features

"The Importance of Good Character to Friendships," p. 253

COMMUNICATION SKILLS

INTRODUCING VOCABULARY

- Ask students to explain how the following terms are related to one another: *relationship, friendship, role*.

- Have students complete the Chapter 10 Study Guide in the *Student Activity Workbook*.

VOCABULARY
- **relationship**
- **friendship**
- **citizenship**
- **role**
- **communication**
- **cooperation**
- **compromise**

YOU'LL LEARN TO

- Analyze how relationships with peers, family, and friends affect physical, mental/emotional, and social health.

- Demonstrate strategies for communicating needs, wants, and emotions in healthy ways.

- Identify the qualities and character traits that promote healthy relationships with peers, family, and friends.

QUICK START List five characteristics you think are needed for healthy relationships. Rank the characteristics in order of importance, and explain why you ranked each item as you did.

A Shared values and mutual respect are essential in healthy relationships.

As you learned in Chapter 7, human beings are social creatures with a need to belong and be loved. We also need to feel safe, secure, valued, and recognized. These needs are met when we form healthy relationships with others. A **relationship** is *a bond or connection you have with other people.*

Healthy Relationships

All of your relationships can have effects on your physical, mental/emotional, and social health. Healthy relationships are based on shared values and interests and mutual respect. You are naturally drawn to those who encourage and support your own best qualities. A healthy relationship is one in which both people benefit and feel comfortable.

248 **Chapter 10** Skills for Healthy Relationships

Lesson 1 *Resources*

Teacher Classroom Resources
- Concept Mapping Activity 35
- Decision-Making Activity 10
- Guided Reading Activities 35
- Lesson Plan 35
- Lesson Quiz 35

- Parent Letter and Activities 10
- Reteaching Activity 35

Student Activity Workbook
- Applying Health Skills 35
- Chapter 10 Study Guide

Multimedia

- Transparency 26

The roles you play in relationships with family, with friends, and in the community are part of your everyday life. *Name several different relationships and roles that you experience each day.*

Family Relationships

Family relationships, which involve both immediate family (parents or guardians and siblings) and extended family (grandparents, aunts, uncles, and cousins), last your entire life. Healthy family relationships enhance all sides of your health triangle. For example, your parents or guardians provide for your physical health with food, clothing, and shelter. They build your social health by teaching you the values that will guide you throughout your life. The love, care, and encouragement you receive from family members also contribute to your mental/emotional health.

Friendships

A **friendship** is *a significant relationship between two people that is based on caring, trust, and consideration.* Your friends can be of any age, and you can choose them for different reasons. For example, a friend may be someone with whom you share confidences, interests, hobbies, or other friends. Good friends share similar values. They can positively influence your self-concept and behavior and help you resist negative influences. Maintaining a good friendship can sometimes be hard work, but it is well worth the effort.

Community Relationships

Citizenship is *the way you conduct yourself as a member of the community.* Members of a community work together to promote the safety and well-being of the entire community. Citizens may volunteer at hospitals or work to provide food, clothing, or shelter to the homeless. You can demonstrate good citizenship by obeying laws and rules, by being a friendly and helpful neighbor, and by contributing to efforts to improve your school and community.

hot link

family relationships For more information on family relationships, see Chapter 11, page 272.

Did You Know ?

Your friends can influence your self-concept greatly. When choosing a friend, ask yourself these questions:

- Does this person have the qualities I admire most?
- Is this someone I can trust with my thoughts and confidences?
- How does this person affect my health triangle?
- What interests and values do we have in common?
- What can I offer in this friendship? What can the other person offer?

Lesson 1 Foundations of Healthy Relationships **249**

2 TEACH

Cooperative Learning

Divide students into discussion groups. Have the members of each group brainstorm and record two lists, one of the benefits of spending time alone and the other of the benefits of having relationships with other people. Ask: Which list is longer? Why? L1

hot link

Everyone needs family relationships because they contribute to a person's total health. Have students consider the ways in which their family members contribute to their health. Ask volunteers to share their thoughts with the class.

ACTIVE READING

Main Idea

Explain to students that paragraphs often contain a main idea. The main idea may be stated in a sentence that gives the most important idea about the topic, or readers may have to figure out the main idea on their own. Have students reread the paragraph on this page about family relationships. Ask them to identify the sentence that states the main idea and explain why they have chosen that sentence. The main idea is expressed in the second sentence, "Healthy family relationships enhance all sides of your health triangle." That sentence gives the most important idea about the topic: family relationships. The other sentences give reasons that support the main idea. For more strategies, see the *Guided Reading Activities* booklet.

HEALTH LITERACY

Friendships and Self-Esteem Friends have a major impact on a teen's self-esteem. Tell students to think about TV shows, movies, or books that depict characters having strains in their friendship. Ask them to share why the characters did not make good friends or why there was trouble. Ask students to explain how the other characters felt about the situation and what they did to recover from it. Discuss general strategies for choosing friends who share your values as well as ways to decrease the risk of getting into a friendship with someone who is a negative influence or who does not promote your self-concept.

Discussing

Have students list all the roles they play in their relationships during an average week. Have a few volunteers write their lists on the board. As a class, go through the lists, and discuss the behavior that is expected in each role. Encourage students to identify which roles have clearly defined behaviors and expectations and which are more ambiguous or dependent on the situation. Explain that roles help relationships go more smoothly by guiding our behavior and helping us to understand the behavior of others. **L2**

Critical Thinking

Ask: Do all your friends have to be other teens? What are some of the special benefits of having friends younger or older—perhaps much younger or much older—than you are? Encourage volunteers to share some of their experiences with friends of different ages. **L1**

Reinforcing Concepts

Allow students to brainstorm the personal qualities they feel are important in a friend. List these on the board as students call them out. Narrow down the list to about ten qualities that the class agrees are the most important. Ask: Why do you think these particular qualities are important to have in a friend? **L1**

HEALTH Online

To learn more about building healthy relationships through communication, click on Web Links at **health.glencoe.com**.

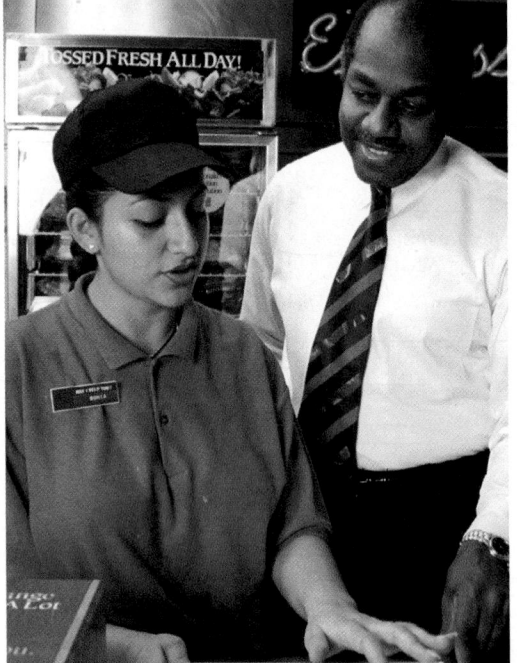

This teen has a working relationship with her employer. *What other relationship roles might be part of this teen's life?*

Roles with Family and Friends

What roles do you play as you interact with others? A **role** is *a part you play in a relationship.* You may be a daughter or son; a sister or brother; a granddaughter or grandson; a member of the school band or volleyball team; a volunteer at a homeless shelter; an employee; a member of a church, synagogue, or mosque; a best friend; and a girlfriend or boyfriend. You probably play many of these roles—all at the same time!

The role you play in a relationship may be obvious. For example, you know that when you baby-sit a neighbor's child, you are an employee. Sometimes your roles are less clear, and they may change gradually or even suddenly. For example, your relationship with a fellow choir member may change if you begin dating. Such role changes can be confusing and can make it difficult to know how to act.

Building Healthy Relationships

For a relationship to succeed, the people involved need certain skills. Three of these skills are communication, cooperation, and compromise—the Three Cs of healthy relationships.

Communication

Communication refers to *your ways of sending and receiving messages.* These messages may be exchanged in words or through gestures, facial expressions, and behaviors. You communicate to let others know your feelings, thoughts, and expectations. Communication also lets you discover the feelings, needs, wants, and knowledge of others. You will learn more about skills for effective communication in the next lesson.

Cooperation

Have you ever helped someone move a heavy object, such as a large piece of furniture? Such activities are almost impossible without **cooperation**, *working together for the good of all.* Working together through cooperation helps build strong relationships. For example, Susan helps prepare dinner each evening because her parents don't get home from work until 6 p.m. Because of her help, Susan's family is able to eat together and enjoy one another's company. Her contribution benefits the entire family.

250 Chapter 10 Skills for Healthy Relationships

Curriculum Connections

Foreign Language Invite a French or Spanish language teacher to discuss the different forms and uses of the word *you.*

Drama Select students to write and perform a skit based on the following scenario: *Carlos and Jenna are both running for class president. Each has accused the other of destroying his or her campaign signs. Kelly is* friends with both Carlos and Jenna. She doesn't want to take sides, but she would like her friends to resolve their differences. Kelly decides to talk to Carlos and Jenna at the same time in hopes of finding a fair solution. After the skit, ask students to evaluate the actions of all three characters.

Compromise

Three friends can't agree on how they'll spend the afternoon: Thomas and Elise want to go biking, but Serena wants to play miniature golf. Have you ever been in a similar situation? If so, you probably used compromise to solve the problem. **Compromise** is *a problem-solving method that involves each participant's giving up something to reach a solution that satisfies everyone.* It can be used to create a win-win situation for everyone involved.

The "give and take" of effective compromise strengthens relationships. By your willingness to give up something in order to reach a solution, you show the other person that you value the relationship. Remember, however, that compromise involves seeking a solution that is acceptable to *all* persons involved. Therefore, it should not lead to a decision that goes against your values or beliefs. In such situations, it's important that you use refusal skills to stand your ground. Learning when—and when *not*—to compromise is a vital relationship skill.

Characteristics of Healthy Relationships

By practicing the Three Cs, you make positive contributions to healthy relationships. In addition, all good relationships—whether with family members, friends, or other members of your community—have certain recognizable characteristics. Some of these characteristics are described below.

▶ **Mutual Respect and Consideration.** In healthy relationships, people show mutual respect even when they disagree. This involves accepting one another's tastes and opinions and being tolerant of different viewpoints. Furthermore, each person shows consideration by being thoughtful about the rights and feelings of others.

▶ **Honesty.** Because of their mutual respect and consideration, participants in a healthy relationship have the confidence to be open and honest about their actions, thoughts, and feelings. Dishonesty can seriously weaken or even destroy a relationship.

▶ **Dependability.** Participants in a healthy relationship are dependable. They are trustworthy and reliable. Each is there for the others when they are needed.

▶ **Commitment.** Healthy relationships require commitment. The participants are willing to work together and make sacrifices that benefit everyone involved. They are loyal to each other, and they are committed to strengthening the relationship.

Isn't compromise really a matter of one person giving in or losing?

If two people can't agree on a compromise between two choices, they should look for a third choice that both can agree on. If there really are only two choices, the compromise might be for one person to "win" this time with the understanding that the next time it will be the other person's turn to "win." If only one person is always giving up something, there is no compromise.

Discussing

Have students describe instances where teens show respect for one another in their daily activities. Afterward, ask how it feels when someone fails to consider their feelings or to respect them in other ways. **L2**

hotlink

Guide students in a discussion of character. You may want to have them refer to pages 252 and 253 to read more about the topic. Ask: What does the word *character* mean to you? How do people show good character? Why is good character an important trait in a friend? Tell students that they can review the information about character in Chapter 2.

VISUAL LEARNING

Figure 10.1 Guide students in reading and discussing the six traits of good character on page 252. Then divide students into six groups. Write each of the six traits on a separate slip of paper, and give one slip to each group. Have group members write and perform a short skit that illustrates how their trait can be demonstrated in a healthy relationship. Then ask the rest of the class to guess which trait is being portrayed and to explain their choice.

Lesson 1 Foundations of Healthy Relationships **251**

⟋⋁⋀⋁⟍ HEALTH LITERACY

Compromising Have students write down descriptions of several recent incidents during which they said or did something that they would not ordinarily do in order to be fair, comply with a rule, keep the peace, protect someone's feelings, or maintain a friendship.

Suggest that they relate these compromises to the abilities, qualities, and understandings humans need to develop in order to form sucessful friendships and relationships. Call on volunteers to share parts of their entries.

hotlink

character For more information about character, see Chapter 2, page 37.

Real-Life Application

THE IMPORTANCE OF GOOD CHARACTER TO FRIENDSHIPS

NHES Standard 5 Students will demonstrate the ability to use interpersonal communication skills to enhance health.

Objectives

- Identify the qualities and character traits that promote healthy relationships with friends.
- Demonstrate communication skills in maintaining healthy relationships.

Motivator

Survey the class on how many students communicate with their friends through e-mail messages. Ask them how they think e-mail communication helps them to maintain their friendships.

Teaching Strategies

1. Review effective communication skills.
2. Advise students to use effective communication techniques in developing their reply.

Assessment

Using a rubric, student work should provide comprehensive evidence of the following criteria to achieve the highest score:

✔ demonstration of at least four character traits in their reply.
✔ paragraph explaining how the character traits could strengthen the friendship.

Character and Healthy Relationships

Your **character**—the way you think, feel, and act—has the greatest influence on your relationships with others. Think about the people with whom you enjoy spending time. These people probably have values similar to yours. Your values are the beliefs and ideals that guide the way you live.

You can build a foundation for healthy relationships by demonstrating the six main traits of good character. These traits are described in **Figure 10.1.** Think about ways you can demonstrate each character trait.

FIGURE 10.1

DEMONSTRATING CHARACTER IN RELATIONSHIPS

Trustworthiness	Fairness
You show trustworthiness when you are honest, reliable, and loyal. Trustworthy people don't cheat, steal, or deceive; they have the courage to do what's right. • *Example:* Hector finds a wallet containing $300. He uses the name on the driver's license and the phone book to call the owner so that he can return the wallet.	You show fairness when you play by the rules, take turns, and share. You also don't blame or take advantage of others. A fair person listens to others and is open-minded. • *Example:* Maria shows fairness by telling the referee that the volleyball was on the line and the opposing team won the point.
Respect	**Caring**
You show respect by using good manners, being considerate of others, and being tolerant of differences. You are also respectful when you deal with anger and disagreements in a peaceful way and treat other people and property with care. • *Example:* Sid knows that his dad brought a lot of work home from the office. Sid turns down the volume of his music so he won't disturb his father.	You show that you are caring when you are kind and compassionate. Caring means putting in time and energy to help others. • *Example:* Juanita is entering a store. She holds the door open for a man whose arms are filled with packages.
Responsibility	**Citizenship**
You show that you are responsible when you do what is expected of you and are accountable for your choices. Being responsible also means that you use self-control, think before you act, and always try your best. • *Example:* Sarah's drama rehearsal runs late. She calls her parents to let them know she is going to be late.	You show good citizenship by cooperating and doing your share to improve your school and community. You obey laws and rules and respect authority. Staying informed about issues that affect you and your neighbors, voting when you are of age, and doing your part to protect the environment are other ways to demonstrate good citizenship. • *Example:* Brad sees that someone has left an empty juice bottle on a table in the school cafeteria. He picks up the bottle and puts it in a recycling bin.

252 Chapter 10 Skills for Healthy Relationships

Promoting Coordinated School Health

Measuring Progress Assessment

Evaluating the committee's progress will help identify what works, what has been successfully changed, and how the community is instrumental in the process of change. Assessment might take any of the following forms: ongoing evaluation of the action plan, a comparison of the program against a set of voluntary guidelines or statewide objectives, review of the health statistics in the community, or questioning of committee members to retake the survey that originally led to the priority list of problems. For more information, consult *Planning a Coordinated School Health Program.*

Real-Life Application

The Importance of Good Character to Friendships

Discuss how the e-mail below demonstrates good character traits.

> Dear Lola,
>
> I'm sorry I didn't invite you to go with me to the grand opening of the new music store. I didn't think you were interested, so I was surprised when I found out that you were angry about not being invited. I'm not making excuses—I should have thought of you before we left. I don't blame you for feeling hurt and angry.
>
> I care about our friendship and I hope you'll forgive me. I'll try to be more considerate next time.
>
> Your friend (I hope),
>
> Mieko

Trustworthiness: apologizing, being honest, not making excuses.

Fairness: not blaming Lola.

Caring: saying that she is grateful for the friendship.

Responsibility: realizing that she should have thought before she acted.

ACTIVITY

Write a reply to the e-mail above. Show at least four traits of good character. Next, write a paragraph explaining how the character traits demonstrated in your message can strengthen the friendship.

Lesson 1 Review

Reviewing Facts and Vocabulary

1. Define *relationship*, and evaluate the positive effects of family relationships on your emotional health.

2. What are the Three Cs of healthy relationships?

3. List the six traits of good character.

Thinking Critically

4. **Evaluating.** Identify specific examples of how the roles you play with family and friends differ from those you play in other social groups.

5. **Applying.** Give an example of how you demonstrate consideration, respect, commitment, honesty, and dependability in your relationships with family members.

Applying Health Skills

Advocacy. Design a flip book for children about the six traits of good character. The book should demonstrate the importance of good character and persuade children to develop these traits.

WORD PROCESSING Make use of clip art, graphics, and fonts in your word-processing software. See **health.glencoe.com** for tips on using your word-processing program.

Lesson 1 Foundations of Healthy Relationships **253**

3 ASSESS

EVALUATING THE LESSON

Assign and discuss the Lesson 1 Review; then administer, grade, and discuss Lesson Quiz 35 in the TCR. 📁

RETEACHING

- Ask students to examine and write about a relationship they have with a relative or close friend. Have them describe situations in which they have used communication, cooperation, and compromise to improve the relationship.

- Have the class complete Reteaching Activity 35 in the TCR. 📁

ENRICHMENT

Sociology is the scientific study of human relationships or group life. Provide several books, journals or textbooks on the topic for students to browse through and expand their knowledge of relationships and social responsibility.

4 CLOSE

Summarize the lesson by reviewing the traits of a healthy relationship.

Lesson 1 Review

Answers to Reviewing Facts and Vocabulary

1. A relationship is a bond or connection you have with other people. Examples will vary but may include the following: Family relationships have a positive effect on emotional health by providing love, care, and encouragement.

2. Communication, cooperation, compromise.

3. Trustworthiness, respect, responsibility, fairness, caring, citizenship.

Answers to Thinking Critically

4. Responses will vary but should describe different roles in different situations.

5. Responses will vary.

Communicating Effectively

FOCUS

Communicating Effectively

QUICK START Allow time for students to list ways in which people communicate. Have volunteers share some of their responses, and as a class, discuss which methods are used most often.

TYING TO PRIOR KNOWLEDGE

Ask volunteers to share something they communicated about today and the method of communication they used. As a class, discuss how body language might have strengthened these messages.

VOCABULARY
"I" message
active listening
body language
prejudice
tolerance
constructive criticism

YOU'LL LEARN TO

- Classify forms of communication as passive, aggressive, or assertive.

- Demonstrate communication skills needed to build and maintain healthy relationships with family, friends, peers, and others.

- Apply communication skills that demonstrate consideration and respect for oneself, one's family, and others.

QUICK START On a sheet of paper, make a list of eight different ways in which people communicate with one another. Place a check mark beside each communication method you have used in the past two days.

Health Skills Features

"Demonstrating Empathy," p. 258

PRACTICING HEALTHFUL BEHAVIORS

"Expressing Disapproval of Bullying," p. 259

COMMUNICATION SKILLS

INTRODUCING VOCABULARY

- Have students work with partners to quiz each other on the vocabulary definitions.

- Ask students to complete the Chapter 10 Study Guide in the *Student Activity Workbook*.

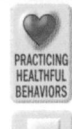 Writing a note or letter can be an effective way to communicate your feelings. *In what other ways do you communicate with your family, friends, and peers?*

H ow often have you given or received a shrug, a raised eyebrow, or a grin in reply to a comment or question? Although you may not have thought about it at the time, these responses are all forms of communication. Most of the time, you probably talk to let others know about your feelings, wants, and needs. Sometimes you may convey your feelings by writing notes or letters. People also show their feelings through gestures, facial expressions, and behaviors. There are many ways to exchange ideas with others. All of the ways in which you send and receive messages are forms of communication.

Effective Communication

C ommunication is critical to healthy relationships. When you communicate effectively, the messages you send to others are clear. Being an effective communicator also means that you correctly interpret the messages you receive and respond appropriately.

Three basic skills are needed for effective communication: speaking, listening, and body language. Learning to use these skills well takes practice, but the effort is worthwhile because effective communication helps you form and maintain healthy relationships with others. It is a skill from which you will benefit for your entire life.

Lesson 2 Resources

Teacher Classroom Resources

Concept Mapping Activity 36

Cross-Curriculum Activity 10

Current Health Issues 10

Enrichment Activity 10

Guided Reading Activities 36

Health Lab 10

Lesson Plan 36

Lesson Quiz 36

Reteaching Activity 36

Student Activity Workbook

Applying Health Skills 36

Chapter 10 Study Guide

Multimedia

Transparency 27

Communication Styles

Do you have any friends who always just "go along" with what others decide to do, never saying what they would prefer? Perhaps you know someone who is "pushy," always insisting on getting his or her own way. These examples reflect two of the three styles of communication.

▶ **Passive.** Passive communication involves the inability or unwillingness to express thoughts and feelings. Passive communicators do not stand up for themselves or defend their attitudes or beliefs. They will often do something they'd prefer not to do rather than say how they really feel.

▶ **Aggressive.** Aggressive communicators often try to get their way through bullying and intimidation. They do not consider the rights of others. In disagreements, they attack the other person, not the problem.

▶ **Assertive.** Assertive communication involves expressing thoughts and feelings clearly and directly but without hurting others. Assertive communicators stand up for themselves. They defend their attitudes and beliefs, but they also respect the rights of others. In disagreements, they attack the problem, not the other person.

Assertive communication, which involves effective speaking and listening skills as well as appropriate body language, is an important asset in all healthy relationships.

Speaking Skills

Having good communication skills means that you do not assume that others can read your mind or know your needs and expectations. When you interact with others, you are responsible for making your thoughts and feelings known. For example, you need to say when your feelings have been hurt or when you've been disappointed. You demonstrate good speaking skills when you clearly say what you mean. This is the first step in healthy communication.

Changes in the tone, pitch, or loudness of your voice can affect communication. Kind words spoken in a sarcastic tone, for example, may not be interpreted as kind. Speaking loudly may make you seem bossy or arrogant. Saying "no" too softly can make you sound insincere or uncertain. These examples show that *how* you say something is as important as *what* you say.

Good communication skills can strengthen a friendship. *List some strategies for effectively communicating your thoughts to a listener.*

---

❷ TEACH

Discussing

Help students discuss the steps in the communication process: When you and a friend have a face-to-face conversation, which one sends messages? both Which person receives messages? both What happens to the communication process if your friend stops paying attention while you are talking? It breaks down because messages are no longer being received. How is the communication process altered when you and the same friend talk on the phone? Facial expressions and gestures no longer help to send the intended messages. What happens when you and the same friend communicate by e-mail? Facial expressions, gestures, and tone of voice are not available to help send messages. **L1**

Activity

Ask students to watch one or more TV programs such as a sitcom, a documentary, or a movie. Lead a discussion of the means of communication portrayed and the communication styles used. Have students evaluate the effectiveness of each type. **L2**

Activity

Have volunteers do research on the latest developments in voice-recognition systems. What functions do these systems perform? How do they help improve communication? Who might benefit most from these systems? Have students share their findings with the class. **L3**

— *School to Work* —

Communication at Work Have students choose an occupation that demands good relationship and communication skills. If students need suggestions, provide the following list of jobs: a doctor, a store manager, the press secretary to the president, a police officer, a real estate agent, and a receptionist in a busy office.

Ask students to write a help-wanted ad for the position they have chosen. Have them check for spelling and grammar and make sure that their ad is error-free. In the ad, they should describe the position and communication skills desired.

Figure 10.2 Guide students in comparing and contrasting each aggressive message with its corresponding assertive "I" message. Have pairs of volunteers role-play one of the aggressive messages and a possible response from the receiver. Then have the same pair role-play the assertive "I" message and a possible response. Ask: How did the two responses differ? Which type of message prompted a more positive response? Why? Was it difficult using an "I" message? Why?

Explaining

Frequently, students are unaware that there are several different types of listening. Introduce and compare attentive listening and selective listening. Selective listening is used to hear only enough of what is spoken to allow the listener to argue or to support a previously held point of view. Attentive listening allows listeners to hear not only what is spoken but also the feelings that are being communicated. **L1**

Health Skills Practice

Family Communication
To enhance good listening skills at home, have students ask their family about the possibility of turning the TV off during mealtime so that family communication can take place with fewer distractions. Ask volunteers to share their experiences with the class.

COMMUNICATION SKILLS

FIGURE 10.2

STATING YOUR FEELINGS EFFECTIVELY

Compare the messages and the probable results of these scenes.

Aggressive Messages (What *not* to say)	Assertive "I" Messages (What to say)
"You idiot! You took my favorite jacket and got paint all over it! You ruined it, and you'll have to pay for it."	"I'm upset that my favorite jacket was borrowed without my knowledge."
"Why are you always late? It's really annoying."	"I worry about you when you don't show up."
"Why do you always have to get what you want? You never do what I suggest."	"I'll agree to have Mexican food today if I can pick the restaurant the next time we go out."

Did You Know ?

About 45 percent of the average person's communication time is spent listening, and 30 percent is spent speaking.

Reading, on average, occupies about 16 percent of a person's communication time, and writing accounts for only 9 percent of this time.

When you want to deliver messages that have strong emotional content, consider using "I" messages. An **"I" message** is *a statement in which a person describes how he or she feels by using the pronoun "I."* As shown in **Figure 10.2,** using "I" messages can help you communicate your feelings positively, without blame or name-calling. Blaming and name-calling always put people on the defensive because they feel that they are being attacked.

Listening Skills

Speaking is an important communication skill, but listening is equally important. You can make use of **active listening**, *paying close attention to what someone is saying and communicating,* to improve your communication skills. Active listening involves giving your full attention to whatever the speaker is saying without interrupting or making judgments. **Figure 10.3** illustrates some ways of becoming a more active listener.

Meeting Individual Needs

Hearing-Impaired Students Although some people with hearing impairments communicate verbally with words, many others use sign language to communicate their thoughts and ideas. Much like spoken languages, such as English and Spanish, sign language varies depending on where a person lives. American Sign Language (ASL) is one of the most commonly used languages in the United States. ASL combines hand gestures with facial expressions and body movements to communicate words and concepts. Have students find out more about ASL. How does a person learn sign language? Where are classes available in the community?

TECHNIQUES FOR ACTIVE LISTENING

Being a good listener is important to healthy relationships. When you listen to others, you show them that you care about what they have to say and how they feel. Active listeners use several techniques to show others that they are listening. These techniques include:

▶ **Reflective listening.** In reflective listening, you rephrase or summarize what the other person has said. This allows you to be sure you have understood what was intended.

▶ **Clarifying.** Clarifying involves asking the speaker what he or she thinks or how he or she feels about the situation being discussed. It also involves asking questions to help you understand more fully what is being said.

▶ **Encouraging.** You encourage the speaker when you signal that you are interested and involved. You can show your interest by nodding your head or saying "I see," "Uh-huh," or "I understand."

▶ **Empathizing.** When you have **empathy**, you are able to imagine and understand how someone else feels. Empathizing is feeling what the other person feels as you listen. For example, if a friend tells you how disappointed he was when he didn't make the baseball team, you are likely to share his disappointment. Keep in mind that sometimes empathy is not appropriate, such as when what the person is saying goes against your values.

hot link

empathy For more information on empathy, see Chapter 7, page 186.

FIGURE 10.3

TIPS FOR ACTIVE LISTENING

Practicing active listening skills can improve your relationships.

- Make direct eye contact.

- Use body language, such as leaning in toward the speaker, which shows you are listening and giving your full attention.

- Use signals, such as nodding, to show that you are involved and interested.

- Don't interrupt the speaker.

- Put away prejudices, images, or assumptions that you have of the other person so that you can focus on what he or she is saying.

Lesson 2 Communicating Effectively **257**

---

hot link

Have students review the definition of *empathy*. Ask: How might showing empathy make you a good listener? Have volunteers give examples of situations in which a listener might empathize with another person.

VISUAL LEARNING

Figure 10.3 Discuss the tips in Figure 10.3 and other listening skills discussed in the lesson. Then allow groups of four to share what they would do on the perfect vacation. As one person shares his or her vacation plans, a second person should evaluate the other two members of the group's listening skills. As students rotate roles, have them share their evaluations as feedback.

Cooperative Learning

Divide the class into groups of three: a speaker, an active listener, and an observer. Assign topics for the groups to talk about. Use time limits. Have the observer determine whether active listening rules are being followed. After the speaker has spoken and the listener has paraphrased what has been said, have the observer tell them what he or she observed that was done well and where improvements could be made. Have students take turns until each has performed every role. **L2**
Interpersonal Intelligence

More About...

Using Good Listening Skills Jumping to conclusions is a common fault among listeners. By assuming they know what is coming next, they can seriously damage their understanding of what is actually being said at that very moment and for the rest of the conversation. Instead of continuing to listen, they become mired in their own thoughts.

Since people can think much faster than most people can usually talk, a listener's thoughts can sometimes race ahead of the speaker. Good listeners use the extra time to summarize the speaker's ideas, evaluate the strength and logic of the speaker's arguments, and respond nonverbally to what they hear.

Hands-On Health

DEMONSTRATING EMPATHY

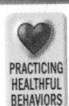

PRACTICING HEALTHFUL BEHAVIORS

NHES Standard 3 Students will demonstrate the ability to practice health-enhancing behaviors and reduce health risk.

Objectives

- Demonstrate how friends can show empathy for each other.

- Apply communication skills that demonstrate consideration and respect for self, family, and others.

Motivator

Review the meaning of the word *empathy.*

Teaching Strategies

1. Remind students that when expressing empathy, especially in difficult situations, they may not know what to say; it is okay to admit this to the other person.

2. Have the class generate additional ways to show empathy as you list these on the board. Students can incorporate them into their role-plays.

✔Assessment

Using a rubric, student work should provide comprehensive evidence of the following criteria to achieve the highest score:

✔ demonstrate several different techniques that show empathy for others

✔ use techniques appropriate for the situation

Hands-On Health ACTIVITY

Demonstrating Empathy

One way to be a good friend is to express empathy. Here are some tips:

- Maintain eye contact as you listen.
- Rephrase or summarize what the person has said.
- Avoid judging or offering advice.
- If a loss has been experienced, avoid trying to minimize the sense of loss by stating that it is not that bad.

In this activity you will role-play situations in which friends express empathy for each other.

What You'll Need

- index cards
- pen or pencil

What You'll Do

1. In groups of six, brainstorm three situations that could cause teens to feel sad. Write each one on a separate index card.

2. Your teacher will assign one situation to you and a partner in your group.

3. Practice and then role-play the situation for the class, demonstrating several different ways a friend can show empathy.

Apply and Conclude

Demonstrating empathy during happy moments is just as important as being empathetic during sad times. Make a list of situations in which you might share in a friend's joy or excitement. Explain how showing empathy during these situations can strengthen your friendship.

Nonverbal Communication

Many of the messages you send to others do not involve words. Such messages involve **body language**, *nonverbal communication through gestures, facial expressions, behaviors, and posture.* You use body language when you nod or shake your head to show that you agree or disagree with something that is said. When you hold yourself in a tense posture, you silently communicate that you're feeling nervous or worried.

Nonverbal communication can be subtle, taking place at an unconscious level. For example, if you feel embarrassed or ashamed, you may look at the ground instead of at the person to whom you are speaking. If you are greatly interested in what someone is saying, you may find yourself leaning toward the speaker.

You can help send clearer messages by being aware of your body language. If your words and your body language seem to contradict each other, the person you are speaking to may be confused or unsure of what to believe.

258 **Chapter 10** Skills for Healthy Relationships

Home and Community

Relationships and Society Learning and practicing good social skills can help people to have and maintain strong relationships. However, learning to perceive others as individuals with feelings and rights is a long and difficult process that some people never complete. The socialization process helps humans learn to get along with others in society. Ask students to privately list the relationship skills they have learned and decide whether they learned each skill from their family, school, or community. Have them identify which skills children and teens are usually taught and which ones are usually learned by observation.

Eliminating Communication Barriers

Have you ever heard the saying, "A chain is only as strong as its weakest link"? The same is true of communication. If one person in a relationship has good communication skills but the other person does not, the entire communication process suffers. Sometimes a person's beliefs or attitudes can make communication difficult. Examples of obstacles to clear communication include:

▶ **Image and identity issues.** Many teens spend at least part of their teen years searching for an **identity**—a sense of who they are and their place in the world. If someone is unsure of his or her values, the uncertainty can complicate the communication process.

hot link

identity For more information about the search for identity during the teen years, see Chapter 7, page 178.

Health Skills Activity

Communication: Expressing Disapproval of Bullying

Walking in the school hallway, Marya and Ramone witness Matt intentionally bump into a boy walking the other way. The boy drops his books and papers.

"Hey!" Matt says rudely, "Watch where you're going!"

"Sorry," the boy apologizes, scrambling to pick up his things.

Matt places his foot on one of the boy's papers. "Looking for this?"

Ramone starts to laugh, but Marya frowns. "Matt is just having a little fun," Ramone says.

Marya shakes her head. She wonders how to let Matt know that she disapproves of his bullying.

What Would You Do?

Marya uses body language to communicate to Ramone that she disapproves of Matt's bullying behavior. Now it is important to verbally communicate this message to Matt. Use the following communication skills to role-play a dialog between Marya and Matt that clearly communicates that his behavior is not acceptable.

1. Present a clear, organized statement.
2. Use "I" statements.
3. Show appropriate body language.
4. Listen carefully.
5. Be firm and direct, but avoid being rude or insulting.

Cooperative Learning Activity

Advice Column Divide the class into groups. Have each member bring an advice column about a family or peer relationship problem to class. Stress that the topic should relate to chapter content and be appropriate for class discussion. Tell them to separate the description of the problem from the columnist's advice. Have members take turns reading aloud the descriptions of the problems. Then have other group members discuss the problems and agree upon the advice. Then have a student read the columnist's advice. Ask other members to compare their advice with that of the columnist.

Health Skills Activity

EXPRESSING DISAPPROVAL OF BULLYING

NHES Standard 5 Students will demonstrate the ability to use interpersonal communication skills to enhance health.

Objectives

- Analyze ways to show disapproval of inconsiderate and disrespectful behavior.
- Apply communication skills that demonstrate consideration and respect for self, family, and others.

Motivator

Ask volunteers to share their experiences of witnessing someone being bullied and how they responded to the situation.

Teaching Strategies

1. Ask students why it is important not to respond to a bully in a rude or insulting manner.
2. Tell students to complete their dialogues by specifying how they will report this incident to a trusted adult.

✓ Assessment

Using a rubric, student work should provide comprehensive evidence of the following criteria to achieve the highest score:

✔ interactions among individuals
✔ a clear, organized statement
✔ use of "I" statements to convey the appropriate point of view
✔ appropriate body language
✔ firm, direct message that is not rude or insulting

Discussing

Ask: How do people communicate their chosen identities to others? What does an individual's appearance say about who he or she is? Do most people project different images under different circumstances or with different people? Have students describe examples of the different images they project. **L1**

Activity

Assign students to watch a television drama or situation comedy. Have students identify and discuss specific examples of obstacles to effective communication among the TV characters. **L2**

Cooperative Learning

Have students work in small groups to generate a list of situations in which a teen is disappointed in or disapproves of another person's behavior. Record their ideas on the board. Then have groups suggest constructive criticism the teen might use in each situation. **L1**

Fairness Lead students in a discussion of the importance of fairness in all relationships. Ask volunteers to describe a real or fictional situation in which someone was treated unfairly. Ask: How do you think the other person felt? What might have been a better way to handle the situation so that the other person was treated fairly?

CHARACTER CHECK

Fairness. Fairness is an important quality in any relationship. Whether you are facing an opponent in a student council election or competing with a friend on the tennis court, fairness is a principle that respects the abilities, needs, and contributions of all parties. **Describe three ways that you demonstrate fairness in your relationships.**

Accept constructive feedback positively. This is one way you can learn from others and improve yourself. *Give an example of how a critical statement can be turned into constructive feedback.*

► **Unrealistic expectations.** Avoid imposing unrealistic expectations on your listener; this may cause the individual to become frustrated or defensive.

► **Lack of trust.** Good communication is built on trust between two people. If you don't trust a person—if you believe that you can't count on him or her to tell you the truth or to keep a confidence—communication is very difficult.

► **Prejudice.** Some individuals have a **prejudice** or *an unfair opinion or judgment of a particular group of people.* Prejudice prevents a person from having an open mind and listening to new information. To avoid developing prejudices, you can demonstrate **tolerance**, or *the ability to accept others' differences and allow them to be who they are without your expressing disapproval.* Being tolerant helps you understand the differences among people and recognize the value of diversity.

► **Gender stereotyping.** Gender stereotyping is a type of prejudice that involves having an exaggerated or oversimplified belief about people of a certain gender. Assuming that all males like sports and that all females enjoy cooking are examples of gender stereotyping. Such assumptions make it difficult to communicate effectively.

Constructive Feedback

No one, not even your best friend or your teacher, is perfect. It's only realistic to be disappointed in a relationship occasionally. Imagine that you are meeting a friend to see a movie. Your friend is late, causing you to miss the beginning of the show. How would you react in this situation? Some people might resort to name-calling or placing blame. However, when someone lets you down, you may find that giving the person feedback in a more positive manner helps him or her *and* your relationship. The feedback you provide should take the form of **constructive criticism**, *non-hostile comments that point out problems for the purpose of helping a person improve.*

Constructive criticism is intended to bring about positive changes. Consequently, it should not be given in an aggressive way. Verbally attacking the other person will only make things worse. It is very important to begin your discussion by using an "I" message to explain how you feel. Point out what the person is doing or has done, and suggest a better way to do it. For example, you might deal with your friend's lateness by saying in a neutral voice, "I really don't like missing the opening scene of a movie. Let's get here early next time, okay?"

HEALTH LITERACY

Communication Skills Have students work in groups to brainstorm a list of situations that require active listening skills. If they need help, suggest these examples: (1) one person wants a loan from a friend who does not like lending money, (2) two teens are going steady and one wants to break up, (3) one teen wants to get ice cream with a friend who is trying to stick to healthy food choices, (4) one teen tells another about a problem at home. Ask students to role-play the situations using effective communication skills.

Acknowledgements and Compliments

How do you feel when someone thanks you for being a good friend or tells you how much he or she admires your honesty? Hearing such acknowledgements and compliments probably makes you feel good about yourself and your relationship with the person who made the comments. Expressing and receiving respect, admiration, and appreciation with grace and sincerity can help you maintain healthy relationships.

Acknowledgements and compliments take many forms. For example, you might tell a parent how much you enjoyed a meal that he or she prepared. You might also tell a friend that she is a good artist or congratulate the team that defeated yours in a play-off game. Gestures such as these can strengthen relationships and enhance your social health. It shows that you do not take the relationship for granted, and it demonstrates good sportsmanship and good character.

Acknowledging accomplishments is a way to show others that you care about them. *What are some other benefits of giving acknowledgements and compliments?*

Discussing

Ask: Why are acknowledgments and compliments so effective in improving the health of a relationship? Why do so many people find it difficult to accept compliments? What are some appropriate responses to sincere compliments? **L1**

③ ASSESS

EVALUATING THE LESSON

Assign and discuss the Lesson 2 Review; then administer, grade, and discuss Lesson Quiz 36 in the TCR.

RETEACHING

- Ask students to give to others ten constructive criticisms, acknowledgements, or compliments over the next day. Ask students to note how it felt to say this and how the other person reacted.

- Have students complete Reteaching Activity 36 in the TCR.

ENRICHMENT

Ask students to research differences in the use of body language in other cultures. For example, direct eye contact may be considered disrespectful in some cultures. Have students present the information in a written or oral report to the class. Remind them to proofread for errors and develop several drafts of their writing.

 Lesson 2 *Review*

Reviewing Facts and Vocabulary

1. What are the three basic skills needed for effective communication?

2. List four ways to show that you are actively listening to another person.

3. Define the term *body language*, and give three examples of it.

Thinking Critically

4. **Contrasting.** Compare the different ways in which passive and aggressive communication interfere with the effective expression of thoughts and feelings.

5. **Applying.** List three ways to demonstrate consideration and respect for self, family, and others through communication skills.

Applying Health Skills

Refusal Skills. In a group, develop a skit that includes both dialogue and body language to show how teens can demonstrate refusal strategies in resisting pressure to take part in an unhealthful activity.

WEB SITES Use your skit to make a PSA (public service announcement) or video that is part of a Web page you develop on refusal skills. See health.glencoe.com for help in planning and building your own Web site.

Lesson 2 Communicating Effectively **261**

 Lesson 2 *Review*

Answers to Reviewing Facts and Vocabulary

1. Speaking, listening, and body language.
2. Any four of the tips shown in Figure 10.3 or techniques identified on page 257.
3. See page 258 for definition. Examples will vary.

Answers to Thinking Critically

4. Passive communication avoids

expressing thoughts and feelings, whereas aggressive communication attempts to silence others.

5. Answers will vary but may include using "I" messages, listening actively, eliminating communication barriers, and giving acknowledgments and compliments.

④ CLOSE

Ask students to summarize the most important concepts learned in the lesson.

Resolving Conflict

1 FOCUS

QUICK START Ask volunteers to share their responses for encouraging better understanding and avoiding conflict. Write some of the responses on the board. Then ask: Which of these responses would work best to diffuse a tense situation? Why?

TYING TO PRIOR KNOWLEDGE

Ask students to list some conflicts that they observed or read about recently. Tell them to put a check mark beside each conflict that was resolved peacefully. Have volunteers share their responses. Ask: How are these conflicts similar? How are they different? Tell students that this lesson will focus on causes of conflict and conflict resolution skills.

Health Skills Features

"What Causes Conflicts to Escalate?" p. 265

INTRODUCING VOCABULARY

- Have students review and discuss the vocabulary terms. Ask them to use the terms in original sentences.

- Ask students to complete the Chapter 10 Study Guide in the *Student Activity Workbook*. 📁

Resolving Conflict

VOCABULARY
conflict
interpersonal conflicts
conflict resolution
negotiation
mediation
confidentiality
peer mediators

YOU'LL LEARN TO
- Analyze the causes of conflict.
- Analyze the relationship between the use of refusal skills and the avoidance of unsafe situations.
- Demonstrate healthful strategies for resolving conflicts, and evaluate the effectiveness of conflict resolution techniques in various situations.

QUICK START Write three things you could say or do in a tense situation that would encourage better understanding and avoid conflict.

▼ Unresolved conflicts can interfere with healthy relationships. *What communication skills can help teens deal with everyday conflicts?*

Two drivers argue over a parking space; fans of opposing soccer teams brawl in the stadium parking lot; a shoving match occurs as students wait in line in the cafeteria. All of these events have something in common—they involve conflict. **Conflict** is *any disagreement, struggle, or fight.* Conflicts are a normal part of life. They often occur when one person's wants, needs, wishes, demands, expectations, or beliefs clash with those of another person.

Understanding Conflict

The types of conflicts that impact relationships are **interpersonal conflicts**. These are *disagreements between groups of any size, from two people to entire nations.* Interpersonal conflicts can begin over minor problems, such as when siblings argue over what to watch on television. They can also affect large groups of people, such as a dispute over how to spend community funds.

Lesson 3 *Resources*

Teacher Classroom Resources
📁 Concept Mapping Activity 37
📁 Guided Reading Activities 37
📁 Lesson Plan 37
📁 Lesson Quiz 37
📁 Reteaching Activity 37

Student Activity Workbook
📁 Applying Health Skills 37
📁 Chapter 10 Study Guide

Multimedia
💾 Transparency 28

As you learn more about conflict, keep in mind that disagreements are normal in healthy relationships and that not all conflicts are harmful. A beneficial result of some conflicts is that they require people to come together to work out problems. Learning to recognize how conflict builds and knowing how to deal with conflict effectively can have a direct impact on your total health and well-being.

What Causes Conflicts?

Conflicts can begin in many ways and for many reasons. Some conflicts begin innocently, such as when one person accidentally bumps another's lunch tray. Other conflicts are the result of deliberate acts or remarks that provoke another person—for example, purposely tripping someone or making a derogatory comment. In personal relationships, conflicts can occur when one person wants to control the actions, opinions, or decisions of another person. Such conflicts may be *chronic*, or ongoing. **Figure 10.4** identifies other common causes of conflicts.

Understanding the causes of conflict in relationships may help you keep conflict from developing. If you see that a conflict is building, it is often wise to walk away. Doing so may prevent the conflict from escalating, or growing, into a situation that is unhealthful or unsafe for everyone involved.

How are internal conflicts different from interpersonal conflicts? Internal conflicts take place within an individual. For example, if a friend's birthday party and a sibling's championship soccer game occurred on the same day, you might feel conflicted about which event to attend. Using an effective decision-making model and seeking advice from parents or other trusted adults will often help you resolve these struggles in a positive, healthful way.

FIGURE 10.4

COMMON CAUSES OF CONFLICT

Situations such as these often lead to conflict.

Power struggles
Now that he is a teen, Terrence thinks that he, rather than his parents, should decide what time he will come home at night.

Loyalty
Manuel and Fred have always been best friends. When Fred takes Julio's side in an argument with Manuel, Manuel feels betrayed.

Jealousy/Envy
Keiko feels a little envious when she does not make the softball team but her best friend Meagan does.

Property disputes
Jan gets angry when Lisa borrows her clothes without asking permission.

Territory and space
Troy gets annoyed when his brother Sam uses Troy's room to watch television and play video games.

Conflict often occurs over power, property, loyalty, territory, or issues of envy or jealousy. *What are some sources of conflict that you have observed?*

---

② TEACH

Activity

Select students to role-play (in the form of a monologue) teens who are dealing with an internal conflict such as whether or not to lie; whether to return lost money; or if they should help a friend cheat on a test. Then have each student write a short letter to one of the teens, offering advice in dealing with their conflict. Remind them to check their letters for spelling and grammatical errors. Encourage them to write several drafts before their final draft. Choose some of the letters to share with the class. **L2**

Cooperative Learning

Have students work in small groups to design and complete a mural, display, or mobile illustrating conflicts in everyday life. Display students' artwork in the classroom. Then lead the class in a discussion of conflicts depicted in the projects. **L2** **Visual/ Spatial Intelligence**

VISUAL LEARNING

Figure 10.4 Ask for volunteers to read the common causes of conflict among teens as well as the examples provided in Figure 10.4. Have students work in small groups to think of additional examples that illustrate each of the causes. Ask students: What are common causes of conflict among adults? Among young children? Are they the same or different from the common causes of conflict among teens?

Curriculum Connections

Language Arts Prepare by choosing one or more poems, songs, or short stories ahead of time, and identifying the conflicts or tensions in each piece. Divide students into small groups and hand out each selection. Ask them to determine how the conflicts were handled. Who handled the conflicts?

Art Many artists capture feelings of conflict in their work. Have students identify paintings, photographs, or sculptures that depict conflict within an individual or among others. Ask students to share some of their findings with the class.

Health Minute

Discuss the importance of not allowing feelings to build up. Remind students that talking out their negative feelings lessens the chances that they will have the urge to act them out. Ask volunteers to describe a situation in which they used communication to avoid conflict.

Community Involvement

Select students to observe young children at play. Students might observe younger siblings, cousins, or neighbors. Ask them to complete anecdotal records of conflicts observed among the children. Have them also note the related actions taken by the children and/or their caregivers to resolve the conflict. Ask the students to share their observations with the class. **L3**

VISUAL LEARNING

Figure 10.5 Ask for a volunteer to read aloud the strategies for resolving conflicts. Guide students in discussing the value of using the Three Cs in conflict resolution: What can happen when individuals who disagree fail to communicate? How can cooperation help resolve conflicts? Have groups of students work together to apply the strategies to a specific conflict. Group members may record their ideas in a short essay, or plan and present a skit illustrating the steps.

Health Minute

Using Communication to Resolve Conflict

To communicate effectively:

► Talk about what is *really* troubling you.

► Practice being assertive. Learn to speak up for yourself and tell others how you feel.

► When you feel hurt or offended, use "I" messages to state your feelings clearly.

► Avoid keeping your feelings bottled up. Not stating your feelings can worsen the conflict.

Responding to Conflict

When a conflict arises, you have a choice: face the conflict or ignore it. As you decide which action to take, remember the following:

► Your primary concern should be your health and safety.

► Walking away from a potentially dangerous situation is a mature, healthful choice. It does not make you a coward. It is the smart and safe thing to do.

Minor conflicts can often be resolved by a simple compromise. If you and a sibling want to watch different television programs at the same time, for example, you might compromise by watching one program while taping the other. A compromise may be difficult to reach if the differences of opinion are strong or concern serious matters. Sometimes it can be inappropriate to compromise, such as when the compromise would go against your values or lead to harmful consequences. You must evaluate each conflict to decide whether a safe, agreeable solution can be reached or whether you should simply walk away. It is often helpful to seek the advice of a parent, guardian, teacher, or other trusted adult.

Conflict Resolution

You can learn and practice conflict resolution skills to prepare yourself for unexpected situations. **Conflict resolution** is *the process of solving a disagreement in a manner that satisfies everyone involved.* **Figure 10.5** shows some strategies for resolving conflicts peacefully.

FIGURE 10.5

STRATEGIES FOR RESOLVING CONFLICTS

1. Take time to calm down and think over the situation.
2. When discussing the conflict, take turns explaining each person's side of the conflict without interruption. Use "I" messages.
3. Ask for clarification so that each person understands the other's position.
4. Brainstorm solutions.
5. Agree on a solution that benefits both sides.
6. Follow up to see whether the correct solution was chosen and whether that solution worked for each person.

More About...

Conflict Ask students to describe conflicts they have experienced or observed that ended with a positive outcome. Remind students that many conflicts can have positive results, depending on how they are handled. For example, a conflict can encourage change by preventing people from getting into ruts and keeping old habits that they need to review and discard. Conflicts can make life more interesting by causing people to look more deeply into an issue, particularly from a new perspective. A conflict can even help to deepen and improve a relationship by strengthening each person's belief that the bond between the individuals is stronger than any one issue.

Respect for Oneself and Others

To resolve a conflict fairly and effectively, you must show respect for yourself and others. Having respect for yourself means that you recognize that you have a right to your own opinions and values. When you respect yourself, you can stand up for your beliefs. When you respect others, you can listen to them with an open mind, consider their thoughts and feelings, and honor their values.

The views and ideals of others may be different from your own. Even though you may not agree, you can demonstrate respect and tolerance. When you are tolerant of different viewpoints or ideas, fewer conflicts arise. Therefore, tolerance is crucial to preventing conflict and promoting peace.

What Causes Conflicts to Escalate?

Conflicts can occur at any time or place. The important thing is to keep them from escalating. What are some elements that can worsen a conflict? Here are two points of view.

Viewpoint 1: Marsela W., age 15

I think most conflicts escalate because of poor communication. A lot of times, people get angry and say things without considering the consequences. When there's a conflict, people also tend to forget to practice good listening skills. They ignore signs that the conflict is getting worse because they're so busy saying their piece. If people remember to use effective communication skills, they can prevent most minor conflicts from escalating.

Viewpoint 2: Annalise D., age 16

I agree that good communication skills are important, but I think the biggest reason that conflicts escalate is because of people's attitudes and emotions. If people don't know how to deal with their feelings, it's not enough to have effective communication skills. Learning to manage emotions like anger is as important as having good speaking and listening skills. In some cases, it's even more important because emotions can prevent people from thinking before they act.

(ACTIVITY)

Do you think Marsela's and Annalise's viewpoints are valid? What other elements may cause conflicts to escalate? What strategies can people use to prevent conflicts from escalating?

Lesson 3 Resolving Conflict **265**

Discussing

Have students relate how their friends deal with disagreements in peaceful ways. Discuss the need to resolve minor differences before they grow into major conflicts. **L1**

Activity

Using online and newspaper sources, have one group of students research and write a report on conflicts around the world, addressing issues such as where conflicts have occurred most frequently as well as the reasons for and consequences of the conflicts. Have another group of students research and write a report on various individuals, groups, or programs that are addressing conflicts in healthy and peaceful ways. Remind students to develop several drafts of their writing and to proofread for errors. Encourage them to produce a final error-free draft. Ask for representatives from each group to summarize their research for the class. **L3**

Exploring Issues

WHAT CAUSES CONFLICTS TO ESCALATE?

Direct students to read the Exploring Issues feature and pick a viewpoint they agree with. Have them explain why Marsela's or Annalise's viewpoint is valid. Help students identify strategies people can use to prevent conflicts from escalating.

Guest Speaker

Invite the school counselor to come to class. Ask students to prepare lists of questions about common conflicts they have experienced or observed at school or off campus. Have students ask their questions and get advice from the counselor about how some of the conflicts might have been prevented. **L2**

Community Involvement

Have students interview adult family members and friends, teachers, and/or community leaders to generate a list of ways these adults dealt with sources of conflict when they were younger. Ask students to submit their lists anonymously and read aloud to the class those ways that exemplify creative and effective conflict-resolution techniques. **L3**

Reinforcing Concepts

Choose students to role-play situations in which teens resolve conflicts by negotiating with one another. Ask the class to critique the role-plays by asking: How realistic are the conflict situations? How successful would the negotiations likely be in real life? **L2**

 Kinesthetic Intelligence

Discussing

Have students discuss some of the reasons that peer mediation is increasing in popularity on school campuses. **L1**

FYI

Conflict resolution has become such an important skill that hundreds of universities throughout the country and world now offer courses and advanced degrees in conflict analysis and resolution.

Successful negotiation requires the two parties involved to work together to find a satisfactory solution. *How did you use negotiation to resolve a recent conflict?*

Negotiating During Conflict Resolution

Even if people demonstrate respect and tolerance, they may find it difficult to resolve their conflict. It is then necessary to try **negotiation**, *the use of communication and often compromise to settle a disagreement.* The negotiation process involves talking, listening, considering the other person's point of view, compromising if necessary, and devising a plan for working jointly to resolve the conflict.

PREPARING FOR NEGOTIATION

To prepare yourself for a successful negotiation process, keep the following points in mind:

▶ Make sure the issue is important to you.

▶ Check your facts. Make sure the disagreement is not based on incorrect information.

▶ Remind yourself that your goal is to find a solution, not to fight or prove who is "in control."

▶ Rehearse what you will say, even if you have to script it out in advance.

STEPS TO TAKE WHEN NEGOTIATING

You can become a better negotiator through practice. Follow these steps to negotiate effectively.

▶ **Select a time and place suited to working out problems.** Arrange to meet when you are calm, not impatient or rushed. Choose a quiet meeting place.

▶ **Work together toward a solution.** Do not approach the other person as an enemy. Instead, work together to reach a solution.

▶ **Keep an open mind.** Remember that there are two sides to every story. Listen carefully to what the other person has to say.

▶ **Be flexible.** Be willing to meet the other person halfway.

▶ **Take responsibility for your role in the conflict.** Apologize if you know that you have hurt the other person.

▶ **Give the other person an "out."** If the other person seems embarrassed or uncomfortable, suggest continuing the conversation at a later time.

Home and Community

Mediators Have students investigate their community to find people or agencies that act as mediators. Find out if your school has a peer mediation program. Encourage students to discuss the program, evaluate its effectiveness, and make suggestions for improvement. If your school does not have such a program, ask for volunteers to try to establish one. In addition, have students find out what mediation resources are available in the community for families or neighbors in conflict. Have students make posters advertising these services.

The Mediation Process

Even with negotiation, it's not always possible for two parties in conflict to reach an agreement. When this happens, it may be time for **mediation**, *a process in which specially trained people help others resolve their conflicts peacefully.*

Mediation sessions take place in a neutral location. During the mediation process, the mediator maintains strict **confidentiality**. This involves *respecting the privacy of both parties and keeping details secret.* The process has well-defined ground rules that are set by the mediator and explained to both sides. The mediator begins by asking each person to describe the disagreement. The mediator then summarizes each side, asking for clarification of any points that are inaccurate. Each side is then given the opportunity to talk to the other under the supervision of the mediator. The mediator may then ask the parties to sign an agreement to work out the problem within a certain time frame.

Today, many schools offer peer mediation programs for settling conflicts that take place at school. These programs have **peer mediators**, *students trained to help other students find fair resolutions to conflicts and disagreements.* You will learn more about peer mediation programs in Chapter 13.

 Peer mediation is often effective in settling disputes and resolving conflicts. *What qualities would an effective peer mediator have?*

Activity

Select students to research and write articles about the school's peer mediation system to submit to the school newspaper. **Verbal/Linguistic Intelligence**

3 ASSESS

EVALUATING THE LESSON

Assign and discuss the Lesson 3 Review; then administer, grade, and discuss Lesson Quiz 37 in the TCR.

RETEACHING

- Divide students into small groups. Have them write short lessons for elementary students, using the main ideas of this lesson. Have them combine groups and present their lessons to one another.

- Ask students to complete Reteaching Activity 37 in the TCR.

ENRICHMENT

Direct students to interview a speech or drama teacher about different ways in which tone of voice can be used to avoid or reduce conflict. Have them report their findings to the class.

4 CLOSE

Ask students to summarize the most important concepts in this lesson. Remind them that conflicts can be resolved peacefully.

 Lesson 3 *Review*

Reviewing Facts and Vocabulary

1. What is an *interpersonal conflict*? What are some causes of interpersonal conflicts?

2. What are the benefits of walking away from a situation when a conflict is building?

3. What are some healthful ways of resolving conflicts?

Thinking Critically

4. **Synthesizing.** Conflicts are not always negative. Describe a situation in which a conflict can be positive. Explain why the conflict is positive.

5. **Analyzing.** Describe a conflict you have had with another person. Explain how you resolved the conflict, and evaluate the effectiveness of your conflict resolution techniques.

Applying Health Skills

Conflict Resolution. Luke wants to go to a basketball game with his friends this Saturday, but his parents want him to attend the family picnic. Write a skit in which Luke and his parents use conflict resolution techniques to solve their problem.

 TECHNOLOGY *OPTION*

VIDEO PRODUCTION Make a video of your skit. For help in planning and producing your video, see **health.glencoe.com**.

Lesson 3 Resolving Conflict **267**

 Lesson 3 *Review*

Answers to Reviewing Facts and Vocabulary

1. A disagreement between groups of any size; power struggles, loyalty, jealousy, disputes over property or territory.

2. Walking away may prevent the conflict from escalating. It is also a mature, healthful action.

3. Using communication, cooperation, compromise, negotiation, and mediation.

Answers to Thinking Critically

4. Responses will vary but should include the idea that a conflict can be positive when it brings people together to work out problems.

5. Responses will vary.

Internet Etiquette and Relationships

NHES Standard 4 Students will analyze the influence of culture, media, technology, and other factors on health.

Objective

Evaluate problems in online communication, identify strategies to resolve these problems, and practice Internet etiquette.

Motivator

Ask students if they frequently use e-mail or instant messaging to communicate with others.

Teaching Strategies

Ask students to think about whether they have experienced problems with unsolicited e-mail.

Awareness Explain to teens that there are appropriate uses of e-mail technology.

Analysis After students have completed their own charts identifying problems and solutions, ask them what issues may still exist for teens who use proper Internet etiquette rules.

Reflection Ask students to think about ways families might agree on certain rules and guidelines when using e-mail.

Take Action Ask students to come up with effective strategies to keep online communications safe and respectful.

✔Assessment

Comprehensive lists should include potential problems and effective solutions. Internet Etiquette Rules should apply good communication skills for using the Internet.

Internet Etiquette and Relationships

Technology such as e-mail has made it easy to keep in touch with family and friends who are far away. Like strong speaking and listening skills, strategies for effective online communication can strengthen relationships. In this activity, you will develop a list of Internet etiquette strategies that promote healthy, respectful communication.

Problems with Online Communication	Possible Solutions
Privacy issues	• Avoid sending e-mails dealing with private or sensitive issues. They can be forwarded to anyone.
Chain e-mails	• Do not send or forward such e-mails to others. • Politely ask friends and relatives not to send or forward them to you.
Viruses in attachments	• Make sure antivirus software is installed. • Do not open attachments from unknown or unreliable sources.

ACTIVITY

In a group, brainstorm potential problems with online communication and ways to resolve those problems. Use the chart above as a model, and try to come up with as many issues and solutions as possible. You might consider how traditional communication strategies (such as specific speaking and listening skills) can apply to online activities like e-mail and instant messaging. After completing your chart, use it to develop a list of Internet Etiquette Rules.

Make copies of your list, and share it with family and friends.

EXPRESS YOUR VIEWS

Write a one-page essay explaining the importance of online etiquette. Discuss how its use impacts relationships with family, friends, and peers. Your essay should promote communication strategies that maintain and strengthen healthy relationships.

More About...

Internet Safety The Federal Bureau of Investigation has developed a Web site dedicated to Internet. The site is specifically designed for parents and adults and lists things adults can do to make sure that youth do not fall victim to Internet harassment. Some of these suggestions include communicating and talking to the teen or child about potential dangers online; spending time with the teen while he or she is online; using parental controls that block dangerous content; and teaching children how to use the Internet responsibly. As a teacher, inquire as to what assurances are in place for keeping students safe on the Internet at your school.

CROSS-CURRICULUM CONNECTIONS

Write a Story. Conflict—that tug of war between your wishes and someone else's—arises even in the healthiest of relationships. Write a narrative about two friends who have a disagreement. Show how the characters use effective communication skills to resolve their conflict. As you write your story, consider the characters' words, tone, and body language.

Write an Essay. In the give and take of negotiating the terrain of any relationship, communication and compromise are key. Negotiation has a long history in the United States, especially the arbitration between labor unions and business management. Research and write an analytical essay on how negotiation became crucial as conflicts between workers and management grew in the early 1900s. In your essay, also consider what you can learn about negotiations that could be useful in your own relationships.

Calculate Chance. Joe wants to go to a concert, and Florence wants to go to a movie. They decide to settle the dispute amicably by flipping a coin, with the loser getting to choose the activity the next time. What are the odds that Joe will have to see a movie this time?

Research and Report. Physiologists have discovered that the primitive sections of our brains are hard-wired to protect us. The chemical activity produced by perceived threats has been called the "fight-or-flight" response. It raises blood pressure, heart rate, and respiration to increase oxygen supply and produces endorphins to fight pain. Investigate this natural response to danger, and discuss it in light of the modern need for peaceful conflict resolution.

Professional Mediator

Are you a good listener? Are you the person in your group of friends who most often helps the others reach a compromise? These skills may indicate that you are suited to a career as a professional mediator. Professional mediators often work for corporations, schools, or government agencies. They help others work together to settle disputes peacefully.

To become a professional mediator, you'll need to attend a four-year college and receive training in mediation. You can find out more about this and other health-related careers by clicking on Career Corner at **health.glencoe.com**.

Chapter 10 Review **269**

Portfolio Assessment

Self-Evaluation Direct students to review the Health Skills Activities and other activities completed in the chapter. Encourage each student to select one finished product or activity that demonstrates his or her best work for the chapter and that represents the student's learning goals. Have students explain what they have learned and how the examples they have selected demonstrate their growth in health literacy, knowledge, and skills.

Teacher Classroom Resources Assign Performance Assessment 10, "Hurrah for Volunteers," in the TCR.

Chapter 10 *Review*

CHECKING COMPREHENSION

- Assign and discuss the chapter review.
- Use the Chapter 10 MindJogger Videoquiz to review the chapter. 📼

CHAPTER 10 REVIEW ANSWERS

Exploring Health Terms

1. friendship
2. role
3. communication
4. cooperation
5. "I" messages
6. body language
7. active listening
8. conflict
9. conflict resolution
10. confidentiality

Recalling the Facts

1. Responses may include that at home, the teen plays the role of child and sibling; at school, the teen plays the roles of student, peer, friend, and possibly teammate. Accept all reasonable responses.

2. Compromise makes each person feel that she or he has been heard and stresses the importance of the relationship over the needs of the individuals involved.

3. You can demonstrate responsibility by doing what is expected of you, doing your best, using self-control, thinking before you act, and being accountable for your choices.

4. You communicate effectively when the messages you send and receive are interpreted correctly.

➤ EXPLORING HEALTH TERMS   *Answer the following questions on a sheet of paper.*

Lesson 1   *Match each definition with the correct term.*

cooperation	citizenship
compromise	role
friendship	relationship
communication	

1. A significant relationship between two people based on caring, trust, and consideration.
2. A part you play in a relationship.
3. The ways in which you send and receive messages.
4. A process of working together for the good of all.

Lesson 2   *Fill in the blanks with the correct term.*

body language	constructive criticism
tolerance	"I" messages
active listening	prejudice

Tara is annoyed because Liz is late. To avoid placing blame, she uses (_5_) to let Liz know how she feels. Liz shows she is listening to Tara by using appropriate (_6_), such as nodding her head. Using (_7_) skills helps Liz understand why Tara is upset, and she apologizes for being late.

Lesson 3   *Replace the underlined words with the correct term.*

negotiation	peer mediators
conflict resolution	interpersonal conflict
mediation	confidentiality
conflict	

8. Any disagreement or struggle is a <u>negotiation</u>.
9. Mediation and negotiation are two processes used for <u>interpersonal conflict</u>.
10. Mediators must demonstrate <u>conflict</u>, respect for the rights and privacy of others.

➤ RECALLING THE FACTS   *Use complete sentences to answer the following questions.*

Lesson 1

1. Name three roles you play in your relationships with others. Explain when you play each role.
2. How can compromise help strengthen a relationship?
3. What are some ways you can demonstrate the character trait of responsibility?

Lesson 2

4. How do you know when you are communicating effectively?
5. What is reflective listening?
6. How does prejudice set up a barrier to effective communication?

Lesson 3

7. List the strategies for conflict resolution.
8. What two things should you consider when deciding how to respond to conflict?
9. Define negotiation.
10. When might it be necessary to have a mediator help settle a conflict?

---

5. Reflective listening is rephrasing or summarizing what the speaker says to make sure you understand what is intended.

6. Prejudice prevents a person from having an open mind and listening to new information.

7. Take time to calm down and think over the situation; take turns explaining each person's side of the conflict without interruption; ask for clarification so that each person understands the other's position; brainstorm solutions; agree on a solution that benefits both sides; follow up to see whether the correct solution was chosen.

8. When deciding how to respond to conflict, you should always remember that your primary concern should be your health and safety and that walking away from a potentially dangerous situation is a mature, healthful choice.

9. The use of communication and often compromise to settle a disagreement.

10. Mediation may be necessary if the two parties are unable to find a solution for the problem causing the conflict.

➤ THINKING CRITICALLY

1. **Evaluating.** Kate always decides what she and her friend Suki will do when they go out together. What trait or skill is missing in this relationship? How might the situation be changed? *(LESSON 1)*

2. **Synthesizing.** Explain how you would use reflective listening, clarifying, and encouraging techniques to demonstrate active listening skills if your friend tells you the following: "I'm sorry I missed the game last night. My mother fell and we had to take her to the hospital for stitches. It was really scary." *(LESSON 2)*

3. **Analyzing.** Making compromises is not always a good way of resolving a situation. Describe the types of situations in which you should not be willing to compromise or negotiate. *(LESSON 3)*

➤ HEALTH SKILLS APPLICATION

1. **Analyzing Influences.** Think about a relationship you have with a family member or a friend. Evaluate and describe the positive and negative effects of this relationship on each side of your health triangle. *(LESSON 1)*

2. **Communication Skills.** Imagine that you have a friend who frequently borrows things and returns them in poor condition. Explain how you could use constructive criticism to help the person change this pattern of behavior. *(LESSON 2)*

3. **Advocacy.** Write a persuasive letter to the principal of your school to advocate the use of peer mediators. In your letter, explain why peer mediation is important. Describe the steps involved in this process and the types of situations in which it might be used. *(LESSON 3)*

BEYOND *the* Classroom

Parent Involvement

Advocacy. Learn more about community mediation programs. With your parents, find out how your family can become involved in raising awareness about the existence and usefulness of such programs in your community. If mediation programs do not already exist in your community, learn how you can help create one.

School and Community

Overcoming Prejudice. Speak with a law enforcement official in your community who has helped victims of hate crimes—offenses against an individual or group that are a direct or indirect result of prejudice. Ask the official what communication skills a person would need to help victims of hate crimes. Report to your class what you have learned.

Chapter 10 Review **271**

Lessons	Standards		Features
	National	**State/Local**	
1 **The Role of the Family** *pages 274–279*	National Health Education Standards 1.4, 3.1, 3.4, 5.4		**Hands-On Health** • Making Time for Family Fun *(Practicing Healthful Behaviors)*, page 277
2 **Change and the Family** *pages 280–285*	National Health Education Standards 3.4, 3.7, 5.1, 5.3, 5.7		**Health Skills Activity** • That's What Friends Are For *(Communication)*, page 284
3 **Dealing with Family Crises** *pages 286–290*	National Health Education Standards 3.4, 3.6, 5.7		**Exploring Issues** • What Are the Benefits of Individual and Family Counseling? page 288
4 **Community Support Systems** *pages 291–295*	National Health Education Standards 1.4, 2.4, 2.6, 6.2		**Real-Life Application** • Family Support Services *(Accessing Information)*, page 293

Chapter 11 Planning Guide

Reproducible Resources	Assessment	Technology
Student Activity Workbook for use with each chapter	📁 Lesson Quiz 38	🕹️ Transparency 29
📁 Concept Mapping Activity 38		💿 TeacherWorks®
📁 Cross-Curriculum Activity 11		💻 Internet Activities
📁 Current Health Issues 11		
📁 Enrichment Activity 11		
📁 Guided Reading Activities 38		
📁 Health Lab 11		
📁 Lesson Plan 38		
📁 Parent Letter and Activities 11		
📁 Reteaching Activity 38		
📁 Concept Mapping Activity 39	📁 Lesson Quiz 39	🕹️ Transparency 30
📁 Decision-Making Activity 11		💿 TeacherWorks®
📁 Guided Reading Activities 39		
📁 Lesson Plan 39		
📁 Reteaching Activity 39		
📁 Concept Mapping Activity 40	📁 Lesson Quiz 40	💿 TeacherWorks®
📁 Guided Reading Activities 40		
📁 Lesson Plan 40		
📁 Reteaching Activity 40		
📁 Concept Mapping Activity 41	📁 Lesson Quiz 41	🕹️ Transparency 31
📁 Guided Reading Activities 41		💿 TeacherWorks®
📁 Lesson Plan 41		
📁 Reteaching Activity 41		

0:00 OUT OF TIME

If time does not permit teaching the entire chapter, use:

- Hands-On Health, p. 277
- Health Skills Activity, p. 284
- Figure 11.2, p. 289
- Real-Life Application, p. 293

Language Diversity

- 🎧 English Audio CD Program
- 🎧 Spanish Audio CD Program
- 📁 English Summaries, Quizzes, and Activities
- 📁 Spanish Summaries, Quizzes, and Activities
- 📁 Spanish Parent Letters and Activities

End of Chapter Assessment

Blackline Masters

- 📁 Chapter 11 Test
- 📁 Performance Assessment Activity 11

Technology

- 💿 Vocabulary PuzzleMaker
- 📼 MindJogger Videoquiz
- 💿 **Exam***View*® Pro Testmaker

Professional Health Series

Dealing with Sensitive Issues
Planning a Coordinated School Health Program
Promoting Character Education
Home, School, and Community Involvement

CHAPTER OVERVIEW

Chapter 11 explores the area of family relationships. The chapter emphasizes the importance of strengthening relationships and seeking support during times of crisis.

Lesson 1 The family is the basic unit of society. A family is responsible for the physical, mental/emotional, and social health of its members. Parents, grandparents, and other family members play a part in promoting a healthy family.

Lesson 2 Changes in family structure, such as divorce, can cause stress in families. Changes in family circumstances, such as financial problems, can also be stressful. It is important to learn how to deal with stress in healthy ways.

Lesson 3 The breakdown of a family system can result in violence. Domestic violence can involve emotional, physical, or sexual abuse. Using the three Rs—recognize, resist, and report—can help people avoid and prevent domestic violence.

Lesson 4 Professional health services are available to assist members of families facing crises. Sources of help include community services, support groups, counseling, and mediation.

Health Skills Features

- Hands-On Health (*Practicing Healthful Behaviors*), p. 277
- Health Skills Activity (*Communication*), p. 284
- Exploring Issues, p. 288
- Real-Life Application (*Accessing Information*), p. 293

272

Chapter 11

Family Relationships

Lesson 1
The Role of the Family

Lesson 2
Change and the Family

Lesson 3
Dealing with Family Crises

Lesson 4
Community Support Systems

272

MEETING STUDENT DIVERSITY

Language Diversity Use the following suggestions to help students who have difficulty with English:

- Pair English language learners with native speakers of English who can restate the Chapter Summary in language that helps students comprehend important concepts.

- Direct auditory learners or those students with language diversity to the *Glencoe Health Audio CD Program.* Available in English and Spanish, this component provides an audio and written summary of the chapter.

- Use photographs, drawings, or magazine clippings to help students visualize the important concepts of the chapter.

Personal Health Inventory ✓

What's Your Health Status?

Read each statement below and respond by writing *yes*, *no*, or *sometimes* for each item. Write *yes* only for items that you practice regularly.

1. I spend time with my family.
2. I demonstrate love and respect for members of my family.
3. I communicate effectively with family members.
4. When there's a disagreement, I try to see the points of view of other family members.
5. I share household responsibilities with my family.
6. I share my thoughts, feelings, dreams, accomplishments, and disappointments with family members.
7. I ask for help from family members when I need support.
8. I am a loyal and trustworthy member of my family.
9. I provide positive input that helps other family members feel appreciated and supported.
10. I am committed to healthy family relationships.

Keep this personal inventory for review later in the chapter. When you complete the chapter, review your answers and identify two or three behavior changes you could make to improve your relationship with your family.

Quick *Write*

Using Visuals. List some of the ways you interact with and support the members of your family. What actions do you and other family members take to promote the health and well-being of the entire family?

273

INTRODUCING THE CHAPTER

Personal Health Inventory ✓

Let students read and briefly discuss the Personal Health Inventory statements. Then have them record their responses to these statements in their private health journals. Remind students that they should respond honestly and openly, and avoid comparing their own families with the families of friends and neighbors or those seen on TV programs.

Tell students that members of a family affect one another economically, socially, emotionally, and in some ways, physically. As the basic unit of society, the family plays a critical role in the healthy growth and development of the individual. Remind students that this material is not intended to delve into their private lives; rather, it is meant to create an awareness of the importance of the family unit and an understanding of what constitutes a healthy family. Tell students that they will learn more about families and family relationships as they read Chapter 11.

Quick *write*

Using Visuals Direct students to look at the photographs. Ask: What do these scenes show or suggest about family relationships? Have volunteers share some of the ways in which they interact with and support their family members. As a class, discuss ways in which family members promote the health and well-being of the family.

TECHNOLOGY OPTIONS

MINDJOGGER
VIDEOQUIZ

To preview or review chapter content, you may wish to use the Chapter 11 MindJogger Videoquiz.

HEALTH *Online* **Online Resources for the Teacher** For a fresh approach to health topics and an in-depth look at health issues, use these online resources found under Teacher Resources at **health.glencoe.com:**

• Block Schedule Lesson Plans
• Technology Projects
• Health Updates

FOCUS

 QUICK START On the board, draw three columns labeled *Physical Health*, *Mental/Emotional Health*, and *Social Health*. Ask volunteers to share the ways in which family members contribute to each aspect of health, and write their responses in the appropriate columns. Lead the class in a discussion of the important role of family in a person's total health.

TYING TO PRIOR KNOWLEDGE

Have students share what they already know about families. Ask: What are some of the roles of family members? What are some of their responsibilities? Explain that the lesson will focus on the roles and responsibilities of family members and the traits of a healthy family.

Health Skills Features

"Making Time for Family Fun," p. 277

PRACTICING HEALTHFUL BEHAVIORS

INTRODUCING VOCABULARY

- Have students write a sentence describing what the word *family* means to them. Ask volunteers to read their sentences to the class.
- Ask students to complete the Chapter 11 Study Guide in the *Student Activity Workbook*. 📁

274

Lesson 1

The Role of the Family

VOCABULARY
family
extended family
sibling
affirmation

YOU'LL LEARN TO
- Evaluate the effects of family relationships on physical, mental/emotional, and social health.
- Describe the roles of parents, grandparents, and other family members in promoting a healthy family.
- Analyze the dynamics of family roles and responsibilities relating to health behavior.

 QUICK START List the different ways that members of your family contribute to your physical, mental/emotional, and social health.

H ow would you describe your family? How has your family influenced your behaviors and goals? In what ways have family members contributed to your sense of security and belonging? Because the family plays an important part in all aspects of a person's health, it's important to learn about family dynamics and ways of promoting a healthy family.

What Is a Family?

T he **family**, *the basic unit of society*, provides a safe and nurturing environment for its members. Because the health of society is directly related to the health of the family, promoting healthy families contributes to a healthy society.

A healthy family freely expresses mutual love and respect. Its members communicate effectively with one another, providing support and encouragement. Through caring family relationships, teens develop the values and self-confidence that help them make responsible decisions and work to achieve their goals. In addition, a strong family foundation can serve as an important **protective factor**, helping children and teens to avoid risky behaviors.

hot link

protective factors For more information about protective factors and how they empower you to practice healthful behaviors and make responsible decisions, see Chapter 8, page 216.

274 **Chapter 11** Family Relationships

Lesson 1 Resources

Teacher Classroom Resources
📁 Concept Mapping Activity 38
📁 Cross-Curriculum Activity 11
📁 Current Health Issues 11
📁 Enrichment Activity 11
📁 Guided Reading Activities 38
📁 Health Lab 11
📁 Lesson Plan 38

📁 Lesson Quiz 38
📁 Parent Letter and Activities 11
📁 Reteaching Activity 38

Student Activity Workbook
📁 Applying Health Skills 38
📁 Chapter 11 Study Guide

Multimedia
 Transparency 29

The Importance of Family

Although families differ in size and makeup, a healthy family strives to promote the physical, mental/emotional, and social health of its members. Some of the ways in which the family meets these needs are shown in **Figure 11.1.**

Meeting Physical and Other Basic Needs

Most parents and guardians work hard to provide for their family's basic physical needs, including food, clothing, and shelter. Adult family members also make certain that children get medical and dental checkups, receive immunizations, and learn to practice healthful behaviors. The family is responsible for teaching children the skills needed to live safely in their environment. For example, children need to be taught how to cross streets safely and not to get into a car with a stranger. As they grow and mature, children learn more life skills from older members of the family. These skills may range from making healthful food choices to setting goals and making decisions.

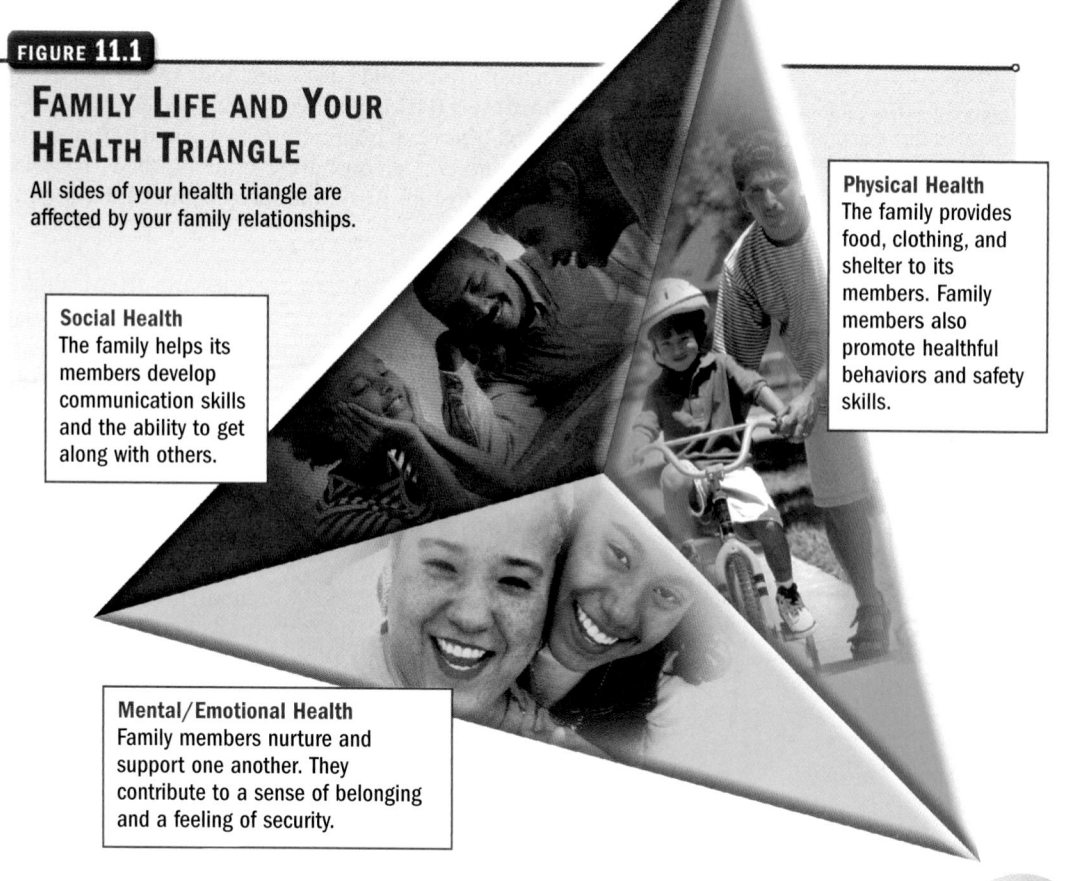

FIGURE 11.1

FAMILY LIFE AND YOUR HEALTH TRIANGLE

All sides of your health triangle are affected by your family relationships.

Social Health
The family helps its members develop communication skills and the ability to get along with others.

Physical Health
The family provides food, clothing, and shelter to its members. Family members also promote healthful behaviors and safety skills.

Mental/Emotional Health
Family members nurture and support one another. They contribute to a sense of belonging and a feeling of security.

② TEACH

VISUAL LEARNING

Figure 11.1 Direct students to review the information shown in Figure 11.1. Divide the class into three groups, and assign each group one side of the health triangle. Have each group write down additional examples of ways in which family relationships promote the assigned area of health. Then ask volunteers to use the lists from each group to create a poster depicting some of the examples.

Discussing

On the board, list the names of some popular family dramas or situational comedies. Discuss the strengths portrayed in these TV families. Ask questions such as: Why are these families successful (or unsuccessful)? How do family members meet one another's physical, mental/emotional, and social needs? Are the portrayals realistic? Conclude by saying that all families are different, and each one has its strengths and weaknesses. ◀

Cooperative Learning

Divide the class into two groups. One group will list ways the family can affect that person's self-concept. The other group will list the ways in which a person's self-concept can affect his or her family's health. ◀

Home and Community

Homeless Families Females who are single parents account for a rapidly increasing percentage of homeless and impoverished people in the United States. Have students conduct research about homeless or poverty-stricken families in their community or state. How many are single women with children? What factors account for their homelessness? (inadequate or minimum wages for women, teen pregnancy, or lack of child support) What services does the community offer to help low-income and homeless families? Encourage students to discuss problems and solutions.

Discussing

Have students name some of the values that parents teach their children. Ask: How do these values help children develop good character? How do they help children become responsible adults? Have students give specific examples.

Activity

Assign volunteers to plan and carry out an activity for a family night, holiday, or vacation. Afterward, have them write a short paper about the family experience. Make sure students identify the values that were reinforced by the activities they had chosen. **L2** **Verbal/Linguistic Intelligence**

Community Involvement

Ask students to interview someone they know about the roles and responsibilities in that person's family. Have them find answers to questions such as: How does the family divide household responsibilities? Who is the "head" of the household? Who cares for the children? What household responsibilities do the children share? What roles do the other family members have? **L2**

Meeting Mental/Emotional Needs

The family provides a safe, comforting environment in which all members can express thoughts and emotions freely. By providing emotional support and unconditional love, families promote positive self-concepts in their members. A positive self-concept, the view a person has of himself or herself, gives individuals a sense of confidence, helping them become healthy, happy adults.

Meeting Social Needs

In the first few years of life, children learn from family members how to communicate and get along with others. Families also play a major role in children's social growth by helping them develop a value system, by instilling religious beliefs, and by raising them with cultural and family traditions. A healthy family helps children become team players and teaches them to accept differences in others. Families prepare their members to survive and function independently in the world.

DEVELOPING A VALUE SYSTEM

You learn your values—your beliefs and feelings about what is important—from your family. Developing a good value system helps you in making responsible decisions. Your values also determine your **character.** Having positive values helps you become a good citizen who obeys laws, respects authority, and contributes to school and community. Demonstrating traits of good character improves your relationships with other people and contributes to society in a positive way.

hotlink

character For more information on traits that demonstrate character, see Chapter 2, page 37.

▶ Families enhance social health by passing family and cultural traditions on to their children. *What are some of your family's traditions?*

SHARING CULTURE AND TRADITIONS

Does your family have special traditions, such as participating in Chinese New Year celebrations or lighting candles at Hanukkah? By observing traditions such as these, adult family members pass their culture and history on to children. Sharing a cultural heritage enriches the lives of family members and helps individuals develop a sense of pride in who they are.

School to Work

Childcare Provider Childcare workers nurture and teach children of all ages in childcare centers, nursery schools, preschools, public schools, private households, family childcare environments, and before- and after-school programs. These workers play an important role in a child's development by caring for the child when the parents are at work or for other reasons.

Have students research careers as childcare providers in a variety of settings. Encourage them to list the advantages and challenges of a career as a childcare provider. Follow the activity with a class discussion about the importance of childcare workers to families.

Dynamics of Family Roles and Responsibilities

Your family is more than just the people who live in your home. It also includes your **extended family**, that is, *your immediate family and other relatives such as grandparents, aunts, uncles, and cousins.* What are some of the benefits that you enjoy from your extended family? Have you learned about your family's history from a grandparent or vacationed with cousins who live in another part of the country? Perhaps an aunt or an uncle has helped your immediate family during times of need or has acted as your mentor. Each family member has roles and responsibilities in a healthy family. The adults are usually in charge of providing basic comforts and fulfilling basic needs such as food and shelter. They also set limits and make rules that protect the health and safety of their children.

Family members can spend quality time together by sharing knowledge and interests. *What are some ways you spend time with your extended family?*

Hands-On Health

MAKING TIME FOR FAMILY FUN

PRACTICING HEALTHFUL BEHAVIORS

NHES Standard 3 Students will demonstrate the ability to practice health-enhancing behaviors and reduce health risks.

Objective

Develop strategies to improve or maintain family health.

Motivator

Give students one minute to share activities they like to participate in with their families.

Teaching Strategies

1. Suggest that students consider the interests of their family members. This will help them think of an activity that will appeal to all members.
2. Tell students to choose a variety of activities in which family members interact, and encourage activities that also promote physical activity.

✓ Assessment

Using a rubric, student work should provide comprehensive evidence of the following criteria to achieve the highest score:

✔ explanation of how activities promote the physical, mental/emotional, and social health of family members
✔ identification of strategies that strengthen family relationships

Hands-On Health ACTIVITY

Making Time for Family Fun

Busy schedules can make it difficult for family members to spend quality time together, but it is important to make time to strengthen family relationships. In this activity, you will develop a plan to spend more quality time with your family.

What You'll Need

- paper and markers
- ruler

What You'll Do

1. Brainstorm a list of activities you and your family enjoy doing together. Examples might include weekend outings or trips, recreational activities, family game night, and roundtable discussions.

2. Consider other ways you can strengthen family relationships. You might suggest projects such as putting together a memory album or starting a new family tradition like pizza night every Wednesday.

3. Using your ideas, create a chart of strategies that promote the physical, mental/emotional, and social health of family members.

Apply and Conclude

Show your chart to family members, and discuss how spending quality time together promotes healthy family relationships. Ask them for other suggestions, and then put your ideas into action.

Curriculum Connections

Family and Consumer Sciences Hand out to each student or small group a magazine that features one or more stories about a particular family or family life. Have students read the articles about the family and ask them to circle information in the articles about the following: sharing culture and traditions, communication, family roles and responsibilities, family crises, and coping with crises. Collect the articles, and share some of them with the class. Point out instances that spotlight families sharing culture and traditions, good communication, family members who share household responsibilities, and family members who are coping with crises.

Critical Thinking

Have volunteers share some of the responsibilities they have in caring for a younger brother, sister, or cousin. Ask students: How can teens act as role models for younger relatives? How might they show support and caring for younger family members? In what ways does this positive behavior promote the health of the entire family? **L2**

Discussing

Talk about some of the responsibilities that teens can assume to help a family function smoothly. Survey the class to see what responsibilities students are currently assuming. Ask: Why is it important for teens to have family responsibilities? **L1**

HEALTH Online

Have students read about techniques for improving communication in families. Ask: Which methods do you think would work best? Why?

Reinforcing Concepts

Instruct students to keep a log of the number of hours they spend with each member of their family in one week. Have them specify the activities they share with each family member during these times. Then ask them to analyze their findings and tell how they might improve the quality or the quantity of time spent with family members. **L1**

HEALTH Online

Click on Web Links at health.glencoe.com to learn more about ways to improve family communication.

Affirming family members' achievements demonstrates love and pride. *How do you show family members that they are appreciated and supported?*

Like the adults in a healthy family, children and teens also have responsibilities in the household. They respect the authority of parents or guardians and may take on tasks such as washing dishes or cleaning. Teens may be asked to care for a younger **sibling**—*a brother or sister*—while a parent is at work. Sharing such tasks helps the family run smoothly. It also helps boost your self-esteem and gives you a greater sense of responsibility.

Strengthening Family Relationships

Good communication is one of the most important traits of a healthy family. Sharing thoughts, feelings, experiences, and concerns helps strengthen family bonds. Every member of the family plays a role in promoting the health of the entire family. You can help strengthen your family in the following ways.

▶ **Demonstrate care and love.** Family members show that they care about and love one another through words and actions. You can give affirmation for a job well done, for example, through a compliment or a pat on the back. **Affirmation** is *positive feedback that helps others feel appreciated and supported.* You can also show empathy for a family member who is feeling down to remind that person that he or she is loved.

▶ **Show support, especially during difficult times.** Whether the difficulty is something minor (such as getting a low grade on a quiz) or a traumatic experience (such as a death in the family), talking about your feelings can help you feel better. Remember to be a good listener when others want to talk.

▶ **Demonstrate trust.** Members of a healthy family trust one another. Parents earn their children's trust by caring for them, being honest, and keeping promises. Children show that they can be trusted when they are honest, reliable, and loyal.

▶ **Express commitment.** Building a strong, healthy family requires commitment—the willingness to work together and make necessary sacrifices for the benefit of the entire family.

▶ **Be responsible.** Thinking before you act, avoiding risky behaviors, asking for permission, and being accountable for your actions demonstrate respect for self and family members.

278 Chapter 11

Curriculum Connections

Language Arts Have students write an essay describing the kind of family they would like to have when they are adults. Have them describe such elements as how they would like their family members to interact and what traditions or rituals they might share.

Social Studies Have students select and research family life in two cultures. Have them compare and contrast the roles and responsibilities of family members in each culture. Ask them to write a comparative report on their findings.

- ► **Spend time together.** Eating meals together, playing games or sports, and planning fun activities and trips all contribute to strong family relationships.

- ► **Respect individuality.** Strong families have respect for each other. They accept individual tastes, talents, and opinions.

- ► **Work together to solve problems.** Healthy families try to identify and work out problems before they become serious. If necessary, they seek outside help to resolve their conflicts. Working together can also mean planning events together, such as having a surprise party, choosing a pet, or going on vacation.

- ► **Be sensitive to others' needs.** Pay attention to how others feel. You can help relieve the stress of daily life by using good communication skills and helping with household tasks. Respecting the privacy of others is also a way to demonstrate sensitivity.

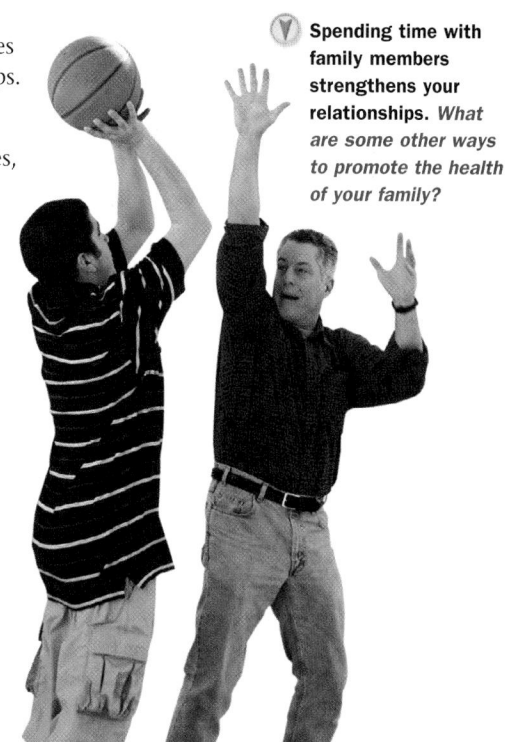

Spending time with family members strengthens your relationships. *What are some other ways to promote the health of your family?*

 Lesson 1 *Review*

Reviewing Facts and Vocabulary

1. List two ways that families help their members develop social health.

2. What is an *extended family*?

3. Why is it important for family members to give affirmation to one another?

Thinking Critically

4. **Analyzing.** Explain how family roles and responsibilities influence health behaviors.

5. **Synthesizing.** Identify three traits of a healthy family, and describe the roles your immediate and extended family members play in promoting the health of the family.

Applying Health Skills

Communication Skills. Work with class-mates to list ways families can improve communication. Include the elements of effective communication, such as "I" messages, active listening, and appropriate body language. Write and perform a skit to demonstrate your ideas.

WEB SITES Videotape your skit as part of a Web page you develop on promoting healthy families. See health.glencoe.com for help in planning and building your Web site.

Lesson 1 The Role of the Family   **279**

 Lesson 1 *Review*

Answers to Reviewing Facts and Vocabulary

1. See page 276.
2. The immediate family plus other relatives such as grandparents, aunts, uncles, and cousins.
3. To show care and consideration.

Answers to Thinking Critically

4. By following and adopting the skills, values, and traditions taught to them by adults, children take on healthful behaviors and support the family.
5. Answers will vary.

---

3 ASSESS

EVALUATING THE LESSON

Assign and discuss the Lesson 1 Review; then administer, grade, and discuss Lesson Quiz 38 in the TCR. 📁

RETEACHING

- Ask students to describe the roles they have in their own family. Then, have students discuss their responsibility in contributing to their family's health.

- Ask students to complete Reteaching Activity 38 in the TCR. 📁

ENRICHMENT

Help students analyze media representations (and misrepresentations) of family life portrayed on television. Have them choose a television show that depicts family life and have them write an analysis of the family based on information presented in this lesson.

4 CLOSE

Review the traits of a healthy family with the class. Discuss how each trait helps promote the physical, mental/emotional, or social health of family members. If any area of the health triangle is neglected, the health of the family or individual members could be affected. Stress the importance of individuals assuming responsibility for one another in maintaining a healthy family.

Change and the Family

1 FOCUS

QUICK START Write *Stress That Affects a Family* in the center of the board. As students complete their word webs, ask volunteers to share their responses, and write them on the board. As a class, discuss ways in which these stresses might affect the health of a family.

TYING TO PRIOR KNOWLEDGE

Ask students to write a paragraph describing a change, such as moving to a new area or the death of a grandparent. Then have them write a paragraph describing how individuals can cope with the change. Tell the class that this lesson will focus on ways in which changes affect the family and discuss methods of coping with these changes.

Health Skills Features

"That's What Friends Are For," p. 284

COMMUNICATION SKILLS

INTRODUCING VOCABULARY

- Have students work in pairs. Have one student of each pair write a few sentences that use the vocabulary terms in context. Have the other student look up the words in the Glossary to confirm the definitions.

- Ask students to complete the Chapter 11 Study Guide in the *Student Activity Workbook.*

Change and the Family

VOCABULARY
separation
divorce
custody
grief
resiliency

YOU'LL LEARN TO

- Evaluate positive and negative effects of family relationships on physical and emotional health.

- Discuss how significant family events can impact health.

- Examine issues related to death and grieving.

- Examine causes and effects of stress within families and develop strategies for managing stress.

QUICK START All families, including healthy ones, experience stress from time to time. Create a word web with the words *Stress That Affects a Family* at the center of a sheet of paper; around it, write the causes of stress that any family might face.

Some family events, such as moving to a new home, can be stressful. *What are some healthy ways to deal with the stress of moving?*

Minor problems and irritations are normal when people are living together. Usually, good communication and problem-solving skills can help family members work out such conflicts. Significant changes in family dynamics, however, can threaten the health of a family. It is important that all family members develop coping skills for dealing with problems that may arise.

Families and Change

Change, a normal part of life, can be a major cause of stress within families. The sudden loss of a job, for example, may cause a financial hardship, making it difficult to provide food, clothing, and other basic physical needs. Serious or chronic illness in a family member can result in long-term stress for the whole family. Life events perceived as positive can also cause stress. For example, buying a new car, moving, or the marriage of an older sibling are positive events that may cause stress.

The changes that cause stress in families are of two main types. The first type involves changes in the structure, or makeup, of the family. The second involves changes in the family's circumstances.

Lesson 2 Resources

Teacher Classroom Resources

- Concept Mapping Activity 39
- Decision-Making Activity 11
- Guided Reading Activities 39
- Lesson Plan 39
- Lesson Quiz 39
- Reteaching Activity 39

Student Activity Workbook

- Applying Health Skills 39
- Chapter 11 Study Guide

Multimedia

 Transparency 30

Changes in Family Structure

Family structure changes when someone new joins the family or when a member of the family moves out of the home. To accommodate a new family member, you may have to get along with less space in your home. A new family member also brings a new personality that may change the character of the family. Some changes may be joyful, such as the birth or adoption of a child. Other changes may be sorrowful, such as the breakup of a marriage or the death of a family member. Losing a family member can mean losing the love and care he or she provided, as well as the sharing of experiences with that person. Whatever the reason or nature, any change in family structure can cause stress.

Separation and Divorce

Marriage is an agreement between two people to commit to sharing life's joys, struggles, and challenges. Usually, married couples find ways to work out their problems. However, if conflicts become too difficult to work out, the couple may decide to separate or divorce. A **separation** is *a decision between married individuals to live apart from each other.* A couple may separate until they resolve their differences and believe that they can live together again. If they can't work out their problems, the couple may decide to divorce. A **divorce** is *a legal end to a marriage contract.*

MEETING THE NEEDS OF CHILDREN

When parents divorce, it must be decided where the children will live. **Custody** is *a legal decision about who has the right to make decisions affecting the children in a family and who has the responsibility of physically caring for them.* Custody may be granted to only one parent (sole custody) or divided so that both parents share in the child-rearing (joint custody).

FAMILY ADJUSTMENTS

Adapting to divorce requires emotional adjustments for the whole family. Teens and children often find it difficult to live apart from one parent and not see that parent for long periods of time. Some may experience some of the stages of grief, including denial or numbness; anger (at one or both parents); bargaining; depression; and finally, acceptance.

Did You Know ?

▶ Family structure has become more diverse in past decades. Some teens live with only one parent, and others live with a grandparent or relative. In blended families, teens live with stepparents, stepbrothers, and stepsisters. There are also many teens who live with adoptive families. In fact, more than 100,000 children are adopted in the United States each year. Belonging to different family structures may cause difficult feelings in some teens. In these situations, it is helpful to discuss feelings and concerns with family members.

ⓨ Separation and divorce can put a strain on the family unit. *What can family members do to support one another through such a change?*

② TEACH

Service Learning

Choose students to write positive public service announcements about the changing family system. Have them present their public service announcements to the class. L2 🔲 **Verbal/ Linguistic Intelligence**

Health Skills Practice

Family Support Services Ask several students to investigate local sources of support for families going through a divorce. Have them find out the kinds of services provided and how someone in need could get involved. Invite the students to prepare a small bulletin board to share their findings. L3

ACCESSING INFORMATION

Community Involvement

Select students to interview one or more single-parent heads of households. Have students ask about ways the parents deal with increased responsibilities and stress while playing multiple roles to maintain the home and family. L2

⟩*More About...*

Divorce Divorce can be a result of troubled families. About one in two marriages ends in divorce. When divorce involves children, it can put extreme emotional stress on family members when children are caught in a battle between parents. They may blame themselves or fear abandonment and loss of love. Children and all family members experiencing the loss may experience stages of

grieving before they finally accept the finality of divorce. The process may take years.

Divorce may also create a financial crisis. Without child support, it is difficult to rear children on one income. For the parent with custody, being a single parent can be both physically and emotionally exhausting, frustrating, and lonely.

Community Involvement

Suggest that students interview adults who have adopted new roles, such as a career change; caring for a sick or aging family member; or the addition of new family members because of a birth, remarriage, or adoption. What challenges do the new roles bring? What strategies help the adult manage these new responsibilities? **L3**

Activity

Have students interview their grandparents or an adult of their grandparents' generation about their family and its members' roles and responsibilities. Encourage volunteers to share their findings. Discuss the changes in today's families and some of the reasons for the changes. **L3**

Critical Thinking

Of the following changes affecting families today, have students identify which they think are the most significant: families living away from extended family; both parents working outside of the home; or single-parent households. Ask them to give reasons for their choices. **L1**

Grief is a natural emotion when you lose someone you love. *What might be a healthy way for this teen to deal with the loss of her loved one?*

Keep in mind that parents divorce each other, not their children. Although the feelings that divorced parents have for each other change, their love for their children can stay the same. Below are some suggestions for managing emotional stress when parents get divorced.

▶ Remind yourself that you did not cause the problem.

▶ Do not feel that you have to choose sides.

▶ Communicate your feelings about the divorce with your parents and other trusted, supportive adults.

▶ Take care of yourself by eating nutritious foods, getting physical activity, and managing your stress.

▶ Consider joining a support group for children of divorce. Doing so will help you realize that you are not alone.

Remarriage

The remarriage of a parent can also be stressful. Stepparents and children need time to adjust to one another. If the stepparent has children from a previous marriage, everyone in the blended family needs time to adjust to the change and to develop the communication skills and respect needed for healthful family relationships.

Death of a Family Member

A death in the family can be an extremely difficult experience. Feelings of **grief**, *the sorrow caused by the loss of a loved one,* can be intense. When a death occurs, each family member needs time to grieve, but the length of time needed for grieving is different for each person. Here are some strategies for coping with the death of a loved one.

▶ **Focus on happy memories.** Remember good times and the qualities that made the person special.

▶ **Accept your feelings.** It's normal to feel hurt when you lose someone. Don't try to deny your pain.

▶ **Join a support group.** Grief support groups allow people who have suffered a loss to share their pain with others. Local religious institutions or other organizations may sponsor these groups.

▶ **Seek help from a grief counselor.** If feelings of grief interfere with a person's life for an extended period of time, it is necessary to seek professional help.

282 **Chapter 11** Family Relationships

More About...

Blended Families Many students may be part of blended families. The term "blended" can be misleading. Even though teens may be part of a new "blended" family, they still may continue to be connected to their other biological parent. While every stepfamily is different, teens need to understand that adjusting to a new family structure requires patience and flexibility. If teens appear to be having difficulty adjusting to a new stepfamily, you may want to share with them the following tips:

• Remember that your feelings are normal and that help is available.

• If you are angry or upset, try expressing your feelings in healthy ways, such as writing in a journal or drawing pictures.

Changes in Family Circumstances

Changes in circumstances can also cause difficulties for families. Often, honest and open communication can help families deal with such changes in healthful ways.

Moving

When a family moves, its members may miss their old friends and the familiar surroundings of their old home. Teens may be anxious about making new friends and adjusting to a new school. If a move follows the breakup of a marriage, children may miss the parent who no longer lives with them.

Financial Problems

Meeting a family's financial needs is not easy. Loss of a job, medical emergencies, and overdue bills can cause anxiety about how to support family needs. Impulse buying or poor planning may also cause financial problems. *Credit card abuse*, the overuse of credit cards, can be a serious problem for those who pay the bills, and it often leads to arguments about spending habits.

Illness and Disability

A serious illness or disability can disrupt a family's normal activities. One or more family members may need to change their schedules to care for the sick or disabled person. In addition to worry and concern for the person who is ill, family members may also experience the stress of making major medical decisions about types of care or treatments. Some of this stress can be relieved if all members of the family share in the responsibility of caring for the person who is sick or disabled.

Drug and Alcohol Abuse

Substance abuse within the family threatens the health of the entire family. Without intervention and outside help, this problem can cause the family system to break down. If a family member has a substance abuse problem, seek immediate help from trusted adults, school personnel, or organizations such as Alateen. These resources can help you understand the problem and guide you in getting additional assistance.

▲ When a family member becomes ill or disabled, the rest of the family assumes responsibility for his or her care. *What are some ways that teens can help in the care of a family member who is ill or disabled?*

....

Caring. When you seek help for a problem that affects the health of the family, you are demonstrating caring. **Make a list of people you think you could approach for assistance if a family member has a substance abuse problem.**

Community Involvement

Select students to interview representatives from the local chapter of the Alzheimer's Association. Ask students to request information about ways in which family members can deal with stress when caring for a patient with Alzheimer's disease. **L3**

Cross Curriculum Activity

Language Arts Have students write a story about a fictional family undergoing a major change in their family. Have students address how the family deals with the change (or changes) in circumstances while maintaining a healthy family. Have students exchange papers with a partner and critique each other's work, examining them for both mechanics and content. Then have them return the papers to the original writer for revisions. **L2**

Caring Ask students to create a list of adults who could offer help and advice if a family member had a substance abuse problem. Then have students compile a list of community resources for people with substance abuse problems. Ask: How does seeking help for a family member with a problem demonstrate that you care about that person as well as the rest of your family?

Curriculum Connections

Language Arts Assign students to read a short story or novel about a troubled family. You may want to provide suggestions, or work with the school librarian to collect titles. Have students write a one-page report, analyzing the family's problems and suggesting strategies to help the family cope with stress.

Math Present students with this scenario: A two-income family recently took out a 30-year mortgage on a $150,000 home. Have students research current mortgage rates and then consult a mortgage calculator online to determine the family's monthly mortgage payment. Lead the class in discussing the impact that a job loss might have on this family.

Health Skills Activity

THAT'S WHAT FRIENDS ARE FOR

NHES Standard 5 Students will demonstrate the ability to use interpersonal communication skills to enhance health.

Objectives

- Discuss how significant family events can impact health.
- Demonstrate empathy toward others.

Motivator

Give students two minutes to make a list of how a teen's life might change if his or her parents divorced.

Teaching Strategies

1. Have students work in pairs to assume the roles of Craig and Robert as they work out the dialogue.
2. Tell students to use their list to help them understand what Robert is going through and to empathize with him.

✓Assessment

Using a rubric, student work should provide comprehensive evidence of the following criteria to achieve the highest score:

✔ effective listening skills
✔ use of "I" statements
✔ respectful tone of voice
✔ appropriate body language, including eye contact

Health Skills Activity

Communication: That's What Friends Are For

"Are you okay?" Craig asked his friend Robert after school one day. "You seem down."

Robert hesitated before admitting, "My parents have decided to get a divorce. My dad's going to move across town soon. One of these days, I know that they're going to ask me who I want to live with. I feel close to both my mom and dad, and I don't want to have to choose sides. Everything is changing. I want to talk to my parents about my feelings and worries, but I'm afraid I'll add to their problems."

What Would You Do?

How would you respond if you were Craig? Finish the rest of this dialogue, incorporating effective communication skills to demonstrate how Craig shows support and empathy.

1. Listen attentively.
2. Use "I" statements.
3. Speak in a respectful tone of voice.
4. Display appropriate body language.

Coping with Family Changes

It is important to manage the stress caused by family changes. In some cases, this may be as simple as turning to a family member for help. Talking with family members can often reduce the stress and lead to a successful solution. If a parent is unavailable, find another adult who can help, such as a teacher, guidance counselor, member of the clergy, or a member of your extended family. Additional strategies for coping with family stress include the following.

▶ **Do what you can to help.** For example, if your parents are feeling stressed, you might be able to reduce their burden by taking on added chores and responsibilities. Knowing that you are helping out can make you feel better.

▶ **Read books about or talk to people who have faced a similar problem.** You may find strategies for managing the problem.

▶ **Use stress-management techniques.** Engage in physical activity, get adequate sleep, eat nutritious meals, and find a way to relax, such as listening to soothing music.

hotlink

stress-management techniques To learn more about managing stress, see Chapter 8, page 209.

284 Chapter 11 Family Relationships

∿ HEALTH LITERACY

Listening and Empathy Much family conflict and stress could be minimized if family members really listened to and empathized with one another. Encourage students to make a point of listening carefully to at least one member of the family or household each day and putting themselves in that family members' position. Suggest that they make daily notes in their private health journals for at least two weeks. Ask: How did their understanding of family members change? How did the relationship with family members change? How could they increase the amount of time they spend really listening and empathizing?

Resiliency Within the Family

Resiliency is an important trait of a healthy family. **Resiliency** is *the ability to adapt effectively and recover from disappointment, difficulty, or crisis.* Resilient people can call upon their own strengths to deal with changes. Resilient families pull together to cope with changing circumstances. Keeping a family healthy takes planning, compromise, and effort. When problems occur, family members must identify the problem, evaluate how the problem is affecting the entire family, discuss what can be done to handle the problem, and draw upon family unity and strength to resolve the problem together. If the family cannot resolve problems on their own in a healthful way, resources to which families can turn for help are available. You will learn more about these resources in Lesson 4.

 Resilient families work through problems and difficulties while maintaining strong, healthy relationships. *What are some ways you can cope with stress during times of family difficulties?*

 Lesson 2 *Review*

Reviewing Facts and Vocabulary

1. What are the two main types of stress that affect families?
2. What is *grief*?
3. What is *resiliency*?

Thinking Critically

4. **Applying.** Causes of stress may be positive or negative in nature. Give examples of a positive event and a negative event that have caused stress within your family. Explain how you handled this stress.
5. **Synthesizing.** Why might children whose parents have recently divorced experience the stages of grief? How might a young child express these feelings?

Applying Health Skills

Stress Management. All families face changes that result in stress. Imagine a change in your family that would cause you or other family members significant stress. Make a list of stress-management techniques you would employ in such a situation.

WORD PROCESSING Word processing can help you prepare a list that is neat and easy to follow. See **health.glencoe.com** for tips on how to get the most out of your word-processing program.

---

③ ASSESS

EVALUATING THE LESSON

Assign and discuss the Lesson 2 Review; then administer, grade, and discuss Lesson Quiz 39 in the TCR.

RETEACHING

- Encourage students to use the headings within the lesson to create graphic organizers. The organizers should illustrate the important points and provide a summary of the lesson at a glance.

- Ask students to complete Reteaching Activity 39 in the TCR.

ENRICHMENT

Assign each student to read a newspaper article or book or to watch a television show or movie that depicts an American family in the 1940s or 1950s. Ask: What problems were most common for families during that time period? How have American families changed?

④ CLOSE

Write the lesson's major concepts on numbered, separate slips of paper. Place the slips into a box, and invite each student to draw one. Reading the slips in numerical order, have students define and summarize the concept they have selected.

 Lesson 2 *Review*

Answers to Reviewing Facts and Vocabulary

1. Changes in the family's structure or changes in family circumstances
2. Sorrow caused by the loss of a loved one.
3. The ability to adapt effectively and recover from disappointment, difficulty, or crisis.

Answers to Thinking Critically

4. Answers will vary.
5. Children who must live apart from one parent may experience a feeling of loss and express sorrow. Possible descriptions may include denial or numbness, anger, bargaining, and depression.

Dealing with Family Crises

① FOCUS

QUICK START Have students create a list of crises that families might experience. After students have completed their lists, lead the class in a discussion of healthy ways in which families might cope with these crises.

TYING TO PRIOR KNOWLEDGE

Have students write a paragraph about a fictional family experiencing a crisis. Perhaps they can draw upon a newspaper account or television news report of a real family crisis. Tell the class that the lesson will focus on healthy strategies for preventing abuse and avoiding violence within the family.

Health Skills Features

"What Are the Benefits of Individual and Family Counseling?" p. 288

INTRODUCING VOCABULARY

- Have students write their own definitions for two of the vocabulary words in this lesson. Then have them check their definitions against the Glossary.

- Ask students to complete the Chapter 11 Study Guide in the *Student Activity Workbook*. 📁

286

Lesson 3

Dealing with Family Crises

VOCABULARY
domestic violence
emotional abuse
physical abuse
sexual abuse
spousal abuse
child abuse
neglect
cycle of violence

YOU'LL LEARN TO
- Analyze the importance of healthy strategies that prevent emotional, physical, and sexual abuse.
- Evaluate and apply strategies for avoiding violence within the family.
- Discuss the importance of seeking advice and help in breaking the cycle of violence.

QUICK START Make a list of crises that families may experience. In what healthy ways might families cope with these crises?

▼ Striking out at others and destroying property are unhealthful ways to deal with conflict. *What are some healthful strategies for resolving conflict?*

Some families experience problems that can interfere with the normal, healthy conduct of family life. It may be a teen getting into trouble at school, a parent losing a job, or a disagreement over household rules. Most problems are resolved through effective communication and conflict resolution. However, sometimes negative and even dangerous situations may develop in families undergoing conflict and stress. It is critical to know how to recognize and deal with unhealthy cycles of family behavior.

Family Violence

When conflict occurs and family members react in out-of-control ways, violence may result. Violence can be emotional, physical, or sexual in nature. No matter what form it takes, it is destructive to family health. **Domestic violence**, *any act of violence involving family members,* is a criminal act that can be prosecuted by law.

All types of domestic violence involve abuse. Abuse includes any mistreatment of one person by another. The main forms of abuse in the home include the following:

286 Chapter 11 Family Relationships

Lesson 3 Resources

Teacher Classroom Resources
📁 Concept Mapping Activity 40
📁 Guided Reading Activities 40
📁 Lesson Plan 40
📁 Lesson Quiz 40
📁 Reteaching Activity 40

Student Activity Workbook
📁 Applying Health Skills 40
📁 Chapter 11 Study Guide

- **Emotional abuse** is *a pattern of behavior that attacks the emotional development and sense of worth of an individual.* Yelling, bullying, name-calling, and threats of physical harm are examples of emotional abuse.

- **Physical abuse** is *the intentional infliction of bodily harm or injury on another person.* Slapping, punching, kicking, pinching, and throwing objects at another person are all forms of physical abuse.

- **Sexual abuse** involves *any sexual contact that is forced upon a person against his or her will.* Sexual abuse includes making unwelcome comments of a sexual nature to another person as well as actually touching the person in an unwelcome sexual way.

Spousal Abuse

Domestic violence directed at a spouse is called **spousal abuse**. Spousal abuse may occur in all kinds of families, regardless of education level, income, or ethnicity. Often, this mistreatment results when one partner uses physical strength to try to control the other. However, the abuse may also be emotional or sexual in nature.

Spousal abuse can seriously harm the victim's physical, social, and mental/emotional health. Physical abuse, for example, can result in serious injury or even death. A victim's social health suffers when he or she avoids friends and family to hide evidence of the abuse. Often, the mental/emotional trauma of spousal abuse, such as feelings of fear and shame, remains long after physical injuries have healed. Spousal abuse also harms the health of other family members. It is critical for victims of spousal abuse and their children to leave the dangerous situation and seek help.

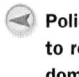 **Police are often the first to respond to reports of domestic violence.** *Learn what resources are available in your community to help victims of abuse.*

What are the elements of a safety plan against abuse?

People in abusive situations should develop a safety plan that includes:

- **Places and situations to avoid.** Avoid locations that have only one exit. Try not to be around the abuser when he or she has been drinking or using drugs.
- **Possible escape routes.** Doors, first-floor windows, basement exits, elevators, and stairwells are options.
- **A place to go.** Go somewhere safe, such as a friend's or relative's home, a shelter, or a hotel.
- **Telephone numbers.** Know the number of the domestic violence hot line. Use it to get help or information.

② TEACH

Explaining

Tell students that abuse in a family is a very serious problem. Stress the availability of help for both the children and the parents. Explain that the children are not at fault in these situations and that they should not feel guilty. **L1**

Discussing

Ask students to identify situations in which a teen may face the danger of physical or emotional abuse. List their responses on the board. Then have the class discuss how some of the situations might be avoided. **L1**

ACTIVE READING

Text Organization

Studying how text is organized will help students read and process information more quickly. Students should be able to see that the bulleted text can be read and referred to quickly. Ask the class to explain how this format can be useful when reading for the first time or when studying for a test. Point out that key points are often presented as bulleted lists. As a helpful study technique, have students search for sections of bulleted text or lists in their textbook and create a new heading for them. Creating headings helps students organize the key points of a lesson. For more strategies, see the *Guided Reading Activities* booklet. 📂

Cooperative Learning Activity

Abuse, Values, and Media At one time, spousal and child abuse may have been tolerated or ignored in the United States. People have tended to write off family abuse as parental, spousal, or cultural prerogatives. More recently, the media has raised public awareness and shifted societal attitudes. Have students choose two news stories from magazines or newspapers about child abuse or spousal abuse. One story should be from twenty years ago, and the other should be from a fairly recent source. Have them compare and contrast the coverage. Ask: How is the coverage different? Why? How do you think the media affects the public's opinions about special issues such as these?

Exploring Issues

WHAT ARE THE BENEFITS OF INDIVIDUAL AND FAMILY COUNSELING

Encourage students to discuss the kinds of issues for which a family might seek counseling. After a brief discussion, point out that family and individual counseling each have advantages and drawbacks. For example, a person in individual counseling might feel more comfortable sharing personal feelings, but in family counseling, the counselor can see how family members interact. Have students read the feature. Then have them meet in discussion groups to share, compare, and defend their responses to the first Activity questions. After students have researched other methods of helping families, have volunteers share their findings with the class.

Guest Speaker

Invite a police officer, other community worker, or a school counselor to address the class about the problems of young runaways in today's society. Have the speaker talk about the reasons why some young people run away, the ages of young runaways, the dangers they face on the street, where runaways can go for help, and the percentage of runaways who return home to their families.

Exploring Issues

What Are the Benefits of Individual and Family Counseling?

Individual and family counseling are two ways to cope with family crises. What are the benefits and drawbacks of each method of counseling? Here are two points of view.

Viewpoint 1: Sheila K., age 14

The family is a unit and should be treated as one. Sending one family member to counseling sends a message that he or she is the problem that needs fixing. Besides, "fixing" one person isn't going to resolve problems that involve the whole family. Family counseling is the best way to make sure that everyone takes responsibility for what's going on in the home.

Viewpoint 2: Jay S., age 16

Sure, families are a unit, but they're made up of individuals with their own issues. And let's face it, not all family members are willing to get help. In that situation, it would be helpful for a family member to have a one-on-one outlet. Away from other family members, individuals may feel more comfortable and be more honest. It can help them better handle whatever happens at home.

ACTIVITIES

1. **What are additional benefits and drawbacks of each type of counseling? Under what circumstances do you think one type of counseling might be more appropriate than another?**

2. **Access information about other methods of helping families. For example, one form of counseling uses both group and individual sessions.**

Did You Know?

Domestic violence costs the nation $5–10 billion a year. These costs include:
- medical expenses
- police and court costs
- shelters and foster care
- sick leave, absenteeism, and nonproductivity

Child Abuse

Child abuse is *domestic abuse directed at a child*. Like spousal abuse, the abuse of a child can be emotional, physical, or sexual. Child abuse may also include **neglect**, the *failure to provide for a child's physical or emotional needs*. Physical needs include adequate food, clothing, shelter, and medical care. Emotional neglect may take the form of indifference or withholding love and support.

A child who lives in an abusive home may try to escape the abuse by running away. Runaways often become victims of exploitation because they do not have the money, job skills, or means to support themselves. In fact, they are prime targets for people dealing in pornography and prostitution. Running away from home is not a good solution for dealing with child abuse. The best solution for children suffering abuse is to ask for help from trusted adults.

288 Chapter 11 Family Relationships

Myths & Reality

MYTH. Child abuse occurs only among lower income families.

FACT. Child abuse can and does occur in families of all economic levels.

MYTH. If a child misbehaves, he or she may be to blame for physical abuse by an adult.

FACT. Children are never to blame for abuse.

MYTH. If a child's physical needs are being met, the child is not being neglected.

FACT. Children, like all human beings, have emotional needs. If these needs are not being met, the child may be suffering from emotional neglect.

Effects of Abuse

Victims of domestic abuse experience feelings of shame, fear, humiliation, and guilt. They often feel powerless to change their circumstances. Long-term effects of domestic abuse may include:

▶ Inability to trust or establish healthy personal relationships

▶ Chronic physical pain

▶ Neglect of or injury to oneself, including suicide attempts

▶ Depression, anxiety, sleep disorders, and eating disorders

▶ Abuse of alcohol and other drugs

It is critical that victims of domestic violence get outside help to deal with this extremely dangerous situation. Getting to a safe place is the first priority.

Breaking the Cycle of Violence

Involvement in domestic violence is often a learned behavior. A child who suffers or who witnesses abuse may view violence in the home as a normal way of life. As a result, the child may be more likely to become an adult who abuses others. In this way, domestic violence can cycle from one generation to the next. This *pattern of repeating violent or abusive behaviors from one generation to the next* is called the **cycle of violence**. The only way to break this cycle is to stop all forms of violence and abuse. **Figure 11.2** provides suggestions for breaking the cycle of violence.

FIGURE 11.2

BREAKING THE CYCLE OF VIOLENCE

You can help break the cycle of abuse. If you or someone you know is being abused . . .

• Tell a trusted adult (parent, other family member, teacher, school nurse or counselor, doctor). Ask this person to help you find a way to resolve the problem.

• Contact an abuse hot line or crisis center that can assist you in finding counselors or other forms of help.

• Report the abuse to the police. It may also be appropriate to contact child welfare or youth services.

The Cycle of Violence

STOP

Source: Office of Justice Programs, US Department of Justice

Health Minute
Preventing Domestic Violence

To encourage an atmosphere of nonviolence at home:

▶ Don't provide violence-oriented toys to small children, such as toy guns or knives.

▶ Don't provide children with video games that focus on violence, such as attacks on property, people, or animals.

VISUAL LEARNING

Figure 11.2 Ask volunteers to read aloud the information shown in Figure 11.2. Then present the class with a fictional scenario in which a witness to child abuse decides to break the cycle of abuse by contacting a trusted adult, hotline worker, or police officer. Have students work in pairs to role-play the scenario using one of the methods provided in Figure 11.2. Afterward, ask: How would these actions help break the cycle of abuse?

Health Minute

Read aloud the tips for encouraging an atmosphere of nonviolence at home. Have volunteers describe specific toys or video games they have seen that focus on violence. Ask: What message might these materials send to children and teens? Have students provide examples of toys or video games that might send a more positive message to young children.

Dealing with Sensitive Issues

Offering Support Given the widespread problem of child abuse, it is highly likely that some students in your class have been physically, emotionally, or sexually abused by a family member or other adult. Your role, as a teacher, is to identify students in need, offer the students support, and refer them to other sources of help. Be prepared, in advance, with brochures and/or business cards from appropriate local resources.

The first step in helping a student you suspect has been abused is showing the student you care. If you broach the problem with the student, be sure to do so privately. Also, take care to avoid conveying value judgments about the issue. Refer to Glencoe's professional booklet, *Dealing with Sensitive Issues*, for more information.

3 ASSESS

EVALUATING THE LESSON

Assign and discuss the Lesson 3 Review; then administer, grade, and discuss Lesson Quiz 40 in the TCR. 📁

RETEACHING

- Ask students to list the forms of abuse. For each one, have them provide a strategy for preventing or avoiding the abuse.

- Ask students to complete Reteaching Activity 40 in the TCR. 📁

ENRICHMENT

Ask students to conduct research, using online and print sources, to find out more about the cycle of violence and how it can be broken. Have them prepare a brief report about what they have learned, citing specific examples or statistics. Remind students to check their writing for spelling and grammar usage. Encourage them to write several drafts and evaluate their writing for both mechanics and content. Ask volunteers to share their findings with the class.

4 CLOSE

Instruct students to list on a sheet of paper five important concepts that they have learned from the lesson.

Seeking help is the first step to take when dealing with domestic violence issues. *What strategies might help individuals avoid violence within the family?*

Avoiding Domestic Violence

There are several strategies that can help you avoid and prevent domestic abuse. You can recall these strategies by remembering the three Rs.

▶ **Recognize.** Become aware of acts that are abusive. Remember that abuse takes many forms, including physical abuse, verbal and emotional abuse, sexual abuse, and neglect.

▶ **Resist.** If anyone tries to harm you physically or abuse you in a sexual way, resist in any way you can. Be assertive and stand up for yourself. Run away from the abuser, and seek help from a trusted adult.

▶ **Report.** If someone treats you in an abusive manner, get away and tell someone about the incident as soon as you can. If you witness someone else being abused, report the abuse to the authorities or tell an adult who can help you.

Victims of domestic abuse need help. Their abusers also need help. Being a child victim or witness of abuse does not justify becoming an abusive adult. All forms of domestic abuse are unacceptable, and most of these acts are illegal. In the next lesson, you will learn more about sources of help for victims of abuse.

▶ Lesson 3 Review

Reviewing Facts and Vocabulary

1. What are the effects of spousal abuse?
2. What is *neglect*? Explain how neglect affects each part of a child's health triangle.
3. What is the *cycle of violence*? What are some ways of breaking this cycle?

Thinking Critically

4. **Synthesizing.** One of the effects of abuse is the victim's feeling of worthlessness. How could you help a victim of abuse to feel better about himself or herself?
5. **Evaluating.** Some say that the long-term effects of abuse are worse than the short-term effects. Explain why this statement might be true for many victims.

Applying Health Skills

Advocacy. Write an article discussing the serious problem of domestic abuse. Describe the effects of abuse, and urge victims of any form of domestic violence to seek help immediately. Ask the school newspaper to print your article.

TECHNOLOGY *OPTION*

WORD PROCESSING Use a word-processing program to write your article. See **health.glencoe.com** for tips on how to get the most out of your word-processing program.

▶ Lesson 3 Review

Answers to Reviewing Facts and Vocabulary

1. See page 287.
2. The failure to provide for a child's physical or emotional needs. Examples will vary.
3. The pattern of repeating violent or abusive behavior from one generation to the next. Tell a trusted adult or call the police or a hotline.

Answers to Thinking Critically

4. Encourage the abused person to seek help and offer support.
5. Long-term effects may include inability to trust; chronic pain; neglect or injury to oneself; poor mental health; sleep and eating disorders; abuse of drugs.

Community Support Systems

VOCABULARY

crisis center
foster care
family counseling
mediator

YOU'LL LEARN TO

• Demonstrate knowledge about personal and family health concerns.

• Identify family situations requiring professional health services and explain how to access those services.

• Evaluate appropriate and effective conflict resolution techniques for various family situations.

 QUICK START List some types of health resources available to families facing crises. For each resource, give an example of when individual family members or an entire family may need to seek such professional health services. Add to or revise your list as you read this lesson.

Throughout this chapter, you've learned how the health of the entire family depends on the health of its individual members. You have seen how important it is to manage stress and conflict to prevent problems from escalating. However, sometimes families must turn to outside help to deal with problems.

Help for Families

The most appropriate resource for a family in crisis depends on the seriousness of the problem. Some problems, such as domestic violence, may require the intervention of law enforcement agencies. Problems such as substance abuse may require medical help. Victims must recognize that help is needed in order to find a solution. Members of a troubled family can call a **crisis center**, *a facility that handles emergencies and provides referrals to an individual needing help.* Many communities also have crisis hot lines, special telephone numbers people can call to receive help 24 hours a day. People who work at crisis centers and hot lines are often able to guide individuals toward solutions to their problems. The solution may include a referral to one of the resources described in **Figure 11.3** on the next page.

 Crisis centers can provide help and support for families facing difficult situations. *What other resources offer help for families in crisis?*

Lesson 4 *Resources*

Teacher Classroom Resources

📁 Concept Mapping Activity 41

📁 Guided Reading Activities 41

📁 Lesson Plan 41

📁 Lesson Quiz 41

📁 Reteaching Activity 41

Student Activity Workbook

📂 Applying Health Skills 41

📂 Chapter 11 Study Guide

Multimedia

🖱 Transparency 31

Lesson 4

Community Support Systems

① FOCUS

→ **QUICK START** Have students create a list of health resources that could help families facing crises. Ask volunteers to share their responses, and write them on the board. Guide students in a discussion of ways in which these health resources might help troubled families.

TYING TO PRIOR KNOWLEDGE

Remind the class that there are many threats to the health of today's families. Ask students to make a list of some specific actions that they can take to help strengthen their family. Tell students that, as they read this lesson, they will learn about where families can go for help in times of crisis.

Health Skills Features

"Family Support Services," p. 293   ACCESSING INFORMATION

INTRODUCING VOCABULARY

• Have students create a fill-in-the blank activity. Ask students to write sentences using each vocabulary term. Then have them omit the terms. Tell students to exchange papers with a partner and have them complete the sentences by writing in the correct terms.

• Ask students to complete the Chapter 11 Study Guide in the *Student Activity Workbook*. 📂

② TEACH

VISUAL LEARNING

Figure 11.3 Direct students to review the information presented in Figure 11.3. Then divide the class into nine groups, and assign each group one of the sources of help for families. Have each group use the telephone book and other resources to find local organizations that fit the assigned category. Encourage each group to create a list that includes the organizations' name, address, phone number, services, and other relevant information. Then ask volunteers to compile all nine lists into one handy reference guide.

Health Minute

Have students read aloud the tips to follow before calling a hot line for help and those to follow when making the call. Ask: What kinds of phone calls are difficult for you—or for other teens—to make? What can you do to overcome your worries and make those difficult calls? Let volunteers role-play various hot line calls, asking for help. Close by explaining that many people have trouble using the phone to find help with a difficult family situation. In what ways would the techniques listed here help a person make that kind of call?

FIGURE 11.3

SOURCES OF HELP FOR FAMILIES

Many agencies offer help to families in need.

Faith Communities • Community Services • Police • Hospital/Clinics • **Source of Help for Families** • Hospital/Clinics • Shelters • Support Groups • Family Counseling • Mediation

Health Minute

Calling a Hot Line for Help

Before you call:

▶ **State the problem to yourself.** Write out the problem and what you will say.

▶ **List all of the questions you have.** Don't dismiss a topic because you think it's trivial.

▶ **Practice.** Rehearse what you will say.

When you make the call:

▶ **Have paper and a pencil handy.** Record the names and numbers of people the counselor suggests you call.

▶ **Consider the counselor's suggestions.** Decide on the best course of action.

Community Services

Most communities offer a variety of services to families who need help. Parenting and conflict resolution classes may be offered by both public and private agencies. Many services can help families get food, clothing, and shelter. Some agencies provide financial aid, medical care, job training, and help in finding employment.

HELP FOR CHILDREN

Sometimes parents are unable to care adequately for their children. Children whose basic needs are not being met or who live in abusive situations may be placed in **foster care**, *a temporary arrangement in which a child is placed under the guidance and supervision of a family or an adult who is not related to the child by birth.* Foster families provide havens for abused or neglected children by giving care and support. Sometimes, foster families adopt the children they have been caring for.

HELP FOR VICTIMS OF SPOUSAL ABUSE

Victims of spousal abuse can seek help by contacting an organization dealing with domestic violence. Many communities provide shelters and a network with other safe houses throughout the United States. These organizations offer shelter, food, clothing, and counseling for women in crisis and their children. Some also help victims strengthen their employment skills by teaching them interviewing techniques and providing them with job training.

Promoting Coordinated School Health

Adults as Models You can use resources in the immediate school environment to stress the importance of lifelong responsibility for personal health. Since most school sites involve employees from a wide spectrum of age groups, students can witness how employees model healthful behaviors. For example, faculty and staff can be encouraged to participate in a student-teacher volleyball game. Above all, everyone of all ages should be encouraged to recognize their role in making the school community function positively. For more information, consult *Planning a Coordinated School Health Program*.

Support Groups

Some people find help through **support groups,** meetings in which individuals share their problems and get advice from others facing similar issues. Participants discuss their concerns and often take comfort in knowing that they are not alone. Support groups help many people cope on a day-to-day basis.

The purpose of support groups is to deal with various types of personal or family health concerns. For example, there are groups for personal health issues such as substance abuse, eating disorders, domestic violence, dealing with grief, and coping with a family member's long-term illness.

hotlink

support groups For more information about support groups and other treatment methods, see Chapter 9, page 237.

Real-Life Application

Family Support Services

There are many community resources that provide help for families facing difficulties.

 Al-Anon 555-2666
Support for family members of people addicted to substances such as alcohol and other drugs

 Alateen 555-8336
A support group for teens who live with someone addicted to alcohol or other drugs

 Conflict Resolution Center 555-1234
Offers counseling, mediation, and training to help resolve conflicts

 Family Resource Center 555-9876
Provides support for families, including counseling services

 Family Services 555-5671
Provides counseling for individuals, couples, and families

 Teens in Transition 555-8485
Offers resources for teens seeking help for difficult life problems, such as coping with divorce or death

 ACTIVITY

Using the above flyer as a guide, search your telephone directory to identify similar health-related services in your community. In small groups, compile a Community Family Support Directory that describes each agency. Include the services, hours, and locations. Target the directory toward teens. Use clip art to make it visually appealing.

∿ HEALTH LITERACY

Self-Directed Learner Invite students to use online and print sources to examine research suggesting that patterns of relating formed with siblings may determine adult patterns of relating with peers, coworkers, and spouses. Some experts believe that in many cases, siblings influence patterns of relating to peers even more than parents do. They may wish to look for specific information such as which patterns of relating with siblings are most likely to be repeated in relationships with adult peers, which have healthy or unhealthy effects, and what the articles say about only children. Have them summarize their findings in a brief written report.

Real-Life Application

FAMILY SUPPORT SERVICES

 ACCESSING INFORMATION

NHES Standard 2 Students will demonstrate the ability to access valid health information and health-promoting products and services.

Objectives

- Identify, describe, and assess available health-related services in the community that relate to sources of help for families.
- Demonstrate knowledge about family health concerns.

Motivator

Ask: If a teen's family were going through a crisis, where could he or she turn for help in the community?

Teaching Strategies

1. Before this activity, collect pamphlets from family support agencies or access information online.
2. Suggest that students place their directories in the media center, counseling office, and office of the school nurse.

✓ Assessment

Using a rubric, student work should provide comprehensive evidence of the following criteria to achieve the highest score:

✔ ability to access appropriate community resources to meet specific needs
✔ rationale for the appropriateness of the source
✔ type of help available from the sources

Discussing

Lead students in brainstorming a list of factors that might deter families from seeking outside support or help with problems. Examples might include embarrassment, denial that a problem exists, fear of the unknown, lack of knowledge about what help is available, refusal to admit failure or inadequacy, cost of professional services, fear of a breach of confidentiality, etc. **L1**

Reinforcing Concepts

Pose the question: Who could you go to if your family were in trouble? Consider friends and other people with whom you have regular contact. Have students list the names of some people who would help. **ELL**

Explaining

Discuss with the class the many sources of support available for members of a family in trouble. Explain, however, that it is important that members recognize the problem and seek help early, before the problem worsens. Any concerns should be discussed with a parent or trusted adult. **L1**

Service Learning

Ask each student to create a poster that illustrates one of the ways to strengthen family relationships. Display student posters in the classroom. Ask: How can strong family relationships prevent domestic violence? **L1**

Visual/Spatial Intelligence

Counseling

Family counseling, *therapy to restore healthy relationships in a family*, is another source of help for families facing problems. Family members meet regularly with counselors to discuss issues and to try to find solutions. Such counseling often provides families with the skills they need to resolve future conflicts on their own.

In some cases, a family member may benefit from individual counseling. When dealing with issues of domestic violence, one-on-one sessions with a counselor, a psychologist, or a psychiatrist may help an abuser see that he or she learned abusive family patterns in childhood. The cycle of violence may then be broken as the individual learns to recognize the abusive patterns and replace them with healthful behaviors.

Mediation

Families often have difficulty working out problems that involve divorce, including custody of children or disbursement of property. In such cases, mediation may help. A **mediator** is *a person who helps others resolve issues to the satisfaction of both parties*. The mediator sets ground rules and aids in effective communication that permits each party to speak and be heard. The mediation process encourages family members to communicate, cooperate, and compromise. Mediators often help both parties find the resources and make the emotional connections that will result in mutual agreement.

Maintaining Healthy Families

Each family member can do his or her part to keep the family healthy. Through communication and awareness, people can become knowledgeable about their own health and the health of family members. Spend time with other members of your family, and find out what's going on in their lives. Show an interest, ask questions, and offer help if you think it's needed.

Because a family lives together in a household, it is important to respect one another's personal space and feelings. Be considerate of other people in the family. Keeping the noise level down, for example, may prevent you from invading a family member's space. Here are some additional ways to strengthen family relationships:

Family counselors can help teens and their parents learn to communicate their feelings and find ways to resolve differences.
What strategies might counselors use to help improve communication in a family?

294 Chapter 11 Family Relationships

School to Work

Family Mediator During a divorce, some families need the help of a mediator to solve problems. Ask students to research careers in the field of mediation. If possible, have students interview a mediator who works with families or ask one to speak to the class about his or her job. Encourage students to find answers to these questions: In what settings do mediators work? What educational level is required to become a mediator? What skills do mediators typically use on the job? What are the benefits and drawbacks of a career in this field? Have students use the information they acquired to create a help-wanted ad for a family mediator.

▶ **Cooperate.** Respond politely to requests or questions. Meet your responsibilities without being asked or reminded.

▶ **Show appreciation.** Avoid taking family members for granted, and remember to say "Thank you" when appropriate. Be supportive and encouraging.

▶ **Be a good communicator.** Avoid interrupting, daydreaming, or jumping to conclusions when someone is speaking. Try not to raise your voice if you disagree with something.

▶ **Offer help.** Show concern, and offer support and help.

▶ **Be empathetic.** Try to see the situation from the family member's point of view.

▶ **Work to resolve conflicts.** Remember the Three Cs: communication, cooperation, and compromise. If appropriate, use **conflict resolution** strategies.

▶ **Know when to get outside help.** Be able to identify situations that require professional help, and know how to access these services.

hot link

conflict resolution To review the steps of conflict resolution, see Chapter 10, page 264.

 You can often help family members feel better by simply listening to what they have to say.

▶ Lesson 4 Review

Reviewing Facts and Vocabulary

1. Identify some family situations that require help from professional health services.

2. When might a child be placed in foster care?

3. What are three things you can do to help maintain the health of your family?

Thinking Critically

4. **Applying.** Look at the resources for families in Figure 11.3. Give an example of a personal or family health concern that might be addressed by each resource.

5. **Synthesizing.** Explain how crisis centers and crisis hot lines are similar. How are the two health services different?

Applying Health Skills

Accessing Information. Research to find out what resources in your community help families in crisis. Make a list of the health services you identify, and learn how to access each resource. Create a handbook of the information you gather that can be distributed to classmates.

WORD PROCESSING Word processing can help you prepare a handbook that is easy to follow. See health.glencoe.com for tips on how to get the most out of your word-processing program.

▶ Lesson 4 Review

Answers to Reviewing Facts and Vocabulary

1. Substance abuse, eating disorders, domestic violence, dealing with grief, coping with long-term illness.

2. Children whose basic needs are not being met or who live in abusive situations may be placed into foster care.

3. See pages 294–295 for answers.

Answers to Thinking Critically

4. Answers will vary.

5. Both services can provide advice and referrals. At a crisis center, however, people seeking help speak to someone in person rather than over the phone.

EVALUATING THE LESSON

Assign and discuss the Lesson 4 Review; then administer, grade, and discuss Lesson Quiz 41 in the TCR. ▱

RETEACHING

• Have students write a letter of advice to a fictional teen whose family is in crisis. Tell students to include information about the sources of help for families that they learned about in this lesson.

• Ask students to complete Reteaching Activity 41 in the TCR. ▱

ENRICHMENT

Have students review what services are available in the community to assist families. Ask them to interview one of the sources to determine the most common family problems and possible reasons for the problems. Allow them to share their findings with the class.

❹ CLOSE

Select students to act out situations involving a friend who is a victim of abuse or neglect. Have them practice encouraging the friend to seek help from one of the resources described in this lesson. Ask students to explain their choice of resources.

Family Dramas

NHES Standard 4 Students will analyze the influence of culture, media, technology, and other factors on health.

Objective

Critique a story from a film or television series considering content from this chapter on how family members relate to one another and how they deal with change and crises.

Motivator

Ask students to recall a movie or TV series they have seen that centered on struggles and conflicts within a family.

Teaching Strategies

Awareness Popular films and novels often portray family relationships to create dramatic storylines.

Analysis Students should include as many incidences as they can recall.

Reflection Prompt students to compare the examples they found in the book or movie with the positive descriptions and strategies in the chapter.

Take Action Explain to students that they can form an opinion on how their book or movie depicts family relationships and illustrates positive family dynamics.

✓Assessment

Students' charts should contain numerous examples that give descriptions of how characters illustrated the concepts in the chapter. Analyses should contain a general opinion about how well the book or movie illustrates positive family dynamics.

Eye ON THE Media

Family Dramas

Family dynamics, particularly during challenging times, is a topic often explored in literature and on film. In the activity below, you will analyze an example of a family drama and discuss how it portrays family relationships, changes, and crises.

How do the family members meet each other's physical, mental/emotional, and social needs?	Parents work hard to meet family's needs.	Siblings listen to each other's problems.
How do they demonstrate good communication skills, respect, trust, love, and responsibility?	Family discussions at the dinner table	Hugs, encouragements, comforting words
What do they do to adapt to changes and difficulties?	Everyone works to solve the problem.	Family members make sacrifices.
What strategies do they use to avoid or deal with violence, abuse, or neglect?	The family accesses community resources.	They discuss violence prevention strategies.

ACTIVITY

Select or recall a book you have read or a movie you have seen that centers on a family undergoing a change or crisis. Use the chart above as a model to help you analyze the ways in which the book or movie reflects the lessons about family relationships discussed in this chapter. Jot down examples from the book or movie that answer the questions.

EXPRESS YOUR VIEWS

Write a two-page analysis of the family drama you read or watched. Evaluate how the book or movie presents the dynamics of family relationships. Consider whether family dramas reinforce positive models of family interactions, and whether the book or movie you selected lives up to that challenge.

More About...

Families on TV In the early 1960s, the majority of television programs were comedies that depicted families as suburban, white, and middle-class. Sensitive issues such as divorce and abuse were almost never addressed. The 1970s and 1980s brought a more diverse view of the world to television and its viewing audience. By the end of the twentieth century, television programming provided greater opportunities for dealing with change and conflict in family relationships. Television increasingly seeks to include the stories of single parents, working mothers, blended families, and intergenerational families. Television has always strived to reflect, however accurately or inaccurately, the realities of our day and times.

CROSS-CURRICULUM CONNECTIONS

Create a Family Tree Poem. The strong bonds of family form a foundation for a healthy, happy life. Sketch a family tree of your immediate family. Next to each family member, write a short poem describing how he or she contributes to strong, healthy family relationships. You might discuss how the person contributes to feelings of love and warmth or how he or she provides physical and emotional support for other family members. Include illustrations, sketches, or clip art to give your work an artistic look.

Analyze Family Dynamics. The impact of major historical events has shaped the American family. Through research, analyze how one of the following events or eras changed or had an effect on the American family: the Civil War, the Industrial Revolution, World War II, or the Civil Rights movement. Write an analysis in which you consider how the event or era had an impact on the family structure, how family members related to one another, and how family members took care of one another financially.

Calculate Demographics. U.S. Census figures for 1990 showed that married couples with children made up 26.3 percent of U.S. households. Figures for 2000 showed that married couples with children made up 24.1 percent of U.S. households. Assuming the same rate of decline, what percentage of U.S. households will be married couples with children in the year 2010? If the number of households in 2000 was 104,705,000, how many of those households consisted of married couples with children?

Research a Topic. There has been much debate over whether genetics or the environment has a stronger impact on an individual's development. The family unit is at the center of this "nature vs. nurture" debate. What roles do heredity and upbringing play in a child's development? Research theories on both sides of this debate, and present your findings in a report. Include your own thoughts and opinions on this topic.

Family Therapist

Depression, marital problems, and parent-child conflicts can strain family relationships. A family therapist can help families find ways to work out their problems and communicate more openly and honestly. To become a family therapist, you'll need a master's degree in couples and family therapy. Learn more about this and other health careers by clicking on Career Corner at **health.glencoe.com**.

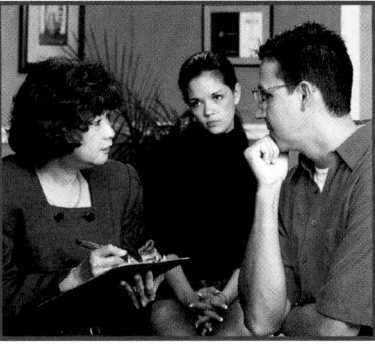

Portfolio Assessment

Self-Evaluation Direct students to review the Health Skills Activities and other activities completed in the chapter. Encourage each student to select one finished product or activity that demonstrates his or her best work for the chapter and that represents the student's learning goals. Have students explain what they have learned and how the examples they have selected demonstrate their growth in health literacy, knowledge, and skills.

Teacher Classroom Resources Assign Performance Assessment 11, "Strengthening Family Relationships," in the TCR. 📁

CROSS-CURRICULUM CONNECTIONS

Enrich student learning by connecting the topic of family relationships to one of the four subject areas presented on this page. The activity may be completed individually or with a partner.

Language Arts Encourage students to think up creative rhymes. Suggest that they include small illustrations or clipart of items that symbolize what the family members contribute. For example, a heart can symbolize love, and a book can symbolize knowledge.

Social Studies Students should explore how family dynamics were affected by the events. For example, during the Industrial Revolution, many families moved from an agricultural life to a city-dwelling, factory life. Another example is the shift after World War II, when women who had been working in the factories were sent home after men returned from war.

Math Answer #1: 26.3% − 24.1% = 2.2%; 24.1% − 2.2% = 21.9% in 2010. Answer #2: 104,705,000 × .241 (or 24.1%) = 25,233,905 households were married couples with children in 2000.

Science Direct students toward resources in the library or on the Internet that discuss the "nature vs. nurture" debate.

Have students read and discuss the Career Corner information on family therapists. Ask interested students to explore the Glencoe Health Web site at **health.glencoe.com** for more information on this career.

Chapter 11 *Review*

CHECKING COMPREHENSION

- Assign and discuss the chapter review.
- Use the Chapter 11 MindJogger Videoquiz to review the chapter.

CHAPTER 11 REVIEW ANSWERS

Exploring Health Terms

1. sibling
2. affirmation
3. family
4. divorce
5. separation
6. custody
7. child abuse
8. domestic violence
9. emotional abuse
10. foster care
11. family counseling
12. crisis center

Recalling the Facts

1. provide food, clothing, and shelter; teach children to practice healthful behaviors, and safety skills; make sure children get medical check-ups and receive immunizations.

2. The health of society is directly related to and dependent upon the health of families.

3. Traits include commitment, spending time together, trust, good communication, love, respect, and the ability to solve problems.

4. Any three: divorce of parents, death of a family member, birth or adoption of a child, sibling leaving home for college or marriage, a member of the extended family (for example, a grandparent, aunt, or uncle) coming to live with the family.

298

➤ EXPLORING HEALTH TERMS *Answer the following questions on a sheet of paper.*

Lesson 1 *Match each definition with the correct term.*

affirmation	family
extended family	sibling

1. A brother or sister.
2. Positive feedback that helps individuals feel appreciated and supported.
3. The basic unit of society.

Lesson 2 *Fill in the blanks with the correct term.*

custody	resiliency
divorce	separation
grief	

Dan's parents fight a lot. They have considered ending their marriage through (__4__) but decided instead on a (__5__), a period in which they will live apart from each other, to see whether they can resolve their differences. During this time, Dan's mom and dad have joint (__6__), so they care for and make decisions about Dan together.

Lesson 3 *Replace the underlined words with the correct term.*

sexual abuse	emotional abuse
cycle of violence	physical abuse
domestic violence	child abuse

7. Neglect of a baby is a form of spousal abuse.
8. Three forms of exploitation are emotional, physical, and sexual abuse in the home.
9. Calling someone names or attacking his or her self-worth is physical abuse.

Lesson 4 *Match each definition with the correct term.*

crisis center	foster care
mediator	family counseling

10. A temporary arrangement in which a child is placed under the guidance or supervision of a family or adult not related by birth.
11. Therapy to restore healthy relationships in a family.
12. A facility that handles emergencies and provides referrals to persons who need help.

➤ RECALLING THE FACTS *Use complete sentences to answer the following questions.*

Lesson 1

1. List three ways that parents promote the physical health of their children.
2. Why is the family considered the basic unit of society?
3. List five traits of a healthy family.

Lesson 2

4. Identify three situations that may result in a change in the family structure.
5. What events may lead to a change in a family's financial situation?
6. List three ways to cope with stress within the family.

Lesson 3

7. What constitutes sexual abuse?
8. Why is a child who runs away from home to escape an abusive situation often at risk of exploitation?
9. What are the three Rs for preventing and avoiding domestic violence?

5. Causes of financial change may include loss of a job, medical emergencies, overdue bills, and impulse buying or poor planning.

6. Speaking with a parent, another trusted adult, or siblings about the problem; making an effort to help relieve family members' stress by helping out; reading books about or talking to people who have gone through similar situations; use stress-management techniques.

7. Sexual abuse involves any sexual contact that is forced upon a person against his or her will.

8. Runaways have no money, job skills, or means for supporting themselves. This places them at risk of being taken advantage of by others who promise to meet these needs.

9. The three Rs are strategies for avoiding and preventing domestic violence. They include recognizing the types of behaviors that are abusive, resisting these behaviors, and reporting incidents of abuse to authorities or someone who can help.

10. Besides crisis centers and hot lines, list three resources to which families in crisis can turn for help.

11. What is the main difference between a support group and counseling?

12. What are three skills that mediators use to help families solve problems?

➤ THINKING CRITICALLY

1. **Analyzing.** Serena cooks dinner for her family when her parents work late. How does Serena benefit from her considerate behavior? How do the members of her family benefit? *(LESSON 1)*

2. **Synthesizing.** What stresses might a family experience when a child goes off to college? *(LESSON 2)*

3. **Applying.** Carlos frequently tries to speak with his mother about problems he is having at school, but she tells him that she doesn't have time to listen to his problems. This pattern of behavior might be a signal of what kind of family crisis? *(LESSON 3)*

4. **Synthesizing.** A teen has parents who abuse alcohol. What type of resource might best provide help to this teen? Explain your choice. *(LESSON 4)*

➤ HEALTH SKILLS APPLICATION

1. **Practicing Healthful Behaviors.** Make a list of specific actions that family members can take to strengthen their relationships with each other. Explain how these behaviors can improve family health. *(LESSON 1)*

2. **Communication Skills.** Write a skit in which one teen demonstrates active listening skills and empathy when a friend reveals that his or her parent is suffering from an illness or a disability. *(LESSON 2)*

3. **Advocacy.** Develop a poster or a PSA that can be used to make others aware of what they can do to break the cycle of abuse. *(LESSON 3)*

4. **Decision Making.** Carol thinks that her older sister has a drug problem. Use the steps of decision making to help Carol decide how to get help for her sister. *(LESSON 4)*

★ BEYOND the Classroom

Parent Involvement

Advocacy. With your parents, learn about shelters in your area that provide victims with a safe place to recover from abuse. Determine what needs the shelter has and what your family can do to help support the shelter's efforts. You might collect materials such as clothing, books, toys, and blankets for the shelter.

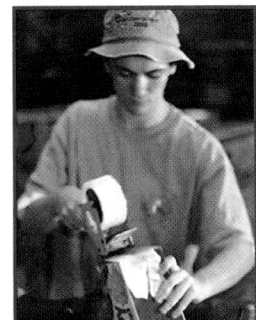

School and Community

Community Events. Identify events and programs in your community that are geared toward students and their families. Contact the organizations sponsoring the activities to find out how you, your classmates, and your family members can get involved.

Chapter 11 Review **299**

---

10. Any three: police, hospitals/clinics, shelters, family counseling, faith communities, support groups, mediators, community services, substance abuse and treatment facilities.

11. Members of support groups meet to share their problems and get help from others who are struggling with similar issues; counseling involves meeting with a professional counselor who provides therapy and guides people to find solutions to their problems—often by teaching them skills they need for specific purposes.

12. Communication, cooperation, compromise.

Thinking Critically

1. Possible answer: Helping out may give Serena a sense of self-worth and allow her to spend more time with her family; it also shows responsibility and caring. Her family benefits by having a meal ready, thereby reducing stress.

2. Possible answer: The makeup of the family changes when a child goes to college. Family members may be saddened by the person's absence. The situation may also place financial stresses on the family.

3. Failure to listen to a child having a problem is a sign of emotional neglect.

4. Possible responses: The teen may benefit from a support group for family members of alcoholics. A support group, such as Al-anon, can provide the teen with people to talk to about the problem and help the teen recognize that he or she is not alone.

Health Skills Application

1.–4. Answers will vary.

Evaluate

- Use the reproducible Chapter 11 Test in the TCR, or construct your own using the Testmaker software. 🗁 ⊙

- Use Performance Assessment 11 in the TCR. 🗁

ENRICHMENT

Ask students to complete Enrichment Activity 11 in the TCR. 🗁

Keep students involved in the community, and encourage parent participation by assigning the activities on this page for students to work on outside of class.

Lessons	Standards		Features
	National	State/Local	
1 **Safe and Healthy Relationships** *pages 302–306*	National Health Education Standards **1.4, 5.1, 5.4, 5.5**		**Health Skills Activity** • When Best Friends Disagree *(Conflict Resolution)*, page 304
2 **Peer Pressure and Refusal Skills** *pages 307–312*	National Health Education Standards **1.4, 3.6, 5.6**		**Hands-On Health** • Assert Yourself *(Refusal Skills)*, page 311
3 **Dating and Setting Limits** *pages 313–317*	National Health Education Standards **1.4, 3.6, 5.1, 5.3**		**Exploring Issues** • What Are the Benefits of Group Dating and Individual Dating? page 314
4 **Abstinence: A Responsible Decision** *pages 318–323*	National Health Education Standards **1.1, 3.4, 5.3, 6.1, 6.3**		**Real-Life Application** • Abstinence Pledges: A Growing Trend *(Advocacy)*, page 321

Reproducible Resources	Assessment	Technology
Student Activity Workbook for use with each chapter	📁 Lesson Quiz 42	🕹 Transparency 32
📁 Concept Mapping Activity 42		💿 TeacherWorks®
📁 Cross-Curriculum Activity 12		💻 Internet Activities
📁 Decision-Making Activity 12		
📁 Guided Reading Activities 42		
📁 Lesson Plan 42		
📁 Parent Letter and Activities 12		
📁 Reteaching Activity 42		
📁 Concept Mapping Activity 43	📁 Lesson Quiz 43	🕹 Transparency 33
📁 Current Health Issues 12		💿 TeacherWorks®
📁 Enrichment Activity 12		
📁 Guided Reading Activities 43		
📁 Health Lab 12		
📁 Lesson Plan 43		
📁 Reteaching Activity 43		
📁 Concept Mapping Activity 44	📁 Lesson Quiz 44	🕹 Transparency 34
📁 Guided Reading Activities 44		💿 TeacherWorks®
📁 Lesson Plan 44		
📁 Reteaching Activity 44		
📁 Concept Mapping Activity 45	📁 Lesson Quiz 45	🕹 Transparency 35
📁 Guided Reading Activities 45		💿 TeacherWorks®
📁 Lesson Plan 45		
📁 Reteaching Activity 45		

0:00 OUT OF TIME

If time does not permit teaching the entire chapter, use:
- Health Skills Activity, p. 304
- Hands-On Health, p. 311
- Health Minute, p. 317
- Real-Life Application, p. 321

Language Diversity

- 🎧 English Audio CD Program
- 🎧 Spanish Audio CD Program
- 📁 English Summaries, Quizzes, and Activities
- 📁 Spanish Summaries, Quizzes, and Activities
- 📁 Spanish Parent Letters and Activities

End of Chapter Assessment

Blackline Masters
- 📁 Chapter 12 Test
- 📁 Performance Assessment Activity 12

Technology
- 💿 Vocabulary PuzzleMaker
- 📼 MindJogger Videoquiz
- 💿 **Exam**View® Pro Testmaker

Professional Health Series

Dealing with Sensitive Issues
Planning a Coordinated School Health Program
Promoting Character Education
Home, School, and Community Involvement

CHAPTER OVERVIEW

Chapter 12 focuses on the types of peer relationships and the positive and negative influence of peer pressure. Dating relationships and the benefits of abstinence until marriage are also discussed.

Lesson 1 A friendship is a significant relationship between two people. Working to build and maintain healthy friendships is an important social skill to develop during the teen years.

Lesson 2 Peer pressure can have a positive or negative influence on a person's actions and behaviors. To resist negative peer pressure, teens need to be assertive and effectively use refusal skills.

Lesson 3 During adolescence, teens often develop new feelings toward people of the opposite gender. Dating can be a fun way to develop social skills and learn more about oneself.

Lesson 4 Abstinence from sexual activity is the only 100 percent sure way to prevent pregnancy and sexually transmitted diseases. Abstinence is a safe and responsible choice for teens.

Health Skills Features

- Health Skills Activity *(Conflict Resolution)*, p. 304
- Hands-On Health *(Refusal Skills)*, p. 311
- Exploring Issues, p. 314
- Real-Life Application *(Advocacy)*, p. 321

Chapter 12
Peer Relationships

Lesson 1
Safe and Healthy Friendships

Lesson 2
Peer Pressure and Refusal Skills

Lesson 3
Dating and Setting Limits

Lesson 4
Abstinence: A Responsible Decision

300

MEETING STUDENT DIVERSITY

Language Diversity Use the following suggestions to help students who have difficulty with English:

- Pair English language learners with native speakers of English who can restate the Chapter Summary in language that helps students comprehend important concepts.

- Direct auditory learners or those students with language diversity to the *Glencoe Health Audio CD Program*. Available in English and Spanish, this component provides an audio and written summary of the chapter.
- Use photographs, drawings, or magazine clippings to help students visualize the important concepts of the chapter.

Derek's Story

Derek is 15. His father, who is in the military, is often transferred from one location to another. This means that Derek's family has to move every few years. The family has just moved from Alaska to Texas. For the third time, Derek is in a new school and surrounded by people he doesn't know.

"Everybody knows everyone else, except me. The people at school are polite to me, but it's difficult becoming good friends with them. They already have people to hang out with, and they don't need me. It's really tough for a new person."

Things seemed easier for Derek the last time he changed schools. "I was just a kid then. It's different now." For the first time in his life, Derek feels shy about approaching new people and making new friends.

"After spending about a month sitting by myself in the cafeteria, I decided I had to do something, so I joined the Community Service Club. I found out that a few people in the club play tennis. So do I."

What can you learn from Derek's story? Write a sentence or two describing what else Derek could do to make friends in his new school. In what ways could you help someone who is new to your school or community? What behaviors and actions help you build and maintain healthy peer relationships?

301

Quick **Write**

Using Visuals. Write five sentences, each one beginning with the words: *A true friend is someone who . . .* Discuss your descriptions with your classmates.

INTRODUCING THE CHAPTER

Case Study

Invite students to read and discuss Derek's story. Ask: What other steps could Derek take to make friends at his new school? Ask two volunteers to role-play a conversation between Derek and other members of the Community Service Club who play tennis. Ask: What might Derek do to encourage a friendship with these teens? Lead the class in discussing ways to help new students or new members of the community.

Review how family relationships provide the foundation for emotional health. Introduce how peer relationships increasingly take on importance and contribute to the emotional needs of the individual as the person matures.

Quick **write**

Using Visuals Direct students to look at the photographs. Ask: What do these scenes show or suggest about friendships? Ask volunteers to share some of their sentences describing a true friend. Have students write a song or poem illustrating the qualities of a good friend.

TECHNOLOGY OPTIONS

MINDJOGGER
VIDEOQUIZ

To preview or review chapter content, you may wish to use the Chapter 12 MindJogger Videoquiz.

 HEALTH *Online*

Online Resources for the Teacher For a fresh approach to health topics and an in-depth look at health issues, use these online resources found under Teacher Resources at **health.glencoe.com:**

• Block Schedule Lesson Plans
• Technology Projects
• Health Updates

Safe and Healthy Friendships

Safe and Healthy Friendships

1 FOCUS

QUICK START Ask volunteers to share examples of ways in which friends contribute to their lives. Then guide the class in a discussion of the importance of friendships.

TYING TO PRIOR KNOWLEDGE

Have students make a list of the benefits of a close friendship, and ask volunteers to share some of the entries on their lists.

Health Skills Features

"When Best Friends Disagree," p. 304

CONFLICT RESOLUTION

INTRODUCING VOCABULARY

- Have students determine the meanings of the terms *clique* and *stereotype* and then write a brief paragraph using the terms. Ask volunteers to share their paragraphs.

- Ask students to complete the Chapter 12 Study Guide in the *Student Activity Workbook.*

VOCABULARY

**peers
friendship
platonic friendship
clique
stereotype**

YOU'LL LEARN TO

- Evaluate the positive and negative effects of peers and friends on physical, mental/emotional, and social health.

- Evaluate the dynamics of peer groups.

- Demonstrate strategies for communicating needs, wants, and emotions.

- Develop management strategies to improve or maintain your health and that of peers.

QUICK START In what ways do friends contribute to your life? List as many examples as you can.

 You may know many classmates and peers, but only a few may be your good friends. *What qualities set a friend apart from other peers?*

302 **Chapter 12** Peer Relationships

During your teen years, you begin a search for a personal identity. This identity will be shaped, at least in part, by your **peers**—*people of similar age who share similar interests.* Your relationships with friends and peers not only contribute to your identity but can also affect your health and well-being.

Types of Peer Relationships

As you get older, the dynamics of your social groups change. For example, instead of attending a small local school, you may now go to a large school attended by students from many neighborhoods. Perhaps you have a part-time job or a volunteer position in which you and your peers have a work-based relationship. Such situations can benefit your social health by giving you opportunities to meet people of all ages, races, religions, and backgrounds. Interacting with diverse peers can enrich your life and contribute to personal growth. Some of the friendships you form in high school may last throughout your life.

Lesson 1 *Resources*

Teacher Classroom Resources

- Concept Mapping Activity 42
- Cross-Curriculum Activity 12
- Decision-Making Activity 12
- Guided Reading Activities 42
- Lesson Plan 42
- Lesson Quiz 42

- Parent Letter and Activities 12
- Reteaching Activity 42

Student Activity Workbook

- Applying Health Skills 42
- Chapter 12 Study Guide

Multimedia

- Transparency 32

Friendships

A **friendship** is *a significant relationship between two people.* Healthy friendships are based on caring, respect, trust, and consideration. Friends are people with whom you share hobbies, interests, and other friends. They may also become people with whom you are comfortable sharing your needs, wants, emotions, and confidences. Healthy friendships can give you a sense of belonging and help you define and reinforce your values.

Your friends probably include both males and females. A **platonic friendship** is *a friendship with a member of the opposite gender in which there is affection but the two people are not considered a couple.* Such relationships can help you understand and become comfortable with individuals of the opposite gender. In addition, such friends can be a valuable source of advice concerning dating issues. Platonic friendships help you realize that all people, regardless of gender, have similar feelings, needs, and concerns.

Friendships vary in importance and commitment. If you have a best friend, you already know that not all friendships are the same. In fact, there are several kinds of friendships.

CASUAL FRIENDSHIPS

A casual friendship is a relationship between peers who share something in common. You may form a casual friendship with a classmate, a teammate, or someone who attends your place of worship. You may sit with casual friends in the cafeteria or at school events. Casual friends are usually people with whom you share some interests but are not necessarily people with whom you form deep emotional bonds.

CLOSE FRIENDSHIPS

Some casual friendships may develop into close friendships. Close friends have strong emotional ties and feel comfortable sharing their thoughts, experiences, and feelings. They trust and support each other, acting with kindness, courtesy, and loyalty. When problems arise in the relationship, close friends will try to work them out together.

Ⓨ **These teens have a casual friendship based on a common interest.** *What interests do you share with the peers you think of as casual friends?*

② TEACH

Reinforcing Concepts

Have students write private health journal entries recalling the small circle of peers they had as very young children. Ask: Who were your peers? How did you relate to them? Are you still friends? Why or why not? **L1**

Discussing

Pose these questions: What are some examples of platonic friendships between characters in TV programs or current movies? How can you tell the relationships are platonic friendships? What special benefits do you think this kind of friendship offers teens? **L1**

Critical Thinking

Ask: How are casual friendships and close friendships alike? What are the most important differences? Why is it important to have both kinds of friendships? **L1**

Cross-Curriculum Activity

Language Arts Remind students of the old English proverb: *A friend in need is a friend indeed.* Ask volunteers to share their interpretations of this quote. Then have students use library or online resources to find other proverbs or quotations about friendship. Ask volunteers to share their quotes with the class, and then have a class discussion about their meanings. **L2**

Cooperative Learning Activity

Relationships in Fiction Divide the class into several groups and tell them that they will analyze a peer relationship in a film, TV show, short story, or poem. Have each group decide what form of media they will examine. Then have each group report on the fictional relationship in the film, TV show, story or poem, and analyze the messages it sends about relationships. Whenever possible, have students use quotations from the chosen media to defend his or her interpretation. Suggest that they follow up with a discussion about the value of peer relationships.

Health Skills Activity

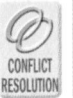

WHEN BEST FRIENDS DISAGREE

CONFLICT RESOLUTION

NHES Standard 5 Students will demonstrate the ability to use interpersonal communication skills to enhance health.

Objectives

- Evaluate the positive and negative effects of peers and friends on physical, mental/emotional, and social health.
- Demonstrate skills for communicating effectively with family, peers, and friends.

Motivator

Ask students to think of a clique to which they belong or that they know of and to list positive and negative aspects of being in a clique.

Teaching Strategies

1. Review the characteristics of close friendships, and advise students to consider these when creating their scenario.
2. Have students work in pairs to take on the roles of Marissa and Julia and experiment with different dialogues until they reach a satisfactory solution.

✓ Assessment

Using a rubric, student work should provide comprehensive evidence of the following criteria to achieve the highest score:

✔ explaining each side of the conflict without interruption
✔ use of "I" messages
✔ listening skills and appropriate questions
✔ solution that benefits both sides

True friendships have several common attributes:

- ▶ Similar values, interests, beliefs, and attitudes on basic issues
- ▶ Open and honest communication
- ▶ Sharing of joys, disappointments, dreams, and concerns
- ▶ Mutual respect, caring, and support
- ▶ Concern about each other's safety and well-being

Cliques

Does your school have cliques? A **clique** is *a small circle of friends, usually with similar backgrounds or tastes, who exclude people viewed as outsiders.* Clique members may share the same attitudes, wear similar clothing, meet regularly in an area identified as their "turf," or engage in other behaviors that identify them as a clique.

Health Skills Activity

Conflict Resolution: When Best Friends Disagree

"Guess what?" Marissa asked excitedly when she saw her best friend, Julia. "Nicole and Dave asked us to join their group!"

"But I like the friends we have right now," Julia frowned. "Why do you want to be part of their group?"

"Because they're the most popular people in school!" Marissa answered. "It'll be great!"

"I've heard that they make fun of people who are different from them," Julia said.

"I'm sure that's just a rumor," Marissa insisted. "Come on, you never want to do anything fun."

Julia doesn't want to lose Marissa as a best friend, but she also doesn't feel comfortable joining Nicole and David's group. She wonders how to respond.

What Would You Do?

Write an ending to the scenario in which Julia and Marissa resolve their conflict in a healthful way. Use the following tips as a guideline.

1. **Take turns explaining each side of the conflict without interruption.**
2. **Use "I" messages.**
3. **Listen carefully, and ask appropriate questions.**
4. **Brainstorm solutions.**
5. **Agree on a solution that benefits both sides.**

304 Chapter 12 Peer Relationships

Home and Community

Cliques There are varying opinions on the nature and value of cliques. Some people feel that exclusive social groups, or cliques, should be banned. Others feel that some cliques, including college fraternities and sororities, are worthwhile—especially when organizing around a good cause. Encourage students to find out how members of their community feel about cliques.

Suggest that they interview friends, relatives, and neighbors by asking questions such as: What groups do you consider to be cliques? Do cliques determine social, economic, or political success in your school or community? Then divide the class into two groups, those favoring cliques and those opposing cliques, and hold a class debate.

Cliques can have both positive and negative influences on peers. Being part of a clique, for example, may provide members with a sense of belonging. However, cliques are a negative influence if members are discouraged from thinking for themselves or acting as individuals.

Clique membership is often limited—not everyone who wants to belong is welcome. Often, the beliefs and actions clique members use to exclude others are prejudicial and based on stereotypes. **Prejudice** is making assumptions or judgments about an individual without really knowing him or her. A **stereotype** is *an exaggerated and oversimplified belief about an entire group of people, such as an ethnic or religious group or a gender.*

Forming Healthy Friendships

Relationships with friends may become more complex as you begin sharing thoughts and feelings that are more serious in nature than those you experienced in childhood. Working to build and maintain healthy friendships is an important social skill to develop during the teen years.

Choosing Friends

Throughout your life you have many opportunities to choose friends. Positive people with healthy attitudes can support you emotionally, reinforce your values, and motivate you. For example, if your friends think education is important, you're likely to take education seriously and do well in school. Often, friends encourage each other to make healthy, responsible decisions. They might inspire each other to engage in more physical activity or participate in community service. They can also serve as mutual protective factors, helping each other avoid unsafe or unhealthy situations. For example, a friend may encourage you to walk away from a fight.

Some friends, however, may try to influence you to participate in risky activities or behaviors that go against your values and the values of your family. In such cases, it's probably best to end the relationship. Healthy relationships are based on mutual respect and caring. If a friendship isn't contributing to your life in a positive way, it's time to reevaluate that relationship.

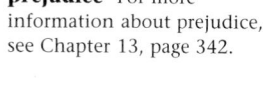

prejudice For more information about prejudice, see Chapter 13, page 342.

Group outings with friends can provide you with a sense of belonging.
Evaluate other positive effects of friends on mental/emotional health.

Lesson 1   Safe and Healthy Friendships   **305**

Community Involvement

Suggest that students talk with their parents or other close adults about cliques. Students might ask questions such as these: What kinds of cliques existed at your school? Which—if any—did you belong to? How did you feel about cliques at school? Why? What do you think about cliques now? **1**

Discussing

Have the class name some commonly held stereotypes about particular groups of people, such as males, females, cheerleaders, and football players. Ask: What prejudices do individuals face because of stereotypes? How might you feel if you were judged based on a stereotype? **2**

hotlink

Have students notice that *prejudice* is similar to a word they already know, *prejudge*. Ask: How does knowing similar words help you understand a word's meaning? Ask volunteers to cite examples of prejudice.

Discussing

Discuss with students ways to respond to stereotypical comments made by a friend. Ask: Should a comment be ignored, or should you draw your friend's attention to the comment? What would you say to him or her? How do you think stereotyping leads to prejudicial treatment. How do you think stereotypes arise? Are all people guilty of stereotyping? **2**

More About...

Friendship Being best friends does not necessarily mean being constant companions. People can maintain close relationships while also spending time with other people. It is possible to be best friends and not see the other person every day or even every week. A friendship with someone who has moved to a new town, a different state, or even another country can still be a close relationship. With today's communication technology, such as e-mail and instant messages, and even old standbys like the telephone and letter writing, friends can easily keep in touch even when they are far apart.

❸ ASSESS

EVALUATING THE LESSON

Assign and discuss the Lesson 1 Review; then administer, grade, and discuss Lesson Quiz 42 in the TCR. 📁

RETEACHING

- Have students make a list of the various types of peer relationships along with the characteristics of each type.
- Ask students to complete Reteaching Activity 42 in the TCR. 📁

ENRICHMENT

Have students write a short story about a teen who is having a major disagreement with a friend. The story could involve working to solve the problem or deciding to end the friendship because of dissimilar values and a lack of respect and caring. Encourage students to proofread for organization, content, style, and conventions of grammar and spelling. Ask volunteers to share the final drafts of their stories with the class. 💻

❹ CLOSE

Prepare by writing each lesson concept on a separate numbered index card. Place the cards in a box, and have a volunteer each draw one. Going in numerical order, have the students define and summarize the concept written on the card they have selected.

▼ Mutual respect helps friends feel comfortable sharing their needs, wants, and emotions.

Building and Strengthening Friendships

Positive friendships are built on common values and interests. Having common values means friends won't pressure each other to engage in unhealthy risk behaviors. Having common interests gives friends something to talk about and do together. There are many ways to strengthen a healthy friendship.

▶ **Be loyal.** Friends can trust and depend on each other. They don't purposely do anything to hurt each other, and they always speak respectfully of each other.

▶ **Encourage each other.** A good friend is supportive and makes you feel good about yourself. Friends acknowledge each other's accomplishments and help each other through difficult times.

▶ **Respect each other.** Common courtesy helps keep friendships strong. Avoid taking friends for granted. Being on time and keeping your promises will let your friends know that you care about and respect them.

▶ Lesson 1 Review

Reviewing Facts and Vocabulary

1. What are *peers*?
2. Define *friendship*. Identify four character traits on which friendships are based.
3. List two ways to strengthen a friendship.

Thinking Critically

4. **Evaluating.** Interactions with friends and peers can have both positive and negative effects on all sides of your health triangle. Evaluate and provide examples of the positive and negative effects of peers and friends on physical, mental/emotional, and social health.
5. **Comparing and Contrasting.** Evaluate the dynamics of social groups consisting of casual friends, close friends, and platonic friends. What qualities do these groups share? How do they differ?

Applying Health Skills

Communication Skills. With a classmate, role-play two scenarios. In the first, demonstrate skills that close friends would use to communicate needs, wants, and emotions. In the second, show how peers might express disagreement about an issue while still showing respect for themselves and each other.

PRESENTATION SOFTWARE Use presentation software to develop a slide show that demonstrates strategies for communicating needs, wants, and emotions to peers. Find help in using presentation software at **health.glencoe.com**.

306 Chapter 12 Peer Relationships

▶ Lesson 1 Review

Answers to Reviewing Facts and Vocabulary

1. Peers are people of similar age who share similar interests.
2. A friendship is a significant relationship between two people. Caring, respect, trust, consideration.
3. Any two: loyalty, encouragement, respect

Answers to Thinking Critically

4. Examples will vary.
5. All involve relationships between people with similar interests who care about and respect each other. Differences lie in the degree of care, respect, and trust between the participants.

Peer Pressure and Refusal Skills

VOCABULARY

peer pressure
harassment
manipulation
assertive
refusal skills
passive
aggressive

YOU'LL LEARN TO

• Demonstrate refusal strategies and apply skills for making responsible decisions under pressure.

• Classify forms of communication as passive, aggressive, or assertive.

• Analyze the relationship between the use of refusal skills and the avoidance of unsafe situations.

QUICK START Make a two-column chart. In the left column, list examples of positive peer pressure. In the right column, list examples of negative peer pressure.

I magine that you are out with friends and someone suggests going to a party a few miles away. Most of your friends agree, but you aren't sure because you don't know the person who's throwing the party. Your friends spend the next few minutes trying to persuade you to join them. What will you do?

Peer Pressure

P erhaps you have been in a situation similar to the one above. Your peers can sometimes influence how you think, feel, and act. *The influence that people your age may have on you* is called **peer pressure**.

Peer pressure can have a positive or negative influence on your actions and behaviors. Because it can occur in many types of relationships, it is useful to learn to evaluate forms of peer pressure and develop healthful strategies for responding to it.

Peer pressure may make some decisions more difficult. *What strategies can help you make healthful, responsible decisions when faced with peer pressure?*

Lesson 2 Peer Pressure and Refusal Skills **307**

Peer Pressure and Refusal Skills

1 FOCUS

QUICK START On the board, create two columns labeled *Positive Peer Pressure* and *Negative Peer Pressure*. As students create their own lists, ask volunteers to share some of their examples of positive and negative peer pressure, and write their responses on the board.

TYING TO PRIOR KNOWLEDGE

Explain that pressure may or may not be intended when a person influences a friend, but it often has that effect because of the nature of peer relationships and the need for acceptance. Tell students that this lesson will examine peer relationships and ways to deal with negative peer pressure.

Health Skills Features

"Assert Yourself," p. 311

REFUSAL SKILLS

INTRODUCING VOCABULARY

• Have students work in small groups to define *peer pressure, harassment,* and *manipulation* in their own words. Then have them check their definitions against the Glossary.

• Ask students to complete the Chapter 12 Study Guide in the *Student Activity Workbook.*

307

Lesson 2 Resources

Teacher Classroom Resources

📁 Concept Mapping Activity 43
📁 Current Health Issues 12
📁 Enrichment Activity 12
📁 Guided Reading Activities 43
📁 Health Lab 12
📁 Lesson Plan 43

📁 Lesson Quiz 43
📁 Reteaching Activity 43

Student Activity Workbook

📁 Applying Health Skills 43
📁 Chapter 12 Study Guide

Multimedia

💾 Transparency 33

> Positive peer pressure can motivate you to try new activities that can benefit all sides of your health triangle. *What are some examples of positive peer pressure that you have experienced?*

② TEACH

hotlink

Have volunteers tell the class about a role model in their life. Ask them to describe how their role model has inspired them in a positive way.

Cooperative Learning

Divide the class in half. Ask half of the class to write a description of a hypothetical case of positive peer pressure and the other half to write a case about negative peer pressure. Have each group share its case with the rest of the class. **L2** 📀

Cross-Curriculum Activity

Language Arts Guide students in writing a short essay about strategies for dealing with negative peer pressure. Have them write several drafts of their essays. Remind them to proofread for organization, content, style and conventions of spelling and grammar. Have volunteers share their essays with the class. **L2** 📀

hotlink

role model For more information about role models, see Chapter 2, page 40.

Cooperative Learning

Select pairs of volunteers to write scenarios that demonstrate manipulation in a relationship. Have the students role-play their scenarios for the class. For each skit, ask the class to decide who is being manipulated, what methods are used (such as mockery or bribery), and what the manipulator hopes to gain. Have the class brainstorm ways to respond to the manipulation in each scenario. **L3** 📀
Bodily/Kinesthetic Intelligence

Positive Peer Pressure

Peers can influence you in many positive ways. For example, they might encourage you to participate in a cleanup campaign to clear away trash from a roadside. Agreeing to work with your peers in this campaign benefits your social health because you have the opportunity to interact with others in positive ways. It also benefits the community by providing a cleaner environment. Volunteering to serve food at a homeless shelter or working at a Special Olympics event because a friend does so are other examples of positive peer pressure.

Positive peer pressure may also involve *not* participating in risky behaviors or activities. For instance, having friends who do not use tobacco, alcohol, or other drugs may positively influence you to avoid these harmful substances.

You can also use positive peer pressure to influence others in healthful ways. You can be a **role model** by inspiring peers to take part in a positive act or a worthwhile cause.

Negative Peer Pressure

Peers sometimes pressure others to take part in behaviors or accept beliefs that have negative consequences. The members of a clique, for example, may be disrespectful toward people they do not consider acceptable to their group. Such behavior may involve **harassment**, or *persistently annoying others*. Harassment may include name-calling, teasing, or bullying. Negative peer pressure may also lead some teens to engage in behaviors that go against their values. For instance, a peer might pressure a classmate to help him or her cheat on a test.

Manipulation is another way of exerting negative peer pressure on others. **Manipulation** is *an indirect, dishonest way to control or influence others*. Some examples of the ways people manipulate one another are listed in **Figure 12.1.** It's important to discourage this kind of hurtful behavior and encourage the victim to report the problem to a trusted adult.

School to Work

Work Relationships In some jobs, the ability to relate well to peers accounts for 90 percent of job performance and success. In other jobs, relating to others is not quite as essential. List a variety of careers on the board such as a police officer, physician, gardener, telemarketer, computer programmer, writer, teacher, hair stylist, or lab technician. Then divide students into groups or pairs. For each career, have students list the factors that affect job performance, such as skills and knowledge, punctuality, dependability, honesty, physical strength, efficiency, and social skills. Have them rank the qualities for each job. Invite groups to share their rankings, and discuss where they placed social skills on their list and why.

FIGURE 12.1

COMMON METHODS OF MANIPULATION

- Mocking or teasing another person in mean or hurtful ways
- Using "guilt trips" to get desired results
- Bargaining—offering to make a deal to get what one wants
- Using flattery or praise to influence another person
- Bribing—promising money or favors if the person will do what is asked
- Making threats—promising violence or some other negative consequence if the person does not do what is asked
- Using blackmail—threatening to reveal some embarrassing or damaging information if the person does not do what is asked

Resisting Negative Peer Pressure

Peer pressure doesn't stop at the end of the teen years. Throughout your life, you may experience many instances in which peers, including friends and coworkers, make requests or demands of you. In some cases, your responses to these requests or demands will directly affect your health. For example, refusing to use tobacco, alcohol, or other drugs is a decision that will promote your overall health. At times there may be instances in which your response to peer pressure could seriously impact your life. For example, agreeing to get into a car with friends who have been drinking can place your life in danger.

One way to resist negative peer pressure is to avoid it. Develop friendships with people who share your values and interests. Friends who have respect for your health and well-being will be less likely to pressure you into doing something that goes against your values. You will find that it's much easier to resist negative peer pressure from someone else when you have friends who stand by you and support your decision.

Sometimes, however, the pressure to participate in unsafe or potentially harmful activities can be intense. When pressured by a friend, many teens worry about hurting the person's feelings or jeopardizing the relationship. Refusing to go along with a group may make some people concerned about appearing "uncool." Even though these situations may be difficult, it is important to remain firm and stay true to yourself. Remember, you have the responsibility to make decisions that have the best possible effect on your well-being. When making decisions that involve potentially risky consequences, your health and safety come first. Respect yourself, stand by your values, and be assertive in your refusal.

HEALTH Online

Learn more about dealing with negative peer pressure by clicking on Web Links at health.glencoe.com.

Lesson 2 Peer Pressure and Refusal Skills **309**

VISUAL LEARNING

Figure 12.1 Read aloud the common methods of manipulation shown in Figure 12.1. Have volunteers give examples of each form of manipulation. Ask students: How do you think this type of manipulation would make someone feel? What are other ways for a person to get what he or she wants—ways that are more direct, honest, and respectful?

Reinforcing Concepts

Pose this question: Who could you go to if you felt you were being pressured or manipulated by someone? Why? Have students list the names of some people who might encourage them to make their own decisions and not to be overly influenced by others. **ELL**

Activity

Select students to design and distribute a campus-wide questionnaire about the influence of peer pressure on teen behavior. Have students summarize and submit the results of the questionnaire in an article to the school newspaper. **L3** **Verbal/Linguistic Intelligence**

HEALTH Online

Have students read about techniques for dealing with negative peer pressure. Ask volunteers to role-play scenarios in which these techniques are used.

Promoting Coordinated School Health

Desired Results for Students As a measurement of the success of a coordinated school health program, an exiting student should demonstrate the following: is self-directed as a learner and an individual; has high self-esteem as a learner and an individual; is able to solve problems, make decisions, and understand cause-and-effect relationships; accepts responsibility for his or her own physical, mental/emotional, and social well-being; has academic skills essential to being a productive member of society. For more information, consult *Planning a Coordinated School Health Program*.

⏱ Health Minute

Ask volunteers to read aloud the strategies for resisting negative peer pressure. For each one, have students give an example of a situation in which that strategy would be an appropriate response.

Discussing

Have students write a paragraph explaining a situation in which being able to use refusal skills is necessary to withstand negative peer pressure. Ask them to explain how this refusal could be handled in an assertive manner. Why would this be an effective approach? Ask: What might happen if the refusal was handled passively? Aggressively? **L2**

Cooperative Learning

Ask volunteers to give examples of risk behaviors teens are often pressured to engage in, and record their ideas on the board. Then have students form small discussion groups. Assign each group one of the listed risk behaviors. Let group members explain how they would apply the three steps of effective refusal skills to resist the negative peer pressure. Ask each group to summarize its discussion for the rest of the class. **L2**

VISUAL LEARNING

Figure 12.2 Have volunteers read and demonstrate each example of body language shown in Figure 12.2. Ask: What type of message would be sent if the word *no* was combined with an approving nod of the head? A smile? Shrugging of the shoulders? How would this type of body language lessen the effectiveness of the refusal?

310

⏱ Health Minute

Resisting Peer Pressure

To resist negative peer pressure:

▶ Stand your ground by stating your values and beliefs.

▶ Consider the consequences of unsafe behavior.

▶ Decide whether the source of pressure is from yourself or from others.

▶ Be assertive, and use refusal skills to say no to risky activities.

▶ Leave the scene if necessary.

Assertive Refusal

Being **assertive** means *standing up for your rights in a firm but positive way.* When you are assertive, you state your position and stand your ground while acknowledging the rights of the other individuals. This is the most effective approach when facing negative peer influences. Assertive teens are often role models for others because most people respect individuals who stay true to themselves.

REFUSAL SKILLS

An important aspect of being assertive is the ability to use appropriate refusal skills. **Refusal skills** are *techniques and strategies that help you say no effectively when faced with something that you don't want to do or that goes against your values.* Effective refusal skills involve a three-step process. Learning and practicing these steps will help prepare you for dealing with high-pressure situations.

▶ **Step 1: State Your Position.** The first step in resisting negative peer pressure is to say no. You need to state your position simply and firmly. Make sure your "no" sounds as though you really mean it. Combining your words with nonverbal messages, such as those shown in **Figure 12.2,** will make your statement more effective. Having said no, give an honest reason for your response. Your reason may be as simple as, "It goes against my values." Offering a legitimate reason will help strengthen your refusal.

FIGURE 12.2

BODY LANGUAGE AND ASSERTIVE REFUSAL

Reinforce the meaning of your words with appropriate body language.

 Shaking your head is one way to communicate no.

 Raising your hand in a "Stop" or "No way" signal tells others that you are not interested.

 If the other person continues to pressure you, walk away from the situation.

〜 HEALTH LITERACY

Responsible, Productive Citizen Eating nutritious foods can be a challenge for teens when attending social events or parties. Encourage students to design a club that organizes healthful activities for teens, such as weekend hikes, bicycle trips, skating or swimming events, or charity marathons.

Students may wish to design a club that takes part in organic gardening or meets monthly for healthy vegetarian dinners. Whatever the event, nutritious foods should be served or available. Have students make a calendar of events as well as a menu of foods served.

Hands-On Health ACTIVITY

Assert Yourself

Learning to be assertive can help you maintain your commitment to a healthful lifestyle. By practicing assertiveness, you will find it easier to live by your values. In this activity, you will role-play assertive communication skills.

What You'll Need

- large index cards
- pen or pencil and paper

What You'll Do

1. With a partner, think of a realistic scenario in which you are being pressured by one or more peers to do something against your values.

2. Write your scenario on an index card, and swap cards with another pair of partners.

3. Role-play the scenario you've received, using the checklist shown here to make sure you have included the elements of assertive communication.

Apply and Conclude

Write a short reflective paper describing how being assertive can help protect your physical, mental/emotional, and social health.

▶ **Step 2: Suggest Alternatives.** When a peer asks you to take part in an activity with which you are uncomfortable, try suggesting another activity. For example, if a friend wants to go to a party where there is no adult supervision, you might say, "No, let's go to the movies instead." By offering an alternative, you create an opportunity for your friend to be with you in a way that makes you comfortable. Keep in mind that your suggestion is most effective if it takes you away from the dangerous or unpleasant situation.

▶ **Step 3: Stand Your Ground.** Even after you've refused, peers may continue trying to persuade you to join in. Make it clear that you mean what you've said. Use strong body language and maintain eye contact. If this doesn't work, remove yourself from the situation. Simply say, "I'm going home."

When faced with negative peer pressure, it's critical to stay true to yourself and do what's best for your health and well-being. Knowing that you made the decision to protect your safety and uphold your values will make you feel good about resisting the pressure.

Checklist: Assertive Communication Skills

 "I" messages

 Respectful but firm tone of voice

 Alternatives to the action

 Clear, simple statements

Appropriate body language

Lesson 2 Peer Pressure and Refusal Skills **311**

Hands-On Health

ASSERT YOURSELF REFUSAL SKILLS

NHES Standard 5 Students will demonstrate the ability to use interpersonal communication skills to enhance health.

Objective

Demonstrate refusal strategies, and apply skills for making responsible health decisions in high-pressure situations.

Motivator

Think of a situation that would require a teen to use refusal skills to stay healthy.

Teaching Strategies

1. Review the elements of assertive communication.
2. Ask volunteers to recall and share assertive responses they have used.
3. Approve rough drafts of the role-plays before giving out the index cards.

✓Assessment

Using a rubric, student work should provide comprehensive evidence of the following criteria to achieve the highest score:

✔ interactions among individuals
✔ use of "I" messages
✔ respectful but firm tone of voice
✔ alternatives to the action
✔ clear, simple statements
✔ appropriate body language

Cooperative Learning Activity

Refusal Skills Present the class with several scenarios involving negative peer pressure. For example, a teen might pressure a peer to stay out past curfew. Divide the class into groups. For each scenario, have one group provide a passive refusal, another group an aggressive refusal, and the third group an assertive refusal. For example, the passive refusal might include students dropping their shoulders or hanging their heads while the aggressive refusal might include crossed arms and an angry expression. After groups have responded to several scenarios, discuss the effectiveness of each type of refusal. Ask students to explain why assertive refusal is the most effective response.

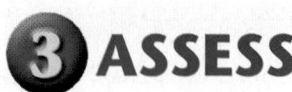

③ ASSESS

EVALUATING THE LESSON

Assign and discuss the Lesson 2 Review; then administer, grade, and discuss Lesson Quiz 43 in the TCR. 📁

RETEACHING

- Instruct students to write a brochure for teens entitled "Manipulation—Don't Let It Happen to You." In the brochure, have students identify methods of manipulation and ways to respond to manipulation. 📁

- Ask students to complete Reteaching Activity 43 in the TCR. 📁

ENRICHMENT

Ask students to find and read a news article about a crime involving teens or young adults. Have students write a one-page report summarizing the incident and speculate on how negative peer pressure may have contributed to the outcome.

④ CLOSE

Summarize the lesson by reviewing the important concepts.

▼ Practicing refusal skills will help you deal with negative peer pressure. *Give examples of passive, aggressive, and assertive ways to respond to peer pressure. Which method is most effective? Why?*

Passive and Aggressive Responses

Being assertive may take some practice. To some people, a passive response to negative peer pressure seems more natural and therefore easier. People who are **passive** have a *tendency to give up, give in, or back down without standing up for their own rights and needs.* Teens who respond passively to peer pressure may believe they are making friends by going along. However, being passive may cause others to view them as pushovers who aren't worthy of respect.

Some people may feel more comfortable with an aggressive response. **Aggressive** people are *overly forceful, pushy, hostile, or otherwise attacking in their approach.* An aggressive way of resisting peer pressure may involve yelling, shouting, shoving, or insulting others or the use of other kinds of verbal or physical force. Aggressive people may get their way, but most people react to aggressive behavior by avoiding the individual or by fighting back. Either reaction can result in emotional or physical harm to both parties.

Learning and practicing assertive responses is the most effective way to deal with peer pressure. Being assertive will help you resist negative peer pressure today, and it will also serve as a useful skill throughout your life.

▶ Lesson 2 *Review*

Reviewing Facts and Vocabulary

1. What is *peer pressure*?
2. Identify two examples of manipulation.
3. How might a friend help you resist negative peer pressure?

Thinking Critically

4. **Analyzing.** Suppose a group of friends constantly teases a student in your school. How can you show disapproval of this inconsiderate and disrespectful behavior?
5. **Comparing and Contrasting.** Explain the differences between passive, aggressive, and assertive forms of communication.

Applying Health Skills

Refusal Skills. With a classmate, develop a scenario in which peers use pressure to try to get you to use tobacco or alcohol. Demonstrate strategies for resisting the negative peer pressure.

SPREADSHEETS Use spreadsheet software to develop a table that provides examples of how refusal skills might make use of passive, aggressive, and assertive forms of communication. Find help in using spreadsheet software at **health.glencoe.com**.

312 **Chapter 12** Peer Relationships

▶ Lesson 2 *Review*

Answers to Reviewing Facts and Vocabulary

1. Peer pressure is the influence people your age may have on you.
2. Any two from Figure 12.1 on page 309.
3. Possible answer: A friend who shares your values and interests is less likely to pressure you; having a friend support your decisions makes resisting easier.

Answers to Thinking Critically

4. Responses will vary but should demonstrate appropriate communication skills.
5. Passive is giving in to pressure, aggressive is being pushy or hostile, and assertive is standing up for your own rights in a firm but positive way.

Dating and Setting Limits

VOCABULARY

infatuation
affection
curfew

YOU'LL LEARN TO

• Analyze behavior that will enhance dignity, respect, and responsibility in a dating relationship.

• Examine strategies for maintaining safe and healthy dating relationships.

QUICK START Give examples of health-related goals and limits you have set for yourself. How do the goals and limits benefit each side of your health triangle?

During adolescence it's natural to experience a change in attitude toward the opposite gender. Teens may find themselves feeling attracted to people they'd only thought of as classmates or friends before. These feelings of attraction may cause you to begin—or at least to begin thinking about—dating.

Dating

Dating can be an enjoyable learning experience. It provides opportunities to develop social skills, such as communicating and interacting with a person of the opposite gender. Dating also allows people to learn more about themselves. Through dating, some people discover new interests, reaffirm their values, and even start thinking about the type of person with whom they might like to build a future.

Sometimes when a teen is attracted to someone, an **infatuation**, or *exaggerated feelings of passion for another person*, develops. Although such feelings are natural, it is important not to mistake them for genuine affection. **Affection**, *a feeling of fondness for someone*, comes when you know another person well. Friendship and caring are essential for building an affectionate, close relationship with a dating partner. Teens who are dating can express affection by communicating with and listening to each other, holding hands, hugging, and spending quality time together.

Dating teens can express their affection in healthy, respectful ways. *List three positive ways for teens to show affection for a dating partner.*

Lesson 3 Dating and Setting Limits **313**

Dating and Setting Limits

1 FOCUS

QUICK START Ask volunteers to share their health-related goals and the limits they have set for themselves. Record their responses on the board. Lead the class in discussing the benefits of each goal or limit on the three sides of the health triangle.

TYING TO PRIOR KNOWLEDGE

Have volunteers share their thoughts on dating during the teen years. Ask: What are some benefits of dating? What are some drawbacks? Why is it important to set limits before dating? Explain that this lesson will focus on dating relationships and strategies for keeping them safe and healthy.

Health Skills Features

"What Are the Benefits of Group Dating and Individual Dating?" p. 314

INTRODUCING VOCABULARY

• Ask students to write a brief paragraph explaining the difference between *infatuation* and *affection*. Have them check their explanations against the definitions in the Glossary.

• Ask students to complete the Chapter 12 Study Guide in the *Student Activity Workbook*.

Lesson 3 *Resources*

Teacher Classroom Resources

- 📁 Concept Mapping Activity 44
- 📁 Guided Reading Activities 44
- 📁 Lesson Plan 44
- 📁 Lesson Quiz 44
- 📁 Reteaching Activity 44

Student Activity Workbook

- 📁 Applying Health Skills 44
- 📁 Chapter 12 Study Guide

Multimedia

- 🕹 Transparency 34

2 TEACH

Discussing

Ask: What are some healthful ways in which teens who are dating can show affection for one another? Students may share responses such as writing letters or poems, giving cards or small gifts, offering encouragement and support, helping whenever it is needed, and giving compliments.

Critical Thinking

Ask: What are additional reasons some teens might choose not to date? Which family traditions or values might cause a teen to decide against dating? How could you show respect for a friend's decision not to date? **L2**

Exploring Issues

WHAT ARE THE BENEFITS OF GROUP DATING AND INDIVIDUAL DATING?

Encourage students to share and compare their ideas about group and individual dating. Ask: Which dating situation and activities are likely to allow teens to have a good time without facing undue pressure to engage in sexual activity? Why is it important to plan dates that avoid high-pressure situations? After a brief discussion, have students read the feature and then write the essay. Remind students to proofread their essays. They may need to develop several drafts before handing in an error-free, final draft. Invite volunteers to read their essays to the class, and provide time for other students to respond to their essays.

Deciding to Date

Not everyone dates. Some teens choose not to date because they're shy around persons of the opposite gender. Others may choose not to date because they have other interests or time commitments. Still others may not date because of family traditions or values. Everyone is unique. There's no reason to let anyone pressure you into dating if you're not ready for it.

As a way of easing into dating, many teens go out with groups of friends of both genders. Being part of a group allows teens to develop and practice their social skills without having the pressure of focusing on only one person. Going out in a group takes some of the attention away from the individual, helping him or her relax and feel less self-conscious. Group dates or double dates can also relieve the pressure of being alone with someone new.

Exploring Issues

What Are the Benefits of Group Dating and Individual Dating?

There are benefits to both group dating and individual dating. What are your thoughts on these dating situations? Here are two viewpoints.

Viewpoint 1: Daphne L., age 15

I think group dating is the best choice for teens who are just beginning to date. Dating for the first time can be nerve-racking. It helps when you have the support of other friends. Going out on group dates makes the situation more comfortable and helps teens get used to dating. It's also a lot of fun.

Viewpoint 2: Ted R., age 16

Yeah, group dates can be fun, but it's hard to get to know a person better when you are surrounded by other friends. Going out in a group may make it seem less like a date. To really get comfortable with dating relationships, people need to go on individual dates. It's important to learn to communicate on a one-on-one basis with your date.

What do you think about group dating and individual dating? What other issues should teens consider before they start dating? Summarize your views in a one-page essay.

More About...

Dating Students need to recognize that not all persons desire to date at the same age or desire to date at all. In addition, some parents discourage or even forbid their children from dating until they reach a certain age. In some traditional cultures, dates are arranged and supervised by parents or other adult family members. Because of this diversity, care must be taken so that teens who do not date, for whatever reason, are never singled out in a discussion.

What to Do on a Date

What you decide to do on a date depends on the person you are with and your common interests. If you don't know the person well, a movie might be a good choice. Going out to dinner or to a school dance are also good options. You might also try attending a sports event such as a baseball or basketball game. When you get to know each other and have a better idea of your interests, you will probably find activities that both you and your date enjoy.

SPORTS OR ATHLETIC ACTIVITIES

If you and your date like sports, you might want to consider a date that includes athletic activities. In-line or ice skating, tennis, miniature golf, cycling, hiking, bowling, skiing, and horseback riding are all fun activities you can try on a date. Athletic activities such as these promote health and provide a way for dates to share and develop common interests. They also allow dates to get to know each other better in a friendly, relaxed atmosphere.

COMMUNITY ACTIVITIES

Consider going to the zoo or a local museum. If you and your date enjoy music or theater, you can attend concerts or plays being held in your community. You may also sign up for a painting, dancing, or photography class together at a local community center. Find out whether your community has any tourist attractions that you have overlooked. Learn what's available by asking friends and family, reading the local newspaper, and looking through the telephone book. Then, choose an event or activity that interests both you and your date, and go explore together. For example, you might attend a community festival or a stargazing party hosted by a local astronomy club.

CHARITABLE ACTIVITIES

Volunteering together can help build strong friendships and dating relationships. You can help build a house for Habitat for Humanity, participate in a charity walk-a-thon, volunteer to maintain a local park or beach, or attend a fund-raising event. Such activities allow you and your date to contribute to the community in positive ways. Volunteering is also a great option for group dates!

Many teens enjoy athletic activities during dates.
Why are athletic activities a good option for dating?

What can I do to make a good impression on a first date?

- **Relax and be yourself.** You want your date to like you for who you are, not who you're pretending to be.
- **Be honest.** There are no "rules" about who calls whom or about telling someone how you feel.
- **Plan your date.** Come up with something you'll both enjoy doing.
- **Be courteous.** Be on time, and treat your date with kindness and respect.

Lesson 3 Dating and Setting Limits **315**

Discussing

Ask students to interview their friends and peers regarding their views on dating. Share these responses in a class discussion. What are the similarities and differences among the views? What might account for them? **L2**

Activity

Ask students to check local resources to find places in the community that are appropriate locations for teen dates. Have them list several local activities that fit within each of the three categories presented on this page. Encourage students to include helpful information such as addresses, phone numbers, and hours of operation. They might also highlight activities that are good choices for group dates. Ask volunteers to compile all of the lists into a brochure for all dating teens. **L2**

Community Involvement

Through a series of interviews with parents, grandparents, or older friends, have students determine the changes that have taken place in dating behaviors. For example, encourage students to find out what types of dating activities were popular in the past. Ask students to try to explain why they think the changes have taken place. Have them share what they have learned with the class through oral presentations. **L2**
Verbal Intelligence

Meeting Individual Needs

Physically Challenged Students with physical challenges might be called upon to participate in a discussion on social health and dating. The discussion can focus on the difficulties encountered in dating relationships and on common misconceptions people have toward those with physical challenges. Information could also be presented about the variety of dating activities that many people with physical challenges enjoy.

Discussing

Initiate a discussion of what is meant by a dating relationship. Ask: What do you regard as a dating relationship versus casual dating? **L1**

Critical Thinking

Ask students to describe ways in which dating relationships differ from friendships. Can friendships turn into dating relationships and vice versa? In their opinion, how does each type of relationship help prepare them for relationships in their adult lives? **L1**

Cooperative Learning

Divide the class into two groups. Write *Pros* on one side of the board and *Cons* on the other. Have the first group brainstorm the pros of serious dating in high school and have a volunteer write the responses in the appropriate column. Have the other group do the same with their arguments against serious dating and record their responses. **L1**

CHARACTER CHECK

Trustworthiness Ask students to create a list of ways in which they can demonstrate trustworthiness to their parents and other family members. Have volunteers share their responses with the class. Ask students: How does resisting pressure and avoiding risk behaviors demonstrate trustworthiness? How do the qualities of self-control and self-discipline help teens resist negative pressure?

CHARACTER CHECK

Trustworthiness. When parents permit their teens to date, they show that they trust their children to make responsible decisions. A teen who has the self-control and self-discipline to resist peer pressure and avoid high-risk behaviors demonstrates trustworthiness. **What are some other ways you can demonstrate trustworthiness?**

 A curfew is a limit that many parents set for their teens. *What are some other examples of limits that help keep you safe?*

Avoiding Risk Situations

Some dating situations may increase the chance of being pressured to participate in sexual activity or some other high-risk behaviors. Before you go on a date, know where you're going and what you will be doing. Find out who else will be there, and discuss with your parents what time they expect you home. If you're going to a party, for example, know where the party is being held and whether there will be adult supervision. Regardless of where you go on a date, make sure you have money with you in case something goes wrong and you need to call home for a ride.

Below are more tips for avoiding high-risk dating situations:

▶ **Avoid places where alcohol and other drugs are present.** The use of alcohol or other drugs interferes with judgment. People under the influence of these substances are more likely to engage in unsafe or high-risk behaviors. Prevent such situations by not using alcohol or other drugs and avoiding those who are using these substances.

▶ **Avoid being alone with a date at home or in an isolated place.** You may find it more difficult to maintain self-control when you are home alone or in an isolated place with a date. Being isolated from others also increases your risk of being forced into a sexual act against your will.

Dating Relationships

Some teens choose to have an ongoing dating relationship with only one person. This type of relationship may help you develop skills and behaviors that will someday prepare you for the dignity, respect, and responsibility required in a marriage. However, keep in mind that dating only one person during adolescence may limit your chances for socializing with others. This may prevent you from developing other positive relationships.

Your teen years are a time for trying many different roles and relationships. Although beginning and ending dating relationships can be difficult, such experiences help you mature emotionally. Staying in a relationship because you don't know how to leave it gracefully or clinging to a person who wishes to end the relationship are common dating problems. Honesty and open communication will help resolve such difficulties.

∿ HEALTH LITERACY

Poems and Song Lyrics Relationships are the topic of many song lyrics and poems. Lovers, friends, family members, and even enemies have been immortalized in verse. Encourage students to list in their private health journals their favorite songs or poems about relationships. Have them check any that have influenced their thoughts, feelings, or images of what love is and make notes about how they have been influenced. Have them consider how their image of an ideal partner may be shaped by the words of a poet or songwriter. Invite them to write songs or poems about relationships and to share them if they choose.

Setting Limits

Your parents or guardians may set limits regarding your dating relationships. Such limits are intended to protect your health and safety. For example, your parent or guardian might insist on a **curfew**, *a set time at which you must be home at night.* A curfew is a limit that many parents establish for their teens. Limits should be established ahead of time and agreed upon by both teens and their families before the date.

As you mature, you'll need to know how to set your own limits. Remember, your parents or guardians can guide and support you through this process. For example, it's a good idea to set a limit on the age of the person you date. You also need to set limits with your date regarding places you'll go, how you'll get there, and what you will do. Setting such limits and making them clear before a date helps you avoid potentially risky situations.

When you communicate your limit on sexual activity, you need to be clear and firm about your decision to practice abstinence. You can make this task easier by developing and rehearsing avoidance techniques and refusal skills—including specific actions and phrases—that you can use. You will learn more about these skills in the next lesson.

Health Minute

Healthful Dating Expectations

When in a dating relationship, remember:

► You deserve to be treated with consideration and respect.

► Your partner should recognize and respect your values.

► If pressured by your date, you can say no to drugs or other high-risk activities without apologizing or offering an explanation.

► No one has the right to force or pressure you into doing anything that goes against your values or your family's values.

Health Minute

Ask a volunteer to read aloud the list of healthful dating expectations. Ask students to name other expectations that should be added to the list.

3 ASSESS

EVALUATING THE LESSON

Assign and discuss the Lesson 3 Review; then administer, grade, and discuss Lesson Quiz 44 in the TCR. 🗁

RETEACHING

• Have students write a few paragraphs describing a fun and safe date. Ask them to discuss where they would go on the date. Have them also explain how they would avoid risk situations.

• Ask students to complete Reteaching Activity 44 in the TCR. 🗁

ENRICHMENT

Have students watch a television show or movie involving teens in a dating relationship. Initiate a class discussion of the media's portrayal of teen dating.

▶ Lesson 3 Review

Reviewing Facts and Vocabulary

1. What is *affection*? How can teens show affection in a dating relationship without participating in sexual activity?

2. What are some ways to avoid high-risk dating situations?

3. Why is it important to set limits in a dating relationship?

Thinking Critically

4. **Synthesizing.** List the personal benefits that establishing a curfew can have for your health.

5. **Analyzing.** Explain the role that substance abuse plays in increasing the risk of unsafe behaviors such as sexual activity.

Applying Health Skills

Analyzing Influences. Watch several television programs that portray characters involved in dating relationships. Observe the interaction among the characters, and identify what message the program communicates to teens about peer pressure and sexual activity. Summarize your observations in a written report.

TECHNOLOGY OPTION

WORD PROCESSING Word processing can give your report a more polished look. Visit **health.glencoe.com** for tips on using your word-processing program.

Lesson 3 Dating and Setting Limits **317**

4 CLOSE

Summarize the lesson by reviewing the strategies for maintaining safe and healthy dating relationships.

▶ Lesson 3 Review

Answers to Reviewing Facts and Vocabulary

1. A feeling of fondness for someone; communicating and listening to each other, holding hands, hugging, and spending quality time together.

2. Avoid places where alcohol and drugs are present; avoid being alone with a date at home or in an isolated place.

3. Setting limits helps avoid risk.

Answers to Thinking Critically

4. Possible answer: Curfews ensure that a teen gets sufficient rest and reduces the chance of engaging in risky behaviors.

5. Use of such substances affects judgment and might lead individuals to participate in unsafe activities.

Abstinence: A Responsible Decision

①FOCUS

QUICK START   Ask volunteers to share some of the consequences they have listed. Write their responses on the board. Guide the class in discussing the ways in which these consequences affect all three aspects of health for both the individual and his or her family members. Ask: How could these consequences be avoided?

TYING TO PRIOR KNOWLEDGE

Have volunteers name some of the benefits of abstinence from sexual activity during the teen years. Discuss the challenges that sexual activity places on teen relationships and how it can be harmful to both individuals and the relationship. Tell students that this lesson will further discuss the possible consequences of teen sexual activity and present ways to support a decision to practice abstinence.

Health Skills Features

"Abstinence Pledges: A Growing Trend," p. 321

INTRODUCING VOCABULARY

- Ask students to define *priorities*. Next, have students write down some priorities that they have established.
- Ask students to complete the Chapter 12 Study Guide in the *Student Activity Workbook*. ☞

318

Abstinence: A Responsible Decision

VOCABULARY
- **abstinence**
- **sexually transmitted diseases (STDs)**
- **priorities**
- **self-control**

YOU'LL LEARN TO
- Analyze the importance of abstinence from sexual activity as the preferred choice of behavior for teens.
- Discuss the legal implications regarding sexual activity as it relates to minors.
- Discuss abstinence as the only method that is 100 percent effective in preventing pregnancy and sexually transmitted diseases.

QUICK START   On a sheet of paper, list several consequences of being sexually active. Explain how each consequence could affect the health of the individual and the health of his or her family members.

These teens have chosen to make abstinence from sexual activity a priority in their relationship. *Why is abstinence the best choice for teens?*

Many of the sexual feelings teens experience are brought on by the body's release of chemicals. You don't have control over the feelings caused by your hormones, but you do have complete control over how you respond to them.

Abstinence Until Marriage

Each year, more and more teens make the safe and responsible choice of abstinence from sexual activity until marriage. **Abstinence** is *a deliberate decision to avoid high-risk behaviors, including sexual activity before marriage and the use of tobacco, alcohol, and other drugs.* Many teens choose to practice abstinence because it is the only 100 percent sure way to eliminate health risks associated with sexual activity. These risks include unplanned pregnancy and **sexually transmitted diseases (STDs)**—*infections spread from person to person through sexual contact.*

318   Chapter 12   Peer Relationships

Lesson 4 *Resources*

Teacher Classroom Resources
- 📁 Concept Mapping Activity 45
- 📁 Guided Reading Activities 45
- 📁 Lesson Plan 45
- 📁 Lesson Quiz 45
- 📁 Reteaching Activity 45

Student Activity Workbook
- 📁 Applying Health Skills 45
- 📁 Chapter 12 Study Guide

Multimedia
- 🖇 Transparency 35

Committing to Abstinence

The teen years are a time for physical, mental/emotional, and social growth. Part of this growth process involves setting goals for the future and establishing priorities. **Priorities** are *those goals, tasks, and activities that you judge to be more important than others.* A priority for many teens, for example, is to get good grades and succeed in school. Think about your plans for the future. How might an unplanned pregnancy or a **sexually transmitted disease** (STD) affect your plans? Making abstinence from sexual activity a priority can eliminate these risks and help you achieve your goals.

Practicing abstinence requires planning and self-control. **Self-control** is *a person's ability to use responsibility to override emotions.* Use the following tips as a guide to commit to abstinence.

▶ **Establish your priorities.** Think about your goals, and set priorities that will help you reach them. Consider your values and those of your family, such as respect, honesty, integrity, and morality.

▶ **Set personal limits on how you express affection.** Base your limits on your priorities. Set your limits before you are in a situation where sexual feelings begin to build.

▶ **Share your thoughts with your partner.** One sign of a mature, responsible relationship is being able to communicate with your partner openly and honestly. Discuss your priorities, and clearly define your limits.

▶ **Talk with a trusted adult.** Parents and other trusted adults are often able to suggest safe and healthful ways for you to manage your feelings.

▶ **Avoid high-pressure situations.** When possible, go out on dates in a group. Stay away from unsupervised parties and dark rooms. Avoid parking in secluded spots.

▶ **Do not use alcohol or other drugs.** Using alcohol or other drugs interferes with the ability to think clearly. It is also wise to avoid people who are using these substances.

hot link

sexually transmitted disease For more information about specific sexually transmitted diseases, see Chapter 25, page 646.

Ⓥ **Choosing a safe, supervised area for a date helps you uphold your values.** *What other strategies can help you maintain your commitment to abstinence?*

Lesson 4 Abstinence: A Responsible Decision **319**

② TEACH

ACTIVE READING

Study Skills

Reading the review questions at the back of each lesson, before reading the material, will help students identify specific information as they read. It also helps them to process information better as they anticipate what they can expect to read. As students read the lesson and take notes, tell them to include the answers to the review questions in their notes. When finished reading, students should use the lesson review to determine how well they recall, or remember, the information. For more strategies, see the *Guided Reading Activities* booklet. 📂

Discussing

Talk about some of the pressures teens may experience in making decisions about sexual activity. Examples might include peers, music, movies, television, etc. 🔳

Critical Thinking

Ask: Why do you think some young people choose not to brag about choosing abstinence? Suppose a group of teens at your school began talking proudly about their own abstinence and pressuring others to choose abstinence. What effect do you think they would have? Explain. 🔳

Home and Community

Readings for Teens Suggest that students visit local libraries and examine the selection of fiction and nonfiction books that deal with dating relationships and other issues teens face. First, they should find out how their libraries classify the young adult section. Have students survey the teen situations explored in the books that the young adult section offers. Suggest that students read recent book reviews and make a list of books they think the library should carry for adolescents. Encourage them to provide the librarian with the list.

Service Learning

Have students write a public service announcement about the importance of abstinence until marriage for teens. Encourage students to include information about the negative consequences of sexual activity on an individual's physical health. Ask volunteers to read their public service announcements to the class.

Guest Speaker

Ask a physician, school nurse, or other health care professional to speak to your class about the health risks associated with teen sexual activity. Encourage students to write down any questions they may have for the speaker. Before the day of the discussion, pass around a box in which students can anonymously submit their questions. 🔲 ▭

Cooperative Learning

Have students brainstorm the roles and responsibilities of being a parent. Write these on the board. Discuss how teens are not prepared to adopt these roles. 🔲

h⊙t link

Have students use classroom or library resources to learn more about AIDS, including the ways in which it is and is not transmitted. Ask volunteers to share their findings with the class.

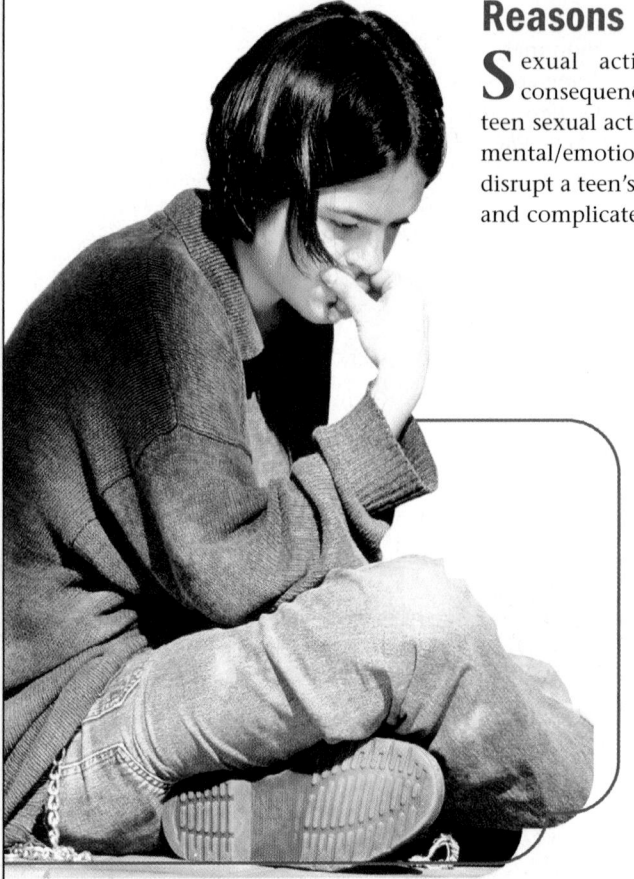

⚠️ **Careful consideration of the negative consequences associated with sexual activity will reinforce the decision to practice abstinence until marriage.** *What are your reasons for practicing abstinence?*

h⊙t link

acquired immune deficiency syndrome (AIDS)
For more information on the problems associated with the AIDS epidemic, see Chapter 25, page 658.

320 Chapter 12 Peer Relationships

Reasons to Practice Abstinence

Sexual activity has many short-term and long-term consequences. In addition to having legal consequences, teen sexual activity can seriously harm an individual's physical, mental/emotional, and social health. These negative effects can disrupt a teen's life, interfere with his or her goals for the future, and complicate his or her relationships with others.

Legal Implications

It is illegal for an adult to have sexual contact with anyone under the age of consent, which varies from state to state. In many states, it is illegal for unmarried minors to engage in sexual activity. For example, if the age of consent in a state is 18, two seventeen-year-old teens who engage in sexual activity would be breaking the law. People who are arrested for and convicted of breaking sexual laws can go to jail. Depending on the situation, they may be identified as sex offenders—a label that will follow them for the rest of their lives. This label can harm their careers and future relationships.

Effects on Physical Health

Teen sexual activity can affect the physical health of both females and males in significant ways.

UNPLANNED PREGNANCY

For many teens, unplanned pregnancy is the consequence of sexual activity. Teen pregnancy risks the health of both the teen mother and her child. Often, the body of a teen is not sufficiently mature to sustain a healthy pregnancy. This can lead to complications that threaten the lives of mother and baby.

SEXUALLY TRANSMITTED DISEASES (STDS)

Teens from 15 to 19 years of age are at the greatest risk of contracting STDs. Each year, about 3 million teens in the United States contract some form of STD. If diagnosed early, many STDs can be treated and cured. However, some of these diseases have no cure and can have lifelong consequences. For example, chlamydia can cause sterility if left untreated, making it impossible for a person ever to have a child. Other STDs, such as **acquired immune deficiency syndrome (AIDS),** can be fatal.

Dealing with Sensitive Issues

Being Supportive Studies indicate that nearly half of American high school students say they have been sexually active. Your role as a teacher is to emphasize to all students that it is never too late to choose abstinence even if they have already participated in sexual activity. Too often, teens who have had some sexual experience—or who have experimented with tobacco, alcohol, and other drugs—feel they cannot go back. Remind students that each instance of sexual activity—like each use of tobacco, alcohol, or other drugs—is a choice. In discussing this issue, however, take care to avoid conveying value judgments. Refer to Glencoe's professional booklet *Dealing with Sensitive Issues* for more information.

Real-Life Application

Abstinence Pledges: A Growing Trend

Teens who take a pledge to delay sexual activity until marriage are far less likely than their peers to become pregnant or to contract a sexually transmitted disease. How can teens strengthen their commitment to abstinence?

Abstinence Pledge

A Commitment to Myself and Others

On this day, I make a commitment to myself, my family, my friends, and to those I date, to abstain from sexual activity until marriage.

My reasons include: upholding family values, wanting to attend college, safeguarding my self-worth and self-concept, wanting to have healthy children when I marry.

People who will support me in my pledge include:

☆ my parents/guardian   ☆ my family doctor

☆ my best friend   ☆ my school counselor

I hereby sign this pledge as an indication of my personal commitment to remain abstinent until marriage.

My signature: _____

○ How can teens' goals be compromised by sexual activity? What are the most important reasons for you to practice abstinence?

○ Which people in your life can help support your decision to practice abstinence?

ACTIVITY

Work with a small group. Use your answers to the questions to create a poster advocating that high school teens practice abstinence. Communicate the importance and benefits of practicing abstinence. Make your poster persuasive and attention-getting, and include a memorable phrase or slogan.

Effects on Emotional Health

Establishing and following a strong value system leads teens to healthy feelings of self-respect. Engaging in sexual activity outside of marriage goes against the values and religious beliefs of many people. Often, the fear of being caught leads teens who engage in such activity to begin lying to parents or others about their whereabouts. This dishonesty can cause emotional distress by bringing on feelings of guilt and regret that are harmful to a teen's self-concept.

For teens facing unplanned pregnancy, the demands of being a parent can cause great emotional strain. Pregnancy followed by the birth and care of an infant is extremely demanding. Parenthood is a serious, full-time, lifelong responsibility that teens are not ready for.

Lesson 4 Abstinence: A Responsible Decision   **321**

Real-Life Application

ABSTINENCE PLEDGES: A GROWING TREND

 ADVOCACY

NHES Standard 7 Students will demonstrate the ability to advocate for personal, family, and community health.

Objectives

- Analyze the importance of abstinence from sexual activity as the preferred choice of behavior for teens.
- Communicate the importance of practicing abstinence.

Motivator

Ask: How can sharing your pledge with supportive friends help you to honor it?

Teaching Strategies

1. Allow students to work in small groups to clarify their ideas on how abstinence helps teens to reach personal goals.
2. Encourage students to discuss in their groups ways that friends can support one another in their decision to abstain from sexual activity until marriage and incorporate these ideas into their posters.

✓ Assessment

Using a rubric, student work should provide comprehensive evidence of the following criteria to achieve the highest score:

✔ clear, health-enhancing stand
✔ support for the position with relevant information
✔ awareness of the audience
✔ encouragement of others to make healthful choices
✔ passion/conviction

Cooperative Learning Activity

Teens Portrayed in the Media Have students work in groups to study the power of the media to shape teens' self-images and behavior. The media may project images that teens try to emulate, but the images may or may not align with the health triangle. Instruct students to bring to class advertisements, stories, and photographs that exemplify media portrayal of teens. Ask: What teens in films and on TV are projected as "cool"? Are these positive role models? Are the teens sexually active? How does the media promote the idea that teens are supposed to be sexy? Encourage each group to create a visual that classifies types of images the media portrays. If possible, each type should be illustrated with a photograph, headline, or other example of media portrayal.

Discussing

Select students to debate the statement: *A real friend would not pressure you into doing something you do not want to do.* ◼

Reinforcing Concepts

Stress that pressure from peers and the media can be strong influences. Remind students of the importance of being able to identify their personal values and goals when they feel pressured by these outside influences. Encourage them to base decisions, especially those about sexual activity, on their values rather than on peer pressure. ◼

Health Skills Practice

Avoidance Techniques and Refusal Skills Present students with a fictional scenario in which a teen resists pressure to engage in sexual activity. Have students point out the avoidance techniques and refusal skills used by the teen. Discuss other possible ways in which a person could avoid or resist being pressured into sexual activity.

Discussing

Talk about instances in which facial expressions and body language or gestures—instead of words—are used to pressure others. Have volunteers demonstrate examples of this kind of silent pressure. Ask students how they feel when they are pressured like this. How effective is this kind of pressure? Ask whether there are other nonverbal means of pressure. ◼

Teens who choose sexual abstinence safeguard their reputations. *What are some other benefits of abstinence?*

Effects on Social Health

Sexually active teens risk their reputations. Being labeled by peers as "easy" can make it difficult for a teen to build new and healthy relationships. For example, to eliminate the risk of being pressured into sexual activity, some teens refuse to date those who are sexually active. Also, partners may view each other differently when a relationship involves sexual activity. In some cases, the pressure and expectations caused by sexual activity may lead to the breakup of a relationship.

Engaging in sexual activity can also harm a teen's relationship with family members. When teens decide to become sexually active, they go against their family's values. They go beyond the limits that their parents or guardians set to protect them. In failing to demonstrate responsible and healthful dating behavior, these teens break their parents' trust. Parents who discover that their teen is sexually active often feel disappointed and betrayed. Such feelings can cause tension among family members.

When faced with an unplanned pregnancy, many teen parents drop out of school to support their child. By law, the teen father is required to support his child financially until the child reaches the age of 18. Frequently, teen parents sacrifice plans for college and job training. They may also give up their social lives to meet the needs of the child. Unmarried teens are not prepared to assume the responsibilities of parenthood. Committing to abstinence is the safe and healthy choice for teens.

Using Avoidance Techniques and Refusal Skills

To reduce the risk of being pressured into sexual activity, learn avoidance techniques—actions or phrases you can use to avoid risky situations. For example, if your date wants to go to a party that will not be supervised by adults, you might suggest going to a restaurant instead. If a boyfriend or girlfriend wants to come over when your parents or guardians aren't at home, you might suggest going skating or biking instead.

HEALTH LITERACY

Effective Communicator Remind students that being able to communicate effectively is essential for resisting pressure to engage in sexual activity. Help students practice using refusal skills to say no to sexual activity. Write their refusals on the board. Then ask students to comment on the effectiveness of each refusal. Stress the importance of learning refusal skills.

FIGURE 12.3

SAYING NO TO SEXUAL ACTIVITY

If someone uses pressure lines to persuade you to break your commitment to abstinence, use refusal statements to communicate your stance firmly.

Pressure Line	Refusal Statement
• If you love me, you will. • Everyone's doing it. • Don't be such a baby. • My feelings won't change. I'll still respect you.	• If you care about me, you won't pressure me. • No, everyone's not. I'm sticking to my values. • It's the mature, responsible decision to wait. • Maybe, but I won't respect myself.

Share your commitment to abstinence with your girlfriend or boyfriend, stating your position simply but firmly. After you have discussed your decision to practice abstinence, you will find it easier to exercise self-control. If a situation seems to be getting out of control, insist on stopping. Then, back away and explain why you want to stop. If your girlfriend or boyfriend tries to pressure you, become more assertive. You might use refusal statements similar to those in **Figure 12.3.** Make sure your body language supports your verbal message. Don't be afraid of hurting the other person's feelings. It's possible to say no and still remain friends.

 Lesson 4 *Review*

Reviewing Facts and Vocabulary

1. What is *abstinence*?
2. Discuss the legal implications regarding sexual activity as it relates to minors.
3. What are effective ways to avoid being pressured into sexual activity?

Thinking Critically

4. **Evaluating.** Write a paragraph describing the short-term and long-term benefits of abstinence for the emotional and social health of both the individual and the family.
5. **Analyzing.** How can practicing abstinence benefit a teen's self-image? Explain your answer.

Applying Health Skills

Refusal Skills. With a classmate, role-play situations in which teens use refusal skills to avoid participating in sexual activity. Have classmates analyze the effectiveness of these refusal skills.

WEB SITES Create a Web page that advocates for teen abstinence. See **health.glencoe.com** for help on planning and building your own Web page.

Lesson 4 Abstinence: A Responsible Decision **323**

 Lesson 4 *Review*

Answers to Reviewing Facts and Vocabulary

1. A deliberate decision to avoid high-risk behavior, including sexual activity before marriage and the use of drugs.
2. It is illegal for an adult to engage in sexual activity with a minor. In many states, it is illegal for unmarried minors to engage in sexual activity.

3. Use of avoidance techniques and refusal skills.

Answers to Thinking Critically

4. Responses will vary.
5. Answers may include feeling good about staying true to self and values, being confident in identity, and having high self-esteem.

Figure 12.3 Have a volunteer read each pressure line shown in Figure 12.3, followed by another volunteer reading each refusal statement. Ask: How are these pressure lines a form of manipulation? How are they intended to make the other person feel?

3 ASSESS

EVALUATING THE LESSON

Assign and discuss the Lesson 4 Review; then administer, grade, and discuss Lesson Quiz 45 in the TCR.

RETEACHING

- Have students outline the steps involved in making a decision to practice abstinence.

- Ask students to complete Reteaching Activity 45 in the TCR.

ENRICHMENT

Ask a group of students to survey classmates about whether they would or would not want to be parents now, in five years, or in ten years.

4 CLOSE

Remind students that abstinence is one of the most important decisions they can make during their teen years. Stress how maintaining a person's values and goals should be the basis when making any decision. Then discuss how a person should communicate the reasons for his or her personal decision when faced with peer pressure.

Screenplays for Healthy Peer Relationships

NHES Standard 4 Students will analyze the influence of culture, media, technology, and other factors on health.

Objective

Write a screenplay for a new teen television show that presents healthful messages about peer relationships.

Motivator

Ask students to think about teen or family television shows they watch and consider how peer pressure and friendship issues are presented in those shows.

Teaching Strategies

Awareness Ask students to share their responses to the Motivator.

Analysis Students should place themselves in the shoes of each character in order to empathize with how that character feels.

Reflection Instruct students to compose at least three scenes in which action will take place. Just as in their own lives, suggest that central characters might consult other people they trust, such as parents, guardians, teachers, or school counselors, in order to figure out the right course of action.

Take Action Encourage students to critique a television show they watch regularly for its messages regarding peer relationships.

✓ Assessment

Student screenplays should follow the format given. The characters should employ refusal skills and/or display healthy friendship traits depicted in the chapter.

Eye ON THE Media

Screenplays for Healthy Peer Relationships

Drawing from the chapter content, write a screenplay for a new teen television show that presents healthful messages about peer relationships. Use the following example as a guide for formatting your screenplay.

```
                  ACT I
                 SCENE 1
        INT. (INTERIOR) SCHOOL CAFETERIA, NOON
   TWO BEST FRIENDS, JUDY AND GREG, WALK INTO THE BUSY
    CAFETERIA AND SIT DOWN AT THEIR FAVORITE TABLE.

                  JUDY
    I think Sara is upset about something. She's been
    keeping to herself all day. I wonder what's wrong.

                  GREG
   I don't know. Do you think she and her boyfriend had
            an argument about something?

                 SCENE 2
          INT. SCHOOL HALLWAY, 3:30 PM
   SARA IS AT HER LOCKER, LOOKING SAD AND DISTRACTED.
```

ACTIVITY

Choose one of the following scenarios, and write a screenplay with three scenes. Apply what you have learned in this chapter about healthy peer relationships.

Scenario 1: Three teen boys who have been friends for years are having a conversation about girls. Two of them are taunting the third for choosing abstinence.

Scenario 2: Four teen girls who are close friends are at a school dance. Two of them are making fun of a classmate whom they consider overweight.

EXPRESS YOUR VIEWS

Review the healthful ways you resolved the situation in your screenplay. Using what you have learned from this chapter, write a friendship or behavior pledge that incorporates the elements of healthy friendships and positive peer pressure.

324 Chapter 12 Review

More About...

Addressing Teen Males Although the choice of abstinence and the use of refusal skills to counter negative peer pressure are lessons aimed at both male and female teens, it can be said that, historically, addressing these issues meant addressing predominantly female teens. In other words, it was up to the female to refuse the advances of the male. Recently however, many programs have been created that directly address teenage male behavior regarding sexual activity choices and peer pressure. These programs are aimed at helping male youths understand their direct responsibility in decisions to engage in sexual activity and their responsibility for the consequences of such activity.

CROSS–CURRICULUM CONNECTIONS

Write a Journal Entry. Nurturing healthy friendships means taking responsibility for your actions and understanding the roles others play in your life. Brainstorm a list of important decisions you have made that were influenced by peer pressure. Write a journal entry about the decision on your list that stands out as the most significant. Describe the incident. Reflect on why it was a positive or negative experience.

Explore Dating Customs. Dating customs for teens vary from culture to culture. As a class, brainstorm a list of cultures whose dating customs you would be interested in studying. Your teacher will organize the class in teams and assign you a culture to research. Each team should report back to the class. Then, have a class discussion comparing and contrasting the different customs.

Practice Problem Solving. Bob had three friends with whom he socialized almost exclusively. When he got a job, he struck up friendships with four people at work and got invited to a party. One of his new friends brought three people that Bob liked immediately. His other three coworkers brought one friend each, but Bob didn't have anything in common with two of them. How many friends does Bob have now?

Research a Topic. Chemicals called *pheromones* contribute to the physical attraction to others that many people begin to experience during the teen years. Many animal species secrete pheromones as a means of communication. Because of the complexity of mammalian behavior, studies on pheromones have focused largely on insects. Research the ways social insects use pheromones to communicate and send messages. Summarize your findings in a one-page report.

School Social Worker

School social workers deal with a wide range of social, emotional, cultural, and economic concerns among students. They help students overcome problems that may be interfering with their education. School social workers also help improve students' decision-making skills, motivation, attendance, and self-concept.

To become a school social worker, you need a bachelor's or a master's degree in social work and a license or certificate from your state. Learn more about this and other health careers by clicking on Career Corner at **health.glencoe.com**.

CROSS–CURRICULUM CONNECTIONS

Enrich student learning by connecting the topic of peer relationships to one of the four subject areas presented on this page. The activity may be completed individually or with a partner.

Language Arts Explain to the students that journal entries provide an opportunity to analyze personal decisions and behaviors. Review the use of first-person pronouns.

Social Studies Help teams assign roles to each member, such as researcher, fact checker, recorder, and presenter.

Math Answer: $3 + 4 + 3 + (3-2) = 11$

Science Many insects produce pheromones that attract the opposite sex or increase sexual maturation. Research in this field has led to attempts to use pheromones to control insect behavior (e.g., to prevent mating).

Have students read and discuss the Career Corner information on school social workers. Ask interested students to explore the Glencoe Health Web site at **health.glencoe.com** for more information on this career.

Portfolio Assessment

Self-Evaluation Direct students to review the Health Skills Activities and other activities completed in the chapter. Encourage each student to select one finished product or activity that demonstrates his or her best work for the chapter and that represents the student's learning goals. Have students explain what they have learned and how the examples they have selected demonstrate their growth in health literacy, knowledge, and skills.

Teacher Classroom Resources
Assign Performance Assessment 12, "Qualities of a Friend," in the TCR.

CHECKING COMPREHENSION

- Assign and discuss the chapter review.
- Use the Chapter 12 MindJogger Videoquiz to review the chapter. ▷ ◁

CHAPTER 12 REVIEW ANSWERS

Exploring Health Terms

1. platonic friendship
2. clique
3. stereotype
4. Manipulation
5. refusal skills
6. aggressive
7. infatuation
8. curfew
9. sexually transmitted disease
10. priorities
11. self-control

Recalling the Facts

1. Peers are the people with whom you are likely to have casual friendships.

2. Platonic friendships can help teens understand and become comfortable with individuals of the opposite gender.

3. Similar values, interests, beliefs, and attitudes on basic issues; open and honest communication; sharing of joys, disappointments, dreams, and concerns; mutual respect, caring, and support; concern about each other's safety and well-being.

4. Peer pressure that influences you to do something positive, such as doing well on a test, getting involved in volunteer work, or not using drugs.

5. Body language can be used to back up words. For example, shaking your head as you say no reinforces your message.

▶ EXPLORING HEALTH TERMS *Answer the following questions on a sheet of paper.*

Lesson 1 *Match each definition with the correct term.*

clique	friendship
peers	platonic friendship
stereotype	

1. A relationship with a member of the opposite gender in which there is affection but the people are not considered a couple.
2. A small circle of friends that excludes people viewed as outsiders.
3. An exaggerated or oversimplified belief about an entire group of people.

Lesson 2 *Replace the underlined words with the correct term.*

aggressive	assertive
harassment	manipulation
passive	peer pressure
refusal skills	

4. <u>Harassment</u> is an indirect and dishonest way to control someone.
5. An important aspect of being assertive is to use effective <u>manipulation</u>.
6. Being overly pushy and hostile is being <u>assertive</u>.

Lesson 3 *Fill in the blanks with the correct term.*

affection	curfew
infatuation	

Shane's parents worry about his (_7_), or exaggerated feelings of passion, with his girlfriend. To help Shane avoid situations that could involve him in high-risk behaviors, his parents set guidelines for him, including an early (_8_), or time by which he must be at home.

Lesson 4 *Match each definition with the correct term.*

abstinence	self-control
sexually transmitted disease	priorities

9. A risk associated with not choosing abstinence.
10. Goals, tasks, and activities you judge as more important than others.
11. A person's ability to use responsibility to override emotions.

▶ RECALLING THE FACTS *Use complete sentences to answer the following questions.*

Lesson 1

1. What is the relationship between peers and casual friendships?
2. What are the benefits of a platonic friendship?
3. Identify five attributes of a true friendship.

Lesson 2

4. What is positive peer pressure?
5. How can body language be used to communicate refusal?
6. Describe an aggressive response to peer pressure.

Lesson 3

7. What are some benefits of dating?
8. Why do some teens choose not to date?
9. What are some advantages of group dating over individual dating?

Lesson 4

10. Identify three risks associated with sexual activity during the teen years.
11. Analyze the importance of abstinence from sexual activity as the preferred choice of behavior for teens.
12. Describe a problem that can result from an unplanned teen pregnancy.

---

6. An aggressive response is overly forceful, pushy, hostile, or otherwise attacking.

7. Possible answers: Develop social skills, discover new interests, reaffirm values, have fun, get to know another person better, learn what type of person you might like to build a future with.

8. Possible answers: They're shy around persons of the opposite gender, they have other interests or time commitments, they are not ready, dating goes against family traditions or values.

9. Possible answers: Group dating may make shy teens feel more comfortable around persons of the opposite gender; going out in groups helps teens avoid risky situations.

10. Risks include unplanned pregnancies; exposure to sexually transmitted diseases, including HIV; and loss of self-respect or the respect of others.

► THINKING CRITICALLY

1. **Evaluating.** Describe both the advantages and disadvantages of being a member of a social group such as a clique. *(LESSON 1)*

2. **Analyzing.** Suggest ways you can stand up to peers to show disapproval of inconsiderate and disrespectful behavior such as harassment of others. *(LESSON 2)*

3. **Applying.** Marriage is a long-term commitment. Getting married means that a person is deciding to spend the rest of his or her life with another person. How can the behaviors you practice in a dating relationship help prepare you for the responsibility of marriage? *(LESSON 3)*

4. **Summarizing.** Unplanned pregnancy among teens affects the teens involved, their families, and society as a whole. Write a paragraph explaining the negative consequences teen pregnancy holds for individuals, families, and society. *(LESSON 4)*

► HEALTH SKILLS APPLICATION

1. **Practicing Healthful Behavior.** Develop a plan for demonstrating to your friends each of the traits that characterize a healthy friendship. Over the span of a week, keep a log to describe how you demonstrated each trait. *(LESSON 1)*

2. **Analyzing Influences.** Locate a magazine or newspaper article about a teen who has set a positive example in the community. Write a brief summary of the article, and identify how the actions of that teen might be a positive influence on other teens. *(LESSON 2)*

3. **Communication Skills.** Write a skit that depicts a responsible, healthful dating relationship between two teens. The teens should demonstrate effective communication skills to show their respect for each other and their commitment to practicing abstinence. *(LESSON 3)*

4. **Advocacy.** Write a letter to the editor of your school newspaper in which you discuss abstinence from sexual activity as the only method that is 100 percent effective in preventing pregnancy, STDs, and the sexual transmission of HIV/AIDS. *(LESSON 4)*

✳ BEYOND *the* Classroom

Parent Involvement

Practicing Healthful Behaviors. Many communities have programs that provide drug-free places where teens can socialize under adult supervision. Such programs help teens avoid pressure to participate in high-risk behaviors. With your parents, learn about the programs for teens in your area. If such programs do not exist in your community, find out how one might be created.

School and Community

Stopping Harassment. Speak with a law enforcement official in your community to learn the legal definition of harassment and what penalties exist for teens found guilty of harassment. Share your findings with the class. Discuss actions that students, faculty, and community members can take to help stop harassment.

Chapter 12 Review **327**

Thinking Critically

1. Answers should discuss an advantage of a sense of belonging and a disadvantage of limiting social contacts and discouraging independent thinking.

2. Answers should discuss assertive ways of showing disapproval.

3. Possible answer: You learn how to communicate and interact with a person of the opposite gender and how to demonstrate affection and respect for another person.

4. Answers will vary.

Health Skills Application

1.–4. Answers will vary.

EVALUATE

• Use the reproducible Chapter 12 Test in the TCR, or construct your own using the Testmaker software. 📁 ⊙

• Use Performance Assessment 12 in the TCR. 📁

ENRICHMENT

Ask students to complete Enrichment Activity 12 in the TCR. 📁

✳ BEYOND *the* Classroom

Keep students involved in the community, and encourage parent participation by assigning the activities on this page for students to work on outside of class.

---

11. Responses should reflect an understanding that teens are not prepared for the negative consequences that may result from engaging in sexual activity and that practicing abstinence is the only 100 percent effective way to protect themselves from these consequences.

12. Possible answers: health risks to mother and baby, dropping out of school, giving up plans for future, being held responsible by law for child support.

Lessons	Standards		Features
	National	**State/Local**	
1 **Personal Safety** *pages 330–334*	National Health Education Standards **1.4, 3.1, 3.4, 3.6**		**Hands-On Health** • Practicing Safety Strategies *(Practicing Healthful Behaviors)*, page 333
2 **Keeping Schools Safe** *pages 335–340*	National Health Education Standards **1.4, 3.4, 3.6, 5.6**		**Exploring Issues** • School Safety—What Works? page 339
3 **Protecting Yourself from Violence** *pages 341–347*	National Health Education Standards **1.4, 4.2, 5.7, 7.2**		**Real-Life Application** • Stopping Sexual Harassment *(Advocacy)*, page 345
4 **Preventing and Overcoming Abuse** *pages 348–353*	National Health Education Standards **1.4, 2.6, 3.3, 3.5, 3.6**		**Health Skills Activity** • Helping a Victim of Dating Violence *(Communication)*, page 351

Reproducible Resources	Assessment	Technology
Student Activity Workbook for use with each chapter 📁 Concept Mapping Activity 46 📁 Decision-Making Activity 13 📁 Enrichment Activity 13 📁 Guided Reading Activities 46 📁 Lesson Plan 46 📁 Parent Letter and Activities 13 📁 Reteaching Activity 46	📁 Lesson Quiz 46	🕹 Transparency 36 💿 TeacherWorks® 🖥 Internet Activities
📁 Concept Mapping Activity 47 📁 Current Health Issues 13 📁 Guided Reading Activities 47 📁 Lesson Plan 47 📁 Reteaching Activity 47	📁 Lesson Quiz 47	🕹 Transparency 37 💿 TeacherWorks®
📁 Concept Mapping Activity 48 📁 Cross-Curriculum Activity 13 📁 Guided Reading Activities 48 📁 Health Lab 13 📁 Lesson Plan 48 📁 Reteaching Activity 48	📁 Lesson Quiz 48	🕹 Transparency 38 💿 TeacherWorks®
📁 Concept Mapping Activity 49 📁 Guided Reading Activities 49 📁 Lesson Plan 49 📁 Reteaching Activity 49	📁 Lesson Quiz 49	🕹 Transparency 39 💿 TeacherWorks®

0:00 OUT OF TIME

If time does not permit teaching the entire chapter, use:

- Hands-On Health, p. 333
- Figure 13.2, p. 337
- Real-Life Application, p. 345
- Health Skills Activity, p. 351

Language Diversity

🎧 English Audio CD Program
🎧 Spanish Audio CD Program
📁 English Summaries, Quizzes, and Activities
📁 Spanish Summaries, Quizzes, and Activities
📁 Spanish Parent Letters and Activities

End of Chapter Assessment

Blackline Masters

📁 Chapter 13 Test
📁 Performance Assessment Activity 13
📁 Unit 4 Test

Technology

💿 Vocabulary PuzzleMaker
📼 MindJogger Videoquiz
💿 **Exam*View*® Pro Testmaker**

Professional Health Series

Dealing with Sensitive Issues
Planning a Coordinated School Health Program
Promoting Character Education
Home, School, and Community Involvement

Key to Ability Levels

Teaching strategies that appear throughout the chapter have been identified by one of the following codes to give teachers an idea of their suitability for students of varying learning styles and abilities.

L1 Strategies should be within the ability range of all students. Full class participation is often required. Teacher direction is usually needed.

L2 Strategies are designed for average to above-average students or for small groups. Some teacher direction is needed.

L3 Strategies are designed for students able and willing to work independently. Minimal teacher direction is needed.

ELL Strategies should be within the ability range of students learning the English language.

📁 Block scheduling strategies are useful in a block scheduling format.

Violence Prevention

CHAPTER OVERVIEW

Chapter 13 identifies ways to keep oneself safe from violence at home, in the community, and at school. It also discusses strategies for preventing and overcoming abuse.

Lesson 1 Taking precautions against risky situations and developing safety habits can enhance personal safety. Engaging in responsible behaviors will help maintain safety at home.

Lesson 2 Bullying, sexual harassment, and involvement in gangs are factors that play a role in school violence. Students, school faculty, and parents can take a stand to help keep schools safe.

Lesson 3 Although the nature of violence is complex, one's personal safety depends on the ability to recognize potential sources of violence. This ability can help in the prevention of violence.

Lesson 4 Abuse can take many forms. Of particular concern for teens is the incidence of abuse in dating relationships. Victims of abuse should seek counseling in dealing with the trauma.

Health Skills Features

- Hands-On Health (*Practicing Healthful Behaviors*), p. 333
- Exploring Issues, p. 339
- Real-Life Application (*Advocacy*), p. 345
- Health Skills Activity (*Communication*), p. 351

Chapter 13

Violence Prevention

Lesson 1 Personal Safety

Lesson 2 Keeping Schools Safe

Lesson 3 Protecting Yourself from Violence

Lesson 4 Preventing and Overcoming Abuse

KEEP OUR COMMUNITIES SAFE

328

MEETING STUDENT DIVERSITY

Language Diversity Use the following suggestions to help students who have difficulty with English:

- Pair English language learners with native speakers of English who can restate the Chapter Summary in language that helps students comprehend important concepts.

- Direct auditory learners or those students with language diversity to the *Glencoe Health Audio CD Program*. Available in English and Spanish, this component provides an audio and written summary of the chapter.

- Use photographs, drawings, or magazine clippings to help students visualize the important concepts of the chapter.

Myth or Fact?

What Do You Know About Youth Violence?

Read each statement below and respond by writing *Myth* or *Fact* for each item.

1. About one-third of teens in grades 9–12 are involved in at least one physical fight each year.

2. Teens are more likely to be victims of violence than adults are.

3. By age 13, the average American child has watched 100,000 acts of violence on TV.

4. Joining a gang is not an effective way of protecting oneself from violent activities.

5. Homicide, or murder, is the leading cause of death among teens.

6. Use of alcohol and other drugs is a contributing factor in incidents of violent crime.

7. Programs intended to treat violent behavior are ineffective.

8. Nearly half of all rapes and sexual assaults are committed by acquaintances of the victim.

9. Schools can promote effective ways to prevent violence.

10. Of the industrialized nations in the world, the United States has the highest rates of homicide and firearm-related deaths among adolescents.

Keep your responses for review later in the chapter. When you complete the chapter, review your answers and change or modify them based on what you have learned.

Quick Write

Using Visuals. Community involvement and advocacy can contribute to safer environments for everyone. What can you do to help keep your neighborhood safe?

329

INTRODUCING THE CHAPTER

Myth or Fact?

Ask volunteers to read the statements aloud. For each one, have students write down *Myth* or *Fact* and a reason for their response. Then discuss the answers with students.

1. Fact.
2. Fact.
3. Fact.
4. Fact.
5. Myth. Homicide is the second leading cause of death among teens. Motor vehicle accidents are the leading cause.
6. Fact.
7. Myth. Several effective prevention and intervention programs for treating violent behavior have been developed.
8. Fact.
9. Fact.
10. Fact.

Quick write

Using Visuals Direct students to look at the photographs. Discuss ways in which community members can promote safety for all residents. Ask: What can teens do to advocate for safe neighborhoods?

TECHNOLOGY OPTIONS

MINDJOGGER
VIDEOQUIZ

To preview or review chapter content, you may wish to use the Chapter 13 MindJogger Videoquiz. ▶◀

HEALTH *Online*

Online Resources for the Teacher For a fresh approach to health topics and an in-depth look at health issues, use these online resources found under Teacher Resources at **health.glencoe.com:**

- Block Schedule Lesson Plans
- Technology Projects
- Health Updates

Personal Safety

①FOCUS

QUICK START Have students make a list of actions they can take to keep safe. Ask volunteers to share their responses, and write some of them on the board. Guide students in discussing ways in which these safety habits help provide personal protection.

TYING TO PRIOR KNOWLEDGE

Ask students to make a list of situations that they would try to avoid because of concerns about safety. Have volunteers share some of their responses. Ask: If the place or situation was unavoidable, what else might you do to protect yourself?

Health Skills Features

"Practicing Safety Strategies," p. 333

PRACTICING HEALTHFUL BEHAVIORS

INTRODUCING VOCABULARY

• Discuss the meanings of the terms. Then have volunteers use the vocabulary terms in original sentences.

• Ask students to complete the Chapter 13 Study Guide in the *Student Activity Workbook.*

Personal Safety

VOCABULARY
body language
self-defense
assertive

YOU'LL LEARN TO

• Identify behaviors and strategies that enhance personal safety.

• Demonstrate ways of avoiding and reducing threatening situations.

• Examine strategies for promoting safety at home and in the community.

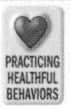

QUICK START On a sheet of paper, list five actions you can take to keep yourself safe. Then, write a paragraph explaining how these safety habits would help protect you.

Being confident and not looking like a victim can help keep you safe. *How can you project self-confidence?*

The key to personal safety is to be able to recognize potentially dangerous situations and learn strategies to avoid them. In addition, simple safety habits that you practice everyday can decrease your exposure to risk. Being aware of your surroundings, not walking alone, staying away from dark or isolated areas, and looking alert and confident are all behaviors that can protect you. In this lesson, you will learn about the factors that affect your personal safety and the actions you can take to keep yourself safe.

Your Protective Factors

Although you may not be conscious of them, you already have many assets that increase your chances of staying safe. The list of personal traits and environmental conditions that reduce teens' risk of violence is shown in **Figure 13.1** on the next page. These traits and conditions are specific protective factors that can help shield you from harm. Everyone can work to strengthen his or her protective factors and help to reduce the risk of violence. Doing so will contribute to personal safety.

Lesson 1 *Resources*

Teacher Classroom Resources

📁 Concept Mapping Activity 46

📁 Decision-Making Activity 13

📁 Enrichment Activity 13

📁 Guided Reading Activities 46

📁 Lesson Plan 46

📁 Lesson Quiz 46

📁 Parent Letter and Activities 13

📁 Reteaching Activity 46

Student Activity Workbook

📁 Applying Health Skills 46

📁 Chapter 13 Study Guide

Multimedia

🔊 Transparency 36

FIGURE 13.1

INDIVIDUAL AND SOCIAL PROTECTIVE FACTORS AGAINST VIOLENCE

These protective factors decrease the likelihood of teen violence.

Individual	Family	Peer/School	Community
• No history of aggressive behavior • Positive social skills; gets along with others • Intelligent • Antiviolence attitude • Being female	• Parents monitor child's behavior • Parents positively evaluate peers • Warm, supportive relationship with parents or other adults	• Peers and friends avoid high-risk behaviors • Commitment to school • Good attitude	• Strong economic opportunity • Involvement in community activities

Source: Youth Violence: A Report of the Surgeon General

Strategies for Staying Safe

In addition to strengthening your **protective factors,** there are behaviors you can practice to stay safe. These actions include taking precautions against risky situations and developing safety habits.

Smart Precautions

The first step in taking responsibility for your personal safety is to consider preventive behaviors that will help protect you. Many safety precautions that can prevent your becoming a victim are commonsense actions. Here are some preventive measures to follow.

▶ Avoid unsafe areas, including places with high crime rates.

▶ Don't carry your wallet or purse in a conspicuous, easy-to-grab place.

▶ Walk briskly and confidently. *Always* look as though you know where you are going and what you are doing.

▶ Avoid walking alone at night, in wooded areas, or in dark alleys. If you must walk at night, avoid doorways and walk under lights near the curb.

▶ If you drive, park your car in a well-lit area. Have your keys out and ready as you approach your parked car. Before getting into your car, look to make sure that no one is inside. Lock the doors as soon as you get in.

hot link

protective factors For more information on protective factors, see Chapter 8, page 216.

Taking safety precautions is particularly important when you are out at night. *What behaviors demonstrated by these teens help keep them safe?*

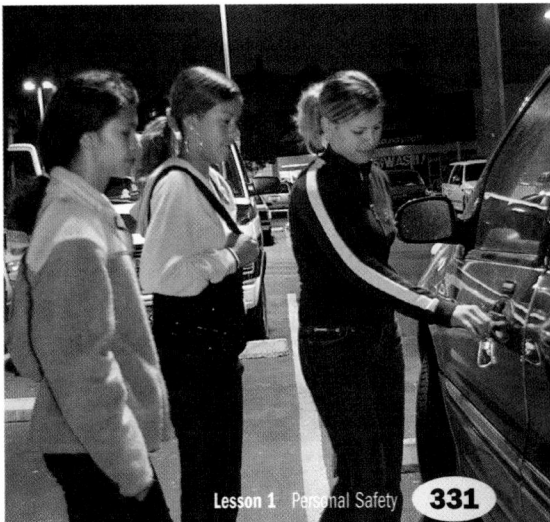

Lesson 1 Personal Safety **331**

More About...

What to Do If Attacked Escape to a safe place if you can. Negotiate when possible. Talking may help dissipate the violence. These are the key rules for dealing with an attacker. Precisely what you do depends on your strength, confidence, and willingness to fight back, and your assessment of the assailant. An assailant who is drunk or using other drugs acts impulsively, so you can't predict what will happen if you try to defend yourself.

If you fight your attacker, strike as swiftly and as hard as you can, and be ready to repeat the blow. Always scream for help as you fight. Ask volunteers to investigate self-defense courses available in the community and report their findings to the class.

2 TEACH

VISUAL LEARNING

Figure 13.1 Ask volunteers to read the protective factors listed under each category in Figure 13.1. Divide the class into four groups, and assign one category to each. Have group members discuss the protective factors within their assigned category and reasons that the factors decrease the likelihood of teen violence. Ask one member of each group to summarize the group's discussion for the rest of the class.

hot link

Have students make a list of their personal protective factors. Ask them to rank these factors in order of importance—from the most important for decreasing the risk of violence to the least important.

Discussing

Ask: What are several common sense measures you should practice in order to avoid being the victim of an attack? 🔟

Service Learning

Have students work in groups to create a poster that helps people remember preventive behaviors they can practice to protect themselves from harm. Encourage students to illustrate two or three of the measures noted on pages 331–332. 🔟 🔲 **Visual/Spatial Intelligence**

Quick Demo

Ask students to demonstrate how they can use body language as a self-defense strategy. **ELL** **Bodily/Kinesthetic Intelligence**

Explaining

Explain why assertive, self-assured behavior is a good self-defense strategy. Assertive people are not easy targets because they are proactive in protecting their health and safety. Ask: Why do you think aggressive and passive behaviors are not good self-defense strategies? **L1**

Critical Thinking

Pose this question: How is a self-protective attitude related to self-esteem? Give examples. How would you describe the level of self-esteem of a person who is continually a victim or target of violence? **L3**

Reinforcing Concepts

Ask students to make a list on the board of mental self-defense strategies that will help protect them from becoming victims of violence and explain each one. Have them privately identify which of these strategies they practice on a routine basis. Ask them to identify one strategy that they do not routinely practice and that they will work on to improve. **L1**

HEALTH Online

Instruct students to read about strategies for enhancing their personal safety. Have volunteers describe real or fictional scenarios in which these strategies could be used. Ask: How might practicing these strategies now help you in the future?

HEALTH Online

To learn more about personal safety strategies, click on Web Links at **health.glencoe.com.**

▶ Let your family know where you're going and when you'll return.

▶ Do not get into an elevator alone with a stranger.

▶ Get on and off buses in well-lit areas.

▶ If someone you know gives you a ride, ask the person not to leave until you have safely entered a building.

▶ Do not hitchhike or give rides to hitchhikers.

▶ Avoid the use of alcohol or other drugs. These substances impair your judgment and reduce your ability to protect yourself.

Body Language and Self-Defense

You can protect yourself from harm by communicating to others that you are worthy of being treated with respect and that you have a right to be safe and secure. You can project this information through the use of **body language,** *nonverbal communication through gestures, facial expressions, behaviors, and posture.* Making direct eye contact, using a strong voice, holding your head high, and walking with a deliberate stride demonstrate that you are in charge of your safety.

Key self-defense strategies can also protect you from becoming a victim of violence. **Self-defense** includes *any strategy for protecting oneself from harm.* Many people of all ages have taken self-defense classes to increase their sense of personal safety. A range of self-defense classes, including various martial arts courses, is available. Signing up for such a class is an effective way to enhance your confidence and sense of preparedness. Although physical strategies can be a useful part of self-defense, mental strategies are also important. In some communities, law enforcement officials teach personal safety classes on awareness and preparedness. Often, they stress the importance of projecting self-confidence and assertiveness. Being **assertive** means *standing up for your rights and beliefs in firm but positive ways.* Through words and actions, assertive people show that they are not easy targets. They are proactive in protecting their health and safety.

⚠ Taking a self-defense class can increase your sense of personal safety. *What other strategies can help protect your health and safety?*

Cooperative Learning Activity

Martial Arts Many people enjoy practicing martial arts as a way to engage in physical activity. Studying martial arts is also an excellent way to learn self-defense techniques. Divide the class into several groups. Assign each group one form of martial arts, such as karate, judo, tae kwon do, aikido, and jujutsu. Have each group conduct research to learn more about the assigned martial art. Encourage them to find the art's origins, philosophies, techniques and movements. Have each group find out where the assigned martial art is being taught in their community. Ask each group to prepare and present a report on their findings.

Hands-On Health ACTIVITY

Practicing Safety Strategies

Staying safe doesn't mean living in fear. It means learning and applying strategies that will reduce your risk of becoming a victim of violence. In this activity, you will role-play some strategies for staying safe.

What You'll Need

- pencil and notebook paper

What You'll Do

1. With a partner or in a small group, brainstorm several unsafe situations that teens may face. For example, a stranger in a car tells you that he is lost and asks you to approach the window to look at his map. Record your scenarios on a sheet of paper.

2. For each situation, discuss safe ways for teens to respond. If necessary, refer to the tips given in this lesson.

3. Role-play a situation from your list.

4. As a class, discuss the situations that were role-played. Which did you think were the most realistic? Why? What safety strategies might be effective?

Apply and Conclude

Using what you learned from the role-plays you observed, compose a short essay for the school paper informing teens how to stay safe in various situations. The article should include three or four safety tips and be relevant to teens in high school.

Keeping Homes Safe

A home should be a nurturing haven in which family members feel secure. The entire family can engage in responsible behaviors that will help maintain the safety of the home environment. Here are some tips for you to follow.

▶ Lock doors with a bolt. All family members should make an effort to keep all doors, including sliding doors and French doors, secure and in good repair.

▶ Make sure windows have locks. Keep windows locked at night and when no one is home. Repair broken windows immediately.

▶ Never open the door to someone you don't know or trust. Don't let strangers use your phone.

▶ Do not tell unknown callers that you are home alone.

▶ Do not give out personal information over the telephone or computer.

Keeping your doors and windows locked can help keep you and your family safe. *What are some other strategies for keeping your home secure?*

Lesson 1 Personal Safety **333**

Hands-On Health

PRACTICING SAFETY STRATEGIES

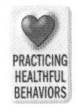
PRACTICING HEALTHFUL BEHAVIORS

NHES Standard 3 Students will demonstrate the ability to practice health-enhancing behaviors and reduce health risks.

Objectives

- Analyze and apply strategies for avoiding violence.
- Demonstrate ways to avoid and reduce threatening situations.

Motivator

Have students think of and describe a situation in which they might feel unsafe. Briefly discuss their responses.

Teaching Strategies

1. Read aloud some of the safety tips given in this lesson. Ask different students to explain the rationale behind each one.

2. Suggest that students use the Motivator to develop their role-plays.

✓Assessment

Using a rubric, student work should provide comprehensive evidence of the following criteria to achieve the highest score.

✔ identification of potentially unsafe situations and specific protective behaviors to reduce the risks of danger in these situations

✔ demonstration of behaviors to avoid becoming a victim of violence

---

Home and Community

Responsible Citizen Suggest that students find out about neighborhood crime prevention programs. If students are interested in starting a crime watch program in their neighborhoods, invite a local police officer or sheriff to discuss the concept. You may also want to extend the invitation to interested parents so that they can become involved in the program. At the intial meet-

ing, discuss needs, the level of interest, possible challenges, and the concept of neighborhood watch. Brainstorm tasks for teens and for adult members. For example, teens may remove grafitti. Adult members may gather information such as names, addresses, and phone numbers of participating households.

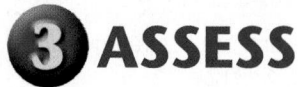

Citizenship Have volunteers give examples of ways they can demonstrate good citizenship to help reduce crime in their community. Ask: How does this type of behavior benefit everyone in the community?

③ ASSESS

EVALUATING THE LESSON

Assign and discuss the Lesson 1 Review; then administer, grade, and discuss Lesson Quiz 46 in the TCR. 📁

RETEACHING

- Have students apply what they have learned in this lesson by describing some unsafe situations. For each situation, ask students to discuss ways the situation could have been avoided and, if it could not be avoided, how the situation could best be handled.
- Ask students to complete Reteaching Activity 46 in the TCR. 📁

ENRICHMENT

Tell students to research about body language in their own culture and in other cultures. Ask the class to discuss how misunderstandings could arise because of differences in body language among people of different cultures.

④ CLOSE

Review with students ways to reduce their risk of becoming victims of violence.

334

CHARACTER ✔ CHECK

Citizenship. Teens who obey laws and respect authority demonstrate good citizenship. Good citizenship also involves doing your part to make your community safer. **What are some ways you can demonstrate good citizenship to help reduce crime in your community?**

Safety in the Community

How safe a community is has a significant impact on personal safety. Many communities have taken steps to make neighborhoods safer. Some of the strategies include:

▶ **Increased police patrol.** Some communities have increased the number of law enforcement officers on street patrol.

▶ **Neighborhood Watch programs.** Residents have joined the crime prevention effort by looking for signs of suspicious activity and reporting such incidents to the police. It is also a good idea to report suspicious vehicles in the neighborhood.

▶ **After-school programs.** Academic, cultural, or recreational programs after school provide safe environments where teens can use their time productively.

▶ **Improved lighting in parks and playgrounds.** Better lighting can discourage crime by making it more difficult to commit crimes without being seen.

By supporting and participating in efforts such as these, residents can contribute to making communities safer for everyone.

▶ Lesson 1 Review

Reviewing Facts and Vocabulary

1. What is *body language*? Give three examples.
2. Define the term *assertive*, and use it in a sentence.
3. List two ways to keep your home safe.

Thinking Critically

4. **Evaluating.** Assess the value of avoiding potentially dangerous situations, even if you know how to defend yourself.
5. **Analyzing.** How can involvement in community activities serve as a protective factor against violent behavior?

WORD PROCESSING You can set up your plan in a word-processing program. See health.glencoe.com for tips on using word-processing software.

Applying Health Skills

Practicing Healthful Behaviors. Develop a list of strategies that you and other members of your family can use to promote personal and family safety. Discuss these safety behaviors with your family, and put your plan into action.

334 **Chapter 13** Violence Prevention

▶ Lesson 1 Review

Answers to Reviewing Facts and Vocabulary

1. Nonverbal communication through gestures, facial expressions, and posture. Examples will vary.
2. Standing up for your rights and beliefs in firm but positive ways. Sentences will vary.
3. See page 333 for possible answers.

Answers to Thinking Critically

4. Possible answer: The safest defense is to avoid dangerous situations altogether.
5. Possible answer: Community involvement provides opportunities for residents to spend their time in safe, productive ways.

Keeping Schools Safe

VOCABULARY
- violence
- bullying
- sexual harassment
- gang
- peer mediation

YOU'LL LEARN TO
- Examine factors that play a role in school violence.
- Analyze and apply strategies for avoiding school violence.
- Identify actions that individuals, schools, and communities can take to reduce violence.

 QUICK START What are some causes of conflict that lead to violence among high school students? How do you think violence affects the students involved? How does it affect others in the school community? Write a paragraph summarizing your views.

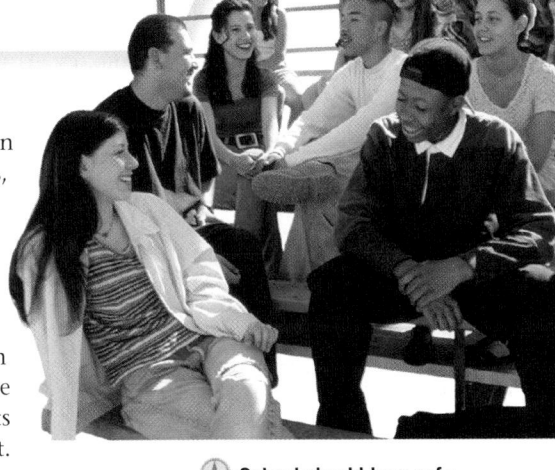

School should be a safe place for students to learn and engage in fun, healthy activities. *How does your school help ensure the safety of students and school personnel?*

In recent years, the media has focused attention on acts of violence in schools, including gang activities, physical attacks, and shootings. However, despite the publicity given to violent incidents, schools are generally safe places. According to the Centers for Disease Control and Prevention (CDC), the trend has been toward *less* violence in schools since 1991. For example, the number of students who participated in physical fights at school has dropped nine percentage points. During that same time, the number of students who carried weapons decreased from 26.1 to 17.4 percent.

Issues of School Safety

Although schools are generally safe, some violence may occur on or near school grounds. **Violence** is *the threatened or actual use of physical force or power to harm another person or to damage property.* The 2001 Youth Risk Behaviors Surveillance Survey found that 33.2 percent of teens in grades 9–12 had been in at least one physical fight at school in the previous year. In the same year, 8.9 percent of students were threatened or injured with a weapon at school.

Lesson 2 *Resources*

Teacher Classroom Resources
- 📂 Concept Mapping Activity 47
- 📂 Current Health Issues 13
- 📂 Guided Reading Activities 47
- 📂 Lesson Plan 47
- 📂 Lesson Quiz 47
- 📂 Reteaching Activity 47

Student Activity Workbook
- 📂 Applying Health Skills 47
- 📂 Chapter 13 Study Guide

Multimedia
- 🖥 Transparency 37

Lesson 2

Keeping Schools Safe

1 FOCUS

QUICK START After students have finished writing their paragraphs, ask volunteers to share their responses. Discuss how school violence affects everyone in the school community.

TYING TO PRIOR KNOWLEDGE

Ask students to write a paragraph or two summarizing their feelings about safety at school. Have them answer questions such as: Do you feel safe at school? Why or why not? Are you concerned about violence at school? If so, what issues concern you? Explain to students that this lesson will discuss school safety and strategies for reducing the risk of school violence.

Health Skills Features

"School Safety—What Works?" p. 339

INTRODUCING VOCABULARY

- Write the terms *violence, bullying,* and *sexual harassment* on the board. Ask the class to discuss how the terms are related.
- Ask students to complete the Chapter 13 Study Guide in the *Student Activity Workbook.* 📂

335

② TEACH

Cooperative Learning

Ask students to interview their parents about what their biggest fears or concerns were when they were teens in high school. They should also interview other students in their school to find out what teens today fear or are most worried about. Then have groups of two or three students each compile the concerns into two lists—one for their parents' generation and one for their own generation. Ask a representative from each group to share their lists with the rest of the class. Generate class discussion by asking whether today's teens have more or less to fear than their parents' generation. How are the concerns different? What do they think account for these concerns? How do they think their fears as teens might affect them as adults? **L1**

Discussing

Discuss the criteria for bullying. Ask: How does bullying differ from simply joking? How do you think it feels to be the target of bullying? Have students describe the prevalence of bullying at school and ways that students currently deal with the problem. Encourage students to give reasons for why a victim of bullying should report the problem. **L1**

Reinforcing Concepts

What is sexual harassment? Ask students to give examples of comments and behaviors they consider to be sexually harassing. Is there disagreement among class members? If so, why? What are some things you can do if you are experiencing sexual harassment? **L1**

Bullies use words and physical force to seek power or attention. *What are some ways you can let bullies know that you don't approve of their actions?*

Did You Know ?

Sexual harassment occurs more frequently than many people realize. Behaviors that constitute sexual harassment include

- making sexual comments or jokes.
- writing sexual messages on notes or walls.
- spreading sexual rumors.
- spying on someone dressing or showering.
- pulling off someone's clothes.
- exposing body parts.
- inappropriate touching.

336　**Chapter 13** Violence Prevention

Because any violence threatens the safety of everyone in the school community, national health goals have been set to reduce physical fighting by adolescents and to reduce carrying of weapons by adolescents on school property. In order to meet these goals, it's important to look at factors that play a role in school violence. Three of these factors are bullying, sexual harassment, and involvement in gangs.

Bullying

Have you ever witnessed students teasing or taunting others? Perhaps you've seen a classmate shove another student or make offensive gestures at her or him. These activities are forms of **bullying**, *the act of seeking power or attention through the psychological, emotional, or physical abuse of another person.* Bullies come in all ages and genders, and they sometimes act in groups. Bullying may cause victims to become depressed, withdrawn, fearful, or angry. Sometimes, victims may try to strike back. Bullying is unacceptable, harmful behavior. You can take a stand against bullying by not joining in and by discouraging this kind of behavior.

Bullies often try to cause anger or fear in their victims. By walking away from a bully and encouraging others to walk away, you deny the bully this victory. In some instances, ignoring a bully can help stop the behavior. However, most cases of bullying require adult intervention. If you witness or experience bullying, report the problem to teachers, counselors, parents, or other adults. No one should tolerate bullying; witnesses can join together with school personnel to stop this behavior.

Sexual Harassment

Sexual harassment is *uninvited and unwelcome sexual conduct directed at another person.* Words, jokes, gestures, or touching of a sexual nature are all forms of sexual harassment. Harassment causes embarrassment, discomfort, and emotional pain for the victim. Federal law states that sexual harassment is illegal. Incidents of sexual harassment should be reported to school personnel at once. After a complaint has been made, school officials will investigate and take action to solve the problem.

What Teens Want to Know

Why do some teens bully? Teens can bully for a variety of reasons. Although bullies may appear strong and powerful on the surface, many actually feel insecure and vulnerable underneath. They may tease, taunt, and put down other people as a way to boost their own egos and make themselves feel superior. Bullies are often so focused on themselves that they have trouble empathizing with other people. For some bullies, their behavior is a form of retaliation for hurt or abuse that may have been inflicted on them—sometimes even by other bullies—in the past.

Gangs

Some violence in schools is related to gang activity. A **gang** is *a group of people who associate with one another to take part in criminal activity.* Common gang activities include vandalism, robbery, defacing public property with graffiti, and selling drugs. Some gang activities are unpredictable and place innocent people in harm's way. Random shootings, for example, can injure or kill non-gang members. Gang members may bring weapons or drugs to school, endangering the safety of other students.

Reducing the Risk of Violence

Students and faculty have the right to feel safe at school. Being worried about personal safety in the school environment hinders the teaching and learning process. Keeping schools safe is a priority shared by communities across the nation.

Recognizing Warning Signs

Being able to recognize the warning signs of violence can help members of a school community address potentially threatening situations before they occur. **Figure 13.2** lists some common warning signs of violence. Evidence of these signs may indicate that a person is near to acting in a dangerous manner. If you observe any of these signs in a student and suspect that he or she may become violent, inform a teacher, counselor, or other faculty member immediately.

You can help keep your school safe by reporting any behaviors that may lead to violence. *What other actions can you take to contribute to school safety?*

FIGURE 13.2

WARNING SIGNS OF VIOLENCE

- Has difficulty controlling anger
- Disobeys school rules
- Frequently engages in risk behaviors
- Creates violent artwork or writing
- Constantly talks about weapons or violence
- Vandalizes and destroys property
- Uses alcohol or other drugs
- Harms animals
- Makes threats or detailed plans to hurt others
- Brings or talks about bringing a weapon to school

Guest Speaker

Ask a police officer or youth counselor who is knowledgeable about gang violence to speak with your class. You may want the speaker to address topics such as how students can avoid the recruitment of gangs and the ways in which schools can deter gangs. Prepare the class for the speaker by asking students: What role does the community serve in preventing gangs? What risks do gang members face? **L1**

Cross-Curriculum Activity

Social Studies Have students use online or library resources to research the issue of gang violence in the United States. Lead students in a discussion of what they have learned about ongoing conflicts and violence between rival gangs. Ask: What do you think causes this kind of conflict? Why does it often lead to violence? What special dangers are associated with gang violence? **L2**

VISUAL LEARNING

Figure 13.2 Read aloud to the class the warning signs of violence presented in Figure 13.2. Guide students in discussing how each of these warning signs could escalate into an act of violence. Ask students: How might a potentially dangerous situation turn violent if two or more people with these warning signs banded together?

Cooperative Learning Activity

Gangs Gangs and gang activities are sometimes glorified or glamorized in movies, songs, and music videos. Have students read a non-fiction book or magazine article about the life of someone who succeeded in leaving a gang. Then have students work together in groups to create a song, short story, or one-act play that presents a realistic portrayal of gang life. If students choose to write a first person narrative, remind them to share their ideas in a voice and style appropriate to the speaker and audience. Ask each group to share their completed project with the class.

What You Can Do

Making your school safe begins with building a culture of respect among all students and faculty members. You are empowered to contribute to a safe and healthy school environment. Nationwide, teens are pledging to avoid violence and are encouraging their peers to do the same. To take a stand and help keep schools safe, you can

► refuse to carry weapons and report people who do carry them.

► report any violent acts or threats of violence to school authorities or police.

► practice **conflict resolution** skills and help others settle disputes peacefully.

► use refusal skills to resist negative peer pressure and avoid unsafe situations and behaviors.

► choose your friends carefully. Having friends who share similar values, such as caring about school, can help protect you from violence.

► avoid spending time with people who show warning signs of violent behavior.

► tell a parent, teacher, or other adult about your fears if you suspect that your safety is in danger. Avoid being alone.

► join or develop a S.A.V.E. chapter (Students Against Violence Everywhere).

hot link

conflict resolution For more information on conflict resolution, see Chapter 10, page 264.

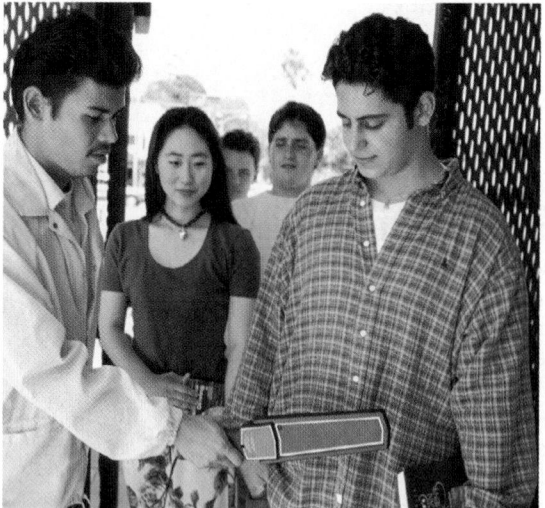

Some schools use metal detectors to reduce the threat of violence. *What other measures might schools adopt to promote safety?*

What Schools Are Doing

Schools have procedures and policies to ensure the safety of students. For example, some schools have adopted a *zero-tolerance policy,* which can require expulsion of students who participate in violence or who are found with drugs or weapons. Zero-tolerance policies apply equally to all students with no exceptions. Other efforts to reduce school violence include using metal detectors, examining students' backpacks, or searching lockers for weapons or drugs. Some schools have "closed" campuses, keeping all doors except the main entrance locked. This helps prevent unauthorized persons from coming into the school. Security guards may also be hired to patrol hallways and grounds while classes are in session.

Home and Community

S.A.V.E. Students Against Violence Everywhere (S.A.V.E) is a program that promotes nonviolence within schools and communities. Run by students, S.A.V.E. educates people about the risks and consequences of violence. It also provides safe activities including nonviolence pledge drives, conflict management programs, fund-raisers, and community volunteer work. Ask students to learn more about S.A.V.E. by finding out answers to these questions: Who started S.A.V.E. and why? What are the goals of the program? Why does S.A.V.E. use orange and purple as its official colors? Have students find out whether there is a S.A.V.E. chapter at their school. If not, encourage them to learn more about starting one.

School Safety—What Works?

Though violence in schools remains low, there is a public perception that schools need to be safer. Some schools are employing crisis drills, security guards, and metal detectors. Do these measures work? Read what two teens have to say about one such measure—metal detectors.

Viewpoint 1: Lori M., age 16

The metal detectors create more hassles than they're worth. Sometimes we get to our first class late because all our bags have to be scanned. Besides, if students want to bring in weapons, they'll find a way. I think we should use school money for something else, like classes on conflict resolution skills. Also, we could have stricter discipline policies for those students who do cause problems.

Viewpoint 2: Jason C., age 16

I feel safer with the extra security that metal detectors provide. I think they do act as a deterrent for carrying weapons, and the policy sends the message that our school does not tolerate weapons. It shows that the school cares about our safety and well-being. As far as the cost goes, anything that can save a life is worth it.

ACTIVITY

Do you think that metal detectors and other measures, such as security guards, decrease the risk of violence in schools? Are they necessary to keep schools safe? How do you think limited funds should be spent to enhance school safety? Is technology or education the answer?

PEER MEDIATION

Many schools use peer mediation to help reduce the risk of violence that may stem from unresolved conflicts. **Peer mediation** is *a process in which trained students help other students find fair ways to resolve conflict and settle their differences.* Such programs are successful because they are confidential and do not punish the students involved. Peer mediation sessions typically follow these steps:

► **Making introductions.** The mediator explains that he or she will remain neutral and that the session will be confidential.

► **Establishing ground rules.** The parties agree to the rules of the process, such as listening without interrupting, maintaining respect and honesty, and being willing to accept the adopted solutions. Then, the mediator decides who talks first.

Lesson 2 Keeping Schools Safe **339**

Promoting Coordinated School Health

Violence and School Safety School policies can be an important step in addressing the problems of violence. To develop an atmosphere of safety in your school, you must consider addressing such issues with a coordinated approach. A committee or task force on school safety should include representatives from parent groups, community members, business representatives, and local law enforcement officials, as well as teachers, counselors, and administrators. For more information, consult *Planning a Coordinated School Health Program.*

③ ASSESS

EVALUATING THE LESSON

Assign and discuss the Lesson 2 Review; then administer, grade, and discuss Lesson Quiz 47 in the TCR. 📁

RETEACHING

- Have students use the information in the lesson to answer these questions: Why is it important to recognize warning signs of violence? What are two actions teens can take to help keep schools safe?

- Ask students to complete Reteaching Activity 47 in the TCR. 📁

ENRICHMENT

Have volunteers interview school administrators to learn about school policies on bullying, sexual harassment, and gang involvement. Encourage students to find out how the problem is handled and what punishment is involved. Ask the class whether they have additional ideas for school policies. Have volunteers write up the class ideas and present them to school administrators.

④ CLOSE

Ask students to complete the following statements: *Since studying about school violence, I have learned... Three factors that play a role in school violence are... The steps followed in a peer mediation session are...*

▶ **Hearing each side.** The mediator allows each party to speak. He or she may ask questions and take notes.

▶ **Exploring solutions.** After all parties have spoken, the mediator asks for possible solutions. A list is made of the suggestions, and each one is discussed. The mediator helps the parties compromise until a solution is agreed upon.

▶ **Closing the session.** The mediator summarizes the agreement and asks participants to discuss their feelings about the process. The parties are encouraged to use these skills to solve future conflicts.

 These teens are holding a rally to promote safe schools in their community. *What are some ways that communities can promote school safety?*

Parent and Community Involvement

Parents can work with police officers, social workers, and business leaders to promote safety in schools. Community members can help by taking part in school events and by volunteering to monitor hallways, rest rooms, cafeterias, and other areas where students gather. Developing and supporting programs and activities that provide teens a safe place to gather can also help reduce violence.

▶ Lesson 2 *Review*

Reviewing Facts and Vocabulary

1. Define *gangs*. How might gang members endanger the safety of other students?

2. List two warning signs that a person may be close to acting in a dangerous manner.

3. Identify three policies or procedures that schools use to ensure safety for students and faculty.

Thinking Critically

4. **Analyzing.** Explain the similarities and differences between bullying and sexual harassment.

5. **Applying.** What are some ways of avoiding unsafe or threatening situations at school?

Applying Health Skills

Refusal Skills. Write a scenario in which a student applies refusal skills to avoid participation in a situation that may become violent. Include both verbal and nonverbal messages in your scenario.

WORD PROCESSING Use a word-processing program to write your scenario. See **health.glencoe.com** for tips on using word-processing software.

340 **Chapter 13** Violence Prevention

▶ Lesson 2 *Review*

Answers to Reviewing Facts and Vocabulary

1. A group of people who associate with one another to take part in criminal activity. They may bring weapons to school, endangering other students.

2. See Figure 13.2 for possible answers.

3. See page 338 for possible answers.

Answers to Thinking Critically

4. Both involve annoying another person, sometimes through teasing or jokes. Sexual harassment differs in that the actions or words involve sexual content.

5. Possible responses: Don't be alone with a person you think may be violent. Tell someone about your concerns.

Protecting Yourself from Violence

VOCABULARY
assailant
prejudice
assault
random violence
homicide
sexual violence
sexual assault
rape

YOU'LL LEARN TO
- Identify the causes and effects of violence.
- Evaluate how messages from the media influence violent behavior.
- Explain the role that alcohol and other drugs play in violent behaviors.
- Examine different types of violence and develop strategies for violence prevention.

QUICK START List three television shows or movies you have seen that showed some form of violence. What messages do they send to teens about violence?

The nature of violence is complex. For years, psychologists have investigated the question of why people commit violent acts. Experts have not yet reached a conclusion that they can all agree on. Regardless of the nature of violence, your personal safety depends on your ability to recognize possible sources of violence in your environment. This awareness will help you choose behaviors that minimize your chances of being a victim.

Why Violence Occurs

Violence may occur for many reasons. Some people use violence as a means of dealing with conflicts. In such cases, the victim may know his or her **assailant**—*a person who commits a violent act against another.* Violence may also result from anger or frustration. No matter what causes violence, people can be injured or killed during violent criminal acts.

Going out in groups and being aware of your surroundings are two ways of reducing your risk of violence. *What are some other strategies you can use to avoid unsafe situations?*

Lesson 3 Resources

Teacher Classroom Resources
- Concept Mapping Activity 48
- Cross-Curriculum Activity 13
- Guided Reading Activities 48
- Health Lab 13
- Lesson Plan 48
- Lesson Quiz 48
- Reteaching Activity 48

Student Activity Workbook
- Applying Health Skills 48
- Chapter 13 Study Guide

Multimedia
- Transparency 38

Lesson 3

Protecting Yourself from Violence

1 FOCUS

QUICK START Ask students to name three television shows or movies that contain violent scenes. Guide students in discussing the messages being sent by the media to teens about violence.

TYING TO PRIOR KNOWLEDGE

Ask students to write a few sentences describing a situation they have witnessed, taken part in, or heard about that involved violence or the potential for violence. Tell students that in this lesson, they will learn why violence occurs and how they can protect themselves from it.

Health Skills Features

"Stopping Sexual Harassment," p. 345

ADVOCACY

INTRODUCING VOCABULARY
- Discuss the meanings of the terms. Have students write a paragraph in which they describe a call coming over a police radio about an emergency situation. Remind students that they need to use every term in their paragraph.
- Ask students to complete the Chapter 13 Study Guide in the *Student Activity Workbook.*

② TEACH

Discussing

Initiate a discussion of the long-lasting emotional damage caused by violence by having students imagine a violent act, such as a mugging. Ask them what emotions they think the victim would experience both during and after the attack. How do they think the victim's self-confidence and self-esteem would be affected over the long run by the violent act? Ask students for suggestions of actions the victim may take to recover from the emotions caused by the experience of the violent act. **L3**

Reinforcing Concepts

Have students use classroom or library resources to find news articles about acts of violence. Ask several volunteers to each summarize one article for the class. After each summary, have students determine the likely cause of the violence. **L2** 🖦

Cooperative Learning

Divide the class into groups of two or three students. Assign each group a factor to discuss that may contribute to violence in our society, such as: availability of weapons, the media, use of alcohol and other drugs, mental/emotional issues, breakdown of the family, racial prejudice, and poverty. Have a representative from each group explain to the class why the factor they were assigned may contribute to violence. At the end of the presentations, have the class decide which factor or factors they think are the most significant and why. Have the class brainstorm ways in which society can address these factors to lessen their negative impact. **L2** 🖦

Other common causes of violence include the following:

▶ **Need to control others.** Some people use violence to control others or to get something they want.

▶ **Way of expressing anger.** People who are unable to manage their anger may strike out against others in a violent way.

▶ **Prejudice.** Some acts of violence are crimes of hate that stem from **prejudice**—*an unfair opinion or judgment of a particular group of people.*

▶ **Retaliation.** People sometimes use violence to retaliate against—or get back at—others who have hurt them in some way. The retaliation may be directed at individuals or groups.

Influences on Violence

In addition to motives for violent behavior, several factors may also contribute to violence. These include weapons availability, media messages, substance abuse, and mental/emotional health issues such as low self-concept.

Weapons Availability

Most homicides that occur among 15- to 19-year-olds involve firearms. A recent survey sponsored by the CDC found that almost one-fifth of responding high-school students reported carrying a weapon in the month proceeding the survey. Most of these weapons are conventional weapons such as handguns, knives, and clubs. However, newer, more dangerous weapons, including assault rifles, are finding their way into teens' hands—especially teens with gang affiliations.

Strategies exist to reduce accidents and intentional injuries caused by firearms. Efforts have been made to control gun ownership through stronger laws. People must now undergo background checks in order to purchase guns from licensed dealers. In some states, they must also register their handguns. People who own guns legally can install safety devices, such as trigger locks, on their firearms. In addition, owners are encouraged to keep guns unloaded and securely stored when not in use and to store ammunition in a separate, secure location.

Working together to stop prejudice can help reduce violence. *How can individuals and communities contribute to a tolerant, peaceful environment?*

Curriculum Connections

Social Studies You may want to work with the school librarian to select and copy short stories for students that deal with people who have suffered violence because of prejudice. Then divide students into small groups, hand out the stories, and have students share their stories with one another.

Language Arts Have students write a short story from the viewpoint of an individual who has experienced violence because of an untrue rumor. Ask them to include information about the origin of the rumor, the people who spread it, the effects of the rumor, and how the individual felt.

The Media

By age 13, most American children have seen 100,000 acts of violence on television, including about 8,000 murders. Violence is also a common theme in movies, video games, song lyrics, and music videos. The role of the media in contributing to violent behavior is a matter of great debate. Some critics think that exposure to violence may provide a "recipe" for violence. They point to increased occurrences of violent acts following extensive media coverage of such events. Other experts think that young people become desensitized, or emotionally indifferent, to acts of violence when they see such images repeatedly. People who become desensitized are no longer bothered or upset when they witness violent acts. As a result, they may be less inclined to take action to prevent or stop violence.

Alcohol and Other Drugs

Use of alcohol and other drugs may contribute to incidents of violent crime. Drug users often turn to illegal activities, such as robbery, to obtain money to purchase drugs. Many drive-by shootings involve disputes between gangs or individuals who sell drugs.

People using alcohol or other drugs cannot think clearly and have difficulty making safe, healthful decisions. Accidents caused by people driving under the influence of drugs or alcohol result in thousands of injuries and deaths each year. Use of these substances also makes it difficult for an individual to control his or her emotions. This may cause a person to behave violently.

Mental/Emotional Issues

Some studies have found a direct correlation between engaging in violent behavior and having a low self-concept. People who feel unvalued may use violence in an attempt to prove their self-worth. Some violent behaviors are acts of revenge by people who have never learned any other way of dealing with disagreements. Also, some people have a very low tolerance for frustration or inconvenience. These people may lash out at others, including those who are not the source of the frustration. **Anger management** workshops and counseling are available in most communities for people who have problems controlling their anger.

Man held up in drive-by shooting

Green City — Tuesday night there was a do' the new development in the case was re the sheriff's office was going to iss

Violence breaks out at a Community Concert
Thursday, June 16

Three suspects sought in convenience store robbery

 Headlines focusing on violent acts are common in local and national newspapers. *Find three news stories that center on acts of violence. Analyze the messages delivered by these stories.*

h⊕t link

anger management For more information on anger management, see Chapter 7, page 190.

Lesson 3 Protecting Yourself from Violence **343**

Activity

Have students research and write a report on the rise of random violence in our society today. They should address issues such as: reasons for the increase in random violence and what can be done to avoid being involved in a random crime. Have students write several drafts of their report and proofread for spelling and grammatical errors. **L3**
Verbal/Linguistic Intelligence

Cooperative Learning

Have the class work in groups of four or five to make bulletin board displays titled "Teens and Violence in the United States Today." They should collect information of violent situations involving teens as victims and as perpetrators as well as teens preventing violence. Their objective should be to increase awareness of the risk of violence faced by today's youth. **L1**

Activity

Have the class research using online and library sources what happens when teens are arrested for committing violent crimes. In particular, they should investigate whether teens are tried as adults and given adult sentences. They also should address the age at which a teen is considered an adult in this context and whether the nature of the crime plays a role. Have students present oral reports upon completion of their research. **L2** **Verbal/Linguistic Intelligence**

Did You Know ?

➤ Understanding statistics can help dispel misconceptions about incidents of violence.

- In about 75 percent of teen homicides, the victim and person who committed the crime know each other.
- Most homicides are not hate crimes based on race. In 90 percent of homicides, the victim and killer are of the same race.
- Among adolescents injured by guns, 35 percent report carrying a gun when they were shot.
- More than half of all violent acts involve someone who is under the influence of alcohol or other drugs.

➤ **Police are among the first to arrive at a crime scene.** *What can citizens do to help law enforcement officers keep the community safe?*

Types of Violence

Youth violence is violence directed toward or carried out by persons under the age of 19. Many violent acts today involve teens. In fact, teens are two and a half times more likely to be crime victims than adults are. According to a recent report of the Surgeon General, the proportion of young people involved in violent crimes has actually leveled off during the past decade. Nonetheless, about 100,000 teens are arrested each year for violent crimes. The crimes for which teens are often arrested include assault, homicide, and sexual violence.

Assault and Homicide

Each day in the United States, about 18,000 people survive an assault. An **assault** is *an unlawful attack on a person with the intent to harm or kill.* Some assaults involve people who do not know one another. For example, **random violence** is *violence committed for no particular reason.* Innocent bystanders can become victims of both intended and random violence. For instance, innocent bystanders are sometimes injured in store robberies.

Assault may sometimes result in **homicide**, *the willful killing of one human being by another.* After automobile accidents, homicide is the second leading cause of death among individuals who are in the 15–24 age group. Most of these deaths involve firearms. To protect yourself from assault and homicide, follow the general safety tips outlined in Lesson 1 as well as the suggestions listed here.

▶ If an attacker wants your money or jewelry and you are in danger, throw your purse, wallet, or jewelry away from you. Then run in the opposite direction. It's better to lose possessions than risk injury or death.

▶ If you are being followed, go to a place where there are other people.

Meeting Individual Needs

Gifted Students Suggest to gifted students that they present a debate to the rest of the class. Each student should adopt one of the following points of view in the debate.

- Violence should be permitted at any time on television because censoring violence would be a violation of freedom of speech.

- The networks should reduce violence during prime-time hours, but it is up to parents to control their children's exposure to violence on television at other times.

- The networks should take an active role in protecting children from violence by keeping violence to a minimum in all television programming.

Real-Life Application

Stopping Sexual Harassment

Sexual harassment is illegal behavior that may result in violence. Use this graph to help you develop a campaign against sexual harassment.

Impact of Sexual Harassment on Students

Source: based on American Association of University Women Educational Foundation study

- How is sexual harassment related to truancy and dropout rates?

- How can being sexually harassed affect a student's ability to graduate from high school? To get a college scholarship?

- How might being sexually harassed affect a teen's ability to form friendships?

ACTIVITY

In small groups, create a poster or a public service announcement (PSA) that informs students about the harmful effects of sexual harassment. Make a clear statement showing disapproval of these behaviors and encouraging healthful, respectful behaviors.

Sexual Violence

Sexual violence is *any form of unwelcome sexual conduct directed at an individual, including sexual harassment, sexual assault, and rape.* Sexual assault and rape differ from sexual harassment in that physical attacks are involved. These are acts of violence rather than acts of passion. The attacker is generally motivated not by sexual desire but by the desire to force another person to do something he or she does not want to do. All forms of sexual violence are illegal.

Lesson 3 Protecting Yourself from Violence **345**

Real-Life Application

ADVOCACY

STOPPING SEXUAL HARASSMENT

NHES Standard 7 Students will demonstrate the ability to advocate for personal, family, and community health.

Objectives

- Analyze ways to show disapproval of inconsiderate and disrespectful behavior.
- Demonstrate the ability to adapt health messages and communication techniques to the characteristics of a particular audience.

Motivator

Give some examples of sexual harassment. Ask: Why do people engage in this type of behavior? How does this behavior show a lack of respect?

Teaching Strategies

1. Guide students to recognize how sexual harassment negatively affects school performance and confidence in one's academic ability.
2. Tell students to use realistic examples of sexual harassment in their poster or PSA.

✓Assessment

Using a rubric, student work should provide comprehensive evidence of the following criteria to achieve the highest score:

✔ clear, health-enhancing stand
✔ support for the position with relevant information
✔ awareness of the audience
✔ encouragement of others to make healthful choices
✔ passion/conviction

Curriculum Connections

Language Arts Have students write a short essay on a victim of crime. The essay should explore the personal feelings of the persons involved and the effects of the crime on their lives. Have students write in the voice or style of the victim or family member. Remind them to develop several drafts, and share their final draft with the class.

Social Studies Have students research violence in other countries and write an essay of comparison and contrast. They may choose to focus their research on violence among teens, assault and homicide, as well as how other countries punish offenders.

Explaining

Explain the similarities and differences among assault, murder, homicide, battery, sexual assault, and rape. **L1**

Discussing

Ask students to identify behaviors and situations they should avoid to reduce the risk of rape. **L1**

Quick Demo

Have students describe the best way to deal with an attacker in a variety of situations. If possible, ask a physical education teacher or self-defense instructor to demonstrate to the class some basic ways to physically disable or stun an attacker. **L1**

Guest Speaker

Invite a counselor from a rape crisis center or hot line to class to discuss where, when, and why rapes occur; how best to avoid rape; and what one should do if raped. Ask the speaker to conclude by discussing how to help a friend who has been raped or sexually assaulted. **L1**

Community Involvement

Guide the class in a discussion of alternatives to gang activity or other destructive behaviors offered in your area. Have students identify several different school, community, or private organizations and find ways to publicize their activities. **L2**

Did You Know **?**

→ **S**exual violence affects many children and teens. Data show that

- 51 percent of rape victims are under the age of 18, and 29 percent of victims are under the age of 12.
- friends or acquaintances are involved in nearly half of all rapes reported by women.

Sexual assault is *any intentional sexual attack against another person.* Sexual assault is often accompanied by battery or the beating of the victim. **Rape** is *any form of sexual intercourse that takes place against a person's will.* It is also one of the least reported crimes. In fact, of the estimated 683,000 rapes taking place each year, only about 16 percent are reported to police.

Most sexual violence is directed at females, but males may also be victims. Often, sexual violence among teens occurs within a dating relationship. Currently, 8 percent of teens report being victims of sexual violence during dating by the time they reach the ninth grade. In some states, sexual intercourse between a male of any age and a female under the age of 18 is considered rape unless the two are married. Penalties for this crime may include going to prison as well as a life-long record as a sex offender. In the next lesson, you will learn more about preventing sexual abuse during dating.

ESCAPING AND SURVIVING A SEXUAL ATTACK

Sexual attacks can happen anywhere. They can even happen in someone's home—your own or the home of a friend or an acquaintance. However, as with other forms of physical attack, there are measures you can take to prevent sexual assaults. If you do become the target of a sexual attack, try to run for help. If it's not possible to run, try something else, such as screaming or yelling "Fire!" If possible, try to physically disable or stun your attacker. Be alert to moments when you might catch the attacker off guard and escape. Use your wits and try different approaches. Don't assume that you can't get away—you have a better chance of escaping than you might think. As in any encounter with violence, it's important to keep in mind that your ultimate survival is of the utmost importance.

➤ **Many law enforcement departments offer instructions in basic self-defense and techniques for escaping attackers.** *What resources in your community provide self-defense instruction?*

Myths & Reality

MYTH. Rape can't happen between a boyfriend and girlfriend or husband and wife.

FACT. Being in a relationship does not give anyone the right to force another person to have sex. Sexual intercourse that takes place against a person's will is rape regardless of whether or not the people involved are dating or even married.

MYTH. Women who are sexually assaulted were "asking for trouble" by the way they looked, dressed, or acted.

FACT. No one ever asks for or deserves to be raped. The responsibility for the rape lies with the rapist, never with the victim.

Gang-Related Violence

Many crimes committed by teens are gang-related. These crimes often include the sale of drugs, physical assaults on rival gang members, and homicide. Teens may join gangs because of peer pressure or to gain a sense of identity or belonging. Some join to be with their friends. Others join gangs to gain protection from violence in their neighborhoods.

However, because most gangs are involved in violent activities, joining a gang increases one's risks of being arrested, hurt, or killed. The U.S. Department of Justice reports that in large cities, most acts of gang-related violence are committed against members of rival gangs. In smaller towns, most gang-related violence is directed at individuals not involved in a gang. You can avoid risks associated with gang membership by resisting pressure to join a gang and leaving when you see gang members.

 People who feel a part of their community are less inclined to commit acts of violence, including vandalism. *How can you and your community work together to promote nonviolence?*

 Lesson 3 *Review*

Reviewing Facts and Vocabulary

1. Identify four common causes of violence.
2. Define *prejudice,* and explain how it can lead to violence.
3. Explain the role that alcohol and other drugs play in violent behaviors.

Thinking Critically

4. **Analyzing.** Explain how tolerant attitudes can help reduce violence.
5. **Evaluating.** How might messages from the media influence violent behavior?

Applying Health Skills

Analyzing Influences. Find three different media sources, such as movies, rap music, and video games, that contain messages involving violence. Analyze the message delivered in each media source you choose. How do you think these messages affect teens?

TECHNOLOGY *OPTION*

WEB SITES You might want to search the Internet for some of your media sources. Find help in conducting Internet searches at **health.glencoe.com.**

Lesson 3 Protecting Yourself from Violence **347**

 Lesson 3 *Review*

Answers to Reviewing Facts and Vocabulary

1. See pages 341–342 for answers.
2. An unfair opinion or judgment of a particular group of people; being prejudiced can lead to hate crimes.
3. Use of alcohol or other drugs can make it difficult for a person to control emotions, which may lead to violence.

Answers to Thinking Critically

4. Answers may discuss how racial and ethnic tolerance or ability to tolerate frustration or inconvenience can reduce violence.
5. Answers should discuss the desensitizing effect of media images.

 ASSESS

EVALUATING THE LESSON

Assign and discuss the Lesson 3 Review; then administer, grade, and discuss Lesson Quiz 48 in the TCR. ☞

RETEACHING

- Divide the class into four groups. Assign each group one of the factors that contribute to violence. Have each group compose a public service announcement about its assigned factor. Post the announcements for others to read.
- Ask students to complete Reteaching Activity 48 in the TCR. ☞

ENRICHMENT

Ask students to research and present orally the controversy over the legality of handguns. Make sure they present both sides of the issue and conclude with their own opinion. Remind students to use information from the text to support their responses.

4 CLOSE

Sum up this lesson for students by reminding them that teens are affected by much of the violence in today's society, including violence in schools. Emphasize that it is important for them to know what causes violence, how to prevent it, and how to protect themselves from it.

Preventing and Overcoming Abuse

Lesson 4

❶ FOCUS

QUICK START Have volunteers share examples of behaviors they consider abusive. Find out whether the rest of the class agrees or disagrees that these behaviors are abusive. Ask: What constitutes abuse? Guide the class in discussing strategies for preventing abusive behaviors.

TYING TO PRIOR KNOWLEDGE

Have students make a list of cases of abuse that they have heard or read about recently in the news. Discuss the prevalence of abuse in our society. Tell students that this lesson will focus mainly on abuse in dating relationships—how it happens and ways to prevent it.

Health Skills Features

"Helping a Victim of Dating Violence," p. 351

COMMUNICATION SKILLS

INTRODUCING VOCABULARY

• Have students define in their own words the term *abuse* and identify the many forms of abuse.

• Ask students to complete the Chapter 13 Study Guide in the *Student Activity Workbook*. 📁

Preventing and Overcoming Abuse

VOCABULARY
abuse
physical abuse
verbal abuse
stalking
date rape

YOU'LL LEARN TO

• Recognize threats to personal safety and analyze strategies for responding to abusive situations.

• Analyze the importance of healthy strategies that help prevent physical, sexual, and emotional abuse, including date rape.

• Examine the legal and ethical ramifications of unacceptable behaviors such as sexual abuse and acquaintance rape.

QUICK START On a sheet of paper, give two or three examples of behaviors you would consider abusive and suggest strategies that might help prevent these behaviors. Add to or revise your examples as you study this lesson.

Some people abuse others by yelling or mistreating them with angry words. *What strategies can help a person manage his or her anger?*

A healthy relationship is one in which both parties feel valued. The health of some relationships can be threatened by violence in the form of abusive behavior. You can protect yourself from such relationships by becoming aware of what behaviors are abusive and learning how to protect yourself from abuse.

Types of Abuse

A buse is *the physical, mental/emotional, or sexual mistreatment of one person by another.* Like other types of violence, abuse takes many forms and affects people of all economic, racial, and ethnic groups. Abuse also affects both males and females of all ages. Unlike many other forms of violence, abuse is most common between people involved in close relationships. Types of abuse include physical abuse, emotional abuse, and sexual abuse. All forms of abuse are illegal.

348 Chapter 13 Violence Prevention

Lesson 4 *Resources*

Teacher Classroom Resources

📁 Concept Mapping Activity 49

📁 Guided Reading Activities 49

📁 Lesson Plan 49

📁 Lesson Quiz 49

📁 Reteaching Activity 49

Student Activity Workbook

📁 Applying Health Skills 49

📁 Chapter 13 Study Guide

Multimedia

🕹 Transparency 39

Physical Abuse

Physical abuse is *the intentional infliction of bodily harm or injury on another person.* This form of abuse includes behaviors such as slapping, punching, kicking, biting, shaking, beating, or shoving another person. It may also involve inflicting injury by using items such as belts or weapons. Often, the person inflicting abuse tries to make the victim feel deserving of the mistreatment. However, abuse is not the victim's fault; no one deserves to be abused. Such behavior is not only physically harmful to the victim, but harmful to the mental/emotional health of everyone involved.

Emotional Abuse

Have you ever witnessed one person screaming insults at another? This behavior is an example of **verbal abuse**, *using words to mistreat or injure another person.* Name-calling, hurling insults, and yelling in a threatening way are all forms of verbal abuse. Such abuse harms the victim's mental/emotional health by making the person feel stupid, worthless, or helpless. Anger caused by such behavior may result in physical violence.

Verbal abuse is a type of *emotional abuse,* a pattern of behavior that attacks an individual's emotional development and sense of worth. Emotional abuse may be used to gain a sense of power over another person or to make victims feel that they deserve to be punished. Emotional abuse may serve as a warning of future physical abuse.

Stalking is *the repeated following, harassment, or threatening of an individual to frighten or cause him or her harm.* Following a person, standing outside his or her home, making repeated phone calls, and destroying property are common stalking behaviors. Stalking is a form of emotional abuse. Victims are often made to feel anxious, nervous, and unsafe. Stalking is a growing problem. In fact, each year in the United States, as many as 200,000 people are victims of stalking.

Q&A

Is neglect a form of abuse? How is it related to violence?
Neglect is a form of abuse that involves the failure to meet a person's basic needs, such as adequate food, clothing, shelter, love, and support. Although neglect is not violent in nature, it can result in future violence. Children who are victims of neglect may be at an increased risk of violent behavior, gang membership, and criminal activities.

Ⓥ Teen victims of abuse should seek help immediately from a trusted adult. *What other steps might help someone put a stop to abuse?*

② TEACH

Critical Thinking

Pose these questions: Which is more harmful to an individual's health—physical abuse or emotional abuse? Why? Have students present arguments to support their choice. ▣

Guest Speaker

Invite representatives from the local center for battered women, rape crisis center, and/or community mental health clinic to speak with the class about abuse and violence prevention. Ask the speakers to discuss the role of refusal skills and assertive behavior in preventing and dealing with conflict, abuse, and violence. Have them share the services of the center and any ways in which the students can become involved. ▣ ⬛▭

Activity

Have students find the definition of *statutory rape.* Ask volunteers to research the state laws regarding sexual activity between a teen and a person who is older than the teen. What age difference is considered statutory rape? What are the penalties for this crime? Have students share their findings with the class. ▣

— *School to Work* —

Child Welfare Worker When a case of child abuse or suspected child abuse is reported, county agencies need to act. Counties employ social workers charged with investigating reports of child abuse. When they find abuse has occurred, they report their findings and make recommendations about the appropriate course of action. If an abused child is left in the home or returned to the home after a period of parent or guardian rehabilitation, child welfare workers usually monitor the progress of the child and the family. Have students learn about the duties of child welfare workers and the qualifications for such a position.

Explaining

Explain why people who do not know healthy ways to manage their emotions may be prone to dating violence and other types of abusive behavior. **L1**

Discussing

What are *date rape* and *acquaintance rape?* How do they differ from rape by a stranger? What actions can someone take to lessen their risk of date or acquaintance rape? **L2**

FYI

The most frequent victims of date rape are girls and young women between the ages of 15 and 25.

Explaining

Explain how and why rape victims are often made to feel guilty or ashamed of what has happened to them. Elaborate on how this leads to underreporting of rapes and fewer convictions of rapists. Ask students to find out what state laws protect rape victims. **L2**

Health Minute

Ask volunteers to read aloud the tips for avoiding date rape. Have students explain how each action can help prevent date rape. Encourage students to share additional suggestions for staying safe on a date.

Health Minute

Tips for Avoiding Date Rape

To protect yourself:

▶ Do not go out with a person whom you do not know well.

▶ Date people who are close to your own age.

▶ Set clear sexual boundaries, and communicate them assertively.

▶ Avoid being completely alone with your date—for example, at home or in a car.

▶ Do not use alcohol or drugs or date anyone who does. Avoid places where alcohol or drugs may be present.

▶ Watch your food and drink. Do not allow an opportunity for someone to give you a date rape drug.

▶ **Issues of jealousy or control may lead to an unhealthy relationship.** *What are healthful ways to resolve such issues before they become violent?*

Dating Violence

Abuse in dating relationships, or *dating violence,* is on the rise. Dating violence includes all forms of abuse—physical, emotional, and sexual. Sometimes, teen victims may accept abuse as part of a relationship. Some teens, for example, mistake dominant treatment by a girlfriend or boyfriend as an expression of caring. These teens may see jealousy as an expression of love. However, true caring involves kindness, gentleness, and respect, *not* control and abuse.

Signs indicating that an unhealthy dating relationship may be headed toward abusive behavior include

▶ expressions of jealousy.

▶ attempts to control a partner's behavior.

▶ use of insults or put-downs to manipulate a partner.

▶ use of guilt to manipulate a partner.

Anyone in such a relationship should seek advice from parents or other trusted adults about ending the relationship. Remember that in healthy relationships, people respect and care about each other. They hold each other in high esteem, acting with consideration and kindness.

Date and Acquaintance Rape

Rape occurs whenever one person is forced into participating in any form of sexual intercourse. Often, a victim of rape knows the attacker. For example, **date rape** occurs *when one person in a dating relationship forces the other person to participate in sexual intercourse.* Although most reported cases of date rape are committed against young women, both males and females may be victims. Another form of rape, called *acquaintance rape,* occurs when someone known casually or considered a friend forces a person to have sexual intercourse. All forms of rape may traumatize victims and leave lasting emotional scars. It is critical to take preventive measures to protect yourself from rape.

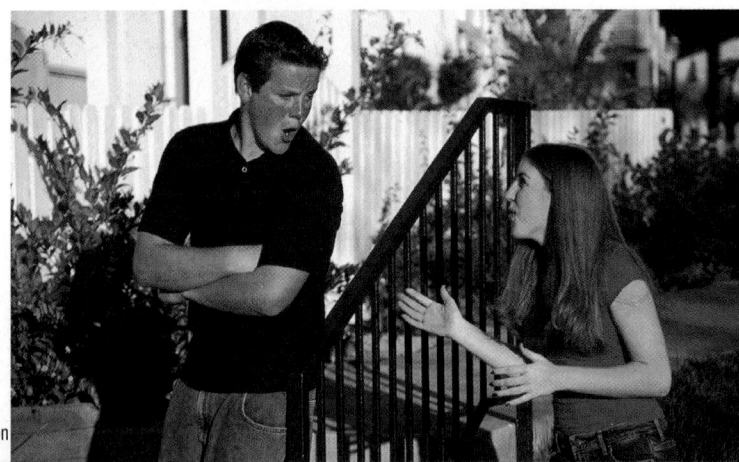

HEALTH LITERACY

Effective Communicator Some perpetrators of date rape genuinely disbelieve a rape has occurred. Knowing how to communicate effectively and assertively can help prevent date rape and unwanted sexual activity or physical intimacy. Have students make two anonymous lists—one labeled "Verbal Signals" and the other labeled "Body Language Signals." Under the appropriate heading, students should list verbal or body language signals that say no to sexual activity. Have students discuss the responses, including how messages might be more assertive. Help students understand that no means no, regardless of other signals. Discuss reasons why setting limits before and during a date can be helpful.

Health Skills Activity

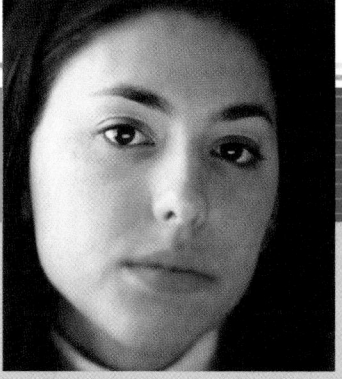

Communication: Helping a Victim of Dating Violence

Dyann became concerned when her friend Raye began dating an older boy from another school. Dyann thought he was possessive and controlling. It seemed that whenever Dyann and Raye had a chance to talk, Raye's boyfriend would call her cell phone, demanding to know where she was and what she was doing.

Now, Dyann feels as if Raye is avoiding her. Today, she notices that one of Raye's eyes is swollen and discolored. When Dyann tries to speak to her, Raye barely nods and rushes off in the opposite direction. Dyann suspects that Raye's boyfriend has been hitting her. Dyann would like to help her friend, but she's not sure how.

What Would You Do?

Apply the following communication skills to Dyann's situation. Write a dialogue that Dyann could use to persuade Raye to seek help.

1. Use "I" messages to show concern.
2. Use appropriate listening skills to encourage the other person to talk.
3. Provide facts or data about why it is important to get help.
4. Demonstrate conviction about the urgency of getting help.

ALCOHOL, DRUGS, AND DATE RAPE

Research shows that alcohol use is involved in as many as two-thirds of date-rape cases involving teens and college students. In recent years, the **drugs** GHB and Rohypnol, sometimes called "date rape drugs," have also become common in such cases. These drugs are sometimes placed in a victim's food or drink without that person's knowledge. The victim who consumes the substance may black out, becoming an easy target for rape. You can help protect yourself from rape by avoiding the use of alcohol or other drugs and situations in which these substances are present. When at a party or another social situation, get your own beverage, keep the beverage container covered, and never leave your beverage unattended. Pairing with a trustworthy friend to keep tabs on each other is also a good strategy for staying safe in such social situations.

hot link

drugs For more information about the dangers of drug use, see Chapter 23, page 594.

More About...

Rohypnol Rohypnol is a strong depressant drug that is sometimes used in treating insomnia, or the inability to sleep. Although it is a legal prescription drug in certain countries, most Rohypnol currently found in this country has been illegally smuggled here or produced in makeshift laboratories.

Often referred to by the street name "roofies," Rohypnol has become a popular club drug among teens and young adults. Because it has no taste or odor, Rohypnol can be put in a victim's drink without the person's knowledge. Rohypnol is sometimes used in date rape because it can cause not only a blackout but also a form of amnesia so that the victim may not remember what happened. Ask: How can you protect yourself from this situation?

Health Skills Activity

HELPING A VICTIM OF DATING VIOLENCE

COMMUNICATION SKILLS

NHES Standard 5 Students will demonstrate the ability to use interpersonal communication skills to enhance health.

Objectives

- Analyze the importance of healthy strategies that prevent physical, sexual, and emotional abuse.
- Apply communication skills that demonstrate consideration and respect for others.

Motivator

Ask students to discuss the traits of a healthy dating relationship. What might indicate an unhealthy relationship?

Teaching Strategies

1. Tell students to approach Raye with a discussion of what constitutes a healthy dating relationship (e.g., no violence, respecting opinions, wanting each other to maintain other friendships).
2. Advise students not to be judgmental or critical of Raye in their dialogues.

✓ Assessment

Using a rubric, student work should provide comprehensive evidence of the following criteria to achieve the highest score:

✔ use of "I" messages
✔ listening skills
✔ respectful tone of voice
✔ reasons to get help
✔ conviction about the urgency of getting help

Critical Thinking

Focus students' attention on the importance of recognizing abuse. Ask: How should a person respond if he or she recognizes abuse in a relationship? **L1**

Reinforcing Concepts

Remind students of the steps that should be taken if they or someone they know have been raped or sexually assaulted. The first step is to get away from the rapist and to a safe place. There, the victim should call local law enforcement to report the crime. The person should also call a friend or family member who can provide emotional support. In addition, it is essential for the rape victim to seek immediate medical attention. **L1**

VISUAL LEARNING

Figure 13.3 Have a volunteer read aloud the sources of help for victims of abuse or rape as shown in Figure 13.3. Ask students: Which of these resources do you think teen victims of abuse or rape would be most likely to use? Why? Have volunteers compile a list of sources of help for victims of abuse or rape in their community, including addresses, phone numbers, and other contact information.

hotlink

STDs For more information about sexually transmitted diseases, see Chapter 25, page 652.
HIV For more information about HIV and AIDS, see Chapter 25, page 658.

Overcoming Abuse

It is important for people who have suffered abuse or rape to remember that they are victims and have not done anything wrong. All forms of abuse, including rape, are illegal and should be reported to authorities. Reporting such incidents may help prevent future abuse. Today, all states have laws that require health care professionals to report child abuse. Many states also require anyone who suspects or knows of an abusive situation to report the problem.

Help for Victims

If you or someone you know is raped, call law enforcement officials immediately. Next, seek medical attention and be sure to get tests for pregnancy, **STDs,** and **HIV** infection. These actions may help prevent further illness or injury and may provide physical evidence that will be useful in the conviction of the rapist.

A teen victim of abuse or rape should speak with a caring, trusted, and knowledgeable adult, such as a parent. The trusted adult can provide emotional support and aid the teen in getting help. **Figure 13.3** identifies resources that can provide help, including support and counseling, for abuse or rape victims.

In cases of child abuse, counseling is available and recommended for both the abused child and his or her parents or guardians. With help, most people can recover from the trauma of abuse, violence, or rape. However, the recovery requires patience and time.

FIGURE 13.3

SOURCES OF HELP FOR VICTIMS OF ABUSE OR RAPE

Many sources of help are available for people in abusive situations.
- Parents or guardians
- Teacher, coach, guidance counselor
- Clergy member
- Police
- Private physician, hospital emergency room
- Battered women's shelter
- Rape crisis center
- Private therapist/counselor
- Support groups

WomanLine
CRISIS CENTER

Let our caring and supportive staff of counselors help you.
Call our 24-Hour **HELPLINE**
1-800-555-1234

Dealing with Sensitive Issues

Providing Support With the increasing incidence of dating violence, a student in your class may have been sexually assaulted or raped. Your role as a teacher is to identify students in need, offer the students support, and refer them to other sources of help. Have a list of local support services and their phone numbers readily available. Rape victims should be strongly encouraged to contact law enforcement and to seek counseling.

The first step in helping a student you suspect has been assaulted or raped is showing the student you care. If you broach the problem with the student, be sure to do so privately. Refer to Glencoe's professional booklet, *Dealing with Sensitive Issues,* for more information.

Help for Abusers

In cases of abuse, both the victim and the abuser need help. Abusive behavior is learned. Often, individuals who abuse others were themselves victims of abuse. Thus, abusers may see violence and abuse as a normal way of life. This is one reason why the **cycle of violence** may continue from one generation to the next. Abusers need intense counseling to succeed at breaking this harmful cycle.

To break the cycle of violence, long-range prevention of abuse is needed in society as a whole. One solution may be to provide parents and prospective parents with opportunities to learn about family life, child development, and parent-child relationships. Another is to provide counseling for all victims of abuse and violence. Support and counseling can help victims recover from abuse and learn prevention strategies. People convicted of abuse are required to participate in treatment programs conducted by mental health professionals. To prevent and overcome abuse, all individuals need to learn skills for developing and maintaining healthy relationships.

 h⬛t link

cycle of violence For more information about how to break the cycle of violence, see Chapter 11, page 289.

Ⓥ **Counseling can help break the cycle of violence.** *Why is it important for both abusers and their victims to seek counseling?*

 Lesson 4 *Review*

Reviewing Facts and Vocabulary

1. What is *verbal abuse*, and how does it harm the victim?

2. List two signs that may indicate an unhealthy dating relationship.

3. What is *date rape*?

Thinking Critically

4. **Applying.** What strategies can help a person avoid date or acquaintance rape in social situations? Analyze the importance of such strategies.

5. **Evaluating.** Why might victims of rape be reluctant to tell others what has happened to them? What should these victims keep in mind to help them overcome their fears and report the crime?

Applying Health Skills

Advocacy. Design a pamphlet that informs teens how to recognize the signs of an abusive situation. Provide strategies for avoiding or dealing with such situations, stressing the importance of seeking help.

 TECHNOLOGY | *OPTION*

DESKTOP PUBLISHING You can use desktop publishing to produce your pamphlet. Find help in using desktop publishing software at **health.glencoe.com.**

Lesson 4 Preventing and Overcoming Abuse **353**

---

③ ASSESS

EVALUATING THE LESSON

Assign and discuss the Lesson 4 Review; then administer, grade, and discuss Lesson Quiz 49 in the TCR. 📁

RETEACHING

• Have students prepare a detailed lesson outline using the lesson's headings.

• Ask students to complete Reteaching Activity 49 in the TCR. 📁

ENRICHMENT

Have students research the cycle of abuse where victims can become abusers themselves. Provide time for discussion of their findings.

④ CLOSE

Summarize the most important concepts in the lesson. Write the lesson's major concepts on separate, numbered slips of paper. Place the slips into a box, and have each student draw one. Going in numerical order, ask each student to use his or her own words to summarize the concept written on the slip of paper.

 Lesson 4 *Review*

Answers to Reviewing Facts and Vocabulary

1. Using words to mistreat or injure another person. It harms mental/emotional health.
2. Jealousy, control, insults, guilt
3. When one person in a dating relationship forces the other person to participate in sexual intercourse.

Answers to Thinking Critically

4. Answers will vary.
5. Possible answer: Victims of rape may feel ashamed or may not wish to undergo the exams that are necessary to gather evidence. They should remember that they are not to blame and should report the crime.

Eye ON THE Media

Antiviolence Media Campaign

NHES Standard 4 Students will analyze the influence of culture, media, technology, and other factors on health.

Objective

Help reduce the risk of violence by creating a media campaign that focuses on violence prevention.

Teaching Strategies

Ask students if they have ever seen media that promote violence prevention.

Awareness Ask students if they think a youth-centered violence prevention program is more effective than one that doesn't include youth. Why or why not?

Analysis Ask students how a youth-centered approach to a teen violence prevention program might be different. What components of a program could teens be more effective in developing?

Reflection Ask: What are the most effective ways to get a media message out to fellow students at their school?

Take Action Have students write letters to community leaders describing their media campaign and discussing the importance of antiviolence efforts that include schools and community working together.

✓ Assessment

Students should actively participate in groups to develop media focusing on preventing youth violence. Media items should include violence prevention strategies such as refusal skills or conflict resolution skills.

Eye ON THE Media

Antiviolence Media Campaign

Teens around the country are taking steps to prevent violence by initiating teen-run, antiviolence programs in their communities and schools. One of the most important components of any successful violence prevention program is a media strategy that educates people about violence prevention strategies and protective factors.

STOMP OUT VIOLENCE

ACTIVITY

For this activity, you will develop a media campaign as part of a violence prevention program in your school. Your media campaign should focus on reducing the risk of violence by encouraging the use of prevention strategies, refusal skills, conflict resolution skills, and protective factors.

- As a class, brainstorm ideas for a slogan for your campaign.

- In groups of three or four, create media strategies to bring awareness to this issue. One group might design an antiviolence advertisement for the school

paper. Another group might develop a poster to hang in the school cafeteria. Other components might include brochures, public service announcements, fact sheets, T-shirts, bulletin board designs, and Web pages.

EXPRESS YOUR VIEWS

Evaluate your media campaign. Write an analysis of each component, and discuss the effectiveness of the campaign in bringing awareness to the problem of youth violence. What makes an item effective or ineffective?

More About...

Youth Violence Programs One of the most frequently asked questions about youth violence prevention programs is: "What works for teens?" Research has shown that any antiviolence program must include a comprehensive approach that includes the family, the school, the community, and teens.

Programs need to be long-term and must actively involve adult role models and mentors. Discuss with the class other initiatives being taken in your school, community, and nation that are helping to combat teen violence.

CROSS-CURRICULUM CONNECTIONS

Teach Conflict Resolution. Learning conflict resolution skills can prevent violence. Write an essay describing how to use conflict resolution skills to settle a disagreement. Discuss the steps people can take to resolve disagreements in an assertive yet positive manner. Create a visual aid, such as a diagram or chart, to help illustrate the process.

Create a Time Line. "Nonviolence is a powerful and just weapon," stated Dr. Martin Luther King, Jr. During the Civil Rights movement in the United States, Dr. King taught people how to use passive resistance by organizing nonviolent protests such as marches, boycotts, and sit-ins to fight segregation. Research key events in the Civil Rights movement and create a time line of the nonviolent events that led to the end of segregation.

Calculate Percentage. Suppose that during a given year in the United States, 35 percent of high school students reported being involved in a fight. Officials at Anytown Senior High School want to use the national average to estimate how many of their students are likely to be involved in a fight. If the school has 2,200 students, how many are likely to be involved in a fight during the school year?

Research a Topic. Traumatic events may cause individuals to experience a variety of psychological and biological changes. These reactions constitute what has come to be called Post-Traumatic Stress Disorder (PTSD). The disorder can be induced by any number of events, from neglect to physical assault. Research PTSD and write an essay discussing the possible causes, symptoms, and treatment methods for this disorder.

Social Worker

Helping people in need—including victims of abuse—can be rewarding. Social workers are among the many resources to which victims of abuse can turn for help. Social workers can be found in hospitals, nursing homes, governmental agencies, and community service agencies. Social workers can help people find alternative housing or other resources that will help them escape abusive situations.

To obtain a job as a social worker, you'll need to complete a four-year college program followed by a master's degree program in social work. Find out more about this and other health careers by clicking on Career Corner at **health.glencoe.com**.

Chapter 13 Review **355**

CROSS-CURRICULUM CONNECTIONS

Enrich student learning by connecting the topic of violence prevention to one of the four subject areas presented on this page. The activity may be completed individually or with a partner.

Language Arts Advise students to start the essay with a clear thesis statement and divide the process into manageable parts.

Social Studies Demonstrate through example that a time line needs to include clear images and captions with pertinent information.

Math Answer: $2200 \times 0.35 = 770$

Science All the events discussed in this chapter can trigger PTSD. Encourage students to recognize the causes and symptoms with a focus on what can be done to prevent or limit exposure to these stressors.

Have students read and discuss the Career Corner information on social workers. Ask interested students to explore the Glencoe Health Web site at **health.glencoe.com** for more information on this career.

Portfolio Assessment

Self-Evaluation Direct students to review the Health Skills Activities and other activities completed in the chapter. Encourage each student to select one finished product or activity that demonstrates his or her best work for the chapter and that represents the student's learning goals. Have students explain what they have learned and how the examples they have selected demonstrate their growth in health literacy, knowledge, and skills.

Teacher Classroom Resources Assign Performance Assessment 13, "Peer Mediation," in the TCR. 🗁

CHECKING COMPREHENSION

- Assign and discuss the chapter review.
- Use the Chapter 13 MindJogger Videoquiz to review the chapter. 〉〈

CHAPTER 13 REVIEW ANSWERS

Exploring Health Terms

1. self-defense
2. assertive
3. body language
4. violence
5. bullying
6. peer mediation
7. Assault
8. sexual violence
9. assailant
10. homicide
11. abuse
12. stalking
13. Date rape

Recalling the Facts

1. Any two: having no history of aggressive behavior, having positive social skills, being intelligent, having an antiviolent attitude, being female.

2. Any five: Avoid unsafe areas; don't carry your wallet or purse in an easy-to-grab place; walk briskly and with confidence; park in well-lit area and have car keys ready; avoid walking alone at night; when walking at night, avoid doorways and walk under lights near curb; let people know where you are going and when you will return; don't get into an elevator with a stranger; get on and off buses in well-lit areas; ask the person driving you home not to leave until you have safely entered a building; don't hitchhike or pick up hitchhikers; avoid using alcohol or other drugs.

➤ **EXPLORING HEALTH TERMS** *Answer the following questions on a sheet of paper.*

Lesson 1 *Fill in the blanks with the correct term.*

assertive	body language
self-defense	

1. Any physical or mental strategies used to protect oneself from harm are forms of _____ .

2. When you protect yourself by clearly stating your intentions and displaying confidence, you are being _____ .

3. Making direct eye contact or walking with a deliberate and confident stride are examples of _____ .

Lesson 2 *Match each definition with the correct term.*

bullying	gang
peer mediation	sexual harassment
violence	

4. Threatened or actual use of physical force or power to harm another person or to damage property.

5. Seeking power or attention through the psychological or physical abuse of another person.

6. Process in which trained students help other students find fair ways of resolving conflict and settling differences.

Lesson 3 *Fill in the blanks with the correct term.*

assailant	assault
homicide	prejudice
random violence	rape
sexual assault	sexual violence

(_7_) is an unlawful attack on a person with the intent to harm or kill. Rape, sexual harassment, and sexual assault are all forms of (_8_). The person who commits any of these acts against another person is known as the (_9_). If a person is killed during an assault, the crime is known as (_10_).

Lesson 4 *Replace the underlined words with the correct term.*

date rape	abuse
physical abuse	stalking
verbal abuse	

11. Any physical, mental, or emotional mistreatment of one person by another is <u>physical abuse</u>.

12. The repeated following, harassment, or threatening of an individual to frighten or cause harm to him or her is known as <u>verbal abuse</u>.

13. <u>Stalking</u> occurs when one person in a relationship forces the other to have sexual intercourse.

➤ **RECALLING THE FACTS** *Use complete sentences to answer the following questions.*

Lesson 1

1. List two individual protective factors that can help keep you from harm.

2. List five precautions that might keep you from becoming a victim of violence.

3. What are three strategies that communities use to increase safety in their neighborhoods?

Lesson 2

4. What are two ways of dealing with a bully?

5. Identify three strategies you can use to avoid school violence. Analyze how applying these strategies can help keep you safe.

6. What are the steps used in peer mediation?

Lesson 3

7. Identify two safety tips that can help protect an individual from assault.

8. Define sexual violence.

9. How can teens avoid the risks associated with gang membership?

3. Any three: increased police patrols; Neighborhood Watch programs; after-school programs; improved lighting in parks and playgrounds.

4. Ignore the bully, and encourage others to do the same; inform teachers, counselors, parents, or other adults of the problem.

5. Any three: Refuse to carry weapons and report others who do carry them, report any threat of violence to authorities, practice conflict resolution skills, use refusal skills to resist negative peer pressure, choose your friends carefully, don't spend time with people who show warning signs of violent behavior, develop a S.A.V.E. chapter. Analysis will vary but should mention how preventive behaviors can reduce violence.

6. Make introductions, establish ground rules, hear each side, explore solutions, close session.

7. Tips include if an attacker wants money or jewelry, throw the items away from you and

10. Why is verbal abuse considered a form of emotional abuse?

11. Explain the role that the use of alcohol and other drugs plays in abusive situations such as date rape.

12. Name two strategies for breaking the cycle of violence.

▶ THINKING CRITICALLY

1. **Analyzing.** Explain how family protective factors can decrease the likelihood of teen violence. *(LESSON 1)*

2. **Evaluating.** Many schools have adopted zero-tolerance policies for bullying and other forms of harassment. How might these policies positively affect the mental and emotional health of students? *(LESSON 2)*

3. **Analyzing.** Retaliation is a cause of violence. How might retaliation create an environment in which the level of violence tends to escalate continually? *(LESSON 3)*

4. **Synthesizing.** Examine the legal and ethical ramifications of unacceptable behaviors such as acquaintance rape and sexual abuse. *(LESSON 4)*

▶ HEALTH SKILLS APPLICATION

1. **Analyzing Influences.** Using Figure 13.1 as a reference, write a short story describing how peer and school protective factors help protect a teen from violence. *(LESSON 1)*

2. **Accessing Information.** Find out what policies your school has for protecting students from sexual harassment. Develop a presentation to make others in your school aware of these policies. *(LESSON 2)*

3. **Practicing Healthful Behaviors.** Analyze strategies you might apply in your selection of friends as a means of avoiding violence, gangs, weapons, and drugs. *(LESSON 3)*

4. **Accessing Information.** Research the resources available to victims of abuse and violence in your community. Make a flyer that includes these resources, their contact information, and details about the services they provide. *(LESSON 4)*

Thinking Critically

1. Answers should discuss the supportive environment created by adults in the family, the accountability of having to answer to adults who monitor teens' behavior, and the role of adult approval of teens' friends.

2. Students in these schools would know that they were safe and that if bullying did occur, it would be dealt with by school officials.

3. Retaliation usually sets up the need for the "other side" to retaliate against the retaliation.

4. Unacceptable behavior such as acquaintance rape and sexual abuse are illegal and punishable by law. These abusive actions can severely harm all aspects of the victims' health, often leaving psychological and emotional scars long after the incident.

Health Skills Application

1.–4. Answers will vary.

EVALUATE

- Use the reproducible Chapter 13 Test in the TCR, or construct your own using the Testmaker software. 📂

- Use Performance Assessment 13 in the TCR. 📂

ENRICHMENT

Ask students to complete Enrichment Activity 13 in the TCR. 📂

BEYOND *the* Classroom

Parent Involvement

Accessing Information. With a parent, contact your local police department to determine whether there is a Neighborhood Watch program in your community. If there is such a program, obtain information on how the program works and how your family can become involved. If no program exists, discuss with local law enforcement officials how you might start such a program.

School and Community

Crisis Centers and Shelters. Contact a local rape crisis center or battered women's shelter. Arrange for an interview with a worker at the facility to discuss the services the agency provides, how the services are accessed, and how the agency is funded. Share this information with your class. If possible, arrange for a speaker from the agency to talk to your class.

BEYOND *the* Classroom

Keep students involved in the community, and encourage parent participation by assigning the activities on this page for students to work on outside of class.

run in the opposite direction and if you are being followed, go to a place where there are other people.

8. Any form of unwelcome sexual conduct directed at an individual, including sexual harassment, sexual assault, and rape.

9. By resisting pressure to join a gang and leaving when they see gang members.

10. Verbal abuse can harm the mental and emotional health of its victim.

11. Use of alcohol and other drugs greatly increase the risk of abusive situations. Alcohol use is involved in as many as two-thirds of date rape cases involving teens and college students. "Date rape drugs," such as GHB and Rohypnol, have also become common in such cases.

12. Strategies include provide parents and prospective parents with opportunities to learn about family life, child development, and parent-child relationships; provide counseling for all victims of abuse and violence as well as perpetrators of abuse.

Lessons	Standards		Features
	National	**State/Local**	
1 **Healthy Skin, Hair, and Nails** *pages 360–366*	National Health Education Standards **1.1, 2.3, 3.3, 6.1**		
2 **Care of Teeth and Mouth** *pages 367–370*	National Health Education Standards **1.1, 2.3, 3.1**		**Real-Life Application** • Examining Product Claims *(Accessing Information)*, page 339
3 **Eye Care** *pages 371–375*	National Health Education Standards **1.3, 2.6, 3.1, 4.3**		
4 **Ears and Hearing Protection** *pages 376–379*	National Health Education Standards **1.1, 1.3, 3.1, 7.4**		**Exploring Issues** • Should Noise Levels at Concerts Be Controlled? page 378

Reproducible Resources	Assessment	Technology
Student Activity Workbook for use with each chapter 📁 Concept Mapping Activity 50 📁 Current Health Issues 14 📁 Decision-Making Activity 14 📁 Enrichment Activity 14 📁 Guided Reading Activities 50 📁 Lesson Plan 50 📁 Parent Letter and Activities 14 📁 Reteaching Activity 50	📁 Lesson Quiz 50	🖨 Transparency 40 💿 TeacherWorks® 🖥 Internet Activities
📁 Concept Mapping Activity 51 📁 Guided Reading Activities 51 📁 Lesson Plan 51 📁 Reteaching Activity 51	📁 Lesson Quiz 51	🖨 Transparency 41 💿 TeacherWorks®
📁 Concept Mapping Activity 52 📁 Guided Reading Activities 52 📁 Lesson Plan 52 📁 Reteaching Activity 52	📁 Lesson Quiz 52	🖨 Transparency 42 💿 TeacherWorks®
📁 Concept Mapping Activity 53 📁 Cross-Curriculum Activity 14 📁 Guided Reading Activities 53 📁 Health Lab 14 📁 Lesson Plan 53 📁 Reteaching Activity 53	📁 Lesson Quiz 53	🖨 Transparency 43 💿 TeacherWorks®

⏱ OUT OF TIME

If time does not permit teaching the entire chapter, use:
- Figure 14.2, p. 365
- Real-Life Application, p. 369
- Exploring Issues, p. 378
- Eye on the Media, p. 380

Language Diversity

🎧 English Audio CD Program
🎧 Spanish Audio CD Program
📁 English Summaries, Quizzes, and Activities
📁 Spanish Summaries, Quizzes, and Activities
📁 Spanish Parent Letters and Activities

End of Chapter Assessment

Blackline Masters
📁 Chapter 14 Test
📁 Performance Assessment Activity 14

Technology
💿 Vocabulary PuzzleMaker
📼 MindJogger Videoquiz
💿 Exam*View*® Pro Testmaker

Professional Health Series
Dealing with Sensitive Issues
Planning a Coordinated School Health Program
Promoting Character Education
Home, School, and Community Involvement

Personal Care and Healthy Behaviors

CHAPTER OVERVIEW

Chapter 14 discusses personal care. It helps students understand how the skin, teeth, eyes, and ears function and explains how teens can promote the health of these important body structures.

Lesson 1 Skin, the largest organ in the human body, protects internal organs and is the first line of defense against pathogens that might enter the body. Proper care can help keep the skin healthy. Hair and nails are part of the same body system as the skin.

Lesson 2 The teeth and gums make important contributions to physical health and to appearance. Proper care includes brushing, flossing, and regular dental checkups.

Lesson 3 Eyes are the most important receptors of information from the environment. Eating a healthy diet, wearing eye protection, and having regular eye exams are all important in promoting eye health.

Lesson 4 Ears, our organs of hearing and balance, should be protected from injury and loud noises.

Health Skills Features

- Real-Life Application *(Accessing Information)*, p. 369
- Exploring Issues *(Advocacy)*, p. 378

Chapter 14

Personal Care and Healthy Behaviors

Lesson 1
Healthy Skin, Hair, and Nails

Lesson 2
Care of Teeth and Mouth

Lesson 3
Eye Care

Lesson 4
Ears and Hearing Protection

358

MEETING STUDENT DIVERSITY

Language Diversity Use the following suggestions to help students who have difficulty with English:

- Pair English language learners with native speakers of English who can restate the Chapter Summary in language that helps students comprehend important concepts.

- Direct auditory learners or those students with language diversity to the *Glencoe Health Audio CD Program.* Available in English and Spanish, this component provides an audio and written summary of the chapter.

- Use photographs, drawings, or magazine clippings to help students visualize the important concepts of the chapter.

Myth or Fact?

What Do You Know About Healthy Skin, Teeth, Eyes, and Ears?

Read each statement below and respond by writing *Myth* or *Fact* for each item.

1. There is a safe way to tan.

2. Skin cancer is never fatal.

3. As long as I brush my teeth every day, I do not need to floss.

4. Eating foods that contain vitamin A can help keep my eyes healthy.

5. Exposure to loud noises does not damage hearing.

6. Tattooing or piercing can result in serious infection transferred by nonsterile needles.

7. Regular breaks can keep your eyes from becoming fatigued when using a computer.

8. People with dry skin are more likely to develop wrinkles.

Keep your responses for review later in the chapter. When you complete the chapter, review this list of myths and facts again. If necessary, change your answers according to what you have learned.

Quick Write

Using Visuals. Many routine tasks, such as brushing and flossing your teeth or caring for your skin, are behaviors that positively affect your long-term health. What are some simple behaviors you can practice each day to protect your health?

359

INTRODUCING THE CHAPTER

Myth or Fact?

Have students read each statement and identify it as myth or fact. Then have volunteers read their responses aloud, and ask students to share their ideas about each.

1. Myth. There is no safe way to tan.

2. Myth. Melanoma is a type of skin cancer that, if not removed early, spreads internally and is usually fatal.

3. Myth. Flossing removes plaque from between teeth and at the gum line, where periodontal disease often begins.

4. Fact. Vitamin A is essential for good eyesight.

5. Myth. More than 35 percent of the 28 million cases of hearing loss in the United States are caused, at least in part, by exposure to loud noise.

6. Fact. Both procedures involve breaking the skin. Bacteria or viruses can be introduced.

7. Fact. Resting your eyes reduces eye strain.

8. Myth. Wrinkles are simply more noticeable in dry skin.

Quick Write

Using Visuals Have students describe the teens in the pictures. What actions can these teens take to protect their health? Then give students a few minutes to list actions they take every day to protect their physical health.

TECHNOLOGY OPTIONS

MINDJOGGER
VIDEOQUIZ

To preview or review chapter content, you may wish to use the Chapter 14 MindJogger Videoquiz. ▶◀

HEALTH *Online*

Online Resources for the Teacher For a fresh approach to health topics and an in-depth look at health issues, use these online resources found under Teacher Resources at **health.glencoe.com**:

- Block Schedule Lesson Plans
- Technology Projects
- Health Updates

① FOCUS

QUICK START Have students record the time they spend in daily care of their skin, hair, and nails. Then encourage them to describe what they do to care for their skin, hair, and nails and to discuss how these actions affect their health.

TYING TO PRIOR KNOWLEDGE

Refer to the Quick Start activity, and point out that students already know a great deal about caring for their skin, hair, and nails. Tell students they will learn more about these kinds of care and about protecting the health of their skin, hair, and nails.

INTRODUCING VOCABULARY

- Have students define each term in their own words and then use the Glossary to check their definitions. Then ask students to write three sentences, using at least three of the vocabulary terms.

- Ask students to complete the Chapter 14 Study Guide in the *Student Activity Workbook.* 🗁

360

Healthy Skin, Hair, and Nails

VOCABULARY
- epidermis
- dermis
- melanin
- sebaceous glands
- sweat glands
- melanoma
- hair follicle
- dandruff

YOU'LL LEARN TO
- Examine the structure of the skin.
- Identify the functions of the skin.
- Examine the effects of health behaviors on skin, hair, and nails.
- Relate the importance of early detection of skin diseases to healthy life.

QUICK START Divide a sheet of paper into three columns labeled "Skin," "Hair," and "Nails." Record how much time you spend over the course of one day on personal grooming in these areas. How do these personal grooming habits affect your health?

⚠ **Washing your face regularly keeps skin free of dirt, bacteria, and perspiration.** *How does keeping your face and hands clean affect your overall health?*

Beads of perspiration form on your forehead while you are exercising or when you are outside on a hot day. Your skin, the largest organ of your body, produces perspiration in order to help keep your body cool. Skin is the main organ of the integumentary system, which also includes hair, nails, and glands found in your skin. Your skin serves as a physical barrier between the outside world and your internal organs. It shields them from injury, and it is the first line of defense against pathogens entering your body.

Structure and Function of the Skin

The skin consists of two main layers, as shown in **Figure 14.1**. The **epidermis** is *the outer, thinner layer of the skin that is composed of living and dead cells.* The **dermis** is *the thicker layer of the skin beneath the epidermis that is made up of connective tissue and contains blood vessels and nerves.*

The epidermis is composed of several layers. The top layer consists of dead cells that are constantly being shed and replaced. In the deeper layers of the epidermis, living cells continually divide and replace dying cells, which are pushed toward the surface layer.

Lesson 1 *Resources*

Teacher Classroom Resources
- 🗁 Concept Mapping Activity 50
- 🗁 Current Health Issues 14
- 🗁 Decision-Making Activity 14
- 🗁 Enrichment Activity 14
- 🗁 Guided Reading Activities 50
- 🗁 Lesson Plan 50
- 🗁 Lesson Quiz 50

- 🗁 Parent Letter and Activities 14
- 🗁 Reteaching Activity 50

Student Activity Workbook
- 🗁 Applying Health Skills 50
- 🗁 Chapter 14 Study Guide

Multimedia
- 🕹 Transparency 40

FIGURE 14.1

STRUCTURE OF THE SKIN

The two main layers of skin, the epidermis and the dermis, are attached to bones and muscles by the subcutaneous layer, a layer of fat and connective tissue located beneath the dermis.

hair
dead epidermis
living epidermis
sweat pore

sebaceous gland
hair follicle
muscle
duct of sweat gland
sweat gland
artery
vein
nerve

fat tissue

Epidermis

Dermis

Subcutaneous Layer

Certain cells in the epidermis make a substance called *keratin*, a protein that toughens nails. These same cells also produce substances called lipids, which make your skin waterproof. This waterproofing helps the body maintain a proper balance of water and electrolytes. Other cells produce **melanin**, *a pigment that gives the skin, hair, and iris of the eyes their color*—the more melanin, the darker the skin. People with fair skin have less melanin and are at risk of damage from harmful ultraviolet (UV) radiation.

The dermis is a single thick layer composed of connective tissue, which gives the skin its elastic qualities. **Sebaceous glands**, *structures within the skin that produce an oily secretion called sebum*, are also found in the dermis. Sebum helps keep skin and hair from drying out.

Blood vessels in the dermis supply cells with oxygenated blood and nutrients and facilitate the removal of cellular wastes. These blood vessels also function in temperature regulation. When body temperature begins to rise, the blood vessels in the skin dilate. This allows heat to escape through the skin's surface. If body temperature begins to drop, the blood vessels in the skin constrict, decreasing the amount of blood and heat loss at the skin's surface. **Sweat glands**, *structures within the dermis that secrete perspiration through*

Lesson 1 Healthy Skin, Hair, and Nails **361**

More About...

Diagnosing Allergies In addition to its many other functions, the skin remains one of the most reliable diagnostic tools in the treatment of hay fever and other seasonal allergies. When sensitivity to an allergen is suspected, a doctor will administer a scratch test. The test consists of a series of surface injections of plant extracts and other possible immunosensitive culprits. Depending on the substance, a positive response registers in the form of a blotch or bump; either one is a sign that immunotherapy (treatment or prevention of disease by attempting to induce immunity) is needed.

---

2 TEACH

Discussing

Help students consider the relationship between the words *epidermis* and *dermis*. Ask: What do you think the prefix *epi-* means? over Have students look up *–dermis* in their dictionaries. Then ask students to think of other words related to *dermis*. Examples include *dermatitis, dermatology,* and *pachyderm.*

VISUAL LEARNING

Figure 14.1 Have students work with partners to study the picture and read the labels in Figure 14.1. Encourage partners to identify the function of each labeled feature.

ACTIVE READING

Overview

Help students recognize that any chapter or lesson is easier to understand once they have an overview of the contents. Suggest that students use the two pages of a chapter opener to find out about the chapter contents; the chapter title, the listed lesson titles, and the photographs give reliable clues. They should read the lesson title, the objectives, and all the headings and subheadings. These will help students recognize the organization of the lesson and identify the most important concepts. For more strategies, see the *Guided Reading Activities* booklet in the TCR.

Activity

Explain that one of the functions of the skin is to help the body make vitamin D. This vitamin is produced in the skin when it is exposed to sunlight. The amount of vitamin D produced depends on the length of exposure to sunlight and on the color of your skin. People with darker skin tend to produce less vitamin D than those with lighter skin. Have interested students determine other sources of vitamin D. fortified milk, cereals, eggs, sardines, salmon, beef, and margarine

Have a volunteer read the question and answer aloud, and encourage students to discuss their experiences with sunscreen. How can they identify broad-spectrum sunscreens? Who has used a broad-spectrum sunscreen? With what results?

Explaining

Explain to students that for adequate protection, a sunblock with an SPF (sun protection factor) of 15 or greater is recommended. SPF, which is rated from 2 to 15 or greater, indicates how long a person can stay in the sun without getting burned. If you normally burn after 15 minutes in the sun, for example, an SPF of 8 will allow you to stay out for 8 times 15, or 120 minutes (2 hours).

A diet rich in vitamin A will contribute to healthy skin. *Which foods do you enjoy that are a good source of vitamin A?*

What is UVA and UVB radiation?

Ultraviolet rays come in different wavelengths—UVA and UVB. UVB rays cause most sunburn; thus, most sunscreens block these rays. However, UVA rays penetrate the skin more deeply than UVB, causing more damage. Now that dermatologists know about UVA, they recommend sunscreens that block both UVA and UVB rays.

ducts to pores on the skin's surface, *also are involved in temperature regulation. Sweat glands produce perspiration on the surface of the skin. Body heat is lost as the sweat evaporates.*

Touch a hot stove, and your hand immediately pulls back. Why? The skin is a major sense organ. Nerve cells in the dermis act as receptors, which are stimulated by changes in the outside environment. These receptors enable you to feel sensations such as pressure, pain, hot, and cold.

Healthy Skin

Keeping your skin healthy should be an important part of your daily routine. Wash your face every morning and evening with mild soap and water. Daily washing, bathing, or showering helps remove and slow the growth of bacteria that cause body odor. Avoid touching your face with your hands. This can introduce new bacteria to the skin's surface. Carefully choose personal skin care products, such as moisturizers, shaving cream, or cosmetics, to help keep your skin from becoming irritated or having an allergic reaction. Follow a well-balanced diet that is rich in vitamins and minerals. Foods such as milk, green and yellow vegetables, and liver are rich in vitamin A—a vitamin that is particularly important for healthy skin.

Skin and the Sun

Understanding the effects of UV radiation on the skin and knowing some preventive behaviors can help you protect your skin now and throughout your life. When skin is exposed to UV rays, whether from the sun, a tanning booth, or another source, melanin production is increased. This self-protective mechanism is the skin's attempt to protect its cells from UV rays. Fair-skinned people whose skin has little melanin, and thus little natural protection from UV radiation, burn in the sun. People with more melanin will tan.

The symptoms of sunburn will disappear, and a tan will fade. The long-term effects, however, are cumulative and the damage is permanent. UV rays damage the genetic material in skin cells and cause it to undergo changes. These changes can eventually result in the formation and growth of cancerous cells. Exposure to UV radiation is the leading cause of certain types of skin cancer. UV radiation also breaks down the elastic fibers that support your skin and allow it to be flexible yet retain its shape. The skin will become wrinkled or hard and leathery with repeated exposure to UV radiation.

— School to Work —

Working Outdoors Have students interview an adult who works all or most of the day in the sun. For example, they might speak to lifeguards, physical education teachers, or coaches, farm laborers, gardeners, or construction workers. Then have students write handbooks for workers in a given occupation or create posters that could be displayed in the workplace, listing the precautions that might protect workers from sun damage. Have them proofread their writing for spelling and grammatical errors and make sure their information is presented in a clear and coherent way. Also, encourage students to develop several drafts before turning in their final drafts.

PROTECTING YOUR SKIN FROM UV RAYS

Protecting your skin from the damaging rays of the sun is as simple as following a few protective steps.

▶ **Always wear sunscreen on exposed areas of skin.** Use an SPF 15 or higher sunscreen that blocks both UVA and UVB rays. Apply it 15 to 30 minutes before going outside. Use it even on cloudy days and while participating in winter sports.

▶ **Wear protective clothing.** Hats, long-sleeved shirts, and long pants can help prevent sun exposure. Don't forget your sunglasses. Exposure to UV rays can damage the eyes, causing burns, cataracts, and even blindness. Avoid outdoor activities when sunlight is most intense, between 10:00 a.m. and 4:00 p.m.

Body Piercing and Tattooing

Ear piercings and tattooing are practices that have been around for thousands of years. Unlike decorating the body with make-up or changing hair color, however, these changes to the body are permanent, and both carry potential health risks.

Both procedures result in the physical barrier of the skin being broken, so the possibility of bacteria or viruses entering the body increases. Bacteria that are normally found on the surface of the skin can cause a localized infection if they enter deeper layers of tissue. New bacteria can be introduced through nonsterile needles. Of special concern is the transfer of blood-borne pathogens such as the viruses **hepatitis B, hepatitis C,** and **HIV** through nonsterile needles used during tattooing.

Tattooing and piercings can threaten your social health as well. Imagine dating someone who is tattooed with the name of a past boyfriend or girlfriend. Body piercings may make a poor impression on a future employer or in-law.

A tattoo can be removed by using a laser procedure. However, the procedure can cause skin discoloration and infection and can leave scars. Consider the long-term consequences when you think about tattooing and piercing.

Health and Beauty

SUNSCREEN

SPF
30

SPF 30 provides UVA and UVB Protection.
It is water and perspiration resistant and PABA Free. Weightless, nongreasy lotion provides 30 times the skin's natural protection against sunburn.

⊙ **A broad-spectrum sunscreen protects against both UVA and UVB radiation.** *Why is it important to protect against both forms of ultraviolet radiation?*

hot link

hepatitis B and **hepatitis C** For more information on these communicable diseases, see Chapter 24, page 638.
HIV For more information on HIV and other sexually transmitted diseases, see Chapter 25, page 646.

Explaining

Emphasize that UV rays affect all kinds and shades of skin. All individuals need to protect themselves from the sun. 🔟

Discussing

Ask the class to identify sporting activities during which it is especially important to protect skin from the harmful effects of the sun. Be sure they include sports that take place in or on water, and those that take place on snow. 🔟

Critical Thinking

Ask students how they would respond to a teen who says: "I'm already 17 years old, and I've spent every day of every summer out in the sun. The damage has already been done—there's no point in starting to protect my skin from the sun now." 🔟

Discussing

Have students consider the long-term consequences of having a tattoo. Ask: Will you be proud of that tattoo years from now? How could it work against you when you look for a job? Also explain that it's expensive to get rid of a tattoo. A $50 tattoo can cost $1000 to remove.

Dealing with Sensitive Issues

Teens and Acne Although nearly all teens are affected by acne to some degree, certain students may feel especially self-conscious about this skin problem.

A teen's perception of his or her acne condition, even if an objective observer sees "just a mild case," can lead to withdrawal from social contacts, anger, loneliness, confusion, and depression.

As with other sensitive issues, it is best to keep class and group discussions of acne quite general and avoid singling out students.

Critical Thinking

Tell students that, in many American communities, ear piercing is accepted and even common for females; but other forms of piercing may be less acceptable, at least to most adults. Ask: What do you think accounts for these different attitudes? How do you think most adults' disapproval of certain kinds of piercing might affect teens' attitudes toward those same types of piercing? How might chances for parental approval, dating, scholarships, and employment be affected? **L1**

Activity

Many communities offer tattoo-removal services for young adults who are trying to find employment. Invite a group of volunteers research such programs in your area: Is there a tattoo-removal program? If so, who offers it? How is it done? What does it cost? If not, is there an interest or need? Have these volunteers share their findings with the rest of the class. **L3**

FYI

The National Institutes of Health report that about 85 percent of 12 to 24 year olds develop acne.

Did You Know?

➤ Acne is often blamed on intake of greasy foods or chocolate, but according to researchers at the National Institutes of Health, foods have little to do with the cause of acne for most people.

• Doctors believe hormonal changes during puberty may be an important factor in the development of acne.

• Dermatologists specialize in skin problems and treat severe cases of acne. They may recommend over-the-counter medicines, prescription medicines, and sometimes antibiotics to treat moderate to severe acne problems.

hotlink

skin cancer For more information on skin cancer, see Chapter 26, page 683.

Skin Problems

Many problems of the skin are not life threatening. They can, however, affect a person's self-image. Some common skin problems include:

▶ **Acne,** a common skin problem among teens, is caused when pores in the skin get clogged and the sebum produced by sebaceous glands cannot reach the skin's surface. One type of bacteria normally found on the skin thrives in the trapped sebum. The surrounding area becomes inflamed, and pus may form. Washing your face gently twice a day, applying over-the-counter treatment creams, and avoiding the use of oily products can help control breakouts. Touching and picking at acne only aggravates the condition and may cause scarring.

▶ **Warts** are caused by a virus that infects the surface layers of the skin. They are usually noncancerous growths that can appear anywhere on the body, but they are most commonly found on the hands, feet, and face. The virus that causes warts can be acquired through contact with infected skin.

▶ **Vitiligo** is a skin condition in which patches of skin have lost all pigment. For reasons not yet known, the melanin-producing cells in the affected areas of the skin are destroyed. With no melanin, these patches of skin are extremely susceptible to burning when exposed to UV light. Sunscreen should be applied or protective clothing should be worn over these areas to avoid severe sunburn. Although treatments involving repigmentation are available, there is no known cure for vitiligo.

▶ **Boils** form when hair follicles become infected with bacteria that are normally found on the surface of the skin. The tissues around a boil become inflamed, and pus forms. Treatment can include draining the pus and taking a course of antibiotics. Some boils may heal without treatment. Never squeeze or burst a boil because this can spread the infection. Keeping skin clean can help prevent boils.

▶ **Moles** are spots that contain extra melanin. They can appear anywhere on the body; most moles are harmless. Certain types of moles may develop into **melanoma**, *the most serious form of skin cancer,* which can be deadly. Early detection and treatment are critical to controlling the spread of **skin cancer** throughout the body. Monitoring the appearance of moles, as described in **Figure 14.2,** and reporting any changes to a dermatologist are essential to the early detection of melanoma.

More About...

Skin Cancers The National Cancer Institute reports that nearly half of all Americans who live to the age of 65 experience at least one case of skin cancer. The most common form of skin cancer is basal cell carcinoma. This cancer grows slowly and very rarely spreads to other parts of the body.

Basal cell carcinoma can cause a lot of damage to the skin — often leading to disfigurement and the need for surgery. This distinguishes it from melanoma, the most dangerous and fastest spreading skin cancer. With all forms of cancer, early detection provides the best opportunity to avoid spreading.

FIGURE 14.2

THE ABCDs OF MELANOMA

Regularly checking the appearance of your moles is important for the early detection of melanoma.

A = **Asymmetry**
An imaginary line drawn through the center of the mole does not produce matching halves.

B = **Border irregularity**
Noncancerous moles have smooth edges. Suspect moles often have irregular edges.

C = **Color**
Look for moles that are intensely black, possibly with a bluish tint, or that have an uneven color.

D = **Diameter**
Check for moles that are wider across than a pea.

Your Hair

Except for the palms of your hand and the soles of your feet, you have hair on almost every skin surface. You have between 100,000 to 200,000 hairs on your head alone! Although hair itself is composed of dead cells that contain keratin, living cells in the epidermis make new hairs and cause hair growth. A **hair follicle** is *a structure that surrounds the root of a hair.* Hair helps protect the skin, especially the scalp, from exposure to UV radiation. The eyes are protected from dust or other particles by the eyebrows and eyelashes. Hair also reduces the amount of heat lost through the skin of the scalp.

The foundation of healthy hair is a well-balanced diet. Hair can become thin and dry without proper nutrients. Regular shampooing is a must to keep your hair healthy. Daily brushing keeps dirt from building up and helps distribute the natural hair oils evenly. Limit the use of treatments such as permanents, dyes, or bleach. Overexposure to these harsh chemicals can cause hair to become dry and brittle.

Hair Problems

Normally, oil produced by sebaceous glands protects the skin from drying out and keeps hair soft and shiny. **Dandruff** is *a condition that can occur if the scalp becomes too dry and dead skin cells are shed as sticky, white*

Ⓨ **Give your hair daily attention to keep it clean and healthy.** *How do you choose hair care products that are right for your hair?*

Cooperative Learning

Divide the class into five groups, and assign each group one of the following common skin problems: acne, moles, warts, vitiligo, or boils. Ask the members of each group to read and discuss the information about their assigned skin problem. Then let them present that information to the rest of the class. [L2]

Activity

Ask interested students to use library and/or online resources to learn about the structure of a healthy strand of hair. Have them draw and label a large picture, and let them show their picture to the rest of the class. [L2] **Visual/Spatial**

Cooperative Learning

Divide the class into three groups, and assign each group one kind of product: acne skin cleansers, dandruff treatments, or shampoos for controlling head lice. Let group members work together to compare at least three different brands of their assigned product, noting differences in price, ingredients, and advertising claims. Have each group draw and label a graph to summarize its findings. [L2]

VISUAL LEARNING

Figure 14.2 Have volunteers describe the four pictured moles and read the labels that go with them. Help students discuss the importance of checking moles regularly.

Cooperative Learning Activity

Analyzing Ads Prepare by clipping ads from magazines or videotaping commercials ahead of time about various shampoos. In small groups, have students examine the shampoo ads. Discuss techniques used to sell the products. For example, which of the shampoo ads use testimonials? Trendy or popular images? Celebrity endorsements?

Have group members compare the claims in their ads with the ratings for each product in a publication, such as *Consumer Reports*. Then have them compare the products that received high ratings with their actual cost. Encourage groups to share their findings.

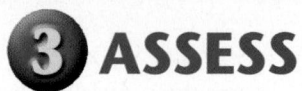

③ ASSESS

EVALUATING THE LESSON

Assign and discuss the Lesson 1 Review; then administer, grade, and discuss Lesson Quiz 50 in the TCR. 📁

RETEACHING

- Have students work with partners to draw and label concept maps that show ways to care for the skin, hair, and nails.

- Ask students to complete Reteaching Activity 50 in the TCR. 📁

ENRICHMENT

Ask students to research careers that involve care of the skin, hair, or nails. Have them consider the following: What education and training are needed? What is the outlook for employment? What does an average working day involve? What salary can be expected? What would be the advantages—and disadvantages of this job for me?

④ CLOSE

Have each student identify, either orally or in writing, one habit he or she plans to develop to protect the health of their skin, hair, or nails.

Keeping nails neatly clipped and filed improves your overall appearance. *List three other grooming habits that contribute to a healthy appearance.*

flakes. Dandruff can usually be treated by washing hair with an over-the-counter dandruff shampoo. If itching or scaling persists, consult a health care professional.

Head lice are tiny parasitic insects that live in the scalp hair of humans. They feed on blood by biting through the skin of the scalp. Lice are transmitted mainly by head-to-head contact and can infect anyone. They can also be acquired by using objects such as combs or hats that have been used by an infected person. These insects can be eliminated by washing hair with a medicated shampoo that kills the organisms. Washing sheets, pillowcases, combs, and hats in hot water with soap can help prevent the spread of head lice or a repeat infection.

Your Nails

Your fingernails and toenails are made of closely packed dead cells that contain keratin. Nails function to protect and support the tissues of the fingers and toes. Keeping your nails healthy should be part of your daily routine. Good care includes keeping nails clean and evenly trimmed. Use a nail file to shape and smooth nails, and keep cuticles pushed back. Trim toenails straight across and just slightly above skin level to reduce the risk of infection and ingrown nails.

▶ Lesson 1 *Review*

Reviewing Facts and Vocabulary

1. Define the terms *epidermis* and *dermis*.
2. Why is early detection of skin cancer important to your overall health?
3. What is a *hair follicle*?

Thinking Critically

4. **Applying.** Consider your daily activities in the sun. Compose a list of ways you can protect your skin from the sun for each activity.
5. **Synthesizing.** Explain how your overall appearance makes a statement about how you care for your skin, hair, and nails.

Applying Health Skills

Decision Making. With a partner, role-play deciding whether to get a tattoo. Include the steps of the decision-making model in a discussion on why someone might want a tattoo and discuss the consequences to physical health. Include some dialogue on tattoo removal.

TECHNOLOGY *OPTION*

INTERNET RESOURCES Find information about the complexities of tattoo removal in Health Updates at **health.glencoe.com**.

▶ Lesson 1 *Review*

Answers to Reviewing Facts and Vocabulary

1. Epidermis: the outer, thinner layer of skin, composed of living and dead cells. Dermis: the thicker layer of skin beneath the epidermis, made up of connective tissue and containing blood vessels and nerves.
2. Reduces risk of the cancer spreading.

3. The structure surrounding the hair root.

Answers to Thinking Critically

4. Answers may include sunscreen; avoiding intense sunlight; and wearing tight-knit clothes, a hat, and sunglasses.
5. Your overall appearance indicates whether you take the time to care for yourself.

Care of Teeth and Mouth

VOCABULARY
- periodontium
- pulp
- plaque
- periodontal disease
- tartar

YOU'LL LEARN TO
- Identify the parts of a tooth.
- Examine the effects of health behaviors on prevention of diseases of the teeth and mouth.
- Relate the importance of early detection and warning signs that prompt individuals to seek dental care.

QUICK START On a sheet of paper, make a list of ways to keep your teeth healthy. Circle the behaviors you do regularly. Put a star next to the ones you would like to improve.

M aintaining healthy teeth is important not only for your appearance but also for your overall health. Your teeth allow you to chew foods properly and help form the shape and structure of your mouth. In this lesson you will learn about the structure and function of the teeth and how to prevent tooth decay.

Your Teeth

Y ou may remember losing your teeth when you were younger, only to have new, permanent teeth grow in their place. Although your permanent teeth have different shapes, depending on their exact role in chewing food, they all have the same structure.

Parts of a Tooth

The **periodontium** (per-ee-oh-DAHN-tee-uhm) is *the area imme- diately around the teeth*. It is made up of the gums, periodontal ligament, and the jawbone. The structures of the periodontium support the teeth and hold them in place.

A tooth itself is made up of three main parts: the crown, the neck, and the root, as shown in **Figure 14.3.** The crown is the visible portion of the tooth. It is covered with enamel, a hard substance made of calcium that protects the teeth.

Healthy teeth are a result of good oral hygiene. *Explain why it is important to brush and floss after meals.*

Lesson 2 Care of Teeth and Mouth **367**

Lesson 2

Care of Teeth and Mouth

1 FOCUS

QUICK START Give students three or four minutes to write and mark their lists. Then have stu- dents meet in small groups to share and compare their responses.

TYING TO PRIOR KNOWLEDGE

Let volunteers share a few familiar facts about teeth and tooth care. Then tell students they will learn more about this topic as they study Lesson 2.

Health Skills Features

"Examining Product Claims," p. 369

ACCESSING INFORMATION

INTRODUCING VOCABULARY

- Ask students to sort the vocabulary terms into two groups— parts of the mouth and problems within the mouth. Remind students to use the Glossary to check the correct meanings of the terms if necessary.

- Ask students to complete the Chapter 14 Study Guide in the *Student Activity Workbook.*

Lesson 2 Resources

Teacher Classroom Resources
- Concept Mapping Activity 51
- Guided Reading Activities 51
- Lesson Plan 51
- Lesson Quiz 51
- Reteaching Activity 51

Student Activity Workbook
- Applying Health Skills 51
- Chapter 14 Study Guide

Multimedia
- Transparency 41

❷ TEACH

Reinforcing Concepts

Ask how many students have had the noncommunicable disease tooth decay. Help students compare the percentage in their class with the national average of 80 percent. **L1**

Activity

Ask a small group of students to find out about the removal of wisdom teeth. Why do some teens need to have their wisdom teeth removed? What is the usual procedure? What are impacted wisdom teeth? How are they removed? Let these students discuss their findings with the rest of the class. **L2**

VISUAL LEARNING

Figure 14.3 Have groups of students work together to examine and discuss the diagram in Figure 14.3. Ask group members to take turns reading the labels and describing the parts.

✓ Health Minute

Guide students in reading and discussing the suggestions for proper brushing and flossing. Then ask volunteers to mime (without props) correct brushing and flossing techniques. To encourage students to brush longer, try playing a radio in the background, and have students "brush" through the length of one song.

✓ Health Minute

Brushing and Flossing

Removing plaque from teeth requires two minutes of proper brushing followed by flossing.

Effective brushing and flossing:

► Hold the bristle tips at a 45-degree angle against the gumline.

► Brush back and forth in short strokes. Use a gentle, scrubbing motion.

► Brush the outer surfaces of each tooth, the inner surfaces, and then the chewing surfaces.

► To clean the inside surfaces of the front teeth, tilt the brush vertically and make up-and-down strokes.

► Floss not only between the surface of each tooth but also beneath the gum line.

Beneath the enamel is dentin, a layer of connective tissue that contributes to the shape and hardness of a tooth and acts as a barrier to protect the pulp. The **pulp** is *the tissue that contains the blood vessels and nerves of a tooth.* Pulp extends into the root canal and provides nourishment to the tooth.

Healthy Teeth and Mouth

Thorough, regular oral hygiene is necessary for healthy, clean teeth. One of the main threats to the health of your teeth is the bacteria that inhabit your mouth and live on the sugar found in foods you eat.

Plaque is *a sticky, colorless film that acts on sugar to form acids that destroy tooth enamel and irritate gums.* As plaque coats a tooth, it prevents your saliva, which has substances that protect teeth from bacteria, from reaching the tooth surface. In areas where plaque accumulates, bacteria thrive and the acids from the bacteria break down enamel. If the breakdown of enamel continues, a hole, or cavity, is formed in a tooth. The tooth can continue to decay to the pulp and may have to be removed if left untreated.

Tooth decay and other diseases can be easily prevented by practicing good oral hygiene. Brushing teeth after eating removes plaque from the surface of the teeth, before bacteria can produce the acid that harms teeth. Flossing between teeth removes plaque in areas that cannot be reached with the bristles of a toothbrush.

FIGURE 14.3

CROSS-SECTION OF A TOOTH

A protective layer of enamel covers the crown of a tooth. Inside the tooth, blood vessels supply the living tissue with oxygen and nutrients.

enamel
dentin
pulp cavity with nerves and vessels
gum
gingiva
cementum
periodontal ligaments
periodontal membrane
root canal
bone

Crown
Neck
Root

368 Chapter 14 Personal Care and Healthy Behavior

〜〜 HEALTH LITERACY 〜〜

Consumer Health Some toothpastes and mouthwashes contain additives that claim to fight dental disease. Fluoride, for example, is reported to make teeth more resistant to cavity-causing acids. Other substances, such as sanguinaria extract, inhibit plaque formation. Encourage students to examine ads for toothpastes and mouthwashes and to read the labels of various brands in stores. Have them list substances represented as "cavity fighters" or "plaque inhibitors" and note which brands are supported by the American Dental Association (ADA). Suggest that students also research the negative effects of such substances, and decide whether they want to use dental products containing these ingredients.

Real-Life Application

Examining Product Claims

Tooth whitening products work either by removing surface stains or by bleaching the natural tooth color. The FDA does not regulate these products, but the American Dental Association (ADA) approves products that meet certain standards for safety and effectiveness.

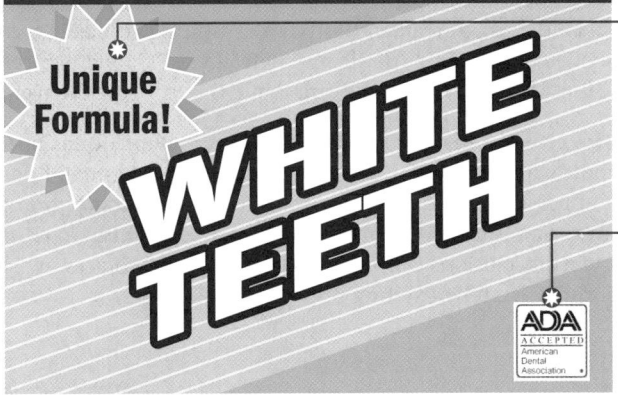

Whiter Teeth in just 24 Hours! ✳

Unique Formula! ✳

WHITE TEETH

Manufacturers may make exaggerated or misleading claims about a product or fail to explain the way the product works.

Some products use peroxide-based whiteners, others contain mild abrasives and polishing agents. Gum irritation, tooth sensitivity, and possible tooth damage can occur if products are not used correctly.

Although there are many products available, only those bearing the ADA seal are considered safe. Patients are encouraged to consult a dentist for the most appropriate whitening treatment.

ACTIVITY

Identify at least two types of over-the-counter tooth whitening products. Compare marketing claims with facts from the American Dental Association. How can you determine which products are safe and which ones may cause damaging side effects? Report your findings to the class. Cite your sources and explain how you know that they are reliable.

Regular visits to a dental care professional are the next most important part of maintaining dental health. These professionals will clean your teeth and examine them for signs of decay. Dentists may treat children's teeth with sealants to prevent tooth decay.

Following a well-balanced diet that includes foods containing phosphorus, calcium, and vitamin C helps keep your teeth strong and your gums healthy. Reducing the number of sugary snacks eaten between meals also helps protect your teeth from decay. Avoid all tobacco products. These items stain teeth and cause gums to recede. They also increase the risk of oral cancer.

Lesson 2 Care of Teeth and Mouth **369**

Cooperative Learning Activity

Evaluating Tooth-Care Products Have groups of students work together to learn about the quality and prices of various brands of toothbrushes. Group members should begin by reading evaluations of toothbrushes in publications such as *Consumer Reports*. Encourage representatives of each group to contact local dentists and ask for information about recommended toothbrush shape, bristles, and so on. Have students discuss: Do the dentists agree on all points? Are the dentists' recommendations in line with consumer publications? Based on their findings, which kind of toothbrush would students purchase? Why?

Real-Life Application

EXAMINING PRODUCT CLAIMS

ACCESSING INFORMATION

NHES Standard 2 Students will demonstrate the ability to access valid health information and health-promoting products and services.

Objectives

- Analyze the health messages delivered through media.
- Demonstrate the ability to evaluate resources from home, school, and community that provide valid health information.

Motivator

Display several ads from magazines for different whitening agents. Ask students to explain which of the claims they most believe and why.

Teaching Strategies

1. Have students work in small groups to apply evaluation criteria to their chosen products.

2. Tell students to identify any unfamiliar ingredients and research negative health effects.

✓Assessment

Using a rubric, student work should provide comprehensive evidence of the following criteria to achieve the highest score:

✔ citation of specific sources
✔ evaluation of the validity of the source
✔ rationale for the appropriateness of the source
✔ identification of type of help available from the sources

Reinforcing Concepts

Have volunteers sketch pictures that show malocclusions on the board. Help students discuss the dental problems that might result.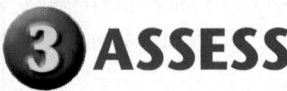

③ ASSESS

EVALUATING THE LESSON

Assign and discuss the Lesson 2 Review; then administer, grade, and discuss Lesson Quiz 51 in the TCR. 📁

RETEACHING

- Have students work together to make one poster showing the progression of periodontal disease and another showing the steps necessary to prevent it.

- Ask students to complete Reteaching Activity 51 in the TCR. 📁

ENRICHMENT

Have interested students interview a local dentist about the most common dental problems he or she sees in teen patients: What are the primary causes of these problems? How might they be prevented? How can they be treated once they occur? Have these students summarize their findings and share them with the rest of the class.

④ CLOSE

Have students write private health journal entries describing the health of their own teeth and identifying any changes they plan to make in caring for their teeth and mouth.

Did You Know ?

Fluoride has been found to be an effective way to reduce tooth decay. Fluoride can be applied to teeth in several ways.

- Many communities add fluoride to water supplies.
- Brushing twice a day with a fluoride toothpaste applies fluoride directly to the teeth.
- Fluoride treatments can be applied directly to teeth in a dental office or be prescribed for home use.

Problems of the Teeth and Mouth

Many oral problems are caused by poor hygiene. Others result from poorly aligned teeth.

▶ **Halitosis,** or bad breath, can be caused by eating certain foods, poor oral hygiene, smoking, bacteria on the tongue, decayed teeth, or gum disease. If halitosis is caused by tooth decay or disease, treatment by a dental professional is needed.

▶ **Periodontal disease**, *an inflammation of the periodontal structures*, is caused by bacterial infection. Often called gum disease, periodontal disease begins with the buildup of plaque. *The hard, crustlike substance formed when plaque hardens is* **tartar**. Plaque and tartar cause the gums to become irritated and swollen. In this early stage, called gingivitis, the disease is reversible through regular, thorough brushing and flossing. Early detection is important since, left untreated, periodontal disease can destroy the bone and tissue that support the teeth.

▶ **Malocclusion** means "bad bite." Sources of a malocclusion include extra teeth, crowded teeth, and the misalignment of the upper and lower jaws. Malocclusion can lead to decay and disease, and it can affect a person's speech and ability to chew. Some malocclusions can be corrected by wearing braces, which reposition teeth by exerting pressure on them.

▶ Lesson 2 Review

Reviewing Facts and Vocabulary

1. Define the terms *periodontium* and *pulp*.
2. How does plaque affect the teeth?
3. Examine the effects of health behaviors and list three health behaviors that help prevent tooth decay and periodontal disease.

Thinking Critically

4. **Evaluating.** How can early detection of gum disease affect your long-term health?
5. **Synthesizing.** How might you be able to distinguish between a person who practices good oral hygiene and one who does not?

Applying Health Skills

Accessing Information. Research library or Internet resources to learn more about how braces can help a person with misalignment of the jaw or malocclusion. Collect brochures to share with the class.

INTERNET RESOURCES Use Web Links at health.glencoe.com to get more information on how braces work and options for teens who wear braces.

▶ Lesson 2 Review

Answers to Reviewing Facts and Vocabulary

1. Periodontium—the area immediately around the teeth. Pulp—the tissue that contains the blood vessels and nerves of a tooth.
2. Plaque coats the teeth, making it difficult for saliva to protect against bacteria.
3. Any three: brushing and flossing, going to dentist twice a year, reducing sugary snacks, using fluoride toothpaste or mouth rinse, avoiding tobacco.

Answers to Thinking Critically

4. Could help prevent infection, extensive damage to gums, and losing one's teeth.
5. A person who practices poor oral hygiene has decay, receding gums, bad breath.

Eye Care

VOCABULARY

lacrimal gland
sclera
cornea
choroid
retina

YOU'LL LEARN TO

- Identify the parts of the eye.
- Understand how the eye forms visual images.
- Examine the effects of health behaviors on the eye.
- Describe different types of eye problems.

QUICK START Make a list of activities during which some type of eye protection should be worn. Consider both recreational and sport activities, such as playing hockey, and tasks such as mowing the lawn.

M ore than 70 percent of the sensory informa-tion your brain receives comes to it by way of your eyes. The function of the eye is to gather light. The images formed in the eye are sent to the brain, which interprets those images. The amount of light that enters the eye is controlled by the size of the pupil. When light hits the retina, light-sensitive cells are stimulated and an image is formed.

Like the click of a camera lens, in the blink of an eye, images are formed in the process of vision. *What structures help protect the eye?*

Your Eyes

Y our eyes sit in bony sockets, called orbits, in the front of your skull. A layer of fat surrounds each eyeball and cushions it inside its socket. The eyebrows, eyelashes, and eyelids protect the eyes from foreign particles and bright light. Each eye has a group of structures that make and allow drainage of tears. One of these structures is the **lacrimal gland**, *the gland that secretes tears into ducts that empty into the eye.* As you blink, tears are moved across the surface of the eye. On average, most humans blink about 6,205,000 times a year! Tears keep the surface of the eyeball moist and clear of foreign particles. Tears consist of water, salts, and mucus that protect the eye against infection.

Lesson 3 Eye Care **371**

Lesson 3

Eye Care

1 FOCUS

QUICK START Have a volunteer read the Quick Start assignment aloud, and have students jot down their lists. Then guide students in discussing their responses and identifying effective eye protec-tion for each example.

TYING TO PRIOR KNOWLEDGE

Refer to the Quick Start discus-sion, and point out that students already know several ways to care for their eyes. They will learn more about eye care as they read this lesson.

INTRODUCING VOCABULARY

- Have students meet in groups of five. Have each group member look up one of the vocabulary terms in the Glossary and then explain it to the rest of the group.

- Ask students to complete the Chapter 14 Study Guide in the *Student Activity Workbook.*

Lesson 3 *Resources*

Teacher Classroom Resources

- Concept Mapping Activity 52
- Guided Reading Activities 52
- Lesson Plan 52
- Lesson Quiz 52
- Reteaching Activity 52

Student Activity Workbook

- Applying Health Skills 52
- Chapter 14 Study Guide

Multimedia

- Transparency 42

2 TEACH

Discussing

Ask students who are familiar with photography to explain specific similarities between the functioning of a camera and the functioning of the eye. **L1**

Reinforcing Concepts

As students read about the parts of the eye, ask: When people ask about eye color, which part of the eye are they talking about? iris **L1**

VISUAL LEARNING

Figure 14.4 Have students work with partners to study the diagram and read all the labels. Then have the partners list and describe the structures shown in the figure. ◀▢▶

Activity

Use this experiment to help students determine whether they are right- or left-eye dominant. Give the following directions:

1. Point your index finger up, and hold it out in front of you.

2. Line it up with an object across the room.

3. Close your left eye. Now, open your left eye and close your right. Notice when your finger appears to jump to the side. If your finger stays lined up with the object when your right eye is open, you are right-eye dominant. If it stays lined up when your left eye is open, you are left-eye dominant.

FIGURE **14.4**

THE EYE

The optic nerve connects the eye with the brain to produce images.

sclera, choroid, vitreous humor, optic nerve, retina, cornea, iris, pupil, lens, aqueous humor

Parts of the Eye

The eye is made up of two main parts, shown in **Figure 14.4,** the optic nerve and three layers of the eyeball wall.

▶ The outermost layer of the eye is made up of the sclera and the cornea. The **sclera** (SKLEHR-uh), *the tough, white part of the eye,* is composed of tough, fibrous tissue that protects the inner layers of the eye and supports and shapes the eyeball. At the front of the eye is the cornea. The **cornea** is *a transparent tissue that bends and focuses light before it enters the lens.*

▶ Within the middle layer of the eyewall is the **choroid,** (KOHR-oid), *a thin structure that lines the inside of the sclera.* Also within the middle layer of the eye is the iris, the colored portion of the eye that contains the pupil. The pupil is the hole through which light reaches the inner eye. The muscles of the iris control the size of the pupil. In bright light the pupil constricts; in dim light it enlarges to let in more light.

▶ The **retina** is *the light-sensitive membrane on which images are cast by the cornea.* The light-sensitive cells in the retina are called rods and cones, each named for its basic shape. Rods are very sensitive to light and allow us to see in dim light. Cones function in bright light and allow us to see color. When light stimulates these cells, a nerve impulse travels to the brain via the optic nerve, which is located at the back of the eye.

More About...

Sunglasses Unfortunately, many sunglasses available for sale do not carry labels that indicate whether they are safe for exposure to UV radiation. These rays can damage the eyes if they are not protected by sunglasses that block or absorb the full range of UV-B and UV-A. Because sunglasses darken the eye area, the pupils dilate, allowing for more absorption of UV light.

Sunglasses with UV protection should be worn in bright sunlight to prevent radiation damage and future incidence of cataracts. While prescription sunglasses provide the necessary lenses to block or absorb UV radiation, it can be difficult to determine which nonprescription sunglasses have adequate UV protection.

Behind the iris and the pupil is the lens of the eye. Like the cornea, the lens is transparent and functions to refine the focus of images on the retina. The area between the cornea and the lens is filled with a watery fluid called *aqueous humor*. Aqueous humor provides nutrients to the structures of the eye. Between the lens and retina is a cavity that is filled with a gelatin-like substance called *vitreous humor*. Vitreous humor helps the eyeball stay firm.

Vision

Image formation begins as light passes through the cornea, pupil, and lens and reaches the retina. Light rays are first focused by the curved cornea, and then the focus is refined by the lens. Muscles attached to the lens contract or relax to change its shape. The lens becomes more curved to focus the eye on a near object; it becomes flatter to focus the eye on a distant object. Light stimulates rods and cones in the retina, and a **nerve impulse** is transmitted to the brain through the optic nerve. In humans both eyes focus on the same set of objects. This allows our brains to interpret depth and judge distances.

If your vision is normal, a sharp image will be produced on the retina. The sharpness of vision can be measured by reading an eye chart. If you have 20/20 vision, you can stand 20 feet away from an eye chart and read the top eight lines. If you have 20/60 vision, you can see the chart from 20 feet the way a person with normal vision would see it from 60 feet. In other words, a person with 20/60 vision is "nearsighted." Reading an eye chart measures only one aspect of vision. Other components of vision include eye coordination, peripheral or side vision, and depth perception.

Healthy Eyes

There are several health behaviors you can practice every day to help keep your eyes healthy.

▶ **Follow a well-balanced diet.** Include foods that contain vitamin A. Deficiency in vitamin A could result in night blindness, reducing a person's ability to see well in dim light.

▶ **Protect your eyes.** Wear safety goggles or a mask when participating in activities in which the eye could be damaged. Keep dirty hands or other objects away from your eyes to reduce the risk of eye infections and injury. Wear sunglasses that block UV light, and never look directly into the sun or bright lights.

▶ **Have regular eye exams.** Routine eye exams allow certain eye diseases to be detected and treated in their early stages.

Experience a virtual view of the makeup of the eye in Web Links at health.glencoe.com.

hotlink

nerve impulse For more information on nerve impulses and the nervous system, see Chapter 15, page 400.

Having vision problems diagnosed and treated reduces the risk of future eye problems. *What are some signs that you may need corrective lenses?*

Lesson 3 Eye Care **373**

Discussing

Have students share and discuss their own experiences with eye charts and other vision tests. Ⓛ1

Explaining

Remind students that vitamin A is also important for keeping skin healthy. Have students recall foods that are rich in vitamin A. milk, green and yellow vegetables, liver

Activity

Ask a group of volunteers to collect different kinds of protective eyewear appropriate for various sports, hobbies, and work activities. Have these volunteers show the eyewear to the rest of the class, explaining when and how each should be worn. Ⓛ2

Discussing

Guide students in discussing specific vision problems. Let volunteers identify and describe their own vision problems—myopia, hyperopia, astigmatism, or strabismus. How was the problem identified? How is it being corrected? Ⓛ1

HEALTH Online

Encourage students to "tour" the eye online. Have students describe what they see. Ask: How does this virtual view add to your understanding of the eye?

Meeting Individual Needs

Diabetics Diabetic retinopathy is a condition that damages the small blood vessels nourishing the retina; it occurs as a result of the inadequate or faulty insulin production caused by diabetes.

It is essential for anyone with diabetes to pay attention to the following warning signs: loss, distortion, or dimness of vision; pain in or around the eyes; excessive tearing or discharge from the eye; swelling of the eyelids or protrusion of the eye; double vision; flashes of light, halos around lights, or floating spots; a sudden crossing or deviation of one eye; a change in color of an eye.

Activity

Have students create a book for elementary-school children that teaches them how to protect and care for their eyes. Suggest that they sketch out illustrations and outline the text beforehand. Remind them to use examples that will appeal to their target audience. Have students proofread their work for spelling and grammatical errors. Then have them staple the pages together to form a book.

Explaining

Tell students that Laser-Assisted *In Situ* Keratomileusis (LASIK) is an increasingly popular surgical procedure that uses the excimer laser, a cold beam of ultraviolet light that destroys problem cells on the cornea, to improve vision. LASIK has been performed in the United States since 1995 and is considered safe and effective. The procedure takes just minutes and the patient remains awake. LASIK is generally not considered appropriate for people whose vision is still changing—and is therefore not recommended for children and teens.

Cross-Curriculum Connections

Science Explain to students that as often as five times a year, the moon passes between the sun and the earth, causing a solar eclipse. If you want to observe a solar eclipse, you must protect your eyes. Regular glasses do not provide enough protection. You need a special solar light filter. Have students use online sources to find out more about these special filters and tell them to be prepared for the next eclipse.

374

▶ **Rest your eyes regularly.** Take regular breaks while working on the computer or when reading. Looking up and away from close work every 10 minutes or so reduces eyestrain.

Eye Problems

Eye problems can occur, despite good health practices. These problems can be classified as vision problems and diseases of the eye.

Vision Problems

Two common vision problems reflect the inability of the eye to properly focus light on the retina. *Myopia*, or nearsightedness, results in a person not being able to see distant objects clearly. For a person diagnosed with *hyperopia*, or farsightedness, distant objects can be seen clearly; however, near objects appear blurry. These conditions can be corrected with glasses or contact lenses. In recent years, laser surgery has become an option for correcting vision problems. In this procedure, a laser is used to reshape the cornea in order to change its focusing power. Other vision problems include:

▶ **Astigmatism.** Because of an irregularly curved cornea or lens, the eye is not able to focus properly, resulting in images that appear blurry. This condition can usually be corrected with glasses, contact lenses, or laser surgery.

▶ **Strabismus.** If the muscles of the eyes are weak or don't function properly, strabismus may result. One or both eyes may appear to be off-center, turned inward, or turned outward. Treatment includes corrective lenses, vision therapy, and surgery.

Diseases of the Eye

Diseases of the eye range from easily treated infections such as sties and pinkeye to conditions that can threaten sight. A sty is an inflamed swelling of a sebaceous gland near the eyelash. *Conjunctivitis*, also known as pinkeye, is an inflammation of the conjunctiva, a thin membrane that covers the sclera lining of the eyelids.

A serious threat to vision results from a detached retina. This occurs if a portion of the retina is separated from the choroid as a result of natural aging or from an injury. Warning signs include blurred vision or seeing bright flashes of light. Treatment includes using a laser to repair a tear or surgery to reattach the retina. Three other serious eye diseases are described on the next page.

Did You Know

▶ The titles referring to people who work with eyes are very similar:

• **optician**—technician who provides technical and patient services
• **optometrist**—doctor of optometry (OD) who examines, diagnoses, treats, and manages diseases and disorders of the visual system
• **ophthalmologist**—medical doctor who specializes in the medical and surgical care of the eyes and visual system

More About...

Eye Care Pinkeye, or conjunctivitis, may result from allergic reactions, from exposure to cosmetics or chlorinated water, or from a bacterial infection or virus. If students get pinkeye, they should follow these steps:

• Avoid touching the eye. Use tissues when wiping away secretions.
• Avoid wearing eye makeup and contact lenses until the condition clears up.

• Avoid using other people's washcloths and towels, and warn them not to use yours.
• *Do not* attend school during the contagious period.
• Use warm washcloth compresses on your eyes.
• If your eyes feel pain and/or are light sensitive, call your doctor. It may require a prescription drug.

▶ **Glaucoma.** The pressure inside the eye is normally maintained by the aqueous and vitreous humor. In glaucoma, abnormally high pressure leads to irreversible damage of the retina and the optic nerve and can result in loss of sight. Regular eye checkups can lead to early detection and treatment to control the condition.

▶ **Cataracts.** In this condition the normally transparent lens becomes cloudy. The formation of a cataract interferes with the lens' ability to focus light rays, making images appear blurry or vision seem foggy. Treatment of a cataract is typically the surgical removal of the old lens and replacement of it with a new, artificial lens.

▶ **Macular Degeneration.** This condition occurs when the light-sensing cells of the macula, the portion of the retina directly opposite the lens, begin to malfunction. Macular degeneration is the leading cause of vision loss for individuals over 60. There is no cure, and treatment is limited.

Ⓨ **This simple test is used to identify people with color blindness.** *What other types of vision problems can be identified through regular eye exams?*

Lesson 3 *Review*

Reviewing Facts and Vocabulary

1. List the structures that make up the three layers of the eyeball wall.
2. Give three examples of healthy behaviors you can practice to care for your eyes.
3. Explain the difference between myopia and hyperopia.

Thinking Critically

4. **Analyzing.** How might having night blindness affect a person's activities?
5. **Applying.** How could you demonstrate the effect of cataracts on vision?

Applying Health Skills

Accessing Information. Research programs such as Unite for Sight that provide vision screenings for young children. Find out why it's important to identify vision problems as early as possible. Make a pamphlet that can be used as a reference on the availability and costs of these community services.

TECHNOLOGY | **OPTION**

PRESENTATION SOFTWARE Using presentation software, you can include art and graphics to make an electronic slideshow. See **health.glencoe.com** for tips on how to use presentation software.

Lesson 3 Eye Care **375**

Lesson 3 *Review*

Answers to Reviewing Facts and Vocabulary

1. Outer: sclera and cornea. Middle: choroid, iris, pupil. Inner: retina.
2. Any three behaviors listed on page 373.
3. Myopia is nearsightedness; near objects are clear and distant objects are blurry. Hyperopia is farsightedness; near objects are blurry, distant objects are clear.

Answers to Thinking Critically

4. The person will not see well at night or in the dark; may not be able to drive at night or see well in a poorly lighted room.
5. Possible answers: looking through glass lenses coated with petroleum jelly, squinting to blur vision, looking though frosted glass.

③ ASSESS

EVALUATING THE LESSON

Assign and discuss the Lesson 3 Review; then administer, grade, and discuss Lesson Quiz 52 in the TCR. 📁

RETEACHING

- Have students sketch and label a simple drawing of the eye. Then have them list five things teens should do to care for their eyes.
- Ask students to complete Reteaching Activity 52 in the TCR. 📁

ENRICHMENT

Have students research, using online and/or library resources, the training and work of ophthalmologists, optometrists, and opticians. Ask them to summarize their findings by drawing Venn diagrams. Alternately, students may choose to write a short report. If so, remind them to proofread their work and develop several drafts. Encourage students to turn in a final error-free draft to share with the class.

④ CLOSE

Have students write private health journal entries describing the health of their own teeth and identifying any changes they plan to make in caring for their teeth and mouth.

Ears and Hearing Protection

1 FOCUS

QUICK START Have students work with partners to write their lists. Then have volunteers read their lists aloud, and help students discuss how important hearing is in their daily lives.

TYING TO PRIOR KNOWLEDGE

Remind students of the importance of their own hearing, and have volunteers identify a few healthy habits that help protect a person's ears and hearing. Then tell students that, as they read Lesson 4, they will learn more about these topics.

Health Skills Features

"Should Noise Levels at Concerts Be Controlled?" p. 378

INTRODUCING VOCABULARY

- Have a student look up in the dictionary and share with the class the derivation of the word *auditory*. It comes from the Latin word *audire*, to hear. Then have students identify other familiar words with the same root. *audition*, *audiovisual*, and *auditorium*

- Ask students to complete the Chapter 14 Study Guide in the *Student Activity Workbook*.

Lesson 4

Ears and Hearing Protection

VOCABULARY
external auditory canal
auditory ossicles
labyrinth
tinnitus

YOU'LL LEARN TO
- Identify the parts of the ear.
- Examine the effects of health behaviors on the ears and hearing.
- Describe some problems of the ear.

QUICK START List at least three situations you've experienced in the last week that involved exposure to loud noises that put your hearing at risk. Review your list, and then explain how you can protect your ears from the damaging effects of loud noise.

A health care professional will check your ears in a routine physical examination.

When you attend a sporting event, you can hear the crowd cheering, whistles blowing, athletes yelling, and music playing. All of these stimuli add to the excitement and perhaps to your enjoyment of the game. Your ears and brain, working together, allow you to hear and interpret sounds and form a response, such as turning your head when you hear a friend calling your name.

Parts of the Ear

The ear has three main sections, each with its own unique structures. The parts of the ear are shown in **Figure 14.5.**

▶ **The Outer Ear.** The outer ear begins with the visible part of the ear, the auricle. The auricle helps channel sound waves into the **external auditory canal**, *a passageway about one inch long that leads to the remaining portion of the outer ear, the eardrum.* The external auditory canal is lined with tiny hairs and glands that produce wax to protect the ear from dust and foreign objects. The eardrum, also called the *tympanic membrane*, is a thin membrane that acts as a barrier between the outer and middle ear.

Lesson 4 Resources

Teacher Classroom Resources
- 📁 Concept Mapping Activity 53
- 📁 Cross-Curriculum Activity 14
- 📁 Guided Reading Activities 53
- 📁 Health Lab 14
- 📁 Lesson Plan 53

- 📁 Lesson Quiz 53
- 📁 Reteaching Activity 53

Student Activity Workbook
- 📁 Applying Health Skills 53
- 📁 Chapter 14 Study Guide

Multimedia

- Transparency 43

FIGURE 14.5

INNER, MIDDLE, AND OUTER EAR

The ear has two functions: hearing and balance. Identify the parts of the ear involved in hearing.

▶ **The Middle Ear.** Directly behind the eardrum are the **auditory ossicles**, *three small bones linked together that connect the eardrum to the inner ear.* The auditory ossicles are the smallest bones in the body. The middle ear is connected to the throat by the eustachian tube. This tube allows pressure to be equalized on either side of the eardrum when you swallow or yawn.

▶ **The Inner Ear.** *The inner ear,* or **labyrinth**, consists of a network of curved and spiral passages with three main parts. The cochlea is the area of hearing in the inner ear. The vestibule and semicircular canals are where balance is controlled.

Hearing and Balance

When receptors in your inner ear are stimulated by a sound wave, a nerve impulse is sent to your brain. Your brain interprets the impulse as a sound. Sound waves enter the external auditory canal and cause the eardrum to vibrate. The vibrations cause fluid in the cochlea to move, which stimulates receptor cells to send a nerve impulse to the brain where sounds are interpreted. Receptor cells in the vestibule and the semicircular canals send messages to the brain about your sense of balance. Tiny hairs located in the crista sense movement and send nerve impulses to the brain. The brain then signals muscles to make adjustments to maintain balance.

How does the brain know where the source of a sound is located?
The ear that is closer to the sound hears it louder and a little sooner than the other ear. The brain picks out this difference and uses it to figure out where the sound is coming from. This is known as *binaural hearing.*

② TEACH

Reinforcing Concepts

Help students discuss the importance of hearing. Ask: How do sounds contribute to your appreciation and understanding? Which sounds do you most enjoy hearing? Why? **L1**

VISUAL LEARNING

Figure 14.5 Have students meet in cooperative groups to study and discuss the diagram in Figure 14.5. Have group members read and point to each of the labeled structures. Then have them work together to identify the parts that are involved in hearing.

Activity

Have interested volunteers research the relationship between motion sickness and the balance functions of the ears. Have these students summarize their findings for the rest of the class. **L2**

Before reading, have two volunteers stand on opposite sides of the room. Ask the rest of the students to close their eyes, and listen as one of the volunteers claps his or her hands. Help students recognize that they had no trouble identifying which of the two volunteers made the sound. Then have students read the Q & A explanation to understand how they could tell.

More About...

Acuity and Range of Human Hearing
When the energy of audible sound waves is compared with the energy of visible light waves, human hearing is about ten times more sensitive than human vision. In fact, if our hearing were much more acute, it would result in our experiencing a constant buzzing or hissing sensation.

Human ears can detect sound waves from 20–20,000 cycles per second (or hertz), which is a range of over ten octaves. Human voices range from 500–4,000 hertz; so it's not surprising that our greatest acuity falls within that range, occurring between 1,000–2,000 hertz.

Exploring Issues

SHOULD NOISE LEVELS AT CONCERTS BE CONTROLLED?

Direct students to read the feature. Point out that two common potential sources of excessive noise are the workplace and public events, such as sporting events and rock concerts. The Occupational Safety and Health Administration (OSHA) sets legal standards for noise in the workplace, but no federal laws exist regulating noise levels at concerts, which often exceed OSHA standards for the workplace. Have students discuss the role of legislation in other health and safety matters, such as requiring drivers to wear safety belts. Guide students to draw conclusions as they do the activities. Then have them share their responses in a classroom discussion.

Activity

Have students work with partners to make posters showing practices that help protect the health of ears. **ELL**

Reinforcing Concepts

Help students discuss the difference between conductive hearing loss and sensorineural hearing loss. Ask volunteers to give specific examples. **L1**

Activity

Have students do online or library research or conduct personal interviews to learn about the experiences of people who have tinnitus. **L2**

Exploring Issues

Should Noise Levels at Concerts Be Controlled?

A major concern at concerts is the risk of hearing loss from exposure to loud music. Although outdoor sound levels are monitored by law enforcement to prevent a public nuisance, indoor sound levels usually go unchecked. Should indoor sound levels at public events be regulated?

Viewpoint 1: Kyle T., 16

From what I've learned about hearing loss, I feel a limit on indoor noise at concerts should be set. It's impossible to talk to anyone with the music so loud. I have trouble hearing for hours afterward. I'd like to enjoy the music without worrying that my hearing might be permanently damaged. No wonder hearing loss among musicians is so high!

Viewpoint 2: Starr L., 16

I agree that loud noise can affect your hearing, but I think passing a law is extreme. Most hearing loss can be avoided if people use common sense. For example, you don't have to sit or dance right in front of the speakers. If it's really loud, I think dance organizers should make earplugs available. A lot of musicians and DJs wear earplugs, and they hear the music just fine.

ACTIVITIES

1. Do you think sound levels inside establishments should be monitored to protect against hearing loss? Why or why not?

2. Should earplugs be made available at indoor events? Would teens use them?

Healthy Ears

To keep your ears healthy, clean them regularly and always protect the outer ear from injury and extreme cold. Wear protective gear such as batting helmets when playing sports. A hat that covers both the auricles and the earlobes should be worn in cold weather. Keep foreign objects, including cotton-tipped swabs, out of the ear. Ear infections can damage ear structures and should be treated immediately by a health care professional. Have your ears examined and your hearing tested to detect any problems.

An important step you can take to protect your hearing is to avoid loud noise. Exposure to loud noise over time can lead to temporary, and sometimes permanent, hearing loss or **deafness.**

hotlink

deafness For more information on deafness, see Chapter 26, page 696.

Home and Community

The Hearing Impaired Encourage students to investigate how their community provides for individuals with impaired hearing. Are signers present to translate at town meetings? Are signers present at other community events? Do most public telephones have volume adjustments? How easy is it to contact community agencies through access operators for the hearing impaired? Have students write a letter to the editor of a local newspaper, commending community provisions for the hearing impaired or suggesting needed changes. Remind them to be aware of their reader by showing knowledge of the situation. Have students proofread for clarity and logic as well as for spelling and grammar.

Problems of the Ear

Hearing loss can be divided into two categories: conductive and sensorineural.

Conductive Hearing Loss

In conductive hearing loss, sound waves are not passed from the outer to the inner ear. Middle-ear infections may lead to rupture of the eardrum. Persistent buildup of fluid within the middle ear, often caused by infection, is most common in children.

Sensorineural Hearing Loss

Sensorineural hearing loss results from damage to the cochlea, the auditory nerve, or the brain. **Tinnitus** is *a condition in which a ringing, buzzing, whistling, roaring, hissing, or other sound is heard in the ear in the absence of external sound.* Tinnitus can occur as a result of natural aging, or health conditions such as high blood pressure, or overexposure to loud noise. To protect your ears from this condition, lower the volume of the source of the noise. Wear earplugs in noisy environments, when operating machinery, and at loud concerts or sporting events. Limit the length of time you are exposed to loud noise to reduce the chance of permanent damage.

CHARACTER CHECK

Consideration. Treating all people with consideration and respect is the first step toward forming a friendship with someone you have just met. These qualities are just as important when meeting and communicating with a person with a disability, such as hearing impairment. **Consider the difficulties a hearing impairment would cause. List suggestions for communicating with a hearing-impaired person in ways that would show consideration and respect.**

Lesson 4 *Review*

Reviewing Facts and Vocabulary

1. Identify the three main parts of the ear and the structures that can be found in each part.
2. Define the term *tinnitus*.
3. Examine the effects of health behaviors on hearing: What effect can loud noises have on hearing?

Thinking Critically

4. **Analyzing.** What activities might cause the inner ear to send mixed messages to the brain and result in dizziness and nausea?
5. **Synthesizing.** Under what circumstances might you need to protect yourself from sensorineural hearing loss? How might you do so?

Applying Health Skills

Advocacy. Work with classmates to create a campaign that raises awareness about hearing loss. Brainstorm ways teens can reduce exposure to damaging noise levels and protect their hearing. Use effective strategies to promote hearing protection.

TECHNOLOGY OPTION

WORD PROCESSING Use a word-processing program to record ideas and plan your campaign. See **health.glencoe.com** for tips on how to get the most out of your word-processing program.

Lesson 4 Ears and Hearing Protection **379**

CHARACTER CHECK

Consideration Have students meet in groups to read and discuss the information on respect. Then have group members work together to write their list of suggestions.

③ ASSESS

EVALUATING THE LESSON

Assign and discuss the Lesson 4 Review; then administer, grade, and discuss Lesson Quiz 53 in the TCR. 📁

RETEACHING

- Ask students to make a drawing of the ear and trace the path of sound through the ear.
- Ask students to complete Reteaching Activity 53 in the TCR. 📁

ENRICHMENT

Have students read about Gallaudet University in Washington, D.C., the nation's only institution of higher learning for the deaf. What resources does it offer its hearing-impaired students? Have students write about or discuss their findings and opinions.

④ CLOSE

Have students list five rules for ear care they are willing to follow for life.

Lesson 4 *Review*

Answers to Reviewing Facts and Vocabulary

1. Outer ear: auricle, external auditory canal, eardrum. Middle ear: auditory ossicles, oval window. Inner ear: cochlea, vestibule, semicircular canals.
2. See page 379 for definition.
3. Exposure to loud noises can result in hearing loss and tinnitus.

Answers to Thinking Critically

4. Possible answer: Activities that move the body side to side or up and down.
5. Possible answers: when listening to music through headphones, when at a live concert, when near loudspeakers. Reducing volume, using earplugs.

Media Technologies for People with Disabilities

NHES Standard 4 Students will analyze the influence of culture, media, technology, and other factors on health.

Objective

Explore assistive and adaptive technologies and discover how media technologies are adapted for people with disabilities.

Motivator

Have students think about the types of devices disabled people use for everyday tasks.

Teaching Strategies

Awareness Have students focus on media technologies such as screen readers that convert text on a computer to speech and screen enlargers that enable vision-impaired people to see a computer screen better.

Analysis Ask students how government legislation such as the Americans with Disabilities Act might encourage the development of assistive technologies.

Reflection Remind students that showing respect is the number one way in which they can assist classmates with disabilities.

Take Action Ask students to survey their own school for types of assistive and adaptive technologies available.

✓Assessment

Students' oral reports should be informative in nature. They should thoroughly explain the device or technology they researched and where possible, use visual aids.

Media Technologies for People with Disabilities

Assistive media technologies are devices that assist individuals who are hearing-impaired or vision-impaired. Examples include radio reading services and the closed caption option on televisions. Voice recognition software is an example of an adaptive media technology. Other examples of adaptive technologies are large-print computer keyboards or joysticks that enable physically disabled people to use a computer. Use the activity below to explore these assistive and adaptive technologies and discover how media technologies are adapted to service or be used by people with disabilities.

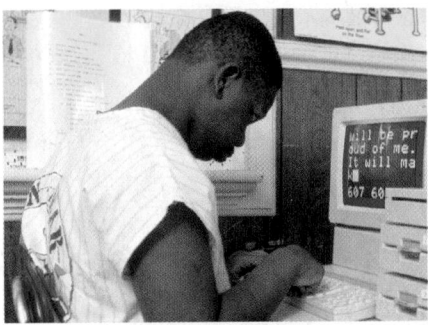

ACTIVITY

Using your school or public library as a resource, research how a particular media technology is used to assist disabled people, or research how a technological device, such as a computer, has been adapted for use by vision- or hearing-impaired individuals. Prepare an oral report that explains how the technology works, how it is used, and by whom. Include visual aids that help illustrate the technology or device you researched. Present your oral report to the rest of the class.

EXPRESS YOUR VIEWS

What can you do to assist a fellow student who is vision- or hearing-impaired? Consider providing reading or writing services for someone who is vision impaired, or learning some basic sign language to help you communicate with hearing-impaired classmates. Write a one-page proposal that suggests how you and your classmates can provide assistance to students with disabilities.

More About...

Disabilities in the Workplace According to the Americans with Disabilities Act (ADA), an employer can be accused of discrimination if reasonable accommodations are not made to the known physical or mental limitations of an otherwise qualified individual with a disability who is an applicant or employee. Also, employers cannot deny employment to a qualified applicant based solely on the fact that the employer would have to make such reasonable accommodations in order to employ the disabled person. Students interested in pursuing this topic further should be directed to research the Americans with Disabilities Act to see what other provisions it contains.

CROSS-CURRICULUM CONNECTIONS

Create a Poem. Taking good care of your eyes, nose, skin, and teeth help you better appreciate your surroundings. Using a chart, make an account of details from a day you have spent at an event that appealed to your five senses. Then use some of these details to write an imagist poem, which is a poem that presents a picture in words.

Research Braille. Braille, a system using the sense of touch to read, helps visually impaired people function in the everyday world. Write a short research report on the recent progress to improve the quality of life of the visually impaired. Include information on groups such as the American Council of the Blind that have fought to improve conditions for the visually-impaired.

Measure the Speed of Sound. Your ears and brain can calculate the direction of a sound. If a man's head is 7 inches wide and the speed of sound at his location is 741.82 miles per hour, how much later, in seconds, does a sound coming from the right side reach the left ear? Hint: First convert inches to feet and miles/hour to feet/sec.

Examine Effects of Color Blindness. Research the various type of color blindness and their physiological causes. Locate illustrations depicting actual colors compared with those perceived by people with different types of color blindness to share with the class.

CAREER Corner

Dental Hygienist

Regular dental care includes more than just seeing the dentist. Most dental offices rely on dental hygienists to provide some routine dental care. A dental hygienist can take your dental and medical history, clean your teeth, and teach you how to achieve and maintain good oral health.

To become a dental hygienist, you will need a high school diploma or its equivalent. Taking biology, chemistry, and math classes is recommended. After high school, hygienists complete a two-year training program in which they earn an Associate's degree. You can find out more about this and other health careers by clicking on Career Corner at **health.glencoe.com**.

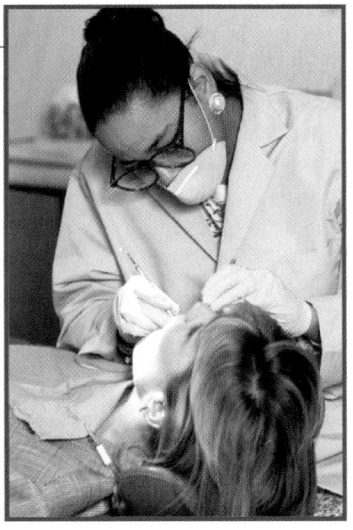

Portfolio Assessment

Self-Evaluation Direct students to review the Health Skills Activities and other activities completed in the chapter. Encourage each student to select one finished product or activity that demonstrates his or her best work for the chapter and that represents the student's learning goals. Have students explain what

they have learned and how the examples they have selected demonstrate their growth in health literacy, knowledge, and skills.

Teacher Classroom Resources Assign Performance Assessment 14, "Tattoos and Piercing—Risky Business," in the TCR.

CROSS-CURRICULUM CONNECTIONS

Enrich student learning by connecting the topic of personal care and healthy behaviors to one of the four subject areas presented on this page. The activity may be completed individually or with a partner.

Language Arts Help students create a sensory chart. Ask them to list these headings: sight, sound, touch, taste, and smell. Then for each category, they should list details.

Social Studies Remind students that when writing a research report they should refer to several different sources.

Math First convert inches to feet and miles/hour to feet/sec. (5,280 feet in a mile; 3600 seconds in an hour) $7in/12in = 0.583$ ft $5280/3600 = 1.4666$ ft/sec $0.583/1088 = .0005$ seconds

Science Colorblindness is a gender-linked genetic trait passed on from the female primarily to male children. The various types are Anomalous Trichromacy, Protanomaly, Deuteranomaly, Trinomaly, Dichromacy, Protanopia, Deuteranopia, Tritanopia, and Monochromacy. They are caused by weak, damaged or missing light receptors on the retina with different combinations of rod and cone failure accounting for type.

CAREER Corner

Have students read and discuss the Career Corner feature. Ask interested students to explore the Glencoe Health Web site at **health.glencoe.com** for more information on career possibilities for dental hygenists.

CHECKING COMPREHENSION

- Assign and discuss the chapter review.
- Use Chapter 14 MindJogger Videoquiz to review the chapter. ▷◁

CHAPTER 14 REVIEW ANSWERS

Exploring Health Terms

1. melanin
2. sweat glands
3. sebaceous glands
4. dandruff
5. plaque
6. periodontal disease
7. sclera
8. cornea
9. retina
10. external auditory canal
11. auditory ossicles
12. labyrinth

Recalling the Facts

1. Skin creates a physical barrier between outside environment and internal organs. It helps protect against water loss and overheating. Melanin in skin helps protect the body from UV rays.
2. Possible answer: Wash face/bathe/shower daily, eat a balanced diet that includes vitamin A, take precautions in the sun.
3. Because the procedure results in the physical barrier of the skin being broken, the possibility of bacteria or viruses entering the body increases.
4. Chew food and contribute to the shape and structure of your mouth.
5. Eating a well-balanced diet that includes foods with calcium, phosphorous, and vitamin C can help keep teeth and gums

382

> **EXPLORING HEALTH TERMS** *Answer the following questions on a sheet of paper.*

Lesson 1 *Match each definition with the correct term.*

dermis	**epidermis**
dandruff	**hair follicle**
melanin	**sebaceous glands**
sweat glands	**melanoma**

1. A pigment that gives skin, hair, and eyes their color.
2. Structures within the skin that produce perspiration through ducts to pores on the skin's surface.
3. Structures within the skin that produce sebum.
4. A condition that can occur if the scalp becomes too dry and dead skin cells are shed as sticky, white flakes.

Lesson 2 *Replace the underlined words with the correct term.*

periodontium	**pulp**
tartar	**plaque**
periodontal disease	

5. <u>Tartar</u> is a sticky, colorless film that acts on sugar to form acids that destroy tooth enamel and irritate gums.
6. <u>Periodontium</u> is completely preventable.

Lesson 3 *Fill in the blanks with the correct term.*

choroid	**cornea**
lacrimal gland	**retina**
sclera	

The outer layer of the eyewall consists of the (_7_), the white part of the eye, and the (_8_), the transparent tissue in the front of the eye. The (_9_) is the inner layer of the eyewall.

Lesson 4 *Match each definition with the correct term.*

auditory ossicles	**labyrinth**
external auditory canal	**tinnitus**

10. A passageway in the outer ear that leads to the eardrum.
11. Three small bones in the middle ear.
12. Another name for the inner ear.

> **RECALLING THE FACTS** *Use complete sentences to answer the following questions.*

Lesson 1

1. Explain how the skin protects your body.
2. List three steps you can take to keep your skin healthy.
3. Why may getting a tattoo be hazardous to your health?

Lesson 2

4. Name two functions of the teeth.
5. How do the foods you eat and your eating habits affect the health of your teeth?
6. List three strategies for reducing bad breath.

Lesson 3

7. How do the lacrimal glands contribute to the health of your eye?
8. Explain how the iris and pupil regulate the amount of light entering the inner eye.
9. Describe what 20/60 vision means.

---

healthy. Limiting the number of sugary snacks also helps protect teeth from decay.

6. Any three: brushing teeth and tongue after meals, flossing every day, avoiding use of tobacco products, using a mouthwash.

7. Lacrimal glands make tears, which keep the eye moist and wash away foreign particles from the surface of the eye.

8. The muscles of the iris cause the pupil to constrict or dilate in response to the amount of external light.

9. A person with 20/60 vision can see at 20 feet what a person with normal vision can see at 60 feet.

10. Allows pressure to be equalized on either side of the eardrum.

11. Any three: protect outer ear from injury and cold, do not allow foreign objects to enter the external auditory canal, protect ears from loud noise, see a doctor for an ear infection, get regular checkups including an ear exam and hearing test.

10. What is the function of the eustachian tube?
11. List two actions you can take to keep your ears healthy.
12. What are three causes of hearing loss?

➤ THINKING CRITICALLY

1. **Applying.** What strategies can you use to keep track of changes in the appearance of moles on your skin? *(LESSON 1)*
2. **Analyzing.** How could having advanced stages of periodontal disease affect other areas of your life? *(LESSON 2)*
3. **Evaluating.** Resting the eyes while reading or working on the computer can help reduce eyestrain. During which other activities should you periodically rest your eyes? *(LESSON 3)*
4. **Applying.** You have developed an ear infection from swimming. Examine the effects of health behaviors on the health of the ears. What precautions could you take to prevent reinfection? *(LESSON 4)*

➤ HEALTH SKILLS APPLICATION

1. **Communicating.** A young child refuses to have a bath or wash his or her hair. How can you encourage him or her to change this behavior? *(LESSON 1)*
2. **Goal Setting.** Set a goal to brush and floss your teeth every morning and every evening. Use the goal-setting steps to help you identify behaviors that will help you meet this goal. *(LESSON 2)*
3. **Accessing Information.** Imagine that you have just been told that you need corrective lenses. Research the advantages and disadvantages of glasses and contact lenses. Make a chart that lists the pros and cons of each. Use this information along with the decision-making steps to determine which you would prefer. *(LESSON 3)*
4. **Communicating.** You suspect that a close family member is experiencing hearing loss, but he or she is not asking for help. What clues might make you think this is the case? How can you talk to this person about what is happening? *(LESSON 4)*

BEYOND the Classroom

Parent Involvement

Advocacy. With a parent or guardian, learn more about the services available for hearing-impaired individuals in your community. Are there any services that are unavailable in your community? Discuss with family members the possible reasons for this lack. What can you do to raise awareness about services for the hearing impaired?

School and Community

Volunteering. Locate an agency that works with individuals with hearing or sight impairments. Ask whether there are any opportunities for volunteer work within the agency. Report to your class on what you have learned.

12. Any three: build up of earwax in the external auditory canal, buildup of fluid within the middle ear, injury, prolonged exposure to loud noise.

Thinking Critically

1. Answers will vary but may include checking moles regularly, noticing color changes, noting size, having moles checked by a doctor.

2. Answers will vary but could include not being able to eat certain foods because teeth are loose or missing, having to spend extra time and money on treatment, risking lower self-esteem caused by embarrassment about losing teeth.

3. Answers could include any activity that requires focusing on detail—such as sewing, cross-stitching, painting or drawing fine detail, or looking through a microscope.

4. Possible answers: Put earplugs in ears, or wear swim cap to prevent water entering the ears; choose activities that do not submerge the head.

Health Skills Application

1.–4. Answers will vary.

EVALUATE

- Use the reproducible Chapter 14 Test in the TCR, or construct your own using the Testmaker software. 📁 💿
- Use Performance Assessment 14 in the TCR. 📁

ENRICHMENT

Ask students to complete Enrichment Activity 14 in the TCR. 📁

BEYOND the Classroom

Keep students involved in the community, and encourage parent participation by assigning the activities on this page for students to work on outside of class.

Lessons	Standards		Features
	National	**State/Local**	
1 The Skeletal System *pages 386–389*	National Health Education Standards 1.3, 3.1, 6.1		
2 Care and Problems of the Skeletal System *pages 390–393*	National Health Education Standards 1.3, 1.6, 2.6, 3.3		**Real-Life Application** • Are You Getting Enough Calcium? *(Goal Setting),* page 392
3 The Muscular System *pages 394–398*	National Health Education Standards 1.3, 3.1, 3.3, 6.4		**Hands-On Health** • Training Safety Checklist *(Practicing Healthful Behaviors),* page 397
4 The Nervous System *pages 399–405*	National Health Education Standards 1.2, 1.3, 7.4		
5 Care and Problems of the Nervous System *pages 406–409*	National Health Education Standards 1.3, 3.6, 6.3, 2.6		**Health Skills Activity** • Riding Smart *(Decision Making),* page 407

Reproducible Resources	Assessment	Technology
Student Activity Workbook for use with each chapter 📁 Concept Mapping Activity 54 📁 Guided Reading Activities 54 📁 Lesson Plan 54 📁 Parent Letter and Activities 15 📁 Reteaching Activity 54	📁 Lesson Quiz 54	🕹️ Transparency 44 💿 TeacherWorks® 🖥️ Internet Activities
📁 Concept Mapping Activity 54 📁 Cross-Curriculum Activity 15 📁 Decision-Making Activity 15 📁 Guided Reading Activities 55 📁 Lesson Plan 55 📁 Reteaching Activity 55	📁 Lesson Quiz 55	🕹️ Transparency 45 💿 TeacherWorks®
📁 Concept Mapping Activity 56 📁 Current Health Issues 15 📁 Guided Reading Activities 56 📁 Health Lab 15 📁 Lesson Plan 56 📁 Reteaching Activity 56	📁 Lesson Quiz 56	🕹️ Transparency 46 💿 TeacherWorks®
📁 Concept Mapping Activity 57 📁 Enrichment Activity 15 📁 Guided Reading Activities 57 📁 Lesson Plan 57 📁 Reteaching Activity 57	📁 Lesson Quiz 57	🕹️ Transparency 47 💿 TeacherWorks®
📁 Concept Mapping Activity 58 📁 Guided Reading Activities 58 📁 Lesson Plan 58 📁 Reteaching Activity 58	📁 Lesson Quiz 58	💿 TeacherWorks®

0:00 OUT OF TIME

If time does not permit teaching the entire chapter, use:
- Figure 15.1, p. 388
- Real-Life Application, p. 392
- Figure 15.2, p. 396
- Hands-On Health, p. 397
- Figure 15.4, p. 401

Language Diversity

🎧 English Audio CD Program
🎧 Spanish Audio CD Program
📁 English Summaries, Quizzes, and Activities
📁 Spanish Summaries, Quizzes, and Activities
📁 Spanish Parent Letters and Activities

End of Chapter Assessment

Blackline Masters
📁 Chapter 15 Test
📁 Performance Assessment Activity 15

Technology
💿 Vocabulary PuzzleMaker
📼 MindJogger Videoquiz
💿 **Exam***View*® Pro Testmaker

Professional Health Series
Dealing with Sensitive Issues
Planning a Coordinated School Health Program
Promoting Character Education
Home, School, and Community Involvement

CHAPTER OVERVIEW

Chapter 15 discusses these important body systems: the skeletal system, the muscular system, and the nervous system.

Lesson 1 The skeletal system provides the basic framework for the human body. The system includes four kinds of bones, which meet at five different kinds of joints.

Lesson 2 Eating a balanced diet, engaging in regular physical activity, and wearing appropriate protective gear are all behaviors that help protect the health of the skeletal system.

Lesson 3 The body has three kinds of muscles. Those that control involuntary processes are always at work. Practicing good posture and exercising regularly are important steps in protecting the health of the muscular system.

Lesson 4 The nervous system—which includes the brain, the spinal cord, and a complex system of nerves—coordinates all the activities in the human body.

Lesson 5 Protecting the health of the nervous system involves eating a well-balanced diet, exercising regularly, getting enough sleep, avoiding risk behaviors, and avoiding alcohol, tobacco, and other drugs.

Health Skills Features

- Real-Life Application (*Goal Setting*), p. 392
- Hands-On Health (*Practicing Healthful Behaviors*), p. 397
- Health Skills Activity (*Decision Making*), p. 407

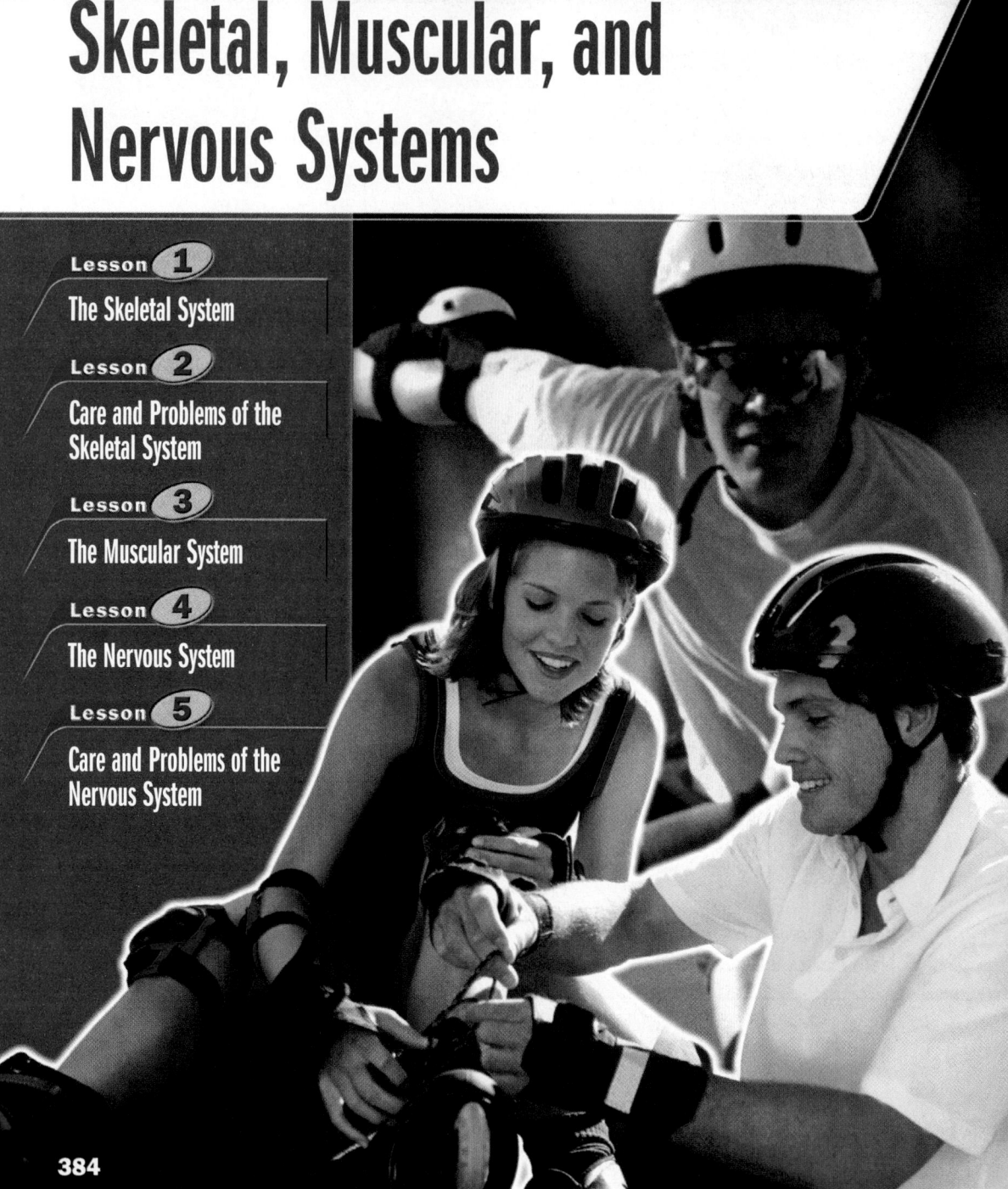

Skeletal, Muscular, and Nervous Systems

Lesson 1
The Skeletal System

Lesson 2
Care and Problems of the Skeletal System

Lesson 3
The Muscular System

Lesson 4
The Nervous System

Lesson 5
Care and Problems of the Nervous System

384

MEETING STUDENT DIVERSITY

Language Diversity Use the following suggestions to help students who have difficulty with English:

- Pair English language learners with native speakers of English who can restate the Chapter Summary in language that helps students comprehend important concepts.

- 🎧 Direct auditory learners or those students with language diversity to the *Glencoe Health Audio CD Program*. Available in English and Spanish, this component provides an audio and written summary of the chapter.

- Use photographs, drawings, or magazine clippings to help students visualize the important concepts of the chapter.

Personal Health Inventory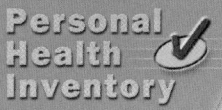

What's Your Health Status?

Read each statement below and respond by writing *yes*, *no*, or *sometimes* for each item. Write *yes* only for items that you practice regularly.

1. I follow a well-balanced diet that includes foods rich in calcium and vitamin D.

2. I incorporate weight-bearing exercises into my physical activities.

3. I practice good posture in order to strengthen my back muscles.

4. I take frequent breaks while working on a computer to avoid injury from repetitive motion.

5. I engage in aerobic activity at least three times each week.

6. I incorporate a warm-up, a cool-down, and stretching in my exercise routine.

7. When I perform weight or resistance training, I follow safety precautions.

8. When participating in contact sports, I wear appropriate safety gear and a helmet.

9. When participating in recreational activities such as biking, skateboarding, or in-line skating, I wear a helmet and other protective gear.

10. I wear a safety belt when driving or riding in a vehicle.

Keep this personal inventory for review later in the chapter. When you complete the chapter, review your answers and identify two or three behavior changes you could make to improve your health.

Quick *Write*

Using Visuals. The skeletal, muscular, and nervous systems are fine-tuned to work together, allowing the body to perform a variety of coordinated actions. What steps do you take in your day-to-day activities to keep these systems functioning and to protect them from injury?

385

INTRODUCING THE CHAPTER

Personal Health Inventory

To promote students' understandings, ask students the following questions:

- What constitutes a well-balanced diet?
- Which foods are good sources of calcium and vitamin D?
- What are some examples of weight-bearing exercises?

Then guide students in reading and discussing each statement in the Personal Health Inventory. Have them record their personal responses by writing *yes*, *no*, or *sometimes* in their journals. Remind students that their responses are private and to save them for review when they have finished studying Chapter 15.

Quick *write*

Using Visuals Let students describe the teens in the photographs:

- What safety equipment are they wearing?
- How will that equipment protect their skeletal, muscular, and nervous systems?

Then have students list the steps they take to protect their own skeletal, muscular, and nervous systems from injury.

TECHNOLOGY OPTIONS

MINDJOGGER
VIDEOQUIZ

To preview or review chapter content, you may wish to use the Chapter 15 MindJogger Videoquiz.

HEALTH *Online*

Online Resources for the Teacher For a fresh approach to health topics and an in-depth look at health issues, use these online resources found under Teacher Resources at **health.glencoe.com**:

- Block Schedule Lesson Plans
- Technology Projects
- Health Updates

The Skeletal System

1 FOCUS

QUICK START Invite students to jot down their lists of healthy behaviors. Then have volunteers share their ideas and discuss how each behavior helps to maintain strong bones.

TYING TO PRIOR KNOWLEDGE

Have students brainstorm a quick list of facts about the skeletal system. Record these facts on the board. Then explain that as they read Lesson 1, students will learn more about their bones and skeletal system.

INTRODUCING VOCABULARY

- Go over the vocabulary terms with the class. Invite volunteers to share what they already know about each term. Then have students find and read the term definitions in the Glossary.

- Ask students to complete the Chapter 15 Study Guide in the *Student Activity Workbook.* 📁

The Skeletal System

VOCABULARY

axial skeleton
appendicular skeleton
cartilage
ossification
ligament
tendon

YOU'LL LEARN TO

- Identify the functions of the skeletal system.

- Describe the main divisions and types of bones of the skeletal system.

- Recognize how understanding the functions of the skeletal system is important for maintaining personal health.

QUICK START Write three health behaviors that you think are important for keeping your skeletal system healthy. How do these behaviors help maintain strong bones?

▲ The interaction of bones and muscles allows you to perform all kinds of motions. *List three functions of the skeletal system.*

You reach out your arm and hit the snooze button; it's 6:00 a.m.—time to rise and shine. As you roll out of bed, you reach your arms above your head, stretching your arms and back and rolling your shoulders. You are able to start your day thanks to the interrelationships of your skeletal, muscular, and nervous systems. In this lesson you'll learn about the system that provides the basic framework for your body, your skeletal system.

Functions of the Skeletal System

Your skeletal system provides a living structure for your body. Strong bones, including the vertebrae of your spine, support your upper body and head. The skeleton plays a crucial role in movement by providing a strong, stable, and mobile framework on which muscles can act. Your skeletal system also protects your internal tissues and organs from trauma. The skull, vertebrae, and ribs create protective cavities for the brain, the spinal cord, and the heart and lungs, respectively. Bones store minerals such as calcium and phosphorus, which are important to the health and strength of the skeleton and to various essential processes in your body. Bone marrow, a connective tissue within bones, produces new red blood cells and white blood cells.

386 **Chapter 15** Skeletal, Muscular, and Nervous Systems

Lesson 1 *Resources*

Teacher Classroom Resources

📁 Concept Mapping Activity 54

📁 Guided Reading Activities 54

📁 Lesson Plan 54

📁 Lesson Quiz 54

📁 Parent Letter and Activities 15

📁 Reteaching Activity 54

Student Activity Workbook

📁 Applying Health Skills 54

📁 Chapter 15 Study Guide

Multimedia

🔊 Transparency 44

Structure of the Skeleton

Your skeletal system consists of 206 bones that can be classified in two main groups. The **axial skeleton** consists of *the 80 bones of the skull, spine, ribs, vertebrae, and sternum, or breastbone.* The **appendicular skeleton** is composed of the remaining *126 bones of the upper and lower limbs, shoulders, and hips.* The bones of these two groups are shown in **Figure 15.1** on page 388.

Types of Bones

All bones are covered with an outer layer of hard, densely packed, compact bone. Beneath the compact bone is spongy bone, a less dense bone with a network of cavities filled with red bone marrow. Almost every bone in the body can be placed in the following categories by shape, as shown in the illustration:

▶ **Long Bones.** Examples of long bones include the bones in your legs and arms. The *humerus* is the bone in your upper arm. The *diaphysis,* or main column of a long bone, is composed of compact bone. Within the diaphysis is a narrow cavity that contains yellow bone marrow, a type of connective tissue that stores fat. The end of a long bone is called the *epiphysis.* The epiphyses form joints with other bones and contain red bone marrow, where new blood cells are produced.

▶ **Short Bones.** Short bones are almost equal in length and width. Examples include the bones of the hands, wrists, feet and ankles.

▶ **Flat Bones.** Flat bones are somewhat thinner and much flatter than other bones. Flat bones, such as those in the skull, protect organs. The scapula, or shoulder blade, is another example of a flat bone.

▶ **Irregular Bones.** Irregularly shaped bones, such as some facial bones or the vertebrae, have unusual shapes and do not fit into the other categories.

Cartilage

Cartilage, *a strong, flexible connective tissue,* is another component of your skeletal system. Cartilage can be found in many areas of the body: at the ends of long bones, at the end of the nose, and within the outer ear. In some joints, such as the knee, cartilage acts as a cushion, reducing friction and allowing smooth motion.

An embryo's skeleton consists mostly of cartilage that serves as a template from which bones will form. Early in embryonic development, the cartilage hardens. This **ossification** (ah-suh-fuh-CAY-shun) is *the process by which bone is formed, renewed, and repaired.*

▼ Bone tissue consists of living cells embedded in a hard matrix of calcium, phosphate, and other calcium minerals.

cartilage
marrow
cavity
compact bone
spongy bone

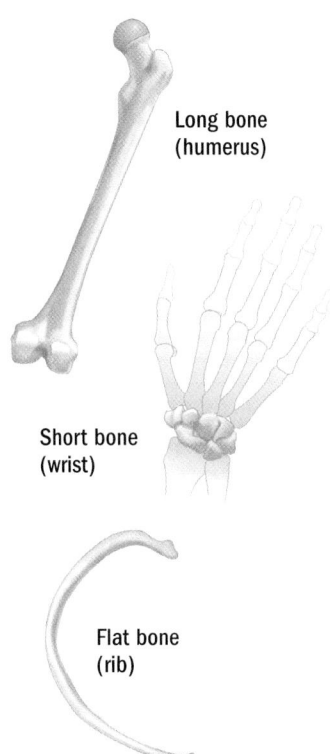

▼ Bones are shaped according to their function: long, short, flat, or irregular. *Give an example of each of these types of bones.*

Long bone (humerus)

Short bone (wrist)

Flat bone (rib)

② TEACH

Discussing

Guide students in discussing the functions of the skeletal system. Ask:

- What are some specific bones (or specific locations of bones) that support the upper body and head?
- What are some examples of bones that protect internal tissues and organs?
- Why do you think healthy bone marrow is especially important to good health? **L1**

Explaining

Help students recognize that the word *appendicular* is similar to other words they may know such as *append,* meaning to attach, and *appendage,* any part, such as a limb, that is joined to an axis or trunk. **L1**

Activity

Ask students to use online or library sources to find answers to these questions:

- How many bones does a newborn baby have?
- How does the number of bones change as the baby grows? **L2**

FYI

The smallest bone in the human body is the stirrup bone (or stapes) in the middle ear. In an adult, this bone is about the size of a grain of rice.

More About...

Bone Growth Bone tissue grows and expands from conception until early adulthood. The bones of newborns are made up primarily of cartilage as well as some spongy bone. The marrow cavities of the bones contain red marrow, which is used to manufacture red blood cells, white blood cells, and platelets. As a child grows, some of the cartilage continues to grow while a portion of the cartilage and spongy bone gradually hardens into what is called true bone. By the time an individual reaches late adolescence, red marrow is located in fewer bones, and the rate of new cartilage growth has begun to slow. By this time, the growth of long bones is nearly complete.

ACTIVE READING

Webbing

Students may be familiar with creating webs as part of the writing process. In this strategy, students place the main ideas within the larger shapes while the smaller, attached shapes show supporting facts and details. Help students practice webbing to record main ideas and supporting facts presented in the text. Read a section of the lesson together. Ask:

• What is the main idea of this section?

• Which facts support that idea and are important enough to remember?

Draw a web on the board, recording students' ideas. Encourage students to practice webbing on their own. Point out that it can be an effective note-taking technique to use in place of, or in addition to, outlining. For more strategies, see the *Guided Reading Activities* booklet in the TCR. 📂

VISUAL LEARNING

Figure 15.1 Guide students in describing the shape and features of the axial skeleton and of the appendicular skeleton. Then, if a skeletal model is available, invite students to take turns identifying the bones named in the figure and finding them on the model.

Activity

Explain that the skeleton of a male is different from that of a female. Invite a small group of students to research, using online and print sources, how the skeletons differ. Have them present their findings with the rest of the class. 📘2

388

FIGURE **15.1**

THE SKELETAL SYSTEM

Your bones continue to grow both in length and in thickness until you are about 25 years old. At this age bones usually stop growing, but may continue to thicken.

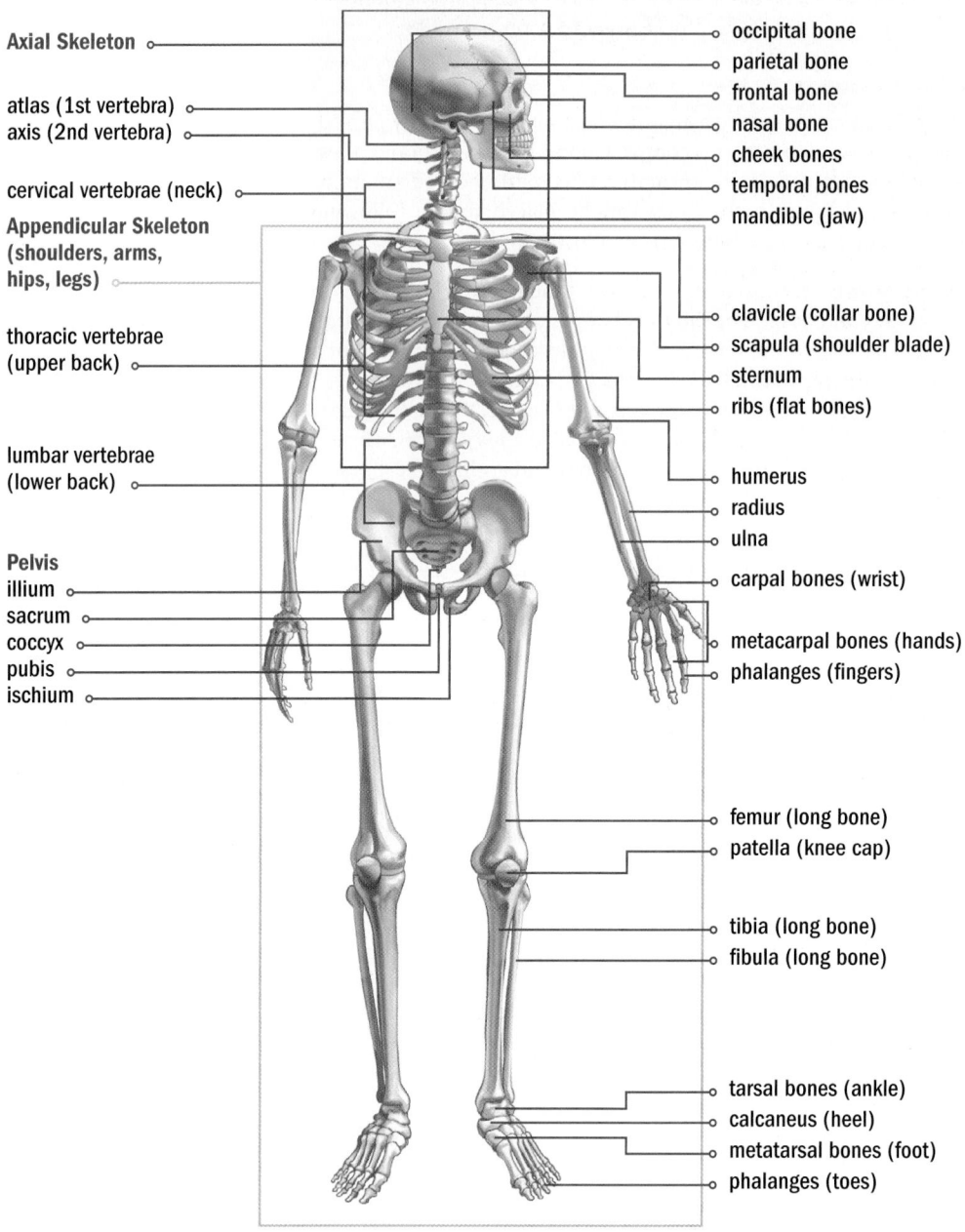

Axial Skeleton

atlas (1st vertebra)
axis (2nd vertebra)

cervical vertebrae (neck)

Appendicular Skeleton
(shoulders, arms, hips, legs)

thoracic vertebrae (upper back)

lumbar vertebrae (lower back)

Pelvis
illium
sacrum
coccyx
pubis
ischium

occipital bone
parietal bone
frontal bone
nasal bone
cheek bones
temporal bones
mandible (jaw)

clavicle (collar bone)
scapula (shoulder blade)
sternum
ribs (flat bones)

humerus
radius
ulna
carpal bones (wrist)
metacarpal bones (hands)
phalanges (fingers)

femur (long bone)
patella (knee cap)

tibia (long bone)
fibula (long bone)

tarsal bones (ankle)
calcaneus (heel)
metatarsal bones (foot)
phalanges (toes)

388 **Chapter 15** Skeletal, Muscular, and Nervous Systems

Curriculum Connections

Science In a science lab, cut cross sections of the bones of a pig, cow, lamb, and chicken. Have students compare the structures for differences and similarities. The bone sections should be comparable in function, e.g., long bones of the legs.

Family and Consumer Science Ask a home economics teacher to present

information on the history of rickets. Have him or her discuss how rickets was diagnosed, treated, and prevented.

Physical Education Invite a physical education teacher to speak with the class about how growth spurts affect the ability to coordinate body movements. How long do these difficulties usually last? 💊

Joints

Joints are points at which bones meet. Some joints, such as those between the bones of the skull, do not move. Others, including the joints between vertebrae, have limited movement.

More flexible joints are classified by type:

► **Ball-and-socket joints** are formed when the rounded head of one bone fits into the rounded cavity of an adjoining bone, as in a hip or shoulder joint. These joints allow the widest range of movement in all directions.

► **Hinge joints,** found at the elbow, knee, ankle, and fingers, allow a joint to bend and straighten, promoting rotation.

► **Pivot joints** allow limited rotation or turning of the head.

► **Ellipsoidal joints,** such as the one in your wrist, have an oval-shaped part that fits into a curved space. Gliding joints allow bones to slide over one another.

A **ligament** is *a band of fibrous, slightly elastic connective tissue that attaches bone to bone.* Ligaments help stabilize the movements of bones at a joint. A **tendon** is *a fibrous cord that attaches muscle to the bone or other muscle.* Movement is produced because muscles are attached to bones by tendons and ligaments.

 Joints allow a wide range of motions. *What is another example of a ball-and-socket joint?*

Hip (ball-and-socket joint)

Knee (hinge joint)

 Lesson 1 *Review*

Reviewing Facts and Vocabulary

1. What are the functions of the skeletal system?
2. Define the terms *cartilage* and *ossification.*
3. Name and give examples of each type of joint.

Thinking Critically

4. **Analyzing.** The ligament that holds the bones in your forearm together and helps form the pivot joint there has been torn. How might this affect your ability to move the hand and arm? What movements might be affected?

5. **Comparing and Contrasting.** Recognize how knowledge of the skeletal system is important for maintaining personal health. How are the bones in the axial skeleton similar to those in the appendicular skeleton?

Applying Health Skills

Decision Making. Hector's friends have invited him to go mountain biking. He is hesitant because he thinks this activity would pose some risks to his bones or joints. Using the decision-making steps, role-play with a friend the process of Hector's decision.

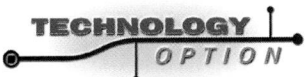 **TECHNOLOGY** *OPTION*

WORD PROCESSING Use a word-processing program to list options for Hector's decision. See health.glencoe.com for tips.

Lesson 1 The Skeletal System **389**

Quick Demo

As they read about joints, have students identify examples of each kind of joint. Then let students work in pairs to demonstrate and observe the functioning of the wrist, an ellipsoidal joint.

③ ASSESS

EVALUATING THE LESSON

Assign and discuss the Lesson 1 Review; then administer, grade, and discuss Lesson Quiz 54 in the TCR. 🗁

RETEACHING

• Working with small groups, help students recall the functions of the skeletal system. Then help students discuss the relationships among bones, cartilage, and joints.

• Ask students to complete Reteaching Activity 54 in the TCR. 🗁

ENRICHMENT

Have students use online and library sources to research the differences and similarities between the skull of an infant and an adult. Have students summarize their findings in a one-page report. Have them proofread for errors before handing in an error-free final draft.

 Lesson 1 *Review*

Answers to Reviewing Facts and Vocabulary

1. See page 383 for functions.
2. Cartilage is a strong, flexible connective tissue. Ossification is the process by which bone is formed, renewed, and repaired.
3. Ball-and-socket: hip, shoulder; Hinge: elbow, knee, ankle, fingers; Pivot: top two vertebrae; Ellipsoidal: wrists.

Answers to Thinking Critically

4. May be unable to turn palms to face up or down; Possible answer: turning a doorknob, etc.
5. They are similar in that they are made of the same kinds of material and are bone tissue. They differ in shape and function.

④ CLOSE

Have each student identify an interesting new fact he or she has learned about the skeletal system.

389

Care and Problems of the Skeletal System

Lesson 2

1 FOCUS

QUICK START Ask several volunteers to identify the kinds of situations that could cause a bone or joint injury. Write these on the board. Then, record students' suggestions for preventing bone or joint injury.

TYING TO PRIOR KNOWLEDGE

Tell students that this lesson will focus on how they can care for their skeletal system. It also discusses a variety of problems associated with the system, including fractures, as well as injuries to joints and repetitive motion injuries. Have students briefly share any prior knowledge they may have about the topic.

Health Skills Features

"Are You Getting Enough Calcium?" p. 392

GOAL SETTING

INTRODUCING VOCABULARY

- Have students work with partners to find, read, and discuss the Glossary definitions of the vocabulary terms.

- Ask students to complete the Chapter 15 Study Guide in the *Student Activity Workbook.*

390

Care and Problems of the Skeletal System

VOCABULARY
- osteoporosis
- scoliosis
- repetitive motion injury

YOU'LL LEARN TO
- Examine strategies to prevent injuries that damage the skeletal system.
- Analyze the relationship between health promotion and prevention of bone disorders.
- Identify different types of joint injuries and situations requiring professional health services.

QUICK START Write a paragraph describing a situation that could cause a bone or joint injury. List ways of preventing the injury.

 Getting enough calcium during your teen years is essential for a lifetime of healthy bones. *Name two foods you enjoy that provide calcium, phosphorus, and vitamin D.*

The overall health of your body very much depends on the health of your skeletal system. If your skeletal system cannot perform its functions properly, your freedom of movement may be limited and other areas of your health and lifestyle may also be affected.

Care of the Skeletal System

Caring for your skeletal system is something you can do every day. Eating foods that contain calcium, vitamin D, and phosphorus, can help prevent the development of certain skeletal disorders. Phosphorus can be found in dairy products, beans, whole grains, and liver. Dark green, leafy vegetables are a source of calcium. Milk is fortified with vitamin D and also provides calcium. Regular physical activity, including weight-bearing exercise, helps keep bones strong. Wearing protective gear such as a helmet and padding when you participate in sporting or recreational activities reduces the risk of bone fractures.

390 Chapter 15 Skeletal, Muscular, and Nervous Systems

 Lesson 2 *Resources*

Teacher Classroom Resources
- Concept Mapping Activity 55
- Cross-Curriculum Activity 15
- Decision-Making Activity 15
- Guided Reading Activities 55
- Lesson Plan 55

- Lesson Quiz 55
- Reteaching Activity 55

Student Activity Workbook
- Applying Health Skills 55
- Chapter 15 Study Guide

Multimedia
- Transparency 45

Problems of the Skeletal System

Skeletal system disorders and bone injuries can be the result of many factors, including poor nutrition, infections, sports and recreational injuries, and poor posture. The skeletal system is also affected by degenerative disorders such as osteoporosis.

Fractures

A fracture is any type of break in a bone. Fractures can be either compound or simple. A compound fracture is one in which the broken end of the bone protrudes through the skin. A simple fracture is one in which the broken bone does not protrude. Fractures are also classified by the pattern of the break:

▶ **Hairline fracture.** The fracture is incomplete, and the two parts of the bones do not separate.

▶ **Transverse fracture.** The fracture is completely across the bone. A transverse fracture may result from a sharp, direct blow or from stress caused by prolonged running on an already damaged bone.

▶ **Comminuted fracture.** The bone shatters into more than two pieces, usually as a result of severe force.

Osteoporosis

You can build bone mass only during the time you are growing. Health behaviors that you practice now, during your teen years, can reduce your risk of developing osteoporosis later in life. **Osteoporosis** is *a condition in which progressive loss of bone tissue occurs.* It is a very serious bone disease that affects millions of older Americans and has no warning signs in its early stages. Bones are weakened and become brittle, causing them to break easily. Adequate amounts of calcium, vitamin D, and phosphorus help bones remain strong and healthy. Regular weight-bearing physical activities, such as walking and weight training, stimulate bone cells to increase bone mass, thereby reducing the risk of osteoporosis. Early detection is essential to treatment and to slowing loss of bone tissue. A bone scan (in which X rays measure bone density) can be performed at regular intervals later in life.

Scoliosis

Scoliosis is *a lateral, or side-to-side, curvature of the spine.* Scoliosis may exist at the time of birth, or it can develop during childhood. The curvature of the spine worsens as growth continues and may proceed even after growth stops. Early detection is important in the treatment of scoliosis. Treatment includes wearing a brace to help straighten the spine and, in more severe cases, surgery.

 A break like the comminuted fracture shown here might be avoided by keeping bones strong through good nutrition and following safety precautions. *What steps do you take to keep your bones and joints healthy?*

Lesson 2 Care and Problems of the Skeletal System **391**

2 TEACH

Reinforcing Concepts

Ask students to identify protective gear worn for sporting or recreational activities. Have them identify the bones that each item helps to protect.

Activity

Many broken bones result from accidents in the home. Have students research potential safety hazards in the home, such as throw rugs, loose cords, and blocked stairways. Invite them to make a checklist to be used when conducting a home safety check.

Discussing

Ask students to use online and library resources to learn more about osteoporosis:

• Who is considered most at risk? Why?

• Is the condition considered hereditary?

• How is osteoporosis treated?

Let students meet in groups to discuss their findings. **L2**

Cooperative Learning

Let students form five groups, and assign each group a typical joint injury, such as dislocation, torn cartilage, bursitis, bunion, and arthritis. Have group members read and discuss the information on their assigned injury and then present the information to the class. **L1**

More About...

Fractures Broken bones may not heal as easily as we assume. Circumstances often influence the healing process. Younger people heal more quickly than older people. Mental stress, fatigue, and other physical problems, as well as some medications, may influence healing rates. Any serious disease can cause healing problems, as we know, but people who seem reasonably healthy sometimes find that a break just won't heal.

Techniques to assist the healing process include placement of pins and replacement of an entire joint or bone with synthetic bones.

Real-Life Application

ARE YOU GETTING ENOUGH CALCIUM?

GOAL SETTING

NHES Standard 6 Students will demonstrate the ability to use goal-setting and decision-making skills to enhance health.

Objectives

• Analyze the relationship between health promotion and prevention of bone disorders.

• Implement a plan for attaining a personal health goal.

Motivator

Have students brainstorm food sources of calcium.

Teaching Strategies

1. Have students discuss ways foods in the chart might be incorporated into a day's eating plan.

2. Have students access other sources to identify foods relatively high in calcium.

Assessment

Using a rubric, student work should provide comprehensive evidence of the following criteria to achieve the highest score:

✔ clear progression through a goal-setting process
✔ inclusion of a clear goal statement
✔ identification of a realistic goal
✔ plan for reaching the goal
✔ evaluation or reflection on the action

Real-Life Application

Are You Getting Enough Calcium?

During the teen years it is very important to choose calcium-rich foods to build maximum bone density. Building strong bones during adolescence will help prevent osteoporosis and bone fractures later in life. You should have at least 3 servings of milk, cheese, or yogurt daily to meet your calcium needs. If you don't drink milk, then choose other foods high in calcium, such as yogurt, kale, or fortified fruit juices. The Recommended Dietary Allowance of calcium for teens between the ages of 11 to 18 is 1,300 mg. The following table shows the approximate calcium content in a single serving of some common calcium-rich foods.

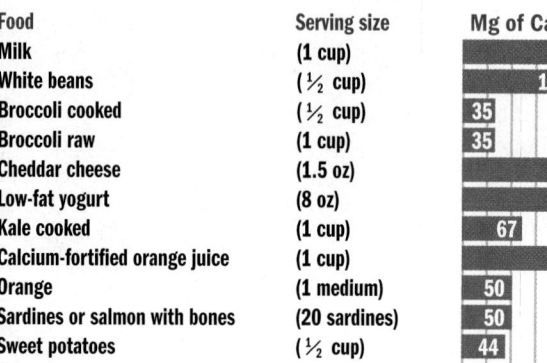

Food	Serving size	Mg of Calcium per Serving
Milk	(1 cup)	300
White beans	(½ cup)	113
Broccoli cooked	(½ cup)	35
Broccoli raw	(1 cup)	35
Cheddar cheese	(1.5 oz)	300
Low-fat yogurt	(8 oz)	300-415
Kale cooked	(1 cup)	67
Calcium-fortified orange juice	(1 cup)	300
Orange	(1 medium)	50
Sardines or salmon with bones	(20 sardines)	50
Sweet potatoes	(½ cup)	44

ACTIVITY

List all the calcium-rich foods you eat over the next 24 hours, and record the amount or serving size you eat. Compare your calcium intake to the amounts of calcium shown on the chart to see whether you are getting at least 1,300 mg of calcium daily. Create a written plan describing how you will maintain or increase your calcium intake. Include specific actions you will take.

Injuries to Joints

Injuries to joints can occur for such reasons as overuse, strain, or disease. The following are typical joint injuries.

▶ **Dislocation** results when the ligaments that attach the bone at the joint are torn as the bone slips out of place. Never attempt to replace a dislocated joint; get immediate medical help. Treatment includes having the joint reset and immobilized while the ligaments heal.

▶ **Torn cartilage** can result from a sharp blow or the twisting of a joint. Injuries are treated with arthroscopic surgery.

392 Chapter 15 Skeletal, Muscular, and Nervous Systems

Cooperative Learning Activity

Lifestyle Risks for Osteoporosis Students have learned that a sedentary lifestyle and inadequate calcium intake can increase the risk of osteoporosis. Have students work in small groups to research other lifestyle factors that contribute to osteoporosis. For example, one group member might investigate the effects of dieting and weight loss on bone loss. Another might research the effects of alcohol, while a third examines caffeine and its effects. After groups have completed their research, have students conduct a panel discussion about risk factors and make lifestyle recommendations for preventing osteoporosis.

- **Bursitis** results from the inflammation of a fluid-filled sac called the bursa. Certain joints, such as the elbow, have bursae that help reduce friction between their movable parts. When the bursa becomes inflamed, pain and swelling can occur at the joint.

- **A bunion** is a painful swelling of the bursa in the first joint of the big toe. Wearing ill-fitting shoes can make bunions worse. Large bunions may require surgery.

- **Arthritis** is the inflammation of a joint. The condition can result from an injury, natural wear and tear, or autoimmune disease. The most common form of arthritis, osteoarthritis, results from wear and tear on the joints.

Repetitive Motion Injury

A **repetitive motion injury** is *damage to tissues caused by prolonged, repeated movements* such as in computer work, sewing, or assembly line work. One of the most common repetitive motion injuries is carpal tunnel syndrome. This condition occurs when swollen ligaments and tendons in the wrist cause numbness, a burning or tingling sensation in the thumb and forefinger, pain, and weakness in the hand. Treatment includes wearing a splint to reduce wrist movements, medication to reduce swelling and, in a small percentage of cases, surgery.

Health Minute
Reduce the Risk of Carpal Tunnel Syndrome

Use these tips to reduce your risk of developing repetitive motion injuries.

While using a computer:

- Rest your hands and wrists from repetitive motion by taking frequent breaks.

- Use a keyboard or other equipment designed to reduce strain and pressure.

- Adjust chair height, so that your forearms will be level with your wrists and so reduce the angle of your bent wrists when you are typing.

Health Minute

Ask volunteers to demonstrate or describe how to apply each of the suggestions to avoid damage to the skeletal system.

③ ASSESS

EVALUATING THE LESSON

Assign and discuss the Lesson 2 Review; then administer, grade, and discuss Lesson Quiz 55 in the TCR. 📂

RETEACHING

- Have students work with partners to list and discuss four ways to protect the health of their bones.

- Ask students to complete Reteaching Activity 55 in the TCR. 📂

ENRICHMENT

Have students plan and present an effective approach to making younger students aware of possible dangers to the skeletal system.

▶ Lesson 2 *Review*

Reviewing Facts and Vocabulary

1. Name three behaviors that help keep your bones and joints healthy.

2. What should you do if you think someone has a fractured bone or dislocated joint?

3. Define the term *repetitive motion injury*. Explain how to prevent this type of injury.

Thinking Critically

4. **Analyzing.** A dislocated or injured joint is often immobilized by putting a rigid cast around the affected area. How might this procedure affect the health of the surrounding muscle tissue?

5. **Evaluating.** Analyze how health promotion during your teen years relates to the prevention of developing osteoporosis later in life.

Applying Health Skills

Accessing Information. Research more about keeping the skeletal system healthy. Choose a category such as injury prevention, nutritional needs, or building bone mass to focus your research. Then prepare a pamphlet of step-by-step strategies you and your peers can use to promote the health of bones during the teen years.

TECHNOLOGY OPTION

SPREADSHEETS Use spreadsheet software to organize your lists. See **health.glencoe.com** for tips on how to use spreadsheets to build tables.

Lesson 2 Care and Problems of the Skeletal System **393**

④ CLOSE

Ask: What changes could you make to protect the health of your skeletal system? Invite students to write their responses in a paragraph. Have students exchange their paragraphs with a partner for proofreading. Then have them incorporate their partner's comments into a final draft. Encourage volunteers to share their paragraphs with the class.

▶ Lesson 2 *Review*

Answers to Reviewing Facts and Vocabulary

1. Balanced diet, physical activity, protective gear

2. Get medical help immediately.

3. Damage to tissues caused by prolonged, repeated movements. Take frequent breaks, adjust chair height, use special equipment.

Answers to Thinking Critically

4. Muscles lose their tone if not used, which leads to a loss of muscle mass, which must be rebuilt after the injury.

5. Practicing healthful behaviors in your teen years will help build muscle mass and reduce risk for osteoporosis later in life.

The Muscular System

Lesson 3

1 FOCUS

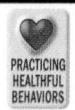**QUICK START** Have a volunteer read the Quick Start assignment aloud, and let several students explain the importance of muscle tone. Then let students work with partners to write their lists of benefits and problems associated with poor muscle tone.

TYING TO PRIOR KNOWLEDGE

Ask students to share a few familiar facts about muscles and the muscular system. If necessary, refer them to their Quick Start lists. Then explain that, as they read Lesson 3, students will expand their understanding of the human muscular system.

Health Skills Features

"Training Safety Checklist," p. 397

PRACTICING HEALTHFUL BEHAVIORS

INTRODUCING VOCABULARY

- Divide the class into eight groups, and assign each group one of the vocabulary terms. Have group members read the Glossary definition of their term and explain the term to the rest of the class.

- Ask students to complete the Chapter 15 Study Guide in the *Student Activity Workbook*. 📁

The Muscular System

VOCABULARY

smooth muscles
skeletal muscles
flexors
extensors
cardiac muscle
muscle tone
tendonitis
hernia

YOU'LL LEARN TO

- Explain the functions of the muscular system.
- Describe the different types of muscles in the body.
- Examine the effects of health behaviors on the muscular system.
- Identify problems of the muscular system.

QUICK START List five benefits of having good muscle tone. Next to each benefit, list a problem that might be caused by not having good muscle tone.

 Proper warm-up and stretching before and cool-down after any physical activity keeps your muscles flexible and strong.

The action of a slingshot is the result of two interdependent parts—a forked stick and a rubber band or other elastic material. The same is true of the human body. The role of the stick is played by the skeleton. The role of the rubber band is played by the muscular system. Muscles are elastic; they stretch to allow a wide range of motion.

Functions of the Muscular System

Certain muscles in your body are always at work. Even when you sleep, muscles help you breathe, make your heart beat, and move food through your digestive system. These involuntary processes happen without your consciously controlling them. At other times, such as when you play the piano or a video game, make a dash toward first base, or throw a ball, you are using muscles that are under conscious, or voluntary, control. Without the use of both voluntary and involuntary muscles, you would be unable to perform any of these activities.

Lesson 3 *Resources*

Teacher Classroom Resources

📁 Concept Mapping Activity 56
📁 Current Health Issues 15
📁 Guided Reading Activities 56
📁 Health Lab 15
📁 Lesson Plan 56
📁 Lesson Quiz 56

📁 Reteaching Activity 56

Student Activity Workbook

📁 Applying Health Skills 56
📁 Chapter 15 Study Guide

Multimedia

🕹 Transparency 46

Structure of the Muscular System

A muscle is made up of hundreds of long cells called fibers. Major muscles in the body are made up of hundreds of bundles of these fibers. Muscles work by means of two complementary, or opposing, actions. These are contraction, the shortening of a muscle, and extension, the stretching of a muscle. Muscle contraction is triggered by nerve impulses. Some nerves provide impulses for many muscle fibers, especially to large muscles such as the calf muscle or biceps. In other areas, such as your eyes, a single nerve may provide impulses to only two or three muscle fibers.

Types of Muscles

The body contains three types of muscle tissue: smooth muscle, skeletal muscle, and cardiac muscle.

▶ **Smooth muscles** *act on the lining of passageways and internal organs.* These muscles can be found in the lining of the blood vessels, the digestive tract, the passageways that lead into the lungs, and the bladder. Smooth muscles are under involuntary control.

▶ **Skeletal muscles** *are attached to bone and cause body movements.* Skeletal muscle tissue has a striated, or striped, appearance under a microscope. Most of your muscle tissue is made up of skeletal muscle, and almost all skeletal muscles are under voluntary control. Skeletal muscles often work together, undergoing opposing actions to produce movement. One muscle contracts while the other muscle extends. An example of this can be seen in the diagram at the right, which shows the biceps and triceps muscles of the upper arm. To bend and straighten your arm at the elbow, these muscles oppose each other's action. The **flexor** is *the muscle that closes a joint.* In this example the biceps is the flexor. The **extensor** is *the muscle that opens a joint.* In this case the triceps is the extensor. Identify other opposing skeletal muscles that appear in **Figure 15.2** on page 396.

▶ **Cardiac muscle** is *a type of striated muscle that forms the wall of the heart.* The involuntary cardiac muscles are responsible for the contraction of your heart, the most important part of the cardiovascular system. The heart contracts rhythmically about 100,000 times each day to pump blood throughout your body.

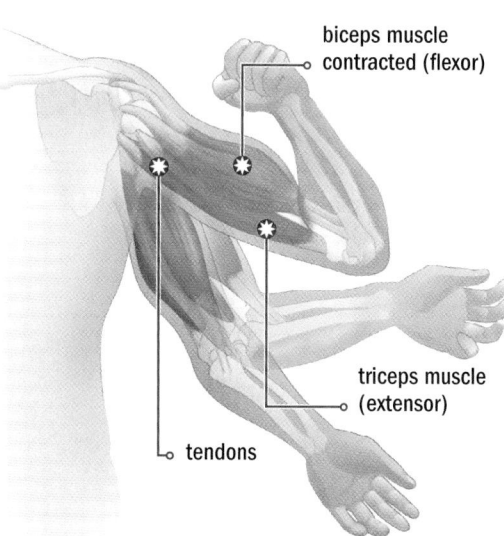

ⓥ **Skeletal muscles produce movement by working in pairs. One muscle contracts while the other extends.** *Try holding your thigh as you bend your leg at the knee. Identify the flexor and the extensor muscles as you perform this action.*

Muscle Movement

biceps muscle contracted (flexor)

triceps muscle (extensor)

tendons

❷ TEACH

Reinforcing Concepts

After students have read Functions of the Muscular System, ask:

- What is the difference between voluntary and involuntary muscles?
- Why are both kinds of muscles vital in your daily life? ⬛

Activity

Prepare by bringing skeins of yarn or raffia to class. Invite interested students to use the material to recreate models of muscles. Ask these students to share their models with the rest of the class. ⬛ ◖

Cooperative Learning

Ask students to form three groups, and assign each group one of the types of muscle tissue: smooth, skeletal, or cardiac. Have group members read about their assigned type of muscle, discuss the information, and consider how they can most effectively share it with the rest of the class. Then let the members of each group describe and explain their assigned muscle type. ⬛

Activity

Have students describe and discuss the picture on this page. Then ask students to try the activity discussed in the photo caption, identifying both the flexor and the extensor.

❯ *More About...*

Anaerobic and Aerobic Processes
Adenosine triphosphate (ATP) is a molecule that results in the breakdown of glucose. ATP stores energy in cells. When ATP is broken down chemically, energy is released. ATP is not stored in large quantities in muscle cells. Therefore, it must be replaced. When glucose is broken down, it is stored as glycogen in the liver and in the muscles, and it provides some ATP molecules. This process does not require the presence of oxygen and, therefore, is called anaerobic. In the presence of oxygen, however, a glucose molecule is completely broken down, producing 18 to 20 times more ATP than does the anaerobic process. This aerobic process results in a higher yield of energy.

Activity

Ask volunteers to describe and demonstrate a few exercises that help keep specific muscles healthy. ▣ **Bodily/Kinesthetic**

Quick Demo

Have students demonstrate examples of good and poor posture. You may also want to research examples or print examples from online sources. Encourage students to discuss the benefits of good posture. Ask: How is practicing good posture like exercising?

VISUAL LEARNING

Figure 15.2 Have students meet in groups to examine and discuss the labeled muscles in the drawings. If possible, give each group a small model of the human skeleton and have group members point out the location of each muscle on the model.

Discussing

Encourage students to discuss their own experiences with bruises, muscle strain, and tendonitis:

- How was the problem identified?
- How was it treated?
- How well and how quickly did the treatment relieve the problem? ▣

hotlink

physical activity For more infomation about the benefits of physical activity, see Chapter 4, page 75.

Care of the Muscular System

Regular physical activity is the best way to keep your muscles strong and healthy. Muscles that remain unused for long periods of time will *atrophy,* or decrease in size and strength. **Muscle tone** is *the natural tension in the fibers of a muscle.* Regular **physical activity** helps keeps muscles toned and healthy. Practicing good posture strengthens back muscles. Wearing safety equipment and appropriate clothing can protect muscles during physical activity.

FIGURE 15.2

THE SKELETAL MUSCLES

Major muscle groups include the arms, legs, back, abdomen, shoulders, and chest.

extensor muscles (dorsal surface)
teres
trapezius
rhomboid
triceps
biceps (of arm)
latissimus dorsi
gluteus maximus
abductor muscles (pull legs away from body)
biceps (of thigh)
semitendinosus
peroneus
gastrocnemius
Achilles tendon

Facial Muscles
frontalis
temporalis
orbicularis oculi
masseter
orbicularis oris

adductor muscles (pull legs toward body)
gastrocnemius
soleus

sternocleidomastoid
flexor muscles (inside of arm)
biceps
deltoid
pectoralis major
serratus oblique
external oblique (muscle of abdomen)
sartorius
adductor muscles (pull legs toward body)
quadriceps muscles
patella (kneecap)
peroneus
anterior tibial

Home and Community

Protecting the Skeletal and Muscular Systems Some students live with older adult family members. The older the individual, the greater the risk of injury to or disease of the muscular and skeletal systems. Suggest that students share the information in this chapter with adults at home. If family members tend to engage in repetitive motion activities, students may research

and inform them of exercises to prevent injuries. Regular stretching helps keep the body flexible and can help prevent injuries to the skeletal and muscular systems. Suggest that students find out whether the local recreation department offers flexibility or stretch classes. If so, they might recommend these classes to family members.

Hands-On Health ACTIVITY

Training Safety Checklist

Participating in weight-bearing exercise throughout life is important to maintain muscle tone and to keep bones strong and healthy. As with any physical activity, however, safety comes first. In this activity you will create safety checklists for teens doing weight or resistance training.

What You'll Need

- paper and pen or pencil
- textbook and other sources of information

What You'll Do

1. In your group, identify at least one weight-bearing exercise for every major muscle group.

2. Use a separate sheet of paper for each exercise. Describe the exercise, and then list the following: appropriate clothing, when and where to work out, safe exercise procedures, and how to use equipment properly. Refer to your textbook and other reliable sources to develop your checklist.

3. For each exercise, include at least five easy-to-remember tips for practicing safe weight training. Create an acronym that teens can recall easily.

4. Staple the pages together to make a guide. If your classroom has a computer, input the text and print copies. Place the guides in the gymnasium and in other areas around the school.

Apply and Conclude

Write a paragraph explaining what you have learned about the benefits of weight-bearing exercise. Note the importance of following safety procedures while keeping your muscles healthy.

Problems of the Muscular System

When you are exercising, your muscles are working very hard. They might be sore after strenuous activity, such as going for an all-day hike or bike ride. Although they can be painful, sore muscles are usually temporary. However, other problems of the muscular system are far more serious and can affect a person's overall health and lifestyle. The recovery time for injury-related muscle problems varies with the type and severity of the injury.

School to Work

Protection on the Job Ask each student to choose a job that involves risk to skin, bones, tendons, joints, or muscles. For example, gardeners are exposed to sun and must bend and pull in ways that could injure muscles or joints if they did not exercise care. Factory workers and word processors may repeat motions all day. Movers lift heavy and often bulky objects. Plumbers work in cramped spaces and sometimes move from awkward positions. Have each student write a page for a worker safety manual, describing potential injuries for the specific job and listing preventive measures for the worker. Let a small group of volunteers compile the pages into a book. Then make the book available in the classroom.

Hands-On Health

TRAINING SAFETY CHECKLIST

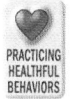
PRACTICING HEALTHFUL BEHAVIORS

NHES Standard 3 Students will demonstrate the ability to practice health-enhancing behaviors and reduce health risks.

Objectives

- Examine the effects of health behaviors on the muscular system.
- Develop injury prevention and management strategies for personal and community health.

Motivator

Ask students why safety is so important in resistance training.

Teaching Strategies

1. Remind students that major muscle groups include arms, legs, back, abdomen, shoulders, and chest.
2. Have students prepare a first draft on scrap paper first. Verify the accuracy of the information in each group's guide before they prepare the final version.

Assessment

Using a rubric, student work should provide comprehensive evidence of the following criteria to achieve the highest score:

✔ identification and description of at least one weight-bearing exercise for every major muscle group
✔ list of appropriate clothing along with when and where to work out
✔ identification of safe exercise procedures and proper use of exercise equipment
✔ utilization of textbook and other reliable sources of information
✔ at least five easy-to-remember safety tips in acronym form

Activity

Ask a group of volunteers to learn more about hernias and the surgeries performed to correct them. Let the volunteers share their findings with the rest of the class.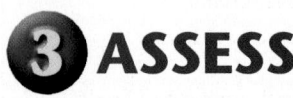

③ ASSESS

EVALUATING THE LESSON

Assign and discuss the Lesson 3 Review; then administer, grade, and discuss Lesson Quiz 56 in the TCR. ▱

RETEACHING

- Ask students to recall the three types of muscles. Have them describe any similarities and differences and provide an example and location of each type.
- Ask students to complete Reteaching Activity 56 in the TCR. ▱

ENRICHMENT

Have students discuss specific muscles known to cramp. Ask: What are the most effective stretches for relieving a cramp in that muscle? Let students describe and demonstrate their findings.

④ CLOSE

Have students meet in small groups to reread and discuss the first paragraph of the lesson. Ask: How has your understanding of this description changed?

Did You Know ❓

Muscles produce heat when they contract. Shivering is an involuntary contraction of skeletal muscles in an effort to warm the body.

- Smooth muscles located in the skin at the base of hairs contract involuntarily, raising the hair and producing "goose bumps" in response to cold or fear.
- A muscle spasm occurs when a single muscle involuntarily contracts. A tic is the twitching that results when muscles involuntarily contract in a repeated spasm.

▶ **Bruise.** A bruise is an area of discolored skin that appears after an injury causes the blood vessels beneath the skin to rupture and leak. Swelling can be reduced with an ice pack.

▶ **Muscle strain or sprain.** A strained muscle results when a muscle is stretched or partially torn as a result of overexertion. Strains are usually treated by using the R.I.C.E. (rest, ice, compression, elevation) procedure. A sprain is an injury to the ligament in a joint, and it requires medical treatment.

▶ **Tendonitis. Tendonitis**, or *the inflammation of a tendon,* can be caused by injury, overuse, or natural aging. Signs of tendonitis include joint pain or swelling that worsens with activity. Treatment includes rest, anti-inflammatory medication, or ultrasound.

▶ **Hernia.** A **hernia** occurs *when an organ or tissue protrudes through an area of weak muscle.* This condition can result from straining to lift a heavy object. Hernia repair usually requires surgery.

▶ **Muscular dystrophy.** Muscular dystrophy is an inherited disorder in which skeletal muscle fibers are progressively destroyed. There is no cure, but with early detection muscle weakness can be delayed through exercise programs.

▶ Lesson 3 Review

Reviewing Facts and Vocabulary

1. Give examples of how muscles work together with other body systems.
2. Describe *cardiac muscle.*
3. What is *tendonitis*? Why does it occur?

Thinking Critically

4. **Applying.** Examine the effects of health behaviors on the muscular system. Which muscles are most involved in your favorite physical activities? What behaviors can help you protect the health of these and other muscles?
5. **Analyzing.** Describe two types of muscle injury, and suggest strategies that can prevent them.

Applying Health Skills

Goal Setting. Set a goal to begin a program of strengthening your muscles. Decide on a weight-training program or another physical activity that will increase muscle strength. On which muscle groups will you focus? Use the steps of goal setting to develop your plan.

SPREADSHEETS Design a table with spreadsheet software to help you organize your training plan. See **health.glencoe.com** for information on how to use a spreadsheet.

▶ Lesson 3 Review

Answers to Reviewing Facts and Vocabulary

1. Muscles work with respiratory, cardiovascular, and digestive systems.
2. Cardiac muscle is a striated muscle that forms the wall of the heart.
3. The inflammation of a tendon caused by injury, overuse, or aging.

Answers to Thinking Critically

4. Answers will vary.
5. Answers should include two of the following: strain, bruise, tendonitis, or hernia. Prevention strategies will vary, but should include treatments from lesson content.

The Nervous System

VOCABULARY
- neurons
- cerebrum
- cerebellum
- brain stem
- reflex

YOU'LL LEARN TO
- Differentiate between the central nervous system and the peripheral nervous system.
- Identify the structure and function of neurons.
- Describe the areas of the brain and the function of each.
- Demonstrate knowledge and research more about personal health concerns related to the nervous system.

QUICK START Compare the nervous system with a technology we use today, for example, the telephone system. How are the two systems similar?

Your nervous system is a complex network that allows communication between the brain and all other areas of the body. It also enables you to remember your part in a play or the time to meet your friends for a movie on Friday night.

Function and Structure of the Nervous System

Your nervous system coordinates all of the activities in your body—from breathing or digesting food to sensing pain or feeling fear. The brain, spinal cord, and nerves work together. Nerves transmit messages back and forth to every organ, tissue, and cell.

The nervous system has two main divisions. The *central nervous system (CNS)* consists of the brain and spinal cord. The *peripheral nervous system (PNS)* gathers information from inside and outside your body. It includes nerves that extend from the brain, spinal cord, and sensory receptors, such as those in the skin that sense pressure, temperature, or pain. The central nervous system receives messages from the nerves in the peripheral nervous system, interprets them, and sends out a response. Impulses can be carried at speeds of up to 280 miles per hour, which means, for example, that you can let go of a hot pan before you are badly burned.

A Computed Tomography (CT) scan is used to diagnose problems that can affect the function of the nervous system. *Name a type of injury that can cause damage to the brain.*

Lesson 4 Resources

Teacher Classroom Resources
- Concept Mapping Activity 57
- Enrichment Activity 15
- Guided Reading Activities 57
- Lesson Plan 57
- Lesson Quiz 57
- Reteaching Activity 57

Student Activity Workbook
- Applying Health Skills 57
- Chapter 15 Study Guide

Multimedia
- Transparency 47

The Nervous System

1 FOCUS

QUICK START Invite students to work together to brainstorm comparisons between the nervous system and various forms of current technology. Then give students four minutes to write out their own comparisons, including as many supporting details as possible. Ask students to save their paragraphs for use at the end of the lesson.

TYING TO PRIOR KNOWLEDGE

Guide students in recognizing some of the facts they already know about the nervous system. Explain that this lesson presents further information about the structure and the function of the nervous system.

INTRODUCING VOCABULARY

- Have students work with partners to read the vocabulary terms and discuss what they already know about each. Then ask partners to work together in looking up, reading, and discussing the Glossary definitions of the terms.

- Ask students to complete the Chapter 15 Study Guide in the *Student Activity Workbook.*

②TEACH

Reinforcing Concepts

Have several volunteers explain, in their own words, the difference between the CNS and the PNS. Ask: How are the two related? [L1]

Activity

Point out that nerve impulses, which travel at speeds up to 280 miles per hour, do not travel distances of miles or for periods of an hour or more. Invite a group of volunteers to calculate how many feet per minute and how many inches per second nerve impulses can travel. Let them share the results of their calculations with the rest of the class. [L2] **Logical/ Mathematical**

Reinforcing Concepts

As students read about the parts of a neuron, have them identify each part in Figure 15.3. [L1]

VISUAL LEARNING

Figure 15.3 Have students work in cooperative groups to examine and discuss the illustration. Ask group members to trace with their fingers the route that a nerve impulse travels. Have group members take turns identifying and describing each aspect of the nervous system along that route.

Explaining

Let students share what they may have read or heard about surgeries to reattach or transplant limbs. Be sure students understand that such surgeries involve connecting parts of the skeletal, muscular, and nervous systems. [L1]

400

Neurons

Messages are transmitted to and from the spinal cord and brain by **neurons**, or *nerve cells*. Neurons are classified by their function: sensory neurons, motor neurons, and interneurons. Interneurons communicate with and are found between other neurons. **Figure 15.3** illustrates the nerve impulse.

A neuron consists of three main parts:

▶ **Cell body.** The cell body of a neuron contains the nucleus, the control center of the cell. The nucleus regulates the production of proteins within the cell. Unlike other cells in the body, neurons have limited ability to repair damage or replace destroyed cells.

▶ **Dendrites.** Dendrites are branched structures that extend from the cell body in most neurons. Dendrites receive information from other neurons or sensory receptors and transmit impulses toward the cell body.

▶ **Axons.** Axons transmit impulses away from the cell body and toward another neuron, muscle cell, or gland. Some axons are surrounded by a covering called a myelin sheath and can transmit impulses more quickly than axons without coverings.

FIGURE 15.3

THE NERVE IMPULSE

A nerve impulse begins when a sensory receptor is stimulated. The impulse travels to the CNS and is interpreted with the help of an interneuron. Then a motor neuron carries the message to a muscle cell or gland in response to the stimulus.

Sensory Neuron
interneuron dendrites (receptors)
interneuron cell body
skin
receptors
axon
cell body of sensory neuron

Motor Neuron
motor neuron dendrites
motor neuron cell body
axon
synapse
skeletal muscle

More About...

Sensory Neurons Sensory neurons in the cerebrum allow a sensation—seeing, hearing, feeling, smelling, or tasting—to trigger the re-creation of a past experience.

Sensory neurons located in muscles are triggering mechanisms for the stretch reflex. The body reacts to overstretching with muscle contractions and pain.

Sensory neurons in the walls of the stomach send us "hunger pangs" when the stomach is empty and ready to be filled.

Sensory neurons in the esophagus and pharynx signal the gag reflex when contacted, causing the stomach to contract and possibly regurgitate its contents.

The Central Nervous System

Impulses in the body are carried to and from either the spinal cord or the brain, the two organs that make up the central nervous system, as shown in **Figure 15.4.**

FIGURE **15.4**

THE NERVOUS SYSTEM

Nerves extend to various parts of the body along the length of the spinal cord.

cerebrum

cerebellum

spinal cord

vertebra

Spinal Cord Cross Section
white matter
spinal cord
gray matter

Spinal Meninges
spinal nerve
pia mater
arachnoid
dura mater
vertebra (bone)

12 pairs of cranial nerves

8 pairs of cervical nerves

12 pairs of thoracic nerves

5 pairs of lumbar nerves

5 pairs of sacral nerves

1 pair of coccygeal nerves

The Spinal Cord

The spinal cord is a long column of nerve tissue about the thickness of your index finger, extending about 18 inches down your back. Vertebrae are the bones that make up your spine. Connective tissue called the spinal meninges, along with the vertebrae, help protect the spinal cord. The spinal cord is also bathed in cerebrospinal fluid that absorbs shock and nourishes nerve tissue.

Discussing

Have students describe the spectrum of sensations that produce pleasure or pain from the receptor of sensory neurons. For example: favorite music and loud sirens; the aroma of baking bread and the smell of a skunk. **L1**

Cooperative Learning

Invite students to meet in groups to discuss the following situation: *You are attending a concert featuring your favorite music group. At the end of the concert, you are so excited that you jump to your feet and applaud loudly.* Have group members list all the processes involved in the nervous system that are related to this kind of reaction. **L2**

VISUAL LEARNING

Figure 15.4 Let volunteers read aloud the title of the figure and the label for each part. Have the other students point to each part as it is named. Ask: Which labeled parts belong to the CNS? Which belong to the PNS?

Then focus students' attention on the cross section of the spinal cord. Help them recognize the complexity as they name and point to the various sections.

Quick Demo

Using a skeletal model, help students locate the cervical (neck), thoracic (chest), and lumbar (lower back) vertebrae that are the origin of nerves. **L1**

Cooperative Learning Activity

Optical Illusions Explain that we experience optical illusions when our nervous system "tricks" our eyes into seeing something that is not really there. Let students work in cooperative groups to learn more about optical illusions. Have group members use online and library resources to explore the topic. Then have them select a specific optical illusion to share and explain. Suggest that groups make posters presenting both an optical illusion and the explanation of how and why that illusion works. Or let group members plan and use another method of presenting their example and research findings to the rest of the class.

Encourage students to work with partners in checking the Web Links. Suggest that partners generate a list of questions that interest them and then use the links to find the answers to their questions.

Activity

Give students two minutes to list specific activities that involve the brain. At the end of the time, ask: How many activities did you list?

Then let volunteers read aloud some of the items on their lists. Encourage students to discuss how the brain is involved in each. 🔲

Reinforcing Concepts

Ask students:

- What is the significance of the fact that the brain can last without oxygen only four to five minutes before suffering serious and irreversible damage?

- In which kinds of situations can this time period be critical? 🔲

Discussing

Guide students in discussing the drawing of a brain. Ask: What can you learn about the location and relative size of the parts of the brain? 🔲

Understand more about how scientists can trace activities in the brain. Check Web Links at **health.glencoe.com.**

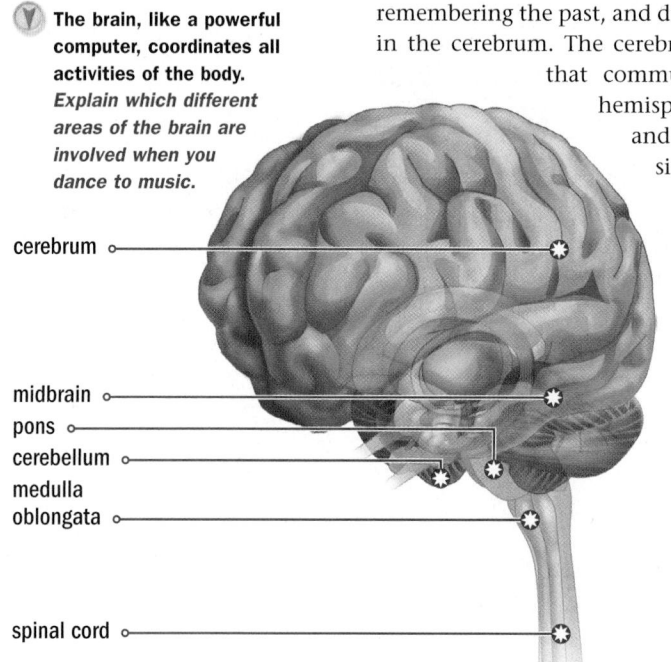

The brain, like a powerful computer, coordinates all activities of the body. *Explain which different areas of the brain are involved when you dance to music.*

cerebrum

midbrain
pons
cerebellum
medulla
oblongata

spinal cord

The Brain

The brain, shown in the illustration, integrates and controls the activities of the nervous system. Your brain helps you receive and process messages; think, remember, and reason; and coordinate muscle movements. Breathing, digesting food, learning math, running a race, and remembering a family vacation are all processes accomplished by the brain. It is involved in emotions and all of your senses.

An adult human brain weighs up to three pounds and sits in the protective cavity formed by the bones of the skull. Like the spinal cord, the brain is covered with layers of cranial meninges and surrounded by cerebrospinal fluid. Both help protect the tissues of the brain from injury. Although the brain makes up only about 2 percent of a person's total body weight, it uses more than 20 percent of the oxygen inhaled. Without oxygen, the brain can last for only four to five minutes before suffering serious and irreversible damage.

The brain has three main divisions: the cerebrum, the cerebellum, and the brain stem.

THE CEREBRUM

The **cerebrum** is *the largest and most complex part of the brain.* It is covered with a thin layer of gray matter. The billions of neurons in the cerebrum are the center for conscious thought, learning, and memory. Learning how to use language, creating art and music, remembering the past, and dreaming about the future all take place in the cerebrum. The cerebrum is divided into two hemispheres that communicate with each other. The right hemisphere controls the left side of the body, and the left hemisphere controls the right side of the body. Both hemispheres contain centers for different processes that take place in the brain. The left hemisphere is the center for language, reasoning, and the ability to analyze and think critically about mathematical or scientific problems. The right hemisphere is the center for processing music and art and comprehending spatial relationships.

Each hemisphere has four lobes, and each lobe is named after the skull bone that protects it:

402 Chapter 15 Skeletal, Muscular, and Nervous Systems

More About...

Adolescent Brain Development
Recent research shows that the brains of preadolescents and adolescents undergo a series of growth spurts that actually encourage learning, especially of foreign languages and mathematics. Although learning can and does continue throughout life, adolescence may present a particular "key period" for learning opportunities.

Different areas of the brain experience greatest growth during different periods of childhood. From 3 to 6 years of age, the frontal circuits are the sites of particular brain growth. Between the ages of 7 and 15, the primary areas of brain development are the temporal and parietal lobes. These are the areas involved in memory and manual skills.

- **The frontal lobe** controls voluntary movements and has a role in the use of language. The prefrontal areas are thought to be involved with intellect and personality.

- **The parietal lobe** is involved with sensory information such as heat, cold, pain, touch, and body position in space.

- **The occipital lobe** controls the sense of vision.

- **The temporal lobe** controls the senses of hearing and smell; it is also involved with memory, thought, and judgment.

THE CEREBELLUM

The **cerebellum** is *the second largest part of the brain*. Its principal function is to coordinate the movement of skeletal muscles. This area of the brain continually receives messages from sensory neurons in the inner ear and muscles, and it uses this information to maintain the body's posture and balance. Being able to complete a complex series of muscle movements, such as serving a volleyball, dancing, or playing the violin, is made possible by the cerebellum.

THE BRAIN STEM

The **brain stem** is *a three-inch stalk of nerve cells and fibers that connects the spinal cord to the rest of the brain*. Incoming sensory impulses and outgoing motor impulses pass through the brain stem. It consists of three main parts—the medulla oblongata, the pons, and the midbrain—and two smaller regions—the thalamus and the hypothalamus.

- **Medulla oblongata.** Rising from the top portion of the spinal cord, the medulla oblongata is the lowest part of the brain stem. Within the medulla are centers that regulate heartbeat and respiratory rates as well as reflexes such as coughing, sneezing, and vomiting. The medulla also receives input and sends motor impulses to the cochlea of the inner ear for hearing and to the tongue for movement during speech and swallowing.

- **Pons.** Approximately one inch in length, the pons is just above the medulla. The pons is the pathway connecting nerve impulses to other areas of the brain; it also helps regulate breathing. The pons controls the muscles of the eyes and face.

- **Midbrain.** The highest portion of the brain stem, the midbrain is involved in such functions as controlling eyeball movement and pupil size. The reflexive response of turning your head when you hear an unexpected loud noise is also initiated by the midbrain.

- **Thalamus.** The thalamus is an important relay center for incoming sensory impulses. Nerve cells within the thalamus

How do scientists learn about the brain?
Recent advances in technology have enabled scientists to "see" inside a living brain. Brain imaging techniques help scientists understand the functions of the brain, locate areas affected by neurological disorders, and develop new strategies to treat brain disorders. These techniques include:

- CT, or "CAT" scans, in which a series of X rays are beamed through the head, producing an image that shows the structure of the brain.
- PET scans, in which a machine detects and images radioactive material that is either injected into or inhaled by the patient. This type of scan provides information on brain function.
- MRI, which uses radio waves and magnetic fields to produce an anatomical view of the brain.

Lesson 4 The Nervous System **403**

Cooperative Learning

Divide the class into three groups. Assign each group one of the main divisions of the brain. Ask group members to read about that part of the brain and, if time permits, to further research its structure and functions. Then have students plan and present a poster, a skit, a song, or another instructional aid summarizing the information about the brain part for the rest of the class. **L2**

Activity

Have interested volunteers use dictionaries to find out about the derivation of the words *cerebrum* and *cerebellum*. How are the two words related? **L2 Verbal/Linguistic**

Ask a volunteer to read the question aloud, and invite other students to share what they have read in the news or heard about brain research. Then guide students in reading and discussing the brain imaging techniques scientists use. Encourage interested students to learn more about these techniques and to discuss their findings with the rest of the class.

Curriculum Connections

Psychology Suggest that interested students research the right-brain and left-brain theory. Have students make a notebook about the theory. They should include articles from newspapers, magazines, or the Internet relating to the theory. Then ask each student to determine whether he or she is right-brain or left-brain dominant. Have students provide an assessment from their research to determine right- or left-brain dominance.

In their notebooks, have students consider the validity of the precept that *we can all draw*. Ask: What does this imply for people who are not comfortable with drawing? They have not developed that part of the brain.

Cooperative Learning

Let students work in small cooperative groups to learn more about brain size. Have the members of each group select four animals, living or extinct. How large is each animal's brain? How does it compare in size and weight to the human brain? Ask group members to prepare and share posters or other displays that present their conclusions. **L2 Visual/Spatial**

Activity

Have each student choose a body part—such as heart, lungs, or intestines—and write a paragraph describing the functions of the sympathetic and parasympathetic nervous systems on this organ: What are the physical signs that show the effects of the nervous system response? **L2**

Discussing

Guide students in discussing the relationship between the actions of the sympathetic and parasympathetic nervous systems. Why is balance between these two systems important? **L1**

Quick Demo

Have students work with a partner to demonstrate the knee-jerk reflex. One student sits in a chair crossing his or her legs. The other student uses the side of an extended hand to gently strike the soft area just below the kneecap. Ask: What happened? What caused this to happen? Then have students switch roles.

hotlink

pituitary gland For more information about the work of the pituitary gland, see Chapter 18, page 465.

▼ **When you are nervous about taking a big test, increased heart rate and sweaty palms are signs that your sympathetic nervous system is at work.** *Name another situation that will cause a response from your sympathetic nervous system.*

receive information from different sense organs such as the eyes and ears. Through the spine the thalamus also receives information from touch and pressure receptors in the skin.

▶ **Hypothalamus.** The hypothalamus controls and balances various body processes to regulate body temperature, stimulate appetite for food and drink, and regulate sleep. The hypothalamus also controls secretions from the **pituitary gland** that control metabolism, sexual development, and emotional responses.

The Peripheral Nervous System

The peripheral nervous system (PNS) consists of all of the nerves that are not part of the CNS. The PNS carries messages between the CNS and the rest of the body. The PNS can be divided into two sections, the autonomic nervous system and the somatic nervous system.

The Autonomic Nervous System

The autonomic nervous system (ANS) controls such involuntary functions as digestion and heart rate. The ANS consists of a network of nerves divided into two parts: the sympathetic nervous system and the parasympathetic nervous system.

THE SYMPATHETIC NERVOUS SYSTEM

You may have felt the effects of the sympathetic nervous system the last time you were startled. Messages from the sympathetic nervous system cause your heart rate to increase and the blood vessels leading to your muscles to dilate, allowing greater blood flow. This is the "fight or flight" response that prepares your body to react to what may be a dangerous situation. You also have experienced a **reflex**, *a spontaneous response of the body to a stimulus,* as when a doctor tests the knee-jerk reflex by tapping the ligament below the knee. **Figure 15.5** on page 405 shows the steps of a reflex action.

THE PARASYMPATHETIC NERVOUS SYSTEM

During periods of rest and relaxation, the parasympathetic system opposes the action of the sympathetic system by slowing body functions. It slows down the heartbeat, opens blood vessels, and lowers blood pressure.

Somatic Nervous System

The somatic nervous system consists of sensory neurons that relay messages from receptors in the eyes, ears, nose, tongue, and skin to the CNS and motor neurons that carry impulses from the CNS to skeletal muscles.

404 Chapter 15 Skeletal, Muscular, and Nervous Systems

School to Work

Help for Damaged Nervous Systems
Have students conduct research about the function that crawling and opposite arm-and-leg movements play in the development of infants' and children's nervous systems. Then ask students to relate this research to modern rehabilitation techniques. Have students research the work of physical therapists and occupational therapists. Have them consider: What are the similarities and differences? What are the qualifications for each? Encourage students to find out about what such therapists can do, in partnership with neurologists, to help victims of brain or nerve damage recover part or all of their functions.

FIGURE 15.5

STEPS OF A REFLEX ACTION

Reflexes can prevent injuries. For example, when you touch something hot, your hand jerks away before you feel your finger being burned.

1. **Stimulus:** the hand touches a hot stove.

2. The **sensory neuron** makes contact with a **connecting neuron** in the spinal cord.

3. The **connecting neuron** contacts a **motor neuron** that sends an impulse to the muscles.

4. **Reflex:** The muscle responses by pulling the hand away from the stove.

Lesson 4 Review

Reviewing Facts and Vocabulary

1. What is the main function of the brain?

2. Define the term *neuron*. What are the parts of a neuron?

3. What is a *reflex*? How does having quick reflexes benefit your health?

Thinking Critically

4. **Analyzing.** After sustaining a head injury, a patient is having trouble understanding language and controlling movement on the right side of his or her body. What parts of the brain could be damaged?

5. **Evaluating.** Why is an injury to the brain stem considered critical?

Applying Health Skills

Advocacy. Research additional material on the benefits of wearing a helmet when biking, skating, or skateboarding. Make an informative pamphlet that outlines helmet laws and explains the importance of protecting the brain from injury. Make your pamphlet available to your classmates.

PRESENTATION SOFTWARE Use presentation software to illustrate your pamphlet. See health.glencoe.com for tips on using presentation software.

VISUAL LEARNING

Figure 15.5 Ask several students to explain, in their own words, an example of a reflex response. Then guide students in reading and studying Figure 15.5 to understand how a reflex response works.

③ ASSESS

EVALUATING THE LESSON

Assign and discuss the Lesson 4 Review; then administer, grade, and discuss Lesson Quiz 57 in the TCR. 📁

RETEACHING

- Have students work with partners to draw diagrams showing the related parts of the nervous system. (CNS—spinal cord, brain; PNS—autonomic, somatic)

- Ask students to complete Reteaching Activity 57 in the TCR. 📁

ENRICHMENT

Have students research phantom limbs or phantom pain. Ask students to summarize their findings in written reports. Have the students proofread and revise their writing. You may need to encourage them to write several drafts before handing in a final error-free draft.

④ CLOSE

Have students review their responses to the Quick Start assignment for this lesson. What changes would they make to their paragraphs?

Lesson 4 Review

Answers to Reviewing Facts and Vocabulary

1. The brain integrates and controls the activities of the nervous system.
2. Neuron is a nerve cell; cell body, dendrites, and axons.
3. A reflex is a spontaneous response of the body to a stimulus. Reflexes allow you to withdraw from dangerous situations.

Answers to Thinking Critically

4. The damage could have occurred in the left cerebral hemisphere and possibly in the part of the cerebellum that coordinates muscle movements.
5. It controls many vital functions in the body, such as heart and respiration rates; serious injury can result in death.

Care and Problems of the Nervous System

Lesson 5

❶ FOCUS

QUICK START Let students work with partners to list common activities that could cause head or spinal injuries. Then invite volunteers to read their lists aloud. Encourage students to discuss how they protect themselves from accidents and injuries.

TYING TO PRIOR KNOWLEDGE

Refer to the Quick Start assignment to help students recognize that they are already familiar with practices that help them protect the health of their nervous system. Explain that this lesson presents more information on such care as well as potential problems of the nervous system.

Health Skills Features

"Decision Making: Riding Smart," p. 407

DECISION MAKING

INTRODUCING VOCABULARY

- In a brief class discussion, have students share what they know about epilepsy and cerebral palsy. Then let students work with partners to find, read, and discuss the Glossary definitions of these terms.

- Ask students to complete the Chapter 15 Study Guide in the *Student Activity Workbook*. 📁

Care and Problems of the Nervous System

VOCABULARY
epilepsy
cerebral palsy

YOU'LL LEARN TO
- Examine the effects of health behaviors that prevent injury to the nervous system.
- Identify different types of head and spinal cord injuries.
- Describe different diseases and disorders of the nervous system.

QUICK START Make a list of how often you engage in activities in which there is a risk of head or spinal injury. What do you do to protect these areas during the activity?

▼ Take care of your nervous system by protecting your head. Wear an approved helmet when participating in outdoor activities and certain sports.

Proper use of helmets and safety belts protects the brain and spinal column from injury. Your nervous system interacts and coordinates with all other body systems so that your body will remain internally balanced and functioning properly. Any injury to the nervous system affects the immediate tissues and may lead to dysfunction in other areas of the body.

Care of the Nervous System

Your overall health habits, such as eating a well-balanced diet, exercising regularly, and getting enough sleep, contribute to the health of your nervous system. Keep your nervous system healthy by protecting it from injury. To protect your head and spine, wear a helmet and protective gear while riding a bike, motorcycle, or other open vehicle or when playing a contact sport or engaging in activities such as skateboarding. Before diving, always check water depth and look along the bottom for protruding logs or rocks. Wear a safety belt when driving or riding in a motor vehicle. Avoid the use of alcohol and drugs, which can cause permanent damage.

406 Chapter 15

Lesson 5 *Resources*

Teacher Classroom Resources
📁 Concept Mapping Activity 58
📁 Guided Reading Activities 58
📁 Lesson Plan 58
📁 Lesson Quiz 58
📁 Reteaching Activity 58

Student Activity Workbook
📁 Applying Health Skills 58
📁 Chapter 15 Study Guide

Problems of the Nervous System

Problems of the nervous system can result from damage to nerve cells or injury to the head or spinal cord. Nerve tissue can also be damaged by degenerative diseases. Using **drugs** and **alcohol** can destroy brain cells and cause nervous system disorders.

Head and Spinal Cord Injuries

In the United States each year, over one million people sustain head injuries and an estimated 11,000 new cases of spinal cord injury occur. These injuries may result from falls, sports or recreational activities, motor vehicle crashes, physical assaults, or gunshot wounds.

HEAD INJURIES

Although the brain is protected by the bones of the skull, any direct blow to the head can cause injury. A concussion, the mildest

hot link

drugs For more information on how drugs damage the nervous system, see Chapter 23, page 604.
alcohol For more information on the effects of alcohol, see Chapter 22, page 569.

Health Skills Activity

Decision Making: Riding Smart

When Alfonso's friend Noah wants to give him a ride home from school on his motorcycle, Alfonso hesitates. An avid dirt bike rider, Alfonso knows the importance of wearing a helmet. Unfortunately, Noah doesn't have a spare one.

"Hop on, Alfonso," Noah says, "there's a thunderstorm coming. The sooner we get home, the better."

"I'd really like to," Alfonso replies, "but you don't have an extra helmet. I never ride without one."

"Don't worry," Noah says. "We're going only a couple of miles and I know a short cut. Nothing can happen in that short distance."

As the thunderstorm nears, Alfonso wonders what he should do.

What Would You Do?
Apply the six steps of the decision-making process to help Alfonso make a health-enhancing decision.
1. State the situation.
2. List the options.
3. Weigh the possible outcomes.
4. Consider values.
5. Make a decision and act.
6. Evaluate the decision.

More About...

Injuries to the CNS Concussion occurs when the brain absorbs external forces and collides with the cranium, causing the brain to bruise. The bruise usually occurs on the side opposite the initial impact. Symptoms normally become evident within 24 hours of the injury and include loss of memory, disorientation, loss of balance, blurred vision, and minor to extreme levels of unconsciousness.

Research efforts are opening up exciting new recovery possibilities for those with spinal cord injury. In 2002, Christopher Reeve, who had been completely paralyzed from the neck down due to a horseback riding accident, achieved the ability to move some of his fingers and toes and to distinguish between hot and cold sensations.

---

② TEACH

Health Skills Activity

RIDING SMART

NHES Standard 6
Students will demonstrate the ability to use goal-setting and decision-making skills to enhance health.

Objectives
- Identify health behaviors that help prevent injury to the nervous system.
- Identify decision-making skills that promote individual health.

Motivator
Bring a bicycle or a motorcycle helmet to class, and review how helmets decrease the risk of serious head injury in a collision.

Teaching Strategies
1. Tell students that head injuries are the major cause of death in motorcycle collisions.
2. Point out that Alfonso has two safety decisions to make: whether to ride without a helmet and how to avoid exposure to lightning. Students should arrive at a decision that represents options for avoiding both risks.

✓Assessment

Using a rubric, student work should provide comprehensive evidence of the following criteria to achieve the highest score:
✔ clear description of the situation
✔ several options with possible outcomes of each
✔ influence of values on possible decisions
✔ health-enhancing decision and an evaluation of it

Discussing

Help students discuss how avoiding alcohol, tobacco, and other drugs can help protect the health of their nervous systems. Emphasize that alcohol, tobacco, and other drugs can do direct damage to nerve cells; in addition, they put individuals at greater risk of injury.

FYI

The Spinal Cord Injury Information Network estimates that every year, 11,000 Americans suffer from spinal cord injuries.

Activity

Ask students to use online or library resources to learn more about current research into the treatment of Parkinson's disease, multiple sclerosis, or Alzheimer's disease. Suggest that students look into the efforts and attention generated by celebrities and figures such as Michael J. Fox and Ronald Reagan. **L3**

CHARACTER CHECK

Caring Guide students in reading and discussing the suggestions for showing care for those who are disabled. Encourage students to share their own experiences and plans for helping others.

CHARACTER CHECK

Caring. When you understand the effects a nervous system disease can have, you can find ways to help others through a difficult time. **Offering your companionship; reading aloud; or helping with small tasks such as letter writing, watering plants, grocery shopping, or meal delivery are meaningful ways to help those who are disabled.**

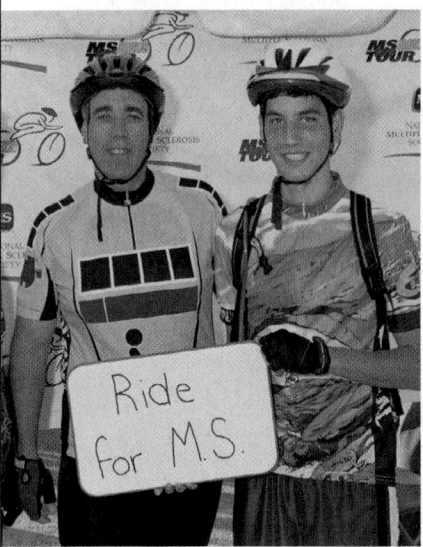

Bicycle tours and races are often held to fund research on degenerative diseases such as multiple sclerosis. *Participating in a fund-raising event can be a rewarding experience. Find out more about such opportunities in your community.*

and most common type of brain injury, results in a temporary loss of consciousness, sometimes lasting only a few seconds. A more serious brain injury is a contusion, a bruising of the brain tissues that can result in dangerous swelling. A major trauma to the brain can result in a coma, a state of unconsciousness from which a person cannot be roused.

SPINAL INJURIES

Any injury to the spine must be considered serious and should be evaluated by a health care professional. Some spinal injuries are mild, and full recovery is possible. Swelling of the spinal cord or the tissue around it in response to trauma can result in temporary loss of nerve function. Without treatment, this can lead to permanent nerve damage. If the spinal cord has been severed or damaged beyond repair, paralysis usually results. An injury to the upper part of the spinal cord may result in *quadriplegia,* or paralysis of both upper and lower limbs. *Paraplegia,* paralysis of both lower limbs, can be caused by an injury that occurs at a lower point in the spinal column.

Degenerative Diseases

Degenerative diseases cause affected cells and tissues to break down or deteriorate over time. Common degenerative ailments of the nervous system are listed below.

▶ **Parkinson's disease** results in the destruction of nerve cells in an area of the brain that helps coordinate skeletal muscle movement. Parkinson's is a progressive disorder, meaning that it gradually involves more and more nerves. As the cells are destroyed, muscle function is impaired. Symptoms include uncontrolled muscle tremors and increased muscle rigidity. There is no known cause or cure at present.

▶ **Multiple sclerosis** involves the destruction of the myelin sheath that surrounds the axons of neurons in the CNS. The scar tissue that remains on the neuron interferes with the conduction of nerve impulses, and voluntary control of muscles gradually decreases. With each attack, loss of nerve function increases. Multiple sclerosis is an autoimmune disease in which the body attacks its own tissues.

▶ **Alzheimer's disease** results when neurons are destroyed. If neurons become clogged with protein deposits, they are unable to transmit impulses. The result is confusion, loss of memory, and gradual mental deterioration. Currently, the cause of Alzheimer's disease is unknown, but the search to find prevention methods continues.

Dealing with Sensitive Issues

Epilepsy It is important to be prepared to respond in case a student has an epileptic seizure in the classroom. Talk to the class about how to deal with the situation. Stress that the individual needs support.

During a seizure, do the following:

• Move all items that may cause injury to the affected student.

• Loosen all restrictive clothing.
• Try to keep the student on his or her side.
• Do not try to retrieve the tongue if it lodges in the throat.
• Send for medical help.
• When the seizure is over, reassure the student that everything is okay.
• Contact parents and medical personnel.

Other Disorders and Problems

Other disorders of the nervous system may not be progressive or degenerative. In some cases a cause may never be identified. These disorders include the following:

▶ **Epilepsy** is *a disorder of the nervous system that is characterized by recurrent seizures—sudden episodes of uncontrolled electrical activity in the brain.* Epilepsy can be caused by several different factors, including brain damage before or during birth, infections, head injury, withdrawal from drugs or alcohol, or exposure to toxins. Seizures may be small and brief, involving little body movement; or they may be quite severe, involving muscle contractions throughout the entire body. Medications can help control seizures so that a person with epilepsy can lead a normal, healthy life.

▶ **Cerebral palsy** refers to *a group of nonprogressive neurological disorders that are the result of damage to the brain before, during, or just after birth or in early childhood.* Some causes of cerebral palsy may include infections such as encephalitis or meningitis, head injury, or exposure to radiation before birth. Physical therapy, braces to enable walking, and medication can help cerebral palsy patients be independent and participate in everyday activities.

Ⓨ **Many people lead full, independent lives in spite of nervous system disorders.** *How would you encourage a close friend or family member who is coping with a nervous system disorder?*

Lesson 5 Review

Reviewing Facts and Vocabulary

1. What precautions should you take before diving into water?
2. Explain the difference between a concussion and a coma.
3. How does multiple sclerosis affect the nervous system?

Thinking Critically

4. **Analyzing.** Examine the effects of health behaviors you can practice to prevent injury to the nervous system. Give a specific example.
5. **Evaluating.** Most states have enacted laws requiring that children under a certain age be restrained by car seats, booster seats, or safety belts. How do such laws benefit the health of small children?

Applying Health Skills

Accessing Information. Write a one-page report on research that is being done to treat spinal cord injuries. Which treatments have had the most success? Why is it so difficult to restore function to the spinal cord after it has been injured?

INTERNET RESOURCES Find more information about spinal cord injuries in Web Links at health.glencoe.com.

Discussing

Guide students in discussing the causes of epilepsy. Ask:

- What can individuals do to protect themselves from factors that can cause epilepsy?
- Which factors cannot be controlled by the individual who might be affected by epilepsy? L1

③ ASSESS

EVALUATING THE LESSON

Assign and discuss the Lesson 5 Review; then administer, grade, and discuss Lesson Quiz 58 in the TCR.

RETEACHING

- Working with small groups, help students recall specific habits that contribute to and help protect the health of the nervous system.
- Ask students to complete Reteaching Activity 58 in the TCR.

ENRICHMENT

Have students research, using online and print sources, the use of acupuncture to calm nerves and ease pain without any risk of the side effects associated with drugs. Let students discuss their findings and their opinions about acupuncture.

Lesson 5 Review

Answers to Reviewing Facts and Vocabulary

1. Check water's depth and look for protruding objects.
2. A concussion results in a temporary loss of consciousness. A coma is a state of unconsciousness from which the person cannot be roused.
3. The myelin sheath that surrounds the axons is destroyed. The resulting scar tissue interferes with nerve impulses.

Answers to Thinking Critically

4. Answers will vary.
5. Possible answer: Such laws help reduce head and spinal injuries.

④ CLOSE

Have each student list two short-term and two long-term advantages of making choices that promote the health of the nervous system.

409

Soft Drink versus Milk Advertisements

NHES Standard 4 Students will analyze the influence of culture, media, technology, and other factors on health.

Objective

Compare the differences between soft drink and milk advertisements.

Motivator

Ask students if they have ever seen an advertisement for milk.

Teaching Strategies

Ask a couple of students to share their responses to the Motivator. Ask them to describe the ad and where they saw it.

Awareness Tell students that while soft drink companies use different media outlets for ads, milk ads are often seen on billboards or in magazines.

Analysis Ask students what other generic food products could be advertised that would help ensure bone health.

Reflection Some milk ads use celebrities to sell their product. Ask students what the impact is of using celebrities to sell products.

Take Action Ask students to create an advertisement for another generic food product that is rich in calcium. Encourage them to get permission to hang the ads in the school cafeteria or near school vending machines.

✓Assessment

Students should have extensive lists of where soft drink ads appear. Essays should indicate that milk ads often make health claims about the benefits of drinking milk.

410

Eye ON THE Media

Soft Drink versus Milk Advertisements

Advertisements for soft drinks appear on shopping carts, video games, billboards, cups, scoreboards, and nearly everywhere people gather. Because milk consumption by youth has decreased dramatically in recent years, the National Dairy Council launched an advertising campaign that encourages teens and young adults to continue to drink milk. The milk campaign, however, is very different from the soft drink campaigns. Use the activity below to compare milk ads and soft drink ads.

Soft Drink Ads	Milk Ads
1. bus stop	1. poster in school cafeteria
2.	2.

ACTIVITY

Using a table similar to the one above, list the different commercial areas where soft drink ads appear. Then list places where milk ads can be seen. Compare the lists. Which beverage ad appears in more places and is more likely to appeal to teens? Does one type of beverage tend to advertise primarily in electronic or print media? How does the type of media attract certain age groups?

EXPRESS YOUR VIEWS

Choose one soft drink ad and one milk ad. Write a short essay comparing the two ads. Does either ad make health claims about its product? If the ad makes health claims, is the information accurate? Explain, basing your answers on what you've learned in the chapter.

More About...

Building Stronger Bones Recent studies have shown that young people should get calcium from a number of sources, not just dairy products. In fact, some studies have shown that diets high in animal protein have an adverse effect on calcium absorption. Calcium absorption from milk is approximately 30 percent while absorption from vegetables such as brussel sprouts, mustard greens, turnip greens, kale, green beans and some other leafy green vegetables range between 40 percent and 64 percent. Studies also show that children need to strengthen their bones by getting regular exercise and getting vitamin D from sunlight.

CROSS-CURRICULUM CONNECTIONS

Concrete Poem. A concrete poem is one in which words are arranged on the page to produce a picture. Write and design a concrete poem with the shape of a skeleton and words that explain how the skeletal system works. Before writing your poem, brainstorm with classmates some appropriate adjectives and adverbs, and discuss such poetic devices as alliteration and assonance to use in your poem.

Fitness in History. Physical activity benefits skeletal and muscular health. In recent years, fitness and aerobics classes have gained popularity in the United States. However, fitness and exercise is not new. In fact, many cultures, such as the Mayan or ancient Greek cultures, have a tradition of sports, games and fitness techniques. Write a short research report on a sport or game from one cultural or historical period. Create a poster that shows how that sport or game works as a form of physical fitness.

How Many Fingers? Each hand contains 27 bones: 8 carpal bones, 5 metacarpal bones, and 14 phalanges. Given that the body has 206 bones, what percentage of these are phalanges? What percentage of the total bones in your body do your hands contain?

Biomechanics. People in the field of biomechanics study how the muscular and skeletal systems function. Biomechanics seeks to improve the efficiency of muscle use in order to improve performance, particularly in sports. Biomechanics is the basis for the field of ergonomics, the design of work spaces that provide the most comfort and efficiency. Investigate and discuss how advances in these fields may impact the future of manufacturing, sports, and everyday life.

Physical Therapy Assistant

Do you enjoy seeing people make progress and reach goals? Physical therapy assistants work with people to help them recover mobility after an injury or reduce the impact of a progressive condition such as multiple sclerosis.

To become a physical therapy assistant, you need a high school diploma or its equivalent. After high school, physical therapy assistants complete a two-year program and receive an associate's degree. Find out more by clicking on Career Corner at **health.glencoe.com**.

Chapter 15 Review **411**

Portfolio Assessment

Self-Evaluation Direct students to review the Health Skills Activities and other activities completed in the chapter. Encourage each student to select one finished product or activity that demonstrates his or her best work for the chapter and that represents the student's learning goals. Have students explain what they have learned and how the examples they have selected demonstrate their growth in health literacy, knowledge, and skills.

Teacher Classroom Resources Assign Performance Assessment 15, "No Bones About It," in the TCR.

CROSS-CURRICULUM CONNECTIONS

Enrich student learning by connecting the three body systems covered in this chapter to one of the four subject areas presented on this page. The activity may be completed individually or with a partner.

Language Arts Review with students definitions for the following terms: adjective, adverb, and alliteration.

Social Studies Remind students to explore the topic by gathering factual information from several different sources.

Math Answers: $(14 \times 2) \times 100/206 = 13.59\%$ of the body's bones are phalanges $(27 \times 2) \times 100/206 = 26.21\%$ of the body's bones are in the hands

Science Questions such as "What are the limits to human performance?" are dealt with in this field. The most visible use of ergonomics is in the design of computer stations and equipment, but is also applied to the construction of shoes, furniture, automobiles and assembly lines.

Have students read and discuss the Career Corner information on physical therapy assistants. Ask interested students to explore the Glencoe Health Web site at **health.glencoe.com** for more information on this career.

CHECKING COMPREHENSION

- Assign and discuss the chapter review.
- Use Chapter 15 MindJogger Videoquiz to review the chapter. ▶◀

CHAPTER 15 REVIEW ANSWERS

Exploring Health Terms

1. axial skeleton
2. appendicular skeleton
3. ligament
4. tendon
5. osteoporosis
6. scoliosis
7. smooth muscles
8. cardiac muscle
9. muscle tone
10. hernia
11. brain stem
12. cerebellum
13. cerebrum
14. epilepsy
15. cerebral palsy

Recalling the Facts

1. Axial skeleton consists of the skull, spine, ribs, vertebrae, breastbone. Appendicular skeleton consists of the upper and lower limbs, shoulders, hips.

2. Long bones have a long column covered with compact bone (arms and legs); short bones are almost equal in length and width (wrists, hands, feet); flat bones are thinner and flatter than other bones (scapula); irregular bones' shapes do not fit into the other categories (facial bones).

3. Tendons attach muscles to bones. Muscles push and pull on bones, creating movement.

4. Early detection is important because scoliosis is a progressive disorder.

412

Chapter 15 *Review*

➤ EXPLORING HEALTH TERMS *Answer the following questions on a sheet of paper.*

Lesson 1 *Match each definition with the correct term.*

appendicular skeleton	ligament
axial skeleton	ossification
cartilage	tendon

1. A division of the skeletal system that includes the bones of the skull and face, the vertebrae, and the ribs.
2. A division of the skeletal system that includes the bones of the upper and lower limbs and the shoulders and hips.
3. A band of fibrous, slightly elastic connective tissue that attaches bone to bone.
4. A fibrous cord that attaches muscle to bone.

Lesson 2 *Identify each statement as True or False. If false, replace the underlined term with the correct term.*

| osteoporosis | scoliosis |
| repetitive motion injury | |

5. A condition in which there is a progressive loss of bone tissue is called <u>scoliosis</u>.
6. <u>Osteoporosis</u> is a lateral or side-to-side curvature of the spine.

Lesson 3 *Match each definition with the correct term.*

smooth muscles	skeletal muscles
flexors	extensors
cardiac muscle	muscle tone
tendonitis	hernia

7. The muscles that act on the lining of passageways in the body and on internal organs.
8. A type of striated muscle that forms the wall of the heart.
9. The natural tension in the fibers of a muscle.
10. A condition created when an organ or tissue protrudes through an area of weak muscle.

Lesson 4 *Fill in the blanks with the correct term.*

| brain stem | cerebrum | reflex |
| cerebellum | neurons | |

The (_11_) is a stalk of nerve cells and fibers that connects the spinal cord to the rest of the brain. The second largest part of the brain is the (_12_). The (_13_) is the largest and most complex part of the brain.

Lesson 5 *Replace the underlined words with the correct term.*

| epilepsy | cerebral palsy |

14. A disorder of the nervous system that is characterized by recurrent seizures is <u>cerebral palsy</u>.
15. <u>Epilepsy</u> is a group of nonprogressive neurological disorders that are the result of damage to the brain before, during, or just after birth.

➤ RECALLING THE FACTS *Use complete sentences to answer the following questions.*

Lesson 1

1. Compare and contrast the axial and appendicular skeletons.
2. Describe and give examples of each type of bone.
3. Explain how tendons are involved in movement.

Lesson 2

4. Why is the early detection of scoliosis important?
5. Explain the association between dislocated joints and torn ligaments. Identify situations that may require professional medical services.
6. Explain the difference between bursitis and arthritis.

---

5. Ligaments attach bone to bone and help stabilize bones at a joint. If a bone is pushed so far out of joint it is dislocated, the ligament holding that bone in place is likely to tear under the pressure. Answers will vary.

6. Bursitis is an inflammation of the bursa. It can result from overuse or injury. Arthritis is an inflammation of the joint itself.

7. The muscular system allows voluntary movement of the skeletal muscle. Smooth and cardiac muscles move food through the digestive system, regulate the diameter of blood vessels and respiratory passages, and keep the heart beating. Muscles also produce heat.

8. Good posture strengthens back muscles.

9. Muscular dystrophy is an inherited disorder that destroys skeletal muscle.

10. Meninges, layers of connective tissue; cerebrospinal fluid, which absorbs shock; and the bones of the skull and vertebrae

11. The brain stem consists of the medulla oblongata, the pons, and the midbrain. The

Lesson 3

7. Describe the functions of the muscular system.

8. Examine the effects of health behaviors on the muscular system. Why is good posture important to the health of your muscles?

9. What is muscular dystrophy?

Lesson 4

10. What natural protective mechanisms exist in the body for the brain and spinal cord?

11. Identify and describe the three parts of the brain stem.

12. Explain the difference between the autonomic nervous system and the somatic nervous system.

Lesson 5

13. Examine the effects of health behaviors, and name three ways to prevent spinal cord injury.

14. What are some symptoms that result from neuron damage caused by Alzheimer's disease?

15. What is quadriplegia? What is paraplegia?

16. What is a degenerative disease?

17. Compare and contrast Parkinson's disease and Alzheimer's disease.

nerves that help control skeletal muscle movements are destroyed. Alzheimer's disease results when neurons are destroyed, and/or become clogged with protein deposits.

Thinking Critically

1. Possible answers: eating a well-balanced diet that includes calcium, vitamin D, and phosphorus; getting regular physical activity including weight-bearing exercise; wearing protective gear (helmets, padding) when participating in sports or recreational activities.

2. Health behaviors that are practiced now can help prevent the development of some disorders later. Getting enough calcium and vitamin D and avoiding injury can help keep bones strong and healthy throughout life.

3. Involuntary control of important body processes enables them to continue even when a person is sleeping or thinking about other things.

4. The automatic and central nervous system.

5. Swelling of the brain or spinal tissues increases pressure in the confined space of the skull or vertebrae, compressing and damaging the tissues.

Health Skills Application

1.–5. Answers will vary.

► THINKING CRITICALLY

1. **Evaluating.** Describe what lifestyle choices you can make to protect your bones and skeletal system from damage or injury. *(LESSON 1)*

2. **Analyzing.** Although some bone and joint problems, such as osteoporosis and arthritis, seldom occur until later in life, why is it important to think about these conditions now? *(LESSON 2)*

3. **Applying.** What advantage is involuntary muscle control to processes such as the contraction of the heart and the movement of food through the digestive tract? *(LESSON 3)*

4. **Synthesizing.** After you run, your heart rate slows. Which parts of your nervous system are involved in this function? *(LESSON 4)*

5. **Evaluating.** How can swelling of the brain or spinal cord result in damage to these tissues? *(LESSON 5)*

► HEALTH SKILLS APPLICATION

1. **Communicating.** Your younger brother loves to in-line skate. However, he never wears protective gear while skating. List some strategies you can use to teach him about the importance of preventing injury and encourage him to change his behavior. *(LESSON 1)*

2. **Advocacy.** Find out how often screening for scoliosis is offered in your community. To which age groups does it apply? Is there a cost? Raise community awareness by making and displaying a poster that advertises the next screening. *(LESSON 2)*

3. **Analyzing Influences.** A healthy muscular system depends on physical activity. Even when people are aware of this connection, they may fail to get the physical activity they need. List factors that may positively influence someone's decision to engage in physical activity. *(LESSON 3)*

4. **Accessing Information.** Use the Internet to find brain images made with Positron Emission Tomography (PET) scanners. Compare images of drug users' brains to those of individuals who have never used drugs. How could you use these images to explain the effects of drug use on the nervous system? *(LESSON 4)*

5. **Refusal Skills.** Alicia and her friends are exploring a lake in which they have not swum before. Someone spots a rock beneath the water's surface but suggests that it is probably safe to dive anyway. Write a dialogue between Alicia and her friends, demonstrating how she refuses to take this unnecessary risk. *(LESSON 5)*

EVALUATE

• Use the reproducible Chapter 15 Test in the TCR, or construct your own using the Testmaker software. 📁 💿

• Use Performance Assessment 15 in the TCR. 📁

ENRICHMENT

Ask students to complete Enrichment Activity 15 in the TCR. 📁

medulla connects the spinal cord to the brain and regulates heart and respiratory rates. The pons is involved in the regulation of breathing. The midbrain controls eye movement and pupil size.

12. The ANS consists of sensory neurons that bring impulses from receptors in internal organs and tissues to the CNS and motor neurons that transmit impulses from the CNS to smooth muscle, cardiac muscle, and glands. Somatic nervous system consists of sensory neurons and motor neurons.

13. Wear protective gear, check water before diving, avoid drug and alcohol use.

14. Confusion, memory loss, deterioration.

15. Quadriplegia is paralysis of both upper and lower limbs. Paraplegia affects the lower limbs.

16. A degenerative disease causes affected cells and tissues to break down or deteriorate over time.

17. Both are progressive, degenerative diseases of the CNS. Parkinson's disease occurs when

Lessons	Standards		Features
	National	**State/Local**	
1 The Cardiovascular System *pages 416–422*	National Health Education Standards 1.1, 1.3, 3.1, 6.6		
2 Care and Problems of the Cardiovascular System *pages 423–427*	National Health Education Standards 2.6, 3.2, 4.3, 7.1		
3 The Respiratory System *pages 428–431*	National Health Education Standards 1.1, 1.3, 3.1, 1.6		**Hands-On Health** • Seeing the Effects of Smoking *(Advocacy)*, page 430
4 Care and Problems of the Respiratory System *pages 432–435*	National Health Education Standards 1.5, 2.6, 5.1, 6.3		**Health Skills Activity** • Asthma and Physical Activity *(Communication)*, page 434

Reproducible Resources	Assessment	Technology
Student Activity Workbook for use with each chapter 📁 Concept Mapping Activity 59 📁 Current Health Issues 16 📁 Guided Reading Activities 59 📁 Health Lab 16 📁 Lesson Plan 59 📁 Parent Letter and Activities 16 📁 Reteaching Activity 59	📁 Lesson Quiz 59	🖨 Transparency 48 💿 TeacherWorks® 💻 Internet Activities
📁 Concept Mapping Activity 60 📁 Decision-Making Activity 16 📁 Guided Reading Activities 60 📁 Lesson Plan 60 📁 Reteaching Activity 60	📁 Lesson Quiz 60	🖨 Transparency 49 💿 TeacherWorks®
📁 Concept Mapping Activity 61 📁 Enrichment Activity 16 📁 Guided Reading Activities 61 📁 Lesson Plan 61 📁 Reteaching Activity 61	📁 Lesson Quiz 61	🖨 Transparency 50 💿 TeacherWorks®
📁 Concept Mapping Activity 62 📁 Cross-Curriculum Activity 16 📁 Guided Reading Activities 62 📁 Lesson Plan 62 📁 Reteaching Activity 62	📁 Lesson Quiz 62	💿 TeacherWorks®

0:00 OUT OF TIME

If time does not permit teaching the entire chapter, use:
- Figure 16.1, p. 418
- Figure 16.2, p. 420
- Figure 16.4, p. 429
- Health Skills Activity, p. 434
- Eye on the Media, p. 436

Language Diversity

- 🎧 English Audio CD Program
- 🎧 Spanish Audio CD Program
- 📁 English Summaries, Quizzes, and Activities
- 📁 Spanish Summaries, Quizzes, and Activities
- 📁 Spanish Parent Letters and Activities

End of Chapter Assessment

Blackline Masters
- 📁 Chapter 16 Test
- 📁 Performance Assessment Activity 16

Technology
- 💿 Vocabulary PuzzleMaker
- 📼 MindJogger Videoquiz
- 💿 **Exam**View® Pro Testmaker

Professional Health Series
Dealing with Sensitive Issues
Planning a Coordinated School Health Program
Promoting Character Education
Home, School, and Community Involvement

Key to Ability Levels

Teaching strategies that appear throughout the chapter have been identified by one of the following codes to give teachers an idea of their suitability for students of varying learning styles and abilities.

L1 Strategies should be within the ability range of all students. Full class participation is often required. Teacher direction is usually needed.

L2 Strategies are designed for average to above-average students or for small groups. Some teacher direction is needed.

L3 Strategies are designed for students able and willing to work independently. Minimal teacher direction is needed.

ELL Strategies should be within the ability range of students learning the English language.

📖 Block scheduling strategies are useful in a block scheduling format.

CHAPTER OVERVIEW

Chapter 16 discusses the structure, functioning, potential problems, and care of the cardiovascular and respiratory systems.

Lesson 1 The cardiovascular system moves blood through the body. This system includes the heart, blood vessels, and blood. The action of the heart is critical to cardiovascular function as it pumps blood through two major pathways, allowing for pulmonary and systemic circulation.

Lesson 2 Lifestyle choices and behaviors—such as maintaining a healthy weight; eating a balanced, low-fat diet; and engaging in regular physical activity—can protect the health of the cardiovascular system.

Lesson 3 The respiratory system functions externally to take in oxygen and give off carbon dioxide. Internally, it exchanges gases between the blood and body cells, releasing oxygen and taking in carbon dioxide.

Lesson 4 Not smoking is the most important step anyone can take to protect the health of the respiratory system. Avoiding secondhand smoke and engaging in regular physical activity are also important behaviors in promoting respiratory health.

Health Skills Features

- Hands-On Health *(Advocacy)*, p. 430
- Health Skills Activity *(Communication)*, p. 434

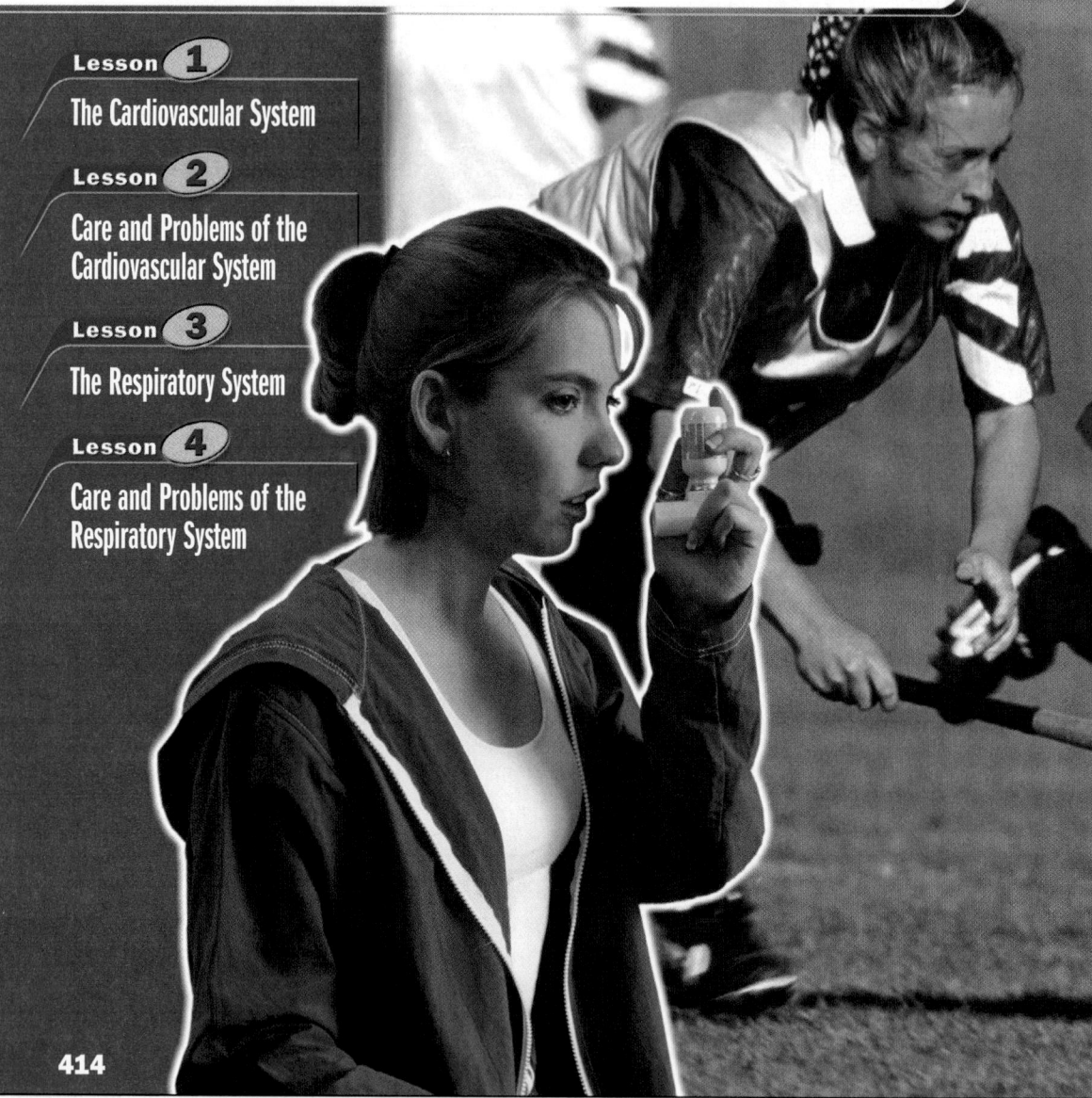

Chapter 16

Cardiovascular and Respiratory Systems

Lesson 1
The Cardiovascular System

Lesson 2
Care and Problems of the Cardiovascular System

Lesson 3
The Respiratory System

Lesson 4
Care and Problems of the Respiratory System

414

MEETING STUDENT DIVERSITY

Language Diversity Use the following suggestions to help students who have difficulty with English:

- Pair English language learners with native speakers of English who can restate the Chapter Summary in language that helps students comprehend important concepts.

- Direct auditory learners or those students with language diversity to the *Glencoe Health Audio CD Program.* Available in English and Spanish, this component provides an audio and written summary of the chapter.

- Use photographs, drawings, or magazine clippings to help students visualize the important concepts of the chapter.

Personal Health Inventory

What's Your Health Status?

Read each statement below and respond by writing *yes, no,* or *sometimes* for each item. Write *yes* only for items that you practice regularly.

1. I eat a well-balanced diet that is low in saturated fat, salt, and cholesterol.

2. I maintain a weight appropriate for my height.

3. I participate in aerobic physical activity at least three times a week for at least 30 minutes at a time.

4. I do not smoke or use tobacco products.

5. I eat foods that are high in iron, such as dark green leafy vegetables, dried fruits, and fortified cereals, every day.

6. I wash my hands regularly to reduce the risk of communicable disease.

7. I limit my exposure to pollutants in the air, including tobacco smoke.

8. I study, work, and exercise in well-ventilated areas.

9. I get at least eight to ten hours of sleep each night.

10. I get regular medical checkups that include monitoring the health of my cardiovascular and respiratory systems.

Keep this personal inventory for review later in the chapter. When you have completed the chapter, review your answers again and identify two or three behavior changes you could make to improve your health.

Quick Write

Using Visuals. Write a short paragraph describing how the cardiovascular and respiratory systems are important for participation in active sports. How might a respiratory condition such as asthma affect a person's ability to participate?

415

INTRODUCING THE CHAPTER

Personal Health Inventory

Have students work with partners to read and discuss the Personal Health Inventory statements. Encourage partners to share what they understand about each practice:

- Why is this important?
- What factors can make this difficult for teens?
- How does this practice affect physical health?
- What effects can it have on mental/emotional and social health?

After these partner discussions, have students work independently to record their responses. Assure students that their responses are confidential.

Quick Write

Using Visuals Have students look at the photographs and describe what the pictured teens are doing:

- What activity are these teens participating in?
- How do you think their cardiovascular and respiratory systems are involved?
- What piece of medical equipment is the teen in the smaller picture using?

After a discussion of the pictures, have students read and respond to the Quick Write assignment.

TECHNOLOGY OPTIONS

MINDJOGGER
VIDEOQUIZ

To preview or review chapter content, you may wish to use the Chapter 16 MindJogger Videoquiz. ▷◁

HEALTH Online

Online Resources for the Teacher For a fresh approach to health topics and an in-depth look at health issues, use these online resources found under Teacher Resources at **health.glencoe.com:**

- Block Schedule Lesson Plans
- Technology Projects
- Health Updates

The Cardiovascular System

The Cardiovascular System

1 FOCUS

QUICK START Let a volunteer read the Quick Start assignment aloud. Then ask other volunteers to demonstrate effective methods for taking one's own pulse, either at the neck or at the wrist. Caution students to take their pulse with fingers rather than thumbs since the thumb usually has a discernible pulse. When students are prepared, announce the beginning and end of a 60-second period during which they can count their own pulse. Then have them calculate their number of heartbeats in 24 hours. Encourage students to share and compare their numbers.

TYING TO PRIOR KNOWLEDGE

Let students summarize what they have learned about their cardiovascular systems from the Quick Start activity. Explain that they will learn more about this body system as they study Lesson 1.

INTRODUCING VOCABULARY

- Have students form eight groups, and ask each group to pick a different vocabulary term. Let group members work together to find their term in the lesson and in the Glossary; have them read and discuss the definition. Then ask each group to explain its term to the rest of the class.

- Ask students to complete the Chapter 16 Study Guide in the *Student Activity Workbook*. 📁

416

VOCABULARY

plasma
hemoglobin
arteries
capillaries
veins
platelets
lymph
lymphocytes

YOU'LL LEARN TO

- Identify the functions and structures of the cardiovascular system.
- Describe the circulation of blood throughout the heart and body.
- Identify the structures and functions of the lymphatic system.
- Recognize how knowledge of the cardiovascular system is important for maintaining personal and family health.

QUICK START Use a digital timer or the second hand on a watch to take your pulse for 60 seconds. Use this number to calculate how many times your heart beats in 24 hours. What can cause your heart rate to increase or decrease?

Any physical activity that raises your heart rate will help strengthen your cardiovascular system. *What is the main function of the cardiovascular system?*

When you look at a road map, you see a series of interconnected roads—some small, others large—that connect cities and towns. Vital goods are transported into and out of central areas on these roads. Similarly, your cardiovascular system consists of vessels, both large and small, that transport life-supporting materials to cells of your body. Your heart, one of the main organs of your cardiovascular system, is the central point from which these vessels branch.

Functions of the Cardiovascular System

The cardiovascular system is composed of the heart and all the blood vessels of the body. Its function is to circulate blood, thereby maintaining an internal environment in which all the cells of your body are nourished. As your heart pumps blood, blood vessels carry oxygen and nutrients to body cells. At the same time, carbon dioxide is carried, along with waste matter, from your cells. Oxygen is delivered to your lungs and waste products to the kidneys for removal from the body.

416 Chapter 16 Cardiovascular and Respiratory Systems

Lesson 1 *Resources*

Teacher Classroom Resources

📁 Concept Mapping Activity 59
📁 Current Health Issues 16
📁 Guided Reading Activities 59
📁 Health Lab 16
📁 Lesson Plan 59
📁 Lesson Quiz 59

📁 Parent Letter and Activities 16
📁 Reteaching Activity 59

Student Activity Workbook

📁 Applying Health Skills 59
📁 Chapter 16 Study Guide

Multimedia

💿 Transparency 48

Structure of the Cardiovascular System

The cardiovascular system consists of the heart; blood; and blood vessels, including arteries, capillaries, and veins, which transport blood throughout the body.

The Heart

The heart and the brain are perhaps the most important organs in your body. Your heart is the pump that makes the cardiovascular system work. It never rests. Most of the heart is made of muscle tissue called the myocardium, which contracts and relaxes constantly and rhythmically. Your heart rate adjusts automatically in response to an increase or decrease in physical activity. In an average life span, a person's heart beats more than 2.5 billion times.

CHAMBERS OF THE HEART

Inside the heart are four chambers. Each of the two smaller chambers is called an *atrium*. The two lower, larger chambers are called *ventricles*. A wall of tissue called the *septum* separates the right and left atria, as well as the right and left ventricles, from one another.

At the top of the right atrium is an area of muscle that acts as a natural pacemaker for the rest of the heart. Regular electrical impulses generated from this area stimulate the muscles of each atrium to contract, forcing blood into the ventricles. Within milliseconds each electrical impulse travels through the heart to an area between the two ventricles. There it stimulates the muscles of the ventricles to contract, pumping blood out of the heart.

Valves between the atria and ventricles allow blood to flow through the chambers of the heart. These valves are "one-way" valves, opening to allow blood to flow from the atria into the ventricles. When the ventricles contract, the valves close again to keep blood from flowing back into the atria. The sounds heard as the heart beats are produced by the closing of the valves.

CIRCULATION IN THE HEART

The circulation of blood through the heart and lungs is shown in **Figure 16.1** on page 418. Blood that has been depleted of oxygen but contains carbon dioxide and waste matter is carried to the heart by two large blood vessels called the *vena cava*. This deoxygenated blood enters the right atrium and is transferred to the right ventricle. The blood is then pumped to the lungs. In the lungs the blood releases carbon dioxide and picks up oxygen from inhaled air. This newly oxygenated blood is returned from the lungs to the left atrium of the heart. The left atrium pumps the oxygenated blood into the left ventricle, which then pumps the blood out of the heart to the rest of the body by way of a large artery called the aorta.

Health Minute

Get the Most from Your Physical Activity

Aerobic activities can reduce your risk of developing cardiovascular diseases later in life.

Exercising within your target heart range:

▶ Sit quietly for five minutes, and then take your pulse. This is your resting heart rate.

▶ Subtract your age from the number 220 to find your maximum heart rate.

▶ Subtract your resting heart rate from your maximum heart rate.

▶ Multiply the number you arrived at by 60 percent and again by 85 percent. Round off these numbers.

▶ Add your resting heart rate to the numbers you just calculated. These two new numbers represent your target heart range.

② TEACH

Reinforcing Concepts

Ask several students to explain, in their own words, the functions of the cardiovascular system. Ask: How are those functions related to each other? ◀1

Critical Thinking

Ask students to evaluate this statement from the text: "The heart and the brain are perhaps the most important organs in your body." Encourage volunteers to explain whether they agree or disagree. Have them also explain the reason for their response. ◀1

Health Minute

Guide students in reading and discussing the first paragraph in the Health Minute activity. Ask: In addition to reducing your risk of cardiovascular disease later in life, what are some other benefits of aerobic activities?

Then go over the directions for calculating the target heart rate. Be sure students understand that resting heart rates and target heart ranges are individual; they should not expect to have rates exactly like those of others. Let students work with partners to identify their own resting heart rate and target heart range. When they have finished, ask volunteers to share their numbers.

～∧∧～ HEALTH LITERACY

Self-Directed Learner Students should be capable of taking their own pulse in various situations. Present them with these instructions:

You can feel your pulse in places where arteries are close to the skin, such as on the carotid artery in the neck and the brachial artery in the arm. The most convenient spot for getting a clear pulse rate however, is your wrist. Begin by sitting quietly. Place two fingers gently against the inside of your wrist until you feel your pulse. Use your first and second fingers or your two middle fingers; do not use your thumb. Using the second hand on a watch, clock, or stopwatch to measure time, count the number of beats for 30 seconds. Multiply the number of beats by two to obtain your pulse in beats per minute.

Figure 16.1 Guide students in examining the drawing and reading the labels in Figure 16.1. Help them refer to this drawing as they read about the chambers of the heart and circulation in the heart.

Quick Demo

If a model of the heart is available, use it to help students understand the direction of blood flow through the heart. Let volunteers point out the direction of blood flow. Then ask: Which chamber has the thickest wall for pumping blood to the body? left ventricle Explain that heart valves permit blood to flow only in one direction: atrium to ventricle, ventricle to vessels. **1**

Discussing

Have students share what they know about blood types. Ask:

- When and how are you most likely to find out which blood type you have?

- Under what circumstances can it be important to know your blood type?

- How are the blood types of children related to those of their biological parents?

FIGURE 16.1

PULMONARY CIRCULATION

The circulation of the blood between the heart and lungs is called pulmonary circulation.

right lung
pulmonary artery
superior vena cava
capillaries
pulmonary veins
right atrium
right ventricle
inferior vena cava

left lung
pulmonary artery
aorta
left atrium
left ventricle

What is blood type?

There are four blood types: A, B, AB, and O. Blood type is determined by the presence or absence of certain substances, called antigens, that stimulate an immune response. Type A has antigen A, type B has antigen B, type AB has both those antigens, and type O has neither. Most blood also carries another substance called the Rh factor. Blood that doesn't have the Rh factor is called *Rh negative.*

Blood

Blood delivers oxygen, hormones, and nutrients to the cells and carries away wastes that the cells produce. About 55 percent of total blood volume consists of **plasma**, *the fluid in which other parts of the blood are suspended.* Plasma, which is mostly water, contains nutrients, proteins, salts, and hormones. Red blood cells make up about 40 percent of blood. White blood cells and platelets together make up the remaining 5 percent of blood. One milliliter of blood contains millions of each of these types of cells.

RED BLOOD CELLS AND WHITE BLOOD CELLS

Red blood cells transport oxygen to the cells and tissues of the body. Formed in bone marrow, red blood cells contain hemoglobin. **Hemoglobin** is *the oxygen-carrying protein in blood.* Hemoglobin contains iron that binds with oxygen in the lungs and releases the oxygen in the tissues. Hemoglobin also combines with carbon dioxide, which is carried from the cells to the lungs.

The main role of white blood cells is to protect the body against infection and fight infection when it occurs. White blood cells, which are part of the body's immune system, are also produced in bone marrow. Production of these cells increases when an infection is present. Some white blood cells surround and ingest disease-causing microbes. Others are involved in allergic reactions. A third type of white blood cell forms antibodies that provide immunity.

More About...

The Blood Variation in ABO and Rhesus blood types is studied through immunological reactions, which can best be understood by considering a specific example.

If someone has type A blood, the red blood cells bear the A antigen and the serumcontains anti-B antibodies. Someone with type B blood has the B antigen and anti-A antibodies.

When red blood cells with A antigen (from the type A individual) are mixed with serum containing anti-A antibodies (from the person with type B blood), an antigen-antibody reaction occurs. Pairs of antibodies and antigens each fit together like a key in a lock, leading to agglutination, or clumping, of the red blood cells.

Blood Vessels

The network of more than 60,000 miles of blood vessels that transports blood is shown in **Figure 16.2** on page 420. There are three main types of blood vessels: arteries, capillaries, and veins.

ARTERIES

The *blood vessels that carry blood away from the heart* are called **arteries**. Arteries have thick elastic walls that contain smooth muscle fibers. The elastic fibers in the walls of arteries allow them to withstand the pressure exerted by the blood as the heart beats.

Pulmonary arteries carry deoxygenated blood from the right ventricle to the lungs. Systemic arteries, such as the aorta, carry oxygenated blood from the left ventricle to all areas of the body. As arteries move away from the heart, they branch into progressively smaller vessels called *arterioles*. Arterioles deliver blood to capillaries.

CAPILLARIES

Capillaries are *small vessels that carry blood between arterioles and small vessels called venules*. Capillaries form an extensive network throughout tissues and organs in the body, reaching almost all body cells. The exchange of gases, nutrients, and wastes between blood and cells takes place through the ultra-thin walls of capillaries. Capillaries also play a role in body temperature regulation. As body temperature rises, capillaries near the skin's surface dilate, allowing heat to escape the body through the skin. If body temperature begins to drop below normal, the capillaries constrict, reducing heat loss.

VEINS

The *blood vessels that return blood to the heart* are called **veins**. Although the walls of veins are thinner and less elastic than those of arteries, veins are still able to withstand the pressure exerted by blood as it flows through them. The large veins called the *vena cava* carry deoxygenated blood from the body to the right atrium of the heart. Pulmonary veins carry oxygenated blood from the lungs to the left atrium. Many veins throughout the body, especially those in the legs, have valves that help prevent the backflow of blood as it is pumped under lower pressure back to the heart. Pressure on the vessel walls from the contraction of surrounding muscles helps move blood through the veins. The venules collect blood from capillaries and empty it into larger veins.

The blood regulates body temperature. *Explain how these swimmers' bodies adjust to cold water temperature.*

Lesson 1 The Cardiovascular System **419**

Activity

Have students work independently or with partners to draw a picture of the heart. Ask them to label the aorta, the ventricles, and the layers of heart muscle. **L1**

Quick Demo

Students can simulate the work a heart does by squeezing a tennis ball 70 times in one minute. The force needed to squeeze the tennis ball is about the same as the force needed to squeeze blood from the heart, which the heart does about 70 times a minute. **L2**

ACTIVE READING

Flow Chart

Creating their own flow charts can help students comprehend and recall important sequential information. In this lesson, facts about the circulation of blood throughout the body are presented. Suggest that students work with partners to make flow charts identifying the stages through which one drop of blood might flow. For more strategies, see the *Guided Reading Activities* booklet.

Discussing

Let students explain, in their own words, the differences among arteries, capillaries, and veins. Ask:

- Why is each essential?
- How do the three types of vessels work together? **L1**

∿ HEALTH LITERACY

Critical Thinker and Problem Solver

Encourage students to study the basic blood types. Provide information about the antigens and antibodies in type A and type B blood and how blood is tested for type using antigen-antibody reactions. After they learn about antigens and antibodies in type A and type B blood, have them explain why type O individuals are universal donors and type AB are universal recipients, given compatible Rh factors. Encourage students to research and examine strategies people use when they are anticipating an operation that will require transfusions. For example, some people plan long in advance, donating pints of their own blood. Others have friends and family of compatible blood types donate blood for their use during the operation.

Discussing

Encouarge students to discuss their experiences with injuries and the ability of blood to clot. Ask:

- How should small injuries be treated to prevent infection and encourage clotting?
- Which kinds of injuries usually require medical attention? **L1**

VISUAL LEARNING

Figure 16.2 Have students work with partners to study the drawing and read the labels that explain the cardiovascular system. Suggest that students use their fingers or the eraser end of their pencils, to trace the routes that blood travels through the circulatory system.

Cooperative Learning

Have interested students plan and produce a skit about circulation. Students should plan their performance to help elementary school students understand the circulation process. Suggest, for example, that the performers act out the circulation of a blood cell through the body. Students might identify and label specific areas as the left atrium, the left ventricle, the aorta, branching arteries, capillaries, veins, the right atrium, the right ventricle, the lungs, and the pulmonary vein. Each should be introduced and briefly explained to the younger students. Small pieces of red and blue paper could be used to represent oxygen and carbon dioxide and picked up and dropped off appropriately through the system. **Bodily/Kinesthetic L2**

PLATELETS

Platelets are *cells that prevent the body's loss of blood*. Platelets gather at the site of an injury and release chemicals that make them sticky, causing them to clump together with other cells. The chemicals released by platelets also stimulate the blood to produce small thread-like fibers called *fibrin*. Fibrin threads continue to trap platelets along with red and white blood cells. A mass of fibrin, platelets, and red and white blood cells forms a sticky mass until a clot is formed. This stops the loss of blood from the injury site. A scab is formed on a healing wound as the surface of the clot dries.

FIGURE 16.2

THE CARDIOVASCULAR SYSTEM

A network of arteries, veins, and capillaries moves blood throughout the body, providing cells with oxygen and nutrients and removing wastes.

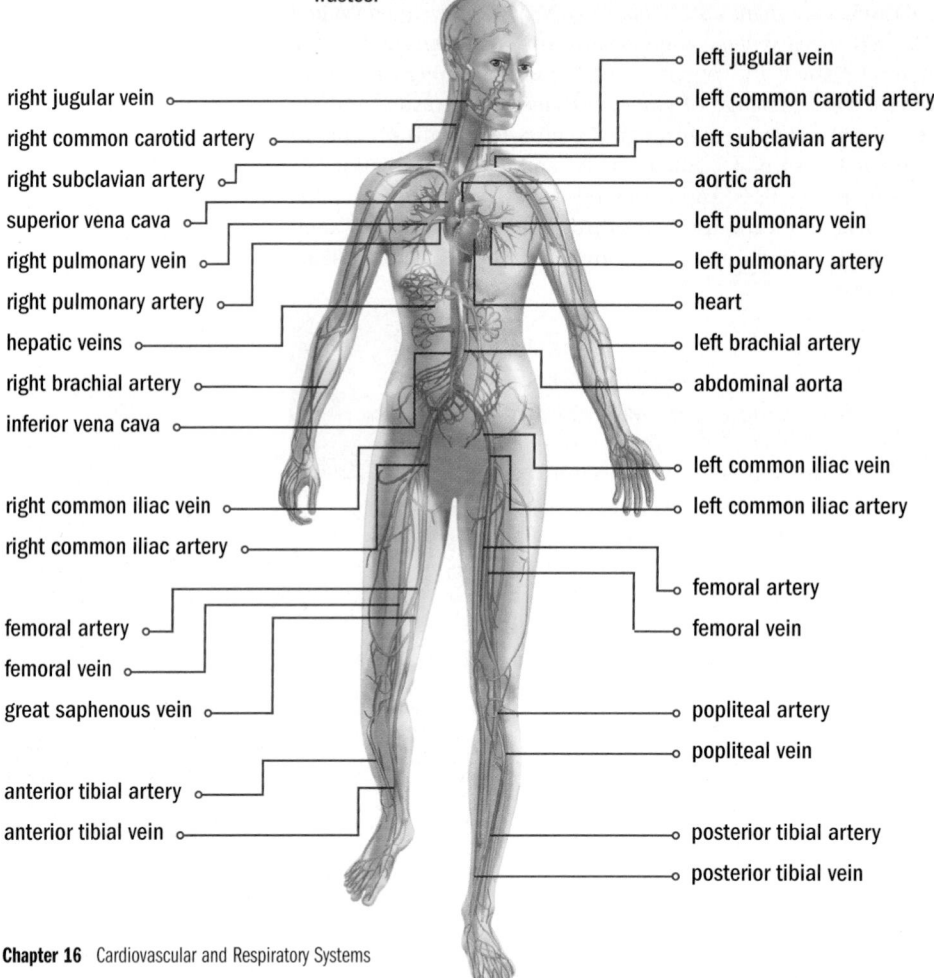

right jugular vein
right common carotid artery
right subclavian artery
superior vena cava
right pulmonary vein
right pulmonary artery
hepatic veins
right brachial artery
inferior vena cava
right common iliac vein
right common iliac artery
femoral artery
femoral vein
great saphenous vein
anterior tibial artery
anterior tibial vein

left jugular vein
left common carotid artery
left subclavian artery
aortic arch
left pulmonary vein
left pulmonary artery
heart
left brachial artery
abdominal aorta
left common iliac vein
left common iliac artery
femoral artery
femoral vein
popliteal artery
popliteal vein
posterior tibial artery
posterior tibial vein

More About...

Reducing Heart Attack Risks The heart is a muscle. Like other muscles, it needs regular exercise and care to thrive. Teens are likely to think that they can start paying attention to heart attack risks when they reach middle age. Unfortunately, that may be too late to protect the health of the heart and the rest of the cardiovascular system. Healthful behaviors during the teen years promote good health now and establish healthy habits to be followed in the future.

The National Heart, Blood, and Lung Institute, a part of the National Institutes of Health, emphasizes the importance of aerobic exercise. This kind of physical activity, which can be as simple as walking briskly, makes the heart muscle stronger and more efficient.

The Lymphatic System

The lymphatic system also helps fight infection and plays an important role in the body's immunity to disease. This system, shown in **Figure 16.3**, is a network of vessels that helps maintain the balance of fluids in the spaces between the cells. The lymphatic system supports the cardiovascular system. All body tissues are bathed in a watery fluid that comes from the blood. Although much of this fluid returns to the blood through capillary walls, some excess remains and is carried to the heart through the lymphatic system.

Lymph

Lymph is *the clear fluid that fills the spaces around body cells.* It is transported by the lymphatic system to the heart and eventually returns to the blood. Lymph is similar to plasma in content, consisting of water and proteins along with fats and lymphocytes. **Lymphocytes** are *specialized white blood cells that provide the body with immunity* and protect the body against pathogens. A pathogen is an organism that causes disease. There are two types of lymphocytes, **B cells** and **T cells.**

B CELLS

B cells are lymphocytes that are stimulated to multiply when they come in contact with a pathogen. Some of the new B cells form plasma cells, which produce antibodies that attack the pathogen. Other B cells form memory cells that are activated if the body is exposed to the same pathogen a second time, creating immunity.

T CELLS

Like B cells, T cells are lymphocytes that are stimulated to enlarge and multiply when they encounter a pathogen. There are two main types of T cells, killer cells and helper cells. Killer T cells stop the spread of disease within the body by releasing toxins that destroy abnormal and infected cells. Helper T cells aid in the activation of B cells and killer T cells and control the body's immune system.

FIGURE 16.3

THE LYMPHATIC SYSTEM

The lymphatic system is a network of vessels, much like the cardiovascular system, that helps protect against pathogens.

- tonsils
- thymus gland
- lymphatic duct
- lymphatic vessel
- spleen
- lymphatic node
- lymphatic vessel

hotlink

B cells and **T cells**   For more information about how the immune system works, see Chapter 24, page 628.

VISUAL LEARNING

Figure 16.3 Let students meet in small groups to examine and discuss Figure 16.3. Have group members take turns reading the labels while other students point to each section of the drawing. Encourage students to discuss how the lymphatic system is similar to—and different from—the circulatory system.

Activity

Point out that the tonsils are part of the lymphatic system. Ask what function students think the tonsils serve. Then have several volunteers research the tonsils, focusing on what they are, how they function, when and how they can be removed, and how tonsil removal is likely to affect a patient. Let these volunteers summarize their findings in written or oral reports. **L3**

Explaining

Tell students that B cells mature in bone marrow and T cells mature in the thymus gland. **L1**

Activity

Ask volunteers to research the role of helper T cells in HIV/AIDS. Let them discuss their findings with the rest of the class. **L2**

Discussing

Refer students to the sentence near the top of this page: "The lymphatic system supports the cardiovascular system." Ask volunteers to explain how the two systems are related and how they support each other. **L1**

Curriculum Connections

History Claudius Galenus, known to the world of science as Galen, is often called the father of experimental physiology. Born in the second century A.D., Galen became a physician to the gladiators and, eventually, to the Roman emperor Marcus Aurelius. Since Roman laws prevented him from dissecting humans, Galen used the bodies of monkeys and apes to learn about body systems and functions. One discovery was that arteries carry blood, not air as had been previously thought. Though many of Galen's observations were later disproved, his theories were believed and accepted for nearly 1,200 years.

③ ASSESS

EVALUATING THE LESSON

Assign and discuss the Lesson 1 Review; then administer, grade, and discuss Lesson Quiz 59 in the TCR. 📁

RETEACHING

- Have students work with partners to write questions about the key concepts presented in the lesson. Compile these questions, and use them as the basis for discussion.
- Ask students to complete Reteaching Activity 59 in the TCR. 📁

ENRICHMENT

Have interested students research blood donations and pheresis donations. Suggest that they find answers to questions such as these:

- How and why are these donations made?
- How are the blood and blood products used?
- Can they be stored? If so, how and for how long?
- Who is qualified to make these donations?
- What motivates people to donate blood and blood products?

Let these students discuss their findings with the rest of the class.

④ CLOSE

Have students write and then share two- or three-sentence summaries of the lesson.

▼ Lymph is moved through the body by the contraction of skeletal muscles during physical activity. *Name the structures of the lymphatic system.*

Structure of the Lymphatic System

The lymphatic system consists of a network of vessels and tissues that are involved in the movement and filtering of lymph. Much like the capillaries and arterioles in the cardiovascular system, small lymph vessels collect lymph and combine to form larger vessels. Lymph is moved toward the heart both by the contraction of smooth muscles that line the walls of lymph vessels and by the contraction of surrounding skeletal muscles.

Two large lymphatic ducts empty lymph into veins close to the heart, where it is returned to the blood. As it is moved through the body, lymph is filtered by lymph nodes, small, bean-shaped organs that are found in lymph vessels. White blood cells within lymph nodes trap and destroy foreign organisms such as bacteria and viruses to keep them from spreading throughout the body. Other structures of the lymphatic system include the spleen, thymus gland, and tonsils, all of which play a role in immunity, protecting the body from infection.

▶ Lesson 1 *Review*

Reviewing Facts and Vocabulary

1. What are the functions of the cardiovascular system?
2. Describe the functions of arteries, capillaries, and veins.
3. Define *lymph* and *lymphocytes*.

Thinking Critically

4. **Comparing and Contrasting.** Compare and contrast the lymphatic and cardiovascular systems.
5. **Evaluating.** What might swollen lymph nodes indicate?

Applying Health Skills

Advocacy. Research and demonstrate knowledge about behaviors that benefit personal and family health. Examine the effects of sedentary behavior on the cardiovascular system. Create an informative brochure about the relationship between an active lifestyle and a healthy heart. Share the brochure with your family.

TECHNOLOGY | O P T I O N

INTERNET RESOURCES Use information and links found at **health.glencoe.com** to help with your research.

▶ Lesson 1 *Review*

Answers to Reviewing Facts and Vocabulary

1. Transports materials, nourishes cells, regulates fluid balance and body temperature, and carries wastes away from cells.
2. See page 419 for functions.
3. Lymph is the clear fluid that fills the spaces around body cells. Lymphocytes are white blood cells that provide immunity.

Answers to Thinking Critically

4. Possible answer: Both systems maintain fluid and chemical balance. The cardiovascular system provides nutrients to cells, while the lymphatic system fights infection.
5. Swollen lymph nodes can indicate infection. Lymph nodes become inflamed as they trap and destroy invading microbes.

Care and Problems of the Cardiovascular System

VOCABULARY
- blood pressure
- congenital
- anemia
- leukemia
- Hodgkin's disease

YOU'LL LEARN TO
- Analyze the relationship between health promotion and the prevention of cardiovascular disease.
- Examine the effects of health behaviors on the cardiovascular and lymphatic systems.
- Relate the importance of early detection and warning signs that prompt individuals of all ages to seek health care.

QUICK START Think about the last time you were examined by a medical professional. Which parts of the examination focused on the health of your cardiovascular and lymphatic systems?

These coronary arteries are partially blocked. Blood supply to the heart is reduced if blood cannot flow through arteries. *What health behaviors will help you avoid cardiovascular system problems?*

Most problems of the cardiovascular and lymphatic systems can be prevented with proper care and by healthy decisions you make during your teen years. These involve physical activity, adequate rest, proper diet, and regular medical checkups. Some problems may be hereditary. If you know that heart disease runs in your family or if you have other traits that may lead to heart disease, you need to make careful choices now to promote a lifetime of cardiovascular health.

Health Behaviors and the Cardiovascular and Lymphatic Systems

Healthful habits can help reduce many of the risk factors associated with problems of the cardiovascular and lymphatic systems. Here are some healthful behaviors that should become part of your life.

Lesson 2   Care and Problems of the Cardiovascular System   **423**

Lesson 2 *Resources*

Teacher Classroom Resources
- Concept Mapping Activity 60
- Decision-Making Activity 16
- Guided Reading Activities 60
- Lesson Plan 60
- Lesson Quiz 60
- Reteaching Activity 60

Student Activity Workbook
- Applying Health Skills 60
- Chapter 16 Study Guide

Multimedia
- Transparency 49

Lesson 2

Care and Problems of the Cardiovascular System

FOCUS

QUICK START   Read the Quick Start assignment aloud, and give students three minutes to jot down their responses. Then ask volunteers to share what they have written.

TYING TO PRIOR KNOWLEDGE
Refer to the title of the lesson, and ask students to identify some of the things they already do to care for their own cardiovascular systems. Explain that this lesson presents more detailed information on promoting and protecting cardiovascular health and avoiding problems.

INTRODUCING VOCABULARY
- Guide students in discussing the vocabulary terms. Let volunteers explain what they understand about each term and, when possible, identify the source of their information. Then have other volunteers look up each term and read the Glossary definition aloud.

- Ask students to complete the Chapter 16 Study Guide in the *Student Activity Workbook.*

② TEACH

Reinforcing Concepts

Guide students in discussing the importance of making choices now, as teenagers, to protect cardiovascular health. Most people who develop problems with their cardiovascular system do not have symptoms or diagnoses until middle age. Still in many cases, lifestyle habits established during childhood and the teen years contribute to the development of those disorders. Explain that individuals who are genetically predisposed may develop heart disease even though they do everything right. **L1**

Cooperative Learning

Divide the class into five groups, and assign each group one of the healthful behaviors that reduce the risks of problems with the cardiovascular and lymphatic systems. Have the members of each group work together to plan and share a brief presentation—such as a skit, a rap, or a simulated news broadcast—to persuade others of the importance of adopting their assigned behavior. **L2** ⬛

Quick Demo

If a sphygmomanometer, an instrument for measuring blood pressure in the arteries, is available, ask the school nurse or another teacher to demonstrate its use. Emphasize the procedure rather than the reading. **L2**

hot link

cholesterol For more information on heart disease and cholesterol, see Chapter 26, page 675.

illegal drugs For more information about how illegal drugs can damage the cardiovascular system, see Chapter 23, page 594.

Ⓨ **Medical professionals check your heart and blood pressure during regular medical examinations. What measurements are taken during blood pressure readings?**

hot link

healthful eating plan For more information on eating right for cardiovascular health, see Chapter 5, page 113.

▶ Follow a well-balanced diet that is low in saturated fats, **cholesterol,** and salt.

▶ Maintain a healthy weight to reduce stress on the heart, blood vessels, and lymph vessels.

▶ Participate in regular aerobic exercise for at least 30 minutes three to four times per week.

▶ Avoid the use of tobacco products and exposure to secondhand tobacco smoke.

▶ Avoid **illegal drugs,** including stimulants, marijuana, and Ecstasy (MDMA).

Blood Pressure

Maintaining pressure in the cardiovascular system is important for proper blood circulation. Pressure in arteries is created as the ventricles contract. As blood is forced into the arteries that exit the heart, arterial walls stretch under the increased pressure. When the ventricles relax and refill with blood, arterial pressure decreases. **Blood pressure** is *a measure of the amount of force that the blood places on the walls of blood vessels, particularly large arteries, as it is pumped through the body.*

Blood pressure can be measured with an instrument called a sphygmomanometer (sfig-mo-muh-NAH-muh-ter) and a stethoscope. A cuff is placed around the upper arm and inflated until the pressure from the cuff blocks the flow of blood. As the cuff is deflated, the health care professional listens through the stethoscope for blood flow. As your heart contracts to push blood into your arteries, the maximum pressure, called *systolic* pressure, is measured. This is recorded as the upper number of the fraction representing your blood pressure. As the ventricles relax to refill, blood pressure is at its lowest point, called the *diastolic* pressure. This is the lower number of the fraction in a blood pressure reading.

Blood pressure is an indicator of cardiovascular health. Although a healthy person's blood pressure will vary with physical activity or emotional stress, it should remain within a normal range. Blood pressure above 140/90 is considered high, and if chronic, places a strain on the heart as it pumps. Chronic high blood pressure is associated with several cardiovascular system problems including hardening of the arteries and heart attacks. Prevention of high blood pressure includes maintaining a healthy weight, staying physically active, managing stress, avoiding tobacco and drugs, and following a **healthful eating plan** that is low in salt.

∿ HEALTH LITERACY

Health Information Unlike your heartbeat, which is likely to slow gradually as you mature and age, your blood pressure typically rises over the course of your life. A newborn baby may have a systolic pressure of about 40, which rises to an average of about 100 by the age of 10. In older adults, systolic pressure may rise to an average of 140 by age 60 and go up to 160 by the age of 80.

The range of blood pressure for teens at rest is considered to be 100-120/60-80. While under stress, teens' blood pressure is likely to rise to 140/90; after vigorous exercise, it may go up to 180/100.

Cardiovascular System Problems

Disorders of the cardiovascular system can interfere with blood flow through the heart or body, reduce the amount of oxygen that reaches the cells, or keep the blood from clotting properly. Some problems are inherited; others result from illness.

Congenital Heart Defects

A condition that is present at birth is said to be **congenital**. One common type of congenital heart defect is a septal defect, in which a hole in the septum allows oxygenated blood to mix with deoxygenated blood and affects the pumping efficiency of the heart. In other cases of congenital heart defects, valves may not function properly, or the aorta may be abnormally narrow, reducing the amount of blood flowing to the body.

Some congenital heart defects are less serious than others, but most require medication and possibly surgery to repair the affected portion of the heart. In many cases the cause of a congenital defect may remain unknown. Use of alcohol and other drugs during pregnancy is associated with heart defects in newborns. Certain infections during pregnancy can also increase the risk of congenital heart defects. Some cases may be hereditary.

Cardiovascular Disease

Cardiovascular disease (CVD) is actually a group of diseases of the cardiovascular system that includes hypertension, heart disease, and stroke. CVD is the number one killer of both men and women among all racial and ethnic groups in the United States. According to the Centers for Disease Control and Prevention, about 95,000 Americans die of CVD each year. Many of these diseases are associated with lifestyle behaviors. Early detection is important for reducing the risk for CVD.

Heart Murmur

Heart murmurs are abnormal sounds that are made as blood flows through the heart. Some heart murmurs may be very slight and disappear without treatment. Other murmurs can be an indication of problems in the heart, such as the valve between the left atrium and ventricle not closing properly, and may require surgery.

Varicose Veins

Varicose veins form if valves in the veins do not close tightly enough to prevent backflow of blood. Varicose veins become enlarged and can be painful. They most commonly occur in veins in the legs. Weakened valves can be the result of a congenital defect or natural aging. Physical activity helps prevent varicose veins. Treatment includes reducing standing time, exercise, elevating legs when sleeping, and in severe cases, surgery to remove the affected vein.

Did You Know ?

➤ Substances taken into the body can have serious effects on the heart and cardiovascular system—including consequences that can result in death.

- Ephedra, which is used by some people as a diet aid, stimulates the cardiovascular system. As a result, its use has been linked to heart attacks and strokes.
- Stimulant drugs including cocaine and amphetamines can cause rapid heart rate, high blood pressure, and damage to blood vessels.
- Marijuana use has been linked to heart and lung damage.

hot link

cardiovascular disease
For more information on CVD and lifestyle behaviors, see Chapter 26, page 678.

Community Involvement

Suggest that volunteers learn about local efforts of organizations such as March of Dimes to reduce the risks of congenital heart defects and other congenital problems. Ask these volunteers to report their findings to the rest of the class. **L2**

Activity

Ask a group of interested students to research the sounds of a healthy heartbeat and the sounds of a heart with a murmur. Then have them create an original way of sharing those sounds—perhaps through a short musical composition or a series of percussive performances. **L2 Musical/Rhythmic**

Discussing

Have students identify kinds of work that might put people at particular risk for varicose veins. Ask: What would you recommend for a friend or family with one of those jobs? **L1**

Explaining

Ask volunteers to share situations in which they've heard the term *cardiovascular disease (CVD)* used. What did they understand the term to mean?

Explain that the term can be confusing because it refers not to one specific disorder but to a whole group of diseases affecting the cardiovascular system. Ask: What are the lifestyle behaviors that are often associated with CVD? Why is it important for teens to avoid those behaviors?

More About...

Angina Angina is actually a symptom rather than a disease in itself. A recurring pain in the chest and/or left arm and shoulder may be angina. If this pain occurs during and after physical exertion or emotional stress, it is likely to be angina.

Angina is the body's way of signaling that something is happening to the heart. It is a warning that a heart attack may be next.

During angina, the heart muscle cells are being deprived of oxygen-carrying blood. Years of overeating or eating high-fat foods may be the cause for many angina attacks. Such diets cause plaque and cholesterol to line the interior of the coronary arteries. Smoking is also a contributing factor to the risks of heart attack—and thus the risks of angina.

Activity

Have interested students research bone marrow transplants as treatments for leukemia. Suggest they look for answers to questions such as these:

- Which other treatments are often attempted before this kind of transplant?

- How are transplant donors identified?

- What are the particular risks and benefits of this treatment?

Ask the volunteers to discuss their findings with the rest of the class. **L2**

Explaining

Explain to students that the gene for hemophilia is on the X chromosomes. A female with this disease must inherit two copies of the gene, which is extremely unlikely. Males need to inherit only one copy of the gene; so hemophilia is much more common in males than in females. **L1**

CHARACTER CHECK

Respect Guide students in reading and discussing the Character Check assignment. Be sure they recognize its two parts: first, select an appropriate and appealing program of diet and physical activity; second, discuss that program with a doctor. When students have completed both those steps, encourage them to keep diet and activity journals to record their progress.

 Individuals in good health who are from 17 to 70 years of age can donate blood. *Name one way donated blood can be used.*

hot link

iron deficiency For more information on nutrition for individual needs, see Chapter 6, page 157.

CHARACTER CHECK

Respect. Making healthful decisions about diet and incorporating physical activity into your daily routine are ways to demonstrate responsibility and respect for your body. **Determine what type of eating plan and physical activity program would be best suited for you. With the advice of a health care provider, make a plan to maintain your cardiovascular health.**

Anemia

Anemia is *a condition in which the ability of the blood to carry oxygen is reduced.* Anemia can result from low numbers of red blood cells or from low concentrations of hemoglobin in the blood. Both of these conditions interfere with the blood's ability to carry oxygen. The most common cause of anemia is **iron deficiency,** which can be avoided by eating foods high in iron, such as dark green leafy vegetables, red meat, liver, egg yolks, and fortified cereals. Taking an iron supplement also may be recommended by a medical professional.

Leukemia

Leukemia is *a form of cancer in which any one of the different types of white blood cells is produced excessively and abnormally.* The abnormal white blood cells cannot function properly, making the leukemia patient very susceptible to infection. Because all blood cells are produced in the bone marrow, the uncontrolled production of white blood cells can hinder the production of red blood cells and platelets. The result is infection, severe anemia, or uncontrolled bleeding. Childhood leukemia is often curable, and in adults leukemia can go into remission. Chemotherapy and radiation are among the treatment options. Also, some forms of leukemia have been successfully treated with bone marrow transplants.

Hemophilia

Hemophilia is an inherited disorder in which the blood does not clot properly. Certain proteins, called clotting factors, are absent. This may cause uncontrolled bleeding that can occur spontaneously or as a result of injury. Bleeding can take place internally in muscles, tissues of the digestive and urinary tract, and the joints. It may also occur externally as a result of injury or surgery. Treatment for hemophilia includes injections that introduce the missing clotting factors into the blood. These clotting factors can be extracted from blood donated by healthy individuals.

Cooperative Learning Activity

Vitamin E Have students use reliable online and library resources to examine reports on the role of vitamin E in reducing heart disease. Let students work in pairs to conduct research and determine the amount of vitamin E that has been correlated with lower incidence of heart disease. Then assign one partner to use a nutrition chart to plan a day's meals that supply the recommended dietary intake of vitamin E without exceeding the recommended dietary guidelines for fat. The other partner is to attempt to plan a day's meals that supply as much vitamin E as has been shown to reduce heart disease without exceeding dietary fat guidelines. Ask partners to discuss whether a vitamin E supplement is advisable.

Lymphatic System Problems

Problems can be the result of infection or heredity and may range in severity from mild to life-threatening.

▶ **Immune Deficiency.** Immune deficiencies occur when the immune system can no longer protect against infection. Some immune deficiencies may be congenital, and others can be caused by **HIV,** the virus that causes AIDS. A weakened immune system may be the result of natural aging or of the side effects of chemotherapy.

▶ **Hodgkin's Disease. Hodgkin's disease**, or Hodgkin's lymphoma, is *a type of cancer that affects the lymph tissue* found in lymph nodes and the spleen. Early detection and treatment, as in all types of **cancer,** is essential for recovery. Treatment may include removal of lymph nodes, radiation, and chemotherapy.

▶ **Tonsillitis.** Tonsils are part of the immune system and help reduce the number of pathogens entering the body through the respiratory system. Infected tonsils, or *tonsillitis,* can be common in children. The condition is most often treated with antibiotics. Chronic cases may call for surgical removal of the tonsils.

hot link

HIV For more information on how HIV affects the immune system, see Chapter 25, page 658.

cancer To learn about cancer and how it affects the body, turn to Chapter 26, page 681.

Health Skills Practice

Influences on Behavior
Let students meet in small groups to review the important health behaviors that can help them protect their cardiovascular health. Have group members identify and discuss factors, both internal and external, that encourage those health behaviors. Which factors sometimes discourage students from practicing those behaviors?

Lesson 2 Review

Reviewing Facts and Vocabulary

1. Analyze the relationship between health behaviors and diseases of the cardiovascular system. List three health behaviors you can practice to help prevent cardiovascular problems.

2. What is *blood pressure*?

3. Name and describe two problems that can occur in the lymphatic system.

Thinking Critically

4. **Applying.** What symptoms might indicate that a person is suffering from anemia?

5. **Analyzing.** Explain why early detection of cardiovascular disorders is important in prompting individuals with symptoms to seek health care.

Applying Health Skills

Communication Skills. Imagine that you are worried about a close family member who has unhealthy eating and fitness habits. Write a dialogue in which you encourage this person to incorporate positive health behaviors into his or her lifestyle. Examine and include the positive effects such a change would have on his or her cardiovascular and lymphatic systems.

SPREADSHEETS Design a table that can be used to record foods eaten and periods of physical activity. See **health.glencoe.com** for information on how to use a spreadsheet.

Lesson 2 Care and Problems of the Cardiovascular System **427**

3 ASSESS

EVALUATING THE LESSON

Assign and discuss the Lesson 2 Review; then administer, grade, and discuss Lesson Quiz 60 in the TCR. 📁

RETEACHING

- Let students work with partners to write informal outlines of the lesson.

- Ask students to complete Reteaching Activity 60 in the TCR. 📁

ENRICHMENT

Have students make a pamphlet on the mission, programs, and activities of the American Heart Association. Encourage students to proofread their pamphlets before handing them in.

 ## Lesson 2 Review

Answers to Reviewing Facts and Vocabulary

1. Any three: Eat a well-balanced diet that is low in saturated fat, cholesterol and salt; maintain weight; exercise; avoid tobacco and illegal drugs.

2. A measure of the amount of force that the blood places on the walls of blood vessels, particularly large arteries, as it is pumped through the body.

3. Immune deficiency, Hodgkin's disease, tonsillitis.

Answers to Thinking Critically

4. Fatigue, weakness, shortness of breath.

5. Early detection is essential to treatment and control of cardiovascular disorders.

4 CLOSE

Ask each student to identify one important habit he or she plans to develop or strengthen to protect cardiovascular health.

1 FOCUS

QUICK START Have a volunteer read the Quick Start assignment aloud, and point out that a change in rate may involve speeding up or slowing down any activity. Give students two minutes to list situations, and then ask volunteers to share their responses.

TYING TO PRIOR KNOWLEDGE

Remind students that the lungs are the principal organs of the respiratory system, and ask volunteers to describe the relationship of the lungs to the circulatory system. Then tell students that, as they study Lesson 3, they will learn more about the lungs and the rest of the respiratory system.

Health Skills Features

"Seeing the Effects of Smoking," p. 430

ADVOCACY

INTRODUCING VOCABULARY

- Have students meet in small groups to read and discuss the vocabulary terms. Then let them work together in looking up and reading the Glossary definition of each term.

- Ask students to complete the Chapter 16 Study Guide in the *Student Activity Workbook.*

Lesson 3

The Respiratory System

VOCABULARY

respiration
diaphragm
pharynx
trachea
bronchi
larynx

YOU'LL LEARN TO

- Identify the functions and structures of the respiratory system.

- Describe the process of breathing.

- Recognize how knowledge of the respiratory system is important for maintaining personal and family health.

QUICK START List situations in which your breathing rate changes. Why does this happen?

Your lungs and chest expand like a balloon as you inhale. As you exhale, your lungs deflate slightly. *Name the structures of the respiratory system involved in breathing.*

Without your conscious control, your lungs rhythmically first fill with air and then are emptied. This rhythm varies with changes in your level of activity. Breathing is regulated by certain areas of the brain that send impulses that stimulate the muscles involved in respiration to contract automatically.

Functions of the Respiratory System

The main function of the respiratory system is **respiration**, *the exchange of gases between the body and the environment.* The process of respiration can be divided into two parts. *External respiration* is the exchange of oxygen and carbon dioxide that takes place between air and blood in the lungs. Oxygen moves from the lungs into the blood, and carbon dioxide moves from the blood into the lungs. *Internal respiration* is the exchange of gases between blood and body cells. Oxygen moves from the blood into the cells, and carbon dioxide moves from the cells into the blood. The continual exchange of gases in both external and internal respiration is essential for survival. Oxygen fuels the brain and allows your body to metabolize food for energy to move muscles.

428 Chapter 16

Lesson 3 *Resources*

Teacher Classroom Resources

 Concept Mapping Activity 61

 Enrichment Activity 16

Guided Reading Activities 61

Lesson Plan 61

Lesson Quiz 61

Reteaching Activity 61

Student Activity Workbook

Applying Health Skills 61

Chapter 16 Study Guide

Multimedia

 Transparency 50

Structure of the Respiratory System

The respiratory system, shown in **Figure 16.4,** consists of the lungs and a series of passageways through which air travels. The nose and throat make up the upper respiratory system. The lower respiratory system contains the larynx, trachea, bronchi, and lungs.

The Lungs

The lungs are the principle organs of the respiratory system and the site of external respiration. They are found within the chest cavity and are protected by the ribs. The **diaphragm** is *the muscle that separates the chest from the abdominal cavity.*

The structure of the lungs can be compared to the structure of a branching tree. Air moves into the lungs through the trachea, or the windpipe. The trachea branches out into the bronchi, the main airways that reach into each lung. The airways that lead into the lungs divide and subdivide to form a network of tubes called *bronchioles.* At the end of each bronchiole are groups of microscopic structures called *alveoli,* thin-walled air sacs covered with capillaries. Gas exchange takes place as oxygen and carbon dioxide diffuse across capillary and alveolar walls.

FIGURE 16.4

THE RESPIRATORY SYSTEM

The lungs are the principle organs of the respiratory system.

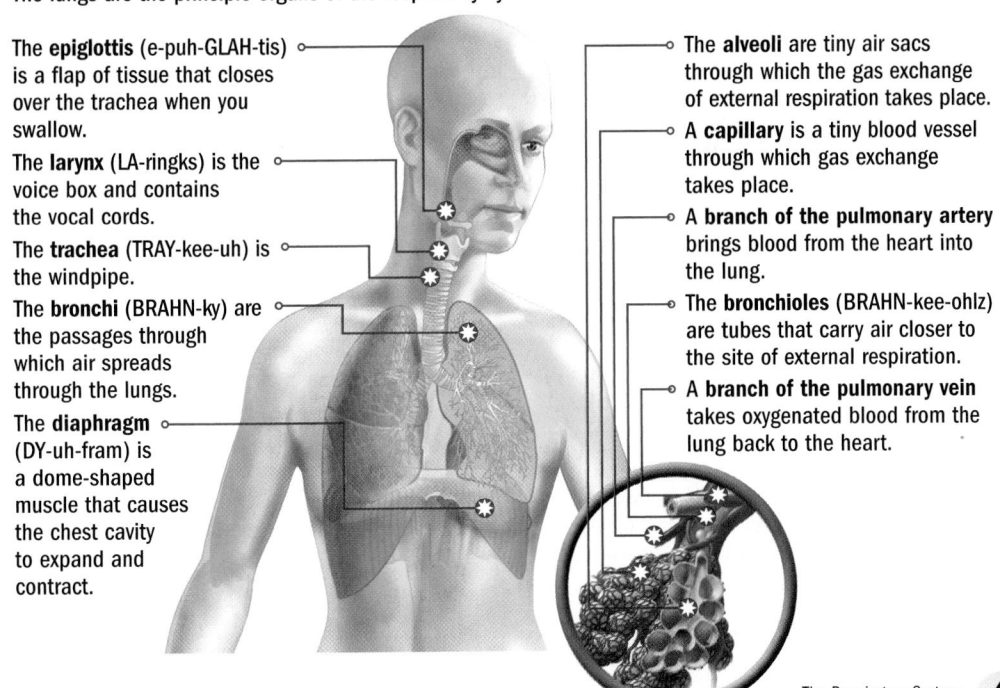

The **epiglottis** (e-puh-GLAH-tis) is a flap of tissue that closes over the trachea when you swallow.

The **larynx** (LA-ringks) is the voice box and contains the vocal cords.

The **trachea** (TRAY-kee-uh) is the windpipe.

The **bronchi** (BRAHN-ky) are the passages through which air spreads through the lungs.

The **diaphragm** (DY-uh-fram) is a dome-shaped muscle that causes the chest cavity to expand and contract.

The **alveoli** are tiny air sacs through which the gas exchange of external respiration takes place.

A **capillary** is a tiny blood vessel through which gas exchange takes place.

A **branch of the pulmonary artery** brings blood from the heart into the lung.

The **bronchioles** (BRAHN-kee-ohlz) are tubes that carry air closer to the site of external respiration.

A **branch of the pulmonary vein** takes oxygenated blood from the lung back to the heart.

The Respiratory System **429**

— HEALTH LITERACY —

Health Information Hyperventilation means overbreathing. People sometimes hyperventilate when they are frightened or otherwise stressed, drawing in more oxygen than the body needs. This condition can cause a number of symptoms, ranging from numbness of the tongue and lips to tightness in the chest or fainting. When a hyperventilation attack occurs, consciously slowing the rate of breathing and taking smaller breaths can help. Exhaling into a paper bag and then inhaling the contents of the bag back into the lungs can also help. This restores carbon dioxide to its more normal levels.

---

2 TEACH

Critical Thinking

Ask: Do you think the muscles involved in respiration are voluntary or involuntary? Let students who respond explain their thinking. **L1**

Activity

Have students draw diagrams to illustrate the exchange of gases that takes place in external respiration and internal respiration. **L2**
Visual/Spatial

VISUAL LEARNING

Figure 16.4 Have students work with partners to examine and discuss the drawings in Figure 16.4. Ask partners to point to each part of the respiratory system as they read the label for that part. Ask: How do all these parts work together to facilitate the exchange of gases?

Quick Demo

Have volunteers (or all students) compare their lung capacities by taking in as much air as possible and then exhaling into balloons. Compare the sizes of the balloons. Ask: What factors might account for differences in lung capacity? **L2**

Discussing

Ask students: What is the difference between inhaling through your nose and inhaling through your mouth? Mucus and cilia in the nose filter air inhaled through nose. Under what circumstances can you feel that difference? **L1**

Hands-On Health

SEEING THE EFFECTS OF SMOKING

ADVOCACY

NHES Standard 7 Students will demonstrate the ability to advocate for personal, family, and community health.

Objectives

- Analyze the harmful effects of tobacco.
- Demonstrate the ability to influence and support others in making positive health choices.

Motivator

Ask students to guess how much tar accumulates in the lungs of a person who smokes one pack of cigarettes a day for one year and write their estimates on the board.

Teaching Strategies

1. Review facts about tar and how it affects health (from Chapter 21).
2. Point out that it takes up to 15 years for the lungs of a smoker to become fully free of tar.

✓ Assessment

Using a rubric, student work should provide comprehensive evidence of the following criteria to achieve the highest score:

✔ clear, health-enhancing stand
✔ support for the position with relevant information
✔ awareness of the audience
✔ encouragement of others to make healthful choices
✔ passion/conviction

Did You Know ?

Hiccups occur as a result of the diaphragm contracting in a spasm, quickly followed by the closure of the vocal cords. This sudden closure produces the unmistakable sound of a hiccup.

THE BREATHING PROCESS

The breathing process is made possible by creating a pressure difference between the lungs and the outside of the body. When you inhale, the diaphragm and muscles between your ribs contract, expanding your chest cavity and your lungs. When your lungs expand, the pressure inside them becomes lower than the pressure outside your body. Air naturally flows into your lungs to equalize the pressure. When you exhale, the same muscles relax and the volume of your chest cavity decreases, making the pressure in your lungs higher than the pressure outside your body. Air naturally flows out of your lungs to the area of lower pressure.

Other Respiratory Structures

The upper respiratory system includes structures such as the nose and mouth. Air enters and exits your body through the nose and mouth. The membranes of the nose are lined with hair-like structures called *cilia* and with cells that produce mucus. Together, the cilia and mucus trap and remove foreign particles, such as dust, bacteria, and viruses, that would otherwise move farther into the respiratory system.

Hands-On Health ACTIVITY

Seeing the Effects of Smoking

What You'll Need

- glass jar with a lid
- one cup of dark brown corn syrup
- packaging tape
- poster board and markers

What You'll Do

1. Pour the cup of corn syrup into the jar, put on the lid, and secure it with packaging tape to prevent leaks.
2. Examine the contents of the jar. The liquid represents the amount of tar that gets into a smoker's lungs during a single year of smoking one pack of cigarettes each day.

3. Discuss your response to this activity with the class. Are you surprised by the amount of "tar" in the jar? How do you think this affects a smoker's health?
4. Create a poster that highlights the dangers of tar, a carcinogen. Write a convincing statement about why teens should avoid tobacco. Present your information in a clear, concise manner.

Apply and Conclude

Present this activity and your poster to a class of younger students. Is it effective in persuading others to avoid tobacco? Why or why not?

430 Chapter 16 Cardiovascular and Respiratory Systems

More About...

Benefits of Deep Breathing Professionals such as voice teachers, many exercise coaches, and people who teach stress management say most people breathe too shallowly. They believe in the value of slow, deep breathing from the diaphragm or abdomen. Suggest that students study a system of breathing techniques and exercises taken from a class or book on speech therapy, voice training, or stress management. Have them examine the physical, mental, and emotional benefits of systematic diaphragm or abdominal breathing as well as each breathing technique they learn. Encourage them to choose a few breathing exercises to practice each day.

In addition to being filtered, air is warmed and moistened as it moves through the nasal passages. Air continues through the respiratory system to the **pharynx**, or *throat*, and into the **trachea**, or *windpipe*, which is located in front of the esophagus. Like the nasal passages, the tissue that lines the trachea is covered with mucus and cilia to trap particles and prevent them from going deeper into the respiratory system. As the trachea reaches the lungs, it branches into two tubes called **bronchi**, *the airways that connect the trachea and the lungs.*

The Larynx and the Epiglottis

Other structures that are not directly involved in respiration but have important functions in the respiratory system are the larynx and the epiglottis. The **larynx**, or *voice box*, connects the throat and the trachea. The larynx contains the vocal cords, two bands of tissue that produce sound when air forced between them causes them to vibrate.

The epiglottis is a flap of cartilage located above the larynx. It folds down to close off the entrance to the larynx and trachea when you swallow, keeping food or drink from entering the respiratory system. If you eat too quickly or laugh while eating, food may go down the "wrong pipe." The cough reflex is then stimulated in an attempt to expel the material from the respiratory system.

Your voice may be affected by health behaviors. For example, smoking irritates structures in the throat and can cause hoarseness. What are some other factors that can affect your voice?

Lesson 3 *Review*

Reviewing Facts and Vocabulary

1. What is the function of the respiratory system?
2. Explain the relationship among the trachea, the pharynx, and the larynx.
3. What role does the diaphragm play in respiration?

Thinking Critically

4. **Evaluating.** Explain the relationship between oxygen and carbon dioxide in the respiration process.
5. **Analyzing.** Demonstrate knowledge of the respiratory system functions. Explain why it is important that the lungs are elastic.

Applying Health Skills

Advocacy. Tobacco use is associated with several types of cancer that occur in the upper respiratory system, most notably the throat. Research the effects of tobacco use on the structures of the upper respiratory system. Use what you learn to produce an educational pamphlet.

WORD PROCESSING Word processing can give your pamphlet a professional look. See health.glencoe.com for tips on how to get the most out of your word-processing program.

Lesson 3 The Respiratory System **431**

Reinforcing Concepts

Help students discuss what they can do when food that "goes down the wrong pipe" results in a choking emergency. (You may want to refer students to Chapter 28, Lesson 2.)

③ ASSESS

EVALUATING THE LESSON

Assign and discuss the Lesson 3 Review; then administer, grade, and discuss Lesson Quiz 61 in the TCR. 📁

RETEACHING

- Have students draw and label simple sketches of the respiratory system. Then have them meet in groups to discuss the function of each part.
- Ask students to complete Reteaching Activity 61 in the TCR. 📁

ENRICHMENT

Have students research the effects of high altitudes, space travel, and deep-sea diving on respiration. What adaptations are required in each situation? Have students report and discuss their findings with the rest of the class.

④ CLOSE

Ask students to describe the interdependence of the cardiovascular and respiratory systems.

Lesson 3 *Review*

Answers to Reviewing Facts and Vocabulary

1. Respiration, or exchanging gases between the body and environment.
2. The larynx, or voice box, connects the trachea (windpipe) and the pharynx (throat).
3. See The Breathing Process on page 430.

Answers to Thinking Critically

4. Answers should discuss that gas exchange takes place and that the blood picks up carbon dioxide from the cells and leaves oxygen and then reverses the exchange in the lungs.
5. They must be able to expand and shrink in order for air to move in and out.

Care and Problems of the Respiratory System

Lesson 4

Care and Problems of the Respiratory System

① FOCUS

QUICK START   Let volunteers suggest several problems with the respiratory system. Then give students a few minutes to jot down their responses to the Quick Start questions. If time permits, have students share and discuss their responses.

TYING TO PRIOR KNOWLEDGE

Let volunteers recall some of the facts they have learned about the respiratory system. Tell the class that this lesson presents information about caring for the respiratory system.

Health Skills Features

"Communication: Asthma and Physical Activity," p. 434

COMMUNICATION SKILLS

INTRODUCING VOCABULARY

- Have students work with partners to create their own vocabulary flash cards. Ask students to write each vocabulary term on a separate flash card; on the other side of the card, have them write the Glossary definition of the term.

- Ask students to complete the Chapter 16 Study Guide in the *Student Activity Workbook.*

VOCABULARY
- **bronchitis**
- **pneumonia**
- **pleurisy**
- **asthma**
- **sinusitis**
- **tuberculosis**
- **emphysema**

YOU'LL LEARN TO

- Analyze the relationship between health promotion and the prevention of respiratory disorders.

- Examine the effects of health behaviors on the respiratory system.

- Relate the importance of warning signs that prompt individuals to seek care for respiratory problems.

QUICK START   Think about a time when you experienced a problem with your respiratory system. How did it affect your daily activities? What treatment did you receive?

 Imagine not being able to perform so simple an act as climbing a single flight of stairs without having to stop to catch your breath. *What are some reasons for shortness of breath?*

For your body to function properly, all your body systems must be healthy and working together. Respiratory system problems can affect the functioning of other body systems.

Health Behaviors and the Respiratory System

Many respiratory system disorders can be prevented by practicing positive health behaviors. The single most important decision you can make for respiratory health is not to smoke. Smoking damages the respiratory system and is the main cause of lung cancer. Tobacco use has also been connected with cancers of the mouth, pharynx, and larynx. It can cause bronchitis, emphysema, and an increase of asthma in children and adults. In teens smoking reduces the rate of lung growth. Avoiding the use of tobacco and all secondhand smoke, including smoke from cigarettes, cigars, pipes, and marijuana, greatly reduces your risk of all these effects.

Lesson 4 *Resources*

Teacher Classroom Resources
- 📁 Concept Mapping Activity 62
- 📁 Cross-Curriculum Activity 16
- 📁 Guided Reading Activities 62
- 📁 Lesson Plan 62

- 📁 Lesson Quiz 62
- 📁 Reteaching Activity 62

Student Activity Workbook
- 📁 Applying Health Skills 62
- 📁 Chapter 16 Study Guide

Regular physical activity is also important to the health of the respiratory system. Increased respiration during exercise improves the capacity of the lungs to diffuse oxygen into the blood. Exercise also increases the total amount of air moved into and out of the lungs per minute.

Although the mucus and cilia that line the nasal passages and trachea work to keep out foreign particles, the respiratory system is still vulnerable to infection from bacteria and viruses. Pathogens can be transmitted easily to the respiratory system by contaminated hands touching the nose or mouth. Washing your hands regularly helps prevent infection.

Air pollution contributes to lung diseases, including respiratory tract infections, **asthma,** and lung **cancer.** Limiting your exposure to pollutants in the air, including **environmental tobacco smoke,** can also reduce your risk of developing respiratory disorders.

Respiratory System Problems

Problems of the respiratory system range from mild infections to disorders that can damage lung tissue or interfere with respiration. Colds and influenza are common infections of the upper respiratory system. Other infections and disorders affect the lower respiratory tract.

Bronchitis

Bronchitis is *an inflammation of the bronchi caused by infection or exposure to irritants such as tobacco smoke or air pollution.* In this condition the membranes that line the bronchi produce excessive amounts of mucus in the airways. Decreased airway diameter leads to symptoms such as coughing, wheezing, and shortness of breath that worsens with physical activity. Treatment includes medication that dilates the bronchial passages. Chronic bronchitis, a more serious form of the disease, is often caused by smoking. If not detected and treated early, the disease can cause irreversible tissue damage. Treatment includes eliminating exposure to the irritant.

Pneumonia

Pneumonia, *an inflammation of the lungs commonly caused by a bacterial or viral infection,* actually describes several types of lung infections. In a common type of pneumonia, the alveoli swell and become clogged with mucus, decreasing the amount of gas exchange. Symptoms of pneumonia include cough, fever, chills, and chest pain. Bacterial pneumonia is treated with antibiotics. **Pleurisy** (PLUR-uh-see), *an inflammation of the lining of the lungs and chest cavity,* causes chest pain when breathing and coughing.

hot link

asthma and **cancer** More information about asthma, cancer, and other noncommunicable diseases can be found in Chapter 26, page 674.
environmental tobacco smoke For more information on the effects of tobacco use on the respiratory system, see Chapter 21, page 540.

Health Minute

Reduce Your Exposure to Air Pollution

Know the dangers:

► The air quality index (AQI) is a daily measure of the air quality in an area. Information about the levels of pollutants such as carbon monoxide, fine particles, and ozone is usually included in the report.

► Check the AQI for your area in the newspaper, television or radio weather forecasts, or on the Internet.

Respond to alerts:

► If the AQI measurement for the day is very high or if you are sensitive to certain air pollutants, avoid participating in strenuous outdoor activities.

2 TEACH

Discussing

Guide students in discussing the importance of protecting their health—and the health of family and friends—by avoiding all tobacco products. Ask:

- How does cigarette smoke affect the health of the respiratory system?

- What are the effects of smoke from cigars, pipes, and marijuana?

- What factors can influence teens to smoke in spite of the health risks?

- How can teens focus on positive influences that help them avoid smoking?

Service Learning

Have volunteers find and share information about local tobacco-cessation programs.

Discussing

Guide students in discussing bronchitis and pneumonia. What are the essential similarities and differences between these two diseases?

Health Minute

Guide students in reading and discussing the information about air quality index (AQI):

Suggest that volunteers report the local daily AQI to the class for the next several weeks. Each day, ask students to evaluate the AQI and discuss how they think they should respond to it.

More About...

Colds Researchers have found that colds are caused by hundreds of different viruses, not a single virus as was once thought. The rhinovirus family of viruses is predominant in the winter but is active all year. Occurrence is more frequent when school starts and students gather in closed spaces. Research on prevention has included covering the nose with masks to keep the viruses from entering the main receptor. The use of antiviral drugs in nasal sprays and attempts to block proteins that may produce cold symptoms have opened new possibilities. Because the rhinovirus is spread through air particles, some research is being done to develop an air-filtering system that interrupts the spread of the viruses.

Health Skills Activity

COMMUNICATION: ASTHMA AND PHYSICAL ACTIVITY

NHES Standard 5 Students will demonstrate the ability to use interpersonal communication skills to enhance health.

Objectives

- Demonstrate communication skills in maintaining healthy relationships.
- Demonstrate strategies for communicating emotions.

Motivator

Have volunteers come up with situations in which a teen would need to convey that his or her feelings were hurt. Ask: What might be some effective strategies for communicating hurt feelings?

Teaching Strategies

1. Discuss the role that effective communication plays in healthy relationships.
2. Review with the class communication skills from Chapters 2 and 10.

✓Assessment

Using a rubric, student work should provide comprehensive evidence of the following criteria to achieve the highest score:

✔ use of "I" messages
✔ appropriate body language
✔ respectful tone of voice
✔ clear, simple statements

Health Skills Activity

Communication: Asthma and Physical Activity

Todd and Rohan are friends and are happy to be in the same gym class this semester. Todd is a captain and has to choose teammates for the next few weeks. He is aware that Rohan has recently been suffering from asthma attacks. Todd decides not to choose Rohan to be on his team, but he does not explain why.

Rohan is disappointed and a little hurt. He suspects that his asthma is Todd's reason for not choosing him. Rohan has been to his doctor and knows that it's perfectly okay to participate in physical activity as long as he uses his medication. His performance should not be affected by his asthma.

Rohan sees Todd at lunch. He wants to explain how he feels and let his friend know what the doctor said.

"Hey, Todd," Rohan calls out. "Can we talk about gym class?" Todd looks a little embarrassed, but he comes over to sit with his friend.

What Would You Do?

Finish the dialogue showing how Rohan can let Todd know how he feels.

1. Use "I" messages.
2. Use appropriate body language.
3. Maintain a respectful tone of voice.
4. Use clear, simple statements.

Asthma

Asthma (AZ-muh) is *an inflammatory condition in which the trachea, bronchi, and bronchioles become narrowed, causing difficulty in breathing.* An asthma attack is characterized by the involuntary contraction of smooth airway muscles that leads to wheezing, chest tightness, and difficulty in breathing. Acute asthma attacks can be relieved with the use of an inhaler that contains a bronchodilator, a medicine that dilates, or widens, the airways. Long-term treatment of asthma includes using medication that reduces inflammation and avoiding substances that can trigger an attack, such as pollen, dust, animal dander, and tobacco smoke. Certain food preservatives, aspirin, and inhalation of cold air can also trigger asthma attacks.

434 **Chapter 16** Cardiovascular and Respiratory Systems

Cooperative Learning Activity

Asthma Information and Support Let students form cooperative groups, and have each group identify a major organization that provides information about asthma and/or support to asthma patients and their families. Ask group members to work together, using online and/or library sources to learn about the purpose and activities of their chosen organization. Then have them create a brochure or informational flyer about one of the following organizations:

- American Academy of Allergy and Immunology
- American Lung Association
- Asthma and Allergy Foundation of America
- Allergy and Asthma Network Mothers of Asthmatics
- National Heart, Lung, and Blood Institute

Sinusitis

An inflammation of the tissues that line the sinuses, air-filled cavities above the nasal passages and throat, is called **sinusitis**. Symptoms include nasal congestion, headache, and fever. Treatment includes nasal decongestant drops or sprays and antibiotics.

Tuberculosis

Tuberculosis is *a contagious bacterial infection that usually affects the lungs.* When a person is infected with tuberculosis, the immune system surrounds the infected area and isolates it. In this inactive stage, symptoms do not appear. This stage can last for many years. If the immune system is weakened by illness or advancing age, the infection can become active. Symptoms of active tuberculosis include cough, fever, fatigue, and weight loss. Treatment involves antibiotics and hospitalization. Numbers of reported cases of tuberculosis have increased in the United States in recent years.

Emphysema

Emphysema is *a disease that progressively destroys the walls of the alveoli.* Symptoms include difficulty breathing and chronic cough. Although the symptoms of emphysema can be treated, tissue damage is irreversible. Eventually the lungs cease to function. Emphysema is almost always caused by smoking.

Anti-inflammatory medications keep bronchial tubes open and reduce swelling to help control asthma before an attack. *What other treatment can be used to relieve symptoms during an asthma attack?*

 Lesson 4 *Review*

Reviewing Facts and Vocabulary

1. Explain the effects of smoking on the health of the respiratory system.
2. Define *bronchitis* and describe its symptoms.
3. List three things you can do to help keep your respiratory system healthy.

Thinking Critically

4. **Applying.** Your friend is having trouble with shortness of breath during everyday activities. How can you encourage him or her to be examined by a health care professional?
5. **Analyzing.** Why is early detection important in the treatment of respiratory disorders?

Applying Health Skills

Accessing Information. Analyze the relationship between health promotion and the prevention of respiratory system disorders. Draw a diagram of the respiratory system, and label each part with health behaviors that will help teens avoid respiratory problems.

TECHNOLOGY *OPTION*

INTERNET RESOURCES Find information on the Internet about smoking and its effects by visiting Web links at **health.glencoe.com.**

Lesson 4 Care and Problems of the Respiratory System **435**

Activity

Have volunteers research tuberculosis, focusing on methods of prevention and treatment. Ask these volunteers to share their findings in brief oral reports. **L2**

③ ASSESS

EVALUATING THE LESSON

Assign and discuss the Lesson 4 Review; then administer, grade, and discuss Lesson Quiz 62 in the TCR. 📁

RETEACHING

- Have partners list at least five behaviors that protect the health of the respiratory system.
- Ask students to complete Reteaching Activity 62 in the TCR. 📁

ENRICHMENT

Have students work in groups to plan and prepare messages that will encourage elementary school students to protect their respiratory health. Their messages may take the form of skits, posters, songs, picture books, games—anything students feel will engage the children's attention. If possible, arrange to have students share their messages with an elementary school class.

 Lesson 4 *Review*

Answers to Reviewing Facts and Vocabulary

1. Damages respiratory system, causes cancer, bronchitis, emphysema, and increases the incidence of asthma.
2. Inflammation of the bronchi. Symptoms include inflammation and excess mucus resulting in coughing, wheezing, and shortness of breath.
3. Any three: regular physical activity, avoid tobacco, secondhand smoke, contaminants in air; wash hands regularly.

Answers to Thinking Critically

4. Answers will vary.
5. Disorders can be slowed, stopped, or even reversed.

④ CLOSE

Have students list the steps they plan to take to protect the health of their respiratory system.

Healthy Hearts and Lungs Week

NHES Standard 4 Students will analyze the influence of culture, media, technology, and other factors on health.

Objective

Explore the media outlets in your school and plan a variety of events for a "Healthy Hearts and Lungs Week."

Motivator

Have students brainstorm creative ways to teach fellow students about cardiovascular health and fitness.

Teaching Strategies

Awareness Running and walking events educate, involve, and inform the public. National media coverage gives these creative events a larger audience and far-reaching impact.

Analysis Suggest that students scan local media such as newspapers, magazines, television and radio for news of special charitable events in their local area. How are these events promoted?

Reflection Ask them to include in their projects suggestions on how to promote their event in local media outlets.

Take Action Have students put their ideas together as a proposal to the appropriate school authority for permission to implement their "Healthy Hearts and Lungs Week" at your school.

✓ Assessment

Student proposals and projects should be clear, contain factual information from the chapter, and be fully developed.

436

Healthy Hearts and Lungs Week

Health advocacy organizations use special events and the media to promote awareness of their programs. For instance, the American Heart℠ Walk, a noncompetitive walking event, promotes awareness of and raises funds for the American Heart Association. Use the activity below to explore the media outlets available in your school, and plan a variety of events for a "Healthy Hearts and Lungs Week."

ACTIVITY

As a class, brainstorm a list of the media outlets available in your school, such as a public announcement (PA) system, bulletin boards, school newspapers, and school sporting events. Work in groups to create a project or an event that promotes awareness of heart and lung health issues, using the media assigned to you. For instance, one group might write short tips on heart and lung health to be read over the PA system during morning announcements. Another group might create fact sheets on asthma and allergies and distribute them at school sporting events. Be creative in your use of the media and how you present the information.

EXPRESS YOUR VIEWS

Research local events such as the American Heart℠ Walk or the American Lung Association's Christmas Seals® program. Then write an open letter to the student body, promoting these charitable events. Include information on upcoming local events, and encourage fellow students to get involved.

More About...

Publicizing Your Event Contacting local media and trying to get them interested in covering an event can be a tricky business. Local media outlets are always looking for a "hook" that they believe will make their audience want to see or read about your event. A student-run, week-long promotion for good heart and lung health might be very attractive to local media outlets. Students who are attempting to implement the "Healthy Hearts and Lungs Week" should start by making a local media contact list. They can do this by contacting local media outlets and obtaining the names of those individuals that cover the "health beat" or "education beat" for that particular media.

CROSS-CURRICULUM CONNECTIONS

Writing a Heartbeat Poem. The steady thump of a beating heart and the rhythm of pumping lungs often take on symbolic meaning. For example, in Edgar Allan Poe's "The Tell-Tale Heart," the beating heart represents the narrator's guilty conscience. Write a poem using either a heartbeat or a breathing rhythm to symbolize something other than itself. Use rhyme or rhythm to suggest the sound of a beating heart or the illusion of someone's breathing in your poem.

Measuring Gallons of Blood. Assume that the average human heart rate is 72 beats per minute. If the average human heart pumps 4300 gallons of blood per day, how many gallons of blood does the heart pump every time it beats?

Researching Organ Transplants. Every 27 minutes someone in the world receives an organ transplant. The first lung and heart transplants were performed in the 1960s. Research and report on the development of either heart or lung transplants over the last four decades. Include information on legislation that affects transplants, such as the National Organ Transplant Act.

Examining Sound Physics. The lungs are the primary organs used to produce sound. Whether you are whispering, singing, shouting, or humming, control of the flow of air from the lungs is essential. Research the physics of vocal sound production, and list or diagram the various muscles and body structures that produce and shape sounds.

CAREER Corner

Medical Laboratory Technician

If you are interested in biology, chemistry, math, and computer science, and if you enjoy working in the laboratory, consider a career as a medical laboratory technician (MLT). MLTs discover information about a patient's health by analyzing tissue samples and using the latest laboratory technology and techniques.

To become an MLT, you need a high school diploma or its equivalent to enter a college-level course of study. Successful completion of an associate's degree program and a national certification exam are required for employment. You can find out more about this and other health careers by clicking on Career Corner at **health.glencoe.com**.

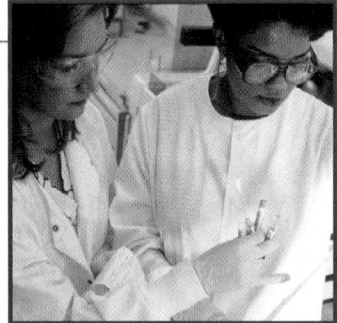

Chapter 16 Review **437**

Portfolio Assessment

Self-Evaluation Direct students to review the Health Skills Activities and other activities completed in the chapter. Encourage each student to select one finished product or activity that demonstrates his or her best work for the chapter and that represents the student's learning goals. Have students explain what they have learned and how the examples they have selected show their growth in health literacy, knowledge, and skills.

Teacher Classroom Resources Assign Performance Assessment 16, "Promoting Healthy Hearts," in the TCR.

CROSS-CURRICULUM CONNECTIONS

Enrich student learning by connecting the topic of the cardiovascular and respiratory systems to one of the four subject areas presented on this page. The activity may be completed individually or with a partner.

Language Arts Review the definitions of these literary devices: symbolism, rhyme, and rhythm.

Social Studies Direct students to Web sites like those of the U.S. Department of Health and Human Services and the United Network of Organ Sharing.

Math Answer: 4300 gals per day/24 hours per day = 179.1667 gals/hr; 179.1667 gals per hr/60 min per hr = 2.986 gals per min 2.986 gals per min/72 beats per min = 0.0415 gals per beat

Science The size of the vocal cords, larynx and the mouth and sinus cavities affect resonance and base pitch of the voice. Lung capacity and pressure assist in sustained tone and volume.

CAREER Corner

Have students read and discuss the Career Corner information on medical laboratory technicians. Ask interested students to explore the Glencoe Health Web site at **health.glencoe.com** for more information on this career.

CHECKING COMPREHENSION

- Assign and discuss the chapter review.
- Use Chapter 16 MindJogger Videoquiz to review the chapter. 🔲

CHAPTER 16 REVIEW ANSWERS

Exploring Health Terms

1. plasma
2. hemoglobin
3. platelets
4. veins
5. False—Anemia
6. True
7. False—Hodgkin's disease
8. respiration
9. diaphragm
10. bronchi
11. trachea
12. larynx
13. pneumonia
14. asthma
15. pleurisy

Recalling the Facts

1. All are components of blood, and all are formed in bone marrow. Red blood cells carry oxygen and nutrients to cells and contain hemoglobin; mature red blood cells do not have nuclei. White blood cells protect the body against infection. Platelets are fragments of cells that help form clots at injury sites to reduce blood loss from the body.

2. B cells produce antibodies that attack pathogens; they also produce memory cells that protect against a second infection by the same organism. Killer T cells attack and kill pathogens by releasing toxins. Helper T cells are involved in other aspects of immunity,

---

▶ **EXPLORING HEALTH TERMS** *Answer the following questions on a sheet of paper.*

Lesson 1 *Match each definition with the correct term.*

arteries	lymphocytes
capillaries	plasma
hemoglobin	platelets
lymph	veins

1. The fluid in which other parts of the blood are suspended.
2. The oxygen-carrying protein in blood.
3. Cells that prevent the body's loss of blood.
4. Blood vessels that carry blood to the heart.

Lesson 2 *Identify each statement as True or False. If false, replace the underlined term with the correct term.*

anemia	Hodgkin's disease
blood pressure	leukemia
congenital	

5. <u>Leukemia</u> is a condition in which the ability of the blood to carry oxygen is reduced.
6. A <u>congenital</u> condition is present at birth.
7. <u>Anemia</u> is a type of cancer that affects the lymphatic system.

Lesson 3 *Replace the underlined words with the correct term.*

bronchi	pharynx
diaphragm	respiration
larynx	trachea

8. The exchange of gases between the body and the environment is known as <u>bronchi</u>.
9. The <u>pharynx</u> is a muscle that separates the chest from the abdominal cavity.
10. The <u>diaphragm</u> are airways that connect the trachea and the lungs.
11. The windpipe is also referred to as the <u>pharynx</u>.
12. The voice box is the <u>trachea</u>.

Lesson 4 *Match each definition with the correct term.*

asthma	pneumonia
bronchitis	sinusitis
emphysema	tuberculosis
pleurisy	

13. An inflammation of the lungs commonly caused by a bacterial or viral infection.
14. An inflammatory condition in which the trachea, bronchi, and bronchioles become narrowed, causing difficulty breathing.
15. An inflammation of the lining of the lungs and chest cavity.

▶ **RECALLING THE FACTS** *Use complete sentences to answer the following questions.*

Lesson 1

1. Compare and contrast red blood cells, white blood cells, and platelets.
2. Differentiate between B cells and T cells.
3. What is the purpose of the lymphatic system?

Lesson 2

4. What are some possible causes of congenital heart disease?
5. What causes anemia, and how can it be avoided?
6. What can cause a deficiency of the immune system?

Lesson 3

7. What is the difference between external and internal respiration?
8. Explain how the process of breathing occurs.
9. What is the function of the epiglottis?

---

helping with the activation of B cells and killer T cells.

3. Possible answer: It is part of the immune system, and it helps maintain the balance of fluids in the spaces between the body's cells.

4. Use of alcohol and other drugs during pregnancy; infections during pregnancy; heredity; the cause for many cases may remain unknown.

5. Possible cause: low number of red blood cells or low concentration of hemoglobin.

Possible avoidance: eating foods high in iron or taking an iron supplement if recommended by a health care professional.

6. Chemotherapy, natural aging, an illness such as HIV; may also be congenital.

7. External respiration is the exchange of oxygen and carbon dioxide that takes place between air and blood in the lungs; internal respiration is the exchange of gases between blood and body cells.

8. During inhalation, the diaphragm and the muscles between ribs contract, increasing

10. How is physical activity related to the health of your respiratory system?

11. What is pneumonia? What causes it?

12. What effects does emphysema have on the respiratory system?

THINKING CRITICALLY

1. **Analyzing.** How would the improper functioning of the valve between the left atrium and ventricle affect the movement of blood through this area of the heart? *(LESSON 1)*

2. **Analyzing.** How could having hemophilia affect a person's everyday activities? *(LESSON 2)*

3. **Synthesizing.** Describe the process of respiration, including both internal and external respiration. Identify each body structure involved, and explain how these work together in respiration. *(LESSON 3)*

4. **Evaluating.** Review the information provided for each respiratory disease. How many of the diseases are linked to smoking? How can you use this information to persuade a family member not to smoke? *(LESSON 4)*

HEALTH SKILLS APPLICATION

1. **Analyzing Influences.** Explain the effect technology has had on cardiovascular health. Evaluate both the positive and negative effects of technologies such as the automobile, elevators, and medical equipment. *(LESSON 1)*

2. **Decision Making.** You are sick with tonsillitis and your friends want you to go hiking. Your doctor has advised you to avoid physical activity and get plenty of rest. Using the steps in the decision-making process, role-play with a friend how you will make your decision. *(LESSON 2)*

3. **Accessing Information.** Find information about abdominal thrusts. Why is it important to properly perform this maneuver? What agencies in your community offer training in first aid for choking? *(LESSON 3)*

4. **Advocacy.** An antibiotic-resistant strain of tuberculosis is increasing in frequency in the United States. Find out how often testing for tuberculosis is offered in your community. For which age groups does it apply? Is there a cost? Raise community awareness by making a poster that encourages individuals to get tested. *(LESSON 4)*

Thinking Critically

1. If the valve does not close properly, blood flows back into the atrium, reducing the amount of blood that flows to the aorta and increasing the pressure in the atrium and pulmonary veins.

2. Possible answer: The person may have to avoid activities that involve the risk of bruising or injury.

3. Answers should include description of internal and external respiration as described on pages 428–429, and the breathing process on page 430.

4. Diseases related to smoking include cancer, bronchitis, asthma, and emphysema; smoking is also related to a general reduction of function of the respiratory system. Persuasive statements will vary.

Health Skills Application

1.–4. Answers will vary.

EVALUATE

- Use the reproducible Chapter 16 Test in the TCR, or construct your own using the Testmaker software.

- Use Performance Assessment 16 in the TCR.

ENRICHMENT

Ask students to complete Enrichment Activity 16 in the TCR.

 BEYOND *the* Classroom

Parent Involvement

Practicing Healthful Behaviors.
Brainstorm with parents or guardians ways your family can practice healthful behaviors to maintain the health of your cardiovascular and respiratory systems. Find ways to incorporate low-fat, low-cholesterol foods, including fresh fruits, into your family's daily eating plan.

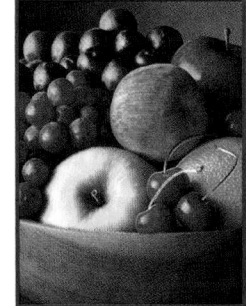

School and Community

A Smoke-Free Community. Find information about the Great American Smoke Out. What does your community do to participate in this event? Share the information you learn with your classmates, and brainstorm ideas about how your school can become involved with this event.

the volume of the chest cavity and decreasing the pressure in the lungs. Air flows into the lungs naturally. During exhalation, the diaphragm and rib muscles relax, decreasing the volume of the chest cavity and increasing the pressure in the lungs. Air flows out of the lungs as a result.

9. It closes off the entrance to the larynx and trachea, which prevents food or liquid from entering the respiratory system.

10. Regular exercise increases the capacity of the lungs to diffuse oxygen into the blood.

Exercise also increases the total amount of air moved into and out of the respiratory system per minute.

11. Pneumonia is an inflammation of the lungs. It can be caused by bacterial or viral infection.

12. In emphysema the walls of the alveoli are progressively destroyed, resulting in a reduced amount of gas exchange between the lungs and blood and a loss of elasticity of lung tissue. Damage is irreversible.

BEYOND *the* Classroom

Keep students involved in the community, and encourage parent participation by assigning the activities on this page for students to work on outside of class.

Lessons	Standards		Features
	National	State/Local	
1 The Digestive System *pages 442–446*	National Health Education Standards 1.1, 1.3, 3.1		
2 Care and Problems of the Digestive System *pages 447–452*	National Health Education Standards 1.3, 2.6, 3.1, 3.4		**Hands-On Health** • Avoiding Stress for Healthy Digestion *(Stress Management)*, page 449
3 The Urinary System *pages 453–457*	National Health Education Standards 1.1, 1.3, 2.6, 3.1		**Exploring Issues** • Bottled Water, Health or Hype? page 455

Reproducible Resources	Assessment	Technology
Student Activity Workbook for use with each chapter 📁 Concept Mapping Activity 63 📁 Current Health Issues 17 📁 Enrichment Activities 17 📁 Guided Reading Activities 63 📁 Health Lab 17 📁 Lesson Plan 63 📁 Parent Letter and Activities 17 📁 Reteaching Activity 63	📁 Lesson Quiz 63	🕹 Transparency 51 💿 TeacherWorks® 💻 Internet Activities
📁 Concept Mapping Activity 64 📁 Decision-Making Activity 17 📁 Guided Reading Activities 64 📁 Lesson Plan 64 📁 Reteaching Activity 64	📁 Lesson Quiz 64	💿 TeacherWorks®
📁 Concept Mapping Activity 65 📁 Cross-Curriculum Activity 17 📁 Guided Reading Activities 65 📁 Lesson Plan 65 📁 Reteaching Activity 65	📁 Lesson Quiz 65	🕹 Transparency 52 💿 TeacherWorks®

⏱ OUT OF TIME

If time does not permit teaching the entire chapter, use:
- Figure 17.1, p. 444
- Hands-On Health, p. 449
- Figure 17.3, p. 454
- Exploring Issues, p. 455

Language Diversity

- 🎧 English Audio CD Program
- 🎧 Spanish Audio CD Program
- 📁 English Summaries, Quizzes, and Activities
- 📁 Spanish Summaries, Quizzes, and Activities
- 📁 Spanish Parent Letters and Activities

End of Chapter Assessment

Blackline Masters

- 📁 Chapter 17 Test
- 📁 Performance Assessment Activity 17

Technology

- 💿 Vocabulary PuzzleMaker
- 📼 MindJogger Videoquiz
- 💿 **Exam***View*® Pro Testmaker

Professional Health Series

Dealing with Sensitive Issues
Planning a Coordinated School Health Program
Promoting Character Education
Home, School, and Community Involvement

Key to Ability Levels

Teaching strategies that appear throughout the chapter have been identified by one of the following codes to give teachers an idea of their suitability for students of varying learning styles and abilities.

L1 Strategies should be within the ability range of all students. Full class participation is often required. Teacher direction is usually needed.

L2 Strategies are designed for average to above-average students or for small groups. Some teacher direction is needed.

L3 Strategies are designed for students able and willing to work independently. Minimal teacher direction is needed.

ELL Strategies should be within the ability range of students learning the English language.

🔲 Block scheduling strategies are useful in a block scheduling format.

CHAPTER OVERVIEW

Chapter 17 discusses the structure, function, potential problems, and care of the digestive and urinary systems.

Lesson 1 The digestive system changes food into smaller nutrients that can be absorbed and used by cells throughout the body. Digestion involves both mechanical and chemical changes. The digestive process begins with ingestion and includes digestion, absorption, and elimination.

Lesson 2 Behaviors that protect the health of the digestive system include eating a well-balanced diet with foods that are low in fat and high in fiber, washing hands before preparing or eating food, eating slowly, and drinking at least eight 8-ounce glasses of water each day.

Lesson 3 The urinary system, consisting of two kidneys, two ureters, a bladder, and the urethra, removes water-soluble waste from the blood, tissues, and cells.

Health Skills Features

- Hands-On-Health *(Stress Management)*, p. 449
- Exploring Issues, p. 455

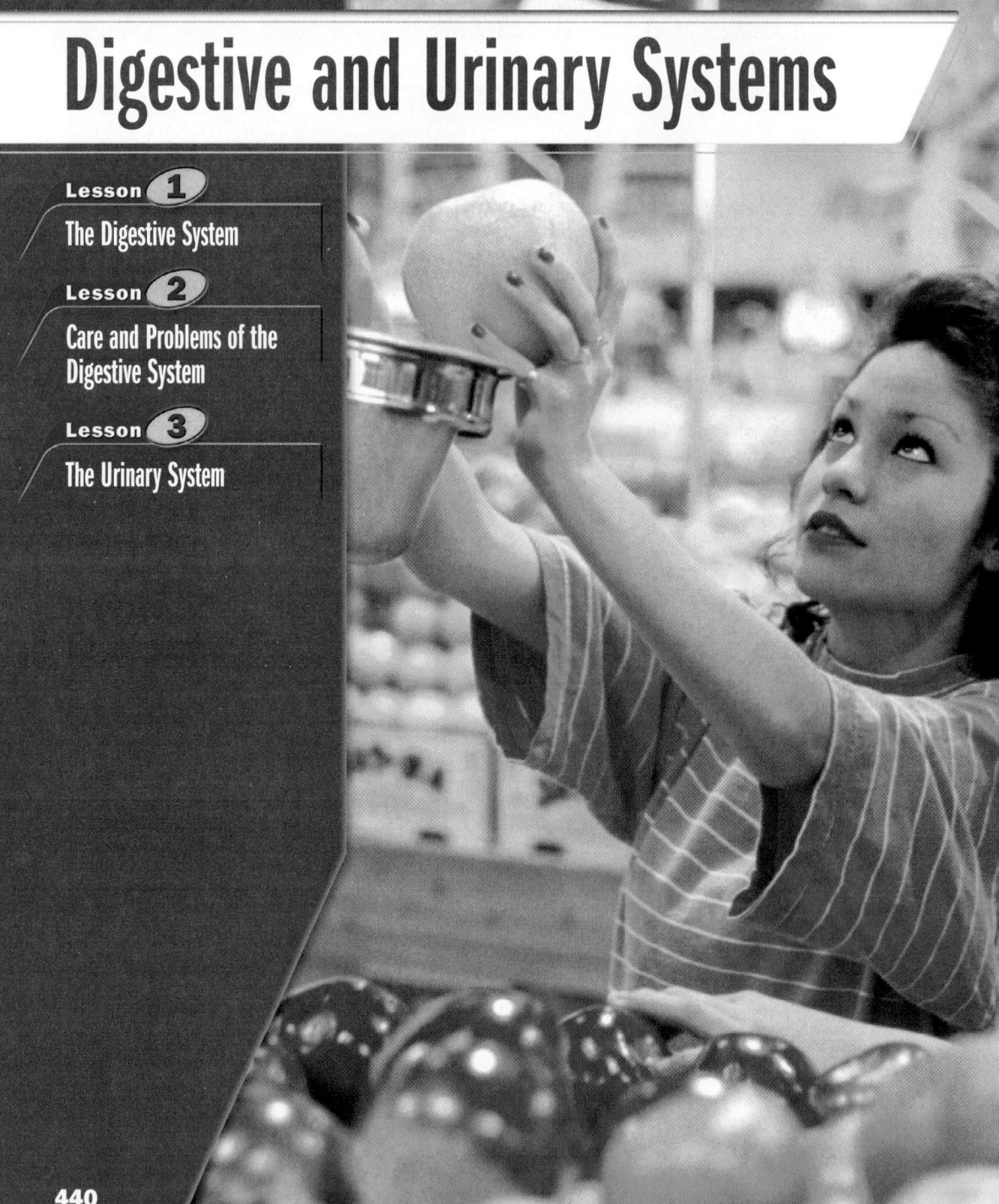

Chapter 17

Digestive and Urinary Systems

Lesson 1
The Digestive System

Lesson 2
Care and Problems of the Digestive System

Lesson 3
The Urinary System

440

MEETING STUDENT DIVERSITY

Language Diversity Use the following suggestions to help students who have difficulty with English:

- Pair English language learners with native speakers of English who can restate the Chapter Summary in language that helps students comprehend important concepts.

- Direct auditory learners or those students with language diversity to the *Glencoe Health Audio CD Program.* Available in English and Spanish, this component provides an audio and written summary of the chapter.

- Use photographs, drawings, or magazine clippings to help students visualize the important concepts of the chapter.

Personal Health Inventory

What's Your Health Status?

Read each statement below and respond by writing *yes, no,* or *sometimes* for each item. Write *yes* only for items that you practice regularly.

1. I eat foods that are low in fat and high in fiber, such as oatmeal, lettuce, and bran, every day.

2. I limit my intake of salty foods, high-sugar snacks, and soft drinks.

3. I avoid using food as a way of coping with my emotions.

4. I brush my teeth at least twice a day and floss at least once a day.

5. I chew each bite of food thoroughly before swallowing.

6. To reduce the risk of spreading bacteria, I wash my hands before preparing food or eating.

7. I do not use laxatives except when recommended by a health care professional.

8. I drink at least eight 8-ounce glasses of water per day.

9. I seek medical attention when diarrhea persists for more than 48 hours.

10. If necessary, I would discuss with a health care professional any changes in urine color or odor, as well as any changes in frequency of urination.

Keep this personal inventory for review later in the chapter. When you have completed the chapter, review your answers and identify two or three behavior changes you could make to improve your health.

441

Quick *Write*

Using Visuals. The foods you eat provide nutrition for all of the body's systems. Healthful choices are important for the proper functioning of your digestive and urinary systems. List ways you and your family can incorporate a variety of nutritious foods into your meal plans.

INTRODUCING THE CHAPTER

Personal Health Inventory

Guide students in reading and discussing the Personal Health Inventory statements. Have volunteers share their ideas about each behavior. Ask:

- How does this practice protect and promote physical health?

- What effects is it likely to have on mental/emotional and social health?

After the discussion, remind students that this Personal Health Inventory is for their own use only. Encourage them to respond openly and honestly to each statement. Ask students to mark the item on which they want to focus to improve their health. Have students keep their responses for review at the end of Chapter 17.

Quick *Write*

Using Visuals Have volunteers describe the scenes in the photograph. Ask:

- What food choices are these people making?

- What are the benefits of those choices?

- How do their food choices compare to the food choices you usually make?

After a brief discussion, have students read and respond to the Quick Write assignment.

MINDJOGGER
VIDEOQUIZ

To preview or review chapter content, you may wish to use the Chapter 17 MindJogger Videoquiz.

HEALTH *Online*

Online Resources for the Teacher For a fresh approach to health topics and an in-depth look at health issues, use these online resources found under Teacher Resources at **health.glencoe.com:**

- Block Schedule Lesson Plans
- Technology Projects
- Health Updates

The Digestive System

The Digestive System

❶ FOCUS

QUICK START Have a volunteer read the Quick Start assignment aloud. Give students about three minutes to record their responses, including as much detail as they can. Then encourage students to share and discuss their responses.

TYING TO PRIOR KNOWLEDGE

Referring to their responses to the Quick Start assignment, help students recognize that they already know some basic facts about the digestive system. Ask: What questions about the digestive system do you hope to have answered as you read this lesson? Record students' questions on the board, if possible in an area where they won't be erased during the study of Lesson 1. Encourage students to look for answers to their questions as they read the lesson.

INTRODUCING VOCABULARY

- Have students work with partners to make flash cards for the vocabulary terms. Suggest that students write each term on a separate index card and record the Glossary definition on the opposite side of the card.

- Ask students to complete the Chapter 17 Study Guide in the *Student Activity Workbook.* 📁

VOCABULARY
- **digestion**
- **absorption**
- **elimination**
- **mastication**
- **peristalsis**
- **gastric juices**
- **chyme**
- **bile**

YOU'LL LEARN TO
- Identify the structures and functions of the digestive system.
- Describe the pathway of food through the digestive system.
- Recognize that knowledge of the functions of the digestive system is important for maintaining personal and family health.

QUICK START On a sheet of paper, describe the path that food takes from the time you ingest it until it is eliminated from the body.

 Digestion begins when you take your first bite of food.
What are three functions of the digestive system?

You may not give much thought to the digestive process as you enjoy a meal with friends or family. However, the foods you eat are not in the form that the body can use as nourishment. Food and drink must be changed into smaller nutrients before they can be absorbed into the blood and carried to cells in the body.

Functions of the Digestive System

The functions of the digestive system can be divided into three main processes:

▶ **Digestion**, *the mechanical and chemical breakdown of foods for use by the body's cells.*

▶ **Absorption**, *the passage of digested food from the digestive tract into the cardiovascular system.*

▶ **Elimination**, *the expulsion of undigested food or body wastes.*

Digestion includes both mechanical and chemical processes. The mechanical portion involves chewing, mashing, and breaking food into smaller pieces. The chemical process involves digestive juices

442 Chapter 17 Digestive and Urinary Systems

Lesson 1 *Resources*

Teacher Classroom Resources
📁 Concept Mapping Activity 63
📁 Current Health Issues 17
📁 Enrichment Activities 17
📁 Guided Reading Activities 63
📁 Health Lab 17
📁 Lesson Plan 63
📁 Lesson Quiz 63

📁 Parent Letter and Activities 17
📁 Reteaching Activity 63

Student Activity Workbook
📁 Applying Health Skills 63
📁 Chapter 17 Study Guide

Multimedia
🕹 Transparency 51

that change food into simpler substances. Digestive juices are secretions produced by various organs in the digestive system. These secretions contain chemicals that help break down the food.

The nervous system and the cardiovascular system also play major roles in digestion. The nervous system triggers the digestive process to begin at the sight or smell of food and controls the muscles that move food through the digestive system. After food has been broken down, nutrients, including carbohydrates, proteins, fats, vitamins, and minerals, are absorbed into the blood and delivered to all cells of the body by the cardiovascular system.

Structures of the Digestive System

The digestive process begins in the mouth. Ingestion, the first stage of the process, is the taking of food into the body. Structures involved in ingestion include your teeth, salivary glands, and tongue. These structures are shown in **Figure 17.1** on page 444.

▶ **Teeth.** The primary function of the teeth is to break the food you eat into smaller pieces. **Mastication** (MAS-tuh-KAY-shuhn) is *the process of chewing,* which prepares food to be swallowed.

▶ **Salivary glands.** The salivary glands in the mouth produce the first digestive juices used in the digestive process. Saliva produced by these glands contains an enzyme that begins to break down the starches and sugars in food into smaller particles. Saliva also lubricates food, making it easier to swallow.

▶ **Tongue.** The tongue forms chewed food into a size and shape that can be swallowed. As you swallow, muscular contractions force food into the pharynx, or throat. The uvula, a small flap of muscular tissue at the back of the mouth, closes the opening to the nasal passages. The epiglottis, the flap of tissue covering the throat, closes the opening to the trachea, or windpipe, to prevent food from entering the respiratory system.

The Esophagus

When food is swallowed, it enters the esophagus, the muscular tube about 10 inches long that connects the pharynx with the stomach. Food is moved through the esophagus, stomach, and intestines by a process called **peristalsis** (PER-uh-STAWL-suhs), *a series of involuntary muscle contractions that move food through the digestive tract.* The action of peristalsis is like a wave moving through the muscle to push food and fluid through each hollow organ. The peristaltic action begins as soon as food is swallowed and enters the esophagus. A sphincter muscle at the entrance to the stomach allows food to move from the esophagus into the stomach.

▼ Your salivary glands respond to the smell of foods before you begin to eat. *How does saliva help in the digestion process?*

CHARACTER CHECK

Respect. Making healthful choices about what you eat and how you eat is a demonstration of responsibility and respect for your body. Using food to cope with emotions or to relieve boredom can lead to overeating or indigestion. **Follow the Dietary Guidelines and the Food Guide Pyramid to be sure that you are getting the right balance of nutrients each day. Take time to eat slowly to help your body digest foods properly.**

Lesson 1 The Digestive System **443**

② TEACH

Activity

As students discuss the three main functions of the digestive system, have volunteers look up the three identifying words: *digestion, absorption, elimination.* Ask:

- From which Latin word is each term derived?
- What suffix is part of all three words? To what verbs has that suffix been added? **L2**

Discussing

Guide students in discussing ingestion as the first step in the digestive process. Ask:

- What choices do you have about ingestion?
- How do those choices affect your health? **L1**

CHARACTER CHECK

Respect Let students meet in small groups to discuss how commitment to healthful eating demonstrates responsibility and respect. Then ask group members to read the Character Check assignment. Suggest that they review the Dietary Guidelines and the Food Guide Pyramid (found in Chapter 5, Lesson 4) and then share their responses to questions such as these:

- What changes can you make to improve the balance of nutrients in your daily diet?
- How can you make sure you have time to eat in a relaxing setting?
- What are healthful ways to handle stress and boredom?

More About...

The Role of Teeth in Digestion In humans, as well as in most other mammalian species, teeth are the prime agents of mechanical digestion. Unlike other animals with dentition, mammals have teeth that reflect their specialization for chewing. Most mammals have several different types of teeth, each type suited for a particular function. In general terms, incisors shear food, canines rip, and molars grind.

For most mammals, the volume of food is not reduced significantly by chewing. However, by breaking up food into small particles, chewing greatly increases the surface area of food that is exposed to digestive juices. This makes mammals very efficient at getting the greatest amount of energy from what they eat.

Discussing

Hold up an apple, or let students imagine an apple. Then ask students to explain how one bite of the apple is affected by these steps in the digestive process:

- Biting
- Chewing
- Addition of saliva
- Peristalsis through the esophagus. **L1**

VISUAL LEARNING

Figure 17.1 Have volunteers describe the location, size, and shape of the digestive system within the body. Then guide students in studying the drawings and reading the labels of The Digestive System. Suggest that students refer back to this drawing as they read about the various organs of the digestive system.

Explaining

Explain that the stomach is a flexible organ. It expands when you eat; then, as chyme moves out of the stomach into the small intestine, the stomach contracts again. **L1**

Reinforcing Concepts

Ask volunteers to explain which parts of the digestive process are voluntary and which involve involuntary muscles. Digestion in the mouth, including chewing and swallowing, is voluntary. After food has been swallowed, it is moved through the digestive system by peristalsis, a series of involuntary muscle contractions. **L1**

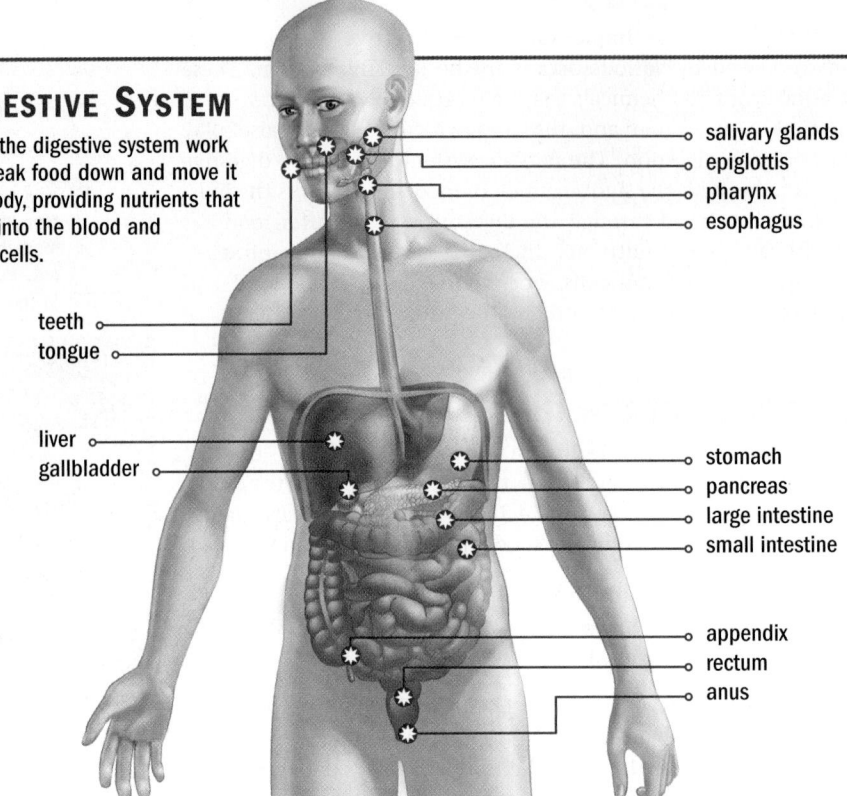

FIGURE 17.1

THE DIGESTIVE SYSTEM

The organs of the digestive system work together to break food down and move it through the body, providing nutrients that are absorbed into the blood and transferred to cells.

salivary glands
epiglottis
pharynx
esophagus

teeth
tongue

liver
gallbladder

stomach
pancreas
large intestine
small intestine

appendix
rectum
anus

The Stomach

The stomach is a hollow, saclike organ enclosed in a muscular wall. These flexible muscles allow the stomach to expand when you eat. The stomach, shown in **Figure 17.2,** has three tasks in digestion.

▶ **Mixing foods with gastric juices. Gastric juices** are *secretions from the stomach lining that contain hydrochloric acid and pepsin, an enzyme that digests protein.* Hydrochloric acid in the stomach kills bacteria taken in with food and creates an acidic environment for the pepsin to do its work. The hydrochloric acid is strong enough to dissolve metal. Mucus produced in the stomach forms a protective lining so that the strong gastric juices do not digest the stomach.

▶ **Storing swallowed food and liquid.** The stomach holds food and liquid for further digestion before they move into the small intestine.

▶ **Moving food into the small intestine.** As food is digested in the stomach, it is converted to **chyme** (kym), *a creamy, fluid mixture of food and gastric juices.* Peristalsis moves the chyme into the small intestine.

Myths & Reality

MYTH. An individual cannot live without all the parts of the digestive system.

FACT. An individual can live a healthy life if certain parts of the digestive system have to be removed surgically. For example, a person can digest food even if the stomach has been removed because most of the digestive process occurs after food leaves the stomach area. Individuals can even live with just one-third of their small intestine. Some patients may have sections of the colon removed. Surgery to remove the gallbladder is also not uncommon and generally carries few health risks. In each of these cases, individuals usually have to make adjustments in their eating habits, but they can still live healthy lives.

FIGURE 17.2

THE STOMACH

Digestion continues in the stomach. Each of the three layers of stomach muscles moves in a different direction. These movements aid both mechanical and chemical digestion.

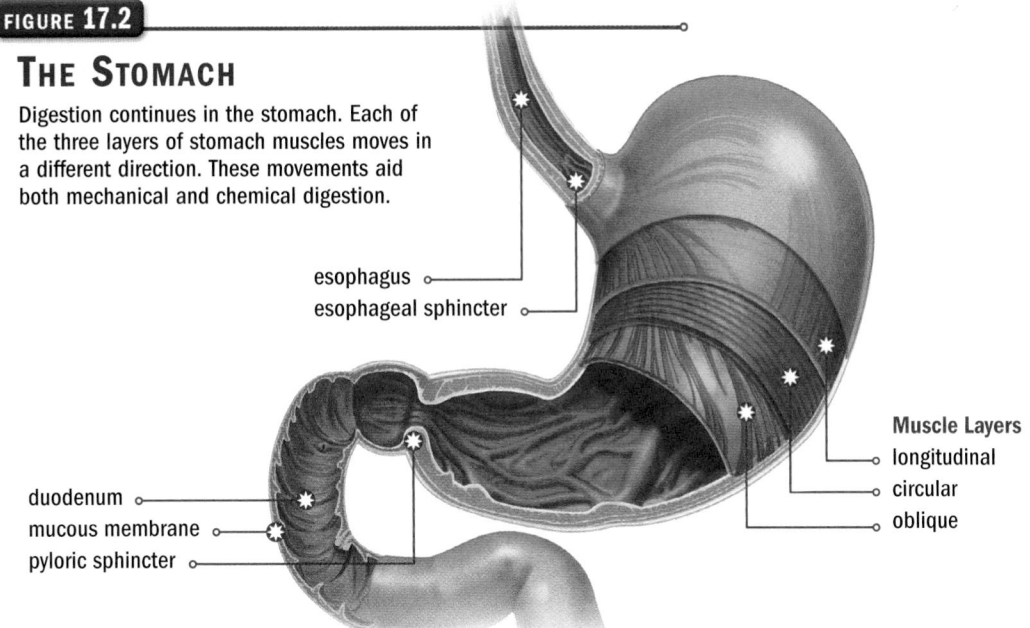

esophagus
esophageal sphincter

duodenum
mucous membrane
pyloric sphincter

Muscle Layers
longitudinal
circular
oblique

The Pancreas, Liver, and Gallbladder

In the small intestine, the juices of two other digestive organs mix with the food to continue the process of digestion. One of these organs is the pancreas. It produces enzymes that break down the carbohydrates, fats, and proteins in food. Other enzymes that are active in the process come from glands in the wall of the intestine.

The liver produces another digestive juice—**bile**, *a yellow-green, bitter fluid important in the breakdown and absorption of fats.* Between meals, the bile is stored in the gallbladder. At mealtime, it is secreted from the gallbladder into the bile ducts to reach the intestine and mix with the fats in food. Bile acids dissolve the fats into the watery contents of the intestine. After the fat is dissolved, it is digested by enzymes from the pancreas and from the lining of the intestine.

The Small Intestine

The small intestine is 20 to 23 feet in length and 1 inch in diameter. It consists of three parts, the duodenum (doo-uh-DEE-nuhm), the jejunum (juh-JOO-nuhm), and the ileum (IL-lee-uhm). As chyme enters the duodenum from the stomach, it includes partially digested carbohydrates and proteins and undigested fats. This mixture is further dissolved by digestive juices secreted from glands in the lining of the small intestine, along with secretions from the liver and the pancreas.

Did You Know?

The liver is the body's heaviest gland and largest organ after the skin. It produces bile and removes toxic substances such as alcohol from the blood.

The pancreas produces three digestive enzymes: *amylase*, which breaks down carbohydrates; *trypsin*, which breaks down proteins; and *lipase*, which breaks down fats. These enzymes are carried to the small intestine by a tube leading from the pancreas to the small intestine.

VISUAL LEARNING

Figure 17.2 Have students meet with partners to study the drawing and labels of The Stomach. Ask both partners to point to the appropriate parts of the stomach as they read the labels together. Ask: Why does the stomach have so many muscle layers?

Explaining

Tell students that food may stay in the stomach two to six hours. Only protein begins digestion in the stomach. Carbohydrates leave the stomach first; proteins leave next; fats remain longest.

Quick Demo

Ask a group of students to measure a section of the classroom wall 23 feet long and 1 inch wide. Explain that this is the approximate size of the small intestine.

Bodily/Kinesthetic

ACTIVE READING

K-W-L Charts

Many students find K-W-L charts useful tools for studying and reviewing content. At the beginning of a lesson or chapter, suggest that students set up their own three-column charts. In the first column, *K*, students list what they already know about the topic of the lesson or chapter. In the second column, *W*, they list questions they want to have answered about that topic. As they study the lesson or chapter, they record in the third column, *L*, important facts they have learned. For more strategies, see the *Guided Reading Activities* booklet in the TCR.

Cooperative Learning Activity

Informative Display Have the entire class work together to create posters showing the best foods and health practices for a healthy digestive system. Guide students by asking what information they want to communicate, to whom they want to communicate, and how they can communicate that information most effectively. Then let students plan how many groups they need to complete the planned project and what responsibilities each group should have. Let students form the appropriate number of groups (or divide the class into groups). Have the members of each group work cooperatively to complete their section of the project. Help students display their completed posters in a public area of the school.

③ ASSESS

EVALUATING THE LESSON

Assign and discuss the Lesson 1 Review; then administer, grade, and discuss Lesson Quiz 63 in the TCR. 📁

RETEACHING

- Have students work in groups to draw and label their own charts showing the parts of the digestive system. Guide groups in discussing the function of each digestive organ.

- Ask students to complete Reteaching Activity 63 in the TCR. 📁

ENRICHMENT

Have each student research the digestive system of a specific kind of animal such as a cow, chicken, goat, or deer:

- What foods does the animal eat?

- How is the animal's digestive system designed to digest those particular foods?

- What are the most important similarities and differences between that animal's digestive system and the human digestive system?

Ask students to summarize their findings in oral reports and/or posters.

④ CLOSE

Have each student write a short response to this question: How does understanding your digestive system help you take better care of your health? Encourage students to use examples from their textbooks to support their responses.

Did You Know

▶ The small intestine is named for its diameter, not its length. It is about 1 inch wide and 20 to 23 feet long.

- It takes three to five hours for material to move through the small intestine.

- The small intestine is the main site of nutrient absorption. Ninety percent of all nutrients are absorbed through this organ.

The inner wall of the small intestine contains millions of finger-like projections called villi (VIL-eye). The villi are lined with capillaries. Nutrients entering these capillaries are absorbed and carried throughout the body by the cardiovascular system. Unabsorbed material leaves the small intestine in the form of liquid and fiber and moves by peristalsis into the large intestine.

The Large Intestine

The undigested parts of food pass into the colon, or large intestine. The large intestine is about 2.5 inches in diameter and 5 to 6 feet in length. Its main functions are to absorb water, vitamins, and salts, and to eliminate wastes.

REMOVING WASTES FROM THE BODY

The body produces wastes in the form of solids, gases, and liquids. Solid wastes are eliminated through the large intestine. Bacteria that live in the large intestine convert the undigested food materials into a semisolid mass called feces. Feces are excreted from the body through the anus during a bowel movement. The skin excretes some wastes through the pores by perspiration. The lungs expel carbon dioxide, a gaseous waste, when you exhale. Liquid wastes are filtered through the urinary system, described in Lesson 3.

▶ Lesson 1 *Review*

Reviewing Facts and Vocabulary

1. What are the functions of the digestive system?
2. Define *peristalsis*.
3. Describe the pathway of food and undigested wastes through the digestive system.

Thinking Critically

4. **Synthesizing.** Explain how the digestive system interacts with the cardiovascular system.
5. **Evaluating.** Assess the importance of the role of the pancreas in the digestive process.

Applying Health Skills

Advocacy. Prepare a booklet that demonstrates how knowledge of the functions of the digestive system is important to maintaining health. Your booklet should outline the organs of the digestive system, describe the function of each organ, and list behaviors that contribute to the health of these organs. Share the booklet with your family.

WORD PROCESSING Use word-processing software to create your booklet. See **health.glencoe.com** for information on how to use word-processing software.

▶ Lesson 1 *Review*

Answers to Reviewing Facts and Vocabulary

1. Mechanically and chemically breaks down food, absorbs nutrients, eliminates wastes.
2. A series of involuntary muscle contractions that move food through the digestive tract.
3. Mouth, esophagus, stomach, small intestine, large intestine, anus.

Answers to Thinking Critically

4. Capillaries in villi absorb nutrients into the blood and lymph to be delivered to cells of the body.
5. Without the enzymes produced by the pancreas, digestion could not occur.

Care and Problems of the Digestive System

VOCABULARY
indigestion
heartburn
hiatal hernia
appendicitis
peptic ulcer

YOU'LL LEARN TO
* Examine the effects of health behaviors on the digestive system.
* Identify and describe problems of the digestive system.
* Analyze the relationship between health promotion and disease prevention.

QUICK START Recall the last time you experienced a problem with your digestive system. What effects did the problem have on your eating patterns? Was a cause determined? If so, what was it?

Do you often rush through your day without giving much thought to your next meal? Part of having good digestive health includes taking the time to prepare and eat a variety of nutrient-rich foods. Practicing health behaviors that include healthy eating habits can reduce the risk of developing problems with digestion or with the organs of the digestive system.

Health Behaviors and the Digestive System

Taking care of your digestive system begins with the choices you make about which foods to eat and how you eat them. The reward for maintaining good eating habits may well be a lifetime free of digestive problems or habits that may lead to disease. The following health behaviors will keep your digestive system healthy.

▶ Follow a well-balanced diet that includes a variety of foods that are low in fat and high in fiber. Such foods contribute to the proper functioning of the digestive system.

Choose high-fiber foods such as whole grain breads and vegetables to help keep your digestive system healthy. *What are some other healthful habits that might benefit your digestive system?*

Lesson 2 Care and Problems of the Digestive System **447**

Lesson 2 Resources

Teacher Classroom Resources
📁 Concept Mapping Activity 64
📁 Decision-Making Activity 17
📁 Guided Reading Activities 64
📁 Lesson Plan 64
📁 Lesson Quiz 64
📁 Reteaching Activity 64

Student Activity Workbook
📁 Applying Health Skills 64
📁 Chapter 17 Study Guide

Multimedia
📱 Transparency 64

Lesson 2

Care and Problems of the Digestive System

1 FOCUS

QUICK START Have a volunteer read the Quick Start assignment aloud, and give students three minutes to jot down their responses.

TYING TO PRIOR KNOWLEDGE

Invite students to briefly discuss what they already know about possible problems with the digestive system. Then tell the class that this lesson presents more information about such problems as well as explanations of how to care for the digestive system.

Health Skills Features

"Avoiding Stress for Healthy Digestion," p. 449

STRESS MANAGEMENT

INTRODUCING VOCABULARY

* Have students work with partners to read and discuss the vocabulary terms. Encourage students to explain to one another what they already know about these words. Then ask partners to find, read, and discuss the Glossary definition of each term.

* Ask students to complete the Chapter 17 Study Guide in the *Student Activity Workbook*. 📁

② TEACH

Quick Demo

Display eight 8-ounce glasses of water. Ask:

- Why is it important to drink this much water every day?
- What kind of planning might be involved in drinking this much water over the course of a day? **L1**

Health Skills Practice

Washing Hands Have students meet in groups to discuss the importance of washing hands before preparing food and before eating. Then ask:

PRACTICING HEALTHFUL BEHAVIORS

- Why is it sometimes inconvenient to practice this healthful behavior?
- What do you think you can do to make hand-washing a regular habit?
- How do you think you could encourage friends and family members to wash hands before preparing food or eating?

After the group discussions, have each student write a private journal entry describing his or her plan for improving hand-washing habits.

Activity

Suggest that interested students research the various kinds of hepatitis and discuss their findings with the rest of the class.

Incorporate physical activity into your day. *How does physical activity enhance the health of your digestive system?*

How does viral hepatitis affect the liver?

Hepatitis, an inflammation of the liver, is caused by viral infections. Several different viruses exist, including hepatitis A, B, and C. Hepatitis A is spread by contaminated food or water and by the feces of infected people. Hepatitis B and C can be spread by sexual contact, by contact with infected blood, and by sharing needles with infected drug users. Hepatitis B and C viruses can cause chronic hepatitis, a disease that can last a lifetime.

- Wash your hands before preparing a meal or before eating to reduce the risk of introducing harmful bacteria into your digestive system.
- Eat slowly and chew your food thoroughly. Do not wash food down with liquid.
- Drink at least eight 8-ounce glasses of water each day to help your digestive system function properly.
- Avoid using food as a way of dealing with your emotions. Instead, take a walk or write in a journal when you feel stressed.

Problems of the Digestive System

Problems of the digestive system include the minor discomfort caused by indigestion or an upset stomach, more serious bacterial infections or foodborne illness, and conditions that need immediate medical attention, such as appendicitis.

Functional Digestive System Problems

Problems such as indigestion, heartburn, gas, constipation, nausea, or diarrhea may result from illness, stress, or eating certain foods.

- **Indigestion** is *a feeling of discomfort in the upper abdomen.* This feeling of fullness can sometimes be accompanied by gas and nausea. Indigestion can be caused from eating too much food, eating too quickly, or eating foods that are spicy or high in fat. Stomach disorders and stress can contribute to indigestion.

- **Heartburn** is *a burning sensation in the center of the chest that may rise from the bottom, or tip, of the breastbone up to the throat.* It results from acid reflux, or the backflow of stomach acid into the esophagus. As the acid enters the esophagus, it irritates the tissues, causing a burning feeling. Heartburn can also be a symptom of a **hiatal hernia** (hy-AY-tuhl HER-nee-uh), *a condition in which part of the stomach pushes through an opening in the diaphragm.* Because frequent or prolonged heartburn can be an indication of more serious digestive disorders, it is important to discuss the symptoms with a medical professional. He or she may recommend the use of an antacid or prescribe medications to help relieve symptoms.

- **Gas.** Although a certain amount of gas in the stomach and intestines produced from the breakdown of food is normal, excessive gas can result in cramps or an uncomfortable feeling of fullness in the abdomen. Foods that produce gas in one person may not cause gas in another. Most foods that contain carbohydrates or complex sugars, such as beans, cabbage, broccoli, onions, and starches can cause gas. Fats and proteins produce less gas than carbohydrates.

Promoting Coordinated School Health

Working Together As a health teacher and a member of the school community, you are concerned about all aspects of your students' health. You recognize that, even working with other teachers and school personnel, you cannot meet all the health needs of every student. Still schools have an essential role to play. They can work collaboratively with other groups, families, city and county government, local businesses, social agencies, and religious organizations to develop and implement a coordinated health program that will foster teen health and development. For more information, consult *Planning a Coordinated School Health Program.*

▶ **Constipation** is a condition in which feces become dry and hard and bowel movements are difficult. Constipation can be caused by not drinking enough water or consuming enough **fiber** to move wastes through the digestive system. Some medications can also cause constipation. Following a diet that includes fruits and vegetables, drinking at least eight 8-ounce glasses of water each day, and getting regular physical activity are the best ways to avoid constipation.

When recommended by a health care professional, laxative drugs may be used to treat constipation. Laxatives can cause diarrhea, abdominal cramps, and gas. Some types of laxatives coat the intestine.

hotlink

fiber For more information on how fiber affects the digestion of food, see Chapter 5, page 115.

Hands-On Health ACTIVITY

Avoiding Stress for Healthy Digestion

What does stress have to do with digestion? More than you might think! Stress can affect how your digestive system functions. Plus, stress can lead to poor eating habits. Chronic stress can cause poor absorption of vitamins and minerals, which can lead to nutritional deficiencies. In this activity, you will design a poster displaying stress-management strategies to aid healthy digestion.

What You'll Need

- pencil and paper
- markers
- poster board

What You'll Do

1. Divide a piece of paper into four sections.
2. Write one of the following concepts in each section:
   - Eat regular meals, with a variety of foods, instead of over- or undereating.
   - Limit comfort foods, which are frequently full of fat and sugar.
   - Limit caffeine, which is a stimulant.
   - Don't rush through meals; sit down and relax.
3. Under each concept, list 5–10 positive stress-management strategies. For example, under "Limit comfort foods" you may write, "When I'm stressed, I will take a long walk instead of eating cookies." Under "Don't rush through meals," you may write, "I will get up ten minutes early every morning so I have time to eat a leisurely breakfast."
4. Working with a small group, create a poster about one of these four concepts, showing how teens can avoid stress and maintain digestive system health. Make your poster colorful and attractive. Be sure to include tips for stress-management techniques.

Apply and Conclude

Present your stress-management poster to the class. Consider displaying the posters in the cafeteria or other areas of the school.

Lesson 2 Care and Problems of the Digestive System **449**

Hands-On Health

AVOIDING STRESS FOR HEALTHY DIGESTION

STRESS MANAGEMENT

NHES Standard 3 Students will demonstrate the ability to practice health-enhancing behaviors and reduce health risks.

Objectives

- Examine the effects of health behaviors on the digestive system.
- Implement plan for reducing stress.

Motivator

Have volunteers list on the board food items that teens are likely to consume when they are feeling stressed. Ask other students to circle those foods that are nutritious and draw a line through those that are high in sugars, salt, or fats.

Teaching Strategies

1. Review with students the functions of the digestive system, and ask volunteers to explain the process of absorption. Ask: Why is proper absorption important during the digestion process?
2. After completing their posters, have students present their ideas. Arrange to display posters in the school cafeteria.

✓Assessment

Using a rubric, student work should provide comprehensive evidence of the following criteria to achieve the highest score:

✔ recognition of healthful behaviors
✔ demonstration of support system
✔ plan for positive alternatives
✔ application of stress management techniques

Cooperative Learning Activity

Medicines for the Digestive System
Invite students to work in groups to gather information about a variety of products sold over the counter or by prescription as remedies for digestive problems such as ulcers, indigestion, constipation, heartburn, and diarrhea. Have them investigate side effects and long-term effects of prolonged use. They can find such information in the *Physicians' Desk Reference* or abridged versions, literature on labels or in package inserts from the manufacturer upon request, or from pharmacists and health care professionals. Have each group choose five products and list the side effects and consequences of overuse or misuse.

Cooperative Learning

Divide the class into six groups, and assign each group one of these functional digestive problems: indigestion, heartburn, gas, constipation, nausea, diarrhea. Have group members work together to discuss the information about that problem presented in the text and to research it further. Have group members write paragraphs explaining the problem, its cause, its prevention, and suggested treatments. **L2**

Discussing

As students consider each of the six functional digestive problems discussed in the lesson, ask:

- Under what circumstances do you think it best to deal with these problems on your own? With the advice of a parent or guardian?
- What might lead a person to seek professional medical care for one of these problems? **L1**

Reinforcing Concepts

Guide students in discussing gallstones and appendicitis:

- Why is it important to be familiar with the symptoms of these structural problems?
- How are the symptoms for these two problems alike? **L1**

Health Minute

Let students meet in small groups to read and discuss the Health Minute information and tips. Have the members of each group write a realistic schedule for a school day, listing times for meals, snacks, and physical activities.

Health Minute

Reducing Digestive Discomfort

It is natural for indigestion, heartburn, and gas to occur occasionally. There are several things you can do to avoid these problems.

Tips for avoiding digestive discomfort:

- Avoid lying down immediately after finishing a meal. If possible, wait two to three hours before going to bed after eating the last meal of your day.
- Eat smaller, more frequent meals.
- Avoid fried foods and other foods that are high in fat.
- Participate in regular physical activity, which helps regulate the flow of materials through the digestive system.

This may prevent vitamin absorption. The body may also become dependent on laxatives and fail to function on its own.

▶ **Nausea** is the feeling of discomfort that sometimes precedes vomiting. Motion sickness, pathogens, some medications, and dehydration can cause nausea. Vomiting is a reflex in which the contents of the stomach are brought back up the esophagus and out of the mouth. Powerful contractions of the abdominal muscles compress the stomach, while the esophageal sphincter relaxes to allow the contents to exit the stomach.

▶ **Diarrhea** is the frequent passage of watery feces. When digested food passes too quickly through the large intestine, water cannot be absorbed and diarrhea results. Diarrhea may result from changes in eating style, overeating, emotional turmoil, or nutritional deficiencies. Bacterial or viral infections and certain medications can cause diarrhea. One of the greatest concerns about diarrhea, especially when it occurs in infants and young children, is dehydration. To avoid dehydration during an episode of diarrhea, drink plenty of water and other fluids. Fluids that contain electrolytes help maintain the body's fluid and chemical balance. Medical attention should be sought if diarrhea persists for more than 48 hours.

Structural Problems of the Digestive System

Although some digestive system problems are temporary or easily treated, others are very serious, requiring immediate medical attention.

GALLSTONES

Gallstones are formed when cholesterol in bile crystallizes and blocks the bile duct between the small intestine and the gallbladder. Symptoms include pain in the upper right portion of the abdomen, nausea, vomiting, and fever. Treatment includes taking medication that dissolves the stones or having the stones broken down by high-intensity ultrasound waves. Surgical removal of the stones and possibly the gallbladder itself is an option when symptoms are severe.

APPENDICITIS

Appendicitis is *the inflammation of the appendix,* a tube from three to four inches long that extends from the beginning portion of the large intestine. The appendix becomes swollen and inflamed if it is blocked or clogged by bacteria or other foreign matter that prevent the release of its secretions. Symptoms of appendicitis include pain in the lower right portion of the abdomen, fever, loss of appetite, nausea and vomiting, and tenderness in the area of the appendix. The appendix may burst, spreading infection throughout the abdomen, making the condition extremely serious. Medical care is essential. Treatment involves surgical removal of the appendix.

Dealing with Sensitive Issues

Diabetics It is important to recognize that any class may include one or more students with diabetes and that these students have special needs in order for their digestive systems to function properly. They may need to take daily doses of insulin, usually by injection, to lead healthy lives. Modern technology has now produced an "artificial pancreas" in the form of an insulin pump for these individuals. The pump supplies insulin to their bodies continuously, eliminating the need for daily injections. The insulin pump is a small device that is embedded beneath the skin. A tube connects the pump to a large vein, where the insulin is injected into the bloodstream. Every two weeks, the patient returns to the hospital to have the pump refilled with insulin.

GASTRITIS

Gastritis, one of the most common disorders of the digestive system, is an inflammation of the mucous membrane that lines the stomach. An increase in the production of stomach acid, the use of tobacco or alcohol, infections caused by bacteria and viruses, and medications such as aspirin can irritate the stomach lining. Symptoms of gastritis include pain, indigestion, decreased appetite, and nausea and vomiting. Treatment includes avoiding irritants and taking medications or antibiotics to eliminate infection.

LACTOSE INTOLERANCE

Lactose, a type of sugar found in milk and other dairy products, is normally broken down by the enzyme lactase. People who are lactose intolerant do not produce enough lactase, so undigested lactose remains in the small intestine. Bacteria in the digestive tract ferment ingested lactose, producing such symptoms as abdominal cramps, bloating, gas, and diarrhea. Chewing lactase enzyme tablets can reduce symptoms. People with lactose intolerance should choose alternate sources of calcium including dark green vegetables such as broccoli and kale, fortified soymilk, and yogurt with active cultures.

PEPTIC ULCER

A **peptic ulcer** is *a sore in the lining of the digestive tract.* Peptic ulcers can be caused by regular use of anti-inflammatory drugs such as aspirin and by a bacterial infection caused by *Helicobacter pylori (H. pylori).* Symptoms include nausea, vomiting, and abdominal pain that worsens when the stomach is empty. Ulcers can cause bleeding in the stomach, and without treatment, they may perforate, or break through, the stomach wall. Treatment includes medications that neutralize acid or eliminate infection and avoiding irritants such as aspirin, cigarette smoke, and alcohol.

CIRRHOSIS

Destruction of liver tissue, usually caused by prolonged and heavy alcohol use, results in cirrhosis, or scarring of the liver tissue. Alcohol interferes with the liver's ability to break down fats. Excess fat in the liver blocks the flow of blood in the liver cells. Liver tissue is destroyed and replaced with useless scar tissue, preventing normal liver function. Cirrhosis can lead to liver failure and may cause death unless a liver transplant is performed.

CROHN'S DISEASE

Crohn's disease causes inflammation of the lining of the digestive tract. Symptoms include diarrhea, weight loss, fever, and abdominal pain. Although no cause has yet been discovered, the disease seems to be associated with problems in the immune system.

People with lactose intolerance can meet their calcium needs by choosing yogurt, fortified soymilk, and certain green vegetables that are high in calcium.

HEALTH Online

Find more information about how to keep your digestive system healthy in Web Links at health.glencoe.com.

Cooperative Learning

Have students work in groups to write two lists of foods that provide a teen's daily requirements for calcium. One list should include dairy products; the other should be suitable for someone with lactose intolerance. **L2**

Reinforcing Concepts

As students discuss cirrhosis, ask: What is the best way to prevent this destruction of liver tissue? Avoid alcohol. Explain that people who do not drink alcohol can still get cirrhosis. Anything that stresses the liver and its ability to process substances is a danger. **L1**

HEALTH Online

Let students work in groups to brainstorm a list of questions about keeping the digestive system healthy. Then have group members use the Web Links to find answers to their questions.

School to Work

Dietitian and Diet Technician A registered dietitian is a professional trained in food and nutrition. Dietitians may work for hospitals, health maintenance organizations, weight-reduction centers, food service companies, or company cafeterias. Some work in private practice with medical or other health care professionals. They develop diets to meet special needs and counsel groups or individuals in making food choices. A dietitian needs a bachelor's degree in food and nutrition, followed by a one-year internship at an approved institution. He or she must pass a registered examination for dietitians. Students who do not wish to complete a four-year program often pursue two-year programs for diet technicians as assistants to dietitians.

Discussing

Guide students in discussing tooth decay as a problem of the digestive system.

- How do the foods and drinks ingested affect the health of a person's teeth?
- How does the health of a person's teeth affect his or her digestion?

3 ASSESS

EVALUATING THE LESSON

Assign and discuss the Lesson 2 Review; then administer, grade, and discuss Lesson Quiz 64 in the TCR. 📁

RETEACHING

- Have students work with partners to list the types of digestive disorders discussed in this lesson. Then guide students in discussing how each disorder can be avoided or eliminated.

- Ask students to complete Reteaching Activity 64 in the TCR. 📁

ENRICHMENT

Have students use online and library sources to research digestive disorders caused by food contamination. Let them share their findings in brief written reports.

4 CLOSE

Have students identify, either orally or in writing, specific steps they plan to take to protect the health of their digestive system.

 The teeth are an important part of your digestive system. *What health behaviors do you practice every day to promote the health of your teeth?*

COLON CANCER

Cancer of the colon and rectum is the second leading cause of cancer deaths in the United States. This cancer usually develops in the lowest part of the colon, near the rectum. As the cancer grows larger, it either blocks the colon or causes bleeding, often during elimination. Cancers of this type are usually slow to spread. Seeking early medical help greatly increases a person's chance of survival.

COLITIS

Colitis is an inflammation of the large intestine or colon. It may be caused by bacterial or viral infections. Symptoms may include fever, abdominal pain, and diarrhea that can contain blood.

HEMORRHOIDS

Hemorrhoids are veins in the rectum and anus that are swollen as a result of increased pressure. Hemorrhoids may occur with constipation, during pregnancy, and after childbirth. Signs of hemorrhoids include itching, pain, and bleeding. Regular physical activity and a diet high in fiber can help prevent hemorrhoids.

TOOTH DECAY

Teeth are very important to the digestive process. Brushing and flossing teeth daily is the best way to prevent tooth decay and to keep your teeth healthy.

▶ Lesson 2 Review

Reviewing Facts and Vocabulary

1. Examine the effects of health behaviors, and list three behaviors that help prevent digestive system problems.
2. Define *indigestion* and describe its symptoms.
3. Name and describe two structural problems of the digestive system.

Thinking Critically

4. **Synthesizing.** How does fiber contribute to the health of the digestive system?
5. **Analyzing.** Why is early detection and treatment of digestive system disorders important?

Applying Health Skills

Goal Setting. Analyze the relationship between health promotion and disease prevention. Make a list of health behaviors you could practice to improve the health of your digestive system. Choose one behavior from your list and use the goal-setting steps to develop a plan to incorporate this behavior into your daily life.

SPREADSHEETS Making a list is easy when you use spreadsheet software. See **health.glencoe.com** for tips on using a spreadsheet program.

▶ Lesson 2 Review

Answers to Reviewing Facts and Vocabulary

1. Any three of the behaviors identified on page 447 and 448.
2. A feeling of discomfort in the upper abdomen. Feeling of fullness that may be accompanied by gas and nausea.
3. Any two listed on pages 450–452.

Answers to Thinking Critically

4. Fiber is indigestible material that helps move food through the digestive system. Too little fiber can result in constipation.
5. Early detection and treatment can stop or reverse the progression of peptic ulcers and gallstone and of life-threatening problems such as colon cancer.

The Urinary System

VOCABULARY

urine
nephrons
ureters
bladder
urethra
cystitis
urethritis
hemodialysis

YOU'LL LEARN TO

* Identify the structures and functions of the urinary system.

* Examine the effects of health behaviors on the health of the urinary system.

* Identify and describe problems of the urinary system.

* Relate the importance of early detection and warning signs that prompt individuals of all ages to seek health care for urinary system problems.

1 FOCUS

QUICK START Give students a few minutes to write their own lists of familiar filters. Then let volunteers share their responses, and create a class list on the board. Guide students in discussing how the listed filters are used.

QUICK START The kidneys use filtration to cleanse the blood. List several examples of filters used in everyday life. As you read this lesson, compare these examples of filtering with the way the urinary system filters the blood.

TYING TO PRIOR KNOWLEDGE

Refer to the list of filters on the board, and remind students that the kidneys also function as filters. Explain that students will learn more about the kidneys and other parts of the urinary system as they read Lesson 3.

W hile the digestive system removes solid wastes from the body, the urinary system functions to filter and remove liquid waste. A healthy urinary system helps maintain balance within the internal environment of the body. Because of this important role, problems in the urinary system, if left untreated, can affect the entire body and may result in death.

Function of the Urinary System

T he main function of the urinary system is to filter waste and extra fluid from the blood. **Urine** is *liquid waste material* excreted from the body through the process of urination. Urine consists of water and body wastes that contain nitrogen. These wastes become toxic to cells if they remain in the body for too long.

The Kidneys

The kidneys, shown in **Figure 17.3** on the next page, are bean-shaped organs about the size of a fist. They are near the middle of the back, just below the rib cage.

(A) **Avoid caffeine drinks, drink at least eight glasses of water daily, and include other healthful sources of fluids to help maintain the function of your urinary system.**

Health Skills Features

"Bottled Water: Health or Hype?" p. 455

INTRODUCING VOCABULARY

* Divide students into groups. Encourage group members to explain what they already know about each term. Then have them look up each term in the Glossary.

* Ask students to complete the Chapter 17 Study Guide in the *Student Activity Workbook*.

Lesson 3 *Resources*

Teacher Classroom Resources

📁 Concept Mapping Activity 65

📁 Cross-Curriculum Activity 17

📁 Guided Reading Activities 65

📁 Lesson Plan 65

📁 Lesson Quiz 65

📁 Reteaching Activity 65

Student Activity Workbook

📁 Applying Health Skills 65

📁 Chapter 17 Study Guide

Multimedia

 Transparency 52

② TEACH

Reinforcing Concepts

After students have read about the function of the urinary system, invite volunteers to explain in their own words how the urinary system is similar to the lungs, skin, and intestines. **L1**

VISUAL LEARNING

Figure 17.3 Ask volunteers to describe the size and location of the urinary system shown in Figure 17.3. Then have volunteers read the labels aloud as other students point to the appropriate part of the urinary system.

Activity

Let students work with partners to draw and label diagrams of a nephron. Have them label the glomerulus and the renal tubule in their diagrams. **L1 Visual/Spatial**

Reinforcing Concepts

Ask students to explain in their own words what happens in their blood, kidneys, and brain when they feel thirsty. **L1**

Activity

Have a small group of interested students create their own model of the ureters and the bladder. Ask students to use as a bladder a container that can hold about two cups of liquid. Have these students demonstrate their model, passing a small amount of water into the bladder every 15 seconds. **L3 Bodily/Kinesthetic**

The kidneys remove waste products from the blood through tiny filtering units called **nephrons** (NEH-frahnz), *the functional units of the kidneys*. Each kidney contains over 1 million nephrons. Each nephron consists of a ball formed of small capillaries, called a glomerulus (gluhm-ER-ruh-luhs), and a small tube called a renal tubule that functions as a filtering funnel.

FIGURE 17.3

THE KIDNEY

The kidney, part of the urinary system, performs the vital function of removing wastes from the blood.

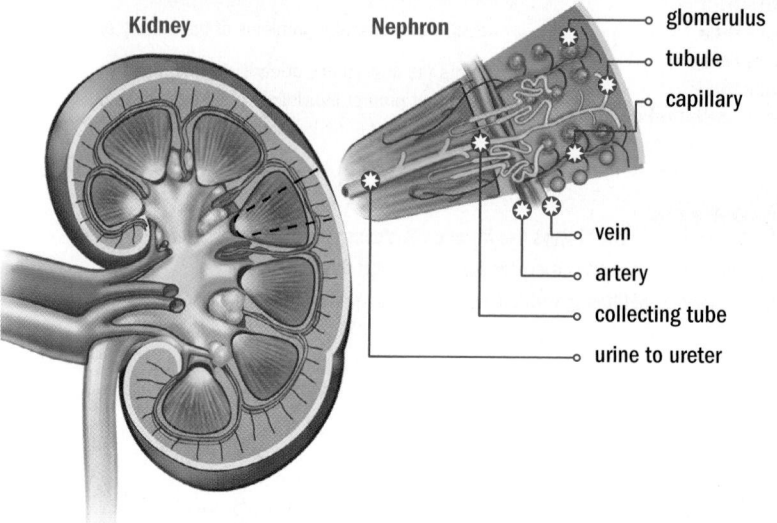

Kidney Nephron glomerulus tubule capillary vein artery collecting tube urine to ureter

Did You Know?

The urinary system filters about 50 gallons of blood and produces one to two quarts of urine each day.

As part of the filtering process, the kidneys adjust the amount of salts, water, and other materials excreted in the urine according to the body's needs. They monitor and maintain the body's acid-base and water balances. When the blood and body fluids become too acidic or too alkaline, the kidneys alter the acidity of the urine to restore the balance. When the body becomes dehydrated, the pituitary gland releases antidiuretic hormone (ADH), stimulating thirst and allowing the kidney to balance the fluid levels in the body.

The Ureters, Bladder, and Urethra

From the kidneys urine travels to the bladder through the ureters. The **ureters** are *tubes that connect the kidneys to the bladder*. Each ureter is 8 to 10 inches long. Muscles in the ureter walls tighten and relax to force urine down and away from the kidneys. The ureters are constantly working. Some amount of urine is passed from the ureters to the bladder about every 15 seconds.

454 **Chapter 17** Digestive and Urinary Systems

Home and Community

Analgesics and Kidney Health Over-the-counter (OTC) analgesics, or painkillers, can, in some cases, pose a danger to kidney health. Although aspirin, acetaminophen, ibuprofen, and naproxen sodium are generally considered safe, they can cause kidney damage in people with conditions that put them at risk for kidney failure such as advanced age, lupus, and recent alcohol bingeing. Analgesics may also pose some risk to kidney health among the general population if taken every day over a period of years. Painkillers that combine two or more analgesics (such as aspirin and acetaminophen) with caffeine are considered most risky.

The Bladder

The **bladder** is *a hollow muscular organ that acts as a reservoir for urine.* Located in the pelvic cavity, the bladder is held in place by ligaments attached to other organs and to the pelvic bones. Until the bladder is ready to be emptied, sphincter muscles close tightly, like a rubber band, around the opening into the **urethra**, *the tube that leads from the bladder to the outside of the body.*

Health Behaviors and the Urinary System

Proper urinary function is important because wastes that are not removed from the body quickly become toxic. There are several behaviors that can help keep your urinary system healthy.

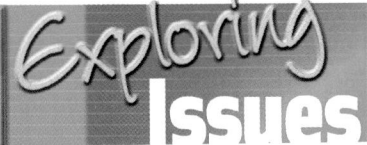

Bottled Water: Health or Hype?

Drinking enough water each day is essential to maintaining the health of your urinary system. Many people choose bottled water because they think it's safer than tap water. Others view bottled water as a healthful alternative to soft drinks or other sugary beverages. Read how two teens view the issue.

Viewpoint 1: Andrea B., 16

My friends and I drink bottled water because tap water doesn't seem to be as safe as it used to be. I've read articles about possible contamination of water supplies, and it scares me. Although I'll drink tap water if I have to, drinking bottled water gives me greater peace of mind. Plus, I know it's better for me than a soft drink.

Viewpoint 2: Damien J., 15

While I agree with Andrea that water is better for you than soft drinks, I don't feel bottled water is any cleaner than tap water. My uncle works for the health department, and he said that municipal water undergoes the same safety tests as bottled water. Besides, tap water is practically free!

ACTIVITIES

1. Do you think bottled water is safer than tap water? Do you think that many teens drink bottled water because it's more healthful than soft drinks?

2. Government and industry estimate that about 25 percent of the bottled water sold in the U.S. comes from tap water; sometimes with further treatment, sometimes not. What does this say about the safety of tap water?

Exploring Issues

BOTTLED WATER: HEALTH OR HYPE?

Survey the class to see how many students drink bottled water. How many drink water only in the form of bottled water? For what reasons do they drink bottled water? Students may answer that they think it's safer, more convenient, or tastes better. Let students meet in small groups to read the feature, then access print or online sources that discuss the safety of bottled water versus tap water. The FDA is a good source because it regulates interstate sales of bottled water. Have students find out whether their state regulates the sale of intrastate bottled water. Students should use their sources to write responses to the questions, then hold a class debate.

Cooperative Learning Activity

Weight-Reduction Aids: What's Being Lost? Many weight-loss aids contain such substances as caffeine, diuretics, laxatives, and nervous system stimulants such as ephedra-containing herbs. It is important to note that any products containing ephedra may involve risks of stroke, heart attacks, seizures, and even death.

Have students form cooperative groups, and let each group member choose a different weight-loss formula to evaluate. Have students list the ingredients in the products and look up each substance in reference sources. Then have groups discuss the benefits and risks of using each product.

Discussing

Guide students in discussing the importance of drinking at least eight 8-ounce glasses of water each day. Ask:

- What are some examples of drinks with caffeine?
- Why should you drink more than eight glasses of water if you drink those beverages? **L1**

Reinforcing Concepts

Help students discuss and compare cystitis and urethritis:

- How are the two disorders similar? How do they differ?
- Why do both require care from a medical professional? **L1**

Activity

Have students use online or library sources to find articles by patients that discuss the experience of hemodialysis. How does this treatment affect the patient's daily life and sense of well-being? Let students meet in groups to share and discuss their findings. **L2**

Critical Thinking

Guide students in reading and discussing the information on organ transplants included in the photo caption and the Did You Know? feature. Ask:

- Why do you think an organ donor must be healthy?
- Why must a donor under age 18 have consent from a parent or guardian?
- What is the procedure in this state for getting and carrying an organ donation card?

If students are not sure about the answer to the last question, ask a volunteer to find out and share the information with the rest of the class. **L1**

A healthy individual who wishes to become an organ donor carries a card stating that preference. An organ donation card such as the one shown here is often carried with the person's driver's license.

Did You Know?

According to the U.S. Department of Health and Human Services, about 63 people receive a successful organ transplant each day. Most people who wish to do so may become tissue or organ donors. Anyone under the age of 18 must have the consent of a parent or guardian.

- Drink at least eight 8-ounce glasses of water each day, and limit your intake of caffeine and soft drinks. Caffeine drinks can interfere with kidney function and increase the amount of water lost through urination.

- Eat a well-balanced diet.

- Practice good hygiene and personal health care to help prevent harmful bacteria from causing infection.

- Have regular medical checkups. Reporting to your doctor any changes in the frequency of urination and in the color or odor of urine is important to the early detection and treatment of urinary system disorders.

Problems of the Urinary System

Urinary system problems can result from several different conditions, including infection and blockage of urine. **Cystitis** is *an inflammation of the bladder,* most often caused by a bacterial infection, which can spread to the kidneys. **Urethritis**, *the inflammation of the urethra,* can be caused by a bacterial infection. Symptoms of both conditions include burning pain during urination, increased frequency of urination, fever, and the presence of blood in the urine. Treatment includes antibiotics to eliminate infection.

Kidney Problems

Kidney disorders, some of which can be life threatening, should be treated and monitored by a medical professional. Kidney problems include the following conditions.

- **Nephritis** is the inflammation of the nephrons. Symptoms include fever, tissue swelling, and changes in urine production.

- **Kidney stones** form when salts in the urine crystallize into a solid stone, usually containing calcium. Small stones can pass through the urinary system naturally, with treatment to relieve symptoms. Treatment for larger stones includes a procedure in which high-intensity sound waves are used to break stones apart so they can pass through the urethra.

- **Uremia** is a serious condition associated with a decrease in blood filtration by the kidneys. As a result of decreased filtration, abnormally high levels of nitrogen waste products remain in the blood and can cause tissue damage.

More About...

Kidney Problems Kidney disorders are most commonly caused by diabetes and/or by high blood pressure. If a person with diabetes does not regulate diet, exercise, and/or medication successfully, glucose may stay in the blood rather than be broken down by digestion. This can damage the nephrons, resulting in kidney disorders.

High blood pressure can cause kidney disorders by placing too much pressure on the blood vessels in the kidneys. This is just one of the reasons for keeping blood pressure down—by choosing a healthful diet and engaging in regular physical activity.

KIDNEY FAILURE

Kidney failure can be acute, meaning sudden onset, or chronic, in which case the kidneys progressively lose their ability to function. Treatment includes reducing symptoms and slowing the progression of the disease. If kidney damage is extensive, dialysis or a kidney transplant may be required.

▶ **Hemodialysis** (HEE-moh-dy-AL-uh-suhs) is *a technique in which an artificial kidney machine removes waste products from the blood.* A needle connected to plastic tubing passes blood from the patient to a machine that filters the blood and returns it in much the same manner that a healthy kidney would.

▶ **Peritoneal dialysis** uses the peritoneum, a thin membrane that surrounds the digestive organs, to filter the blood. A catheter, a tube that provides a passageway for fluids, is inserted into the abdominal cavity to remove toxins.

▶ **Kidney transplant** is a third treatment option for chronic kidney failure. This involves the replacement of a nonfunctional kidney with a healthy kidney from a donor.

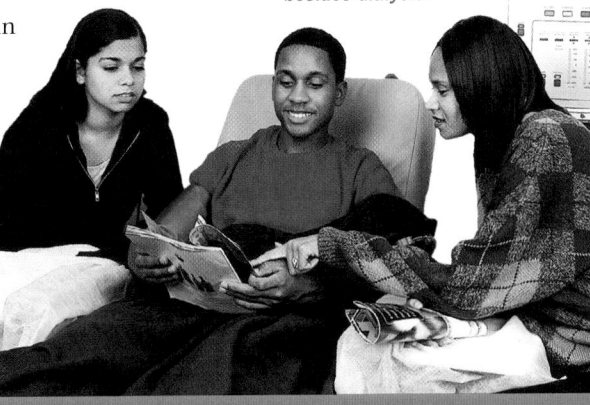

Kidney failure is treated by using medical technology to filter the blood artificially. *What options might a person with kidney failure have besides dialysis?*

 Lesson 3 *Review*

Reviewing Facts and Vocabulary

1. Describe the main function of the urinary system.
2. What is a *ureter* and what is a *urethra*?
3. Examine three health behaviors that affect the health of the urinary system, and explain how these behaviors help reduce the risk of developing a urinary system disorder.

Thinking Critically

4. **Analyzing.** Explain why coffee, tea, or cola drinks should not be counted as part of your daily recommended eight glasses of water.
5. **Applying.** Relate the importance of early detection and warning signs that prompt individuals of all ages to seek health care for urinary system problems. What might a change in the appearance of one's urine indicate?

Applying Health Skills

Accessing Information. Research and discuss the social issues regarding organ donation and kidney transplants. How are donors matched with potential recipients? What type of follow-up care is needed? Share with your classmates what you learned about organ donation and transplants.

 INTERNET RESOURCES Find more information about kidney transplants by visiting **health.glencoe.com.**

Lesson 3 The Urinary System **457**

③ ASSESS

EVALUATING THE LESSON

Assign and discuss the Lesson 3 Review; then administer, grade, and discuss Lesson Quiz 65 in the TCR. 📁

RETEACHING

- Have students refer to Figure 17.3 to review the major urinary system organs and their functions.
- Ask students to complete Reteaching Activity 65 in the TCR. 📁

ENRICHMENT

Ask a group of interested students to learn more about portable dialysis machines. Suggest they work together to answer these questions:

- How do they function?
- What problems can be associated with their use?

Let these students discuss their findings and conclusions with the rest of the class.

④ CLOSE

Have students recall their responses to the Quick Start assignment for this lesson. Ask:

- How are kidneys similar to the other filters you have listed?
- How are kidneys different from those other filters?

Lesson 3 Review

Answers to Reviewing Facts and Vocabulary

1. To filter waste and extra fluids from the blood.
2. See pages 454 and 455 for descriptions.
3. See pages 455 and 456 for possible answers.

Answers to Thinking Critically

4. Caffeine increases water lost through urination; consuming these beverages reduces the amount of water in the body.
5. A person may prevent damage that can lead to dialysis, a transplant, or death. A change in the appearance of urine might indicate a urinary infection. A change in the amount of urine production might indicate nephritis among other problems.

Dietary Supplement Advertising

NHES Standard 4 Students will analyze the influence of culture, media, technology, and other factors on health.

Objective

Analyze claims made in advertisements for dietary supplements.

Motivator

Ask students what they think dietary supplements are. Are vitamins considered dietary supplements? How about "sport bars" or "sport drinks"? The FDA considers all of these products to be dietary supplements.

Teaching Strategies

Awareness Emphasize that the FDA does not test the safety and effectiveness of dietary supplements before they are marketed.

Analysis Note that an advertisement that looks like a magazine article might imply that it is written by an objective third party.

Reflection In their summary paragraphs, ask students to consider the dangers of leaving out crucial information about ingredients.

Take Action Encourage students to take a trip to a pharmacy or health food store, examine a container of a dietary supplement, and write down the ingredients that appear on the label. Then have them research each of those ingredients to discover their possible side effects.

✔ Assessment

Students' grids should demonstrate their understanding of the difference between implied and expressed claims and should contain examples.

Eye ON THE Media

Dietary Supplement Advertising

Dietary supplements include vitamins, plant extracts, amino acids, and combinations of such ingredients. Advertisements for these products may make claims about weight loss, alleviating pain, and even curing diseases. The U.S. Food and Drug Administration (FDA) does not test these products in the same way that it tests pharmaceutical medicines. Some of these products can have adverse effects on the digestive system, kidneys, and other organs. Use the following activity to analyze claims made in advertisements for dietary supplements.

Name of Product	
Expressed Claims	**Implied Claims**

ACTIVITY

Visit your school or public library and select several different fitness, exercise, or health magazines. Choose two different advertisements for dietary supplements, and use a chart like the one above to help you analyze the claims made in each ad. List the "expressed" and "implied" claims about the product's effectiveness and safety. An expressed claim is a statement such as "This product will help you lose weight." An implied claim is conveyed in a more subtle way, such as the display of before-and-after photos that imply the amount of weight loss achieved by a customer.

EXPRESS YOUR VIEWS

Write a paragraph for each ad, summarizing your overall impressions of it. Is it misleading? Does it make claims about scientific studies on the product? Does the ad appear to be a magazine article rather than an advertisement? Does the ad give warnings about possible adverse side effects associated with the product?

More About...

Supplement Testing A botanical ingredient called *aristolochic acid* has been found to cause permanent kidney damage, complete kidney failure, and in some cases cancer in the urinary tract. Aristolochic acid is a natural ingredient found in a plant called *Aristolochia*, and it is found in a variety of dietary supplements. Nonetheless, this ingredient is a known carcinogen. In 2001, the FDA issued consumer warnings and asked manufacturers to make sure their products are free of this ingredient. However, because dietary supplements are not tested and approved by the FDA, consumers have to rely on the manufacturer to ensure this ingredient is not present.

CROSS-CURRICULUM CONNECTIONS

Write About Flavor. Sweet, salty, sour, or bitter: the 10,000 microscopic taste buds located on the tongue help us pick up these four basic flavor sensations. Choose a favorite food and freewrite about it, focusing on a description of the food's taste. Read the description to classmates without revealing the food item's name. Using listening skills, your classmates will try to guess the food item.

Measure the Intestine. The average small intestine is 1 inch in diameter and 21 feet long. The average large intestine is 2.5 inches in diameter and 5 to 6 feet long. What is the difference in their volumes in cubic feet?

(Hint: The area of a circle is πr^2.)

Trace Water Consumption. Drinking eight glasses of water each day is recommended as a way of keeping your digestive and urinary systems healthy. People are listening. Consider that more than 12 gallons of bottled water are consumed per person per year in the United States. Although drinking bottled water is not a new practice, it has reached a new level of popularity. In a short report, trace the recent trend in the use of bottled water. From your research, explain your conclusions about this trend.

Investigate Artificial Kidneys. The oldest artificial organs are kidney dialysis machines. Unfortunately, these machines are very large, not portable, and extremely expensive to purchase and operate. Over the last 30 years, the use of dialysis has grown steadily in developed countries and the cost has risen along with the demand. Research is currently underway to solve these problems and to produce a small, portable (or implantable) artificial kidney at a significantly lower cost. Investigate the latest developments in this field.

Urologist

A urologist is a doctor who specializes in treating diseases of the urinary tract. About 60,000 Americans die every year from causes related to kidney failure. This number is expected to grow in the near future as the American population ages. In order to meet this demand for medical services, more young people will be needed to pursue careers in this special field.

To become a urologist, you'll need a four-year college degree followed by five years of medical school. You can find out more about this and other health careers by clicking on Career Corner at **health.glencoe.com**.

Chapter 17 Review **459**

CROSS-CURRICULUM CONNECTIONS

Enrich student learning by connecting the topic of the digestive and urinary systems to one of the four subject areas presented on this page. The activity may be completed individually or with a partner.

Language Arts Remind students that listening, like speaking, is an active process. Suggest that they mentally process what they hear as well as take notes.

Social Studies Explain to students that analysis of a topic requires examination of information gathered from various sources.

Math Answer: Small intestine: $17\text{ft} \times (.5\text{ in.}/12\text{ in/ft})^2 \times 3.14 = 0.093\text{ft}^3$

Large intestine: $5.5\text{ft} \times (1.25\text{in}/12\text{in/ft})^2 \times 3.14 = 0.187\text{ ft}^3$

The difference in volume: $0.187\text{ ft}^3 - 0.093\text{ ft}^3 = 0.094\text{ ft}^3$

Science There are two approaches being considered: mechanical filtering devices and bioengineered devices.

CAREER Corner

Have students read and discuss the Career Corner information on urology. Ask interested students to explore the Glencoe Health Web site at **health.glencoe.com** for more information.

Portfolio Assessment

Self-Evaluation Direct students to review the Health Skills Activities and other activities completed in the chapter. Encourage each student to select one finished product or activity that demonstrates his or her best work for the chapter and that represents the student's learning goals. Have students explain what they have learned and how the examples they have selected demonstrate their growth in health literacy, knowledge, and skills.

Teacher Classroom Resources Assign Performance Assessment 17, "Write a True/False Test," in the TCR.

- Assign and discuss the chapter review.
- Use Chapter 17 MindJogger Videoquiz to review the chapter. ▶◀

CHAPTER 17 REVIEW ANSWERS

Exploring Health Terms

1. digestion
2. absorption
3. bile
4. elimination
5. heartburn
6. hiatal hernia
7. appendicitis
8. peptic ulcer
9. nephrons
10. urine
11. bladder
12. urethra

Recalling the Facts

1. In the mouth; saliva.
2. A creamy, fluid mixture of food and gastric juices. It is formed during digestion in the stomach.
3. Villi increase the surface area for absorption of nutrients through capillaries into the blood.
4. To absorb water, salts, and vitamins.
5. Constipation is a condition in which feces become dry and hard and bowel movements are difficult. It is caused by not consuming water or fiber so that wastes move slowly through the lower intestine.
6. Diarrhea, abdominal cramps, and gas.
7. Gastritis is an inflammation of the stomach lining. It can have a variety of causes including

460

▶ EXPLORING HEALTH TERMS
Answer the following questions on a sheet of paper.

Lesson 1 *Replace the underlined words with the correct term.*

absorption	bile
chyme	digestion
elimination	gastric juices
peristalsis	mastication

1. The mechanical and chemical breakdown of foods for use by the body's cells is <u>peristalsis</u>.
2. The process of <u>elimination</u> is the passage of food from the digestive tract into the cardiovascular and lymphatic systems.
3. <u>Chyme</u> is a yellow-green bitter fluid important in the breakdown and absorption of fats.
4. <u>Digestion</u> is the expulsion of undigested food or body wastes.

Lesson 2 *Match each definition with the correct term.*

appendicitis	indigestion
heartburn	peptic ulcer
hiatal hernia	

5. A burning sensation in the center of the chest that may rise from the bottom, or tip, of the breastbone up to the pharynx.
6. A condition in which part of the stomach pushes through an opening in the diaphragm.
7. An inflammation of the appendix.
8. A sore in the lining of the digestive tract.

Lesson 3 *Fill in the blanks with the correct term.*

cystitis	urethra
hemodialysis	urethritis
nephrons	bladder
urine	ureters

(_9_) are the functional units of the kidneys. The (_10_) produced in the kidneys is carried to the (_11_), where it is stored until it exits the body through the (_12_).

▶ RECALLING THE FACTS
Use complete sentences to answer the following questions.

Lesson 1

1. Where does the process of digestion begin, and which digestive juice is involved?
2. Define the term *chyme*. In which part of the digestive process is it formed?
3. What is the purpose of villi?
4. What is the main function of the large intestine?

Lesson 2

5. What is constipation? What causes it?
6. What are some problems that can be caused by overusing laxatives?
7. How do gastritis and a peptic ulcer differ?
8. Explain the causes and risks of cirrhosis of the liver.

Lesson 3

9. Define the term *urine*. What are the main components of urine?
10. What is the function of the bladder?
11. Compare and contrast cystitis and urethritis.
12. Describe the two types of dialysis available for patients with chronic kidney failure.

the increased production of stomach acid, tobacco or alcohol use, infections, and certain medications. A peptic ulcer is a sore in the lining of the digestive tract. Causes of peptic ulcers include the use of anti-inflammatory drugs and infection by *Helicobacter pylori.*

8. Heavy alcohol use can cause cirrhosis of the liver. It can lead to liver failure and death.
9. Urine is the liquid waste material produced by the kidneys. It consists of water and body wastes that contain nitrogen.
10. The bladder stores urine until it is ready to be emptied.
11. Cystitis is an inflammation of the urinary bladder; urethritis is an inflammation of the urethra. Both are caused by bacterial infection, and both have symptoms that include pain during urination, increased frequency of urination, fever, and the presence of blood in urine. Both are treated with antibiotics.
12. Hemodialysis involves the blood being passed through a machine that artificially

► THINKING CRITICALLY

1. **Analyzing.** If the duct that brings pancreatic juices to the small intestine were blocked, how would the digestive process be affected? *(LESSON 1)*

2. **Applying.** Relate the importance of early detection and warning signs and explain why seeking early medical help is important for the treatment of colon cancer. *(LESSON 2)*

3. **Evaluating.** Fresh urine is sterile, or free of bacteria or viruses, in a healthy person. Why might a health care professional check urine for bacteria if a person were suffering from reduced urine flow and fever? *(LESSON 3)*

2. **Communicating.** You are worried about a close family member who appears to be using food as a coping mechanism for dealing with his or her emotions. Write a dialogue that includes how you could encourage this person to use more positive health behaviors to manage his or her emotions. Use "I" messages and active listening techniques in your dialogue. *(LESSON 2)*

3. **Accessing Information.** Research more about the elimination of waste products from the body. Identify the different types of wastes and which organs and body functions are responsible for eliminating each type. Make a poster that shows the results of your research. *(LESSON 3)*

► HEALTH SKILLS APPLICATION

1. **Goal Setting.** Examine the effects and benefits of physical activity for coping with stress and helping reduce the risk of developing certain digestive disorders. Use the steps of goal setting to develop a plan to incorporate 30 minutes of physical activity into each day. Make a table to help you organize your time to fit the activity into your day. *(LESSON 1)*

BEYOND *the* Classroom

Parent Involvement

Advocacy. With a parent, learn more about the services available for patients suffering from digestive or urinary problems in your community. Are there groups for people with colitis or irritable bowel syndrome, for example? Where do patients receive dialysis? Investigate programs that raise awareness of these services, and ask how you and your parents can participate.

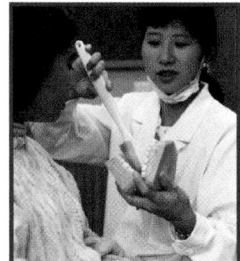

School and Community

Tooth Care. Contact a dentist, and ask him or her to talk to your class about oral health. Ask the dentist to describe the specific role of teeth in digestion and how different teeth are shaped to carry out different functions.

filters the blood. Peritoneal dialysis involves using the peritoneum as a filter while adding solution to the abdominal cavity to promote filtration. The solution is removed after filtration is complete.

Thinking Critically

1. Blocking these secretions from the pancreas could result in slower, less efficient digestion of food and the absorption of fewer nutrients.

2. Possible answer: Because this type of cancer usually spreads slowly, if it is detected and treated early, your chances of survival are greatly increased.

3. The presence of bacteria in the urine would indicate an infection that can be treated with antibiotics.

Health Skills Application

1. Answers will vary.

2. Answers will vary but may include suggestions for how to reduce stress such as exercising, writing in a journal, or talking to a friend.

3. Answers will vary but should include solid wastes, gaseous wastes, and liquid wastes.

EVALUATE

- Use the reproducible Chapter 17 Test in the TCR, or construct your own using the Testmaker software.

- Use Performance Assessment 17 in the TCR.

ENRICHMENT

Ask students to complete Enrichment Activity 17 in the TCR.

BEYOND *the* Classroom

Keep students involved in the community, and encourage parent participation by assigning the activities on this page for students to work on outside of class.

Lessons	Standards		Features
	National	**State/Local**	
1 The Endocrine System *pages 464–467*	National Health Education Standards 1.3, 3.1, 3.2		
2 The Male Reproductive System *pages 468–473*	National Health Education Standards 1.2, 1.3, 3.1, 3.3, 7.1		**Hands-On Health** • Monthly TSE Reminder Card *(Practicing Healthful Behaviors),* page 471
3 The Female Reproductive System *pages 474–479*	National Health Education Standards 1.2, 1.3, 3.1, 3.3, 7.1		**Health Skills Activity** • Asking Difficult Questions *(Communication),* page 478

Reproducible Resources	Assessment	Technology
Student Activity Workbook for use with each chapter	📁 Lesson Quiz 66	🕹 Transparency 53
📁 Concept Mapping Activity 66		💿 TeacherWorks®
📁 Enrichment Activities 18		💻 Internet Activities
📁 Guided Reading Activities 66		
📁 Lesson Plan 66		
📁 Parent Letter and Activities 18		
📁 Reteaching Activity 66		
📁 Concept Mapping Activity 67	📁 Lesson Quiz 67	🕹 Transparency 54
📁 Cross-Curriculum Activity 18		💿 TeacherWorks®
📁 Decision-Making Activity 18		
📁 Guided Reading Activities 67		
📁 Health Lab 18		
📁 Lesson Plan 67		
📁 Reteaching Activity 67		
📁 Concept Mapping Activity 68	📁 Lesson Quiz 68	🕹 Transparency 55
📁 Current Health Issues 18		💿 TeacherWorks®
📁 Guided Reading Activities 68		
📁 Lesson Plan 68		
📁 Reteaching Activity 68		

0:00 OUT OF TIME

If time does not permit teaching the entire chapter, use:
- Figure 18.1, p. 465
- Figure 18.2, p. 470
- Hands-On Health, p. 471
- Figure 18.3, p. 475
- Health Skills Activity, p. 478

Language Diversity

- 🎧 English Audio CD Program
- 🎧 Spanish Audio CD Program
- 📁 English Summaries, Quizzes, and Activities
- 📁 Spanish Summaries, Quizzes, and Activities
- 📁 Spanish Parent Letters and Activities

End of Chapter Assessment

Blackline Masters
- 📁 Chapter 18 Test
- 📁 Performance Assessment Activity 18
- 📁 Unit 5 Test

Technology
- 💿 Vocabulary PuzzleMaker
- 📀 MindJogger Videoquiz
- 💿 Exam*View*® Pro Testmaker

Professional Health Series
Dealing with Sensitive Issues
Planning a Coordinated School Health Program
Promoting Character Education
Home, School, and Community Involvement

Key to Ability Levels

Teaching strategies that appear throughout the chapter have been identified by one of the following codes to give teachers an idea of their suitability for students of varying learning styles and abilities.

L1 Strategies should be within the ability range of all students. Full class participation is often required. Teacher direction is usually needed.

L2 Strategies are designed for average to above-average students or for small groups. Some teacher direction is needed.

L3 Strategies are designed for students able and willing to work independently. Minimal teacher direction is needed.

ELL Strategies should be within the ability range of students learning the English language.

🔲 Block scheduling strategies are useful in a block scheduling format.

Endocrine and Reproductive Systems

CHAPTER OVERVIEW

Chapter 18 discusses the endocrine system and the male and female reproductive systems.

Lesson 1 The endocrine system is made up of glands that secrete hormones. These hormones affect the nervous system and control growth and other body functions. Good health habits can help maintain the endocrine system.

Lesson 2 When a male reaches puberty, hormones stimulate the production of testosterone, initiating sperm production and the development of secondary sex characteristics. Care of the male reproductive system includes monthly testicular self-exams and practicing abstinence.

Lesson 3 When a female reaches puberty, hormones stimulate the production of estrogen and progesterone. As a result, secondary sex characteristics develop. During the reproductive years, one ovum a month matures, allowing an opportunity for fertilization. Care of the female reproductive system includes monthly breast self-exams and practicing abstinence.

Health Skills Features

- Hands-On Health *(Practicing Healthful Behaviors)*, p. 471
- Health Skills Activity *(Communication)*, p. 478

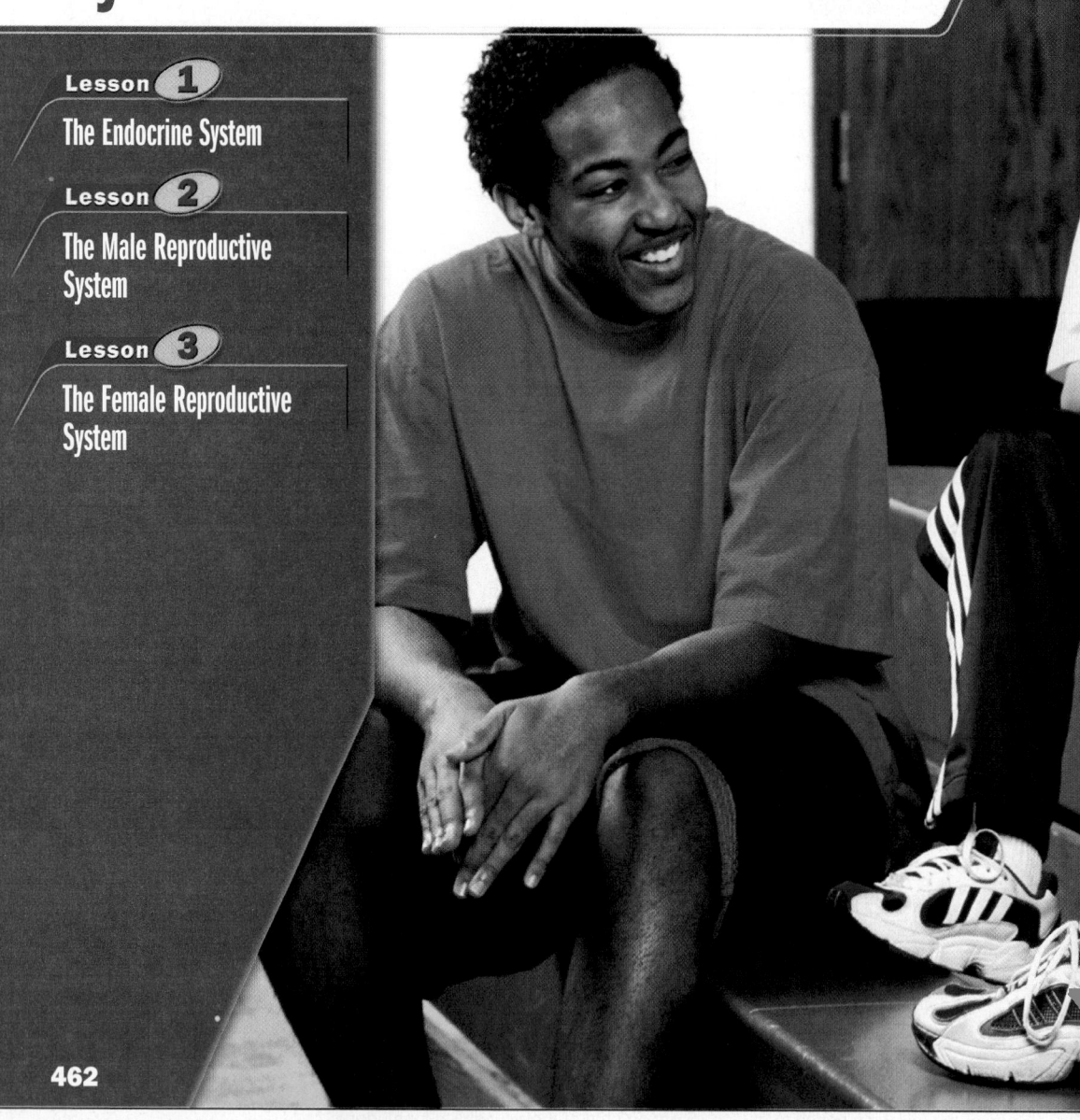

Chapter **18**

Endocrine and Reproductive Systems

Lesson 1
The Endocrine System

Lesson 2
The Male Reproductive System

Lesson 3
The Female Reproductive System

462

MEETING STUDENT DIVERSITY

Language Diversity Use the following suggestions to help students who have difficulty with English:

- Pair English language learners with native speakers of English who can restate the Chapter Summary in language that helps students comprehend important concepts.

- Direct auditory learners or those students with language diversity to the *Glencoe Health Audio CD Program.* Available in English and Spanish, this component provides an audio and written summary of the chapter.
- Use photographs, drawings, or magazine clippings to help students visualize the important concepts of the chapter.

Personal Health Inventory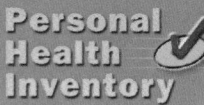

What's Your Health Status?

Read each statement below and respond by writing *yes*, *no*, or *sometimes* for each item. Write *yes* only for items that you are sure of.

1. I understand how hormones affect my body during adolescence and adulthood.

2. I eat a well-balanced diet.

3. I include physical activity in my daily routine.

4. I have regular medical checkups.

5. For males: I do a monthly testicular self-exam.

6. For females: I do a monthly breast self-exam.

7. I follow strategies for practicing abstinence.

8. I avoid situations that might put me at risk of contracting STDs.

9. For males: I wear a protective cup or supporter when participating in sports or a strenuous physical activity.

10. For females: I avoid the use of feminine products such as douches and sprays.

Keep this personal inventory for review later in the chapter. When you complete the chapter, review your answers and identify two or three behavior changes you could make to improve your health.

Quick Write

Using Visuals. Many changes take place during the teen years. Some of these changes are controlled by hormones produced by the endocrine system. Describe how the endocrine and reproductive systems are related.

463

INTRODUCING THE CHAPTER

Personal Health Inventory

Have the males and females meet in separate groups to read and discuss the Personal Health Inventory statements that apply to their gender. Ask:

- What is involved?
- Why is this important?

Then as a whole class, have students discuss their responses to the remaining questions. Encourage each student to respond to the inventory, writing *yes, no,* or *sometimes* for every applicable statement. Remind students that the inventory is for their own use and that they can use it to guide their learning and to shape their own health habits. Ask students to keep their inventory responses so they can review them at the end of Chapter 18.

Quick Write

Using Visuals Have students describe the photographs, focusing on the teens in the pictures. Ask:

- What do all these teens have in common?
- How are individual teens different from the others?
- What do you think accounts for these differences?

Then let a volunteer read the Quick Write assignment aloud, and give students about three minutes to jot down their responses.

TECHNOLOGY OPTIONS

MINDJOGGER

VIDEOQUIZ

To preview or review chapter content, you may wish to use the Chapter 18 MindJogger Videoquiz.

HEALTH Online **Online Resources for the Teacher** For a fresh approach to health topics and an in-depth look at health issues, use these online resources found under Teacher Resources at **health.glencoe.com:**

- Block Schedule Lesson Plans
- Technology Projects
- Health Updates

Lesson 1

The Endocrine System

QUICK START Have students work with partners to read, discuss, and respond to the Quick Start. Then ask several volunteers to read their responses aloud.

TYING TO PRIOR KNOWLEDGE

Referring to the Quick Start assignment, point out that students already have some familiarity with the endocrine system. Ask volunteers to contribute other facts about hormones and endocrine glands. Then explain that students will learn more about the endocrine system as they read Lesson 1.

INTRODUCING VOCABULARY

- Divide the class into eight groups, and assign each group one of the vocabulary terms. Have group members discuss the Glossary definition of their term. Also, have them scan the lesson and read the paragraph in which that term is introduced. Then let each group present and explain its term to the rest of the class.

- Ask students to complete the Chapter 18 Study Guide in the *Student Activity Workbook.* 📁

VOCABULARY

- **endocrine glands**
- **hormones**
- **thyroid gland**
- **parathyroid glands**
- **pancreas**
- **pituitary gland**
- **gonads**
- **adrenal glands**

YOU'LL LEARN TO

- Identify the glands of the endocrine system and explain the function of each.

- Examine the effects of health behaviors on the endocrine system.

- Appraise the significance of body changes during adolescence.

QUICK START *Endo* means "within" and *crine* means "to separate." How does this information help you understand one of the characteristics of the endocrine system?

When the brain recognizes a stressful situation, the endocrine system reacts by releasing the hormone adrenaline. *How do these changes help prepare the body to react under stress?*

All the cells in your body respond to messages sent by three of your major body systems—the nervous system, the immune system, and the endocrine system. These three systems work closely together to coordinate the functions of the body. The endocrine system is especially important during the teen years because one of its main functions is to regulate growth and development.

Structure of the Endocrine System

The endocrine system consists of a network of endocrine glands located throughout the body. **Endocrine glands** are *ductless—or tubeless—organs or groups of cells that secrete hormones directly into the bloodstream.* **Hormones** are *chemical substances that are produced in glands and help regulate many of your body's functions.* Hormones are secreted by the endocrine glands and then carried to their destinations in the body by the blood. These chemical messengers influence physical and mental responses. Hormones produced during puberty trigger physical changes in the body. **Figure 18.1** describes the major glands of the endocrine system and the body functions they regulate.

Lesson 1 *Resources*

Teacher Classroom Resources

📁 Concept Mapping Activity 66

📁 Enrichment Activities 18

📁 Guided Reading Activities 66

📁 Lesson Plan 66

📁 Lesson Quiz 66

📁 Parent Letter and Activities 18

📁 Reteaching Activity 66

Student Activity Workbook

📁 Applying Health Skills 66

📁 Chapter 18 Study Guide

Multimedia

🖳 Transparency 53

FIGURE 18.1

THE ENDOCRINE SYSTEM

The glands of the endocrine system are located throughout the body. Each gland has at least one particular function.

Thyroid The **thyroid gland** *produces hormones that regulate metabolism, body heat, and bone growth.* The thyroid produces thyroxine, which regulates the way cells release energy from nutrients.

Parathyroid Glands The **parathyroid glands** *produce a hormone that regulates the body's calcium and phosphorus balance.*

Testes The testes are the male reproductive glands.

Ovaries The ovaries are the female reproductive glands.

Besides playing a role in reproduction (as described in Lessons 2 and 3), the ovaries and testes control the development of secondary sex characteristics during puberty.

Pineal Gland This gland produces the hormone melatonin, which helps regulate sleep cycles and is thought to affect the onset of puberty.

Pituitary Gland The pituitary regulates and controls the activities of all other endocrine glands.

Hypothalamus The hypothalamus links the endocrine system with the nervous system and stimulates the pituitary gland to secrete hormones.

Adrenal Glands These glands produce hormones that regulate the body's salt and water balance. Secretions from the adrenal cortex and the adrenal medulla control the body's emergency response.

Pancreas The **pancreas** is *a gland that serves both the digestive and the endocrine systems.* As an endocrine gland, the pancreas secretes two hormones that regulate the level of glucose in the blood—glucagon and insulin.

Pituitary Gland

The **pituitary gland** *regulates and controls the activities of all of the other endocrine glands.* The pituitary is known as the master gland. It has three sections, or lobes—anterior, intermediate, and posterior.

▶ **Anterior lobe.** The anterior, or front, lobe of the pituitary gland produces six hormones. Somatotropic, or growth, hormone stimulates normal body growth and development by altering chemical activity in body cells. Thyroid-stimulating hormone (TSH) stimulates the thyroid gland to produce hormones. Adrenocorticotropic (uh-DREE-noh-kawr-ti-koh-TROH-pik) hormone (ACTH) stimulates production of hormones in the adrenal glands.

More About...

Glands The human body contains several other glands, including the exocrine glands, that are not a part of the endocrine system. While the endocrine glands release their hormones into the bloodstream, the exocrine glands deliver secretions directly onto the body's surface through a duct or tube. Examples of exocrine glands include the salivary glands, which produce saliva in the mouth; the sweat and oil glands of the skin; and the tear glands of the eye.

② TEACH

Discussing

Guide students in discussing why the pituitary gland is called the master gland. Ask: Which other parts of the endocrine system does the pituitary gland control? How does it affect other body systems? Which part of the brain stimulates the pituitary gland? hypothalamus **L1**

VISUAL LEARNING

Figure 18.1 Have students meet in cooperative groups to study the illustration and to read and discuss the information in Figure 18.1. Ask group members to describe, in their own words, the location and function of each labeled gland.

Activity

Prepare by bringing colored construction paper, scissors, and poster board to class. You may also want to bring in some photos or diagrams of the lobes of the pituitary gland to share with students. Have a group of interested students create representations of the three lobes. Then ask them to cut out and glue the shapes onto a poster and to label each lobe with its function. **L2** **Visual/Spatial**

ACTIVE READING

Flash Cards

Flash cards can be a useful comprehension and study aid for some students. Suggest that, as they read, students prepare a separate flash card for each key term or concept. Then encourage students to use their cards to review the main concepts of the lesson. For more strategies, see the *Guided Reading Activities* booklet.

Discussing

Guide students in discussing the importance of the adrenal glands. Ask:

- Why are the adrenal glands essential to good physical health?

- What health conditions might be associated with adrenal problems? problems associated with metabolism and high blood pressure **L1**

Reinforcing Concepts

Ask students to compare Graves' disease, or hyperthyroidism, and hypothyroidism. Ask:

- How are the two disorders related?

- What is the essential difference between them?

- How can the two prefixes *hyper-* (in great amount) and *hypo-* (abnormally low) help you understand the underlying problems of these disorders? **L1**

Activity

Have students use online and library sources to research growth disorders:

- How are they identified?

- How are they treated? With what results?

Let students meet in groups to discuss their findings. **L2**

HEALTH *Online*

Let students work in groups to brainstorm lists of questions about the endocrine system. Then have group members work together to use the Web Links to find answers to their questions.

Hormones produced by the pituitary gland play a role in determining height. *Locate the pituitary gland in Figure 18.1. Name two other important functions of the pituitary gland.*

HEALTH *Online*

Discover more about the endocrine system and its function in Web Links at health.glencoe.com.

diabetes For more information on different types of diabetes and the risk factors for this disease, see Chapter 26, page 691.

Two hormones that stimulate production of all other sex hormones are secreted by the pituitary's anterior lobe during adolescence. Follicle-stimulating hormone (FSH) and luteinizing hormone (LH) control the growth, development, and functions of the **gonads**, another name for *the ovaries and testes*.

- In females, FSH stimulates cells in the ovaries to produce estrogen, a female sex hormone that triggers the development of ova. LH is responsible for ovulation and stimulates ovarian cells to produce progesterone. The hormone prolactin stimulates milk production in females who have given birth.

- In males LH stimulates cells in the testes to produce the male hormone testosterone. FSH controls the production of sperm.

▶ **Intermediate lobe.** The intermediate, or middle, lobe of the pituitary secretes melanocyte-stimulating hormone (MSH), which controls the darkening of the skin by stimulating skin pigments.

▶ **Posterior lobe.** The posterior, or rear, lobe of the pituitary gland secretes antidiuretic hormone (ADH), which regulates the balance of water in the body. ADH also produces oxytocin, which stimulates uterine contractions during the birth of a baby.

Adrenal Glands

The **adrenal glands** are *glands that help the body recover from stress and respond to emergencies*. They each have two parts.

▶ The **adrenal cortex** secretes a hormone that inhibits the amount of sodium excreted in urine and serves to maintain blood volume and pressure. It also secretes hormones that aid the metabolism of fats, proteins, and carbohydrates. These hormones play a role in immunity and the body's response to stress.

▶ The **adrenal medulla** is controlled by the hypothalamus and the autonomic nervous system. It secretes the hormones epinephrine (also called adrenaline) and norepinephrine. Epinephrine increases heartbeat and respiration, raises blood pressure, and suppresses the digestive process during periods of high emotion.

Problems of the Endocrine System

Factors such as stress, infection, and changes in the balance of fluid and minerals in the blood can cause hormone levels to vary. Often these situations will correct themselves. More serious problems, including those described here, may require medication.

▶ **Diabetes mellitus** is a disorder in which the pancreas produces too little or no insulin, resulting in high blood glucose levels. Symptoms include fatigue, weight loss, thirst, and frequent urination.

More About...

Hormones When a hormone, such as cortisone, is taken in amounts larger than that produced by the body, it can act as a drug. It may reduce swelling, but it might also suppress the immune system. Short-term use can be beneficial in a variety of conditions, but long-term use may lead to lowered immunities, weakening of the bones, and high blood pressure. Doctors have recently discovered that serious side effects can be avoided by prescribing low doses or by giving higher doses on alternate days.

- **Graves' disease,** also called *hyperthyroidism,* is a disorder in which an overactive and enlarged thyroid gland produces excessive amounts of thyroxine. Symptoms include nervousness, weight loss, increased thirst, rapid heartbeat, and intolerance for heat. Low thyroxine production, called *hypothyroidism,* causes fatigue, dry skin, weight gain, constipation, and sensitivity to cold.

- **Cushing's disease** results from the overproduction of adrenal hormones. Symptoms include round face, humped upper back, thin and easily bruised skin, and fragile bones.

- **Goiter,** an enlargement of the thyroid gland, is caused mainly by a lack of iodine in the diet. Since the introduction of iodized salt, goiters have become rare in the United States.

- **Growth disorders** are caused by abnormal amounts of growth hormone. With early diagnosis and proper treatment, a child with a growth disorder can reach a normal height.

Care of the Endocrine System

To keep your endocrine system functioning at peak performance, take care of all of your body systems. Eat nutritious meals, get enough sleep, and avoid stress. A health care professional can perform medical tests to determine whether your endocrine function is normal.

Staying physically active is one way of reducing stress and keeping your endocrine system healthy. *What other healthy behaviors help ensure the health of this system?*

Lesson 1 Review

Reviewing Facts and Vocabulary

1. What is an *endocrine gland*?
2. What are the two parts of the adrenal glands, and what do they do?
3. What are the functions of FSH and LH?

Thinking Critically

4. **Evaluating.** Do you agree with the statement that the pituitary gland is the "master gland"? Explain your reasoning.
5. **Analyzing.** Which endocrine glands become more active during puberty? Name the hormones these glands produce, and appraise their effects on changes in the body during adolescence.

Applying Health Skills

Self Management. On a sheet of paper, write the names of two endocrine glands. List one important function of each gland. Then write a statement examining the effects of health behaviors on the endocrine system.

TECHNOLOGY *OPTION*

WORD PROCESSING Use the bullet feature of your word-processing program to make your list. For help with word-processing software, go to **health.glencoe.com.**

Lesson 1 The Endocrine System **467**

EVALUATING THE LESSON

Assign and discuss the Lesson 1 Review; then administer, grade, and discuss Lesson Quiz 66 in the TCR. 📁

RETEACHING

- Have students work with a partner to make a two-column chart about the endocrine system. In the left column, have students list the names of the glands in the endocrine system. In the right column, have them list the function of each gland.

- Ask students to complete Reteaching Activity 66 in the TCR. 📁

ENRICHMENT

Have each student select one gland in the endocrine system and learn more about its function.

What happens when the gland malfunctions? How are problems with the gland treated? Have students summarize their findings in written reports. Remind them to proofread their reports, checking for organization, content, style and conventions. Have them develop several drafts before turning in a final, error-free draft.

④ CLOSE

Have each student identify a health habit he or she intends to improve to protect the health of his or her endocrine system.

Lesson 1 Review

Answers to Reviewing Facts and Vocabulary

1. Ductless—or tubeless organs—or group of cells that secrete hormones directly into the bloodstream.
2. Adrenal cortex and adrenal medulla; see page 466 for functions.
3. They control the growth, development, and function of ovaries and testes.

Answers to Thinking Critically

4. Students should recognize that the pituitary gland regulates and controls the other endocrine glands.
5. The pituitary gland begins secretion of FSH and LH, stimulating the ovaries to produce estrogen and progesterone and the testes to produce testosterone.

The Male Reproductive System

The Male Reproductive System

①FOCUS

QUICK START

Ask a volunteer to read the Quick Start assignment aloud, and give students three minutes to record their responses. Then have volunteers share their ideas, and help the class discuss the importance of protecting the health of the reproductive system.

TYING TO PRIOR KNOWLEDGE

Have students recall what they learned about hormones in the previous lesson. Ask: Which hormones affect the male reproductive system? How? Then tell students that, in Lesson 2, they will learn more about the male reproductive system.

Health Skills Features

"Monthly TSE Reminder Card," p. 471

PRACTICING HEALTHFUL BEHAVIORS

INTRODUCING VOCABULARY

- Let students meet in groups to discuss what they already know about the vocabulary terms. Then have group members work together to find and read the Glossary definition of each term. Ask: How does that definition change your understanding of the term?

- Ask students to complete the Chapter 18 Study Guide in the *Student Activity Workbook.* 📂

VOCABULARY

reproductive system
sperm
testosterone
testes
scrotum
penis
semen
sterility

YOU'LL LEARN TO

- Describe the parts of the male reproductive system and explain the function of each part.

- Relate the importance of early detection and warning signs that prompt males of all ages to seek health care for the male reproductive system.

- Identify situations requiring professional health services for preventive care.

- Analyze the importance of abstinence as it relates to the prevention of STDs.

QUICK START

Why is it important to protect your reproductive system? List two ways you can safeguard this system.

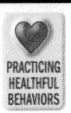 **There are 300 million to 400 million sperm in each ejaculation, but only one can fertilize an ovum.** *What is the relationship of testosterone to sperm?*

An essential function of all living things is reproduction, the process by which life continues from one generation to the next. In humans, as in many other animal species, reproduction results from the union of two specialized sex cells—one from the male and one from the female. These cells are made by the **reproductive system**, *the system of organs involved in producing offspring.*

Structure and Function of the Male Reproductive System

The male reproductive system includes both external and internal organs. The two main functions of the male reproductive system are the production and storage of **sperm**, *the male reproductive cells,* and transfer of sperm to the female's body during sexual intercourse. During the early teen years, usually between the ages of 12 and 15, the male reproductive system reaches maturity.

468 Chapter 18 Endocrine and Reproductive Systems

Lesson 2 *Resources*

Teacher Classroom Resources

📂 Concept Mapping Activity 67

📂 Cross-Curriculum Activity 18

📂 Decision-Making Activity 18

📂 Guided Reading Activities 67

📂 Health Lab 18

📂 Lesson Plan 67

📂 Lesson Quiz 67

📂 Reteaching Activity 67

Student Activity Workbook

📂 Applying Health Skills 67

📂 Chapter 18 Study Guide

Multimedia

 Transparency 54

At that time hormones produced in the pituitary gland stimulate the production of **testosterone**, *the male sex hormone*. Testosterone initiates physical changes that signal maturity, including broadening of the shoulders, development of muscles and facial and other body hair, and deepening of the voice. Testosterone also controls the production of sperm. A physically mature male is capable of producing sperm for the rest of his life.

External Male Reproductive Organs

The testes, the penis, and the scrotum are external structures involved in the process of reproduction. The **testes**, (singular, *testis*) also called testicles, are *two small glands that produce sperm*. These glands secrete testosterone. The testes are located in the **scrotum**, *an external skin sac*. The **penis** is *a tube-shaped organ that extends from the trunk of the body just above the testes*. It is composed of spongy tissue that contains many blood vessels. When blood flow to the penis increases, it becomes enlarged and erect. This normal body function is called an *erection*. Males experience erections easily and frequently during puberty. Erections can occur for no reason. Sometimes an erection results when clothing the male is wearing causes friction.

The penis releases semen. **Semen** is *a thick fluid containing sperm and other secretions from the male reproductive system*. At the height of sexual arousal, a series of muscular contractions known as *ejaculation* may occur. **Fertilization**—the joining of a male sperm cell and a female egg cell—can result if ejaculation occurs during sexual intercourse.

At birth a male has a covering of thin loose skin, called the *foreskin*, over the tip of the penis. Some parents choose *circumcision*—surgical removal of the foreskin of the penis—for their male children. Circumcision is often performed for cultural or religious reasons, but is not generally considered medically necessary today.

Sperm cannot live in temperatures higher than the normal body temperature of 98.6°F. The scrotum protects sperm by keeping the testes slightly below the normal body temperature. When body temperature rises, muscles attached to the scrotum relax, causing the testes to lower away from the body. If body temperature lowers, the muscles tighten and the testes move closer to the body for warmth. Tight clothing that holds the testes too close to the body may interfere with sperm production.

When a male begins to produce sperm, he may experience nocturnal emissions, or ejaculations that occur when sperm is released during sleep. This is a normal function that relieves the buildup of pressure as sperm begin to be produced during puberty.

Development of facial hair is one of the changes that occurs during a male's early teens. Another change is the ability to produce sperm. *Which hormone stimulates physical changes in a maturing male?*

hot link

Fertilization To learn more about fertilization, see Chapter 19, page 486.

CHARACTER CHECK

Responsibility. Here are some ways a teen can show that he or she is mature and responsible.

- Demonstrate respect for yourself and others.
- Control sexual urges, and never impose them on others.
- Practice abstinence from sexual activity before marriage.

② TEACH

Discussing

Guide students in discussing the relationship between the endocrine system, specifically the pituitary gland, and the male reproductive system. **L1**

CHARACTER CHECK

Responsibility Let students meet in groups to read and discuss the list of ways that teens can demonstrate responsibility. Ask:

- Why is it important for males—and females—to avoid imposing their sexual urges on others?
- What are the benefits of practicing abstinence from sexual activity?

Activity

Ask interested students to learn more about circumcision. Encourage some to research various religious and cultural traditions of circumcision. Encourage others to research current understandings of the benefits and risks of the practice. Then have students share their findings and discuss their ideas. **L2**

) More About...

Prenatal Gender Differentiation It appears that the female is the "basic" gender into which embryos develop if not stimulated to do otherwise. When the gonads first appear in a developing embryo, they look the same in both sexes. But by eight weeks after fertilization, they become recognizable as testes in male embryos, presumably because of genes in the Y chromosome. For female embryos, the gonads develop into ovaries by week nine.

Shortly after the male embryo's testes develop, they start secreting testosterone, which causes the previously undifferentiated external genitalia to form the penis and scrotum. In the absence of testosterone, the external genitalia develop into those of the female.

Figure 18.2 Have students meet in groups to study the illustrations and to read and discuss the labels in Figure 18.2. Have group members restate, in their own words, the function of each internal structure.

Activity

Provide simple unlabeled drawings of the male reproductive system. Let students work with partners or with their Figure 18.2 groups to label the internal structures and to review the function of each. **L2**

Cooperative Learning

Divide the class into five groups, and assign each group one of the paragraphs on the care of the male reproductive system. Have group members read and discuss their assigned section and then present that information to the rest of the class. **L1**

Health Skills Practice

Self-exams Have students meet in groups to discuss the importance of talking about testicular self-exams and other practices that help protect the health of the reproductive system. Ask:

COMMUNICATION SKILLS

- Why is it sometimes difficult to discuss these topics?

- Why is it important for teens to share reliable information about these health practices?

Have group members plan what they can do to improve communication on these topics.

470

Internal Male Reproductive Organs

Although sperm are produced in the testes, which are suspended outside the body, they must travel through several structures inside the body before they are released. These structures include the vas deferens, the urethra, the seminal vesicles, and the prostate and Cowper's glands. **Figure 18.2** shows the path taken by sperm cells from the testes until they are released from the body.

FIGURE 18.2

MALE REPRODUCTIVE SYSTEM

The internal structures of the male reproductive system play a role in the delivery of sperm.

bladder

Seminal Vesicle As sperm move through the vas deferens, they are combined with a nourishing fluid produced by the seminal vesicles.

Prostate Gland and Cowper's Glands Secretions from the prostate gland and Cowper's glands combine with the sperm-containing fluid to form semen.

penis

scrotum

Epididymis The tubes in each testis join the epididymis, a larger coiled tube where sperm mature and are stored.

Testis Each testis is divided into tiny tubules in which sperm are formed.

Urethra The urethra is the passageway through which both semen and urine leave the male body.

Vas Deferens The vas deferens are tubes that extend from each epididymis to the urethra.

Cooperative Learning Activity

Effects of Environmental Factors Let students work with partners or in groups to investigate environmental factors that can affect reproductive systems. For example, pesticides called endocrine disruptors alter sex characteristics such as sperm count and breast development in animals. Scientists have investigated the proliferation of endocrine-disrupting chemicals as a possible cause of declining human sperm count as well as rising incidence of cancers and developmental problems in humans. Studies are available from the EPA and the National Coalition Against the Misuse of Pesticides. Have students research and share ideas about protecting reproductive systems from environmental damage.

Hands-On Health ACTIVITY

Monthly TSE Reminder Card

It's important for males to do a testicular self-exam (TSE) every month. However, not all males are accustomed to performing it. In this activity you will create a reminder card for yourself or the males in your family.

What You'll Need

- paper
- colored pens
- lamination supplies (optional)

What You'll Do

1. Cut the paper into a wallet-sized card.
2. On one side of the card, write out the steps in performing a TSE (see page 472).
3. On the other side of the card, create a message that will remind and persuade you or males in your family to do a monthly exam. The exam could be scheduled for the same time each month, such as the first day of every month.
4. Laminate the card so that it will last.

Apply and Conclude

Keep the reminder card in a location where you (or males in your family) will see it often. Because the best time to examine yourself is after a warm bath or shower, consider placing the card in the bathroom. Explain the importance of taking responsibility for regularly performing a TSE.

Care of the Male Reproductive System

Caring for the male reproductive system involves medical checkups, hygiene, protection, and self-examination.

▶ **Get regular checkups.** All males should have regular checkups by a physician every 12 to 18 months.

▶ **Bathe regularly.** Males should shower or bathe daily, thoroughly cleansing the penis and scrotum. Uncircumcised males should take care to wash under the foreskin.

▶ **Wear protective equipment.** Use a protective cup or supporter during **physical activities** to shield external organs.

▶ **Perform regular self-examinations.** Check the scrotum and testicles for signs of cancer. Report any change to a physician.

▶ **Practice abstinence.** Abstain from sexual activity before marriage to avoid contracting **STDs.**

hot link

sexually transmitted diseases (STDs) For more information on STDs and how they affect the male reproductive system, see Chapter 25, page 652.

Hands-On Health

MONTHLY TSE REMINDER CARD

PRACTICING HEALTHFUL BEHAVIORS

NHES Standard 3 Students will demonstrate the ability to practice health-enhancing behaviors and reduce health risks.

Objectives

- Examine the effects of health behaviors on the reproductive system.
- Analyze the role of individual responsibility for enhancing health.

Motivator

Discuss with the class why many males do not regularly examine themselves for testicular abnormalities. How do they think a reminder card would help them practice this habit?

Teaching Strategies

1. Review with students the steps of a testicular self-exam.
2. Tell students that, because this is a reminder card, they should write the steps in their own words and make each step short and easy to remember.

✓ Assessment

Using a rubric, student work should provide comprehensive evidence of the following criteria to achieve the highest score:

✔ identification of all steps of performing a testicular self-exam
✔ correct sequence of steps

Promoting Coordinated School Health

Creating a Team Sometimes, school health policies respond to state mandates and programs and services of the past regardless of their appropriateness, adequacy, or effectiveness. To develop or clarify the vision for school health, the entire system of public school education must be considered. School health committees should consist of representatives of the following:

parents, community members, and business representatives; teachers, counselors, nurses, and other school staff; religious groups; state, county, or local health agency representatives; human services representatives; and volunteer health organizations. For more information, consult *Planning a Coordinated School Health Program*.

Reinforcing Concepts

When students discuss abstinence as a practice that protects teens from STDs, remind them that HIV/AIDS is also transmitted through sexual contact. **L1**

Activity

Have each student choose one of the named STDs to research. Have students find out about the treatment, effectiveness and side effects of the treatment, and long-term results of the disease with and without treatment. Ask students to summarize their findings in brief written reports. You may want to have them evaluate their own writing for mechanics and content. If so, have them write their comments on their reports. **L2**

Health Minute

Guide students in reading and discussing the procedure for performing a testicular self-exam. Then help students discuss the importance of performing this self-exam every month:

• How can this exam lead to early detection of any possible problems?

• Why is the early detection of cancer so important?

Activity

Point out that lifting heavy objects incorrectly can cause inguinal hernia. Invite two or three students to work together to find out the correct way to prepare for and lift a heavy or bulky object. Then ask these students to demonstrate, using an imaginary object, what they have learned. **L2**

472

Health Minute

Steps for Performing a Testicular Exam

The American Cancer Society recommends that males perform a self-exam for testicular cancer once a month.

Follow this procedure:

▶ Stand in front of a mirror. Check for any swelling on the scrotum skin. Examine each testicle with both hands. Roll the testicle gently between the thumbs and fingers.

▶ Find the epididymis, the soft, tubelike structure behind the testicle that collects and carries sperm. Become familiar with this structure so that you won't mistake it for a lump.

▶ Cancerous lumps usually are found on the sides of the testicle but can also appear on the front.

▶ Although lumps do not always indicate the presence of cancer, be sure to consult a health care professional if you do find a lump.

Source: American Cancer Society

hot link

steroids For more information about the harmful effects of anabolic-androgenic steroids, see Chapter 23, page 601.

Sexually Transmitted Diseases (STDs)

Listed below are some of the STDs that affect the male reproductive system. More information about STDs can be found in Chapter 25. The primary means of transmission of all STDs is sexual activity. Teens who practice abstinence from sexual activity greatly reduce or even eliminate their risk of contracting these diseases:

▶ **Chlamydia** and **gonorrhea** are bacterial infections that cause discharge from the penis and burning upon urination; both conditions can damage reproductive health. Treatment includes a course of antibiotics.

▶ **Syphilis** is another bacterial infection. Initially, a painless, reddish sore appears at the site of infection. If left untreated, syphilis can spread and damage internal organs. It is treated with antibiotics.

▶ **Genital herpes** is a virus that causes periodically occurring blisterlike sores in the genital area. Medication relieves symptoms, but the virus remains in the body for life.

Problems of the Male Reproductive System

The organs of the male reproductive system can be affected by functional and structural problems. Infections from sexually transmitted diseases (STDs) also affect these organs.

Inguinal Hernia

An inguinal (IN-gwuh-nuhl) hernia is a separation of tissue that allows part of the intestine to push into the abdominal wall near the top of the scrotum. Straining the abdominal muscles or lifting heavy objects can cause a tear in this tissue. Symptoms of inguinal hernia may include a lump in the groin near the thigh, pain in the groin or, in severe cases, partial or complete blockage of the intestine. Surgery is usually necessary to repair the opening in the muscle wall.

Sterility

Sterility is *the inability to reproduce.* In males it can result from too few sperm—fewer than 20 million per milliliter of seminal fluid—or sperm of poor quality. Sterility can result from environmental hazards, including exposure to X rays or other radiation, toxic chemicals, and lead. Hormonal imbalance, certain medications, or use of drugs, including anabolic **steroids,** can damage sperm. Some diseases, including STDs, and contracting mumps as an adult also can result in sterility.

School to Work

Medical Technicians Physicians and nurses are not the only medical personnel who can detect problems of the reproductive system. Instead, many medical technicians perform diagnostic procedures. Technicians may have special training in administering X rays, ultrasound, and mammograms. While some positions require a four-year college degree, others require no college at all. All positions, however, require some special training. Have students learn about the responsibilities assumed by medical technicians in their area. Then have students choose a technical position of interest and conduct research into the range of duties, qualifications, and training required for the job.

Testicular Cancer and Problems of the Prostate

Testicular cancer can affect males of any age but occurs most often in males between the ages of 14 and 40. These factors increase the risk of developing the disease: undescended testicle, abnormal testicular development, and family history of testicular cancer. A monthly testicular self-exam is recommended by the American Cancer Society. Males should see a health care professional if they notice any changes or symptoms, such as a painless lump or swelling in either testicle or pain or discomfort in a testicle or in the scrotum. With early detection most testicular cancer is treatable through surgery, radiation therapy, or chemotherapy.

The prostate gland can become enlarged as a result of an infection, a tumor, or age-related problems. An enlarged gland presses against the urethra, resulting in frequent or difficult urination. Symptoms may also indicate more serious conditions, including prostate cancer. Prostate cancer screening is usually done during routine physical exams for males over age 50. Early detection increases the chance of survival. Treatment includes surgery, radiation, and hormone therapy.

National and world champion cyclist Lance Armstrong is a survivor of testicular cancer.
Why are testicular self-exams important for male reproductive health?

 Lesson 2 *Review*

Reviewing Facts and Vocabulary

1. What is the function of the testes?
2. Describe the path that sperm follow from the time they form until they leave the body.
3. What are the symptoms of testicular cancer? Identify conditions requiring professional health services for preventive care.

Thinking Critically

4. **Analyzing.** Why would knowing the correct way to lift a heavy object be an important behavior to protect the health of the male reproductive system?
5. **Synthesizing.** Analyze the importance of abstinence as it relates to the prevention of STDs. How can problems related to STDs affect the male reproductive system?

Applying Health Skills

Practicing Healthful Behaviors. Analyze the relationship between unsafe behaviors related to drug use and the harmful effects of these substances on the male reproductive system. Write a paragraph stating how avoiding drugs, including steroids, can ensure the health of your reproductive system.

WORD PROCESSING Word-processing software can help you record your healthy behaviors. For tips go to health.glencoe.com.

Lesson 2 The Male Reproductive System **473**

③ ASSESS

EVALUATING THE LESSON

Assign and discuss the Lesson 2 Review; then administer, grade, and discuss Lesson Quiz 67 in the TCR. 📁

RETEACHING

- Have students work with partners to write informal outlines of the information presented in this lesson.
- Ask students to complete Reteaching Activity 67 in the TCR. 📁

ENRICHMENT

How does the use of tobacco, alcohol, and other drugs affect the male reproductive system? Have students use online and library resources to explore that question. Then have students meet in groups to discuss their findings and any implications associated with them.

④ CLOSE

Have each student write a sentence about one new fact he or she has learned about the male reproductive system. To extend the activity, you may want to have them rewrite their sentences using more complex grammatical elements such as gerunds, particles, and infinitives.

 Lesson 2 *Review*

Answers to Reviewing Facts and Vocabulary

1. To produce sperm and secrete testosterone.
2. From the testes, sperm go to the epididymis, the vas deferens, and the urethra before leaving the body.
3. Painless lump or swelling; pain or discomfort in the testicle or scrotum.

Answers to Thinking Critically

4. Incorrect lifting can cause an inguinal hernia.
5. Sexual contact can spread STDs, which can harm the reproductive organs, sometimes causing sterility. Teens who practice abstinence from sexual activity avoid the risk of contracting STDs.

The Female Reproductive System

Lesson 3

①FOCUS

QUICK START Have a volunteer read the Quick Start assignment aloud, and give students three minutes to write their sentences. Then have students meet with partners to share and discuss their sentences.

TYING TO PRIOR KNOWLEDGE

Let students share a few facts about the female reproductive system. Explain that, as they read this lesson, students will learn about the female reproductive system.

Health Skills Features

"Asking Difficult Questions," p. 478

COMMUNICATION SKILLS

INTRODUCING VOCABULARY

- Have each student make a separate flash card for each of the vocabulary terms. Ask students to write the term on one side of an index card and the Glossary definition on the other side of the card.

- Ask students to complete the Chapter 18 Study Guide in the *Student Activity Workbook*. 📁

The Female Reproductive System

VOCABULARY
- **ova**
- **uterus**
- **ovaries**
- **ovulation**
- **fallopian tubes**
- **vagina**
- **cervix**
- **menstruation**

YOU'LL LEARN TO
- Describe the parts of the female reproductive system and explain the function of each part.
- Relate the importance of early detection and warning signs that prompt females of all ages to seek health care for the female reproductive system.
- Identify situations requiring professional health services for preventive care.
- Analyze the importance of abstinence as it relates to the prevention of STDs.

QUICK START Write a short paragraph that contains the words *reproductive system*, *responsibility*, and *health*. Share these sentences with your classmates.

 The female reproductive system stores ova that unite with sperm in the process of reproduction. *Name another function of the female reproductive system.*

The female reproductive system has several functions. It produces female sex hormones and stores *female reproductive cells,* called **ova** (singular, *ovum*). The **uterus,** *a hollow, muscular, pear-shaped organ inside a female's body,* nourishes and protects the fertilized ovum from conception until birth.

Structure and Function of the Female Reproductive System

The female reproductive system includes several organs and glands. **Ovaries** are *the female sex glands that store the ova and produce female sex hormones.* At birth a female's ovaries contain more than 400,000 immature ova, or eggs. At puberty, the pituitary gland produces hormones that cause these ova to mature. **Ovulation** is *the process of releasing a mature ovum into the fallopian tube each month.* The right ovary will release a mature ovum one month, and the left ovary will release one the next month.

Lesson 3 *Resources*

Teacher Classroom Resources
📁 Concept Mapping Activity 68
📁 Current Health Issues 18
📁 Guided Reading Activities 68
📁 Lesson Plan 68
📁 Lesson Quiz 68
📁 Reteaching Activity 68

Student Activity Workbook
📁 Applying Health Skills 68
📁 Chapter 18 Study Guide

Multimedia
🖱 Transparency 55

Female Reproductive Organs

Figure 18.3 shows the structures of the female reproductive system. Notice the tube that lies next to each ovary. When a mature ovum is released from the ovary, it moves to one of the **fallopian tubes**, *a pair of tubes with fingerlike projections that draw in the ovum.*

Tiny hairlike structures called cilia work, along with muscular contractions in the fallopian tubes, to move the ovum along. Sperm from the male enter the female reproductive system through the **vagina**, *a muscular, elastic passageway that extends from the uterus to the outside of the body.*

If sperm are present in the fallopian tubes, a sperm cell may unite with an ovum, resulting in fertilization. The fertilization of an egg by a sperm produces a cell called a *zygote.* When the zygote leaves the fallopian tube, it enters the uterus. There, the zygote attaches itself to the uterine wall and begins to grow. In preparation for receiving the zygote, the uterine wall has thickened and is rich in blood, which enables the uterus to nourish the zygote. The developing fetus will remain attached to the uterine wall until **birth.**

hot link

birth For more information on prenatal development and birth, see Chapter 19, page 486.

2 TEACH

Reinforcing Concepts

Ask students to suggest examples to help demonstrate the magnitude of a number such as 400,000. Emphasize that, at birth, a female has all the ova she will ever have. Ask: How is this different from the sperm a male produces? **L1**

Activity

Have students use dictionaries to explore the relationships among the words *ovum, ova, ovary,* and *ovulation.* **L2**

VISUAL LEARNING

Figure 18.3 Have students meet in groups to study the illustrations and read the labels in Figure 18.3. Ask group members to describe the location of each labeled feature and to restate, in their own words, the feature's function. Also, ask group members to describe the path that an ovum follows to the uterus.

Explaining

Remind students that the uterus is a muscular organ that enlarges and contracts. Normally, the uterus is about the size of a pear. During pregnancy, it increases to about 20 times its size. Approximately three to six weeks after the birth of a baby, the uterus returns to its prepregnancy size. **L1**

FIGURE 18.3

FEMALE REPRODUCTIVE SYSTEM

The female reproductive system produces sex cells called ova and provides a place for a fertilized ovum to grow.

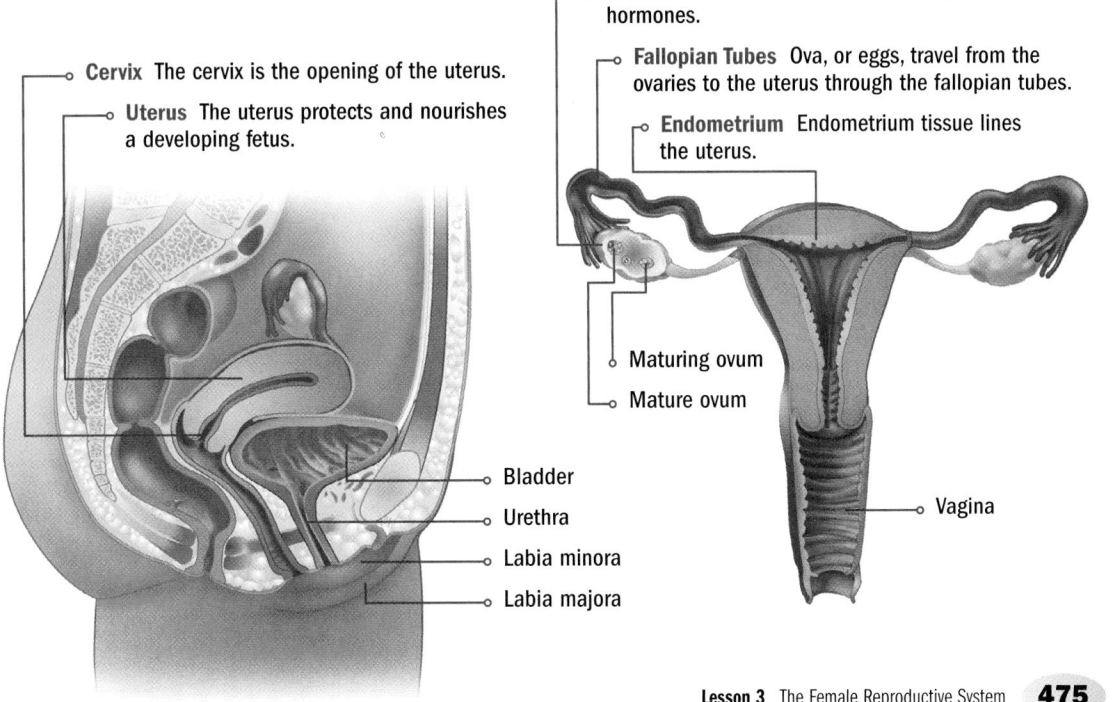

Ovaries The ovaries contain ova and produce hormones.

Fallopian Tubes Ova, or eggs, travel from the ovaries to the uterus through the fallopian tubes.

Endometrium Endometrium tissue lines the uterus.

Cervix The cervix is the opening of the uterus.

Uterus The uterus protects and nourishes a developing fetus.

Maturing ovum

Mature ovum

Bladder

Urethra

Labia minora

Labia majora

Vagina

Lesson 3 The Female Reproductive System **475**

More About...

Conception Conception is unpredictable. Although many couples conceive unintentionally, many married couples who want children are unable to conceive a baby.

Fertilization of the ovum can occur only during a two- to three-day time period when the cervical mucus forms small channels that allow sperm cells to enter the uterus.

Once in the mucus, the sperm can live up to 48 hours. So fertilization could theoretically occur two days after sexual intercourse. Females of fertile couples in their 20s have a 20 percent chance each month of conceiving. Females of couples in their late 30s have about an 8 percent chance per month of getting pregnant.

Cooperative Learning

Have students work with partners or in small groups to research the effects of poor nutrition, stress, or illness on the menstrual cycle. Encourage some students to select eating disorders as the focus of their research. Have students share and discuss their findings. **L2**

Activity

Have interested students calculate the number of ova a female might release during a lifetime. Suggest that these students assume the female has a regular 28-day cycle. Then have them propose the ages at which she starts and stops menstruating and the number of pregnancies she has had. Once they have calculated a number of ova this fictional woman has released in her lifetime, ask: What percentage is that of the total 400,000 ova a female has at birth? **L2 Logical/ Mathematical**

Discussing

Guide students in discussing the benefits of practicing abstinence. Ask:

• How does abstinence protect the health of the female reproductive system?

• How does abstinence promote good mental/emotional and social health? **L1**

FIGURE 18.4
THE MENSTRUAL CYCLE

Days 1–13	Day 14	Days 15–20	Days 21–28
A new egg is maturing inside the ovary.	The mature egg is released into one of the fallopian tubes.	The egg travels through the fallopian tube to the uterus.	After seven days, if the egg is not fertilized, menstruation begins.

Eating nutritious foods and avoiding caffeine can often reduce discomfort related to menstruation. *What other health behaviors will keep your reproductive system healthy?*

Menstruation

In a mature female, each month the uterus prepares for possible pregnancy. If pregnancy doesn't occur, the thickened lining of the uterus, called the *endometrium,* isn't needed, and it breaks down into blood, tissue, and fluids. These materials pass through the **cervix,** *the opening to the uterus,* and into the vagina. This *shedding of the uterine lining* is called **menstruation** and is part of the menstrual cycle, which is summarized in **Figure 18.4.** Females wear either sanitary pads or tampons to absorb the blood flow. After the menstrual period ends, usually within five to seven days, the entire cycle begins again in preparation for receiving a fertilized ovum the next month.

Most females begin their first menstrual cycle between the ages of 10 and 15. The cycle may be irregular at first. As a female grows and matures, her menstrual cycle usually becomes more predictable. Endocrine hormones control the cycle, but poor nutrition, stress, and illness can influence it.

Care of the Female Reproductive System

Good hygiene is important for maintaining the health of the female reproductive system. In a mature female, cells in the lining of the vagina are constantly being shed, causing a slight vaginal discharge. Cleanliness will help eliminate odors.

▶ **Bathe regularly.** It is especially important to shower or bathe daily during the menstrual period. During menstruation, change tampons or sanitary pads every few hours. Feminine deodorant sprays and douches are not necessary and may cause irritation or infection in the sensitive tissues around the vagina.

▶ **Practice abstinence.** Abstain from sexual activity before marriage to avoid unplanned pregnancy and STDs.

Cooperative Learning Activity

Gender Roles Group students to discuss historical and modern gender roles. Suggest they distinguish between gender role differences that are inevitable because of physiological distinctions between males and females and gender role differences that are not. Encourage them to briefly discuss their feelings about gender roles. Ask: Are they more comfortable with strictly defined gender roles? Why or why not? Would they prefer more equality? To what extent do they feel nature imposes restrictions on gender roles? Suggest that students set up a panel discussion about gender roles in our society, with different group members expressing different points of view.

BREAST SELF-EXAM

Breast cancer is the most common cancer and the second leading cause of death, after lung cancer, for women in the United States. The American Cancer Society recommends that females examine their breasts once a month, right after the menstrual period, when breasts are not tender or swollen. Early detection is an important factor in the successful treatment of breast cancer.

► Lie down and place a pillow under the right shoulder. Place the right arm behind the head. Use the fingers of the left hand to feel for lumps or thickening in the right breast. Move around the breast first in a circle, then up and down, and be sure to go over the entire breast area. Repeat the procedure the same way each month. Examine the left breast with the right hand.

► Repeat the examination of both breasts while standing, with one arm behind the head. In the upright position, check the upper and outer parts of the breasts, toward the armpit. Standing in front of a mirror, inspect the breasts for any dimpling of the skin, changes in the nipple, redness, or swelling.

Problems of the Female Reproductive System

Several disorders can affect the female reproductive system. Problems related to menstruation can range from minor discomfort to life-threatening illness.

► **Menstrual cramps** sometimes occur at the beginning of a menstrual period. Light exercise or applying a heating pad to the abdominal area may help relieve symptoms. A health care professional may recommend medication for pain relief. Severe or persistent cramping, called dysmenorrhea, may be an indication that medical attention is needed.

► **Premenstrual syndrome (PMS)** is a disorder caused by hormonal changes. Its symptoms, which may be experienced one to two weeks before menstruation, include nervous tension, anxiety, irritability, bloating, weight gain, depression, mood swings, and fatigue. Regular physical activity and good nutrition may reduce the severity of symptoms.

► **Toxic shock syndrome (TSS)** is a rare but serious bacterial infection that affects the immune system and the liver, and can be fatal. To reduce the risk of TSS, use tampons with the lowest possible absorbency and change tampons often. Symptoms of TSS include fever, vomiting, diarrhea, a sunburn-like rash, red eyes, dizziness, and muscle aches. Any female with these symptoms should contact a physician immediately.

Did You Know?

→ The American Cancer Society recommends that females have pelvic exams by age 18 or when recommended by their physician. A pelvic exam is not painful.

• During a pelvic exam, a health care professional checks the shape, size, and position of pelvic organs and checks for any tumors or cysts.

• An examination of cells collected from the cervix, called a *Pap test*, can detect early changes in cells that may indicate a risk of cervical cancer.

• The health care professional also may test for certain sexually transmitted diseases.

Community Involvement

Suggest that interested students obtain copies of brochures explaining the steps in giving a breast self-exam. These may be available in local medical offices and/or from organizations such as the American Cancer Society. **L2**

Activity

Recent research has indicated a direct connection between smoking and an increased risk of breast cancer. Ask a group of volunteers to use online resources to learn more about the link between smoking and this form of cancer. Then have them share and discuss their findings with the rest of the class. **L3**

Discussing

Guide students in discussing the reasons for having regular pelvic exams. Explain that a female should have this kind of checkup yearly with her pediatrician's recommendation. Stress the importance of doing this even though she may not suspect a problem. **L1**

FYI

Toxic shock syndrome (TSS) was much more common several decades ago. In 1980, there were 813 cases of TSS in the United States. In 1998, for example, only 3 cases of TSS were confirmed.

More About...

Menstrual Cramps Among female teens, painful menstrual cramps, or dysmenorrhea, is the leading cause of short-term absences from school. About 75 percent of adolescent girls experience these painful cramps, but only about 25 percent of them consider it disabling.

The principal symptom of dysmenorrhea is sharp, cramping abdominal pain that begins just before, or at the onset of, menstrual flow. Other symptoms can include headache, nausea, vomiting, fatigue, irritability, dizziness, and fainting. Over-the-counter pain medications may relieve symptoms.

Health Skills Activity

ASKING DIFFICULT QUESTIONS

NHES Standard 5 Students will demonstrate the ability to use interpersonal communication skills to enhance health.

Objectives

- Appraise the significance of body changes occurring during adolescence.
- Demonstrate strategies for communicating health concerns.

Motivator

Ask: Is it or would it be hard for you to talk to an adult about concerns related to body changes you are experiencing? Why or why not?

Teaching Strategies

1. Have students work with a partner; provide the option of working with a partner of the same gender.
2. When students have finished writing their dialogues, collect them and choose several to read and discuss with the class. Assure students ahead of time that their dialogues will remain anonymous.

Assessment

Using a rubric, student work should provide comprehensive evidence of the following criteria to achieve the highest score:

✔ interactions among individuals
✔ use of "I" messages
✔ respectful tone of voice
✔ appropriate body language including eye contact
✔ clear, organized message

Communication: Asking Difficult Questions

"Hello, Brooke," says Dr. Morgan, "How are you? I see we're doing a basic summer camp physical."

Brooke smiles and nods. She has been coming to Dr. Morgan for years and feels comfortable with her.

"Before we begin," Dr. Morgan continues, "do you have any questions for me? Everything okay?"

"Well," Brooke begins, "about a week before my period, I get depressed. It seems much worse than the everyday blues. Once my period starts, I'm okay."

"It's important to ask about your concerns," Dr. Morgan replies. "Many girls and women feel a little blue before their periods, but if your depression is severe, there are treatments we can try. Let's talk more about your symptoms."

What Would You Do?

How would you bring up a reproductive health topic with your parents or guardian or a health care professional? Use the following guidelines for effective communication to help you develop a dialogue.

1. Use "I" messages.
2. Speak in a respectful tone.
3. Make eye contact.
4. Show appropriate body language.
5. Express clear, organized ideas.

Problems Related to Infertility

Infertility, the inability to conceive a child, can have several causes.

▶ **Endometriosis.** This painful, chronic disease occurs when tissue that lines the uterus migrates and grows in the ovaries, fallopian tubes, the uterus, or the lining of the pelvic cavity. Treatments include pain medications, hormone therapy, and surgery.

▶ **Pelvic inflammatory disease (PID).** PID is an infection of the fallopian tubes, ovaries, and the surrounding areas of the pelvis. It can damage a female's reproductive organs. PID usually is caused by **sexually transmitted diseases (STDs).**

▶ **Sexually transmitted diseases** are the most common causes of infertility and other disorders of the reproductive system. Often symptoms of STDs are not evident in females unless a medical examination is performed. Avoiding sexual contact until marriage is the one sure way to prevent STDs.

hot link

STDs For more information on STDs and how they affect the female reproductive system, see Chapter 25, page 652.

⌇⌇ HEALTH LITERACY

Effective Communicator As a precaution, students should examine themselves regularly for signs of cancer in their reproductive systems; however, they may not be prepared if they find something wrong. Discovering a lump or other symptom of possible cancer can be frightening for anyone. Teens should know that the first step in such a situation is confiding in a parent, guardian, or other trusted adult. Then they should consult their family doctor immediately. Understanding and remembering a doctor's explanation and advice can be especially difficult in this kind of stressful situation. It is up to the individual to ask questions and address concerns. Most patients—adults as well as teens—benefit from having a family member attend such consultations.

Other Female Reproductive Disorders

Other reproductive disorders include the following:

▶ **Vaginosis** is the most common vaginal infection in women of childbearing age, and it is sometimes accompanied by discharge, odor, pain, itching, or burning. If not treated with antibiotics, vaginosis can sometimes lead to PID.

▶ **Blocked fallopian tubes,** the leading cause of infertility, may result from PID, abdominal surgery, STDs, or endometriosis.

▶ **Ovarian cysts** are fluid-filled sacs on the ovary. Small, noncancerous cysts usually disappear on their own. Larger cysts may require surgery.

▶ **Cervical, uterine, and ovarian cancer** occur in the female reproductive system. Early sexual activity and STDs such as human papillomavirus (HPV) are related to an increased incidence of cervical cancer. Regular checkups and pelvic exams are important for early detection and treatment.

 Did You Know

➤ Untreated STDs put women at risk for infertility, chronic pelvic pain, and cancer.

- Chlamydia is the most common bacterial STD in the United States. Symptoms, when present, include vaginal discharge or unexpected bleeding, burning upon urination, and abdominal pain.

- HPV is probably the most common viral STD among sexually active young people. Infection with certain types of HPV can lead to cervical cancer. This STD has no known cure.

❸ ASSESS

EVALUATING THE LESSON

Assign and discuss the Lesson 3 Review; then administer, grade, and discuss Lesson Quiz 68 in the TCR. 🗁

RETEACHING

- Provide a simple, unlabeled drawing of the female reproductive system. Have students work with partners to label the parts and to describe the path an ovum follows.

- Ask students to complete Reteaching Activity 68 in the TCR. 🗁

ENRICHMENT

Have interested students use online and library resources to learn about the treatment options currently available to females diagnosed with breast cancer. Let these students explain their findings to the rest of the class. Then help students discuss the factors a female might consider in choosing a treatment procedure.

❹ CLOSE

Have students brainstorm a list of the most important concepts presented in this lesson.

▶ Lesson 3 Review

Reviewing Facts and Vocabulary

1. How do the structures in the fallopian tubes help move the ovum from the ovaries to the uterus?
2. Explain *ovulation, fertilization,* and *menstruation.*
3. List three causes of infertility in females.

Thinking Critically

4. **Synthesizing.** Analyze the importance of abstinence as it relates to the prevention of STDs. What behaviors can female teens practice to protect the health of their reproductive systems?

5. **Analyzing.** Relate the importance of early detection and warning signs for problems of the female reproductive system. Why is it important for every female to have regular pelvic exams starting at age 18 or when recommended by her physician?

Applying Health Skills

Advocacy. Make a card reminding yourself or the females in your family to perform a monthly breast self-exam. Provide step-by-step instructions. Add a catchy phrase that will remind users of the importance of early detection, and include warning signs that should prompt females to seek professional health services.

 TECHNOLOGY *OPTION*

PRESENTATION SOFTWARE You can use presentation software to combine text and graphics on your reminder card. For help in using presentation software, go to **health.glencoe.com.**

Lesson 3 The Female Reproductive System **479**

▶ Lesson 3 Review

Answers to Reviewing Facts and Vocabulary

1. Cilia draw in and move the ovum.
2. The release of an ovum; when a sperm and ovum join; shedding of the uterine lining.
3. Endometriosis, PID, STDs.

Answers to Thinking Critically

4. Abstinence eliminates the possibility of STDs. Regular bathing, proper diet, exercise, and pelvic exams.
5. Regular pelvic exams can detect abnormalities in internal and external reproductive organs. Doctors may also test for STDs during a pelvic exam.

Gender Representation in the Media

NHES Standard 4 Students will analyze the influence of culture, media, technology, and other factors on health.

Objective

Recognize potential gender bias in the media by examining types of news stories written by male and female reporters.

Motivator

Ask students if they ever watch the national news on network television. Ask them if the news anchor for the program is typically male or female.

Teaching Strategies

Awareness Ask students why they think news outlets are slower to include women.

Analysis Have students consider these questions: What kinds of stories were written by men and what kinds by women? Which forms tended to favor one gender over the other?

Reflection Explain that soft news tends to be more entertainment and personality centered than does hard news.

Take Action Ask students to write a letter to the media outlet they surveyed giving their results. Tell them to ask the owners of the media to take steps to ensure that both genders cover hard and soft news equally.

✓Assessment

In their essays, students should reflect on why there still continues to be some gender bias in these media forms.

480

Eye ON THE Media

Gender Representation in the Media

Studies have shown that although the numbers of males and females represented in the media are becoming more equal, women continue to be less visible in news reporting and news magazine writing. For instance, women often cover human interest stories, sometimes called "soft news," while male reporters cover "hard news," such as world and local news. In this activity you will look for potential gender bias in the media by examining types of news stories presented by male and female reporters.

	Male Reporters / Writers	Female Reporters / Writers
Number of Stories/ Resource	3/television 5/newspaper 2/news magazine	1/television 3/newspaper 5/news magazine
Kinds of Stories	1. 2. 3. 4.	1. 2. 3. 4.

ACTIVITY

Use a chart similar to the one shown to survey the number of stories you see on television, in newspapers, or news magazines. Count the number of stories presented by male reporters and the number of stories presented by female reporters. Then, in each column, describe the kinds of stories that males and females present. Discuss your findings with the class.

EXPRESS YOUR VIEWS

Write a brief analysis of the results of your survey on the types of stories presented primarily by men or primarily by women. Which gender was most represented by feature or lead articles? Which was most represented by "soft news" items?

More About...

Women in the News There is little debate that newspapers and news magazines have changed in their treatment of women's stories as well as their inclusion of hard-core reporting by women. In the past, newspapers often featured a "women's section" that would include garden club meeting announcements, recipes and other stories with a domestic theme. Today, although much has changed, women still continue to struggle to be taken seriously as reporters of hard news. Subtle gender bias in news reporting still exists. In the U.S., only 10 percent of journalists working for newspapers are female, while 37 percent of magazine writers are women.

CROSS-CURRICULUM CONNECTIONS

Create a Mood Poem. During puberty both males and females experience sudden emotional changes. These fluctuations can produce intense feelings. As a class, brainstorm different emotions associated with mood swings. Pick one of these emotions and write a metaphor or simile that communicates how you feel about that emotion beyond its literal meaning. Use your metaphor or simile as the basis for a poem about that emotion.

Research Health Advances. Although many married couples can conceive a child easily, some who desire children are infertile, meaning that they cannot conceive at all. Infertility was considered an insurmountable misfortune until the development of in vitro fertilization techniques. More than 20,000 babies have been born worldwide through in vitro procedures. In a research report, trace the significant advances in reproductive health over the last few decades.

Find Percentages of Infertility. About 12 percent of all couples experience infertility. Forty percent of these cases are primarily male problems, 40 percent female, and the remaining 20 percent are the result of problems stemming from both partners. What percentage of all couples are infertile as a result of problems stemming from both partners?

Research Adrenal Gland Functions. The adrenals produce adrenaline for the "fight or flight" response and help the body recover from stress. Recent research indicates that they may play a role in memory. Research the adrenal glands and write a report explaining their many functions. Include information on adrenal disorders such as Addison's Disease.

School Nurse

Are you caring and sympathetic, and are you concerned with the physical and mental/emotional needs of others? If so, a career as a school nurse may be right for you. School nurses perform screenings, provide emergency first aid, monitor state immunization laws, develop health-related curricula to meet the needs of students and teachers, and counsel students on personal health issues.

Nursing students need a strong background in science and mathematics. To become a registered nurse, a student must graduate from an accredited nursing school and pass a national licensing exam. For more information, click on **health.glencoe.com**.

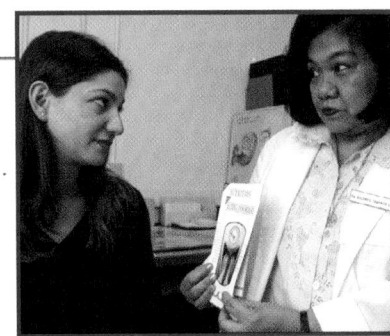

Chapter 18 Review **481**

Portfolio Assessment

Self-Evaluation Direct students to review the Health Skills Activities and other activities completed in the chapter. Encourage each student to select one finished product or activity that demonstrates his or her best work for the chapter and that represents the student's learning goals. Have students explain what they have learned and how the examples they have selected demonstrate their growth in health literacy, knowledge, and skills.

Teacher Classroom Resources Assign Performance Assessment 18, "Care of the Reproductive System," in the TCR.

CROSS-CURRICULUM CONNECTIONS

Enrich student learning by connecting the topic of the endocrine and reproductive systems to one of the four areas presented on this page. The activity may be completed individually or with a partner.

Language Arts Tell students that both metaphors and similes are used to compare unlike things to create an image in the reader's mind. Also, explain that each word in a poem should be selected for a particular reason.

Social Studies Remind students they should gather factual information from several different sources when writing a research report.

Math Answer: $(12/100) \times (20/100) \times 100 = 2.4\%$

Science Direct students to reliable resources in the library or through **health.glencoe.com**. Suggest that they explore recent research into the relationship between stressful situations such as test taking and memory function.

CAREER Corner

Have students read and discuss the Career Corner information on school nursing. Ask interested students to explore the Glencoe Health Web site at **health. glencoe.com** for more information on this career.

CHECKING COMPREHENSION

- Assign and discuss the chapter review.
- Use Chapter 18 MindJogger Videoquiz to review the chapter. ▶◀

CHAPTER 18 REVIEW ANSWERS

Exploring Health Terms

1. pituitary gland
2. thyroid gland
3. parathyroid gland
4. adrenal glands
5. false; Sperm
6. false; scrotum
7. true
8. ovaries
9. vagina
10. uterus

Recalling the Facts

1. To regulate body functions.
2. The hormones secreted by these glands control the development of secondary sex characteristics during puberty.
3. It increases heartbeat and respiration rates, raises blood pressure, and suppresses the digestive process during periods of high emotion.
4. Goiter is often caused by lack of iodine. In the United States, iodine is added to table salt.
5. Any three: broadening of the shoulders, development of muscles, facial and body hair, deepening of the voice, production of sperm.
6. Any three: Get regular checkups; bathe regularly; wear protective equipment; perform regular self-examinations; practice abstinence.
7. A tissue separation that allows part of the intestine to push into the lower abdominal wall.

▶ EXPLORING HEALTH TERMS
Answer the following questions on a sheet of paper.

Lesson 1 Match each definition with the correct term.

adrenal glands	pituitary gland
endocrine glands	parathyroid glands
hormones	thyroid gland
pancreas	gonads

1. The gland that regulates activities of all the other endocrine glands.
2. The gland that produces hormones that regulate metabolism and bone growth.
3. Glands that produce a hormone that regulates the body's calcium and phosphorus balance.
4. Glands that help the body recover from stress and respond to emergencies.

Lesson 2 Identify each statement as True or False. If false, replace the underlined term with the correct term.

penis	sperm
reproductive system	semen
scrotum	testes
sterility	testosterone

5. Semen is the male reproductive cell.
6. The testes are contained in the penis.
7. Testosterone is the male sex hormone.

Lesson 3 Fill in the blanks with the correct term.

cervix	ovulation
fallopian tubes	ovum
menstruation	uterus
ovaries	vagina

8. Ova mature in the _____ .
9. The _____ is a muscular, elastic passageway that extends from the uterus to the outside of the body.
10. The hollow, pear-shaped organ inside a female's body where a fetus is nourished is the _____ .

▶ RECALLING THE FACTS
Use complete sentences to answer the following questions.

Lesson 1

1. What is the function of hormones?
2. Why are the ovaries and testes considered endocrine glands?
3. What is epinephrine and what function does it have?
4. Why is a goiter an uncommon problem in the United States?

Lesson 2

5. What are three physical changes initiated by testosterone in the male?
6. What are three ways to care for the male reproductive system?
7. What is an inguinal hernia?
8. Relate the importance of early detection and warning signs of prostate cancer that prompt males of all ages to seek health care.

Lesson 3

9. Name and describe the two processes that are part of the menstrual cycle.
10. How can menstrual cramps be relieved?
11. Relate the importance of early warning signs for seeking health care. Why should a female with symptoms of TSS contact a health care professional immediately?
12. Identify situations requiring professional health services for preventive care. What is PID, and what usually causes it?

---

8. Frequent or difficult urination should prompt males of all ages to seek advice from a health care professional. Such symptoms can indicate an enlarged prostate gland or, in some cases, prostate cancer. Early detection of prostate cancer simplifies treatment and increases the chance of survival.
9. The menstrual cycle includes both ovulation, the release of a mature egg each month, and menstruation, the flow of the uterine lining out of the body.
10. Light exercise or the applying of a heating pad to the abdominal area may help relieve menstrual cramps.
11. TSS can be fatal if not treated.
12. PID is an infection of the fallopian tubes, ovaries, and surrounding areas in the pelvis. It is usually caused by STDs.

➤ THINKING CRITICALLY

1. **Synthesizing.** Compare and contrast the symptoms of Graves' disease, also known as hyperthyrodism, and hypothyrodism. Why might you infer that the thyroid plays a role in internal temperature regulation? *(LESSON 1)*

2. **Summarizing.** Relate the importance of early detection and warning signs that prompt males to seek health care for the reproductive system. Suppose that a friend tells you he won't perform a testicular self-exam because it is too embarrassing. What advice would you give him? *(LESSON 2)*

3. **Analyzing.** In what ways are PMS, TSS, and PID similar to and different from one another? *(LESSON 3)*

➤ HEALTH SKILLS APPLICATION

1. **Practicing Healthful Behaviors.** Excessive weight has been shown to be a contributing factor for developing diabetes mellitus. Identify three things you can do each day to help maintain a healthy weight for life. *(LESSON 1)*

2. **Accessing Information.** Some athletes use anabolic-androgenic steroids—chemicals similar to testosterone—to increase muscle size and improve overall performance. Research and list the harmful effects of steroids on the body. Then create a visual presentation that informs others of the dangers of steroid use. *(LESSON 2)*

3. **Advocacy.** Annual Pap tests are important for all women over the age of 18. Relate the importance of early detection and warning signs that prompt females to seek health care. Prepare an informative, accurate, and persuasive pamphlet to encourage women to have an annual Pap test. *(LESSON 3)*

 BEYOND *the* Classroom

Parent Involvement

Advocacy. Share the information about breast and testicular self-exams with a parent. Work together to find a place to display the reminder cards you made. Then discuss will all family members the importance of these exams for early detection of cancers. Discuss also the warning signs that should prompt persons of any age to seek medical attention.

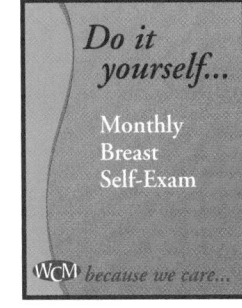

Do it yourself...

Monthly
Breast
Self-Exam

WCM *because we care...*

School and Community

School Health Services. Ask the school nurse to talk to your class about the importance of proper hygiene and care of the reproductive systems. Also, have the nurse describe the health services available through his or her office. How can students access these services? Which services require the approval of a parent?

Thinking Critically

1. A symptom of hypothyroidism is sensitivity to cold; a symptom of hyperthyroidism is intolerance to heat. From this, a person could infer that temperature regulation is one function of the thyroid gland.

2. Answers should emphasize the importance of regular self-exams to ensure early detection of testicular cancer.

3. All are disorders of the female reproductive system. PMS and TSS are problems related to menstruation; PID is a problem usually associated with STDs. PMS is caused by hormonal changes; TSS and PID are infections caused by outside agents. PMS can be very uncomfortable but is not life threatening; TSS can be fatal if left untreated. PID can damage the reproductive organs and lead to blocked fallopian tubes; it is the primary cause of infertility in women.

Health Skills Application

1.–3. Answers will vary.

EVALUATE

- Use the reproducible Chapter 18 Test in the TCR, or construct your own using the Testmaker software. 📁 💿

- Use Performance Assessment 18 in the TCR. 📁

ENRICHMENT

Ask students to complete Enrichment Activity 18 in the TCR. 📁

 BEYOND *the* Classroom

Keep students involved in the community, and encourage parent participation by assigning the activities on this page for students to work on outside of class.

483

Lessons	Standards		Features
	National	**State/Local**	
1 The Beginning of the Life Cycle *pages 486–491*	National Health Education Standards **1.4, 1.6, 2.3**		**Real-Life Application** • Fetal Ultrasound Technology *(Accessing Information)*, page 490
2 Prenatal Care *pages 492–497*	National Health Education Standards **1.1, 1.3, 3.4, 7.1**		**Hands-On Health** • Tips for a Healthy Pregnancy *(Advocacy)*, page 495
3 Heredity and Genetics *pages 498–503*	National Health Education Standards **1.8, 2.4, 3.2, 6.3**		**Exploring Issues** • Should People Undergo Genetic Testing? page 502
4 Infancy and Childhood *pages 504–507*	National Health Education Standards **1.4, 2.6, 5.2, 6.2, 7.6**		**Health Skills Activity** • Choosing Toys *(Decision Making)*, page 506

Reproducible Resources	Assessment	Technology
Student Activity Workbook for use with each chapter 📁 Concept Mapping Activity 69 📁 Guided Reading Activities 69 📁 Lesson Plan 69 📁 Parent Letter and Activities 19 📁 Reteaching Activity 69	📁 Lesson Quiz 69	🕹 Transparency 56 💿 TeacherWorks® 💻 Internet Activities
📁 Concept Mapping Activity 70 📁 Guided Reading Activities 70 📁 Lesson Plan 70 📁 Reteaching Activity 70	📁 Lesson Quiz 70	🕹 Transparency 57 💿 TeacherWorks®
📁 Concept Mapping Activity 71 📁 Cross-Curriculum Activity 19 📁 Current Health Issues 19 📁 Decision-Making Activity 19 📁 Guided Reading Activities 71 📁 Health Lab 19 📁 Lesson Plan 71 📁 Reteaching Activity 71	📁 Lesson Quiz 71	💿 TeacherWorks®
📁 Concept Mapping Activity 72 📁 Enrichment Activity 19 📁 Guided Reading Activities 72 📁 Lesson Plan 72 📁 Reteaching Activity 72	📁 Lesson Quiz 72	🕹 Transparency 58 💿 TeacherWorks®

0:00 OUT OF TIME

If time does not permit teaching the entire chapter, use:
- Figure 19.2, p. 488
- Real-Life Application, p. 490
- Figure 19.4, p. 501
- Figure 19.5, p. 505
- Eye on the Media, p. 508

Language Diversity

- 🎧 English Audio CD Program
- 🎧 Spanish Audio CD Program
- 📁 English Summaries, Quizzes, and Activities
- 📁 Spanish Summaries, Quizzes, and Activities
- 📁 Spanish Parent Letters and Activities

End of Chapter Assessment

Blackline Masters

- 📁 Chapter 19 Test
- 📁 Performance Assessment Activity 19

Technology

- 💿 Vocabulary PuzzleMaker
- 📺 MindJogger Videoquiz
- 💿 Exam*View*® Pro Testmaker

Professional Health Series

Dealing with Sensitive Issues
Planning a Coordinated School Health Program
Promoting Character Education
Home, School, and Community Involvement

Prenatal Development and Birth

CHAPTER OVERVIEW

Chapter 19 explores life from its initial stage as a single cell through the developmental stages of childhood. The process of heredity is also explained.

Lesson 1 Human development begins as one microscopic cell, formed by the union of an egg cell and a sperm cell. This zygote, then embryo, and later fetus develops in the uterus in regular stages for about 40 weeks.

Lesson 2 Prenatal care is essential to protect the health of a pregnant woman and of her developing baby. Good prenatal care includes regular visits with a health care professional; proper nutrition; and the avoidance of alcohol, tobacco, other drugs, and environmental hazards.

Lesson 3 Chromosomes carry the codes for inherited traits. At fertilization, a developing baby inherits traits from both the mother and the father. Genetic disorders can sometimes be detected by prenatal procedures.

Lesson 4 Infancy and childhood are periods of rapid sequences of physical, mental, and emotional growth.

Health Skills Features

- Real-Life Application (*Accessing Information*), p. 490
- Hands-On Health (*Advocacy*), p. 495
- Exploring Issues, p. 502
- Health Skills Activity (*Decision Making*), p. 506

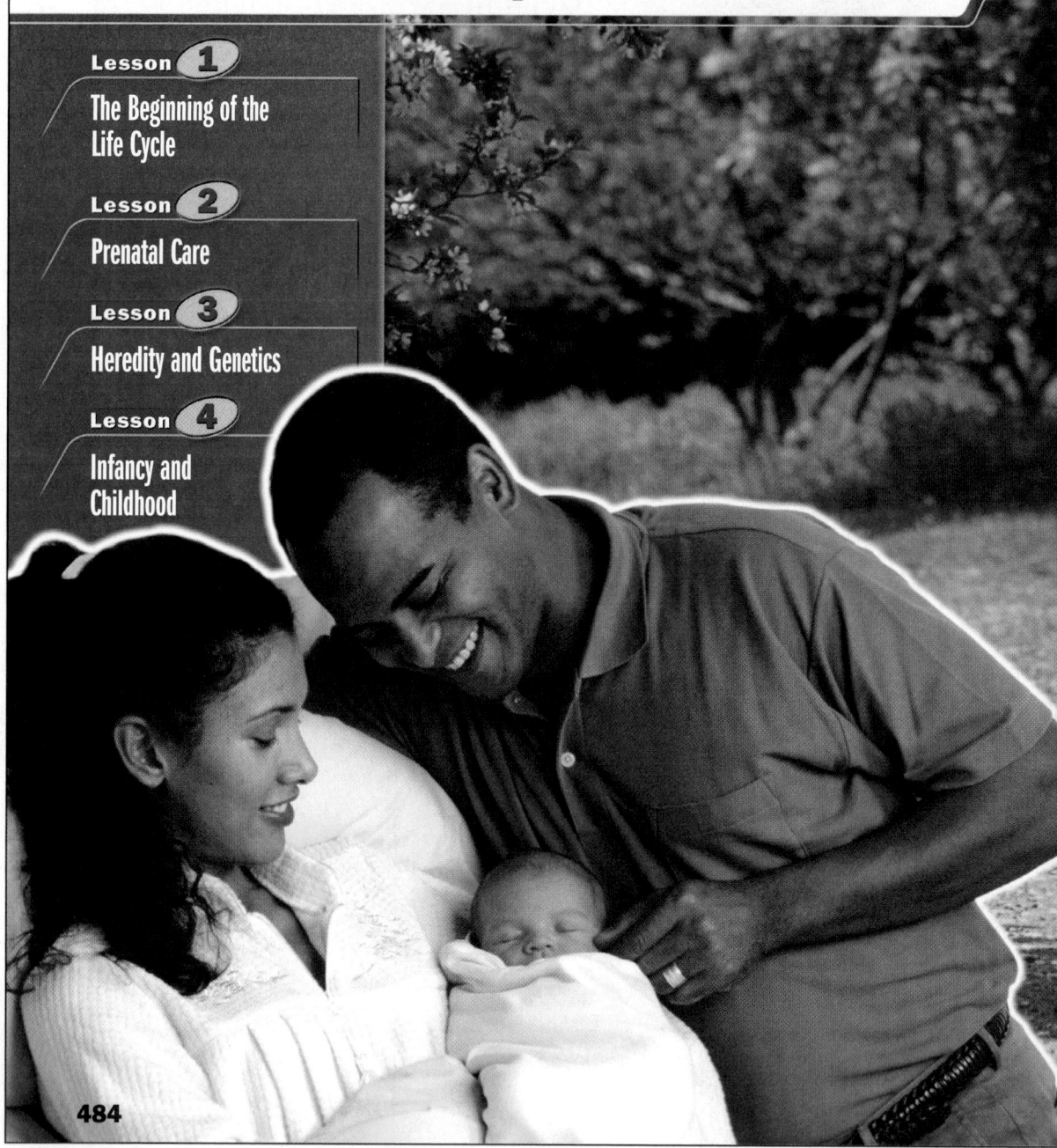

Chapter 19

Prenatal Development and Birth

Lesson 1
The Beginning of the Life Cycle

Lesson 2
Prenatal Care

Lesson 3
Heredity and Genetics

Lesson 4
Infancy and Childhood

484

MEETING STUDENT DIVERSITY

Language Diversity Use the following suggestions to help students who have difficulty with English:

- Pair English language learners with native speakers of English who can restate the Chapter Summary in language that helps students comprehend important concepts.

- Direct auditory learners or those students with language diversity to the *Glencoe Health Audio CD Program*. Available in English and Spanish, this component provides an audio and written summary of the chapter.

- Use photographs, drawings, or magazine clippings to help students visualize the important concepts of the chapter.

Myth or Fact?

What Do You Know About Prenatal Development?

Read each statement below and respond by writing *Myth* or *Fact* for each item.

1. The egg from the mother determines a baby's gender.

2. Twins result when more than one sperm fertilizes a single egg.

3. A fetus usually remains in the uterus for about nine months.

4. If a pregnant female uses tobacco, alcohol, or other drugs, these substances can harm the fetus.

5. A female should gain as much weight as possible during pregnancy.

6. Both prescription and over-the-counter drugs can harm a fetus.

7. A pregnant female should never exercise.

8. Genes carry the hereditary traits of an individual.

9. Balanced nutrition is especially important during pregnancy because the nutrients a female ingests affect her baby's development.

10. A female who wants children does not need to take special care of herself until she knows for sure that she is pregnant.

Keep your responses for review later in the chapter. After you complete the chapter, review your answers again and change or modify them on the basis of what you have learned.

485

Quick**Write**

Using Visuals. Both parents have the responsibility to provide for the health of their unborn child. What steps can parents-to-be take to maximize the chances of having a healthy baby?

INTRODUCING THE CHAPTER

Myth or Fact?

Have students work independently to read the statements and identify each as fact or myth.

1. Myth. Chromosomes in the father's sperm determine the sex of a baby.

2. Myth. Fraternal twins result when two different sperm fertilize two different eggs. Identical twins result when a fertilized egg forms two embryos.

3. Fact.

4. Fact.

5. Myth. Most health care professionals suggest that females gain 25–35 pounds during pregnancy.

6. Fact.

7. Myth. Moderate physical activity is considered beneficial for most pregnant women and their babies.

8. Fact.

9. Fact.

10. Myth. She should avoid caffeine, tobacco, alcohol, and other drugs and take folic acid.

Quick**write**

Using Visuals Let volunteers describe the couples in the photographs and tell how each parent might be preparing for the baby they are expecting. Then have students jot down their responses to the Quick Write. Ask volunteers to read their responses aloud.

The Beginning of the Life Cycle

FOCUS

 QUICK START Give students two or three minutes to write their responses to the Quick Start question. Then let volunteers read their answers aloud. Help students discuss the ideas presented, and correct any misconceptions.

TYING TO PRIOR KNOWLEDGE

Ask students to recall some basic facts about the body systems (respiratory system, digestive system, and so on). Explain that, in this lesson, students will learn how these body systems develop before birth.

Health Skills Features

"Fetal Ultrasound Technology," p. 490

ACCESSING INFORMATION

INTRODUCING VOCABULARY

• Divide students into cooperative groups. Have group members work together to find, read, and discuss the vocabulary term definitions in the Glossary.

• Ask students to complete the Chapter 19 Study Guide in the *Student Activity Workbook*. 📁

486

The Beginning of the Life Cycle

VOCABULARY
fertilization
implantation
embryo
fetus
amniotic sac
umbilical cord
placenta
labor

YOU'LL LEARN TO
• Explain the stages of fetal development from conception through pregnancy and birth.
• Recognize how nutrients and other substances are transferred from a pregnant female to her fetus.

 QUICK START A developing baby grows rapidly inside its mother's body. How is an unborn baby nourished? Write down your ideas.

 This human egg cell is surrounded by sperm. Chemical changes take place in the egg's surface so that only one sperm can fertilize it.

486 Chapter 19 Prenatal Development and Birth

Did you know that your body is made of trillions of cells? These cells form the tissues and organs in your body. Yet your heart, lungs, skin, bones, and other body organs all begin as a single cell that is smaller than the period at the end of this sentence.

Conception and Implantation

The entire complex human body begins as one microscopic cell that is formed by the union of an egg cell, or ovum, from a female and a sperm cell from a male. The *union of a male sperm cell and a female egg cell* is called **fertilization**, which is also known as *conception*. The resulting cell is called a *zygote* (ZY-goht).

Look at **Figure 19.1** on page 487. Notice that within a day after the zygote forms, it begins dividing as it travels down the fallopian tube. By the time it reaches the uterus, the zygote has divided many times to form a cluster of cells with a hollow space in the center. Within a few days, *the zygote attaches to the uterine wall* in the process called **implantation**. After this, the cluster of cells is known as an **embryo** (EM-bree-oh), *the developing child from the time of implantation until about the eighth week of development*. The *developing embryo in the uterus* is called a **fetus** (FEE-tuhs).

Lesson 1 Resources

Teacher Classroom Resources
📁 Concept Mapping Activity 69
📁 Guided Reading Activities 69
📁 Lesson Plan 69
📁 Lesson Quiz 69
📁 Parent Letter and Activities 19
📁 Reteaching Activity 69

Student Activity Workbook
📁 Applying Health Skills 69
📁 Chapter 19 Study Guide

Multimedia
💾 Transparency 56

Embryonic Growth

As the embryo grows, its cells continue to divide, forming three tissue layers that later become various body systems. One layer becomes the respiratory and digestive systems. A second layer develops into muscles, bones, blood vessels, and skin. A third layer forms the nervous system, sense organs, and mouth.

During this time two important structures form outside the embryo:

▶ The **amniotic** (am-nee-AH-tik) **sac** is *a thin, fluid-filled membrane that surrounds and protects the developing embryo.* It also insulates the embryo from temperature changes.

▶ The **umbilical** (uhm-BIL-uh-kuhl) **cord** is *a ropelike structure that connects the embryo and the mother's placenta.* The **placenta** (pluh-SEN-tuh) is *a thick, blood-rich tissue that lines the walls of the uterus during pregnancy and nourishes the embryo.*

Although the blood supply of the mother and the developing embryo are kept separate, materials diffuse from one blood supply to the other through the umbilical cord. Nutrients and oxygen pass from the mother's blood to the embryo, and wastes from the embryo diffuse into the mother's blood. The wastes are excreted from the mother's body along with her body wastes.

Substances that are harmful to the developing embryo can pass through the umbilical cord, too. If a pregnant female uses harmful substances, such as tobacco, alcohol, or other drugs, they can cross the placenta and harm the developing embryo.

How do twins form?
Identical twins result when a single egg that has been fertilized by a single sperm divides and forms two embryos. Because they develop from the same zygote, identical twins have the same genetic information, are the same gender, and look almost exactly the same.

Fraternal twins form when a female's ovaries release two eggs. Separate sperm fertilize each egg, and two embryos develop. Each twin has a different genetic makeup, and may or may not be the same gender. Fraternal twins do not resemble each other any more than other brothers and sisters do. Fraternal twins are much more common than identical twins.

FIGURE 19.1

IMPLANTATION

Fertilization and implantation occur after an egg is released from the ovary.

Cell Division
As the zygote travels down the fallopian tube toward the uterus, it divides many times.

Fertilization
Only one sperm can fertilize an egg.

Implantation
About six days after fertilization, the zygote burrows into the lining of the uterus.

---

2 TEACH

Reinforcing Concepts

Ask students to explain, in their own words, the relationship among a zygote, an embryo, and a fetus. **L1**

Discussing

Be sure students understand that, even though the mother's blood supply is never mixed with the embryo's, every nutrient and drug the mother introduces into her body is also introduced into the body of the developing baby. Ask: What does this suggest about the kinds of foods a pregnant woman should eat? What medicines and drugs should she avoid? **L1**

VISUAL LEARNING

Figure 19.1 Guide students in studying the illustration. Let volunteers read aloud the captions and labels as the rest of the class follows along. Have other volunteers restate, in their own words, the information about fertilization, cell division, and implantation.

Guide students in reading and discussing the information on twins. Encourage volunteers to describe any pairs of twins they might know. Ask: Are they identical twins or fraternal twins? How can you tell?

Curriculum Connections

Math Have students use public records, available either in a local library or online, to gather statistics on local births during a recent three-year period. How many babies were born during each year? For each year, how many babies born alive did not survive their first birthday (infant mortality)? Ask students to plan and draw graphs summarizing their findings.

Language Arts Invite students to recall and discuss stories or movies in which a husband and wife prepare for the birth of a child. How accurate do students consider the facts? What impression of the emotional experience of pregnancy is presented?

Fetal Development

The time from conception to birth is usually about nine full months. These nine months are divided into three 3-month periods called *trimesters*. Read about the changes that take place during each trimester in **Figure 19.2**. Compare the images to see the growth of the fetus in each trimester.

FIGURE 19.2

STAGES OF EMBRYONIC AND FETAL DEVELOPMENT

First Trimester (0 to 14 weeks)	Major Changes
0–4 weeks	A zygote may float freely in the uterus for 48 hours before implanting. The spinal cord grows faster than the rest of the body. The brain, ears, and arms begin to form. The heart forms and begins to beat.
5–8 weeks	The fetus is about 1 inch long at 8 weeks. The mouth, nostrils, eyelids, hands, fingers, feet, and toes begin to form. The nervous system can respond to stimuli. The cardiovascular system is fully functional.
9–14 weeks	The fetus develops a human profile. Sex organs, eyelids, fingernails, and toenails develop. By week 12 the fetus makes crying motions but no sound and may suck its thumb.

Promoting Coordinated School Health

On-Site Health Services One characteristic of a successful coordinated school health program is an adequate level of staffing, with personnel committed to screening, surveillance, and management of health problems. Traditionally, the school nurse serves as the primary source of health information both inside and outside the classroom, with support from administration, parents, and community members. The nurse addresses the specific health needs of students and reinforces positive health concepts. For more information, consult *Planning a Coordinated School Health Program*.

During the period of growth in the uterus, the fetus develops in preparation for living outside the mother's body. Organs develop and become ready to function on their own. The fetus grows and gains weight. After about the seventh month, fat deposits are added under the skin to help the baby maintain body heat after birth. The fetus stores nutrients and builds immunity and protection from diseases and infections.

Second Trimester (15 to 28 weeks)	Major Changes	
15–20 weeks	The fetus can blink its eyes. The body begins to grow, growth of the head slows, and the limbs reach full proportion. Eyebrows and eyelashes develop. The fetus can grasp and kick and becomes more active.	
21–28 weeks	The fetus can hear conversations and has a regular cycle of waking and sleeping. Weight increases rapidly. The fetus is about 12 inches long and weighs a little more than 1 pound. Fetus may survive if born after 24 weeks but will require special medical care.	
Third Trimester (29 weeks to birth)	Major Changes	
29–40 weeks	The fetus uses all five senses and begins to pass water from the bladder. Brain scans have shown that some fetuses dream during their periods of sleep in the eighth and ninth months of development. Approximately 266 days after conception, the baby weighs 6 to 9 pounds and is ready to be born.	

Lesson 1   The Beginning of the Life Cycle   **489**

Discussing

Ask students to compare an 8-week-old embryo with an 18-week-old fetus. Consider:

- What are the most important changes that take place during those intervening weeks?
- What changes do you imagine take place in the mother's perceptions of her pregnancy? In the perceptions of family members and friends? **L1**

FYI

In one recent year, about 4 million babies were born in the United States. Of those, just over 8,500 were born to girls under the age of 15. Though still numerous, teen birth rates have declined steadily over the past decade.

Activity

Ask interested students to learn more about the survival rate for fetuses born at 24 weeks. Encourage them to use print and online sources to gather information. Have them consider:

- How much do babies born at this time usually weigh?
- What special medical procedures are used with these babies?
- What risks do they face?

Have the students discuss their findings with the rest of the class. **L3**

More About...

The Delivery Process A cesarean delivery is the surgical removal of the fetus through the mother's abdominal wall. The most common reason for cesarean delivery is that the baby is too large or the pelvis too small for a safe vaginal delivery. Certain medical conditions in the mother, including diabetes and high blood pressure, may sometimes necessitate a cesarean delivery. Fetal distress is another common reason. In the case of multiple births, a cesarean delivery is sometimes planned. Recovery from a cesarean delivery, which is major surgery, is longer than from a vaginal delivery. Vaginal delivery remains an option for future pregnancies.

Real-Life Application

FETAL ULTRASOUND TECHNOLOGY

ACCESSING INFORMATION

NHES Standard 2 Students will demonstrate the ability to access valid health information and health-promoting products and services.

Objectives

- Explain how technology has impacted the health status of individuals and families.
- Explain the importance of the role of prenatal care.

Motivator

Ask students: *Is there a way to determine the sex of a baby before it is born?*

Teaching Strategies

1. Tell students to obtain at least two different sources for each technology and explain why the technology is used.
2. Have volunteers report their findings to the class.

✔Assessment

Using a rubric, student work should provide comprehensive evidence of the following criteria to achieve the highest score:

✔ citation of specific sources
✔ evaluation of the validity of the source
✔ rationale for the appropriateness of the source
✔ type of help available from the sources

Did You Know ?

Immediately after birth a newborn is given an *Apgar score.* The Apgar test is used to assess an infant's physical condition at birth. The score measures appearance, heart rate, reflex irritability, activity, and respiration.

Stages of Birth

In the final weeks of pregnancy, the fetus becomes more and more crowded in the uterus and puts increased demands on its mother's body. Most often the baby's head moves to the lower part of the uterus. Many females experience weak, irregular muscular contractions of the uterus for weeks or even months before the baby is born. As the time approaches for the baby to be born, however, these contractions become regular, stronger, and closer together. The stronger contractions induce **labor,** *the final stage of pregnancy in which the uterus contracts and pushes the baby out of the mother's body.* The stages of labor are summarized in **Figure 19.3.**

Real-Life Application

Fetal Ultrasound Technology

Ultrasound is a nonintrusive technology used to monitor a fetus in the uterus using the reflection of sound waves. A moving image of the developing fetus can be viewed on a monitor. Doctors can measure how the fetus is growing and whether organs such as the heart are developing properly. Ultrasound is used to determine the position of the fetus before birth.

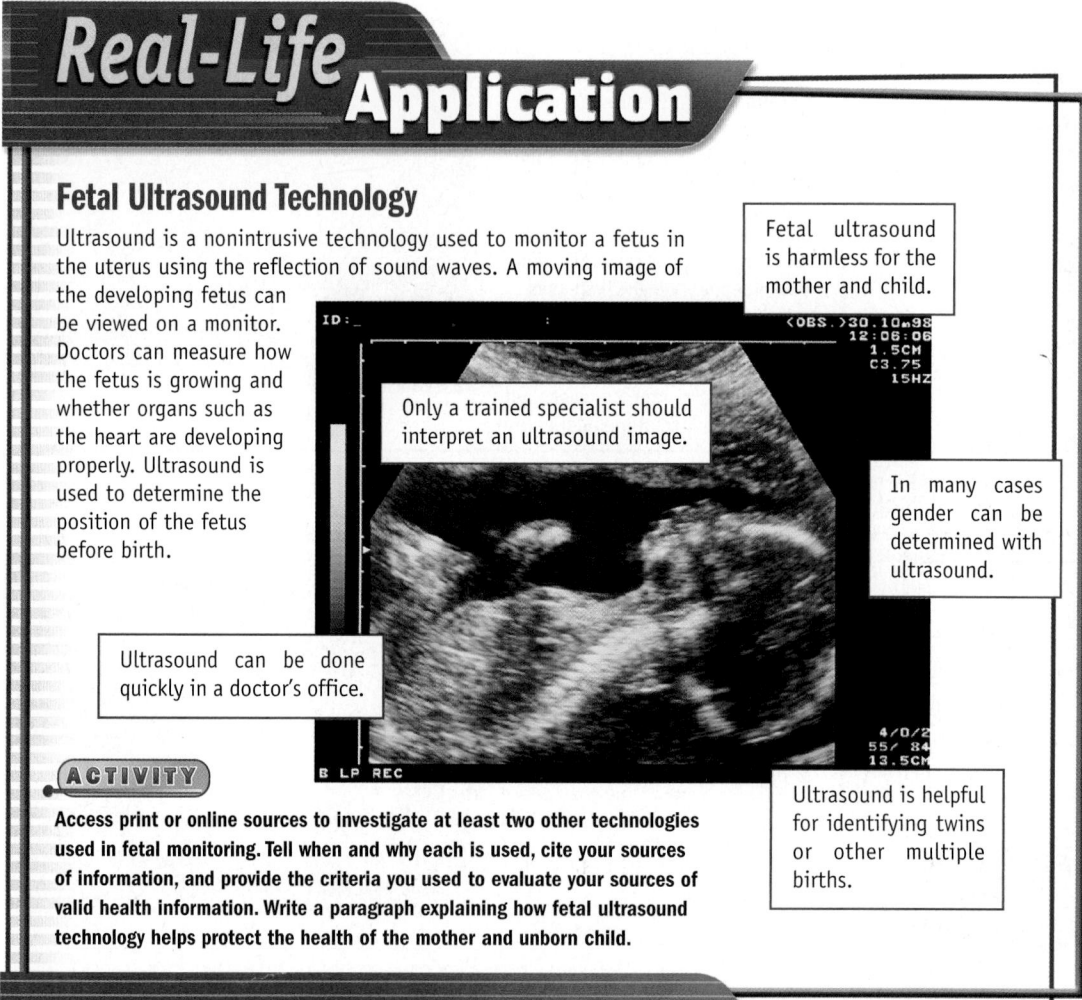

Fetal ultrasound is harmless for the mother and child.

Only a trained specialist should interpret an ultrasound image.

In many cases gender can be determined with ultrasound.

Ultrasound can be done quickly in a doctor's office.

Ultrasound is helpful for identifying twins or other multiple births.

ACTIVITY

Access print or online sources to investigate at least two other technologies used in fetal monitoring. Tell when and why each is used, cite your sources of information, and provide the criteria you used to evaluate your sources of valid health information. Write a paragraph explaining how fetal ultrasound technology helps protect the health of the mother and unborn child.

490 **Chapter 19** Prenatal Development and Birth

Cooperative Learning Activity

Frequency of Cesarean Deliveries

Some people feel cesarean deliveries are performed too frequently. Invite students to work in groups to research the frequency of cesarean deliveries in their city or county. They may wish to consider:

- What percentage of births in a recent year were by cesarean delivery?

- How do local statistics compare to state and national rates?
- What reasons are most commonly given for performing cesarean deliveries?

Then have students from all groups share and discuss their findings. What opinions do students hold about the frequency of local cesarean deliveries?

FIGURE 19.3

LEAVING THE WOMB

A female goes through three stages of labor to deliver a baby. Labor can last from a few hours to several days.

Stage 1: Dilation	Stage 2: Passage Through Birth Canal	Stage 3: Afterbirth
The contractions of the uterus cause the cervix, the opening to the uterus, to begin to dilate, or widen. In about 95 percent of pregnancies, the baby's head is resting on the cervix. Toward the end of this stage, contractions break the amniotic sac that surrounds the baby.	When the cervix is fully dilated, the baby passes through the birth canal and emerges from the mother's body. Right after birth the baby takes its first breath and cries to clear the lungs of amniotic fluid.	The placenta is still attached to the baby by the umbilical cord. Contractions continue until the placenta, now called the *afterbirth*, is pushed from the mother's body. The umbilical cord will be cut to separate the placenta from the baby.

Lesson 1 *Review*

Reviewing Facts and Vocabulary

1. Define *fertilization* and *implantation*.
2. Explain the relationship between a zygote, an embryo, and a fetus.
3. How is a developing fetus nourished?

Thinking Critically

4. **Synthesizing.** Considering what you learned about the female reproductive system in Chapter 18, explain what would happen if the zygote did not implant in the uterus after leaving the fallopian tube.
5. **Applying.** Explain how harmful substances taken in by a pregnant female can be transferred to a developing fetus. How might fetal development be affected?

Applying Health Skills

Accessing Information. Research the changes that occur in a female's body during the nine months of pregnancy. Make an informative pamphlet that summarizes this information by trimester. Illustrate the pamphlet with pictures that show fetal development during each trimester.

PRESENTATION SOFTWARE Create a slide show that describes changes during pregnancy and fetal development. For help in making a computer slide show, see **health.glencoe.com**.

Lesson 1 The Beginning of the Life Cycle **491**

Prenatal Care

1 FOCUS

QUICK START To get students started on the Quick Start assignment, have volunteers name a few positive health behaviors that should be practiced daily. Then ask students to write their own lists and circle the behaviors that, when practiced by a pregnant female, would benefit the developing fetus.

TYING TO PRIOR KNOWLEDGE

Let students briefly recall what they have learned about the development of a fetus within the uterus. Explain that students will learn what an expectant mother can do to protect and promote the health of her developing baby.

Health Skills Features

"Tips for a Healthy Pregnancy," p. 495

ADVOCACY

INTRODUCING VOCABULARY

• Have students meet in groups to analyze the vocabulary terms. What roots and/or familiar words can be identified in each? Then have group members use the Glossary to check the definition of each vocabulary term.

• Ask students to complete the Chapter 19 Study Guide in the *Student Activity Workbook*. 🗀

492

Prenatal Care

VOCABULARY

prenatal care
birthing center
fetal alcohol syndrome
(FAS)
miscarriage
stillbirth

YOU'LL LEARN TO

• Explain the importance of prenatal care and proper nutrition in promoting optimal health for both mother and baby.

• Analyze the harmful effects of tobacco, alcohol, and other drugs on the fetus.

• Identify and analyze the effects of environmental hazards on the fetus.

• Explain why seeking prenatal care early in pregnancy is important.

 QUICK START List five positive health behaviors that a person should practice each day. Circle any that you think would also benefit a developing fetus.

 Regular physical activity under the guidance of a health care professional, along with good nutrition, contribute to a healthy pregnancy.

Although most pregnancies proceed with few or no complications, a female should begin prenatal care as soon as her pregnancy is confirmed. **Prenatal** (pree-NAY-tuhl) **care** refers to *steps that a pregnant female can take to provide for her own health and the health of her baby.*

Importance of Prenatal Care

One of the first decisions a pregnant female must make is who will provide her prenatal care. An *obstetrician* (ahb-stuh-TRI-shuhn) is a doctor who specializes in the care of a female and her developing child. A *certified nurse-midwife* is an advanced practice nurse who specializes in prenatal care and the delivery of babies. The mother-to-be must also decide where the birth will take place. In the United States, most births take place at a hospital, but some women may choose to have the delivery at home or in a **birthing center**, *a facility in which women with low-risk pregnancies can deliver their babies in a homelike setting.* Regardless of where the birth takes place, a doctor or certified nurse-midwife should be present.

492 Chapter 19 Prenatal Development and Birth

Lesson 2 *Resources*

Teacher Classroom Resources

🗀 Concept Mapping Activity 70
🗀 Guided Reading Activities 70
🗀 Lesson Plan 70
🗀 Lesson Quiz 70
🗀 Reteaching Activity 70

Student Activity Workbook

🗀 Applying Health Skills 70
🗀 Chapter 19 Study Guide

Multimedia

🔖 Transparency 57

During prenatal visits the female will have a complete physical that includes blood tests and a pelvic exam. The purpose of the exam is to identify problems so that they can be corrected or treated as early as possible. The obstetrician or nurse-midwife will monitor the mother's weight and blood pressure. Often the developing baby will be viewed with an ultrasound machine. These visits also give the parents-to-be the opportunity to ask questions and to learn about important behaviors that can help ensure the health of the baby.

Proper Nutrition During Pregnancy

An unborn baby depends on its mother for nourishment. For this reason, a pregnant female needs more nutrients than at any other time in her life. To ensure the health of the developing fetus, increased amounts of many nutrients, including those below, are needed.

▶ **Calcium** helps build strong bones and teeth and healthy nerves and muscles. It is also important in developing heart rhythm.

▶ **Protein** helps form muscle and most other tissue.

▶ **Iron** makes red blood cells and supplies oxygen to cells.

▶ **Vitamin A** aids in cell and bone growth and eye development.

▶ **Vitamin B complex** aids in forming the nervous system.

▶ **Folic acid** is a critical part of spinal fluid and helps close the tube that contains the central nervous system. This neural tube forms 17 to 30 days after conception, so neural tube defects can occur before a female knows that she is pregnant. Health care providers suggest that all females of childbearing age consume 400–600 micrograms of folic acid daily to prevent these defects.

Although a pregnant female's nutritional requirements may increase, she must be careful not to gain too much weight. Most pregnant females need only 300 additional calories each day—about the number of calories found in two and a half cups of low-fat milk. Most health care professionals suggest that females who are at a healthy pre-pregnancy weight gain between 25 and 35 pounds during pregnancy. Excess weight can be a health risk for both mother and baby.

Choosing nutritious foods such as fruits and vegetables, and drinking milk during pregnancy can ensure that a mother-to-be receives the optimal amount of nutrients. *What nutrients are especially important for proper development of the fetus?*

Lesson 2 Prenatal Care **493**

2 TEACH

Discussing

Guide students in discussing the kinds of health care professionals who provide prenatal care. What are the advantages of each? What might lead a female to choose one over the other? **L1**

Activity

Point out that a birthing center is appropriate only for females with low-risk pregnancies. Ask a volunteer to research what constitutes a low-risk pregnancy. Which factors can exclude a pregnant female from the low-risk category? Let this volunteer share his or her findings with the rest of the class. **L2**

Critical Thinking

Ask: What special care do you think a female should take to prepare for pregnancy? Why? **L1**

Activity

Ask a group of volunteers to find out about the early signs of pregnancy. Have these students share their findings with the rest of the class. Ask: Why is it important to be aware of pregnancy as soon as possible? **L2**

Activity

Ask students to identify foods that are good sources of calcium, protein, iron, vitamin A, vitamin B complex, and folic acid. **L2**

Home and Community

Prenatal Care Careful monitoring and thoughtful counseling from a doctor or other health care professional should be an essential part of prenatal care. Some females receive this kind of care from a private obstetrician or midwife; others go to health clinics supported by private or public agencies in their community.

Have students work together to compile information about local prenatal clinics and other sources of help and support for pregnant women. Ask them to publish this information in an illustrated flyer. Remind students to proofread their flyers. They may need to write several drafts before turning in a final error-free draft.

493

Community Involvement

Hospitals and other health care centers may offer special exercise programs for pregnant females. Ask interested students to find out about such programs:

- Where and when are they offered?
- What is the cost, if any?
- What training do the exercise leaders have?
- What kinds of exercises are taught and practiced? **L2**

Discussing

Guide students in reading and discussing the information about fetal alcohol syndrome (FAS), including the lifelong consequences listed in Did You Know. Ask: Why is avoiding alcohol altogether the only safe choice for a woman who is pregnant? **L1**

Discussing

Present the following situation to the class: Norma has just confirmed that she is pregnant, but she and her husband have decided not to share the news for a few more weeks. They go to a family party at Norma's aunt's house; several people are smoking indoors. Ask:

- What do you think Norma should do? Why?
- What do you think her husband should do? Why? **L1**

Smokers inhale nicotine and carbon monoxide, both of which reach the fetus through the umbilical cord, preventing the fetus from getting enough nutrients and oxygen. *How might this affect fetal development?*

h⊙tlink

FAS For more information about alcohol and FAS, see Chapter 22, page 575.

Did You Know ?

Children with FAS suffer lifelong consequences, including

- mental retardation.
- learning disabilities.
- serious behavior problems.
- slowed growth.
- physical deformities including a small skull, abnormal facial features, and heart defects.

Weight reduction diets during pregnancy can harm the developing fetus. Such diets should be undertaken only under the guidance of an experienced health care provider.

Caffeine, present in coffee, tea, chocolate, and many cola drinks, can affect the developing fetus. A high intake of caffeine during pregnancy has been linked to an increased risk of birth defects and low birth weight.

Physical activity can be beneficial to the pregnant female and developing child. Before starting any exercise program, the expectant mother should discuss the matter with her health care provider.

The Health of the Fetus

A pregnant female must be very careful about the substances she takes into her body. Tobacco, alcohol, and other drugs can enter the body of the developing fetus and have serious effects.

Alcohol and Pregnancy

Any alcohol consumed during pregnancy quickly passes through the umbilical cord to the fetus. The fetus breaks down alcohol much more slowly than an adult does, so the alcohol level in the fetus's blood can be higher than that of the mother and remain higher for a longer period of time. An elevated alcohol level can result in permanent damage to the fetus and a condition known as **fetal alcohol syndrome (FAS)**, a *group of alcohol-related birth defects that includes both physical and mental problems.* The serious, lifelong consequences of FAS are listed at the left.

The tragedy of **FAS** is that it is entirely preventable. Because even small amounts of alcohol can be harmful, especially early in pregnancy, the safe decision for pregnant females and females considering pregnancy is not to drink any alcoholic beverages.

Tobacco and Pregnancy

Smoking during pregnancy is estimated to account for up to 30 percent of low birth weight babies, 14 percent of premature births, and 10 percent of all infant deaths. Studies suggest that a pregnant female's smoking may also affect the growth, mental development, and behavior of her child until he or she is 11 years old. The only sure way to protect the developing fetus and child from the negative effects of tobacco is not to smoke.

The responsibility to provide a smoke-free environment extends beyond the expectant mother. According to the American Lung Association, pregnant females exposed repeatedly to secondhand smoke also have an increased risk of having a low birth weight baby. Low birth weight is a leading cause of death for children under 12 months old.

⟩ *More About...*

Preventing Fetal Alcohol Syndrome
The National Organization on Fetal Alcohol Syndrome (NOFAS) is a nonprofit organization with the mission of eliminating birth defects caused by FAS and helping families with children who have FAS. NOFAS's list of goals and objectives include the following:

- To increase public awareness about the range of consequences associated with

prenatal alcohol exposure
- To promote preconception health among all childbearing age females who use alcohol
- To train youth as peer educators in their schools and communities
- To develop prevention and education messages and strategies for implementation among diverse populations nationwide

Medicines, Other Drugs, and Pregnancy

Using **drugs** when pregnant can have serious consequences. During pregnancy even prescription and over-the-counter **medicines** should be taken only with the approval of a doctor or other qualified health care provider.

Using illegal drugs when pregnant poses a serious health threat to both the mother and the fetus. Drug abuse can harm the mother's health and make her less able to support the pregnancy. Drugs also can directly harm fetal development. The use of certain illegal drugs during pregnancy can cause serious birth defects, premature labor, or miscarriage. In addition, a baby can be born addicted to the drugs the mother uses during pregnancy. The infant will suffer withdrawal when it no longer receives the drugs after birth. The baby may be hypersensitive and irritable and may cry for hours. It may tremble and jerk. A baby born addicted to drugs may fail to bond with its parents as normal babies do.

hot link

drugs and **medicines** For more information about the effects of medicines and drugs on the body, see Chapter 23, page 594.

Hands-On Health ACTIVITY

Tips for a Healthy Pregnancy

In this activity you will write and design a brochure with tips to help ensure a healthy pregnancy. Keep in mind that prenatal care isn't just the responsibility of the mother-to-be. Expectant fathers, for example, can buy and prepare healthful food and accompany their wives to medical visits and childbirth classes.

What You'll Need
- construction paper
- colored markers or pens
- magazines or newspapers

What You'll Do
1. Fold the construction paper to make a three-panel pamphlet.
2. Using the information in this chapter, write at least five tips for a healthy pregnancy. Under each tip, include actions both parents should take to ensure that their baby is healthy.
3. Illustrate your pamphlet with photos from magazines or newspapers, or draw your own illustrations. Make your pamphlet persuasive, and target it to expectant parents.
4. Share your pamphlet with the class.

Apply and Conclude

As a class, combine the best features of all the pamphlets to create one pamphlet. Make copies, and give them to family members who are expecting a child or planning a family.

Lesson 2 Prenatal Care **495**

School to Work

Parental Leave Have students research the parental leave policies of several major employers in their area. These might include government agencies and large corporations. Ask students to find out about both maternity and paternity leave. Is paternity leave allowed? Are maternity and paternity leaves paid or unpaid? How long can parents take leave without risk of job loss?

What benefits are provided during the leave? Have students share their findings and discuss their views on this topic. Ask: Do you think the leave provides adequate time for the mother to regain her strength after childbirth? Is there time for the parents to adjust to the new infant? Will the parents be able to be with their newborn during important early stages of development?

Hands-On Health

TIPS FOR A HEALTHY PREGNANCY

ADVOCACY

NHES Standard 7 Students will demonstrate the ability to advocate for personal, family, and community health.

Objectives
- Explain the importance of prenatal care and proper nutrition in promoting optimal health for both mother and baby.
- Demonstrate the ability to adapt health messages to the characteristics of a particular audience.

Motivator
Review with students healthful behaviors a pregnant female should practice.

Teaching Strategies
1. Display prenatal care brochures from a doctor's office or health department. Then have students review the brochures and summarize the key points.

2. Encourage students to use software programs for designing brochures.

✓Assessment

Using a rubric, student work should provide comprehensive evidence of the following criteria to achieve the highest score:

✔ clear, health-enhancing stand
✔ support for the position with relevant information
✔ awareness of the audience
✔ encouragement of others to make healthful choices
✔ passion/conviction

Critical Thinking

Guide students to consider the issue of responsibility regarding fetal exposure to drugs, such as alcohol and cocaine.

- Should pregnant females who knowingly damage their developing babies through drug use be held criminally accountable? Why or why not?

- Should bartenders be required by law to withhold alcoholic beverages from customers who are obviously pregnant? Why or why not? **L1**

Health Skills Practice

Share Information Allow students to meet in groups to discuss how they can encourage healthful behaviors in friends and relatives who are pregnant. Ask each group to write and share a list of helpful actions and attitudes.

ADVOCACY

Cooperative Learning

Divide the class into four groups, and assign each group one of the listed environmental hazards. Have group members read and discuss the information in the text and then present it to the rest of the class. **L1**

▲ **Although most pregnancies progress without complications, certain environmental factors can affect the healthy development of a fetus.** *What steps can a mother-to-be take to protect the health of her unborn child?*

Environmental Hazards

Harm to the fetus can result when a pregnant female is exposed to some common substances in the environment. Being familiar with these substances can help a female avoid exposing her unborn child to their harmful effects.

▶ **Lead.** Lead exposure has been linked to miscarriage, low birth weight, mental disabilities, and behavior problems in children. Lead can be found in the paint of houses built before 1978 and can leach from old pipes into tap water.

▶ **Smog.** Recent studies have linked air pollution with birth defects, low birth weight, premature birth, stillbirth, and infant death. The greatest risk occurs during the second month of pregnancy when most organs and facial features develop.

▶ **Radiation.** Ionizing radiation—the type found in X rays—can affect fetal growth and cause mental retardation. Other types of radiation, such as that from video displays, color television sets, and microwave ovens, have not been shown to be harmful.

▶ **Cat Litter.** Cat feces may contain a parasite that can cause a disease called toxoplasmosis (tahk-suh-plaz-MOH-suhs). This disease can result in miscarriage, premature labor, and health problems in a newborn. Pregnant females should wash their hands after petting a cat, have others clean the cat litter box, and wear gloves when gardening where cats may be present.

In addition, when using household chemicals, pregnant females should read the cautions on cleaning products, wear gloves, and work in well-ventilated areas.

Complications During Pregnancy

Most pregnancies proceed with few problems. However, complications can arise, some of them serious. One complication is **miscarriage**, *the spontaneous expulsion of a fetus that occurs before the twentieth week of a pregnancy. A dead fetus expelled from the body after the twentieth week* is called a **stillbirth**. Women who use tobacco or drugs during pregnancy are more likely to experience a miscarriage or stillbirth than those who abstain from these substances. A miscarriage or stillbirth doesn't necessarily mean that the mother did something wrong. Receiving the proper prenatal care during pregnancy can reduce the risk or severity of any problems that do arise.

Home and Community

Support Groups The complications of miscarriage and stillbirth can be devastating experiences for expectant parents. Many health care facilities and other organizations provide support groups for parents who have suffered this kind of loss. Suggest that students gather information about local support groups, such as:

- Where do they meet?

- Whom do they serve?
- What are the goals of their meetings?
- How do they share information with people who might want to join them?

  Let students share and discuss what they learn about these groups. If possible, have one of the students invite a support group leader to speak to the class.

Ectopic Pregnancy

Ectopic (ek-TAH-pik) pregnancies result when the zygote implants in the fallopian tube, the abdomen, the ovary, or the cervix. Ectopic pregnancy can occur when the fertilized egg can't pass to the uterus, sometimes because of inflammation or scar tissue that has developed as a result of **sexually transmitted diseases.** The fetus can't get the nourishment it needs to grow normally. The situation is a threat to the pregnant female's life. Ectopic pregnancy is the number one cause of death of females in the first trimester of pregnancy. The treatment of ectopic pregnancy is removal of the fetus from the female's body.

Preeclampsia

Preeclampsia (pree-ee-CLAMP-see-ah), also called toxemia, can prevent the placenta from getting enough blood. The condition may result in low fetal birth weight and problems for the mother. Symptoms of preeclampsia in a pregnant female include high blood pressure, swelling, and large amounts of protein in the urine. Treatment includes reducing blood pressure through bed rest or medicines. In some cases, hospitalization is necessary.

hot link

sexually transmitted diseases Read more about STDs in Chapter 25, page 648.

Did You Know?

► Two to five percent of pregnant females in the United States are diagnosed with Gestational Diabetes Mellitus, or GDM. It usually disappears after the baby's birth.

Activity

Ask students to research and write short reports on one complication related to pregnancy. Remind students to proofread their writing for spelling and grammatical errors. Then have them develop and turn in an error-free final draft. L2

③ ASSESS

EVALUATING THE LESSON

Assign and discuss the Lesson 2 Review; then administer, grade, and discuss Lesson Quiz 70 in the TCR. 📁

RETEACHING

- In small groups, have students explain why prenatal care is important. Then have students sketch pictures to depict four guidelines for mothers-to-be.

- Ask students to complete Reteaching Activity 70 in the TCR. 📁

ENRICHMENT

Have interested students learn more about midwives. What education and training do they receive? What are the licensing requirements? What relationships do local midwives maintain with physicians and hospitals in the community?

▶ Lesson 2 Review

Reviewing Facts and Vocabulary

1. Explain the importance of *prenatal care* and describe what it involves.
2. Define the term *stillbirth*.
3. Analyze the effects of certain substances on the fetus. Why should pregnant females avoid drugs, alcohol, and tobacco?

Thinking Critically

4. **Evaluation.** Suppose someone told you that pregnancy is a natural process so prenatal care is not important. What information would you give such a person?
5. **Synthesizing.** Analyze the harmful effects of environmental hazards on the fetus. Over which factors that affect a developing fetus does a pregnant female have control?

Applying Health Skills

Stress Management. Pregnancy causes extra stress on the body of the mother. Along with these physical stresses come concerns about the health of the baby and about parenthood. Make a list of healthy "stress-busters" pregnant females could use. Share your list with families who are expecting a child.

TECHNOLOGY *OPTION*

INTERNET RESOURCES Use the Internet to find information on stress management techniques. See **health.glencoe.com** for links to help your research.

Lesson 2 Prenatal Care **497**

---

④ CLOSE

Ask each student to complete this sentence: *During pregnancy, a woman should . . .*

▶ Lesson 2 Review

Answers to Reviewing Facts and Vocabulary

1. Steps a pregnant female can take to provide for her own health and for the health of her baby.
2. The birth of a dead fetus after the 20th week of pregnancy.
3. Harmful substances in alcohol, drugs, and tobacco can be passed to the fetus through the umbilical cord, causing problems with fetal development.

Answers to Thinking Critically

4. Answers should suggest that prenatal care is important for identifying problems.
5. Answers should include the quality of prenatal care, nutrition, physical fitness, and the substances taken into her body.

Heredity and Genetics

Lesson 3

Heredity and Genetics

1 FOCUS

QUICK START   Give students about four minutes to jot down their lists. Then ask volunteers to read their lists aloud. Which traits are more likely to be considered similar? Which are more likely to be identified as different within a family?

TYING TO PRIOR KNOWLEDGE

Have students recall what they have learned about fertilization. Explain that students will learn more about what the male sperm cell and the female egg cell contribute to the developing baby.

Health Skills Features

"Should People Undergo Genetic Testing?" p. 502

INTRODUCING VOCABULARY

- Divide the class into eight groups. Have the members of each group look up one of the vocabulary terms in the Glossary and discuss its definition. Then have group members explain the term to the rest of the class.

- Ask students to complete the Chapter 19 Study Guide in the *Student Activity Workbook.*

VOCABULARY

heredity
chromosomes
genes
DNA
genetic disorder
amniocentesis
Chorionic villi
  sampling
gene therapy

YOU'LL LEARN TO

- Explain the significance of genetics and its role in determining human traits.

- Identify common genetic disorders.

- Explain how genetic research has impacted the health status of families and those with genetic disorders.

QUICK START   Fold a sheet of paper in half. Think of a family you know. Make two columns, one listing ways family members are alike and one listing ways they are different.

Family members often share a strong physical resemblance. *What inherited characteristics are visible in this family?*

N o two individuals are exactly alike. Even identical twins have some differences. What accounts for this variety of traits? A number of factors influence the way an individual develops. One significant factor is heredity.

Heredity

T he *passing of traits from parents to their children* is called **heredity**. Examples of traits that you inherited from your parents are your eye and hair color and the shape of your earlobes. Environment can also influence inherited traits. For example, height is an inherited trait, but poor nutrition may stunt a child's growth.

498   Chapter 19   Prenatal Development and Birth

Lesson 3 *Resources*

Teacher Classroom Resources

 Concept Mapping Activity 71
Cross-Curriculum Activity 19
Current Health Issues 19
Decision-Making Activity 19
Guided Reading Activities 71
Health Lab 19

Lesson Plan 71
Lesson Quiz 71
Reteaching Activity 71

Student Activity Workbook

Applying Health Skills 71
Chapter 19 Study Guide

Chromosomes and Genes

Most cells of your body contain a nucleus—the cell's control center. Inside each nucleus is a set of **chromosomes** (KROH-muh-sohmz), *threadlike structures found within the nucleus of a cell that carry the codes for inherited traits.* Most cells in the body contain 46 chromosomes arranged as 23 pairs.

Sections of chromosomes, called genes, carry codes for specific traits. **Genes** are *the basic units of heredity.* Like chromosomes, genes occur in pairs. One gene from each pair is inherited from each parent. You have thousands of genes in every cell of your body.

DNA

The chemical unit that makes up chromosomes is called **DNA**, or deoxyribonucleic (dee-AHK-si-REYE-boh-nyoo-KLEE-ik) acid. All living things are made of DNA. Chemical compounds, called bases, make up the structure of DNA. The arrangement of the bases along each DNA molecule differs. Because several thousand pairs of bases are in each gene, countless numbers of arrangements are possible. The order of the bases is called the *genetic code.* Cells use the genetic code to make proteins. Proteins help to build and maintain body tissues. Different kinds of proteins will result in various individual traits. All the characteristics that you have—the color of your eyes and the amount of curl in your hair—are determined by your genetic code. Unless you have an identical twin, your DNA is different from that of any other person.

Genetics and Fetal Development

Every living organism has a certain number of chromosomes. Although most human cells contain 46 chromosomes —23 pairs—sperm and egg cells have only half that amount, or 23 chromosomes. When a sperm and an egg unite, the resulting zygote will have 46 chromosomes—23 from each parent. These chromosomes carry the hereditary traits of the parents.

As you learned in Lesson 1, a zygote divides many times, producing the trillions of cells that make up the human body. Between each cell division, each chromosome in the cell nucleus duplicates itself, producing two sets of 46 chromosomes. As the cell divides, the two sets of chromosomes separate. Each new cell will contain one set of 46 chromosomes that are identical to those in the first cell of the zygote.

DNA resembles a long twisted helix, with ladder-like chains. Nitrogen bases make up the rungs of the ladder. *Give an example of a trait that is determined by genes.*

2 TEACH

Discussing

Ask students to identify several examples of heredity, perhaps referring to the traits they listed in their Quick Start assignments. Then ask students to explain, in their own words, the relationships between heredity, chromosomes, and genes.

Reinforcing Concepts

Help students recall that cells, the basic unit of life, form all tissues in the human body. The nucleus is the central unit within the cell. To help students understand the relationships, have a volunteer draw a large circle on the board. Explain that this circle represents a cell. Have the volunteer draw a smaller circle to represent the nucleus inside the large circle. Then have the volunteer draw lines within the nucleus circle to represent chromosomes. Ask: Where should our representation of genes be drawn? on the chromosome lines

Activity

Ask a group of interested students to find out (or recall) the meaning of the term *helix* in geometry, anatomy, and architecture. Have these students prepare a display to be shared and explained to the rest of the class. L2

Dealing with Sensitive Issues

Inherited Traits Keep in mind that any discussion of inherited traits may make some students uncomfortable. Teens who were adopted in infancy and who have never seen their birth parents may be especially curious about inherited traits—and especially reluctant to discuss them. Other students may not remember, or may never have known, both parents. These issues may be especially difficult for students living in foster families or group homes. To facilitate discussions of inherited traits, describe fictional families and present photographs or drawings of family members.

Reinforcing Concepts

Have students discuss their responses to these questions:

- Can two brown-eyed parents have a blue-eyed child? Why or why not?
- Can two blue-eyed parents have a brown-eyed child? Why or why not? **L1**

Activity

Suggest that interested students use online or library sources to find specific information about Mendel's experiments with pea plants. Then have these students conduct their own experiments with pea plants, following the same general procedures Mendel used. Ask them to record their observations with charts and/or drawings and then to share those observations with the rest of the class. **L3**

Community Involvement

Specific organizations offer information and support to families who may have a member with a birth defect. Ask: Which of these organizations is established in your community? What kinds of services do they offer? Let volunteers explore them and share the information with the rest of the class. **L2**

Human X and Y chromosomes determine gender. Each of the body cells in a male has an X and a Y chromosome. Each body cell of a female has two X chromosomes. *Explain why the sperm, not the ovum, determines the gender of a fetus.*

Dominant and Recessive Genes

At least one pair of genes is responsible for each human trait. Some genes are *dominant,* and others are *recessive.* The traits of dominant genes generally appear in offspring whenever they are present. The traits of recessive genes usually appear only when dominant genes are not present. For example, suppose an individual receives two genes for eye color—one for brown eyes and one for blue eyes. The resulting individual will have brown eyes because the gene for brown eyes is dominant and the gene for blue eyes is recessive. An individual with blue eyes must have two recessive genes for blue eye color.

The situation is more complex than in the example above because traits that express a quantity or an extent—such as height, weight, or color—usually depend on many gene pairs, not just one.

Genes and Gender

In humans one pair of chromosomes determines the gender of an individual. If you are female, these two chromosomes look exactly alike and are called X chromosomes. If you are male, the two chromosomes differ—one is shorter than the other. The shorter chromosome is the Y chromosome. The longer one is the X chromosome.

Remember that sperm and egg cells contain only half the chromosomes of other cells, or one sex chromosome, not two. Sperm contain an X or a Y chromosome. Eggs have only an X chromosome. The gender of a child is determined by which type of sperm—X or Y—unites with an egg.

Genetic Disorders

Sometimes the genes that an individual inherits contain a *mutation,* or abnormality, in the base sequence of the genetic code. Often the mutation has little or no effect on the individual, but sometimes the mutation can result in defects or other health problems. **Genetic disorders** are *disorders caused partly or completely by a defect in genes.* Some genetic disorders, such as those that cause birth defects, are apparent right away. One example of such a defect is cleft palate. However, other genetic disorders do not show up until later in life. **Figure 19.4** gives information about some common genetic disorders.

500 Chapter 19 Prenatal Development and Birth

More About...

Prenatal Technology Amniocentesis is usually used to test amniotic fluid for birth defects during the second trimester. This procedure can also be used during the third trimester to diagnose uterine infections and to determine whether the fetus's lungs are mature for delivery. Ultrasound (or sonography) is a technique that converts sound waves bouncing off the fetus to an image called a sonogram. It is used throughout pregnancy to evaluate fetal growth, to diagnose certain birth defects, and for other reasons. Fetal pulse oximetry is a technology used during labor and delivery; it indicates how much oxygen is in the blood of the fetus. A low reading can alert doctors that a cesarean section may be necessary.

FIGURE 19.4

COMMON HUMAN GENETIC DISORDERS

Disorder	Characteristics
Sickle-cell anemia	Red blood cells have a sickle shape and clump together; may result in severe joint and abdominal pain, weakness, kidney disease, restricted blood flow
Tay-Sachs disease	Destruction of nervous system; blindness; paralysis; death during early childhood
Cystic fibrosis	Mucus clogs many organs, including lungs, liver, and pancreas; nutritional problems; serious respiratory infections and congestion
Down syndrome	Varying degrees of mental retardation, short stature, round face with upper eyelids that cover inner corners of the eyes
Hemophilia	Failure of blood to clot

Although most genetic disorders cannot be cured, in some cases they can be treated, especially if they are diagnosed early—often before birth. Two common procedures used to test for genetic disorders are amniocentesis (am-nee-oh-sen-TEE-sis) and chorionic villi (kor-ee-ON-ik VIL-eye) sampling.

▶ **Amniocentesis** is *a procedure in which a syringe is inserted through a pregnant female's abdominal wall into the amniotic fluid surrounding the developing fetus.* Doctors can examine the chromosomes in fetal cells taken from amniotic fluid for genetic abnormalities or to determine the gender and age of the fetus. Amniocentesis is usually performed 16 to 20 weeks after fertilization.

▶ **Chorionic villi sampling**, or **CVS**, is *a procedure in which a small piece of membrane is removed from the chorion, a layer of tissue that develops into the placenta.* The tissue can be examined for genetic disorders or to determine fetal age and gender. The procedure is done around the eighth week of fetal development.

Tests for genetic disorders may also be done after a child is born. For example, many states require the testing of all newborns for phenylketonuria (PKU). If PKU is diagnosed soon after birth, a baby's diet can be altered to stop possible mental retardation caused by this genetic disorder.

Ⓥ **Health care professionals can check the health of a fetus using a variety of testing procedures.** *How can the age of a fetus be determined?*

─/\/\/─ HEALTH LITERACY ────

Self-Directed Learner Have you ever noticed the warnings on most diet soft drinks regarding phenylalanine? Probably not unless you or a family member has PKU. Individuals with PKU must follow a strict diet to avoid phenylalanine because it accumulates in their blood. Accumulation can result in learning disabilities, behavior problems, and personality disorders. Since the mid-1960s, all states routinely test newborn infants. Children diagnosed with PKU can now lead normal lives if they maintain a strict diet. Ask volunteers to investigate, using print and online sources, the cause and incidence of PKU. Though the condition is rare, one of every 50 people is a carrier.

Exploring Issues

SHOULD PEOPLE UNDERGO GENETIC TESTING?

Ask students to discuss what they have heard about genetic testing. Explain that tests exist to determine whether an individual is genetically predisposed to develop certain diseases or pass them on to offspring. Have students express their opinions on this topic. Then let students work in groups to read the feature, discuss the viewpoints, and share their responses to the activities.

Activity

Ask a pair of volunteers to learn about the history and the mission of the March of Dimes. How does this organization work to prevent and treat genetic birth defects? Have the volunteers discuss with the rest of the class what they have learned about the March of Dimes. **L2**

Service Learning

Encourage interested students to learn about—and participate in—opportunities to support the local March of Dimes. **L2**

Should People Undergo Genetic Testing?

In the past few years, researchers have linked specific genes or gene mutations with particular diseases. People can be tested to find out whether they are genetically predisposed to those diseases. Some people feel that the disadvantages of genetic testing outweigh the advantages. Others think the opposite is true. Here are two points of view.

Viewpoint 1: Neil S., age 15

I don't think that people should undergo genetic testing. What if they have the gene for a disease for which there's no cure? They would probably worry about it all the time and not be able to do anything about it. A positive test doesn't necessarily mean that the person will develop the disease, but it could cause the person to lose his or her health insurance.

Viewpoint 2: Jan P., age 16

I think genetic testing should be available for those who want it. A person who carries the gene for a particular disease may be able to take additional precautions such as more frequent screenings to reduce the risk of developing the disease. Also, I think that having genetic testing is a personal choice. People can choose not to have it if they don't want to know.

ACTIVITIES

1. Research some diseases or conditions for which people can undergo genetic testing.

2. After researching, list some legal and ethical questions to consider before having a genetic test. How do you think these issues might influence someone's decision about whether to be tested?

Genetic Counseling

Research for diagnosing, preventing, and treating genetically related diseases has resulted in a wide variety of programs. Genetic counselors can advise families about the probability of having a child with a genetically related disease. They also can guide families of children with genetic disorders about possible treatment options.

Genetic Research to Cure Disease

Scientists have taken an important step in understanding and treating genetic disorders. The Human Genome Project is an international effort that has successfully identified the approximately 30,000 genes on the 46 human chromosomes. Gene maps can be used to diagnose genetic disorders.

HEALTH LITERACY

Drugs and Embryonic Development

Through genetic research, causes and cures for genetic disorders are being identified. Females can take steps to control other factors that cause defects during prenatal development. Much important development takes place in an embryo before a female is aware that she is pregnant. Harmful substances ingested before the pregnancy is discovered can have damaging results. Have students write a paragraph about substances that should be avoided to reduce risking the healthy development of an embryo. Drugs can inflict the same harm whether obtained illegally, by prescription, or over-the-counter. Encourage students to research drugs sold by prescription or over-the-counter that could be harmful to the embryo.

Gene Therapy

Many disorders result when an individual lacks a functioning gene. Without the functioning gene, certain substances that the body needs are not produced. **Gene therapy** is *the process of inserting normal genes into human cells to correct genetic disorders.* When the defective gene is replaced with a normal one, the cells with the new gene begin to make the missing substance. Most often, viruses are the carriers used to insert the new gene into a person's cells. The practice of placing fragments of DNA from one organism into another is called *genetic engineering,* and it is considered highly experimental. Genetic diseases for which scientists are researching gene therapies include cystic fibrosis and various types of cancer.

Genetically Engineered Drugs

Genes used to treat disease aren't usually inserted directly into human beings. Instead they are placed into other organisms, causing them to produce substances that can be used to treat human diseases and disorders. Genetically produced medicines include treatments for burns and ulcers, growth defects, and for ovarian and breast cancers. Factor VIII medicines treat hemophilia. Genetic engineering also is used to produce some vaccines that prevent diseases.

Did You Know

Two purposes of the Human Genome Project are to identify all of the genes in human DNA and to determine the sequences of the 3 billion base pairs that make up human DNA. A working draft of the entire human genome sequence was announced in June 2000. Scientists hope to use the information from the project to improve diagnosis and treatment for approximately 4,000 human genetic disorders.

Discussing

Have students discuss the uses of gene therapy and genetic engineering. Let several volunteers explain the processes in their own words. Discuss the latest findings about the success of gene therapy. **L1**

3 ASSESS

EVALUATING THE LESSON

Assign and discuss the Lesson 3 Review; then administer, grade, and discuss Lesson Quiz 71 in the TCR. 📁

RETEACHING

- Help small groups of students work together to review the lesson content. Suggest that group members identify each main heading in the lesson and state, in their own words, one or two main ideas from that heading along with supporting details.

- Ask students to complete Reteaching Activity 71 in the TCR. 📁

ENRICHMENT

Have students explore genetic engineering. Ask students to summarize their findings in written reports. Remind students to check for spelling and grammatical errors. They may need to develop several drafts before handing in a final error-free draft of their findings.

▶ Lesson 3 *Review*

Reviewing Facts and Vocabulary

1. What is *heredity*?

2. Name three human genetic disorders.

3. Explain the difference between *amniocentesis* and *chorionic villi sampling (CVS).*

Thinking Critically

4. **Analyzing.** Explain how chromosomes, genes, and DNA are significant in determining human traits.

5. **Synthesizing.** Explain how genetic research technology has impacted the health status of families. How might a genetic counselor help a family that has just learned that their child may have inherited a genetic disorder?

Applying Health Skills

Accessing Information. Research a particular genetic disorder. Prepare a presentation that summarizes the cause, symptoms, and treatment of the disorder and the latest research being conducted. Explain how technology has impacted the health status of communities throughout the world.

TECHNOLOGY *OPTION*

PRESENTATION SOFTWARE Use presentation software to combine text, photos, and illustrations in an interesting summary of a genetic disorder. Find help in using presentation software at **health.glencoe.com.**

Lesson 3 Heredity and Genetics **503**

▶ Lesson 3 *Review*

Answers to Reviewing Facts and Vocabulary

1. The passing of traits from parents to their children.

2. Any three: sickle-cell anemia, Tay-Sachs disease, cystic fibrosis, Down syndrome, hemophilia, PKU.

3. See page 501 for differences.

Answers to Thinking Critically

4. Each chromosome is made up of chemical units called DNA. DNA base pairs form genes. Genes determine physical characteristics in humans.

5. A genetic counselor can guide the family in understanding the disorder and the possible treatment options.

4 CLOSE

Have each student write one sentence identifying the most important new fact he or she has learned from this lesson.

1 FOCUS

Lesson 4

Infancy and Childhood

QUICK START   Have students list the specific activities and behaviors they have observed in young children. Then let volunteers share items from their lists, noting the ages of children appropriate to each activity or behavior. Help students identify which behaviors are included on many lists.

VOCABULARY
developmental tasks
autonomy
scoliosis

YOU'LL LEARN TO
- Identify and explain the developmental tasks of childhood.
- Analyze the influence of laws and policies in regard to health screenings for children.
- Identify school and community health services that offer vision and hearing screenings and immunization programs for children.

TYING TO PRIOR KNOWLEDGE

Point out that everyone knows something about childhood since everyone has experienced it. Explain that, as students read this lesson, they will learn more about infants and children.

QUICK START   Do you or any of your friends have younger brothers or sisters? List activities and behaviors you have noticed about younger siblings. Look for patterns among children of similar ages.

Health Skills Features

"Choosing Toys," p. 506

DECISION MAKING

 Children often imitate the behavior of adults. *What are some examples of positive behaviors adults can display when they are around children?*

Dramatic physical and mental changes take place as an infant grows through childhood. Many scientists have studied these changes, and they have developed different theories about them. One of the most widely accepted theories of development is that of psychologist Erik Erikson.

Childhood Development

According to Erikson, each individual passes through eight developmental stages during his or her life. Each stage is characterized by **developmental tasks**, *events that need to happen in order for a person to continue growing toward becoming a healthy, mature adult.* Success in each stage is dependent on an individual's experiences during that stage. Partial development at one stage can be overcome by developmental successes in following stages. The four stages that apply to infancy and childhood are summarized in **Figure 19.5.**

Infancy

Infancy is the period of fastest growth in a person's life. During this time a child's weight may triple, and his or her height may

INTRODUCING VOCABULARY

- Have students work with partners to discuss their current understanding of each vocabulary term. Then have them look each term up in the Glossary and discuss its definition.

- Ask students to complete the Chapter 19 Study Guide in the *Student Activity Workbook.*

Lesson 4 *Resources*

Teacher Classroom Resources
- Concept Mapping Activity 72
- Enrichment Activity 19
- Guided Reading Activity 72
- Lesson Plan 72
- Lesson Quiz 72
- Reteaching Activity 72

Student Activity Workbook
- Applying Health Skills 72
- Chapter 19 Study Guide

Multimedia
- Transparency 58

FIGURE 19.5

STAGES OF INFANCY AND CHILDHOOD

Each stage of development is associated with a developmental task that involves a person's relationship with other people.

Stage 1	Stage 2	Stage 3	Stage 4
			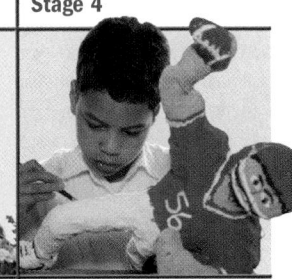
Infancy: Birth to 1 year **Task:** To develop trust **Description:** Infant is completely dependent on others to meet his or her needs. Must be able to trust others to provide for needs.	**Early Childhood:** 1 to 3 years **Task:** To develop ability to do tasks for oneself **Description:** Child learns to walk, talk, and dress and feed himself or herself. Self-control and confidence begins to develop, and child begins a desire for independence.	**Middle Childhood:** 4 to 6 years **Task:** To develop responsibility, take initiative, to create one's own play **Description:** Child becomes more engaged in interactions with others. Models adult behavior by helping with household chores. Learns to control impulses.	**Late Childhood:** 7 to 12 years **Task:** To develop an interest in performing activities **Description:** Child completes transition from home to school; learns to make things, use tools, and acquire skills.

increase by 50 percent. Infancy is a time of learning—how to eat solid food and how to sit, crawl, and walk. An important task for an infant is developing trust. Infants of parents who are attentive—who play with and talk to the infant and give comfort—learn to view the world as a safe place. These children see people as being dependable. If parents ignore a child's needs, the child may learn to be distrustful.

Early Childhood

Children in early childhood begin to feel proud of their accomplishments, and they become eager to learn more. During this time children develop many new skills. They learn to talk, climb, push, and pull. They increase their vocabulary and begin talking in sentences. If parents accept the child's need to do whatever he or she is capable of, the child will develop a sense of **autonomy**, *the confidence that a person can control his or her own body, impulses, and environment.* If parents are overprotective or critical of the child's behaviors, the child may develop doubts about his or her abilities.

Lesson 4   Infancy and Childhood   **505**

More About...

Personality Development Many anthropologists, including John and Beatrice Whiting, question the universality of Erikson's stages of development. They believe that adult personality depends on the specific child-rearing practices found in a given society and that these, in turn, have their roots in a society's ways of meeting the basic physical needs of its members. Autonomy,

for example, may be an important trait to develop in complex societies such as our own, where self-reliance and independence help ensure social and economic success. In many other societies, however, particularly farming societies, such traits conflict with the need of individuals to work for the benefit of the group.

VISUAL LEARNING

Figure 19.5 Divide the class into four groups, and assign each group one of Erikson's stages of infancy and childhood. Have group members read the presented information and discuss examples of behavior they may have observed. Then have members of each group explain their assigned stage to the rest of the class.

Discussing

Encourage students to recall positive interactions they have observed between parents (or older siblings) and infants. Ask: How do you think the infants were affected by those interactions? **L1**

Service Learning

Suggest that students volunteer in local preschool programs. Ask these students to discuss their observations and experiences. **L3**

Critical Thinking

Ask students how elementary schools are designed to meet the developmental needs of late childhood. **L1**

CHARACTER ✔ CHECK

Caring Let students meet in groups to discuss the importance of showing caring toward children as outlined in the character check on the next page. Have group members work together to write a list of specific actions teens can take to show caring to younger siblings and other children.

Health Skills Activity

CHOOSING TOYS

DECISION MAKING

NHES Standard 6 Students will demonstrate the ability to use goal-setting and decision-making skills to enhance health.

Objectives

- Identify and explain the developmental tasks of childhood.
- Apply decision-making skills to make a health-promoting decision.

Motivator

Show the class a box from a child's toy that displays a recommended age and/or a warning that the item may be unsuitable for children under a certain age.

Teaching Strategies

1. Ask students who have young siblings at home to share with the class the kinds of toys their siblings play with and how those toys were chosen.
2. Have students brainstorm potential sources of valid information on age-appropriate toys, and list these on the board.

✓ Assessment

Using a rubric, student work should provide comprehensive evidence of the following criteria to achieve the highest score:

✔ clear description of the situation
✔ several options with possible outcomes of each
✔ influence of values on possible decisions
✔ health-enhancing decision and an evaluation of it

CHARACTER ✓ CHECK

Caring. When a child feels understood and has physical and emotional needs taken care of, he or she will thrive. Take the time to listen attentively and show that you care whenever you have a chance to help a toddler or young child. **Think of ways you demonstrate caring with younger siblings or other children.**

Middle Childhood

During middle childhood children learn to initiate play activities rather than merely following the lead of others. Children of this age display their intelligence by asking many questions. They must learn to recognize emotions and practice expressing them in appropriate ways. If parents show approval of these new abilities and encourage questions, children learn creativity, initiative, and the ability to start something on their own. Children of parents who are impatient with the child may develop a sense of guilt about self-initiated activities, resulting in low self-esteem.

Late Childhood

During late childhood school becomes an important part of a child's life. Children develop skills in reading, writing, and math.

Health Skills Activity

Decision Making: Choosing Toys

Colleen is buying a gift for her sister's second birthday. She and her friend, Amanda, are in the toy store. "What about this puzzle?" asks Amanda.

"That's cute," Colleen replies, "but it looks complicated. What if she chokes on the small pieces?"

"Maybe a ride-on toy?" Amanda suggests. "My little brother loves his tricycle."

"Those are fun," Colleen agrees. "But you have to make sure they're stable, so the child doesn't tip over. There are a lot of safety issues to consider when you get a toy for a child."

Amanda sighs. "Maybe we need to do some research to find out what two-year-olds can play with."

"The party is tomorrow," Colleen replies. "I don't have a lot of time for research."

What Would You Do?

How can Colleen find out more about age-appropriate toys? Apply the six steps of the decision-making process to Colleen's situation.

1. State the situation.
2. List the options.
3. Weigh the possible outcomes.
4. Consider values.
5. Make a decision and act.
6. Evaluate the decision.

Cooperative Learning Activity

Photo Collections Have students bring to class photographs from magazines of newborn babies, babies at the age of one year, and babies at several stages in between. Then divide the class into cooperative groups. Have students examine the photographs in their groups and discuss their observations about physical development at various ages. At what age do babies have teeth? How much do babies grow between birth and the end of the first year? How does their appearance change within the first year? Invite each group to create a poster using the photos of babies at various ages. Have them include summaries of what they have learned about development based on this chapter and their observations.

Children learn to get along with peers, learn appropriate roles in society, and develop a conscience. If their efforts are rewarded and appreciated, their pride in their work increases. Children who are scolded for making a mess, getting in the way, or not following directions may develop feelings of self-doubt.

Health Screenings in Childhood

Vision and hearing impairments can affect a child's development as much as social factors do. Immunizations and health screenings can prevent many problems.

Vision and Hearing

According to the CDC, nearly one in every 1,000 children in the United States has low vision or is legally blind. The American Academy of Ophthalmology recommends that vision screenings be given to newborns and regularly throughout childhood. Schools often provide regular vision screenings for students.

In the United States, two to three of every 1,000 infants are born with a hearing impairment severe enough to affect a child's language development. Some states require that newborns be screened at birth for hearing loss. Schools often provide periodic screenings.

Scoliosis

Scoliosis, an *abnormal lateral, or side-to-side, curvature of the spine,* may begin in childhood and go unnoticed until the teen years. Its exact cause is unknown, though it is more common in girls. Many public schools check for scoliosis in middle school.

HEALTH Online

Keeping up with childhood immunizations is important for protection against disease. Visit Web Links at **health.glencoe.com**, and examine the schedule recommended by the American Academy of Family Physicians.

Lesson 4 Review

Reviewing Facts and Vocabulary

1. Define *developmental tasks.* List three developmental tasks of infancy and childhood.
2. What developmental task must be accomplished in early childhood?
3. Which health screenings are usually provided by schools?

Thinking Critically

4. **Synthesizing.** How do the actions of parents contribute to the developmental tasks of their children?
5. **Evaluating.** Do you think that all states should have laws requiring regular health screenings for children? Explain your answer.

Applying Health Skills

Accessing Information. Research where individuals in your community can get free or low-cost vision and hearing screenings or immunizations. Post your findings on a class Web site.

TECHNOLOGY OPTION

WEB SITES Go to **health.glencoe.com** for help in building your Web site.

Lesson 4 Infancy and Childhood **507**

Lesson 4 Review

Answers to Reviewing Facts and Vocabulary

1. Events that need to happen in order for a person to continue growing toward becoming a healthy, mature adult. Any three from page 505.
2. The ability to do tasks for oneself; develop a sense of autonomy.
3. Vision, hearing, and scoliosis screenings.

Answers to Thinking Critically

4. Vision and hearing impairments can affect the normal development of a child.
5. Positive responses at each stage give the child confidence to develop in healthy ways.

Reading Programs for Children

NHES Standard 4 Students will analyze the influence of culture, media, technology, and other factors on health.

Objective

Research and select print media sources for children that illustrate or reinforce the developmental tasks discussed in this chapter.

Motivator

Have students review the developmental tasks outlined in Lesson 4.

Teaching Strategies

Awareness Have students brainstorm a list of activities or skills that would reinforce developmental tasks of childhood.

Analysis Students should assess their selections for how the stories reinforce the developmental tasks for that age group.

Reflection Encourage students to consider the variety of ways media choices might affect the development of childhood skills.

Take Action Encourage students to get involved in their community by volunteering to aid in public library reading programs or after-school literacy programs.

✓Assessment

For each story they select, students should submit a brief synopsis that includes an explanation of how the story reinforces or illustrates one of the developmental tasks outlined in the chapter. Students' letters to the editor should be persuasive and should contain concrete ideas on how teens can get involved in literacy and summer reading programs in their area.

Reading Programs for Children

Some experts suggest that children should read or be read to for at least 20 to 30 minutes each day. For school age children, reading skills are essential for achieving a sense of competence about their own abilities. For preschoolers, being read to fosters the desire to read and teaches them cooperation and listening skills. In the activity below, you will research and select print media sources for children that illustrate or reinforce the developmental tasks discussed in Lesson 4 of this chapter.

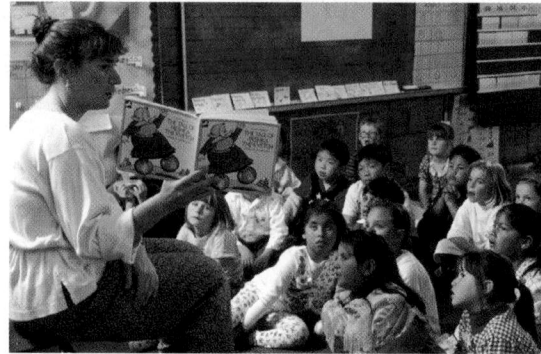

ACTIVITY

You have been asked by your local library to develop a summer reading program for children. Pick one of two age groups for your project, children ages 3 to 5 or children ages 6 to 11. For children ages 3 to 5, research and select five stories to be read aloud to the children. For children ages 6 to 11, identify five books or stories for the children to read themselves.

Using your school or local library as a resource, research and select the five stories you will recommend for your summer reading or storytelling program. For each selection you make, write a brief synopsis of the story that explains how the selection illustrates or reinforces the developmental tasks for that age group.

EXPRESS YOUR VIEWS

Research summer reading and literacy programs in your area. Write an editorial for your school newspaper that encourages teens to volunteer for these programs. Your editorial should state why reading is important, give information about local programs, and contain suggestions for how to get involved.

More About...

Literacy Programs Literacy and reading programs exist in almost every community. The strength and effectiveness of these programs is a result of strong partnerships developed among schools and universities, libraries, parents, community leaders, area businesses, community organizations, the media, or local zoos or museums. The National Center for Educational Statistics conducted a nationwide study of student reading skills in 2000. They found that the gap between high performing students and low performing students has widened since 1992. Many reading and literacy programs are making great efforts to recruit below average readers at a young age in order to reverse this trend.

CROSS-CURRICULUM CONNECTIONS

Create a Futuristic Story. As a result of scientific breakthroughs in genetic research, scientists predict they can make even greater strides in treating and curing illnesses. From what you have learned about genetics, write a science fiction story of how the human genome-mapping project might further impact the future. Remember that although science fiction contains the possibilities of the imagination, the plot must reflect in some way the laws of science.

Examine Theories of Development. Understanding the physical and mental stages of human development helps parents guide their children toward adulthood. Select and study the work of a psychologist or scientist, such as Sigmund Freud, who has theorized about early childhood development. Using a Venn diagram, compare and contrast this researcher's stages to Erik Erikson's theory outlined in Lesson 4 of this chapter.

Calculate Percentage of Births and Deaths. The number of live births in the U.S. in 1999 was 3,959,417, and the total number of deaths was 2,391,399. What was the percentage by which births outnumbered deaths?

List Discoveries in Health. A general map of the human genetic code was completed in June 2000 through the Human Genome Project. Enormous potential exists for the correction of birth defects and the production of highly specific medications. Investigate the progress made by the Human Genome Project. Make a list of current technologies that use the information and future uses proposed.

CAREER Corner

Pediatrician

Being a physician who specializes in treating children from birth through the teen years takes patience, understanding, and a lot of education. Pediatricians get a four-year college degree and then complete four years of medical school. This is followed by three or more years of residency training in pediatrics. Some pediatricians have additional training in specialties such as neonatal care or heart diseases in children. Find out more about this and other health careers by clicking on Career Corner at **health.glencoe.com**.

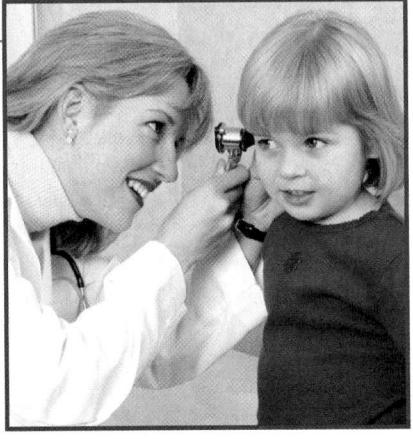

CROSS-CURRICULUM CONNECTIONS

Enrich student learning by connecting the topic of prenatal development and birth to one of the four areas presented on this page. The activity may be completed individually or with a partner.

Language Arts Encourage students to use suspense, one element common to science fiction.

Social Studies To use a Venn diagram, draw two intersecting circles, labeling each. Where the circles overlap, list common traits. In the areas not overlapping, write the differing traits.

Math Answer: $(3,959,417 - 2,391,399)/3,959,417 \times 100 = 39.6\%$

Science Primary uses will be for medicines and therapies for inherited disorders.

CAREER Corner

Have students read and discuss the Career Corner information on pediatricians. Ask interested students to explore the Glencoe Health Web site at **health. glencoe.com** for more information on this career.

Portfolio Assessment

Self-Evaluation Direct students to review the Health Skills Activities and other activities completed in the chapter. Encourage each student to select one finished product or activity that demonstrates his or her best work for the chapter and that represents the student's learning goals. Have students explain what they have learned and how the examples they have selected demonstrate their growth in health literacy, knowledge, and skills.

Teacher Classroom Resources Assign Performance Assessment 19, "Genes Count," in the TCR.

CHECKING COMPREHENSION

- Assign and discuss the chapter review.
- Use Chapter 19 MindJogger Videoquiz to review the chapter. ▷◁

CHAPTER 19 REVIEW ANSWERS

Exploring Health Terms

1. labor
2. umbilical cord
3. placenta
4. birthing center
5. fetal alcohol syndrome (FAS)
6. miscarriage
7. chromosomes
8. genes
9. DNA
10. genetic disorder
11. developmental task
12. Autonomy
13. scoliosis

Recalling the Facts

1. From the sperm cell and the egg cell.
2. To protect and insulate the fetus.
3. Dilation, passage through the birth canal, afterbirth.
4. The pregnant woman will have a complete physical that includes blood tests and a pelvic exam.
5. Nutrition in pregnancy is a balancing act of eating the right food without overeating; each woman has unique nutritional requirements, as does the fetus.
6. Lead, smog, radiation, cat litter.
7. Brown.
8. Males have an X chromosome and Y chromosome. Females have two X chromosomes.

510

➤ **EXPLORING HEALTH TERMS** *Answer the following questions on a sheet of paper.*

Lesson 1 *Replace the underlined words with the correct term.*

amniotic sac	implantation
embryo	labor
fertilization	placenta
fetus	umbilical cord

1. The final stage of pregnancy, in which the uterus contracts and pushes the baby out of the mother's body, is <u>fertilization</u>.
2. The ropelike structure that connects the embryo and the placenta is the <u>fetus</u>.
3. The <u>amniotic sac</u> is the thick, blood-rich tissue that lines the walls of the uterus and nourishes the embryo during pregnancy.

Lesson 2 *Match each definition with the correct term.*

birthing center	prenatal care
stillbirth	fetal alcohol syndrome (FAS)
miscarriage	

4. A facility in which females with low-risk pregnancies can deliver their babies in a homelike setting.
5. A group of alcohol-related birth defects.
6. The spontaneous expulsion of a fetus that occurs before the twentieth week of a pregnancy.

Lesson 3 *Fill in the blanks with the correct term.*

CVS	genetic disorder
DNA	chromosomes
genes	heredity
gene therapy	amniocentesis

7. The threadlike structures found within the nucleus of a cell that carry the codes for inherited traits are called _____.
8. The basic units of heredity are _____.
9. The chemical units that make up chromosomes are called _____.
10. A defect in genes can result in a(n) _____.

510 Chapter 19 Review

Lesson 4 *Fill in the blanks with the correct term.*

autonomy	scoliosis
developmental tasks	

11. _____ is/are a series of events that must happen in order for an individual to continue growing toward becoming a healthy, mature adult.
12. _____ is/are the confidence that a person can control his or her own body, impulses, and environment.
13. An abnormal sideways curvature of the spine is _____.

➤ **RECALLING THE FACTS** *Use complete sentences to answer the following questions.*

Lesson 1

1. From where does a zygote's DNA originate?
2. What is the function of the amniotic sac?
3. Summarize the three stages of labor.

Lesson 2

4. What happens during a prenatal visit to a doctor or certified nurse midwife?
5. Why is nutritional counseling during pregnancy important?
6. List four environmental hazards that can harm a fetus.

Lesson 3

7. Explain the role of genetics in human development. If a baby boy receives a dominant gene for brown eyes and a recessive gene for blue eyes, what color will his eyes be?
8. How does the genetic makeup of a male differ from that of a female?

---

9. The child might develop low self-esteem.
10. At birth.
11. In middle school.

Lesson 4

9. How might impatience toward someone in middle childhood affect the development of that child?

10. How soon after birth should an infant have a hearing screening?

11. When is a child commonly checked for scoliosis?

▶ THINKING CRITICALLY

1. **Summarizing.** Make a booklet to explain the process of fetal development to young children. Share your booklet with a young child you know. *(LESSON 1)*

2. **Synthesizing.** Suppose you observed a pregnant female drinking an alcoholic beverage. How might you inform her about the effects of her drinking on her unborn child? *(LESSON 2)*

3. **Applying.** Identify and survey occurrences of an easily observed genetic trait such as hair color. From your data, decide whether the trait you observed is dominant or recessive. Research the trait to confirm or disprove your decision. *(LESSON 3)*

4. **Evaluating.** You observe a parent interacting with a child in the grocery store. The child is pushing a mini-cart and mimicking the motions of "shopping." Periodically the child asks, "Why?" and wants to examine everything in the store. Which stage of childhood is the child displaying? What clues help you make this determination? *(LESSON 4)*

▶ HEALTH SKILLS APPLICATION

1. **Accessing Information.** Choose a human body system. Research its development before birth. Prepare a visual report of your findings. *(LESSON 1)*

2. **Communicating.** Research and analyze the effects of secondhand smoke on a developing fetus. Write a dialogue in which a pregnant woman uses this factual information and "I" messages to communicate her desire for a person not to smoke in her presence. *(LESSON 2)*

3. **Advocacy.** Research a genetic disorder that interests you. Find out what organizations are currently doing research on the disease and how this research is funded. Write a letter to the funding organization urging them to continue their support. *(LESSON 3)*

4. **Practicing Healthful Behaviors.** Identify screening and immunization programs in your community. What screenings and immunizations are required by your state? By your school district? Check with your parents about whether your own family's immunizations are up to date. *(LESSON 4)*

BEYOND the Classroom

Parent Involvement

Analyzing Influences. Talk with a parent or other adult family member about the responsibilities of parenthood. Share Erikson's stages of infancy and early, middle, and late childhood, and discuss how your family helped you move successfully from one stage to another.

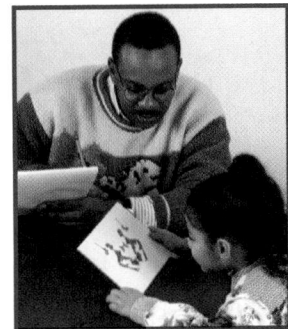

School and Community

Child Care. Invite a child psychologist to your school to discuss the developmental tasks of children. Have the person explain the positive behaviors that caregivers can use to help ensure that the children they care for become healthy, mature adults. Then use the information to prepare a pamphlet for all babysitters to read.

Chapter 19 Review **511**

Thinking Critically

1. Booklets and presentations will vary.

2. Answers will vary. Students should stress the dangers of FAS in a polite, respectful manner.

3. Freckles, unattached earlobes, widow's peaks are some dominant traits students may name.

4. Early childhood. Answers will vary.

Health Skills Application

1.–4. Answers will vary.

EVALUATE

- Use the reproducible Chapter 19 Test in the TCR, or construct your own using the Testmaker software.

- Use Performance Assessment 19 in the TCR.

ENRICHMENT

Ask students to complete Enrichment Activity 19 in the TCR.

BEYOND the Classroom

Keep students involved in the community, and encourage parent participation by assigning the activities on this page for students to work on outside of class.

Lessons	Standards		Features
	National	State/Local	
1 Adolescence— Understanding Growth and Change *pages 514–519*	National Health Education Standards **1.2, 1.4, 3.4, 5.3, 6.5**		**Exploring Issues** • Should High School Classes Start Later in the Day? page 518
2 **Moving Toward Adulthood** *pages 520–523*	National Health Education Standards **1.4, 1.6, 3.2, 4.1, 6.6**		**Health Skills Activity** • Exploring Careers *(Decision Making)*, page 522
3 **Marriage and Parenting** *pages 524–528*	National Health Education Standards **1.2, 1.4, 3.4, 5.2, 5.4**		**Hands-On Health** • Skills for a Healthy Marriage *(Conflict Resolution)*, page 525
4 **Health Through the Life Span** *pages 529–533*	National Health Education Standards **2.4, 4.3, 6.6, 7.5**		**Real-Life Application** • Government Spending for Health Research *(Advocacy)*, page 532

Reproducible Resources	Assessment	Technology
Student Activity Workbook for use with each chapter 📁 Concept Mapping Activity 73 📁 Decision-Making Activity 20 📁 Enrichment Activity 20 📁 Guided Reading Activities 73 📁 Health Lab 20 📁 Lesson Plan 73 📁 Parent Letter and Activitie 20 📁 Reteaching Activity 73	📁 Lesson Quiz 73	🕹 Transparency 59 💿 TeacherWorks® 🖥 Internet Activities
📁 Concept Mapping Activity 74 📁 Guided Reading Activities 74 📁 Lesson Plan 74 📁 Reteaching Activity 74	📁 Lesson Quiz 74	🕹 Transparency 60 💿 TeacherWorks®
📁 Concept Mapping Activity 75 📁 Guided Reading Activities 75 📁 Lesson Plan 75 📁 Reteaching Activity 75	📁 Lesson Quiz 75	🕹 Transparency 61 💿 TeacherWorks®
📁 Concept Mapping Activity 76 📁 Cross-Curriculum Activity 20 📁 Current Health Issues 20 📁 Guided Reading Activities 76 📁 Lesson Plan 76 📁 Reteaching Activity 76	📁 Lesson Quiz 76	💿 TeacherWorks®

⏱ OUT OF TIME

If time does not permit teaching the entire chapter, use:

- Figure 20.1, p. 515
- Figure 20.2, p. 516
- Figure 20.3, p. 521
- Health Skills Activity, p. 522
- Hands-On Health Activity, p. 525

Language Diversity

🎧 English Audio CD Program
🎧 Spanish Audio CD Program
📁 English Summaries, Quizzes, and Activities
📁 Spanish Summaries, Quizzes, and Activities
📁 Spanish Parent Letters and Activities

End of Chapter Assessment

Blackline Masters

📁 Chapter 20 Test
📁 Performance Assessment Activity 20
📁 Unit 6 Test

Technology

💿 Vocabulary PuzzleMaker
📼 MindJogger Videoquiz
💿 **Exam***View*® ProTestmaker

Professional Health Series

Dealing with Sensitive Issues
Planning a Coordinated School Health Program
Promoting Character Education
Home, School, and Community Involvement

CHAPTER OVERVIEW

Chapter 20 discusses the life stages that follow childhood: adolescence, early adulthood, middle adulthood, and late adulthood.

Lesson 1 Adolescence, the stage between childhood and adulthood, is a period of rapid growth, involving physical, mental/emotional, and social changes.

Lesson 2 Adulthood is marked by both physical and emotional maturity. During the stage of young adulthood, one of the primary goals is to establish intimate relationships.

Lesson 3 Marriage is a long-term commitment made by two people who intend to spend the rest of their lives together. Most teens do not yet have the maturity needed to accept the responsibilities that marriage involves. Parenting is both challenging and rewarding; it involves huge, ongoing responsibilities.

Lesson 4 During middle adulthood, from the ages of 40 to 65, individuals contribute to society, look outside themselves and care for others, and take an active concern for young people. In late adulthood, individuals often evaluate the events of their lives and their achievements.

Health Skills Features

- Exploring Issues, p. 518
- Health Skills Activity (*Decision Making*), p. 522
- Hands-On Health (*Conflict Resolution*), p. 525
- Real-Life Application (*Advocacy*), p. 532

Chapter 20

Adolescence and the Life Cycle

Lesson 1 Adolescence—Understanding Growth and Change

Lesson 2 Moving Toward Adulthood

Lesson 3 Marriage and Parenting

Lesson 4 Health Through the Life Span

512

MEETING STUDENT DIVERSITY

Language Diversity Use the following suggestions to help students who have difficulty with English:

- Pair English language learners with native speakers of English who can restate the Chapter Summary in language that helps students comprehend important concepts.

- ⌒ Direct auditory learners or those students with language diversity to the *Glencoe Health Audio CD Program.* Available in English and Spanish, this component provides an audio and written summary of the chapter.

- Use photographs, drawings, or magazine clippings to help students visualize the important concepts of the chapter.

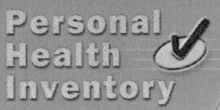

Personal Health Inventory

What's Your Health Status?

Read each statement below and respond by writing *yes*, *no*, or *sometimes* for each item. Write *yes* only for items that you practice regularly or feel sure about.

1. I have loving, caring relationships with other people.

2. I understand the changes my body goes through during adolescence.

3. I have my own ideas, beliefs, and sense of individuality.

4. I am able to think through problems and weigh possible solutions.

5. I have a close family member or friend with whom I can share my innermost feelings.

6. I am involved in and concerned about my community.

7. I am setting goals for my future and have short-term plans to achieve my goals.

8. I am beginning to understand the responsibilities of caring for children.

9. I have a general understanding of the physical, mental/emotional, and social changes that occur in adulthood.

10. Some older adults are part of my circle of relationships.

Keep this personal inventory for review later in the chapter. When you complete the chapter, review your answers again and identify two or three behavior changes you could make to improve your health.

513

Quick*Write*

Using Visuals. Write sentences that describe each of these stages of life: adolescence, early adulthood, middle adulthood, and late adulthood. How can the healthy behaviors you practice now positively affect your health at each stage of adulthood?

INTRODUCING THE CHAPTER

Personal Health Inventory

Have students meet in small groups to read and discuss each of the Personal Health Inventory statements. Have them consider:

- What does this statement reflect about an individual's health?

- Is it most closely related to physical health, mental/emotional health, or social health?

After group discussions, have each student independently write *yes*, *no*, or *sometimes* about each statement. Remind students to keep their inventory responses and to review them at the end of this chapter.

Quick*Write*

Using Visuals Guide students in describing and discussing the people shown in the photograph:

- Which person in the photograph is probably in the life stage of late childhood?

- Which person seems to be in about the same stage of life you are in?

- How would you describe the stage of life of the other people in the picture?

Then have a volunteer read the Quick Write assignment aloud. Give students about five minutes to jot down their responses. If time allows, ask several students to read their responses aloud to the rest of the class.

TECHNOLOGY OPTIONS

MINDJOGGER
VIDEOQUIZ

To preview or review chapter content, you may wish to use the Chapter 20 MindJogger Videoquiz.

Online Resources for the Teacher For a fresh approach to health topics and an in-depth look at health issues, use these online resources found under Teacher Resources at **health.glencoe.com:**

- Block Schedule Lesson Plans
- Technology Projects
- Health Updates

Adolescence—Understanding Growth and Change

1 FOCUS

QUICK START

Invite a volunteer to read the Quick Start assignment aloud, and give students two minutes to write their lists. Then have students read their lists aloud. Record differences on the board, noting how many times each difference is repeated. Which changes did students list most often?

TYING TO PRIOR KNOWLEDGE

Referring to the Quick Start assignment, point out that students already recognize some of the important differences between childhood and adolescence. Explain that, as they study Lesson 1, they will learn more about those differences.

Health Skills Features

"Should High School Classes Start Later in the Day?" p. 518

INTRODUCING VOCABULARY

- Let students meet in groups to compare and discuss what they already know about each of the vocabulary terms. Then have group members check the definitions in the Glossary.

- Ask students to complete the Chapter 20 Study Guide in the *Student Activity Workbook*. 📁

514

Adolescence—Understanding Growth and Change

VOCABULARY
- adolescence
- puberty
- hormones
- sex characteristics
- gametes
- cognition

YOU'LL LEARN TO
- Appraise the significance of physical changes of adolescence.
- Identify the mental, emotional, and social changes that occur during adolescence.
- Recognize the advantages of seeking advice and feedback regarding the use of decision-making and problem-solving skills during adolescence.

QUICK START Adolescence is a time of physical, mental/emotional, and social changes. List three ways that adolescents differ from children.

 Learning to cope with the changes of adolescence can help to make your teen years happy and fulfilling.

The *period from childhood to adulthood,* called **adolescence**, is a time of many exciting challenges and changes. One of the most noticeable of these changes is physical growth. Many of your friends have gotten taller. Voices are changing and bodies are filling out. After infancy, adolescence is the fastest period of growth. Changes are also taking place in your mental/emotional and social life.

Puberty

Sometime between the ages of 12 and 18, individuals go through Erikson's fifth stage of development—**puberty**, *the time when a person begins to develop certain traits of adults of his or her own gender.* Puberty marks the beginning of adolescence. **Hormones** are *chemical substances that are produced in glands and help regulate many of your body's functions.* The male hormone, testosterone, and the female hormones, estrogen and progesterone, are responsible for the changes that affect teens during puberty.

514 **Chapter 20** Adolescence and the Life Cycle

Lesson 1 *Resources*

Teacher Classroom Resources
📁 Concept Mapping Activity 73
📁 Decision-Making Activity 20
📁 Enrichment Activity 20
📁 Guided Reading Activities 73
📁 Health Lab 20
📁 Lesson Plan 73

📁 Lesson Quiz 73
📁 Parent Letter and Activities 20
📁 Reteaching Activity 73

Student Activity Workbook
📁 Applying Health Skills 73
📁 Chapter 20 Study Guide

Multimedia
 Transparency 59

Physical Changes During Adolescence

Growth isn't the only physical change that happens during puberty. Perhaps the most important physical change that takes place is the development of **sex characteristics**, *the traits related to a person's gender*. Some sex characteristics, called primary sex characteristics, are related directly to the production of *reproductive cells*, called **gametes**. The male gametes are **sperm**. In males the production of sperm by the testes begins in puberty. The female's gametes are the **eggs**, or *ova*. All eggs are present at birth, but they don't mature until puberty, when ovulation begins. In females the uterus and ovaries enlarge at this time. Other changes during puberty are those associated with secondary sex characteristics, which are described in **Figure 20.1.**

Look at any group of teens, and you'll notice great variation in the size and shape of adolescents of the same age. This variation can be a source of concern among teens who sometimes compare themselves with others. For example, since boys tend to start their growth spurts later, girls who grow taller than their classmates may feel self-conscious about their height. A boy may be embarrassed when his voice "cracks" because of the growth of the larynx.

Each individual goes through the changes of puberty at his or her own rate. You may experience the changes sooner or later than others, and you may feel uncomfortable about the differences. Just remember that every teen experiences these changes, which are completely normal and will resolve themselves as time passes.

hot link

sperm and **eggs** Learn more about the functions of the male and female reproductive systems in Chapter 18, pages 468 and 474.

Health Minute

Strategies for Avoiding Acne

Acne is caused by a bacterial infection in the oil glands, which can cause pimples.

Tips for dealing with acne:

► Avoid oil-based makeup and greasy lotions.
► Keep your face and hair clean.
► Change washcloths and towels often.
► Don't squeeze or scratch pimples.
► In cases of severe acne, consult your family health care professional or a dermatologist, a doctor who specializes in problems of the skin.

FIGURE 20.1

SECONDARY SEX CHARACTERISTICS

The exact age at which puberty begins is primarily determined by heredity. These changes do not occur overnight but gradually unfold over several months or years.

In females:
- Breasts develop
- Waistline narrows
- Hips widen
- Body fat increases
- Menstruation starts

In males:
- Facial hair appears
- Voice deepens
- Shoulders broaden
- Muscles develop
- Hairline begins to recede

In both:
- Body hair appears
- All permanent teeth grow in
- Perspiration increases

515

---

② TEACH

Reinforcing Concepts

Help students discuss the relationship between puberty and adolescence. Be sure students understand that both involve processes—the process of developing adult traits and the process of transition from childhood to adulthood. **L1**

VISUAL LEARNING

Figure 20.1 Guide students in reading and discussing the information about secondary sex characteristics. Stress that these changes occur gradually and can begin over a wide range of ages. Ask: How might teens feel when they are among the first—or the last—of their peers to experience these physical changes?

Health Minute

Let a volunteer read aloud Strategies for Avoiding Acne, and help students discuss the information. Then guide students in reading and discussing Tips for Dealing with Acne. Ask:

- What are some ways that products for preventing or treating acne are advertised?
- How could teens evaluate those products effectively?

Dealing with Sensitive Issues

Individual Differences Adolescence is a time of physical changes. These changes begin at various times in different individuals and proceed at various rates. Adolescence is also a time of emotional sensitivity. For these reasons, refrain from citing individuals as examples in discussions of adolescent changes. Instead, have students refer to the photographs in the text as examples of individual differences. Prepare a collage of photographs of teens, cut from magazines, and use those photos as points of reference. Include photographs of teens from a wide variety of backgrounds; if possible, include photos of teens with physical disabilities as well.

brain Find more information about the structure of the brain and nervous system in Chapter 15, pages 402–404.

HEALTH
Online

Visit **health.glencoe.com** and link to discoveries about the human brain and its development.

ACTIVE READING

Paraphrasing

Explain to students that paraphrasing—rewriting or restating ideas in your own words—is a useful aid to understanding and remembering information. Have students work with study partners to select and paraphrase important sections from a lesson they are studying. For more strategies, see the *Guided Reading Activities* booklet. 📁

HEALTH
Online

Encourage students to use the online resources to learn more about the human brain and its development. Suggest that they share and discuss their findings in cooperative groups.

Discussing

Help students discuss the importance of brain development during adolescence. Ask: What kinds of problems can you solve now that were beyond your abilities a few years ago? **L1**

Reinforcing Concepts

Have students identify and discuss examples of their own expanding vocabularies. Ask: How can you foster the development of your own language skills and enhance your vocabulary? **L1**

Mental Changes During Adolescence

Not only does your body grow during adolescence, but so does your **brain.** By the time a person reaches the age of six, his or her brain is 95 percent of its adult size. However, the cerebrum—the thinking part of the brain—continues to develop in adolescence, increasing memory and **cognition**, *the ability to reason and think out abstract solutions.* As a child you could see only limited solutions to a problem; but as an adolescent, you become increasingly capable of solving problems in more complex ways. This new ability enables you to anticipate the consequences of a particular action, think logically, and understand different points of view.

As you are making the transition from child to adult, your vocabulary will grow to enable you to express your new ways of thinking. Expanding on the limited language of childhood will help you express yourself better as an adult.

What specific changes take place in your brain that enable you to develop these new skills? Examine **Figure 20.2,** and read what scientific research is uncovering about the brain during adolescence.

FIGURE 20.2

BRAIN DEVELOPMENT IN TEENS

Over the past 25 years, neuroscientists have discovered a great deal about the human brain. Recent imaging techniques have enabled scientists to examine the brains of people throughout their life spans—including the teen years.

Cerebellum
The cerebellum coordinates muscles and physical movement. Recently scientists have found evidence that it is also involved in the coordination of thinking processes. The cerebellum undergoes dramatic growth and change during adolescence.

Amygdala
The amygdala is associated with emotion. New studies suggest that teens use this part of the brain rather than the more analytical frontal cortex that adults use in emotional responses. Scientists think this might explain why teens sometimes react so emotionally.

Frontal Cortex
The frontal cortex is responsible for planning, strategizing, and judgment. The area undergoes a growth spurt when a child is 11 to 12 years of age. This is followed by a growth period when new nerve connections form.

Corpus Callosum
The corpus callosum connects the two sides of the brain. It is thought to be involved in creativity and problem solving. Research suggests that it grows and changes significantly during adolescence.

Source: National Institute of Mental Health

516 **Chapter 20** Adolescence and the Life Cycle

VISUAL LEARNING

Figure 20.2 Divide the class into four groups, and assign each group one of the areas of the brain discussed in the figure. Have group members read and discuss the information for their assigned area and then explain it to the rest of the class.

Cooperative Learning Activity

Teens Portrayed in the Media Have students work in groups to study how the power of the media shapes the behaviors and self-images of teens. What does the media tell adolescents—and other members of society—about how they should look and act? How do those messages conform to, or conflict with, messages about healthful behaviors? Have students work in groups to explore these questions. Ask group members to bring to class advertisements, magazine articles, stories, and photos that typify media portrayal of teens. Have group members discuss the messages these portrayals send and consider how teens can counteract the more negative messages.

Emotional Changes in Adolescence

Teens often experience bursts of energy and waves of strong emotions in addition to the physical and mental changes taking place. Teens may feel that puberty is like being on a roller coaster, with constantly changing feelings that go up and down quickly. You may feel on top of the world one day and down in the dumps the next. The intensity of these feelings can be overwhelming, but it is important to know that every teen experiences these changing feelings. Support and love from family and friends are especially important and can give you a sense of security when you need it. This support can help you become more confident both emotionally and socially.

Social Changes During Adolescence

During adolescence teens also experience social changes. The need to make friends and be accepted into a peer group becomes important. Close friends are a major part of your social experience. Expanding your circle of friends can be rewarding and fun. For example, you are meeting new people in high school and being exposed to different groups. By taking a variety of classes, and through extracurricular activities, you will meet people from many cultural and social backgrounds. Peers may challenge what you stand for, what you believe, and what you think is right or wrong. Good friends, however, will not ask you to do something that goes against your personal values. Strong friendships generally begin when people realize that they have the same goals, experiences, and values.

Developmental Tasks of Adolescence

You have read about some of the physical, mental/emotional, and social changes teens experience. Adolescents don't move through these changes separately. At any given time a teen may be dealing with several of them at once. Robert Havighurst, a well-known sociologist, identified more specific tasks connected to the transition from adolescence to adulthood. Some of these developmental tasks include achieving emotional independence from parents, developing your identity, and adopting a personal value system. You will begin to establish goals for a career, and you will find that practicing appropriate behaviors will help you achieve these goals.

As you recognize the adjustments you are going through, evaluate your progress by asking yourself the questions that follow each task on the next two pages to help you assess your personal growth.

Discovering who you are is a lifelong process. *How can having close friendships be a positive experience in your development?*

Discussing

Help students discuss the emotional changes of adolescence. Ask:

- What makes these emotional changes difficult?
- How can friends help teens deal with emotional swings?
- How can family members help?
- What are some steps teens can take to help themselves deal with these changes? **L1**

Reinforcing Concepts

Ask students to write private health journal entries in response to these questions:

- What are your four most important beliefs or values?
- How would you stand up for your beliefs and values with your friends? **L1**

Activity

Have volunteers use online and/or library sources to learn more about the life and work of Robert Havighurst. Ask them to share their findings in a brief oral report. **L2**

Cooperative Learning

Ask interested students to form cooperative groups to learn more about the theories of Erik Erikson and Robert Havighurst. What are their similarities? What are their major differences? Ask students to discuss their findings with the rest of the class. **L3**

Home and Community

Teen Volunteer Opportunities Help students identify situations outside the school environment where they can make responsible contributions appropriate to their age, talents, and interests. For example, many retirement homes, skilled-care facilities, and hospitals have programs for teen volunteers. Your community may have a local youth job corps that helps young people find part-time jobs or volunteer work. Suggest that students refer to local phone directories, guidance counselors, and social workers for additional sources. Remind students to get permission from home before taking on any volunteer commitment or job.

Exploring Issues

SHOULD HIGH SCHOOL CLASSES START LATER IN THE DAY?

Survey students to find out times they commonly sleep and wake up. Invite them to meet in small groups to read the feature and discuss their views. Then have students gather information about studies on adolescent sleep cycles as well as the success or failure of later start times in schools. In their papers they will need to defend their views about the subject. Remind students to proofread their papers for spelling and grammar. They may also need to develop several drafts before sharing their final drafts with the class. Afterwards, have the groups meet again to discuss how their views may have changed after researching the issue and hearing the views of others.

Discussing

Guide students in discussing the establishment of emotional and psychological independence:

- Why is it important for teens to establish their independence gradually?

- Do you think older teens and young adults continue to benefit from the security of family support? If so, do you believe that means they are not truly independent?

▶ **Establish emotional and psychological independence.** You may move back and forth between the desire for independence and the security of knowing your family supports you. Teens who have an ongoing, open communication with their parents learn the advantages of advice and feedback when making decisions. When parents or guardians discuss and explain situations, rules, or reasons in the decision-making process, teens can learn from their modeling of problem-solving skills. You will discover ways that your family's support and guidance can help you become more emotionally and socially independent. *In what ways is your relationship with your parents or guardians changing for the better?*

Exploring Issues

Should High School Classes Start Later in the Day?

Scientists have found that, in late puberty, the body secretes the sleep-related hormone melatonin at a different time of day than during other stages of life. This means that teens may not be able to fall asleep until very late. They may not get adequate sleep if the school day starts early. Some schools have decided to start school an hour later. Do you think this is a good idea? Here are two points of view.

Viewpoint 1: Alexa J., age 17

For the past couple of years, I haven't been able to fall asleep until late. Then I'm really drowsy in the morning—I have a hard time paying attention in class. Getting an extra hour of sleep would make a real difference. In addition, we wouldn't have to wait in the dark for the school bus. It's time high schools synchronized their clocks with our body clocks!

Viewpoint 2: Ray S., age 16

I don't think starting later in the day is going to change anything. Some people will just stay up later. Also, I have a job in the afternoons. If the school day starts later, we get out later and I lose an hour of work time. Maybe people who have trouble falling asleep should practice a routine to help wind down. My routine seems to work. By the time ten o'clock rolls around, I'm ready to hit the sack.

ACTIVITIES

1. Do you think the benefits of starting school later in the day would make a difference in academic achievement? Do you agree that establishing a routine for falling asleep earlier is the way for teens to get adequate rest?

2. Research the issue of sleep cycles in adolescents. Write a short paper explaining your own views.

518 **Chapter 20** Adolescence and the Life Cycle

School to Work

Education and Careers Adolescents often make choices that will shape the rest of their lives. For example, some leave high school to work full time. Others graduate and immediately take full-time jobs, marry, and/or become parents. Others continue their education in college or business school. Encourage students to survey the number and variety of jobs available for teens and adults without a high school education, with a high school education, with a technical or trade school degree, and with a four-year college degree. Have them gather salary information for each job. Then suggest students create a graphic showing job opportunities and earnings of workers in each category.

► **Develop a personal sense of identity.** Your identity began to develop when you were a child and your parents were your role models. During adolescence you develop confidence and become more independent. *In what ways are you a different person than you were two years ago?*

► **Adopt a personal value system.** When you were a young child, your parents provided you with a set of rules for appropriate and inappropriate behavior. As an adolescent you can begin to assess your own values when they differ from the values expressed by your peers and others. *Have you begun to establish personal beliefs and values that enhance your health and well-being? Are you acting in ways that support those standards?*

► **Establish adult vocational goals.** The teen years are the time during which you begin to identify your vocational goals. *Have you set long-term goals and identified steps to reach your goals?*

► **Develop control over your behavior.** Adolescents make decisions daily about whether to participate in risk behaviors that may harm their health. Considering your values and your short-term and long-term goals will give you a firm idea on the importance of making healthy decisions and avoiding risky situations. *Consider two recent events that challenged you to show emotional maturity and avoid a risk behavior.*

Explore opportunities and find ideas to help you establish educational and vocational goals. *Where can you get information that will help you make important decisions about your future?*

 Lesson 1 *Review*

Reviewing Facts and Vocabulary

1. What is *adolescence*?
2. Describe and appraise two physical changes that take place in males and two that take place in females during adolescence.
3. What is *cognition*?

Thinking Critically

4. **Synthesizing.** Choose one developmental task of adolescence. Explain what steps you might take to accomplish this task.
5. **Analyzing.** Summarize the advantages of seeking advice and feedback as you make decisions and solve problems during adolescence.

Applying Health Skills

Analyzing Influences. Make a two-column chart. In the first column, list changes other than physical changes that you have observed in yourself since you became an adolescent. In the second column, identify any person, event, or idea that influenced the change.

TECHNOLOGY *OPTION*

SPREADSHEETS Making a table with a spreadsheet program will help you organize and edit your list. See **health.glencoe.com** for tips on spreadsheets.

Lesson 1 Adolescence—Understanding Growth and Change **519**

Community Involvement

Ask a pair of volunteers to learn about local career fairs. When and where are they held? How can students arrange to attend? Let the volunteers share this information with the rest of the class. If an upcoming fair seems appropriate for a large portion of your school's students, have a group make posters with information about the fair and display them in the school's hallways.

③ ASSESS

EVALUATING THE LESSON

Assign and discuss the Lesson 1 Review; then administer, grade, and discuss Lesson Quiz 73 in the TCR.

RETEACHING

- Have students work with partners to list the physical, mental/emotional, and social changes that take place during adolescence.

- Ask students to complete Reteaching Activity 73 in the TCR.

ENRICHMENT

Have students write an analysis of the ways in which a teen in a current TV show or movie demonstrates working on the developmental tasks of adolescence.

 Lesson 1 *Review*

Answers to Reviewing Facts and Vocabulary

1. The period between childhood and adulthood.
2. Answers will vary but should include changes noted in Figure 20.1.
3. The ability to reason and think out abstract solutions.

Answers to Thinking Critically

4. Answers will vary.
5. Answers should indicate that physical changes during adolescence could affect how a person thinks about himself or herself and how he or she interacts with others.

④ CLOSE

Have each student identify a new fact he or she learned about growth and development during adolescence.

Moving Toward Adulthood

1 FOCUS

Let a volunteer read the Quick Start assignment aloud, and give students several minutes to write their responses. Then encourage students to share and discuss their paragraphs.

TYING TO PRIOR KNOWLEDGE

Ask students to recall some of the changes involved in adolescence; emphasize that these changes prepare an individual for adulthood. Then explain that, in this lesson, students will learn more about the early stage of adulthood.

Health Skills Features

"Exploring Careers," p. 522

DECISION MAKING

INTRODUCING VOCABULARY

- In a brief class discussion, let volunteers share their ideas about the meanings of the three vocabulary terms. Then have students use the Glossary to look up the definition of each term.

- Ask students to complete the Chapter 20 Study Guide in the *Student Activity Workbook*.

Moving Toward Adulthood

VOCABULARY

physical maturity
emotional maturity
emotional intimacy

YOU'LL LEARN TO

- Evaluate positive and negative effects of relationships with peers, family, and friends on physical and emotional health.

- Identify and explain the developmental tasks of adulthood.

QUICK START Teens spend a lot of time thinking about what they'll be like when they are adults. Write a short paragraph that begins "My vision of myself as an adult is . . . ."

 Physical maturity is just one component of adulthood. *What other changes took place as this individual became a healthy, emotionally mature adult?*

Many of the changes that occur in adolescence prepare you for the role of an adult. What does it mean to be an adult? Clearly adulthood isn't something that suddenly appears on the morning of your twenty-first birthday. There is much more than chronological age to be considered. One term often used when defining adulthood is *maturity.* Maturity has several components, including both physical and emotional aspects.

Physical and Emotional Maturity

In late adolescence or the early twenties, most people reach **physical maturity**, *the state at which the physical body and all its organs are fully developed.* However, an adult physique doesn't mean that you are an adult. To be an adult, you'll need to develop emotionally.

Emotional maturity is *the state at which the mental and emotional capabilities of an individual are fully developed.* An emotionally healthy person not only has a strong personal identity but also has developed close relationships. The individual possesses positive values and goals. He or she has the ability to give and receive love, the ability to face reality and deal with it, and the capacity to relate positively to life experiences and learn from them. Peers, family, and friends can make a positive contribution by strengthening your resiliency and helping you get through difficult and challenging times.

Lesson 2 *Resources*

Teacher Classroom Resources

- Concept Mapping Activity 74
- Guided Reading Activities 74
- Lesson Plan 74
- Lesson Quiz 74
- Reteaching Activity 74

Student Activity Workbook

- Applying Health Skills 74
- Chapter 20 Study Guide

Multimedia

- Transparency 60

Considering the Entire Life Cycle

Human growth and development have intrigued many people over the years. Psychologist Erik Erikson's theory of social development covers the entire life span. Each stage of adulthood is characterized by its own accomplishments as shown in **Figure 20.3.**

Young Adulthood

Erikson's stages of life illustrate that as a person progresses through life, his or her goals continue to evolve. Although physical growth occurs automatically, emotional maturity develops as each individual focuses on four major aspects of life: personal independence, occupational choices, intimate relationships, and contributions to society.

FIGURE 20.3

ERIKSON'S STAGES OF ADULTHOOD

The adult years are made up of three major stages. Each stage is associated with a goal that involves a person's relationships with other people.

Stage 6 – Young Adulthood 19 to 40 years	Stage 7 – Middle Adulthood 40 to 65 years	Stage 8 – Late Adulthood 65 years to death
Goal: To develop intimacy **Description:** Person tries to develop close personal relationships. **Positive Outcomes:** Individual can form close relationships and share with others; families are started. **Negative Outcomes:** Individual may fear commitment, feel isolated, and be unable to depend on others.	**Goal:** To develop a sense of having contributed to society **Description:** Individual looks outside self and cares for others, often through grandparenting or volunteering. **Positive Outcomes:** Individual helps others and the next generation. **Negative Outcomes:** Person may remain self-centered and have little involvement with others.	**Goal:** To feel satisfied with one's life **Description:** Person tries to understand meaning of own life. **Positive Outcomes:** Adult will have a sense of fulfillment and satisfaction with life choices. **Negative Outcomes:** Person may feel disappointment with life's achievements.

Lesson 2 Moving Toward Adulthood **521**

Myths & Reality

MYTH Once you reach adulthood, you have the freedom to do whatever you want.

REALITY Being an adult involves being responsible to yourself and to others. Often, adults are responsible for being supportive and caring as well as for the security and well-being of their spouses and children. They may look back on their teen years as a "carefree" time.

MYTH Since it is legal to buy and drink alcohol at the age of 21, it must be a good idea to start drinking then.

REALITY The health risks of alcohol continue to be dangerous, even after you reach the age of 21.

② TEACH

Discussing

Let students share their responses to these questions:

• What is maturity?

• How can you tell whether you are mature?

• How do you judge whether another person is mature? **L1**

Explaining

Explain how the developmental tasks of adulthood differ from many of the tasks that are achieved in earlier stages of life. The developmental tasks of adulthood take longer to achieve. They are less related to physical maturation and more involved with learning and gaining insight. **L1**

VISUAL LEARNING

Figure 20.3 Have students meet in small groups to read and discuss the information about Erikson's Stages of Adulthood.

• How are the three stages related?

• What are the most important differences among them?

Community Involvement

Have each student interview at least three adults about their careers, focusing on when and how career choices were made and (in some cases) altered. What—if anything—would the adults have done differently? Then have students meet in groups to discuss what they have learned from these interviews. **L2**

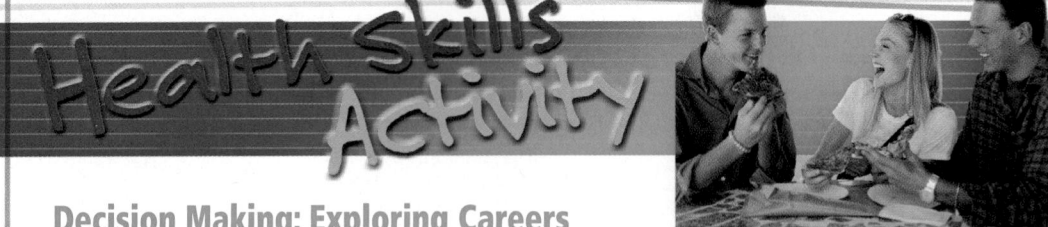

Health Skills Activity

EXPLORING CAREERS

DECISION MAKING

NHES Standard 6 Students will demonstrate the ability to use goal-setting and decision-making skills to enhance health.

Objectives

- Identify and explain the developmental task of making an occupational choice.
- Identify decision-making skills that promote individual health.

Motivator

Have volunteers explain how they have taken steps to investigate possible careers.

Teaching Strategies

1. Point out that Jason's decision is not simply how he will spend his summer. His major decision, as he progresses towards adulthood, is whether he will be influenced by his peers or by his own values and beliefs.
2. Have volunteers share and discuss their decisions with the class.

✓Assessment

Using a rubric, student work should provide comprehensive evidence of the following criteria to achieve the highest score:

✔ clear description of the situation
✔ several options with possible outcomes of each
✔ influence of values on possible decisions
✔ health-enhancing decision and an evaluation of it

Health Skills Activity

Decision Making: Exploring Careers

"I just had a talk with the school counselor," Jason says to his friends over lunch. "He gave me tips on how to decide on a career. I'm glad summer is almost here so I can get started!"

"You mean you're going to spend your summer exploring careers?" Kim asks. "Just what did the counselor say?"

Jason replies, "Well, because I'm interested in health care, the counselor advised that I volunteer at the hospital. In fact, the hospital has a Medical Explorers Club that I can get involved in."

"What's the rush?" Lonnie asks, "You've got plenty of time to do these things, right, Kim?" "Lonnie's right," Kim agrees. "Just take it easy this summer and hang out with us. What's your hurry, anyway?"

Jason wonders what he should do.

What Would You Do?

Apply the six steps of the decision-making process to Jason's dilemma. Identify a health-promoting decision that will positively affect Jason's future.

1. State the situation.
2. List the options.
3. Weigh the possible outcomes.
4. Consider values.
5. Make a decision and act.
6. Evaluate the decision.

Developing Personal Independence

The desire for independence during adolescence is a part of the quest for *self-actualization,* which includes developing one's capabilities to the fullest. When leaving home or beginning to work full-time, young adults may substitute the emotional support of friends for the support they once received from parents. As they mature, however, they become more self-sufficient.

Making Occupational Choices

As a teen you probably are giving some thought to what you want your life to be like when you are an adult. Part of that thought process may include your ideas about a career or occupation. Your ideas may be influenced by a part-time job, a role model, or the amount of education beyond high school required for a specific career.

522 **Chapter 20** Adolescence and the Life Cycle

Curriculum Connections

English/Language Arts Have students select a TV show or current movie that focuses on the lives of young adults. Let them meet in groups to discuss how accurately the characters portray young adulthood. Ask: What are the indications of emotional maturity? How do the characters demonstrate personal independence? How do they contribute to society?

Have each student select one character from the show or movie and write an essay explaining how the character's actions and dialogue could be revised to more accurately portray the real lives of young adults. Encourage students to develop several drafts of their writing before sharing their final drafts with the class.

Establishing Intimate Relationships

As individuals grow into adulthood, they begin to develop emotional intimacy with other individuals. **Emotional intimacy** is *the ability to experience a caring, loving relationship with another person with whom you can share your innermost feelings.* During this time, some people may have several successive romantic relationships. This may result in marriage when individuals are ready for a permanent commitment. Individuals who are occupied with establishing a career or determining their own identity may decide to seek romantic relationships later or not at all. Some people choose to remain single. Practicing abstinence until marriage gives a person freedom from sexually transmitted disease and maintains options for a healthy future.

Contributing to Society

Another task of young adulthood includes determining where and how a person fits into society. You have probably already developed some of your own political ideas and religious views. Voting in elections and taking part in community projects is a way of increasing self-esteem and confidence and of contributing to society in a positive and effective manner.

 Forming intimate relationships allows two people to spend time together enjoying shared interests. *How might a close, committed relationship help a person throughout later adulthood?*

 Lesson 2 *Review*

Reviewing Facts and Vocabulary

1. When do most people reach physical maturity?
2. What is the difference between *emotional maturity* and *emotional intimacy*?
3. What are the four developmental tasks of adulthood?

Thinking Critically

4. **Analyzing.** What does Erickson say is the goal of young adulthood? Why might this goal be the most challenging? Explain your reasoning.
5. **Synthesizing.** Evaluate positive and negative ways that relationships with peers, family, and friends might affect a person's physical and emotional health.

Applying Health Skills

Goal Setting. Identify two occupations of interest to you. Using the goal-setting process discussed in Chapter 2, list steps you can take as an adolescent to prepare for each occupation. Share these steps with a parent or your school counselor, and incorporate into your plan any additional steps they suggest.

INTERNET RESOURCES Use the Internet to find information about different careers. See Career Corner at **health.glencoe.com**.

Lesson 2 Moving Toward Adulthood **523**

Discussing

Ask students how contributing to society is related to making occupational choices. Ask: Which kinds of work do you think are most likely to give individuals a sense of making an important contribution? ⬛

3 ASSESS

EVALUATING THE LESSON

Assign and discuss the Lesson 2 Review; then administer, grade, and discuss Lesson Quiz 74 in the TCR. 📁

RETEACHING

- Have students review the four aspects of emotional maturity by identifying examples of each.
- Ask students to complete Reteaching Activity 74 in the TCR. 📁

ENRICHMENT

Discuss with students the concept of a generation gap, differences in ideas and perceptions based largely on differences in age and experience. Have students work in cooperative groups to list specific examples of a generation gap between themselves and older individuals. Have them write a second list of steps they can take to help bridge that gap.

4 CLOSE

Have students review, discuss, and revise their Quick Start paragraphs.

 Lesson 2 *Review*

Answers to Reviewing Facts and Vocabulary

1. In late adolescence or their early 20s.
2. See pages 520 and 523 for definitions.
3. Developing personal independence, making occupational choices, establishing intimate relationships, and contributing to society.

Answers to Thinking Critically

4. The development of intimacy with another person. Many individuals choose to focus on their career or their own identity.
5. Possible answer: Family support helps a person's physical growth and maturity. Positive values, caring, and intimacy help a person grow and mature.

Marriage and Parenting

①FOCUS

Marriage and Parenting

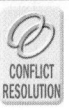

QUICK START Have students work with partners to list five responsibilities of parenthood. Then encourage students to share and discuss their ideas.

TYING TO PRIOR KNOWLEDGE

Ask students: How do you think marriage and parenthood fit into the stage of young adulthood? Tell students they will explore that question more fully as they study Lesson 3.

Health Skills Features

"Skills for a Healthy Marriage," p. 525

CONFLICT RESOLUTION

INTRODUCING VOCABULARY

- Write the following words on the board: *commit, marry, adjust, direct, condition.* Ask students to discuss the relationship between the words and the vocabulary terms. Then have students look up the terms in the Glossary.

- Ask students to complete the Chapter 20 Study Guide in the *Student Activity Workbook.* 📁

VOCABULARY
commitment
marital adjustment
adoption
self-directed
unconditional love

YOU'LL LEARN TO
- Distinguish between a dating relationship and a marriage.
- Demonstrate how married couples use effective communication skills in maintaining healthy relationships.
- Describe the roles of parents, grandparents, and other family members in promoting a healthy family.

QUICK START Marriage and parenting involve many responsibilities. List five responsibilities of parenthood.

When two people decide to marry, they sometimes attend premarital counseling sessions to build skills for a healthy, lasting relationship. *Why is making a commitment for life important to a successful marriage?*

According to the U.S. Census Bureau, nearly 9 of every 10 people expect to marry in their lifetime. Although close to half of first marriages end in divorce, most individuals who marry begin with the intent of making a lifetime commitment. A **commitment** is *a promise or a pledge* that a couple makes to each other. Marriage is a long-term commitment.

Marriage

People marry for different reasons. Most people marry because they fall in love and are ready to enter into a lasting, intimate relationship. Couples in a marriage are able to share togetherness and give each other support in hard times as well as good times.

Choosing Marriage

There are several differences between a dating relationship and a marriage. When two individuals understand that marriage is their eventual goal, their relationship becomes more thoughtful, they make deeper commitments to each other, and they consider long-term consequences when making decisions. If an individual has any doubts or questions about a partner's reasons for marrying, these questions should be fully explored before the marriage takes place.

524 **Chapter 20** Adolescence and the Life Cycle

Lesson 3 *Resources*

Teacher Classroom Resources
📁 Concept Mapping Activity 75
📁 Guided Reading Activities 75
📁 Lesson Plan 75
📁 Lesson Quiz 75
📁 Reteaching Activity 75

Student Activity Workbook
📁 Applying Health Skills 75
📁 Chapter 20 Study Guide
Multimedia
 Transparency 61

Hands-On Health ACTIVITY

Conflict Resolution Skills for a Healthy Marriage

Good communication is critical for a successful marriage. Spouses who share feelings and express concerns in a respectful way are more likely to settle conflicts effectively. In this activity you will role-play a solution to a challenging marital situation using good communication and conflict resolution skills.

What You'll Need

- scenarios provided by your teacher
- paper and pencils or pens

What You'll Do

1. Each group will be given a scenario that poses a potential challenge to a marriage. Topics may include moving because of a spouse's job, struggling to pay the mortgage, or caring for a sick relative.

2. Using content from this chapter, brainstorm several ways that the conflict can be resolved successfully. For example, for moving because of a spouse's job the couple may work together to find a new home both spouses love; budget for long-distance phone calls; agree to visit old friends and family often.

3. Plan a dialogue or skit showing ways the situation can be resolved. Use conflict resolution skills that include "I" messages, listening skills, and agreeing on a solution that benefits both sides. Present your skit to the class.

Apply and Conclude

Write a paragraph explaining what you have learned about the importance of good communication and problem-solving skills in a marital relationship.

Successful Marriages

Making a life commitment is only the first step in a successful marriage. **Marital adjustment**—*how well a person adjusts to marriage and to his or her spouse*—depends on these factors:

▶ **Good communication.** Couples need to be able to share their feelings and express their needs and concerns. Couples in well-adjusted marriages know how to demonstrate affection.

▶ **Emotional maturity.** People who are emotionally healthy try to understand their partners' needs and are willing to compromise. They don't always think of themselves first; they consider what is best for the relationship.

▶ **Similar values and interests.** When couples share attitudes about the importance of good health, religious beliefs, cultural heritage, family, and friendships, they spend more time together, which strengthens a marriage.

Lesson 3 Marriage and Parenting **525**

MEETING STUDENT DIVERSITY

Cultural Perspectives In some cultures, marriage and the establishment of a family are considered too important to be carried out by young people. Marriages are arranged for the economic, social, and political advantage of the family. Among some cultural groups, arranged marriages preserve traditional values—values that might be lost if children married outside the group. Ask interested students to research marriage traditions in various cultures and to share their findings with the rest of the class. Then guide the class in discussing these various approaches to marriage. What are the advantages and benefits of each?

---

2 TEACH

Hands-On Health

CONFLICT RESOLUTION SKILLS FOR A HEALTHY MARRIAGE

NHES Standard 5 Students will demonstrate the ability to use interpersonal communication skills to enhance health.

Objectives

- Demonstrate strategies for communicating needs, wants, and emotions.
- Demonstrate communication skills in building and maintaining a healthy marriage relationship.

Motivator

Ask: What factors do you think are necessary for a successful marriage? List answers on the board and point out that effective communication skills are necessary to resolve marriage conflicts.

Teaching Strategies

1. Prepare the scenarios ahead of time and make them as specific as possible.
2. Have students work in groups of mixed gender.

✓ Assessment

Using a rubric, student work should provide comprehensive evidence of the following criteria to achieve the highest score:

✔ interaction between "spouses"
✔ respectful tone of voice
✔ appropriate language (without "put downs")
✔ strategies such as "I" statements and standing up for one's beliefs

Discussing

Have students share their responses to these questions:

- What are some reasons that people choose to marry?
- What do you consider the best reasons for choosing marriage?
- What might lead individuals to remain single?

Reinforcing Concepts

Ask students how long they think the period of marital adjustment might last. Help them recognize that, since individuals continue to grow and change, some aspects of adjustment can last throughout marriage; the factors that support a successful adjustment definitely remain important throughout marriage.

Activity

Have each student interview a couple that has been married at least five years. Students should ask couples about the skills they consider most important in making their marriage work. Then have students write paragraphs, presenting the conclusions they have drawn. Remind students to proofread their paragraphs for spelling and grammatical errors. You may also need to remind them to keep names out of their paragraphs.

Discussing

Help students discuss the issues that commonly cause problems in marriages. Ask:

- How do you think couples can prepare for these problems before they marry?
- What steps do you think couples can take to deal with these problems after marriage?

hotlink

conflict resolution Find out what strategies can help in solving a conflict by reading Chapter 10, page 264.

Teens have the responsibility to finish school and set personal goals before considering marriage. *What added responsibilities come with a marriage commitment?*

Resolving Conflicts in Marriage

Even in the best marriages, conflict occasionally results because no two people will always agree on everything. Some common issues that cause problems in marriages include the following:

▶ Differences in spending and saving habits

▶ Conflicting loyalties involving family and friends

▶ Lack of communication

▶ Lack of intimacy

▶ Jealousy, infidelity, or lack of attention

▶ Decisions about having children and arranging child care

▶ Abusive tendencies or attitudes

In a successful marriage both partners respect, trust, and care for each other. Conflicts are resolved fairly without damaging the self-esteem of either partner. Couples can reduce the impact of conflict by developing good communication and **conflict resolution** skills. Sometimes resolving marital conflict requires that a couple seek counseling.

Teen Marriages

One of the most important factors for a successful marriage is maturity. Emotional maturity enables partners to deal with the problems and decisions of marriage. Most teens are still struggling to figure out their own identity and to set goals for their own future. It is unlikely that they have had a chance to determine what is important to them or what they want in a marriage partner. That's one reason that about 60 percent of marriages involving teens end in divorce. Statistics from the CDC indicate a high probability that a teen marriage will end in its first few years.

Once in a marriage relationship, teens begin to realize that they have increased responsibilities that may interfere with personal freedoms and educational or career goals. They also recognize that they do not have enough life experience to make this important and lasting life choice. Overwhelming financial pressures add stress to the relationship. Marriage difficulties arise as the newness wears off and teens recognize the responsibilities required to make the marriage succeed.

Curriculum Connections

Math Have students use online or library sources to gather statistics on teen marriage in your city, county, or state. In a recent year, how many teens married? How many couples who married as teens divorced? Have group members work together to plan and draw a graph that summarizes their findings.

Drama/Language Arts Ask interested students to plan a short play about teens considering marriage. Students may want to include dialogue between the couple, between the prospective bride and her friends, and between the prospective groom and his friends. Have students practice and then perform their play.

Responsibilities of Parenthood

After marriage, many couples decide to start a family. Some couples choose to adopt a child. **Adoption** is *the legal process of taking a child of other parents as one's own.* Mature couples also may make a choice to bring foster children into their lives. Becoming a parent can be an exciting experience. Most parents find raising a child to be both challenging and rewarding, and they take great joy in loving and caring for their children. Parents watch with pride and joy as the child grows and develops within a healthy family environment. Parenting is a serious, ongoing responsibility. Parents must provide protection, food, clothing, shelter, education, and medical care. Parenting also involves providing guidance, instilling values, setting limits, and giving unconditional love.

Providing Guidance

Parenting involves providing guidance and teaching children that each individual is responsible for his or her own successes and failures. One way to do this is by encouraging children and helping them develop a sense of pride in their accomplishments. Another aspect of parenthood is guiding and protecting children while teaching them to make their own decisions. Watching children learn to get along with others and solve their own problems is a satisfying experience for a parent. When parents are joined by the extended family—grandparents and other family members—in providing good examples and role models, the joy of raising children becomes a shared experience. When children see family members interacting in a mature, loving, and caring manner, they are more likely to grow up to be healthy and productive.

Instilling Values

Parents with a strong commitment to their value system and spirituality wish to pass on these important aspects of life to their children. As children grow, they develop a set of *values,* the system of beliefs and standards of conduct that they find important and that will guide the way they live. Values help children develop strong character and resiliency to resist the negative influences they may encounter. Parents who teach positive values help their children become happy, mature adults.

Did You Know ?

For teens the challenges of parenthood are especially difficult. The consequences of teen parenthood include
- financial problems.
- restraints on educational and career plans.
- emotional stress.
- limitations on personal and social life.

▼ A child can bring pride and joy, but he or she also brings new responsibilities. *What responsibilities does this father have to his new child?*

Discussing

Guide students in discussing the problems of teen marriages. Let them describe teen marriages they have seen depicted in TV shows and movies. Ask: How realistic do you think those depictions are? **L1**

Critical Thinking

Have students share their responses to this question: When do you think the responsibilities of parenthood end? Encourage students to explain and defend their responses. **L1**

Discussing

Have students recall the factors involved in marital adjustment. Ask: How do you think a couple's adjustment to marriage is affected when they have to adjust to parenthood at the same time? **L1**

Cooperative Learning

Ask students to bring to class photographs from magazines showing parents and their young children. Then have students meet in groups to discuss what the pictures portray.

- Which aspects of parenting are emphasized?
- Which responsibilities of parenthood are shown?
- Why do you think most pictures do not emphasize the responsibilities of parenthood? **L2**

More About...

Teen Parenthood Having a child as a teen poses serious risks:

- Teen mothers are less likely than others to complete their educations. Less than one-third of women who have their first baby before the age of 18 ever complete high school.

- Teen pregnancy is closely linked to poverty. In one recent study, more than half of all teenage mothers began receiving welfare within five years of the birth of their first child.
- Babies of teen mothers have a higher rate of low birth weight than babies born to young adult mothers.

Discussing

Help students discuss the relationship between unconditional love and setting limits. How can parents place restrictions on their children's behavior and, at the same time, show those children love without limitation? **L1**

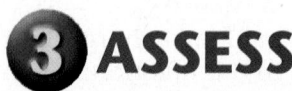

3 ASSESS

EVALUATING THE LESSON

Assign and discuss the Lesson 3 Review; then administer, grade, and discuss Lesson Quiz 75 in the TCR. 📁

RETEACHING

- Have students work with partners to list, in their own words, the factors that affect marital adjustment and the responsibilities of parenthood.

- Ask students to complete Reteaching Activity 75 in the TCR. 📁

ENRICHMENT

Have students research premarital counseling. Who usually offers this form of counseling? What kinds of issues are addressed? Have students write short essays summarizing their findings. Remind them to proofread their writing. They may need to develop several drafts before handing in a final, error-free draft.

4 CLOSE

Have each student complete the following sentence: *Before I get married, I want to . . .*

Unconditional love is an important responsibility of parenthood. *How can unconditional love contribute to a healthy childhood experience?*

Setting Limits

One way parents can help their children develop positive values is to set limits and establish a clearly defined set of rules. When children learn limits, they become **self-directed**, or *able to make correct decisions about behavior when adults are not present to enforce rules*. When children must be disciplined, parents should follow these guidelines:

▶ Act quickly so that children understand the link between misbehavior and consequences.

▶ Distinguish between the behavior and the child so that children think of themselves as people who sometimes misbehave rather than as bad children.

▶ Be consistent with rules and consequences so that children can easily establish a connection between certain behaviors and resulting consequences. Praise positive behavior.

Giving Unconditional Love

One of the most important responsibilities of parenthood is providing children with **unconditional love**, *love without limitation or qualification*. Parents need to show their children love at all times—whether the child is well-behaved, happy, sad, sick, or afraid. Receiving unconditional love helps a child thrive.

▶ Lesson 3 Review

Reviewing Facts and Vocabulary

1. What commitment do couples make to each other when they marry?

2. What are two communication skills that help determine a successful marital adjustment?

3. Describe how parents, grandparents, and others contribute to a healthy family.

Thinking Critically

4. **Analyzing.** Explain why choosing to become a parent is one of the most serious decisions a person can make.

5. **Synthesizing.** Distinguish between a marriage and a dating relationship. Discuss ways that responsibilities of marriage are different from dating.

528 **Chapter 20** Adolescence and the Life Cycle

Health Skills Activity

Advocacy. List important techniques and responsibilities involved in raising a healthy, happy child. Create a pamphlet of parenting tips for married couples thinking of starting a family.

TECHNOLOGY *O P T I O N*

INTERNET RESOURCES Learn more online about parenting. See health.glencoe.com for Web Links that offer tips for parents and families.

▶ Lesson 3 Review

Answers to Reviewing Facts and Vocabulary

1. They promise to spend their lives together and care for each other throughout their lives.

2. To be able to share their feelings and express their needs and concerns.

3. They provide examples as role models and share in loving and caring.

Answers to Thinking Critically

4. Possible answer: He or she is deciding to be responsible for another individual who is totally dependent on others.

5. Marriage requires deeper commitment and has long-term consequences. Dating is a time to explore goals and reasons for being together.

Health Through the Life Span

VOCABULARY
transitions
empty-nest syndrome
integrity

YOU'LL LEARN TO

- Describe the physical, mental, and social transitions that occur during middle and later adulthood.

- Identify and analyze lifestyle behaviors that promote health and prevent disease throughout the life span.

- Analyze the influence of laws, policies, and practices on health-related issues, including those related to disease prevention.

 QUICK START Think about some happy, healthy older adults you know. What characteristics do they share? How do these characteristics contribute to their positive attitude?

If you had been born in the United States in 1900, your life expectancy would have been only about 45 years. Today life expectancy in the United States is almost 77 years, and it continues to rise. What has contributed to this increase? Part of the answer is the advances in health care that occurred throughout the twentieth century. Along with those advances is the public's increased awareness about the importance of practicing healthful behaviors at all ages.

Middle Adulthood

In the first three lessons of this chapter, you read about the many changes that take place during adolescence and young adult-hood. Erikson's seventh developmental stage is middle adulthood, encompassing the ages from 40 to 65. These years are often full of **transitions**, *critical changes that occur at all stages of life.* It can be a time of family and individual accomplishments, such as children graduating from college, the arrival of the first grandchild, achievement of a satisfying career goal, or recognition of the individual's contributions to community and friends. Enjoyment of these accomplishments is more fulfilling when people are in good health.

1900	47.3
1920	54.1
1940	62.9
1960	69.7
1980	73.7
2000	76.9

10 20 30 40 50 60 70 80
Average Age

 The average life expectancy in the United States has almost doubled in the last 100 years. *Why has life expectancy risen?*

Lesson 4 Health Through the Life Span **529**

Lesson 4

Health Through the Life Span

1 FOCUS

 QUICK START Give students a few minutes to list the characteristics of happy, healthy older adults they know. Then have students share their ideas and discuss how the listed characteristics contribute to the positive attitudes of these older adults.

TYING TO PRIOR KNOWLEDGE

Ask students to review, briefly, what they have learned about the earlier stages in the life span. Explain that, as they study Lesson 4, they will learn more about the later stages of life: middle and late adulthood.

Health Skills Features

"Government Spending for Health Research," p. 532 ADVOCACY

INTRODUCING VOCABULARY

- Divide the class into three groups, and assign each group one of the vocabulary terms. Have group members look up the term in the Glossary. Then have them explain the term to the rest of the class.

- Ask students to complete the Chapter 20 Study Guide in the *Student Activity Workbook.* 📁

Lesson 4 Resources

Teacher Classroom Resources
📁 Concept Mapping Activity 76
📁 Cross-Curriculum Activity 20
📁 Current Health Issues 20
📁 Guided Reading Activities 76
📁 Lesson Plan 76

📁 Lesson Quiz 76
📁 Reteaching Activity 76

Student Activity Workbook
📁 Applying Health Skills 76
📁 Chapter 20 Study Guide

② TEACH

Discussing

Let students share their own ideas about middle adulthood. Ask:

- How do you imagine yourself in middle adulthood?
- What do you see yourself doing?
- What challenges might you face in this part of your life?
- What benefits might you enjoy? **L1**

Reinforcing Concepts

Ask students what kinds of transitions are part of adolescence. How do these transitions compare with the transitions of middle adulthood? **L1**

Cooperative Learning

Have students find and read magazine articles that deal with middle adulthood (often called middle age). Then have students meet in groups to discuss the information and advice in the articles. How accurate do they consider the information? How healthful do they consider the advice? **L2**

VISUAL LEARNING

Figure 20.4 Let students meet with partners to read and discuss the information in Figure 20.4.

Physical Transitions

Change doesn't stop when adolescence ends; it continues throughout the life span. People in middle adulthood experience physical changes as their bodies begin to age. Skin loses its elasticity, the functioning of the body's organs slows, and the body's immune system becomes less effective. Females experience menopause around ages 45–55. This is the stopping of ovulation and menstruation, after which a female cannot get pregnant. Hormonal changes during menopause often cause physical effects that may include hot flashes.

FIGURE 20.4

KEEPING YOUR BODY HEALTHY THROUGH THE LIFE SPAN

Many of the health habits you develop as an adolescent will affect the way you feel as you grow older. Practicing healthful behaviors and avoiding tobacco, alcohol, and other drugs during your teen years will reduce your risk of developing serious problems such as diabetes or heart disease in the future.

Eyes Eyesight changes with age. The eyes have more difficulty bringing images into focus. Eating plenty of leafy green vegetables, controlling blood pressure, and avoiding tobacco use promotes eye health. Sunglasses protect your eyes from damaging UV rays.

Brain Scientists say that like your muscles, your brain needs exercise to stay healthy. Read and keep learning to exercise your brain.

Mouth Teeth and gums can become decayed and diseased without proper care. Brush and floss regularly. See a dentist every six months.

Ears Loud sounds take a toll on your hearing. Limit your exposure to noise. Keep the stereo at a low volume. Use earplugs when operating noisy equipment.

Heart Lack of physical activity and a diet high in saturated fats are known risk factors for heart disease. Engaging in regular aerobic activity and choosing foods low in saturated fats greatly reduces the risk of heart disease.

Muscles and Joints Arthritis affects half of those over age 65. Maintaining a healthy weight and being physically active can help keep joints healthy and pain free.

Skin Aging skin may become wrinkled, spotted, and dry. Reduce exposure to harmful UV rays by covering up and wearing a sunscreen. Avoid using tanning beds.

530 Chapter 20 Adolescence and the Life Cycle

School to Work

Age Discrimination on the Job Even as the percentage of older adults has grown, the media continue to report that some workers in middle and late adulthood have faced discrimination in the workplace. Although laws prohibit age discrimination, reports indicate that some older workers have been laid off or have had difficulty finding jobs. Older job seekers often include women reentering the workforce after raising children, divorcing, or being widowed. They also include workers whose jobs had been cut or who had been terminated. Have students research age discrimination in the workplace. They may consider: How widespread is age discrimination? How can it continue in spite of laws prohibiting it? Let students summarize their findings in oral reports.

Research indicates that most people who have practiced healthy behaviors such as weight management, nutritious eating, and regular physical activity as teens and young adults find these changes to be less severe. Adults who have developed lifelong healthy habits and continue to be active stay healthy by eating low-fat, high-fiber diets, and avoiding tobacco, alcohol, and other drugs. Strength training has been proven to provide significant benefits to most adults. Those benefits include increasing muscle mass, preserving bone density, and protecting the major joints from injury. **Figure 20.4** on page 530 describes some healthy behaviors you can begin now to reduce your risk of developing the illnesses and disabilities that historically have been common among older adults.

Mental Transitions

Just as exercise strengthens the muscles of people at any age, mental activities strengthen the brain. Solving puzzles, reading, or playing board games provides mental stimulation. An adult who "exercises" his or her brain remains mentally active. Learning is a lifelong pursuit. At midlife many adults start new careers, return to school, and learn new hobbies. The use of computers gives older adults opportunities to broaden their access to information. People reach middle adulthood with a great deal of knowledge and experience, which they can use to pursue new interests.

Emotional Transitions

The emotional transitions for some people in middle adulthood are much like the "growing pains" of adolescence. Most people have by this time experienced many of life's greatest joys, including children, pride in their personal accomplishments, as well as some disappointments. The midlife crisis for some individuals results from questions and concerns about whether they have met their goals, feel loved and valued, or have made a positive difference in the lives of others. Keeping the health triangle in balance and continuing to set goals along the way will help people avoid these concerns.

Social Transitions

Most social transitions during middle adulthood focus on the family. Many adults of this age are faced with the death of a parent or the need to adjust to their children's growing up and leaving home. *The feelings of sadness or loneliness that accompany children's leaving home and entering adulthood* is called **empty-nest syndrome**.

People who maintain healthy relationships with family and friends have less difficulty adjusting to these changes. For many, this is a time to apply their talents and life experience to community and social programs. They use their time to pursue new interests and make new friends. Developing good social skills as an adolescent helps ease these transitions.

ⓥ **Meeting new challenges is just one way to maintain physical health.** *How can your actions as a teen help prepare you for the physical, mental, and social transitions of adulthood?*

Discussing

Let students describe the depictions of midlife crises they may have seen in TV shows or movies or may have read about in novels or short stories. Ask:

- How accurate do you think these depictions are?
- Why do you think many people face a crisis or make a major change in middle adulthood?
- What form do you think it takes? 🔳

CHARACTER ✓ CHECK

Respect Have students meet in small groups to read and discuss the information about respect. Ask: What have you learned from older adults that you probably would not be able to learn from younger people? Then have group members work together to list specific things teens can do to show respect to older adults.

Activity

Have students collect photographs from magazines of people in late adulthood. Suggest that they organize the photos, as a collage or display, to present a single idea or mood. Encourage them to add writing and illustrations as necessary. ELL 🖼

Critical Thinking

Have students share what they know about specially designed communities exclusively for older adults. Ask: What are the advantages and disadvantages of such communities? 🔳

More About...

Societal Perceptions In previous decades, the American population was dominated by large numbers of young people. They had had a tremendous influence on the way our society perceived aging and the elderly. As the baby boom generation ages however, society is increasingly dominated by individuals who are middle-aged and older. As a result, our attitudes toward aging and older adulthood are also changing. More and more, mass media, consumer products, and advertising are slanted toward people over the age of 40—people in middle adulthood—who are increasingly portrayed in a positive way.

Late Adulthood

Erikson's final stage of development, late adulthood, occurs after age 65. One of the goals of people at this stage is to look at life with satisfaction and a sense of fulfillment. Older adults evaluate the events of their lives and their achievements. If they have lived their life with **integrity**, making their decisions with *a firm adherence to a moral code*, they are likely to be satisfied. For example, a person who considered family a high priority may have also succeeded in a career while providing for their family. Older adults who have maintained intimate relationships and remained committed to a system of values will have a sense of satisfaction. They can look back without regret and feel content with their accomplishments.

GOVERNMENT SPENDING FOR HEALTH RESEARCH

NHES Standard 7 Students will demonstrate the ability to advocate for personal, family, and community health.

Objectives
- Analyze the influence of laws, policies, and practices on health-related issues, including those related to disease prevention.
- Express information and opinions about health issues.

Motivator
Discuss with students the fact that funding for health research is not unlimited; governmental and other agencies must choose how to allocate money.

Teaching Strategies
1. Advise students that their letters may be easier to compose if they include specific examples.
2. Give students the option of sending their letters via e-mail.
3. Access **health.glencoe.com** for a link to the NIH Web site.

Assessment

Using a rubric, student work should provide comprehensive evidence of the following criteria to achieve the highest score:
- ✔ clear, health-enhancing stand
- ✔ support for the position with relevant information
- ✔ awareness of the audience
- ✔ encouragement of others to make healthful choices

Government Spending for Health Research

The National Institutes of Health (NIH) gathers information from many sources to establish research priorities for the prevention and treatment of diseases, including those that affect older people. Study the illustration and captions. Then complete the activity to advocate for one of the following aging-related health issues.

Source: National Institutes of Health, 2002

Advocacy groups
The Alzheimer's Association advocates increased funding for **Alzheimer** research.

Volunteer groups
Stroke survivors have testified to Congress about increased funding for **stroke** and heart research.

Professional groups
The American Academy of Orthopaedic Surgeons advocates increases in NIH funding for **osteoarthritis** and other musculoskeletal disorders.

ACTIVITY
Choose one disease related to aging that you believe should receive additional research funding from the NIH. Then compose a letter to a voluntary health organization, a member of Congress, or a patient advocacy group. Write with conviction, and target your letter to the people who will be reading it. Support your letter with data from your research.

HEALTH LITERACY

Responsible/Productive Citizen
Encourage students to find ways of helping older adults in the community. Some students can start with their own older relatives, taking the time to visit, helping a grandparent or other relative shop, and so on. Other students might want to visit retirement centers or volunteer with programs that deliver meals to housebound seniors.

Some libraries recruit older adults to read stories and tutor students. Once students have identified opportunities for senior involvement, have them create informational flyers to leave in places such as local senior centers and housing complexes for seniors.

Expanding Opportunities in Late Adulthood

Because of the increase in life expectancy in the United States, most adults can enjoy many years of late adulthood. Many look forward to retirement so that they can pursue new interests. Others choose to continue to work or even change careers. For many, volunteering is another way of staying active. However they choose to do it, adults who remain mentally and physically active enjoy their later years more than those who don't challenge themselves.

Public Health Policies and Programs for Older Adults

The Social Security system, first created in 1935, provides benefits to older adults, as well as people with disabilities. To assist retirees with their health care needs, the government offers Medicare to people 65 years of age and older and Medicaid to people with low incomes and limited resources.

Because of better health care, people can now expect to live longer after retirement. For this reason, financial planning is essential. Although some companies provide retirement benefits, many workers must plan for their own retirement with personal or company-run long-term savings plans. Through use of these funds in conjunction with Social Security benefits, the poverty rate for older adults has been reduced. Many older adults are finding that, because of a lifetime of healthy behaviors, the years after retirement are their best.

What are Social Security credits?
As you work and pay taxes, you earn "credits" that count toward eligibility for future Social Security benefits. You can earn a maximum of four credits each year. Most people need 40 credits (10 years of work) to qualify for benefits.

Have students read the question and share their ideas about the answer. Then let students read the answer and discuss what it means to them, to people of their parents' generation, and to older Americans.

3 ASSESS

EVALUATING THE LESSON

Assign and discuss the Lesson 4 Review; then administer, grade, and discuss Lesson Quiz 76 in the TCR.

RETEACHING

- Ask students to work in small groups to write informal outlines of the lesson.
- Ask students to complete Reteaching Activity 76 in the TCR.

ENRICHMENT

Have interested students research and write a report on the stages of middle and late adulthood in other cultures. How do the attitudes toward age and aging differ from those common in the United States? Remind them to proofread for spelling and grammatical errors, and develop several drafts, if necessary. Have them hand in their error-free final drafts.

Lesson 4 Review

Reviewing Facts and Vocabulary

1. What transitions do people in middle adulthood face?
2. What causes empty-nest syndrome?
3. What is *integrity*?

Thinking Critically

4. **Analyzing.** Name specific examples of the relationship between health decisions you make as a teen and disease prevention later in life.
5. **Evaluating.** How have programs such as Social Security and personal retirement plans changed the lifestyles of older adults? Analyze how laws providing Social Security and Medicare benefits can enhance health and prevent disease in older adults.

Applying Health Skills

Goal Setting. Write a list of goals indicating where you would like to be when you reach middle and late adulthood. The list should include physical, mental, emotional, and social goals. Next to each goal, write a healthful behavior that you can start now to ensure that you will reach your goal.

WORD PROCESSING Use a word-processing program to set up a table listing your goals. Go to **health.glencoe.com** for help using your word-processing program.

Lesson 4 Health Through the Life Span **533**

4 CLOSE

Ask students to complete this sentence in writing:

- My plans for middle adulthood include . . .

Lesson 4 Review

Answers to Reviewing Facts and Vocabulary

1. Physical, mental/emotional, and social transitions.
2. Children growing up and leaving home.
3. A firm adherence to a moral code.

Answers to Thinking Critically

4. Possible answer: People can maintain good health by managing their weight and by exercising both the brain and the body.
5. With both Social Security and retirement plans, the poverty rate has been reduced. People live longer and with better treatments for disease.

Representation of Older Adults in the Media

NHES Standard 4 Students will analyze the influence of culture, media, technology, and other factors on health.

Objective

To analyze representations of older adults in various media forms and to challenge negative stereotypes of this group.

Motivator

Ask students if they can recall television shows that center on the relationships between older adults.

Teaching Strategies

Awareness Ask students if older adults are seen in a variety of roles in the media. What kinds of activities are seniors performing?

Analysis Often older adults are represented as being cared for by younger family members. Ask students how this image might limit how seniors are perceived.

Reflection Have students reflect on older adults in their own family, neighborhood, school, or community. Encourage students to think of occupations and roles seniors participate in.

Take Action Ask students to draft a letter to senior advocacy groups about their research findings. Have students ask the organization to put pressure on media outlets to make changes that show seniors in more positive roles.

✔Assessment

Student groups should consider several examples. Student essays should speculate on why a particular media form might have more images of seniors.

Eye ON THE Media

Representation of Older Adults in the Media

Although older adults make up 17 percent of the population, they make up only 5.4 percent of all network prime-time characters and 4 percent of characters on daytime television, according to one study. TV programs often place older adults in supporting roles, but seldom portray them as leading characters. For this activity you will analyze representations of older adults in various media forms.

ACTIVITY

As a class, brainstorm a list of magazines, newspapers, radio, or music you will examine for images of seniors. Then list types—for instance, under *magazines* you might list newsmagazines, health magazines, hobby and home decorating magazines. Try to get a representative sample of each media form.

Work in groups to research one of the media forms. One group should examine magazines, one music, and so on. Tally the numbers of times an older adult appears in the media form you are researching. Add up your group's tallies, and then compare the results with those of other groups. Which media form most accurately represents the percentage of older adults in our population?

EXPRESS YOUR VIEWS

Write a short essay discussing which media form represents older adults in more balanced numbers. Which media form shows older adults more frequently? What suggestions can you make for portraying older adults in positive roles?

▶ More About...

AARP Groups such as the National Council on Aging and AARP (formerly known as the American Association of Retired Persons) are dedicated to helping change traditional images of older adults as dependent, inactive, and frail. AARP's slogan is "To Serve, Not to be Served," a testament to their commitment to changing senior stereotypes. But other groups too make it a point to expand the images of older adults by showing them embarking on new careers, having new interests, and concentrating on healthy images of seniors. For the "Take Action" activity, point students to groups such as state and area agencies on aging as well as community groups that encourage intergenerational participation.

CROSS-CURRICULUM CONNECTIONS

Shape a Poem. Learning to fulfill a promise to yourself, to a friend, or to your family helps you as an adolescent build toward a successful future. Make a list of the promises you have made to yourself and others. From this list, write a vertical poem using the word "promise." A vertical poem is one in which the letters of a word appear down the page, and each letter starts a line of the poem.

Calculate Life Expectancy. According to Lesson 4, page 529, the average lifespan in 1900 was 45 years but has risen to a current life expectancy of 77 years. Assuming that figure to be valid for the year 2004, if the life expectancy continues to rise at the same rate, how long should a person born in the year 2050 expect to live?

Debate on Change. Historians debate whether adolescence is a modern concept. They note that in medieval England, few common people lived past the age of 40, which denied them the pleasures of youth and instead forced them into apprenticeships or to begin life's work as a teen. Research and make a time line of changes that took place in the nature of adolescence in the industrialized Western culture during the twentieth century. Have a class discussion of what you learned.

Compare Self-Sufficiency. For humans, the responsibilities of caring for offspring last through adolescence and sometimes young adulthood. This is not so for many animal families. Research the development of one type of animal. Find out how soon the offspring of this animal are physically developed enough to survive on their own. Compare and contrast the self-sufficiency of human offspring with the animal you researched.

 C A R E E R Corner

Gerontologist

If you get along well with older adults, you might want to consider a career as a gerontologist. A gerontologist often works with other professionals, such as occupational and physical therapists, dietitians, or lawyers, to improve the quality of life for older persons. Some gerontologists work in nursing homes, senior centers, and other community facilities. Still others teach or work in research facilities. Because the population of the United States is aging, the job outlook for individuals working in gerontology is excellent. Find out more about this and other careers in Career Corner at **health.glencoe.com**.

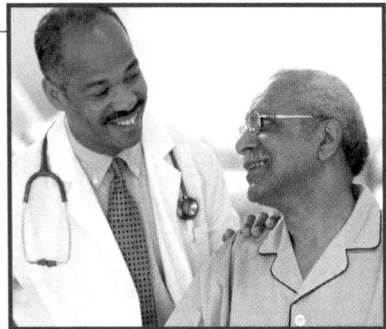

Chapter 20 Review **535**

CROSS-CURRICULUM CONNECTIONS

Enrich student learning by connecting the topic of adolescence and the life cycle to one of the four areas presented on this page. The activity may be completed individually or with a partner.

Language Arts Tell students that although there are no set rules to writing poetry, most poems share two elements: creative use of language and emphasis on sound.

History Illustrate through a model that time lines need to include engaging photographs and drawings as well as relevant text.

Math Answer: $77 + [(77 - 45)/100 \times 46] = 91$. The current life expectancy + the difference in expectancy per the number of years over which it occurred times the number of years projected.

Science Each animal offspring develops to meet particular evolutionary needs and a specific range of adaptability to its environment.

 C A R E E R Corner

Have students read and discuss the Career Corner information on gerontologists. Ask interested students to explore the Glencoe Health Web site at **health. glencoe.com** for more information on this career.

Portfolio Assessment

Self-Evaluation Direct students to review the Health Skills Activities and other activities completed in the chapter. Encourage each student to select one finished product or activity that demonstrates his or her best work for the chapter and that represents the student's learning goals. Have students explain what they have learned and how the examples they have selected demonstrates their growth in health literacy, knowledge, and skills.

Teacher Classroom Resources Assign Performance Assessment 20, "The Journey Ahead," in the TCR.

CHECKING COMPREHENSION

- Assign and discuss the chapter review.
- Use Chapter 20 MindJogger Videoquiz to review the chapter. ▶◀

CHAPTER 20 REVIEW ANSWERS

Exploring Health Terms

1. puberty
2. Hormones
3. sex characteristics
4. physical maturity
5. emotional maturity
6. marital adjustment
7. self-directed
8. unconditional love
9. False: transitions
10. True

Recalling the Facts

1. Any two: The frontal cortex undergoes a growth spurt, followed by growth of new nerve connections. The corpus callosum grows and changes. The cerebellum undergoes growth and change. Teens use the amygdala rather than the frontal cortex to interpret emotional information.

2. The language of children is insufficient to deal with the more complex concepts of adolescence.

3. The value system of a child is determined by his or her parents; adolescents begin to form their own value systems.

4. Any two: ability to give and receive love, ability to face reality and deal with it, capacity to relate positively to life experiences and learn from them, desire to strive to be the best you can be.

▶ **EXPLORING HEALTH TERMS** *Answer the following questions on a sheet of paper.*

Lesson 1 *Replace the underlined words with the correct term.*

adolescence	hormones
cognition	puberty
gametes	sex characteristics

1. A person begins to develop sex characteristics during <u>cognition</u>.
2. <u>Gametes</u> are produced in glands and help regulate many of the body's functions.
3. During adolescence, <u>puberty</u>, the traits related to a person's gender, develop.

Lesson 2 *Match each definition with the correct term.*

emotional intimacy	physical maturity
emotional maturity	

4. The state in which the physical body and all its organs are fully developed.
5. The state in which the mental and emotional capabilities of an individual are fully developed.

Lesson 3 *Fill in the blanks with the correct term.*

commitment	self-directed
marital adjustment	unconditional love
adoption	

6. When someone adjusts to marriage or to his or her spouse, that person makes a _____ .
7. Making decisions about behavior when adults are not present to enforce the rules is an indication that a child is _____ .
8. When parents show their child love at all times without limitation or qualification, the parents are giving _____ .

Lesson 4 *Identify each statement as True or False. If false, replace the underlined term with the correct term.*

empty-nest syndrome	transitions
integrity	

9. The critical changes that take place during adulthood are called <u>integrity</u>.
10. <u>Empty-nest syndrome</u> may result when children move from home.

▶ **RECALLING THE FACTS** *Use complete sentences to answer the following questions.*

Lesson 1

1. What are two physical changes that take place in the teen brain? How are these changes significant?
2. Why is it important for adolescents to expand their verbal skills?
3. How does the value system of an adolescent differ from that of a child?

Lesson 2

4. What are two characteristics of an emotionally mature person?
5. Why does emotional maturity take longer to achieve than physical maturity?
6. What are some ways that young adults can contribute to society?

Lesson 3

7. Why do most people marry?
8. How can couples reduce the impact of conflict on their marriage?
9. Why are teen marriages often unsuccessful?
10. How can a parent help a child become self-directed?

5. Because it comes from experiencing relationships and situations throughout adulthood.

6. Answers may include volunteering.

7. Most people marry because they fall in love and are ready to enter into a lasting, intimate relationship.

8. By developing good communication skills and good conflict resolution skills.

9. Most teens are not mature enough to handle the responsibilities of marriage.

10. By correcting misbehavior, praising positive behavior, and being consistent with rules and consequences.

11. These activities exercise, or strengthen, the brain.

12. Answers may include the fact that older adults can pursue interests and expand social activities or start new careers.

13. People want to be healthier and more active during their retirement years.

Lesson 4

11. How do mental activities such as reading or solving puzzles help older adults?

12. What are some ways in which older adults can use the freedom that comes from having children move away from home?

13. How has increased life expectancy affected the way people view retirement?

➤ THINKING CRITICALLY

1. **Synthesizing.** In a private health journal, answer each of the questions asked in the developmental tasks section of Lesson 1. Reflect on your answers and identify the areas that need attention. Determine the steps you could take to accomplish those particular tasks. *(LESSON 1)*

2. **Summarizing.** Interview three adults about their contributions to society, and make a list indicating how that contribution met a need in their lives. Write a short report summarizing your findings. *(LESSON 2)*

3. **Evaluating.** In some cultures parents arrange the marriages of their children. How do you think this would work in today's American society? *(LESSON 3)*

4. **Applying.** What advice would you give to someone who is suffering from empty-nest syndrome? Write a letter to a friend or relative with this problem. *(LESSON 4)*

➤ HEALTH SKILLS APPLICATION

1. **Analyzing Influences.** Adolescence is a stage marked by change. List three changes teens experience. Appraise and explain how each influences and contributes to personal growth for a healthy life. *(LESSON 1)*

2. **Refusal Skills.** You have your sights set on a career goal, but your friends want you to go against a school rule that might cause you to jeopardize that goal. Write three refusal statements that are based on your goals. *(LESSON 2)*

3. **Accessing Information.** Poll friends and acquaintances who want to get married about why they would like to do so. Identify similar reasons, and use the information to create a graph showing the number of individuals choosing each reason. *(LESSON 3)*

4. **Practicing Healthful Behaviors.** Analyze the dynamics of family roles and responsibilities relating to health behaviors. Work with an older adult in your family to identify one health behavior that you can do together.

BEYOND *the* Classroom

Parent Involvement

Advocacy. Find out about community resources available to help parents with their parenting roles and child-care options. Are there programs associated with local schools or colleges? Find out how you and your parents can become involved in such programs.

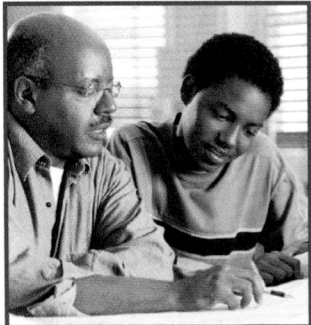

School and Community

Active Older Adults. Visit a senior center in your community. Meet some of the older adults who use the center. Find out why they visit the center and what other resources they use. If possible, volunteer at the center.

Thinking Critically

1. Journal entries will vary.

2. Reports will vary, but should include some connection to the stages of adulthood in lesson 2.

3. Answers will vary, but should be positive and contain an advocacy message that emphasizes health-enhancing behaviors adults can practice.

4. Letters will vary.

Health Skills Application

1.–4. Answers will vary.

EVALUATE

- Use the reproducible Chapter 20 Test in the TCR, or construct your own using the Testmaker software. 📁 💿

- Use Performance Assessment 20 in the TCR. 📁

ENRICHMENT

Ask students to complete Enrichment Activity 20 in the TCR. 📁

BEYOND *the* Classroom

Keep students involved in the community, and encourage parent participation by assigning the activities on this page for students to work on outside of class.

Lessons	Standards		Features
	National	**State/Local**	
1 **The Effects of Tobacco Use** *pages 540–545*	National Health Education Standards **1.1, 1.3, 1.7, 3.1, 7.2**		*Exploring* **Issues** • Are Tobacco Warning Labels Effective? page 544
2 **Choosing to Live Tobacco Free** *pages 546–550*	National Health Education Standards **3.1, 3.3, 6.1, 7.4**		*Real-Life* **Application** • Help a Friend STOP Using Tobacco *(Advocacy)*, page 549
3 **Promoting a Smoke-Free Environment** *pages 551–555*	National Health Education Standards **1.1, 1.7, 2.1, 6.1, 7.4**		Health Skills *Activity* • Avoiding Environmental Tobacco Smoke *(Communication)*, page 553 Hands-On Health • Smoking Out Underage Tobacco Sales *(Advocacy)*, page 554

Reproducible Resources

Student Activity Workbook for use with each chapter

- 📁 Concept Mapping Activity 77
- 📁 Current Health Issues 21
- 📁 Decision-Making Activity 21
- 📁 Enrichment Activity 21
- 📁 Guided Reading Activities 77
- 📁 Health Lab 21
- 📁 Lesson Plan 77
- 📁 Parent Letter and Activities 21
- 📁 Reteaching Activity 77

- 📁 Concept Mapping Activity 78
- 📁 Guided Reading Activities 78
- 📁 Lesson Plan 78
- 📁 Reteaching Activity 78

- 📁 Concept Mapping Activity 79
- 📁 Cross-Curriculum Activity 21
- 📁 Guided Reading Activities 79
- 📁 Lesson Plan 79
- 📁 Reteaching Activity 79

Assessment

- 📁 Lesson Quiz 77

- 📁 Lesson Quiz 78

- 📁 Lesson Quiz 79

Technology

- 🕹 Transparency 62
- 💿 TeacherWorks®
- 💻 Internet Activities

- 🕹 Transparency 63
- 💿 TeacherWorks®

- 💿 TeacherWorks®

0:00 OUT OF TIME

If time does not permit teaching the entire chapter, use:
- Figure 21.1, p. 543
- Exploring Issues, p. 544
- Real Life Application, p. 549
- Health Skills Activity, p. 553
- Eye on the Media, p. 556

Language Diversity

- 🎧 English Audio CD Program
- 🎧 Spanish Audio CD Program
- 📁 English Summaries, Quizzes, and Activities
- 📁 Spanish Summaries, Quizzes, and Activities
- 📁 Spanish Parent Letters and Activities

End of Chapter Assessment

Blackline Masters
- 📁 Chapter 21 Test
- 📁 Performance Assessment Activity 21

Technology
- 💿 Vocabulary PuzzleMaker
- 📼 MindJogger Videoquiz
- 💿 **Exam**View® Pro Testmaker

Professional Health Series

Dealing with Sensitive Issues
Planning a Coordinated School Health Program
Promoting Character Education
Home, School, and Community Involvement

Key to Ability Levels

Teaching strategies that appear throughout the chapter have been identified by one of the following codes to give teachers an idea of their suitability for students of varying learning styles and abilities.

L1 Strategies should be within the ability range of all students. Full class participation is often required. Teacher direction is usually needed.

L2 Strategies are designed for average to above-average students or for small groups. Some teacher direction is needed.

L3 Strategies are designed for students able and willing to work independently. Minimal teacher direction is needed.

ELL Strategies should be within the ability range of students learning the English language.

🔲 Block scheduling strategies are useful in a block scheduling format.

CHAPTER OVERVIEW

Chapter 21 examines the dangers of using tobacco in any form. The chapter also discusses the risks and rights of nonsmokers, provides strategies for quitting tobacco use, and presents ideas for advocating for smoke-free environments.

Lesson 1 All forms of tobacco, including cigarettes, pipes, cigars, and smokeless tobacco, pose serious risks to the user's physical health. Tobacco use damages the nervous, respiratory, cardiovascular, digestive, and excretory systems.

Lesson 2 Increasing numbers of Americans, including teens, are choosing a tobacco-free lifestyle. Teens who have already become addicted to nicotine can turn to such resources as nicotine substitutes and consultations with health care professionals for help in quitting tobacco use.

Lesson 3 Air contaminated by tobacco smoke endangers the health of nonsmokers, especially unborn children, infants, and young children. Teens can take an active role in protecting their health and the health of others from secondhand smoke.

Health Skills Features

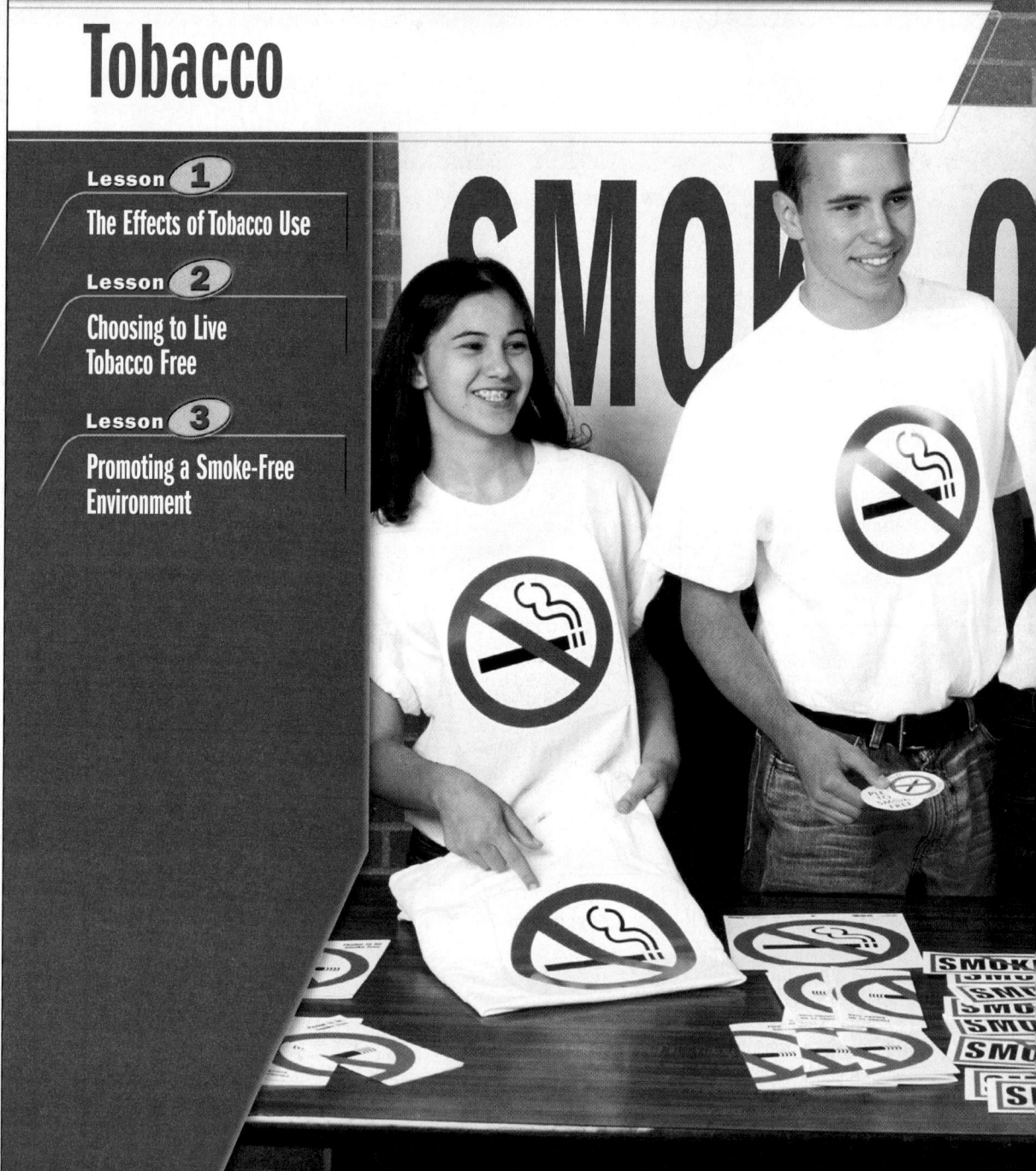

Chapter 21

Tobacco

Lesson 1
The Effects of Tobacco Use

Lesson 2
Choosing to Live Tobacco Free

Lesson 3
Promoting a Smoke-Free Environment

538

MEETING STUDENT DIVERSITY

Language Diversity Use the following suggestions to help students who have difficulty with English:

- Pair English language learners with native speakers of English who can restate the Chapter Summary in language that helps students comprehend important concepts.

- 🎧 Direct auditory learners or those students with language diversity to the *Glencoe Health Audio CD Program*. Available in English and Spanish, this component provides an audio and written summary of the chapter.

- Use photographs, drawings, or magazine clippings to help students visualize the important concepts of the chapter.

Case Study

Make a Difference

Mike is an advocate for a smoke-free environment. He and his friends are active members of Teens Against Tobacco Use (TATU), a national peer education program sponsored by the American Lung Association. The group's goal is to help its members and others understand the dangers of tobacco and prevent its use.

Mike says, "I got involved with TATU because you get to teach young people about the harmful effects of smoking—a big health issue. We went to an elementary school and taught the facts and consequences of smoking. We used a metal bowl and a bunch of metal BBs to teach our lesson. Each BB represented a certain number of people who had died because of a specific condition, such as AIDS or car crashes. When we dropped those BBs into the bowl, they made a pretty loud sound. When we dropped the BBs representing the 450 thousand people a year, however, who die of smoking-related diseases—more than all the other causes combined—the students were stunned!

We also put on a skit, teaching refusal skills to use if someone offers them cigarettes. Helping people choose to live tobacco free has made a difference in my life and, I hope, in the lives of others."

Write a few sentences describing how Mike's involvement with TATU promotes a healthy community. Reread this story and your response when you complete the chapter. Identify some ways you could teach others about the harmful effects of tobacco.

539

Quick *Write*

Using Visuals. Using tobacco can seriously damage a person's health. What strategies can you use to prevent the use of tobacco?

INTRODUCING THE CHAPTER

Case Study

Write the acronym *TATU* on the board, and let students share what they know about this organization (Teens Against Tobacco Use).

Then have students work with partners to read and discuss the Case Study. Have partners describe some of the benefits Mike gets out of his volunteer work and how his activity influences the younger students. Collect student responses. Return the responses after students have completed Chapter 21. Allow time for students to review their responses.

Quick *Write*

Using Visuals Ask volunteers to describe the photograph. Then have students work independently to think of other strategies teens can use to prevent tobacco use. Ask several volunteers to read their lists aloud, and encourage students to add to their own lists as they recognize new ideas.

TECHNOLOGY OPTIONS

MINDJOGGER
VIDEOQUIZ

To preview or review chapter content, you may wish to use the Chapter 21 MindJogger Videoquiz. ▶◖

HEALTH *Online*

Online Resources for the Teacher For a fresh approach to health topics and an in-depth look at health issues, use these online resources, found under Teacher Resources at **health.glencoe.com:**

• Block Schedule Lesson Plans
• Technology Projects
• Health Updates

The Effects of Tobacco Use

1 FOCUS

QUICK START Help students discuss what they already know about the harmful effects of tobacco. Have them jot down their responses to the Quick Start question, and then meet in groups to discuss their responses.

TYING TO PRIOR KNOWLEDGE

Guide students in recalling and discussing basic facts about the respiratory and cardiovascular systems. Then let volunteers explain how tobacco smoke might affect the healthy functioning of those systems.

Health Skills Features

"Are Tobacco Warning Labels Effective?" p. 544

INTRODUCING VOCABULARY

- Have students use at least three of the vocabulary terms in a paragraph that discusses the effects of tobacco. Ask volunteers to read their paragraphs aloud.

- Ask students to complete the Chapter 21 Study Guide in the *Student Activity Workbook.* 📂

540

Lesson 1

The Effects of Tobacco Use

VOCABULARY
- **addictive drug**
- **nicotine**
- **stimulant**
- **carcinogen**
- **tar**
- **carbon monoxide**
- **smokeless tobacco**
- **leukoplakia**

YOU'LL LEARN TO
- Describe the harmful substances contained in tobacco and in tobacco smoke.
- Examine the harmful effects of tobacco use on body systems.
- Analyze the physical, mental, social, and legal consequences of tobacco use.

QUICK START Most people know that using tobacco is harmful. Why do you think some people continue to use tobacco products? Write your response on a sheet of paper.

V Tobacco products, which are made from the leaves of tobacco plants, contain nicotine. Experts say that nicotine is more addictive than heroin or cocaine. *List some harmful effects of nicotine.*

Trends in tobacco use are changing, and that's good news for public health, according to the American Lung Association. The public is becoming more aware of the health costs of tobacco use, and more individuals are making the choice to be tobacco free.

Tobacco Use—A Serious Health Risk

According to the Surgeon General, tobacco use, particularly smoking, is the number one cause of preventable disease and death in the United States. Because tobacco use has been linked to many health risks, the government requires all tobacco products to carry warning labels. Avoiding *all* forms of tobacco can prevent many serious health problems. Still, every day some teens begin to smoke, chew, or dip tobacco. Many people begin to use tobacco products thinking that they can quit whenever they want to. Once a person has formed the habit, however, it's very difficult to quit.

Nicotine

One of the reasons that tobacco users find it difficult to quit is that tobacco contains an **addictive drug**, *a substance that causes*

540 Chapter 21 Tobacco

Lesson 1 *Resources*

Teacher Classroom Resources
- 📂 Concept Mapping Activity 77
- 📂 Current Health Issues 21
- 📂 Decision-Making Activity 21
- 📂 Enrichment Activity 21
- 📂 Guided Reading Activities 77
- 📂 Health Lab 21
- 📂 Lesson Plan 77

- 📂 Lesson Quiz 77
- 📂 Parent Letter and Activities 21
- 📂 Reteaching Activity 77

Student Activity Workbook
- 📂 Applying Health Skills 77
- 📂 Chapter 21 Study Guide

Multimedia
- Transparency 62

physiological or psychological dependence. All tobacco products contain **nicotine**, *the addictive drug found in tobacco leaves.* Nicotine is classified as a **stimulant**—*a drug that increases the action of the central nervous system, the heart, and other organs.* Nicotine raises blood pressure, increases heart rate, and contributes to heart disease and stroke. Once addicted, people need more and more tobacco to satisfy the craving for nicotine.

Cigarette Smoke—A Toxic Mixture

Not only is tobacco addictive, but the smoke from burning tobacco is toxic. In 1992 the Environmental Protection Agency classified environmental tobacco smoke, or secondhand smoke, as a Group A carcinogen. This is the most dangerous class of carcinogen. A **carcinogen** is *a cancer-causing substance.* Other compounds in tobacco smoke are described below.

Tar and Carbon Monoxide

Cigarette smoke contains **tar**, *a thick, sticky, dark fluid produced when tobacco burns.* As tar penetrates the smoker's respiratory system, it destroys cilia, tiny hairlike structures that line the upper airways and protect against infection. Tar damages the alveoli, or air sacs, which absorb oxygen and rid the body of carbon dioxide. It also destroys lung tissue, making the lungs less able to function. Lungs damaged by smoking are more susceptible to diseases such as bronchitis, pneumonia, emphysema, and cancer.

Carbon monoxide, another compound found in cigarette smoke, is *a colorless, odorless, and poisonous gas* that is taken up more readily by the blood than oxygen is. Carbon monoxide replaces oxygen in the blood, thereby depriving the tissues and cells of oxygen. It also increases the risk of high blood pressure, heart disease, and hardening of the arteries.

Harmful Effects of Pipes and Cigars

Like smoking cigarettes, smoking pipes or cigars presents major health risks. Cigars contain significantly more nicotine and produce more tar and carbon monoxide than cigarettes do. One cigar can contain as much nicotine as a pack of cigarettes. Pipe and cigar smokers have an increased risk of developing cancers of the lip, mouth, and throat.

▶ **S**pecialty cigarettes carry many health risks.

- Testing has shown that imported cigarettes contain two to three times the amount of tar and nicotine found in American cigarettes.
- Smokers of low-nicotine, low-tar cigarettes smoke more and inhale more deeply to maintain their body's accustomed nicotine level.
- Bidis and clove cigarettes can contain up to seven times as much nicotine and twice as much tar as regular cigarettes.

🔺 **Cigarettes contain 43 known carcinogens, including cyanide, formaldehyde, and arsenic. They also contain poisonous chemicals used in insecticides, paint, toilet cleaners, antifreeze, and explosives.** *How can you use this knowledge to help others stay tobacco free?*

Lesson 1 The Effects of Tobacco Use **541**

② TEACH

Discussing

Have students think about the people they know who use tobacco products. Ask: How does the use of tobacco products affect these people's health, appearance, behavior, and social activities? Are these people aware of the effects tobacco has on their lives? Why or why not? 🔲

Cooperative Learning

Divide the class into groups of four or five. Have the members of each group work together to design and make a poster showing the chemicals in cigarettes. On their posters, they should list the major chemicals and describe the function or effect of each chemical. Encourage students to make posters that are both creative and informative. Let each group share their poster with the rest of the class. If possible, display the posters in a school hallway or other public area. 🔲 **Visual/Spatial**

FYI

The National Academy of Pediatrics reports that nine out of ten American smokers began using tobacco before they were 19 years old. Teens who do not start smoking before high school graduation are unlikely to begin smoking at all.

⟩ More About...

Nicotine and Smoking It only takes 5–7 seconds for nicotine to reach the brain after a person inhales tobacco smoke. In those seconds, the nicotine is absorbed into the bloodstream through the lining of the mouth and through the lungs. The smoker's blood pressure goes up; heart rate increases by up to 20 beats per minute; oxygen supply to body tissues decreases; and blood circulation to the arms, hands, legs, and feet decreases. The first "rush" of stimulation in the brain is followed by depression and fatigue, leading the smoker to seek even more nicotine— another cigarette.

542

ACTIVE READING

Synonyms

Exploring word meanings through the use of synonyms helps readers understand new vocabulary and distinguish subtle differences in word meanings. Have students brainstorm to identify as many synonyms or close synonyms as possible for *smokeless tobacco* and *cigarette.* Examples are smokeless tobacco—*spit, chew, dip, chaw; cigarette–light, smoke, drag, cig.* Then encourage discussion by asking students to compare the following terms that are close synonyms: *smoke free* and *designated nonsmoking.* Have students use a dictionary or thesaurus to research the terms to determine the slight differences. For more strategies, see the *Guided Reading Activities* booklet. 📂 🔲

Quick Demo

Use a smoking machine (available free from the American Cancer Society) to demonstrate tar residue left in the lungs after smoking one cigarette. If no machine is available, hold a clean white tissue or handkerchief over the smoke, and let it flow through the cloth. The cloth should show a yellowish brown stain. Ask: Who is exposed to more carcinogens, the smoker or the nonsmoker who is in the room with the smoker? Why? What does the filter at the end of the cigarette look like after the cigarette has been smoked? Why do you think cigarette companies began adding a filter to cigarettes? 🔲

🔻 **Your decision not to smoke can help keep your lungs healthy.** *Compare the healthy lung (top) with the one damaged from smoking (bottom). Discuss how tar and other components in tobacco smoke affect the lungs and their function.*

Harmful Effects of Smokeless Tobacco

Smokeless tobacco is tobacco that is *sniffed through the nose, held in the mouth, or chewed.* These products are *not* a safe alternative to smoking. Like tobacco that is smoked, smokeless tobacco contains nicotine in addition to 28 carcinogens, all of which are absorbed into the blood through the mucous membranes or the digestive tract.

Because smokeless tobacco is often held in the mouth for a length of time, it delivers both nicotine and carcinogens to the body at levels that can be two to three times the amount delivered by a single cigarette. As a result, people who chew eight to ten plugs of tobacco each day take in the same amount of nicotine as a two-pack-a-day smoker. Smokeless tobacco is as addictive as smoked tobacco. In addition, it irritates the mouth's sensitive tissues, causing **leukoplakia**, or *thickened, white, leathery-looking spots on the inside of the mouth that can develop into oral cancer.* Cancers of the throat, larynx, esophagus, stomach, and pancreas are also more common among users of smokeless tobacco.

How Tobacco Affects the Body

For several decades health officials have warned the public about the health risks of tobacco. The chemicals in tobacco products can cause damage to many body systems. **Figure 21.1** on page 543 illustrates some of the effects of tobacco on the body.

Short-Term Effects of Tobacco Use

Some effects of tobacco use can occur immediately after using the product. Here are some of these short-term effects:

▶ **Changes in brain chemistry.** The addictive properties of nicotine cause the body to crave more of the drug. The user may experience withdrawal symptoms such as headaches, nervousness, and trembling as soon as 30 minutes after his or her last tobacco use.

▶ **Increased respiration and heart rate.** Breathing during physical activity becomes more difficult; and in some cases, nicotine may cause an irregular heart rate.

▶ **Dulled taste buds and reduced appetite.** Tobacco users often lose much of their ability to enjoy food.

▶ **Bad breath and smelly hair, clothes, and skin.** These unattractive effects may cause people to avoid the tobacco user.

Long-Term Effects of Tobacco Use

Over time, tobacco use takes a serious toll on many body systems, including the respiratory, cardiovascular, and digestive

School to Work

Smoking in the Workplace Some states and communities have laws governing smoking in the workplace. Beyond local or state laws, many companies have no-smoking policies or designated smoking areas. Have students find out what state or city laws govern smoking in local workplaces in your community.

Then have students read newspaper employment columns. Ask them to calculate the percentage of ads that make reference to a nonsmoking environment. You might also suggest that students read want ads for domestic help and see how many specify nonsmokers.

FIGURE 21.1

Chapter 21 • Lesson 1

HEALTH RISKS OF TOBACCO

Tobacco use damages several important body systems, causing severe health problems that may result in death.

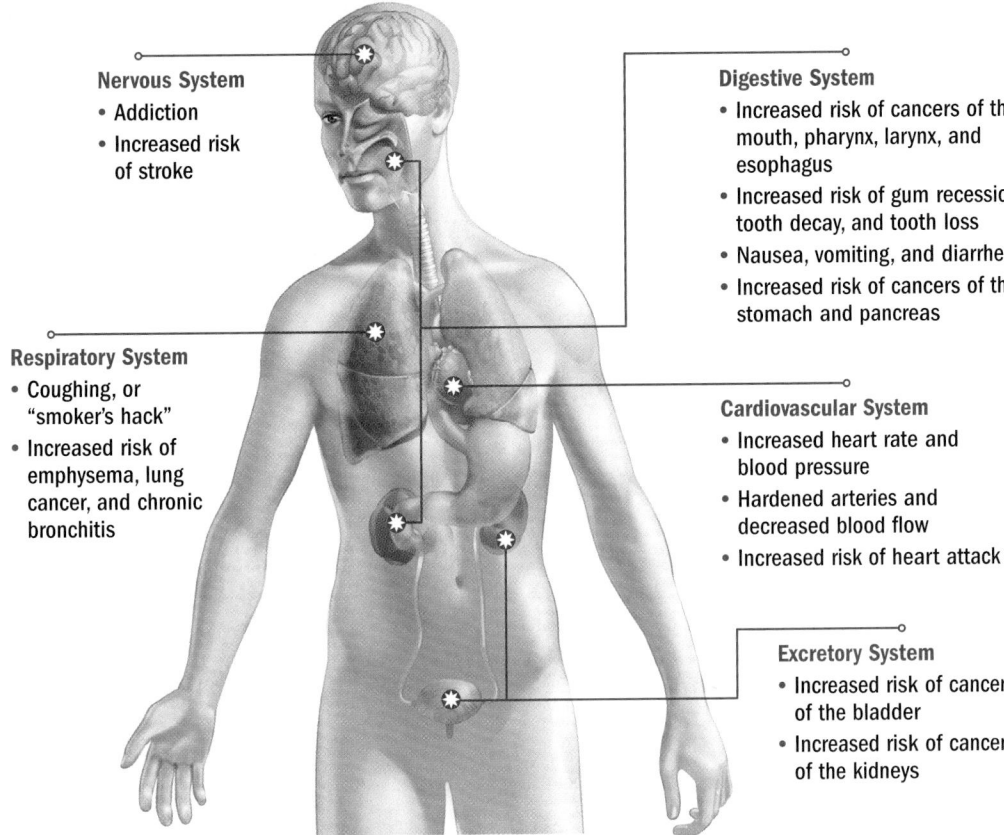

Nervous System
- Addiction
- Increased risk of stroke

Respiratory System
- Coughing, or "smoker's hack"
- Increased risk of emphysema, lung cancer, and chronic bronchitis

Digestive System
- Increased risk of cancers of the mouth, pharynx, larynx, and esophagus
- Increased risk of gum recession, tooth decay, and tooth loss
- Nausea, vomiting, and diarrhea
- Increased risk of cancers of the stomach and pancreas

Cardiovascular System
- Increased heart rate and blood pressure
- Hardened arteries and decreased blood flow
- Increased risk of heart attack

Excretory System
- Increased risk of cancer of the bladder
- Increased risk of cancer of the kidneys

systems. The immune system is weakened, making the body more vulnerable to disease. Long-term tobacco use can lead to health problems such as:

▶ **Chronic bronchitis.** Repeated tobacco use can damage the cilia in the **bronchi** until they no longer function. This leads to a buildup of tar in the lungs, causing chronic coughing and excessive mucus secretion.

▶ **Emphysema.** This is a disease that destroys the tiny air sacs in the lungs. The air sacs become less elastic, making it more difficult for the lungs to absorb oxygen. A person with advanced emphysema uses up to 80 percent of his or her energy just to breathe.

ho🔥link

bronchi For more information about the respiratory system functions, see Chapter 16, page 428.

Lesson 1 The Effects of Tobacco Use **543**

VISUAL LEARNING

Figure 21.1 Divide the class into five groups, and assign each group one of the body systems shown in Figure 21.1. Have the members of each group read and discuss the listed health risks for their assigned system; if necessary, refer them to other chapters in the text to review the organs and functions of that system. Then have each group present its information to the rest of the class.

Explaining

Tell students what happens to the body when a person uses tobacco. Explain why, after about 30 minutes, the tobacco user wants more. The constriction of the blood vessels causes a mild high. When the vessels return to normal, there is a sensation of restlessness and irritation. The smoker or oral tobacco user does not like the discomfort and will repeat the behavior that produced pleasure. This causes a cycle of use that becomes habitual. The frequent use builds up an addiction to nicotine. **L1**

Discussing

On a diagram of the human body, follow the pathway of smoke when it is inhaled and exhaled. Have students identify all the body parts that are exposed to the inhaled and exhaled smoke. Ask: If a person did not inhale, what areas of the body would still be vulnerable? **L1**

Critical Thinking

Pose the following questions: What is the reason a person with heart disease is told to avoid smoke? Why does the heart have to work harder in a smoker than in a nonsmoker? What happens to the heart when it works overtime? **L1**

Curriculum Connections

Math Ask students to calculate the cost of smoking one pack of cigarettes a day beginning at age 15 through age 65. Have them base their calculations on the current price of cigarettes for the first five years, and increase it 5 percent for each five-year period.

Ask: What else could have been purchased with that amount of money? Encourage students to use the advertisements in the local paper to find costs of other articles such as stereo equipment, a car, and even a house. Have them compare costs.

▶ **Lung cancer.** When the cilia in the bronchi are destroyed, extra mucus cannot be expelled. Cancerous cells can grow in these conditions, block the bronchi, and move to the lungs. Unless detected early, lung cancer causes death.

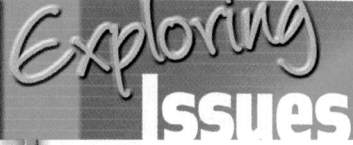

hotlink

blood vessels For more information on the cardiovascular system, see Chapter 16, page 416.
arteriosclerosis To learn more about arteriosclerosis see Chapter 26, page 675.

▶ **Coronary heart disease and stroke.** Nicotine constricts **blood vessels,** which cuts down on circulation, or blood flow. Nicotine also contributes to plaque buildup in the blood vessels, which can lead to hardened arteries, a condition called **arteriosclerosis.** Arteries may become clogged, increasing the risk of heart attack and stroke. The risk of sudden death from

Exploring Issues

ARE TOBACCO WARNING LABELS EFFECTIVE?

Before students read and discuss the two viewpoints, present these findings:

- 44 percent of smokers said the new warnings increased their motivation to quit smoking.

- 48 percent of nonsmokers said the new warnings made them feel better about being a nonsmoker.

- 27 percent of smokers said they smoke less inside their homes because of the new warnings.

- 24 percent of smokers said they have transferred their cigarettes to another container or put a cardboard sleeve over the pack to avoid seeing the images.

Have students read the Exploring Issues feature, and discuss the two viewpoints as a class. Then have students form small groups. Ask the members of each group to choose one of the viewpoints; have them gather additional facts and examples to support that position. If time permits, allow opposing groups to debate the issue.

Exploring Issues

Are Tobacco Warning Labels Effective?

The Canadian government requires tobacco companies to place full-color pictures and warning labels on all cigarette packages. Do you think such labels are effective in influencing people to practice healthful behaviors?

Viewpoint One: Hillary F., age 16

I don't think that warning labels on cigarette packages are effective. People who smoke know the dangers—they've heard it all before, from newspapers, magazines, and doctors. If they haven't quit before this, a message and a picture on a pack of cigarettes isn't going to have much influence. Labels like these lose their impact after a while anyway. Smokers get used to seeing them and eventually ignore them.

WARNING:
CIGARETTES CAUSE LUNG CANCER

85% of lung cancers are caused by smoking. 80% of lung cancer victims die within 3 years.

Health Canada

Viewpoint Two: Gary H., age 15

The labels on these cigarette packages are effective media messages. Smokers see them every time they pull a cigarette out of the pack. It will cause some of those people to think about quitting, and some will quit. Sure, smokers hear about the health risks of smoking from other sources, but that doesn't mean the labels aren't effective. Images often have a stronger impact than words.

ACTIVITIES

1. Do you think the Canadian warning labels on cigarette packs are more effective than American labels? Why or why not?

2. Do you agree that people become desensitized to labels? If so, what can health advocates do to make labels promoting healthful behaviors more effective?

HEALTH LITERACY

Responsible/Productive Citizen

Encourage students to conduct an anonymous poll of students to find out how many are nonsmokers and how the nonsmokers react to their peers who are smokers. Have students begin by planning the yes/no questions they want to use in their questionnaire. For example, they might include questions such as these: Do you smoke? Do you object to the smell of smoke in a smoker's hair or clothes? Are you bothered when a friend or date smokes around you? Students might enlist the help of teachers to distribute and collect the questionnaires. Have students tabulate and graph the results. Display graphs to raise awareness of how teens really feel about smoking.

heart disease is three times greater for smokers than for nonsmokers.

Other Consequences

Tobacco use brings many other serious consequences especially for teens.

▶ **Legal consequences.** Selling tobacco products to persons under the age of 18 is illegal in all states. Schools prohibit the use of tobacco products on school property, and a student may be suspended or expelled for breaking these rules.

▶ **Social consequences.** Many people find secondhand smoke and the smell of tobacco offensive, so tobacco users may be excluded from social gatherings. Having bad breath, yellowed teeth, and stained fingers may also harm a tobacco user's social life.

▶ **Financial consequences.** Use of tobacco products can be very expensive. Someone who smokes a pack of cigarettes a day can spend more than $2,000 each year just on cigarettes. According to a recent report, the total economic cost of tobacco use to taxpayers in the United States, including medical costs, is about $97 billion a year.

▼ Most teens choose healthy alternatives and avoid the negative consequences of tobacco use.

Lesson 1 Review

Reviewing Facts and Vocabulary

1. What is *nicotine*? Why is it harmful?
2. Explain why cigarette smoke is toxic.
3. List the short-term and long-term effects of tobacco use.

Thinking Critically

4. **Applying.** Examine the effects of tobacco use on the respiratory and cardiovascular systems.
5. **Synthesizing.** Analyze the harmful effects of teen tobacco use. Include physical, mental, social, and legal consequences.

Applying Health Skills

Advocacy. Help others recognize how tobacco use can harm body systems. Write a letter to your parents or adult members of your family explaining what damage can occur as a result of using tobacco products.

TECHNOLOGY OPTION

WORD PROCESSING Word processing can give your report a professional look. Learn more about using word-processing software at **health.glencoe.com**.

Lesson 1 The Effects of Tobacco Use **545**

Lesson 1 Review

Answers to Reviewing Facts and Vocabulary

1. Nicotine is the addictive drug found in tobacco leaves. It is addictive, and it contributes to heart disease and stroke.
2. It contains the poisons found in products such as paint, rat poison, toilet cleaner.
3. Short-term and long-term effects are listed on pages 542–543.

Answers to Thinking Critically

4. See Figure 21.1.
5. Cancer, emphysema, and heart disease; addiction; being excluded from certain social groups; and getting into trouble with the law for illegal possession of tobacco.

3 ASSESS

EVALUATING THE LESSON

Assign and discuss the Lesson 1 Review; then administer, grade, and discuss Lesson Quiz 77 in the TCR. 📁

RETEACHING

- Have students work with partners to write informal outlines of the lesson, noting only the most important facts and ideas.
- Ask students to complete Reteaching Activity 77 in the TCR. 📁

ENRICHMENT

To demonstrate the harmful effects of chemicals in tobacco, find a plant infested with aphids and cut off a twig or leaf cluster which has many insects on it. Remove the paper from several cigarettes. Boil the tobacco in a cup of water for 15 minutes. Strain the solution by pouring it through filter paper or a paper towel into a glass jar. Add a pinch of soap detergent to this tobacco solution to make it easier to spray. Pour the solution into an atomizer or other small spray can. Spray the leaves on top and bottom. (Do not breathe the spray.) Observe what happens to the aphids. (The solution kills the aphids because nicotine, a chemical in tobacco, is poisonous.)

4 CLOSE

Have each student identify the main content of the lesson he or she considers most important. Then help students compare and discuss their ideas about the importance of these facts.

Choosing to Live Tobacco Free

QUICK START After students have written their responses, let volunteers share their ideas. Ask one student to record all the negative effects in a class list on the board. Then have students share and discuss their suggestions for refusal statements. Let the class decide on the three most effective statements, and record those on the board.

TYING TO PRIOR KNOWLEDGE

Ask students to recall some of the already-familiar benefits of not using tobacco. Explain that they will learn more about the benefits of choosing a tobacco-free lifestyle as they study this lesson.

Health Skills Features

"Helping a Friend STOP Using Tobacco," p. 549

ADVOCACY

INTRODUCING VOCABULARY

- Have students discuss the vocabulary terms and use what they already know to define the terms informally. Then have them use the Glossary to check their definitions.

- Ask students to complete the Chapter 21 Study Guide in the *Student Activity Workbook.*

Choosing to Live Tobacco Free

VOCABULARY
nicotine withdrawal
nicotine substitute

YOU'LL LEARN TO
- Explain the benefits of a tobacco-free lifestyle.
- Develop strategies for preventing the use of tobacco products.
- Identify health services in the community that help prevent tobacco-related diseases and promote a tobacco-free lifestyle.

QUICK START On a sheet of paper, list all of the negative effects of tobacco use that you can recall. Then write three refusal statements you can use to avoid tobacco use.

 After peaking in 1997, teen smoking has fallen sharply. *What has contributed to the drop in teen smoking in recent years?*

High school students who reported smoking a cigarette in the last 30 days

Source: Centers for Disease Control and Prevention, 2001

Knowing the health risks of tobacco use has helped people make the healthful decision to stay tobacco free. In fact, the number of people in the United States who don't smoke, either because they never started or because they have quit, has been rising steadily.

Reduced Tobacco Use Among Teens

According to the Centers for Disease Control and Prevention (CDC), smoking rates among teens have fallen sharply in recent years. Reports show that nationally 28 percent of high school students smoke. This is down from 36 percent in 1997. Some factors contributing to this ongoing trend include:

▶ **Antismoking campaigns.** In 1998, tobacco companies and 46 states reached a legal settlement that restricted tobacco advertising and promotion. Tobacco companies are now required to fund ads that discourage young people from smoking.

▶ **Financial cost.** Tobacco use is expensive. Many teens find that they would rather spend their money on healthier alternatives.

▶ **Societal pressures.** Legislative acts have limited smoking in public places. More young people are growing up in an environment that is less tolerant of secondhand smoke.

▶ **Family influence.** Many teens avoid tobacco use because their parents strongly disapprove of the use of tobacco products.

546 Chapter 21 Tobacco

Lesson 2 *Resources*

Teacher Classroom Resources
- Concept Mapping Activity 78
- Guided Reading Activities 78
- Lesson Plan 78
- Lesson Quiz 78
- Reteaching Activity 78

Student Activity Workbook
- Applying Health Skills 78
- Chapter 21 Study Guide

Multimedia
- Transparency 63

Benefits of Living Tobacco Free

People who have never used tobacco and people who have quit enjoy the many benefits of a tobacco-free lifestyle. Avoiding tobacco lowers the risk of lung cancer, heart disease, and stroke. It improves cardiovascular endurance and lung function, which increases physical fitness and enhances athletic performance.

Living tobacco free has mental, emotional, and social benefits, too. Tobacco-free people have a sense of freedom because they know that they are not dependent on an addictive substance. They experience less stress because they don't have to worry about health-related problems caused by tobacco use. A tobacco-free lifestyle will also help a person look and feel better. Having higher energy levels, healthier skin, fresher breath, and better-smelling clothes and hair will increase confidence in social situations.

Strategies for Preventing Tobacco Use

The best way to avoid the negative consequences of tobacco use is never to start using tobacco products. Nearly 90 percent of all adult smokers started when they were teens, so if you avoid tobacco use during middle school and high school, you are likely to stay tobacco free throughout your life. Below are some strategies to help you stick to your decision to live tobacco free.

▶ **Choose friends who don't use tobacco.** Being around people who share your values and beliefs will strengthen your commitment to lead a tobacco-free life.

▶ **Avoid situations where tobacco products may be used.** By staying away from such situations, you reduce the chance of being pressured to use tobacco.

▶ **Practice and use refusal skills.** Prepare in advance what you will say if someone offers you tobacco. Your refusal may be a simple "No thanks," or you may give a reason, such as, "No, I need to stay fit for the track competition." Be assertive, and leave the situation if the pressure continues.

A tobacco-free lifestyle improves heart and lung function, which helps your athletic performance. *List some other benefits of living tobacco free.*

Lesson 2 Choosing to Live Tobacco Free **547**

Chapter 21 • Lesson 2

② TEACH

Discussing

Peer pressure is often thought of as having only negative influences. Ask students:

- What are some ways in which peer pressure can be positive?
- What are some approaches students could take to help someone kick a tobacco habit? **L1**

Activity

Have volunteers interview adults who do not smoke. Ask them to find out whether the adult ever smoked, if so, when and how the adult quit; if not, why the adult chose not to smoke; when and where the adult felt most pressured to smoke; how the adult feels now about smoking and smokers. Have the students share their findings with the class. **L2**
Interpersonal

Critical Thinking

Ask: Why could it be difficult for a nonsmoker to be good friends with a smoker? What kinds of pressure are the two friends likely to exert on each other? How do you think good friends would react to those kinds of pressures? **L1**

Service Learning

Ask a group of interested volunteers to plan and write a rap about refusing tobacco. Have them perform their rap for the class and, if they are willing, for a larger teen audience. **L3**
Musical/Rhythmic

Promoting Coordinated School Health

The Cost of Prevention It is widely recognized that schools cannot afford the costs of problems stemming from the following: low self-esteem; dropout rate from school; participation in high-risk behaviors, such as those that may result in sexually transmitted diseases or unplanned pregnancy; health costs associated with poor prenatal care; malnutrition; and poor mental health. One approach schools can use to improve the health of their students, faculty, and staff is the coordinated school health program. For more information, consult *Planning a Coordinated School Health Program.*

Critical Thinking

Ask students to imagine that a friend or family member is trying to stop smoking and struggling with an addiction to nicotine. Advise them not to use names as they discuss these "imaginary" smokers. Have them share their ideas in response to these questions:

- What symptoms of physiological addiction would you expect that person to show?

- What symptoms of psychological addiction would you expect?

- What do you think you could do to help a friend or family member deal with those symptoms?

- What do you think you should avoid saying or doing? Why? **L2**

Cooperative Learning

Organize students who want to stop smoking into a support group that meets each morning before school. Train peers to be supporters. Have participants post the number of days they have been smoke free. **L1 Interpersonal**

Health Minute

Have students meet in small groups to read and discuss the Benefits of Quitting. Ask: Why might a smoker feel better as soon as he or she stops using tobacco? When do you think an ex-smoker would begin to notice improvements in his or her physical health?

548

Health Minute

What Happens When a Smoker Quits?

Benefits of Quitting:

▶ **Within 20 minutes** blood pressure and pulse rates drop. Body temperature in limbs returns to normal.

▶ **Within eight hours** oxygen levels return to normal.

▶ **In 24 hours** the chance of heart attack begins to decrease.

▶ **In 48 hours** nerve endings begin to regrow. Senses of taste and smell improve.

▶ **In three days** breathing becomes easier as lung capacity increases.

▶ **Within two weeks to three months** lungs function up to 30 percent better.

▶ **Within one to nine months** lung cilia regrow and coughing, sinus congestion, and shortness of breath decrease.

▶ **In one year** the risk of coronary heart disease is cut in half.

▶ **In five years** the risk of lung cancer and cancers of the mouth, throat, and esophagus is reduced by 50 percent. Stroke risk is also decreased.

▶ **In ten years** the risk of cancer of the bladder, kidney, cervix, and pancreas decreases.

Why Some Teens Use Tobacco

In spite of the many benefits of a tobacco-free lifestyle, some teens choose not to resist the pressure to start smoking. Some teens think that smoking will help them control their weight or cope in times of stress and crisis. Other teens believe that smoking will make them seem mature and independent. These beliefs are far from the truth about tobacco use. Because smoking reduces the body's capacity for physical activity, it may actually lead to weight gain. In addition, health problems and nicotine dependency will increase the tobacco user's stress level.

Other reasons for teen tobacco use are peer pressure and media influences. Some teens try their first cigarette with a friend who already smokes. Other teens may try tobacco to imitate, or model, celebrities or other adults who smoke. Some teens are influenced by ads that depict tobacco use as glamorous and sophisticated.

Being aware of these influences and being informed about the harmful effects of tobacco can help teens resist the pressure to use tobacco products. Teens who analyze these influences realize that most people who use tobacco products suffer from health problems and wish they could quit the habit.

Reasons to Give Up Tobacco Use

Many teens who start using tobacco do decide to quit. Here are just a few of the reasons they cite:

▶ They begin to have health problems, such as asthma or respiratory infections.

▶ They have the desire, will, and commitment to stop.

▶ They realize how expensive the habit is.

▶ They realize that using tobacco can lead to other risky behaviors, such as the use of alcohol and other drugs.

▶ They find it difficult to purchase tobacco products because selling tobacco products to persons under the age of 18 is illegal in all 50 states.

▶ They realize the damaging effects of secondhand smoke and don't want to harm their families and friends.

Stopping the Addiction Cycle

Millions of people have succeeded in their effort to quit tobacco use. Overcoming nicotine addiction can be difficult, but it's not impossible. Most people who stop using tobacco will experience symptoms of **nicotine withdrawal**, *the process that occurs in the body when nicotine, an addictive drug, is no longer used.* The cravings

---

More About...

Keeping the Proper Focus It is important to avoid implying that marketing or advertising is unethical or dishonest. Remember that some students probably know people who work in these professions. Rather, emphasize that some advertising techniques can be misleading and that students must, therefore, be aware of the strategies used to lure them to use tobacco products.

Advertising Techniques You may wish to review with students some of the various advertising techniques:

- Bandwagon
- Rich and famous
- Good times
- Testimonials

See page 49 for descriptions.

and discomfort caused by these symptoms are temporary, and smokers trying to quit should remember that success will lead to better health.

Withdrawal

Symptoms of nicotine withdrawal include irritability, difficulty concentrating, anxiety, sleep disturbance, and cravings for tobacco. To relieve the symptoms, some people use a **nicotine substitute**, *a product that delivers small amounts of nicotine into the user's system while he or she is trying to give up the tobacco habit.* Many nicotine substitutes are available, including gum, patches, nasal sprays, and inhalers. Nicotine gum is an over-the-counter product; the other nicotine substitutes require a doctor's prescription. Users who are trying to quit should take the process one step at a time. They might begin by seeking help from a health care professional.

Real-Life Application

Help a Friend STOP Using Tobacco

Studies have shown that most people who try to quit have a greater success rate if they have support from others. Use the **STOP** approach to help someone stop using tobacco.

Show concern. Approach the person in a caring, nonjudgmental manner. Use "I" messages to let the person know that you care about his or her health.

Take time to plan. Putting a plan on paper makes it easier to set objectives. You may need to help the person create a physical activity program. Set a date to quit, locate formal tobacco cessation programs, and devise strategies to cope with tobacco cravings.

Offer support. Put the plan into action. For example, you might bring the person sugarless gum. Ride a bike, shoot hoops, or take a walk together to help him or her get physical activity. Arrange to attend a class together to learn relaxation techniques.

Promote success. Let the person know that you are proud of him or her for quitting. Celebrate each week of abstinence. If the person relapses, continue to encourage him or her. Keep in touch with the person after he or she has quit.

> **ACTIVITY**
>
> **Write a plan that addresses each of the STOP guidelines. If you have a family member or a friend who uses tobacco, create the plan for that person, or work with a classmate who knows someone who uses tobacco. Make sure that your plan contains messages that promote the health benefits of stopping tobacco use. Consider the person, and tailor the plan to that person's needs and interests.**

Real-Life Application

Help a Friend STOP Using Tobacco

NHES Standard 7 Students will demonstrate the ability to advocate for personal, family, and community health.

Objectives

- Recognize strategies to help people who wish to become tobacco free.

- Demonstrate the ability to influence and support others in making positive health choices.

Motivator

Ask students to write about a habit that they wanted to stop, such as biting their nails or waiting until the last minute to study for a test.

Teaching Strategies

1. Have students discuss their responses to the Motivator.
2. Ask students to identify and include in their plans other sources of help, such as health care professionals and specific agencies that provide tobacco cessation programs.

✔Assessment

Using a rubric, student work should provide comprehensive evidence of the following criteria to achieve the highest score:

✔ clear, health-enhancing stand
✔ support for the position with relevant information
✔ awareness of the audience
✔ encouragement of others to make healthful choices
✔ passion/conviction

More About...

Tobacco and Youth In 1998, the major American tobacco companies reached an agreement with 46 states regarding cigarette marketing and underage smoking; the companies had previously reached similar settlements with the remaining four states.

This settlement prohibits tobacco companies from directing any marketing or advertising campaigns at teens or children. It bans specific forms of tobacco promotion, including cartoon characters in ads and brand-name sponsorship of team sports events and other public events.

In addition, the settlement requires tobacco companies to pay the states $246 billion over a period of 25 years. These funds are intended to support antismoking education programs for youth.

3 ASSESS

EVALUATING THE LESSON

Assign and discuss the Lesson 2 Review; then administer, grade, and discuss Lesson Quiz 78 in the TCR. 📁

RETEACHING

- Have students work with partners to write two lists: one identifying the problems teens might have in resisting the pressures to use tobacco, and the second identifying the problems teens might have in quitting tobacco use. Then guide a group discussion, sharing and discussing these lists.

- Ask students to complete Reteaching Activity 78 in the TCR. 📁

ENRICHMENT

Have interested students gather information about specific tobacco cessation programs in your community. Ask these students to plan and make useful handouts with facts to be shared with other students.

4 CLOSE

Have students write short answers to this question: What do you consider the most important benefit of living tobacco free?

HEALTH Online

Learn more about the American Lung Association's programs to help people quit smoking. Click on Web Links at **health.glencoe.com**.

Getting Help—Tips for Quitting

People who are trying to give up tobacco use can try the following strategies.

► **Prepare for the day.** Set a target date for quitting.

► **Get support and encouragement.** Support from family, friends, and peers will increase a person's chance of success.

► **Access professional health services.** It may be necessary to seek advice from a doctor, enroll in a tobacco cessation program, or join a support group. Other helpful resources include the American Lung Association, the Centers for Disease Control and Prevention (CDC), and local hospitals.

► **Replace tobacco use with healthier alternatives.** Sugarless gum, carrots, and cinnamon sticks are substitutes that people can use when they feel an urge to have a cigarette.

► **Change daily behavior.** Avoiding other tobacco users, preparing one's environment for a tobacco-free life, and changing daily routines can also help smokers avoid their tobacco triggers.

► **Engage in healthful behaviors.** Physical activity, good nutrition, stress management techniques, and abstinence from alcohol and other drugs will help people through the withdrawal process.

▶ Lesson 2 Review

Reviewing Facts and Vocabulary

1. List three benefits of staying tobacco free.
2. List four strategies for preventing tobacco use.
3. What is *nicotine withdrawal*, and what are *nicotine substitutes*?

Thinking Critically

4. **Evaluating.** Why might tobacco advertisements target teens?
5. **Synthesizing.** Identify services in your community that help to prevent tobacco-related diseases and explain how helping people quit tobacco use promotes a healthy community.

Applying Health Skills

Refusal Skills. Make a two-column chart. In the first column, write five situations in which a teen might be pressured to use tobacco. In the second column, develop effective refusal statements and strategies the teen can use to avoid tobacco use.

TECHNOLOGY OPTION

SPREADSHEETS Use a spreadsheet to draft and finalize your lists. Using this type of program makes it easy to make revisions, and it produces a product that is easy to read. See **health.glencoe.com** for tips on how to use a spreadsheet.

550   **Chapter 21** Tobacco

▶ Lesson 2 Review

Answers to Reviewing Facts and Vocabulary

1. See page 547.
2. Choose friends who don't use tobacco, avoid situations where tobacco products may be used, practice and use refusal skills.
3. The process that occurs in the body when nicotine is not present; products that deliver small amounts of nicotine.

Answers to Thinking Critically

4. Possible answer: Tobacco companies know that people are more likely to start smoking as teens than as adults.
5. Possible answer: Support groups, doctors, Amercan Lung Association, hospitals; eliminates tobacco-related illness.

Promoting a Smoke-Free Environment

VOCABULARY

environmental tobacco smoke (ETS)
mainstream smoke
sidestream smoke

YOU'LL LEARN TO

• Analyze the harmful effects of tobacco on the health of fetuses, infants, and young children.

• Analyze the influence of laws, policies, and practices on preventing tobacco-related disease.

• Relate the nation's health goals and objectives for reducing tobacco-related illnesses to the individual, family, and community.

QUICK START Many communities encourage a smoke-free environment in which people can live, work, and play. What places in your community are smoke free? List the benefits of a smoke-free environment.

As more and more people become aware of the harmful effects of tobacco, efforts to curb tobacco use in public places are gaining ground.

Risks for Smokers and Nonsmokers

Both smokers and nonsmokers who breathe air containing tobacco smoke are at risk for health problems. **Environmental tobacco smoke (ETS)**, or secondhand smoke, is *air that has been contaminated by tobacco smoke.* Environmental tobacco smoke is composed of **mainstream smoke**, *the smoke exhaled from the lungs of a smoker*, and **sidestream smoke**, *the smoke from the burning end of a cigarette, pipe, or cigar.* Sidestream smoke is more dangerous than mainstream smoke because it has higher concentrations of carcinogens, nicotine, and tar.

The dangers of ETS have prompted some states to pass laws that prohibit all tobacco use in public buildings. *What other measures can be taken to protect the health and well-being of nonsmokers?*

Lesson 3 Promoting a Smoke-Free Environment **551**

Lesson 3 *Resources*

Teacher Classroom Resources

📂 Concept Mapping Activity 79

📂 Cross-Curriculum Activity 21

📂 Guided Reading Activities 79

📂 Lesson Plan 79

📂 Lesson Quiz 79

📂 Reteaching Activity 79

Student Activity Workbook

📂 Applying Health Skills 79

📂 Chapter 21 Study Guide

Lesson 3

Promoting a Smoke-Free Environment

1 FOCUS

QUICK START Have students work with partners to brainstorm a list of local smoke-free environments. Let students share their responses and briefly discuss the benefits these smoke-free environments provide.

TYING TO PRIOR KNOWLEDGE

Help students discuss the everyday choices they make to avoid smoke and to help others avoid smoke. Then explain that, as they study Lesson 3, students will add to their understanding of how they can promote a smoke-free environment.

Health Skills Features

"Avoiding Environmental Tobacco Smoke," p. 553 COMMUNICATION SKILLS

"Smoking Out Underage Tobacco Sales," p. 554 ADVOCACY

INTRODUCING VOCABULARY

• Have students differentiate *mainstream smoke* and *sidestream smoke.* How do these terms relate to *environmental tobacco smoke?*

• Ask students to complete the Chapter 21 Study Guide in the *Student Activity Workbook.* 📂

② TEACH

Activity

Have volunteers visit or call at least ten local restaurants and ask whether each restaurant has a "no smoking" section. If so, how long has the practice been in effect? Which area—smoking or non-smoking—attracts more customers? Are there restaurants that do not allow smoking at all? Then have the volunteers plan and draw a graph that summarizes their findings; ask them to display and explain the graph. (If your state has banned all smoking in restaurants, how long has the law been in effect?) **L3**

Logical/Mathematical

Service Learning

Have students form small groups. Let the members of each group choose an elementary grade level (from K to 5) and write and develop a lesson on the dangers of tobacco for that grade level. Lessons might include a skit, discussion questions, student activities, charts, or displays. If possible, arrange to have the members of each group share their lesson with an elementary school class. **L3**

Discussing

Guide students in discussing the impact of such problems as premature delivery, low birth weight, and growth and developmental problems on parents and other family members. **L1**

Parents protect the health of their children by staying tobacco free. *What specific healthful behaviors should pregnant females practice?*

Effects of Smoke on Nonsmokers

Environmental tobacco smoke from cigarettes, cigars contains more than 4,000 different chemical compounds, 43 of which are identified as carcinogens. Inhaling this smoke either by smoking or by breathing in ETS brings these carcinogens into the body. ETS affects people of all ages, causing eye irritation, headaches, ear infections, and coughing. It worsens asthma conditions and other respiratory problems. Three thousand people every year are diagnosed with lung cancer caused by secondhand smoke.

Effects of Smoke on Unborn Children and Infants

Choosing to live tobacco free is one of the best things a pregnant woman can do to make sure that her baby will be born healthy. Smoking during pregnancy can seriously harm the developing fetus. Nicotine passes through the placenta, constricting the blood vessels of the fetus. Carbon monoxide reduces the oxygen levels in the mother's and the fetus's blood. These negative effects increase the risk of impaired fetal growth, miscarriage, prenatal death, premature delivery, low birth weight, deformities, and stillbirths. The infant may also suffer from growth and developmental problems throughout early childhood. Babies of smokers are two and a half times more likely to die of sudden infant death syndrome (SIDS). One study found that nearly 60 percent of all SIDS cases could be prevented if babies and pregnant females were protected from tobacco smoke. Infants exposed to ETS have an increased risk of asthma, tonsillitis, and respiratory tract infections.

Effects of Smoke on Young Children

Young children are also particularly sensitive to environmental tobacco smoke. Children of smokers are nearly twice as likely to be in poor health as those of nonsmokers. Consider these facts:

▶ Children of smokers tend to have a higher incidence of sore throats, ear infections, and upper respiratory problems than children of nonsmokers.

▶ Children who live with smokers have double the risk of developing lung cancer than children of nonsmokers.

Because children learn by example, it's not surprising that children of smokers are nearly three times as likely to smoke as children of nonsmokers. Being a positive role model is another good reason to make the choice to be tobacco free.

552 **Chapter 21** Tobacco

More About...

Secondhand Smoke Affects Children's Learning Ability A new study shows that even a small amount of secondhand smoke can hinder a child's learning ability, affecting reading, math, and reasoning skills. Researchers at the Cincinnati Children's Hospital examined data compiled over several years for the National Health and Nutrition Examination Survey. In particular, the researchers looked at levels of cotinine, a substance produced when nicotine is broken down by the body. The researchers determined that the more cotinine children had in their bodies, the lower their reading, math, and reasoning scores. What steps can be taken to protect children from exposure to environmental tobacco smoke?

Reducing Your Risks

What can you do to protect yourself from ETS? If you and your family want your home to be smoke free, politely ask visitors to refrain from smoking inside. If someone in your household smokes, open windows to allow fresh air to circulate and request that certain rooms remain smoke free. Consider using air cleaners to help remove contaminants from the air. If you are visiting a home in which someone smokes, go outside or to another room. Ask to open the window slightly to provide fresh air. Suggest meeting elsewhere, such as in your home or at a library. In restaurants and other public places, request seating in a nonsmoking area. If no smoke-free area is available, go to another restaurant.

Health Skills Activity

AVOIDING EVIRONMENTAL TOBACCO SMOKE

NHES Standard 6 Students will demonstrate the ability to use communication skills.

Objectives

- Identify reasons to avoid second-hand smoke.
- Practice interpersonal communication skills to avoid secondhand smoke.

Motivator

Ask students to write about a time when someone smoked around them and they asked the person to stop. How did the other person respond?

Teaching Strategies

1. After students have read the scenarios and practiced communication skills, encourage students to share their responses.
2. Remind students to use a respectful tone when requesting the person to stop smoking.

✓Assessment

Using a rubric, student work should provide comprehensive evidence of the following criteria to achieve the highest score:

✔ use of "I" messages
✔ respectful tone
✔ appropriate body language
✔ reason(s) for their request

Health Skills Activity

Communication: Avoiding Environmental Tobacco Smoke

You can protect your health and the health of others by asking smokers not to light up in your presence. Read the scenarios below, and practice communication skills by stating polite requests for a smoke-free environment.

Situation 1

You are at a wedding rehearsal dinner with relatives. Your favorite cousin, whom you haven't seen for a long time, is seated next to you. As you begin catching up on family news, your cousin lights a cigarette.

Situation 2

You and your friends have been waiting for 30 minutes to be seated in a restaurant. A table becomes available in the smoking section, where several people are smoking heavily. Your friends want to take it.

What Would You Do?

Using the communication skills you have learned, write a response to each scenario. Be prepared to role-play your response for the class.

1. Use "I" statements.
2. Keep your tone respectful.
3. Maintain appropriate body language.
4. Give reasons for your request.

Lesson 3 Promoting a Smoke-Free Environment **553**

Curriculum Connections

History Ask individual students to choose a decade from the past century of American history and research tobacco-related attitudes and practices during that decade. Have all these students share their findings, in chronological order, with the rest of the class. Then help the class discuss identifiable trends in these attitudes and practices. What changes do students predict for the decades ahead?

Music Challenge students to identify popular songs that include anti-tobacco messages, however subtle. Let students play these songs for the rest of the class, and help the class discuss the use and impact of such messages.

Hands-On Health

SMOKING OUT UNDERAGE TOBACCO SALES

HEALTH ADVOCACY

NHES Standard 7 Students will demonstrate the ability to advocate for personal, family, and community health.

Objectives

- Analyze the influence of laws and policies on health-related issues.

- Design materials for health advocacy.

Motivator

Ask: Have you ever witnessed an underage teen trying to buy tobacco products? Did the person succeed?

Teaching Strategies

1. After sharing responses to the Motivator, ask students whether they are aware that 90 percent of all regular smokers begin smoking at or before the age of 18.
2. Encourage students to include a positive health message in their posters.

✓ Assessment

Using a rubric, student work should provide comprehensive evidence of the following criteria to achieve the highest score:

- ✔ citation of specific sources
- ✔ evaluation of the validity of the source
- ✔ rationale for the appropriateness of the source
- ✔ ability to access appropriate community resources to meet specific needs
- ✔ type of help available from the sources

Did You Know ?

Statewide antismoking campaigns are effective in reducing smoking. For example, the number of smokers in California was reduced by 16 percent in the first four years of that state's campaign. The number of smokers in Massachusetts was reduced by 20 percent.

Toward a Smoke-Free Society

As people realize that smoking causes diseases and harms not only their own health but also the health of others, the drive to become a smoke-free society increases. Many states have taken steps to prohibit smoking in all public buildings and private workplaces. In the past the law required only that "no smoking" areas be available to those who wished to avoid ETS. Now, however, many people are promoting laws that would ban smoking and eliminate ETS in public places such as restaurants, civic buildings, business offices, and lobbies. Laws prohibiting the sale of tobacco products to minors are being strictly enforced. Tobacco licenses are being revoked when stores sell tobacco products to people under the age of 18.

Hands-On Health ACTIVITY

Smoking Out Underage Tobacco Sales

Federal law prohibits the sale of tobacco products to all persons under 18. In some states, buyers must be 21. The easier it is to buy tobacco products, the more likely it is that teens will experiment with tobacco and become addicted. Promote health in your community by reminding peers that it's illegal for stores to sell tobacco products to minors.

What You'll Need

- information provided by your teacher
- poster board
- masking tape
- markers

What You'll Do

1. In a small group, use the information your teacher has provided on tobacco control in your state to answer these questions:
   - What is the legal age to purchase tobacco products?
   - What is the penalty for minors who use or possess tobacco products?
   - What are the penalties for merchants who sell tobacco to minors?
   - What is your state doing to curb underage tobacco sales?
2. With your group, discuss your findings. Recall signs you have seen that explain store policies regarding the sale of tobacco products. How do you think these signs affect teens who wish to purchase tobacco products?

Apply and Conclude

With your group, create a poster that is targeted at teens who wish to purchase tobacco products even though it is against the law. Include the responses to at least two of the questions you answered in the activity. Your poster should be attention-getting, persuasive, and accurate. Ask a local merchant to display your poster.

Myths & Reality

MYTH Tobacco-related health problems are generally limited to the United States.

FACT Worldwide, some 3 million people die each year from tobacco-related diseases. That number is expected to reach 10 million by the year 2025.

MYTH Smokers only hurt themselves.

FACT Smokers do hurt themselves—and other people. In the past decade, 30,000 non-smoking Americans died from lung cancer caused by ETS, or secondhand smoke.

Increasingly, the law is taking into consideration the rights of the nonsmoker. Certain states have successfully sued tobacco companies to recover the cost of treating tobacco-related diseases. The money awarded in these cases is often used to fund statewide antismoking campaigns or to offset the medical costs related to tobacco use.

Working Toward National Health Goals

The Department of Health and Human Services has launched a program, called *Healthy People 2010*, to promote health and prevent disease nationwide. One of the goals of *Healthy People 2010* is to reduce the number of people who use tobacco and the number of deaths associated with tobacco use. Decreasing tobacco use and reducing exposure to secondhand smoke are important steps in increasing the years of healthy life among people in the United States.

You, your family, and your community can join in the national effort to take a stand against tobacco. Become involved in activities that promote a healthy lifestyle, and encourage others to practice healthful behaviors, too. You can start a tobacco prevention program at school or join a youth group campaigning for stricter government control of tobacco and its availability.

 These teens are asking the storeowner to remove a tobacco ad because their state prohibits such ads from appearing within 1,000 feet of a school. *What other actions can teens take to promote health in their community?*

HEALTH Online

Set aside time for students to view the *Healthy People 2010* slide show at the Web site.

3 ASSESS

EVALUATING THE LESSON

Assign and discuss the Lesson 3 Review; then administer, grade, and discuss Lesson Quiz 79 in the TCR.

RETEACHING

- Have students work in small groups to list the dangers of environmental tobacco smoke. Give the groups about four minutes to list as many dangers as possible; then have the groups share and compare their lists.

- Ask students to complete Reteaching Activity 79 in the TCR.

ENRICHMENT

Have volunteers work together to develop an antismoking ad campaign aimed at expectant parents and parents of young children. The campaign might include TV ads, radio ads, magazine ads, and/or billboards.

Lesson 3 Review

Reviewing Facts and Vocabulary

1. Define *mainstream smoke* and *sidestream smoke*. Explain what they have in common.

2. Explain how the tobacco settlement money helps disease prevention and health promotion.

3. What strategies can you use to limit the amount of ETS you breathe?

Thinking Critically

4. **Evaluating.** Analyze the influence of laws on teen tobacco use and explain how this influence relates to prevention of disease.

5. **Analyzing.** Analyze the harmful effects of environmental tobacco smoke on fetuses, infants, and young children.

Applying Health Skills

Advocacy. You can help others make the decision to stay tobacco free. Using the goals of *Healthy People 2010*, create a pamphlet that will educate people about the harmful effects of tobacco use and secondhand smoke. Relate the nation's health goals and objectives for reducing tobacco-related illnesses in your pamphlet.

WEB SITES Instead of a pamphlet, create a Web site advocating a tobacco-free lifestyle and a smoke-free environment. See **health.glencoe.com** for help in planning and building your Web site.

Lesson 3 Promoting a Smoke-Free Environment **555**

Lesson 3 Review

Answers to Reviewing Facts and Vocabulary

1. Smoke exhaled from the lungs of a smoker; smoke from a burning cigarette, pipe, or cigar; components of environmental smoke.

2. The money funds antismoking campaigns and offsets medical costs related to tobacco use.

3. Possible answers: Sit in a nonsmoking section of public places; sit outside.

Answers to Thinking Critically

4. Stronger enforcement of laws prohibiting the sale of tobacco products to minors is leading to reduced teen tobacco use.

5. Increases risk of miscarriage, low birth weight, deformities, and stillbirths.

4 CLOSE

Have students work with partners to share their ideas about the most effective steps teens can take to promote better health through tobacco-free environments.

Which Antismoking Ads Are More Effective with Teens?

NHES Standard 4 Students will analyze the influence of culture, media, technology, and other factors on health.

Objective

Students will identify different techniques in antismoking advertisements and analyze the effectiveness of these advertisements on teen audiences.

Motivator

Ask students to recall a specific antismoking advertisement they have seen.

Teaching Strategies

Awareness Ask students to read the opening paragraph and identify techniques used in antismoking ads.

Analysis Students should recognize that the image in the text focuses on the health risks of tobacco use.

Reflection Encourage students to be specific when describing why certain techniques might be more effective than others.

Take Action Have students write to their congressman or senator advocating for funding antismoking advertisements.

✅Assessment

Students' one-page analyses should compare the two ads discussed and give supporting evidence for their viewpoint on which is more effective.

556

Which Antismoking Ads Are Most Effective with Teens?

Studies show that antismoking ads aimed at teen audiences are effective in helping teens make the healthful decision to avoid tobacco use. Antismoking advertisements may be sponsored by health organizations, by nonprofit companies, or by tobacco companies. Some ads use satire or humor while others give hard facts about the health risks of tobacco use. Use the activity below to help you identify different techniques in antismoking ads and analyze the effectiveness of these ads on teens.

 ACTIVITY

Read the script of the television ad. Using the Internet and your library as resources, find an antismoking advertisement created by a tobacco company. Compare the tobacco company ad with the ad pictured above.

1. How do the messages of each ad differ?

2. What techniques are used in each ad? Does either ad use satire or humor? Does either ad use dramatic visuals to convey its message?

3. Does each ad contain credible information? How do you know it is credible?

4. How does each ad explain or show the harmful effects of smoking?

EXPRESS YOUR VIEWS

Write a letter to the editor of your local newspaper advocating for citizens to take action to promote a tobacco-free society. Include your views on which antismoking ads you find most effective for teens and why.

More About...

Legacy Foundation The language within the Master Settlement Agreement reached between the tobacco companies and 46 states in 1998 set aside money to form The Legacy Foundation, a national organization formed to combat tobacco use, sponsored the ad in the activity. It was created by a panel of teens working with an advertising firm. The 46 states that entered into the settlement agreement with the tobacco companies also receive money earmarked for smoking cessation and prevention programs. Have students research what their state is doing with the tobacco settlement money. Have groups create a proposal to send to a state representative or state senator, detailing a plan on how to spend the tobacco settlement money in their state.

CROSS-CURRICULUM CONNECTIONS

Write a Story. Tobacco ads once used cartoon characters intended to be appealing to young people. Relying on the same appeal, work with a group to write a story in which the main character, the wily coyote, tricks another character into quitting tobacco use, and teaches him an important life lesson. Personify a cigarette, making it the villain of your story and the target of the trick.

Warnings Against Tobacco. Opposition to tobacco use dates back to its early cultivation. For example, in 1604 King James I of England pronounced in his "Counterblast to Tobacco" that smoking was "loathsome to the eye, hatefull to the Nose, harmfull to the brain, [and] dangerous to the lungs." Research and write a report on the fight against tobacco, citing warnings throughout history. Show how similarities in these warnings support medical evidence about the health risks of tobacco use.

Lung Cancer Deaths. From 1995 to 2000, a community averaged 1,126.7 deaths per 100,000 people. Lung cancer accounted for an average of 115.3 of those deaths. What percent of all deaths was the result of lung cancer?

Diagram the Lungs. All the blood in your body passes through the lungs. This allows the red blood cells to absorb oxygen and release carbon dioxide. The lungs are made up of a number of structures that allow the exchange of gases and prevent infection. Diagram the lungs, and show the various parts and their functions. Demonstrate how inhalation of tobacco smoke affects each function, and explain how this might affect related systems, particularly circulation.

Respiratory Therapist

Do you enjoy interacting with people of all ages? Are you interested in working in a medical field? A respiratory therapist works with patients who need respiratory care. Therapists may provide temporary relief to patients suffering from asthma or emphysema or provide emergency care to patients who are suffering from a heart attack, stroke, drowning, or shock.

Formal training is required to enter this profession. Training programs vary in length and in the credentials or degrees awarded. Find out more about this and other health careers by clicking on Career Corner at **health.glencoe.com**.

Chapter 21 Review **557**

CROSS-CURRICULUM CONNECTIONS

Enrich student learning by connecting the topic of tobacco use to one of the four subject areas presented on this page. The activity may be completed individually or with a partner.

Language Arts Point out to students that a good trickster tale entertains and teaches through action and comic relief.

Social Studies Instruct students to gather factual information from several different sources when writing a research report.

Math $115.3/1126.7 \times 100 = 10.23\%$

Science The students should be able to outline the basic system down to the alveoli and show how the presence of foreign substances impedes gas exchange and causes excess mucous production.

Have students read and discuss the Career Corner information on respiratory therapists. Ask interested students to explore the Glencoe Health Web site at **health.glencoe.com** for more information on this career.

Portfolio Assessment

Self-Evaluation Direct students to review the Health Skills Activities and other activities completed in the chapter. Encourage each student to select one finished product or activity that demonstrates his or her best work for the chapter and that represents the student's learning goals. Have students explain what they learned and how the examples they selected demonstrate their growth in health literacy, knowledge, and skills.

Teacher Classroom Resources Assign Performance Assessment 21, "Implied Messages," in the TCR.

CHECKING COMPREHENSION

- Assign and discuss the chapter review.
- Use Chapter 21 MindJogger Videoquiz to review the chapter. ▷◁

CHAPTER 21 REVIEW ANSWERS

Exploring Health Terms

1. nicotine
2. stimulant
3. carcinogen
4. tar
5. Nicotine withdrawal
6. nicotine substitute
7. Environmental tobacco smoke (ETS)
8. Mainstream smoke
9. Sidestream smoke

Recalling the Facts

1. It destroys the cilia that keep the respiratory tract clear; damages alveoli and reduces lung function.

2. Carbon monoxide replaces oxygen in the blood depriving the tissues and cells of oxygen. It increases the risk of high blood pressure, heart disease, hardening of the arteries, and other circulatory problems.

3. Answers may include increased risk of cancers of the mouth, pharynx, larynx, esophagus, stomach, pancreas, bladder, and kidneys; increased risk of gum recession, tooth decay, and tooth loss; nausea, vomiting, and diarrhea.

4. Tar in cigarettes destroys lung tissue and makes the body more susceptible to disease.

5. Possible answers: Tobacco companies use ads that target young people, place their promotional signs at the eye level

---

► EXPLORING HEALTH TERMS
Answer the following questions on a sheet of paper.

Lesson 1 *Match each definition with the correct term.*

stimulant	carcinogen
addictive drug	smokeless tobacco
carbon monoxide	nicotine
tar	leukoplakia

1. The addictive drug in tobacco.
2. A drug that increases the action of the central nervous system, the heart, and other organs.
3. A cancer-causing substance.
4. A thick, sticky, dark fluid produced when tobacco burns.

Lesson 2 *Fill in the blanks with the correct term.*

nicotine withdrawal
nicotine substitute

(**_5_**) is the process that occurs in the body when nicotine is no longer used. A (**_6_**) can be used to ease the side effects associated with this process.

Lesson 3 *Replace the underlined words with the correct term.*

mainstream smoke
sidestream smoke
environmental tobacco smoke (ETS)

7. Sidestream smoke is another name for secondhand smoke.
8. Environmental tobacco smoke is the smoke exhaled from the lungs of a smoker.
9. Mainstream smoke is tobacco smoke from the burning end of a cigarette, pipe, or cigar.

► RECALLING THE FACTS
Use complete sentences to answer the following questions.

Lesson 1

1. What effect does tar in cigarette smoke have on the respiratory system.
2. What effect does carbon monoxide have on the body?
3. How does tobacco use harm the digestive and excretory systems?
4. How does smoking lead to lung cancer?

Lesson 2

5. How do tobacco companies encourage teen tobacco use?
6. List two refusal skills you can use to say no to tobacco.
7. What are some reasons why teens stop using tobacco?
8. Identify three sources of help for people who want to quit tobacco use.

Lesson 3

9. List three health problems associated with environmental tobacco smoke.
10. How does ETS harm infants and young children?
11. How do state laws discourage teen smoking?
12. Describe the goals of *Healthy People 2010* that relate to tobacco use.

---

of children, pay to feature their products in movies, and give away promotional items.

6. Answers will vary. Students should use simple, clear statements and be assertive.

7. Possible answers: health problems, financial cost, wish to avoid other risky behaviors, difficulty purchasing tobacco products because such sales are illegal, desire to protect the health of family and friends.

8. Any three: doctor, tobacco cessation program, support group, American Lung Asso-

ciation, Centers for Disease Control and Prevention, local hospitals.

9. ETS contains 43 known carcinogens. Any three: eye irritation, headaches, ear infections, coughing, asthma and other respiratory problems, lung cancer.

10. Babies of smokers are two and a half times more likely to die of sudden infant death syndrome; have greater risk of growth and developmental problems, asthma, tonsillitis, and respiratory infections. Young

➤ THINKING CRITICALLY

1. **Explaining.** Why would a smoker tend to inhale more deeply and smoke more cigarettes when he or she switches to low-nicotine cigarettes? *(LESSON 1)*

2. **Analyzing.** What factors influence a teen's decision to use tobacco? *(LESSON 2)*

3. **Evaluating.** How do laws that prohibit smoking in specified areas contribute to community health? *(LESSON 3)*

4. **Synthesizing.** Relate the nation's health goals for reducing tobacco-related illness in your community. Explain how smoke-free zones in your community support *Healthy People 2010*. *(LESSON 3)*

➤ HEALTH SKILLS APPLICATION

1. **Decision Making.** What would you do if a close friend wanted to use tobacco to relieve stress? Use the six steps of decision making to form a plan of action. *(LESSON 1)*

2. **Accessing Information.** Conduct research to identify, describe, and assess health services in the community that provide tobacco cessation programs to prevent disease. Make a list of resources that will provide help for tobacco users who want to quit. *(LESSON 2)*

3. **Communication Skills.** What would you say to a pregnant female to encourage her to live tobacco free? *(LESSON 3)*

4. **Advocacy.** Write a letter to a state or local official expressing your opinions on what the government should do to promote the health of its citizens. Include in your letter information on the benefits of a smoke-free environment for all people. *(LESSON 3)*

BEYOND *the* Classroom

Parent Involvement

Advocacy. With your parents, brainstorm ways your family can help promote a smoke-free environment in your community. What actions can you take to contribute to a healthy environment for all people in your community?

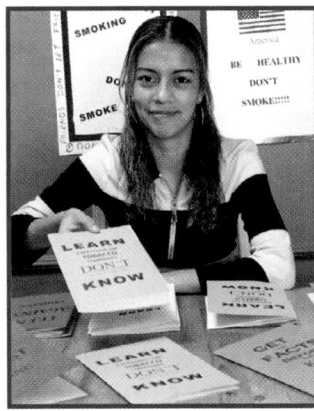

School and Community

Antitobacco Programs. Work with classmates, teachers, and administrators to start a Teens Against Tobacco Use (TATU) program at your school. As a group, design a plan for promoting health in your school and community by reducing tobacco use. Ask members of the community to support your goals.

children exposed to ETS have an increased risk of sore throats, ear infections, upper respiratory infections, and lung cancer.

11. Laws prohibit the sale of tobacco products to minors; stores that sell tobacco products to anyone under 18 have their tobacco licenses revoked.

12. *Healthy People 2010* has set a goal to reduce the number of people who use tobacco and to reduce the number of tobacco-related deaths.

Thinking Critically

1. The body becomes dependent on a certain amount of nicotine. When the smoker switches to low-nicotine cigarettes, he or she subconsciously tries to get the same amount of nicotine.

2. Possible answers: stress, weight control, desire to appear mature and independent, peer pressure, role models, advertising.

3. Answers should mention that such areas protect the health of nonsmokers by reducing their exposure to ETS.

4. Answers may mention that national health goals can influence individuals, families, and communities to work toward a healthier environment and lifestyle.

Health Skills Application

1.–4. Answers will vary.

EVALUATE

- Use the reproducible Chapter 21 Test in the TCR, or construct your own using the Testmaker software. 📁 💿

- Use Performance Assessment 21 in the TCR. 📁

ENRICHMENT

Ask students to complete Enrichment Activity 21 in the TCR. 📁

BEYOND *the* Classroom

Keep students involved in the community, and encourage parent participation by assigning the activities on this page for students to work on outside of class.

Lessons	Standards		Features
	National	**State/Local**	
1 Choosing to Be Alcohol Free *pages 562–567*	National Health Education Standards **1.2, 1.4, 3.3, 4.2, 6.3**		**Real-Life Application** • Seeing Through Alcohol Advertising, *(Analyzing Influences)*, page 564 **Health Skills Activity** • Avoiding Alcohol, *(Refusal Skills)*, page 566
2 Harmful Effects of Alcohol Use *pages 568–573*	National Health Education Standards **1.3, 3.2, 3.3, 5.6**		**Hands-On Health** • Saying No to a Driver Who Has Been Drinking, *(Refusal Skills)*, page 572
3 Alcohol, the Individual, and Society *pages 574–579*	National Health Education Standards **1.7, 2.3, 2.5, 2.6, 3.1**		

Reproducible Resources	Assessment	Technology
Student Activity Workbook for use with each chapter	📁 Lesson Quiz 80	💿 TeacherWorks®
📁 Concept Mapping Activity 80		🖥 Internet Activities
📁 Current Health Issues 22		
📁 Enrichment Activity 22		
📁 Guided Reading Activities 80		
📁 Lesson Plan 80		
📁 Parent Letter and Activities 22		
📁 Reteaching Activity 80		
📁 Concept Mapping Activity 81	📁 Lesson Quiz 81	🕹 Transparency 64
📁 Cross-Curriculum Activity 22		💿 Teacher Works®
📁 Decision-Making Activity 22		
📁 Guided Reading Activities 81		
📁 Lesson Plan 81		
📁 Reteaching Activity 81		
📁 Concept Mapping Activity 82	📁 Lesson Quiz 82	🕹 Transparency 65
📁 Guided Reading Activities 82		💿 TeacherWorks®
📁 Health Lab 22		
📁 Lesson Plan 82		
📁 Reteaching Activity 82		

⏱ OUT OF TIME

If time does not permit teaching the entire chapter, use:
- Real-Life Application, p. 564
- Figure 22.1, p. 569
- Health Skills Activity, p. 566
- Hands-On Health, p. 572
- Figure 22.3, p. 575

Language Diversity

- 🎧 English Audio CD Program
- 🎧 Spanish Audio CD Program
- 📁 English Summaries, Quizzes, and Activities
- 📁 Spanish Summaries, Quizzes, and Activities
- 📁 Spanish Parent Letters and Activities

End of Chapter Assessment

Blackline Masters

- 📁 Chapter 22 Test
- 📁 Performance Assessment Activity 22

Technology

- 💿 Vocabulary PuzzleMaker
- 📼 MindJogger Videoquiz
- 💿 **Exam***View*® Pro Testmaker

Professional Health Series

Dealing with Sensitive Issues
Planning a Coordinated School Health Program
Promoting Character Education
Home, School, and Community Involvement

Key to Ability Levels

Teaching strategies that appear throughout the chapter have been identified by one of the following codes to give teachers an idea of their suitability for students of varying learning styles and abilities.

L1 Strategies should be within the ability range of all students. Full class participation is often required. Teacher direction is usually needed.

L2 Strategies are designed for average to above-average students or for small groups. Some teacher direction is needed.

L3 Strategies are designed for students able and willing to work independently. Minimal teacher direction is needed.

ELL Strategies should be within the ability range of students learning the English language.

⬛▶ Block scheduling strategies are useful in a block scheduling format.

CHAPTER OVERVIEW

Chapter 22 discusses the risks alcohol poses to all three aspects of the health triangle. It helps students identify and practice useful strategies for refusing alcohol.

Lesson 1 Alcohol is a powerful and addictive drug that poses serious risks to physical, mental/emotional, and social health. Refusal skills can help teens avoid alcohol use and thus enjoy the benefits of being alcohol free.

Lesson 2 Alcohol has immediate negative effects on the nervous, cardiovascular, digestive, and respiratory systems. Driving under the influence of alcohol poses special risks; it is the leading cause of death among American teens.

Lesson 3 Alcohol use has negative long-term effects on physical health. Alcoholism is a serious disease involving physical or psychological dependence on alcohol. Alcoholics and their families can get support for treatment.

Health Skills Features

- Real-Life Application (*Analyzing Influences*), p. 564
- Health Skills Activity (*Refusal Skills*), p. 566
- Hands-On Health (*Refusal Skills*), p. 572

Chapter 22

Alcohol

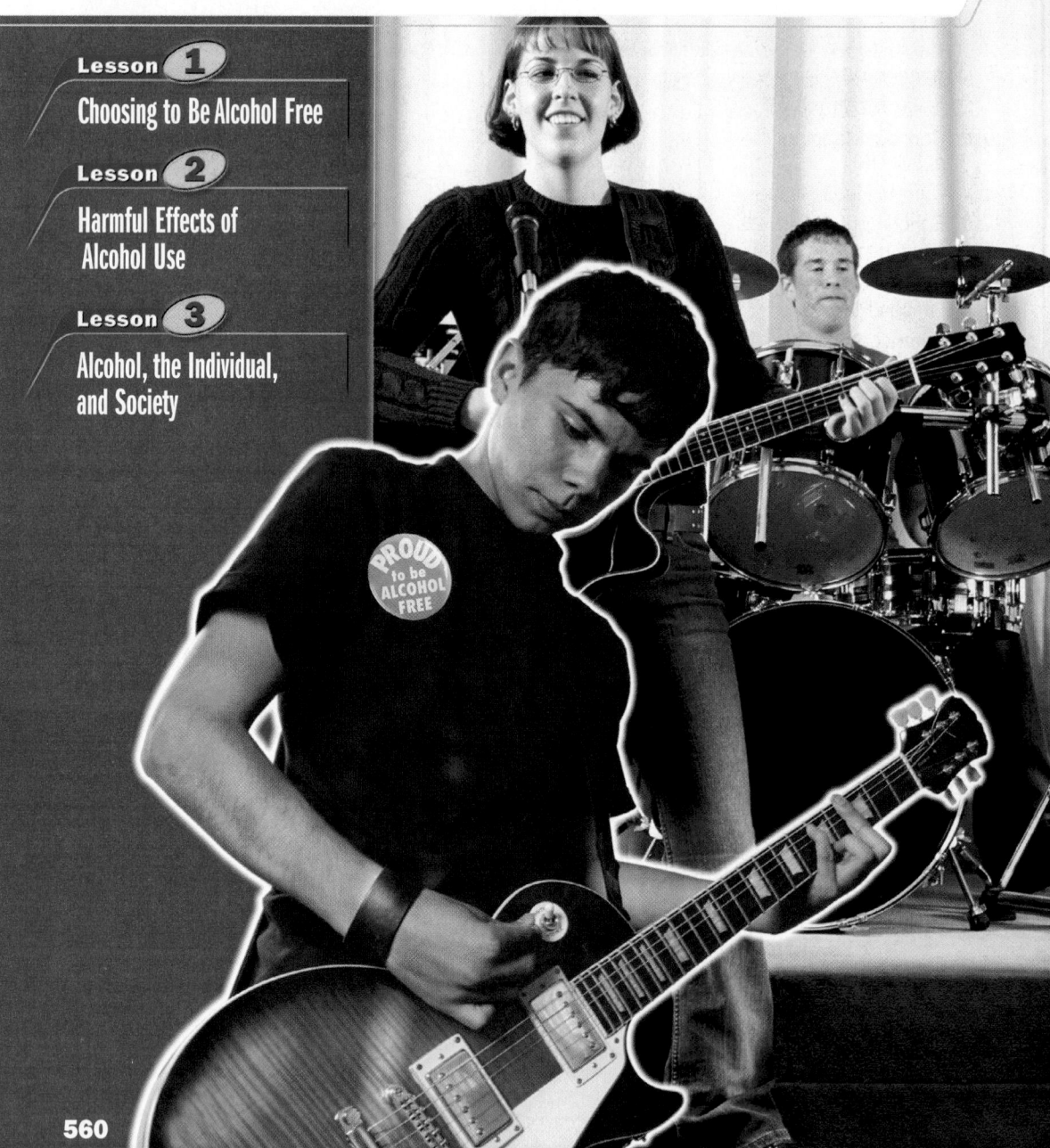

Lesson 1
Choosing to Be Alcohol Free

Lesson 2
Harmful Effects of Alcohol Use

Lesson 3
Alcohol, the Individual, and Society

560

MEETING STUDENT DIVERSITY

Language Diversity Use the following suggestions to help students who have difficulty with English:

- Pair English language learners with native speakers of English who can restate the Chapter Summary in language that helps students comprehend important concepts.

- Direct auditory learners or those students with language diversity to the *Glencoe Health Audio CD Program*. Available in English and Spanish, this component provides an audio and written summary of the chapter.

- Use photographs, drawings, or magazine clippings to help students visualize the important concepts of the chapter.

Noon Concert

Sponsored by: Students Against Alcohol Use!

Quick Write

Using Visuals. Teens who make the decision to avoid the use of alcohol enjoy safe and healthy activities. How can you and your peers make a statement about your decision to stay alcohol free?

Myth or Fact?

Do You Know Which Is a Myth and Which Is a Fact About Alcohol?

Read each statement below and respond by writing *Myth* or *Fact* for each item.

1. Alcohol has the same chemical and physical effects on everyone who drinks.

2. Someone who doesn't act drunk isn't drunk.

3. When a person is intoxicated, coffee, a cold shower, or fresh air will sober him or her up.

4. Alcohol impairs judgment and social behaviors.

5. People can get into serious health, legal, and social problems *anytime* they use alcohol.

6. Drinking alcohol on weekends or once in a while is not harmful.

7. No amount of alcohol is safe for a pregnant woman to drink.

8. Binge drinking has no long-term effects.

Keep your responses for review later in the chapter. When you complete the chapter, review this list of myths and facts again. If necessary, change your answers on the basis of what you have learned.

INTRODUCING THE CHAPTER

Myth or Fact?

Let a volunteer read aloud the title of the feature on this page. Have students write and then discuss their responses.

1. Myth: Females lack a specific enzyme to metabolize alcohol and become intoxicated faster than males of the same size. Also, alcohol has a stronger effect on teens and older people than on young adults and middle-aged adults.

2. Myth: Some people can become drunk without showing obvious signs.

3. Myth: These practices do not speed up the liver's ability to break down the alcohol; so they don't help to sober a person up.

4. Fact

5. Fact

6. Myth: It is illegal for teens to drink any amount of alcohol.

7. Fact

8. Myth: Binge drinking can result in alcohol poisoning, which can be fatal.

Quick Write

Using Visuals Direct students to look at the photograph. Ask: How are these teens assuring that their activities are safe and healthy? What problems would develop if one of these teens decided to drink alcohol? Then have students write their responses to the Quick Write assignment.

TECHNOLOGY OPTIONS

MINDJOGGER
VIDEOQUIZ

To preview or review chapter content, you may wish to use the Chapter 22 MindJogger Videoquiz.

HEALTH *Online*

Online Resources for the Teacher For a fresh approach to health topics and an in-depth look at health issues, use these online resources found under Teacher Resources at **health.glencoe.com**:

- Block Schedule Lesson Plans
- Technology Projects
- Health Updates

Choosing to Be Alcohol Free

 FOCUS

QUICK START Give students three minutes to list the risks of alcohol use and another three minutes to list alternatives to alcohol use. Then have students share and discuss their responses.

TYING TO PRIOR KNOWLEDGE

Ask several volunteers to share a few facts they already know about alcohol. After a brief discussion, explain that students will learn more about alcohol as they study this lesson.

Health Skills Features

"Seeing Through Alcohol Advertising," p. 564

 ANALYZING INFLUENCES

"Avoiding Alcohol," p. 566

 REFUSAL SKILLS

INTRODUCING VOCABULARY

- Have students look in their Glossaries or dictionaries for the definition of *intoxication*. Then have them use the term in a sentence. Discuss behaviors associated with drinking alcohol.

- Ask students to complete the Chapter 22 Study Guide in the *Student Activity Workbook*. 📁

Choosing to Be Alcohol Free

VOCABULARY
ethanol
fermentation
depressant
intoxication
alcohol abuse

YOU'LL LEARN TO

- Identify factors, such as the media, that influence decisions about alcohol use and your health.

- Analyze the physical, mental, social, and legal consequences of alcohol use.

- Explain the relationship between alcohol use by adolescents and the role alcohol plays in unsafe situations.

- Develop strategies for preventing the use of alcohol.

- Demonstrate refusal strategies regarding alcohol use and the benefits of choosing to be alcohol free.

QUICK START Fold a sheet of paper in half. On the left side of the paper, list reasons why drinking alcohol is risky for teens. On the right side, list alternatives to alcohol use.

🔺 Recognizing the health risks of alcohol will help you make the decision to stay alcohol free. *How can avoiding alcohol use help you succeed in school?*

For many people the image is a familiar one: energetic young adults playing sports, cooking out, living life to the fullest. The purpose of this attractive advertisement scene is to promote and sell a drug—alcohol—that is addictive, physically damaging, and often an entry into other drug use. In reality, alcohol is a lethal drug with harmful physical, mental, social, and legal consequences. These consequences can result in serious health problems to the drinker and those around him or her and even death caused by disease, violence, or vehicle crashes.

The Facts About Alcohol

Alcohol, or, more accurately, **ethanol**—*the type of alcohol in alcoholic beverages*—is a powerful and addictive drug. Ethanol can be produced synthetically or naturally through the fermentation of fruits, vegetables, and grains. **Fermentation** is *the chemical*

Lesson 1 *Resources*

Teacher Classroom Resources
📁 Concept Mapping Activity 80
📁 Current Health Issues 22
📁 Enrichment Activity 22
📁 Guided Reading Activities 80
📁 Lesson Plan 80

📁 Lesson Quiz 80
📁 Parent Letter and Activities 22
📁 Reteaching Activity 80

Student Activity Workbook
📁 Applying Health Skills 80
📁 Chapter 22 Study Guide

action of yeast on sugars. Water, flavoring, and minerals are mixed with ethanol to produce a variety of beverages, such as beer and wine. Alcohol also can be processed to create spirits, or liquors, such as whiskey, rye, and vodka.

Immediate Effects of Alcohol Consumption

At first drinking alcohol may provide a kind of energy "rush." This initial reaction masks alcohol's true effects as a **depressant**, *a drug that slows the central nervous system.* Alcohol quickly affects a person's motor skills by slowing reaction time and impairing vision. Clear thinking and good judgment also diminish. A variety of factors, including a person's body size and stomach contents, determines alcohol's effect. For this reason, the amount of alcohol that leads to intoxication varies from person to person. **Intoxication** is *the state in which the body is poisoned by alcohol or another substance and the person's physical and mental control is significantly reduced.*

Factors That Influence Alcohol Use

Despite the many problems associated with alcohol use, many teenagers still choose to drink. Why? Several reasons influence teens in their choice to use—or not use—alcohol:

▶ **Peer pressure.** It's normal for teens to want to feel accepted within a group. The desire to fit in is strong. Teens who choose friends who avoid alcohol use are more likely to be alcohol free than teens whose friends accept alcohol use.

▶ **Family.** Family members can help teens be alcohol free. Parents who discourage and avoid the use of alcohol are more likely to have teens who do the same. In fact, teens cite parental disapproval as the number one reason for not using alcohol.

▶ **Media messages.** Many media messages on TV and radio and in movies make alcohol use appear exciting, attractive, and fun. Many of these messages feature elements targeted to a teen audience, such as young, attractive people engaging in problem-free drinking in a partylike atmosphere. The message of many ads is "To fit in, drink alcohol." However, teens who recognize these messages and their meanings are more likely to resist negative influences.

Your family, friends, and peers influence your decisions about avoiding the use of alcohol. *How does your family support you in your healthy choice to be alcohol free?*

Did You Know ?

Through the media teens are exposed to alcohol use in many forms.
- By the time teens reach ninth grade, most will have seen more ads for beer or wine than for any other product.
- A recent study found that 93 percent of the 200 most popular movie rentals depicted alcohol use.
- A review of top-selling rap recordings found alcohol mentioned in 47 percent of the songs.

② TEACH

Critical Thinking

Have students share their responses to these questions:

- Why do you think some teens experiment with alcohol even though underage drinking is illegal and unsafe?

- What can adults do to discourage drinking among teens?

- What responsibility do you think teens have to discourage their friends from drinking? Their classmates? Other teens who they might not even know?

Health Skills Practice

Considering Consequences Read aloud the following: A group of friends are driving out to the lake. You heard people are bringing alcohol. You are trying to decide whether or not to go. With a partner, list all the considerations you might go through to make a responsible decision.

DECISION MAKING

More About...

Teen Health In an average month, 9 million American teens drink alcohol. In a nationwide survey, 32 percent of students in grades 9 through 12 reported that they had first drunk alcohol (more than a few sips) before age 13. Signs of a problem with drinking (besides seeing the person drinking or drunk) include lying about things, avoiding friends, giving up activities, taking risks, and feeling depressed. People with a drinking problem often deny it and don't get help on their own. Teens who suspect a friend has a problem should tell a trusted adult. They can let the person know they care and encourage the person to talk to a trusted adult.

SEEING THROUGH ALCOHOL ADVERTISING

ANALYZING INFLUENCES

NHES Standard 4 Students will analyze the influence of culture, media, technology, and other factors on health.

Objectives

• Recognize the hidden messages in advertisements for alcohol.

• Identify alcohol-related facts that are not presented in advertisements.

Motivator

Ask: How do advertisers make alcohol seem attractive? Which ads are especially appealing to teens? Why?

Teaching Strategies

1. Bring in a sample ad from a newspaper or magazine. Let students work together to read and discuss the ad.

2. Be sure students recognize that the three questions they will answer about each ad are the same three questions answered for the sample ad.

✓ Assessment

Using a rubric, student work should provide comprehensive evidence of the following criteria to achieve the highest score:

✔ identification and analysis of external and internal factors
✔ attention to interrelationships and complexity of influences
✔ variety of influences as appropriate

Advertising Techniques

Companies that produce alcoholic beverages spend billions of dollars each year and use various strategies to advertise and sell their products. Advertisements appear on billboards, can be seen or heard on television and radio, and fill magazines and newspapers. Alcohol companies sponsor sporting events, music concerts, art festivals, exhibits, and other community events. They do this to

Real-Life Application

Seeing Through Alcohol Advertising

What media images come to mind when you think of advertisements for alcohol? Many advertisers appeal to emotions and desires to influence people to buy their products. By understanding the ways in which advertisers market alcohol, teens can make the informed choice to avoid using it.

JOIN THE FUN!

ACTIVITY

Use a critical eye when looking at advertisements in magazines and newspapers and on billboards, television, and the Internet. Select three examples of alcohol advertising. For each example, ask yourself these questions:

1. **What is really being advertised?** Write a paragraph that analyzes how the ad appeals to an emotion or a desire in a particular audience.

2. **What is the hidden message?** Create a caption that describes what the advertisers want the intended audience to believe about drinking alcohol.

3. **What is the truth?** Explain why the ad is misleading, using at least three facts about alcohol use that the ad does not mention.

Demonstrate what you have learned from your analysis by writing a statement on the truthfulness of alcohol advertising.

What is really being advertised?
The ad is "selling" physical attractiveness. It appeals to an internal influence that most people share: the desire to be among friends who enjoy being together.

What is the hidden message?
"You need our beer to have fun with your friends."

What is the truth?
Drinking beer is not the reason people are enjoying the party. This picture is staged. In fact, drinking alcohol impairs coordination; the ability to play volleyball would be affected. None of the risks of alcohol use are shown.

Home and Community

Community Resources As students discuss activities that they consider attractive alternatives to alcohol use, encourage them to explore local centers and organizations where those activities might be available. For example, they might investigate a basketball league at the local recreation center, afternoon classes at a nearby youth organization or community college, or volunteer opportunities at a neighborhood hospital. Encourage them to find as many community resources as possible. Also, if they have an interest that is not met by community groups, they might consider starting an after-school club for that activity.

associate their products with attractive and healthy people having fun. It is important to thoroughly analyze and interpret media messages that encourage the consumption of alcohol.

Avoid Alcohol: Avoid Unsafe Situations

Alcohol use can be dangerous and even deadly. Alcohol-related traffic collisions are the number one cause of death and disability among teens. Alcohol use also is linked with deaths by drowning, fire, suicide, and homicide. Even if you are not drinking but are around people who are, you have an increased risk of being seriously injured, involved in a vehicle crash, or affected by violence. Alcohol-related incidents can be damaging to the health and safety of the user and those associated with the user.

Alcohol and the Law

If you are under 21, it is illegal to buy, possess, or consume alcohol. For teens who break the law, the costs can be very high. Teens can be arrested, fined, and sentenced to a youth detention center. By breaking the law, the offender risks both damaging his or her reputation and losing the trust and respect of friends and family members.

Alcohol, Violence, and Sexual Activity

Teens can protect their health by avoiding situations where alcohol is present. Teens who drink alcohol are more likely to be victims or perpetrators of violent crimes such as rape, aggravated assault, and robbery. They are also more likely to become involved in fights, resulting in school or police action.

Alcohol use and sexual activity are a dangerous mixture. Alcohol impairs a person's judgment, lowers his or her inhibitions, and compromises his or her moral standards. Teens who use alcohol are more likely to become sexually active at earlier ages, to engage in sexual activity more often, and to engage in unprotected sexual activity more often than teens who do not use alcohol. Such careless sexual activity can lead to unplanned pregnancy, sexually transmitted diseases, and emotional scars that don't heal easily.

Alcohol Abuse

Most young people do not live in families in which alcohol abuse is a problem. However, it is estimated that 25 percent of all youth *are* exposed to family **alcohol abuse**—*the excessive use of alcohol*—at some time before they reach the age of 18. Young people who live in a household in which a family member abuses alcohol are at a high risk for neglect, abuse, economic hardship, and social isolation. Sometimes, these problems can lead a young person to try alcohol

CHARACTER CHECK

Responsibility. Demonstrate your commitment to a lifestyle that does not include alcohol use by taking responsibility for your decisions. **Write and sign a pledge to stay alcohol free. Share your pledge with your parents and friends. Encourage your friends to sign pledges, too.**

Did You Know ?

Alcohol use is a serious matter. It is a key factor in

- 33 percent of suicides.
- 50 percent of homicides.
- 62 percent of assaults.
- 68 percent of manslaughter cases.
- 50 percent of head injuries.
- 41 percent of traffic fatalities.
- Alcohol also plays a major role in domestic abuse and injury, child abuse and neglect, and workplace injuries.
- More than half of all people who drown have consumed alcohol before entering the water.

Researching

Ask volunteers to learn about your state's laws regarding the purchase, possession, and consumption of alcohol by minors and the sale or delivery of alcohol to minors and share their findings with the class. Then encourage a class discussion in response to the following questions:

- Who needs to know about these laws? Why?
- Who is responsible for adhering to the restrictions included in these laws?
- How do these laws impact you directly?

CHARACTER CHECK

Responsibility Help students discuss why avoiding alcohol demonstrates responsibility as well as respect for themselves and others. Ask students what makes an effective pledge statement. Let them brainstorm a list of possible pledges about staying alcohol free during special events such as homecoming or the prom. Have students write and sign their own pledges. Suggest that students post their pledges and pass out similar versions to the school community during special events.

More About...

Reliable Sources As students consider strategies that can help others make responsible choices about alcohol, they might consult online or printed resources provided by Students Against Destructive Decisions (SADD). Students dedicated to helping other students say no to drinking and driving created this organization.

Today, SADD has expanded its mission to include other high-risk behaviors. The group's goal is "to provide students with the best prevention and intervention tools possible to deal with the issues of underage drinking, drunk driving, drug abuse, and other destructive decisions." More information is available in Web Links at **health.glencoe.com.**

Health Skills Activity

AVOIDING ALCOHOL

NHES Standard 6

Students will demonstrate the ability to use goal-setting and decision-making skills to enhance health.

Objectives

- Identify reasons to avoid using alcohol.
- Apply decision-making skills to make a health-promoting decision.

Motivator

Have students brainstorm a list of reasons not to use alcohol. Then have them brainstorm a list of reasons to avoid situations where other people are using alcohol.

Teaching Strategies

1. Have students work with partners to read and discuss the situation.

2. Let students work independently to write their responses to each step in the decision-making process.

✓ Assessment

Using a rubric, student work should provide comprehensive evidence of the following criteria to achieve the highest score:

✔ progression through a decision-making process
✔ identification of the decision to be made
✔ consideration of options and consequences
✔ taking action or making a decision
✔ evaluation or reflection on the decision

Decision Making: Avoiding Alcohol

Chantelle has been invited to a party at her friend Natasha's house. When Chantelle arrives, she is surprised to see people drinking alcoholic beverages. Natasha's parents are not at home.

Chantelle walks over to Natasha. "What kind of party is this?" she asks.

"It's a *high-school* party," Natasha says. "Here, have a beer."

"No, thanks," Chantelle responds. "Won't your parents be upset if they see this?"

"Don't worry," Natasha says. "They won't be home for hours. Here, have a drink. It'll loosen you up."

Chantelle just stares.

Natasha says, "Come on. It's no big deal."

What Would You Do?

Apply the six steps of the decision-making process to Chantelle's problem.

1. State the situation.
2. List the options.
3. Weigh the possible outcomes.
4. Consider values.
5. Make the decision and act.
6. Evaluate the decision.

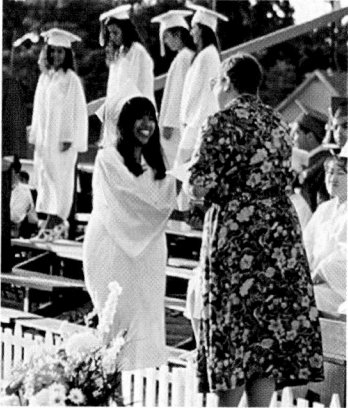

▲ **Choosing to be alcohol free allows you to reach your potential and achieve your goals.**

566 Chapter 22 Alcohol

as an escape. However, drinking only makes the situation worse. Studies indicate that a person who begins drinking as a teen is four times more likely to develop alcohol dependence than an adult is.

Alcohol and Extracurricular Activities

The negative consequences of alcohol use for teens can extend to their eligibility for participation in extracurricular activities, including athletics. Most schools have adopted a zero-tolerance policy for students found using alcohol. If caught, students may become ineligible to participate or may be suspended from their activities or from school. A student's future college and job prospects could be damaged.

Being Alcohol Free

Deciding to be alcohol free is an important step in achieving a healthy lifestyle. Many people, especially teens, make the commitment to stay alcohol free. This commitment helps you:

Cooperative Learning Activity

Alcohol and the Media Divide the class into small groups. Provide a selection of popular magazines and have groups determine which ones have the most advertisements for alcohol. Ask them to draw conclusions about the way alcohol is advertised and the people likely to read the magazine. What is the target audience? Have groups discuss the following: Are the people in the ads having fun? Do they seem sophisticated or not? Are they portrayed as athletic? Have groups discuss what other possible destructive behaviors are often promoted through the media. Have each group cut out the ads for alcohol, and create a binder with plastic sleeves to hold the ads. Each group should include a critique of each of the ads on separate pages in the binder.

- **Maintain a healthy body.** Avoiding alcohol use protects body organs from damage and decreases the chance of injury.

- **Make responsible decisions.** Having a clear head helps you make decisions to protect your health and the health of others.

- **Avoid risky behavior.** Teens who avoid alcohol reduce their risk of participating in unsafe behaviors such as sexual activity or drinking and driving, and of being a victim or perpetrator of a violent crime.

- **Avoid illegal activities.** Purchasing or possessing alcohol is against the law for anyone under the age of 21. You can avoid arrest and legal problems by being alcohol free.

Refusing Alcohol

Even if the pressure to use alcohol becomes intense, saying no is much easier when you're prepared. If you find yourself in a situation in which alcohol is present, be assertive: refuse to drink, leave the situation quickly, and call for a ride home. Remember that your best defense is to avoid situations in which alcohol is present. Avoid parties where alcohol is served. Practice refusal skills at home to build confidence when you are with peers.

Ⓨ **Call home for a ride if you find yourself in a situation where alcohol is present.** *What other strategies can you use to avoid unsafe situations?*

Lesson 1 *Review*

Reviewing Facts and Vocabulary

1. Define the terms *alcohol*, *depressant*, and *intoxication*.

2. Identify and explain ways families can have a positive influence on teens' decisions about alcohol use.

3. Describe two effective refusal strategies for avoiding the use of alcohol.

Thinking Critically

4. **Analyzing.** Explain the depressant effects of alcohol. How might alcohol affect your ability to make healthful decisions?

5. **Synthesizing.** Explain why refusing alcohol will help you avoid unsafe situations such as sexual assault and violence. In what ways will you also be avoiding the risk of exposure to STDs?

Applying Health Skills

Advocacy. Prepare a pamphlet or an article for your school newspaper that advocates an alcohol-free lifestyle. Describe the risks and consequences of alcohol use. Be sure to explain the benefits of being alcohol free and to include examples of effective communication skills when avoiding alcohol use.

TECHNOLOGY | OPTION

WORD PROCESSING Give your pamphlet or article a professional look by using word-processing software. See **health.glencoe.com** for tips on using different features of most word-processing programs.

Lesson 1 Choosing to Be Alcohol Free **567**

Lesson 1 *Review*

Answers to Reviewing Facts and Vocabulary

1. Alcohol is a substance that is produced by a chemical reaction in fruit, vegetables, or grains. A depressant is a drug that slows down the central nervous system. Intoxication is when the body is poisoned by alcohol or another substance, reducing physical and mental control.

2. Family members can influence teens by discouraging teens from drinking and by avoiding alcohol themselves.

3. Possible answers: Be direct, provide personal reasons, or identify values.

Answers to Thinking Critically

4.–5. Answers will vary.

Explaining

Explain to students that if a teen hosts a party where alcohol is present, his or her parents can be held legally responsible for the young people, whether or not they are home. Ⓛ1

③ ASSESS

EVALUATING THE LESSON

Assign and discuss the Lesson 1 Review; then administer, grade, and discuss Lesson Quiz 80 in the TCR. 📁

RETEACHING

- Have students work in small groups to list at least six approaches teens might use to pressure their peers into trying or drinking alcohol. Then have group members identify the inaccuracies in each approach and suggest an effective refusal strategy.

- Ask students to complete Reteaching Activity 80 in the TCR. 📁

ENRICHMENT

Have students work in small groups to plan, practice, and present skits in which teens resist peer pressure to drink alcohol. If possible, arrange to have students perform their skits for younger students, for example, at a local middle school or junior high.

④ CLOSE

Have students write short, private journal entries describing their own best reasons for avoiding alcohol.

Harmful Effects of Alcohol Use

Lesson 2

1 FOCUS

QUICK START Give students several minutes to write their lists of organs affected by alcohol. Ask student volunteers to read from their lists and write these organs on the board. Then have students create their own word webs individually.

TYING TO PRIOR KNOWLEDGE

Help students review some of the risks of drinking alcohol. Explain that students will learn more about the changes that are caused by alcohol and the risk they pose to health.

Health Skills Features

"Saying No to a Driver Who Has Been Drinking," p. 572

REFUSAL SKILLS

INTRODUCING VOCABULARY

- Have students give informal definitions of *binge drinking* and *alcohol poisoning;* then have them check the formal definitions in the Glossary. Ask volunteers to explain the relationship between binge drinking and alcohol poisoning.

- Ask students to complete the Chapter 22 Study Guide in the *Student Activity Workbook.*

Harmful Effects of Alcohol Use

VOCABULARY
metabolism
blood alcohol
    concentration
binge drinking
alcohol poisoning

YOU'LL LEARN TO

- Examine the short-term effects of alcohol use.
- Apply responsible decision making by associating the risks and consequences of drinking and driving.
- Recognize the dangers of alcohol-drug interactions.
- Demonstrate refusal strategies concerning alcohol use.

QUICK START Make a list of all the organs in the body you can think of that are affected by alcohol use. Make a word web of your ideas with the term "alcohol use" in the center.

 Many over-the-counter and prescription drugs carry warning labels about alcohol interactions. *Analyze how these warnings help protect users from health risks.*

S tatistics confirm that drinking alcohol is a high-risk behavior. Nevertheless, some teens feel pressured to drink alcohol. Finding out about the physical effects alcohol has on the body can help you strengthen your commitment to staying alcohol free.

Short-Term Effects of Drinking

T he short-term effects of alcohol are different for each individual. Many of these effects are described in **Figure 22.1.** Some factors that influence the onset of these effects include:

▶ **Body size and gender.** A small person feels the effect of the same amount of alcohol faster than a large person does. In general, alcohol moves into the bloodstream faster in females.

▶ **Food.** Food in the stomach slows down the passage of alcohol into the bloodstream.

▶ **Amount and rate of intake.** As the amount of alcohol consumed increases, the level of alcohol in the bloodstream also rises. When a person drinks alcohol faster than the liver can break it down, intoxication results. When blood alcohol levels become too high, alcohol poisoning can occur.

Lesson 2 *Resources*

Teacher Classroom Resources

📁 Concept Mapping Activity 81

📁 Cross-Curriculum Activity 22

📁 Decision-Making Activity 22

📁 Guided Reading Activities 81

📁 Lesson Plan 81

📁 Lesson Quiz 81

📁 Reteaching Activity 81

Student Activity Workbook

📁 Applying Health Skills 81

📁 Chapter 22 Study Guide

Multimedia

 Transparency 64

Alcohol and Drug Interactions

Alcohol and medications or any other drugs don't mix. Interactions between medications and alcohol can lead to illness, injury, or even death. In fact, alcohol-drug interactions are a factor in about one-fourth of all emergency room admissions. To understand why these interactions occur, you must understand how the body works. When a drug enters the body, it travels through the bloodstream to its target organ or tissue. Over time, the body metabolizes the drug. **Metabolism** is *the process by which the body breaks down substances*. Alcohol travels through the bloodstream to the brain. At the same time, the liver metabolizes the alcohol in the bloodstream and makes it less active. Then the kidneys filter the neutralized particles and other waste products from the blood and produce urine, which is excreted.

The presence of both alcohol and medication or another drug within a person's body can be dangerous. This is because alcohol combined with medicines or other drugs can result in a *multiplier effect*, in which the medication has a greater or different effect than if it were taken alone. Both prescription drugs and over-the-counter medicines, such as aspirin, can alter the way in which alcohol affects the body. Labels on medicines that might cause reactions warn against combining them with alcoholic beverages.

Did You Know

→ Females become intoxicated faster and stay that way longer than do males of comparable size. Why?

- Females have a higher percentage of body fat and less water in their bodies than males. As a result, alcohol in females is less diluted and has a stronger and more lasting effect.
- The enzyme that controls alcohol processing is 70 percent more effective in males than in females.

FIGURE 22.1

SHORT-TERM EFFECTS OF ALCOHOL

Physical and mental impairment begin with the first drink of alcohol and increase as more alcohol is consumed.

Nervous System	Cardiovascular System	Digestive System	Respiratory System
• **Brain.** The brain becomes less able to control the body. Movement, speech, and vision may be affected. • **Memory.** Thought processes are disorganized, and memory and concentration are dulled. • **Judgment.** Judgment is altered and coordination is impaired.	• **Heart.** With a low intake, alcohol causes an increase in heart rate and blood pressure. At higher intake levels, heart rate and blood pressure decrease and heart rhythm becomes irregular. Risk of cardiac arrest increases. • **Blood Vessels.** Alcohol causes the blood vessels to expand. The increased surface area of the blood vessels allows body heat to escape and the body's temperature to drop.	• **Stomach.** Some alcohol passes quickly from the stomach into the bloodstream. Stomach acid production increases and often results in nausea and vomiting. • **Liver.** Toxic chemicals are released as the liver metabolizes alcohol. These chemicals cause inflammation and scarring. • **Kidneys.** Alcohol causes the kidneys to increase urine output, which can lead to dehydration.	• **Lungs.** Carbon dioxide formed by the liver is released from the body through the lungs. • **Breathing.** Alcohol depresses nerves that control involuntary functions such as breathing. If an excessive amount of alcohol is consumed, breathing may slow, become irregular, or stop.

Lesson 2 Harmful Effects of Alcohol Use **569**

---

2 TEACH

Discussing

Ask students what role food plays in slowing the absorption of alcohol in the body. What kinds of food might be more successful in slowing down the absorption process? Stress: Food—no matter what kind—cannot prevent alcohol from affecting the body. **L1**

VISUAL LEARNING

Figure 22.1 Have a student volunteer read aloud the title of Figure 22.1, and emphasize that this chart shows how alcohol affects the body each time an individual drinks. Divide the class into four groups, and assign each group one of the body systems in the chart. Ask the members of each group to work together, reading and discussing the listed effects of alcohol and planning an effective way to share this information with the rest of the class. After 7–10 minutes of preparation, have the groups present the information about alcohol and their assigned body system.

Cooperative Learning

Have small groups of students work together to plan, practice, and perform skits about alcohol's travels through the body. For example, individual students might play the parts of alcohol, the brain, the liver, and the bloodstream. Allow time for each group to perform its skit for the rest of the class. **L2** **Kinesthetic**

Curriculum Connections

Social Studies The financial costs of alcohol's effects on the body are considerable. Ask a representative from a local medical facility to speak to the class about the costs of treating individuals with health problems related to alcohol. Discuss the impact of this expense on society.

Science Ask volunteers to research the types of tests used to check for driving under the influence. Which tests use specific equipment? Which ones are used to check a person's judgment and reaction time? Let volunteers discuss their findings with the class.

Discussing

Ask students:

- How do you think drinking alcohol might affect a student's school work? An athlete's performance?

- What risks does a person take by driving under the influence of alcohol?

- As a passenger, how can you tell whether a driver has drunk too much? Only if the driver has not drunk alcohol at all can you be sure the driver has not had too much. **L1**

Guest Speaker

Ask a representative from Mothers Against Drunk Driving (MADD) or Students Against Destructive Decisions (SADD) to speak with the class about the work the organization does to campaign against drunk drivers. **L1**

Community Involvement

Assign volunteers to interview a local police officer about efforts to crack down on DUI offenders. Have the efforts worked? What age group presents the most serious problem? What can teens do to help fight this problem? Have students share their findings with the rest of the class. **L2**

HEALTH Online

To investigate what Mothers Against Drunk Driving (MADD) is doing about reducing drunk driving crashes, use Web Links at health.glencoe.com.

Alcohol-related vehicle fatalities are a leading cause of death for teens. *What effect does alcohol have on a person's ability to control a vehicle?*

These are some typical alcohol-drug interactions.

▶ Alcohol may slow down a drug's absorption by the body. This increases the length of time that the alcohol or drug is in the body and increases the risk of harmful side effects from the drug.

▶ Frequent drinking may increase the number of metabolizing enzymes in the body. This can cause medications to be broken down faster than normal, decreasing their effectiveness.

▶ Metabolizing enzymes can change some medications into chemicals that can damage the liver or other organs. For example, when taken with alcohol, acetaminophen, a common painkiller and fever reducer, can cause serious liver damage even when it is used in small amounts.

▶ Alcohol can increase the effects of some drugs. For example, antihistamines, which are taken for colds or allergies, react with alcohol and cause excessive dizziness and sleepiness. This effect is especially dangerous if you are operating machinery or driving.

Driving Under the Influence

Drinking alcohol impairs vision, reaction time, and coordination. When drinking is mixed with driving, the results can be disastrous or even deadly. In fact, *driving while intoxicated* (DWI), also known as *driving under the influence* (DUI), is the leading cause of death among teens. A person is said to be intoxicated when his or her blood alcohol concentration exceeds the state's legal limit. **Blood alcohol concentration (BAC)** is *the amount of alcohol in a person's blood, expressed as a percentage.* In most states driving while intoxicated is defined as having a 0.1 percent BAC, although in some states the figure is 0.08. However, signs of intoxication can begin to appear at BACs as low as 0.02. **Figure 22.2** on the next page illustrates the alcohol content of some common alcoholic beverages. Remember that for anyone under 21, there is no acceptable BAC percentage. Medical researchers have found that drinking of any sort

▶ slows reflexes.

▶ reduces a person's ability to judge distances and speeds.

▶ increases risk-taking behaviors.

▶ reduces a person's concentration while increasing forgetfulness.

More About...

Blood Alcohol Concentration One drink is .05 percent blood alcohol concentration (BAC), which can cause sedation and reduced self-control. Two to three drinks is .14 percent BAC, which causes loss of coordination and judgment. Four drinks is .18 percent BAC, which includes intoxication and very slow reaction time. Five to six drinks is .27 percent BAC, which results in a stupor. Seven to eight drinks is .36 percent BAC which leads to unconsciousness and may cause death. Nine or more drinks is .41 percent BAC, which will lead to death.

Ask: If a 120-pound teen drank two beers in an hour, what BAC would he or she likely have? Emphasize that drinking one alcoholic beverage within one hour can be dangerous for anyone.

Consequences of DWI

When a person is stopped for drinking and driving, a police officer will administer a field sobriety test before the person is given a breathalyzer test to measure BAC. The consequences for a teen caught driving while intoxicated or driving under the influence may include

- ▶ harm to the driver and others.
- ▶ severely restricted driving privileges and/or immediate confiscation of a driver's license.
- ▶ alcohol-related injuries, property damage, and death.
- ▶ living with regret and remorse from these consequences.
- ▶ loss of parental trust and respect.
- ▶ arrest, jail time, court appearance, and a heavy fine or bail.
- ▶ a police record and possible lawsuits.
- ▶ higher insurance rates—up to three times higher than those for nondrinking peers.

Like drinking and driving, riding in a vehicle with a driver who has been drinking is also a serious matter. Every day at least a dozen teens are killed in alcohol-related crashes. Never ride in a vehicle with a driver who has been drinking. If you are faced with this situation, find a ride with someone who has not been drinking or call home to have someone come to get you.

Binge Drinking

Recent studies show that **binge drinking**, *drinking five or more alcoholic drinks at one sitting*, is a serious problem among young people. Rapid binge drinking (sometimes done on a bet or dare) is especially dangerous because it is possible to consume a fatal dose of alcohol. Binge drinking can cause alcohol poisoning.

Alcohol Poisoning

It is very dangerous, and can be deadly, to drink a large amount of alcohol. **Alcohol poisoning** is *a severe and potentially fatal physical reaction to an alcohol overdose*. Alcohol acts as a depressant and shuts down involuntary actions such as breathing and the gag reflex that prevents choking. A fatal dose of alcohol will eventually stop these involuntary actions. It's common for a person who has consumed too much alcohol to vomit because alcohol is a stomach irritant. If the involuntary actions are shut down, a person can choke and be asphyxiated by his or her own vomit.

FIGURE 22.2

COMPARING BEER, WINE, AND SPIRITS

Each of these beverages contains the same amount of pure alcohol—about 0.5 ounces.

Drink	Alcohol by Volume	Alcohol Content
Beer 12 oz.	4%	0.4 oz.
Wine 5 oz.	10%	0.5 oz.
Vodka or Whiskey 1.25 oz.	40%	0.5 oz.

Lesson 2 Harmful Effects of Alcohol Use **571**

Researching

Have students work in groups to gather statistics about alcohol-related traffic accidents. Have them find the number of accidents that involve teens, and then calculate the percentage the number represents. Have group members graph their findings. **L3** **Logical/Mathematical**

VISUAL LEARNING

Figure 22.2 Set up an exhibit of three glasses of water; add a bit of food coloring, if possible, to make the contents more visible. Pour 12 ounces (36 ml) into a tall glass, 5 ounces (15 ml) into a short glass, and 1½ ounces (4 ml) into a juice glass. Explain that the glasses represent a serving of beer, a serving of wine, and a serving of vodka or whiskey. Emphasize that all three drinks contain the same amount of alcohol—about 0.5 ounces of pure alcohol. **L2**

Researching

Ask interested volunteers to learn about the particular effects of alcohol on teens. You may want to suggest they research information found in their textbooks, magazines, and other sources. Have them summarize their findings and share information with the rest of the class. Then let students share their responses to these questions: What do you consider the most serious danger of teen alcohol consumption? Why? **L2**

More About...

Alcohol Content Some teens think that beer and wine coolers are "safe" because, ounce for ounce, they contain less alcohol than hard liquor. A can of beer or a bottle of wine cooler contains as much alcohol as a shot of whiskey. Wine coolers are especially dangerous because they taste like sodas; so teens may be unaware of the alcohol content. A couple of beers or wine coolers have the same effects on a teen's body and judgment as the alcohol in two shots of hard liquor. It is essential for teens to recognize that all forms of alcohol are dangerous. Having "just a few beers" or "only wine coolers" puts teens at risk for problems with the law and for unsafe—and even fatal—situations.

Hands-On Health

SAYING NO TO A DRIVER WHO HAS BEEN DRINKING

REFUSAL SKILLS

NHES Standard 5 Students will demonstrate the ability to use interpersonal communication skills to enhance health.

Objectives

- Identify the risks associated with riding in a vehicle whose driver has been drinking.
- Demonstrate appropriate refusal strategies to say no to a ride with a driver who has been drinking.

Motivator

Have students think of times they have driven friends or been driven to a party or a dance. Ask: What responsibilities does a driver have? What might make you feel unsafe with a driver?

Teaching Strategies

1. As students are planning their skits, coordinate the groups so that a variety of drivers (relative, friend, parent of friend) are represented in the skit.
2. List the refusal strategies presented on poster board. Have students add to the list later if they think of new refusals.

✓ Assessment

Using a rubric, student work should provide comprehensive evidence of the following criteria to achieve the highest score:

✔ inclusion of the word no in their response
✔ explanation of why they are refusing
✔ alternatives to the activity
✔ body language

Hands-On Health ACTIVITY

Saying No to a Driver Who Has Been Drinking

You've heard the statement "Don't drink and drive." It's also dangerous to ride in a car if you suspect the driver has been drinking. Here are some ways to refuse that ride.

- Make a firm commitment to yourself not to ride with someone who has been drinking. If you know that alcohol will be available at a party, don't go.
- When you suspect a driver has been drinking, be prepared to make the right choice for your health and safety. Be strong. Find another way home.

Direct Statements: "I am not riding with you. You have been drinking."
Excuses: "I forgot to tell you—my dad is picking me up."
Insults: "You are really crazy to drive after drinking."
Humor: "I'm not getting in that car with you; I value my life."
Alternate suggestion: "Give me the keys; I'll drive."

What You'll Need

- 1 index card per student
- colored pencils or markers
- hole punch
- scissors

What You'll Do

1. Working with a small group, brainstorm a list of refusal strategies a teen can use to avoid riding in a car with a driver who has been drinking.
2. Write and present a skit that has dialogue showing one or more successful refusal skills. Be sure that every group member has a part.
3. Act out your skit for the class. Analyze each skit for the dialogue you think is most effective. Remember

and practice these statements so that you'll be prepared if a drinking driver offers you a ride.

Apply and Conclude

On your own, cut a 3″ × 5″ index card in half so that you have a 3″ × 2½″ card. Punch a hole in one corner. Write "Don't Ride with a Drunk Driver" on the card. Then write at least two statements you can use to refuse such a ride. Use markers to make the card eye-catching. After your teacher laminates the card, place it on your key ring.

Promoting Coordinated School Health

Alcohol Resistance What role does the school play in helping students resist alcohol abuse? In recovering from addiction and other alcohol-related problems? In dealing with alcohol-related problems at home? What role can the school play in supporting teachers and other school staff with alcohol problems? Is there an appropriate role for the school health system in educating and helping other members of the community? These are questions to be considered and resolved in the development of a coordinated school health program. For more information about developing such a program, consult *Planning a Coordinated School Health Program.*

Effects of Alcohol Poisoning

Passing out is a common effect of drinking too much alcohol. Alcohol doesn't stop entering a person's bloodstream after he or she passes out, however. Instead, alcohol in the stomach and intestines continues to enter the bloodstream, and blood alcohol concentration continues to rise. For this reason, it's dangerous to assume that a person who has consumed a lot of alcohol will be fine if left to "sleep it off."

Symptoms that indicate alcohol poisoning include

► mental confusion, stupor, coma, inability to be roused, vomiting, and seizures.

► slow respiration—10 seconds between breaths or fewer than 8 breaths a minute.

► irregular heartbeat.

► hypothermia or low body temperature—pale or bluish skin color.

► severe dehydration from vomiting.

A person who exhibits any of these signs or has passed out may die if left untreated. If you suspect that a person has alcohol poisoning, call 9-1-1 immediately.

The consequences of binge drinking can have serious effects on a person's health. *What should you do if you suspect someone has alcohol poisoning?*

Lesson 2 Review

Reviewing Facts and Vocabulary

1. Define *blood alcohol concentration* and *metabolism*.

2. Examine the short-term effects of alcohol use. List three ways alcohol impairs the functioning of the nervous system.

3. What are the signs of alcohol poisoning?

Thinking Critically

4. **Analyzing.** Explain why it's dangerous to mix alcohol and medications or other drugs.

5. **Synthesizing.** Describe the legal and financial consequences of operating a motor vehicle while under the influence of alcohol. Explain why these are only a few of the risks faced by a person driving under the influence.

Applying Health Skills

Advocacy. Prepare a public service announcement to get the word out about the health risks of binge drinking. Include facts about alcohol's effects on the body, as well as the risks involved with rapid binge drinking and how it can cause alcohol poisoning. Demonstrate effective refusal strategies to avoid these risks.

TECHNOLOGY OPTION

WORD PROCESSING Word processing can help you organize and present your information. See **health.glencoe.com** for tips on how to get the most out of your word-processing program.

Lesson 2 Harmful Effects of Alcohol Use **573**

---

3 ASSESS

EVALUATING THE LESSON

Assign and discuss the Lesson 2 Review; then administer, grade, and discuss Lesson Quiz 81 in the TCR.

RETEACHING

• Work with students to summarize each section of the lesson.

• Ask students to complete Reteaching Activity 81 in the TCR.

ENRICHMENT

Have students research and report on the problems of binge drinking on college campuses. Ask them to share their ideas in response to these questions: What factors might encourage college students, especially those attending college away from home, to engage in binge drinking? What do you think students should learn in high school to help them avoid the risks of college binge drinking?

4 CLOSE

Ask each student to identify one important new fact about alcohol he or she learned in studying this lesson.

Lesson 2 Review

Answers to Reviewing Facts and Vocabulary

1. Blood alcohol concentration (BAC) is the amount of alcohol in a person's blood expressed as a percentage. Metabolism is the process by which the body breaks down substances.

2. Answers will vary. The brain becomes less able to control the body. Heart rate and blood pressure increase. Blood vessels widen and body temperature drops.

3. Mental confusion, stupor, coma, inability to be roused, vomiting, seizures; slow breathing; irregular heartbeat; hypothermia; severe dehydration.

Answers to Thinking Critically

4.–5. Answers will vary.

Alcohol, the Individual, and Society

Lesson 3

Alcohol, the Individual, and Society

①FOCUS

QUICK START Give students about five minutes to jot down their lists. Draw a large triangle on the board; label the sides: physical, mental/emotional, and social health. As volunteers share their responses, record each effect on the appropriate side of the health triangle.

TYING TO PRIOR KNOWLEDGE

Have students recall some of the short-term effects of alcohol and speculate about the long-term effects. Explain that they will learn more about alcohol's long-term effects in Lesson 3.

INTRODUCING VOCABULARY

- Have each student write an original paragraph using at least five of the six vocabulary terms. Suggest that students use the Glossary to check the meaning of the terms.

- Ask students to complete the Chapter 22 Study Guide in the *Student Activity Workbook.* 📁

VOCABULARY
- **fetal alcohol syndrome (FAS)**
- **alcoholism**
- **alcoholic**
- **recovery**
- **detoxification**
- **sobriety**

YOU'LL LEARN TO
- Relate the nation's health goals in *Healthy People 2010* to reducing injury, death, and disease caused by alcohol-related influences.
- Examine the effects of alcohol use on body systems and the risk of disease caused by alcohol use.
- Analyze the harmful effects of alcohol on a fetus.
- Identify and assess community health services for the prevention and treatment of alcoholism and alcohol use.

QUICK START Fold a sheet of paper into three sections. Label the sections "physical," "mental/emotional," and "social." Then list the ways that alcohol use affects each part of the health triangle.

Compare the healthy liver (top) with the liver that has been damaged by alcohol use. *Explain the relationship between a healthy liver and an alcohol-free lifestyle.*

574 Chapter 22 Alcohol

The costs of alcohol use are far-reaching and involve individuals, families, and society. One goal of *Healthy People 2010* is to reduce a number of risk behaviors associated with alcohol. This includes reducing the amount of average annual alcohol consumption, binge drinking, and the total number of alcohol-related deaths and deaths due to alcohol-related vehicle crashes.

Long-Term Effects of Alcohol on the Body

Alcohol use has long-term effects on the user and on others as well. In teens alcohol use can interfere with growth and development. Excessive alcohol use over a prolonged period of time can damage most body systems. These effects are more severe on the body of a young person. **Figure 22.3** shows some of the long-term effects of alcohol abuse.

Lesson 3 *Resources*

Teacher Classroom Resources
- 📁 Concept Mapping Activity 82
- 📁 Guided Reading Activities 82
- 📁 Health Lab 22
- 📁 Lesson Plan 82
- 📁 Lesson Quiz 82
- 📁 Reteaching Activity 82

Student Activity Workbook
- 📁 Applying Health Skills 82
- 📁 Chapter 22 Study Guide

Multimedia
- 🖱 Transparency 65

FIGURE 22.3

LONG-TERM EFFECTS OF ALCOHOL USE

Alcohol affects many of the major organs in the body, and long-term drinking can cause death. The worst damage occurs after years of abuse, but some damage occurs with only moderate drinking.

Changes to the Brain
- **Addiction**—inability to stop drinking.
- **Loss of brain functions**—loss of verbal skills, visual and spatial skills, and memory.
- **Brain damage**—long-term excessive use of alcohol can lead to major brain damage and even to a reduction of brain size. Moderate drinking can destroy brain cells; however, the brain can regain some of its lost abilities over time if a person stops drinking.

Cardiovascular Changes
- **Heart**—damage to heart muscle.
- **Enlarged heart**—from increased workload caused by alcohol.
- **High blood pressure**—damages the heart and can cause heart attack and stroke.

Liver Problems
- **Fatty liver**—fats build up in the liver and cannot be broken down; excess fat blocks the flow of blood to liver cells, leading to cell death.
- **Alcoholic hepatitis**—inflammation or infection of the liver.
- **Cirrhosis**—liver tissue is replaced with useless scar tissue; the disease can lead to liver failure and death unless a liver transplant is performed.

Digestive System Problems
- **Irritation**—digestive lining is damaged; can lead to stomach ulcers and cancer of the stomach and esophagus.

Pancreas Problems
- **Lining of the pancreas**—swells to block the passage from the pancreas to the small intestine. Chemicals the small intestine needed for digestion can't pass through the blocked area. The chemicals begin to destroy the pancreas itself, causing pain and vomiting. A severe case can lead to death.

Alcohol During Pregnancy

When a pregnant female drinks, so, in effect, does her fetus. Alcohol passes from the mother's body into the bloodstream of the fetus. Unlike the adult liver, the fetus's liver is not developed enough to process the alcohol. As a result, a pregnant female who drinks during pregnancy risks permanent damage to the fetus.

Lesson 3 Alcohol, the Individual, and Society **575**

Meeting Individual Needs

Language Diversity A clear understanding of the risks of using alcohol and other drugs is essential for all students. Those who are still acquiring English skills should be encouraged to consult the Glosario, if appropriate, and/or to work in groups, discussing the risks of alcohol and practicing ways to avoid and refuse alcohol.

Learning Styles Students who may have difficulties comprehending alcohol information as presented in the text should be encouraged to work with reading buddies. One student in each pair can be responsible for reading aloud or for helping the other student read aloud. Emphasize that both partners can contribute to learning as they discuss the content.

2 TEACH

VISUAL LEARNING

Figure 22.3 Guide students in reading about and discussing the long-term effects of alcohol on the body systems. For each body system, ask:
- How would this effect change your life?
- If you suffered this effect of alcohol, how would your family and friends be affected?
- How could people you don't know be affected?

Cooperative Learning

Let students work in groups to review the effects of alcohol on the body. Then ask group members to brainstorm responses to these questions:
- How would these physical effects impact the mental/emotional health of the person abusing alcohol?
- How would they affect that person's social health?
- How would the health of that person's family members and friends likely be affected? **L2**

Critical Thinking

Guide students in discussing the risks to the unborn baby when a pregnant female drinks alcohol. Ask:
- What responsibilities does a pregnant female have toward her baby? Toward the father of the baby? Toward other relatives?
- How would you respond if a woman you knew drank alcohol during pregnancy? Why?
- Would your reaction be different if she were your wife? Your sister? Your best friend? **L2**

Concept Map

Build students' vocabulary by asking them to consider what alcohol means to them. Have them list as many details related to the word as they can.

This activity provides a format for students to organize new information about a topic in a meaningful way. Creating a visual display for a complex term helps readers see connections between a word and its meaning. A concept map is a visual representation of the definition of a concept or word. Draw a concept map on the board; write the term *alcohol* in the center. Then ask students to provide details to fill in the corresponding blanks. For more strategies, see the *Guided Reading Activities* booklet.

📁 **L3**

Discussing

Have a volunteer look up the word *disease* in the dictionary and write the definition on the board. Lead students in discussing the reasons alcoholism can be accurately defined as a disease. Alcoholism, like many other diseases, can interfere with a person's normal, day-to-day life. **L1**

hotlink

Ask a group of volunteers to read the information on fetal development and then review it with the rest of the class. Have them emphasize the relationship between maternal health and fetal health, especially as influenced by alcohol. Encourage them to make generalizations when necessary.

hotlink

fetal alcohol syndrome
For more information on fetal development, see Chapter 19, pages 488–489.

GOVERNMENT WARNING: (1)ACCORDING TO THE SURGEON GENERAL, WOMEN SHOULD NOT DRINK ALCOHOLIC BEVERAGES DURING PREGNANCY BECAUSE OF THE RISK OF BIRTH DEFECTS. (2)CONSUMPTION OF ALCOHOLIC BEVERAGES IMPAIRS YOUR ABILITY TO DRIVE A CAR OR OPERATE MACHINERY AND MAY CAUSE HEALTH PROBLEMS.

Avoiding tobacco, alcohol, and other drugs is an important decision a female can take toward a healthy pregnancy. *What other steps can an expectant mother take to protect the health of her unborn child?*

Drinking during the first few weeks of pregnancy—when many women do not yet realize they are pregnant—can be especially harmful to a baby's central nervous system. Infants born to mothers who drink during pregnancy may be at risk of **fetal alcohol syndrome (FAS)**, *a group of alcohol-related birth defects that include physical and mental problems.*

Effects of Fetal Alcohol Syndrome (FAS)

The effects of fetal alcohol syndrome are both severe and lasting. An FAS baby may be born with a small head and deformities of the face, hands, or feet. Heart, liver, and kidney defects, as well as vision and hearing problems, are common. FAS babies experience slow growth and coordination and have difficulties with learning, attention, memory, and problem solving.

FAS is the leading known cause of mental retardation in the United States. The good news is that it's totally preventable—provided that expectant mothers understand two things: there is no safe amount of alcohol to drink and no safe time in which to drink it. Even small amounts of alcohol can harm a fetus.

Alcoholism

One of the most devastating effects of alcohol use is **alcoholism**, *a disease in which a person has a physical or psychological dependence on drinks that contain alcohol.* Alcoholism is characterized by an impaired ability to study, work, or socialize normally.

Alcoholics

An **alcoholic** is *an addict who is dependent on alcohol.* Some alcoholics may display harmful behaviors such as drunken driving and violent or aggressive actions. Others may become quiet and withdrawn. Alcoholism isn't limited to any age, race, ethnic, or socioeconomic group. Alcoholics may be middle-aged business people or high-school athletes. Regardless of background, alcoholics can develop serious health problems, such as cirrhosis of the liver and brain damage. An alcoholic might display these symptoms:

▶ **Craving.** An alcoholic has a compulsion, or strong need, to drink; he or she cannot manage tension or stress without drinking.

▶ **Loss of control.** An alcoholic cannot limit his or her drinking and is preoccupied with alcohol.

HEALTH LITERACY

Influencing Factors Although nobody should consider himself or herself safe from alcoholism, those whose relatives have suffered from alcoholism may be at special risk. There is evidence that alcoholism frequently runs in families, and in 1990, a link was suggested between a particular gene and a susceptibility to alcoholism. It is still not certain whether the connection is hereditary; environmental; or—most likely—a combination. The fact remains that nearly half of all children of alcoholics will develop alcoholism, other drug problems, and/or other serious coping problems.

▶ **Physical dependence.** When not drinking, an alcoholic may experience withdrawal symptoms, such as nausea, sweating, shakiness, and anxiety.

▶ **Tolerance.** An alcoholic experiences a need to drink increasingly greater amounts of alcohol in order to feel its effects.

▶ **Health, family, and legal problems.** An alcoholic often suffers repeated injuries, receives multiple drunk driving citations, and has frequent arguments and generally poor relationships with family members.

Factors Affecting Alcoholics

Growing scientific evidence suggests a genetic link to alcoholism. In fact, the American Academy of Child and Adolescent Psychiatry reports that children of alcoholics are four times more likely than other children to become alcoholics. However, this does not necessarily mean that a person with such a genetic predisposition will become an alcoholic. Other environmental factors, such as family, friends, culture, peer pressure, availability of alcohol, and stress, also put a person at risk for alcoholism. There is, however, one guarantee: You can protect yourself against this disease by making the healthy choice to stay alcohol free.

Stages of Alcoholism

According to the American Medical Association, alcoholism develops in three stages. All alcoholics do not experience each stage equally.

▶ **Stage 1—Abuse.** Typically, alcoholism begins with social drinking in an attempt to relax. Over time, a physical and psychological dependence on alcohol to manage stress develops. At this point a person begins to drink and become intoxicated regularly, which can result in blackouts and memory loss. Often, a person begins to lie or make excuses about his or her drinking. The person needs to consume more alcohol to feel the desired effect. He or she may be a problem drinker.

▶ **Stage 2—Dependence.** The person reaches a point where he or she cannot stop drinking and is physically dependent on the drug. Alcohol becomes the person's central focus. The drinker tries to hide the problem, but performance on the job, at school, or at home soon suffers. The drinker makes excuses and blames others for problems.

Family members of alcoholics also experience the negative effects of alcoholism. *List ways a person can avoid the risks of alcoholism.*

Critical Thinking

Help students consider the stages in the development of alcoholism. Ask:

• Who do you think would be most likely to recognize these stages of developing alcoholism: the alcoholic, a family member, a friend, or an acquaintance? Why?

• Who could intervene most successfully? How?

Applying Life Skills

Have students work in pairs. Instruct each pair to rehearse a situation in which a person is helping a friend with a drinking problem. Every student should have a turn at both parts of the situation. Then have students discuss various tactics used in the activity. What approaches or particular ways of phrasing advice were especially helpful?

Cross-Curriculum Activity

Social Studies Remind students that, from 1920 to 1933, the sale of alcohol to all age groups was illegal throughout the United States. Point out that now the sale of alcohol to people under 21 is illegal in all states. Encourage discussion by asking: Why do you think the government enacts such laws?

Lesson 3 Alcohol, the Individual, and Society **577**

Community Involvement

Have students collect informative brochures from local groups and agencies that work with individuals and families who have difficulty with alcohol. Ask students to make a display of the materials collected. 📙 🔲

hotlink

Recall with students the basic functions of the family—providing a primary support system, meeting emotional needs, instilling values, and so on. Discuss how alcohol use by a parent can prevent normal family functioning and adversely affect a child's development. Explain that situations of abuse in families of an alcoholic affect family members for years, even after the alcoholic has recovered. Discuss counseling for the entire family as a means to treat the trauma associated with alcoholism.

Researching

Have interested volunteers research the process of detoxification for an alcoholic. Let these volunteers share and discuss their findings with the rest of the class. 📗

Discussing

Guide students in reading and discussing the four Steps to Recovery. Ask:

- Do you think these steps have to be taken in order? Why?

- Do you think that each step has to be completed before the next one can be taken? Why not?

hotlink

domestic violence For more information on dealing with family crises, see Chapter 11, page 286.

STEPS TO RECOVERY

Step 1: Admission
The person admits to having a drinking problem and asks for help.

Step 2: Detoxification
The person goes through detoxification, *a process in which the body adjusts to functioning without alcohol.*

Step 3: Counseling
The person receives counseling to help him or her learn to live without alcohol.

Step 4: Recovery
The person takes responsibility for his or her own life.

▶ **Stage 3—Addiction.** In the final stage of alcoholism, drinking is the *most* important thing in a person's life. The person is addicted to the drug and his or her life is out of control, although frequently he or she does not realize or acknowledge this fact. Because liver damage is common at this stage, less alcohol may be required to produce intoxication. If the alcoholic stopped drinking, he or she would experience severe withdrawal symptoms.

Effects on Family and Society

There are an estimated 14 million alcoholics in the United States. Alcohol use is a major factor in the four leading causes of accidental death—car accidents, falls, drownings, and house fires. Alcohol also plays a major role in violent crimes, such as homicide, forcible rape, and robbery. For example:

▶ About 40 percent of violent crimes, totaling about 3 million annually, are alcohol-related.

▶ Two-thirds of victims who encounter **domestic violence** report that alcohol was a factor in the crime.

▶ Nearly half of all homicide victims have alcohol in their bloodstreams.

Often, alcoholism has indirect, as well as direct, effects on people associated with alcoholics. These people may be involved in a process known as *codependency.* Codependents learn to ignore their own needs and focus their energy and emotions on the needs of the alcoholic. In the process codependents lose their trust in others, their self-esteem, and, at times, their own health.

Treatment for Alcohol Abuse

Although alcoholism cannot be cured, it *can* be treated. *The process of learning to live an alcohol-free life* is called **recovery**. As many as two-thirds of all alcoholics who try to recover do so with proper treatment. The goal of treatment programs is to stop or control the intake of alcohol. Counseling and medication can help an alcohol user set goals to deal with problems of alcohol abuse. **Sobriety**, *living without alcohol*, is a lifelong commitment. Many resources are available to help people who have a drinking problem. Help is also available for the families and friends of a problem drinker. Some of these programs are described in **Figure 22.4.**

School to Work

X-Ray and Ultrasound Technologists

Doctors who suspect liver damage from alcohol or alcohol-related cancers may order various tests. Many of these tests are administered by licensed technicians. For example, a patient may be sent for ultrasound, a procedure that uses ultrasonic waves to create a visual image of an internal organ or structure. An ultrasound technologist needs a license and special training from a trade school or medical teaching college. A student without a college degree usually takes four years to complete the program because most candidates complete training as X-ray technicians first. After completing their training, candidates must take a challenging examination to qualify for the state license.

FIGURE 22.4

WHERE TO GET HELP FOR ALCOHOL ABUSE

There are many places to get information about treatment for alcohol dependency. The goal of these programs is to provide support for alcoholics, family members, and friends affected by alcoholism.

Al-Anon/Alateen	Alcoholics Anonymous	National Association for Children of Alcoholics	National Clearinghouse for Alcohol and Drug Information	National Drug and Treatment Referral Routing Service
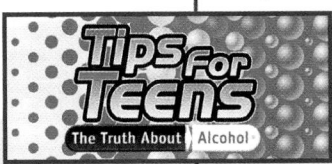 helps families and friends of alcoholics deal with and recover from the effects of living with an alcoholic	provides help for alcohol users of all ages	provides help for children of alcoholics	provides information about alcohol and other drugs	provides treatment referral and information about treatment facilities

It's Not Your Fault!

Lesson 3 Review

Reviewing Facts and Vocabulary

1. Identify three serious effects of alcohol abuse.
2. Define *sobriety*. Explain why sobriety is a lifelong commitment.
3. What steps must an alcoholic take during the recovery process?

Thinking Critically

4. **Analyzing.** Explain how damage can occur in the body of the developing fetus when a pregnant woman drinks alcohol.
5. **Synthesizing.** Alcoholism can have devastating effects on people associated with an alcoholic. Explain ways that these individuals can be affected, and tell how and where those living with an alcoholic can get help.

Applying Health Skills

Accessing Information. Consult your school counselor or use the phone book to identify community resources for families with alcohol-related problems. Research the availability of family counseling. Explain why these sources are valid. Share your information in a flyer or pamphlet.

PRESENTATION SOFTWARE Use presentation software to show the results of your research on community resources to your family and friends. See health.glencoe.com for tips on using presentation software.

Lesson 3 Alcohol, the Individual, and Society **579**

Lesson 3 Review

Answers to Reviewing Facts and Vocabulary

1. Answers will include facts from Figure 22.3, such as addiction, heart muscle damage, and cirrhosis.
2. Sobriety is living without alcohol. Sobriety must become a lifelong commitment because of the addictive qualities of alcohol and alcoholism cannot be cured.

3. Admission, detoxification, counseling, recovery.

Answers to Thinking Critically

4. FAS is caused by a pregnant female drinking alcohol. Mental retardation can be prevented if the mother does not drink alcohol during her pregnancy.
5. Answers will vary.

VISUAL LEARNING

Figure 22.4 Have students read about these sources of help and information. Then divide the class into five groups. Assign each group one of the sources. Ask group members to learn more about their source and report on that program to the class.

3 ASSESS

EVALUATING THE LESSON

Assign and discuss the Lesson 3 Review; then administer, grade, and discuss Lesson Quiz 82 in the TCR.

RETEACHING

- Have students work with partners to list, in their own words, the long-term effects of alcohol use and the four steps to recovery.
- Ask students to complete Reteaching Activity 82 in the TCR.

ENRICHMENT

Have a group of students work together to develop a "Jeopardy"-style game show with questions based on the facts about alcohol.

4 CLOSE

Have students complete the following sentence, either orally or in writing: *The benefits of sobriety are . . .*

Illegal Drugs in the Media

NHES Standard 4 Students will analyze the influence of culture, media, technology, and other factors on health.

Objective

Evaluate Internet resources regarding the issue of teen drinking and driving.

Motivator

Write the following statement on the blackboard: "Youth who start drinking before the age of 15 are four times more likely to develop alcoholism at some point in their lives than those who begin drinking at 21." Ask students to brainstorm ideas on how they could verify this statement.

Teaching Strategies

Awareness Remind students that critical-thinking skills are important when approaching any media source.

Analysis Explain that, generally speaking, credible resources contain factual information supported by independent research institutions, are written by an authority on the subject, and contain current, objective information.

Reflection Students should keep detailed notes to answer the questions in the activity.

Take Action Creating a Web page is an opportunity to reference the research they have gathered on their source.

✓Assessment

Students should give titles of the sources they used to verify the information in the source. The Web page should include the dangers of teen drinking and driving.

580

Researching Alcohol Issues on the Internet

A variety of Internet resources exist that provide information regarding alcohol-related issues. These Web resources may be from a nonprofit advocacy organization, a government institution, a journalist, or even a business. In this activity, you will learn to evaluate Internet resources regarding teen drinking and driving and validate the information contained in those resources.

Criteria

- **Who is the author?** Is the page created by an individual, news organization, or charitable organization?
- **Who is the audience?** Is the page intended for a particular age group or other specific demographic group?
- **How current is the information contained in the source?** What date appears on the page? Can you verify the date from other sources?
- **Is the information provided factual?** Research the source of any statistics, check any references or other sources listed on the page, and check all facts against other sources you know to be reliable.
- **What is the purpose of the page?** Is there a particular viewpoint on the subject matter? If so, what is that viewpoint?

ACTIVITY

Suppose you have been assigned to write a research paper on the subject of teen drinking and driving. Using Web Links at **health.glencoe.com**, choose one Web site or article on the Internet that contains information on the topic of teen drinking and driving. Evaluate the information found in your Web resource by answering the questions in the grid above.

EXPRESS YOUR VIEWS

Working in groups of three or four, create a storyboard for a Web site dedicated to warning teenagers of the dangers of drinking and driving. A storyboard is a mock-up of what each page of your Web site would look like. Include information from the research activity above. Use persuasive language and graphics to illustrate your points. Also, include a list of resources where teens can find further information on the subject.

More About...

Researching When students conduct a detailed evaluation of the usefulness and credibility of a resource, they are doing the work of a research librarian. Part of a research librarian's job is to evaluate all types of different resources. Since the growing Internet has become a favored research source for schools, many people have written papers on evaluating Web resources in order to help both teachers and students become critical Web researchers. Many credible Web-based articles and publications are available that give detailed suggestions for evaluating Web resources.

CROSS-CURRICULUM CONNECTIONS

Create a Campaign. Use your peer pressure in a positive way by organizing an anti-drinking campaign, which will culminate in a class rally. First, put your writing skills to work to appeal to other teens not to use alcohol. Your teacher will divide you into teams and assign each team a different task. Write speeches and skits, create slogans for placards, posters, and bumper stickers. Write a special pledge for students to sign. Devise games to show teens that there are fun alternatives to drinking. Share your final products during the class rally.

Research Alateen. Alcoholics Anonymous, or AA, has helped alcoholics worldwide by introducing them to the 12-step program. Write a short research report on the story of Bill W., who founded the organization in the 1930s, as well as how the organization developed. Then investigate the creation of related groups such as Alateen.

Calculate BAC. The average person's body contains 4 quarts of blood. The standard BAC for intoxication is 0.1 percent. How many ounces of pure alcohol must the average person have in his or her blood to be considered intoxicated?

Find Out More About Addiction. Alcoholism is addiction to alcohol. Recent research has shown that the process of becoming addicted is similar regardless of the substance or activity that is misused. Regular use of the substance alters the neural pathways in the brain. Research the connection between the concentration of neurotransmitters, such as serotonin and dopamine, and addiction to drugs and alcohol.

Substance Abuse Counselor

Do you like helping friends with their problems? Would you enjoy counseling people who need to find help for alcohol abuse problems in their families? As a substance abuse counselor, you would assess and treat people with substance problems and help those who live with alcoholics or substance abusers.

More than half of all counselors in the United States have a master's degree. Most states require some form of credentials, certification, license, or registry before someone can become a counselor. Find out more about this and other health careers by clicking on Career Corner at **health.glencoe.com**.

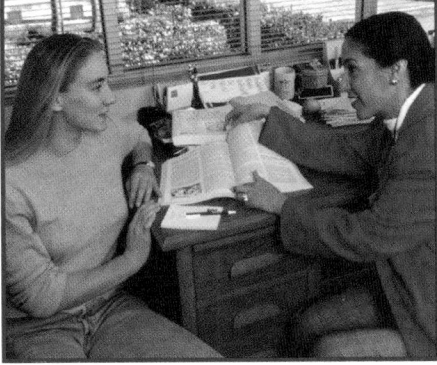

Chapter 22 Review **581**

Portfolio Assessment

Self-Evaluation Direct students to review the Health Skills Activities and other activities completed in the chapter. Encourage each student to select one finished product or activity that demonstrates his or her best work for the chapter and that represents the student's learning goals. Have students explain what they have learned and how the examples they have selected demonstrate their growth in health literacy, knowledge, and skills.

Teacher Classroom Resources Assign Performance Assessment 22, "Script for TV Commercial," in the TCR. 📁

CROSS-CURRICULUM CONNECTIONS

Enrich student learning by connecting the topic of alcohol use to one of the four subject areas presented on this page. The activity may be completed individually or with a partner.

Language Arts Review directions with each team and help them stay on task. Discuss language as propaganda and how it can be put to a positive use.

Social Studies Remind students to verify research by using more than one source when writing a research report.

Math Answer: 4 qt × 32 oz/qt × 0.1/100 = 0.128 oz

Science Addictions to everything from alcohol and food to gambling have been related to blood sugar level and the cascade of hormones and neurotransmitters that affect it. Focus on limbic system responses to stress and the biological predisposition of some people to addictive behaviors. Show that addiction is a process that takes place over time and that choices of behavior become more difficult after actual addiction has occurred.

Keep students involved in the community and encourage parent participation by assigning the activities on this page for students to work on outside of class.

Chapter 22 *Review*

CHECKING COMPREHENSION

- Assign and discuss the chapter review.
- Use Chapter 22 MindJogger Videoquiz to review the chapter. ▶◀

CHAPTER 22 REVIEW ANSWERS

Exploring Health Terms

1. alcohol
2. depressant
3. intoxication
4. alcohol abuse
5. metabolism
6. binge drinking
7. blood alcohol concentration
8. alcohol poisoning
9. Fetal alcohol syndrome
10. alcoholic
11. detoxification

Recalling the Facts

1. Family attitudes toward alcohol, peer pressure, and media messages.

2. Answers may vary but could include drinking and driving, inappropriate sexual activity, or increased risk of being a victim of violent crime.

3. Alcohol is a powerful drug that affects coordination; slows reaction time; and impairs vision, clear thinking, and judgment.

4. Suspension from school; ineligible for graduation; interrupted college or career plans.

5. Possible answer: Alcohol can increase the effects of some drugs, such as antihistamines, causing excessive dizziness and sleepiness.

6. Age, gender, physical condition, the amount of food eaten, and any medications that one is taking.

► EXPLORING HEALTH TERMS
Answer the following questions on a sheet of paper.

Lesson 1 Fill in the blanks with the correct term.

alcohol abuse	fermentation
depressant	intoxication
ethanol	

Drinks that contain (_1_) act as a (_2_) on the central nervous system. Drinking alcohol can lead to physical and mental impairment that is called (_3_). (_4_) puts family members at risk for neglect, physical abuse, or economic hardship.

Lesson 2 Match each definition with the correct term.

blood alcohol concentration	metabolism
	alcohol poisoning
binge drinking	

5. The process by which the body breaks down substances.

6. Drinking five or more alcoholic drinks at one sitting.

7. The amount of alcohol in a person's blood expressed as a percentage.

8. A severe and potentially fatal physical reaction to an alcohol overdose.

Lesson 3 Fill in the blanks with the correct term.

alcoholism	alcoholic
detoxification	fetal alcohol syndrome
sobriety	recovery

9. _____ is a condition in which a fetus has been adversely affected mentally and physically by the mother's alcohol use during pregnancy.

10. A(n) _____ has an addiction to alcohol.

11. _____ is a process in which the body adjusts to functioning without alcohol.

► RECALLING THE FACTS
Use complete sentences to answer the following questions.

Lesson 1

1. List three factors that influence alcohol use.
2. What are some of the risks of alcohol use?
3. Describe the effects that alcohol has on the body.
4. What impact can alcohol use have on a teen's education and career goals?

Lesson 2

5. Describe one typical alcohol-drug interaction.
6. What are some factors that affect an individual's short-term reaction to alcohol?
7. What are some consequences of driving while intoxicated or driving under the influence?
8. Explain how alcohol poisoning can cause a person's blood alcohol concentration to continue to rise even after the person stops consuming alcohol.

Lesson 3

9. What are some specific goals of *Healthy People 2010* for reducing ways in which alcohol affects the family and society?
10. What is a safe amount of alcohol that a mother can drink during pregnancy?
11. Describe the symptoms an alcoholic might display.
12. Describe two programs that offer help to alcoholics and their families. Explain the services they provide.

7. Alcohol is a major factor in the leading cause of accidental death—car accidents; consequences include loss of driver's license, harm to others, police record, others listed on page 571.

8. Alcohol in the stomach and the intestines continues to be absorbed into the bloodstream.

9. Goals of *Healthy People 2010* are to reduce the amount of annual alcohol consumption and the number of alcohol-related deaths due to vehicle crashes.

10. There is no safe amount of alcohol that a pregnant female can drink.

11. Symptoms include craving for alcohol; loss of control over drinking; physical dependence on alcohol; and health, family, and legal problems.

12. Answers will vary, but should include two agencies from Figure 22.4 and describe their primary focus.

▶ THINKING CRITICALLY

1. **Analyzing.** What are some strategies alcohol companies use to target teens in their advertising? *(LESSON 1)*

2. **Synthesizing.** Consider the short-term effects of alcohol on major body systems. How might the organs in the digestive and respiratory systems be damaged by alcohol use over a long period of time? *(LESSON 2)*

3. **Analyzing.** Describe an effective strategy for locating appropriate help and resources available to an alcoholic and his or her family members. *(LESSON 3)*

▶ HEALTH SKILLS APPLICATION

1. **Practicing Healthful Behaviors.** What consequences are faced by students who are caught using or possessing alcohol? *(LESSON 1)*

2. **Communication Skills.** Suppose a friend who has been drinking is going to drive himself or herself and others home. How would you respond to this situation? *(LESSON 2)*

3. **Advocacy.** Find out about groups at your school that advocate for an alcohol-free lifestyle. Get involved with a group, using what you have learned about the consequences of drinking to get local stores to advocate for less advertising of alcohol products. *(LESSON 3)*

BEYOND the Classroom

Parent Involvement

Advocacy. With your parents or guardians, learn more about SADD—Students Against Destructive Decisions. Learn when, where, and why it was founded, what its mission is, and how you and your family can get involved. Draw up a contract for all family members to sign that includes a commitment never to drink and drive and never to ride with any driver who has been drinking— even a family member.

School and Community

Support Programs. Locate an alcohol treatment program in your community. Contact the agency and find out how the program works, what is required of participants, and how people are supported during the recovery process. Report to your class what you have learned.

Thinking Critically

1. They target teens in print and broadcast advertisements that show drinking alcohol to be fun, safe, and exciting.

2. Possible answers: Digestive system—stomach irritation could lead to ulcers, toxic chemicals in the liver could lead to cirrhosis, kidney damage could result from overwork. Respiratory system—depression of the nerves that affect respiration could cause difficulty in breathing.

3. Resources include counseling; medication; and support from family, friends, and alcohol-related groups.

Health Skills Application

1.–3. Answers will vary.

EVALUATE

- Use the reproducible Chapter 22 Test in the TCR, or construct your own using the Testmaker software. 📁 💿

- Use Performance Assessment 22 in the TCR. 📁

ENRICHMENT

Ask students to complete Enrichment Activity 22 in the TCR. 📁

Have students read the Career Corner feature on page 583. Ask interested students to explore the Glencoe Health Web site at **health.glencoe.com** for more information on careers as a substance abuse counselor.

Lessons	Standards		Features
	National	**State/Local**	
1 The Role of Medicines *pages 586–591*	National Health Education Standards 1.1, 1.8, 2.3, 3.2, 6.3		
2 Drug Use—A High-Risk Behavior *pages 592–597*	National Health Education Standards 4.2, 3.1, 3.2, 3.3, 3.6		*Real-Life* **Application** • Analyzing Trends: Drug Prevention Programs *(Analyzing Influences)*, page 593
3 Marijuana, Inhalants, and Steroids *pages 598–602*	National Health Education Standards 1.2, 1.3, 3.3, 5.6, 7.4		*Health Skills* **Activity** • No Means No! *(Refusal Skills)*, page 601
4 Psychoactive Drugs *pages 603–610*	National Health Education Standards 3.1, 3.3, 3.7, 5.6, 6.3		**Hands-On Health** • Refusing Drugs *(Refusal Skills)*, page 607
5 Living Drug Free *pages 611–615*	National Health Education Standards 4.4, 5.4, 7.2, 7.5, 7.6		*Exploring* **Issues** • Drug Testing, Yes or No? page 614

Reproducible Resources	Assessment	Technology
Student Activity Workbook for use with each chapter 📁 Concept Mapping Activity 83 📁 Enrichment Activity 23 📁 Guided Reading Activities 83 📁 Lesson Plan 83 📁 Parent Letter and Activities 23 📁 Reteaching Activity 83	📁 Lesson Quiz 83	🕹 Transparency 66 💿 TeacherWorks® 🖥 Internet Activities
📁 Concept Mapping Activity 84 📁 Cross-Curriculum Activity 23 📁 Current Health Issues 23 📁 Guided Reading Activities 84 📁 Health Lab 23 📁 Lesson Plan 84 📁 Reteaching Activity 84	📁 Lesson Quiz 84	🕹 Transparency 67 💿 TeacherWorks®
📁 Concept Mapping Activity 85 📁 Guided Reading Activities 85 📁 Lesson Plan 85 📁 Reteaching Activity 85	📁 Lesson Quiz 85	🕹 Transparency 68 💿 TeacherWorks®
📁 Concept Mapping Activity 86 📁 Decision-Making Activity 23 📁 Guided Reading Activities 86 📁 Lesson Plan 86 📁 Reteaching Activity 86	📁 Lesson Quiz 86	🕹 Transparency 69 💿 TeacherWorks®
📁 Concept Mapping Activity 87 📁 Guided Reading Activities 87 📁 Lesson Plan 87 📁 Reteaching Activity 87	📁 Lesson Quiz 87	💿 TeacherWorks®

0:00 OUT OF TIME

If time does not permit teaching the entire chapter use:

- Figure 23.1, p. 590
- Health Minute, p. 590
- Figure 23.3, p. 599
- Health Skills Activity, p. 601
- Figure 23.4, p. 604
- Hands-On Health, p. 607
- Exploring Issues, p. 614

Language Diversity

- 🎧 English Audio CD Program
- 🎧 Spanish Audio CD Program
- 📁 English Summaries, Quizzes, and Activities
- 📁 Spanish Summaries, Quizzes, and Activities
- 📁 Spanish Parent Letters and Activities

End of Chapter Assessment

Blackline Masters

- 📁 Chapter 23 Test
- 📁 Performance Assessment Activity 23
- 📁 Unit 7 Test

Technology

- 💿 Vocabulary PuzzleMaker
- ▶◀ MindJogger Videoquiz
- 💿 *ExamView*® Pro Testmaker

Professional Health Series

Dealing with Sensitive Issues
Planning a Coordinated School Health Program
Promoting Character Education
Home, School, and Community Involvement

CHAPTER OVERVIEW

Chapter 23 discusses drugs including both medicines and illegal drugs. Students consider how to use medicines safely and how to avoid the use of illegal drugs.

Lesson 1 Medicines are considered in four categories: those that prevent disease, those that fight pathogens, those that relieve pain, and those that help maintain or restore health and regulate the body's systems.

Lesson 2 Misusing medicines and using illegal drugs are high-risk behaviors. Drug abuse poses risks to physical, mental/emotional, and social health.

Lesson 3 Marijuana, a gateway drug that can lead to the use of other illegal drugs, is in itself dangerous and illegal. Inhalants are substances that are sniffed or inhaled for mind-altering effects. Steroids, drugs with very limited medicinal uses, pose serious risks when misused.

Lesson 4 Psychoactive drugs—which include stimulants, depressants, narcotics, and hallucinogens—affect the central nervous system and alter activity in the brain.

Lesson 5 Teens can make a commitment to a drug-free life and use refusal skills to avoid drug use.

Health Skills Features

- Real-Life Application (*Analyzing Influences*), p. 593
- Health Skills Activity (*Refusal Skills*), p. 601
- Hands-On Health (*Refusal Skills*), p. 607
- Exploring Issues, p. 614

Chapter 23

Medicines and Drugs

Lesson 1
The Role of Medicines

Lesson 2
Drug Use—A High-Risk Behavior

Lesson 3
Marijuana, Inhalants, and Steroids

Lesson 4
Psychoactive Drugs

Lesson 5
Living Drug Free

MEETING STUDENT DIVERSITY

Language Diversity Use the following suggestions to help students who have difficulty with English:

- Pair English language learners with native speakers of English who can restate the Chapter Summary in language that helps students comprehend important concepts.

- Direct auditory learners or those students with language diversity to the *Glencoe Health Audio CD Program*. Available in English and Spanish, this component provides an audio and written summary of the chapter.
- Use photographs, drawings, or magazine clippings to help students visualize the important concepts of the chapter.

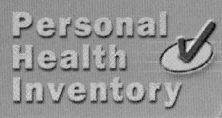

Personal Health Inventory

What's Your Health Status?

Read each statement below and respond by writing *yes*, *no*, or *sometimes* for each item. Write *yes* only for items that you practice regularly.

1. I take medicines as prescribed by my doctor, am careful to follow directions, and never abuse or combine medicines.

2. I use over-the-counter drugs carefully and only as they are intended.

3. I avoid all illegal drug use.

4. I choose friends who avoid using drugs.

5. I would feel comfortable saying no to peers and friends if they offered me drugs.

6. I stay away from areas and events where I know illegal drugs are likely to be used or sold.

7. I never cover for a friend or peer who abuses drugs.

8. I don't attend parties if I know drugs will be used.

9. I know of resources to get help for drug problems and would feel comfortable passing the information along to someone who needed it.

10. I understand the dangers of drugs and am committed to avoiding high-risk situations.

Keep this personal inventory for review later in the chapter. When you complete the chapter, review your answers again and identify two or three behavior changes you can make to improve your health.

585

Quick Write

Using Visuals. Illegal drugs can seriously damage a person's physical, mental/emotional, and social health. In what specific ways can drugs impact an athlete's life?

INTRODUCING THE CHAPTER

Personal Health Inventory

Have volunteers read aloud the ten statements in Personal Health Inventory, and guide students in discussing the statements in general terms. For each statement, ask:

- How does this behavior affect your physical health?

- How does it affect your mental/emotional health?

- How does it affect your social health?

Then remind students of the importance of responding honestly to these statements; assure them that their inventories are confidential. Let students complete the inventory independently. Remind them to keep their responses so they can be considered again when they have completed the chapter.

Quick Write

Using Visuals Let several volunteers describe the teens in the photographs. Ask:

- How do you imagine they feel about what they are doing?

- How do you think they prepared for this competition?

- What do you guess their goals might be for this track meet and for future meets?

Then have students write their responses to the Quick Write question.

TECHNOLOGY OPTIONS

MINDJOGGER
VIDEOQUIZ

To preview or review chapter content, you may wish to use the Chapter 23 MindJogger Video-Quiz. ◗◖

HEALTH *Online* **Online Resources for the Teacher** For a fresh approach to health topics and an in-depth look at health issues, use these online resources found under Teacher Resources at **health.glencoe.com:**

• Block Schedule Lesson Plans
• Technology Projects
• Health Updates

1 FOCUS

QUICK START

Let a volunteer read the Quick Start assignment aloud, and have students suggest several kinds of medicines with which they are familiar. Examples might include cough syrup, sinus tablets, and asthma inhalants. Then have students work independently to write their responses to the Quick Start questions.

TYING TO PRIOR KNOWLEDGE

Point out to students that they are already familiar with various kinds of medicines and that they know at least some guidelines for using medicines carefully. Lesson 1 presents more information about the purposes and uses of medicines.

INTRODUCING VOCABULARY

- Ask students to complete the Chapter 23 Study Guide in the *Student Activity Workbook*. 📁

The Role of Medicines

VOCABULARY
- medicines
- drugs
- vaccine
- analgesics
- side effects
- additive interaction
- synergistic effect
- antagonistic interaction

YOU'LL LEARN TO
- Analyze ways that medicines promote health and prevent disease.
- Describe the difference between prescription and over-the-counter medicines.
- Analyze how laws, policies, and practices influence safe use of medicines.

QUICK START What precautions do you take when you are about to use a medicine? On a separate sheet of paper, write three types of medicine with which you are familiar, tell why each is taken, and explain what you know about proper use of that medicine.

Medicines are taken to fight illness, promote health, prevent disease, or reduce pain. *When was the last time you needed to use some type of medication?*

Medicines are taken for many different reasons. A person may sustain a painful injury while playing a sport or perhaps develop a chest cold accompanied by a hacking cough. To help overcome these ailments and regain their health, people often take medicines.

Classification of Medicines

There are countless medicines that treat a wide range of health problems. **Medicines** are *drugs that are used to treat or prevent disease or other conditions.* **Drugs** are *substances other than food that change the structure or function of the body or mind.* All medicines are drugs, but not all drugs are medicines. Medicines can be sorted into four broad categories: medicines that

▶ help prevent disease.

▶ fight pathogens, or infectious agents that cause disease.

▶ relieve pain.

▶ help maintain or restore health and regulate the body's systems.

Lesson 1 *Resources*

Teacher Classroom Resources
- 📁 Concept Mapping Activity 83
- 📁 Enrichment Activity 23
- 📁 Guided Reading Activities 83
- 📁 Lesson Plan 83
- 📁 Lesson Quiz 83

- 📁 Parent Letter and Activities 23
- 📁 Reteaching Activity 83

Student Activity Workbook
- 📁 Applying Health Skills 83
- 📁 Chapter 23 Study Guide

Multimedia
- 📥 Transparency 66

Medicines That Prevent Disease

One main purpose of medicines is to prevent diseases before they occur. There are two main types of preventive medicines:

▶ **Vaccines.** A **vaccine** is *a preparation introduced into the body to stimulate an immune response.* These medicines contain weakened or dead pathogens that stimulate your body to produce specific **antibodies** against those pathogens. Once the antibodies are produced, they give your body long-lasting protection against these specific pathogens in the future.

▶ **Antitoxins.** These extracts of blood fluids contain antibodies and act more quickly than vaccines. They are produced by inoculating animals, such as sheep, horses, or rabbits, with specific toxins that stimulate the animal's immune system to produce antibodies. In humans, the injection of antitoxins neutralizes the effect of toxins, such as those that cause tetanus and diphtheria.

Medicines That Fight Pathogens

Antibiotics are a class of chemical agents that destroy disease-causing microorganisms while leaving the patient unharmed. Antibiotics work either by killing harmful bacteria in the body or by preventing bacteria from reproducing. The chemical composition of each antibiotic is effective against a particular range of bacteria.

In recent years, strains of bacteria have emerged that are resistant to penicillin and other antibiotics. This drug resistance occurs when a bacterial strain undergoes a change in genetic structure as a result of overexposure to an antibiotic, making the bacterium "immune" to the medicine. For example, a bacteria called *pneumococcus* that causes ear and sinus infections and pneumonia is now resistant to penicillin. The overuse of antibiotics and failure to finish a prescription medication are two reasons why bacteria develop resistance. A new generation of broad-spectrum antibiotics has been developed that kill a wide variety of bacteria, including some penicillin-resistant strains.

ANTIVIRALS AND ANTIFUNGALS

Antibiotics have no effect on viruses. However, a new group of drugs called antivirals has been developed to treat some viral illnesses. Antiviral medicines often only suppress the virus; they don't kill it. Antifungals can cure or suppress infections such as athlete's foot and ringworm.

hotlink

antibodies For more information on antibodies and vaccines, see Chapter 24, page 633.

▽ **Athlete's foot can be controlled with antifungal medicines.** *Why is it important to use the correct medicine for a particular treatment?*

Lesson 1 The Role of Medicines **587**

② TEACH

Reinforcing Concepts

Ask students to share their understanding of this statement: *All medicines are drugs, but not all drugs are medicines.* Ask: What are some examples of drugs that are not medicines? **L1**

Activity

Have each student poll three people about the first thought that comes to their minds when they hear the word *drug*. How many of the responses refer to medicines? How many refer to illegal drugs? Have students share their findings and discuss what these responses suggest. **L2**

Community Involvement

Have a group of volunteers go to the local Health Department clinic. Find out what medicines and vaccines they give, who can receive the medications, the cost of the medications to recipients, and the clinic's daily schedule of service. Allow the volunteers to share their findings with the rest of the class. **L2**

Discussion

Ask students to explain the instructions for taking antibiotics. Explain that instructions for taking antibiotics should be carefully followed. Patients can expect that a specific dosage is prescribed based on the strain of bacteria being treated and the antibiotic chosen for treatment. Emphasize that patients should take the medicine as recommended, for the full period prescribed. **L1**

School to Work

Employer-Provided Vaccines Some employers provide workers with free or low-cost immunizations against influenza and other diseases. Have students find out which companies in the area offer influenza immunizations free or at low cost to workers. Encourage them as well to find out what other immunizations might be provided free in the workplace. Suggest they contact the company that contracts with the employers to administer the injections, and obtain a copy of the release form workers sign when they receive a vaccine. Have them compare any warnings of adverse effects on the form with the adverse effects listed in the *Physicians' Desk Reference*. Do the warnings adequately inform the person receiving the immunization?

Discussing

Explain to students that some medicines may have to be administered for long periods—sometimes even for the rest of the patient's life. Ask:

• Which kinds of medicines are most likely to be taken during a patient's entire life?

• How do you think a lifetime of medicine-taking might affect an individual? **L2**

ACTIVE READING

Paragraph Structure

Remind students that, as they read, they should be looking for main ideas and identifying the details or examples that support each main idea. Recognizing the topic sentence of a paragraph helps readers comprehend subject matter more completely.

Let volunteers answer these questions: What does the topic sentence of a paragraph tell? the main idea In most textbook paragraphs, which sentence is usually the topic sentence? the first sentence of the paragraph What is another common location for the topic sentence within a paragraph? the last sentence of the paragraph

Suggest that students work with partners to identify the topic sentences of paragraphs in one section of the text. Then ask: How did finding the topic sentences help you understand the content of the text? How did it help you take notes on the text?

For more strategies, see the *Guided Reading Activities* booklet.

Ⓐ **Medicines help many people with conditions such as asthma and diabetes live active, normal lives.** *Identify two diseases that are kept under control through the use of medicines.*

Medicines That Relieve Pain

Probably the most common medicines are **analgesics**, or *pain relievers*. Analgesics range from comparatively mild medicines such as aspirin to strong narcotics, such as the opium-based morphine and codeine. Aspirin contains acetylsalicylic (uh-SEE-tuhl-sal-uh-SIL-ik) acid. Aspirin is used to relieve pain, reduce fever, and to treat arthritis.

Because of its widespread use, many people don't realize that aspirin can be dangerous. Even small amounts can irritate the stomach, especially when it's empty. Aspirin can cause dizziness and ringing in the ears. Children who take aspirin are at risk of developing Reye's syndrome, a potentially life-threatening illness of the brain and liver. Aspirin, therefore, should not be given to anyone under the age of 20 unless a health care professional directs otherwise. Some people who are sensitive to aspirin take acetaminophen (uh-see-tuh-MIH-nuh-fuhn) or ibuprofen (eye-byoo-PRO-fuhn) instead. Acetaminophen is the recommended analgesic for children.

Medicines That Promote Health

Medicines that maintain or restore health enable many people with chronic disease to function at increased level of wellness. Such medicines include these:

▶ **Allergy medicines.** Many people rely on antihistamines and other medications to reduce the sneezing, itchy or watery eyes, and runny nose that often accompany allergies.

▶ **Body regulating medicines.** Some medicines maintain health by regulating body chemistry. Insulin is used to treat diabetes. Asthma sufferers use inhalers to relieve the swelling of bronchial tubes. Cardiovascular medicines are taken to regulate blood pressure, normalize irregular heartbeats, or regulate other functions of the cardiovascular system.

▶ **Antidepressant and antipsychotic medicines.** These medicines help normalize brain chemistry. For example, mood stabilizers are often used in the treatment of mood disorders, depression, and schizophrenia. Proper medication can help people with these problems live healthy, productive lives.

▶ **Cancer treatment medicines.** These medicines reduce rapid cell growth and help stop the spread of cancer cells. For instance, chemotherapy is used to kill fast-growing cancer cells. This medication, either applied to the skin or injected, results in serious side effects that usually disappear after treatment stops.

Cooperative Learning Activity

Researching Antibiotics Resistance to antibiotics has become a serious medical problem. Have students work in groups to conduct research about the topic of antibiotic resistance. Then have them research use of antibiotics that could be reduced or eliminated. For example, tell them to investigate findings that most ear infections in children will clear up without antibiotics. Suggest they explore questions such as these: Do patients pressure their doctors to prescribe antibiotics? Do doctors prescribe antibiotics without knowing whether the condition requires them or will respond to them? Have students hold a panel discussion about antibiotic resistance and possible antibiotic abuse, discussing the problems and proposed solutions.

Medicines and the Body

Medicines can have a variety of effects on individuals, or can cause different reactions. A person's reaction to a given medicine depends on how that medicine mixes with the chemicals in his or her body. Most medicines cause **side effects**, *reactions to medicine other than the one intended*. It's important to be aware of your reactions to medicines and report these to your health care provider. Patients should always tell their doctors about any medicines they are already taking when a new medicine is prescribed.

When medicines are taken together or when a medication is taken in combination with certain foods, the combination may produce different effects. In some cases, physicians make use of interactions to increase the effectiveness of a treatment. Other interactions may be harmful.

► **Additive interaction** occurs when *medicines work together in a positive way*. For example, both an anti-inflammatory and a muscle relaxant may be prescribed to treat joint pain.

► **Synergistic effect** is an *interaction of two or more medicines that results in a greater effect than when the medicines are taken alone*—one medicine increases the strength of the other. One medicine may boost the rate of digestion, for example, enabling a second medicine to be absorbed faster.

► **Antagonistic interaction** occurs when *the effect of one medicine is canceled or reduced when taken with another medicine.* For example, someone who receives an organ transplant must take antirejection medicines. If the person is diabetic and takes insulin, the antirejection medicine may decrease the effectiveness of the insulin.

Other Problems

A person may experience other problems when taking medicines:

► **Tolerance** is a condition in which the body becomes used to the effect of a medicine. The body then requires increasingly larger doses of the medicine to produce the same effect. Sometimes a person will experience "reverse tolerance." In this condition, the body requires less of the substance to produce the desired effect.

► **Withdrawal** occurs when a person stops using a medicine on which he or she has a chemical dependence. For example, medicines containing codeine can lead to dependence. Symptoms of withdrawal, which include nervousness, insomnia, severe headaches, vomiting, chills, and cramps, gradually ease over time. Withdrawal sometimes requires medical intervention.

In addition to your health care provider, your local pharmacist is a person who can answer questions about medications. *What questions should you ask your pharmacist before taking a new medication?*

∿∿ HEALTH LITERACY

Self-Directed Learner Have students work individually or in groups to research medications that have been abused specifically for their side effects. In particular, medications may be abused for mood-changing effects. For example, cold medication may be taken to induce sleep. Stimulants prescribed as diet pills may be used to get high or stay awake all night. Some medicines prescribed for respiratory congestion stimulate the central nervous system. For example, ephedrine, used for respiratory ailments, was added to thermogenic weight-loss formulas and herbal combinations to act as mood elevators. Have students complete a chart showing the drugs' intended uses, the negative effects of abuse, and potential consequences.

Quick Demo

Hold up an insert from an OTC medicine. Ask students whether they know what it is and what information it contains. Explain that the Patient Summary Information page indicates directions for use, correct dosage, and warnings for users.

Provide several package inserts from OTC medicines and magazines featuring ads with prescription drug information. Have students create an information page highlighting each of the sections on the insert.

Encourage students to add other information they feel is important, for example, when a person taking the medicine should call his or her physician.

Activity

Write the following on the board and ask students to write their responses: *Should all drugs (even aspirin) carry a warning label that states the possible problems of tolerance?* Divide the class into two teams, and have the teams debate the issue. Note: Students may need time to research the topic before the team debate. Assign the topic as homework and hold the debate the following day, if necessary.

FYI

The National Institute on Drug Abuse reports that, in one recent year, about 4 million Americans used prescription drugs for nonmedical purposes. Among 12–14 year olds, the nonmedical use of a group of drugs including pain killers, tranquilizers, sedatives, and stimulants was the second most common form of drug abuse. This group of drugs is referred to as psychotherapeutics.

VISUAL LEARNING

Figure 23.1 Divide the class into several groups; have group members work together to examine the sample label and discuss the information presented there. If possible, provide each group with an empty container for a prescription medicine. Have group members identify and explain the various parts of the label.

Health Minute

Guide students in reading and discussing the information on medicine safety. Let volunteers give specific examples of how to follow each guideline. Then encourage students to talk with their parents about the medicines kept in their own homes to be certain they are up to date and safely stored. Out-of-date medicines should be safely discarded.

Discussing

Present the following situation and ask how students would respond: You are studying at a classmate's house when you develop a painful headache. Your classmate produces an unmarked capsule—you don't see any container—and says, "We always take these for headaches. They work wonders." Encourage students to give reasons for their responses. **L1**

Service Learning

Encourage students to identify older relatives or close family friends who might need some assistance with checking for out-of-date medicines or storing medicines safely. Suggest that students offer their help as appropriate; let volunteers discuss their experiences with the rest of the class. **L2**

590

Health Minute

Safe Medicine Use

Reduce the risk of inappropriate use of medications by following these tips.

Guidelines for safe medicine use:

► Keep medicine in the container in which it was originally packaged.

► Store medicines in a safe place that is out of the reach of children.

► Never disable or replace the child-resistant cap on a medicine container.

► Flush down the toilet any medicines that have passed their expiration date.

Medicine Safety

To minimize risks to the public, the federal government has established laws and policies for testing and approving new medicines. In the United States, all medicines must meet standards set by the Food and Drug Administration (FDA) before being approved and made available for sale. The FDA requires manufacturers to supply information about a medicine's chemical composition, intended use, effects, and possible side effects. One practice of the FDA is to determine how medicine should be released to the public.

► **Prescription medicines.** The FDA has ruled that certain medicines cannot be used without the written approval of a licensed physician. These prescription medicines are available only by means of a doctor's written instructions and can be dispensed only by a licensed pharmacist. **Figure 23.1** shows the information that must appear on every prescription medicine label.

► **Over-the-counter (OTC) medicines.** This group includes a wide variety of medicines that you can buy without a prescription. Although the FDA considers it safe to use these

FIGURE 23.1

PRESCRIPTION MEDICINE LABEL

Prescription labels must carry certain information about the medicine. In order to use a medicine safely, always read the label carefully and talk to your doctor or pharmacist if you have any questions.

590   Chapter 23 Medicines and Drugs

More About...

The Food and Drug Administration (FDA) As a division of the United States Department of Health and Human Services, the FDA is charged with ensuring the purity and safety of foods, drugs, and cosmetics. It is also responsible for regulating levels of radiation emission of electronic products and the sanitary standards of restaurants.

The federal government maintains regional FDA offices in each federal district. The telephone directory in your area lists the number for the nearest FDA office. Have a volunteer call the office to determine which services the regional FDA offices provide to the public. Then allow the volunteer to share the information with the rest of the class.

medications without medical supervision, any drugs can be harmful if not used properly.

When the FDA approves a medicine, it is saying that the medicine is safe when used as directed. FDA approval also means that a medicine is effective in treating the condition for which it is prescribed.

Medicine Misuse

Medicines can help maintain or improve health, but it is the responsibility of individuals and families to use medicines and supplements as they are prescribed or intended. All medicines are packaged with instructions for use. Failing to follow these instructions is one example of medicine misuse that can have serious health consequences. Other examples include

▶ giving a prescription medicine to a person for whom it was not prescribed or taking another person's medicine.

▶ taking too much or too little of a medicine or taking a medicine for a longer or shorter period than prescribed.

▶ discontinuing use of a medicine without informing the health care professional.

▶ mixing medicines.

Did You Know ?

▶ Ephedrine and creatine are dietary supplements sometimes misused by athletes to enhance performance. Ingredients in these substances produce druglike effects. Medical professionals report that these compounds may be related to increased numbers of heatstroke deaths since 1995. Ephedrine and creatine can seriously affect the heart and CNS. Side effects raise core body temperature to dangerous levels and reduce the body's ability to dissipate heat, resulting in heatstroke.

Lesson 1 Review

Reviewing Facts and Vocabulary

1. What are the four broad categories of medicines?
2. What government organization tests and approves all new medications?
3. List three specific examples of medicine misuse.

Thinking Critically

4. **Synthesizing.** Analyze the influence of laws, policies, and practices on the public release of medicine in the United States.
5. **Evaluating.** Analyze the relationship and use of medicines that promote health and those that prevent disease. Give two examples.

Applying Health Skills

Accessing Information. Using reliable resources, research the known benefits and risks of aspirin. Integrate the information you have found into a poster about safe aspirin use. Make sure your poster explains why dosages vary for infants, children, adults, and the elderly.

SPREADSHEETS Use a spreadsheet to organize information for your poster. See **health.glencoe.com** for tips on how to use spreadsheets.

EVALUATING THE LESSON

Assign and discuss the Lesson 1 Review; then administer, grade, and discuss Lesson Quiz 83 in the TCR. 📁

RETEACHING

- Have students list the four major classifications of medicines presented in this lesson and identify two examples of medicines in each. Then ask students to explain the effects of medicines on the body, including the interaction of combining more than one medicine.
- Ask students to complete Reteaching Activity 83 in the TCR. 📁

ENRICHMENT

Let students work with partners to research familiar OTC analgesics: aspirin, acetaminophen, and ibuprofen. How do the products compare? What are the special benefits of each? What cautions should be used in taking each? Have the partners draw charts or write short reports to summarize their findings.

④ CLOSE

Have students identify specific habits they want to strengthen or develop to avoid misusing medicines.

Lesson 1 Review

Answers to Reviewing Facts and Vocabulary

1. Medicines that prevent disease, that fight pathogens, that relieve pain, that help maintain or restore health and regulate the body's systems.
2. Food and Drug Administration (FDA)
3. Examples are provided on page 591.

Answers to Thinking Critically

4. Laws and policies help ensure medicine safety. For example, medicines must meet standards set by the FDA.
5. Students should note that safe medicine use is an important step in health maintenance.

Drug Use—A High-Risk Behavior

1 FOCUS

QUICK START Give students three or four minutes to record their responses to the Quick Start assignment. Then create three lists on the board, headed *User, Family and Friends,* and *Rest of Society.* Ask volunteers to read their Quick Start lists aloud; record students' ideas in the appropriate lists on the board.

TYING TO PRIOR KNOWLEDGE

Refer to the lists on the board, and point out that students already know quite a bit about the risks of using illegal drugs. They will learn more as they study this lesson.

Health Skills Features

"Analyzing Trends: Drug Prevention Programs," p. 593

ANALYZING INFLUENCES

INTRODUCING VOCABULARY

- Have students use dictionaries to find the precise difference in meaning between the words *use* and *abuse*. Then have students look up all the vocabulary terms in the Glossary, reading and discussing the definition of each.

- Ask students to complete the Chapter 23 Study Guide in the *Student Activity Workbook.*

Drug Use—A High-Risk Behavior

VOCABULARY
- substance abuse
- illegal drugs
- illicit drug use
- overdose
- psychological dependence
- physiological dependence
- addiction

YOU'LL LEARN TO
- Define substance abuse and recognize the health risks involved.
- Analyze the harmful effects of drugs on the fetus.
- Analyze the harmful physical, mental/emotional, social, and legal consequences of drug use.

QUICK START Substance abuse has effects both on individuals and on society as a whole. List as many of the dangerous effects of drugs as you can think of that affect the user, the user's family and friends, and the rest of society.

Substance abuse harms concentration and coordination. You cannot do your best if your body and mind are not functioning properly. *How will you protect your health and avoid substance abuse?*

No one starts using drugs with the intention of causing a drug-related injury or getting hooked on the drug. Substance abuse is a high-risk behavior. Recognizing the difference between drug misuse and substance abuse will help you avoid the risks associated with these potentially dangerous substances.

What Is Substance Abuse?

As you learned in Lesson 1, medicine misuse occurs when people use medicines carelessly or in an improper way. However, some people misuse medicines intentionally to achieve a "high." This is **substance abuse**, *any unnecessary or improper use of chemical substances for nonmedical purposes.* Substance abuse includes overuse or multiple use of a drug, use of an illegal drug, and use of a drug in combination with alcohol or other drugs.

Not all abused substances are medicines. Many are **illegal drugs**, or street drugs, *chemical substances that people of any age may not lawfully manufacture, possess, buy, or sell.* People who use illegal drugs are guilty of a crime called **illicit drug use**, *the use or sale of any substance that is illegal or otherwise not permitted.* This includes the selling of prescription drugs on the street.

Lesson 2 Resources

Teacher Classroom Resources
- Concept Mapping Activity 84
- Cross-Curriculum Activity 23
- Current Health Issues 23
- Guided Reading Activities 84
- Health Lab 23
- Lesson Plan 84

- 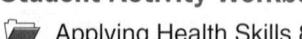 Lesson Quiz 84
- Reteaching Activity 84

Student Activity Workbook
- Applying Health Skills 84
- Chapter 23 Study Guide

Multimedia
- Transparency 67

Factors That Influence Decisions About Drugs

All teens are faced with choices about drug abuse. Many factors influence a teen's response to the opportunities to experiment with drugs, including the following:

▶ **Peer pressure** is the control and urging of friends or social groups to take a particular action. Teens whose friends and acquaintances avoid drug use can say no to drugs more easily than teens whose friends accept and even encourage drug use.

Real-Life Application

Analyzing Trends: Drug Prevention Programs

According to findings by a recent National Household Survey on Drug Abuse (NHSDA) more and more teens are getting involved in drug prevention programs. What effect do you think this has on teens making the decision to avoid drug use?

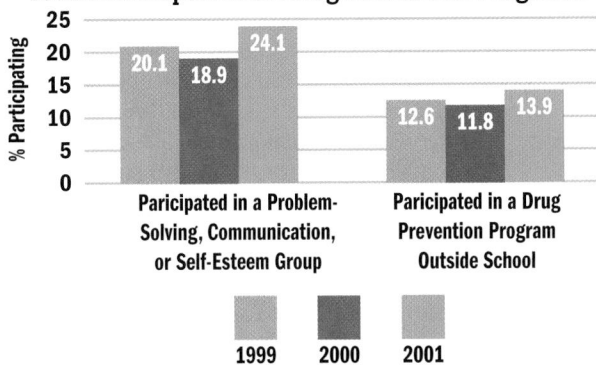

Youth Participation in Drug Prevention Programs

Bar values: Participated in a Problem-Solving, Communication, or Self-Esteem Group — 1999: 20.1, 2000: 18.9, 2001: 24.1. Participated in a Drug Prevention Program Outside School — 1999: 12.6, 2000: 11.8, 2001: 13.9.

Legend: 1999, 2000, 2001

Source: Substance Abuse and Mental Health Services Administration: NHSDA Survey, 2001

- In 2001, 24.1 percent of youths surveyed participated in a problem-solving, communication, or self-esteem group. The percentage of students who had participated in a drug prevention program outside of school was 13.9 percent.

- According to results of this survey, teens reporting an increase in the use of illicit drugs did not participate in such a program. What does this indicate about the influence drug prevention programs can have on a teen's decision to avoid drugs?

- Survey results also showed 55.9 percent of youths aged 12 to 17 indicated that they had talked with a parent in the past year about the dangers of alcohol and drug use. What effect do you think support from parents has on teens' participating in drug prevention programs?

ACTIVITY

Write a newspaper article that describes factors that influence teens' choices about whether to use drugs. Include internal and external influences. How can teens benefit from participating in drug prevention programs and influence others in a positive and healthful way?

Real-Life Application

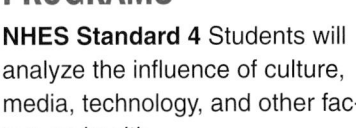

ANALYZING TRENDS: DRUG PREVENTION PROGRAMS

NHES Standard 4 Students will analyze the influence of culture, media, technology, and other factors on health.

Objectives

- Identify factors that influence decisions about drug use.
- Demonstrate strategies for influencing others to make healthful decisions about drug use.

Motivator

Instruct students not to look at their books and to estimate how many teens they think have tried illegal drugs.

Teaching Strategies

1. Guide students into concluding that students may be less likely to try drugs if they actively participate in drug prevention education programs.
2. In small groups, have students brainstorm possible influences on teen drug use.

✓Assessment

Using a rubric, student work should provide comprehensive evidence of the following criteria to achieve the highest score:

✔ identification and analysis of external and internal factors
✔ attention to interrelationships and complexity of influences
✔ variety of influences as appropriate

Cooperative Learning Activity

Conference Agenda Divide students into groups of five, and have them imagine they are members of a steering committee for a conference about drug abuse. Instruct each group to list the issues that should be discussed and rank the issues in order of their importance. Have them prepare a proposed agenda of key topics and issues that should be discussed during the conference. Also,

have them list several experts or leaders who should address the conference. For example, they might specify a representative from a drug abuse treatment center, the surgeon general, an employee of a federal drug enforcement agency or city police force, the head of a university neurology department, etc. Let them explain each choice. Allow time for groups to share their agendas.

Critical Thinking

Help students discuss their responsibility toward friends:

- Do you think teens should be responsible for preventing drug use by their friends? Why or why not?

- Do you expect your friends to discourage you from experimenting with drugs?

- How do you think teens should react when "friends" urge them to experiment with drugs? **L1**

Discussing

Let students share their ideas in response to these questions:

- How do you think parents/caregivers and other adult family members should discuss drugs with teens?

- What other kinds of support can teens find if adult family members do not actively discourage drug use? **L1**

Community Involvement

Have interested students collect current statistics on the use of illegal drugs in their local community. Also, have them find out what the statistics were five years ago. Suggest that they make a bar graph to show the increase or decrease in illegal drug use for different age groups. **L3**
Logical/Mathematical

Activity

Ask a small group of volunteers to design and complete a bulletin board or exhibit portraying some of the possible health risks associated with misuse of supplements. **L2 Visual/Spatial**

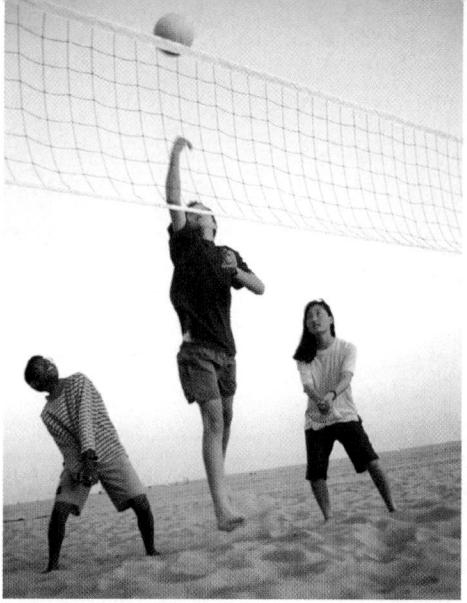

A strong, supportive system of family and friends can help a teen make the healthful decision to avoid drugs. *What other factors help you remain drug free?*

hot link

hepatitis B and **HIV** For more information on hepatitis B and HIV, see Chapters 24 and 25, pages 638 and 662.

▶ **Family members** can help teens resist drugs. Parents and other adults who avoid drug use and who discourage drug experimentation influence their teens to abstain from drugs.

▶ **Role models** are people you admire and want to imitate. Teens who look up to coaches, athletes, actors, and professionals who avoid and discourage drug use have an advantage in resisting drugs.

▶ **Media messages** can influence your impression of drug use. Messages from TV, digital media, film, and music, for example, may be misleading about the harmful effects of drugs.

▶ **Perceptions** of society's drug behavior are often inaccurate. According to the 2001 Youth Risk Behavior Survey, nearly 70 percent of high school students do not use drugs.

The Health Risks of Drug Use

Illegal drugs have serious side effects that can range from minor to deadly. Unlike medicines, these substances are not monitored for quality, purity, or strength. The effects of such drugs is unpredictable. Drug abuse affects all sides of the health triangle.

▶ **Physical health.** Once a drug enters the bloodstream, it can harm a user's brain, heart, lungs, and other vital organs. A serious danger of drug abuse is the risk of overdosing. An **overdose** is *a strong, sometimes fatal reaction to taking a large amount of a drug.* Some drug use involves injecting substances through a needle, which can increase the risk of contracting diseases such as **hepatitis B** and **HIV.**

▶ **Mental health.** Drugs cloud reasoning and thinking, and users lose control of their behavior. As shown in **Figure 23.2** on page 595, the drug Ecstasy alters the brain's structure and function. People who experiment with drugs often lose sight of their values. While under the influence of drugs, teens may no longer recall the positive beliefs, values, and ideals they have used to guide their own conduct.

▶ **Social health.** Even people who are "just experimenting" with drugs do and say things they later regret. Substance abuse can have a negative effect on relationships with friends and family members. It can cause teens to be expelled from school or dropped from a school team, and it often has legal consequences. Substance abuse is a major factor in many crimes, suicides, and unintentional injuries.

Dealing with Sensitive Issues

Protecting Student Privacy It is important to remember that any discussion of the misuse or abuse of drugs may have different effects on students who are themselves experimenting with drugs or who know or fear that a parent, other family member, or friend abuses drugs. In discussing drugs with students, avoid asking questions, even of the class in general, that may seem personal. At the same time, be alert for students who may want or need a private conversation about drugs and drug use. Create opportunities to speak with each of those students alone, or ask a school health provider or counselor to talk with them individually. Provide a list of local resources and phone numbers for students.

FIGURE 23.2

DRUG USE AND THE BRAIN

Ecstasy, a stimulant drug that speeds up the nervous system, affects parts of the brain controlling thinking, mood, memory, and perception.

neocortex — basal ganglia

— amygdala

hypothalamus — hippocampus

Understanding the Addiction Cycle

Teens who experiment with drugs will experience side effects, or unwanted reactions. The side effects can range from nausea and headaches to a loss of consciousness and even death, and can occur with a teen's first use of a drug. What may begin as a seemingly harmless pastime results in serious consequences. These consequences include:

▶ **Tolerance.** The body of the substance abuser needs more and more of the drug to get the same effect.

▶ **Psychological dependence.** *A condition in which a person believes that a drug is needed in order to feel good or to function normally,* **psychological dependence** develops over time. The user has a continuing desire to take the drug for its effect.

▶ **Physiological dependence.** A person who experiences the severe effects of withdrawal when he or she stops taking a drug has a **physiological dependence**, *a condition in which the user has a chemical need for the drug.* Symptoms of withdrawal can include nervousness, insomnia, severe nausea, headaches, vomiting, chills, and cramps. In some cases, death can result.

▶ **Addiction.** Anyone who takes drugs risks one of the most frightening side effects: **addiction**, *a physiological or psychological dependence on a drug.* Addiction causes persistent, compulsive use of a substance known by the user to be harmful. People who are addicted to a substance have great difficulty in stopping without professional intervention.

h⦿t link

addiction For more information on addiction, see Chapter 22, page 578.

Lesson 2 Drug Use–A High-Risk Behavior **595**

CHARACTER CHECK

Courage Have several volunteers share their ideas about the courage it takes to resist pressures to use drugs. Ask: How is resisting drugs part of being a responsible individual? What strengths do you have to help you resist drugs? What responsibilities do you think you have to help others resist drugs? Then let students form groups to carry out the Character Check assignment.

Reinforcing Concepts

Emphasize the connections between drug use and the high risk of contracting HIV. People under the influence of drugs act impulsively, without considering the consequences. Thus they are likely to inject themselves with a used needle or engage in sexual activity even though they might avoid making those choices when not under the influence of drugs. **L1**

Activity

In a few cases, pregnant females have been prosecuted for child abuse because they used illegal drugs while pregnant. Ask a group of interested students to debate the appropriateness of this legal response. **L3 Verbal/Linguistic**

CHARACTER CHECK

Courage. When you resist the pressure to use drugs, you demonstrate that you are responsible and that you have the courage to do the right thing. **Join with friends to visit elementary schools. Share with younger students the positive behaviors and actions you use to stay drug free.**

hot link

STDs For more information about STDs, see Chapter 25, page 646.

Experimenting even once with a drug can quickly lead to a harmful and damaging addiction. *What consequences of drug use affect family and friends?*

Other Consequences of Drug Use

In addition to the physical risks to a person's health, substance abuse can damage a teen's performance in school, in sports, in relationships with friends, and in family life. The abuse of drugs adds pressure and stress to a period of life that is already filled with both.

Consequences to the Individual

Drug use affects all aspects of a person's health. Mental and physical health suffer as tolerance, dependence, and addiction develop. The effects of drug use also influence emotional health. People who experiment with drugs tend to lose control more readily than those who do not. This tendency can lead to violence. Substance abuse is also a major factor in violent crimes, suicides, and both unintentional and intentional deaths. Drug use can lead to a relaxing of inhibitions. As a result, drug users are at risk for engaging in sexual activity, which can lead to unintended pregnancy or exposure to **STDs.**

LEGAL CONSEQUENCES

Teens possessing, using, manufacturing, or selling drugs are committing the crime of illicit drug use. Being arrested leads to court fines and legal fees. Some states automatically suspend the driving privileges of minors convicted of a drug offense. Suspension from school, jail time, or probation also are consequences of arrest and conviction.

Consequences for Family and Friends

Some people believe that their decision about drug use is their business and doesn't involve anyone else. That is not true. When an individual chooses to abuse drugs, the decision affects everyone in the user's life. Teens who become involved with drugs lose their interest in healthy activities and have little time for friends who value a drug-free lifestyle. Family members have a responsibility to be aware of the warning signs of drug use and encourage the individual to seek professional help.

Consequences for Babies and Children

Substance abuse can cause considerable harm to developing fetuses, infants, and children of drug users. A pregnant female who uses drugs passes the drug through the placenta to her unborn child. The baby may be spontaneously aborted or born with birth defects, behavioral problems, or an addiction. If either parent is using injected drugs, the baby may be born with HIV caused by the sharing of infected needles by one or both parents. A nursing mother who uses drugs passes these substances through breast milk to her child. Babies born to mothers who used depressants or other drugs during pregnancy may be physically dependent on drugs and show severe withdrawal symptoms at birth.

Curriculum Connections

Language Arts Have students write a fictional first-person story in which the narrator is the victim of a drug-related crime who needs the help of a detective. Ask them to set the stage of the crime; to describe the persons involved; to depict the specific crime committed; and to explore the feelings and effects of the crime on the victim, the victim's family and friends, and the perpetrator. You may want to read a chapter of a mystery novel to familiarize students with the voice and style of this genre. Have them write drafts of their stories and proofread for errors. Encourage students to read their final drafts aloud.

Children of drug users are often neglected and abused because their addicted parents cannot properly care for them. These children may suffer a lifetime of physical and emotional problems and may need to seek help from health professionals later in life.

Costs to Society

Drug abuse has consequences beyond the individual and family. One of the biggest burdens placed on society is a rise in drug-related crime and violence because the use of drugs decreases inhibitions, increases aggressiveness, and clouds judgment. Driving under the influence of an illegal substance can result in vehicle collisions and cause countless injuries and deaths.

Drug abuse also affects the nation's economy. According to a recent study by the Office of National Drug Control Policy, illegal drugs cost the American economy $160 billion per year. The costs result from lost work hours and productivity caused by drug-related illnesses, jail time, accidents, and deaths; health costs and legal fees resulting from illegal drug use; and law enforcement costs and insurance costs from drug-related damages, injuries, and deaths.

The consequences of drug abuse—physical, mental, social, and legal—are 100 percent preventable. By choosing a drug-free lifestyle, you avoid these consequences.

Teens who use illegal drugs face suspension or expulsion from school as well as legal consequences. *How can these consequences interfere with a teen's goals?*

Lesson 2 *Review*

Reviewing Facts and Vocabulary

1. What are *substance abuse* and *illegal drugs*?
2. What are the factors that influence a teen's decision about substance abuse?
3. Analyze and explain the harmful effects of drugs on the fetus.

Thinking Critically

4. **Synthesizing.** List three costs of drug use to society, and give examples of how each of these costs might affect you.
5. **Evaluating.** What are some of the reasons that a substance abuser may have difficulties in achieving long-term goals?

Applying Health Skills

Advocacy. With classmates, analyze the physical, mental, social, and legal consequences of drug use. Put your ideas in the form of a video or public service announcement to advocate a drug-free lifestyle.

PRESENTATION SOFTWARE

Presentation software can help give your antidrug message a professional look. Find help in using presentation software at **health.glencoe.com.**

Lesson 2 Drug Use—A High-Risk Behavior **597**

Lesson 2 *Review*

Answers to Reviewing Facts and Vocabulary

1. See page 592 for definitions.
2. See "Factors that Influence Decisions About Drugs," pages 593–594.
3. Possible answers: can cause birth defects, infants may be addicted and experience withdrawal symptoms.

Answers to Thinking Critically

4. Possible costs: lost work hours because of illness, accidents, death, jail time, or victims of crime. Effects will vary.
5. Possible answers: legal issues can prevent one from getting or maintaining a job; consequences such as unplanned pregnancy, violence, vandalism, and STDs.

ASSESS

EVALUATING THE LESSON

Assign and discuss the Lesson 2 Review; then administer, grade, and discuss Lesson Quiz 84 in the TCR.

RETEACHING

- Have students work with partners to list the effects of drugs on users and on people around users.
- Ask students to complete Reteaching Activity 84 in the TCR.

ENRICHMENT

Have each student identify a TV show or movie in which positive or negative attitudes toward drug use are depicted. (Remind students that these depictions may be subtle; drug use does not have to be the subject of the show or movie.) Then have students write summaries of the plots and descriptions of the attitudes depicted.

CLOSE

Ask students to state the lesson's most important concepts. Ask for volunteers to share their statements with the class.

Marijuana, Inhalants, and Steroids

1 FOCUS

QUICK START Ask students to suggest one reason for saying no to drugs. Write that reason on the board as an example, and help students recast the reason as an effective refusal statement. Then have students complete the Quick Start assignment on their own.

TYING TO PRIOR KNOWLEDGE

Ask volunteers to share a few facts about marijuana. Tell students they will learn more about marijuana and other drugs as they study Lesson 3.

Health Skills Features

"No Means No!" p. 601

REFUSAL SKILLS

INTRODUCING VOCABULARY

- Ask volunteers to identify the verb from which the noun *inhalants* is formed. Ask other volunteers to look up the terms *anabolic* and *androgenic* and to suggest how that definition describes the effects of steriods. Then have each student use the Glossary to find the definitions of all the vocabulary terms.

- Ask students to complete the Chapter 23 Study Guide in the *Student Activity Workbook*.

Marijuana, Inhalants, and Steroids

VOCABULARY
marijuana
paranoia
inhalants
anabolic-androgenic
    steroids

YOU'LL LEARN TO
- Analyze the physical, mental, social, and legal consequences of using marijuana, steroids, and inhalants.
- Analyze and apply strategies for avoiding the use of marijuana, inhalants, and steroids.
- Explain the negative effects of combining alcohol use with marijuana use.

QUICK START Knowing the risks of substance abuse can help you stay drug free. Write three reasons for saying no to drugs. Then, modify these reasons into effective refusal statements that you could use if someone offered you drugs.

 Marijuana is an illegal drug. It affects your memory, concentration, coordination, and reaction time. *What strategies do you have for avoiding marijuana use?*

Suppose that someone dared you to go into your school's chemistry lab and swallow a mixture of unfamiliar chemicals. You'd think the idea was pretty crazy, wouldn't you? Yet, this is exactly what people do when they experiment with illegal drugs. No government agency inspects these substances, as is done with medicines, to make sure they're safe or pure. People who take illegal drugs are gambling with their lives.

Marijuana

Marijuana, the common name for the Indian hemp plant Cannabis, is *a plant whose leaves, buds, and flowers are smoked for their intoxicating effects.* It is one of the most widely used illegal drugs, and is also known as grass, weed, or pot. It is often the first drug teens experiment with after alcohol. Hashish, or hash, is a stronger form of marijuana. Studies have shown that an individual who uses marijuana is 17 times more likely to use cocaine than one who has never used marijuana. Contrary to popular opinion, this drug is not harmless. All forms of marijuana are mind altering and can damage the user's health. When combined with other drugs, marijuana can be deadly.

598   Chapter 23 Medicines and Drugs

Lesson 3 *Resources*

Teacher Classroom Resources
- Concept Mapping Activity 85
- Guided Reading Activities 85
- Lesson Plan 85
- Lesson Quiz 85
- Reteaching Activity 85

Student Activity Workbook
- Applying Health Skills 85
- Chapter 23 Study Guide

Multimedia
 Transparency 68

Marijuana and Addiction

As with other mood-altering drugs, marijuana raises levels of a brain chemical called dopamine. This chemical produces a pleasurable feeling. In some users, the drug triggers the release of so much dopamine that a feeling of intense well-being or elation is reached. When the drug wears off, however, the pleasure sensation stops, often dramatically. This abrupt letdown is called a "crash." Marijuana contains *more* cancer-causing chemicals than tobacco smoke and carries the same health risks as smoking tobacco. Marijuana also interferes with the immune system, so the user becomes more susceptible to infections. Many of the physical effects of marijuana use are summarized in **Figure 23.3.**

Did You Know ?

➤ Marijuana contains 421 different chemicals, including d-alpha-tetrahydrocannabinol (THC), the main psychoactive ingredient in marijuana. THC is stored in body fat, and traces of it can be present in the blood for as long as a month. It has a lasting effect on the brain. This means that a marijuana user can fail a drug test weeks after using the drug.

FIGURE 23.3

THE HEALTH RISKS OF MARIJUANA

The effects of marijuana use vary from person to person and can be influenced by an individual's mood and surroundings. In all cases, however, marijuana poses serious health risks.

- Hallucinations and paranoia
- Impaired short-term memory, reaction time, concentration, and coordination
- Distorted sense of time, sight, touch, and sound
- Decreased initiative and ambition
- Bloodshot eyes
- Dry mouth

- Lung irritation, coughing
- Heart and lung damage
- Increased risk of lung cancer
- Weakened immunity; increased susceptibility to colds, flu, and viral infections

---

More About...

Marijuana and Addiction Adults rightly fear that marijuana use will lead teens into the use of other, more dangerous drugs. However, it is important to remember that marijuana is itself a dangerous, illegal drug. It is not unusual for marijuana use to cause severe feelings of lethargy, anxiety, or paranoia; users who take very high doses of marijuana may develop psychotic symptoms.

In addition, there is increasing evidence that marijuana can be addictive. Most users reported that they continued using marijuana even after recognizing that it was causing problems in their lives. When heavy users did try to stop, they developed withdrawal symptoms including restlessness, loss of appetite, loss of weight, sleeplessness, and shaky hands.

② TEACH

Activity

Have students use online or library resources to further explore the comparative health risks of marijuana and cigarette smoking. Ask students to draw Venn diagrams to show the similarities and differences. **L2**

VISUAL LEARNING

Figure 23.3 Divide the class into three cooperative groups. Assign each group one of the health risks shown in Figure 23.3. Ask the members of each group to read and discuss the information in their section of the figure and then to present that information to the rest of the class.

Discussing

Ask: How do you think marijuana affects an athlete's performance? Why? **L1**

Health Skills Practice

Planning Ahead Remind students that refusal skills must be practiced; teens can't wait until someone pressures them to use marijuana before deciding how to say no.

Let students meet in groups to brainstorm a list of specific ways someone may pressure them to use marijuana and their refusal to that pressure. Then have students write private journal entries, describing in detail what they plan to say and do if someone urges them to try marijuana.

REFUSAL SKILLS

Discussing

Talk about how personality problems and marijuana use can be a vicious cycle. For example, using marijuana to escape problems may further develop and intensify feelings of paranoia and memory problems. Brainstorm with students actions that would result in reinforcing a teen's self-esteem and would break the cycle. **L2**

Explaining

Help students understand the dangers of driving under the influence of marijuana. Explain that marijuana has these dangerous effects:

- It interferes with the perception of depth and distance.
- It impairs thinking and judgment skills.
- It slows reflexes, affecting a driver's ability to brake, negotiate turns, and respond to unexpected changes.
- It impairs a driver's ability to stay in the proper lane. **L1**

Activity

Ask a group of volunteers to get detailed information about the school's policy regarding marijuana possession and use. What are the consequences for students who are found with marijuana at school? At off-campus school functions? **L2**

hot link

reproductive organs For more information on keeping the reproductive organs healthy, see Chapter 18, pages 470 and 475.

Ⓐ Driving under the influence of marijuana can be dangerous. *What are some effects of marijuana use that could impair a person's ability to drive safely?*

Risks to Mental/Emotional Health

Marijuana users experience slow mental reflexes and suffer sudden feelings of anxiety and **paranoia**, *an irrational suspiciousness or distrust of others.* The user may feel dizzy, have trouble walking, and have difficulty remembering events that just happened. Because short-term memory is adversely affected, problems at school and at work may develop. Users often experience distorted perception, loss of coordination, and trouble with thinking and problem solving.

Risks to Growth and Development

For teens, marijuana poses physical risks to the **reproductive organs.** In males, regular use interferes with sperm production and lowers levels of testosterone, the hormone responsible for the development of adult male characteristics such as voice change, growth of body hair, and broadened shoulders. Females experience the opposite effect—an increase in testosterone levels. This may result in unwanted facial hair and can lead to infertility.

Risks and Consequences of Driving Under the Influence

Driving under the influence of marijuana can be as dangerous as driving under the influence of alcohol because marijuana interferes with depth perception, impairs judgment, and slows reflexes. The penalties and legal consequences of driving under the influence of any drug, including marijuana, are strict. These include suspension of a driver's license, a fine, and often a jail term. Insurance premiums are increased when the driver's license is restored. If injury or death results from a drug-related accident, the impaired driver may face serious legal prosecution.

Inhalants

Inhalants are *substances whose fumes are sniffed and inhaled to achieve a mind-altering effect.* Most inhalants go immediately to the brain, causing damage and actually killing brain cells that will never be replaced. Inhalants include solvents and aerosols such as glues, spray paints, gasoline, and varnishes. They also include nitrates and nitrous oxides, which have medical uses. All inhalants are extremely dangerous, and many are labeled as poisons. These substances were never designed to be taken into the body and cause permanent nervous system and brain damage.

MEETING STUDENT DIVERSITY

Language Diversity A clear understanding of the risks of using drugs is essential for all students. Those who are still acquiring English language skills should be encouraged to consult the Glosario, if appropriate, and/or to work in groups with others who share a common first language, discussing drugs risks and practicing ways to avoid and refuse drugs.

Learning Styles Students who may have difficulties decoding and/or comprehending drug information as presented in the text should work with reading buddies. One student in each pair can be responsible for reading aloud or for helping the other student read aloud. Emphasize that both partners contribute to learning as they consider and discuss the information in the text.

Most inhalants depress the central nervous system and produce effects that include a glassy stare, slurred speech, and impaired judgment. Inhalant use or huffing, inhaling the fumes from aerosol cans, can cause sudden death by increasing heart rate that results in cardiac arrest, or death by suffocation.

Anabolic-Androgenic Steroids

Anabolic-androgenic steroids are *synthetic substances that are similar to the male sex hormone testosterone.* Anabolic refers to muscle building and *androgenic* refers to increased male characteristics. When used under a doctor's guidance, these substances help build muscles in patients with chronic diseases. Steroid use

Refusal Skills: No Means No!

At a recent wrestling competition, Chris lost to an opponent he had beaten several times before.

Afterward, his teammate Josh pulled him aside and said, "You know, that guy has been getting help to build muscles. You need steroids to make State."

Josh held out a pill. Chris shook his head. "No way!"

"You'll definitely take home the title if you just help yourself to a few of these pills," Josh said.

Chris repeated, "I said no and I mean no."

Josh persisted, "If you don't, you won't make State."

"The title is not so important that I should risk my health," Chris reasoned.

"It would just be for this season," Josh continued.

Chris changed the subject, "Hey, look. Jason's match is on. I'm going to check it out." Then Chris walked away.

What Would You Do?

Write your own dialogue for this situation. Analyze and apply at least four refusal strategies for avoiding drugs.

Successful Refusal Techniques:

1. Say no in a firm voice.
2. Explain why you are refusing.
3. Suggest alternatives.
4. Back up your words by using body language.
5. Leave if necessary.

Lesson 3 Marijuana, Inhalants, and Steroids **601**

Health Skills Activity

REFUSAL SKILLS

NO MEANS NO!

NHES Standard 5 Students will demonstrate the ability to use interpersonal communication skills to enhance health.

Objectives

- Analyze the harmful effects of steroids.
- Apply refusal strategies to resist pressure to use steroids.

Motivator

Have students volunteer refusal strategies to resist pressure to use drugs.

Teaching Strategies

1. Have the class identify the refusal strategies used in the feature as you write them on the board.
2. Allow students to work in small groups to write and perform their dialogues or new situations. Encourage them to use additional refusal strategies.

✓ Assessment

Using a rubric, student work should provide comprehensive evidence of the following criteria to achieve the highest score:

✔ inclusion of the word no in their response
✔ an explanation of why they are refusing
✔ alternatives to the proposed activity
✔ body language they would use to back up their words
✔ a description of walking away from the situation, if necessary

More About...

Inhalants The National Institute on Drug Abuse warns that many common household items are misused as inhalants. Such substances are usually within three groups:

- Volatile solvents compose the largest group. They include paint thinners and paint solvent, dry cleaning fluids, gasoline, glues, rubber cement, correction fluid, felt-tip marker fluid, spray paint, nail polish remover, lighter fluid, and hair spray.
- Gases form a second group of inhalants. They include helium, Freon (refrigerant), nitrous oxide, butane lighters, propane tanks, and the propellant used in vegetable cooking spray and whip cream spray.
- Nitrites, including amyl nitrite (available by prescription only) and butyl nitrite (an illegal substance), form the third group.

Activity

Ask interested students to use library and online resources to learn more about specific health problems caused by the illegal use of anabolic-androgenic steroids. Have these students summarize their findings in written or oral reports to be shared with the rest of the class.

3 ASSESS

EVALUATING THE LESSON

Assign and discuss the Lesson 3 Review; then administer, grade, and discuss Lesson Quiz 85 in the TCR. 📁

RETEACHING

- Have students use the charts and photographs to review the lesson with other students.
- Ask students to complete Reteaching Activity 85 in the TCR. 📁

ENRICHMENT

Have students create performances—skits, musical compositions, or dances—that depict the dangers of marijuana use. Allow students to work in pairs or small groups if they want. Let students present their performances to the rest of the class.

4 CLOSE

Go around the room, asking each student to identify one risk of using marijuana, inhalants, or steroids.

---

can cause mood swings; impaired judgment resulting from feelings of invincibility; and paranoia.

Legal and Social Consequences of Steroid Use

All steroid use other than that prescribed by a licensed physician is illegal and dangerous. Although steroids can increase muscle strength, the associated tendons and ligaments don't get stronger. This discrepancy can result in injuries that take a long time to heal and can end an athlete's career. In addition to causing health problems, steroid users often turn to other illegal, addictive drugs to combat the side effects of steroids. Abusers may take anabolic steroids as pills or by injection. If needles are shared or contaminated, steroid users run the risk of exposure to disease-causing bacteria and viruses, including HIV.

Serious health risks are not the only consequences of steroid use. According to the Anabolic Steroids Control Act of 1990, the nonmedical use of steroids is illegal for people of all ages in the United States. As drug testing for athletes becomes more prevalent, athletes who fail a drug test for steroids can face exclusion from an event, expulsion from the team, monetary fines, and jail time.

▼ **Improving athletic performance through hard work and practice shows that you are a healthful, responsible person.**
How could use of steroids harm rather than help an athlete's career?

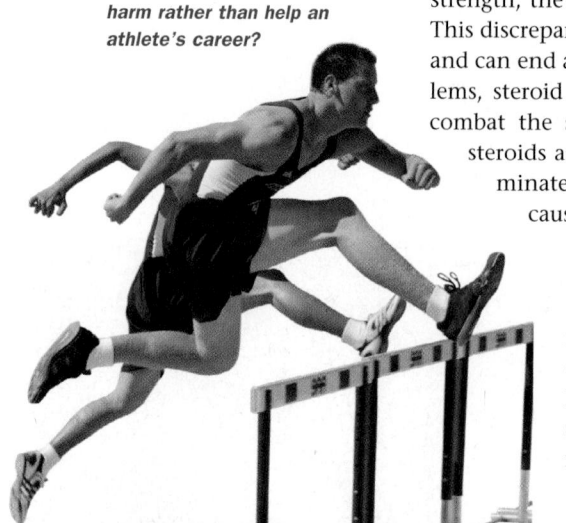

▶ Lesson 3 *Review*

Reviewing Facts and Vocabulary

1. Explain the relationship between marijuana use and alcohol use.
2. How does marijuana interfere with driving ability?
3. Analyze and examine the harmful effects of inhalants and steroids on body systems.

Thinking Critically

4. **Analyzing.** Analyze the physical, mental, social, and legal consequences of using marijuana. What effect can use of this drug have on a teen's future?
5. **Synthesizing.** Why are younger students especially at risk for inhalant use? What can you do to help prevent younger students from trying inhalants?

Applying Health Skills

Practicing Healthful Behaviors. Write a short story in which a teen is being pressured to use one of the drugs discussed in this lesson. Your story should show how the teen effectively analyzes and applies strategies to avoid the dangers associated with drug use.

PRESENTATION SOFTWARE You can use presentation software to incorporate appropriate art and graphics to illustrate your story. Find help in using presentation software at **health.glencoe.com**.

▶ Lesson 3 *Review*

Answers to Reviewing Facts and Vocabulary

1. These are drugs people often use before moving on to other, more dangerous drugs.
2. Marijuana affects concentration, coordination, and the ability to react.
3. See page 602 for psychological effects.

Answers to Thinking Critically

4. Answers will vary, but should include specific examples of physical, mental, social, and legal effects.
5. Because inhalants are often household products, they are more accessible to younger students than are other drugs. Responses should emphasize the dangers of inhalant use and advocate a drug-free lifestyle.

Psychoactive Drugs

VOCABULARY

psychoactive drugs
stimulants
euphoria
depressants
narcotics
hallucinogens
designer drugs

YOU'LL LEARN TO

• Examine the harmful effects of psychoactive drugs on body systems.

• Explain the role psychoactive drugs play in putting teens in unsafe situations that include the risk of HIV, STDs, or unplanned pregnancies.

• Analyze the importance of alternatives to drug use.

• Analyze and apply strategies for avoiding psychoactive drugs.

QUICK START Teens have the opportunity to live healthy lives—to be the healthiest they can be. The best way to make the most of that opportunity is to make wise choices that have a positive effect on your health. On a sheet of paper, write three ways you can safeguard your health and avoid the harmful effects of drug use.

The central nervous system (CNS), which includes the brain and the spinal cord, is an amazingly complex part of the body. Every form of activity, from bending a finger to solving abstract problems, involves the central nervous system. **Psychoactive drugs**, *chemicals that affect the central nervous system and alter activity in the brain*, change the functioning of the CNS.

Classification of Psychoactive Drugs

There are four main groups of psychoactive drugs: stimulants, depressants, narcotics, and hallucinogens (huh-LOO-suhn-uh-juhnz). Some of these drugs have medicinal value when properly used. However, even under a doctor's supervision, they carry risks. When psychoactive drugs are misused or abused, a person's health and the proper function of all body systems are seriously affected. **Figure 23.4** shows the health risks of these drugs on body systems. The effects on the developing brain and body of a teen can be especially damaging.

Your decision to stay healthy and drug free will help you succeed in school.

Lesson 4 *Resources*

Teacher Classroom Resources

📁 Concept Mapping Activity 86
📁 Decision-Making Activity 23
📁 Guided Reading Activities 86
📁 Lesson Plan 86
📁 Lesson Quiz 86
📁 Reteaching Activity 86

Student Activity Workbook

📁 Applying Health Skills 86
📁 Chapter 23 Study Guide

Multimedia

🖱 Transparency 69

Lesson 4

Psychoactive Drugs

FOCUS

QUICK START Have students read the Quick Start assignment, and give them a few minutes to write about two specific choices they have made. Then ask volunteers to read their responses aloud. Help students discuss how and why they made these wise choices.

TYING TO PRIOR KNOWLEDGE

Let volunteers recall what the central nervous system is and does. Then explain that, in this lesson, students will learn about drugs that change the functioning of the central nervous system.

Health Skills Features

"Refusing Drugs," p. 607

REFUSAL SKILLS

INTRODUCING VOCABULARY

• Ask volunteers to identify and define the verbs related to the nouns *stimulant, depressant,* and *hallucinogens*. Ask: How do those verbs help you understand the nouns? Then have students use the verb form to make sentences. Invite students to work in groups to check all the vocabulary term definitions in the Glossary.

• Ask students to complete the Chapter 23 Study Guide in the *Student Activity Workbook.* 📁

2 TEACH

Reinforcing Concepts

Draw students' attention to the statement on the previous page that the effects of psychoactive drugs can be especially damaging for teens. Ask: Why is this true? What is one easy step you can take to protect your central nervous system? **L1**

VISUAL LEARNING

Figure 23.4 Read aloud the title and headings for the figure on psychoactive drugs. Have all students follow the chart as volunteers read aloud the consequences of each drug. Have students identify other names for these drugs. Ask: Why is it important to know the effects each drug has on a person's health? **L1**

Explaining

Stress that people who abuse drugs often become dependent on several different types of drugs. They may take amphetamines to get high and then take a depressant to settle down or to go to sleep. Discuss the implications of this type of abuse on the body's ability to function on its own. **L1**

FYI

The National Institute on Drug Abuse reports that, in one recent year, about 4 million Americans used prescription drugs for nonmedical purposes. Among 12–14 year olds, the nonmedical use of a group of drugs including pain killers, tranquilizers, sedatives, and stimulants was the second most common form of drug abuse.

604

FIGURE 23.4

HEALTH RISKS OF PSYCHOACTIVE DRUGS

Types of Drugs	Consequences to Your Health
STIMULANTS	
Cocaine	• Nausea, abdominal pain, malnutrition • Chest pain, respiratory failure, death • Headache, stroke, seizure, heart attack, death • Exposure to HIV through contaminated needles
Crack (crystallized derivative of cocaine)	• Extreme addiction, with the same effects as pure cocaine • Rapid increase in heart rate and blood pressure can cause death
Amphetamines	• Decreased appetite, weight loss, and malnutrition • High blood pressure, rapid heartbeat, heart failure, death • Loss of muscle coordination, delirium, panic • Aggressiveness, increased tolerance, addiction
Methamphetamine	• Memory loss, heart and nerve damage • Increased tolerance, addiction
DEPRESSANTS	
Barbiturates	• Reduced heart rate and blood pressure • Fatigue, confusion, impaired muscle coordination • Impaired memory, loss of judgment • Reduced respiratory function, respiratory arrest, death
Tranquilizers	• Depression, unusual excitement, fever, irritability • Loss of judgment, dizziness
Rohypnol (date rape drug)	• Confusion, inability to remember what happened • Decreased blood pressure, drowsiness, gastrointestinal disturbances
GHB	• Drowsiness, nausea, vomiting, loss of consciousness • Impaired breathing, coma, death
NARCOTICS	
Opium	• Nausea, constipation
Morphine	• Rapid onset of tolerance, addiction
Heroin	• Confusion, sedation, unconsciousness, coma
Codeine	• Reduced respiratory function, respiratory arrest, death • Exposure to HIV through contaminated needles
HALLUCINOGENS	
PCP	• Loss of appetite, depression • Panic, aggression, violent actions • Increased heart and respiratory function
LSD	• Delusions, illusions, hallucinations, flashbacks, convulsions, coma, and death
Ecstacy (MDMA)	• Confusion, depression, paranoia, muscle breakdown
Ketamine	• Kidney and cardiovascular system failure, death • Memory loss, numbness, impaired motor function • Nausea, high blood pressure, fatal respiratory reaction

---

More About...

Herbal Stimulants Advise students of the risks of another stimulant—ephedrine. This substance is derived from the plant *Ephedra*, a shrub found in desert regions in central Asia. Ephedrine is the active element of *ma huang*, an herb used in Chinese medicine. It stimulates the cardiovascular and central nervous systems. Ephedrine is found in OTC weight-loss products, energy-boosting supplements, and "herbal ecstasy." It has also been used by athletes to enhance athletic performance. The FDA has received reports of adverse reactions including memory loss, nerve damage, liver failure, elevated blood pressure, strokes, and deaths. Ask a volunteer to research online the most recent FDA decisions concerning the use of ephedrine in supplements.

Health Risks of Stimulants

Stimulants are *drugs that speed up the central nervous system.* Some foods, such as coffee, tea, and cola, contain small amounts of a stimulant called caffeine. The **nicotine** in tobacco products is also a stimulant. Sometimes, stimulants are prescribed for specific medical conditions, for example, the medication used to treat hyperactivity. Although some stimulants have medical uses, many of these substances are used illegally. The most dangerous of the illegal stimulants are cocaine, amphetamines (am-FE-tuh-meenz), and methamphetamine (me-tham-FE-tuh-meen).

Cocaine

Cocaine is a rapid-acting, powerful, highly addictive stimulant that interrupts normal functioning of the central nervous system. The purchase and possession of cocaine is illegal everywhere in the United States. Cocaine is a white powder extracted from the leaves of the coca plant. Cocaine users can experience a surge of self-confidence and **euphoria**, *a feeling of intense well-being or elation.* Effects of cocaine use can last from 20 minutes to several hours.

The feeling of confidence induced by cocaine use is followed by an emotional letdown. Regular use can lead to depression, fatigue, paranoia, and physiological dependence. Cocaine use can cause malnutrition and, especially among teens, cardiac problems. When cocaine is snorted, it shrinks the tiny blood vessels in the nose. Repeated use can lead to collapse of the nasal septum, the wall dividing the two halves of the nose. When users inject cocaine, they risk contracting HIV or hepatitis B from infected needles. Overdosing can result in cardiac arrest, respiratory failure, seizures, and death.

Crack

An even more dangerous form of cocaine is crack. Also known as crack cocaine, rock, or freebase rock, crack is one of the most deadly drugs available. It is a very pure form of cocaine that reaches the brain seconds after being smoked or injected. Once in the blood, it causes heart rate and blood pressure to soar to dangerous levels. Death may result from cardiac or respiratory failure. Mixing cocaine and alcohol is extremely dangerous. These substances are combined in the liver, increasing the risk of death from liver failure.

hot link

nicotine For more information on nicotine and tobacco products, see Chapter 21, page 540.

Crack cocaine is a concentrated form of cocaine that can cause death. *What are the dangers of mixing cocaine with other drugs, such as alcohol?*

Cooperative Learning

Let students meet in groups to read and discuss the information on stimulants. Remind students that the medical uses apply to only some of the listed stimulants; others, such as cocaine, are in all cases illegal drugs. Have groups answer the following: Why is it important for everyone to know the indications of possible stimulant use and the symptoms of stimulant overdose?

Activity

Have interested students use online and library resources to learn more about Ritalin in the treatment of hyperactivity: When and why is it prescribed? With what effects? What risks are associated with the use of Ritalin? Have students summarize their findings in written reports. Remind them to proofread for errors before completing a final draft. **L3** **Verbal/Linguistic**

Discussing

Ask students to consider the effects of caffeine found in colas, coffee, and tea:

- Do you think a mild stimulant like caffeine should be legal?
- How and where do you think the division should be made between legal and illegal stimulants? **L1**

Activity

Ask a group of interested students to plan and make a bulletin board display showing the dangers of using cocaine and crack. **L2** **Visual/Spatial**

Curriculum Connections

Language Arts After reviewing literature and personal accounts of people using crack and cocaine, have each student write a short essay on cocaine and crack. The essay should explore the student's personal feelings about this drug and its effects on individuals and the community.

Social Studies Have each student research the history of one psychoactive drug and prepare a one-page report to share with the class. Ask students to consider such questions as these: What effects does this drug produce? What are the risks involved in using this drug? How widespread is the abuse of this drug?

Discussing

Guide students in discussing what might lead a teen to use amphetamines. What are some healthful alternatives for each case? ⬛1

Direct students to work in small groups to find and discuss up-to-date information on the effects of drugs on the brain. Have them put their findings in a table and present it to the class.

Discussing

Help students discuss the cycle that may lead to repeated methamphetamine use: How is a user likely to respond when feelings of euphoria are replaced by depression and paranoia? What kind of help is available for a user who wants to quit? ⬛2

Reinforcing Concepts

Have volunteers explain how depressants affect the central nervous system. Ask: Why might some drug abusers use depressants in combination with stimulants? What do you think happens when someone gets into the habit of using depressants and stimulants? ⬛1

Explaining

Be sure students understand that the most serious health risks of combining depressants—including death—can be caused even by mixing a prescribed tranquilizer with alcohol. ⬛1

Get the latest research and information about the dangerous effects drugs can have on the brain at **health.glencoe.com**.

Source: National Institute on Drug Abuse

⚠ The red areas in the normal brain scan (top) show memory and motor skill control. The brain scan on the bottom, taken one month after the subject's use of methamphetamine, indicates loss of memory and motor control.

Amphetamines

Amphetamines are stimulants used in prescription medicines to reduce fatigue and drowsiness or to suppress the appetite. However, some people use amphetamines illegally to stay awake and alert, to improve athletic performance, or to lose weight. The easily developed tolerance to amphetamines causes a user to ingest more of the substance. Regular use of amphetamines can result in twitching, irregular heartbeat, paranoia, and heart and blood vessel damage.

Methamphetamine

Methamphetamine, or meth, is a stimulant used in treating certain diseases, including Parkinson's disease and obesity. It is a white, odorless powder that easily dissolves in alcohol or water. Because it is produced in makeshift labs, the drug is readily available, but its quality is uncertain. In recent years, this drug has been identified as one of the many dangerous and illegal substances called "club drugs," drugs associated with concerts and all-night parties called raves. Meth may provide a short-term feeling of euphoria. Often the use of this drug results in depression, paranoia, damage to the central nervous system, increased heart rate and blood pressure, and damage to brain cells. It can also cause death.

Health Risks of Depressants

Depressants, or sedatives, are *drugs that tend to slow down the central nervous system.* Depressant drugs relax muscles, relieve feelings of tension and worry, and cause drowsiness. They can be dangerous because they slow the heart rate, lower blood pressure to dangerous levels, and interrupt the normal rate of breathing. One of the most commonly used depressants is alcohol. Two types of sedative medications are barbiturates (bar-BICH-uh-ruhts) and tranquilizers. Other widely-used depressants include Rohypnol and GHB. Combining depressants, even in small amounts, produces a *synergistic* effect. For example, a user combining alcohol and tranquilizers can overdose, causing shallow breathing, weak and rapid pulse, coma, and even death.

More About...

Amphetamines Assign students to research the abuse of amphetamines to stay awake for exams. Have them learn about the disadvantages to such a strategy; for example, the tendency to be careless about test details while on amphetamines. Encourage students to list the effects of such amphetamine abuse. Then have them write an editorial to the school newspaper outlining their findings. Have students proofread one another's work, checking for organization and clarity of argument, as well as spelling and grammatical errors. Finally, encourage students to write several drafts before submitting a final draft to the paper.

Barbiturates

Barbiturates belong to a family of sedative-hypnotic drugs, or drugs that induce sleepiness. Barbiturate use can result in mood changes, sleeping more than normal, and coma. Barbiturates are rarely used for medical purposes. They are used illegally to produce a feeling of intoxication and to counteract the effects of stimulants. Combining barbiturates with alcohol can be fatal.

Tranquilizers

Tranquilizers are depressants that reduce muscular activity, coordination, and attention span. Tranquilizers are prescribed to relieve anxiety, muscle spasms, sleeplessness, and nervousness. However, when tranquilizers are overused, physiological and psychological dependence occurs. Withdrawal from tranquilizers causes severe shaking. In extreme cases, coma or death can result.

Hands-On Health ACTIVITY

Refusing Drugs

Learning to say no to drugs is an important component in maintaining a drug-free life. By practicing refusal skills, you will find it easier to uphold your commitment to a substance-free lifestyle. In this activity you will practice effective ways to say no to drugs.

What You'll Need

- pencil and paper
- one classmate

What You'll Do

1. Divide a sheet of paper into two columns. In the left column, list five pressure lines someone might use to persuade you to use drugs.

2. Trade your paper with a classmate. Read your partner's list. In the right column, write an effective refusal statement responding to each pressure line. Possibilities include: "No thanks, I don't do drugs"; "I'm on medication"; or "That stuff makes me sick."

3. Working with your partner, review your lists and role-play some of the most realistic scenarios. Take turns practicing refusal skills.

4. Which refusal statements did you find to be most effective? Remember and practice them to be prepared when someone tries to offer you drugs.

Apply and Conclude

With your partner, plan a public service announcement that emphasizes the importance of refusal skills. Your announcement should demonstrate how to say no to drugs effectively.

Cooperative Learning Activity

Obesity Drugs Federal health officials have declared obesity a disease that, above a certain level, justified the use of drugs. Have students conduct research about the drugs used to control obesity. Are amphetamines still used? If not, how do the drugs in current use differ from amphetamines? Suggest students use the *Physicians' Desk Reference* or other source, such as medical journals, to research the adverse effects of widely used obesity drugs. Can people stop taking the drugs without regaining the weight? What are the health effects of long-term use? What are the risks for teens using drugs to treat their own obesity? What are more healthful ways teens can treat obesity?

Hands-On Health

REFUSING DRUGS

NHES Standard 5
Students will demonstrate the ability to use interpersonal communication skills to enhance health.

Objectives

- Develop strategies to resist pressure to use drugs.
- Demonstrate refusal skills to resist pressure to use drugs.

Motivator

Display several anti-drug bumper stickers, posters, and/or buttons. Read aloud the messages on display. Ask students to think of other anti-drug messages they have seen or heard.

Teaching Strategies

1. Ask students to brainstorm pressure lines someone might use to try to influence them to use drugs.

2. Have students think of statements to resist pressure to use drugs and write them on the board. Then add other successful refusal techniques to the list.

✓ Assessment

Using a rubric, student work should provide comprehensive evidence of the following criteria to achieve the highest score:

✔ inclusion of the word no in their response

✔ an explanation of why they were refusing

✔ alternatives to the proposed activity

✔ body language to back up their words

✔ a description of walking away from the situation if necessary

Guide students in reading and discussing the information about OxyContin. Stress that this drug has caused an unusually high number of deaths in recent years. Ask volunteers to use online resources to find further facts about the dangers of OxyContin.

Explaining

Remind students that any instance of rape or sexual assault is a criminal act of violence. Also, emphasize that, although teens can take precautions (such as keeping beverage containers covered and not accepting beverages in open containers), victims of rape and sexual assault are never "at fault." Emphasize that they should get to safety first and then get help. **L1**

Discussing

Guide a class discussion of how the effects of heroin use differ from those of cocaine use. Are there any positive uses for either heroin or cocaine? Compare the risks of abusing the two drugs. **L1**

Explaining

Tell students that the life expectancy of heroin addicts is quite short. The risks of overdose, hepatitis, or AIDS are great. The monetary cost of maintaining the habit increases the abuser's risk of bodily harm through association with criminals. Many resort to crime to support their habit. **L1**

hotlink

date rape crimes For more information about protecting yourself from date rape, see Chapter 13, page 350.

Rohypnol

Rohypnol is a widely available club drug. This depressant, which is ten times as strong as tranquilizers, is better known as the date rape drug, used in crimes of dating violence. Rohypnol comes in tablet form and looks like ordinary aspirin. The drug's harmless appearance has made it a dangerously effective drug in **date rape crimes.** The victims may be given the tablets without their knowledge. Rohypnol dissolves in carbonated beverages and may easily be slipped into a soft drink. The victim wakes up much later with no recollection of what may have happened during the last several hours. Unplanned pregnancies or exposure to HIV and STDs can result from such situations.

GHB

Another club drug is gammahydroxy butyric acid (GHB). Like Rohypnol, it has been in used in date rape crimes. GHB is available as a clear liquid, a white powder, and in a variety of tablets and capsules. A person can easily overdose on GHB. The drug leaves the blood relatively quickly, making it hard for emergency room personnel to determine that an overdose has occurred.

Narcotics

What is OxyContin?
OxyContin is a prescription drug that contains oxycodone, a strong narcotic. When used properly under a doctor's supervision, it helps relieve moderate to severe chronic pain. When used illegally and in combination with alcohol or other depressants, however, OxyContin can be deadly. A side effect of this drug is suppression of the respiratory system, which can cause death from respiratory failure.

Narcotics are *specific drugs derived from the opium plant that are obtainable only by prescription and are used to relieve pain.* Morphine, OxyContin, and codeine are examples of narcotics. Morphine is sometimes prescribed by medical professionals, and codeine is an ingredient in some cough medications. These drugs relieve pain by blocking pain messengers in the brain. Narcotic use can cause euphoria, drowsiness, constipation, pinpoint pupils, slow and shallow breathing, convulsions, coma, and death. Abuse of narcotics can cause addiction. Because narcotics are so addictive, pharmacists are required to keep records of all sales of these drugs.

Heroin

Heroin, a highly addictive narcotic, is a processed form of morphine that is injected, snorted, or smoked. Heroin depresses the central nervous system and slows breathing and pulse rate. Heroin abuse can cause infection of the heart lining and valves, as well as liver disease. Infectious diseases such as pneumonia, HIV, and hepatitis B can result from the use of infected needles. Large doses may result in coma or death. Users easily develop tolerance, prompting increased usage. Withdrawal can be very painful. Fetal death may occur if the user is pregnant.

608 Chapter 23 Medicines and Drugs

More About...

Ketamine Ketamine has various street names, including Special K, Vitamin K, Kit Kat, Cat Valium, and Purple. Unlike PCP and LSD, it is legal for use as an animal tranquilizer and anesthetic. Like LSD, it produces hallucinations in its users. Because it is similar to PCP in its molecular structure, Ketamine also has many of the same effects as PCP. Some teens choose to experiment with Ketamine instead of LSD or PCP because its effects typically last only an hour and it is not tested for on standard drug tests. However, the effects of Ketamine are extremely dangerous and can be fatal. It produces hallucinations, confusion, and even psychosis. It can lead to paranoia and violent behavior.

Hallucinogens

Hallucinogens are *drugs that alter moods, thoughts, and sense perceptions including vision, hearing, smell, and touch.* These drugs have no medical use. Phencyclidine (PCP), lysergic acid diethylamide (LSD), ketamine, and Ecstasy are examples of powerful and dangerous hallucinogens. These drugs overload the sensory controls in the brain. The brain then confuses and intensifies sensations and hallucinates. Hallucinogens also impair judgment and reasoning and increase heart and respiratory rates. The altered mental states caused by hallucinogens can last for several hours or several days. The effects are extremely unpredictable, and users sometimes harm themselves physically or demonstrate other violent behaviors.

Ⓥ **Illegal drugs can affect the human body in unpredictable ways.** *What are some of the life-threatening effects of hallucinogens?*

PCP

PCP is considered one of the most dangerous of all drugs, and its effects vary greatly from user to user. Users report distorted sense of time and space, increased muscle strength, and inability to feel pain. Overdoses of PCP can cause death, but most PCP-related deaths are caused by the destructive behavior that the drug produces. PCP users have died in fires because they became disoriented and had no sensitivity to the pain of burning. Flashbacks can occur at any time, causing panic, confusion, and lack of control.

LSD

LSD is an extremely strong hallucinogen. Even a tiny amount can cause hallucinations and severe distorted perceptions of sound and color. Higher doses increase the risk of convulsions, coma, heart and lung failure, and death. Because LSD affects the brain's emotional center and distorts reality, users may experience emotions ranging from extreme euphoria to panic to deep depression. Flashbacks can involve a frightening range of emotions long after actual use of the drug.

Ketamine

Ketamine is an anesthetic used for medical purposes, mostly in treating animals. Misused as a club drug, ketamine is often sold as a white powder to be snorted, like cocaine, or injected. The drug is also smoked with marijuana or tobacco. Ketamine causes hallucinations and dreamlike states. Its use may result in death by respiratory failure. The misuse of ketamine and the use of all other hallucinogens is illegal.

Lesson 4 Psychoactive Drugs **609**

Critical Thinking

Ask students:

- Why do you think a teen or young adult might try hallucinogens?
- What could you say to help a friend or acquaintance avoid experimenting with hallucinogens? Ⅼ

Discussing

Have students read the information on hallucinogens while the rest of the class follows. Be sure students recognize that hallucinogens have no medical uses and that withdrawal from hallucinogens involves chronic recurring hallucinations even after the drugs are no longer being used.

Critical Thinking

Tell students that many teens still think Ecstasy is "safe." Ask:

- Why do you think people continue to be uninformed about this dangerous drug?
- In your opinion, who is responsible for making the facts about Ecstasy clear? Ⅼ

FYI

GHB (gamma-hydroxybutyrate) is an anabolic steroid. It is legal in some countries, used by doctors as a treatment for opiate addiction and sleep disorders. It has never been approved in the U.S. for medical purposes, but during the 1980s it was available at health food stores and used by bodybuilders to stimulate muscle growth.

In 1990, the FDA banned GHB because of its dangerous side effects.

More About...

Ecstasy MDMA—often known as Ecstasy, E, X, or Adam—is a stimulant with hallucinogenic and amphetamine-like effects. It is not a harmless drug. In fact, taking Ecstasy can be fatal. Users may experience high body temperature and potentially fatal dehydration; some users experience confusion, depression, anxiety, and paranoia. Studies of long-term effects of MDMA on rats and other laboratory animals indicate that the drug damages neurons (brain nerve cells), which produce serotonin, a neurotransmitter. Serotonin influences mood, appetite, sleep, and memory. In the studies, damaged neurons regrew abnormally or failed to regrow at all.

Discussing

Help students discuss the importance of avoiding places where drugs are used. Ask:

- Why is it easier not to go to such places than to leave once people start using drugs?
- Why is it safer to leave than to stay and just say no to drugs?
- Beyond the pressure to use drugs, what are the dangers of being in a situation where others are using drugs?

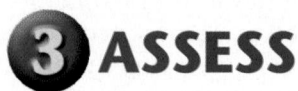 **ASSESS**

EVALUATING THE LESSON

Assign and discuss the Lesson 4 Review; then administer, grade, and discuss Lesson Quiz 86 in the TCR. 📁

RETEACHING

- Let students work with partners to write informal outlines of the lesson.

- Ask students to complete Reteaching Activity 86 in the TCR. 📁

ENRICHMENT

Help students list ideas for sharing drug-awareness with elementary or middle school students. Then have them work together to develop and carry out one of their ideas.

 CLOSE

Have students work with partners to write one-sentence summaries of each group of psychoactive drugs.

610

Did You Know ?

The use of Ecstasy among teens appears to be increasing, probably because teens are being led to think that no significant risks are involved in the use of this drug. However, Ecstasy is extremely dangerous. Over 4,500 visits to the emergency room for Ecstasy-related incidents were reported in one year.

Ecstasy can cause dramatic increases in body temperature and may lead to muscle breakdown, kidney failure, and cardiovascular system damage.

Ecstasy and Other Dangerous Drugs

Designer drugs are *synthetic substances meant to imitate the effects of hallucinogens and other dangerous drugs.* The designer drugs vary greatly in potency and strength. Designer drugs can be several hundred times stronger than the drugs they are meant to imitate. One of the most recognized designer drugs is *Ecstasy,* or MDMA. A combination stimulant and hallucinogen, Ecstasy may give a short-term feeling of euphoria but often causes confusion, depression, paranoia, psychosis, and even long-term damage to brain cells. Overdoses are common. Use can also result in uncontrollable tremors, paralysis, and irreversible brain damage.

Consequences of Drug Use

Illegal drug use is associated with a variety of negative consequences, including health problems, addiction, and difficulties in school. Furthermore, drug use often leads to poor judgment, which may put teens at risk for unintentional injuries, motor vehicle collisions, violence, STDs, unintended pregnancy, and suicide. The best way to avoid these consequences is to refuse to use drugs and to avoid places where they are used. If you find yourself in a situation where drugs are present, leave. Choosing a drug-free life is one of the most important decisions you can make to protect your health.

▶ **Lesson 4** *Review*

Reviewing Facts and Vocabulary

1. Examine and identify the body systems most affected by psychoactive and designer drugs.

2. Examine and explain the harmful effects of stimulants and hallucinogens on the central nervous system.

3. What are the health risks for those who abuse narcotics?

Thinking Critically

4. **Synthesizing.** Analyze the importance of alternatives to drug use. Develop and explain your strategy for preventing the use of addictive substances and for avoiding psychoactive drugs.

5. **Analyzing.** Explain the role psychoactive drugs play in putting teens in unsafe situations.

Applying Health Skills

Accessing Information. Choose one of the drugs you learned about in this lesson. Research to evaluate its medical uses (if any), possible effects, and damage to body systems. Organize your findings in a chart similar to those shown in this lesson. Share the chart with your class.

INTERNET RESOURCES You may want to use the Internet for your research. Be sure to use reliable sources when accessing information on the Web. See **health.glencoe.com** for Internet resources.

▶ **Lesson 4** *Review*

Answers to Reviewing Facts and Vocabulary

1. The central nervous system is most affected. Students may mention other body systems.

2. Stimulants speed up the central nervous system; hallucinogens overload the sensory controls, confusing the brain and intensifying sensations.

3. See page 608 for health risks.

Answers to Thinking Critically

4. Answers will vary.

5. Using psychoactive drugs causes loss of control. Users may make decisions that cause them to be exposed to injury, violence, sexual abuse, health risks, and death.

Living Drug Free

VOCABULARY

drug-free school zones
drug watches

YOU'LL LEARN TO

• Analyze and develop strategies for preventing drug use.

• Examine school and community efforts to curb drug use.

• Identify and assess community health services for getting help with the prevention and treatment of drug addiction and abuse.

• Analyze the importance of alternatives to drug and substance abuse.

⟶ QUICK START Make a word web with statements you can use to refuse drugs. Write and circle the words "Refusal Skills" in the middle of a sheet of paper. Then write refusal statements around the paper, and connect these to the circle with lines.

Public opinion polls and national surveys clearly show that most Americans—children, teens, and adults—have taken a stand against illegal drugs. By working together, you and your family, peers, and community can stop the effects of drug abuse. Your attitudes and decisions about drugs and how you live your life make a statement to others. By deciding not to use drugs, you promote your own health and influence others to do the same.

Resisting Pressure to Use Drugs

Peer pressure can be intense during the teen years, particularly in settings where using alcohol and other drugs may seem the norm. You may be told that "everybody's doing it," but the fact is that illegal drugs never become a part of most teens' lives. In this country almost 58 percent of high school students have never tried marijuana, and more than 90 percent have never tried cocaine. So the claim that "everybody's doing it" is simply not true.

Ⓥ **Let others know your reasons for living drug free.** *What can you do to share your opinion with others?*

Lesson 5 Living Drug Free **611**

Lesson 5 *Resources*

Teacher Classroom Resources

📂 Concept Mapping Activity 87

📂 Guided Reading Activities 87

📂 Lesson Plan 87

📂 Lesson Quiz 87

📂 Reteaching Activity 87

Student Activity Workbook

📂 Applying Health Skills 87

📂 Chapter 23 Study Guide

Lesson 5

Living Drug Free

❶ FOCUS

⟶ QUICK START Draw a sample web on the board showing at least five shapes around the central "Refusal Skills" shape. Have a volunteer suggest one example, and write that sentence or phrase in one of the shapes. Then let students copy the web and complete it independently.

TYING TO PRIOR KNOWLEDGE

Point out that students already know quite a bit about how and why they should say no to drug use. Explain that this lesson will deal with those issues in greater detail.

Health Skills Features

"Drug Testing: Yes or No?"
p. 614

INTRODUCING VOCABULARY

• Let students meet in small groups to discuss what they already know about drug-free school zones and drug watches. Then ask them to read the definitions of those terms given in the Glossary.

• Ask students to complete the Chapter 23 Study Guide in the *Student Activity Workbook.* 📂

② TEACH

Discussing

Ask students: Why is it important to know that most Americans—even most American teens—do not use drugs?

Critical Thinking

Present the following situation to the class: Viviana and Jen have been close friends since third grade. In the past few months, Jen has started experimenting with drugs and pressuring Viviana to try them too. Viviana says, "Jen is my friend. I can't walk away from her just because she's made a bad choice. Besides, maybe I can help her stop before she gets too involved with drugs." Ask: What advice would you give to Viviana? **L1**

Discussing

Encourage students to share their own ideas about drug-free school zones: Is our school in a drug-free zone? Is the drug-free zone enforced? If so, how? How might it be better enforced? What suggestions would you make for keeping our school free of drugs? **L1**

Health Minute

Let students meet in small groups to read and discuss Strategies for Avoiding the Dangers of Substance Abuse. Ask each group member to contribute a simple phrase or sentence that says no to drugs. Then have group members take turns role-playing an individual who says no when the rest of the group offers drugs.

612

Health Minute

Strategies for Avoiding the Dangers of Substance Abuse

If you're offered a drug:

▶ Be firm in saying that you're not interested.

▶ Keep it simple. Say, "No thanks," or "I don't need drugs."

▶ If the pressure continues, walk away.

Protect yourself against risks:

▶ Choose friends who share your commitment to staying drug free.

▶ Maintain your self-respect and be confident about your abilities.

▶ Take pride in your accomplishments.

▶ Use physical activity and relaxation techniques to handle stress.

▶ Stay involved in healthy activities and interests.

▶ Be aware of your surroundings, know what you are drinking, and cover drinks at parties. Never ride with people who are using drugs.

▶ Stay away from parties and places where drugs are present.

Commitment to Be Drug Free

The first step in staying drug free is to make a firm and deliberate decision. The only way to avoid the pitfalls and dangers of substance abuse is to be fully committed to refusing them before drugs are offered. In many cases it also means steering clear of people who use drugs and of places where drugs are likely to be used or offered. Protective factors present in a teen's life can provide the support needed to live a drug-free life.

Making the commitment to abstain from drugs is a life-enhancing decision. It does not mean that you will be deprived of friends or fun. Quite the opposite is true—being drug free means being able to enjoy life and deal with its challenges and problems in healthful ways. It also shows the strength of your values and demonstrates good character and respect for yourself and others.

REFUSAL SKILLS

To honor your commitment to living drug free, you can practice refusal skills. These are techniques that you can use to say no when others pressure you to use drugs. Consider all the harmful effects of drug use and all the benefits of a drug-free lifestyle. Doing so will help you stand up for what you believe without apologizing for or compromising your convictions.

Efforts to Curb Drug Abuse

Individuals are only part of the key to curbing substance abuse. Schools and communities are working together to support students in their efforts to be drug free.

School Efforts

All over the United States, **drug-free school zones** have been established. These are *areas within 1,000 feet of schools and designated by signs, within which people caught selling drugs receive especially severe penalties.* Efforts in and around schools to cut down on drug use include drug education classes, zero-tolerance policies, and expulsion of students found using drugs. In some areas police officers are assigned to patrol campuses. Security guards and locker searches also help protect teens from the dangers of drug abuse.

Community Efforts

Communities across the nation are taking positive action to stop drug abuse. **Drug watches** are *organized community efforts by neighborhood residents to patrol, monitor, report, and otherwise try to stop drug deals and drug abuse.* Becoming involved in anti-drug programs in your community is a good way to protect your family and friends from the dangers and violence associated with drug abuse.

612 Chapter 23 Medicines and Drugs

More About...

Drug-Related Medical Emergencies

Even a first experiment with drugs can be dangerous—even lethal. Students should be aware that a teen who has used any form of a drug is subject to collapse, an indication that he or she is in urgent need of medical care.

If a friend or companion collapses or becomes unconscious, teens should know how to help. Place the ill person in the recovery position, lying on the stomach, with one leg and both arms bent and the head turned to one side. This position provides protection from choking if the victim vomits. Teens should summon medical assistance immediately, dialing 9-1-1 or contacting a qualified adult. Then the ill teen's parents or other family members should be contacted.

Choosing Healthy Alternatives

There are healthier ways to cope with day-to-day problems than turning to drugs. You can find many ways to feel good about yourself without depending on harmful substances. Getting involved in school or community activities and choosing friends who value a drug-free lifestyle can give teens the focus they need to follow through on a commitment toward a more healthful life.

Becoming Drug Free

For those teens already in trouble with drugs, it is never too late to get help. Admitting that there is a problem is the first step, and getting help is the essential next step in overcoming that problem. Teens may turn to individual counseling, support groups, or drug treatment centers for help. Support from parents, guardians, school counselors, or family doctors can guide teens to get help. **Figure 23.5** lists some warning signs of drug abuse. If you know of someone who shows these signs, encourage him or her to seek help. The following steps can guide you in offering help to a friend or family member who is using alcohol or other drugs.

▶ Identify specific sources of help in your community—drug counselors, treatment centers, or support groups.

▶ Talk to the person when he or she is sober. Express your affection and concern for the person, and describe his or her behavior without being judgmental.

▶ Listen to the person's response. Be prepared for anger and denial.

▶ Discuss the sources of help you have found. Offer to go with your friend or family member to a counselor or support group.

Spending time with a parent or trusted adult can reinforce a teen's decision to live drug free.

Health Skills Practice

Looking Toward Your Future Help students discuss goals they may want to reach in the next five or six years. How would any use of drugs make those goals difficult—or impossible—to reach? Then point out that living a healthy, drug-free life can be a goal in itself. For example, students might set the goal of graduating from high school without using drugs at all. Review the steps in a goal-setting action plan. (See Chapter 2.) Then ask students to write their own action plans in their private health journals.

Service Learning

Encourage students to become involved in local drug watches or other antidrug programs in the community. Ask them to discuss their experiences with the rest of the class, including ways the other students may become involved. **L3**

Cooperative Learning

Direct students to work in small groups to identify specific people whom they can ask for help if a friend or family member is using drugs. Ask the groups to brainstorm what they might say or ask these people. **L1 Interpersonal**

FIGURE 23.5

WARNING SIGNS OF DRUG USE

Be alert to these signs that a person may have a drug problem.

- Gets drunk or high regularly, is often hung over
- Lies about the drugs he or she is using, or constantly talks about drugs
- Stops participating in activities that once were an important part of his or her life
- Changes eating or sleeping habits, shows rapid weight loss
- Has difficulty concentrating
- Takes unnecessary risks or participates in unsafe behaviors

- Gets in trouble with authorities, such as school administrators or police
- Seems withdrawn, depressed, tired, and cares less about personal grooming and appearance
- Has red-rimmed eyes and runny nose not related to cold or allergies
- Has "blackouts" and forgets what he or she did while under the influence

Lesson 5 Living Drug Free **613**

VISUAL LEARNING

Figure 23.5 Guide students in reading and discussing each of the Warning Signs of Drug Use.

Myths & Reality

MYTH. "Drug overdoses can't happen to me. I'm always in control of the situation."

FACT. Overdoses aren't due to only carelessness. An overdose may be caused by a drug's uncertain purity or strength. A drug user's tolerance can also lead to an overdose since the user needs more of a drug to get the same effect.

MYTH. Depressants are the safest of all drugs because they just make you relax.

FACT. Depressants are dangerous drugs that can easily cause physical and psychological dependence. Used in combination, depressants can be fatal.

Discussing

Have students compare and contrast the various support services for family and friends of drug abusers. Ask: What do you think determines which service is best for an individual? **L1**

Exploring Issues

DRUG TESTING: YES OR NO?

Ask volunteers to share what they know about drug testing. Ask: Do you know of any local employers who use drug testing? Have students who are employed or have been employed share their experiences. Were they tested for drugs? How often? What are their workplace's policies on drug use? Ask the class to discuss whether they think drug testing is fair and effective. Then have students read the feature to learn more about drug testing and to explore three different viewpoints. Finally, have students meet in small groups to discuss their responses to the activities. Encourage students to offer facts and examples to support their opinions. Have groups hold a classroom debate if time allows.

Service Learning

Have students work together to collect information on local drug hotlines and treatment centers. Have them present this information in a small brochure that can be distributed within the school or the community. Remind students to proofread their work before completing a final draft. **L2**

Getting Help

Drug abuse is a treatable condition. Support groups, counseling services, and treatment centers are available in most communities. For teens, the first step in getting help is talking to a parent, teacher, school counselor, health care provider, or another trusted adult. If an adult is unable to recommend a treatment option, teens can call a toll-free hotline or a drug treatment center.

Treatment Centers

For the most serious addictions, drug users attend treatment centers, facilities that provide medical supervision while a person goes through withdrawal and detoxification, or the removal of drugs from the user's body. Many of these centers provide medications to help with the physical and psychological effects of withdrawal.

Exploring Issues

Drug Testing: Yes or No?

It is estimated that substance abuse costs employers $60 billion a year in decreased productivity, absenteeism, and unintentional injuries. In the interest of health, safety, and economics, many companies are testing employees for illicit drug use. This has triggered a debate over whether people should be tested, who should do the testing, and whether the results are reliable.

Viewpoint 1: Walker J., age 16
Drug testing protects all of us. I wouldn't want a firefighter or police officer who used drugs showing up if there were an emergency. It's not just emergency personnel, either. I wouldn't want a drug user as my mechanic, lawyer, doctor, or anything else. Everyone's job impacts others.

Viewpoint 2: Mackenzie P., age 17
I think drug testing should be restricted to people who are in jobs where public safety is involved—such as pilots or bus drivers—or to cases where there is reason to suspect substance abuse, such as after a workplace accident.

ACTIVITIES

1. **Who, if anyone, do you think should be tested for drugs in the workplace? Why? In what situations?**

2. **When people test positive for drugs, what should be done about it? Why?**

Cooperative Learning Activity

Stress and Drug Abuse Recent studies, especially those conducted after the terrorist attacks on September 11, 2001, show that stressful events lead to a marked increase in drug abuse and in relapse for recovering drug abusers. What are some healthy responses to stressful events? How can teens help one another? How can they help family members? How can they help younger siblings and friends? Have groups of students explore their responses to these questions. Then have the members of each group work together to plan and create a collage, depicting their most important ideas.

Types of drug treatment centers include these:

▶ **Outpatient Drug-Free Treatment.** These programs usually do not include medications and often consist of individual or group counseling.

▶ **Short-Term Treatment.** These centers can include residential, medication, and outpatient therapies.

▶ **Maintenance Therapy.** Intended for heroin addicts, this treatment usually includes medication therapy.

▶ **Therapeutic Communities.** These are residences for people with a long history of drug abuse. The centers include highly structured programs that usually last from 6 to 12 months.

For people who have less serious addictions, or for those who are released from a treatment center, drug counseling is usually recommended. In either a private or a group setting, drug counselors help people adjust to life without drugs. In conjunction with counseling, many recovering drug users attend support groups. These meetings are gatherings of people who share a common problem and who work together to help one another cope and recover. Support groups are confidential and are usually free. Support groups are a popular treatment for addiction because they provide the long-term moral support that the recovering user needs to remain drug free.

 Drug counseling and treatment can help a drug user break the cycle of addiction. *What local resources have counseling and support groups for drug users who want to quit?*

 Lesson 5 *Review*

Reviewing Facts and Vocabulary

1. Identify some strategies that schools and communities have taken to decrease the availability of drugs.

2. List five signs of substance abuse.

3. How do support groups help substance abusers?

Thinking Critically

4. **Analyzing.** Analyze the importance of healthy alternatives to drug use.

5. **Synthesizing.** Develop a list of strategies that might help reduce drug use in your school. Write these in a formal list, and submit your ideas to the school principal or school board.

Health Skills Activity

Refusal Skills. Analyze and develop strategies for preventing the use of drugs. Prepare an insert on drug-refusal strategies for your school newspaper. Explain the dangers of drug abuse, and include examples of appropriate and effective refusal skills to avoid unsafe situations.

WORD PROCESSING Using a word-processing program can help give your work a personalized look. See **health.glencoe.com** for tips on word processing.

Lesson 5 Living Drug Free **615**

 Lesson 5 *Review*

Answers to Reviewing Facts and Vocabulary

1. Schools are adopting drug-free zones, teaching drug education classes, implementing zero-tolerance policies, and expelling drug users. Police officers are assigned to patrol campuses. Security guards and locker searches help protect students from drug danger on campus.

2. Any five from Figure 23.8.

3. Possible answers: These groups provide long-term moral support, offer free service to the community, and are completely confidential.

Answers to Thinking Critically

4. Answers will vary.

5. Answers will vary.

③ ASSESS

EVALUATING THE LESSON

Assign and discuss the Lesson 5 Review; then administer, grade, and discuss Lesson Quiz 87 in the TCR. 📁

RETEACHING

• Have students work with partners to list the benefits of a drug-free life. Give students about five minutes to write their lists. Then let them share and discuss their ideas.

• Ask students to complete Reteaching Activity 87 in the TCR. 📁

ENRICHMENT

Have students work together to identify the most important drug-related facts and attitudes to share with middle-school students. Then let them plan presentations—including skits, raps and other songs, and pictorial displays, for example—to share those facts and attitudes. Arrange to have the class share their presentations at a local middle school. After the presentations, ask students to share what they have learned.

④ CLOSE

Have students identify the value of being committed to a drug-free life and the best ways to keep that commitment.

Interview About Steroid Use

NHES Standard 4 Students will analyze the influence of culture, media, technology, and other factors on health.

Objective

Become an investigative journalist and interview an expert about the problems of steroid use among athletes.

Motivator

Working in pairs, have students interview one another about the class they attended prior to their health class.

Teaching Strategies

Awareness Give suggestions to illustrate the kinds of information gathered in the motivator interview, for example, name of the class, name of the teacher, what was covered.

Analysis Encourage students to research the occupation of the person they are interviewing and research any personal involvement the interviewee might have in the subject.

Reflection Analyzing interviews should help students determine whether or not the information obtained will add credibility and interest to the article.

Take Action Preparing a statement about the dangers of steroid use allows students to not only voice an opinion, but to use his or her research and writing skills to help educate others.

✓ Assessment

Interview charts should show at least 4 questions plus appropriate follow-up questions. Students should have at least one quote.

Interview About Steroid Use

An investigative journalist is a person who thoroughly investigates a particular topic and then writes about it. In this activity, you will become an investigative journalist researching the issue of anabolic-androgenic steroid use among amateur and professional athletes. You will then use your research to conduct an interview on the problems and controversies of steroid use among athletes.

Question 1:
Ask a general question to discover what the person knows about the subject. Remember to prepare several appropriate follow-up questions in advance.

Question 2:
Ask more specific questions, such as whether the person knows of recent studies, events, or legislation regarding the subject.

Question 3:
Ask about any personal experience with the issue. Keep these questions appropriate to the occupation of the person you're interviewing.

Question 4:
Ask for the interviewee's view of the subject. Note any interesting quotes to use in your article.

ACTIVITY

Conduct research on the issue of steroid use among amateur and professional athletes. Cover the following areas in your research: history of steroid use, science of steroid use, how steroids act in the body, and legislation regarding steroid use. After your research, interview a sports physician, an athletic coach, a health teacher, or a law enforcement officer to add credibility to your research. Use the guidelines in the chart shown above to help plan, organize, and write your interview questions. Compose as many questions as you consider appropriate, basing their content on your research. Keep good notes or record the interview.

EXPRESS YOUR VIEWS

Write an article based on your interview. Gear your message toward teens, and warn them about the dangers of steroid use.

More About...

Evaluating Resources Students interested in taking the activity further can work as a group to write an article for the school newspaper based upon their research and interviews. These students will need to closely examine their research by evaluating the validity and credibility of their sources, including their interviewees. Encourage students to seek out the most current resources on the issue, including any recent controversies in professional or amateur athletics. Have students submit their article for consideration in the school newspaper or other local newspaper.

CROSS-CURRICULUM CONNECTIONS

Write a Fable. Accidents, health problems, crime, and violence all result from drug abuse. Yet, many teens succumb to its lure. Write a fable with a moral that shows the dangers of drug use. Like the classic Aesop's fables, your fable should focus on an animal to make a point about risk-taking human behavior. Find out about a drug prevention program in your local elementary school system. Obtain permission to make your class's fables part of the program.

Research and Report. The social costs of drug abuse are so great that some schools have instituted mandatory drug testing for student athletes. However, some teens claim that drug testing is a violation of their constitutional rights. Research the historical writings that have shaped America's government, and write a letter to the editor of your school newspaper. Report on your research, and relate your findings to the social issues of drug abuse.

Figure Drug Usage. According to a recent Monitoring the Future Study, 74.5 percent of students in one year disapproved of marijuana use, and two years later 77.8 percent indicated disapproval. What is the change in percent disapproving over the two years?

Investigate Drug Effects. Narcotics produce their effect on the brain and body by attaching to opioid receptors in the brain. Research the natural function of these receptors. List the similarities and differences between the substances produced by the body and the opiate family of drugs that attach to opioid receptors.

CAREER Corner

Medical Records Technician

Do you enjoy managing information? Do you have strong organizational skills and an eye for detail? If you can keep track of a variety of important data, consider a career as a medical records technician. These professionals maintain medical records of patients in hospitals, clinics, or doctors' offices. They track prescription medicines and other health information to ensure that the right treatments and medications are given to patients.

Medical records technicians are required to have an Associate's degree in information management from a community college or vocational/technical school. Find out more about this and other health careers by clicking on Career Corner at **health.glencoe.com**.

Chapter 23 Review **617**

CROSS-CURRICULUM CONNECTIONS

Enrich student learning by connecting the topic of illegal drugs to one of the four subject areas presented on this page. The activity may be completed individually or with a partner.

Language Arts Define *theme* for students. Explain that the theme of a fable is often an insight that relies on an emotional element tying truth to reality.

Social Studies Direct students to the necessary texts such as the Declaration of Independence and the Bill of Rights.

Math Answer: 77.8% − 74.5% = 3.3%.

Science The opoid receptors are utilized by naturally occurring endorphins produced by the body to regulate the perception of pain. The phenomenon of the "runner's high" is caused by the overproduction of natural endorphins.

CAREER Corner

Have students read and discuss the Career Corner information on medical records technicians. Ask interested students to explore the Glencoe Health Web site at **health.glencoe.com** for more information on this career.

Portfolio Assessment

Self-Evaluation Direct students to review the Health Skills Activities and other activities completed in the chapter. Encourage each student to select one finished product or activity that demonstrates his or her best work for the chapter and that represents the student's learning goals. Have students explain what they have learned and how the examples they have selected demonstrate their growth in health literacy, knowledge, and skills.

Teacher Classroom Resources Assign Performance Assessment 23, "Drug Abuse Education Pamphlets," in the TCR.

Chapter 23 *Review*

CHECKING COMPREHENSION

- Assign and discuss the chapter review.
- Use Chapter 23 MindJogger Videoquiz to review the chapter. ▶◀

CHAPTER 23 REVIEW ANSWERS

Exploring Health Terms

1. medicines
2. analgesics
3. side effects
4. synergistic effect
5. illegal drugs
6. illicit drug use
7. overdose
8. Physiological dependence
9. paranoia
10. inhalants
11. anabolic-androgenic steroids
12. narcotic
13. hallucinogens
14. designer drugs
15. False
16. False

Recalling the Facts

1. Antibiotics kill bacteria directly or prevent them from multiplying; antitoxins are extracts of blood fluids that contain antibodies against a specific toxin.

2. Additive interactions occur when medicines work together in a positive way; antagonistic interactions occur when drugs work against each other.

3. Both must be approved by the FDA. OTC medicines can be bought without a prescription. Prescription drugs are available only with a doctor's written instructions and can be dispensed only by a licensed pharmacist.

▶ **EXPLORING HEALTH TERMS** *Answer the following questions on a sheet of paper.*

Lesson 1 *Match each definition with the correct term.*

analgesics	antagonistic interaction
additive interaction	vaccines
side effects	synergistic effect
drugs	medicines

1. Drugs that are used to treat or prevent disease or other conditions.
2. Pain relievers.
3. Reactions to medicine other than the one intended.
4. An interaction of two or more medicines that results in a greater effect than when each medicine is taken separately.

Lesson 2 *Fill in the blanks with the correct term.*

substance abuse	illegal drugs
illicit drug use	overdose
psychological dependence	addiction
physiological dependence	

When a person uses (**_5_**), he or she is committing the crime of (**_6_**). In addition to legal problems, using drugs carries the risk of (**_7_**), which can be fatal. (**_8_**), a condition in which the body develops a chemical need for a drug, is another health risk of drug use.

Lesson 3 *Match each definition with the correct term.*

anabolic-androgenic steroids	paranoia
marijuana	inhalants

9. An irrational suspicion or distrust of others.
10. Substances whose fumes are sniffed to give a mind-altering effect.
11. Synthetic substances that are similar to male sex hormones.

Lesson 4 *Match each definition with the correct term.*

euphoria	designer drugs
stimulants	narcotics
hallucinogens	psychoactive drugs
depressants	

12. Pain-relieving drugs derived from the opium plant and legally obtainable only by prescription.
13. Drugs that alter moods, thoughts, and sense perceptions, including vision, hearing, smell, and touch.
14. Synthetic substances made to imitate the effects of hallucinogens and other dangerous drugs.

Lesson 5 *Identify each statement as True or False. If false, replace the underlined term with the correct term.*

drug-free school zone	drug watches

15. <u>Drug free school zones</u> are/is organized community efforts by neighborhood residents to patrol, monitor, report, and try to stop drug deals and drug abuse.
16. <u>Drug watches</u> are/is a designated area surrounding schools within which people caught selling drugs receive especially severe penalties.

▶ **RECALLING THE FACTS** *Use complete sentences to answer the following questions.*

Lesson 1

1. Analyze and describe two types of medicines that fight diseases.
2. What is the difference between an additive interaction and an antagonistic interaction?
3. Compare and contrast OTC and prescription medicines.

---

4. Possible answer: Illegal drugs are not monitored by the government for quality, purity, or strength.

5. Any three: Court fines, legal fees, suspended driving privileges, suspension from school, jail time, probation, mandatory community service.

6. Unborn babies exposed to drugs may be spontaneously aborted or born with birth defects, behavioral problems, or an addiction to drugs.

7. Raising the level of dopamine in the brain results in a sense of elation followed by a crash when the drug wears off.

8. Use of inhalants can result in liver damage, blindness, permanent brain damage, numbness or paralysis, lack of oxygen in the blood, possibility of coma or suffocation and death.

9. Athletes failing a drug test will be excluded from sports events, be expelled from the team, lose awards, and face legal consequences.

Thinking Critically

Lesson 2

4. Why are illegal drugs dangerous to the user?
5. List three legal consequences of drug use for teens.
6. Analyze and explain the harmful effects of drugs on a fetus.

Lesson 3

7. Marijuana raises the level of dopamine in the brain. What effect does this have on the body?
8. Examine and describe the physical consequences of inhalant use.
9. What can happen if an athlete uses steroids?

Lesson 4

10. How does a stimulant affect the central nervous system?
11. What are the symptoms of a hallucinogen overdose?
12. List five harmful effects of "club drugs."

Lesson 5

13. List three strategies for staying drug free.
14. How are communities helping in the effort to promote health by stopping drug use?
15. List three types of centers in which drug users can be treated.

➤ THINKING CRITICALLY

1. **Evaluating.** The FDA regulates what manufacturers can say in advertisements for both prescription and OTC medicines. Do you think that such regulation is necessary? Support your answer. *(LESSON 1)*
2. **Analyzing.** What is the relationship between drug use and harmful situations such as violent crimes, HIV and STDs, unplanned pregnancies, and motor vehicle collisions? *(LESSON 2)*
3. **Evaluating.** Marijuana use lowers the level of testosterone in males. How might this fact affect a teen male's development? *(LESSON 3)*
4. **Synthesizing.** In what ways are stimulants and depressants different? In what ways are they similar? *(LESSON 4)*
5. **Summarizing.** The commitment to be drug free can help in achieving personal goals. Make a list of your personal goals. Analyze the importance of alternatives to drug use to help you reach your goals. *(LESSON 5)*

➤ HEALTH SKILLS APPLICATION

1. **Accessing Information.** Research and analyze laws regulating the information that is required to be on all over-the-counter (OTC) medicine labels. Why does the FDA require this information to appear? *(LESSON 1)*
2. **Communication Skills.** Write a skit in which a teen expresses concern for a friend's drug problem. The teen should use effective communication skills to discuss the dangers of drug use and to encourage the friend to seek help. *(LESSON 2)*
3. **Refusal Skills.** Imagine that you are at a party when someone you know suddenly offers you marijuana. Analyze and explain the refusal strategies you could apply. *(LESSON 3)*
4. **Stress Management.** Derek, who has been under a lot of stress, confides in you that he wants to take depressants to relax. What would you say to persuade him not to do so? What healthy alternatives for managing stress would you recommend? *(LESSON 4)*
5. **Goal Setting.** Make a goal to live drug free. Use the goal-setting steps to develop an action plan for honoring your commitment. *(LESSON 5)*

Thinking Critically

1. Answers will vary. Most students will note that FDA regulation helps ensure the safety of medicines available for sale in the United States.
2. Drug use is involved in many harmful situations: Often, either the perpetrator or the victim of violent crimes has been using drugs. Unplanned pregnancies and HIV or STDs may result from sexual activity undertaken when self-control is lowered because of drug use; HIV and STDs may also result from using infected needles when injecting drugs. Some motor vehicle crashes are caused by people under the influence of drugs.
3. Possible answer: Lowered testosterone levels may cause changes in male sex characteristics, which could adversely affect physical development and negatively affect mental/emotional and social health.
4. Possible answer: Both affect the central nervous system (CNS). Stimulants speed up the CNS; depressants slow it down.
5. Answers will vary.

Health Skills Application

1.–5. Answers will vary.

EVALUATE

- Use the reproducible Chapter 23 Test in the TCR, or construct your own using the Testmaker software. 📁 💿
- Use Performance Assessment 23 in the TCR. 📁

ENRICHMENT

Ask students to complete Enrichment Activity 23 in the TCR. 📁

10. It speeds up the central nervous system.
11. Loss of contact with reality, coma, death.
12. Any five: Club drugs damage neurons in the brain, impairing senses, memory, judgment, and coordination; they cause loss of muscle and motor control, blurred vision, and seizures; some increase heart rate and blood pressure and can lead to heart or kidney failure; others cause drowsiness or unconsciousness; some can immobilize a person or cause a type of amnesia; they can cause severe breathing problems, coma, and death.

13. Possible answer: Make a commitment to be drug free, choose friends who are drug free, avoid places where drugs are used.
14. Communities are organizing drug watches, efforts supported by neighborhood residents to patrol, monitor, report, and otherwise try to stop drug deals and drug abuse.
15. Outpatient drug-free centers, short-term treatment centers, therapeutic communities.

Lessons	Standards		Features
	National	**State/Local**	
1 **What Are Communicable Diseases?** *pages 622–626*	National Health Education Standards **1.1, 1.5, 1.6, 3.1, 3.4**		
2 **Preventing Communicable Diseases** *pages 627–634*	National Health Education Standards **1.3, 1.7, 3.2, 4.4, 6.4**		**Health Skills Activity** • Caring for Your Immune System *(Decision Making)*, page 629
3 **Common Communicable Diseases** *pages 635–641*	National Health Education Standards **1.3, 1.6, 2.2, 3.1, 4.3**		**Real-Life Application** • Reducing Your Risk of Lyme Disease *(Analyzing Influences)*, page 639

Reproducible Resources	Assessment	Technology
Student Activity Workbook for use with each chapter 📁 Concept Mapping Activity 88 📁 Decision-Making Activity 24 📁 Guided Reading Activities 88 📁 Lesson Plan 88 📁 Parent Letter and Activities 24 📁 Reteaching Activity 88	📁 Lesson Quiz 88	🕹 Transparency 70 💿 TeacherWorks®
📁 Concept Mapping Activity 89 📁 Current Health Issues 24 📁 Guided Reading Activities 89 📁 Lesson Plan 89 📁 Reteaching Activity 89	📁 Lesson Quiz 89	🕹 Transparency 71 💿 TeacherWorks®
📁 Concept Mapping Activity 90 📁 Cross-Curriculum Activity 24 📁 Enrichment Activity 24 📁 Guided Reading Activities 90 📁 Health Lab 24 📁 Lesson Plan 90 📁 Reteaching Activity 90	📁 Lesson Quiz 90	💿 TeacherWorks®

0:00 OUT OF TIME

If time does not permit teaching the entire chapter, use:
- Figure 24.1, p. 623
- Figure 24.2, p. 628
- Health Skills activity, p. 629
- Figure 24.3, p. 630
- Figure 24.5, p. 640

Language Diversity

🎧 English Audio CD Program
🎧 Spanish Audio CD Program
📁 English Summaries, Quizzes, and Activities
📁 Spanish Summaries, Quizzes, and Activities
📁 Spanish Parent Letters and Activities

End of Chapter Assessment

Blackline Masters

📁 Chapter 24 Test
📁 Performance Assessment Activity 24

Technology

💿 Vocabulary PuzzleMaker
📀 MindJogger Videoquiz
💿 **Exam**View® Pro Testmaker

Professional Health Series

Dealing with Sensitive Issues
Planning a Coordinated School Health Program
Promoting Character Education
Home, School, and Community Involvement

Key to Ability Levels

Teaching strategies that appear throughout the chapter have been identified by one of the following codes to give teachers an idea of their suitability for students of varying learning styles and abilities.

L1 Strategies should be within the ability range of all students. Full class participation is often required. Teacher direction is usually needed.

L2 Strategies are designed for average to above-average students or for small groups. Some teacher direction is needed.

L3 Strategies are designed for students able and willing to work independently. Minimal teacher direction is needed.

ELL Strategies should be within the ability range of students learning the English language.

🔲 Block scheduling strategies are useful in a block scheduling format.

CHAPTER OVERVIEW

Chapter 24 explains what communicable diseases are, their means of transmission, how the risk of infection can be reduced, and how the immune system works. Some common communicable diseases are also described.

Lesson 1 Communicable diseases are spread by pathogens such as viruses, bacteria, fungi, protozoans, and rickettsias. Pathogens are transmitted by direct contact, indirect contact, and airborne transmission. Washing hands and other preventive measures to reduce the risk of getting or spreading communicable diseases are presented.

Lesson 2 Physical and chemical barriers prevent pathogens from entering the body. The process in which immunity to specific pathogens develops is described as well as different types of vaccines.

Lesson 3 The cause, symptoms, and treatment of common communicable diseases and methods to prevent them are presented. Emerging infections are also discussed.

Health Skills Features

- Health Skills Activity (*Decision Making*), p. 629
- Real-Life Application (*Analyzing Influences*), p. 639

Chapter 24
Communicable Diseases

Lesson **1**
What Are Communicable Diseases?

Lesson **2**
Preventing Communicable Diseases

Lesson **3**
Common Communicable Diseases

620

MEETING STUDENT DIVERSITY

Language Diversity Use the following suggestions to help students who have difficulty with English:

- Pair English language learners with native speakers of English who can restate the Chapter Summary in language that helps students comprehend important concepts.

- 🎧 Direct auditory learners or those students with language diversity to the *Glencoe Health Audio CD Program*. Available in English and Spanish, this component provides an audio and written summary of the chapter.

- Use photographs, drawings, or magazine clippings to help students visualize the important concepts of the chapter.

Personal Health Inventory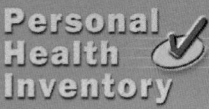

What's Your Health Status?

Read each statement below and respond by writing *yes*, *no*, or *sometimes* for each item. Write *yes* only for items that you practice regularly.

1. I keep my immunizations up to date.

2. I avoid close contact with people who have a cold or the flu.

3. I wash my hands after using the bathroom, before handling food, before meals, and after I blow my nose.

4. I follow a nutritious eating plan.

5. I get at least eight to ten hours of sleep each night.

6. I take precautions to avoid bites from insects and ticks.

7. I prepare and store food in a safe manner.

8. I cover my nose and mouth when I cough or sneeze.

9. I don't use tobacco, alcohol, or other drugs.

10. I get plenty of rest and fluids when I have a cold or the flu.

Keep this personal inventory for review later in the chapter. When you complete the chapter, review your answers again and identify two or three behavior changes you can make to improve your health.

Quick*Write*

Using Visuals. To avoid spreading disease, rest, drink plenty of fluids, and stay home when you are ill. What other measures can you take to prevent communicable diseases?

621

INTRODUCING THE CHAPTER

Personal Health Inventory

Give students time to read the Personal Health Inventory statements. Ask: How do the behaviors identified here relate to your physical health? When you maintain good physical health, how do you affect your mental/emotional health? Your social health? After a brief discussion, have students record their Personal Health Inventory responses in their private health journals.

Ask students how many of them have had to miss school due to a cold or the flu. Have students estimate the number of days missed by the entire class last year as a result of cold or flu symptoms. Discuss the impact of lost days from school and work and the costs of treating the symptoms of cold or flu on our society. Explain that in this chapter, students will learn how to reduce their risk of getting and spreading communicable diseases. They also will gain an understanding of how our bodies defend against diseases.

Quick*write*

Using Visuals Ask students to recall a time when they were ill with a disease that was contagious, such as a cold or strep throat. What precautions did they take to avoid spreading their cold to family members and friends? What did other people do to avoid getting it from them? Have volunteers share their responses.

TECHNOLOGY OPTIONS

MINDJOGGER
VIDEOQUIZ

To preview or review chapter content, you may wish to use the Chapter 24 MindJogger Videoquiz.

HEALTH *Online*

Online Resources for the Teacher For a fresh approach to health topics and an in-depth look at health issues, use these online resources found under Teacher Resources at **health.glencoe.com:**

- Block Schedule Lesson Plans
- Technology Projects
- Health Updates

What Are Communicable Diseases?

1 FOCUS

QUICK START Ask volunteers to share their responses. Write a list of the different symptoms and treatments on the board as students name them. Have students compare and contrast their experiences.

TYING TO PRIOR KNOWLEDGE

Point out that colds and strep throat are just two diseases that a person can catch or give to someone else. Ask students to name other diseases that can be spread from one person to another.

INTRODUCING VOCABULARY

- Instruct students to use a medical dictionary or similar resource to find medical definitions of *communicable disease* and *pathogen* and rewrite the definitions in their own words.

- Ask students to complete the Chapter 24 Study Guide in the *Student Activity Workbook.* 📁

What Are Communicable Diseases?

VOCABULARY
communicable
 disease
pathogen
infection
toxin
vector

YOU'LL LEARN TO
- Identify the types of pathogens that cause communicable diseases.
- Analyze the relationship between healthful behaviors and the ways that communicable diseases are spread.
- Develop and analyze strategies for preventing communicable diseases.

QUICK START Write about the last time you had a cold. Include a list of the symptoms you experienced. Explain how you think you caught the cold and what you did to treat it.

 The HIV virus (top), pneumonia virus, and cold virus (bottom), are pathogens that cause disease.

Most of us don't spend much time thinking about microorganisms, but they often impact our lives. Although most microorganisms—living things too small to be seen without a microscope—are harmless, a few, such as the viruses shown on this page, can cause communicable diseases. A **communicable disease** is *a disease that is spread from one living thing to another or through the environment.* Knowing how communicable diseases spread can help you choose behaviors to reduce your risk of getting them.

Causes of Communicable Diseases

An *organism that causes disease* is called a **pathogen**. Common pathogens include certain viruses, bacteria, fungi, protozoans, and rickettsias (rik-ET-see-uhz). **Figure 24.1** lists some of the diseases caused by each type of pathogen. An **infection** is *a condition that occurs when pathogens enter the body, multiply, and damage body cells.* If the body is not able to fight off the infection, a disease develops.

622 **Chapter 24** Communicable Diseases

Lesson 1 *Resources*

Teacher Classroom Resources
📁 Concept Mapping Activity 88
📁 Decision-Making Activity 24
📁 Guided Reading Activities 88
📁 Lesson Plan 88
📁 Lesson Quiz 88

📁 Parent Letter and Activities 24
📁 Reteaching Activity 88
Student Activity Workbook
📁 Applying Health Skills 88
📁 Chapter 24 Study Guide
Multimedia
 Transparency 70

Viruses

You're already familiar with two diseases caused by viruses—the common cold and influenza, or the flu. Viruses are pieces of genetic material surrounded by a protein coat. By themselves they are inactive. They need living cells to reproduce. Viruses invade all known forms of life—mammals, birds, reptiles, insects, plants, and even bacteria.

After a virus penetrates a cell, called the host cell, the virus takes control of the cell to manufacture more viruses. The new viruses burst from the cell, usually killing it, and take over other cells. Like other pathogens, viruses usually run their course and eventually are killed by the immune system. Antibiotics do not work against viruses.

Bacteria

Bacteria are single-celled microorganisms that live almost everywhere on earth. Most bacteria are harmless, and many types are essential for life. For example, bacteria in your digestive system help digest food and make some of the vitamins you need. When bacteria enter the body, they multiply through cell division. Some bacterial pathogens, such as the ones that cause tetanus, produce a **toxin,** *a substance that kills cells or interferes with their functions.* Like most other microorganisms that enter the body of a healthy individual, bacteria are usually destroyed by the immune system. Most bacterial diseases can be treated with **antibiotics.**

Did You Know

➤ In 1993 four children were killed and hundreds of others sickened by undercooked hamburger from a fast-food restaurant. The culprit was *E. coli O157:H7.* This bacteria causes severe damage to the cells lining the human intestines and can lead to kidney failure and death.

Common sources of the bacteria are undercooked, contaminated ground beef and unpasteurized milk and apple cider.

hotlink

antibiotics For more information about antibiotics, see Chapter 23, page 587.

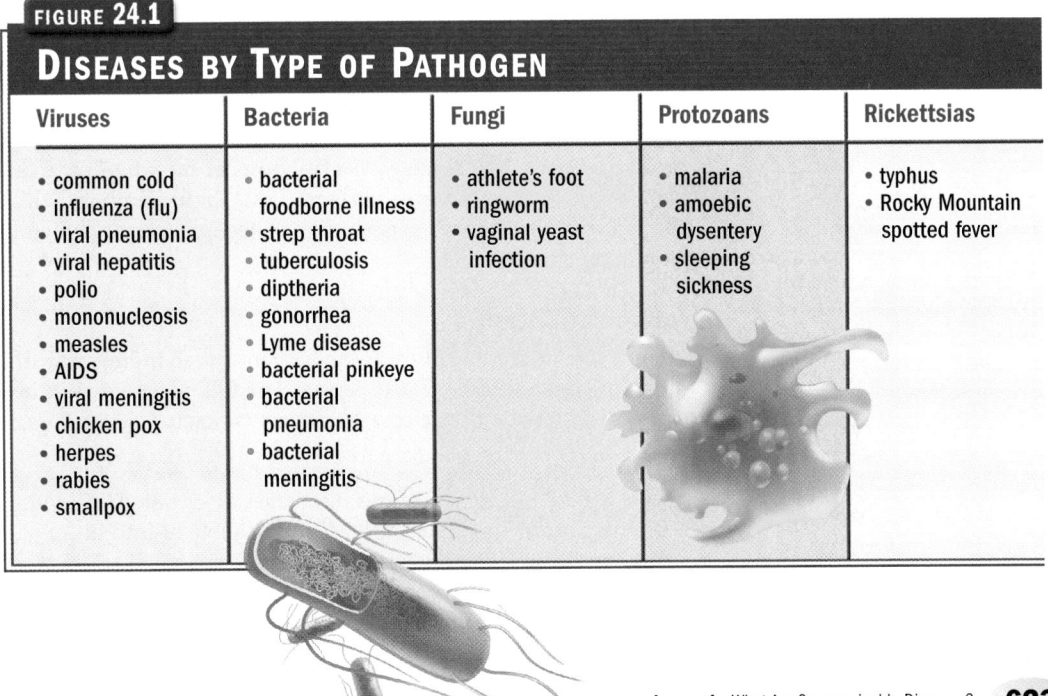

FIGURE 24.1

DISEASES BY TYPE OF PATHOGEN

Viruses	Bacteria	Fungi	Protozoans	Rickettsias
• common cold • influenza (flu) • viral pneumonia • viral hepatitis • polio • mononucleosis • measles • AIDS • viral meningitis • chicken pox • herpes • rabies • smallpox	• bacterial foodborne illness • ringworm • strep throat • tuberculosis • diptheria • gonorrhea • Lyme disease • bacterial pinkeye • bacterial pneumonia • bacterial meningitis	• athlete's foot • ringworm • vaginal yeast infection	• malaria • amoebic dysentery • sleeping sickness	• typhus • Rocky Mountain spotted fever

Lesson 1 What Are Communicable Diseases? **623**

② TEACH

Discussing

Ask students about pathogens. What is their role in communicable diseases? **L1**

VISUAL LEARNING

Figure 24.1 Have students examine the illustrations of bacteria and protozoans. Then ask volunteers to read aloud the lists of diseases caused by each type of pathogen. Tell students that bacteria have three basic shapes: spherical or round, rod-shaped, and spiral or corkscrew. This is one characteristic that helps laboratory workers identify bacteria. **L1**

Activity

Ask students to use classroom and library resources to research some of the bacteria that exist within the body and their functions. **L2**

Explaining

E. coli is a type of bacteria that is normally found in the intestines of all animals and humans. They suppress the growth of harmful bacteria and synthesize some vitamins. *E. coli O157:H7* is one of very few strains that causes illness in humans. **L1**

More About...

Latent Viruses Some viruses become what is known as *latent.* A latent virus enters a cell and becomes part of the cell's hereditary material without immediately destroying the cell or making new viruses. Latent viruses may appear to "hide" inside host cells for many years. Then, at any time, the virus may become active. The viruses that cause cold sores and chicken pox are examples of latent viruses. The appearance of a cold sore is a sign that the virus is active and destroying cells in the lip. The virus that causes chicken pox may appear later in life in a different form called shingles. Most latent viruses stay in the body for life.

Explaining

Remind students that other types of organisms besides the ones mentioned here also can cause disease. For example, roundworms can infect the lungs and gastrointestinal tract. Mites, a form of parasite, can infest the skin, causing a disease called scabies. **L1**

Discussing

Have students discuss how some diseases can be spread in more than one way. Ask them in what different ways the common cold can be spread. Explain that several diseases, including colds, influenza, and chicken pox, can be spread in all three ways (direct contact, indirect contact, and airborne transmission). **L1**

Reinforcing Concepts

Help students visualize the difference between direct contact and airborne transmission. In direct contact, the droplets from a cough or sneeze can travel only within about one meter. The pathogens fall wherever the droplets land. In airborne transmission, the moisture evaporates and the pathogens float on dust particles for longer distances, for example, through recycled air on passenger jets. Pathogens spread by the airborne route can be inhaled deeply into the lungs. **L1**

CHARACTER CHECK

Respect Have students explain why washing hands properly shows respect for others.

Try to reduce your risk of infection when you participate in outdoor activities where vectors are common. *How is this teen protecting himself from deer ticks?*

CHARACTER CHECK

Respect. One simple action can demonstrate your respect for your own health and the health of others. Every time you wash your hands properly you reduce the risk of spreading potential pathogens, especially when you prepare food or when you touch objects that others may put in their mouths. **What other safe food handling habits can you practice?**

Other Types of Pathogens

Other types of organisms also can cause communicable diseases.

▶ **Fungi** are plantlike organisms, such as molds and yeasts. Some types can cause diseases of the skin, such as athlete's foot; diseases of the mucous membranes; or of the lungs.

▶ **Protozoans** are single-celled organisms that are larger and more complex than bacteria. Most are harmless, but some can cause disease, especially in people with weakened immune systems.

▶ **Rickettsias** are pathogens that resemble bacteria. Like viruses, they multiply by invading the cells of another life form. Often these organisms enter humans through the bites of insects such as fleas or lice. Rocky Mountain spotted fever is the most frequently reported illness spread by rickettsias.

How Communicable Diseases Are Transmitted

There are several means of transmission, or the spreading, of pathogens. Transmission can occur through direct or indirect contact or through breathing contaminated air. Some diseases can be transmitted in more than one way. If you know how they are spread you can take precautions and avoid infection.

Direct Contact

Many pathogens are transmitted by direct contact with an infected person or animal or with something in the environment. Direct contact includes touching, biting, kissing, and sexual contact. Sneezing and coughing can spray infectious droplets of saliva or mucus onto a nearby person's eyes, nose, or mouth. A pregnant woman may also transmit an infection to her unborn child through the placenta. A person can get tetanus from a puncture wound by a rusty nail.

Indirect Contact

Some communicable diseases can be transmitted indirectly, without being close to an infected person. The following are ways diseases can be transmitted through indirect contact:

▶ **Contaminated objects.** Inanimate objects can become contaminated with infectious discharges or secretions. Suppose that a person with a cold sneezes onto a table or into his or her hand and then touches the table. The cold viruses can be transmitted to you if you touch the table and then touch your nose or eyes. Use proper handwashing techniques to avoid transmitting infections.

School to Work

Health Inspector Most counties and some cities have regulations designed to prevent the spread of pathogens. City or county health inspectors inspect various public facilities. For example, restaurants may be inspected to check for proper equipment, sanitation procedures, and hygiene among workers. School buildings may be checked for proper plumbing and sewage disposal. Encourage students to find out about the specific duties of health inspectors in their area. They should obtain descriptions of several positions related to public health inspection and the qualifications for each position.

▶ **Vectors.** An *organism, usually an arthropod, such as a tick, that carries and transmits pathogens to humans or other animals* is known as a **vector**. For example, a mosquito may take in pathogens when it feeds on an infected person. The mosquito then injects some of those pathogens into the next person it bites, thus spreading the disease. Common vectors include flies, mosquitoes, and ticks. Lyme disease and malaria are spread by vectors.

▶ **Water and food.** Careless handling and storage of food are major sources of contamination and illness. For example, salmonella (sal-muh-NE-luh) bacteria in undercooked poultry can cause food poisoning. Water supplies that become contaminated with human or animal feces can cause illnesses such as hepatitis A.

Airborne Transmission

Pathogens from a sneeze or a cough may float in the air for a long time and travel long distances. Airborne transmission is different from direct contact because the pathogens don't settle quickly on surfaces. You don't have to be close to an infected person to inhale the pathogens. Diseases that are transmitted this way include chicken pox, tuberculosis, and influenza. A person can get inhalation anthrax by inhaling soil containing the bacteria.

Preventing the Spread of Disease

Reducing your risk of communicable diseases isn't complicated. Practicing healthful behaviors based on good hygiene and common sense will help you avoid infection.

Washing Hands

Handwashing is the single most effective way to prevent the spread of disease. Wash your hands before you prepare food, before you eat, and after you use the bathroom. Clean hands carefully before inserting contact lenses or putting on makeup. After handling animals, especially reptiles, or animal wastes, make it a habit to wash your hands. When someone in your home is ill, keep hands clean to prevent the spread of pathogens.

Handling Food Properly

Foodborne illness occurs in places where food is handled improperly. Always wash your hands before you handle food. Use paper towels, not dishcloths or sponges, to keep surfaces and equipment clean. Separate raw meat from other foods. Cook food to its proper temperature. Chill cold and leftover foods quickly to the proper temperature.

✔Health Minute

Strategies for Avoiding Diseases Transmitted by Vectors

Use these strategies where mosquitoes or ticks are common:

▶ Wear long-sleeved shirts, long pants, socks, and hats.
▶ Tuck shirts in at the waist, and tuck pants into socks.
▶ Wear boots, not sandals.
▶ Apply repellents to clothing, boots, socks, and all exposed skin.
▶ Check yourself and your clothing frequently. Wearing light-colored clothing can help you spot ticks and mosquitoes.

---

hotlink

foodborne illness For more information about foodborne illness and proper food preparation, see Chapter 5, page 134.

✔Health Minute

Have students read and discuss each of the strategies for avoiding vectors that can transmit disease. Explain to students that the most effective insect repellants contain DEET (short for N, N-diethyltoluamide). To apply, hold the container 6–8 inches from the skin or clothing and spray with a slow sweeping motion. Spray shirts, pants, socks, and hats. Do not apply under clothing or on synthetic clothing. Keep it out of the eyes and mouth.

Guest Speaker

Ask a family and consumer sciences teacher or a health official from county extension services to speak with the class about trichinosis and ways to prevent it by proper cooking of pork and other meats. ▱

Promoting Coordinated School Health

Student Organizations School Health Clubs are student organizations that work with teachers and staff to promote a healthy school environment. School Health Clubs may work with custodial staff to identify areas of heavy student traffic where additional soap dispensers and paper towels could be installed. The clubs often organize handwashing campaigns. These campaigns can decrease student absenteeism and help schools save money on substitute teachers. Successful campaigns use the 3 Ps (posters, poems, public service announcements) to communicate humorous and memorable messages that remind students and staff to wash their hands.

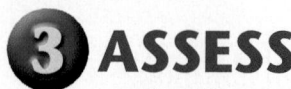

③ ASSESS

EVALUATING THE LESSON

Assign and discuss the Lesson 1 Review; then administer, grade, and discuss Lesson Quiz 88 in the TCR. 📁

RETEACHING

- Have students write a detailed outline of the material in the lesson using the lesson's major headings.

- Ask students to complete Reteaching Activity 88 in the TCR. 📁

ENRICHMENT

Have students research how malaria or Lyme disease is transmitted. Based on their research, they should draw a diagram illustrating the transmission process and the organisms involved (malaria pathogen, mosquito vector, and human host) or (Lyme disease pathogen, tick vector, and human host). They also should provide a brief explanation of the role of each organism in the transmission cycle.

④ CLOSE

Write the lesson's major concepts on separate slips of paper. Place the slips into a box, and let each student draw one. Next, have students define and summarize the concept written on the slip of paper they have selected.

▼ **Handwashing is important since your hands easily pick up and transfer bacteria. List other strategies you can use to avoid the spread of disease.**

Other Prevention Measures

Here are some other strategies that will help you reduce your risk of getting or spreading communicable diseases.

▶ Eat a balanced diet. Participate in regular physical activity. Avoid the use of tobacco, alcohol, and other drugs.

▶ Avoid sharing eating utensils, makeup, combs and brushes, and other personal items.

▶ Prepare and store food safely—keep hot foods hot and cold foods refrigerated or on ice.

▶ Avoid unnecessary contact with people who are ill.

▶ Take care of yourself when you're ill. Cover your mouth when you cough or sneeze. Wash your hands after using a tissue.

▶ Be sure you are vaccinated against particular diseases as recommended by your physician.

▶ Practice abstinence from sexual activity.

▶ Learn to manage stress. Stress makes you vulnerable to illness if you do not find ways to manage it effectively.

▶ Lesson 1 *Review*

Reviewing Facts and Vocabulary

1. List five types of common pathogens, and identify one disease each type of pathogen causes.

2. Describe three ways in which pathogens spread and three healthful behaviors to limit their spread.

3. What are five ways you can reduce your risk of getting a communicable disease?

Thinking Critically

4. **Applying.** The fungus that causes athlete's foot lives in warm, moist places. What can you do to prevent getting this pathogen when you use gym or other common showers?

5. **Analyzing.** You wake up one morning with a headache, body aches, and a fever. You think you might be coming down with something. Analyze the relationship between healthful behaviors you can practice and the ways that communicable diseases are spread. What should you do?

Applying Health Skills

Practicing Healthful Behaviors. Work with a family member to identify ways in which you can reduce your risk of contracting a foodborne illness at home. Explain to family members how you will apply strategies to prevent the spread of food poisoning.

TECHNOLOGY *OPTION*

PRESENTATION SOFTWARE You've probably heard the saying, "a picture is worth a thousand words." Use presentation software to show your plan for reducing the spread of foodborne illness. For tips on using presentation software, see **health.glencoe.com**.

626   **Chapter 24** Communicable Diseases

▶ Lesson 1 *Review*

Answers to Reviewing Facts and Vocabulary

1. Viruses—cold; bacteria—strep throat; protozoans—malaria; fungi—ringworm; rickettsias—typhus.
2. Direct contact, indirect contact, airborne transmission; wash hands, cover mouth when coughing, get vaccinations.
3. Any five of the strategies on this page.

Answers to Thinking Critically

4. Wear shower shoes in the shower, and dry your feet thoroughly.
5. Possible answer: With these symptoms, it would be best to stay home and rest. Going to school risks spreading the disease to others.

Preventing Communicable Diseases

VOCABULARY

immune system
inflammatory response
phagocyte
antigen
immunity
lymphocyte
antibody
vaccine

YOU'LL LEARN TO

- Examine how the body protects itself against invading pathogens.

- Apply strategies for caring for your immune system and preventing disease.

- Explain how technology has impacted the health status of individuals, families, communities, and the world in the prevention of communicable disease.

- Identify community health services that provide vaccines and information on disease prevention.

> ⇒ **QUICK START** Have you ever had a small cut or other injury that became red or painful or developed pus? Write a few paragraphs describing what the area of injury looked like over several days.

You can't see it, but the teen in the picture is waging a battle. The battle is not against other players who are trying to score a point. It's a battle to fight off the pathogens that constantly attack his body. Every day, 24 hours a day, your body is exposed to millions of pathogens. Most of the time, your body manages to stay free of infection because of your immune system. The **immune system** is *a network of cells, tissues, organs, and chemicals that fights off pathogens.*

◁ Compare the protective equipment worn by this goalie to your physical and chemical barriers. *How might behaviors such as wearing appropriate safety equipment help protect you from pathogens?*

Physical and Chemical Barriers

Physical and chemical barriers make up your body's first line of defense, as shown in **Figure 24.2.** They protect against a wide

---

Preventing Communicable Diseases

1 FOCUS

⇒ **QUICK START** Ask students to read the Quick Start and write their responses. Have them share their experiences. Then discuss why they think these changes occurred.

TYING TO PRIOR KNOWLEDGE

Ask students which vaccinations they have received from childhood. Briefly discuss why some vaccinations are required before attending school. Explain that this lesson will teach how vaccines work.

Health Skills Features

"Caring for Your Immune System," p. 629

DECISION MAKING

INTRODUCING VOCABULARY

- Ask students to complete the Chapter 24 Study Guide in the *Student Activity Workbook.* ☞

Lesson 2 *Resources*

Teacher Classroom Resources

☞ Concept Mapping Activity 89

☞ Current Health Issues 24

☞ Guided Reading Activities 89

☞ Lesson Plan 89

☞ Lesson Quiz 89

☞ Reteaching Activity 89

Student Activity Workbook

☞ Applying Health Skills 89

☞ Chapter 24 Study Guide

Multimedia

🖳 Transparency 71

2 TEACH

VISUAL LEARNING

Figure 24.2 After students have read the information, ask:

- What types of infections do you think are prevented by each of the different barriers? Some infections include gastrointestinal infections prevented by gastric juice; respiratory infections prevented by cilia.
- What happens when one of these barriers breaks down? Pathogens are allowed to enter the body through that site.

Activity

Have students use class and library resources to research mucous membranes and where they are found in the body. Follow up with a discussion of the role of mucous membranes in the fight against invading pathogens. **L2**

Explaining

Cilia sweep foreign matter up and out of the respiratory tract. Particles that are missed by cilia are expelled by a cough. If the cilia are damaged or destroyed, a cough is the only way the body can rid the airways of foreign particles. Smoking damages or destroys cilia. This is one reason that most smokers generally have a chronic cough—to compensate for damaged cilia. **L1**

---

variety of invaders. Physical barriers, such as skin and mucous membranes, block pathogens from invading your body. Chemical barriers, such as enzymes in tears, destroy pathogens.

The Immune System

The immune system has two major defense strategies. The inflammatory response is general, or nonspecific; it works against all types of pathogens. Specific defenses work against particular pathogens. Together, these defenses work to prevent disease.

The Inflammatory Response

The **inflammatory response** is *a reaction to tissue damage caused by injury or infection.* Its purpose is to prevent further tissue injury and to halt invading pathogens. Suppose that a splinter enters your finger. Your body immediately reacts to the damage caused by the splinter and to any pathogens on the splinter. If you've ever had the area around an injury become hot, swollen, red, and painful, you've experienced the inflammatory response.

FIGURE 24.2

PHYSICAL AND CHEMICAL BARRIERS— THE BODY'S FIRST LINE OF DEFENSE

These elements work together as your body's first line of defense to prevent pathogens from entering and causing disease.

Skin is the first line of defense against many pathogens. Few pathogens can pass through the tough layer of dead skin cells that surrounds the body.

Tears and saliva contain enzymes that destroy or disable many pathogens.

Mucous membranes line many parts of the body, including your mouth, nose, and bronchial tubes. Cells in these membranes produce *mucus*, a sticky substance that traps pathogens. The mucus then carries the trapped pathogens to other areas of the body for disposal.

Cilia, the hairlike projections that line parts of the respiratory system, sweep mucus and pathogens to the throat, where they can be swallowed or coughed out.

Gastric juice in the stomach destroys many pathogens that enter the body through the nose and mouth.

628 Chapter 24 Communicable Diseases

⌁ HEALTH LITERACY

Self-Directed Learner Have students conduct research about nutrients and other nonmedical substances that have been shown to correlate with improved immune function and/or faster recovery from illnesses such as colds. In some cases, they may wish to include nutrients for which the need is greatly increased during illness or stress. Suggest that they use the FDA as one reliable source of information. Drug studies are usually funded by drug companies, for example, and some herbs or nutrients are studied in hopes of using them in drugs. Suggest students construct a chart listing the substances they have investigated and summarize their findings about each.

In response to invasion by microorganisms or to tissue damage, blood vessels near the site of an injury expand to allow more blood flow to the area. As blood vessels expand, fluid and cells from the bloodstream leak into the area. The collection of fluid and white blood cells causes swelling and pain because of pressure on nerve endings. One type of cell that responds to injury is called a **phagocyte** (FA-guh-site), *a white blood cell that attacks invading pathogens*. Phagocytes engulf pathogens and then destroy them with chemicals. Pus, a collection of dead white blood cells and damaged tissue, may collect at the site of inflammation as a response to bacteria. After the pathogens are killed and tissue damage is under control, tissue repair can begin. However, regardless of whether pathogens survive the inflammatory response, specific defenses are activated. This activation is an effort to prevent this same infection from occurring again.

 Injury and infection caused by this splinter may trigger an inflammatory response. *What immediately happens in the body as a response to injury?*

Health Skills Activity

Decision Making: Caring for Your Immune System

Aaron has been getting a lot of colds lately. Today he woke up with a bad sore throat. Aaron knows that he should stay home and rest, both for his own health and to avoid infecting others at school. However, Aaron plays the lead saxophone in the marching band, and today is the last band practice before the big game. This practice will even be a full-dress rehearsal to make sure everything goes right for the half-time show.

Saturday's game will be the playoff, and everyone is sure the school will win. If Aaron doesn't show up, he thinks he will be letting the band down. Besides, he doesn't want to admit that he is getting sick because then he won't be there on Saturday when the team wins.

Aaron wonders what he should do.

What Would You Do?

Apply the six steps of the decision-making model to Aaron's situation.

1. State the situation.
2. List the options.
3. Weigh the possible outcomes.
4. Consider values.
5. Make a decision and act.
6. Evaluate the decision.

More About...

Symptoms Some symptoms of a disease are actually caused by the immune response rather than the pathogens themselves. For example, one cause of fever is the release of chemicals by macrophages. These chemicals travel in the bloodstream to the brain, where they cause the body's thermostat to be "reset" to a higher level. Many pathogens cannot survive the higher body temperature. These chemicals are also responsible for the runny nose and increased production of mucus when a person has a cold. A fever over 102 degrees Fahrenheit should be treated to prevent convulsions and other complications.

Health Skills Activity

CARING FOR YOUR IMMUNE SYSTEM

DECISION MAKING

NHES Standard 6 Students will demonstrate the ability to use goal-setting and decision-making skills to enhance health.

Objectives

- Examine the effects of health behaviors on the immune system.
- Apply decision-making skills to make a health-promoting decision.

Motivator

Have students recall the last cold they had. Were they stressed or not getting enough sleep right before they became ill?

Teaching Strategies

1. Encourage students to consider what responsibility a person who may be contagious has to prevent spreading the illness.
2. Allow students to work in groups to analyze the consequences and reach a decision. Have each group share with the class the results of their decision-making activity.

✓ Assessment

Using a rubric, student work should provide comprehensive evidence of the following criteria to achieve the highest score:

✔ progression through a decision-making process
✔ identification of the decision to be made
✔ consideration of options and consequences
✔ taking action or making a decision
✔ evaluation or reflection on the decision

Discussing

Ask the class what *specific* means in the phrase *specific resistance to infection*. Continue by asking why it is so valuable to have antibodies that can "remember" a pathogen. **L3**

Cooperative Learning

Divide the class into three or four groups. Have each group produce a diagram that illustrates the action of lymphocytes, including the roles of both T cells and B cells, in fighting off pathogens. Circulate the drawings. Have students give one another feedback on their diagrams to correct errors and misconceptions. **L2**

VISUAL LEARNING

Figure 24.3 Have students follow the four illustrated steps and read all eight steps the body takes to fight pathogens. Ask:

- How do macrophages distinguish between body cells and pathogens? Antigens are on the surface of pathogens.
- What is the function of B cells? To release antibodies

Discussing

Ask students to compare and contrast specific and nonspecific immunity. How are their functions alike and different? How do they work together to fight pathogens? **L1**

HEALTH Online

Find more about how the immune system works in Web Links at health.glencoe.com.

Specific Defenses

Specific defenses react to invasion as a result of the body's ability to recognize certain pathogens and destroy them. The process by which this happens, the immune response, is described in **Figure 24.3**. During the immune response, certain types of white blood cells react to antigens. An **antigen** is *a substance that is capable of triggering an immune response*. Antigens are found on the surfaces of pathogens and in toxins. Macrophages are a type of phagocyte that destroys pathogens by making antigens recognizable to white blood cells. The result of the immune response is **immunity**, *the state of being protected against a particular disease*.

Lymphocytes

A **lymphocyte** (LIMP-fuh-site) is *a specialized white blood cell that coordinates and performs many of the functions of specific immunity*. There are two types of lymphocytes: T cells and B cells.

T CELLS AND B CELLS

There are different types of T cells with different functions. They all work together to protect against infection.

▶ *Helper T cells* trigger the production of B cells and killer T cells.

▶ *Killer T cells* attack and destroy infected body cells. Killer T cells don't attack the pathogens themselves, only the infected cells.

FIGURE 24.3

THE IMMUNE RESPONSE

The immune response is a complex interaction between your body and an invading pathogen. It can be broken down into eight distinct stages.

1. Pathogens invade the body.
2. Macrophages engulf the pathogen.
3. Macrophages digest the pathogen and T cells recognize antigens of the pathogen as an invader.
4. T cells bind to the antigens.
5. B cells bind to antigens and helper T cells.
6. B cells divide to produce plasma cells.
7. Plasma cells release antibodies into the bloodstream.
8. Antibodies bind to antigens to help other cells identify and destroy the pathogens.

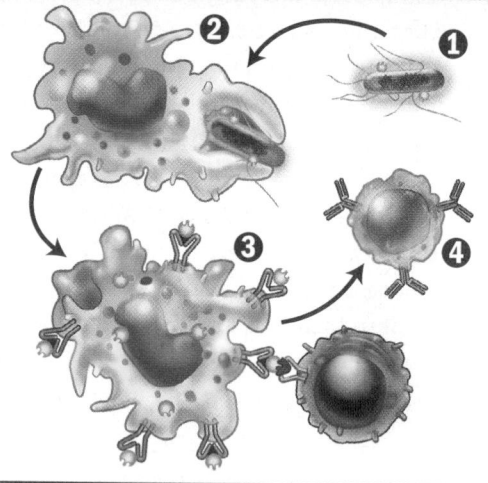

Home and Community

Autoimmune Diseases The immune system is built on the ability to distinguish foreign cells from the body's own cells. If a person has an autoimmune disease, the immune system mistakenly targets and attacks the cells, tissues, and organs of a person's own body. There are dozens of autoimmune diseases that affect millions of Americans. Two examples are rheumatoid arthritis, which affects the lining that covers joints, and multiple sclerosis (MS), in which the immune system targets nerve tissues of the central nervous system. Have students conduct research on one of these diseases. They should find out how the diseases are treated and how they affect the quality of life.

► *Suppressor T cells* coordinate the activities of other T cells. They "turn off" or suppress helper T cells when the infection has been cleared.

In conjunction with the work of T cells, lymphocytes called B cells produce antibodies. An **antibody** is a *protein that acts against a specific antigen.* Each B cell is programmed to make one type of antibody, specific to a particular pathogen. Some antibodies attach to foreign antigens to mark them for destruction. Some destroy invading pathogens. Others block viruses from entering body cells.

The Role of Memory Lymphocytes

Your immune system actually has a "memory." Some T cells and B cells that have been activated by antigens become *memory cells.* These memory cells circulate in your bloodstream and through the lymphatic system, shown in **Figure 24.4** on page 632. When memory cells recognize a former invader, the immune system uses antibodies and killer T cells in a quick defense to stop it. For example, if you have had measles or an immunization against measles, your immune system remembers the antigens for the measles virus. If it enters your body again, antibodies will attack the virus immediately, protecting you from becoming ill.

Active Immunity

The immunity your body develops to protect you from measles or from other diseases is called *active immunity.* Naturally acquired active immunity develops when your body is exposed to antigens from invading pathogens. Artificially acquired active immunity develops in response to a **vaccine**, a *preparation of dead or weakened pathogens, which are introduced into the body to stimulate an immune response.* In this way vaccines cause your body to produce antibodies without actually causing the disease. Today, more than 20 serious human diseases can be prevented by vaccination. Active immunity to many diseases can last a lifetime, but some immunizations need to be repeated to maintain immunity.

Passive Immunity

In active immunity your body produces its own antibodies. You also can be protected from pathogens by *passive immunity*—receiving antibodies from another person or an animal. This immunity is short-lived; it usually lasts only weeks to months. Natural passive immunity occurs when antibodies pass from mother to child during pregnancy or while nursing. Artificial passive immunity results from the injection of antibodies produced by an animal or a human who is immune to the disease.

Is there a vaccine to prevent colds?

Developing a vaccine to prevent colds is difficult. More than 200 different viruses can cause the common cold. This means that more than 200 different vaccines would have to be developed to prevent this illness.

FYI

The number of helper T cells is inversely proportional to stress level, that is, the higher the stress, the lower the T cell count. One of the hormones secreted by the body during stress is cortisol. High levels of cortisol reduce the number of lymphocytes. Other "stress hormones" are norepinephrine and epinephrine, which impair the ability of lymphocytes to fight infection.

ACTIVE READING

Flow Chart

In this strategy, the student logically analyzes and draws a sequence of events. Have students look for key phrases that describe how the body responds to invading pathogens, including physical and chemical barriers, nonspecific responses, and specific responses that lead to the production of a specific antibody. Then have them list the steps and create a flow chart that illustrates each step. Students can work in pairs to produce one chart. For more strategies, see the *Guided Reading Activities* booklet.

Critical Thinking

Why must vaccines be given before exposure to the pathogen against which it protects? It takes time for the body to develop an immune response. Exposure could cause the pathogens to multiply and cause disease before antibodies have a chance to develop. L2

Home and Community

Research Polio Ask students to interview family members, friends, or neighbors who are old enough to remember the threats posed by polio before the vaccine became available. Have them find out what attitudes these people remember about the possibilities of contracting polio. What special precautions were taken? With what results? Did the people interviewed know, or know of, any individuals who did contract polio? If so, how were they affected by the disease? Encourage students to also ask about other diseases, such as tuberculosis, measles, and mumps, before vaccines for those diseases became available. Let students share their interview findings in discussion groups.

Figure 24.4 Have students read the explanations in the figure. Ask: Which structures of the lymphatic system take part in the body's immunity? tonsils, lymph nodes, lymphocytes Have them discuss the roles of lymph nodes and lymphocytes.

Activity

Have interested students find out to which diseases people are given passive immunizations if they are exposed to them but not previously immunized. hepatitis A, chicken pox, and tetanus **L3**

Reinforcing Concepts

Explain that tetanus is a toxin produced by a bacterium in soil. The toxin paralyzes muscles. People who have been actively immunized against tetanus should continue to get active vaccines or "boosters" every ten years to maintain active protection. If a person is potentially exposed to tetanus—for example, through a puncture wound—a booster will be given if five years or more have passed since the last booster. If the person has never had an active vaccine, he or she will be given passive immunity so that the antibodies can go to work right away. **L1**

FIGURE 24.4

IMMUNITY AND THE LYMPHATIC SYSTEM

The lymphatic system circulates antibodies to give you protection against many diseases. This protection can last throughout your life.

The **lymphatic system** is part of your immune system. It includes your tonsils, lymph nodes, and a network of vessels, similar to blood vessels, that transport lymph, or tissue fluid.

Lymph nodes can become enlarged when your body is fighting an infection because of the increased number of lymphocytes. If swelling lasts for three days, see your health care professional.

Lymphocytes are produced by lymph nodes. These nodes occur in groups and are concentrated in the head and neck, armpits, chest, abdomen, and groin.

Care of the Immune System

Your health behaviors can greatly reduce your chance of contracting a disease or getting an infection. When you keep your body strong and healthy, your immune system is better able to fight off pathogens. Taking positive steps in every area of your health will give you the boost needed to reduce your chance of illness.

▶ Follow a sensible eating plan to maintain your overall health and keep your immune system strong. Include whole grains and nutrient-dense foods such as fruits and vegetables, and reduce intake of fats, sugar, and salt. Drink six to eight 8-ounce glasses of water each day.

▶ Get plenty of rest. Fatigue reduces the effectiveness of the immune system. To function at their best, teens should average nine hours of restful sleep each night.

632 **Chapter 24** Communicable Diseases

Cooperative Learning Activity

A Healthful Agreement Divide students into groups of four, and have them discuss each strategy given in the text to care for the immune system. Each student then writes a description of at least two specific behaviors that he or she can practice to support each of the strategies. For example, a specific behavior for a sensible eating plan would be to eat at least five servings of fruits and vegetables daily. Each student creates and signs a behavior health plan that states how and when the student will practice these specific behaviors every day. Members in the group agree to support one another in their efforts.

- ▶ Get about an hour of physical activity each day. This is especially important to relieve stress.

- ▶ Avoid sharing personal items such as towels, toothbrushes, hairbrushes, or makeup.

- ▶ Avoid tobacco, alcohol, and other drugs.

- ▶ Avoid sexual contact. Some **STDs,** such as HIV, actually destroy the immune system.

- ▶ Keep your immunizations up to date.

hot link

STDs For more information on sexually transmitted diseases, including HIV/AIDS, see Chapter 25, page 646.

Vaccines to Aid the Body's Defenses

When a new disease emerges or a familiar one becomes a greater health threat than in the past, health care workers begin to look for ways to prevent the disease. Research and advances in medical technology have allowed scientists to develop vaccines. Today, vaccines prevent diseases that once claimed millions of lives. Vaccines can be one of four types.

- ▶ **Live-virus vaccines** are made from pathogens grown under special laboratory conditions to make them lose most of their disease-causing properties. Although weakened, the organism can still stimulate the production of antibodies. The vaccines for measles, mumps, and rubella (MMR) and for chicken pox are produced in this way.

- ▶ **Killed-virus vaccines** use inactivated pathogens. Even though they are dead, the organism still stimulates an immune response and antibodies are produced. Flu shots, the Salk vaccine for polio, and the vaccines for hepatitis A, rabies, cholera, and plague are all killed-virus vaccines.

- ▶ **Toxoids** are inactivated toxins from pathogens. They are used to stimulate the production of antibodies. Though many pathogens are not harmful themselves, the toxins they produce cause sickness. Toxoids can be used to protect the body against such illnesses. Both tetanus and diphtheria immunizations use toxoids.

- ▶ **New and second-generation vaccines** are being developed by scientists using new technologies. An example is the vaccine for hepatitis B, which is made by genetically altered yeast cells.

These and many other common diseases can be prevented with vaccines:
- Chicken pox
- Hepatitis B
- Measles
- Mumps
- Whooping cough (pertussis)
- Tetanus
- Diphtheria
- Polio
- Rubella

Check with your parents or your health care professional to find out how many of these diseases you have been vaccinated against.

Lesson 2 Preventing Communicable Diseases **633**

Discussing

Ask students to explain the major ways in which the four types of vaccines differ. **L1**

Cooperative Learning

Select students to locate and make a list of all the diseases for which there is a vaccine. Include the ages at which they should be administered. Post the list, and discuss the vaccines for which teens should be up to date. **L3**

Explaining

If possible, have students review their immunization records with their parents or guardians. Discuss the importance of keeping the schedules up to date. Stress that, as the students get older, keeping medical records becomes their responsibility. **L1**

Cross-Curriculum Activity

Science and Technology Have small groups of students research and report on the intranasal flu vaccine. These are nose sprays that are inhaled. Students should include why these vaccines are more effective than those administered with a needle and what impact they think a painless flu vaccine would have on vaccination rates. **L2**

Myths & Reality

MYTH. Only people over 65 and those with chronic diseases need a flu vaccine.

FACT. Everyone, including children and teens who are in good health, need a flu vaccine to stay healthy. A flu vaccine prevents the flu and protects everyone you live with and contact.

MYTH. The vaccine isn't 100 percent effective, so I'm better off getting the flu.

FACT. It is true that no vaccine is 100 percent effective. However, if you get a flu vaccine but still get the flu, you are likely to be far less sick than you would have been without the protection.

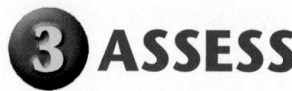

③ ASSESS

EVALUATING THE LESSON

Assign and discuss the Lesson 2 Review; then administer, grade, and discuss Lesson Quiz 89 in the TCR. 📁

RETEACHING

- Suggest that students make a game to be used as a review of the key concepts in the lesson.
- Ask students to complete Reteaching Activity 89 in the TCR. 📁

ENRICHMENT

Ask interested students to research all the communicable diseases for which immunizations have been developed but are not routinely recommended. Have them list the diseases, and for whom or when they are indicated. (For example, rabies vaccine is recommended for veterinarians and people who work with the rabies virus).

④ CLOSE

Divide the class into small groups. As a homework assignment, have each group coordinate rewriting part of this lesson in their own words, using their own case studies or examples. Afterward, duplicate each group's work, and distribute it to the class.

634

Immunization for All

Vaccines benefit more people than just those who receive them. If you are vaccinated against a particular disease, you can't spread that disease to others. In this way vaccination not only protects you but also helps protect those around you, especially your family and friends. One exception is tetanus, which is transmitted through the environment, not from person to person. The tetanus vaccine protects only the individual who receives it.

You should have up-to-date immunizations, including those for tetanus, diphtheria, measles, mumps, rubella, and hepatitis B. Vaccination against chicken pox is recommended if you have not had this disease. Some vaccines require more than one dose over time, or "booster shots." Your family physician or your local health department can advise you on the immunizations you need and provide them for you. Most high schools and colleges require that students show proof of current immunizations before admission. Each state has its own laws governing immunizations and school attendance. Some schools may have additional requirements.

Lesson 2 *Review*

Reviewing Facts and Vocabulary

1. List three physical and chemical barriers that pathogens encounter when they try to enter the human body.
2. What is the difference between active immunity and passive immunity?
3. Where can you go to find out which immunizations you need?

Thinking Critically

4. **Analyzing.** How do you think the development of vaccines for more than 20 communicable diseases has affected the average human life span in areas where these vaccines are available?
5. **Evaluating.** What would you say to someone who says that he or she is careful never to come into contact with pathogens and therefore will not become ill?

Applying Health Skills

Accessing Information. Research those vaccinations suggested for someone your age, and make a table of this information. Work with a parent or guardian to determine which of your immunizations are current, and fill in the information on the table. Plan to get any immunizations you lack. Use this table to track when you should update your immunizations.

SPREADSHEETS Use spreadsheet software to create a chart showing the immunizations suggested for different age groups. You might also include a column listing facilities in the area that offer these vaccinations. See **health.glencoe.com** for information on how to create a spreadsheet.

634 **Chapter 24** Communicable Diseases

Lesson 2 *Review*

Answers to Reviewing Facts and Vocabulary

1. Any three: skin, tears, saliva, gastric juice, cilia, mucous membranes.
2. Active: long-lasting; the body produces antibodies. Passive: lasts only weeks to months; the body receives antibodies.
3. Family physician or local health department.

Answers to Thinking Critically

4. They have reduced deaths caused by communicable diseases, thus lengthening average human life span.
5. Possible answer: Avoiding pathogens is impossible. A healthy immune system can fight off most pathogens but immunization is important.

Common Communicable Diseases

VOCABULARY

pneumonia
jaundice
emerging
    infection

YOU'LL LEARN TO

• Identify the causes, transmission, symptoms, and treatment of several communicable diseases.

• Analyze strategies to reduce the risk of contracting some communicable diseases.

• Explain how technology impacts world health status.

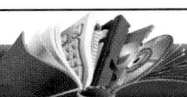 *QUICK START* Make a two-column chart. In the first column, list communicable diseases with which you are familiar and write one fact about each. In the second column, list communicable diseases you have heard of but know little about.

You probably have experienced a fever or the stuffy or runny nose of a cold. In this lesson you'll learn about some common communicable diseases, their symptoms, and how they are treated. Most important, you will learn ways to reduce your risk of contracting these diseases.

Respiratory Infections

The most common communicable diseases are those of the respiratory tract. These infections can occur anywhere from the nose to the alveoli of the lungs. Most are caused by viruses or bacteria. You can reduce your risk of most respiratory illnesses by avoiding close contact with people who are infected, washing your hands often, keeping your hands away from your eyes and nose, and keeping your immune system healthy. Smoking can contribute to illness by damaging cilia and irritating respiratory passages. In addition, symptoms of these diseases may be more severe in smokers. Smoking has also been shown to suppress the immune system.

(A) **When you have a cold, the best thing to do is rest, eat nutritious foods, and drink plenty of fluids such as water or fruit juice.** *How might these strategies help your body fight cold viruses?*

Lesson 3 Common Communicable Diseases **635**

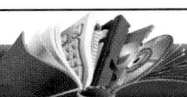
Lesson 3 *Resources*

Teacher Classroom Resources

📂 Concept Mapping Activity 90

📂 Cross-Curriculum Activity 24

📂 Enrichment Activity 24

📂 Guided Reading Activities 90

📂 Health Lab 24

📂 Lesson Plan 90

📂 Lesson Quiz 90

📂 Reteaching Activity 90

Student Activity Workbook

📂 Applying Health Skills 90

📂 Chapter 24 Study Guide

Common Communicable Diseases

1 FOCUS

 QUICK START After students have completed the Quick Start, have them share information. On the board, make a list of questions that students have.

TYING TO PRIOR KNOWLEDGE

Ask students what they think are the most common communicable diseases. Explain that this lesson will focus on some of those diseases.

Health Skills Features

"Reducing Your Risk of Lyme Disease," p. 639
ANALYZING INFLUENCES

INTRODUCING VOCABULARY

• Have students write sentences using each vocabulary term; then have them locate these terms in the chapter and make any necessary adjustments to their sentences.

• Ask students to complete the Chapter 24 Study Guide in the *Student Activity Workbook.* 📂

2 TEACH

Discussing

Ask volunteers to share what they have done when they were ill with a communicable disease: Did they stay home or go to school? On what did they base their decision? Discuss with the class the consequences of staying home from school. What are teachers' policies regarding absence because of illness? Is it possible to make up missed work? Then have students write realistic entries in their private health journals about the pros and cons of staying home when ill.

Health Minute

Have volunteers think about when they have had the flu. Point out that the worst complication from a cold is usually a bacterial infection of the ear or sinuses. This is because the immune system is weakened from fighting the cold. Bacteria that normally live in the nose and throat without causing problems can overcome defenses.

FYI

There is no such thing as "stomach flu." The influenza virus infects respiratory passages, not the gastrointestinal tract. "Stomach flu" is actually gastroenteritis, with symptoms such as nausea, diarrhea, and vomiting.

Common Cold

The common cold is a viral infection that causes inflammation of the mucous membranes that line the nose and throat. Symptoms include a runny nose, sneezing, and sore throat. The most common way of getting a cold is from rubbing your eyes or nose after picking up the virus directly through hand-to-hand contact or indirectly by handling a contaminated object.

There is no cure for the common cold. Treatment is for relief of symptoms, and most colds clear up in a week or so. Often treatment includes the use of **analgesics.** It's important to note that anyone under 20 years of age should avoid use of medications containing salicylates, such as aspirin. Such use is linked to Reye's syndrome, a condition that can be fatal. Avoid these products no matter what disease you might have. Use acetaminophen or ibuprofen instead.

Influenza

Influenza, or the flu, is a viral infection of the respiratory tract. It is most often spread through airborne transmission but also may spread through direct or indirect contact. Symptoms of flu include high fever, fatigue, headache, muscle aches, and cough. The flu can lead to **pneumonia,** (noo-MOH-nyah) *an infection of the lungs in which the air sacs fill with pus and other liquid.* This is a serious disease that is more likely to occur in the elderly and people with lung and heart problems.

Antiviral drugs for treatment of the flu are available but need to be given as soon as the illness arises. Persons who have the flu should get proper nutrition and plenty of rest and fluids. Older adults and persons of any age with chronic health problems should get a flu shot every year. However, anyone who wants to avoid the flu can be given the vaccine.

Pneumonia

Along with influenza, pneumonia is one of the top ten causes of death in the United States. Viral pneumonia is relatively short-lived and produces symptoms similar to those of influenza. Antiviral drugs are used in some cases. Bacterial pneumonia can be treated with antibiotics if diagnosed early. The bacteria that cause pneumonia are often present in healthy throats. When body defenses are weakened in some way, the bacteria can get into the lungs and multiply. For example, if a person is elderly or has influenza, he or she may be more at risk for complications leading to pneumonia.

hot link

analgesics For more information about analgesics, see Chapter 23, page 588.

Health Minute

Is It a Cold or the Flu?

Cold symptoms include:

► Runny or stuffy nose
► Sneezing
► Sore throat
► Headache

Flu symptoms include:

► High fever
► Chills
► Dry cough
► Muscle and joint pain
► Runny nose
► Sore throat
► Extreme fatigue

Home and Community

Preventive Measures at Home Have students work individually or in groups to brainstorm a checklist to use in assessing the home for risks of communicable diseases and adequate preventive measures. In particular, have students assess steps taken to prevent the spread of disease when one member of the household is ill. For example, does the ill person use only certain eating utensils, or are all eating utensils washed in very hot water? What steps are taken to prevent members of the household from touching items contaminated by the infected person? What precautions are taken against spreading infection through airborne particles? Students may wish to recommend additional preventive measures.

Strep Throat

Strep throat is a bacterial infection spread by direct contact, often through droplets that are coughed or sneezed into the air. Symptoms of strep throat include a sore throat, fever, and enlarged lymph nodes in the neck. Untreated, strep throat can lead to serious complications, including inflammation of the kidneys and rheumatic fever, which can cause permanent heart damage. Strep throat can be treated with antibiotics. A doctor cannot always diagnose strep by examination. If a sore throat lasts more than three days, a culture is taken to identify the bacteria.

Tuberculosis

Tuberculosis, or TB, is a bacterial disease that usually attacks the lungs. TB is spread through the air when a person with the disease coughs or sneezes. Most people who are infected carry the bacteria in their lungs but never develop the disease because the body's defenses prevent the bacteria from multiplying and spreading to others. People with weakened immune systems are more likely to develop the active disease with symptoms that include fatigue, coughing (sometimes coughing up blood), fever, night sweats, and weight loss. People with the active disease can spread TB. Prolonged or repeated exposure is usually required for infection. Some strains have developed resistance to antibiotics. Physicians may have to prescribe several antibiotics at one time until tests are conducted to determine which are effective for a particular person.

Hepatitis

Hepatitis is inflammation of the liver and can be caused by chemicals, including drugs or alcohol, or by many different pathogens. The hepatitis A, B, and C viruses are some of the most common causes of this type of liver damage, and there is no cure for them. However, vaccines for hepatitis A and B are available.

Hepatitis A

Hepatitis A is another of the top ten communicable diseases reported in the United States. About 1.5 million people worldwide are newly infected each year. The hepatitis A virus is most commonly spread through contact with feces of an infected person. Infected persons who do not wash their hands properly may contaminate inanimate objects or food or spread the virus through direct contact.

Many employers in the health care industry require applicants to show proof of a negative TB test. *Why may patients in hospitals or in long-term care facilities be at increased risk for tuberculosis?*

Did You Know?

Many people mistakenly believe that tuberculosis is no longer a problem, but experts estimate that about 10 million people in the United States are currently infected with TB bacteria and that about 10 percent of these people will develop the disease.

TB is increasingly a worldwide problem. In 1999, 2 million deaths were attributed to TB; 100,000 of those deaths were among children. The CDC estimates that by 2020 nearly 1 billion people worldwide will become infected with tuberculosis.

Critical Thinking

Ask: Why do outbreaks of hepatitis A occur in child care centers? Many children in child care centers are still in diapers and have not learned personal hygiene. These factors lead to the opportunity for fecal contamination of the environment and direct person-to-person spread. Young children also have the tendency to put toys and other items in their mouths. **L2**

Cross-Curriculum Activity

Math All donated blood in the United States is screened for the presence of hepatitis B and C. The risk of getting these pathogens from the blood supply is very low. However, the risk still exists. Current estimates are that the risk is 1/66,000 screened units of blood for hepatitis B and 1/100,000 for hepatitis C. If 12 million units of blood are donated in the U.S. every year, how many contaminated units containing hepatitis B or C may be undetected? Hepatitis B—182 units; Hepatitis C—120 units **L1**

More About...

E. coli O157:H7 In 1993, four children were killed and hundreds of others sickened by undercooked hamburger from a fast-food restaurant. The culprit was *E. coli O157:H7*, a type of bacteria that produces a toxin that severely damages the intestines and can lead to kidney failure and death. Common sources are undercooked, contaminated ground beef; unpasteurized milk and apple cider. The bacteria also can be transferred from person to person. *E. coli* is a type of bacteria that is normally found in the intestines of all animals and humans. *E. coli* suppresses the growth of harmful bacteria and synthesizes some vitamins. *E. coli O157:H7* is one of very few strains of *E. coli* that causes illness in humans.

Reinforcing Concepts

Emphasize that hepatitis B is a very serious disease—second only to tobacco in known substances that can cause cancer. **L1**

Community Involvement

Select students to investigate the type of mosquito control, if any, used by the local or state health agency. Have students find out which mosquito-borne diseases, if any, have been reported in the city, county, or state within the past two years. **L3**

Discussing

Ask students to compare and contrast the ways that hepatitis B and C are transmitted. What behaviors reduce the risk of both infections? **L1**

Critical Thinking

Remind students that people with any illness should rest and make sure they eat nutritious foods. Ask: Why is it especially important for people to take care of themselves when they are ill with a communicable disease that has no cure? Such actions help the immune system to carry out its function. **L2**

Service Learning

Have students gather information about health clinics and other public sites where free or low-cost flu vaccinations are offered. If appropriate, have a group of volunteers prepare and distribute flyers with up-to-date information on the dates, times, and locations for these vaccination opportunities. **L1** **Interpersonal**

About 30 to 40 percent of people with hepatitis B don't know how they got the infection. *How can you protect yourself from exposure to hepatitis B?*

Symptoms of hepatitis A are generally mild and may include fever, nausea, vomiting, fatigue, abdominal pain, and **jaundice**, a *yellowing of the skin and eyes*. Most infected individuals recover completely. Chronic, or long-lasting, infection is rare. The best way to reduce your risk of hepatitis A is to practice careful handwashing and avoid close contact with people who are infected.

Hepatitis B

Hepatitis B is a more serious disease than hepatitis A. The hepatitis B virus (HBV) is found in most bodily fluids of an infected person, especially blood. It is most often transmitted through sexual contact. It also can be transmitted through needles shared by infected drug users. Though most people who are infected never experience symptoms, the hepatitis B virus frequently causes severe liver damage, including liver failure and cirrhosis, or scarring, of the liver. Hepatitis B may be responsible for up to 80 percent of all cases of liver cancer worldwide. More than two billion people worldwide have been infected with HBV. About 1.25 million people in the United States have chronic HBV infection.

You can reduce your risk of hepatitis B by practicing abstinence from sexual contact and from illegal drug use. Do not share personal items, such as toothbrushes or razors, which could have trace amounts of saliva or blood. Body piercing and tattooing using contaminated needles can spread the disease. The CDC recommends that all children and teens receive the hepatitis B vaccine.

Hepatitis C

Hepatitis C is the most common chronic blood-borne infection in the United States; about four million Americans are infected. It is most often transmitted by direct contact with infected blood through contaminated needles shared by drug users. Hepatitis C can lead to chronic liver disease, liver cancer, or liver failure. It is the leading reason for liver transplants in the United States. Up to 90 percent of those infected with the hepatitis C virus (HCV) don't realize they have the disease until years later when routine tests show liver damage. You can reduce your risk of hepatitis C by practicing abstinence from illegal drug use. In addition, don't share personal care items, such as razors and toothbrushes. As with other viral infections, there is no cure for hepatitis. Treatment includes rest, proper nutrition, and drinking plenty of fluids.

638 Chapter 24 Communicable Diseases

Cooperative Learning Activity

Diagnosis of Communicable Diseases
Divide students into groups of four. Tell each group member to write, on separate cards, symptoms for two specific diseases described in the textbook, with one set of symptoms for each disease. Allow students to use the textbook for reference. Tell them to mix up the cards and place them face-down. Have one member of each group draw a card and examine the symptoms. Next, the student is to identify a disease that fits the symptoms, the type of pathogen that causes it, and the appropriate treatment. Other students will discuss the response and agree, disagree, or suggest modifications. All group members must agree on the diagnosis and treatment before another group member draws a card.

Other Diseases

Several other communicable diseases are common among adolescents and young adults. **Figure 24.5** on page 640 provides a summary of these diseases.

Emerging Infections

Some diseases have been effectively controlled with the help of modern technology such as antibiotics and vaccines. Yet new diseases, such as AIDS and Lyme disease, are constantly appearing. Others, such as malaria and tuberculosis, are occurring in forms

Real-Life Application

Reducing Your Risk of Lyme Disease

In 1982 fewer than 1,000 cases of Lyme disease were reported in the United States. Today, more than 16,000 cases are reported each year. Lyme disease is transmitted to humans by the bite of an infected deer tick. Ticks favor a moist, shaded environment, such as forests. Coastal ticks thrive in areas of high rainfall. Ticks are most active in the spring and summer. Study the graph to help you analyze the environmental and geographical factors that influence the distribution and rate of disease in the United States. Use this information to develop a plan to reduce your risk.

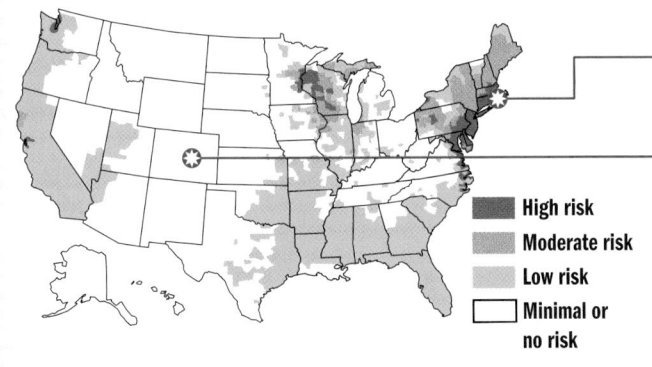

High risk
Moderate risk
Low risk
Minimal or no risk

What does the concentration of cases here tell you about the environment in which ticks live?

What is different about this part of the country that could account for the lower incidence of Lyme disease?

What human activities (leisure and industrial) could have influenced the increase in cases from 1982 to the present?

ACTIVITY

Work with a small group of students. Together, analyze the graph and discuss the questions. Use what you've learned to develop an action plan to decrease your risk of contracting Lyme disease. Include specific steps to protect yourself. Consider clothing, insect repellents, where you live or travel, and the time of year.

Lesson 3 Common Communicable Diseases **639**

Real-Life Application

REDUCING YOUR RISK OF LYME DISEASE

ANALYZING INFLUENCES

NHES Standard 4 Students will analyze the influence of culture, media, technology, and other factors on health.

Objectives

- Describe the factors that influence the incidence of Lyme disease.
- Develop and analyze strategies related to the prevention of Lyme disease.

Teaching Strategies

1. Share possible reasons for the increase in Lyme disease: Building near heavily wooded areas, more people playing outdoors, better tests for detection.
2. Access **health.glencoe.com** to link to CDC Division of Vector-Borne Infectious Diseases.

✓Assessment

Using a rubric, student work should provide comprehensive evidence of the following criteria to achieve the highest score:

✔ identification and analysis of external and internal factors
✔ attention to interrelationships and complexity of influences
✔ variety of influences as appropriate

More About...

Investigating STARI Assign small groups to investigate a rash that has been named the Southern tick-associated rash illness (STARI). This disease is similar to that of Lyme disease and has been found in persons living in southeastern and south-central states such as Texas and Oklahoma.

The pathogens are spread by the bite of the "lone star" tick. Preventive measures are identical to that of Lyme disease. STARI is sometimes treated with antibiotics. Online information on STARI can be found by accessing **health.glencoe.com** for links to the CDC Web site.

Figure 24.5 Have students study the figure. Ask:

- Based on what you know of preventive measures, how would you reduce your risk of encephalitis? Take steps to prevent mosquito bites, such as wearing repellent.
- The number of measles cases has drastically declined over the past few decades. Why is this so? A vaccine is available.

Guest Speaker

Invite a representative from the local or state health department to speak with the class. Ask him or her to discuss special health precautions that are necessary to travel to various parts of the world. Have the speaker list immunizations that are needed and why. ⬛ ▭

FYI

Anthrax is a disease caused by a spore-forming bacterium. Most infections occur when spores enter a cut on the skin (cutaneous anthrax). The risk of death is high when anthrax spores are inhaled (inhalation anthrax) or ingested (gastrointestinal anthrax).

FIGURE 24.5

OTHER COMMON COMMUNICABLE DISEASES

Disease	Cause/Transmission	Symptoms	Treatment/Prevention
Mononucleosis	Virus attacks lymphocytes; spreads through direct contact, including sharing eating utensils and kissing	Chills, fever, sore throat, fatigue, and swollen lymph nodes	Rest if tired
Measles	Virus spreads when an infected person coughs, sneezes, or talks; highly contagious	High fever, red eyes, runny nose, cough, bumpy red rash usually starting on head or face	No definite treatment; vaccine for prevention
Encephalitis	A virus usually carried by mosquitoes; causes inflammation of the brain	Headache; fever; hallucinations; confusion; paralysis; and disturbances of speech, memory, behavior, and eye movement	If caused by herpes simplex virus, antiviral medicine; if caused by another virus, no known treatment
Meningitis	Virus or bacteria cause inflammation of the membranes that cover the brain	Fever, severe headache, nausea, vomiting, sensitivity to light, stiff neck	Viral meningitis: antiviral medicine if severe; bacterial meningitis: antibiotics; vaccine is available

that are resistant to drug treatments. These diseases are known as "emerging." An **emerging infection** is a *communicable disease whose incidence in humans has increased within the past two decades or threatens to increase in the near future.* Many factors are contributing to the development of emerging infections:

▶ **Transport across borders.** Infected people and animals carry pathogens from region to region, often to places where those pathogens previously were not a problem. Two examples of this are the appearance of dengue fever and West Nile encephalitis which is caused by West Nile virus. Dengue fever is found mostly in South and Central America and parts of Asia, and has appeared in the southwestern United States. West Nile encephalitis appears in Asia, Africa, and Europe and is now expanding across the Western Hemisphere, including parts of the United States. Both diseases are carried by mosquitoes.

▶ **Population movement.** A factor in the increase in Lyme disease is the movement of people into heavily wooded areas where ticks are prevalent. Symptoms include a rash, fatigue, fever, headache, stiff neck, sore muscles, and joint pain. Lyme disease can be treated with antibiotics.

More About...

Environmental Changes and Emerging Infections Changes in land use—deforestation, the damming of rivers, the spread of ranching and farming—alter the distribution of disease vectors and bring people in contact with new pathogens. A shift in rainfall patterns may allow mosquito-borne diseases to spread from the tropics into temperate zones. Isolated cases of malaria in New York and New Jersey have already occurred in years that were particularly hot and humid. A hantavirus outbreak in the Four Corners area in the western United States occurred in 1993, a year when heavy rainfall led to an increase in the rodent population. 1993 was the first year in which hantavirus disease was identified. It can cause respiratory failure and death.

► **Resistance to antibiotics.** The widespread use of antibiotics has resulted in pathogens that have become resistant. The pathogens that cause tuberculosis, gonorrhea (a sexually transmitted disease), and a type of pneumonia all have developed resistance to one or more antibiotics.

► **Changes in food technology.** Mass production and distribution of food increases the chance that contaminated food will infect a great number of people. *E. coli* has been responsible for outbreaks affecting thousands.

► **Agents of bioterrorism.** Because of the ease and frequency of travel, a contagious bioterrorist agent such as smallpox can spread rapidly from country to country.

Public health officials in the United States are addressing infectious diseases elsewhere in the world because pathogens can emerge in one region and spread. Information on emerging diseases is widely available—on the Internet, in books and magazines, and through news reports. With health information readily available, individuals can become more proactive and responsible for reducing their risk of communicable diseases, including emerging infections.

Health Minute
What You Can Do

Precautions to avoid emerging or reemerging infections:

► Take all of the antibiotics prescribed by your doctor.
► Eat only fully cooked eggs.
► Avoid swallowing water at water parks.
► Take precautions to prevent bites by vectors such as ticks and mosquitoes.

 Lesson 3 *Review*

Reviewing Facts and Vocabulary

1. Compare and contrast the common cold and the flu.
2. What are three ways you can reduce your risk of getting influenza?
3. What are emerging infections?

Thinking Critically

4. **Synthesizing.** What healthful behaviors can students in your class practice to reduce everyone's risk of respiratory infection?
5. **Analyzing.** Why might emerging infections be an important area to receive funding for research? How can technology impact the reduction of diseases worldwide?

Applying Health Skills

Advocacy. Choose one emerging infection to research. Prepare a script for a public service announcement describing this disease. Be sure to include information on how the disease is transmitted and what the symptoms are. Urge individuals who suspect they may be infected to seek medical attention immediately. Share your script with the class.

TECHNOLOGY *OPTION*

PRESENTATION SOFTWARE Use presentation software to present the information you found on the disease you chose to investigate. Find help in using presentation software at **health.glencoe.com**.

Lesson 3 Common Communicable Diseases **641**

3 ASSESS

EVALUATING THE LESSON

Assign and discuss the Lesson 3 Review; then administer, grade, and discuss Lesson Quiz 90 in the TCR.

RETEACHING

• Have students make sets of flash cards to review the diseases and the pathogens that cause them.
• Ask students to complete Reteaching Activity 90 in the TCR.

ENRICHMENT

Have students research and report on the types of diseases caused by bacteria and on the treatment for these diseases.

4 CLOSE

Assign sections of this lesson to small groups. Have each group summarize the section and present their summary to the class.

 Lesson 3 *Review*

Answers to Reviewing Facts and Vocabulary

1. Both are caused by a virus, but the flu usually has more severe symptoms.
2. Possible answers: Avoid close contact with infected people, wash hands often, keep hands away from eyes and nose.
3. Infectious diseases whose incidence in humans has increased within the past two decades or threatens to increase.

Answers to Thinking Critically

4. Possible answers: Stay home when ill, use a tissue when sneezing, keep hands away from face, get rest.
5. Prevention and treatment of these illnesses can be very difficult; they can spread very rapidly.

Emerging Infections

NHES Standard 4 Students will analyze the influence of culture, media, technology, and other factors on health.

Objective

Analyze potential impact of creating media messages for a target audience, and organize information about communicable diseases for that audience.

Motivator

Ask students whether they can recall any TV news coverage about any communicable diseases.

Teaching Strategies

Awareness In their research on who is at risk for acquiring a disease, point out that students should know where the disease is occurring geographically and among what population.

Analysis Encourage students to think about who the audience is for each type of media and what media their target audience uses. Tell students they may need to use multiple strategies to disseminate information.

Reflection Have each group report to the entire class on their communications plan.

Take Action Have students write health department officials about different ways the department can get the word out about a disease.

✓ Assessment

The press release should contain information on the signs and symptoms of the disease, how the disease is transmitted, and any cures or treatments.

Media Messages on Emerging Infections

Government agencies such as the Centers for Disease Control and Prevention (CDC) are responsible for getting important health information to the public. A particular challenge for these agencies is alerting the public to information about emerging infections, such as dengue fever, West Nile virus, and anthrax. These agencies use press releases as part of a media campaign to pass this information to as many people as possible.

———— DESIGN A LOGO FOR YOUR TEAM AND PLACE HERE

PRESS RELEASE   for immediate release

INCLUDE THE DATE HERE

Name of your City

Your PRESS RELEASE should include all the important information you want people to know about the disease.

————◄— WHOM TO CONTACT IF A REPORTER HAS QUESTIONS OR WANTS TO INTERVIEW SOMEONE SHOULD GO HERE

————◄— INCLUDE A PHONE NUMBER

ACTIVITY

Research one of the emerging diseases that recently have been identified in the United States. Pretend you are on a communications team at the CDC whose job it is to let as many people as possible know about that disease. Begin with a press release, following the example shown above. Design a media campaign to notify the public about the health risks of the disease, what causes the disease, how it is transmitted, and how the disease is treated or prevented.

EXPRESS YOUR VIEWS

Write to your local health department, and ask about its role in responding to the emerging disease you've researched. Find out whether there is a community program that provides information about the disease and whether there is something you and your classmates can do to help spread the word.

More About...

Emerging Infections Some of the emerging diseases could be linked to bioterrorism in the information gathered by the students. For example, the CDC posts information on emerging diseases on a Web page called Public Health Emergency Preparedness and Response. Tell students that they need to be careful about not inducing a sense of panic with their press release.

The tone should be factual. You might guide them if they have picked a disease that is linked to an act or acts of bioterrorism. Suggest that they can include a statement in their press release warning the public: If they believe they have been exposed to such a biological agent, then they should contact their local health department or local law enforcement agency.

CROSS-CURRICULUM CONNECTIONS

Tell a Story. Develop a story that is suitable for retelling aloud and is based on your own experience with one of the common childhood diseases mentioned in this chapter (flu, strep throat, chicken pox, measles, or the common cold). Use the story as a means of teaching your audience about how they can help prevent the spread of such diseases.

Calculate Bacteria Growth. Bacteria can grow rapidly under the right conditions. Some can duplicate themselves every 20 minutes. Calculate how many bacteria would be produced in four hours if a single bacterium reproduced at this rate.

Write a Report. Plague is a communicable disease that had a significant impact on world history, especially European history during the fourteenth century. Using reliable resources, research this disease and its impact during this period of history. Include the plague's causes, symptoms, and effects on society. Be sure to explain how the disease changed people's attitudes and became part of Renaissance folklore.

Create a Visual Display. Choose a vector-borne disease and find out about the life cycle of the pathogen that causes it. Create a display that illustrates the life cycle. Include information about how it is transmitted from host to host. Post the display in your classroom.

Epidemiologist

Did you ever wonder why and how diseases move the way they do? Why is the incidence of a particular disease suddenly on the increase? If these questions interest you, consider a career as an epidemiologist.

Epidemiology is a branch of medical science that deals with the incidence, distribution, and control of disease. Epidemiologists complete at least six years of college, studying science, human behavior, and biostatistics. They usually work in a university, research facility, or public health department. People who want to become epidemiologists should be logical, patient, organized, and curious. Find out more about epidemiology and other health careers by clicking on Career Corner at **health.glencoe.com**.

Chapter 24   Review   **643**

Portfolio Assessment

Self-Evaluation Direct students to review the Health Skills Activities and other activities completed in the chapter. Encourage each student to select one finished product or activity that demonstrates his or her best work for the chapter and that represents the student's learning goals. Have students explain what they have learned and how the examples they have selected demonstrate their growth in health literacy, knowledge, and skills.

Teacher Classroom Resources Assign Performance Assessment 24, "Victory for Vaccines," in the TCR.

CROSS-CURRICULUM CONNECTIONS

Enrich student learning by connecting the topic of communicable diseases to one of the four subject areas presented on this page. The activity may be completed individually or with a partner.

Language Arts Remind students that oral storytelling is not memorizing written words. Instruct students to keep notes rather than writing their stories out word for word. Their note cards should contain pertinent points and should be used only as a reference. Encourage students to practice telling their stories with a partner before sharing with the rest of the class.

Social Studies Direct students to resources such as history books, the Internet, medical journals, and other reliable sources.

Math Answer: 60 min/20 min = 3 duplications per hour 3 × 4 hours = 12

Science Student displays should illustrate the replication of the pathogen and the means of tranmission in the human population. Stages of the life cycle should be clearly labeled.

Have students read the Career Corner feature. Ask interested students to explore the Glencoe Health Web site at **health.glencoe.com** for more information on this topic.

Chapter 24 *Review*

CHECKING COMPREHENSION

- Assign and discuss the chapter review.
- Use Chapter 24 MindJogger Videoquiz to review the chapter. ▣◖

CHAPTER 24 REVIEW ANSWERS

Exploring Health Terms

1. pathogen
2. toxin
3. vector
4. inflammatory response
5. phagocyte
6. immunity
7. pneumonia
8. jaundice
9. True

Recalling the Facts

1. Some help produce vitamins and digest food; others cause disease.

2. Pathogens in saliva or mucus can be deposited directly into another person's eyes, nose, or mouth; the saliva or mucus can evaporate, and the pathogen can be carried in the air.

3. Handwashing will remove pathogens from the hands, reducing the spread of disease by direct contact or through contamination of food or surfaces.

4. They trap pathogens and carry them to areas of the body where they can be disposed.

5. Antibodies are produced in response to antigens.

6. Vaccines cause the body to produce antibodies without actually causing the disease. Vaccines have greatly reduced the incidence of many diseases.

► EXPLORING HEALTH TERMS *Answer the following questions on a sheet of paper.*

Lesson 1 *Match each definition with the correct term.*

| communicable disease | pathogen |
| toxin | vector |

1. A microscopic organism that causes disease.
2. A substance that kills cells or interferes with their function.
3. An organism that carries and transmits pathogens to humans or other animals.

Lesson 2 *Fill in the blanks with the correct term.*

antibody	antigen
immune system	immunity
inflammatory response	lymphocyte
phagocyte	vaccine

4. The swelling and pain that accompanies an injury such as a splinter is part of the body's _____ .
5. A white blood cell that attacks an invading pathogens is a(n) _____ .
6. The state of being protected against a particular disease is _____ .

Lesson 3 *Identify each sentence as True or False. If false, replace the underlined term with the correct term.*

| emerging infection | jaundice |
| pneumonia | |

7. <u>Jaundice</u> can be a complication of the flu.
8. A person with <u>pneumonia</u> will have skin and eyes that are slightly yellow.
9. An <u>emerging infection</u> is an infectious disease that has become more common within the past two decades or that threatens to increase in the near future.

► RECALLING THE FACTS *Use complete sentences to answer the following questions.*

Lesson 1

1. What is one way that some bacteria are helpful to the human body? How do some bacteria harm the body?
2. How do pathogens spread when a person sneezes?
3. Analyze how handwashing can help prevent communicable diseases from spreading.

Lesson 2

4. How do mucous membranes help fight pathogens?
5. How are antibodies and antigens related?
6. Describe how vaccines work, and evaluate their impact on disease prevention.
7. Explain how technology, such as the development of vaccines, has impacted the health status of individuals, families, communities, and the world in the prevention of communicable disease.

Lesson 3

8. With what do the air sacs in the lungs fill in a person infected with pneumonia?
9. What healthful behaviors will reduce your risk of contracting hepatitis A, B, and C?
10. Identify three emerging infections.

7. Vaccines have reduced disabilities, illnesses, and deaths from communicable diseases worldwide, improving the quality of life and increasing the average life span.

8. Pus and other liquids.

9. Hepatitis A: Wash hands and avoid people who are infected; Hepatitis B and C: avoid sexual contact and drug use, sharing personal items that could have trace amounts of blood or saliva, and exposure to contaminated needles.

10. Any three: malaria, tuberculosis, some strains of strep, Dengue fever, smallpox, anthrax, West Nile encephalitis, Lyme disease, Ebola.

➤ THINKING CRITICALLY

1. **Applying.** Imagine that you are a pathogen living in the lungs of an infected person. Write a story about your journey as you leave your host through a sneeze. Tell what happens to you and your fellow pathogens as you travel through the air and land on another individual. *(LESSON 1)*

2. **Analyzing.** Compare and contrast the function of phagocytes in the inflammatory response with the function of specific lymphocytes in the immune response. *(LESSON 2)*

3. **Synthesizing.** Suppose that several people in a community have a disease that is spreading rapidly. If you were a public health worker assigned the task of finding out how the disease is being transmitted, what might you do to find the cause? *(LESSON 3)*

➤ HEALTH SKILLS APPLICATION

1. **Goal Setting.** Identify three things you can do to lower your risk of contracting a communicable disease. Make a plan to incorporate these strategies into your daily life. Prepare a "Staying Healthy" checklist that gives strategies you can use to reduce the number of infections. *(LESSON 1)*

2. **Advocacy.** Check with state and local governments to find out what immunizations are required for admission to schools at various levels from preschool through college. Use this information to create a public service pamphlet that explains why immunizations are important. *(LESSON 2)*

3. **Accessing Information.** Visit **health.glencoe.com** to link to a site on communicable diseases. Choose one of the diseases to research, and create a poster on your chosen disease. Be sure to include information about what symptoms accompany the disease, how it is transmitted, what lasting effects it can have on the body, what the trends are, who is most at risk, and whether a cure or an effective treatment is available. If a vaccination is under development for this disease, include information on that as well. You should also include a section with tips on protecting yourself against this disease. *(LESSON 3)*

BEYOND *the* Classroom

Parent Involvement

Advocacy. Many diseases and emerging infections are spread by vectors. Contact a state or local health department to determine which vector-borne diseases occur most often in the state in which you live. Choose one of these diseases, and interview a local public health official about precautions that can be taken to avoid infection. Be sure to ask what treatments are available to an infected person. Prepare a fact sheet with this information, including a picture of the vector.

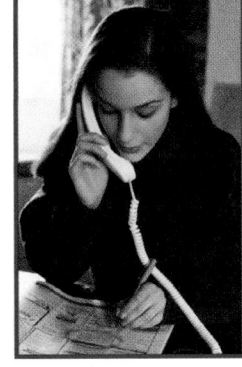

School and Community

Vaccine clinics. Gather information about clinics and other public sites where free or low-cost flu vaccines are offered. Prepare a flyer that explains the need for this immunization. Include the dates, times, and locations for these vaccination opportunities.

Chapter 24 Review **645**

Thinking Critically

1. Students' stories should include examples of direct contact and indirect contact as well as airborne transmission.

2. Both are white blood cells that destroy pathogens. Lymphocytes produce specific antibodies that remain in blood. Phagocytes engulf and destroy pathogens.

3. Possible answers: Determine how the disease is spread, investigate whether the infected individuals shared any common objects or general area, investigate whether vectors were involved in the transmission.

Health Skills Application

1.–3. Answers will vary.

EVALUATE

- Use the reproducible Chapter 24 Test in the TCR, or construct your own using the Testmaker software. ☞ ◉
- Use Performance Assessment 24 in the TCR. ☞

ENRICHMENT

Ask students to complete Enrichment Activity 24 in the TCR. ☞

BEYOND *the* Classroom

Keep students involved in the community, and encourage parent participation by assigning the activities on this page for students to work on outside of class.

Lessons	Standards		Features
	National	State/Local	
1 **The Risks of STIs** *pages 648-651*	National Health Education Standards **1.1, 3.3, 6.1, 7.4**		**Hands-On Health** • The Benefits of Abstinence *(Analyzing Influences)*, page 650
2 **Common STIs** *pages 652-657*	National Health Education Standards **1.6, 1.7, 3.1, 6.3, 7.1**		**Health Skills Activity** • Lines of Defense *(Refusal Skills)*, page 657
3 **HIV and AIDS** *pages 658-661*	National Health Education Standards **1.3, 3.3, 5.6, 6.1**		**Real-Life Application** • HIV in Teens *(Advocacy)*, page 660
4 **Treatment for HIV and AIDS** *pages 662-667*	National Health Education Standards **1.8, 2.5, 3.1, 3.4, 7.2**		**Exploring Issues** • Should More Money Be Spent on AIDS Research and Treatment? Page 666

Reproducible Resources	Assessment	Technology
Student Activity Workbook for use with each chapter	📁 Lesson Quiz 91	🕹 Transparency 72
📁 Concept Mapping Activity 91		💿 TeacherWorks®
📁 Decision-Making Activity 25		💻 Internet Activities
📁 Guided Reading Activities 91		
📁 Health Lab 25		
📁 Lesson Plan 91		
📁 Parent Letter and Activities 25		
📁 Reteaching Activity 91		
📁 Concept Mapping Activity 92	📁 Lesson Quiz 92	🕹 Transparency 73
📁 Cross-Curriculum Activity 25		💿 TeacherWorks®
📁 Enrichment Activity 25		
📁 Guided Reading Activities 92		
📁 Lesson Plan 92		
📁 Reteaching Activity 92		
📁 Concept Mapping Activity 93	📁 Lesson Quiz 93	🕹 Transparency 74
📁 Current Health Issues 25		💿 TeacherWorks®
📁 Guided Reading Activities 93		
📁 Lesson Plan 93		
📁 Reteaching Activity 93		
📁 Concept Mapping Activity 94	📁 Lesson Quiz 94	💿 TeacherWorks®
📁 Guided Reading Activities 94		
📁 Lesson Plan 94		
📁 Reteaching Activity 94		

⏲ OUT OF TIME

If time does not permit teaching the entire chapter, use:
- Hand-On-Health, p. 650
- Figure 25.1, p. 653
- Health Skills Activity, p. 657
- Figure 25.3, p. 659
- Real-Life Application, p. 660
- Figure 25.4, p. 664–665

Language Diversity

- 🎧 English Audio CD Program
- 🎧 Spanish Audio CD Program
- 📁 English Summaries, Quizzes, and Activities
- 📁 Spanish Summaries, Quizzes, and Activities
- 📁 Spanish Parent Letters and Activities

End of Chapter Assessment

Blackline Masters
- 📁 Chapter 25 Test
- 📁 Performance Assessment Activity 25

Technology
- 💿 Vocabulary PuzzleMaker
- 📼 MindJogger VideoQuiz
- 💿 **Exam***View*® Pro Testmaker

Professional Health Series

Dealing with Sensitive Issues
Planning a Coordinated School Health Program
Promoting Character Education
Home, School, and Community Involvement

CHAPTER OVERVIEW

Chapter 25 presents the incidence, symptoms, diagnoses, and treatments for common STIs including HIV/AIDS. Abstinence from sexual activity before marriage as the best means of preventing infection is emphasized.

Lesson 1 Incidence and high-risk behaviors in teens for STIs are presented. STIs can lead to serious consequences. Abstinence is emphasized as the only method that is 100 percent effective in preventing STIs.

Lesson 2 The symptoms, diagnoses, and treatments for several STIs are presented. Infected individuals have a responsibility to get treatment and notify contacts. With HIV it is the law.

Lesson 3 HIV attacks the immune system. Behaviors that transmit HIV and those that reduce the risk are discussed.

Lesson 4 HIV infection progresses through several stages. Testing and treatment is discussed. Teens should practice prevention by staying informed and avoiding high-risk behaviors.

Health Skills Features

- Hands-On Health (*Analyzing Influences*), p. 650
- Health Skills Activity (*Refusal Skills*), p. 657
- Real-Life Application (*Advocacy*), p. 660
- Exploring Issues (*Accessing Information*), p. 666

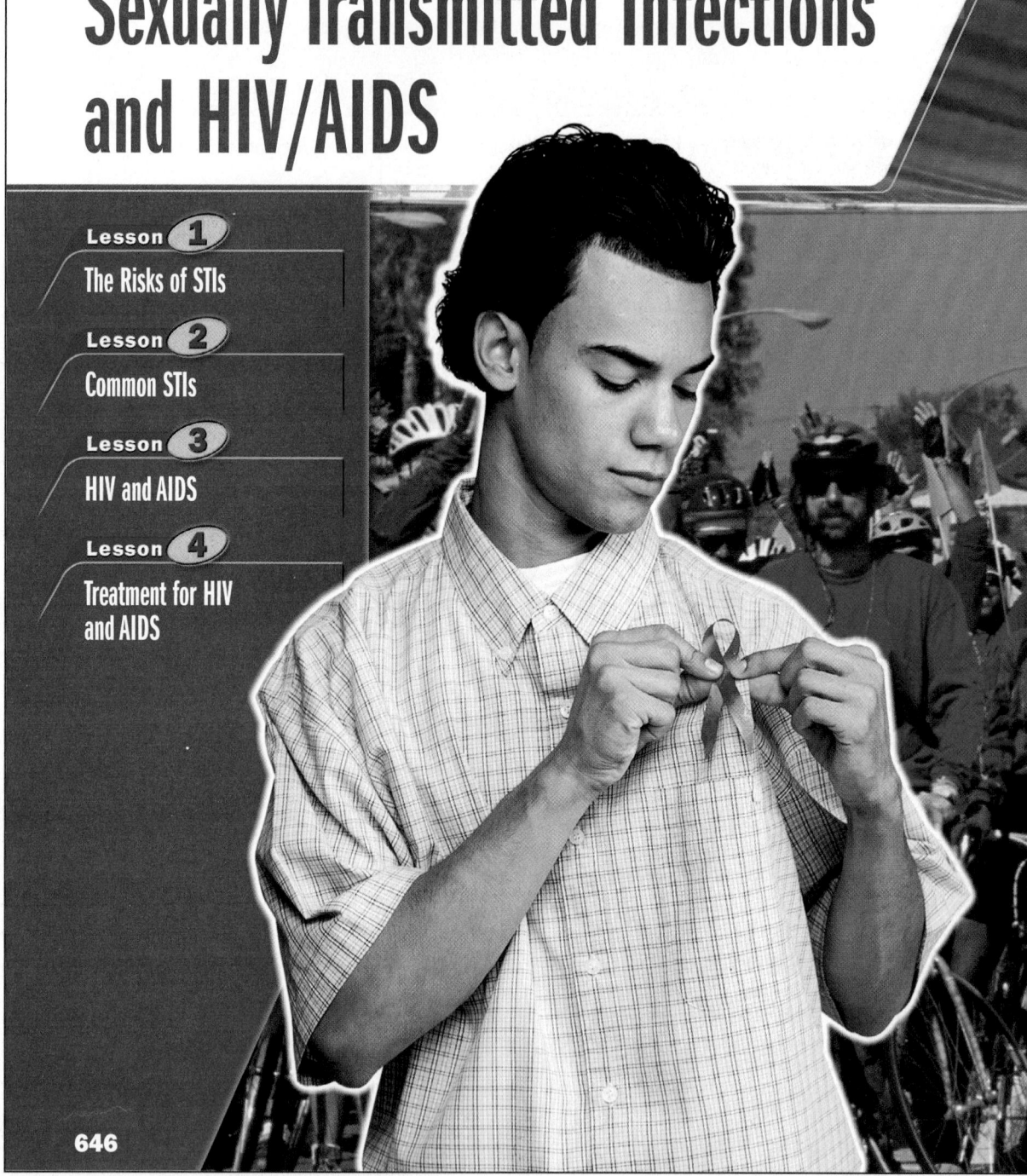

Chapter 25

Sexually Transmitted Infections and HIV/AIDS

Lesson 1
The Risks of STIs

Lesson 2
Common STIs

Lesson 3
HIV and AIDS

Lesson 4
Treatment for HIV and AIDS

646

MEETING STUDENT DIVERSITY

Language Diversity Use the following suggestions to help students who have difficulty with English:

- Pair English language learners with native speakers of English who can restate the Chapter Summary in language that helps students comprehend important concepts.

- 🎧 Direct auditory learners or those students with language diversity to the *Glencoe Health Audio CD Program.* Available in English and Spanish, this component provides an audio and written summary of the chapter.

- Use photographs, drawings, or magazine clippings to help students visualize the important concepts of the chapter.

AIDS Ride

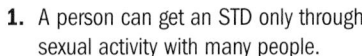

Myth or Fact?

Read each statement below and respond by writing myth or fact for each item.

1. A person can get an STD only through sexual activity with many people.

2. Abstinence from sexual activity is 100 percent effective in preventing STDs and the sexual transmission of HIV and hepatitis B.

3. All STDs can be cured with antibiotics.

4. Anyone with an STD will have symptoms.

5. Many cases of HIV/AIDS go unreported.

6. A person can have only one type of STD at a time.

7. After a person has been treated for an STD, he or she can't get it again.

8. Untreated STDs can lead to difficulty in having children.

9. Some STDs, including HIV/AIDS, can be fatal.

10. Nationwide, STDs are on the rise among teens.

Keep your responses for review later in the chapter. When you complete the chapter, review this list of myths and facts again. If necessary, change your answers according to what you have learned.

Quick Write

Using Visuals. HIV/AIDS awareness and understanding the dangers of STDs can help prevent the spread of these infections. What can you do to participate in fund-raisers and awareness campaigns for HIV/AIDS research?

647

INTRODUCING THE CHAPTER

Myth or Fact?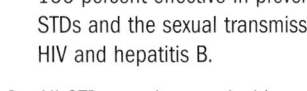

Let a volunteer read aloud the title of the feature on this page. Ask: Why is it important to know the facts about STDs? How can recognizing myths about STDs help you protect your health? Have students write and then discuss their responses.

1. Myth: People can get an STD from one sexual contact.

2. Fact

3. Myth: Some types of STDs are incurable and last a lifetime.

4. Myth: Some STDs have no symptoms, especially early on.

5. Fact

6. Myth: A person can have several STDs at one time.

7. Myth: People do not become immune to most STDs. (Some people do develop immunity to hepatitis B.)

8. Fact

9. Fact

10. Fact

Quick write

Have students write their responses to the QuickWrite question. Guide them in recognizing that, if a person has no symptoms, he or she will not seek medical attention and treatment. The infected person may continue to spread the infection to others.

TECHNOLOGY OPTIONS

MINDJOGGER
VIDEOQUIZ

To preview or review chapter content, you may wish to use the Chapter 25 MindJogger Videoquiz.

HEALTH Online

Online Resources for the Teacher For a fresh approach to health topics and an in-depth look at health issues, use these online resources found under Teacher Resources at **health.glencoe.com:**

• Block Schedule Lesson Plans
• Technology Projects
• Health Updates

The Risks of STIs

1 FOCUS

 QUICK START Have volunteers give examples of high-risk situations a teen may encounter. Then ask them to state specific health skills and behaviors they would use to make a healthful decision in response to each situation.

TYING TO PRIOR KNOWLEDGE

Ask students to identify some of the benefits of abstinence from sexual activity before marriage. Point out that abstinence is the only means to prevent getting an STD. Explain that they will learn more about STDs in this chapter.

Health Skills Features

"The Benefits of Abstinence," p. 651

ANALYZING INFLUENCES

INTRODUCING VOCABULARY

- Have students use their knowledge of the word *epidemic* to write why STDs have become an epidemic in the United States.

- Ask students to complete the Chapter 25 Study Guide in the *Student Activity Workbook.* 📁

The Risks of STIs

VOCABULARY

sexually transmitted diseases (STDs)
sexually transmitted infections (STIs)
epidemics
abstinence

YOU'LL LEARN TO

- Explain the relationship between alcohol and other drugs used by adolescents and the role these substances play in STDs.

- Analyze the importance and benefits of abstinence as it relates to the prevention of STDs.

- Discuss abstinence from sexual activity as the only method that is 100 percent effective in preventing STDs.

- Develop and analyze strategies related to the prevention of STDs.

 QUICK START Your health is affected by the decisions you make regarding risk behaviors. What strategies do you use to help you make responsible decisions?

 STDs are the most common communicable diseases in the United States. *Why do you think this has been called the hidden epidemic?*

Some communicable diseases, such as the cold or flu, can be transmitted through actions as simple as shaking hands. Other communicable diseases are not so easily spread. **Sexually transmitted diseases (STDs)**, also referred to as **sexually transmitted infections (STIs)**, are *infectious diseases spread from person to person through sexual contact*. A person can have an infection, and pass the infection to others, without necessarily having the disease.

STDs: The Hidden Epidemic

Throughout history people have been faced with **epidemics**, *occurrences of diseases in which many people in the same place at the same time are affected*. Today in the United States, we are now facing another epidemic—an epidemic of STDs. An estimated 65 million people in the United States are living with an incurable STD. Many of these cases go undiagnosed and untreated. Why?

Lesson 1 *Resources*

Teacher Classroom Resources

📁 Concept Mapping Activity 91
📁 Decision-Making Activity 25
📁 Guided Reading Activities 91
📁 Health Lab 25
📁 Lesson Plan 91
📁 Lesson Quiz 91

📁 Parent Letter and Activities 25
📁 Reteaching Activity 91

Student Activity Workbook

📁 Applying Health Skills 91
📁 Chapter 25 Study Guide

Multimedia

 Transparency 72

► Many people with STDs are asymptomatic—without symptoms. They do not seek treatment because they don't know they are infected. Individuals who don't know that they are infected can continue to transmit STDs. Some people who suspect they have an STD may be too embarrassed to seek treatment.

► Even when STDs are diagnosed, they may not be reported to health departments so that contacts can be notified and treated. These contacts can continue to unknowingly transmit the disease to others.

High-Risk Behavior and STDs

In the United States teens make up one quarter of the estimated 15 million new cases of STDs each year. That's more than 10,000 young people infected every day. Why are teens at particularly high risk for infection from STDs? Teens who are sexually active are likely to engage in one or more of the following high-risk behaviors:

► **Being sexually active with more than one person.** This includes having a series of sexual relationships with one person at a time. However, being sexually active with even one partner puts a person at risk. Most teens are unaware of a partner's past behavior and whether he or she already has an STD.

► **Engaging in unprotected sex.** Barrier protection is not 100 percent effective in preventing the transmission of STDs, and it is not effective at all against HPV—the human papillomavirus. Abstinence from sexual activity is the only method that is 100 percent effective in preventing STDs.

► **Selecting high-risk partners.** Such partners include those with a history of being sexually active with more than one person and those who have injected illegal drugs.

► **Using alcohol and other drugs.** Alcohol use can lower inhibitions. In a recent survey, more than 25 percent of teens who engaged in sexual activity had been under the influence of alcohol or drug use.

Ⓥ Avoid high-risk behaviors by forming friendships with people who share your commitment to abstinence.

Lesson 1 The Risks of STIs **649**

2 TEACH

Discussing

Guide a class discussion of how STDs are spread from one person to another through sexual contact. Discuss ways to prevent their spread. L1

Activity

Read aloud the following: You and a date go to a party. You become aware that several people at the party are using drugs. Your date says, "I've always been interested in trying that stuff. It would be fun doing it with you." With a partner, list refusal skills you would use in this situation. L1

Discussing

Explain that sexually transmitted diseases are also referred to as sexually transmitted *infections* because the CDC and prevention experts feel that people are more likely to consider themselves susceptible to an infection than a disease. Experts hope the word change might lead to more people seeking testing and treatment. L1

Community Involvement

Suggest that students send for materials from the local health department and area health clinics to prepare posters and a bulletin board on STDs. Students might also download information from the Internet. L1

Promoting Coordinated School Health

Community Support Tapping into local resources is a key to effectively working a comprehensive school health plan. It is important to involve local health agencies, parents, churches, youth groups, and other organizations. By enlisting local groups and individuals, the committee establishes grass roots support. Community involvement provides the resources and support needed to reduce fragmentation of efforts or duplication of programs. Ongoing collaboration and cooperation between the team and other community members prevent unwarranted controversy. For information about community support, consult *Planning a Coordinated School Health Program.*

The Consequences of STDs

Most people, including teens, are not fully aware of the consequences of STDs. These are serious infections that can dramatically change the course of a person's life.

▶ **Some STDs are incurable.** The pathogens that cause these STDs cannot be eliminated from the body by medical treatment, such as antibiotics. The viruses that cause genital herpes and AIDS (the human immunodeficiency virus, or HIV), for example, remain in the body for life.

▶ **Some STDs cause cancer.** The hepatitis B virus can cause cancer of the liver. The human papillomavirus (HPV) can cause cancer of the cervix. These STDs also cannot be cured and may last a lifetime.

Hands-On Health

THE BENEFITS OF ABSTINENCE

ADVOCACY

NHES Standard 7 Students will demonstrate the ability to advocate for personal, family, and community health.

Objectives

• Analyze the importance and benefits of abstinence as it relates to the prevention of STDs.

• Influence peers to practice abstinence.

Motivator

Have students discuss the answer to this question: Can a person get an STD the first time he or she engages in sexual activity?

Teaching Strategies

1. Have students review the consequences of STDs in the text.

2. To make a paper cube, draw the shape shown here. Cut along outside edges. Fold along dotted lines. Glue tabs.

Hands-On Health ACTIVITY

The Benefits of Abstinence

Practicing abstinence from sexual activity can benefit you in many ways. By encouraging your friends to abstain, you can be a positive influence on their health and well-being.

What You'll Need

• paper and pencil
• number cube (one for each group)
• paper cup (one for each group)
• construction paper
• markers

What You'll Do

1. Roll the cube from the cup onto your desk five times and record each number. Complete the following steps at your teacher's instruction.

2. Stand if you rolled one 5. Imagine that you have just found out that you have an STD. Tell how this will affect your life now and in the future.

3. Stand if you rolled a 5 more than once. Tell what you think and how you feel about having more than one STD.

4. As a class, brainstorm reasons for practicing abstinence.

5. Work in small groups to cut out a sheet of construction paper as your teacher instructs.

6. Write a different reason to practice abstinence on each of the six sides of the paper. Target the message to teens and be persuasive.

7. Fold and tape the paper to form a cube, then hang the cube from the ceiling.

Apply and Conclude

Imagine how you want your life to be in five years. Write it down. Be specific. Add how practicing abstinence now can help you achieve the life you want.

650 **Chapter 25** Sexually Transmitted Infections and HIV/AIDS

Assessment

Using a rubric, student work should provide comprehensive evidence of the following criteria to achieve the highest score:

✔ a clear, health-enhancing stand
✔ support for the position with relevant information
✔ awareness of the audience
✔ encouragement of others to make healthful choices
✔ passion/conviction

HEALTH LITERACY

Health Behaviors While most agents that cause STDs die outside the warm, moist environment of the human body, the herpes virus can survive outside the body on surfaces such as toilet seats and towels. Although it can survive for only a few hours, it is not known whether contact with the virus by touching such items can cause infection. Thus, it is better to take precautions, such as using seat covers and washing hands properly, when using public facilities.

▶ **Some STDs can cause complications that affect the ability to reproduce.** Females can develop pelvic inflammatory disease (PID), which damages reproductive organs and can cause sterility.

▶ **Some STDs can be passed from an infected female to her child before, during, or after birth.** STDs can damage the bones, nervous system, and brain of a fetus. Premature births can result, and infants infected with STDs at delivery may become blind or develop pneumonia and some may die.

Preventing STDs Through Abstinence

You may have experienced how an action that has a result demonstrates a cause-and-effect relationship. Touching a hot stove, for example, is the *cause* of sustaining a burn, which is the *result*.

A clear cause-and-effect relationship exists between sexual intercourse in any form and sexually transmitted infection. If you have sexual contact with an infected person, you put yourself at risk of being infected with an STD. Sexual activity is the cause—an STD is the effect.

You can prevent exposure to STDs by practicing **abstinence** from sexual activity and using refusal skills to avoid situations in which you may be at risk. Choose friends who are abstinent and who support your decision to abstain.

HEALTH Online

Investigate facts about the rise in hepatitis B in an article from Health Updates at **health.glencoe.com.**

hot link

abstinence For more information on abstinence, see Chapter 12, page 318.

 ## Lesson 1 *Review*

Reviewing Facts and Vocabulary

1. Identify three reasons why teens are at high risk for getting an STD.

2. Explain the relationship between alcohol use as a high-risk behavior in regard to sexual activity and the risk of STDs.

3. How are refusal skills related to the prevention of STDs?

Thinking Critically

4. **Analyzing.** Analyze, discuss, and communicate the importance and benefits of abstinence as it relates to the prevention of STDs.

5. **Evaluating.** Explain and discuss why abstinence from sexual activity is the only method that is 100 percent effective in preventing STDs.

Applying Health Skills

Advocacy. Write an article for your school newspaper to inform students about the STD epidemic. Include the negative consequences that can affect a person's life, as well as strategies for avoiding STDs.

TECHNOLOGY OPTION

WEB SITES   Use the article you wrote as the basis for a Web page. See **health.glencoe.com** for help in planning and building your own Web site.

Lesson 1 The Risks of STIs   **651**

EVALUATING THE LESSON

Assign and discuss the Lesson 1 Review; then administer, grade, and discuss Lesson Quiz 91 in the TCR. 📁

RETEACHING

• Have students outline the lesson, detailing important facts.

• Direct students to list reasons for practicing abstinence as the only reliable means of avoiding becoming infected with an STD.

• Ask students to complete Reteaching Activity 91 in the TCR. 📁

ENRICHMENT

Have students research influences that have shaped and reshaped society's standards of intimate behavior since the Victorian era and determine changes in health and social structure that resulted.

4 CLOSE

Ask students to explain the importance of abstinence for avoiding exposure to STDs.

 ## Lesson 1 *Review*

Answers to Reviewing Facts and Vocabulary

1. Teens who are sexually active are more likely to be sexually active with more than one person, engage in unprotected sex, select high-risk partners, and use alcohol and other drugs.

2. Alcohol use lowers inhibitions, resulting in people taking risks.

3. Abstinence, a refusal skill, prevents infection with an STD.

Answers to Thinking Critically

4.–5. Answers will vary but should reflect an understanding that STDs are transmitted by sexual contact and abstinence from sexual activity before marriage is the only sure way to prevent infection.

Common STIs

Common STIs

1 FOCUS

QUICK START Have students list at least one reason telling the boyfriend about the STD is a responsible decision. Then let students work in groups to develop a response and share the responses with the class.

TYING TO PRIOR KNOWLEDGE

Ask students to explain why the STD epidemic is hidden and how STDs can be prevented. Tell students they will learn more about the symptoms and treatment of STDs in this lesson.

Health Skills Features

"Lines of Defense,"
p. 656

REFUSAL SKILLS

INTRODUCING VOCABULARY

- Have students look up definitions of the terms in their Glossaries. Then have them work in pairs to use the terms and their definitions to create a crossword puzzle.

- Ask students to complete the Chapter 25 Study Guide in the *Student Activity Workbook*.

VOCABULARY

human papillomavirus (HPV)
chlamydia
genital herpes
gonorrhea
trichomoniasis
syphilis

YOU'LL LEARN TO

- Identify symptoms and treatments for some common STDs.

- Identify community health services for getting help with prevention and treatment of STDs.

- Analyze the influence of public health policies and practices on the prevention and treatment of STDs.

- Analyze the harmful effects of STDs on the developing fetus.

QUICK START Suppose you received a letter from a friend telling you that she may have a sexually transmitted disease. Your friend asks your advice as to whether she should tell her boyfriend. Write a short response to the letter.

Learning about STDs can help you avoid the behaviors that lead to infection. *In addition to having accurate information, what else should you know or do to avoid infection from STDs?*

You have already learned why STDs are referred to as a hidden epidemic in the United States, which has the highest rates of STDs in the industrialized world. The Centers for Disease Control and Prevention (CDC) reports that STDs account for more than 85 percent of the most common communicable diseases in the United States. The estimated incidence and prevalence of STDs is shown in **Figure 25.1.** The most important fact to remember is this: The primary means of transmission of STDs is sexual activity. Teens who practice abstinence from sexual activity greatly reduce their risk of contracting STDs.

Human Papillomavirus

The **human papillomavirus**, or HPV, is *a virus that can cause genital warts or asymptomatic infection.* HPV is considered the most common STD in the United States. The CDC estimates that 50 to 75 percent of sexually active males and females acquire HPV infection at some time during their lives. About 30 different types of HPV can infect the genital area.

652 **Chapter 25** Sexually Transmitted Infections and HIV/AIDS

Lesson 2 *Resources*

Teacher Classroom Resources
- Concept Mapping Activity 92
- Cross-Curriculum Activity 25
- Enrichment Activity 25
- Guided Reading Activities 92
- Lesson Plan 92

- Lesson Quiz 92
- Reteaching Activity 92

Student Activity Workbook
- Applying Health Skills 92
- Chapter 25 Study Guide

Multimedia
- Transparency 73

Most types of HPV infections are asymptomatic. A **Pap test** and other medical examinations may detect changes associated with HPV. There is no treatment. However, most asymptomatic HPV infections appear to be temporary and are probably cleared by the immune system. Almost all cases of cervical cancer are caused by certain types of HPV. HPV also can cause cancers of the penis and anus.

Genital Warts

Genital warts are pink or reddish warts with cauliflowerlike tops that appear on the genitals, the vagina, or the cervix one to three months after infection from HPV. Genital warts are highly contagious, and are spread by any form of sexual contact with an infected person. It may take up to three months for warts to appear, but they often disappear, even without treatment. Diagnosis is determined by a health care worker by examination of the warts. If a person suspects he or she has been infected, examination and treatment are essential, because once infected, a person has the virus for the rest of his or her life. Treatments can rid the body of the warts but not the virus. Complications of HPV and genital warts can result in cervical cancer and cancer of the penis. Infants born to females infected with HPV may develop warts in their throats, obstructing the breathing passages, which can be life-threatening.

hotlink

Pap test For more information about the Pap test and the health of the reproductive systems, see Chapter 18, page 477.

2 TEACH

Explaining

Use the concepts of incidence and prevalence to help students understand the nature of STDs by applying them to a disease that has symptoms and is short-lived, such as measles. Ask students how many people in the class have a cold at least once a year (incidence) and how many have a cold on any given day (prevalence)? Answers will vary, but the incidence should be greater than the prevalence. **L1**

VISUAL LEARNING

Figure 25.1 Direct students to study the figure. Ask:

- What do you notice about the prevalence and incidence of most STDs? The prevalence is greater than the incidence.
- What are the reasons for this? STDs commonly do not have symptoms; so people do not know to seek treatment and may have the infection a long time. Many STDs are incurable; people cannot get rid of them like a cold. **L1**

Cooperative Learning

Ask students to form debate groups. Help them prepare to debate whether tests for STDs should be required during all physical examinations by a physician. **L2** **Verbal/ Linguistic Intelligence**

FIGURE 25.1

ESTIMATED INCIDENCE AND PREVALENCE OF STDs IN THE UNITED STATES

STD	Incidence (Estimated number of new cases every year)	Prevalence (Estimated number of people currently infected)
Human Papillomavirus (HPV)	5.5 million	20 million
Chlamydia	3 million	2 million
Genital Herpes	1 million	45 million
Gonorrhea	650,000	Not Available
Trichomoniasis	5 million	Not Available
Syphilis	70,000	Not Available
Hepatitis B	120,000	417,000

Source: CDC, Tracking the Hidden Epidemics. Trends in STDs in the United States 2000

Lesson 2 Common STIs **653**

More About...

PID Pelvic inflammatory disease is caused by untreated chlamydia or gonorrhea in females. This disease can lead to reproductive damage by causing obstruction and scarring of the fallopian tubes, resulting in involuntary infertility. Thousands of females are affected each year by PID. In addition, females who have had PID are more likely to experience ectopic pregnancies. An ectopic pregnancy occurs when the fallopian tubes are partially blocked and a fertilized egg becomes implanted in one of the tubes rather than in the uterus. As the cells multiply, there is danger of rupturing the fallopian tube. This can result in severe hemorrhaging, and death may result if surgery is not begun immediately.

Critical Thinking

Ask students to compare and contrast the symptoms of chlamydia in males and in females. Have them list reasons a female with chlamydia is less likely than a male to exhibit signs of the disease until it is in an advanced stage. **L1**

Activity

Remind students that, although antibiotics can cure some STDs, some pathogens that cause STDs have developed resistance to certain antibiotics. For example, older, less expensive antibiotics, such as penicillin, are not currently recommended for treating gonorrhea because of widespread drug resistance. Have students write a paragraph about the problems that antibiotic resistance to STDs poses to individuals and to society. Have them proofread their writing for spelling and grammatical errors before submitting a final draft. **L3**

FYI

Genital herpes is more common in women than men, infecting approximately one out of four women versus one out of five men. This difference in gender may be because male-to-female transmission is more efficient than female-to-male transmission.

Community Involvement

Ask students to research the effects of STDs on an unborn child. Contact the March of Dimes for information related to birth defects and other conditions related to STDs and newborns. **L2**

---

hot link

urethra For more information about the male reproductive system, see Chapter 18, page 470.

Mothers have a responsibility to protect their infants from exposure to STDs during pregnancy as well as during breast-feeding. *Which STDs can be transmitted from a mother to her child during pregnancy or birth?*

Chlamydia

Chlamydia is *a bacterial infection that affects the reproductive organs of both males and females.* Forty percent of cases are reported in teens 15 to 19 years old. Chlamydia is asymptomatic, meaning there are no visible symptoms, in 75 percent of infected females and 50 percent of infected males. When symptoms are present, males may experience a discharge from the penis and burning upon urination. Females may have vaginal discharge, burning upon urination, or abdominal pain. Chlamydia is diagnosed by laboratory examination of secretions from the cervix in females or from the **urethra** in males. It can be treated with antibiotics, but no immunity develops, so a person can become infected again.

Because chlamydia is usually asymptomatic, it often goes undetected until serious complications occur. In females who are untreated, the infection can cause pelvic inflammatory disease (PID) and lead to chronic (long-term) pelvic pain or infertility. Untreated chlamydia also can lead to infertility in males. Chlamydia can cause premature birth, and infants born to infected females may develop eye disease or pneumonia.

Genital Herpes

Genital herpes is *an STD caused by the herpes simplex virus (HSV).* There are two types of HSV:

▶ Type 1 usually causes cold sores.

▶ Type 2 usually causes genital sores.

However, both types can infect the mouth and the genitals. Nationwide, about 20 percent of the total adolescent population is infected with the virus. Genital herpes is twice as common in adults from 20 to 29 years old today as it was 20 years ago.

Most individuals who have genital herpes are asymptomatic and are not aware that they are infected. Those who do show symptoms typically have blisterlike sores in the genital area that occur periodically. It is not true that the virus can be spread only when blisters are present; the virus can spread in the absence of symptoms. Diagnosis is made through laboratory tests on the fluid from the blisters. Medication can relieve the symptoms, but cannot cure herpes infection—once contracted, the virus remains in the body for life.

The herpes virus is potentially fatal for infants who contract the virus from their mothers at the time of delivery. The virus may also play a major role in the spread of HIV by making people who are infected with herpes more capable of transmitting or acquiring HIV.

School to Work

Public Health Specialist A person who develops and carries out health education and wellness programs in an effort to reduce communicable diseases is often called a public health specialist. Specialists attend health fairs, support groups, and other gatherings to speak about disease prevention. They perform research on diseases and monitor trends. They also administer surveys and questionnaires. A bachelor's degree in nursing, health care, public relations, marketing, or communications is required. Some specialists hold advanced degrees. Encourage interested students to find out more about the qualifications needed for this career by contacting community groups who may employ specialists and by researching information at their library.

Gonorrhea

Gonorrhea is *a bacterial STD that usually affects mucous membranes*. The highest rates of gonorrhea infection are found in females from 15 to 19 years old and in males from 20 to 24 years old. Symptoms in males include a discharge from the penis and painful urination. Diagnosis in males is made by staining and examining the discharge under a microscope. Approximately 50 percent of females with gonorrhea have no symptoms. Those who do may experience a vaginal discharge and pain or burning upon urination. Diagnosis in females is made by swabbing the cervix and growing the organisms in a laboratory. Gonorrhea can be treated with antibiotics. However, increased resistance to antibiotics can complicate treatment. A person can be reinfected if exposed again to the bacteria. If untreated, gonorrhea can lead to infertility in both males and females. The bacteria can also spread to the bloodstream and cause permanent damage to the joints. Females can pass the infection to their babies during childbirth. Infants born to mothers with gonorrhea can contract eye infections that cause blindness.

Trichomoniasis

Trichomoniasis is *an STD caused by a microscopic protozoan that results in infections of the vagina, urethra, and bladder*. About five million new cases of this disease are estimated to occur every year in the United States. Females may have no symptoms, however the disease may result in **vaginitis,** an inflammation of the vagina characterized by discharge, odor, irritation, and itching. In females trichomoniasis is diagnosed by microscopic examination of the discharge. The organisms can sometimes be seen in a Pap test. Males usually show no symptoms. When symptoms do occur in males, they include mild urethral itching or discharge and burning after urination. Since the disease is difficult to diagnose in males, they are usually treated without laboratory testing if their partners are infected.

Syphilis

Syphilis is *an STD that attacks many parts of the body and is caused by a small bacterium called a spirochete*. The first sign of infection is a painless reddish sore, called a chancre (SHAN-kuhr), at the site of infection. The sore will heal on its own, but if the infection is not treated, it spreads through the blood to other parts of the body. Eventually, the disease can damage internal organs, including the heart, liver, nervous system, and kidneys. If left untreated, the person is at risk of paralysis, convulsions, blindness, and heart disease. Syphilis can be transmitted from a pregnant female to her fetus. An infant infected with syphilis may have a damaged nervous system and can die from the effects.

hot link

vaginitis For more information on diseases of the female reproductive system, see Chapter 18, page 479.

 STDs are caused by bacteria, viruses, and other pathogens. This single-celled protozoan causes trichomoniasis. *Why is it important for people to get tested if they think they may have an STD?*

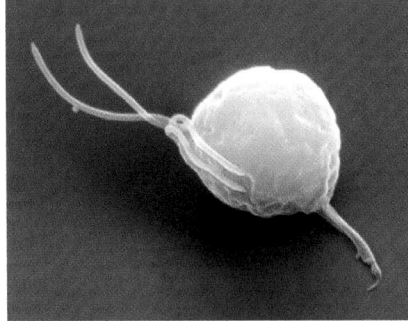

Lesson 2 Common STIs **655**

hot link

Point out that vaginitis often is caused by infections such as bacterial vaginosis; trichomoniasis; and vaginal yeast infection, or candidiasis. Whether yeast infection can be transmitted sexually is unknown. Almost all women have the organism naturally in the vagina, which has made it difficult for researchers to study its transmission. Vaginitis can sometimes have serious complications such as PID and delivery of low-birth-weight infants or premature infants. Assign students to research the different types of vaginitis, their symptoms, and their treatment. **L1**

Reinforcing Concepts

Ask: Why is HSV considered to be a sexually transmitted disease? Sexual activity is the major means of transmission. **L1**

Activity

Have students research how requiring a test for syphilis when applying for a marriage license and during pregnancy has impacted the spread of syphilis in the United States. **L2**

Community Involvement

Instruct students to survey your local area for public health clinics that have facilities for testing for STDs. They should find out which STDs the clinics are required by law to report to the state health department. Have students contact the state health department for the numbers of STDs reported the previous year for the state and for their city or county. **L1**

Home and Community

Educating Peers Have students compile the information about the STDs covered in this chapter into a pamphlet. They should include the symptoms, treatment, and consequences of not getting treatment for an STD. Suggest that the students end with a paragraph about the importance of contacting all present and former sexual partners. The pamphlet should also include a directory of addresses and telephone numbers for local, county, and/or state agencies and free or low-cost clinics that offer confidential treatment for STDs. Encourage them to distribute pamphlets, with permission, in places frequented by teens, such as movie theaters and fast-food restaurants.

FIGURE 25.2

Health Skills Activity

REFUSAL SKILLS

LINES OF DEFENSE

NHES Standard 5 Students will demonstrate the ability to use interpersonal communication skills to enhance health.

Objectives

• Analyze the relationship between the use of refusal skills and the avoidance of unsafe situations such as sexual activity.

• Apply refusal skills to resist peer pressure to engage in sexual activity.

Motivator

Ask students to discuss why the situation suggested by Kyle may make it difficult for Juliana to stick to her decision to practice abstinence.

Teaching Strategies

1. Review examples of refusal skills.
2. Allow students to work in small groups to develop possible responses Juliana could use to refuse Kyle's request. Have groups share their responses.

✓ Assessment

Using a rubric, student work should provide comprehensive evidence of the following criteria to achieve the highest score:

✔ inclusion of the word no in their response
✔ an explanation of why they were refusing
✔ alternatives to the proposed activity
✔ body language they would use to back up their words
✔ a description of walking away from the situation if necessary

OTHER COMMON STDs

Disease (cause)	Symptoms	Treatment	What Could Happen
Chancroid (bacteria)	Sores or bumps on the genitals	Antibiotics	Infection of lymph glands in groin area, and sores
Bacterial vaginosis (bacteria)	Abnormal vaginal discharge, odor, pain, itching, or burning during urination	Antibiotics	In most cases no complications; can lead to PID and premature birth; risk of HIV and STDs
Hepatitis B (virus)	90% of victims are asymptomatic; nausea, vomiting, jaundice, loss of appetite	Antiviral drugs in some cases, but no cure	Chronic infection, cirrhosis of the liver, cancer of the liver
Hepatitis C (blood borne infection)	Often asymptomatic	Antivirual drugs, but no cure	Liver damage, liver disease
Pubic lice (small insects)	Itching, presence of lice and eggs in pubic hair	Medicated soaps; washing all bedding, towels, and clothes	No lasting effects

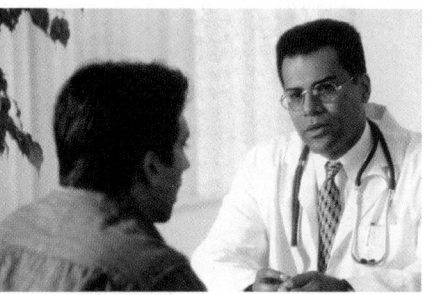

▼ Early detection of STDs is important to avoid serious illness and further spread of the disease. *Why is it important for people not to treat an STD on their own?*

Seeking Treatment

Prevention of STDs is every individual's responsibility. Treatment is also an important personal responsibility. **Figure 25.2** above lists other common STDs, along with their symptoms and the treatment that is usually prescribed for each. As you have read, STDs can cause severe, long-term health problems. Being embarrassed should not stop a person who thinks that he or she may have been exposed to an STD from visiting a private physician or a public health clinic. By law, information about these diseases is kept confidential. Only a health care professional can prescribe the correct treatment, including antibiotics for some STDs.

Individuals also have a social obligation to prevent the spread of infection. Public health clinics sometimes help with contacting current and past partners to make sure they get any needed treatment. Ultimately, however, it is the responsibility of any person infected with an STD to notify everyone with whom he or she has had sexual contact. Informing someone else about the possibility of having an STD could save someone's life.

656 Chapter 25 Sexually Transmitted Infections and HIV/AIDS

Cooperative Learning Activity

Promoting Abstinence Arrange students in small groups, and present this scenario: Imagine that one of your good friends, who is usually talkative and lively, has been quiet and withdrawn lately. Your friend has been dating a classmate. When you ask your friend what's wrong, your friend explains that he or she is being pressured to engage in sexual activity. Ask each group to write a letter to the friend explaining the importance of practicing abstinence. Students should point out the consequences of making high-risk choices and mention the positive goals they want for their friend's future. They should also proofread their letters for errors before submitting a final draft.

Health Skills Activity

Refusal Skills: Lines of Defense

Juliana has been dating Kyle for several months. She has already explained to Kyle that she wants to remain abstinent, and until now he has respected her decision.

Kyle says, "Hey, Jules, let's skip the movie tonight and check out the party at my buddy's house. His folks are gone, and I hear there's going to be a band!"

Juliana responds, "It sounds like fun, but I don't know your buddy and it's pretty far away."

"No problem, I'll protect you!" Kyle laughs. "In fact, we'll finally have a chance to spend some time alone."

Juliana is worried about what might happen.

What Would You Do?

Apply the following refusal skills to write a response to Kyle. Use each refusal skill.

1. Say no in a firm voice.
2. Explain why you are refusing.
3. Suggest alternatives to the proposed activity.
4. Back up your words with body language.
5. Leave if necessary.

 Lesson 2 Review

Reviewing Facts and Vocabulary

1. Which STDs might not present noticeable symptoms?
2. Analyze and explain the harmful effects of two common STDs on fetuses and infants.
3. Where can a person go for treatment of an STD?

Thinking Critically

4. **Compare and Contrast.** Describe symptoms of gonorrhea and genital herpes for males and females.
5. **Analyzing.** Public policies enable health officials to locate and contact sexual partners of people who have been diagnosed with an STD. How do these policies help with the prevention and treatment of STDs?

Applying Health Skills

Refusal Skills. Construct a table similar to the one on page 656. Use this table to list reasons to say no to pressure to engage in sexual activity.

SPREADSHEETS Using spreadsheet software, create a chart to organize the material in your table. See **health.glencoe.com** for information on how to use a spreadsheet.

Lesson 2 Common STIs **657**

 Lesson 2 Review

HIV and AIDS

1 FOCUS

HIV and AIDS

QUICK START   Advise students to think about and write down specific parts of the immune system and explain what happens to each part when potential pathogens enter the body. Then share their responses with the class.

TYING TO PRIOR KNOWLEDGE

Have students recall the reasons for the spread of STDs. Explain that these reasons also apply to the spread of HIV/AIDS. They will learn how the virus that causes AIDS is transmitted and how they can avoid infection.

Health Skills Features

"HIV in Teens,"
p. 660

INTRODUCING VOCABULARY

- Have students use a dictionary to find the meanings of these words or word parts: *acquired, immuno, deficiency, syndrome,* and *opportunistic.*

- Ask students to complete the Chapter 25 Study Guide in the *Student Activity Workbook.*

VOCABULARY
- acquired immune deficiency syndrome (AIDS)
- human immunodeficiency virus (HIV)
- opportunistic infection

YOU'LL LEARN TO
- Explain how HIV affects and destroys the immune system.
- Identify behaviors known to transmit HIV.
- Analyze the relationship between unsafe behaviors, refusal skills, and the risk of HIV.

QUICK START   AIDS is a disease that attacks the immune system. Write two ways that your immune system protects your body from disease.

Health care workers wear goggles, face shields, and disposable gloves whenever they may come in contact with body fluids. *Why are these precautions taken with all patients, not just those known to be infected with HIV?*

In July 1981, an outbreak of a rare form of skin cancer known as Kaposi's (KAY-puh-seez) sarcoma was reported. At the same time, doctors began seeing unusual infections among otherwise healthy individuals. About a year later, the CDC labeled the disease **acquired immune deficiency syndrome** or **AIDS**, *a disease in which the immune system of the patient is weakened.* That year more than 1,600 cases were reported and almost 700 deaths resulted from the newly identified disease. In 1983 the **human immunodeficiency virus**, or **HIV**, *a virus that attacks the immune system*, was confirmed as the cause. In 2000, AIDS was the fifth leading cause of death among adults from 25 to 44 years old.

Teens at Risk

In the United States the overall rate of new cases of HIV infection has fallen slightly since 1985, and new drug therapies help AIDS patients live longer. As a result, some people have a false sense that AIDS is no longer the problem it once was. However, data indicates that although new AIDS cases are declining among the population as a whole, there has been no decline in the number of diagnosed HIV infections among youth from 13 to 24 years old. In fact, teens have one of the fastest growing rates of HIV infection. Many young adults who are currently dying from AIDS were infected in their teens.

Lesson 3 *Resources*

Teacher Classroom Resources
- Concept Mapping Activity 93
- Current Health Issues 25
- Guided Reading Activities 93
- Lesson Plan 93
- Lesson Quiz 93
- Reteaching Activity 93

Student Activity Workbook
- Applying Health Skills 93
- Chapter 25 Study Guide

Multimedia
 Transparency 74

FIGURE 25.3

How HIV Attacks Cells

1. HIV attaches to cell surface.
2. Virus core enters cells and goes to nucleus.
3. Virus makes a copy of its genetic material.
4. New virus assembles at cell surface.
5. New virus breaks away from host cell.

HIV doesn't survive well outside of the human body. *How does this characteristic of HIV affect its transmission?*

Infection with HIV can be prevented. Teens who choose abstinence from sexual activity and from injecting drugs greatly reduce their risk of HIV infection. Making responsible decisions about personal behaviors is the most valuable tool you can use for protection against HIV infection.

HIV and the Human Body

You may recall that lymphocytes are white blood cells that help your body fight pathogens. Your body contains billions of lymphocytes, which are produced in bone marrow and found in the blood, lymph nodes, appendix, tonsils, and adenoids. When HIV enters the blood, it invades certain cells of the immune system, including T cells, which help other lymphocytes identify and destroy pathogens. The viruses take over the cells and cause them to produce new copies of themselves. The newly produced viruses break out of the cells, destroying them. The new viruses infect other cells, and then the process repeats itself, as shown in **Figure 25.3.**

As the number of viruses increases and the number of T cells decreases, the immune system becomes less capable of preventing infections and cancer. The body becomes susceptible to common infections and to **opportunistic infections**, *infections that occur in individuals who do not have healthy immune systems.* These infections are difficult to treat. With a weakened immune system, the infected individual suffers one illness after another.

HIV infection is progressive; that is, it destroys the cells of the immune system over many months or years. Being infected with HIV does not necessarily mean that an individual has AIDS. AIDS is the advanced stage of HIV infection.

Lesson 3 HIV and AIDS **659**

Dealing with Sensitive Issues

Discussing HIV/AIDS Students may be reluctant to discuss HIV and AIDS. For some, AIDS may be too frightening a topic for discussion. For others, it may be a moral issue. Other students may have experienced the pain of watching a family member or friend suffer from and even die of AIDS. As appropriate, remind students that AIDS is a serious disease. Emphasize that HIV is transmitted only through particular behaviors; if students avoid those behaviors, they will virtually eliminate their risk of contracting HIV. Remind them that their best protection is to practice abstinence from sexual activity and injecting illegal drugs, and to stay informed about HIV/AIDS.

2 TEACH

VISUAL LEARNING

Figure 25.3 Ask a volunteer to read the captions for the illustration. Ask the class:

- Which cells are HIV attaching to and entering? T cells
- Explain why the number of T cells decreases over time. As more viruses are made, they infect more T cells. As more infected T cells are destroyed by the virus, fewer are available.

Critical Thinking

What effect does HIV have on the T cell after it enters? It takes over the cell to make copies of itself. The T cell cannot perform its normal functions. **L2**

ACTIVE READING

Metacognition Journal

In this strategy, each student analyzes his or her own thought processes while reading. Have students draw a line down the middle of a page in their private health journal. On the left, they should record what they have learned about each of the ways that HIV is transmitted. On the right, have them record why knowledge of each means of transmission is important. For more activities see the *Guided Reading Activities* booklet in the TCR. 📂 **L1**

Discussing

Discuss how the use of alcohol and illegal drugs, other than injected drugs, is a risk behavior associated with contracting HIV. **L1**

Real-Life Application

HIV IN TEENS

NHES Standard 7

Students will demonstrate the ability to advocate for personal, family, and community health.

Objectives

• Analyze the relationship between unsafe behaviors and attitudes as well as the risk of contracting HIV.

• Demonstrate the ability to influence and support others in making positive health choices.

Motivator

Lead a class discussion on why some teens may be ignoring the health messages that warn of the risks of becoming infected with HIV.

Teaching Strategies

1. Explain that in 1993, the CDC revised its classification system for AIDS. Before 1993, the number of cases was underreported.

2. Ask students to think of possible reasons for the increase in HIV in teens. Student responses may include attitude, such as complacency or denial. Discuss the meanings of these words.

✓Assessment

Using a rubric, student work should provide comprehensive evidence of the following criteria to achieve the highest score:

✔ clear, health-enhancing stand
✔ support for the position with relevant information
✔ awareness of the audience
✔ encouragement of others to make healthful choices
✔ passion/conviction

660

Real-Life Application

HIV in Teens

At least half of all new HIV infections in the United States occur in people under 25 years of age. Although more and more teens are protecting themselves against AIDS by abstaining from sexual activity, this age group still accounts for hundreds of new cases of HIV infection each year.

AIDS in 13- to 19-Year-Olds

Source: CDC, HIV/AIDS Surveillance in Adolescents, 2001
*In 1993 the CDC began using expanded reporting criteria, increasing numbers of reported cases.

ACTIVITY

Work with a small group. Brainstorm reasons that teens continue to become infected with HIV. For every reason, identify a potential solution. For example, if your group believes that using drugs is one reason, then you might identify more health education classes as a potential solution. Share your ideas with the rest of the class. Make a poster that portrays a health-promoting message drawn from this class discussion. Your poster should persuade teens to practice abstinence and emphasize that abstinence is the best way to prevent HIV infection.

How HIV Is Transmitted

The HIV organism lives inside cells and body fluids. However, it doesn't survive well in the air or on surfaces such as toilet seats or telephones. It cannot be transmitted through food. A person is not at risk of HIV infection by working next to or being in the same classroom as a person who is infected nor by merely touching an infected person.

HIV can be transmitted from an infected person to an uninfected person only in certain ways—through blood, semen, vaginal

660 Chapter 25 Sexually Transmitted Infections and HIV/AIDS

Cooperative Learning Activity

Issues About STDs Have students work in pairs or small groups to investigate one of the following controversial issues surrounding STDs: confidentiality of test results, legal suits against people who know they have STDs and intentionally infect others, the laws of the FDA on medicines available to treat STDs and the unavailability of certain experimental medicines, and prejudice against people with the infections. Have students report their findings to the class and, if possible, plan a panel discussion in which several or all of the issues are addressed. Encourage students to assume roles in their groups to divide up the task into manageable parts.

secretions, and breast milk. You can greatly reduce your chances of HIV infection by abstaining from sexual intercourse and avoiding injected drug use.

▶ **Sexual intercourse.** HIV can be transmitted during any form of sexual intercourse. During intercourse, secretions containing HIV can enter a partner's blood through tiny cuts in the body. The risks of HIV infection increase with the number of people with whom a person is or has been sexually active. Having an STD that causes sores, including chlamydia, genital herpes, gonorrhea, or syphilis, increases the risk of HIV.

▶ **Sharing needles.** People who inject drugs and share needles are at high risk for contracting and spreading HIV. If a person who is infected with HIV injects drugs, the needle or syringe can become contaminated with that person's blood. Anyone who uses that same needle or syringe can inject HIV directly into his or her bloodstream. Injections under the skin or in the muscle also can spread HIV.

▶ **Mother to baby.** A pregnant female who is infected with HIV can pass the virus to her baby. HIV in the mother's blood can be transmitted through the umbilical cord or during birth. Because breast milk can contain HIV, a baby can receive HIV while nursing.

Did You Know ❓

▶ The manner in which HIV can be transmitted has been clearly identified through scientific investigations. Yet much false information still exists. HIV has NOT been shown to be spread through
- insect bites.
- sweat.
- sneezing.
- casual physical contact, such as shaking hands or hugging.

③ ASSESS

EVALUATING THE LESSON

Assign and discuss the Lesson 3 Review; then administer, grade, and discuss Lesson Quiz 93 in the TCR. 📁

RETEACHING

- Use an overhead transparency or the board to show the stages out of order of how HIV attacks cells. Have students place the stages in order.
- Tell students to explain how HIV is transmitted and how it is not transmitted.
- Ask students to complete Reteaching Activity 93 in the TCR. 📁

ENRICHMENT

Encourage a group of students to contact the CDC and the state health department. Have them request the latest information on HIV/AIDS.

④ CLOSE

Have students describe responsible behaviors that can prevent a teen from getting HIV/AIDS.

▶ **Lesson 3** *Review*

Reviewing Facts and Vocabulary

1. Describe the HIV/AIDS epidemic in the teen population.
2. How does HIV attack the immune system?
3. How is HIV transmitted?

Thinking Critically

4. **Synthesizing.** Teens have a high rate of contracting HIV, yet more adults from 25 to 44 years old die from AIDS. What characteristic of HIV/AIDS causes this discrepancy?
5. **Analyzing.** Analyze the relationship between unsafe behaviors, refusal skills, and the risk of HIV.

Applying Health Skills

Advocacy. Prepare a script for a public service announcement on the epidemic of HIV/AIDS. Include statistics on numbers infected, diagnosis, and treatment. Be sure to include information on how people can protect themselves from getting HIV/AIDS.

TECHNOLOGY *OPTION*

WORD PROCESSING Use a word-processing program to help you organize the information you want to include in your script. See **health.glencoe.com** for tips on how to get the most out of your word-processing program.

Lesson 3 HIV and AIDS **661**

▶ **Lesson 3** *Review*

Answers to Reviewing Facts and Vocabulary

1. The rate of HIV infection is increasing because of high-risk behaviors such as injecting drugs and engaging in unprotected sexual activity.
2. HIV enters cells of the immune system, where it makes more viruses that break away and attack other cells.

3. Sexual intercourse, sharing contaminated needles, and from mother to baby.

Answers to Thinking Critically

4. HIV can exist undetected for years. It is only after the virus destroys the immune system that death occurs.
5. Unsafe behaviors increase the risk of contracting HIV.

Treatment for HIV and AIDS

Lesson 4

Treatment for HIV and AIDS

①FOCUS

QUICK START Give students one minute to list ways that HIV is and is not transmitted. Advise them to use the list to compose a response; then share it with the class.

TYING TO PRIOR KNOWLEDGE

Have students recall the reasons to get tested for STDs even though a person may not have symptoms. Ask how this information relates to HIV testing. Explain that this lesson discusses testing and treatment for HIV infection.

Health Skills Features

"Should More Money Be Spent on AIDS Research?" p. 666

ACCESSING INFORMATION

INTRODUCING VOCABULARY

- Review the meanings of the words *symptomatic* and *asymptomatic*.

- Ask students to complete the Chapter 25 Study Guide in the *Student Activity Workbook*.

VOCABULARY

asymptomatic stage
symptomatic stage
EIA
Western blot
pandemic

YOU'LL LEARN TO

- Explain how technologies such as new drug treatments have impacted the health status of people with HIV.

- Compare and analyze the cost, availability, and accessibility of health services worldwide for people living with HIV/AIDS.

- Demonstrate strategies to practice abstinence and to refuse pressure to engage in sexual activity or drug use.

QUICK START What would you tell a friend who is afraid of getting HIV from a fellow student who has been diagnosed as HIV positive? Record your ideas.

ⓥ **Even though medicines can slow the progress of HIV infection, there is still no vaccine that prevents the disease.**

Just as many STDs show no symptoms and many infected individuals don't seek treatment, the same is especially true for HIV. Infection can be ignored or overlooked for several years, during which time the virus can still be transmitted.

Stages of HIV Infection

The HIV infection develops in stages over the course of several years. A person is considered infectious immediately after contracting the virus. Approximately half of all persons develop symptoms about three to six weeks after becoming infected with HIV. These symptoms may include fever, rash, headache, body aches, and swollen glands. In general, these symptoms disappear within a week to a month and are often mistaken for another viral infection, such as the flu. After the flu-like symptoms disappear, the person enters the **asymptomatic stage**, *a period of time during which a person infected with HIV has no symptoms*. A person may show no signs of illness for 6 months to 10 years or more. However, the viruses continue to grow and the infected person can still transmit the viruses to others.

Lesson 4 *Resources*

Teacher Classroom Resources

- Concept Mapping Activity 94
- Guided Reading Activities 94
- Lesson Plan 94
- Lesson Quiz 94
- Reteaching Activity 94

Student Activity Workbook

- Applying Health Skills 94
- Chapter 25 Study Guide

Symptomatic HIV Infection

During the asymptomatic stage, the immune system keeps pace with HIV infection by producing billions of new cells. Eventually, though, the numbers of cells in the immune system decline to the point where other infections start to take over. This marks the **symptomatic stage**, *the stage in which a person infected with HIV has symptoms as a result of a severe drop in immune cells*. The infected person may have such symptoms as swollen glands, weight loss, and yeast infections.

AIDS

During the latter stage of HIV infection, more serious symptoms appear until the infection meets the official definition of AIDS. This includes the presence of HIV infection, a severely damaged immune system measured by numbers of helper T cells, and the appearance of one or more opportunistic infections or illnesses. By the time AIDS develops, HIV often attacks brain cells, causing difficulty in thinking and remembering.

Detecting HIV

Individuals who think they may have been exposed to HIV should seek testing from a health care professional immediately. Testing to determine the presence of the virus can be done by a private physician or at a hospital, a health clinic, or a local health department. Most states have laws to protect the confidentiality of test results.

EIA Test

The first test usually performed is an ELISA, or **EIA**—*a test that screens for the presence of HIV antibodies in the blood*. The EIA reacts to even small numbers of HIV antibodies. However, the EIA may give inaccurate results. There are two reasons for this.

▶ **Developing antibodies takes time**—weeks or even months after initial infection. Before antibodies develop, the EIA may give a false negative result. This means the test is negative, but the person is positive; there aren't enough antibodies for the test to detect. Most people will test positive in three to four weeks, but some people take up to six months to test positive.

▶ **Certain health conditions,** such as hemophilia, hepatitis, and pregnancy, can cause the EIA to give a false positive reading. This means that although the test was positive, the person actually does not have the infection.

An EIA test is the first step in determining whether or not an individual is HIV positive. Anyone engaging in risk behaviors should be tested for HIV. *Why is it important for individuals who might be exposed to HIV to be tested even though they aren't experiencing symptoms?*

How do opportunistic illnesses attack?
When the immune system is weakened by the HIV infection, diseases find an *opportunity* to attack the damaged system. There are over 30 common opportunistic illnesses, including Kaposi's sarcoma and Pneumocystis carinii pneumonia (PCP)— a rare form of pneumonia.

---

② TEACH

Discussing

How is a person tested for HIV? Does a negative test always mean that a person is not infected? Can a person who tests positive for HIV actually not be infected? If the first test is negative, what procedure is used next to determine whether a person is infected? Ask students to explain their responses. L2

Community Involvement

Ask students to interview a health professional in a hospital or public health clinic about his or her HIV-related interactions with patients. Under what circumstances does he or she suggest HIV testing? How often does he or she raise the issue of HIV infection and/or HIV risk behaviors with patients? Allow these students to discuss the results of their interviews with the rest of the class. L3

FYI

It is rare for a patient to give HIV to a health care worker (or vice-versa) by accidental sticks with contaminated needles or other medical instruments, but it does occur on average 200 times nationwide each year. Health care professionals are required by federal law to wear protective equipment and to perform certain procedures a certain way with every patient so as to minimize the risk of contracting HIV.

─〰─ HEALTH LITERACY ─

Investigating HIV/AIDS Issues Assign each student to investigate one of the following:

- confidentiality of HIV test results
- mandatory HIV testing
- the FDA and the unavailability of certain experimental drugs
- group homes for children with AIDS
- hospices for people with AIDS

- prejudice against people with HIV/AIDS

Remind students to evaluate the sources of their information and include them in their reports. Group students with the same topics, and have them combine their findings. Then plan a panel discussion in which several or all of these issues are addressed in detail.

VISUAL LEARNING

Figure 25.4 Direct students to examine Figure 25.4. Point out that in 1981, when doctors first noticed the rare disease that today is called AIDS, they did not know the cause. HIV was isolated and identified as the agent of this disease independently by a French research team and in the United States at the National Cancer Institute. In the United States, reporting cases to public health authorities began in 1982.

Have students calculate the magnitude of the increase in numbers of AIDS cases in the United States from 1984 to 1991. About 29 times as many people were reported with AIDS in 1991 as in 1984 (206,000/7,000).

Critical Thinking

Some athletes and celebrities have made public that they are HIV positive. Ask students what influence these admissions may have had and still have on people's attitudes about people with HIV/AIDS. **L2**

Western Blot Test

If the EIA test is positive, it can be repeated to make sure the results are accurate. If the repeat test is also positive, other confirmation tests will be done. The **Western blot**, or WB, is *the most common confirmation test for HIV in the United States*. If done properly, this test is 100 percent accurate. If the results of all three of these tests are positive, a person is determined to have HIV. Often these individuals are referred to as HIV-positive.

Research and Treatment

When HIV was first identified in the early 1980s, there were no treatments for HIV and few treatments for the opportunistic infections associated with the virus. In the years since then, several medications have been developed to treat HIV and to treat and prevent the complications of opportunistic infections. More drugs and vaccines are being researched. For many people these new treatments have extended and improved the quality of life. None of the drugs, however, cures HIV/AIDS. One reason that a cure is so hard to find is that HIV infects the very cells that regulate the immune response. In addition, several new strains of the virus have emerged since it was first discovered, making it even harder to develop an effective treatment. Many treatments have side effects so severe that some people stop treatment or take medicines only once in a while. This can lead to the development of new, drug-resistant strains of the virus. Also, treatment can be costly, exceeding

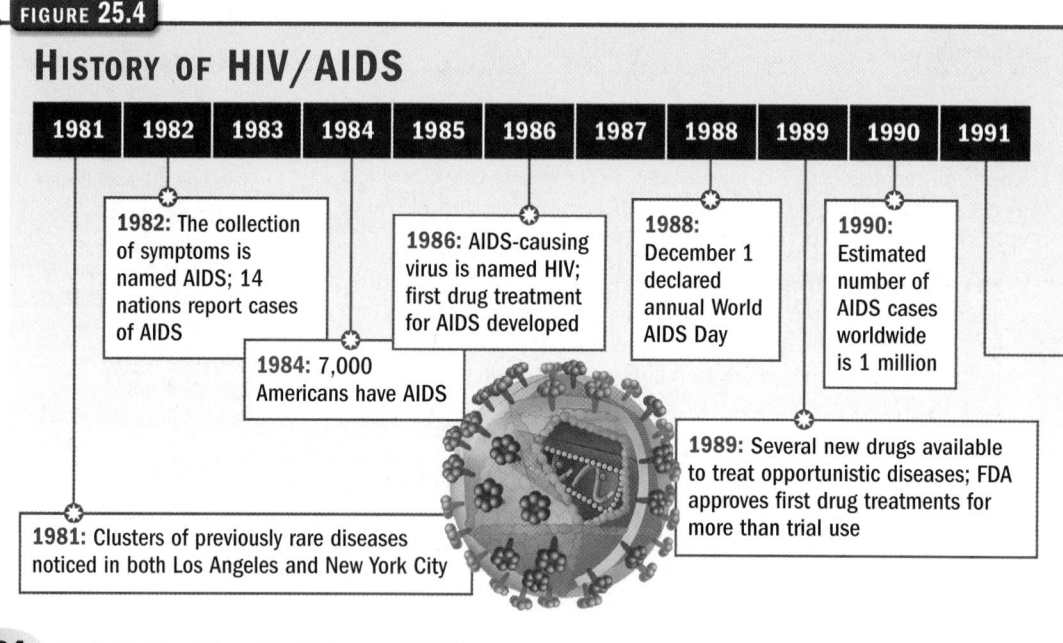

FIGURE 25.4

HISTORY OF **HIV/AIDS**

| 1981 | 1982 | 1983 | 1984 | 1985 | 1986 | 1987 | 1988 | 1989 | 1990 | 1991 |

1982: The collection of symptoms is named AIDS; 14 nations report cases of AIDS

1984: 7,000 Americans have AIDS

1986: AIDS-causing virus is named HIV; first drug treatment for AIDS developed

1988: December 1 declared annual World AIDS Day

1990: Estimated number of AIDS cases worldwide is 1 million

1989: Several new drugs available to treat opportunistic diseases; FDA approves first drug treatments for more than trial use

1981: Clusters of previously rare diseases noticed in both Los Angeles and New York City

664 Chapter 25 Sexually Transmitted Infections and HIV/AIDS

Cooperative Learning Activity

Class Time Line The history of battles waged and won in the area of public health includes many dramatic breakthroughs (e.g., the discovery of bacteria; the development of penicillin and various vaccines; the treatment of diabetes; the cures for pellagra, scurvy, and rickets) as well as heartbreaking setbacks. In the field of HIV/AIDS research, the story is unfolding before our eyes.

Encourage students to start a class time line of current developments in AIDS research. They should summarize articles from a variety of sources onto pieces of construction paper or poster board and arrange these on the walls of the classroom as news and information are published.

$1,000 a month. Worldwide, many infected individuals do not have access to treatment because of high costs and lack of availability. The time line shown in **Figure 25.4** summarizes some of the developments in HIV/AIDS research and treatment.

HIV/AIDS—A Continuing Problem

The number of newly reported AIDS cases in the industrialized world is decreasing. Much of this decrease in AIDS cases results from the success of drug cocktails—combinations of drugs—that slow the progression of HIV infection. This success has brought complacency about the need for HIV prevention. However, this is a false security. Research has identified new, drug-resistant strains of HIV. These strains do not respond to the drug cocktails currently used in the fight against AIDS. The combination of drug resistance and high-risk behaviors could result in HIV strains that are transmitted and spread even more widely. Despite the progress that has been made in development of treatment options, HIV/AIDS is still a fatal disease for which there is no cure.

HIV/AIDS: THE GLOBAL PICTURE

At the end of 2001, an estimated 40 million people worldwide were infected with HIV/AIDS. This statistic means that HIV is now **pandemic**—*a global outbreak of infectious disease.* The number of people living with HIV is growing. It is estimated that in 2001 alone, 5 million people became infected with HIV/AIDS worldwide.

CHARACTER **CHECK**

Responsibility. Each individual can play a role in curbing the spread of HIV by staying informed and spreading the word about this disease. **Take the time to read articles about HIV/AIDS. Share information with family and friends about recent developments in treatment and research to find a cure.**

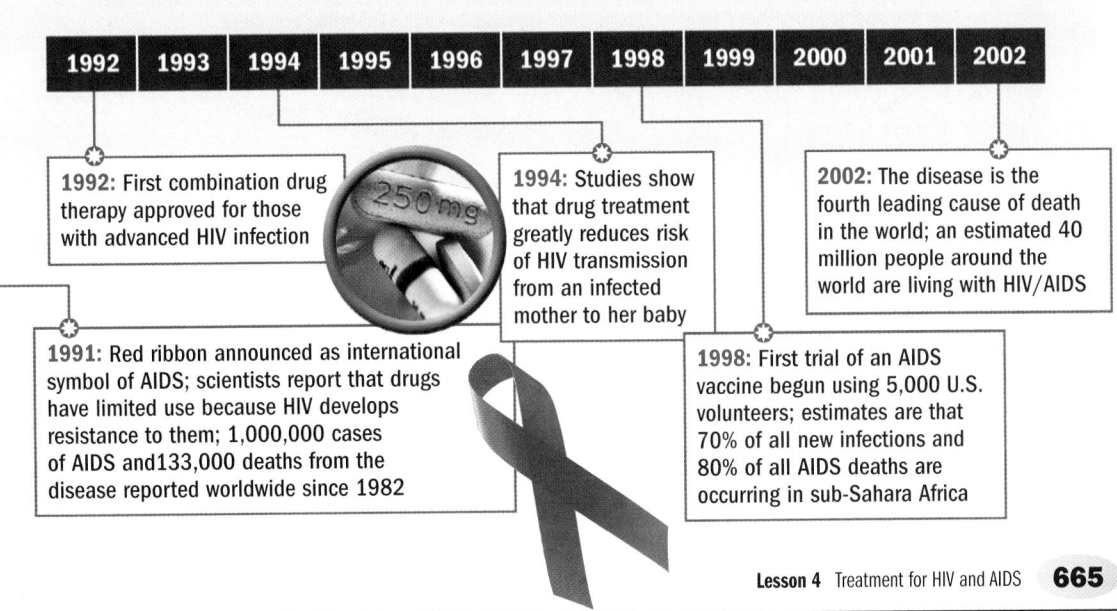

| 1992 | 1993 | 1994 | 1995 | 1996 | 1997 | 1998 | 1999 | 2000 | 2001 | 2002 |

1992: First combination drug therapy approved for those with advanced HIV infection

1994: Studies show that drug treatment greatly reduces risk of HIV transmission from an infected mother to her baby

2002: The disease is the fourth leading cause of death in the world; an estimated 40 million people around the world are living with HIV/AIDS

1991: Red ribbon announced as international symbol of AIDS; scientists report that drugs have limited use because HIV develops resistance to them; 1,000,000 cases of AIDS and133,000 deaths from the disease reported worldwide since 1982

1998: First trial of an AIDS vaccine begun using 5,000 U.S. volunteers; estimates are that 70% of all new infections and 80% of all AIDS deaths are occurring in sub-Sahara Africa

Lesson 4 Treatment for HIV and AIDS **665**

Exploring Issues

SHOULD MORE MONEY BE SPENT ON AIDS RESEARCH AND TREATMENT?

Have students read the feature; then tell them that federal resources for AIDS prevention were first made available to state and local health agencies in 1985. Today, federal funding for research and treatment of AIDS has grown to $13 billion for the federal budget in 2003. As a result, many groups think that tax dollars should be redirected toward diseases and conditions that afflict a greater percentage of the population than does AIDS.

On the other hand, billions of dollars have been lost through lost productivity because many people with AIDS are between 25 and 44 years old; these are among the most productive work years. Ask students to find out what the figure is in economic loss due to HIV-related illness and death. Have students complete the activities, choose a position, and debate it using reliable data.

Exploring Issues

Should More Money Be Spent on AIDS Research and Treatment?

In 1996 the National Institutes of Health (NIH) spent an average of $1,160 on research for every heart disease death, $4,700 on research for every cancer death, and $43,000 on research for every AIDS death. Do you think that more money should be spent on AIDS research and treatment? Here are two points of view.

Viewpoint 1: Parker T., age 17

I don't have a problem with the current level of NIH research money going to AIDS; I know it's a serious disease. I just wish more money were spent researching heart disease, cancer, and other conditions that affect more people. For example, in the last 20 years, 14 million Americans died of heart disease. That's 30 times more than the number who died of AIDS in the same period.

Viewpoint 2: Carmen S., age 16

I agree that heart disease, cancer, and the other diseases should get more funding for research. Unfortunately, however, AIDS is a potentially fatal disease that affects persons of all ages. You can't just look at number of deaths alone. The amount of life-years lost because of AIDS is nearly the same as cancer because many of the people who die of AIDS are young. Also, AIDS is communicable and much of the money spent is to prevent transmission. The preventive measures for AIDS also prevent other STDs, so much of the research money is going toward many diseases, not just AIDS.

ACTIVITY

Take the position of either Parker or Carmen and investigate each supporting argument. Gather additional information to support your point of view using online or print resources and present your viewpoint to the class.

STAYING INFORMED ABOUT HIV/AIDS

Because neither a cure for AIDS nor an effective HIV vaccine is available, knowledge is the first defense against infection. New research can be found in newspapers and magazines and on television, radio, and the Internet. The CDC and state health departments are excellent sources of information. Teachers, school counselors, and physicians can provide guidance on how to find information. By avoiding high-risk behaviors, staying informed, and making responsible decisions, you can protect yourself and others from infection.

666   **Chapter 25**   Sexually Transmitted Infections and HIV/AIDS

Curriculum Connections

Assign students to small groups in which they create a live documentary on the problem of HIV/AIDS.

Language Arts Students should read and use information in the chapter and through research to write a script; then have the students perform their documentary for the class.

Social Studies As part of the documentary, students should include information about HIV/AIDS in the United States and one other country of their choice. Group members should work together to gather information on how HIV is affecting family and social structures and the primary ways HIV is spread in both countries.

Abstinence and HIV/AIDS

During your teen years, you may feel pressure to experiment with new behaviors, such as engaging in sexual activity or using drugs. Consider that your actions today can change the entire course of your life. Choosing to remain abstinent shows that you are taking an active role in caring for your own health and acting responsibly by not jeopardizing the well-being of others. These strategies will help you avoid pressure to engage in sexual activity and use drugs:

▶ Avoid situations and events where drug use or the pressure to engage in sexual activity is likely to occur. If you are at a party where things are getting out of control, leave immediately.

▶ Practice refusal skills. Be firm when you refuse to take part in drug use or sexual activity. Use body language as well as words to get your message across.

▶ Choose your relationships carefully. Avoid forming a dating relationship with someone whom you know to be sexually active. Avoid known drug users or people who approve of drug use.

Each of the more than 44,000 colorful panels in the AIDS Memorial Quilt memorializes the life of a person who died from AIDS. When the entire quilt was in Washington, D.C., it covered the National Mall. *How does the AIDS quilt help educate the public about HIV/AIDS?*

③ ASSESS

EVALUATING THE LESSON

Assign and discuss the Lesson 4 Review; then administer, grade, and discuss Lesson Quiz 94 in the TCR. 📂

RETEACHING

• Assign small groups particular sections of this lesson. Ask them to summarize the content and present it as they would deliver a newscast.

• Ask students to complete Reteaching Activity 94 in the TCR. 📂

ENRICHMENT

Allow students to work in small groups to gather information about opportunistic infections that can affect people who have HIV/AIDS. Have each group prepare a chart, graph, or other graphic summary of their findings to be shared with the rest of the class.

④ CLOSE

Tell students to determine what role they can play in preventing the spread of AIDS.

▶ Lesson 4 Review

Reviewing Facts and Vocabulary

1. What is asymptomatic HIV infection?
2. When is a Western blot test performed?
3. Explain how technologies such as new drug treatments have impacted the health status of people with HIV infection as well as people's attitudes toward the AIDS epidemic.

Thinking Critically

4. **Evaluating.** Why might people in the United States have better access to AIDS treatment than people in developing nations?
5. **Analyzing.** What strategies can you use to resist pressure to engage in sexual activity or drug use and in doing so reduce your risk of HIV infection?

Applying Health Skills

Accessing Information. Research new vaccines that are being developed for HIV/AIDS. Use several different sources of information in your search, such as Web sites, books, and newspaper or magazine articles. Evaluate the validity of your sources to make sure they are reliable and accurate. Then prepare a presentation describing the promise of the new vaccines.

PRESENTATION SOFTWARE Use presentation software to present one of the treatments you researched to your class. Find help in using presentation software at **health.glencoe.com**.

Lesson 4 Treatment for HIV and AIDS **667**

▶ Lesson 4 Review

Answers to Reviewing Facts and Vocabulary

1. When the virus is present in the blood but the person has no symptoms.
2. When two EIA tests are positive.
3. New therapies have extended the lives of people with HIV/AIDS but have caused some to believe that HIV/AIDS is no longer a threat.

Answers to Thinking Critically

4. In contrast to the United States, people in developing nations have few resources to spend on expensive treatments and do not have the same level of access to health care.
5. Students may list any of the strategies found on page 667.

Mock Radio Call-In Program

NHES Standard 4 Students will analyze the influence of culture, media, technology, and other factors on health.

Objective

Stage a mock radio call-in program to talk about and answer questions from listeners on issues surrounding STDs.

Motivator

Ask students what kinds of radio programs they listen to, and make a list on the board. The list could include music programs, news, sports broadcasts, talk radio shows, call-in shows, etc.

Teaching Strategies

Awareness Ask students to think about how much time they spend listening to the radio each day.

Analysis The class activity illustrates how radio might play a part in disseminating important public health information.

Reflection Point out how a program that promotes public dialogue about STDs can disseminate information about different STDs, and promote awareness about curbing the spread of STDs.

Take Action By attempting to be on a live call-in show, students are taking advantage of an opportunity to promote abstinence for youth.

✓Assessment

Each student from Group 2 should ask at least one question of a panelist. Their answers should be supported by facts obtained in their research.

668

Mock Radio Call-In Program

According to the National Association of Broadcasters, people over the age of 12 listen to the radio an average of three hours each day. One of today's popular formats is the radio call-in program. Radio call-in programs are one method of disseminating information to the public and often have a host who invites expert panelists to answer questions from listeners. In the following class activity, you and your classmates will stage a mock radio call-in program to talk about how to prevent the spread of STDs.

ACTIVITY

Group 1 will become the expert panel that answers callers' questions. The panel should consist of:

- **a public health official.** This person should have knowledge of current statistics on STD occurrences and information on prevention and treatment options.

- **a member of a health care organization.** This person provides services and information on community resources for STD diagnosis and treatment.

- **a member of an advocacy group.** This person campaigns for effective methods for control and prevention of STDs.

Group 2 will be the radio show's callers. Each student in Group 2 will research and compose one question for each kind of panelist. Select one person to become the host of the radio call-in show. This person will introduce the panelists and facilitate the discussion by calling on students.

EXPRESS YOUR VIEWS

Compose a short statement for a call-in radio program that promotes abstinence for youth as an effective defense against STDs. Your statement should be persuasive and should contain supporting facts.

668 Chapter 25 Review

More About...

Radio Listeners In a 1999 study, the Kaiser Family Foundation discovered that 70 percent of children between ages 2 and 18 have radios in their bedrooms. Their study also found that children from age 2 to 18 listen to the radio an average of 40 minutes each day. You can extend this lesson by engaging students in a discussion about whether or not they think radio is a valuable medium for getting pertinent health information to a teen audience. Ask students to brainstorm ways in which music stations might help create forums for public debate on pertinent health issues affecting teens.

CROSS-CURRICULUM CONNECTIONS

Prepare a Speech. Making healthy decisions is the key to preventing yourself from being infected with a sexually transmitted disease. Abstinence from sexual activity before marriage and following a drug-free lifestyle are your best choices to avoid the consequences of STDs. Using the facts you have learned in this chapter, plan a short speech on why these lifestyle choices are important for a happy and healthy future.

Research Epidemics. In the 1980s, the HIV/AIDS crisis reached epidemic levels in the United States, and the epidemic continues to heighten worldwide. Throughout history, there have been various diseases that have spread to this dangerous point. For example, in 1918 an influenza outbreak killed 30 million people. Work in groups and choose a major epidemic or plague from history to research.

Calculate AIDS Death Rates. In one recent year, the United States population reached 281,421,906. If there were 14,802 AIDS deaths during that year, what was the rate of death due to AIDS per 100,000 of population?

Investigate Viruses. A master of disguise, the HIV virus keeps changing to evade each new treatment that comes along. Research another type of virus to find out about its structure, life cycle, and characteristics. Create a poster showing how a virus infects cells. Demonstrate how the transmission of the virus can be slowed or prevented.

 CAREER Corner

Health Advocate

Do you like working with people? Can you synthesize information from a variety of sources to come up with innovative solutions to complex problems? If so, you may be interested in a career as a health advocate.

Health advocates work in a wide range of settings. Some are patient representatives and administrators in large health care facilities or at consumer health agencies; others serve on ethics committees and medical policy boards. A community health advocate often provides education and information as a member of a health care team working in clinics and community centers where access to health care is limited. All health advocates work toward one goal: finding innovative ways to improve the delivery of health services.

Health advocates have several levels of certification. Two-year courses are available at some community colleges. Others become advocates through a Master of Arts program following college graduation. Find out more about this and other health careers by clicking on Career Corner at **health.glencoe.com**.

Chapter 25 Review **669**

CROSS-CURRICULUM CONNECTIONS

Enrich student learning by connecting the topic of STDs to one of the four subject areas presented on this page. The activity may be completed individually or with a partner.

Language Arts Explain to students that an extemporaneous speech combines the informality of an impromptu speech with the preparation of a memorized speech. Students may use index cards with chapter notes, but they should not memorize their speeches.

Social Studies Assign each group member a role such as researcher, recorder, or presenter.

Math $14{,}802/281{,}421{,}906 \times 100{,}000 = 5.26$

Science Students should get a basic idea of how a virus is made and the typical characteristics of infection and reproduction in cells.

 CAREER Corner

Have students read the Career Corner feature on page 668. Ask interested students to explore the Glencoe Health Web site at **health.glencoe.com** for more information on careers as a health advocate.

Portfolio Assessment

Self-Evaluation Direct students to review the Health Skills Activities and other activities completed in the chapter. Encourage each student to select one finished product or activity that demonstrates his or her best work for the chapter and that represents the student's learning goals. Have students explain what

they have learned and how the examples they have selected demonstrates their growth in health literacy, knowledge, and skills.

Teacher Classroom Resources Assign Performance Assessment 25, "Knowledge Is Power," in the TCR.

CHECKING COMPREHENSION

- Assign and discuss the chapter review.
- Use Chapter 25 MindJogger Videoquiz to review the chapter. 🔁

CHAPTER 25 REVIEW ANSWERS

Exploring Health Terms

1. sexually transmitted disease (STD) or sexually transmitted infection (STI)
2. epidemic
3. abstinence
4. Chlamydia
5. Genital herpes
6. gonorrhea
7. syphilis
8. False; HIV is the virus that attacks the immune system.
9. False; being infected with HIV does not necessarily mean that a person has AIDS.
10. True
11. asymptomatic stage
12. EIA
13. Western blot

Recalling the Facts

1. Some people are asymptomatic or afraid to seek treatment. Consequently, many cases go undiagnosed and unreported.
2. Use of alcohol or other drugs can lower inhibitions. As a result, teens engage in high-risk behaviors (sexual contact, unprotected sex, use of injected drugs) that increase the risk of infection with an STD.
3. Abstinence from sexual activity or other high-risk behaviors, including use of alcohol and other drugs, is the only 100 percent effective way to prevent STDs.
4. genital herpes, HIV, HPV, HBV

▶ EXPLORING HEALTH TERMS
Answer the following questions on a sheet of paper.

Lesson 1 *Fill in the blanks with the correct term.*

| abstinence | sexually transmitted disease (STD) |
| epidemic | sexually transmitted infection (STI) |

1. An infection that spreads from person to person through sexual contact is called a(n) _____ or a(n) _____ .
2. When a community has a number of cases of an infectious disease larger than would be generally expected, the community is experiencing a(n) _____ .
3. The only 100 percent effective way to avoid STDs is to practice _____ .

Lesson 2 *Replace the underlined words with the correct term.*

chlamydia	syphilis
genital herpes	trichomoniasis
gonorrhea	human papillomavirus (HPV)

4. <u>Gonorrhea</u> can lead to pelvic pain and infertility.
5. <u>HPV</u> is an STD caused by the herpes simplex virus.
6. A bacterial STD that usually affects mucous membranes is <u>chlamydia</u>.
7. The first sign of <u>trichomoniasis</u> infection is a chancre at the site of infection.

Lesson 3 *Identify each statement as True or False. If false, replace the underlined term with the correct term.*

| HIV | AIDS |
| opportunistic infection | |

8. <u>AIDS</u> is the virus that attacks the immune system.
9. Being infected with <u>AIDS</u> does not necessarily mean a person has <u>HIV</u>.
10. <u>Opportunistic infections</u> are rare in a person with a normal immune system, but they easily invade the body of a person with a weakened immune system.

Lesson 4 *Match each definition with the correct term.*

EIA	asymptomatic stage
Western blot	symptomatic stage
pandemic	

11. A period of time during which a person infected with HIV has no symptoms.
12. The first test usually performed to screen for HIV antibodies in the blood.
13. The most common confirmation test for HIV in the United States.

▶ RECALLING THE FACTS
Use complete sentences to answer the following questions.

Lesson 1

1. Why are STDs in the United States considered a hidden epidemic?
2. Explain the relationship between alcohol and other drugs used by adolescents and the role these substances play in STDs.
3. What is the only method that is 100 percent effective in preventing STDs?

Lesson 2

4. Which STDs stay in the body for life?
5. Why is early treatment of STDs important?
6. Explain why an individual diagnosed with an STD should notify contacts.

Lesson 3

7. Why is the risk of HIV infection low for a person whose coworker has tested positive for HIV?
8. Why does having multiple sexual contacts increase the risk of HIV infection?

Lesson 4

9. List and describe the stages of HIV infection.
10. Relate the importance of tests to detect HIV and why early detection is important.

5. Early treatment can help avoid the more serious effects of some STDs and prevent the disease from spreading.
6. Local authorities may not have the resources or be required by law to notify contacts.
7. HIV is transmitted through sexual intercourse, by sharing needles, and from mother to baby. HIV is not transmitted through casual contact, such as touching, and is not transmitted through the air.
8. Having multiple partners increases the probability of coming into contact with a person who has HIV infection.
9. Early infection: symptoms such as fever, rash, headache, body aches, and swollen glands develop three to six weeks after infection and usually disappear within a week to a month. Asymptomatic HIV infection: no symptoms; HIV continues to invade and destroy cells of the immune system. Symptomatic HIV infection:

➤ THINKING CRITICALLY

1. **Analyzing.** Suppose a friend tells you that he or she is considering having a sexual relationship with a boyfriend or girlfriend. Write a letter to your friend explaining the benefits of abstinence as it relates to the prevention of STDs. *(LESSON 1)*

2. **Evaluating.** Some states have laws that require couples who apply for marriage licenses to be tested for particular STDs. Analyze the influence of this public health policy on the prevention and treatment of STDs. *(LESSON 2)*

3. **Synthesizing.** State facts that support this statement: Fighting HIV infection is everyone's responsibility. *(LESSON 3)*

4. **Analyzing.** What makes opportunistic illnesses more dangerous for individuals who are infected with HIV than for those who are not infected? *(LESSON 4)*

➤ HEALTH SKILLS APPLICATION

1. **Advocacy.** Research groups that advocate teen abstinence from sexual activity. Find out what services these groups offer and how you can volunteer to help them. *(LESSON 1)*

2. **Accessing Information.** Identify community health services that help with prevention and treatment of STDs. Discover the types of educational materials they have for educating teens about the risks of STDs. Share your findings with the class. *(LESSON 2)*

3. **Advocacy.** Develop an HIV prevention program aimed at teens entering high school. Emphasize the relationship between unsafe behaviors, such as sexual contact and drug use, and the risk of HIV infection. *(LESSON 3)*

4. **Refusal Skills.** List two suggestions for practicing abstinence when pressured to engage in sexual activity or to use drugs. *(LESSON 4)*

 BEYOND *the* Classroom

Parent Involvement

Advocacy. With your parents, research ways that parents can help their children avoid risky behaviors that might lead to STDs. Work together with your parent or guardian to organize your research, and create guidelines for other parents. If you have access to the Internet, post the guidelines on a Web site.

School and Community

Finding resources. Learn the names of organizations in your community that help people infected with HIV/AIDS. Make a list of these organizations, and describe the services each provides. Create a pamphlet containing the information you have gathered. Make the pamphlet available through the school health office.

Chapter 25 Review **671**

symptoms such as swollen glands, weight loss, and yeast infections; the immune system is no longer able to fight off other diseases. AIDS: the presence of HIV along with a badly damaged immune system (low numbers of T cells) or opportunistic infections indicates full-blown AIDS.

10. Tests allow early detection of HIV, permitting the infected individual to receive treatment that can significantly delay the onset of AIDS. Early detection also alerts the infected individual to the need to inform

partners and to reduce risk behaviors in order to curb the spread of the infection.

Thinking Critically

1. Students should emphasize that abstinence is the only 100 percent effective method of reducing the risk of STDs.

2. Answers will vary. Students should mention that such policies help identify people with STDs and perhaps reduce transmission of these diseases.

3. HIV is a pandemic, a global problem. At the very least, everyone should take precautions to avoid becoming infected.

4. Individuals with HIV have immune systems that do not function properly. Opportunistic infections that do not harm a person with a healthy immune system can be fatal for people with HIV/AIDS.

Health Skills Application

1.–4. Answers will vary and should demonstrate skills knowledge students can apply to reducing the risk of infection with STDs, including practicing abstinence.

EVALUATE

- Use the reproducible Chapter 25 Test in the TCR, or construct your own using the Testmaker software. 📁 💿

- Use Performance Assessment 25 in the TCR. 📁

ENRICHMENT

Ask students to complete Enrichment Activity 25 in the TCR. 📁

 BEYOND *the* Classroom

Keep students involved in the community, and encourage parent participation by assigning the activities on this page for students to work on outside of class.

Lessons	Standards		Features
	National	**State/Local**	
1 **Cardiovascular Diseases** *pages 674–680*	**National Health Education Standards** **1.3, 1.5, 1.6, 3.1, 3.2**		**Hands-On Health** • Start a Healthy Habit *(Practicing Healthful Behaviors)*, page 678
2 **Cancer** *pages 681–687*	**National Health Education Standards** **1.3, 1.8, 3.1, 3.3, 4.3**		**Health Skills Activity** • Being Sun Smart *(Decision-Making)*, page 686
3 **Allergies, Asthma, Diabetes, and Arthritis** *pages 688–694*	**National Health Education Standards** **1.2, 1.5, 2.1, 3.1, 4.3**		**Real-Life Application** • Raising Teen Awareness of Diabetes *(Advocacy)*, page 692
4 **Physical and Mental Challenges** *pages 695–699*	**National Health Education Standards** **1.4, 3.3, 4.4, 5.4, 7.5**		

Reproducible Resources	Assessment	Technology
Student Activity Workbook for use with each chapter 📁 Concept Mapping Activity 95 📁 Cross-Curriculum Activity 26 📁 Enrichment Activity 26 📁 Guided Reading Activities 95 📁 Health Lab 26 📁 Lesson Plan 95 📁 Parent Letter and Activities 26 📁 Reteaching Activity 95	📁 Lesson Quiz 95	🕹 Transparency 75 💿 TeacherWorks® 💻 Internet Activities
📁 Concept Mapping Activity 96 📁 Guided Reading Activities 96 📁 Lesson Plan 96 📁 Reteaching Activity 96	📁 Lesson Quiz 96	🕹 Transparency 76 💿 TeacherWorks®
📁 Concept Mapping Activity 97 📁 Decision-Making Activity 26 📁 Guided Reading Activities 97 📁 Lesson Plan 97 📁 Reteaching Activity 97	📁 Lesson Quiz 97	🕹 Transparency 77 💿 TeacherWorks®
📁 Concept Mapping Activity 98 📁 Current Health Issues 26 📁 Guided Reading Activities 98 📁 Lesson Plan 98 📁 Reteaching Activity 98	📁 Lesson Quiz 98	💿 TeacherWorks®

🕐 OUT OF TIME

If time does not permit teaching the entire chapter use:
- Figure 26.1, p. 676
- Hands-On Health, p. 678
- Figure 26-2, p. 679
- Figure 26.3, p. 683
- Figure 26.5, p. 685
- Health Skills Activity, p. 686

Language Diversity

🎧 English Audio CD Program
🎧 Spanish Audio CD Program
📁 English Summaries, Quizzes, and Activities
📁 Spanish Summaries, Quizzes, and Activities
📁 Spanish Parent Letters and Activities

End of Chapter Assessment

Blackline Masters

📁 Chapter 26 Test
📁 Performance Assessment Activity 26
📁 Unit 8 Test

Technology

💿 Vocabulary PuzzleMaker
📼 MindJogger Videoquiz
💿 ExamView® Pro Testmaker

Professional Health Series

Dealing with Sensitive Issues
Planning a Coordinated School Health Program
Promoting Character Education
Home, School, and Community Involvement

Key to Ability Levels

Teaching strategies that appear throughout the chapter have been identified by one of the following codes to give teachers an idea of their suitability for students of varying learning styles and abilities.

L1 Strategies should be within the ability range of all students. Full class participation is often required. Teacher direction is usually needed.

L2 Strategies are designed for average to above-average students or for small groups. Some teacher direction is needed.

L3 Strategies are designed for students able and willing to work independently. Minimal teacher direction is needed.

ELL Strategies should be within the ability range of students learning the English language.

▥ Block scheduling strategies are useful in a block scheduling format.

CHAPTER OVERVIEW

Chapter 26 discusses the symptoms, causes, treatments, and prevention of common noncommunicable diseases.

Lesson 1 The symptoms and causes of various cardiovascular diseases are presented along with diagnosis and treatment. Prevention is best achieved through lifestyle behaviors.

Lesson 2 Cancers constitute abnormal, uncontrolled cell growth. Diagnosis, treatment, and prevention of several types of cancer are presented. A healthful lifestyle can prevent over half of all cancers.

Lesson 3 This lesson describes the causes, symptoms, treatment, and prevention of allergies, asthma, diabetes, and arthritis. Prevention strategies are emphasized.

Lesson 4 A few of the more common disabilities that result from physical and mental impairments are identified. The importance of eliminating barriers that hinder individuals with a disability is also addressed.

Health Skills Features

- Hands-On Health *(Practicing Healthful Behaviors)*, p. 678
- Health Skills Activity *(Decision Making)*, p. 686
- Real-Life Application *(Advocacy)*, p. 692

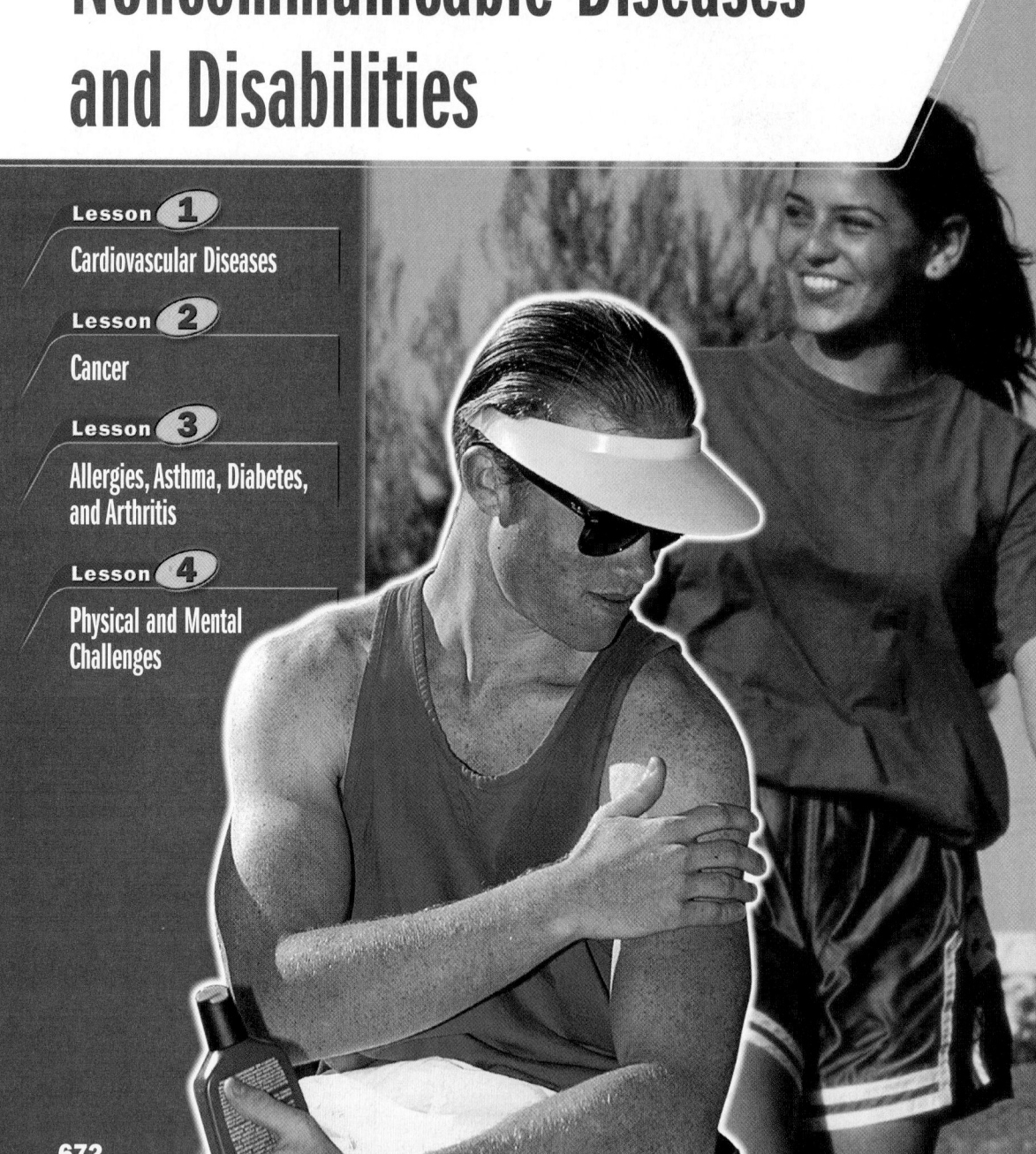

Chapter 26

Noncommunicable Diseases and Disabilities

Lesson 1
Cardiovascular Diseases

Lesson 2
Cancer

Lesson 3
Allergies, Asthma, Diabetes, and Arthritis

Lesson 4
Physical and Mental Challenges

672

MEETING STUDENT DIVERSITY

Language Diversity Use the following suggestions to help students who have difficulty with English:

- Pair English language learners with native speakers of English who can restate the main ideas of the Chapter Summary in language that helps students comprehend important concepts.

- Direct auditory learners or those students with language diversity to the *Glencoe Health Audio CD Program*. Available in English and Spanish, this component provides an audio and written summary of the chapter.

- Use photographs, drawings, or magazine clippings to help students visualize the important concepts of the chapter.

Case Study ✓

Mandy's Story

Mandy is 16. Lately, many of Mandy's friends have begun spending a lot of time at the community pool and at the lake, trying to get the "perfect" tan. They think a tan makes them look healthier and more attractive. Her friends always want her to come along, but Mandy is concerned.

"My skin and hair are very light like my mom's. Mom had some moles removed from her arms and face a few years ago. I was scared when I found out that they were cancerous, but she seems to be okay now. She avoids the sun as much as possible, and she uses a lot of sunscreen."

"Mom wants me to limit my time in the sun and put on sunscreen before I leave the house. I know I should be more careful, but I want to hang out with my friends. If I use sunscreen all the time, I'll be the only one in the group who doesn't have a tan."

What do you think Mandy should do? Write a sentence or two that describes the advice you would give her. Reread this story and your response after you complete the chapter. Identify how tanning can affect your health.

Quick *Write*

Using Visuals. Healthful lifestyle behaviors, including eating nutritious foods and getting regular physical activity, can reduce a person's risk of developing diseases such as heart disease and cancer. Describe one lifestyle behavior that can reduce the risk of skin cancer.

673

INTRODUCING THE CHAPTER

Case Study ✓

Lead a discussion in which students describe what they know about skin cancer, including risk factors and strategies for prevention. List their ideas on the board. Explain that fair-skinned people like Mandy are at high risk for skin cancer from ultraviolet light; but people with darker skin can also get skin cancer. Point out that ultraviolet light, whether from the sun or from sunlamps or tanning beds, is also the primary cause of wrinkles and causing skin to age. This process starts in youth but doesn't show up until years later. However, the damage has already been done. Have students review the list on the board and use the information you have just given them to suggest what Mandy should do. Encourage them to think of several alternatives.

Quick *write*

Using Visuals Allow students to work with a partner to discuss the actions the teens in the photographs could take to reduce the risk of skin cancer. Then have them apply this to their own lives. How can they incorporate these strategies into their everyday routine? Guide them to recognize that reducing the risk of skin cancer and many other noncommunicable diseases is a lifestyle choice.

TECHNOLOGY OPTIONS

MINDJOGGER
VIDEOQUIZ

To preview or review chapter content, you may wish to use the Chapter 26 MindJogger Videoquiz.

HEALTH *Online*

Online Resources for the Teacher For a fresh approach to health topics and an in-depth look at health issues, use these online resources, found under Teacher Resources at **health.glencoe.com:**

• Block Schedule Lesson Plans
• Technology Projects
• Health Updates

Cardiovascular Diseases

1 FOCUS

QUICK START Give students one minute to write their lists; then ask volunteers to share them. On the board, write several habits in one column. Write another column of benefits. Draw connecting lines as students tell you which benefits go with which habits.

TYING TO PRIOR KNOWLEDGE

Ask students to define cholesterol. Explain that a high cholesterol level is a risk factor for heart disease. Explain that they will be learning more about heart disease and how to prevent it.

Health Skills Features

"Start a Healthy Habit," p. 678

PRACTICING HEALTHFUL BEHAVIORS

INTRODUCING VOCABULARY

- Have students look for the definitions of each vocabulary term in their dictionaries or Glossary. Then have them use the terms in sentences.

- Ask students to complete the Chapter 26 Study Guide in the *Student Activity Workbook*. 📁

Cardiovascular Diseases

VOCABULARY

noncommunicable disease
cardiovascular disease (CVD)
hypertension
atherosclerosis
angina pectoris
arrhythmias

YOU'LL LEARN TO

- Examine different types of cardiovascular diseases.

- Recognize the importance of early detection and warning signs that prompt individuals to seek health care.

- Identify risk behaviors and risk factors for cardiovascular diseases.

- Develop, analyze, and apply strategies related to the prevention of cardiovascular diseases.

 QUICK START Brainstorm a list of heart-healthy habits. Briefly explain how you think each one benefits your heart.

 Every day your heart pumps blood through the arteries to all the cells of your body. *Why should you establish and maintain healthful habits to care for your heart?*

A century ago communicable diseases were a leading cause of death in the United States. Since then, the average life span of Americans has nearly doubled, primarily because of public health efforts and new technologies. Today, however, major causes of death, such as heart disease and cancer, come from a different kind of disease. A **noncommunicable disease** is *a disease that is not transmitted by another person, or a vector, nor from the environment.* Medical science has identified certain habits and behaviors that either increase or decrease the risk of many of these diseases.

Cardiovascular Diseases

Your cardiovascular system transports blood to all parts of your body. Without oxygen and other materials that blood carries, your cells would die. Sometimes diseases interfere with the pumping action of the heart or the movement of blood through blood vessels. A **cardiovascular disease (CVD)** is *a disease that*

Lesson 1 *Resources*

Teacher Classroom Resources

📁 Concept Mapping Activity 95
📁 Cross-Curriculum Activity 26
📁 Enrichment Activity 26
📁 Guided Reading Activities 95
📁 Health Lab 26
📁 Lesson Plan 95
📁 Lesson Quiz 95

📁 Parent Letter and Activities 26
📁 Reteaching Activity 95

Student Activity Workbook

📁 Applying Health Skills 95
📁 Chapter 26 Study Guide

Multimedia

 Transparency 75

affects the heart or blood vessels. Approximately 61 million Americans have some form of the disease. CVDs are responsible for more than 40 percent of all deaths in the United States, killing almost a million Americans each year.

Types of Cardiovascular Disease

The heart, blood, and blood vessels are the main parts of the circulatory system. When the parts work together properly, the cardiovascular system runs efficiently. When a problem affects one part, the entire system is threatened. As you read the description of each type of CVD, keep in mind that you can reduce your risk by avoiding tobacco; getting plenty of physical activity; maintaining a healthful weight; and following an eating plan low in saturated fat, cholesterol, and sodium.

Hypertension

Blood pressure is the force of blood created by the heart's contractions and the resistance of the vessel walls. Normal blood pressure varies with age, height, weight, and other factors. **Hypertension** is *high blood pressure*—pressure that is continually above the normal range for a particular person. If high blood pressure continues over a long period, the heart, blood vessels, and other body organs will be damaged. Hypertension is a major risk factor for other types of CVDs. Hypertension can occur at any age, but it is more common among people over the age of 35. Of Americans aged 20–74, 23 percent have hypertension. CVD, considered a "silent killer," often has no symptoms in its early stages, so it's important to get your blood pressure checked regularly. High blood pressure can be lowered with medication, weight management, adequate physical activity, and proper nutrition.

Atherosclerosis

At birth, the lining of blood vessels is smooth and elastic. Over time, factors such as tobacco smoke, high blood pressure, or high cholesterol levels can damage the inner lining of the arteries. Fatty substances in the blood, called plaques, can build up on the artery walls, causing the arteries to thicken and lose their elasticity. *The process in which plaques accumulate on artery walls* is called **atherosclerosis** (a-thuh-roh-skluh-ROH-sis). This buildup is due mainly to food choices—specifically, a high intake of saturated fats and cholesterol. Sometimes, a blood clot forms in the area of plaque. The clot grows until it blocks the artery. If the affected artery feeds the heart or the brain, a heart attack or stroke may result.

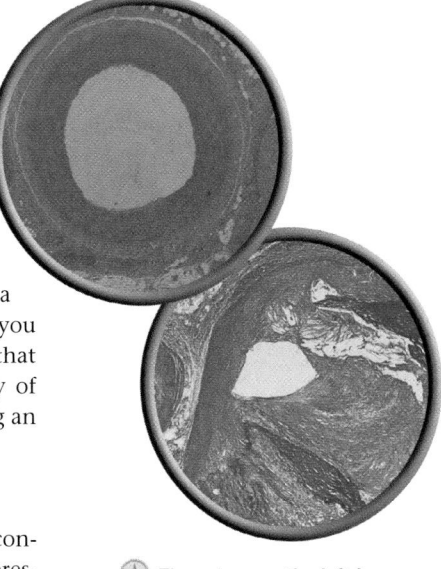

The artery on the left is healthy. The one on the right shows evidence of atherosclerosis. *What dietary choices can you make to lower your risk of atherosclerosis?*

Did You Know

Blood pressure is written as two numbers. The first number is the *systolic* number, which represents the pressure while the heart is beating. The second, or *diastolic*, number represents the pressure when the heart is resting between beats. For example, 122/76 represents a systolic pressure of 122 and a diastolic pressure of 76. High blood pressure in adults is defined as 140/90 or above.

2 TEACH

Reinforcing Concepts

Point out that, as plaques accumulate, the arteries grow narrower. The heart must work harder to push blood through the arteries. It beats more forcefully, and blood pressure is increased even more. Compare this to the flow of water through a hose. Point out that the smaller the nozzle opening is, the more pressure is put on the inside wall of the hose. Similarly, the smaller the arteries, the more pressure is put on the artery walls. **L1**

Discussing

Remind students that the body makes the cholesterol it requires. Consuming saturated fat generally increases blood cholesterol levels more than consuming cholesterol itself. Have students find out why this is true. When cholesterol is taken into the body, manufacture of cholesterol by the body is inhibited, and plasma cholesterol levels usually do not change much. **L3**

Explaining

Explain that excess salt, or sodium, in the diet is a risk factor for hypertension in only 25 percent of Americans with normal blood pressure. However, there is no way at present to tell who is "salt sensitive." This is why a diet low in sodium is recommended for everyone. **L1**

HEALTH LITERACY

Homocysteine as a Risk Factor for CVD High levels of homocysteine, an amino acid circulating in the blood, are associated with an increased risk of CVD. Encourage students to research the evidence for homocysteine as a risk factor and whether lowering homocysteine reduces the risk of CVD. Suggest that they use medical journals to investigate the connection between consumption of meat and other methionine-rich foods with high levels of homocysteine. Have them write a news article summarizing their findings. Encourage students to develop drafts of their writing, and proofread for errors. Display final drafts in the class.

675

hot link

heart For more information about the structure of the heart and the cardiovascular system, see Chapter 16, page 417.

hot link

Bring an anatomical model of a heart to class, and demonstrate the chambers of the heart and how cardiovascular problems can occur. Display a chart of the cardiovascular system, and demonstrate how the blood is pumped throughout the body, carrying oxygen and nutrients to each cell. **L1**

VISUAL LEARNING

Figure 26.1 Have students follow as a student volunteer reads aloud the information in Figure 26.1. Assign students to work in small groups and research one diagnostic tool and one treatment option. Ask them to report on how many people undergo these procedures and treatments every year in the United States and other facts not presented in the table. Have them explain the technology and how it has impacted the health status of individuals with cardiovascular diseases (CVDs).

Diseases of the Heart

Your **heart** pumps about 100,000 times a day *every* day to move blood to all parts of your body. Just like every other organ, your heart needs the oxygen from blood to function. When the blood supply to the heart is insufficient to provide enough oxygen, the result can be pain, damage to the heart muscle, or even sudden death. Methods for diagnosing and treating diseases of the heart and other CVDs are summarized in **Figure 26.1.**

FIGURE 26.1

DIAGNOSTIC TOOLS

EKG	MRI	Radionuclide Imaging	Angiography
An electrocardiogram produces a graph of the electrical activity of the heart. It helps detect the nature of a heart attack and shows heart function.	Magnetic resonance imaging uses powerful magnets to produce images of internal body organs. The images are used to identify heart damage and heart defects.	Radionuclides injected into the blood can be observed on a computer screen as they pass through the heart. This procedure is used to assess the heart's blood supply and to show heart function.	A thin, flexible tube is guided through blood vessels to the heart. Dye is injected and motion X rays are taken to look for heart obstructions.

TREATMENT OPTIONS

Coronary Bypass	Angioplasty	Medications	Pacemaker
Often a healthy vein is removed from the leg or chest and placed elsewhere to create a detour around a blocked artery.	A tube with a balloon is inserted into a blocked artery. The balloon is inflated against the artery walls. Then it is deflated and removed. A metal structure may remain to keep the artery open.	A variety of medications are used to treat CVDs. These include diuretics to aid with the body's fluid balance, cholesterol-lowering drugs, and drugs that slow the blood's clotting mechanisms in order to reduce risk of stroke.	Pacemakers are used to treat an irregular heartbeat. The small device sends steady electrical impulses to the heart to make it beat regularly.

Myths & Reality

MYTH. Most people with heart disease die suddenly.

FACT. Heart disease is a silent killer; the progression of the disease can take years before resulting in a heart attack.

MYTH. Cigarette smokers do not have a higher rate of heart attack than nonsmokers.

FACT. Smoking does increase the risk of heart attack. It causes the blood vessels to constrict, decreasing blood flow to the cells. It increases blood pressure and strains the heart. It releases carbon monoxide into the blood, decreasing the oxygen supply.

ANGINA PECTORIS

Angina pectoris (an-JY-nuh PEK-tuh-ruhs) is *chest pain that results when the heart does not get enough oxygen.* This pain, which usually lasts a few seconds to minutes, is a signal that the heart is temporarily not getting enough blood. The most common cause of angina is atherosclerosis. Angina seldom causes permanent heart damage and sometimes can be treated with medication.

ARRHYTHMIAS

Arrhythmia is a change in the regular beat of the heart. The heart may seem to skip a beat or beat irregularly, very quickly, or very slowly. **Arrhythmias** or *irregular heartbeats,* are common. They occur in millions of people who do not have underlying heart disease, and they usually don't cause problems. However, certain types of arrhythmias are serious. In one type of arrhythmia, called *ventricular fibrillation,* the electrical impulses regulating heart rhythm become rapid or irregular. This is the most common cause of sudden cardiac arrest, in which the heart stops beating without warning. Without immediate emergency help, death follows within minutes.

HEART ATTACK

Each year in the United States, there are more than one million cases of heart attack, and more than 40 percent of those affected die. A heart attack is damage to the heart muscle caused by a reduced or blocked blood supply, usually because of atherosclerosis. Often, ventricular fibrillation occurs seconds to hours or even days following a heart attack and can cause sudden death.

Many heart attacks are sudden and cause intense chest pain, but one in four produces no symptoms and is detected only when routine tests are done later. Most heart attacks start slowly with mild pain or discomfort, which is often mistaken for indigestion. Immediate response to warning signs can often mean the difference between life and death.

CONGESTIVE HEART FAILURE

A heart attack is an immediate response to stress on the heart. Sometimes, however, the heart gradually weakens to the point that it cannot maintain its regular pumping rate and force. The result is a condition called congestive heart failure. This condition can be a result of high blood pressure, atherosclerosis, a heart valve defect, or other factors. Illegal drug use can also bring on this condition by increasing heart rate. Congestive heart failure can be managed with medication and the establishment of healthy lifestyle behaviors, such as a good nutrition and adequate physical activity.

Health Minute
Heart Attack Warnings

These warning signs indicate that a heart attack may be happening and immediate medical attention is needed.

The warning signs of heart attack:

▶ Pressure, fullness, squeezing, or aching in the chest area
▶ Discomfort spreading to the arms, neck, jaw, upper abdomen, and back
▶ Chest discomfort with shortness of breath, lightheadedness, sweating, nausea, and vomiting

In many cases sudden cardiac arrest can be reversed if CPR or electric shock using a defibrillator is applied. *Why is it important to have defibrillators available in many different public places?*

Critical Thinking

Why might some people misinterpret the signs of a heart attack? Other conditions can have the same signs. For example, pain in the chest area might be mistaken for indigestion. **L2**

Health Minute

Direct students to find out the steps of first aid for a person who may be showing signs of a heart attack. Have students make a chart of the ABCs of CPR from information on page 743. Students can contact the American Red Cross or the American Heart Association for materials including posters for the class. Have students share and display the materials.

Service Learning

Encourage students to become involved with an organization such as the American Heart Association. They could join or initiate a fund-raising campaign such as a bike-a-thon or a walk-a-thon. Have them consider involving other classrooms, schools, neighborhoods, or the PTA. **L1**

More About...

Stroke Because of improving diagnosis and treatment of strokes, the survival rate has increased by more than 50 percent in the last 20 years. About 4½ million stroke survivors are alive today. These numbers do not include the millions of spouses and children who care for stroke victims and whose own lives are greatly changed. Strokes are a leading cause of serious, long-term disability in the United States. About 40 percent of people who have strokes will experience moderate to severe impairments requiring special care, even with rehabilitation. Another 10 percent will require care in a long-term care facility, and 15 percent will die shortly after the stroke. Only 35 percent recover or have only minor impairments.

Hands-On Health

START A HEALTHY HABIT

PRACTICING HEALTHFUL BEHAVIORS

NHES Standard 3 Students will demonstrate the ability to practice health-enhancing behaviors and reduce health risks.

Objectives

- Evaluate a personal health assessment to determine strategies for health enhancement and risk reduction.

- Analyze and apply strategies related to the prevention of cardiovascular diseases.

Motivator

Give students one minute to write answers to this question: Are you practicing healthful behaviors to reduce your risk of CVD? If yes, describe. If not, explain.

Teaching Strategies

1. Suggest that students look through other chapters in their textbooks for specific actions.

2. Provide five to ten minutes of class time daily over two weeks for students to share their progress.

✓ Assessment

Using a rubric, student work should provide comprehensive evidence of the following criteria to achieve the highest score:

✔ identification of healthful behaviors to reduce the risk of CVD
✔ incorporation of strategies into a personal routine
✔ evaluation of their progress and obstacles and what they are doing to improve their behavior

---

Hands-On Health ACTIVITY

Start a Healthy Habit

Working prevention strategies into your everyday life is the best way to reduce your risk of cardiovascular diseases. Take the quiz, and then complete the activity.

What You'll Need

- pen or pencil
- paper

What You'll Do

Number a sheet of paper from 1 to 10. Read each statement and write "always," "most of the time," "once in a while," or "never" for each item.

1. I avoid tobacco products and secondhand smoke.
2. I get 60 minutes of physical activity five or more days per week.
3. I get at least 30 minutes of moderate or 20 minutes of vigorous aerobic exercise at least three times a week.
4. I eat plenty of fruits, vegetables, and whole-grain foods.
5. I limit foods that are high in fat and cholesterol.
6. I limit my intake of salt and sodium.
7. I choose nutritious snacks.
8. I maintain a healthful weight.
9. I practice anger-management skills.
10. I practice stress-management skills.

Choose two habits you need to improve. In small groups, brainstorm a list of specific actions to help you practice these habits. Develop strategies to incorporate at least three healthy habits into your routine. Write a paragraph in which you describe your plan. After two weeks, evaluate what obstacles you faced, and what you are doing to improve.

Apply and Conclude

As a group, report on your successes in improving your lifestyle behaviors. Explain why the behaviors are healthful.

Stroke

When arterial blockage interrupts the flow of blood to the brain, a stroke may occur. Stroke can affect different parts of the body, depending on the part of the brain that is deprived of oxygen. Stroke also can occur as a result of a *cerebral hemorrhage*, a condition in which a blood vessel in the brain bursts, causing blood to spread into surrounding brain tissue.

Why Teens Are at Risk

The behaviors established during your teen years and early adult life determine, in large part, your risk of developing CVD. Even though the symptoms of CVD often don't show up until

678 Chapter 26 Noncommunicable Diseases and Disabilities

Curriculum Connections

Physical Education Set aside a time when students can meet in the gym to practice taking their target heart rates. Have them calculate their target heart ranges before leaving the classroom. Use the formula given in the feature in Chapter 4, Lesson 2. Select an aerobic activity for the students. Have them check at intervals to see whether they are performing in the effective, beneficial range. They can check their pulses at the wrist, neck, or use a monitor if it is available from the athletic department.

adulthood, the disease itself starts to develop in childhood, according to the American Heart Association. Autopsy results of adolescents who died from causes other than CVD have revealed that one in six already had evidence of CVD. Those who had a history of known risk factors, such as smoking or diabetes, were more likely to have blood-vessel damage. The health behaviors you practice *now* are affecting your cardiovascular system.

Risk Factors for Cardiovascular Disease

The American Heart Association has identified several factors, such as those in **Figure 26.2,** that increase the risk of cardiovascular disease. The more risk factors you have, the greater your chance of developing cardiovascular disease.

FIGURE 26.2

RISK FACTORS FOR CVDS YOU CAN CONTROL

Although you cannot control all risk factors, the ones listed below are the result of the daily decisions you make about your health and health habits.

Tobacco Use	• **Avoid the use of tobacco.** About 20 percent of the deaths from cardiovascular disease are smoking-related. Tobacco use is the biggest risk factor for teens. • **Avoid secondhand smoke.** Constant exposure to other people's smoke increases the risk of cardiovascular disease even for nonsmokers. About 40,000 nonsmokers exposed to environmental tobacco smoke die from CVDs each year.
High Blood Pressure	• **Have your blood pressure checked periodically.** Maintain normal blood pressure through a healthful diet, regular exercise, and proper weight. If your blood pressure is above normal, follow the advice of your physician to lower it.
High Cholesterol	• **Eat less high-fat foods.** High blood cholesterol can usually be controlled with medication and by practicing healthful lifestyle behaviors. Eat a diet low in cholesterol and saturated fats, and get regular physical activity. These behaviors help keep plaque from forming in your arteries.
Physical Inactivity	• **Get enough physical activity.** Physical inactivity can be a risk factor even if you aren't overweight. Get at least 30 to 60 minutes of physical activity each day. Regular physical activity strengthens your heart and helps you maintain a healthy weight.
Excess Weight	• **Maintain a healthy weight.** Excess weight increases the strain on the heart. It also raises blood pressure and the levels of blood cholesterol.
Stress	• **Reduce stress.** Constant stress can raise blood pressure. Practice stress-management techniques.
Drug and Alcohol Use	• **Avoid the use of alcohol and other drugs.** Drinking too much alcohol can raise blood pressure and cause heart failure or irregular heart beat. Some illegal drugs increase the heart rate and blood pressure and can result in sudden death from heart failure.

VISUAL LEARNING

Figure 26.2 Ask students to read the information in Figure 26.2. Lead a class discussion in which students volunteer what they know about why and how each of these factors can be controlled. Then have students work in small groups to develop an acronym to help them remember healthful behaviors to reduce the risk of CVDs.

Critical Thinking

Ask: Suppose a person consistently gets medical screenings and practices healthful behaviors to reduce his or her risk of CVD. Why is it still important for that person to know whether he or she has a family history of CVD? Answers will vary but sample answers may include that physicians might recommend more frequent screenings for signs of CVD or that the person may be more inclined to take seriously any possible warning signs of heart attack or stroke and seek immediate medical attention if they occur. **L3**

Discussing

Lead a discussion of how the lifestyle choices students make today relate directly to their potential for developing a CVD. **L1**

FYI

About 600,000 people have strokes every year, and 160,000 of them die.

Home and Community

Health Appraisal Ask students to obtain a copy of a health appraisal that assesses the individual's risk of heart disease. Several have been developed by the American Heart Association and other organizations and hospitals. Have students discuss the factors on the health appraisal with their parents or guardians. Tell students to take the health appraisal with their parents or guardian to determine their risk of CVD, and have them urge their parents or guardian to determine their own level of risk. Encourage students to discuss with their parents or guardian ways to reduce their risk of heart disease.

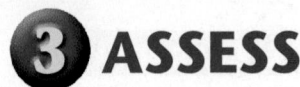

③ ASSESS

EVALUATING THE LESSON

Assign and discuss the Lesson 1 Review; then administer, grade, and discuss Lesson Quiz 95 in the TCR. 📁

RETEACHING

- Ask students to look in their dictionaries or Glossary for the definition of *cardiovascular disease*. Then have them list the types and causes of the disease studied in this lesson.

- Have students relate high blood pressure to heart disease and stroke.

- Ask students to complete Reteaching Activity 95 in the TCR. 📁

ENRICHMENT

Instruct students to research changes in the leading causes of death in the United States since 1900. Ask them to explain how the increase in life expectancy and technological advances have resulted in the decrease in communicable diseases and the increase in noncommunicable diseases.

④ CLOSE

Have students identify the main ideas within the lesson. Encourage them to draw inferences or conclusions as necessary. Clarify any misconceptions.

hot link

heredity To learn more about heredity and genetics, see Chapter 19, page 498.

RISK FACTORS THAT CANNOT BE CONTROLLED

Some risk factors for cardiovascular disease are out of your control, but you should be aware of them and know how they influence your health. These factors include:

▶ **Heredity.** Children whose parents have cardiovascular disease are more likely to develop CVD themselves.

▶ **Gender.** Men have a greater risk of developing cardiovascular disease earlier in life and a greater risk of having a heart attack than women do. However, research indicates that older women are less likely to survive a heart attack than men of the same age.

▶ **Age.** As people become older, they become more likely to develop CVD, as the risk increases with age. About 80 percent of people who die of cardiovascular disease are 65 or older.

Knowing the risk factors you can't control can help you make healthful decisions that protect your cardiovascular system. For example, if you have a family history of hypertension, you should be particularly careful to get the proper medical screenings and to practice preventive strategies, such as maintaining a healthful weight.

 Lesson 1 *Review*

Reviewing Facts and Vocabulary

1. What is *atherosclerosis*? How does it contribute to heart attacks?

2. Define *cardiovascular disease*. How does regular physical activity help prevent CVD?

3. What are five risk factors for CVD that you can control?

Thinking Critically

4. **Evaluating.** Which of the treatments in Figure 26.1 would most likely be used to treat atherosclerosis?

5. **Synthesizing.** How can practicing healthy lifestyle behaviors now help you avoid cardiovascular disease in the future?

Applying Health Skills

Practicing Healthful Behaviors. On a sheet of paper, design a table that lists five of your favorite snacks, and find out which ones are "heart-healthy." For each of the others, think of healthier alternatives that you would enjoy. Enter the alternatives in your table.

TECHNOLOGY *OPTION*

SPREADSHEETS Using spreadsheet software to create your table will help you organize and display your thoughts. See **health.glencoe.com** for tips on how to get the most out of your spreadsheet program.

680 **Chapter 26** Noncommunicable Diseases and Disabilities

 Lesson 1 *Review*

Answers to Reviewing Facts and Vocabulary

1. Process in which plaques accumulate on artery walls; clots that form in the plaques can block the arteries leading to the heart, causing a heart attack.

2. Disease that affects the heart or blood vessels; physical activity strengthens the heart and helps maintain a healthy weight.

3. Any five: tobacco use, high blood pressure, high cholesterol, physical inactivity, excess weight, stress, alcohol or drugs.

Answers to Thinking Critically

4. Bypass, angioplasty, and medications.

5. Many cardiovascular diseases begin at a young age. Practicing healthful behaviors as a teen reduces the risk of CVD.

Cancer

VOCABULARY

cancer
tumor
benign
malignant
metastasis
carcinogen
biopsy
remission

YOU'LL LEARN TO

- Examine the causes and types of and treatments for cancer.

- Relate the importance of early detection and warning signs of cancer that prompt individuals to seek health care.

- Examine the effects of health behaviors that put you at risk for developing cancer.

- Develop, analyze, and apply strategies related to the prevention of cancer.

QUICK START Make a list of any factors or behaviors you know of that can put a person at risk for developing cancer.

The body's cells are constantly growing and dividing. Most new cells are normal, but some are not. Sometimes these abnormal cells reproduce rapidly and uncontrollably, forming masses of abnormal cells inside otherwise normal tissue. This *uncontrollable growth of abnormal cells* is called **cancer**.

▲ Reduce your risk of skin cancer by protecting yourself from the sun's ultraviolet (UV) rays and reducing the amount of time you spend in the sun. *How does each item in the picture help protect you from UV rays?*

How Cancer Harms the Body

An *abnormal mass of tissue that has no natural role in the body* is called a **tumor**. Some tumors are **benign**, or *noncancerous*. Benign tumors grow slowly and are surrounded by membranes that prevent them from spreading from the original site. Although noncancerous tumors don't spread, they can be dangerous if they interfere with normal body functions. For example, a benign brain tumor may block the brain's blood supply.

Tumors that are **malignant**, or *cancerous*, spread to neighboring tissues and through the blood or lymph to other parts of the body. *The spread of cancer from the point where it originated to other parts of the body* is called **metastasis**. As cancer cells spread throughout the body, they divide and form new tumors.

Lesson 2 Cancer **681**

Cancer

① FOCUS

QUICK START Have students work with a partner to generate their lists. After students have completed their lists, lead a discussion in which they share their ideas.

TYING TO PRIOR KNOWLEDGE

Ask students how many of the warning signs of cancer they can name. Explain that over half of all cancers can be prevented. In this chapter, they will learn ways to reduce the risk of cancer.

Health Skills Features

"Being Sun Smart,"
p. 686

DECISION MAKING

INTRODUCING VOCABULARY

- Have students locate the vocabulary terms in the Glossary and define each term.

- Ask students to complete the Chapter 26 Study Guide in the *Student Activity Workbook*. ☞

Lesson 2 *Resources*

Teacher Classroom Resources

☞ Concept Mapping Activity 96

☞ Guided Reading Activities 96

☞ Lesson Plan 96

☞ Lesson Quiz 96

☞ Reteaching Activity 96

Student Activity Workbook

☞ Applying Health Skills 96

☞ Chapter 26 Study Guide

Multimedia

🔌 Transparency 76

2 TEACH

hotlink

Remind students that the immune system can often detect cells that have recently become cancerous and then destroy them just as it would a foreign microorganism. The immune system may start to weaken as people get older or when they have certain immune disorders such as HIV infection.

Explaining

Point out that leukemia is a disease of the parts of the body that make blood, affecting the body's production of white blood cells. Ask students to explain how blood transfusions and bone marrow transplants would benefit persons with leukemia. **L2**

Discussing

Ask students how cancer cells differ from normal cells. What do cancer cells do during their growth process? **L2**

Reinforcing Concepts

Explain that normally, cells divide and grow at a rate just sufficient to replace dying cells (unless they are part of the normal growth of certain tissues in growing children and teens). When a person cuts his or her finger, the cells around the wound divide more rapidly to heal the wound. When the wound is healed, the rate of cell growth and division returns to normal. In contrast, a malignant cell divides without regard for normal control mechanisms and gradually produces a mass of abnormal cells, or a tumor. **L1**

hotlink

immune system For more information about the immune system, see Chapter 24, page 629.

hotlink

tobacco use For more information on the harmful effects of tobacco and **secondhand smoke,** see Chapter 21, page 538.

Many cancers harm the body because they kill normal cells when they compete with them for nutrients. Tumors put pressure on surrounding tissues and organs, interfering with body function. They can also block arteries, veins, and other passages in the body.

Types of Cancer

Cancer can develop in almost any part of the body and in different tissues of each part. **Figure 26.3** shows some types of cancers, grouped according to the body organs where they first develop. Cancers also can be classified according to the tissues they affect.

▶ *Lymphomas* are cancers of the **immune system.**

▶ *Leukemias* are cancers of the blood-forming organs.

▶ *Carcinomas* are cancers of the glands and body linings, including the skin and the linings of the digestive tract and lungs.

▶ *Sarcomas* are cancers of connective tissue, including bones, ligaments, and muscle.

Risk Factors for Cancer

Abnormal cells that have the potential to become cancer cells are produced every day and the immune system destroys most of them. If the immune system becomes weakened or the number of cancer cells becomes overwhelming, cancer may develop. In some cases normal cells change by themselves. In others a faulty gene may have been inherited; between 5 to 10 percent of cancers are hereditary.

The majority of cancers are caused by exposure to certain factors that increase the risk of cell damage. One factor is a **carcinogen** (car-SIN-uh-juhn), *a cancer-causing substance*. Examples of carcinogens are cigarette smoke and ultraviolet light. Several major risk factors for cancer are associated with lifestyle behaviors. It is estimated that about 60 percent of all cancers can be prevented through healthy lifestyle choices.

Tobacco Use

Tobacco use is the major cause of cancer deaths in the United States and the most preventable. Recent studies attribute nearly one in five deaths to smoking or exposure to **secondhand smoke.** About 87 percent of lung cancer deaths are caused by smoking. An additional 25 percent of females who smoke will die of other smoking-related diseases. Tobacco use also increases the risk of bladder, pancreas, and kidney cancers. At least 43 different carcinogens have been identified in tobacco and tobacco smoke.

Home and Community

Assessing Exposure Have students obtain a list of carcinogens from the Environment Protection Agency (EPA) or from online and print sources. Have volunteers contact agencies that monitor water, air, and sanitation in the community for a list of carcinogens that might put residents at risk. Discuss their findings in class. Suggest that students assess their homes with a goal of reducing risk factors. How often are pesticides used inside or outside? What types of chemicals are used? What other factors, such as paint or dry-cleaned clothing, create indoor pollution? Have them suggest improvements such as nontoxic substitutes for pesticides and toxic chemicals.

FIGURE 26.3

TYPES OF CANCER

Organ Affected (new cases/year)	Some Risk Factors	Symptoms	Screening and Early Detection Methods
Skin (1 million) Most common type of cancer in the United States	Exposure to ultraviolet radiation from the sun, tanning beds, sun lamps, or other sources	Change on the skin, especially a new growth, a mole or freckle that changes, or a sore that won't heal	physical exam, biopsies
Breast (205,000) Second leading cause of cancer death for women	Genetic factors, obesity, alcohol use, physical inactivity	Unusual lump; nipple that thickens, changes shape, dimples, or has discharge	self-exam, mammogram
Prostate (189,000) Found mostly in men over age 55	Possible hereditary link, possible link to high-fat diet	Frequent or painful urination; inability to urinate; weak or interrupted flow of urine; blood in urine or semen; pain in lower back, hips or upper thighs	blood test
Lung (169,400) Leading cause of cancer deaths in the United States	Exposure to cigarette smoke, radon, or asbestos	No initial symptoms; later symptoms include cough, shortness of breath, wheezing, coughing up blood, hoarseness	chest X ray
Colon/Rectum (148,000) Second leading cause of cancer deaths in the United States	Risk increases with age; close relative with colorectal cancer	Often no initial symptoms; later, blood in feces; frequent pain, aches, or cramps in stomach; change in bowel habits; weight loss	test for blood in the stool, sigmoidoscopy
Mouth (30,000) Occurs mostly in people over 40	Use of tobacco, chewing tobacco, or alcohol	Sore or lump on mouth that doesn't heal; unusual bleeding; pain or numbness on lip, mouth, tongue, or throat; feeling that something is caught in the throat; pain with chewing or swallowing; change in voice	dental/oral exam
Cervix (15,000)	History of infection with HPV (human papilloma-virus)	Usually no symptoms in early stages; later, abnormal vaginal bleeding, increased vaginal discharge	Pap test
Testicle (7,000) Most common cancer in men ages 15 to 34	Undescended testicle; family history of testicular cancer	Small, hard painless lump on testicle; sudden accumulation of fluid in scrotum, pain in region between scrotum and anus	self-exam

Lesson 2 Cancer **683**

VISUAL LEARNING

Figure 26.3 Ask volunteers to read aloud each row of information in Figure 26.3. Lead a class discussion in which students describe strategies for reducing the risk of each type of cancer and/or actions a person can take for early detection of cancer.

Cross-Curriculum Activity

Geography and Earth Science Review the signs of skin cancer in Figure 26.3. Have students use classroom and library resources to find answers to these questions: What factors influence the total amount of UV radiation that reaches earth at any given time? During which hours of the day should you try to avoid being in the sun? In the United States, which states have the highest incidence of skin cancer? The lowest? Encourage students to check the newspaper daily for UV ratings. L2

Activity

Review with students the three main types of skin cancer. Basal cell and squamous cell carcinomas account for about 95 percent of the skin cancers diagnosed each year. Melanoma is the most dangerous skin cancer because it spreads so rapidly. It is responsible for most deaths from skin cancer. Direct students to access print and online sources to find illustrations of the three different types of skin cancer. L1

What Teens Want to Know

What is it like for a teen to live with cancer? Teens with cancer say one of the most difficult things about living with cancer is the loneliness. They often feel isolated and set apart. They look different—surgical scars, lost weight, lost hair. They may be on medication or in a treatment program. Their lives are different; they may miss school, and there may be restrictions on recreation.

If their friends do treat them differently or ostracize them, it is usually out of ignorance or fear. Friends may be afraid of getting close to someone who is ill, in pain, and possibly going to die. Stress the importance of supporting the person by offering friendship and companionship. Discuss compassion and empathy.

Explaining

Explain to students that excessive use of alcohol can lead to cancer of the liver, larynx, esophagus, and stomach. Alcohol and tobacco (cigarettes or smokeless tobacco) interact as risk factors for oral cancer. The combination of the two multiplies the carcinogenic effect of each substance. Heavy users of both alcohol and tobacco have a risk for oral cancer up to 15 times greater than that of people who don't drink or smoke. **L1**

VISUAL LEARNING

Figure 26.4 Direct students' attention to Figure 26.4. Ask students why the acronym CAUTION is appropriate. Guide students to conclude that, although none of the warning signs are a sure indication of cancer, the appearance of any one should send a person to his or her physician. Emphasize that self-monitoring is the first line of defense against cancer.

Explaining

Explain that the Pap test is used to detect cancer in the female reproductive system. Secretions from the cervix are placed on a slide and examined under a microscope for cancerous cells. **L1**

hot link

HPV and **hepatitis B** For more information on STDs that can cause cancer, see Chapter 25, page 648.
Skin cancer For more information on skin cancer warning signs, see Chapter 14, page 358.

Smokeless tobacco use is a major risk factor in the development of oral cancer, which affects the lips, mouth, and throat. Oral cancer kills roughly one person every hour. You can greatly reduce your risk of cancer by avoiding all forms of tobacco as well as secondhand smoke.

Sexually Transmitted Diseases

Some viruses, such as the human papillomavirus **(HPV)** and the **hepatitis B** virus, cause cervical and liver cancers, respectively. The risk of acquiring these pathogens can be reduced by abstinence from sexual activity and from injecting drugs through infected needles.

Dietary Factors

Approximately 30 percent of all cancer deaths are caused by dietary risk factors. A diet that is high in fat and low in fiber is often linked with cancer. Fats make colon cells more susceptible to carcinogens. Colon cells divide more rapidly if the diet is high in fat, increasing the chance that abnormal cells will form. Choosing foods low in fat and high in fiber reduces the risk of colon, breast, and prostate cancers. Dietary fiber speeds the movement of waste through the intestines, so carcinogens have less time to act on cells.

Radiation

Ultraviolet (UV) radiation from the sun is the main cause of **skin cancer.** Tanning beds and sunlamps also emit UV radiation, which is just as damaging as the sun's rays. A "tan" is the body's response to being injured by UV rays.

About 80 percent of skin cancers can be prevented. Reduce your exposure to UV light by avoiding tanning beds and sunlamps. Limit your time in the sun, especially between 10:00 A.M. and 4:00 P.M. When you must be in the sun, wear protective clothing and use a sunscreen with an SPF (Sun Protection Factor) of at least 15 and that blocks all types of UV radiation. Pay attention to changes in moles on your skin, one of the seven warning signs of cancer, listed in **Figure 26.4.**

FIGURE 26.4

A WORD OF CAUTION ABOUT CANCER

The American Cancer Society recommends that every individual should be alert to the seven warning signs of cancer. Note that their first letters, when combined, spell the word *caution*.

C hange in bowel habits (either loose stools or constipation)

A sore that does not heal

U nusual bleeding or discharge (as from the uterus, bladder, bowels, nipple, or with coughing)

T hickening or a lump in the breast or elsewhere (Let your health care provider decide what the lump means.)

I ndigestion or difficulty swallowing

O bvious change in a wart or mole

N agging cough or hoarseness

Other symptoms include fatigue and unexplained weight loss. The presence of these signs do not necessarily mean a person has cancer. If you experience any of these symptoms, contact a health care professional.

684 **Chapter 26** Noncommunicable Diseases and Disabilities

More About...

Radiation and Cancer Students may be confused by what seems to be a contradiction regarding cancer and radiation. Radiation, including UV light and X rays, is considered a carcinogen; yet radiation also serves as a treatment for cancer. Logically, students may wonder how radiation can be both harmful and beneficial. Explain that radiation is a risk factor for cancer when a person is exposed to large doses of it or for prolonged periods of time. When used as a treatment for cancer, it is targeted directly at cancer cells but may also damage nearby normal cells.

Reducing Your Risk

You can't control some risk factors for cancer, such as heredity, but you can reduce your risk by practicing the healthful behaviors listed in **Figure 26.5.**

FIGURE 26.5

HOW YOU CAN REDUCE YOUR RISK OF CANCER

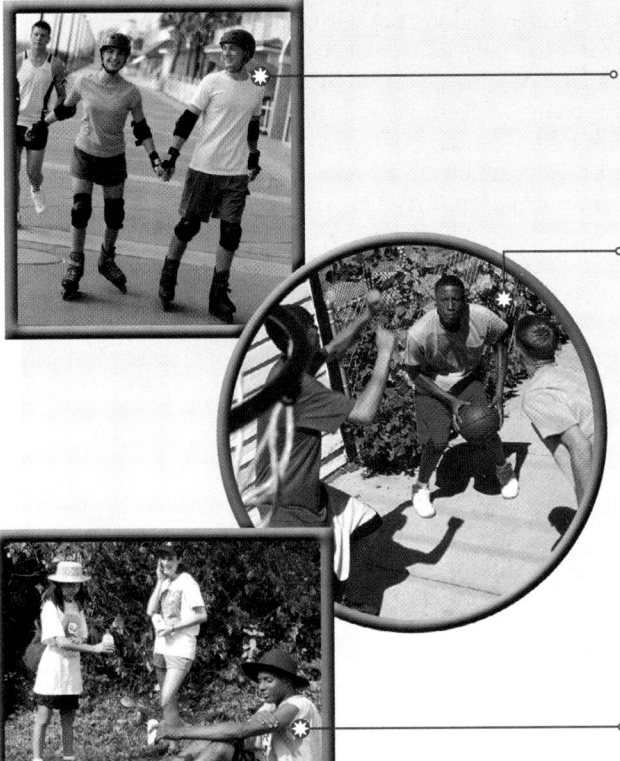

Practice abstinence from sexual activity to reduce the risk of sexually transmitted diseases. Hepatitis B can cause liver cancer, and HPV can cause cancers of the reproductive organs.

Be physically active.

Maintain a healthy weight.

Eat nutritious foods. Include 2–4 serving of fruits and 3–5 servings of vegetables every day. These foods are good sources of fiber, and some contain compounds that act against carcinogens.

Follow an eating plan that is low in saturated fat and high in fiber.

Protect your skin from ultraviolet radiation.

Avoid tobacco and alcohol. Tobacco is the single major cause of cancer death in the United States. Excess alcohol increases the risk of several types of cancer, including mouth and throat cancer.

Recognize the warning signs of cancer. Do regular self-exams to detect cancer early.

Lesson 2 Cancer **685**

Health Skills Activity

BEING SUN SMART

DECISION MAKING

NHES Standard 6 Students will demonstrate the ability to use goal-setting and decision-making skills to enhance health.

Objectives

• Examine the effects of health behaviors on skin safety.

• Apply decision-making skills to make a health-promoting decision.

Motivator

Ask students whether they know the answer to this question: Can one sunburn increase the risk of skin cancer?

Teaching Strategies

1. Tell students that one sunburn during the teen years can increase the risk of skin cancer later in life.
2. Allow students to work in small groups to discuss Amber's options.

✓Assessment

Using a rubric, student work should provide comprehensive evidence of the following criteria to achieve the highest score:

✔ progression through a decision-making process
✔ clear description of the situation
✔ several options with possible outcomes of each
✔ influence of values or possible decisions
✔ health-enhancing decision and evaluation of it

Detecting and Treating Cancer

Many advances have been made in the detection and treatment of cancer, and many more people are successfully living with the disease than ever before. The survival rate for those with cancer depends on the type of cancer and how early it is detected.

Early detection is the most critical factor in successful cancer treatment. Many types of cancer can be detected through self-examination of the **breast, testes,** and skin.

Screening for cancer is examination or testing for early signs of cancer even though a person has no symptoms. Medical screenings can result in early detection of about half of all new cancer cases each year. The current five-year survival rate with early detection is about 80 percent. With regular screenings, the rate could increase to 95 percent.

If cancer is a possibility, a **biopsy**, *the removal of a small piece of tissue for examination*, may be performed. A biopsy is usually

hot link

breast and **testes** For information on testicular and breast self-exams, see Chapter 18, pages 472 and 477.

Health Skills Activity

Decision Making: Being Sun Smart

Amber rushes to meet her friends at the boat dock. "Sorry I'm late," she says breathlessly. "This is going to be great. I love to water-ski. Hey, does anyone have any sunscreen? I was in such a hurry that I forgot mine."

"I never use it. I don't burn," Taylor replies.

"I don't use it either. I like looking tan and healthy," Denise chimes in.

Amber knows that tan skin isn't healthy—it's damaged. "I always wear sunscreen," she says firmly. "I'll just run up the hill to that little corner store and buy some."

"Amber, the boat's in the water. We're ready to go," Denise protests.

What should Amber do?

What Would You Do?

Apply the six steps of the decision-making process to help Amber make a health-enhancing decision.

1. State the situation.
2. List the options.
3. Weigh the possible outcomes.
4. Consider values.
5. Make a decision and act.
6. Evaluate the decision.

686 **Chapter 26** Noncommunicable Diseases and Disabilities

More About...

Cancer Therapies One technological advancement in the war on cancer is the cyberknife. A blend of robotics, computers, and radiation therapy, the cyberknife is used to cut away cancerous tumors deep in the brain. A robotic arm is programmed to fire beams of low-level gamma rays toward specific targets—in this case, tumors. Much like a guided missile, the cyberknife is able to target the tumor with maximum accuracy and without damaging surrounding tissue. The cyberknife automatically and constantly readjusts its fix on the target when patients involuntarily move their heads. Patients no longer have to wear a bulky, uncomfortable metal device to hold their heads in place.

necessary to determine whether cancer is present. X rays and other imaging techniques help determine a tumor's location and size.

Treating Cancer

The methods used to treat cancer depend on several factors, such as the type of cancer, whether the tumor has spread, and the patient's age and health. Treatment might include one or more of the following:

▶ **Surgery** removes some or all of the cancerous masses from the body.

▶ **Radiation therapy** aims rays from radioactive substances at cancerous cells. The radiation kills the cells and shrinks the cancerous mass.

▶ **Chemotherapy** uses chemicals to destroy cancer cells.

▶ **Immunotherapy** activates a person's immune system to recognize specific cancers and destroy them.

▶ **Hormone therapy** involves using medicines that interfere with the production of hormones. These treatments kill cancer cells or slow their growth.

Cancer that responds to treatment or is under control is said to be in **remission**, *a period of time when symptoms disappear.* Cancer in remission is not always cured; it can recur, sometimes years later.

HEALTH Online

Link to the American Cancer Society to discover the latest in cancer research in Web Links at **health.glencoe.com**.

Lesson 2 *Review*

Reviewing Facts and Vocabulary

1. Define *cancer*. Name four risk factors for cancer.
2. What is the difference between a benign tumor and one that is malignant?
3. What are two important means of early cancer detection?

Thinking Critically

4. **Analyzing.** The physician of an adult family member has suggested that the person undergo a certain cancer screening procedure as part of a routine exam. The family member is afraid to have this procedure done. What would you tell this person?
5. **Evaluating.** Why do you think skin cancer is the most common cancer in the United States?

Applying Health Skills

Advocacy. Develop a cancer-awareness booklet that analyzes healthful strategies to reduce cancer risk and encourages people to develop these habits. Include information on technology and new treatments that impact the health status of people with cancer.

TECHNOLOGY OPTION

WORD PROCESSING   Use word-processing software to create your booklet. Use special formats, borders, and art. Click on **health.glencoe.com** for help using word-processing software.

Lesson 2 Cancer   **687**

Chapter 26 • Lesson 2

3 ASSESS

EVALUATING THE LESSON

Assign and discuss the Lesson 2 Review; then administer, grade, and discuss Lesson Quiz 96 in the TCR. 📁

RETEACHING

• Direct students to make lists of the following information: three strategies to reduce the risk of cancer, the seven warning signs of cancer, and three treatments for cancer.

• Ask students to complete Reteaching Activity 96 in the TCR. 📁

ENRICHMENT

Have students research dietary compounds that act against cancer and identify which foods contain them. For example, compounds called carotenoids—found in orange, yellow, and green vegetables—may prevent damage to cells from carcinogens.

4 CLOSE

Have students list the title of each section in this lesson, leaving a few spaces between each one. Direct them to summarize in one sentence the most important concept of that section.

Lesson 2 *Review*

Answers to Reviewing Facts and Vocabulary

1. An uncontrollable growth of abnormal cells. Possible answers: exposure to carcinogens, tobacco use, certain STDs, dietary factors, exposure to radiation.
2. A benign tumor does not spread to other tissue; a malignant tumor does.
3. Medical screenings and self-exams.

Answers to Thinking Critically

4. Possible answer: If a health care professional suggests certain screening tests, it does not mean he or she thinks the patient has cancer. Early detection is important for treatment.
5. Possible answer: Everyone is exposed to UV rays which can cause cancer.

Allergies, Asthma, Diabetes, and Arthritis

1 FOCUS

QUICK START Give students two minutes to make their list. As a class, have students share what they know about why people with these diseases take those measures.

TYING TO PRIOR KNOWLEDGE

Have students brainstorm a list of things that they know or believe to trigger allergies. Explain that in this lesson, they will learn how this process works.

Health Skills Features

"Raising Teen Awareness of Diabetes," p. 692

ADVOCACY

INTRODUCING VOCABULARY

- Without looking up the words, have students write their brief definition of each vocabulary term. They should save the list and correct their definitions as necessary as they study the lesson.

- Ask students to complete the Chapter 26 Study Guide in the *Student Activity Workbook*. 📁

Allergies, Asthma, Diabetes, and Arthritis

VOCABULARY
- allergy
- histamines
- asthma
- diabetes
- autoimmune disease
- arthritis
- osteoarthritis
- rheumatoid arthritis

YOU'LL LEARN TO
- Examine the characteristics, symptoms, causes, and treatments of noncommunicable diseases.
- Describe the importance of taking responsibility for health maintenance to prevent or manage noncommunicable diseases.
- Develop and analyze strategies related to the prevention and management of noncommunicable diseases.

 QUICK START Think of a family member or someone you know who has one of the diseases discussed in this lesson. What does this person do to manage the disease or its symptoms?

 An allergy to pollen, called hay fever, is one of the most common chronic diseases in the United States. Experts estimate that 35 million people suffer from hay fever.

Cardiovascular diseases and cancer are two of the most deadly noncommunicable diseases. Other noncommunicable diseases are chronic, meaning that they are present continuously or recur frequently over a long period time. Allergies, asthma, diabetes, and arthritis are chronic diseases that affect millions of people. Some, such as allergies, asthma, and certain types of diabetes, are caused by a response of the immune system. Others, such as osteoarthritis (ahs-tee-oh-ahr-THRY-tus), cause the breakdown of body cells and tissues.

Allergies

The sneezing and runny nose often associated with a cold are sometimes a response to substances in the air. An **allergy** is *a specific reaction of the immune system to a foreign and frequently harmless substance*. Allergies are among the common causes of illness and disability in the United States, affecting 40 to 50 million people.

688 Chapter 26 Noncommunicable Diseases and Disabilities

Lesson 3 *Resources*

Teacher Classroom Resources
- 📁 Concept Mapping Activity 97
- 📁 Decision-Making Activity 26
- 📁 Guided Reading Activities 97
- 📁 Lesson Plan 97
- 📁 Lesson Quiz 97
- 📁 Reteaching Activity 97

Student Activity Workbook
- 📁 Applying Health Skills 97
- 📁 Chapter 26 Study Guide

Multimedia
- 💾 Transparency 77

Pollen, foods, dust, mold spores, chemicals, insect venom, and medicines are some of the more common *allergens*, substances that cause allergies. The body treats these allergens as foreign invaders. Antigens on the surface of allergens bind to special immune cells in the linings of the nasal passages. These cells release **histamines**, *chemicals that can stimulate mucus and fluid production in an area.*

Histamines produce the sneezing, itchy eyes, runny nose, and other symptoms that make a person with allergies uncomfortable. Some people have an allergic reaction that produces hives—itchy raised bumps on the skin. Others have serious reactions to allergens that can sometimes be life threatening. Severe symptoms include hives, itching or swelling of the stung area or the mouth, difficulty breathing or swallowing. Other severe symptoms might be a raspy voice or swelling of the tongue, or a sharp drop in blood pressure, which can cause dizziness.

If someone you know experiences any of these symptoms after eating foods such as peanuts or shellfish or after being stung by a bee or wasp, seek medical attention immediately.

Diagnosing Allergies

Sometimes you can diagnose an allergy yourself. You may notice that when you are near certain kinds of plants you sneeze or that eating particular foods makes you break out in a rash. In some cases tests are required to determine the cause. Three common methods are used to identify the source of an allergic reaction—a blood test, a food elimination diet, and a skin test. During a skin test, the skin is scratched and small amounts of possible allergens are applied. If a person is allergic to any of the allergens, the skin in the area of the scratch swells and turns red because of the **inflammatory response.**

Treating Allergies

Sometimes allergy treatment can be as simple as avoiding the allergen. This is the best treatment for severe food and insect sting allergies. When avoidance is not possible, medicines, including *antihistamines* that help control the symptoms triggered by histamines, may be suggested. People with long-lasting or severe allergies should seek medical attention. Allergies can irritate the respiratory tract and lead to other health problems, such as asthma. People with severe allergies may receive *immunotherapy*, a series of shots that contain small amounts of the allergen to which the person is sensitive. The injections cause the immune system to become less sensitive to the allergens.

The body's response to allergens can cause a variety of symptoms. *What should you do if you experience more serious allergic reactions?*

hotlink

inflammatory response
For more information about the inflammatory response, see Chapter 24, page 628.

2 TEACH

Discussing

Point out that immune cells that can release histamine are found throughout the body. Ask students to think of possible allergens that may trigger the responses discussed in the text. Possible answers: Eyes: pollen; Respiratory System; pollen, molds, pet dander; Throat: foods, medications; Skin: poison ivy, chemicals; Digestive System: foods.

hotlink

Review with students that histamine is produced in some allergic reactions. This is the result of B cells producing a particular type of antibody that stimulates immune cells to produce histamines. Other allergic reactions involve T cells. For example, the toxin in poison ivy does not in itself cause much harm to tissues. However, in some persons exposed to poison ivy, killer T cells are activated in response to the poison ivy and cause tissue damage.

FYI

The single most important factor in whether a child will develop an allergy is whether a parent or parents have allergies. Approximately 87 percent of people with allergies have a family history of allergies.

Myths & Reality

MYTH. Children with allergies never outgrow them.
FACT. Some children do outgrow allergies, especially food allergies.

MYTH. A person who is allergic to pet dander will not have symptoms around a hairless dog.
FACT. Dander is not the hair or fur of the animal but is old skin scales, which are constantly shed. People with allergies to dogs and cats are allergic to a protein found in dander, urine, and saliva.

Critical Thinking

Explain that the incidence of asthma has nearly doubled in the past two decades in the United States. No one really knows for certain why this is. Some experts think that one reason is an increase in industrial and indoor air pollution. Ask: Why might indoor air pollution be increasing? (Hint: Tell students to think how houses are being built differently today than decades ago.) Possible answer: Houses today have better insulation and, therefore, poorer ventilation. Pollution from dry cleaning and household products is held within the house. **L3**

Reinforcing Concepts

Emphasize that people with asthma can live normal lives. One way to do this is to minimize triggers. Stress that secondhand smoke is a powerful trigger. Even being in a home or car where smoke lingers can trigger an attack as can the smell of smoke on clothing. Teens with asthma need to use effective communication skills to explain why they may not be able to visit in a home or ride in a car where someone smokes and to ask others not to smoke in their presence. **L1**

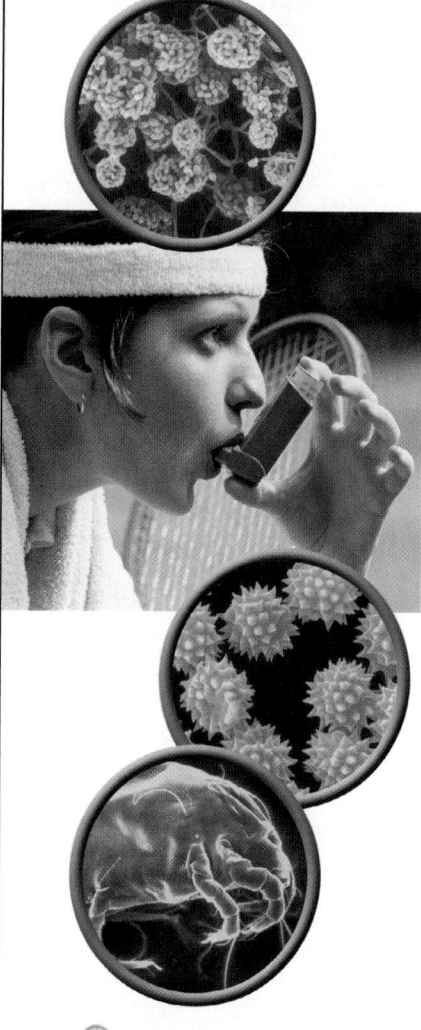

People with asthma can be active if they manage the disease and use proper precautions. *What precautions should a person with asthma take to avoid an attack?*

Experiencing an unpleasant reaction to something you eat does not necessarily mean that you have a food allergy. For instance, lactose intolerance is not an allergy. Because symptoms are similar, this is a common misconception. In reality, only a very small percentage of people actually have proven food allergies. For those who do, the main method of treatment is avoiding the food that causes the allergic reaction. This usually requires diligently reading ingredient lists.

Asthma

Some allergic reactions can lead to **asthma**, *an inflammatory condition in which the small airways in the lungs become narrowed, causing difficulty in breathing.* More than 17 million people in the United States have asthma, and each year more than 5,000 Americans die of this disease. Asthma can develop at any age; however, about one-third of those with asthma are under the age of 18.

The bronchial tubes of people with asthma are sensitive to certain substances called *triggers*. Common asthma triggers include air pollution, pet dander, and tobacco smoke, as well as microscopic mold, pollen, and dust mites, shown on this page. In an asthma attack, the asthma triggers cause the muscles of the bronchial walls to tighten and produce extra mucus. The respiratory passages narrow. The result can range from minor wheezing—breathing with a whistling sound—to severe difficulty breathing. In some cases the condition becomes life threatening.

Managing Asthma

Although asthma has no cure, most people with the condition can lead normal lives by behavior changes and the proper use of medication. People with asthma can lead normal, active lives with proper management that includes the following strategies:

▶ **Monitor the condition.** Recognize the warning signs of an attack: shortness of breath, chest tightness or pain, coughing or sneezing. Treating these symptoms quickly can help prevent attacks or keep an attack from worsening.

▶ **Manage the environment.** Reduce asthma triggers in the environment. Avoid exposure to tobacco smoke, eliminate carpets and rugs when possible, and wash bedding frequently.

▶ **Manage stress.** Stress can trigger an asthma attack. Relaxation and stress-management techniques can be helpful.

▶ **Take medication.** Medications can be used to relieve symptoms, prevent flare-ups, and make air passages less sensitive to asthma triggers. *Bronchodilators* are a type of medication, taken with an inhaler, that relaxes and widens respiratory passages.

Meeting Individual Needs

Project: Have students create a magazine that focuses on promoting healthful lifestyles for teens. ▭▭

Learning Styles: Pair students with special learning needs with those who do not have the same learning need. All students may benefit from working together on a variety of tasks including fact gathering. At the time of assessment, pairs may be evaluated in terms of positive interdependence and individual accountability.

Visually Impaired: Students with visual impairments may want to supervise publication of a large-type version of the magazine. These students should work with illustrators in choosing a typeface that is easy to read.

Diabetes

Diabetes is *a chronic disease that affects the way body cells convert food into energy.* Each year approximately one million new cases are diagnosed. There is no cure for diabetes.

In a person with diabetes, the pancreas produces too little or no insulin, a hormone that helps glucose enter the body's cells. In some diabetics adequate insulin is produced, but cells don't respond normally to it. For the cells in the body to function, they need a constant source of energy—glucose—from foods. If glucose is not converted to energy, it builds up in the blood, and cells do not get the glucose they need to function. The only way to diagnose diabetes is through a blood test. Early detection of diabetes can prevent serious side effects, such as blindness. Diabetes is the main cause of kidney failure, limb amputations, and blindness in adults, as well as a major cause of heart disease and stroke. These effects, however, are not inevitable. If diagnosed, the disease can be successfully managed with medication, a healthful diet, and regular moderate exercise. In many cases, diabetes is preventable.

Type 1 Diabetes

Type 1 diabetes, which accounts for 5 to 10 percent of all diabetes cases, appears suddenly and progresses quickly. The body does not produce insulin, and glucose builds up in the blood, starving cells of the energy they need. Over time, the high blood-sugar level can cause damage to the eyes, kidneys, nerves, and heart.

The cause of type 1 diabetes is not clear. Some scientists suspect an environmental trigger—perhaps an as yet unidentified virus—that stimulates an immune response, destroying the insulin-producing cells of the pancreas in some individuals. For this reason, type 1 diabetes is known as an **autoimmune disease**, *a condition in which the immune system mistakenly attacks itself, targeting the cells, tissues, and organs of a person's own body.* People with type 1 diabetes must take daily doses of insulin, either through injections or through a special pump that is attached to the body by tubing or that is surgically implanted. Today, because of advanced treatment methods, many people with diabetes are able to live near-normal lives.

Type 2 Diabetes

Type 2 diabetes accounts for 90 to 95 percent of all cases of this disease. It most often appears after age 40. However, type 2 diabetes is now being found at younger ages and is even being diagnosed among children and teens. In this form of diabetes, the body is unable to make enough insulin or to use insulin properly. Buildup of glucose in the blood causes many of the same symptoms as type 1 diabetes.

Health Minute

Symptoms of Diabetes

According to the American Diabetes Association, of the estimated 17 million people in the United States who have diabetes, almost 6 million of them don't know it.

Symptoms of diabetes include:

▶ Frequent urination
▶ Excessive thirst
▶ Unexplained weight loss
▶ Extreme hunger
▶ Sudden vision changes
▶ Tingling in hands or feet
▶ Frequent fatigue
▶ Very dry skin
▶ Sores that are slow to heal
▶ More infections than usual

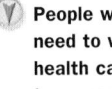 **People with diabetes need to work closely with health care professionals to manage their condition.** *Why is early detection of diabetes important?*

Health Minute

Ask a volunteer to read the list of symptoms. Point out that type 2 diabetes is often asymptomatic in the early stages. Have students access online or print resources to find out when routine screening for diabetes is recommended for people who have risk factors for diabetes and for those who do not.

Cooperative Learning

Divide the class into groups, and give each group a poster board. Assign each group one of the following, and have them create a display for the poster board: (1) List all the types of diabetes and symptoms/characteristics of each. (2) Describe healthful habits, such as diet and exercise, that help to reduce the risk of developing diabetes. (3) Provide pictures of unhealthful habits that contribute to diabetes. (4) Describe ways that people with diabetes manage their disease. **L1**

Discussing

Have students explain how diabetes disrupts normal metabolism. What happens when glucose is unable to enter the body cells? How is this related to weight loss? **L1**

Activity

Have students research the signs of low blood sugar in a person with type 1 diabetes and how this can occur. They should report what first aid should be given in such a situation. **L1**

Cooperative Learning Activity

Party Menu Group students, and have them plan beverages and appetizers for a large party of health-conscious teens. Their goal is to choose foods that reduce the risk of diseases that can be prevented through lifestyle behaviors. Have them obtain information from print and online sources about topics such as food composition and nutrition tables, and list some of the most common party foods. They should choose foods low in sodium, fat, and sugar. Encourage groups to develop menus specifically for this group of teens. Remind them to check for spelling and grammar errors. Then have them illustrate their menus and share them with other groups.

Real-Life Application

ADVOCACY

RAISING TEEN AWARENESS OF DIABETES

NHES Standard 7 Students will demonstrate the ability to advocate for personal, family, and community health.

Objectives

- Analyze the effects of health behaviors on the risk of developing diabetes.

- Demonstrate the ability to influence and support others in making positive health choices.

Motivator

Give students one minute to look at the graph and then answer the question: Why is diabetes considered an epidemic in the United States?

Teaching Strategies

1. Guide students to observe that the rate of diabetes in teens has been increasing along with the rate of obesity.
2. Suggest that students access print and online sources for more strategies on reducing the risk of diabetes.

✓ Assessment

Using a rubric, student work should provide comprehensive evidence of the following criteria to achieve the highest score:

✔ clear, health-enhancing stand
✔ support for the position with relevant information
✔ awareness of the audience
✔ encouragement of others to make healthful choices
✔ passion and conviction

692

Type 2 diabetes is nearing epidemic proportions in the United States because of an increased number of older individuals in the population and a greater prevalence of obesity and inactive lifestyles. A diet high in fat, calories, and cholesterol increases the risk of diabetes. Thus, choosing lower-fat, lower-calorie alternatives can help reduce the risk of this disease. Increased physical activity also reduces risk because it helps control weight and lower blood cholesterol levels.

Treatment of type 2 diabetes includes weight management and regular physical activity. Individuals with this disease must

Real-Life Application

Raising Teen Awareness of Diabetes

Over the last decade, diabetes and obesity have increased dramatically in both adults and teens. Examine the graph and answer the questions. Then use this information to create an advocacy message to encourage others to practice healthful behaviors to control their weight and reduce their risk of diabetes.

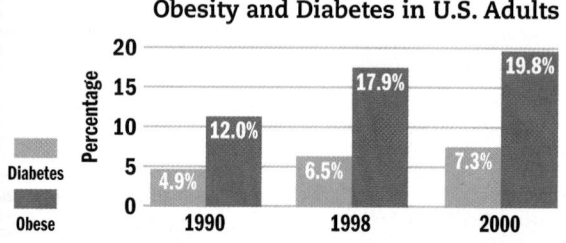

Obesity and Diabetes in U.S. Adults
Diabetes / Obese
1990: 4.9%, 12.0%
1998: 6.5%, 17.9%
2000: 7.3%, 19.8%

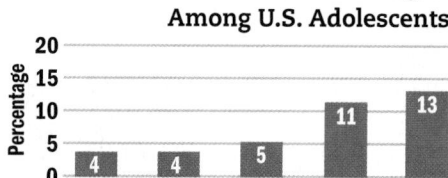

Prevalence of Overweight Among U.S. Adolescents
1963-70: 4
1971-74: 4
1988-94: 5
1976-80: 11
1999: 13

Source: CDC, Behavioral Risk Factor Surveillance System (1991–2000)

1. What do you observe about the relationship between the rates of diabetes and obesity in Graph 1?

2. What do you think would happen to the rate of diabetes if the rate of obesity began to decrease?

3. Look at Graph 2. What can you infer about the rate of diabetes in teens?

4. Why are healthful eating habits and physical activity lifestyle behaviors that reduce the risk of diabetes?

ACTIVITY

In small groups, generate a list of lifestyle behaviors that people can practice to maintain a healthful weight and reduce their risk of diabetes. Create a 60-second public service announcement (PSA) to persuade teens to start good health habits early in life. Include at least one fact about diabetes and one lifestyle behavior that can reduce the risk of diabetes.

692 Chapter 26 Noncommunicable Diseases and Disabilities

Curriculum Connections

Math Tell students that in 1990, 4.9 percent of the U.S. adult population had diabetes. That figure was 7.3 percent in 2000. If the population of the United States was approximately 249 million in 1990 and 281 million in 2000, how many people in each year had diabetes? 1990: 12,201,000; 2000: 20,513,000.

Geography Have students access print and online sources to find out which states have the highest rates of diabetes and obesity. What is the rate in their state? Have them contact their state health department for more information on what state public health agencies are doing to encourage people to adopt healthier lifestyles.

carefully monitor their diet in order to control their blood-sugar levels. In some cases oral medications or injections of insulin are required to manage the disease.

Arthritis

Arthritis is *a group of more than 100 different diseases that cause pain and loss of movement in the joints.* It is one of the most common medical problems in the world and the number one cause of disability in the United States—more than one in six people suffer from the disease. Arthritis is more common in older people, but it can affect anyone, including children and teens. In fact, 8.4 million people between the ages of 18 and 44 have arthritis and millions of others are at risk for it.

Osteoarthritis

Osteoarthritis is *a disease of the joints in which cartilage breaks down.* Cartilage is the strong, flexible tissue that provides cushioning at the joints. In this disease the cartilage becomes pitted and frayed. In time it may wear away completely, and bones may rub against each other. Although osteoarthritis affects primarily the weight-bearing joints of the knees and hips, it can affect any joint—including in the fingers, lower back, and feet—causing aches and soreness, especially when moving.

Osteoarthritis is one of the most common types of arthritis; in fact, it accounts for half of all arthritis cases. It affects about 20 million people in the United States and is most common in women and in people over the age of 45. Many people think that arthritis is an inevitable part of aging. However, several strategies reduce the risk of osteoarthritis:

▶ **Controlling weight.** Maintaining an appropriate weight reduces stress on joints by lessening wear and tear on cartilage.

▶ **Preventing sports injuries.** Warming up before exercising, adding strength training to your physical activities, and using appropriate equipment (including wrist guards and knee pads when necessary) help avoid joint injuries and damage to ligaments and cartilage, thus decreasing the risk of osteoarthritis. Let injuries heal completely before playing again.

▶ **Protecting against Lyme disease.** Lyme disease, which is spread by the bite of infected deer ticks, is associated with the development of osteoarthritis. Using insect repellents, wearing long-sleeved shirts and pants when walking outdoors or in wooded areas, and being educated on tick recognition and removal can help reduce this risk factor.

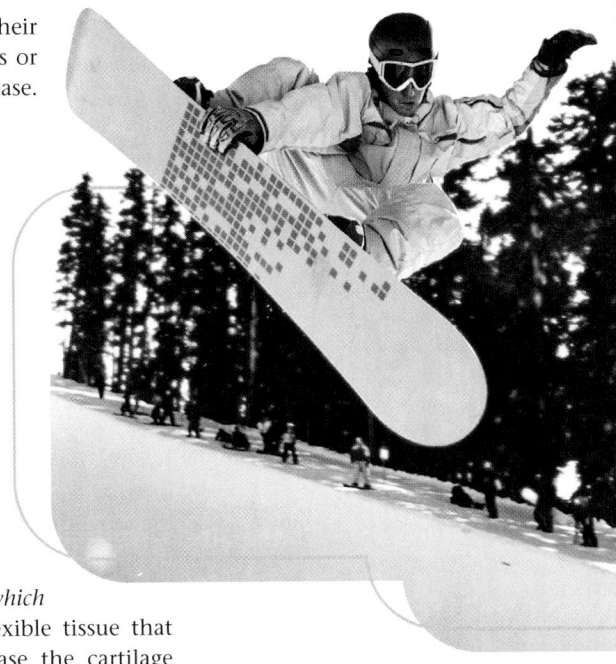

According to the Arthritis Foundation, an arthritis epidemic may result from the number of people who participate in adventure sports. *What can you do to reduce your risk of developing osteoarthritis?*

Cooperative Learning

Divide students into small groups. Have them make a chart of common types of arthritis. They should include ways to reduce the risk of developing arthritis and treatment for each type. **L1** **Visual-Spatial Intelligence**

Explaining

Tell the class that arthritis is seen more often in women than in men. It is likely to strike persons in the age groups of 20–50 years of age. However, it can start at any age. **L1**

Activity

Have students research the use of artificial joints to replace those damaged by arthritis. Have them answer the following question with their research: How successful is this surgery in easing the pain and lack of movement or motion caused by arthritis? **L3**

ACTIVE READING

News Summary

In this strategy, students are given several minutes to summarize, retell, or analyze an activity for an audience. Divide the class into small groups. Have each group develop a two-minute script about osteoarthritis. One group member role-plays a newscaster who is interviewing "expert guests." Advise students to emphasize ways to reduce the risk of developing osteoarthritis. For more strategies, see the *Guided Reading Activities* booklet in the TCR.

More About...

Arthritis In the early 1900s, people who had arthritis had very limited options for treatment. In fact, it was believed that participation in any kind of exercise was the wrong thing to do. It was thought that exercise would aggravate joint problems. As a result, arthritic patients were told that rest was the only option they had. Today, the thinking is much different. Researchers have studied the effects of vigorous exercise on people with arthritis. The results indicate that aerobic exercise is safe and beneficial. Brisk walking is encouraged as an excellent form of exercise for people with arthritis.

③ ASSESS

EVALUATING THE LESSON

Assign and discuss the Lesson 3 Review; then administer, grade, and discuss Lesson Quiz 97 in the TCR. 📁

RETEACHING

- Assign each of four groups one disease studied in this lesson. Using their textbooks, have each group summarize the key points about the disease and give a five-minute presentation.

- Ask students to complete Reteaching Activity 97 in the TCR. 📁

ENRICHMENT

Have interested students find out about noncommunicable diseases or disorders not covered in this chapter and present a report to the class. Examples include lupus, Parkinson's disease, multiple sclerosis, and epilepsy.

④ CLOSE

Have students, without looking at their books, write a paragraph describing the key points they have learned from this lesson. Encourage them to draw conclusions based on their personal experiences as necessary.

Did You Know ?

➤ Arthritis is the leading cause of disability among people age 15 and older. Arthritis and rheumatoid arthritis account for more than 15 percent of all disabilities in the United States.

Rheumatoid Arthritis

Rheumatoid arthritis affects about 2.5 million people in the United States. It is three times more common in women than in men. Symptoms usually first appear between the ages of 20 and 50, but the disease also can affect young children. Juvenile rheumatoid arthritis is the most common form of arthritis in children.

Rheumatoid arthritis is *a disease characterized by the debilitating destruction of the joints due to inflammation*. Like type 1 diabetes, this type of arthritis is caused by an autoimmune disease for which there is no cure. Sufferers are likely to experience joint pain, inflammation, swelling, and stiffness. Eventually the joints may become deformed and cease to function normally. Rheumatoid arthritis affects mainly the joints in the hand, foot, elbow, shoulder, neck, knee, hip, and ankle. Other effects include fever, fatigue, and swollen lymph glands. The effects of this disease are usually symmetrical—both sides of the body develop the same symptoms at the same time and in the same pattern.

Early diagnosis of rheumatoid arthritis is crucial. With the use of medication, in many cases the effects of the disease can be controlled. Treatment methods focus on relieving pain, reducing inflammation and swelling, and keeping the joints moving as normally as possible. A combination of exercise, rest, joint protection, and physical and occupational therapy also can help manage the disease.

▶ Lesson 3 *Review*

Reviewing Facts and Vocabulary

1. What are *histamines*, and what role do they play in allergies?

2. Define *asthma*. What are two strategies for managing this condition?

3. What is *osteoarthritis*? List two ways to reduce the risk of osteoarthritis.

Thinking Critically

4. **Synthesizing.** Why is it difficult to avoid many allergens?

5. **Analyzing.** Why is it important for people with diabetes to take responsibility for managing their condition?

Applying Health Skills

Practicing Healthful Behaviors. Make a table. In the first column, write the names of the noncommunicable diseases in this lesson. In the second column, identify risk factors for each disease. In the third column, describe and analyze strategies for healthful lifestyle behaviors that will reduce your risk for the disease.

TECHNOLOGY *OPTION*

SPREADSHEETS Using a spreadsheet can help you organize and edit your table. For help using spreadsheets, go to **health.glencoe.com**.

694 Chapter 26 Noncommunicable Diseases and Disabilities

▶ Lesson 3 *Review*

Answers to Reviewing Facts and Vocabulary

1. See page 688 for definition; histamines produce many of the typical allergy symptoms.

2. See page 690 for definition; any two: monitor the condition, manage the environment, manage stress, medication.

3. A disease of the joints in which cartilage breaks down; control weight, avoid injuries, protect against Lyme disease.

Answers to Thinking Critically

4. Possible answer: Many allergens are in the air we breathe.

5. Diabetes is a progressive disease with serious consequences.

Physical and Mental Challenges

VOCABULARY
disability
profound deafness
mental retardation
Americans with
   Disabilities Act

YOU'LL LEARN TO
- Identify and recognize the challenges of individuals with disabilities.
- Discuss health-related social issues, and determine ways in which progress has been made to better integrate individuals with disabilities into society.

 QUICK START Make a word web with the word *disability* in the center. List the types of disabilities you know of around it. Add to your web as you study this lesson.

D oes your school have ramps and special rest room facilities to accommodate people in wheelchairs? Are there telephones for people who are hearing or vision impaired? Have you ever seen a closed-captioned television program? All these devices are designed to offset a **disability**, *any physical or mental impairment that limits normal activities, including seeing, hearing, walking, or speaking*. According to the latest U.S. Census Bureau statistics, almost 20 percent of the adult population had some type of disability. People with disabilities sometimes have difficulty doing things that others take for granted. The challenge may be physical, such as climbing stairs, seeing a sign, hearing a conversation, or holding a package, or it may be mental, such as understanding simple instructions.

Physical Challenges

T he most common types of physical challenges affect a person's senses or the ability to move and get around easily. Most physical challenges can be classified as sight impairment, hearing impairment, or motor impairment.

Computers are one of many devices that people with disabilities can use to meet their physical challenges. *List other assistive technologies that help people who have disabilities.*

Lesson 4   Physical and Mental Challenges   **695**

Physical and Mental Challenges

 FOCUS

QUICK START Have students work with partners. Remind them that disabilities can be present at birth or can happen later in life as the result of an accident or disease. Ask volunteers to share their word webs.

TYING TO PRIOR KNOWLEDGE

Have students name all the ways they can think of that public buildings and employers accommodate people who are disabled. Explain that in this lesson, they will learn more about the challenges that individuals with disabilities face and how society is taking steps to better accommodate their needs.

INTRODUCING VOCABULARY
- Give students three minutes to write everything they know about each vocabulary term. Have them add to their list or change it as needed as they study the lesson.
- Ask students to complete the Chapter 26 Study Guide in the *Student Activity Workbook*. 📁

Lesson 4 *Resources*

Teacher Classroom Resources
- 📁 Concept Mapping Activity 98
- 📁 Current Health Issues 26
- 📁 Guided Reading Activities 98
- 📁 Lesson Plan 98
- 📁 Lesson Quiz 98
- 📁 Reteaching Activity 98

Student Activity Workbook
- 📁 Applying Health Skills 98
- 📁 Chapter 26 Study Guide

② TEACH

CHARACTER ✓ CHECK

Caring Ask students why learning sign language demonstrates caring for people who are hearing impaired. Encourage students to investigate opportunities in the community to volunteer working with people who are hearing impaired. Some organizations, including their own school, need people who can tutor in sign language or show people who are hearing impaired how to use computers.

Activity

Have students find out how many people in the United States have each of the conditions discussed on this page. Ask students to interview family members who may have one of these diseases and find out how their diseases are managed or have been treated.

Discussing

Pose these questions: What specific indications do you see that people with disabilities are no longer considered "different"? How do you think this current attitude benefits people with disabilities? People without disabilities? **L1**

CHARACTER ✓ CHECK

Caring. Learning sign language can give you the ability to communicate with the hearing impaired. It is also a way of showing that you care about the needs of others. **Do some research to find organizations in your area that offer classes in sign language. Learn some simple signs so that you can communicate with people who are hearing impaired.**

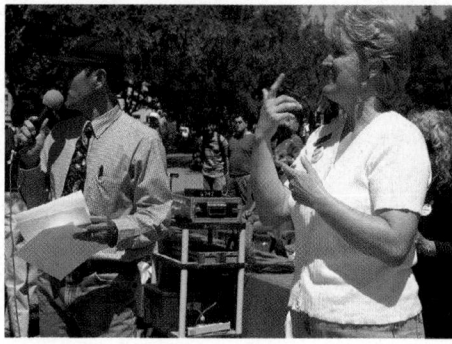

▼ Sign language enables many individuals with hearing impairments to enjoy concerts, plays, and other public events.

Sight Impairment

Like other disabilities, sight impairment can be moderate, as for the more than 5 million Americans who are vision-impaired, or it can be severe, as for the 1.3 million people who are legally blind. In addition, an estimated 1.8 million people in the United States are unable to see words and letters in ordinary print even when wearing glasses or contact lenses. Although visual impairment is more common among older adults, nearly 1 in every 1,000 children has partial vision loss or is legally blind.

The leading cause of blindness is the result of complications of diabetes. Three other common causes of blindness are

▶ **macular degeneration,** a disease in which the retina degenerates. It is the leading cause of blindness in individuals over 55.

▶ **glaucoma,** a disease that damages the optic nerve of the eye.

▶ **cataracts,** a clouding of the lens of the eye.

Regular eye exams are important for people of all ages. The early diagnosis of many conditions can help prevent blindness or slow its progress.

Hearing Impairment

About 20 million adults in the United States have disabilities that affect their ability to hear, and as many as 2 in every 1,000 children have a significant hearing impairment in both ears. Like sight impairment, hearing problems can range from minor to severe. **Profound deafness** is *a hearing loss so severe that a person affected cannot benefit from mechanical amplification, such as a hearing aid.*

One cause of deafness is heredity. Other causes are injury, disease, or obstructions, which can prevent sound waves from traveling to the inner ear. Obstructions may be caused by a buildup of wax, bone blockage, or something stuck in the ear. Some individuals are born with an inherited abnormal bone growth in the inner ear that may cause obstruction. Obstruction usually affects only one ear. Surgery can cure many of these cases.

Hearing impairments caused by nerve damage often occur with age, but also can be the result of repeated exposure to loud noises—such as stereos, traffic, video games, and some machines. Going to one loud concert or blasting the stereo occasionally probably won't hurt your ears, but prolonged exposure to loud music can cause hearing loss. In fact, some experts think that hearing loss is occurring much earlier than it did just 30 years ago possibly because of the increase in environmental noise. This type of hearing impairment can be gradual, so if you have noticed that your hearing has changed, it may be time to visit an audiologist, a specialist in hearing problems.

More About...

Hearing Loss The ability to hear high-pitched and sibilant (hissing) consonant sounds such as *s, z, sh,* and *ch* declines for most people as they age, enough so that hearing loss is now the fourth most common chronic physical disability in the United States. Even by age 35, a person may not hear as well as he or she did at 25. Most people don't notice the progressive muffling until their 60s, when they may begin to have difficulty comprehending speech. These losses may be due to abuse rather than to aging, however. Extremely loud noise, such as from stereo earphones or loud machines, may contribute to hearing loss. A high-fat diet has been linked to clogging of the blood vessels that nourish the hearing organs.

Motor Impairment

Tasks that are simple for most people—tying a shoe, climbing the stairs, opening a jar, lifting a glass—can be a challenge for someone with a motor impairment. Motor impairments result when the body's range of motion and coordination are affected by an injury to the brain or a disorder of the nervous system.

Physical therapy often is used to help those with motor impairment. Through physical therapy, the joints are kept flexible and the muscles stretched, improving the individual's ability to move around. Physical therapists can teach people to use assistive devices. For example, people with limb amputations can be fitted with *prosthetics*, or artificial limbs. Motorized wheelchairs allow many people with motor impairments to get around without assistance. Computers can be adapted in many ways, such as mouth sticks or head sticks for those unable to use their hands or arms.

Mental Challenges

Some challenges affect a person's ability to live independently in society. One such challenge is **mental retardation**, *the below-average intellectual ability present from birth or early childhood and associated with difficulties in learning and social adaptation.* This disability affects about 3 percent of the population, but many of those with this challenge are only mildly affected. Such individuals, who make up 75 percent of the mentally retarded population, cannot be outwardly distinguished from nonretarded people.

Several factors have been found to cause mental retardation, including injury, disease, or a brain abnormality. Some factors are related to **genetic disorders** such as Down syndrome, PKU, Tay-Sachs, and Fragile X syndrome, the most common cause of genetically-inherited developmental disability. Behaviors during pregnancy are another important factor. Pregnant women who use alcohol or other drugs greatly increase the risk that their babies will be born with mental retardation, low birth weight, or conditions such as **fetal alcohol syndrome.** Another preventable risk factor during pregnancy is infection with rubella. Immunization against this disease either during childhood or within three months of becoming pregnant reduces the risk. A restricted supply of oxygen during birth can cause mental retardation. In older children, it can result from a head injury, stroke, or certain infections such as meningitis.

A Advances in technology have benefited people who use assistive devices to perform daily activities. *Name one way your community is improving access and services for individuals with disabilities.*

hot link

genetic disorders Learn more about genetic disorders in Chapter 19, page 500.
fetal alcohol syndrome Learn more about the effects of alcohol use during pregnancy in Chapter 22, page 576.

hot link

Genetic Disorder Have students find out about any research being conducted using current gene therapies such as that being used for cystic fibrosis.

Fetal Alcohol Syndrome Ask students to review what they know about fetal alcohol syndrome. What is it, and how can it be recognized? What causes it, and how can it be avoided? How many babies are born with fetal alcohol syndrome each year?

Service Learning

Explain to students that cerebral palsy is a disorder that affects motor skills. It is one of the most common congenital disorders of childhood, with 10,000 new cases in the United States each year. Explain that there are many organized opportunities for working with children and teens with cerebral palsy. These include helping them with arts and crafts, swimming, games, summer camps, tutoring, and learning computer skills in an organized setting. Suggest that interested students investigate volunteer opportunities. The local chapter of the March of Dimes is a good place to start. 🔳

Cross-Curriculum Activity

History Have students find out the incidence of birth defects that is attributed to rubella before the vaccine was licensed in 1969. 🔳

School to Work

Occupational Hazards Risk factors for illness and disability may be present in the work situation. For example, tobacco smoke may be present in the work environment. Farm laborers, factory workers, and exterminators handle pesticides. Construction workers may be exposed to lead or asbestos. Divide students into groups, and have them pretend that they have been assigned to a congressional subcommittee to study health hazards in the workplace. Have each group choose an area to research and find out what federal laws (through the Occupational Safety and Health Administration) are in place to protect workers; then have each group report its findings. 🔳

Guest Speaker

Invite a person from an organization that trains or sponsors companion dogs for people who are disabled. If possible, have the person bring in a dog. Ask the person to describe some of the things the dogs are trained to do and examples of how the dogs help people who are disabled cope with the challenges of daily living.

Reinforcing Concepts

Emphasize that people with disabilities are people first. Their disability is part of them, but it is not who they are. Sometimes, people are anxious or afraid of saying or doing the wrong thing around people with disabilities and may avoid them for this reason. It is better to make a small mistake than to miss out on the opportunity of making a new friend.

Explaining

Explain that it is okay to offer help to a person who is disabled. Sometimes, they need help, sometimes, not, just as people who are not disabled. Even if they don't need help, they almost always appreciate the offer.

Q&A

How can I show courtesy when I interact with a person who is disabled?

Treating others as you would like to be treated is the best guide for interacting with people, whether or not they are disabled. Speak directly to the person, not to his or her companion. If an individual has a working animal, such as a companion dog, don't call to the animal or pet it—remember, the animal is at work. Distracting the animal may cause it to make mistakes that endanger its handler.

Accommodating Differences

People with physical and mental challenges have the same needs and interests as do the rest of the population. They also have many of the same abilities. Historically people with disabilities have been viewed as a separate population. Fortunately, in recent decades strides have been made toward eliminating the barriers of stereotyping and prejudices. The recent trends have resulted from advocacy efforts by individuals with physical and mental challenges and their supporters who have worked to establish the following important principles:

▶ Society should make certain changes, such as requiring wheelchair access to public transportation and building entrances that allow people with physical and mental disabilities to take part more readily in business and social activities.

▶ People should be evaluated on the basis of individual merit, not on stereotyped assumptions about disabilities.

▶ To the extent that each is able, people with disabilities should have the same opportunities as people who do not have physical or mental challenges.

 Guide dogs are trained to assist the visually impaired by safely navigating around obstacles such as curbs. *Why should you avoid touching or calling a working guide dog?*

Home and Community

Community Report Have students find out what their community does to meet the special needs of its citizens. In small groups, have students develop a checklist of ways the community meets the special needs of people who are physically and mentally challenged. In the form of a letter, have students suggest improvements that the community could make. They could send a written report of their purpose, methods, and conclusions to a local legislator. Remind them of their audience and how to present the information in a clear and organized fashion. Be sure that students check for errors and write several drafts before sending a final draft to their legislator.

A major action toward achieving these goals was the passage by Congress in 1990 of the **Americans with Disabilities Act**, *a law prohibiting discrimination against people with physical or mental disabilities in the workplace, transportation, public accommodations, and telecommunications.* Some provisions of the act require:

▶ employers with 15 or more employees to provide qualified individuals with disabilities an equal opportunity to benefit from of employment-related opportunities available to others.

▶ state and local governments to follow specific architectural standards in the new construction and alteration of their buildings. They also must provide access in inaccessible older buildings and communicate effectively with people who have hearing, vision, or speech disabilities.

▶ telephone companies to establish telecommunications relay services (TRS) that enable callers with hearing and speech disabilities to communicate through a third-party communications assistant.

In addition, the Workforce Investment Act of 1998 ensures that any information posted to a Web site by a government agency must meet certain standards for accessibility by those who are disabled.

This ramp is just one of the many federally required accommodations for people who are disabled. *What other accommodations exist to help those with disabilities?*

③ ASSESS

EVALUATING THE LESSON

Assign and discuss the Lesson 4 Review; then administer, grade, and discuss Lesson Quiz 98 in the TCR. 🗁

RETEACHING

• Have students outline the lesson using Roman numerals for the headings. Ask that they provide at least two facts to support each Roman numeral entry.

• Ask students to complete Reteaching Activity 98 in the TCR. 🗁

ENRICHMENT

Have students form groups to review the contents of the Americans with Disabilities Act of 1990. Assign each group a category such as employment, public transportation, public accommodations, telecommunications, and miscellaneous provisions. Ask each group to summarize the information and prepare a presentation of provisions guaranteed under the law to individuals who are disabled.

④ CLOSE

Have students recall the incidence and causes of common physical and mental disabilities, and discuss the challenges a person with a disability may face.

 Lesson 4 *Review*

Reviewing Facts and Vocabulary

1. What is a *disability*?
2. List three common causes of blindness.
3. Discuss health-related issues and list two laws that help integrate people with disabilities into society.

Thinking Critically

4. **Analyzing.** Identify several different ways that you use the senses of sight and hearing each day. For each item, identify challenges that might be associated with each task for someone with an impairment.

5. **Evaluating.** What loud noises are you subjected to each day? What might you do to reduce your exposure to the noise?

Applying Health Skills

Accessing Information. Go to **health.glencoe.com** to find a link to the Americans with Disabilities Act Web site. Prepare a display showing a summary of the provisions of the act.

PRESENTATION SOFTWARE Make your display professional looking with presentation software. For help with presentation software, access **health.glencoe.com.**

Lesson 4 Physical and Mental Challenges **699**

 Lesson 4 *Review*

Answers to Reviewing Facts and Vocabulary

1. Any physical or mental impairment that limits normal activities, including seeing, hearing, walking, or speaking

2. Any three: complications of diabetes, macular degeneration, glaucoma, cataracts.

3. Possible answer: Passage of legislation such as the Americans with Disabilities Act of 1990 and the Workforce Investment Act of 1998.

Answers to Thinking Critically

4. Lists will vary.
5. Answers will vary.

Prescription Drug Advertising

NHES Standard 4 Students will analyze the influence of culture, media, technology, and other factors on health.

Objective

Research pharmaceutical companies' violations against the FDA's prescription drug advertising policies.

Motivator

Ask students if they know the names of any prescription drugs that treat symptoms of noncommunicable diseases.

Teaching Strategies

Awareness Ask students to recall what they have learned about diseases from prescription drug ads.

Analysis As they read an FDA warning letter, instruct students to briefly paraphrase what the violation is for their charts.

Reflection Before writing, students should take time to analyze the information in their charts and consider the possible health effects on customers.

Take Action Encourage students to learn more about the issue by reading current articles on the Internet, in newspapers, or in other periodicals.

✔Assessment

Each chart should contain at least four entries, each with a brief description of the violation and negative effects. Position papers should state students' position and supporting evidence.

Prescription Drug Advertising

The Federal Drug Administration (FDA) has rules regarding advertisements for prescription drugs used to manage chronic noncommunicable diseases. Yet, every month, the FDA issues warning letters to a number of pharmaceutical companies for violations against the rules for drug advertising. Use the activity that follows to help you identify the effects that might result from misinformation found in prescription drug advertising.

Name of Drug and what it is prescribed for	Violation (in your own words)	Possible effects of violation (health effects, effects on the perception of the medical condition or the use of the drug)
ephedrine	synthetic source, not plant-derived	no evidence that it's safe or effective

ACTIVITY

Working in groups of three or four, research at least four of the warning letters available at the FDA Web site found in the Web links at **health.glencoe.com**. Use the table to help you determine the types of violations against the FDA's prescription drug advertising policies. List the name of the drug, describe the violation, and note possible effects on a person's health if the drug is used.

EXPRESS YOUR VIEWS

Create a one-page paper discussing the rules and regulations that control information in advertisements for prescription drug products. Explain how effective these rules are in protecting the health of individuals who use these products. Consider these questions: How many warnings are issued each month? Can the effects of these violations be life threatening?

▶More About...

Drug Advertising The issue of prescription drug advertising is a topical issue with two very distinct sides. There are those that feel there is potential for serious harm if an advertisement contains misleading information. Researchers for a study done at the University of California's Davis and Los Angeles campuses in 2000 concluded, "Most ads, for instance, failed to offer a clear explanation of wrongly held beliefs about certain medical conditions or pharmaceutical treatments." Some believe that, in general, prescription drug advertising helps raise awareness of the medical condition and possible treatments for it and helps consumers to become more health literate and better able to make informed decisions about their own health care.

CROSS-CURRICULUM CONNECTIONS

Create a Heart Poem. Cardiovascular diseases, including hypertension and atherosclerosis, are diseases that can often be avoided through changes in lifestyle behaviors. Using information from this chapter, write a poem to communicate to teens the importance of maintaining a healthy heart. Include in your poem examples from the list of risk factors that can be controlled. If you wish, create a rap song or put your poem to music to send a positive health message to teens.

Create a Time Line. Although the passage of the Americans with Disabilities Act and other laws in recent years are victories for those with physical and mental challenges, it took years of effort on the legal and social fronts to break down barriers. Research and create a time line focusing on important legislation and events that have moved this cause forward over the decades. Also, include people who have made contributions throughout history—for example, Helen Keller and President Franklin Delano Roosevelt.

Calculate Cancer Deaths. The text states that 87 percent of lung cancer deaths are caused by smoking, and that there are 169,400 new cases of lung cancer every year. How many of these are from causes other than smoking?

Investigate New Technologies. Scientists are constantly researching techniques that will allow doctors to diagnose illnesses more accurately, deliver medication to the exact site of the problem and, in some cases, eliminate the need for surgery. Investigate and report on research programs sponsored by the National Institutes of Health and the National Cancer Institute. Discuss the progress in research for treating diseases such as diabetes and cancer.

Oncologist

Are you interested in helping people who have cancer? If so, you might consider a career as an oncologist, a doctor who studies, diagnoses, and treats cancers. A person who wants to become an oncologist should be ready to deal with the emotional and psychological challenges associated with patients who may be terminally ill. Becoming an oncologist takes many years of formal training: a four-year college degree, a medical degree, a one-year internship, a four-year residency, and a fellowship in oncology. Find out about this and other careers in Career Corner at **health.glencoe.com**.

Chapter 26 Review **701**

Portfolio Assessment

Self-Evaluation Direct students to review the Health Skills Activities and other activities completed in the chapter. Encourage each student to select one finished product or activity that demonstrates his or her best work for the chapter and that represents the student's learning goals. Have students explain what they have learned and how the examples they have selected demonstrate their growth in health literacy, knowledge, and skills.

Teacher Classroom Resources Assign Performance Assessment 26, "Reducing Risk," in the TCR.

CROSS-CURRICULUM CONNECTIONS

Enrich student learning by connecting the topic of noncommunicable diseases to one of the four subject areas presented on this page. The activity may be completed individually or with a partner.

Language Arts Students should include specific information about a disease and its risk factors in their work. Explain to students that they may wish to use narrative verse, which tells a story using poetic devices.

Social Studies Demonstrate through an example that time lines need to include clear images and pertinent information. Direct students toward reliable Internet or library resources.

Math Answer: 169,400 − (169,400 × 87/100) = 22,022

Science Focus on the accurate delivery of chemotherapy drugs and the concurrent reduction of side effects, the use of nanostructures like fullerenes as delivery platforms for new drugs, and the reduction of physically invasive procedures, which require long recovery periods.

Have students read and discuss the Career Corner information on oncology. Ask interested students to explore the Glencoe Health Web site at **health.glencoe.com** for more information on this career.

Chapter 26 *Review*

CHECKING COMPREHENSION

- Assign and discuss the chapter review.
- Use Chapter 26 MindJogger Videoquiz to review the chapter. ▶◎

CHAPTER 26 REVIEW ANSWERS

Exploring Health Terms

1. angina pectoris
2. noncommunicable disease
3. hypertension
4. arrhythmia
5. tumor
6. metastasis
7. carcinogen
8. biopsy
9. allergy
10. diabetes
11. rheumatoid arthritis
12. False; profound deafness
13. False; mental retardation
14. False; Americans with Disabilities Act

Recalling the Facts

1. Hypertension often has no symptoms.

2. Plaques can build up on the arterial walls, causing them to thicken and lose their elasticity.

3. Feelings of pressure, fullness, squeezing, or aching in the chest; discomfort spreading to the arms, neck, jaw, upper abdomen, and back; shortness of breath, lightheadedness; cold sweat; nausea, vomiting.

4. Possible answers: Avoid tobacco, maintain normal blood pressure, eat a healthful diet, maintain low cholesterol, get regular physical activity, maintain a healthy weight, practice stress and anger management, avoid drugs and alcohol.

► EXPLORING HEALTH TERMS
Answer the following questions on a sheet of paper.

Lesson 1 *Match each definition with the correct term.*

angina pectoris	cardiovascular disease
atherosclerosis	hypertension
arrhythmias	noncommunicable disease

1. Chest pain that results when the heart doesn't get enough oxygen.
2. A disease that is not transmitted by another person, or a vector, nor from the environment.
3. High blood pressure.
4. Irregular heartbeats.

Lesson 2 *Fill in the blank with the correct term.*

benign	malignant
biopsy	metastasis
cancer	remission
carcinogen	tumor

5. An abnormal mass of tissue that has no natural role in the body is a _____.
6. The spread of cancer from where it originates is called _____.
7. Cigarette smoke and UV radiation are two examples of a _____.
8. A laboratory analysis of a section of tissue taken from a site where abnormal cell growth is suspected is a _____.

Lesson 3 *Match each definition with the correct term.*

allergy	diabetes
autoimmune disease	histamines
arthritis	osteoarthritis
asthma	rheumatoid arthritis

9. A specific reaction of the immune system to a foreign and frequently harmless substance.
10. A chronic disease that affects the way body cells convert food into energy.
11. A disease characterized by the debilitating destruction of the joints due to inflammation.

Lesson 4 *Replace the underlined words with the correct term.*

Americans with Disabilities Act
disability
mental retardation
profound deafness

12. <u>Disability</u> is hearing loss so severe that a hearing aid doesn't help.
13. <u>Profound deafness</u> is the below-average intellectual ability present from birth or early childhood.
14. <u>Mental retardation</u> is a law prohibiting discrimination against people with physical or mental disabilities.

► RECALLING THE FACTS
Use complete sentences to answer the following questions.

Lesson 1

1. Why is hypertension considered a "silent killer"?
2. How does plaque affect arteries?
3. What are the warning signs of a heart attack?
4. List four ways to prevent cardiovascular diseases.

Lesson 2

5. Which type of cancer is most common in the United States? How can the risk of this cancer be reduced?
6. How does a high-fat diet increase the risk of cancer?
7. What kind of therapy produces antibodies to activate a person's immune system?

Lesson 3

8. Why should people with long-lasting or severe allergies seek medical attention?
9. Why is managing stress important for a person who has asthma?
10. What are two major ways that people can reduce the risk of type 2 diabetes?
11. How does an autoimmune disease harm the body?

5. Skin cancer; protect yourself from the sun.

6. Fats make colon cells more susceptible to carcinogens. In addition, colon cells divide more rapidly if the diet is high in fat, which increases the chance that abnormal cells will form.

7. Immunotherapy

8. Allergies can irritate the respiratory tract and lead to other medical problems, including asthma.

9. Stress can cause or worsen an asthma attack.

10. Weight management and regular physical activity.

11. The immune system mistakenly attacks itself, targeting the cells, tissues, and organs of the person's own body.

12. Possible answers: climbing stairs, reading a sign, hearing a conversation, holding a package, understanding instructions.

12. What are some challenges a person with disabilities might face?

13. What kind of disability would someone with Down syndrome have?

14. What are two of the provisions of the Americans with Disabilities Act?

▶ THINKING CRITICALLY

1. Evaluating. What effect does physical activity have on the cardiovascular system? How does this information affect the goals you set for maintaining health? *(LESSON 1)*

2. Synthesizing. Suppose a friend tells you that she wants to get a tan because people with tans look healthier. What would you tell her? *(LESSON 2)*

3. Summarizing. Type 2 diabetes is becoming more common among children and teens. Write a letter directed to parents of young children that explains how parents can help their children avoid developing the disease. *(LESSON 3)*

4. Analyzing. In the past many people have had misconceptions about individuals with physical and mental challenges. What factors do you think contributed to negative attitudes toward people with disabilities? *(LESSON 4)*

▶ HEALTH SKILLS APPLICATION

1. Practicing Healthful Behaviors. Ask your parents about the history of cardiovascular disease in their families. Use this information to identify any potential risks you might have for developing cardiovascular disease. What steps can you take to reduce your risk? *(LESSON 1)*

2. Analyzing Influences. Look at product ads in a variety of magazines. Identify pictures that show people involved in behaviors that increase the risk of developing cancer. Describe how each of these behaviors puts a person at risk of developing cancer. Summarize your findings and report them to the class. *(LESSON 2)*

3. Accessing Information. Find out about the most common pollen allergens in your community. Gather information about when they are most prevalent and where you can get information about daily pollen counts. Display the information in the classroom. *(LESSON 3)*

4. Advocacy. Survey a local business to see how it might be made more accessible for individuals who have disabilities. Write a letter to the owner of the business making suggestions for improvement. *(LESSON 4)*

BEYOND the Classroom

Parent Involvement

Advocacy. Find out about health fairs or other events in your community that support cancer education. Contact local chapters of the American Cancer Society for information. See how you and your parents can become involved.

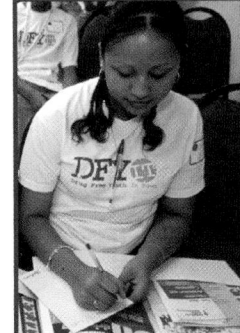

School and Community

CPR Classes. Locate agencies in your community that teach CPR. Arrange for someone from the agency to teach CPR at your school. Help organize the event and prepare posters or flyers to let people know about it.

Thinking Critically

1. Physical activity strengthens the heart; this information should encourage students to get regular exercise.

2. Students should mention the high incidence of skin cancer and the fact that tanning increases the risk of this disease.

3. Students should include the benefits of weight management and regular physical activity.

4. Answers will vary.

Health Skills Application

1.–4. Answers will vary.

EVALUATE

• Use the reproducible Chapter 26 Test in the TCR, or construct your own using the Testmaker software. 🗁 💿

• Use Performance Assessment 26 in the TCR. 🗁

ENRICHMENT

Ask students to complete Enrichment Activity 26 in the TCR. 🗁

BEYOND the Classroom

Keep students involved in the community, and encourage parent participation by assigning the activities on this page for students to work on outside of class.

13. Mental retardation.

14. Possible answers: Employers with 15 or more employees must provide qualified individuals with disabilities an equal opportunity to benefit from employment opportunities; state and local governments must follow specific architectural standards in the new construction and alteration of buildings; telephone companies must establish interstate and intrastate telecommunications relay services.

Chapter 27 *Injury Prevention and Safe Behaviors*

Lessons	Standards		Features
	National	**State/Local**	
1 **Safety at Home and at Work** *pages 706–713*	National Health Education Standards 1.1, 3.2, 3.4, 3.5		**Hands-On Health** • Creating a Fire Safety Plan *(Practicing Healthful Behaviors)*, page 708
2 **Recreation and Water Safety** *pages 714–718*	National Health Education Standards 1.1, 3.2, 3.4, 3.5		**Real-Life Application** • Breaking the Accident Chain *(Practicing Healthful Behaviors)*, page 716
3 **Safety on the Road** *pages 719–724*	National Health Education Standards 3.2, 3.3, 3.4, 3.5		**Exploring Issues** • Should All States Adopt Graduated Licensing for Teen Drivers? page 721
4 **Weather Emergencies and Natural Disasters** *pages 725–729*	National Health Education Standards 1.1, 3.4, 3.5, 6.4		**Health Skills Activity** • Preparing an Emergency Survival Kit *(Goal Setting)*, page 726

Reproducible Resources	Assessment	Technology
Student Activity Workbook for use with each chapter	📁 Lesson Quiz 99	📠 Transparency 78
📁 Concept Mapping Activity 99		💿 TeacherWorks®
📁 Guided Reading Activities 99		🖥 Internet Activities
📁 Lesson Plan 99		
📁 Parent Letter and Activities 27		
📁 Reteaching Activity 99		
📁 Concept Mapping Activity 100	📁 Lesson Quiz 100	📠 Transparency 79
📁 Decision-Making Activity 27		💿 TeacherWorks®
📁 Enrichment Activity 27		
📁 Guided Reading Activities 100		
📁 Lesson Plan 100		
📁 Reteaching Activity 100		
📁 Concept Mapping Activity 101	📁 Lesson Quiz 101	📠 Transparency 80
📁 Cross-Curriculum Activity 27		💿 TeacherWorks®
📁 Current Health Issues 27		
📁 Guided Reading Activities 101		
📁 Health Lab 27		
📁 Lesson Plan 101		
📁 Reteaching Activity 101		
📁 Concept Mapping Activity 102	📁 Lesson Quiz 102	📠 Transparency 81
📁 Guided Reading Activities 102		💿 TeacherWorks®
📁 Lesson Plan 102		
📁 Reteaching Activity 102		

🕐 OUT OF TIME

If time does not permit teaching the entire chapter use:

- Hands-On Health, p. 708
- Figure 27.2, p. 711
- Figure 27.4, p. 717
- Health Minute, p. 722
- Health Skills Activity, p. 726

Language Diversity

- 🎧 English Audio CD Program
- 🎧 Spanish Audio CD Program
- 📁 English Summaries, Quizzes, and Activities
- 📁 Spanish Summaries, Quizzes, and Activities
- 📁 Spanish Parent Letters and Activities

End of Chapter Assessment

Blackline Masters

- 📁 Chapter 27 Test
- 📁 Performance Assessment Activity 27

Technology

- 💿 Vocabulary PuzzleMaker
- 📀 MindJogger Videoquiz
- 💿 **Exam**View® Pro Testmaker

Professional Health Series

Dealing with Sensitive Issues
Planning a Coordinated School Health Program
Promoting Character Education
Home, School, and Community Involvement

Key to Ability Levels

Teaching strategies that appear throughout the chapter have been identified by one of the following codes to give teachers an idea of their suitability for students of varying learning styles and abilities.

L1 Strategies should be within the ability range of all students. Full class participation is often required. Teacher direction is usually needed.

L2 Strategies are designed for average to above-average students or for small groups. Some teacher direction is needed.

L3 Strategies are designed for students able and willing to work independently. Minimal teacher direction is needed.

ELL Strategies should be within the ability range of students learning the English language.

🔲 Block scheduling strategies are useful in a block scheduling format.

Injury Prevention and Safe Behaviors

CHAPTER OVERVIEW

Chapter 27 focuses on ways to prevent unintentional injuries in the home and at work, while participating in recreational activities, and during weather emergencies and natural disasters.

Lesson 1 Safety experts have observed a sequence of events that lead to an unintentional injury. Precautions can be taken to prevent fires, falls, electrical shock, poisonings, and other unintentional injuries that may occur at home and at work.

Lesson 2 Recreational activities can put individuals at risk for injury. People should be aware of possible hazards and follow basic safety rules.

Lesson 3 Vehicular safety involves obeying the rules of the road and using good judgment. Safety considerations for bicycling, skating, and operating motorized vehicles are presented.

Lesson 4 This lesson focuses on strategies to reduce the risk of injury during hurricanes, floods, tornadoes, blizzards, and earthquakes. Students learn how to prepare an emergency survival kit.

Health Skills Features

- Hands-On Health (*Practicing Healthful Behaviors*), p. 708
- Real-Life Application (*Practicing Healthful Behaviors*), p. 716
- Exploring Issues, p. 721
- Health Skills Activity (*Goal Setting*), p. 726

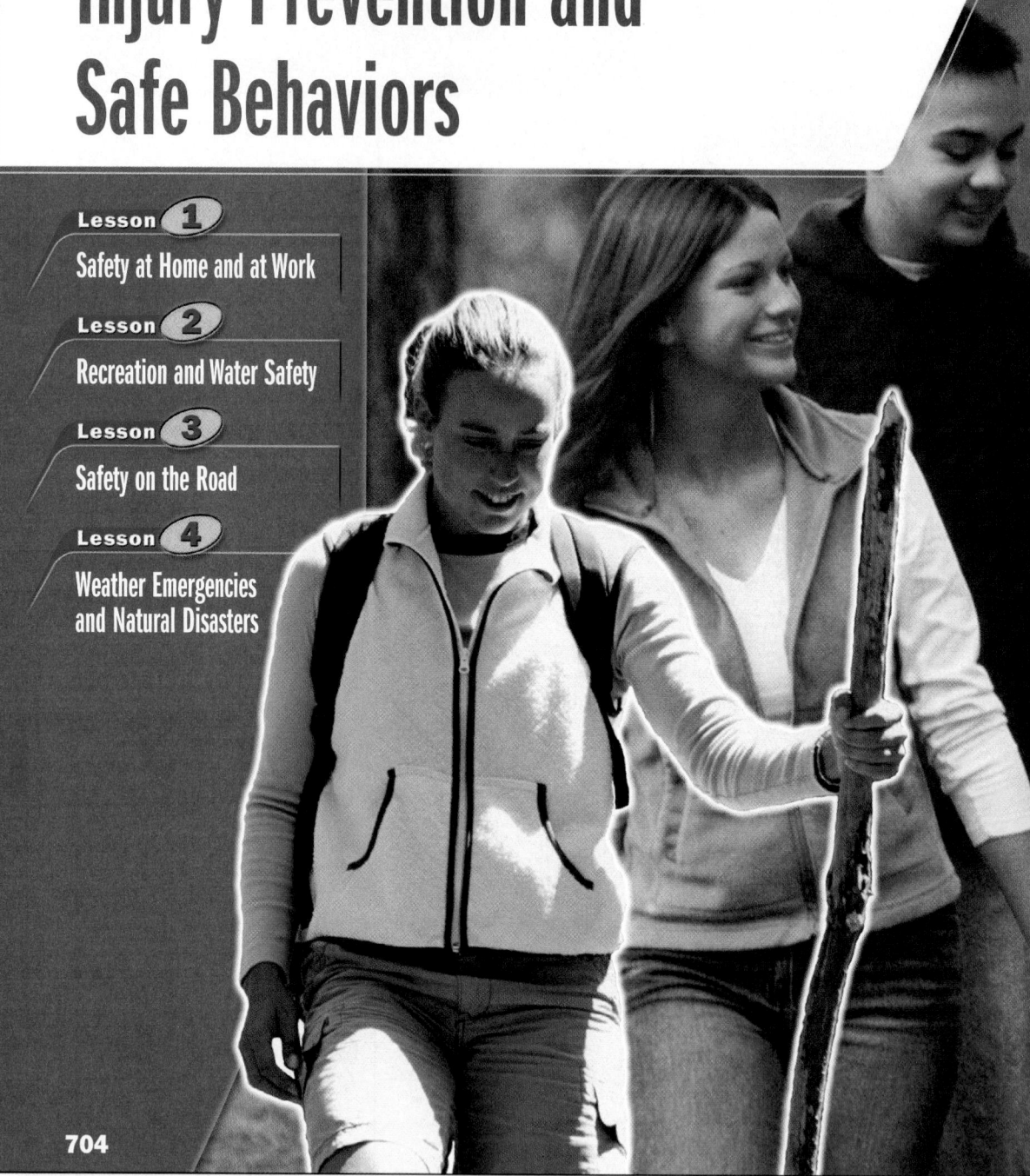

Chapter 27

Injury Prevention and Safe Behaviors

Lesson 1
Safety at Home and at Work

Lesson 2
Recreation and Water Safety

Lesson 3
Safety on the Road

Lesson 4
Weather Emergencies and Natural Disasters

704

MEETING STUDENT DIVERSITY

Language Diversity Use the following suggestions to help students who have difficulty with English:

- Pair English language learners with native speakers of English who can restate the Chapter Summary in language that helps students comprehend important concepts.

- 🎧 Direct auditory learners or those students with language diversity to the *Glencoe Health Audio CD Program.* Available in English and Spanish, this component provides an audio and written summary of the chapter.

- Use photographs, drawings, or magazine clippings to help students visualize the important concepts of the chapter.

Personal Health Inventory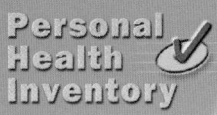

How Do You Rate?

Read each statement below and respond by writing *yes*, *no*, or *sometimes* for each item. Write *yes* only for items that you practice regularly.

1. I do not use an electrical appliance if the floor is wet or if I am near a tub or sink that contains water.

2. I keep all cleaning products and other chemicals in their original containers.

3. I stay within my abilities and limits when taking part in sports and recreational activities.

4. I use a step stool when I need to reach items on high shelves.

5. I don't risk my health or the health of others to show off.

6. I read and follow labels when using cleaning products or other chemicals.

7. I follow traffic guidelines when I drive a vehicle or ride a bike.

8. I follow posted speed limits and other traffic signs and signals when driving.

9. I wear a safety belt.

10. I wear the proper safety equipment when bike riding, skating, and skateboarding.

Keep this personal inventory for review later in the chapter. When you complete the chapter, review your answers and identify two or three behavior changes you could make to improve your health.

705

Quick Write

Using Visuals. Safe behaviors can prevent many unintentional injuries. What are some behaviors that can reduce your risk of unintentional injury while hiking with friends?

INTRODUCING THE CHAPTER

Personal Health Inventory

Have students read and discuss the Personal Health Inventory statements. Ask: How does each behavior relate to protecting your own safety and the safety of others? How can you positively affect each aspect of your health by following basic safety guidelines? After a brief discussion, let students record their inventory responses in their private health journals. Ask students to label this journal page "Safety and Injury Prevention."

Lead a discussion in which students describe their personal responsibility in preventing unintentional injuries both to themselves and to others. Explain that, as they study the chapter, they will explore many safety-related practices in detail.

Quick Write

Using Visuals Ask students to brainstorm safety practices to follow while participating in outdoor activities. List these on the board, and ask how these practices benefit health. Then have students complete the QuickWrite. Tell them to think of safety procedures specific to hiking.

Safety at Home and at Work

1 FOCUS

Safety at Home and at Work

QUICK START When students have completed their lists, lead a five-minute discussion in which they share their ideas. For each precaution, have students explain why it is important.

TYING TO PRIOR KNOWLEDGE

Ask a volunteer to describe an unintentional injury he or she experienced at home or at work. What caused the injury and how could it have been prevented? Tell students that in this lesson they will learn more about preventing injuries at home and at work.

Health Skills Features

"Creating a Fire Safety Plan," p. 708

PRACTICING HEALTHFUL BEHAVIORS

INTRODUCING VOCABULARY

• Review the term *unintentional injury*, and have students give examples of how this differs from an intentional injury. Tell students that *un-* is a prefix meaning "not." Encourage them to brainstorm other words that begin with this prefix.

• Ask students to complete the Chapter 27 Study Guide in the *Student Activity Workbook.*

VOCABULARY
unintentional injury
accident chain
smoke alarm
fire extinguisher
Occupational Safety and Health Administration (OSHA)

YOU'LL LEARN TO

• Analyze strategies for preventing unintentional injuries.

• Examine how proper training at work can prevent unintentional injuries.

• Demonstrate knowledge of strategies to prevent unintentional injuries at home and at work.

QUICK START List five safety precautions that can help reduce the risk of unintentional injuries at home.

 Many unintentional injuries can be prevented by taking precautions such as wiping up spills. *How can this behavior help prevent an unintentional injury?*

Every year thousands of people are injured as a result of accidents in the home. In fact, the National Safety Council reports that a fatal home injury occurs every 18 minutes and a disabling home injury occurs every 4 seconds. One goal of *Healthy People 2010* is to reduce the number of deaths caused by unintentional injuries.

Unintentional Injuries

There are two types of injuries—intentional and unintentional. An intentional injury is the result of a deliberate attempt to cause harm. An **unintentional injury** is *an injury resulting from an unexpected event, or accident.* There are many actions you can take to prevent unintentional injuries.

Preventing Unintentional Injuries

Although unintentional injuries often seem to be random events, experts have observed an **accident chain**, or *a sequence of events that leads to an unintentional injury.* Most unintentional injuries include five steps that are connected, much like the links in a chain. **Figure 27.1** shows these steps.

706 Chapter 27 Injury Prevention and Safe Behaviors

Lesson 1 *Resources*

Teacher Classroom Resources
📁 Concept Mapping Activity 99
📁 Guided Reading Activities 99
📁 Lesson Plan 99
📁 Lesson Quiz 99
📁 Parent Letter and Activities 27
📁 Reteaching Activity 99

Student Activity Workbook
📁 Applying Health Skills 99
📁 Chapter 27 Study Guide
Multimedia
💿 Transparency 78

FIGURE 27.1

PREVENTING UNINTENTIONAL INJURIES: THE ACCIDENT CHAIN

1. The Situation. Mark has overslept and has to rush to get ready for school.

2. The Unsafe Habit. Mark often leaves his books on the stairs.

3. The Unsafe Action. Mark isn't looking where he is going as he races down the stairs.

4. The Accident. Mark trips over his books and falls down the stairs.

5. The Result. When he falls, Mark sprains his wrist. He's also late for school.

Safety at Home

Taking precautions and planning ahead can help prevent injuries from fire, falls, electrical shock, and poisonings.

Preventing Fires

Most household fires are caused by heating equipment, appliances, electrical wiring, and smoking. Three elements—fuel, heat, and oxygen—must be present for a fire to occur. Fuel can be carelessly stored rags, wood, gasoline, or paper. A heat source can be a lighted match, a damaged electrical wire, a smoldering cigarette, or a pilot light. The oxygen in the air feeds and fans the flames. Removing one element will prevent a fire from starting. To avoid unintentional fire injuries:

▶ Never leave a candle burning unattended.

▶ Store matches and lighters out of the reach of children.

▶ Make sure that a person doesn't fall asleep while smoking.

▶ Keep stoves and ovens clean.

▶ Replace frayed electrical cords.

2 TEACH

VISUAL LEARNING

Figure 27.1 Have students study the information presented in Figure 27.1. Ask: What can be done to break the accident chain?

Cross-Curriculum Activity

Language Arts Allow volunteers to write a description of an unintentional injury, including a brief account of the situation, the unsafe habit, the unsafe action, the accident, and the result. **L1**

Explaining

Explain these strategies to students for preventing the spread of fire:

• If a fire starts while something is cooking on a stove, turn off the heat and put a lid on the pan to smother the flames. Never put water on a grease fire — it will make the grease and fire spread.

• Never use water to put out an electrical fire. Instead, use dry materials such as sand, salt, or baking soda.

More About...

Fire Safety Review with students these strategies for surviving a fire:

• If caught in or near a fire, act quickly.
• Smoke rises, so stay low to the floor to escape. Most deaths caused by fire result from smoke inhalation.
• When evacuating a room, cover your mouth and nose with a wet towel or pillowcase to cover the smoke.
• If you cannot escape your room, stuff towels and clothing in door cracks and vents to prevent smoke from entering.
• If your clothes catch fire, remember to stop, drop, and roll.

Hands-On Health

CREATING A FIRE SAFETY PLAN

PRACTICING HEALTHFUL BEHAVIORS

NHES Standard 3 Students will demonstrate the ability to practice health-enhancing behaviors and reduce health risks.

Objectives

- Analyze strategies for preventing unintentional injuries resulting from fire.
- Demonstrate knowledge of strategies to develop a home fire safety plan.

Motivator

Tell students to imagine that a fire has started in their home. What is the first thing they would do?

Teaching Strategies

1. Review conditions during a fire that might impede movement, such as smoke, which obscures visibility, and heat, which can block escape routes.
2. Make sure the plans allow for all possible obstacles, including large, immovable pieces of furniture.

✓ Assessment

Using a rubric, student work should provide comprehensive evidence of the following criteria to achieve the highest score:

✔ identification of strategies to avoid risk of injury from fire
✔ creation of a home fire safety plan showing all escape routes
✔ inclusion of all safety guidelines in the plan

Hands-On Health ACTIVITY

Creating a Fire Safety Plan

In this activity you will create a home fire safety plan with a poster showing escape routes.

What You'll Need

- ruler (optional)
- poster paper and art supplies

What You'll Do

1. Draw a floor plan of your home on poster paper, including doors, hallways, windows, and stairways.
2. Use arrows to point out the fastest way to escape from every room.
3. Identify an alternate escape route for each room in case the first route is blocked by flames or smoke.
4. Indicate the location of smoke alarms and fire extinguishers.
5. Designate a place for your family to meet outside your home and mark it on the escape plan.
6. At the bottom of your plan, write:
   - When escaping, stay low to the floor.
   - Call 911 or the fire department.
   - Never go back inside to retrieve something.

Apply and Conclude

Share the plan with your family and post it in a prominent place in your home. Schedule a home fire drill at least once a month with all family members.

FIRE SAFETY EQUIPMENT

To increase your chances of survival in case of fire, here are two life-saving devices that should be present in every home.

▶ A **smoke alarm** is *an alarm that is triggered by the presence of smoke.* Safety experts recommend that one smoke alarm be located on every floor of a home, preferably outside a sleeping area and near the kitchen. They also advise that the alarm be tested once a month and that batteries be replaced at least once a year.

▶ A **fire extinguisher** is *a portable device that puts out small fires by ejecting fire-extinguishing chemicals.* If your home has a fire extinguisher, check the dial on the equipment periodically to ensure that it still has enough pressure to work in an emergency. When using an extinguisher, stand away from the flames; aim at the source of the fire, not at the flames; and move the spray from side to side. If you are unsure of your ability to put out the fire, forget the extinguisher, get out of the house, and call the fire department.

708 **Chapter 27** Injury Prevention and Safe Behaviors

Home and Community

Smoke Alarm Checklist Write this checklist on the board for students to copy, or reproduce enough copies for each student. Have students take it home and complete it with their parent or guardian.

1. At least one alarm is located on every floor of my home.
2. Detectors are placed near bedrooms, on the ceiling, or 6–12 inches below the ceiling on the wall.
3. Alarms are tested at least once a month and are always in working order.
4. Batteries are replaced at least annually.
5. Batteries are never disconnected.
6. The alarm has a distinct warning signal that can be clearly heard.

Preventing Falls

According to the National Safety Council, one-fifth of injuries that require treatment in an emergency room are the result of falls. A few simple precautions can help reduce the risk of injuries from falls:

▶ Keep stairways well lit, in good repair, free of clutter, and equipped with sturdy handrails and nonskid stair strips.

▶ Keep the floor clean. Mop up any spills immediately.

▶ Use nonskid throw rugs, or place nonskid mats under rugs.

▶ Make sure bathtubs and showers have safety rails and nonskid mats.

▶ Do not run electrical or telephone cords across areas where people walk.

▶ If there are small children in the home, install adjustable safety latches so that windows will open only a few inches. This is especially important for windows above the first floor. Make sure the windows can be opened in case of fire or other emergency.

▶ Use a sturdy step stool when reaching for items in high places.

Preventing Electrical Shock

Electricity can be dangerous if not used correctly. Improper use or maintenance of electrical appliances, wiring, or outlets can cause severe electrical shock. Follow these safety precautions when using electrical appliances to help reduce the risk of injury:

▶ Unplug an electrical appliance immediately if anything seems to be wrong. Always pull on the plug, not the cord.

▶ Inspect cords periodically for signs of cracked insulation. If the cord is frayed, replace it immediately.

▶ Do not run cords under carpets or rugs; they can be damaged when walked on.

▶ Never use an electrical appliance or power tool if your body, clothing, or the floor is wet.

▶ Check outlets and extension cords to make sure they aren't overloaded.

▶ In homes with small children, cover unused outlets with plastic protectors.

 Prevent electrical shocks by using extension cords and electrical outlets correctly. *Why might an overloaded outlet cause a problem?*

CHARACTER ✔ CHECK

Citizenship. Keep your eyes open for potential safety hazards at school. Notice any frayed electrical wires, overloaded outlets, or extension cords stretched across areas where people walk. **Do your part to help make your school a safe environment—report any unsafe situation to the custodian or a teacher.**

CHARACTER ✔ CHECK

Citizenship Ask students why helping to make the school a safe environment shows good citizenship. Answers will vary, but students should recognize that they show good citizenship by cooperating and doing their share to make their school a safer place and by obeying safety rules. Ask students to write down potential safety hazards at school that they notice in one day. Have them include behaviors such as a person who spills a drink on the cafeteria floor but doesn't wipe it up. Encourage students to use their findings to plan a campaign to make the school a safer place.

Critical Thinking

Remind students that falls can occur from walking in dimly-lit areas. What are other safety precautions (besides keeping areas well lit) that people can take to reduce the risk of falls in these situations? Possible answers: Make sure a light switch or a lamp is near the door of every room so a person does not have to walk across a room to turn on a light; use nightlights in bedrooms, halls, and bathrooms. ▣

More About...

Electrical Shock Electrical shock can stop the heart, cause burns, or result in other injuries. Electric current is especially damaging if it flows through the chest cavity or brain. A current flow can disrupt the rhythmic pumping action of the heart, or stop the heartbeat completely. In electrical burns, tissue damage is caused by the heat from the current flow. Touching an overheated electric conductor (such as a very hot electrical cord) can cause a thermal burn. Electrical shock currents can also cause involuntary muscle reactions, which can lead to falls or collisions. This may result in bruises, bone fractures, and even death.

Service Learning

Ask students to develop lists of home and yard childproofing precautions for infants, toddlers, and preschoolers. They may wish to use software programs to create attractive pamphlets for parents that can be placed in child day-care centers or preschools. ⬛

Activity

Have students use library and online resources to research houseplants and seeds that are poisonous. Ask them to bring in pictures and share them with the rest of the class. ⬛ ⬛

Explaining

Tell students that the most common type of poisoning by inhalation is carbon monoxide poisoning. This gas is emitted not only by heating equipment but also by motor vehicles. The effects of exposure to this colorless, odorless gas include headache, blurred vision, and shortness of breath, followed by dizziness, vomiting, and unconsciousness. Carbon monoxide detectors are available for home use. ⬛

Reinforcing Concepts

Emphasize that proper storage of firearms is critical. Never assume that young children cannot fire a gun. About a quarter of children 3–4 years old and three-quarters of children 5–6 years old have enough finger strength to pull a trigger. ⬛

⚠ **Use proper safety precautions for storing household chemicals and medicines, especially if there are small children in the home.** *How should medications be stored?*

Preventing Poisoning

According to the Centers for Disease Control and Prevention (CDC), nearly 900,000 emergency room visits each year are associated with poisonings. About 90 percent of poisonings occur in the home, and more than half involve children under six years of age. Most potentially poisonous products—detergents, disinfectants, paints, polishes, and insecticides—are typically found in the kitchen, bathroom, utility closet, basement, and garage. Here are a few guidelines for preventing poisoning:

▶ Keep medications and other potentially poisonous substances in childproof containers. Store out of the reach of children. Dispose of any expired medications.

▶ Store all household chemicals in their original containers. Never store them in food or drink containers.

▶ Never mix household chemicals. Many household cleaners contain ammonia or bleach, which give off toxic gases when combined.

▶ Use products that give off fumes, such as ammonia, bleach, petroleum products, and paints, in well-ventilated areas.

▶ Make sure there is adequate ventilation when using fuel-burning appliances. These appliances give off carbon monoxide gas while in use. Inhaling this poisonous gas can damage body tissues and cause death from lack of oxygen.

Figure 27.2 summarizes strategies for staying safe in and around your home. Putting these strategies into practice will decrease the likelihood of unintentional injuries.

Firearm Safety

Up to 40 percent of homes in the United States contain firearms. Firearm injuries are one of the top ten causes of death in the United States, and the number of nonfatal firearm injuries is considerable—over 200,000 per year. Following these recommendations can help reduce the risk of injury from firearms.

▶ Never point a firearm at anyone for any reason.

▶ Treat all firearms as if they are loaded. If you find a firearm, leave the area and tell an adult.

▶ Store firearms unloaded and store the ammunition separately. Both should be in locked cabinets that are well out of the reach of children.

Home and Community

Medical Emergency at Home Help students prepare for an emergency at home. Bring index cards to class and give students one index card for every telephone in their home and one for each family member. Instruct students to do the following:

1. Write their phone number and address on one or more cards and post them near each telephone in their home.

2. Have students list information about each family member on a separate card, including birth date, medical history, allergies, current medications, and doctor's name and phone number. The appropriate card should be given to emergency medical technicians when they arrive.

FIGURE 27.2

SAFETY AT HOME

Follow these safety practices to help prevent injuries at home.

Test smoke alarms once a month and change the batteries at least once a year.

Make sure your body and the floor are dry before using electrical appliances such as hair dryers or curling irons.

Store gasoline and other flammable liquids away from hot water heaters or other sources of flames or sparks.

Be sure stairs and hallways are well lit.

Store household products in a secure place, out of the reach of children.

Always turn the handles of pots and pans away from the front of the stove so that they cannot be accidentally knocked or pulled off.

Make sure there is good ventilation when you use chemical products to avoid being overcome by fumes.

Store propane cylinders outdoors to prevent an explosion or a fire.

Lesson 1 Safety at Home and at Work **711**

Critical Thinking

Tell students that approximately 7 million disabling injuries occurred in the home in the year 2000. Ask: Why do you think so many injuries occur in the home? Possible answer: People feel comfortable, safe, and secure in their homes. They might not give much thought to preventing unintentional injuries. Also, people generally spend more time in their homes than in other places, so the chances are greater that an unintentional injury may occur. **L2**

Figure 27.2 Allow students to study Figure 27.2 for a few moments. As you name each area of the house, ask volunteers to read the safety precaution and explain how it can prevent unintentional injuries. Then have students work in pairs or small groups to choose one or two areas shown in the figure. Direct them to use the five steps in the accident chain to write a scenario about an unintentional injury that occurs in that area of the house. They should conclude the scenario by identifying at least two ways that the injury could have been prevented. Each group should present their scenario to the class.

Cooperative Learning Activity

Child Safety in the Home Many students look after younger siblings or have child-sitting jobs. Have groups of students work together to research areas where children are most likely to be injured. Then have them develop a checklist to identify hazards to children in the home. They may want to obtain information from the Centers for Disease Control and Prevention (CDC) or other sources. Invite them to share their findings with the class.

VISUAL LEARNING

VISUAL LEARNING

Figure 27.3 Ask for a volunteer to model the guidelines in Figure 27.3. Have him or her sit in front of a computer if one is available in your classroom. As you read through each guideline, pause and survey the class for the number of students who are aware of and follow this guideline. Ask students what other measures they take to reduce eye or muscle strain while working at the computer.

Discussing

Ask students who have jobs to describe specific safety measures that are taken at their places of work. Point out that many teens are injured on the job as a result of performing a task for which they have not received adequate safety training. By federal law, workers are entitled to ask for and receive safety training. They cannot be fired for requesting this training or for reporting violations to federal authorities. **L1**

Cross-Curriculum Activity

Math Each state maintains data on the types of unintentional injuries that occur on the job. Ask students to contact their nearest Occupational Safety and Health Administration office for data in their state. Have them analyze the data and report on how the most common injuries among working teens can be avoided. **L2**

Did You Know ?

Prolonged typing on the computer keyboard or clicking the mouse can cause repetitive motion injuries (RMIs). RMIs start when the same task is performed repeatedly, straining tissues in the affected area. If these tissues don't get a chance to heal, the damage adds up. Symptoms include pain and tingling. Taking frequent breaks and making sure you're positioned properly at the computer can help prevent RMIs.

Computer and Video Game Safety

Computer tasks often require you to sit in one place for long periods of time and make repetitive motions while staring at the screen. This can cause eyestrain and sore muscles and may even lead to wrist, hand, or arm injuries. To help reduce the risk of injury, take a 10-minute break every hour or so. If you are working intensely for a long period of time, occasionally give your eyes a rest by looking up and focusing on objects that are far away.

Your work area should be a comfortable and healthy place to work. **Figure 27.3** shows the correct way to sit at a computer. Determine whether your computer and chair are adjusted correctly. Here are some other things to consider when setting up a work area:

▶ **Lighting.** Lighting for a computer should be indirect and not too bright. Avoid creating a glare on your computer screen.

▶ **Adjustability.** Chairs, computer monitors, and desks or other work surfaces should be adjustable for the comfort of each user. This is especially important if people of different heights use the same work area.

FIGURE 27.3

COMPUTER WORKSTATION DESIGN

Making your workstation comfortable will reduce fatigue; eyestrain; blurred vision; headaches; and back, neck, and arm cramps.

Use indirect lighting to avoid glare. Arrange the computer so that it is at right angles to windows or other light sources.

Adjust your chair to keep your back straight. This will help keep your body aligned, which reduces muscle strain.

Adjust the height and angle of the monitor so that it is at or slightly lower than eye level. The distance between your eyes and the monitor should be 18–30 inches.

Adjust the chair so that your feet can rest flat on the floor. Use a foot rest if the chair is not adjustable. Your forearms, wrists, and hands should be straight when you are using the mouse or keyboard.

Adjust the height of the computer table so that the keyboard is comfortable, usually slightly higher than waist level. Your forearms should be parallel to the floor when you are using the keyboard.

712 Chapter 27 Injury Prevention and Safe Behaviors

School to Work

Injury Insurance at Work Some worker injury insurance plans are national. Other plans are available only in certain states. Have students investigate employer-provided injury insurance in their state. They should ask: What types of injuries are covered? Are workers covered while traveling from place to place on the job? Are workers covered while working at home or at a client's location?

What circumstances must exist for a claim to be paid? What benefits are paid? What losses are not compensated? Ask students who work to interview their employer about what insurance benefits are offered through their company. Discuss the financial and human costs of work-related injuries that are not compensated.

Safety on the Job

Many teens have part-time or full-time jobs. In fact, the U.S. Department of Labor says that more than 3 million teens earn paychecks during summer vacations alone; others work part-time jobs during the school year. Unfortunately, about 500 of these workers are injured every day. Many of these unintentional injuries could have been avoided if training had been provided before machinery and equipment were used. Teens are permitted to perform certain tasks on the job, but are prohibited from performing others. The Department of Labor prohibits anyone under 18 from doing certain jobs, including roofing or construction work, demolition, driving a forklift or any vehicle, operating power-driven machinery, and handling explosives or radioactive materials.

Both employees and employers must follow safety rules issued by the **Occupational Safety and Health Administration (OSHA)**, *the agency in the federal government that is responsible for promoting safe and healthful conditions in the workplace.* Because many people spend about one third of the day on the job, it's everyone's responsibility to take steps to ensure a healthful and injury-free workplace.

 The U.S. Department of Labor regulates the types of tasks that teens are allowed to perform on the job. *List two types of jobs that the Department of Labor prohibits teens under 18 from doing.*

 Lesson 1 *Review*

Reviewing Facts and Vocabulary

1. What are the five steps in the accident chain?
2. What three elements must be present for a fire to start?
3. Define the term *smoke alarm*.

Thinking Critically

4. **Analyzing.** Why should people always treat a firearm as though it were loaded?
5. **Synthesizing.** Think of a specific job that a teen might have. Analyze strategies for preventing unintentional injuries on that job, and develop a checklist that features these strategies.

Applying Health Skills

Advocacy. Make a poster that encourages family members to practice safety habits. Your poster should include specific safety precautions that family members can take to stay safe in the home. Display your poster at home and discuss with your family any steps that might be taken to improve safety.

 TECHNOLOGY | **OPTION**

PRESENTATION SOFTWARE Use presentation software to illustrate graphically the safety precautions described on your poster. Find help in using presentation software at **health.glencoe.com**.

Lesson 1 Safety at Home and at Work **713**

 ASSESS

EVALUATING THE LESSON

Assign and discuss the Lesson 1 Review; then administer, grade, and discuss Lesson Quiz 99 in the TCR. 📁

RETEACHING

- Have students create a comic book for elementary students, illustrating safety precautions they should take in the home. Remind them to use language and illustrations that will appeal to younger children. Encourage them to develop several drafts, and proofread their writing for errors. Have them share the final drafts of their books with younger students.

- Ask students to complete Reteaching Activity 99 in the TCR. 📁

ENRICHMENT

Have interested students research the causes and treatment of repetitive motion injuries (RMIs).

4 CLOSE

Have students list at least five ways they will apply what they have learned in this lesson to decrease the risk of injury in their homes.

 Lesson 1 *Review*

Answers to Reviewing Facts and Vocabulary

1. Situation, unsafe habit, unsafe action, accident, and result.
2. Fuel, heat source, oxygen.
3. A smoke alarm is an alarm that is triggered by the presence of smoke.

Answers to Thinking Critically

4. Possible answer: If people think that a firearm is loaded, they will handle it carefully and never point it at a person, thereby reducing the risk of injury and death.
5. Checklists will vary.

Recreation and Water Safety

1 FOCUS

QUICK START Give students two minutes to generate their lists. Then ask volunteers to share their ideas and explain how the items reduce the risk of injury or illness.

TYING TO PRIOR KNOWLEDGE

Ask students to volunteer safety guidelines for activities such as swimming, boating, skiing, or camping. Explain that this lesson outlines safety guidelines to reduce the risk of injury during recreational activities.

Health Skills Features

"Breaking the Accident Chain," p. 716

PRACTICING HEALTHFUL BEHAVIORS

INTRODUCING VOCABULARY

- Have students explain what they know about *heat exhaustion* and *hypothermia*.
- Ask students to complete the Chapter 27 Study Guide in the *Student Activity Workbook*. 📁

714

Lesson 2

Recreation and Water Safety

VOCABULARY
heat exhaustion
hypothermia

YOU'LL LEARN TO
- Analyze strategies for preventing accidental injuries that occur during recreational activities.
- Associate risk-taking during recreational activities with consequences such as unintentional injury.

QUICK START If you were planning a day at the beach or lake, what supplies would you need for a safe and healthy outing? List five specific items that you would take.

⚠ **Packing the right supplies will help guarantee that outdoor activities are safe and fun.**

R ecreational activities are fun, but they can be accompanied by the unexpected. Common sense and caution can minimize the risk of unintentional injuries during recreational activities.

Recreational Safety

O utdoor activities are enjoyable and can help you stay fit. To stay healthy and safe during outdoor activities:

▶ **Know your limits.** Stick with tasks that match your level of ability. For example, stay on beginner slopes until you gain experience as a skier.

▶ **Bring supplies.** Take plenty of safe drinking water with you. Never drink from a lake, river, or stream—these bodies of water may contain illness-causing pathogens. Plan simple meals and take any supplies, including coolers and plenty of ice to store foods safely.

▶ **Wear protective clothing.** The proper clothing can protect against the weather and poisonous plants and insects.

▶ **Tell people your plans.** Let them know where you're going and when you plan to return. If possible, carry a cell phone in case of emergencies.

Lesson 2 Resources

Teacher Classroom Resources
- 📁 Concept Mapping Activity 100
- 📁 Decision-Making Activity 27
- 📁 Enrichment Activity 27
- 📁 Guided Reading Activities 100
- 📁 Lesson Plan 100
- 📁 Lesson Quiz 100
- 📁 Reteaching Activity 100

Student Activity Workbook
- 📁 Applying Health Skills 100
- 📁 Chapter 27 Study Guide

Multimedia
- Transparency 79

▶ **Plan ahead for the weather.** Warm days may turn into cold nights and storms may occur suddenly. To avoid heat exhaustion, stay in the shade in hot weather and drink plenty of water. **Heat exhaustion** is *an overheating of the body that results in cold, clammy skin and symptoms of shock.* Use sunscreen to protect the skin from UV rays.

Safety While Camping and Hiking

To prevent injuries when camping and hiking:

▶ Stay in specified campsites, and hike only in approved areas. Never hike or camp alone.

▶ Be knowledgeable about poisonous plants, insects, and snakes. If you'll be in grassy areas, wear socks and long pants tucked into socks or boots to help protect against ticks and mosquitoes.

▶ Be cautious around wildlife. Do not store food in your tent. Store food where animals cannot get to it, such as in a vehicle or suspended from a high tree branch.

▶ Be careful around campfires and observe fire safety rules. Tie back long hair and secure loose clothing. Never cook inside a tent. Smother all campfires with dirt and water.

▶ Never drink water from lakes, rivers, or streams; it may contain disease-causing pathogens.

Winter Sport Safety

When skiing, snowboarding, or participating in other winter sports, dress in layers. Air trapped between layers of clothing helps insulate you from the cold. This can prevent **hypothermia**, *a condition in which body temperature becomes dangerously low.* Make sure the outermost layer is waterproof, and wear a hat. Don't forget to put on sunscreen, especially in high elevations. Always wear the appropriate safety equipment, and make sure it's in good working order and is sized correctly for you.

hot link

heat exhaustion For more information about heat exhaustion, see Chapter 4, page 99.

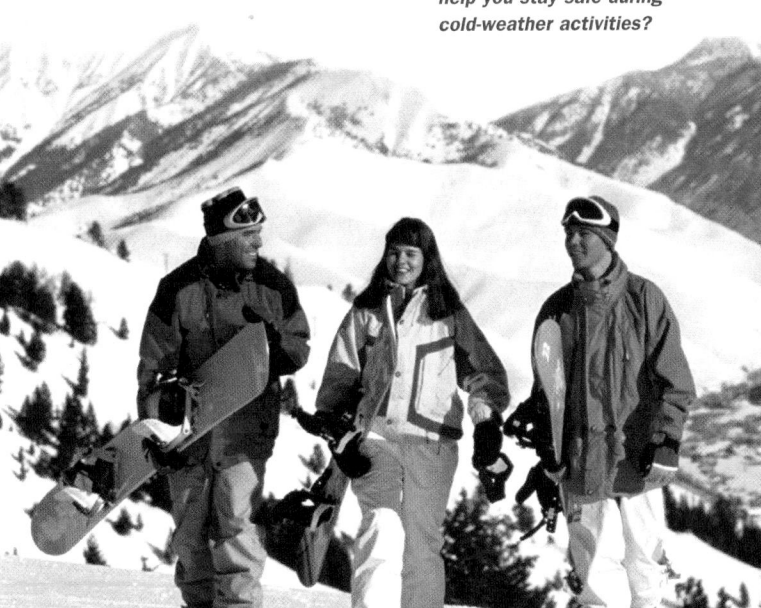

🔻 **Safe participation in winter sports requires proper clothing and equipment.** *How can dressing in layers help you stay safe during cold-weather activities?*

Lesson 2 Recreation and Water Safety **715**

② TEACH

hot link

Have students find out how many people are affected by heat exhaustion each year. What ages of people are these conditions most likely to affect? What are some precautions to prevent heat exhaustion?

Community Involvement

Ask students to research recreational activities that are common in their area. For each activity, ask them to investigate specific rules that regulate the activity, causes of the most common unintentional injuries associated with the activity, and community organizations that provide information on injury prevention. ◾

Explaining

Explain that water from lakes, rivers, and streams can be contaminated with the protozoan *Giardia lamblia*. This pathogen can cause diarrhea, cramps, and nausea. Giardia infection can be treated with antibiotics. ◾

Critical Thinking

Why is sunscreen important at high elevations? The ozone layer is thinner, allowing more UV light to reach the earth; also, if snow is present, it reflects UV rays. ◾

Cooperative Learning Activity

Refusal Skills As a class, discuss reasons individuals might accept dares or other invitations to engage in unsafe behavior. Review refusal skills. Divide the class into groups of four. Have each group brainstorm a scenario in which one teen pressures another to engage in an unsafe behavior, such as diving off a cliff or swimming in heavy surf on an unsupervised beach. Choose two group members to role-play a conversation demonstrating effective refusal skills. The other two members may critique the response and offer constructive suggestions. Have group members switch roles, taking turns until all members have role-played refusal skills.

Real-Life Application

BREAKING THE ACCIDENT CHAIN

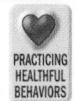
PRACTICING
HEALTHFUL
BEHAVIORS

NHES Standard 3 Students will demonstrate the ability to practice health-enhancing behaviors and reduce health risks.

Objectives

- Analyze strategies for preventing accidental injuries that occur during recreational activities.
- Analyze the consequences of risky or harmful behaviors.

Motivator

Ask students to name safety precautions they take when swimming or diving.

Teaching Strategies

1. Have students draw the accident chain of events as they analyze the clipping in the feature.
2. Lead a class discussion in which students tell how the accident in the feature could have been prevented.

✔ Assessment

Using a rubric, student work should provide comprehensive evidence of the following criteria to achieve the highest score:

✔ identification of risk factors and risk-taking behavior that increases the likelihood of unintentional injuries
✔ identification of strategies to prevent unintentional injuries

---

Real-Life Application

Breaking the Accident Chain

Local Teen Injured in Diving Accident

A Summitville teen is in critical condition after he was recovered from the bottom of a pool Saturday night. Jon Franklin was at the party of a friend where more than 30 people were present. Franklin was found in about six feet of water. The pool had no depth indicators and the area was poorly lit. No one present had training in water safety. Witnesses say alcohol may have been a factor in the accident. A hospital spokesperson has confirmed that Franklin suffered a severe spinal cord injury and that his prognosis is uncertain.

Diving accidents cause more than 850 spinal cord injuries each year. Many of these injuries result in the paralysis of all four limbs. Read the article, and answer the questions below to increase your understanding of how "links" in the accident chain lead to injuries:

- What was the situation?
- What were the unsafe habits that contributed to this accident?
- What was the unsafe action?
- What was the accident?
- What was the result?

ACTIVITY

As a class, discuss the answers to the questions. Individually, bring in a newspaper clipping about a recreational accident. In small groups, identify the situation, the unsafe habits and actions, the accident itself, and the result. Write a paragraph describing how the accident chain could have been broken. Post your clippings and paragraphs on the bulletin board.

Water Safety

Swimming, boating, and other water sports are great summer activities. However, drowning is the second leading cause of injury-related death. The four major causes of drowning are failure to wear a life jacket, alcohol use, lack of swimming skill, and hypothermia. Follow these safety precautions for water-related activities.

SWIMMING

▶ Learn how to swim. Know your abilities, and always swim with a buddy.

▶ Swim only in designated areas where a lifeguard is present.

▶ If you get a muscle cramp, relax, float, and press and squeeze the muscle until it relaxes.

More About...

Drowning Prevention Many drowning victims never intended to go into the water in the first place—they fell in while fishing, walking, playing, boating, or cycling. Because many of us can't swim well enough to save ourselves or others if we do fall into the water accidentally, the best precaution is to avoid falling into the water in the first place. Be cautious when alongside bodies of water—banks are often wet and slippery, and may crumble underfoot. Always pay attention to danger notices, and don't be overconfident—even if you can swim. Swimming in an icy lake is very different from swimming in a warm pool. Finally, never go fishing, boating, or swimming by yourself.

DIVING

▶ Learn the proper diving technique. Always check water depth before diving. The American Red Cross recommends a minimum depth of nine feet.

▶ Never dive in unfamiliar areas or into dark or shallow water. Make sure the area is clear of swimmers and floating objects.

BOATING AND PERSONAL WATERCRAFT

▶ Learn how to handle a boat or personal watercraft (PWC) correctly, and know the laws governing their use.

▶ Always wear approved personal flotation devices on boats and PWC.

▶ At the first indication of bad weather, return to shore.

▶ Never ride in a boat or PWC with an operator who has been using alcohol or other drugs.

Figure 27.4 shows survival techniques you can use if you fall into deep water.

Ⓐ **Always wear a Coast Guard-approved personal flotation device when boating or using a personal watercraft.**

Community Involvement

Survey the class for students who are certified lifeguards. Ask what training they received. If no students are certified, ask volunteers to investigate lifeguard-certifying programs in their community or area. Such programs typically require a certain proficiency in swimming. Training includes surveillance and rescue skills. Allow students to present their findings in class. **L1**

Activity

Tell students that most boating injuries occur when a boat strikes another object, such as another boat. However, most deaths occur when people fall overboard and drown. Alcohol use is a major contributing factor in boating injuries. Have students investigate boating rules in their state. **L1**

VISUAL LEARNING

Figure 27.4 Ask a student volunteer to read the steps to prevent drowning presented in Figure 27.4. Ask: Why is it important to perform these steps slowly? To conserve energy If your school has a pool, arrange for the swimming coach to demonstrate the technique to the class.

FIGURE 27.4

DROWNING PREVENTION

If you fall into cold water while boating, assume one of these positions. They can help you stay afloat and reduce the risk of hypothermia until help arrives.

A. Lessen heat loss by drawing your knees up to your chest and keeping your upper arms close to the sides of your body. You lose a lot of heat through your head, so try to keep it out of the water.

B. If you are with one or more people, huddle close together in a circle to preserve body heat. A child or smaller person who loses heat faster should be placed in the center of the circle.

Lesson 2   Recreation and Water Safety   **717**

More About...

Personal Watercraft Safety A personal watercraft (PWC) is defined by the U.S. Coast Guard as an inboard boat under 16 feet in length. Each year, about 19 million Americans operate PWC. Most injuries on PWC occur when the craft collides with another vessel or with a fixed object such as a dock or a tree stump. About 40 percent of those injured are males 15 to 24 years old.

Behavioral factors associated with injury include operator inexperience, operator inattention, and excess speed or reckless operation. Many states have requirements for operators of PWC, such as age restrictions and mandatory training courses. Have students find out what requirements their state has for PWC operators.

❸ ASSESS

EVALUATING THE LESSON

Assign and discuss the Lesson 2 Review; then administer, grade, and discuss Lesson Quiz 100 in the TCR. 🗁

RETEACHING

- Divide the class into four groups. Assign a topic to each group: camping, winter sports, swimming, and boating safety. Have students create and present a skit that shows strategies for reducing the risk of injury in their assigned activity.

- Ask students to complete Reteaching Activity 100 in the TCR. 🗁

ENRICHMENT

Encourage students to investigate misconceptions people may have about unintentional injuries (for example, "Unintentional injuries cannot be prevented."). Have students write a paragraph explaining why the misconceptions are not true.

❹ CLOSE

Have students recall the major concepts of the lesson. Ask them to analyze their favorite recreational activity, and determine areas of risk and strategies to reduce their risk.

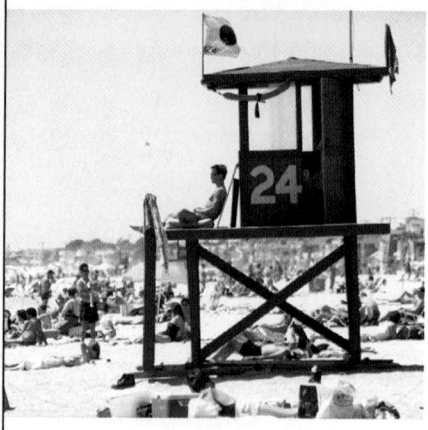

⚠ **Always stay within designated swimming areas that are supervised by a lifeguard.**

Lake, River, and Ocean Safety

Swimming in lakes, rivers, or the ocean presents added safety concerns. Keep these precautions in mind:

▶ **Swim in supervised areas only.** Select an area that is clean and well maintained.

▶ **Enter feet first.** Hidden objects, unexpected drop-offs, and aquatic life may be lurking beneath the surface.

▶ **Watch for marine warnings.** Check to see whether the warning flag is up, or ask the lifeguard whether the water is safe for swimming. If you are at the ocean, check the tides and surf conditions before entering the water. Don't enter the water in an area marked "No Swimming."

▶ **Be aware of surroundings.** Be sure rafts and docks are in good condition. Stay away from piers, pilings, and diving platforms when in the water. Never swim under a raft or dock.

▶ **Plan ahead.** Always make sure that you have enough energy to swim back to shore. If you are pulled offshore by rapid currents or undertows, swim gradually out of the current by swimming across it, often parallel to the shore.

▶ Lesson 2 Review

Reviewing Facts and Vocabulary

1. Why is it risky to drink from lakes, rivers, or streams?

2. Analyze and identify three strategies for preventing accidental injuries while camping or hiking.

3. Define the term *hypothermia*.

Thinking Critically

4. **Synthesizing.** You and your family are taking a boat out on the lake for the afternoon. What supplies and safety equipment should you bring with you?

5. **Analyzing.** You and your friend Jake are skiing. He suggests that you try the advanced slope, even though both of you are beginners. What negative consequences are associated with taking this risk?

Applying Health Skills

Practicing Healthful Behaviors. Choose a sport that you would like to learn, and make a list of the proper equipment and safety precautions associated with that sport. Review your list before you participate. Be sure to incorporate all safety precautions, wear the proper clothing, and use safety equipment.

TECHNOLOGY | **OPTION**

WORD PROCESSING Use word processing to make your list of proper equipment and safety precautions for your chosen sport. Find help in using word-processing software at **health.glencoe.com**.

▶ Lesson 2 Review

Answers to Reviewing Facts and Vocabulary

1. Rivers, lakes, and streams may contain illness-causing pathogens.

2. See page 715 for safety tips.

3. See page 715 for definition.

Answers to Thinking Critically

4. A Coast Guard-approved personal flotation device for each person, plenty of drinking water, sunscreen, sunglasses, healthful food and snacks (packed appropriately for the weather conditions), and a cell phone (if possible).

5. Answers will vary, but should include the likelihood of sustaining a serious injury.

Safety on the Road

VOCABULARY

vehicular safety
graduated driver's
  license
road rage
defensive driver

YOU'LL LEARN TO

- Analyze strategies for preventing accidental injuries while driving or riding in a car or operating another type of vehicle.

- Associate risk-taking while driving a car or operating another type of vehicle with consequences such as unintentional injury.

 QUICK START Make a list of strategies for preventing an unintentional injury while operating a vehicle. Include all of the safety measures that you think apply.

According to the CDC, motor vehicle crashes are the leading cause of death among teens—more than 5,700 teens died in 2001. The fatality rate for teen drivers is about four times higher than the rate for drivers from 25 to 65 years old. The number of teen drivers involved in fatal car crashes is decreasing. However, the percentages are still staggering:

► 14 percent of *all* drivers involved in fatal crashes were between the ages of 15 and 20.

► 21 percent of these drivers were drinking and driving.

► 80 percent of these drivers were not wearing safety belts.

Automobile Safety

When teens are entrusted with driving a car, they have a responsibility to themselves, their families, their passengers, and the people in other vehicles. That responsibility is to behave in a manner that reduces the risk of injury and death. Behaving responsibly means practicing **vehicular safety**—*obeying the rules of the road, as well as practicing common sense and good judgment.* Obeying the rules means driving within the speed limit, yielding the right-of-way when indicated, and observing local traffic regulations.

 Automobile safety begins even before you start the car—buckle up!

Lesson 3 Safety on the Road **719**

Lesson 3

Safety on the Road

❶ FOCUS

 QUICK START Advise students to consider the attitude of the operator and his or her physical state in addition to the rules of the road. Give students a few minutes to share their strategies in a class discussion.

TYING TO PRIOR KNOWLEDGE

Ask students to name behaviors that can contribute to unintentional injuries while driving a car, riding a bicycle, or operating another wheeled vehicle. Explain that this lesson will cover strategies for preventing accidents while driving or riding in or on a wheeled vehicle.

Health Skills Features

"Should All States Adopt Graduated Licensing for Teen Drivers?" p. 721

INTRODUCING VOCABULARY

- Have students list driving habits that may trigger road rage in some drivers. Then have them list the habits of a *defensive driver*.

- Ask students to complete the Chapter 27 Study Guide in the *Student Activity Workbook*. ☞

Lesson 3 *Resources*

Teacher Classroom Resources

- 📁 Concept Mapping Activity 101
- 📁 Cross-Curriculum Activity 27
- 📁 Current Health Issues 27
- 📁 Guided Reading Activities 101
- 📁 Health Lab 27
- 📁 Lesson Plan 101
- 📁 Lesson Quiz 101

- 📁 Reteaching Activity 101

Student Activity Workbook

- 📁 Applying Health Skills 101
- 📁 Chapter 27 Study Guide

Multimedia

- 🖱 Transparency 80

② TEACH

Discussing

Explain that the leading cause of death for older teens and young adults is car crashes. Ask: What do you think are the major contributing factors? speeding, alcohol L1

Service Learning

Tell students that children are at greater risk for injuries and death than adults in car crashes if they are not belted into a car seat. Explain that some public health agencies and other organizations sponsor campaigns to educate parents about the use of child car seats. Have students find out how they can volunteer in such a campaign. L1

ACTIVE READING

Synthesis Journal

In this strategy, students reflect on their own experiences in light of what they are reading and develop a plan for personal application. Have each student divide a piece of paper into three sections. Have them record "What I did," "What I learned," and "How I can use it." Have students write a Synthesis Journal entry related to one or more topics covered in this lesson: driving, bicycling, skating, riding a motorcycle, or riding an all-terrain vehicle (ATV). For more strategies, see the *Guided Reading Activities* booklet in the TCR. 📁

Did You Know ?

Nearly 80 percent of high school students report that they wear safety belts when riding in a car with someone. Female students are more likely than male students to wear safety belts.

Being supervised by an experienced driver can help a teen improve his or her driving skills. *What are three of the common-sense rules of vehicular safety?*

To exercise common sense and good judgment as a driver:

▶ **Pay attention to your vehicle.** Before you start the car, adjust the mirrors and seat to positions that are best for you. Buckle your safety belt. Adjust other items such as the radio, heater, or air conditioner before the car starts moving.

▶ **Pay attention to other drivers.** A popular TV public service announcement sponsored by the National Safety Council advised drivers to "watch out for the other guy." This advice is still sound. At night or when inclement weather reduces visibility, turn on your headlights so that other drivers can see you. In general, drive as though the other driver is going to act irresponsibly. If you do this, you will always be prepared for the unexpected.

▶ **Pay attention to road conditions.** This includes reducing your speed when the road is icy or wet, when a lane narrows, or when there is construction or congestion.

▶ **Pay attention to your physical state.** Don't drive when you are sleepy. If you are tired, do something to refresh yourself, such as rolling down the window or turning on the radio. If you are extremely tired, pull over at the nearest rest stop and call home.

▶ **Pay attention to your emotional state.** If you are angry or feeling other strong emotions, don't drive. Your mental state can affect your judgment and reaction time as much as your physical state can.

Teen Driving Safety

The National Center for Statistics and Analysis reports that 8,155 drivers between 15 and 20 years old were killed in automobile accidents in the year 2000. According to the CDC, teen drivers are more likely than older drivers to speed, run red lights, make illegal turns, ride with an intoxicated driver, and drive after using alcohol or drugs. Teens are also more likely than older drivers to underestimate the dangers in hazardous situations, and they have less experience adjusting to these situations. In an effort to reduce the number of teen deaths in car crashes, some states have adopted a graduated driver's licensing program. A **graduated driver's license** is *a licensing program that gradually increases a new driver's driving privileges over time as experience and skill are gained.* This system allows a new driver to improve his or her driving skills while under the supervision of an older driver. Over time, a teen driver gains more skill, and the driving restrictions are lifted.

720 Chapter 27 Injury Prevention and Safe Behaviors

Home and Community

Public Transit Have students investigate which forms of public transit in their community feature safety restraints. Students may want to consider buses, trains, taxis, and subways, among others. Discuss with students how to minimize the risk of injury in the event of an accident in vehicles without restraints. Also, have them discuss safety precautions for parents of small children,

such as seating the child next to an adult. Encourage students to promote laws that call for safety restraints on public transit by writing to local lawmakers. Remind them to proofread their writing, and develop several drafts before turning in their final draft.

Should All States Adopt Graduated Licensing for Teen Drivers?

Some states have adopted a system of graduated driver licensing (GDL) for teens. This system is based on the idea that a teen with a new driver's license needs time and guidance to gain driving experience and skills in reduced-risk settings. More than half of all states have GDL laws. Should the remaining states also adopt GDL laws for new drivers? Here are two points of view.

Viewpoint 1: Ryan D., age 17
Studies have shown that states with GDL laws have experienced reductions in crashes and traffic violations. I think all states should adopt these laws. When you're behind the wheel, you're responsible for yourself and others.

Viewpoint 2: Shandra L., age 16
I see Ryan's point, but I'm not sure all states need to adopt this system. I think the privilege of driving should be based on skill, not on age, especially in states that don't have high crash rates involving teens.

ACTIVITIES

1. Are graduated licensing laws a good idea for all states?

2. Do you think these laws make a difference or would make a difference in your state in terms of fewer lives lost and reduced number of traffic violations? Explain.

Being a Responsible Driver

As you learn to drive and make decisions behind the wheel, be considerate. Other drivers are trying to anticipate your next move, just as you are trying to anticipate theirs. Follow these safety tips:

▶ Always signal when you are about to make a turn or change lanes. Turn the signal off after the maneuver is complete.

▶ Follow all traffic signals and signs, including speed limits.

▶ Don't tailgate. Following too closely can cause an accident. Other drivers may view tailgating as a hostile act.

▶ Let other drivers merge safely into traffic. Cutting them off or not allowing them to merge is unsafe for you and others.

Lesson 3 Safety on the Road **721**

Exploring Issues

SHOULD ALL STATES ADOPT GRADUATED LICENSING FOR TEEN DRIVERS?

Ask the class: Does our state impose any special restrictions on teen drivers? After a brief discussion, have students read the feature to learn more about the issue of graduated driver licensing for teen drivers. Encourage volunteers to offer additional facts and examples to support the two different viewpoints on this issue. Then have students write their answers to the questions.

Activity

On the board, write the following list of items to keep in the car in the event of an automotive breakdown.

- Flashlight with working batteries
- Notepad and pen or pencil
- Charged cell phone
- Number of a towing service
- Insurance card for the car
- Pump-spray product to fix a flat tire instantly

Encourage students to go over the list with their parents or guardians and collect the necessary items.

More About...

Antilock Braking Systems Antilock braking systems (ABS) prevent cars from skidding by using computers to sense when the car's wheels are going to lock up. When the computer determines that one wheel is beginning to spin more slowly than the others, it automatically releases and applies pressure to the braking mechanism so the wheel does not lock until the car slows down. ABS were designed to improve road safety and prevent automobile accidents. The systems are especially helpful when driving on wet, icy, or snow-covered roads.

Health Minute

Ask a volunteer to read the tips aloud. Let students share their thoughts about road rage, either in groups or as part of a class discussion. Ask: Why do you think people are more likely to feel and express intense anger in their cars? In what sense can road rage be contagious? What can you, as a driver or as a passenger, do to diminish the risks of road rage?

Discussing

Ask students how many of them wear safety belts every time they ride as a passenger or drive a motor vehicle. For those who never wear safety belts or do not wear them all the time, ask them why they do not. **L1**

Explaining

Explain to students that about three-quarters of all motor vehicle collisions occur within 25 miles of home and at speeds lower than 40 miles per hour. These crashes often occur because the driver believes that safety measures are not necessary for short trips. **L1**

Health Minute

Tips for Avoiding Hostility on the Road

Always:

▶ Assume other drivers' mistakes are not meant to annoy you personally.

▶ Be polite, even if the other driver is not.

▶ Avoid conflict if possible.

Never:

▶ Block the right-hand turn lane.

▶ Use high-beams unnecessarily.

▶ Exchange hostile gestures or words with other drivers.

▼ When caught in a traffic slowdown, allow other drivers to merge. Such actions diminish the risks of road rage. *Identify three other actions that could help diffuse road rage.*

ROAD RAGE

Sometimes people who are otherwise emotionally stable become enraged in certain driving situations. **Road rage** is *a practice of endangering drivers by using a vehicle as a weapon.* It can be triggered by a variety of acts, including disputes over a parking space, obscene gestures, loud music, overuse of the horn, and slow driving. A driver consumed with road rage may run red lights, tailgate, or pass on a shoulder. Some enraged drivers have been known to use guns or other weapons. If you see someone who is truly a danger on the road, keep your distance. Get the vehicle's license plate number, and report it promptly to the police.

Other Preventive Measures

Safety belts save lives. Yet according to the CDC's statistics on teen driving, 1 in 5 high school students report that they rarely or never wear safety belts when riding with someone else. Drivers and passengers who fail to use safety belts are more likely to be thrown from the vehicle in a crash. Make sure everyone in the car is buckled up, and take these precautions:

▶ Never engage in high-risk driving behavior such as speeding, drag racing, or daredevil stunts.

▶ Alcohol and other drugs impair judgment, coordination, and reaction time. *Never* use these substances and drive—the consequences could be fatal.

▶ Don't let distractions such as eating or adjusting the radio or CD player take your attention away from the road. Don't use cell phones while driving.

▶ Realize that you have no control over what other drivers are doing, so for the sake of your safety, drive defensively. A **defensive driver** is *a driver who is aware of potential hazards and reacts to avoid them.* A defensive driver acquires driving skills and knowledge to stay safe on the road.

722 Chapter 27

Myths & Reality

MYTH. Safety belts can injure you in a crash.

FACT. Properly worn safety belts seldom cause injuries. In cases when they do, the injury is insignificant compared with the severe injury that may result from not wearing a safety belt.

MYTH. It's better to be thrown out of the car in a crash rather than be strapped in.

FACT. Being thrown clear in a crash is nearly impossible. You will most likely be thrown out of the car through the windshield, or crushed by your own car or the other vehicle.

Safety on Wheels

It is important to use proper safety equipment and common sense when bicycling; skateboarding; riding a scooter; or operating a motorcycle, off-road vehicle, or moped. Almost half of the motorcycle drivers who were killed in the year 2000 were not wearing helmets. Many of these drivers could have survived if they had been wearing helmets.

BICYCLE SAFETY

Bicycles are a main form of transportation in many nations around the world. Their popularity in the United States has grown dramatically in recent years because cycling is a great way to stay fit. For safe cycling:

▶ Always wear a safety-approved, hard-shell helmet that fits properly.

▶ Ride with traffic. Always yield the right-of-way— you will not win against a car or truck.

▶ Watch for cars pulling into traffic and for car doors that swing open suddenly in your path.

▶ Obey the same rules as drivers, such as signaling before you turn and stopping for red lights and stop signs.

▶ Learn to use the hand signals for making turns and stopping.

▶ Except when signaling, keep both hands on the handlebars.

▶ Make sure your bike has a bright headlight and a red rear light and reflector for night riding.

▶ Wear reflective, or at least light-colored, clothing when riding at dawn, dusk, after dark, or in the rain.

△ **By behaving safely and using proper safety equipment, you can avoid injury while riding a scooter, skateboarding, or in-line skating.**

SKATING SAFETY

Skateboarding and in-line skating can be a lot of fun. Follow these tips to help keep these activities safe:

▶ Wear protective equipment—wrist guards, elbow and knee pads, and a safety-approved, hard-shell helmet.

▶ Watch for pedestrians and keep your speed under control.

▶ If you begin to fall, curl up into a ball and roll, staying loose.

▶ Do not hold anything in your hand, such as a portable radio. Doing so will not allow you to fall properly.

~✲✲~ HEALTH LITERACY

Bicycle Helmets Share the following information with students:

1. A bicycle helmet should be brightly colored so that motorists can see the cyclist clearly.

2. A properly fitting helmet should cover the top of the forehead and have straps that prevent it from shifting or falling off.

3. A helmet should be certified by the Snell Memorial Foundation or approved by the American National Standards Institute (ANSI).

Have students use these criteria, along with reliable print and online resources, to research the safest bicycle helmets on the market. 🔒

Discussing

Ask students about bike lanes in the areas around the school and/or their homes. Which major roads have bike lanes? What is the best way to use a bike lane? How should riding in a bike lane affect your adherence to guidelines for safe cycling? ◣

Community Involvement

What special areas have been set aside for trail biking, skateboarding, and/or in-line skating in the community? Let students work together to compile a list with relevant information. Encourage them to share this list with friends, family members, and neighbors. ◣

FYI

Despite the fact that head injuries are involved in about two-thirds of bicycle-related deaths, studies indicate that less than 20 percent of cyclists wear helmets.

Reinforcing Concepts

Tell students that approximately 100,000 people who participate in in-line skating are injured badly enough each year to necessitate a trip to the emergency room. Injuries to the wrist and head are most common; many of these injuries occur because skaters do not wear the appropriate safety gear. Researchers estimate that more than one-third of all serious injuries could be prevented if all skaters wore wrist and elbow protection. ◣

③ ASSESS

EVALUATING THE LESSON

Assign and discuss the Lesson 3 Review; then administer, grade, and discuss Lesson Quiz 101 in the TCR.

RETEACHING

- Divide the class into two teams. Call out a type of wheeled vehicle. Have teams take turns naming one applicable safety strategy until one team cannot think of any more strategies. Repeat with each type of vehicle. The team who names the greatest number of strategies wins.

- Ask students to complete Reteaching Activity 101 in the TCR. 📁

ENRICHMENT

Ask interested students to download multiple-choice format driving tests from the Internet. Have students administer the quiz to at least 10 to 20 adults and teens who drive. What differences, if any, did they find between the answers of teens and adults?

④ CLOSE

Based on their reading, have students write what they think are the three most important safe-driving practices.

When riding ATVs in unfamiliar areas, be alert for wires, fences, and downed trees that can cause serious accidents.

MOTORCYCLES AND ALL-TERRAIN VEHICLES

Motorcycles and mopeds are subject to the same traffic laws as cars. All-terrain vehicles (ATVs) are driven off-road. A driver's license is not required to operate an ATV, but operators still need to use common sense and know the rules of the road. Cyclists and ATV operators can also reduce the likelihood of injury by following these safety tips.

▶ Be aware of potential hazards, such as a car door opening or the presence of pedestrians.

▶ Wear a helmet and proper clothing, including eye protection.

▶ Be cautious in wet weather when tire traction is poor.

▶ Do not carry an additional rider unless you have a second seat and an additional set of safety equipment, including a helmet.

▶ Do not grab onto objects or other vehicles while moving.

▶ Do not use ATVs on paved roads or streets. Ride four-wheeled ATVs only; they are less likely to flip than three-wheeled ones.

▶ Lesson 3 Review

Reviewing Facts and Vocabulary

1. Define the term *vehicular safety*.
2. Analyze and identify three strategies for preventing accidental injuries while driving a car.
3. What is a *defensive driver*?

Thinking Critically

4. **Evaluating.** What does the saying "it's better to be alive than right" mean when it comes to vehicular safety?
5. **Synthesizing.** Drinking and driving can have serious consequences. List three negative consequences associated with this risk behavior.

Applying Health Skills

Advocacy. Choose a type of vehicle you learned about in this lesson. Think of ways to teach teens about the safety rules and equipment that a person must use to operate that vehicle safely. With classmates, create a video, public service announcement, or comic book that encourages teens to stay safe by following the tips in your presentation.

WEB SITES Use your video, public service announcement, or comic book as part of a Web page demonstrating the safety tips for your chosen vehicle. See **health.glencoe.com** for help in planning and building your own Web site.

▶ Lesson 3 Review

Answers to Reviewing Facts and Vocabulary

1. Vehicular safety means obeying the rules of the road, as well as practicing common sense and good judgment.
2. See pages 720–722.
3. A driver who is aware of potential hazards and reacts to avoid them.

Answers to Thinking Critically

4. Answers should reflect an understanding of the importance of safe, defensive driving to prevent injury and death.
5. Answers will vary, but should include the idea that severe injury to the driver and to others is a likely result.

Weather Emergencies and Natural Disasters

Lesson 4

Weather Emergencies and Natural Disasters

VOCABULARY

severe weather
emergency
   survival kit
hurricane
flash flood
tornado
blizzard
earthquake

YOU'LL LEARN TO

* Analyze strategies for preventing accidental injuries during severe weather and natural disasters.

* Explain how technology has impacted the health status of communities by increasing the survival rate during a severe weather event.

* Demonstrate the ability to communicate safety procedures that should be followed during a severe weather event or natural disaster.

QUICK START Identify a natural disaster that is common in your region of the country, and make a list of safety precautions that you should follow during such an emergency.

① FOCUS

QUICK START Give students two minutes to write their lists. Then ask volunteers to share their ideas with the class and tell why each precaution reduces the risk of injury.

TYING TO PRIOR KNOWLEDGE

Have students think of a weather emergency or natural disaster that affected their plans or disrupted their lives for a time. Explain that in this lesson, they will learn more about these events and how to prepare for them.

The sky turns dark, and an ominous funnel appears on the horizon. You're driving home when a sudden thunderstorm strikes, and visibility is drastically reduced. These situations can occur without warning. However, careful planning and preparation can help you survive weather emergencies and natural disasters.

Severe Weather

Familiarize yourself with the types of severe weather that occur in your area. **Severe weather** refers to *harsh or dangerous weather conditions*. Some types of severe weather, such as tornadoes, hurricanes, and blizzards, usually occur in certain regions and at certain times of the year. When severe weather threatens, the National Weather Service (NWS) uses the media to issue watches and warnings. A *watch* means that the weather conditions are right for a specific weather event to occur. A *warning* means that severe weather has been sighted and is heading toward your area.

 Severe weather warnings are broadcast on television and radio stations.

Health Skills Features

"Preparing an Emergency Survival Kit," p. 726   **GOAL SETTING**

INTRODUCING VOCABULARY

* Give students three minutes to write everything they know about *hurricanes, flash floods, tornadoes, blizzards,* and *earthquakes.* Have them add to their list or change it as needed as they study the lesson.

* Ask students to complete the Chapter 27 Study Guide in the *Student Activity Workbook.*

Lesson 4 Weather Emergencies and Natural Disasters   **725**

Lesson 4 Resources

Teacher Classroom Resources
📂 Concept Mapping Activity 102
📂 Guided Reading Activity 102
📂 Lesson Plan 102
📂 Lesson Quiz 102
📂 Reteaching Activity 102

Student Activity Workbook
📂 Applying Health Skills 102
📂 Chapter 27 Study Guide

Multimedia
🕹 Transparency 81

②TEACH

Health Skills Activity

PREPARING AN EMERGENCY SURVIVAL KIT

GOAL SETTING

NHES Standard 6 Students will demonstrate the ability to use goal-setting and decision-making skills to enhance health.

Objectives

- Analyze strategies for preventing accidental injuries during severe weather and natural disasters.
- Develop an emergency survival kit.

Motivator

Ask students why it is important to prepare for severe weather or a natural disaster.

Teaching Strategies

1. Have students make a plan to assemble an emergency survival kit and to develop general steps that family members should take in an emergency.
2. Have students research additional safety precautions.

✓Assessment

Using a rubric, student work should provide comprehensive evidence of the following criteria to achieve the highest score:

✔ clear progression through a goal-setting process
✔ inclusion of a clear goal statement
✔ identification of a realistic goal
✔ plan for reaching the goal
✔ evaluation or reflection on the action

Emergency Survival Preparation

Discuss with your family where to go during an emergency, where to meet if family members get separated, and whom to contact if help is needed. Prepare an **emergency survival kit**—*a group of items that can be used for a short time until an emergency situation has stabilized.* Here are some supplies to collect before disaster strikes:

▶ **Water and food.** Plan on 1 gallon of water per person per day. Store canned and ready-to-eat foods, and a can opener.

▶ **Phone, radio, lighting, and blankets.** A charged cell phone is helpful when phone service is disrupted. Keep a battery-operated radio, flashlights, and extra batteries for each on hand. Blankets can be used for both warmth and shelter.

▶ **Other supplies.** Items such as medications and money may need to be added to your kit at the last minute.

Health Skills Activity

Goal Setting: Preparing an Emergency Survival Kit

Dean and his sister Tara are watching the news about a recent flood in a nearby town.

"I'm glad that's not us!" exclaims Tara. "I'd hate to have our house full of mud. It would ruin my CDs."

"That would be the least of our worries," Dean says. "It wouldn't be safe to drink water from the tap. We wouldn't have food, lights, or a place to sleep."

Tara replies, "I hadn't thought about that. I don't even know Mom's work number without looking it up. Do you?" Tara asks.

"We aren't very prepared, are we? I think we need to put together a survival kit for emergencies," Dean says.

What Would You Do?
Apply the five goal-setting steps to Dean and Tara's situation.

1. Identify a specific goal and write it down.
2. List the steps you will take to reach your goal.
3. Identify potential problems and ways to get help and support from others.
4. Set up checkpoints to evaluate your progress.
5. Reward yourself when you have achieved your goal.

726 **Chapter 27** Injury Prevention and Safe Behaviors

More About...

Emergency Survival Plan The emergency survival plan should specify a place away from the immediate area in which a student lives for the family to meet in case family members cannot return home. Designate an out-of-state friend or family member as the "family check-in contact" for everyone to call if the family gets separated. Be sure everyone has that person's phone number. Keep enough emergency supplies in your home to last for at least three days. Store these supplies in sturdy, easy-to-carry containers such as backpacks or duffle bags. Keep important documents in a waterproof container. Replace stored water and food every six months.

Hurricanes

A **hurricane** is *a powerful storm that originates at sea, characterized by winds of at least 74 miles per hour, heavy rains, flooding, and sometimes tornadoes.* Hurricanes strike mainly on the eastern and southern coasts of the United States and usually occur from June through November, with the peak months being August and September. The NWS tracks hurricanes and issues warnings when they are approaching. If a hurricane watch is issued, secure your property. Bring in items from outside that may blow away in strong winds, such as lawn furniture, children's toys, bicycles, and trash cans. Board up windows and doors, or tape any glass if you are unable to cover it. If a hurricane warning is issued, seek shelter. Evacuate if the NWS instructs you to do so. The farther inland you go, the safer you will be.

Floods

Floods occur throughout the United States and can happen at any time of year. Flooding is often the result of severe rains that accompany hurricanes. If a flood is likely to occur, move valuables and furniture to a safe location or to higher ground. Listen to radio bulletins while you watch for rising water, and be prepared to evacuate. Before leaving, turn off the utilities in your home. Never walk, swim, ride a bike, or drive a car through flood waters. Both drowning and electrocution are risks in flooded areas. Drink only bottled water because floods can pollute the water supply. Learn under what conditions to abandon your home and when it is safer to stay put until help arrives.

FLASH FLOODS

A **flash flood** is *a flood with great volume and of short duration that is usually caused by heavy rainfall.* If you are in an area that is under a flash-flood warning, leave low-lying areas immediately. Do not attempt to drive through floodwaters or to cross police barricades. Stay away from streams, creeks, storm drains, and irrigation ditches, all of which become treacherous during flash floods.

Severe Thunderstorms

Thunderstorms can occur anywhere in the United States. Most thunderstorms include heavy rains, strong winds, lightning, and sometimes hail. Storm clouds and darkening skies indicate that a

Floods are one type of natural disaster. *Why do you need to drink bottled water in the event of a flood?*

Can lightning strike twice in the same place?

Yes! The saying, "Lightning never strikes the same place twice" is a myth. Tall buildings are often hit repeatedly in successive storms. Even the same bolt of lightning can strike the same place multiple times. The flickering effect you sometimes see in a lightning bolt is actually multiple strokes of lightning following the same path.

FYI

America experiences more severe weather than any other country in the world. Most of this severe weather occurs in the Southeastern United States.

Guest Speaker

Invite a speaker from the American Red Cross or other organization that offers disaster relief services. Ask the guest to describe a recent event and how people prepared for it—properly or improperly. Have students prepare a list of questions ahead of time. **L1**

Discussing

Why are hurricane winds so dangerous? They damage structures. Debris is picked up and hurled with massive force. **L1**

Critical Thinking

Why should a person stay away from faucets, sinks, and tubs and not use electrical appliances during a thunderstorm? Appliances and sources of water can conduct electricity from lightning. **L1**

Reinforcing Concepts

Lightning can strike as far as ten miles away from a thunderstorm. If you hear thunder, it means you are within striking distance. Don't wait to see lightning—seek safe shelter immediately. **L1**

Lesson 4 Weather Emergencies and Natural Disasters **727**

Curriculum Connections

Activity Divide the class into small groups, and assign each group one weather emergency or natural disaster. Have them prepare a report. Remind them to proofread their reports for errors and develop several drafts before producing their final drafts.

Science What atmospheric or tectonic phenomena causes the event?

Geography What is the incidence of the

event in your area? Where in the world does the event mostly occur? Why?

History Research at least one account of your event and explain the long-term consequences.

Language Arts Present your report to the class as a group.

Quick Demo

Bring in a National Oceanographic Atmospheric Administration (NOAA) weather radio. These can be purchased at sporting goods stores. Show students how they work. Explain that they sound an alert for the area where you live.

Discussing

Ask students what the difference is between a tornado watch and a tornado warning. A watch means that conditions are such that a severe thunderstorm or tornado may develop. A warning means that a thunderstorm or a tornado has been sighted. When should a person seek shelter from a tornado? When a warning has been issued.

Activity

Tell students that injuries can occur both during and after an earthquake. For example, during an earthquake items can fall out of cabinets. Afterwards, homes and yards may contain broken glass. Have students find out actions to take after an earthquake to reduce the risk of injury.

HEALTH Online

Have students access information from the American Red Cross on safety during natural disasters. Lead a class discussion on the topic.

🅐 **If a tornado warning is issued, seek shelter immediately.** *Where is the best place in your community to seek shelter if a tornado warning is issued?*

HEALTH Online

For information from the American Red Cross on how to prepare for and stay safe during natural disasters, go to **health.glencoe.com.**

thunderstorm is approaching. If you are on the water, go to shore. If you are outdoors, get inside. If you can't get inside, take shelter to avoid being struck by lightning. However, stay away from tall structures and trees, because lightning is attracted to tall objects. As a safety precaution, do not use computers, telephones, or televisions during a severe thunderstorm.

Tornadoes

Tornadoes have occurred in every state and can occur at any time of year. The peak months for tornadoes are March through August. A **tornado** is *a whirling, funnel-shaped windstorm that drops from the sky to the ground and produces a narrow path of destruction on land.* Tornadoes are often associated with severe thunderstorms. The winds of a tornado can reach speeds of up to 200 miles per hour, destroying everything in their path. If a tornado approaches, take these precautions:

▶ If you are outside or in a car, seek shelter inside a sturdy building, not a tent or mobile home. If you cannot get to a shelter, lie down in a ditch or low-lying area. Cover yourself with bulky clothing or a blanket. Protect your head with your hands.

▶ If you are indoors, stay away from windows. A storm cellar, basement, or crawl space is the safest place to be. If such an area is not available, go to an interior room, such as a bathroom, hallway, or closet. Cover yourself and protect your head with a mattress or blanket. As a last resort, get under a piece of heavy furniture and hold onto it.

Winter Storms

A severe winter storm called a **blizzard**, *a snowstorm with winds of at least 35 miles per hour,* is common in the northern areas of the United States. To protect yourself during blizzards or other winter storms, follow these steps:

▶ **Stay inside.** The safest place to be during a blizzard is indoors.

▶ **Wear protective clothing.** If you must go outside, prepare for the extremely cold temperatures and the blowing snow. Put on several layers of loose-fitting, lightweight clothing. Choose an outer layer that is wind- and water-resistant. Use a scarf to protect your mouth and neck. Wear a hat, mittens or gloves to protect your hands and fingers. Wear insulated, water-resistant boots to keep your feet warm and dry.

▶ **Avoid getting lost.** Use landmarks to find your way, or stay where you are until help arrives.

Myths & Reality

MYTH. You can outrun a tornado in a car.

FACT. A tornado is unpredictable. You don't know which way it will go. Tornadoes typically move 10–20 mph but can go as fast as 60 mph. Tornadoes can pick up a car and throw it in the air.

MYTH. In a school, the safest place to be during a tornado is in a large room such as a gymnasium or auditorium.

FACT. During a tornado, the safest place to be in a school (if no underground shelter is available) is an interior hallway on the lowest level away from windows and heavy objects that may be propelled in the windstorm.

Earthquakes

An **earthquake** is *a violent shaking movement of the earth's surface.* Earthquakes can occur in all parts of the United States, but they are most common west of the Rocky Mountains. California alone averages almost 5,000 weak but detectable quakes each year. Most casualties during earthquakes are caused by falling objects or collapsing structures. If you live in an area prone to earthquakes, make sure bookcases and other tall or heavy furniture are bolted to the wall. Follow these safety procedures in the event of an earthquake:

▶ If you are inside a building, stand or crouch in a strongly supported doorway, brace yourself in an inside corner of the building, or get under a piece of sturdy furniture. Cover your head with your arms or a pillow.

▶ If you are outdoors when the earthquake hits, stay away from buildings, trees, and power lines.

▶ Use caution after the tremors have stopped. Stay out of damaged buildings. Be aware that utilities such as electrical or gas lines may be damaged and hazardous. Be prepared for aftershocks—smaller quakes that occur after the main earthquake.

The hazards of an earthquake continue after the shaking has stopped. *Identify measures established in your community to prepare for disasters.*

 Lesson 4 *Review*

Reviewing Facts and Vocabulary

1. Define *severe weather*, and list three examples.
2. What is an *emergency survival kit*?
3. How does a hurricane differ from a tornado?

Thinking Critically

4. **Analyzing.** Imagine that a tornado is approaching your home. What strategies can help prevent accidental injuries during this severe weather event?
5. **Evaluating.** Explain how technology and the media have impacted the health status of communities by improving the chances of surviving a severe weather event. What suggestions might you make to further improve their ability to reach a wide range of the population?

Applying Health Skills

Accessing Information. Use online or print resources to obtain a recommended list of items that should be included in an earthquake emergency kit. Write a PSA detailing the items in the kit. Post the information on a public display board.

 TECHNOLOGY *OPTION*

WEB SITES Post the list of items to be included in an earthquake emergency kit on a Web site. List safety procedures to be followed in the event of an earthquake. See **health.glencoe.com** for help in planning and building your own Web site.

Lesson 4 Weather Emergencies and Natural Disasters **729**

 Lesson 4 *Review*

Answers to Reviewing Facts and Vocabulary

1. See page 725 for definition and examples.
2. A group of items that can be used for a short time until an emergency situation has stabilized.
3. See definitions of terms on pages 727 and 728 for comparison.

Answers to Thinking Critically

4. Answers should include the strategies listed on page 728.
5. Possible answer: Both media and technology give advance warning of severe weather, allowing people to seek shelter and prepare for the event. Suggestions for improvements will vary.

Middle School Safe Behaviors Project

NHES Standard 4 Students will analyze the influence of culture, media, technology, and other factors on health.

Objective

Plan an instructional program on injury prevention and safe behaviors for middle-school students.

Motivator

Ask students to name types of media that might appeal to middle-school students. List these on the board.

Teaching Strategies

Awareness Have students think about how media usage changes as children enter their teens.

Analysis Remind students that media choices should be based not only on what is age-appropriate, but also on what is appropriate for lesson content.

Reflection Before submitting their final proposal ideas, ask students to review their lesson plans for age appropriateness and audience appeal.

Take Action By presenting their projects to a middle school, students contribute to their community.

✓ Assessment

Proposals should contain detailed descriptions of lesson plans. Have students select a lesson plan that can be presented in the time allowed.

Eye ON THE Media

Middle School Safe Behaviors Project

People of different ages respond to different types of media. For instance, recent studies show that, as children become teens, they start to listen to more music whereas younger children spend more time watching television and playing video games. In this activity, you will plan an instructional program on injury prevention and safe behaviors for middle-school students using media that would appeal to their age group.

	Type of Media	Description
Lesson 1: Safety at Home and at Work	Skit	Students will learn what they need to know about fire safety by watching a skit in which a family develops a fire-safety and escape plan for their household.
Lesson 2: Recreation and Water Safety		
Lesson 3: Safety on the Road		
Lesson 4: Weather Emergencies and Natural Disasters		

ACTIVITY

For each lesson, develop a lesson plan that uses a specific form of media to instruct middle-school students on a particular topic. Consider forms such as video games, comic books, skits, print materials, and Web activities. Complete a chart like the one shown above.

EXPRESS YOUR VIEWS

With a partner, select one of your lesson plans and complete the project that you proposed. Pool your projects as a class, and ask permission to present your safety instructional program to a group of middle-school students.

More About...

Middle-School Students and Media

"Children ages 8–13 spend more time with media than kids in any other age group—six and three-quarter hours (6:45) a day. These tweens spend as much or more time with virtually every kind of media except listening to music," states the Kaiser Family Foundation's report on their nationwide study of media usage among children. The report also states that "children in the 8–13 year old age group spend an average of 50 minutes a day reading for fun, including 28 minutes reading books." The results of this study are readily available online and can be used as a reference to help students determine what media choices best appeal to children of middle-school age.

CROSS-CURRICULUM CONNECTIONS

Conduct an Interview. A good way to gather accurate information is to interview knowledgeable people. As a class, brainstorm a list of experts on injury prevention, weather emergencies, and natural disasters, such as health care professionals, driver education teachers, and meteorologists. Your teacher will divide the class into teams and assign each team an expert to interview. Report your findings to the class.

Write a Report. Firefighters, including volunteer firefighters, not only put out fires, they also teach the community how to prevent them. Research the development of the volunteer fire department in American history. Write a brief report that discusses how the demands on volunteer fire departments have changed throughout the years, as well as how fire departments teach fire safety.

Calculate the Magnitude. Earthquakes are measured using the Richter Scale, which was developed in 1935 by Charles Richter at the California Institute of Technology. It is a logarithmic scale, which means that each number represents a power of 10. Therefore a magnitude 4.3 quake can also be written as $10^{4.3}$. How many times more powerful is a magnitude 3 earthquake than a magnitude 1 earthquake?

Research a Topic. Certain activities, such as typing on a computer keyboard, require that specific muscles and tendons perform repetitive motions. This can lead to carpal tunnel syndrome, a condition characterized by varying degrees of numbness, pain, and tingling in the hands and forearms. Research carpal tunnel syndrome and write a report on your findings.

CAREER Corner

Paramedic

Are you interested in helping other people in emergency situations? Paramedics are trained to give immediate and skilled care to people in all types of medical emergencies. These emergencies range from car crashes, heart attacks, and drownings to helping with childbirth. Lives depend upon the quick and competent care of paramedics as they provide assistance to and transport sick or injured people.

Would you like to study to be a paramedic? To enter this profession, you'll need emergency medical training. Find out more about this and other health careers by clicking on Career Corner at **health.glencoe.com**.

Chapter 27 Review **731**

Portfolio Assessment

Self-Evaluation Direct students to review the Health Skills Activities and other activities completed in the chapter. Encourage each student to select one finished product or activity that demonstrates his or her best work for the chapter and that represents the student's learning goals. Have students explain what they have learned and how the examples they have selected demonstrate their growth in health literacy, knowledge, and skills.

Teacher Classroom Resources Assign Performance Assessment 27, "The Deadliest Natural Disasters," in the TCR.

CROSS-CURRICULUM CONNECTIONS

Enrich student learning by connecting the topic of injury prevention and safe behaviors to one of the four subject areas presented on this page. The activity may be completed individually or with a partner.

Language Arts Instruct students on how to prepare questions, make the proper arrangements, and carry out an interview.

Social Studies Remind students that when they write a research report, they should gather factual information from several different sources.

Math Answer: Magnitude 3 = 10^3=1000, Magnitude 1=10^1=10. 1000/10=100

Science Guide students toward reliable sources of information for their research. Direct them to consult current periodicals for recent news and statistics regarding carpal tunnel syndrome. Suggest that they visit government Web sites such as the U.S. Department of Labor for current information on what industries are doing to prevent repetitive motion injuries.

CAREER Corner

Have students read and discuss the Career Corner information on paramedics. Ask interested students to explore the Glencoe Health Web site at **health.glencoe.com** for more information on this career.

CHECKING COMPREHENSION

- Assign and discuss the chapter review.
- Use the Chapter 27 MindJogger Videoquiz to review the chapter. ▷◁

CHAPTER 27 REVIEW ANSWERS

Exploring Health Terms

1. accident chain
2. fire extinguisher
3. unintentional injury
4. Occupational Safety and Health Administration (OSHA)
5. False—heat exhaustion
6. False—Hypothermia
7. defensive driver
8. road rage
9. graduated driver's license
10. earthquake
11. flash flood
12. blizzard

Recalling the Facts

1. These events are linked. If one of the events does not occur, the accident chain is broken and the injury is avoided.
2. Smoke alarms and fire extinguishers increase your odds of surviving a fire. A smoke alarm warns you if there is a fire. The fire extinguisher can be used to put out small fires before they get out of control.
3. Some household chemicals produce toxic gases when mixed.
4. To avoid drowning.
5. Drink plenty of water, dress appropriately for the temperature, and stay in the shade.
6. States are adopting graduated driver's license programs in an effort to reduce the number of teens killed in automobile crashes.

▶ **EXPLORING HEALTH TERMS** *Answer the following questions on a sheet of paper.*

Lesson 1 *Match each definition with the correct term.*

unintentional injury	Occupational Safety
smoke alarm	and Health
fire extinguisher	Administration
accident chain	(OSHA)

1. A sequence of events that leads to an unintentional injury.
2. A portable device that puts out small fires by ejecting fire-extinguishing chemicals.
3. An injury resulting from an unexpected event, or accident.
4. The agency in the federal government that is responsible for promoting safe and healthful conditions in the workplace.

Lesson 2 *Identify each statement as True or False. If false, replace the underlined term with the correct term.*

hypothermia   heat exhaustion

5. An overheating of the body that results in cold, clammy skin and symptoms of shock is known as <u>hypothermia</u>.
6. <u>Heat exhaustion</u> is a condition in which body temperature becomes dangerously low.

Lesson 3 *Match each definition with the correct term.*

vehicular safety	defensive driver
graduated driver's license	road rage

7. A driver who is aware of potential hazards and reacts to avoid them.
8. A practice of endangering drivers by using a vehicle as a weapon.
9. A licensing program that gradually increases a new driver's driving privileges over time as experience and skill are gained.

Lesson 4 *Replace the underlined words with the correct term.*

severe weather	hurricane	tornado
emergency survival kit	flash flood	blizzard
earthquake		

10. A <u>flash flood</u> is a violent shaking movement of the earth's surface.
11. A <u>hurricane</u> is a flood with great volume and of short duration that is caused by heavy rainfall.
12. A <u>tornado</u> is a snowstorm with winds of at least 35 miles per hour.

▶ **RECALLING THE FACTS** *Use complete sentences to answer the following questions.*

Lesson 1

1. Explain why the pattern of events that can lead to an unintentional injury is known as the "accident chain."
2. Why should every home be equipped with smoke alarms and a fire extinguisher?
3. Why is mixing household chemicals an unsafe procedure?

Lesson 2

4. Why should everyone learn to swim?
5. What can you do to protect yourself from heat exhaustion?

Lesson 3

6. Why are some states adopting a graduated driver's license program?
7. Why is it important be aware of your emotional state when driving?
8. What are two safety behaviors that can keep you safe on a skateboard?

7. A person's emotional state can affect his or her judgment and reaction time, which in turn can affect the ability to drive.
8. Possible answers: Wear protective equipment; watch for pedestrians; keep speed under control; don't carry any item in your hands; if you fall, curl into a ball and roll.
9. Possible answers: Secure property; bring in items from outside that may blow away in strong winds; board up windows or doors; tape any glass if you are unable to cover it.
10. Indoors.
11. West of the Rocky Mountains.

9. What precautions should you take if a hurricane watch is issued for your area?

10. Where is the safest place to be during a blizzard?

11. Where do earthquakes occur most often in the United States?

➤ THINKING CRITICALLY

1. Applying. Alicia spends a lot of time working on the computer. Lately, her neck and back have begun to ache, and her eyes often feel tired. What advice would you give her? *(LESSON 1)*

2. Evaluating. Josie lives on a lake and is a good swimmer. On Monday she got home before her parents and decided that she wanted to go for a quick swim. Why is this risky? *(LESSON 2)*

3. Summarizing. Though a driver's license is not required to operate an ATV, all ATV operators should use common sense and have a knowledge of road rules. Write a paragraph summarizing safety rules that all ATV operators should know. *(LESSON 3)*

4. Analyzing. Experts suggest that homeowners bolt heavy household items such as bookcases to the wall in earthquake-prone areas. How might this procedure prevent accidental injuries? *(LESSON 4)*

➤ HEALTH SKILLS APPLICATION

1. Advocacy. Write a letter that stresses the importance of on-the-job training for teen workers in your community. Research your local and state laws and include them in your letter. Submit your letter to your school or local newspaper for publication. *(LESSON 1)*

2. Refusal Skills. Mary is excited to be invited out on a boat for a day of water skiing and swimming. However, when she arrives at the boat, Mary learns that the driver of the boat has been drinking alcohol. What should Mary do? *(LESSON 2)*

3. Decision Making. Imagine that you attended a party that lasted longer than you had planned. Because your license is graduated, you are not allowed to drive your car at this time of night. Use the decision-making steps to determine what to do. *(LESSON 3)*

4. Practicing Healthful Behaviors. Create an informative poster on how to stay safe during severe weather events. Make your poster available to other teens in your school. *(LESSON 4)*

BEYOND
the Classroom

Parent Involvement

Accessing Information. Learning to swim can save your life. Research recreation and water-safety programs in your community. With your parents, find out how your family can become involved in these educational programs. If programs do not already exist in your community, find out how you can bring them to your community.

School and Community

American Red Cross. The American Red Cross helps communities during and immediately after a weather emergency or natural disaster. It also offers first-aid, recreation, and water-safety education classes. Contact the agency and find out what volunteer positions are available. Share your findings with the rest of the class.

Chapter 27 Review **733**

Thinking Critically

1. Possible answers: Take a 10-minute break every hour or so, give eyes a rest by looking up and focusing on distant objects, make sure the computer monitor, desk, and chair are adjusted correctly and that the lighting is appropriate.

2. It is never a good idea to swim alone. You never know when an accident will occur, and you will need a buddy to help you.

3. Answers will vary but should reflect knowledge of road rules, safe driving procedures, and safety precautions such as wearing the appropriate safety gear.

4. It is important to bolt heavy items to the wall so that they do not fall over and cause injuries during an earthquake.

Health Skills Application

1.–4. Answers will vary.

EVALUATE

• Use the reproducible Chapter 27 Test in the TCR, or construct your own using the Testmaker software. 🗁 ⊙

• Use Performance Assessment 27 in the TCR. 🗁

ENRICHMENT

Ask students to complete Enrichment Activity 27 in the TCR. 🗁

BEYOND
the Classroom

Keep students involved in the community, and encourage parent participation by assigning the activities on this page for students to work on outside of class.

Lessons	Standards		Features
	National	**State/Local**	
1 **Providing First Aid** *pages 736–741*	National Health Education Standards **2.6, 3.2, 3.5**		**Health Skills Activity** • How to Handle a Puncture Wound *(Practicing Healthful Behaviors)*, page 739
2 **CPR and First Aid for Shock and Choking** *pages 742–748*	National Health Education Standards **2.6, 3.2, 3.5, 7.2**		**Exploring Issues** • Should Schools Require Teens to Take a CPR Course? page 745
3 **Responding to Common Emergencies** *pages 749–754*	National Health Education Standards **2.6, 3.2, 3.5**		**Hands-On Health** • First-Aid Stations *(Practicing Healthful Behaviors)*, page 753
4 **Treatment for Poisonings** *pages 755–759*	National Health Education Standards **2.4, 2.6, 3.2, 3.5**		**Real-Life Application** • Contacting a Poison Control Center *(Accessing Information)*, page 757

Reproducible Resources	Assessment	Technology
Student Activity Workbook for use with each chapter 📁 Concept Mapping Activity 103 📁 Guided Reading Activities 103 📁 Lesson Plan 103 📁 Parent Letter and Activities 28 📁 Reteaching Activity 103	📁 Lesson Quiz 103	🕹 Transparency 82 💿 TeacherWorks® 💻 Internet Activities
📁 Concept Mapping Activity 104 📁 Current Health Issues 28 📁 Decision-Making Activity 28 📁 Enrichment Activity 28 📁 Guided Reading Activities 104 📁 Lesson Plan 104 📁 Reteaching Activity 104	📁 Lesson Quiz 104	🕹 Transparency 83 💿 TeacherWorks®
📁 Concept Mapping Activity 105 📁 Cross-Curriculum Activity 28 📁 Guided Reading Activities 105 📁 Lesson Plan 105 📁 Reteaching Activity 105	📁 Lesson Quiz 105	🕹 Transparency 84 💿 TeacherWorks®
📁 Concept Mapping Activity 106 📁 Guided Reading Activities 106 📁 Health Lab 28 📁 Lesson Plan 106 📁 Reteaching Activity 106	📁 Lesson Quiz 106	🕹 Transparency 85 💿 TeacherWorks®

⏱ 0:00 OUT OF TIME

If time does not permit teaching the entire chapter use:
- Figure 28.1, p. 737
- Figure 28.3, p. 743
- Figure 28.4, p. 744
- Hands-On Health, p. 753
- Real-Life Application, p. 757

Language Diversity

- 🎧 English Audio CD Program
- 🎧 Spanish Audio CD Program
- 📁 English Summaries, Quizzes, and Activities
- 📁 Spanish Summaries, Quizzes, and Activities
- 📁 Spanish Parent Letters and Activities

End of Chapter Assessment

Blackline Masters
- 📁 Chapter 28 Test
- 📁 Performance Assessment Activity 28

Technology
- 💿 Vocabulary PuzzleMaker
- 📼 MindJogger Videoquiz
- 💿 *ExamView*® Pro Testmaker

Professional Health Series

Dealing with Sensitive Issues
Planning a Coordinated School Health Program
Promoting Character Education
Home, School, and Community Involvement

Key to Ability Levels

Teaching strategies that appear throughout the chapter have been identified by one of the following codes to give teachers an idea of their suitability for students of varying learning styles and abilities.

L1 Strategies should be within the ability range of all students. Full class participation is often required. Teacher direction is usually needed.

L2 Strategies are designed for average to above-average students or for small groups. Some teacher direction is needed.

L3 Strategies are designed for students able and willing to work independently. Minimal teacher direction is needed.

ELL Strategies should be within the ability range of students learning the English language.

🔲 Block scheduling strategies are useful in a block scheduling format.

First Aid and Emergencies

CHAPTER OVERVIEW

Chapter 28 presents first-aid techniques to use during common medical emergencies.

Lesson 1 First aid is the immediate, temporary care given to a person who has become ill or who has been injured. It continues until professional medical help can be rendered.

Lesson 2 CPR is a life-saving procedure that can be administered to a person whose breathing and heartbeat have stopped. The techniques for responding to a person who is choking or in shock are also presented.

Lesson 3 First aid for the following emergencies is presented: muscle, joint, and bone injuries; fainting; concussion; animal bites; nosebleeds; and foreign objects in the eye.

Lesson 4 First aid for different types of poisoning is presented. Poison may enter the body through swallowing, inhalation, skin contact, or insect stings and animal bites.

Health Skills Features

- Health Skills Activity (*Practicing Healthful Behaviors*), p. 739
- Exploring Issues, p. 745
- Hands-On Health (*Practicing Healthful Behaviors*), p. 753
- Real-Life Application (*Accessing Information*), p. 757

Chapter 28

First Aid and Emergencies

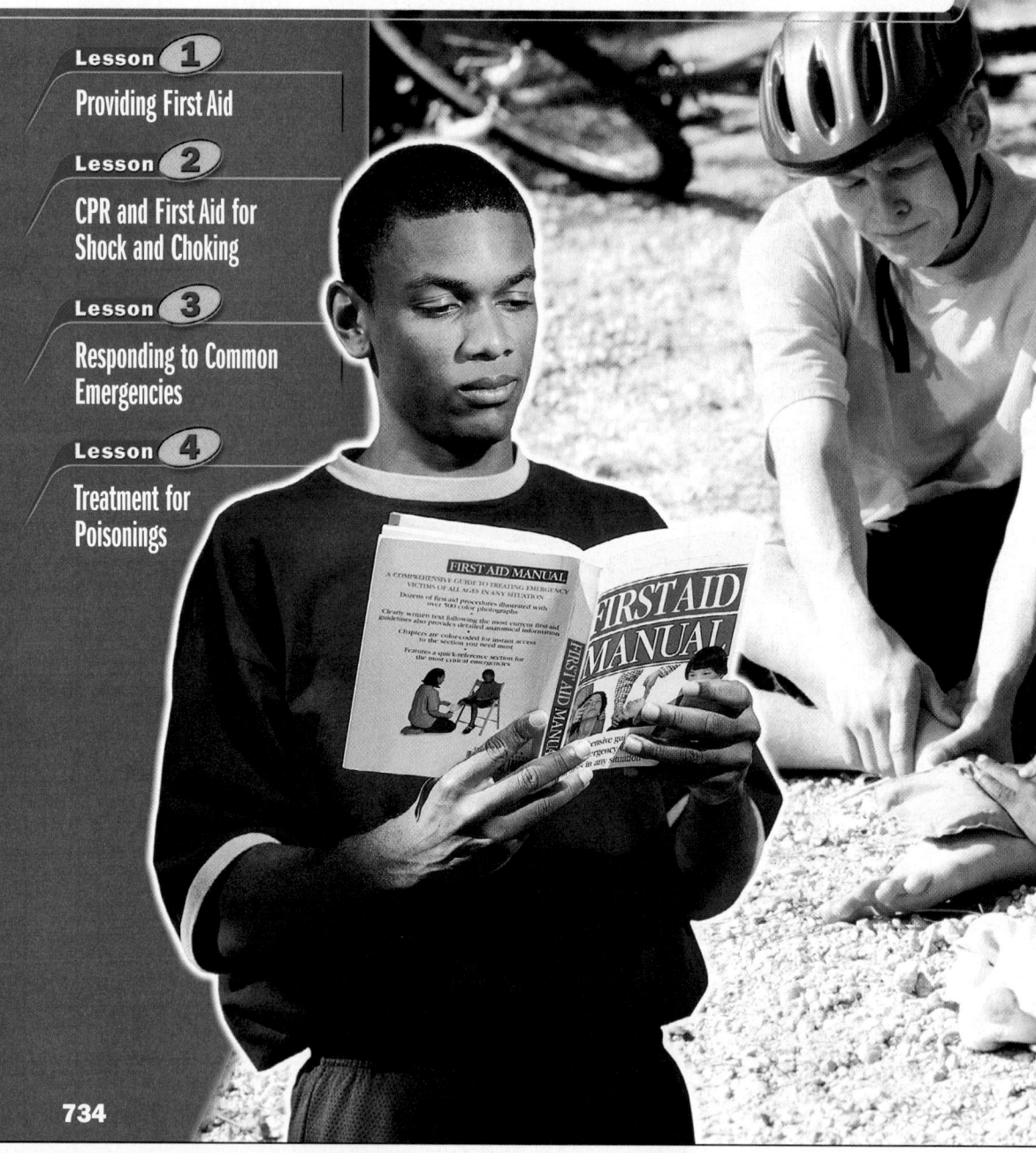

Lesson 1
Providing First Aid

Lesson 2
CPR and First Aid for Shock and Choking

Lesson 3
Responding to Common Emergencies

Lesson 4
Treatment for Poisonings

734

MEETING STUDENT DIVERSITY

Language Diversity Use the following suggestions to help students who have difficulty with English:

- Pair English language learners with native speakers of English who can restate the Chapter Summary in language that helps students comprehend important concepts.

- Direct auditory learners or those students with language diversity to the *Glencoe Health Audio CD Program*. Available in English and Spanish, this component provides an audio and written summary of the chapter.

- Use photographs, drawings, or magazine clippings to help students visualize the important concepts of the chapter.

Personal Health Inventory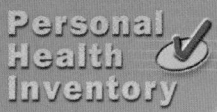

What's Your Health Status?

Read each statement below and respond by writing *yes* or *no* for each item.

1. I have the contact information for my family's health care providers.

2. I keep a list of emergency numbers near a telephone in my home.

3. I can help someone who has swallowed a poison.

4. I take small bites of food when eating and chew each bite thoroughly before swallowing.

5. I know what actions to take to help someone who is choking.

6. I know all of the medications that members of my family take.

7. I am trained and certified to administer CPR.

8. I know what steps to take to stop heavy bleeding.

9. I am able to tell the difference between minor and serious burns and can treat first- and second-degree burns.

10. I know how to help with common emergencies such as nosebleed, fainting, foreign objects in the eye, and insect bites.

Keep this personal inventory for review later in the chapter. When you complete the chapter, review your answers and identify two or three behavior changes you could make to improve your health.

Quick *Write*

Using Visuals. Your response to a medical emergency can be critical to the recovery of an injured person. In what specific ways do you think providing the correct first-aid techniques will help the recovery of this injured person?

735

INTRODUCING THE CHAPTER

Personal Health Inventory

Have students read and discuss the Personal Health Inventory statements. Ask: What first-aid procedures are identified here? How can familiarity with these procedures help you protect your own health and the health of others? After students have shared their ideas, let them record their inventory responses in their private health journals. Have them add the title "First Aid and Emergencies," and remind students that they will revisit this inventory again at the end of the chapter.

Tell students that this chapter will help them learn to administer first aid for common emergencies. As they learn what to do in an emergency, they also should think in terms of how the injury could have been prevented.

Quick *write*

Using Visuals For the Quick Write, ask students to identify the first-aid measure depicted in the photo and explain how it will benefit the victim's recovery. Students should recognize that applying the cold pack helps to reduce swelling.

TECHNOLOGY OPTIONS

MINDJOGGER
VIDEOQUIZ

To preview or review chapter content, you may wish to use the Chapter 28 MindJogger Videoquiz. ◖◗

HEALTH *Online*

Online Resources for the Teacher For a fresh approach to health topics and an in-depth look at health issues, use these online resources found under Teacher Resources at **health.glencoe.com:**

- Block Schedule Lesson Plans
- Technology Projects
- Health Updates

Providing First Aid

Lesson 1

①FOCUS

 QUICK START Give students five minutes to write their paragraphs. Remind them that learning first aid results in understanding not only what to do but also what not to do. Have volunteers share their paragraphs with the class.

TYING TO PRIOR KNOWLEDGE

Ask students to brainstorm medical emergencies that require first aid, such as a deep cut or choking. Explain that this lesson will teach them about the basic rules of first aid.

Health Skills Features

"How to Handle a Puncture Wound," p. 739

PRACTICING HEALTHFUL BEHAVIORS

INTRODUCING VOCABULARY

- Have students write a sentence explaining in their own words what *first aid* means. Review the term *universal precautions* and have students tell where they have observed this practice, such as in dental offices.

- Ask students to complete the Chapter 28 Study Guide in the *Student Activity Workbook.*

Providing First Aid

VOCABULARY
first aid
universal precautions

YOU'LL LEARN TO

- Relate the nation's goals and objectives for improving individual, family, and community health to learning and using appropriate first-aid procedures.

- Understand the importance of learning first aid.

- Analyze strategies for responding to accidental injuries.

QUICK START Write a paragraph explaining the importance of learning first-aid procedures.

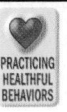 Universal precautions protect both the caregiver and the victim from coming into contact with blood and other body fluids that may contain pathogens.

Imagine that you are taking care of your neighbor's son when he suddenly falls off his bike and cuts his knee. Suppose that you are in the school lunchroom and your best friend begins to choke. Do you know what to do in either of these situations? Your response to an accident or an emergency can minimize injury and might even save a life.

First Aid

First aid is *the immediate, temporary care given to an ill or injured person until professional medical care can be provided.* First aid is administered in the seconds and minutes following an emergency situation in which someone becomes ill or injured. Learning first-aid procedures is an important step in meeting the nation's health goals in *Healthy People 2010.* Using the proper first-aid procedures can reduce the number of people who sustain further injury or die in the absence of early and effective treatment.

736 Chapter 28 First Aid and Emergencies

Lesson 1 *Resources*

Teacher Classroom Resources

- Concept Mapping Activity 103
- Guided Reading Activities 103
- Lesson Plan 103
- Lesson Quiz 103
- Parent Letter and Activities 28
- Reteaching Activity 103

Student Activity Workbook

- Applying Health Skills 103
- Chapter 28 Study Guide

Multimedia

- Transparency 82

Universal Precautions

Some infectious agents, such as the HIV and hepatitis B viruses, can be transmitted through contact with blood and other body fluids. Because of this risk, it is important that you use universal precautions when you administer first aid. **Universal precautions** are *actions taken to prevent the spread of disease by treating all blood and other body fluids as if they contained pathogens.* Universal precautions include wearing protective gloves when there is a possibility of touching blood or other body fluids, using a mouthpiece or other protective ventilation devices for breathing emergencies, and washing your hands before and after providing first aid.

Responding to an Emergency

Recognizing an emergency is the first step in responding to it. Common indicators of an emergency include unusual sights, sounds, odors, and behaviors. If you find yourself at the scene of an emergency, remain calm and follow the steps in **Figure 28.1,** which were developed by the American Red Cross.

FIGURE 28.1

CHECK, CALL, CARE

These are the first steps to take in an emergency situation.

1. Check the scene and the victim.
Look around to be sure that the scene is safe. Be alert for dangers such as spilled chemicals, traffic, fire, escaping steam, downed electrical lines, and smoke. Determine the number of victims. If no immediate danger is evident, do not move the victim. Move the victim only if his or her life is threatened.

2. Call for help.
Call the local emergency number or 911. Answer all of the dispatcher's questions. Do not hang up until the dispatcher does. If possible, have someone else make the call so that you can stay with the victim. If you are the one calling for help, finish the call as quickly as possible, and return to the victim.

3. Provide care for the victim.
If possible, get the victim's permission before giving first aid. Always address life-threatening emergencies first. Take care of anyone who is unconscious; who is not breathing or is having trouble breathing; who shows no signs of circulation, such as moving or coughing; or who is bleeding severely. If you aren't sure that the victim is conscious, tap him or her on the shoulder and ask, "Are you okay?"

Lesson 1   Providing First Aid   **737**

② TEACH

VISUAL LEARNING

Figure 28.1 Give students a few moments to read the information in Figure 28.1. Ask:

- Why is it important not to move a victim unless absolutely necessary? The person could sustain further injury in the process of moving.
- Why is it important that 911 be called only for true emergencies? Nonemergency calls take valuable time away from true emergencies, because the dispatcher must evaluate each call.

Critical Thinking

Ask: Why is it important to wash your hands after administering first aid, even if you wear gloves? Gloves can rip or tear, resulting in potential exposure to pathogens. Inform students that gloves may have tiny holes that you cannot see but that can still permit blood or other body fluids to get through. **L2**

Explaining

Tell students that some people are allergic to the latex in disposable gloves. Vinyl gloves are an alternative. Both types of gloves can be purchased in hardware stores or pharmacies. **L1**

— *School to Work* —

Emergency Medical Technician An emergency medical technician (EMT) must take a comprehensive course in emergency care and pass an examination. Besides providing first aid and CPR, EMTs are allowed to begin such basic treatment as administering oxygen. Encourage interested students to investigate how to become an EMT. What are the training requirements? Where does training take place? What employment opportunities exist? What does an EMT earn? Suggest that students write an employment ad for an EMT, specifying requirements, salary, and duties.

Explaining

Explain to students that puncture wounds are particularly dangerous because of the increased risk of infection. Objects piercing the soft tissues of the body can carry the bacteria that cause tetanus, a disease that can result in paralysis and death. Commonly found in soil, the bacteria that cause tetanus cause problems only when they grow under conditions without air—such as those found in the deep tissues of a puncture wound. Immunization is the best way to prevent tetanus. A person who has sustained a puncture wound and who has previously been immunized against tetanus should get a booster shot if he or she has not had one within the last five years.

Guest Speaker

Invite the school nurse or other medical professional to visit the class to demonstrate basic first-aid treatment for wounds. ⬜

Discussing

All wounds except avulsions can be cleaned unless they are severe. If you cannot hold the wound under cool running water, use a cup to pour cool water over the wound. Use plain soap and a soft washcloth to clean around the wound. Keep soap out of the wound itself. Hydrogen peroxide may also be used. For severe wounds, cover the wound and seek medical help. ⬜

Types of Injuries

Not all injuries are emergencies. Splinters and scrapes, for example, are relatively minor injuries, and the first-aid treatment for them is usually quick and simple. Other injuries are severe enough to endanger life or cause serious physical damage.

Open Wounds

Open wounds are one type of injury. Treatment depends on the severity and type of wound:

Knives and other sharp objects can cause lacerations. When using any sharp tool, pay attention to what you are doing. *What other steps can you take to reduce the risk of lacerations?*

▶ **Abrasion.** If the skin is scraped against a hard surface, tiny blood vessels in the outer layers of the skin break, resulting in an abrasion. Because of the way the injury occurs, dirt and bacteria can easily enter the site. Therefore, it's especially important to clean the wound to prevent infection and speed healing.

▶ **Laceration.** A laceration is a cut caused by a sharp object, such as a knife or broken glass, slicing through the layers of skin. This type of laceration usually has smooth edges. A hard blow from a blunt instrument or the skin being torn may cause lacerations with jagged edges. All lacerations are accompanied by bleeding. Deep lacerations can result in heavy bleeding, as well as damage to nerves, large blood vessels, and other soft tissues. Infection may also occur.

▶ **Puncture.** A puncture wound is a small but deep hole caused by a pin, nail, fang, or other object that pierces the skin. Puncture wounds do not usually cause heavy external bleeding, but they may cause internal bleeding if the penetrating object damages major blood vessels or internal organs. Puncture wounds carry a high risk of infection, including tetanus.

▶ **Avulsion.** An avulsion results when tissue is partially or completely separated from the body. A partially avulsed piece of skin may remain attached, but it hangs like a flap. Heavy bleeding is common. Sometimes a body part, such as a finger, may be severed. With today's medical technology, severed body parts can sometimes be reattached surgically. Pack the severed part in ice or ice water, if possible, to preserve the tissue. Immediately call for professional medical assistance.

Home and Community

First-Aid Kit Have students work in small groups to access print and online sources of information on items to include in a first-aid kit. Then have them prepare a checklist of items and other tips. For example, a first-aid kit should be kept in the home as well as in every vehicle. People should carry a first-aid kit when hiking, biking, camping, or boating.

The container can be a plastic tackle box or a small tote bag; prepared kits can be purchased in pharmacies. Have students share their checklist with their parents or guardians. If their home does not have a first-aid kit, they can work with their family to prepare one.

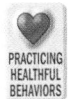

Health Skills Activity

How to Handle a Puncture Wound

Jamie, 16, is looking after Jason, her 7-year-old neighbor, for the afternoon. They are in the backyard playing with toy cars and trucks. After a while, Jason gets up and walks over to the tool shed.

"Jason," Jamie calls, "you're not supposed to go over there. Come back here and pull out my car with your tow truck. I'm stuck in the mud."

Jason starts to walk back, and suddenly starts screaming and holding his foot.

"Oh, my gosh!" Jamie cries. She looks at Jason's foot.

Jason has stepped on a nail, which has punctured his foot. Jamie notes that the wound looks deep but doesn't appear to be bleeding heavily.

What should Jamie do?

What Would You Do?

Describe in detail how you would apply these first-aid steps to Jamie's situation.

1. **Protect yourself from infections** spread by contact with blood.
2. **Control any bleeding.**
3. **Clean the wound.**
4. **Protect the wound.**
5. **Get medical attention if necessary.**

First Aid for Bleeding

To stop blood flow from an open wound, first put on clean protective gloves, if possible. Wash a minor wound with mild soap and running water to remove dirt and debris. Do not attempt to clean a severe injury such as an avulsion. Always wash your hands before and after providing care, even if you wear gloves.

To control bleeding:

▶ Cover the wound with sterile gauze or a clean cloth and press firmly.

▶ If possible, elevate the wound above the level of the heart.

▶ Cover the gauze or cloth dressing with a sterile bandage.

▶ If necessary, cover the dressing with a pressure bandage and/or use pressure point bleeding control (see next page).

▶ Call for help or have someone else do so.

 Applying pressure to a wound will often stop the flow of blood. *What precautions should you take before assisting someone with an open wound?*

Lesson 1 Providing First Aid **739**

More About...

Good Samaritan Law Bring in a copy of the Good Samaritan Law for first aid for your state. Note that the law may be titled differently in your area. Explain that this law is to protect citizens who administer first aid to victims in need of assistance. This law requires that the person remain with the victim, call for help, and/or give basic first aid if they know how. It also protects the citizen from being sued for administering basic first aid. Some states also protect licensed medical personnel from liability if they provide first aid without compensation. However, it usually does not protect against gross or willful negligence, even if the medical professional was not compensated.

Quick Demo

Show an anatomical model that delineates arteries and veins. Point out the major arteries. Leave the model out so individual students can study the location of the arteries and trace their paths. **L1**

Explaining

Explain that a cloth or gauze through which blood has soaked should not be removed from a wound. Instead, more gauze or cloth should be placed over it. **L1**

VISUAL LEARNING

Figure 28.2 Ask a volunteer to read the information about each type of burn described in Figure 28.2 on page 741. Lead a discussion in which students discuss the differences in appearance of each type of burn. Have students compare and contrast first-aid measures that are common to all types and first-aid measures that are different for each type.

Critical Thinking

Have students think about the type of tissue that is affected in each type of burn. Ask: Which type of burn do you think is the most painful and why? Second-degree burns, because the damage is deeper than in first-degree burns, but the nerve endings are still intact. Which type do you think is the least painful and why? At the time of the burn, third-degree burns may not be painful if nerve endings are destroyed. (However, medical treatment for these types of burns is very painful.) **L2**

A pressure bandage may be used to maintain continuous pressure on a wound. *Identify a situation that would require the use of a pressure bandage.*

For severe bleeding, applying pressure at a pressure point will reduce or stop blood flow. *For what type of injury would pressure point bleeding control be necessary?*

How to Apply a Pressure Bandage

Roller bandages can be used to maintain continuous pressure on a wound and control bleeding. A bandage applied snugly to the injured area will hold the dressing in place and facilitate blood clotting. To use a roller bandage:

▶ Place a dressing over the wound.

▶ Secure the roller bandage over the dressing.

▶ Using overlapping turns, cover the dressing completely, as shown in the diagram at the left.

▶ Secure the roller bandage in place by splitting its end into two strips. Tie the split bandage ends tightly over the wound.

▶ Make sure that the bandage is not so tight that it cuts off circulation. It should be just tight enough to maintain pressure on the wound.

Pressure Point Bleeding Control

If elevating the wound and applying a pressure bandage do not stop the bleeding, pressure point bleeding control must be used. This procedure involves pressing the main artery against a bone to stop blood supply to the injured area. Because this technique stops normal blood circulation, it should be used only when absolutely necessary. The diagram at the left shows the location of the points at which pressure should be applied when using this technique.

A person who requires pressure point bleeding control is seriously injured and possibly in shock. Professional medical assistance is necessary and should be consulted before this procedure is applied.

Burns

Heat, radiation from the sun, certain chemicals, and electricity can all burn the skin and soft tissues of the body. Burns caused by heat are the most common. Those caused by chemicals or electricity require special first-aid procedures—for information on treating these types of burns, contact the American Red Cross.

Burns are classified according to depth: first-degree burns are superficial, and second- and third-degree burns are deep. Minor burns can be treated at home. Severe burns, however, require professional medical care. **Figure 28.2** shows the three classifications of burns and the treatment for each.

Home and Community

Emergency Telephone Numbers Give each student an index card for each stationary telephone in their home and make local telephone directories available. Have students find out the telephone numbers for all emergency organizations in their area. This may include the police or sheriff's department, the fire department, the family doctor, the family dentist, the family counselor, and the nearest poison control center. Students should write these numbers on their index cards and write their names on the back of each card. Laminate the cards, and return them to the students to post in their homes.

FIGURE 28.2

TYPES OF BURNS AND TREATMENT

The severity of the burn determines the type of burn and treatment.

First-degree burn	Second-degree burn	Third-degree burn
In a **first-degree burn,** only the outer layer of skin is burned and turns red. Cool the burn with cold running water or by immersing it in cold water (not ice) for 10 minutes. A clean, cold, wet towel will help reduce pain. Pat the area dry, and cover it with a sterile bandage.	A **second-degree burn** is one in which the top several layers of skin are damaged. The skin will have blisters and appear blotchy. Cool the burn with cold water (not ice), and elevate the burned area. Wrap the area loosely with a sterile, dry dressing. Do not pop blisters or peel loose skin. Seek professional medical attention.	A **third-degree burn** is a serious burn in which deeper layers of skin and possibly fat, muscle, nerves, and bone are damaged. Call for professional medical help immediately. Cool the burn with large amounts of cold water (not ice). Cover the area with a dry sterile dressing or clean cloth.

Lesson 1 Review

Reviewing Facts and Vocabulary

1. Define *first aid.*
2. Relate the nation's health goals and objectives to individual, family, and community health: Explain why knowing first-aid procedures can help achieve the goals of *Healthy People 2010.*
3. Why is it necessary to use universal precautions when giving first aid to a person who is bleeding?

Thinking Critically

4. **Synthesizing.** Analyze and develop a strategy for responding to a minor laceration.
5. **Analyzing.** Describe a strategy for responding to a second-degree burn.

Applying Health Skills

Communication Skills. What would you say to a teen who isn't sure why he or she should learn first aid? Write a dialogue in which you use effective communication skills to explain to the teen the importance of knowing first aid.

WORD PROCESSING Use word-processing software to write your dialogue. See health.glencoe.com for tips on using word-processing software.

Lesson 1 Providing First Aid **741**

Lesson 1 Review

Answers to Reviewing Facts and Vocabulary

1. The immediate, temporary care given to an ill or injured person until professional medical care can be provided.
2. It can reduce further injury and possibly prevent death.
3. To prevent the spread of pathogens in blood and other body fluids.

Answers to Thinking Critically

4. Answers should include the strategies featured on page 739.
5. See Figure 28.2 for treatment.

EVALUATING THE LESSON

Assign and discuss the Lesson 1 Review; then administer, grade, and discuss Lesson Quiz 103 in the TCR.

RETEACHING

- Assign each cooperative learning group a different type of injury. Have each group present a one-minute oral summary of the priorities in an emergency and information on responding to their assigned injury.

- Ask students to complete Reteaching Activity 103 in the TCR.

ENRICHMENT

Have interested students set up a display of first-aid information pamphlets and a sample first-aid kit in the cafeteria or other location permitted by school authorities. Students can set up posters showing general procedures to follow in an emergency.

4 CLOSE

Have students summarize the most important concepts studied in this lesson.

CPR and First Aid for Shock and Choking

1 FOCUS

QUICK START
Have students work in pairs and write in their private health journals. Hold a brief discussion in which a few students share their paragraphs. Tell students that at the end of the lesson, they will revise their paragraphs as needed.

TYING TO PRIOR KNOWLEDGE

Ask students to describe how they know a person might be choking and what first-aid measures should be taken. Explain that this lesson outlines first-aid procedures for choking and shock as well as how to perform CPR.

Health Skills Features

"Should Schools Require Teens to Take a CPR Course?," p. 745

INTRODUCING VOCABULARY

• Review what students have learned in Chapter 26 about ventricular fibrillation; then have students explain what they think is the purpose of a *defibrillator*. Also have students tell what they know about *shock*.

• Ask students to complete the Chapter 28 Study Guide in the *Student Activity Workbook*. 📂

742

Lesson 2

CPR and First Aid for Shock and Choking

VOCABULARY
chain of survival
defibrillator
cardiopulmonary resuscitation (CPR)
shock

YOU'LL LEARN TO
• Identify the appropriate steps for responding to life-threatening emergencies.
• Analyze strategies for responding to an emergency situation requiring CPR.
• Analyze strategies for responding to a shock or choking victim.

QUICK START Write a paragraph describing what you know about CPR.

 The increased availability of AEDs has lead to improved survival rates for heart-attack victims.

In an emergency, you need to act quickly—the first few minutes after a medical crisis are usually the most critical. The key is knowing what to do, remaining calm, and making a decision to act.

Life-Threatening Emergencies

If the victim in an emergency is unresponsive, you must begin immediately the **chain of survival**, *a sequence of actions that maximize the victim's chances of survival*. If the victim is an adult, you can begin the first two links in the chain: call 911 and begin CPR. The next two links, early defibrillation and transfer to advanced care, are usually the responsibility of the emergency medical personnel when they arrive. A **defibrillator** is *a device that delivers an electric shock to the heart to restore its normal rhythm*. An automated external defibrillator (AED) is a handheld device that almost anyone can be trained to use. AEDs have not been approved for use on children who are younger than eight years old or who weigh under 55 pounds.

742 Chapter 28 First Aid and Emergencies

Lesson 2 Resources

Teacher Classroom Resources
📂 Concept Mapping Activity 104
📂 Current Health Issues 28
📂 Decision-Making Activity 28
📂 Enrichment Activity 28
📂 Guided Reading Activities 104
📂 Lesson Plan 104

📂 Lesson Quiz 104
📂 Reteaching Activity 104
Student Activity Workbook
📂 Applying Health Skills 104
📂 Chapter 28 Study Guide
Multimedia
🖱 Transparency 83

CPR

A person whose breathing and heartbeat have stopped may need CPR. **Cardiopulmonary resuscitation (CPR)** is *a life-saving first-aid procedure that combines rescue breaths with chest compressions, supplying oxygen to the body until normal body functions can resume.* You must be properly trained by a professional and certified before administering CPR.

CPR for Adults

The steps of CPR are known as the ABCs—airway, breathing, and circulation. If an adult victim is unresponsive, tap him or her and ask in a loud voice, "Are you okay?" If the victim doesn't respond, start the chain of survival. First, call 911 or have someone else do so. Then kneel beside the victim and follow the steps developed by the American Heart Association, which are shown in **Figures 28.3** and **28.4.**

FIGURE 28.3

THE ABCs OF ADULT CPR

A Airway. Look inside the victim's mouth. Remove anything you see blocking the airway. If you don't suspect head or neck injuries, lay the person flat on a firm surface. Gently tilt the head back by lifting the chin with one hand while pushing down on the forehead with the other. If you suspect head or neck injuries, do not move the victim. Open his or her airway by lifting the jaw instead.

B Breathing. Look, listen, and feel for breathing. *Look* for chest movement. *Listen* at the victim's mouth for breathing. *Feel* for exhaled air on your cheek. If the victim is not breathing normally, begin rescue breathing:

1. Keeping the victim's head in the proper position, pinch the nostrils shut.
2. Place your mouth over the victim's mouth, forming a seal. Give 2 slow breaths, each about 2 seconds long. The victim's chest should rise with each breath.

C Circulation. Check for signs of circulation, such as breathing, coughing, or movement. If there are no signs of circulation, a person trained in CPR should begin chest compressions immediately (see **Figure 28.4**). If the victim responds (coughs or moves, for example) but is still not breathing normally, give 1 rescue breath every 5 seconds.

Lesson 2 CPR and First Aid for Shock and Choking **743**

Chapter 28 • Lesson 2

② TEACH

Explaining

Tell students that CPR should be performed only by those who have been trained and certified in the procedure. Persons not certified in CPR should arrange to enroll in a class to learn the procedure. Improperly performed CPR can cause severe injury or even death. **L1**

VISUAL LEARNING

Figure 28.3 Ask a volunteer to read aloud the information in Figure 28.3. Direct the students to study the illustrations. Ask:

- Why is it important not to move the victim if you suspect head or neck injuries? Moving the victim might cause further injury.
- What should you look for to determine whether there is chest movement? if the chest is rising and falling
- What do signs of circulation signify? Why is it important to check for signs of circulation? It means that the heart is beating and that chest compressions should not be performed.

More About...

When to Stop CPR In medical emergencies that require CPR to be performed, those administering first aid should initiate CPR only if they have been trained in the procedure. Resuscitation efforts should continue until one of the following occurs:

- Resuscitation efforts have been transferred to another trained person who continues the efforts.
- Circulation and breathing have been restored.
- A qualified medical professional assumes responsibility.
- The rescuer is exhausted and unable to continue resuscitation.
- The scene becomes unsafe.

VISUAL LEARNING

Figure 28.4 Give students a few moments to read the information and study the illustrations in Figure 28.4. Ask:

- What do you think happens when a chest compression is performed? This forces blood out of the heart and into the blood vessels.
- What do you think happens when the pressure is released? Blood flows back into the heart.

Guest Speaker

Invite a CPR trainer or a nurse to demonstrate CPR on a mannequin for the class. Allow students to practice on the mannequin, but caution them that they should not practice this procedure on someone who has a heartbeat because it will put the heart into fibrillation, which could cause the person to die. Remind students that they should not perform CPR unless they have been trained and certified. **L1**

Community Involvement

Have students investigate the availability, times, and location of CPR courses in their community. Invite them to post these times on a classroom bulletin board or in the school cafeteria or gymnasium to encourage fellow students to learn this vital lifesaving technique. **L1**

Cross-Curriculum Activity

Math Have students find out how many lives are saved each year due to CPR. CPR alone, only 5 percent; CPR with a defibrillator, up to 90 percent **L1**

744

FIGURE 28.4

ADULT CPR CYCLES

1 **Position your hands.** To begin chest compressions, find a spot on the lower half of the victim's breastbone, right between the nipples. Place the heel of one hand on that point, and interlock your fingers with the fingers of the other hand. Don't allow your fingers to rest on the victim's ribs.

2 **Begin chest compressions and rescue breathing.** Lean over the victim so that your shoulders are directly above your arms and hands. Lock your elbows and press straight down quickly and firmly at a rate of about 100 compressions per minute. Allow the chest to spring back between compressions. After every 15 compressions, give 2 rescue breaths. Complete 4 continuous cycles (just over 1 minute) of CPR, then check for signs of circulation. Continue CPR, checking for signs of circulation every few minutes. If the victim begins to respond, stop chest compressions. If the victim coughs or moves but is still not breathing, give 1 rescue breath every 5 seconds until help arrives. If the victim begins breathing normally, turn the victim onto his or her side and wait for professional medical help.

More About...

Rescue Breathing and Choking The following guidelines should only be administered by health care professionals: If a person loses consciousness while attempting to clear an obstructed airway, ease the person to the floor, protecting the head. Open the airway, and attempt to administer a rescue breath. If the airway is obstructed, straddle the person's middle, and give abdominal thrusts. Push forcefully inward and upward just above the navel. After the thrusts, do a finger sweep to remove any object inside the mouth. Tilt the head, and try to administer a breath. If the airway is still obstructed, continue this procedure until help arrives. If the object is removed, continue with rescue breathing as recommended in the ABCs of CPR.

Should Schools Require Teens to Take a CPR Course?

Heart attacks are the most common medical emergencies in the United States. Many deaths could be prevented, however, by people performing CPR. As a result, organizations such as the American Heart Association and the American Red Cross have certified thousands of people in CPR. To increase the number of trained rescuers, many people think CPR certification should be a high-school graduation requirement. Others disagree. Here are two points of view.

Viewpoint 1: Michael P., age 15

I don't think that all high-school students should be required to take a CPR course. It should be a personal choice. Health courses need to focus more on risk behaviors that affect young people, such as using tobacco, alcohol, and other drugs. Teens who want CPR training can go to their local chapter of the Red Cross or American Heart Association.

Viewpoint 2: Sydney J., age 15

Every year in the United States, 350,000 people die of sudden heart attacks. Many of these people could be saved if CPR were administered. It makes sense that the more people who are trained in CPR, the fewer people who may die. Many of these courses are taught by teachers who instruct students in the use of AEDs as well as in oxygen administration. Both of these technologies have improved the survival rates of heart attack victims.

ACTIVITIES

1. Should high schools require teens to take a CPR course? Why or why not?

2. CPR training "obligates" people to use their skills when they witness an emergency situation. How well do you think teens could handle this responsibility?

CPR for Infants and Children

Infants and children in life-threatening emergencies aren't treated in exactly the same way that adults are. For example, you shouldn't use an AED on an infant or a child. Likewise, you can't use the same amount of force in chest compressions. **Figures 28.5** and **28.6** on the next page show how to perform CPR on infants and children. These steps were developed by the American Heart Association. For an infant or child, provide about one minute of CPR *before* calling 911 for help.

Lesson 2   CPR and First Aid for Shock and Choking   **745**

⌁ HEALTH LITERACY ⌁

Responsible/Productive Citizen If your school does not require students to take a first-aid course and you are not certified, help students arrange for a certified instructor to teach a first-aid and CPR course at your school after school hours. If the instructors need to be paid for their time, hold a class fund-raiser so that students may take the course free of charge. Have students make posters to display and create ads to run in the school newspaper. The posters and ads should highlight the benefits and importance of learning first aid and CPR. Assess success by the number of participants, the percentage of participants who certify successfully, and the responses from a student-generated questionnaire to be completed by participants.

Exploring Issues

SHOULD SCHOOLS REQUIRE TEENS TO TAKE A CPR COURSE?

If your school requires CPR training and some students have taken the course, ask them whether they would have taken the course if it had been voluntary and whether they think all students should take the course. If your school does not require CPR training, ask if any students have taken a CPR course and whether they think all teens should take it. After volunteers have expressed their ideas, have students work in small groups to read the feature and discuss their responses to the Activities questions.

Community Involvement

Tell students that the most recent guidelines from the American Heart Association emphasize the importance of using automated external defibrillators (AEDs) to increase survival following cardiac arrest. Have them find out what their community is doing to make these devices available in public places. **L2**

Explaining

Explain that children usually stop breathing before their heart stops. By beginning rescue breathing before calling 911, you may be able to restart a child's breathing before his or her heart stops. **L1**

Activity

Tell students that losing a large volume of blood or other body fluids results in a specific type of shock (*hypovolemic*). Have students research other major types of shock and give an example of each. (Other major types include *cardiogenic, anaphylactic, septic, and neurogenic.*) **L2**

Explaining

If a shock victim lying on his or her back vomits or is drooling and you suspect a spinal or neck injury, "log roll" the victim. Support the neck and spine to keep the head position neutral with the body position while turning the victim onto his or her side. If allowed to remain lying flat, the victim can inhale vomit or blood and suffocate. **L1**

FIGURE 28.5

THE ABCs OF INFANT AND CHILD CPR

A **Airway.** Look inside the victim's mouth. Remove anything you see blocking the airway. If you don't suspect head or neck injuries, lay the victim flat on a firm surface. Gently tilt the head back by lifting the chin with one hand while pushing down on the forehead with the other. If you suspect head or neck injuries, do not move the victim. Instead, open his or her airway by lifting the jaw.

B **Breathing.** Look, listen, and feel for breathing. *Look* for chest movement. *Listen* at the victim's mouth for breathing. *Feel* for exhaled air on your cheek. If the victim is not breathing, begin rescue breathing:

Keep the victim's head in position. For a child, pinch the nostrils shut and seal your mouth over the victim's mouth. For an infant, seal your mouth over the mouth and nose. Give 2 slow breaths, each about 1 to 1½ seconds long. The chest should rise with each breath.

C **Circulation.** Check for signs of circulation, such as breathing, coughing, or movement. If there are no signs of circulation, a person trained in CPR should begin chest compressions immediately (see **Figure 28.6**). If the victim responds (coughs or moves, for example) but is still not breathing normally, give 1 rescue breath every 3 seconds for either a child or an infant.

FIGURE 28.6

INFANT AND CHILD CPR CYCLES

1 **Position your hands.** With one hand, keep the victim's head tilted, unless you suspect head or neck injury. For a child, place the heel of your other hand on the lower half of the breastbone and position your shoulder directly over your straightened arm and hand. For an infant, imagine a line drawn between the nipples. Place two or three fingers of your hand on the lower half of the infant's breastbone, about one finger's width below the imaginary nipple line.

2 **Begin chest compressions and rescue breathing.** Compress the victim's chest downward approximately ⅓ to ½ the depth of the chest at a rate of *about* 100 times per minute for a child, and *at least* 100 times per minute for an infant. Release pressure completely between compressions. After every 5 compressions, give 1 rescue breath (see **Figure 28.5**). Complete 20 continuous cycles (just over 1 minute) of CPR, and then check for signs of circulation. Continue CPR, checking for signs of circulation every few minutes. If the victim shows signs of circulation, stop chest compressions and continue rescue breathing if necessary (1 rescue breath every 3 seconds).

746 Chapter 28 First Aid and Emergencies

More About...

Blood Types Human blood is classified into four types; Type A, Type B, Type AB, and Type O. For transfusions to work, the blood types must match. A person who has Type O blood is referred to as a *universal donor* because that person can give blood to a person with any blood type. A person with Type AB blood is referred to as a *universal recipi-*ent; he or she can receive any type of blood. Rh factor is a protein present in the blood of about 85 percent of the U.S. population. Individuals with Rh-negative blood should not be given Rh-positive blood. Tell students they should know their blood types and have it written on a card they carry in their wallet.

First Aid for Shock

When something happens to reduce blood flow throughout the body, limiting the amount of oxygen carried to the cells, shock may occur. **Shock** is *a failure of the cardiovascular system to keep an adequate supply of blood circulating to the vital organs of the body.* This life-threatening emergency requires immediate medical attention. Common symptoms of shock include restlessness or irritability; altered consciousness; nausea; pale or ashen appearance; cool, moist skin; and rapid breathing and pulse.

If you suspect a head or spinal injury, don't move the victim. Otherwise, have the victim lie down if he or she has not already done so. This position often minimizes pain and keeps the victim calm. You should also

► phone 911 or the local emergency number.

► control any external bleeding.

► elevate the legs about 12 inches, unless you suspect head or back injury or broken bones involving the legs or hips. If you aren't sure, leave the victim lying flat. This helps the blood return to the heart.

► never give the victim anything to eat or drink. Eating or drinking could cause vomiting.

► reassure the victim.

First Aid for Choking

Choking occurs when a person's airway becomes blocked by food or a swallowed object. If the obstruction is not removed, the victim can die from lack of oxygen within a few minutes.

To help someone who is choking, you must first recognize the signs. A person may clutch his or her throat with one or both hands, which is the universal sign for choking. The victim may also cough weakly, make high-pitched sounds, or turn blue in the face. If someone appears to be choking but can cough forcefully or speak, do not attempt first aid. A strong cough can expel the object from the airway.

If you suspect that someone is choking, ask, "Are you choking?" and look for the universal choking sign. Then ask, "Can you speak?" If the person cannot speak in reply, the airway is completely blocked and the victim needs immediate first aid.

Did You Know ?

One cause of shock is losing a large volume of fluid, usually as a result of bleeding. However, shock can result from a significant loss of *any* body fluids. This means that even diarrhea or vomiting, if prolonged and severe, can lead to shock.

Be alert for the universal choking sign.

Reinforcing Concepts

Emphasize that abdominal thrusts can be self-administered if you begin to choke while you are alone. Press your own fist into your upper abdomen and perform quick, upward and inward thrusts. An object such as a sofa arm or the back of a chair can also be used to administer thrusts. Demonstrate how this might be done, and have volunteers demonstrate the maneuver without force. **L1**

Critical Thinking

How can you tell whether an infant is choking? Possible answers: The infant cannot cry, may look panicked, and may gasp or wheeze. His or her eyes may bulge and face may turn purple. **L2**

Explaining

Explain that hand positioning is very important when administering abdominal thrusts. Incorrect positioning of the hands could break ribs, causing internal injury. **L1**

Discussing

Tell students that the most common cause of nonfatal choking in children is foods. Ask: What kinds of foods might cause choking in small children? hot dog bites, whole grapes, nuts, popcorn, hard candies Most cases of fatal choking in children are caused by toys and household items, especially round ones. Ask: What household items might small children choke on? coins, marbles, pen caps, small batteries **L1**

More About...

First Aid for Choking Never hit a choking victim on the back to try to dislodge an object obstructing the airway. This can cause the object to fall deeper into the windpipe, making it more difficult or impossible to dislodge the object. Also, do not give a choking person anything to drink. Liquid can lubricate the throat, allowing the object to slide further down the windpipe. Tell students that they should not administer abdominal thrusts if the victim can cough, speak, or breathe. However, they should stay with the person and watch him or her closely. If they determine that a person is choking, they should direct someone to call 911 and begin abdominal thrusts. **L1**

❸ ASSESS

EVALUATING THE LESSON

Assign and discuss the Lesson 2 Review; then administer, grade, and discuss Lesson Quiz 104 in the TCR. 📁

RETEACHING

- Let volunteers demonstrate first aid for a choking victim. Ask them to role-play an adult choking victim and to use a doll to represent an infant choking victim.

- Ask students to complete Reteaching Activity 104 in the TCR. 📁

ENRICHMENT

Have interested students research the bracelets, necklaces, and charms that list medical conditions such as diabetes, epilepsy, heart conditions, and allergies to medication. Have students design a unique piece of jewelry to indicate a medical condition.

❹ CLOSE

Have students revise the paragraphs they wrote about CPR in the Quick Start for this lesson.

 Use abdominal thrusts on a choking adult, but never on a choking infant. Use back blows alternating with chest thrusts for an infant. *Why do you think different methods are used for adults and infants?*

If the choking victim is an adult or a child, use abdominal thrusts—quick inward and upward pulls to the diaphragm—to force the obstruction out of the airway. To perform this procedure, stand behind the victim and place your arms around him or her. Make a fist with one hand, and grasp it with your other hand. Pull inward and upward just under the rib cage.

If you begin to choke while you are alone, use your own fist and hand to perform the procedure on yourself. You can also try pressing your abdomen forcefully against the back of a chair.

If the choking victim is an infant, hold the baby face down on your forearm. Support the infant's head and neck with your hand and point the head downward so that it is lower than the chest. With the heel of your hand, give the infant five blows between the shoulder blades. If the object is not dislodged, turn the infant over and perform five chest thrusts as described in the CPR section. Alternate the five blows between the shoulders with five chest thrusts until the object is dislodged or the infant begins to breathe or cough. Call 911 if the object is not dislodged within one minute. If the infant loses consciousness, phone 911 and begin CPR if you are trained and certified in the procedure.

▶ Lesson 2 Review

Reviewing Facts and Vocabulary

1. Define *cardiopulmonary resuscitation.*
2. Why should you never give a shock victim anything to eat or drink?
3. What is the universal sign for choking?

Thinking Critically

4. **Evaluating.** Explain why it's important to check the airway before beginning CPR.
5. **Analyzing.** Compare the strategy for responding to a choking adult with the strategy for responding to a choking infant.

Applying Health Skills

Advocacy. Make a video encouraging teens to learn basic first-aid techniques for choking and shock. Make the video available to your class.

TECHNOLOGY *OPTION*

WORD PROCESSING Use word processing to write the script for your video. See **health.glencoe.com** for help in using word-processing software.

748 **Chapter 28** First Aid and Emergencies

▶ Lesson 2 Review

Answers to Reviewing Facts and Vocabulary

1. A lifesaving first-aid procedure that combines rescue breaths with chest compressions, supplying oxygen to the body until normal body functions can resume.
2. Giving food or drink to a shock victim could cause the victim to vomit.

3. Clutching the throat with the hands.

Answers to Thinking Critically

4. Possible answer: You can't get air into the lungs if the airway is blocked.
5. Answers should describe abdominal thrusts for adults and back blows and chest thrusts for infants.

Responding to Common Emergencies

VOCABULARY
fracture
unconsciousness
concussion

YOU'LL LEARN TO

• Analyze strategies for responding to muscle, joint, and bone injuries.

• Analyze strategies for responding to unconsciousness.

• Analyze strategies for responding to animal bites.

• Analyze strategies for responding to nosebleeds and to foreign objects in the eye.

QUICK START Write down three situations that come to mind when you hear the word *emergency.* Next to each situation, describe how you would respond to the emergency.

Suppose that you and a friend are out jogging when your friend falls and sprains an ankle. How can you be sure that the injury is a sprain and not a fracture? Would you know what to do in either case? As with major emergencies, knowing the proper response when dealing with common emergencies can help prevent further injury or complications.

Muscle, Joint, and Bone Injuries

When too much stress is put on an area of the body, an injury may occur. These injuries vary in severity and can affect the bones, muscles, tendons, or ligaments. Some injuries, such as muscle strain, will usually feel better in a few days. Other injuries, such as a broken bone, may take several weeks to heal and require professional medical treatment for a full recovery to occur.

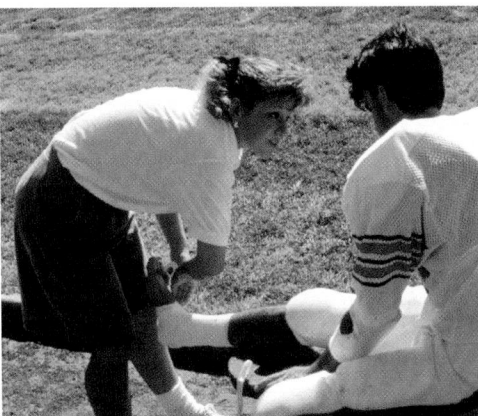

Bone, muscle, and joint injuries can be serious, but they are usually not life threatening.

Lesson 3 Responding to Common Emergencies **749**

Lesson 3 *Resources*

Teacher Classroom Resources

📁 Concept Mapping Activity 105

📁 Cross-Curriculum Activity 28

📁 Guided Reading Activities 105

📁 Lesson Plan 105

📁 Lesson Quiz 105

📁 Reteaching Activity 105

Student Activity Workbook

📁 Applying Health Skills 105

📁 Chapter 28 Study Guide

Multimedia

💾 Transparency 84

1 FOCUS

QUICK START   Before students begin writing, point out that emergencies are not always life threatening or serious. Some, such as minor burns, are common and happen to all of us. Have volunteers share their responses with the class.

TYING TO PRIOR KNOWLEDGE

Ask volunteers who have suffered sprains, broken bones, or other injuries to share their experiences with the class. Tell students that in this lesson, they will learn how to deal with common injuries and emergencies.

Health Skills Features

"First-Aid Stations," p. 753

PRACTICING HEALTHFUL BEHAVIORS

INTRODUCING VOCABULARY

• Have students create a definition for each vocabulary term. Have them look up the terms in the Glossary to verify or correct their definitions.

• Ask students to complete the Chapter 28 Study Guide in the *Student Activity Workbook.* 📁

② TEACH

ACTIVE READING

Jigsaw

In this strategy, students work in groups to become experts on a portion of text and share their expertise with their "home" group. Assign two or three of the emergencies in this lesson to each member of each cooperative learning group. Each student studies his or her topics for 10–15 minutes, summarizes the important points on an index card, and then shares that information with the other group members. For more strategies, see the *Guided Reading Activities* booklet in the TCR. 📁

Quick Demo

Bring X rays of broken bones to class to let students see how they look under the skin. 🔳

Explaining

Explain that there are many causes of unconsciousness, including heart attack, diabetic coma, shock, stroke, hypothermia, and carbon monoxide poisoning. 🔳

Reinforcing Concepts

Tell students that fainting is due to reflexes that slow the heart and dilate blood vessels, resulting in a drop in blood pressure. 🔳

 Applying ice to a sprain reduces swelling and eases pain. *Why is it a good idea to see a health care professional if you suspect that you have a sprain?*

hot link

R.I.C.E. For more information on R.I.C.E., see Chapter 4, page 102.

Muscle Cramps

A muscle cramp is the sudden and painful tightening of a muscle. Muscle cramps can occur when you are physically active or at rest. Some medications can also cause them. If a muscle cramp occurs:

▶ Stretch out the affected muscle to counteract the cramp.

▶ Massage the cramped muscle firmly.

▶ Apply moist heat to the area.

▶ Get medical help if the cramp persists.

Strains and Sprains

A strain is an injury to a muscle, usually resulting from overuse of the muscle. The symptoms of a strain include pain, swelling, bruising, and loss of movement caused by small tears in the muscle. A sprain is an injury to a ligament. Sprains usually result from a sudden twisting force. Sprains also cause pain and swelling from badly stretched or torn ligaments. Although serious sprains require professional medical attention, minor sprains and strains may be treated with the **R.I.C.E.** procedure:

▶ **R**est—Avoid any movements or activities that cause pain, including any use of the affected muscle or joint. Help the victim find a comfortable position.

▶ **I**ce—Ice helps reduce pain and swelling. Place ice cubes in a plastic bag, and wrap a towel or cloth around the bag. Hold the bag on the affected area for 20 minutes, remove it for 20 minutes, and then reapply it. Repeat this process every 3 waking hours over the course of 72 hours.

▶ **C**ompression—Light pressure from wearing an elastic wrap or bandage can help reduce swelling. The wrap should be firm but not uncomfortable.

▶ **E**levation—Raising the affected limb above the level of the heart helps reduce pain and swelling.

Fractures and Dislocations

Fractures and dislocations are similar. A **fracture** is *a break in the bone.* If a joint is under extreme stress, it may dislocate, or disconnect. First-aid procedures are the same for both fractures and dislocations. If possible, keep the victim still and call 911. If the victim must be moved, keep the fractured area immobilized by securing a splint to the body part with clean lengths of cloth. You can fashion a splint from everyday materials such as rolled newspapers and heavy cardboard. Seek professional medical care immediately.

Home and Community

Local Emergencies Have students investigate which emergencies are most likely to occur in the community or immediate area. For example, does heat exhaustion or heatstroke occur frequently because of the hot climate? Suggest that students contact the public relations departments of community hospitals that have emergency rooms to find out more information. Students may need to research first-aid steps for emergencies other than those they have studied to date. Have them create a trifold pamphlet of first-aid measures for emergencies common in the area and share it with family members.

Unconsciousness

Unconsciousness is *a condition in which a person is not alert and aware of his or her surroundings.* There are different levels of unconsciousness, ranging from drowsiness to coma. An unconscious victim can choke to death because of his or her inability to cough, clear the throat, or react to a blocked airway. The primary goal when providing first aid to an unconscious victim is to prevent choking until professional medical help arrives. If the victim is unconscious, place him or her in the recovery position shown in **Figure 28.7** and seek professional medical help immediately.

Fainting

Fainting occurs when the blood supply to the brain is temporarily inadequate. Loss of consciousness is usually brief. Although fainting doesn't always indicate a medical problem, it might be symptomatic of a serious disorder. Treat fainting as a medical emergency until the symptoms are relieved and the cause is known.

If you feel faint, lie down or sit down and place your head between your knees. If someone else faints, position the person on his or her back with legs elevated 8 to 12 inches above the heart unless you suspect head or neck injury. Do not place a pillow under the person's head. This can block airflow. Loosen any tight clothing. Sponge the person's face with water. Do not splash water on the face; this may cause the person to choke. If the person vomits, quickly roll him or her into the recovery position shown in **Figure 28.7** to prevent choking. If the person fails to revive promptly, seek medical help.

CHARACTER CHECK

Citizenship. If you see someone who has just suffered an injury, don't assume that someone else will stop and help. Everyone else might be making that same assumption. **Be a responsible member of your community. If you see someone who needs medical assistance, do what you can to help, even if all you can do is call 911.**

VISUAL LEARNING

Figure 28.7 Have students study the illustration and read the text in Figure 28.7. Tell them that the recovery position should be used if they need to leave the victim to get help or if the victim is breathing but unconscious. The victim should be turned to the other side once every 30 minutes or if the lower arm appears to have lost circulation (the skin will appear pale or gray and feel cool to the touch).

CHARACTER CHECK

Citizenship Have students recall and discuss the three basic steps in an emergency: Check, Call, and Care. Ask: If you do not know how to provide first aid, what else can you do to help an injured person? Answers will vary; students may respond that they can call 911 and stay with the person until help arrives. Ask students how doing all they can for an injured person demonstrates the character trait of citizenship.

Critical Thinking

Ask: If a person is unconscious and is not breathing, what should be the next first-aid step? Begin rescue breathing. **1**

FIGURE 28.7

THE RECOVERY POSITION

The recovery position is the safest placement for an unconscious person because the airway is protected. Put the person in the recovery position only if no spinal or head injury is suspected.

This position helps an unconscious person breathe and allows fluids such as blood and vomit to drain. Do not move a person if you suspect spinal or head injuries. Movement can worsen these injuries.

More About...

First Aid for Seizures Epilepsy is a brain disorder in which neurons sometimes signal abnormally. Persons with epilepsy can have a type of seizure in which the person jerks, goes rigid, and then becomes unconscious. First-aid steps for unconsciousness resulting from seizure include the following: Cushion the head, turn the person on his or her side unless he or she is injured, don't put anything in the person's mouth, don't hold the person's tongue (it cannot be swallowed), and don't give liquids during or after the seizure. Provide rescue breathing only if the person stops breathing. Get medical attention if it is the person's first seizure, if the seizure lasts longer than five minutes, if another seizure occurs, or if the person has difficulty breathing.

Discussing

Tell students that a person who has sustained a head injury should be monitored for 24 hours. Signs of head injury include the following: loss of consciousness, headache, vision disturbances, dizziness, temporary confusion, nausea, memory loss, lump or cut on the head, and temporary drowsiness.

Critical Thinking

Ask: Based on what you know about injuries, what do you think are the major causes of concussions? motor vehicle crashes, falls, contact sports (such as football), and assaults **L2**

Explaining

Explain that almost 5 million people are bitten by dogs each year in the United States. If the bite is superficial and the dog is immunized against rabies, the steps presented in the text should be followed. No further action is usually needed. However, a deep or puncture wound may require a tetanus booster. **L1**

Concussion

A **concussion** is *a jarring injury to the brain that affects normal brain function.* Even if there are no external signs of injury, the brain can strike the inside of the skull and be damaged. To avoid causing spinal injury, do not move an unconscious victim if you suspect a head injury or concussion. Check the person's airway, breathing, and circulation, and get professional medical help immediately. If you suspect that a person has a concussion:

▶ Have a conscious victim lie down.

▶ Use first aid for any bleeding.

▶ If the victim is unconscious and you do not suspect head or neck injury, place him or her in the recovery position, as shown in **Figure 28.7** on page 751. Call 911 immediately.

Animal Bites

One of the most serious possible consequences of an animal bite is rabies, a viral disease of the nervous system that eventually causes paralysis and death if left untreated. There is no cure for rabies after symptoms develop. However, if a person is vaccinated promptly after being bitten, he or she can develop immunity before symptoms appear.

When someone is bitten, report the incident to your community health department or animal control department. It's important to determine whether the animal has rabies. If you find the animal, do not try to capture it. Give its description and location to the proper authorities or the police. The animal will be captured for testing and observation.

Animal bites also carry the risk of infection, including tetanus, an often fatal disease. Although tetanus can be treated, the treatment is long, difficult, and often unsuccessful. Tetanus can be prevented, however, by keeping your immunizations up to date. First aid for animal bites includes the following:

▶ Wash the bite area with mild soap and warm water for five minutes to remove saliva and any other foreign matter.

▶ Use direct pressure or pressure point bleeding control to stop any bleeding.

▶ If the wound is swollen, apply ice wrapped in a towel for 10 minutes.

▶ Cover the wound with a clean dressing or bandage.

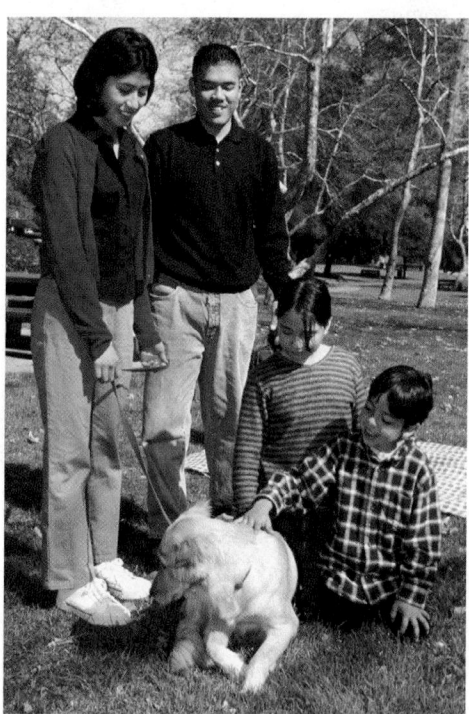

Never approach a strange dog. Always ask the owner's permission before approaching or touching a dog that you do not know. *What two diseases are associated with animal bites?*

752 Chapter 28 First Aid and Emergencies

Cooperative Learning Activity

Safety Around Dogs About 400,000 children are treated in emergency rooms each year because of dog bites. Many children do not know how to behave around a dog. Have students work in small groups to create a poster or pamphlet for younger children with these tips:

• Never go near an unfamiliar dog, even if it is someone's pet or in someone's home.

• Do not disturb any dog, including your own, that is sleeping, eating, or caring for puppies.

• Remain still when an unfamiliar dog comes up to you.

Nosebleeds

Nosebleeds often occur if the nose is struck or if the mucous membranes in the nose dry out from breathing dry air. Seek professional medical attention if nosebleeds occur often.

To treat a nosebleed, keep the person quiet. Walking, talking, and blowing the nose may increase bleeding. Tell the person to breathe through his or her mouth. Have the person sit down and lean forward. Do not tilt the person's head back—doing so may cause the person to choke as blood runs down the back of the throat. Using a protective barrier, press on the bleeding nostril. Maintain pressure for 15 minutes. If the person's nose is still bleeding after 15 minutes, repeat the procedure. If bleeding continues, seek professional medical help.

Applying direct pressure to a nosebleed usually stops the bleeding. *Why might dry air cause a nosebleed?*

Hands-On Health ACTIVITY

First-Aid Stations

In this activity you will set up learning stations for common emergencies and rotate through them.

What You'll Need

- pen or pencil and notebook paper
- poster board and markers
- props (optional)

What You'll Do

1. In small groups, research the following information for the emergency assigned by your teacher:
   - how to recognize it
   - appropriate steps to take in the correct sequence
   - what to do after first aid has been provided
2. Decide on a creative way to present your material at a learning station, such as a poster, a board game, a quiz show, a puzzle, a news story, or demonstrations with props such as bandages.
3. Each group will set up a learning station. One person in each group coordinates the activities at each learning station while all other students rotate through the stations. Group members take turns supervising their station.

Apply and Conclude

Write a script for a skit about a teen or a group of teens who encounter a medical emergency. The script should show one teen experiencing the emergency while the others administer proper first aid.

Lesson 3 Responding to Common Emergencies **753**

Hands-On Health

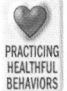

FIRST-AID STATIONS

PRACTICING HEALTHFUL BEHAVIORS

NHES Standard 3 Students will demonstrate the ability to practice health-enhancing behaviors and reduce health risks.

Objectives

- Develop injury-management strategies for personal, family, and community health.
- Analyze strategies for responding to accidental injuries.

Motivator

Ask volunteers to describe creative ways to present information on first aid for emergencies.

Teaching Strategies

1. Divide the class into four groups. Assign one of the following to each group: muscle, joint, and bone injuries; unconsciousness; animal bites; and foreign objects in the eye and nosebleeds.
2. Invite other classes to rotate through the stations during your usual health class period.
3. Allow students to perform demonstrations only on dolls or mannequins.

✓ Assessment

Using a rubric, student work should provide comprehensive evidence of the following criteria to achieve the highest score:

✔ identification of first-aid steps for accidental injuries
✔ listing first-aid steps in the correct sequence

Meeting Individual Needs

Project Have students stage a school-wide expo on first aid.

Visually Impaired Individuals with visual impairments will benefit from large-print versions of printed materials. Students who are visually impaired may oversee the creation of these materials.

Physically Challenged Ask students with physical challenges to head an information unit at the expo, addressing first-aid strategies for people in wheelchairs or with limited muscular function. They can access information from the American Red Cross and organizations for the physically challenged.

754

ASSESS

EVALUATING THE LESSON

Assign and discuss the Lesson 3 Review; then administer, grade, and discuss Lesson Quiz 105 in the TCR. 📁

RETEACHING

- Have students write in their own words the first-aid steps for each type of common emergency discussed in this lesson.

- Ask students to complete Reteaching Activity 105 in the TCR. 📁

ENRICHMENT

Have interested students research and report on the incidence of the injuries discussed in this lesson. They should also include strategies for reducing the risk of these injuries.

CLOSE

Have students summarize the most important concepts learned in this lesson.

To flush an object out of your own eye, gently pour water from a small clean glass into the eye.

Object in the Eye

Foreign objects such as dirt, sand, or slivers of wood or metal that enter the eye are irritating and can cause damage. Encourage the victim not to rub the eye, an action that may scratch the cornea, but to blink several times. If blinking does not dislodge the object, try to find it in the eye. First, wash your hands. Gently pull the lower eyelid down while the person looks up. If you don't see anything, hold the upper lid open and examine the eye while the person looks down. If you see the object on the surface of the eye, lightly touch it with a moistened cotton swab or the corner of a clean cloth.

You can also flush the eye with sterile saline solution or tap water. If the person is wearing contact lenses, do not remove the lens before flushing the eye. To flush the eye, tilt the person's head to the side so that the affected eye is lower than the unaffected eye. Gently hold the eye open with one hand. With the other hand, pour a steady stream of cool water into the eye, from the inside corner toward the outside corner. The water should wash over the surface of the eye. Seek professional medical help if the object is not removed.

▶ Lesson 3 *Review*

Reviewing Facts and Vocabulary

1. What is a *fracture*?
2. What is the primary goal when providing first aid to an unconscious person?
3. What are two common causes of nosebleeds?

Thinking Critically

4. **Analyzing.** While hiking with you, a friend stumbles on a tree root and falls. By the time you get home, her ankle is badly swollen and she can't walk without leaning on you. Analyze and describe the strategy you would use to respond to this accidental injury.

5. **Evaluating.** Why should you seek professional medical care if a sprain or strain doesn't improve or if you suspect that the injury might be a fracture?

Applying Health Skills

Accessing Information. Use online and print resources to find additional information about rabies. Using the information you have obtained, write a newspaper article about giving first aid to someone who has been bitten by an animal, including how to prevent rabies.

TECHNOLOGY *OPTION*

WEB SITES Use your newspaper article as part of a Web site you develop on rabies. See **health.glencoe.com** for help in planning and building your Web site.

▶ Lesson 3 *Review*

Answers to Reviewing Facts and Vocabulary

1. A fracture is a break in the bone.
2. To keep the person from choking.
3. Being hit in the nose or breathing dry air.

Answers to Thinking Critically

4. Answers should include the R.I.C.E.

procedure and seeking medical attention.

5. If a sprain or strain doesn't improve, it could indicate a more serious injury or that tissue damage is severe enough to require medical treatment. If you don't seek medical treatment for a fracture, the bone may not heal properly.

Treatment for Poisonings

VOCABULARY
poison
venom
poison control center

YOU'LL LEARN TO
- Analyze strategies for responding to poisonings.
- Analyze strategies for responding to bites and stings.
- Analyze strategies for preventing and responding to skin irritation caused by contact with poisonous plants.

 QUICK START Accidental poisonings are often associated with toddlers. What are some safety procedures that can help prevent accidental poisoning in a home with young children? Compile a list of at least five tips.

K nowing how to respond to poisoning emergencies is an important part of first aid. A **poison** is *any substance—solid, liquid, or gas—that causes injury, illness, or death when introduced into the body.* Approximately 90 percent of poisonings occur in the home, and more than half of these poisonings involve children under the age of six.

Types of Poisoning

P oisoning results when substances that are not meant to enter the body do so. The substance could be a chemical that is swallowed, a pesticide that is absorbed through the skin, or **venom**, *a poisonous substance secreted by a snake, spider, or other creature,* that is injected into the body through a sting or bite. Even certain plants and foods can be poisonous. Gases or vapors may also be poisonous, such as carbon monoxide from hot water heaters and furnaces, exhaust fumes from automobiles, and fumes from gas- or oil-burning stoves. Your poison control center can tell you the correct procedure to follow in the event of a poisoning. A **poison control center** is *a 24-hour hot line that provides emergency medical advice on treating poisoning victims.*

 Many household products become poisons if they are used incorrectly. *Where can you find information about the toxicity of various household products?*

Lesson 4 Resources

Teacher Classroom Resources
- 📁 Concept Mapping Activity 106
- 📁 Guided Reading Activities 106
- 📁 Health Lab 28
- 📁 Lesson Plan 106
- 📁 Lesson Quiz 106
- 📁 Reteaching Activity 106

Student Activity Workbook
- 📁 Applying Health Skills 106
- 📁 Chapter 28 Study Guide

Multimedia
- 🖱 Transparency 85

 FOCUS

QUICK START Have students work with a partner to create their lists of tips for preventing accidental poisoning in homes with young children. When students have finished their lists, write each tip on the board.

TYING TO PRIOR KNOWLEDGE

Have students think of as many poisonous substances as they can in two minutes. Explain that in this lesson, they will learn more about types of poisonings and how to provide first aid for poisoning.

Health Skills Features

"Contacting a Poison Control Center," p. 757 ACCESSING INFORMATION

INTRODUCING VOCABULARY

- Direct students' attention to the vocabulary terms *poison* and *venom*. Have students write a short explanation of the difference in meaning between these two terms. Then have them look up the definitions in the Glossary to check their work.

- Ask students to complete the Chapter 28 Study Guide in the *Student Activity Workbook.* 📁

❷ TEACH

Activity

Have students use library or online resources to access information on child care from an organization such as the American Red Cross. Then have students prepare written guidelines for handling an emergency situation that arises while babysitting a toddler. When would it be appropriate to contact the child's parents? When would it be appropriate to call 911? When would it be appropriate to call a poison control center? When would calling the child's doctor be the best response? The guidelines should specify how a person left in charge should make decisions in an emergency. 🄻2 🖇

Explaining

Tell students that more than 2 million poisonings occurred in the United States in the year 2000. Point out that some potentially poisonous substances are not typically considered poisons. Overdosing on medications (prescribed or over the counter) or combining medications can be dangerous. Other poisonous substances include cosmetics, nail polish, houseplants, and petroleum-based products. 🄻1

▼ **Poison can enter the body in four ways: ingestion, inhalation, absorption, and injection.** *What can you do to prevent accidental poisonings?*

First Aid for Poisoning

Proper treatment of poisoning requires professional guidance. The best resource in handling poison emergencies is the local poison control center. Have the phone number of your poison control center posted near your phone.

Time is critical when a poisoning has occurred. Some poisoning situations require quick action to minimize the amount of damage to the victim or to prevent death. First, call 911 for help. Then follow these first-aid tips for poisonings.

▶ **Swallowed poisons** vary in their first-aid treatment because the substances that can be swallowed affect the body differently. Quickly try to determine what was swallowed, and call your poison control center. Follow the instructions given to you. It is important that you call the poison control center first. You may be instructed to give the victim something that dilutes the poison, such as milk or water, or you may be directed to induce vomiting. Do not try to induce vomiting unless you are told to do so. Some poisons can be aspirated into the lungs and cause even more damage; others can burn the esophagus if the victim vomits.

▶ **Inhaled poison** is serious because of the damage that can be done to the lungs and other organs of the respiratory system. Quickly get the person to fresh air. Do not breathe in the fumes. If the victim is not breathing, start rescue breathing.

▶ **Poison on the skin** must be removed as quickly as possible to limit the exposure to the body. Remove contaminated clothing. Rinse skin continuously with water for 15 minutes. Then rinse the skin with mild soap and water. Rinse again with fresh water. If possible, have someone call 911 while you are rinsing the skin.

▶ **Poison in the eye** is absorbed quickly. Immediately start flushing the eye with lukewarm water and continue for 15 minutes. Have the victim blink the eye as much as possible while flooding the eye. Do not force the eye open, and do not rub the eye. Have someone call 911 while you are rinsing the eye.

When you call the poison control center:

▶ Be prepared to give your name, location, and telephone number.

▶ Provide the name of the substance, when it was ingested, and the amount involved. If possible, give the brand name of the product and a list of the ingredients.

▶ Describe the state of the victim, as well as his or her age and weight.

▶ Be prepared to follow instructions and answer any questions.

756 Chapter 28 First Aid and Emergencies

▌*More About...*

Swallowed Poison You can suspect that a person has swallowed poison if any of the following are present: a nearby container of a poisonous substance, observing poison ingestion or hearing the victim tell of it, sudden illness or pain, lip or mouth burns, chemical smell on the breath, and/or abnormal pupil size relative to the amount of light.

In the event of poisoning, call the poison control center immediately, even if the container is available and lists the appropriate first-aid steps to take. Knowing the specific poison helps the poison control center give proper instructions to follow. After receiving appropriate first aid, the victim should get professional medical care.

Real-Life Application

Contacting a Poison Control Center

Poisonous products often display warning labels that provide instructions on what to do if someone swallows, inhales, or has skin or eye contact with the product. For cases of poisoning in which the specific product is known, use this information when you contact the poison control center.

The WORKS Toilet Bowl Cleaner

WARNING: KEEP OUT OF REACH OF CHILDREN
CONTAINS: HYDROXYACETIC ACID ⊙

FIRST AID:
If in eyes: Hold eye open and rinse slowly and gently with water for 15–20 minutes.
Remove contact lenses, if present, after the first five minutes, ⊙ and then continue rinsing eye.
If on skin or clothing: Remove contaminated clothing. ⊙
Rinse skin immediately with plenty of water for 15–20 minutes.
If swallowed: Have person sip a glass of water if he or she is able to swallow.
Do not induce vomiting unless told to do so by a poison control center. ⊙
Do not give anything by mouth to an unconscious person. ⊙

- Why is it important for a poison control center to know the specific poison?
- Why should you remove contact lenses if a chemical has entered the eye?
- Why must contaminated clothing be removed at once?
- What is a poison control center? Where is the one nearest you?
- Why is it dangerous to give an unconscious person something to drink?

ACTIVITY

With a partner, role-play a scenario that involves contacting a poison control center when a child has ingested the product shown above. Write your dialogue, and then practice asking and giving information clearly and calmly. One of you will be the caller; the other will be a health professional at the poison control center. The latter will ask for the caller's name and telephone number, as well as questions about

- the child's condition, age, and weight.
- the suspected poison and what instructions/warnings/ingredients appear on the label.
- the time the poisoning may have occurred.
- what first aid the caller may have already provided.

Conclude the role-play with what you think the health professional might tell the caller to do. Then switch roles and repeat the role-play.

Home and Community

Planning a Safe Home Environment
Encourage students to discuss the following guidelines with family members and make any necessary changes in their homes.

- Make sure all potentially poisonous products have child-resistant caps. Even in homes with no small children, these caps can remind family members of a product's potential for poisoning. Also, small children may come to visit.
- Keep household products and medicines out of children's reach. Make sure children are not watching as you open child safety caps or locks.
- Carefully read the directions when using medicines and poisonous products. Reseal containers and store products safely.

Real-Life Application

CONTACTING A POISON CONTROL CENTER

ACCESSING INFORMATION

NHES Standard 2 Students will demonstrate the ability to access valid health information and health-promoting products and services.

Objectives
- Analyze strategies for responding to poisonings.
- Demonstrate the ability to access community health services for self and others.

Motivator
Ask volunteers to explain what a poison control center is. Provide telephone directories and have students locate the nearest poison control center.

Teaching Strategies
1. Discuss with students the answers to the remaining questions in the feature: The center will know the proper first-aid steps to give; even after rinsing contact lenses, hazardous chemicals may still remain; contaminated clothing may continue to irritate the skin; the person could choke.
2. Have volunteers perform their role-plays for the class.

✓ Assessment
Using a rubric, student work should provide comprehensive evidence of the following criteria to achieve the highest score:
- ✔ ability to access appropriate community resources to meet specific needs
- ✔ type of help available from the sources

757

Activity

Have students research poisonous spiders in the United States, such as the black widow spider and brown recluse spider. Ask students to investigate first-aid measures for spider bites Apply an ice pack to the affected area, administer first aid for shock if it occurs, and get the victim to the nearest hospital immediately. **L1**

VISUAL LEARNING

Figure 28.8 Give students a few moments to read the information in Figure 28.8. Ask:

- How can you keep a limb immobilized?
- Why is it important to try to note the appearance of the snake?

Have students find pictures of poisonous snakes. Ask them to find out what regions the snakes are found in and how people can reduce the risk of snakebite.

Reinforcing Concepts

Tell students not to grasp and pull out an insect's stinger in order to remove it. This may cause more venom to enter the skin from the venom sac. **L1**

Quick Demo

Bring to class pictures of common houseplants or yard plants that are poisonous if ingested and discuss them with the class. Then direct students' attention to the photos of poison oak, poison ivy, and poison sumac on page 759. Review techniques for identifying these plants. **L1**

FIGURE 28.8

FIRST AID FOR SNAKEBITE

Use the following steps to administer first aid to a snakebite victim:

- Get the victim to a hospital. This is the most important step. Keep the victim calm and in a reclining position, if possible. The more the victim moves, the greater the risk that venom will circulate throughout the body.

- Keep the bitten area at or below the level of the heart. If the bitten area is on a limb, immobilize that limb.

- Call 911, or have someone else do so. Follow any instructions that are given.

- Do not apply ice or heat. Applying heat will diffuse the venom more rapidly. Applying ice will cause tissue damage. Also, do not give the victim aspirin or other drugs. Some substances can interact dangerously with the venom or thin the blood, causing the venom to spread more rapidly into tissues.

- Maintain breathing and prevent aggravation of the wound. If you are the victim of a snakebite and are alone, walk slowly and rest periodically to help minimize blood circulation.

First Aid for Poisonous Bites and Stings

Insect and animal stings and bites are among the most common sources of injected poisonings. A poisonous bite or sting can come from several sources, including insects, spiders, ticks, scorpions, snakes, marine life, and other animals.

Snakebite

There are about 20 species of venomous snakes in the United States. Most are rattlesnakes, copperheads, coral snakes, and water moccasins (also called cottonmouths). Usually, the bite of a venomous snake is not fatal; however, a bite can cause severe pain, loss of function, and, in rare situations, loss of a limb. The first-aid procedures for snakebite are found in **Figure 28.8.**

Insect Bites and Stings

Some insects, such as the bee, hornet, yellow jacket, wasp, and fire ant, cause painful stings that can produce a strong allergic reaction. For people who are highly allergic to the venom of these insects even one sting can cause a life-threatening condition. These people need immediate medical attention if they are stung. However, for most people, insect bites are uncomfortable but not life threatening. Follow these first-aid procedures for insect bites and stings:

758   **Chapter 28** First Aid and Emergencies

Curriculum Connections

Geography and History Divide the class into small groups, and assign each group one of the following activities. Have groups research the topics and present their findings to the class.

Where are poisonous snakes and spiders most prevalent? What areas of the country have a higher incidence of carbon monoxide poisoning? Why?

How did poisoning affect historical events? For example, the ancient Romans may have experienced lead poisoning from their plumbing pipes.

- Move to a safe area to avoid further harm. Try to remove the stinger by scraping it off with a firm, sharp-edged object such as a credit card or fingernail.

- Wash the area with mild soap and water to help prevent infection. To reduce pain and swelling, apply a cold compress. Apply hydrocortisone cream, calamine lotion, or a baking soda paste to the area several times a day until the pain is gone.

- If the victim was bitten by a venomous spider or scorpion and begins to have trouble breathing or shows other signs of a severe reaction, call 911 immediately.

First Aid for Poisonous Plants

About 85 percent of Americans will develop an allergic skin reaction if exposed to poison ivy, poison oak, or poison sumac. Symptoms include blistering, swelling, burning, and itching at the point of contact, and the person may develop fever.

The first defense against poisonous plants is to recognize and avoid them. If you come into contact with a poisonous plant, remove contaminated clothing. Flush affected areas with water, and then wash thoroughly with soap and water. Certain over-the-counter preparations can be used to wash the affected areas. If a rash develops, use calamine lotion to relieve the itching. For severe discomfort or pain, seek medical attention.

 These are common poisonous plants.

Poison Oak

Poison Ivy

Poison Sumac

❸ ASSESS

EVALUATING THE LESSON

Assign and discuss the Lesson 4 Review; then administer, grade, and discuss Lesson Quiz 106 in the TCR. 📁

RETEACHING

- Have students work in groups to make a collage of poisonous items. Then have each group ask the class what first-aid steps should be provided for the poisons depicted.

- Ask students to complete Reteaching Activity 106 in the TCR. 📁

ENRICHMENT

Encourage interested students to research the beneficial use of venom in medicine. How is venom processed into a serum that is appropriate for medical use?

❹ CLOSE

Have students summarize the first-aid procedures for poisoning and review ways to prevent such emergencies.

▶ Lesson 4 Review

Reviewing Facts and Vocabulary

1. Define the terms *poison* and *venom*.
2. What information should you have ready when you call a poison control center?
3. Analyze and describe the strategy for responding to insect bites and stings.

Thinking Critically

4. **Analyzing.** Analyze and describe a strategy for preventing an accidental poisoning in your kitchen.
5. **Synthesizing.** Develop a list of items needed to administer first aid to a bee-sting victim who is not allergic to bee venom.

Applying Health Skills

Practicing Healthful Behaviors. Prepare a pamphlet that shows the first-aid procedures for responding to poisonings. Include each type of poisoning mentioned in this lesson. Make your pamphlet available to other students in your school.

PRESENTATION SOFTWARE Use the material from your pamphlet and computer software to create a presentation. See **health.glencoe.com** for information on how to create a presentation.

Lesson 4 Treatment for Poisonings **759**

▶ Lesson 4 Review

Answers to Reviewing Facts and Vocabulary

1. See definitions on page 755.
2. Caller's name, location, and phone number; name of the poison and the time and amount involved; details from the poison's label; the age, weight, and state of the victim; any first aid that the rescuer has already provided.

3. See page 759 for strategies.

Answers to Thinking Critically

4. Answers will vary, but might include keeping household chemicals out of reach or in locked cabinets.
5. Possible answer: Credit card; water; mild soap; ice; hydrocortisone cream, calamine lotion, or baking soda paste; bandages.

Emergency and Rescue Workers in the Media

NHES Standard 4 Students will analyze the influence of culture, media, technology, and other factors on health.

Objective

Recognize the positive role of emergency and rescue workers as presented by the media.

Motivator

Ask students if they have ever seen a news item that featured emergency or rescue workers.

Teaching Strategies

Have volunteers share their responses to the Motivator. Ask them to describe the story and indicate where they saw it.

Awareness Ask students if they think there is an increase in media attention for emergency and rescue workers, and why they think that might be so.

Analysis Ask the class to analyze the types of stories that appear in the media about emergency and rescue workers.

Reflection Ask students to reflect on the connection between recent tragic events and the role of emergency and rescue workers as portrayed in the media.

Take Action Have students write a letter to the worker featured in their story thanking them for the important work that they do in the community.

✓Assessment

Student analyses should address each question posed in the activity. Students should also prepare 10 interview questions.

Eye ON THE Media

Emergency and Rescue Workers in the Media

Firefighters, police officers, paramedics, and other emergency and rescue workers are receiving increased media attention for their acts of heroism and bravery. In this activity, you will analyze print media coverage of emergency and rescue workers.

- What kind of story is it? For example, is it a news article about an emergency situation? Is it a human interest piece about the good deeds of the emergency or rescue worker?
- What is the general tone of the article?
- How does the headline help tell the story?
- Where does the story appear in the newspaper or magazine? How does the article's placement help determine what type of story it is?
- Does the story refer to the rescue worker by name, or does it mention only that a rescue worker was on the scene? If a person's name is mentioned, explain why.
- Does a photograph accompany the story? What effect does it have on the story?
- Does the story show the rescue worker in a positive light? If so, identify the specific passages in which his or her deeds are shown positively.
- In what other ways does the story bring recognition to the work of rescue professionals?

ACTIVITY

Search through newspapers or magazines for stories about rescue and emergency workers. Choose an article and analyze it by answering the questions in the chart above. Write your analysis in the form of a report, and share it with the class.

EXPRESS YOUR VIEWS

Prepare a list of ten interview questions for the emergency or rescue worker featured in the article that you analyzed. Questions might focus on background, training, and coping with high-stress situations.

More About...

Rescue Workers in the Spotlight

There have been several analyses written about why emergency and rescue workers are getting so much media attention. Obviously, the tragedy of September 11, 2001 contributed to this trend, but there are also other factors. Technological advances in the media, particularly the rise of digital imaging, have allowed for easier media access to locations that might not have been accessible in the past. Digital technology has lowered media production costs and increased the speed and frequency with which audiences receive information. Today, when disaster strikes, audiences around the globe can see the events unfold and, more importantly, rescue crews and specialists can be mobilized almost instantly.

CROSS-CURRICULUM CONNECTIONS

Write a Dialogue. When a medical emergency occurs, it takes a team to deal with the crisis. Imagine that your job is to calm the injured person. Write a paragraph describing what you would say to reassure the victim. Use descriptive words in your dialogue, and keep in mind that your audience is someone who is scared.

Work in Teams. Developments such as 911 and CPR have improved the chances of survival in the event of an emergency. Organizations such as the American Red Cross have also made contributions to the field of emergency care. Your teacher will divide your class into teams and assign each team a research topic on the subject of emergency care. Present your findings to the class.

Determine the Amount. In the year 2000, there were 172,000 people employed as emergency medical technicians (EMTs) or paramedics in the United States. Of those, 40 percent were employed by private ambulance services, 30 percent were employed by government agencies, and 20 percent were employed by hospitals. How many of the 172,000 EMTs and paramedics were employed by private ambulance services? How many were employed by government agencies?

Research a Topic. In 1628, William Harvey demonstrated that a system of arteries and veins circulated blood throughout the body. Research to learn more about Harvey's findings as well as the theories that his work eventually displaced. Discuss these ideas in light of current concepts of health and first aid.

Emergency Physician

Can you make fast and accurate decisions? As an emergency physician, you often have to make quick diagnoses under extreme conditions. You also need to be able to communicate.

To become an emergency physician, you need a four-year college degree and a medical degree. After finishing medical school, you'll need one year of internship and two to three years of residency. Find out more about this and other health careers by clicking on Career Corner at **health.glencoe.com**.

Portfolio Assessment

Self-Evaluation Direct students to review the Health Skills Activities and other activities completed in the chapter. Encourage each student to select one finished product or activity that demonstrates his or her best work for the chapter and that represents the student's learning goals. Have students explain what they have learned and how the examples they have selected demonstrate their growth in health literacy, knowledge, and skills.

Teacher Classroom Resources Assign Performance Assessment 28, "Administering First Aid," in the TCR.

CROSS-CURRICULUM CONNECTIONS

Enrich student learning by connecting the topic of first aid and emergencies to one of the four subject areas presented on this page. The activity may be completed individually or with a partner.

Language Arts Remind students that descriptive writing should use vivid and precise language.

Social Studies Help the teams assign roles to each member, such as researcher, fact checker, recorder, and presenter.

Math $172,000 \times .40 = 68,800$ employed by private ambulance services; $172,000 \times .30 = 51,600$ employed by government agencies

Science Students' findings should include information on Harvey's work, as well as concepts such as the four humors (blood, phlegm, black bile, and yellow bile) and the ideas of Galen, who thought blood was constantly being created and then consumed. Their discussions should relate these ideas to current concepts about health and first aid.

Have students read and discuss the Career Corner information on becoming an emergency physician. Ask interested students to explore the Glencoe Health Web site at **health.glencoe.com** for more information on this career.

Chapter 28 *Review*

CHECKING COMPREHENSION

- Assign and discuss the chapter review.
- Use the Chapter 28 MindJogger Videoquiz to review the chapter. ▶◀

CHAPTER 28 REVIEW ANSWERS

Exploring Health Terms

1. first aid
2. universal precautions
3. shock
4. defibrillator
5. chain of survival
6. concussion
7. unconsciousness
8. fracture
9. poison control center
10. venom
11. poison

Recalling the Facts

1. Students should list two of the following: using protective gloves when there is a possibility of touching blood or other body fluids, using mouthpieces or other protective ventilation devices for breathing emergencies, washing your hands before and after giving first aid to another person.

2. Answer should discuss checking, calling, and caring.

3. Abrasion, laceration, puncture, and avulsion.

4. Phone 911, begin CPR, early defibrillation, and transfer to advanced care.

5. Airway, breathing, circulation.

6. Symptoms of shock include restlessness or irritability; altered consciousness; nausea; pale or ashen appearance; cool, moist skin; rapid breathing and pulse.

▶ EXPLORING HEALTH TERMS
Answer the following questions on a sheet of paper.

Lesson 1 *Match each definition with the correct term.*

universal precautions   first aid

1. The immediate, temporary care given to an ill or injured person until professional medical care can be provided.

2. Actions taken to prevent the spread of disease by treating all blood and other body fluids as though they contained pathogens.

Lesson 2 *Match each definition with the correct term.*

defibrillator   shock
chain of survival
cardiopulmonary resuscitation

3. A failure of the cardiovascular system to keep an adequate supply of blood circulating to the vital organs of the body.

4. A device that delivers an electric shock to the heart to restore its normal rhythm.

5. A sequence of events that maximize the victim's chances of survival.

Lesson 3 *Fill in the blanks with the correct term.*

concussion   unconsciousness
fracture

A blow to the head can cause a (_6_), which is a jarring injury to the brain, without actually causing (_7_). If the blow is hard enough, it can cause a skull (_8_).

Lesson 4 *Fill in the blanks with the correct term.*

venom   poison
poison control center

A (_9_) provides emergency medical advice on treating poisoning victims. Snake (_10_) is a (_11_) when it is introduced into the human body.

▶ RECALLING THE FACTS
Use complete sentences to answer the following questions.

Lesson 1

1. What are two universal precautions that a person should follow when giving first aid to another person?

2. What are the first three things you should do when you recognize an emergency situation?

3. What are the four types of open wounds?

Lesson 2

4. What is the chain of survival for adults?

5. What are the ABCs of CPR?

6. What are the symptoms of shock?

Lesson 3

7. What is the first-aid procedure for a person who has a muscle cramp?

8. What is the first-aid procedure for a person who has fainted?

9. Why is the recovery position the safest position for a person who is unconscious?

Lesson 4

10. What is the first-aid procedure for a person who has inhaled poison?

11. What is the first-aid procedure for poison in the eye?

12. Why is it important to wash a poisonous bite or sting with mild soap and water?

---

7. Stretch out the affected muscle to counteract the cramp. Massage the cramped muscle firmly. Apply moist heat to the area. Get medical help if the cramp persists.

8. Position the person on his or her back with legs elevated 8 to 12 inches above the heart unless head or neck injury is suspected. Do not place a pillow under the head because this can block airflow. Loosen any tight clothing. Sponge the person's face with water. Do not splash water on the face because this may cause the person to choke.

If the person vomits, quickly roll him or her into the recovery position to prevent choking. If the person fails to revive promptly, seek medical help.

9. The airway is protected, so choking is less likely.

10. Quickly get the person to fresh air. Do not breathe in the fumes. If the victim is not breathing, start rescue breathing. Call 911 for help.

➤ THINKING CRITICALLY

1. **Applying.** While you are jogging through town with some friends, you see that a car has just struck someone on a bicycle. Analyze and describe a strategy for responding to this type of accidental injury. *(LESSON 1)*

2. **Synthesizing.** Why can quick abdominal thrusts dislodge an obstruction in the airway? *(LESSON 2)*

3. **Analyzing.** Explain why you should not try to capture an animal that has bitten someone. *(LESSON 3)*

4. **Evaluating.** Which of the first-aid techniques covered in the chapter would be especially important for a camper or hiker to know? Explain your choices. *(LESSON 4)*

➤ HEALTH SKILLS APPLICATION

1. **Advocacy.** Prepare a talk that encourages younger students in your community to learn first aid. Compile lists of local emergency telephone numbers for distribution. *(LESSON 1)*

2. **Analyzing Influences.** Evaluate the effect of technology on first aid. For example, what techniques and capabilities are available today that were not available 50 years ago? *(LESSON 2)*

3. **Accessing Information.** Research to learn whether your state has a high incidence of rabies and what measures are taken to keep the disease under control. *(LESSON 3)*

4. **Practicing Healthful Behaviors.** Find out which poisonous plants are in your area, how they can be recognized, and what to do in case of exposure to them. Use what you have learned to create a teaching tool, such as a poster or a comic book, for elementary school children. *(LESSON 4)*

BEYOND the Classroom

Parent Involvement

Accessing Information. Learn more about where members of your community can become certified in CPR. With your parents, find out how your family can become involved in promoting CPR certification for everyone. If classes are not available in your community, find out how you can arrange for someone to provide classes in your community.

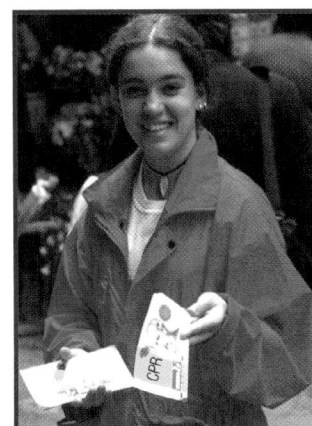

School and Community

CPR Certification. Train to become certified in CPR. Then research to find out how you can volunteer to help teach others the lifesaving techniques of CPR.

11. Immediately start flushing the eye with lukewarm water and continue for 15 minutes. Have the victim blink the eye as much as possible while flooding the eye. Do not force the eye open, and do not rub the eye. Have someone call 911 while you are rinsing the eye.

12. To help prevent infection.

Thinking Critically

1. Answers should include checking the scene and the victim, for example, making sure that no one is in danger from traffic; calling 911; asking permission and administering first aid.

2. The air in the victim's lungs is forced out quickly, a process that usually dislodges the item that is obstructing the airway.

3. Answers will vary but should explain that the animal could bite you or others again while you are trying to capture it or that special equipment is sometimes needed to subdue an animal.

4. Answers will vary.

Health Skills Application

1.–4. Answers will vary.

EVALUATE

- Use the reproducible Chapter 28 Test in the TCR, or construct your own using the Testmaker software. 📂 💿
- Use Performance Assessment 28 in the TCR. 📂

ENRICHMENT

Ask students to complete Enrichment Activity 28 in the TCR. 📂

BEYOND the Classroom

Keep students involved in the community, and encourage parent participation by assigning the activities on this page for students to work on outside of class.

Lessons	Standards		Features
	National	**State/Local**	
1 **Air Quality** *pages 766–771*	National Health Education Standards **1.5, 1.7, 4.3**		*Real-Life* **Application** • Indoor Air Pollution and Asthma: What You Can Do *(Accessing Information)*, page 770
2 **Protecting Land and Water** *pages 772–776*	National Health Education Standards **1.5, 1.7, 4.3**		
3 **Advocating for a Healthy Environment** *pages 777–781*	National Health Education Standards **7.4, 7.5, 7.6**		**Hands-On Health** • One Planet—Your Role *(Advocacy)*, page 780

Reproducible Resources	Assessment	Technology
Student Activity Workbook for use with each chapter	📁 Lesson Quiz 107	🕹️ Transparency 86
📁 Concept Mapping Activity 107		💿 TeacherWorks®
📁 Decision-Making Activity 29		🖥️ Internet Activities
📁 Guided Reading Activities 107		
📁 Health Lab 29		
📁 Lesson Plan 107		
📁 Parent Letter and Activities 29		
📁 Reteaching Activity 107		
📁 Concept Mapping Activity 108	📁 Lesson Quiz 108	🕹️ Transparency 87
📁 Current Health Issues 29		💿 TeacherWorks®
📁 Guided Reading Activities 108		
📁 Lesson Plan 108		
📁 Reteaching Activity 108		
📁 Concept Mapping Activity 109	📁 Lesson Quiz 109	🕹️ Transparency 88
📁 Cross-Curriculum Activity 29		💿 TeacherWorks®
📁 Enrichment Activity 29		
📁 Guided Reading Activities 109		
📁 Lesson Plan 109		
📁 Reteaching Activity 109		

0:00 OUT OF TIME

If time does not permit teaching the entire chapter use:

- Figure 29.1, p. 767
- Figure 29.2, p. 768
- Real Life Application, p. 770
- Health Minute, p. 775
- Hands-On Health, p. 780

Language Diversity

🎧 English Audio CD Program

🎧 Spanish Audio CD Program

📁 English Summaries, Quizzes, and Activities

📁 Spanish Summaries, Quizzes, and Activities

📁 Spanish Parent Letters and Activities

End of Chapter Assessment

Blackline Masters

📁 Chapter 29 Test

📁 Performance Assessment Activity 29

📁 Unit 9 Test

Technology

💿 Vocabulary PuzzleMaker

📺 MindJogger Videoquiz

💿 *ExamView®* ProTestmaker

Professional Health Series

Dealing with Sensitive Issues

Planning a Coordinated School Health Program

Promoting Character Education

Home, School, and Community Involvement

Key to Ability Levels

Teaching strategies that appear throughout the chapter have been identified by one of the following codes to give teachers an idea of their suitability for students of varying learning styles and abilities.

L1 Strategies should be within the ability range of all students. Full class participation is often required. Teacher direction is usually needed.

L2 Strategies are designed for average to above-average students or for small groups. Some teacher direction is needed.

L3 Strategies are designed for students able and willing to work independently. Minimal teacher direction is needed.

ELL Strategies should be within the ability range of students learning the English language.

◧▭ Block scheduling strategies are useful in a block scheduling format.

CHAPTER OVERVIEW

Chapter 29 discusses the forms and consequences of pollution and emphasizes ways that individuals can make a difference by conserving resources, precycling, and recycling.

Lesson 1 Air pollution is caused by gases and particles that enter the atmosphere. Health concerns and ways to manage both outdoor and indoor air pollution are presented. Noise pollution can lead to hearing impairment. Ways to reduce noise pollution are presented.

Lesson 2 Land pollution in the form of solid, hazardous, and nuclear wastes is discussed. Urban expansion and development can have a significant impact on the land. Industrial wastes, polluted runoff, and wastewater contribute to the contamination of the earth's water sources. Ways to reduce land and water pollution are presented.

Lesson 3 Everyone has a responsibility to protect the earth. Individuals can take steps to conserve natural resources. Precycling and recycling can help reduce the quantity of waste.

Health Skills Features

- Real-Life Application
  (Accessing Information), p. 770
- Hands-On Health
  (Advocacy), p. 780

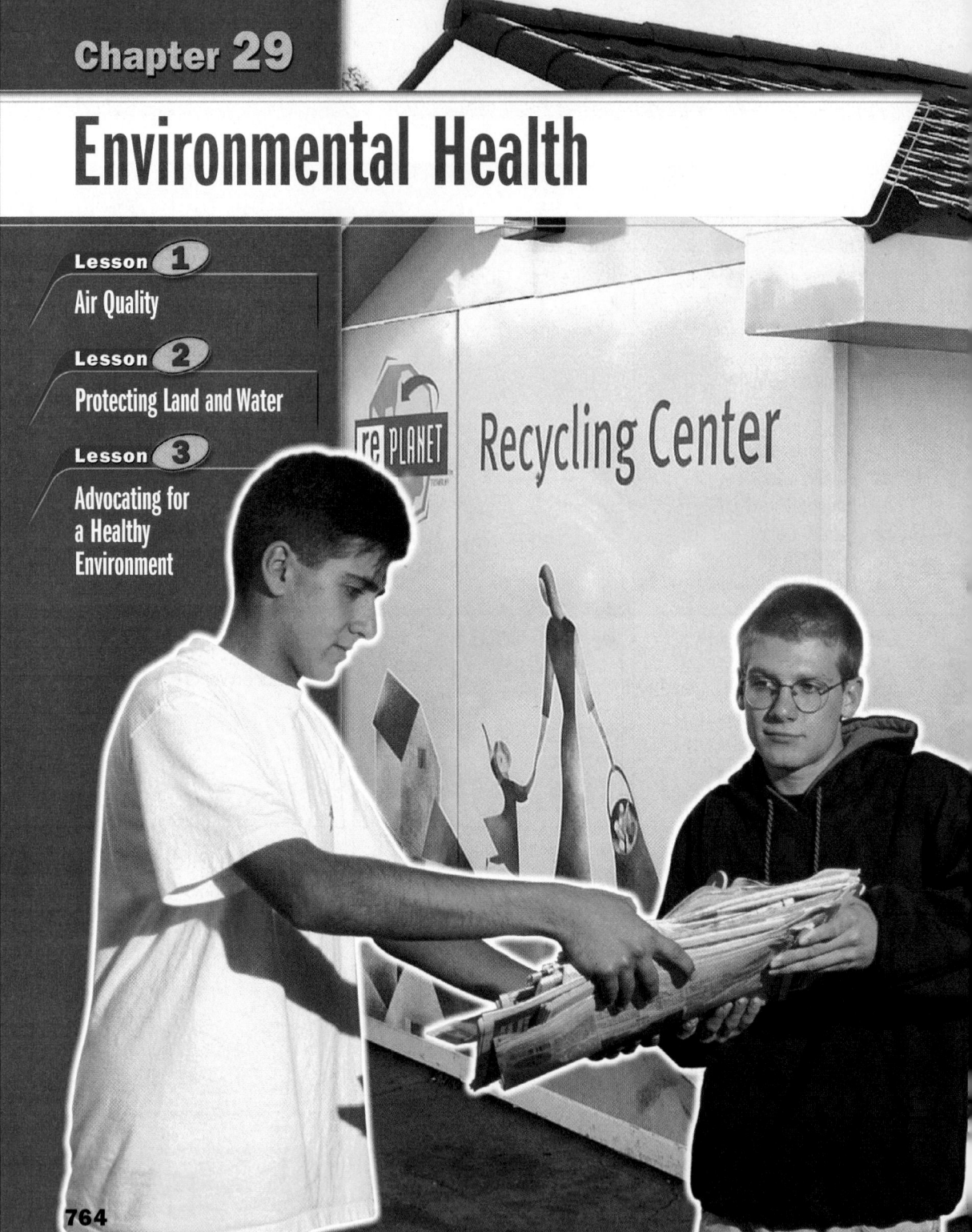

Chapter 29

Environmental Health

Lesson **1**
Air Quality

Lesson **2**
Protecting Land and Water

Lesson **3**
Advocating for a Healthy Environment

Recycling Center

764

MEETING STUDENT DIVERSITY

Language Diversity Use the following suggestions to help students who have difficulty with English:

- Pair English language learners with native speakers of English who can restate the Chapter Summary in language that helps students comprehend important concepts.

- Direct auditory learners or those students with language diversity to the *Glencoe Health Audio CD Program*. Available in English and Spanish, this component provides an audio and written summary of the chapter.

- Use photographs, drawings, or magazine clippings to help students visualize the important concepts of the chapter.

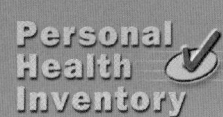

Personal Health Inventory

How Do You Rate?

Read each statement below and respond by writing *yes*, *no*, or *sometimes* for each item. Write *yes* only for items that you practice regularly.

1. I conserve water in my home.

2. I turn out lights when leaving a room.

3. I don't litter.

4. I buy products in refillable containers when possible.

5. I avoid buying disposable products when reusable alternatives are available.

6. I use fans instead of turning on the air conditioning whenever possible.

7. I reuse paper and plastic bags that are brought home from the store.

8. I buy recycled paper products when I have the choice.

9. I actively participate in a recycling program in my community.

10. I put on a second layer of clothing rather than turning up the heat if I feel cold at home.

Keep this personal inventory for review later in the chapter. When you have completed the chapter, review your answers again and identify two or three behavior changes you could make to improve the health of the environment.

Quick*Write*

Using Visuals. Taking care of the environment is everyone's responsibility. In what specific ways do you and your family actively take part in protecting the environment?

765

INTRODUCING THE CHAPTER

Personal Health Inventory

Have students read and discuss the statements in the Personal Health Inventory. Ask: How do the behaviors identified relate to your own health? To the health of others in your community? After a brief discussion, have students record their personal responses to these statements in their health journals.

Then, have students brainstorm environmental threats in their geographic area. Write their ideas on the board. Have them discuss local problems that may have received media coverage, such as landfills, land development, and air pollution. Help students expand their thinking to include environmental problems associated with other localities. Help students recognize that environmental problems in other communities can impact their local area.

Quick*Write*

Using Visuals Lead a class discussion about the scene depicted in the photograph. Then have students write a paragraph describing strategies that they and their families use to reduce air, land, and water pollution. When students have finished writing, ask volunteers to share their ideas with the class.

TECHNOLOGY OPTIONS

MINDJOGGER
VIDEOQUIZ

To preview or review chapter content, you may wish to use the Chapter 29 MindJogger Videoquiz.

Online Resources for the Teacher For a fresh approach to health topics and an in-depth look at health issues, use these online resources found under Teacher Resources at **health.glencoe.com:**

• Block Schedule Lesson Plans
• Technology Projects
• Health Updates

Air Quality

Lesson 1

①FOCUS

 QUICK START Encourage students to include effects not only on the lungs, but also on other organs, such as the brain. Give students three minutes to write their paragraphs. Then have volunteers share their ideas with the class.

TYING TO PRIOR KNOWLEDGE

Ask students to brainstorm as many causes of outdoor and indoor air pollution as they can. Explain that this lesson will focus on air pollution and ways to reduce it.

Health Skills Features

"Indoor Air Pollution and Asthma: What You Can Do," p. 770

ACCESSING INFORMATION

INTRODUCING VOCABULARY

- Divide the class into seven groups. Assign a vocabulary term to each group and have groups look up their term in the Glossary. Direct the first group to write a sentence using the first term. Have remaining groups add subsequent sentences using their terms. Invite a volunteer to read the finished paragraph aloud.

- Ask students to complete the Chapter 29 Study Guide in the *Student Activity Workbook.* 📂

766

Air Quality

VOCABULARY
- air pollution
- smog
- Air Quality Index (AQI)
- asbestos
- radon
- noise pollution
- decibel

YOU'LL LEARN TO
- Relate the nation's environmental health goals and objectives to individual, family, and community health.
- Identify sources of air pollution and strategies for reducing it.
- Develop strategies to evaluate information relating to critical environmental health issues.

 QUICK START Breathing is something you do without thinking. Write a paragraph explaining how you think breathing polluted air could negatively affect your health.

Air quality affects all living organisms, including humans. *Why is it important to alert the public when air pollution levels are extremely high?*

Modern technology has improved the lives of many people in the world. However, the pollution of air, land, and water that may result from technological advances can harm the environment and therefore people's health.

Air Pollution

Air pollution is a serious problem in this nation. It is linked to an estimated 50,000 to 120,000 premature deaths each year. The U.S. health care costs associated with outdoor air pollution range from $40 to $50 billion per year. For this reason, one goal of *Healthy People 2010* is to reduce the proportion of persons exposed to air that does not meet the U.S. Environmental Protection Agency's (EPA) health-based standards for ozone, a major component of air pollution.

Air pollution is *the contamination of the earth's atmosphere by substances that pose a health threat to living things.* The EPA monitors air quality and sets U.S. air quality standards. The agency has identified five major air pollutants whose levels need to be regulated in order to have cleaner air nationwide. These pollutants are described in **Figure 29.1.**

766 Chapter 29 Environmental Health

Lesson 1 *Resources*

Teacher Classroom Resources
- 📂 Concept Mapping Activity 107
- 📂 Decision-Making Activity 29
- 📂 Guided Reading Activities 107
- 📂 Health Lab 29
- 📂 Lesson Plan 107
- 📂 Lesson Quiz 107
- 📂 Parent Letter and Activities 29

- 📂 Reteaching Activity 107

Student Activity Workbook
- 📂 Applying Health Skills 107
- 📂 Chapter 29 Study Guide

Multimedia
- Transparency 86

FIGURE 29.1

FIVE COMMON AIR POLLUTANTS

The EPA has set national air quality standards for these pollutants.

Air Pollutant	Sources	Primary Health Concerns
Ozone (O_3) is a gas composed of three oxygen atoms. Ground-level ozone is a major component of *smog, a yellow-brown haze that forms when sunlight reacts with air pollution.*	O_3 forms from a chemical reaction between nitrogen oxide compounds and volatile organic compounds (VOCs). Motor vehicle exhaust, industrial emissions, gasoline vapors, and chemical solvents are the primary sources of nitrogen oxides and VOCs.	O_3 can irritate and inflame lung airways. It is linked to aggravated asthma, reduced lung capacity, and increased susceptibility to respiratory illnesses such as pneumonia and bronchitis.
Particulate Matter (PM) is a general term for particles such as dust, dirt, soot, smoke, mold, and liquid droplets that are found in the air.	PM may be emitted directly into the air from sources such as motor vehicle exhaust and factories. PM may also form in the air through chemical reactions between gases.	PM is linked to aggravated asthma, chronic bronchitis, decreased lung function, and premature death.
Carbon Monoxide (CO) is a colorless, odorless gas that contains carbon and oxygen. It is formed when carbon in fuel is not burned completely.	Outdoor sources of CO include motor vehicle exhaust and industrial processes. Indoor sources include gas stoves, cigarette smoke, and unvented gas and kerosene space heaters.	CO is poisonous. It prevents the body from receiving the oxygen it needs. It affects people with heart disease and can harm the central nervous system. Large quantities are fatal.
Sulfur Dioxide (SO_2) is a gas made up of sulfur and oxygen. It dissolves in water to form an acid, and it reacts with other gases in the air to form sulfates and other harmful particles.	SO_2 is formed when fuel that contains sulfur (such as coal and oil) is burned, when gasoline is extracted from oil, and when metals are extracted from their ores.	SO_2 contributes to respiratory illnesses and aggravates existing heart and lung diseases.
Nitrogen Oxides (NO_X) is a general term for a group of highly reactive gases that contain varying amounts of nitrogen and oxygen.	These substances form when fuel is burned at high temperatures. Primary sources include motor vehicles and electric utilities.	Nitrogen oxides help form ground-level ozone. They form particles that cause or trigger serious respiratory problems.

Lesson 1 Air Quality **767**

2 TEACH

VISUAL LEARNING

Figure 29.1 Give students a few moments to read the information in Figure 29.1. Have a volunteer read aloud all the ways that air pollution can affect health. Ask:

- Which air pollutants are formed by motor vehicles, either directly or when producing fuel for them? All
- Based on this chart, what do you conclude causes a significant proportion of outdoor air pollution? Motor vehicles

Have students work in pairs to brainstorm at least two actions that industry or individuals can take to reduce emissions of each of the five air pollutants. Students should make a chart that features their findings.

Critical Thinking

Who do you think is most at risk of serious health effects resulting from air pollution? The elderly and people with existing heart or lung diseases such as asthma and congestive heart disease. Why are healthy people who engage in outdoor activity also at risk? Physical activity causes people to breathe faster and more deeply, allowing more polluted air to be inhaled. L2

More About...

Smog A combination of the words *smoke* and *fog,* smog forms when there is little or no wind and a layer of warm air is trapped next to the ground. Without air circulation, pollutants can build up and become visible as smog. One type of smog is photochemical smog, a brown haze that forms with the aid of light. The pollutants get into the air when coal, natural gas, and gasoline are burned by factories and motor vehicles. Another type of smog is sulfurous smog, which results in a blanket of gray haze. This type is created when fossil fuels are burned in electrical power plants and home furnaces. Both types of smog may hang over a city for several days and be hazardous to breathe. For information relevant to your area, check local smog alerts.

Figure 29.2 Bring newspapers to class of the nearest metropolitan area that reports Air Quality Index (AQI). Have small groups of students locate and interpret the AQI, using the information presented in Figure 29.2 as a guide. Ask: What should people do when air quality is poor? **L1**

Explaining

Explain that conserving energy helps to reduce air pollution because power plants give off pollutants in the process of energy production. **L1**

Cross-Curriculum Activity

Math If cars emit 20 pounds of carbon dioxide per gallon of fuel burned, how much more carbon dioxide will a car that gets 20 miles per gallon emit than one that gets 30 miles per gallon if both are driven 18,000 miles per year? 6,000 pounds (18,000 miles/20 mph = 900 gal. 900 gal × 20 lbs = 18,000 lbs; 18,000 miles/30 mph = 600 gal. 600 gal × 20 lbs = 12,000 lbs.) **L2**

Quick Demo

Obtain in advance a radon test kit. Many are available from your local health department or environmental health agency. Have students read the instructions on how to test for radon. Ask students to find out whether their community has high levels of radon. Encourage them to test their homes for radon. **L1**

Reducing Air Pollution

The Clean Air Act of 1990 regulates the five pollutants described in Figure 29.1. Even with such laws in place, air quality can vary. The **Air Quality Index (AQI)**, developed by the EPA, is *an index for reporting daily air quality.* Shown in **Figure 29.2**, the AQI informs the public about local air quality and whether air pollution levels pose health risks.

You and your family can take the following actions to help reduce air pollution.

▶ **Reduce car use.** Walk or bicycle, take public transportation, or carpool to your destination.

▶ **Conserve energy.** Turn off lights when not in use. Set the air conditioner at a higher temperature. Put on extra layers of clothing instead of turning up the heat.

▶ **Use air-friendly machinery.** Small motors such as those found on mowers, chain saws, and leaf blowers emit pollutants. Use manual machinery when possible.

FIGURE 29.2

AIR QUALITY INDEX (AQI)

The AQI alerts people to possible health concerns of breathing polluted air.

Range	Air Quality	Color Code
0 to 50	**Good:** There is little or no health risk.	Green
51 to 100	**Moderate:** Some pollutants may pose a health concern for a small number of individuals.	Yellow
101 to 150	**Unhealthy for Sensitive Groups:** Unless a person has specific health concerns, pollution levels in this range are not likely to cause health problems.	Orange
151 to 200	**Unhealthy:** All individuals may experience some minor negative effects.	Red
201 to 300	**Very Unhealthy:** More serious effects may be felt by all individuals.	Purple
301 to 500	**Hazardous:** Entire population is at risk.	Maroon

School to Work

Reducing Commuter Pollution Encourage students to list strategies they have used to conserve energy when traveling to and from school and work, such as using public transportation, carpooling, walking, or cycling. Then have them research one of the most energy-efficient strategies: telecommuting, or working at home. Tell them to examine the advantages and disadvantages to workers and employers of working at home. Then have students visualize a specific type of business, identify the jobs in which working at home would or would not be feasible, and prepare a work-at-home proposal for company managers.

Indoor Air Pollution

Most people spend about 90 percent of their time indoors. EPA studies indicate that indoor levels of certain pollutants may be 2 to 5 times—and on occasion more than 100 times—higher than outdoor levels. Sources of indoor air pollution include building and furnishing materials such as carpeting and furniture made of certain pressed woods. Another source is old insulation containing **asbestos** (as-BES-tuhs), *a fibrous mineral that has fireproof properties*. When materials containing asbestos deteriorate, tiny fibers of the mineral are released into the air. Household cleaning products and other chemicals also contribute to indoor air pollution. Another major source is the particles and gases that form as a result of combustion. Stoves, furnaces, fireplaces, heaters, and tobacco smoke can all contaminate indoor air. Inadequate ventilation increases the problem. Energy-efficient homes may have so little air exchange that pollutants build up to dangerous levels.

Health Concerns of Indoor Air Pollution

The effects of indoor air pollution depend on the contaminant and the length of exposure. Immediate health concerns include irritation of the eyes, nose, and throat; headaches; dizziness; and fatigue. Long-term exposure to some pollutants can cause asthma. Exposure to lead, especially in children, can damage the kidneys, liver, brain, and nerves. Asbestos has been linked to lung cancer, especially in people who smoke. High levels of carbon monoxide can cause death.

The EPA estimates that **radon**, *an odorless, radioactive gas,* causes at least 14,000 lung cancer deaths per year. Radon is produced during the natural breakdown of the element uranium in soil, rocks, and water. It can seep into a house through cracks in the foundation. Home testing is the only way to assess exposure to radon. Homes with high levels of radon require increased indoor-outdoor air exchange. Some may need structural work to reduce radon levels.

Managing Indoor Air Pollution

To manage indoor air pollution, you must first identify the contaminants. Often, removing or replacing an object or appliance and providing sufficient indoor-outdoor air exchange will solve the problem. Make sure that hot water heaters and furnaces are properly vented and operating efficiently to avoid a buildup of carbon monoxide. Many families have installed carbon monoxide detectors to warn of a toxic buildup. Similar detectors are available for radon. Homeowners who discover the presence of asbestos or lead should seek professional help in removing these contaminants.

What is sick building syndrome?

The term *sick building syndrome* (SBS) refers to a situation in which the occupants of a building experience health problems that seem to be linked to the atmosphere within the building. Symptoms of SBS include headache; itchy and irritated eyes, throat, or nose; dizziness and nausea; fatigue; inability to concentrate; and a sensitivity to odors. SBS sufferers often report relief soon after leaving the building.

HEALTH Online

For more information on ways to minimize indoor air pollution, click on Web Links at **health.glencoe.com**.

Ask: Based on what you know about indoor air pollution in the home, why might people working in a building experience sick building syndrome? poor ventilation and the presence of various sources of indoor air pollution What sources of indoor air pollution might be present in a commercial building? Possible answer: particles and gases from office furniture, carpet, and cleaning products; tobacco smoke

Explaining

Explain that the removal of lead from gasoline has reduced the amount of lead in the environment. However, lead is still found in many other places, such as painted surfaces, dirt, dust, industrial air pollution, colored newsprint, pottery, and water. While lead is not in paint that is sold today, the paint used in older homes may contain lead. When people are sanding away old paint from walls or other surfaces, they and anyone nearby should take precautions against inhaling paint dust. **L1**

Cooperative Learning Activity

Types of Indoor Air Pollution Divide the class into four groups. Assign each group one of the following topics: tobacco smoke and carbon monoxide, volatile organic compounds (from household products), biological pollutants (such as dust mites, mold, and animal dander), and asbestos and radon. Groups should research the sources, health effects, and management strategies for their assigned pollutants. Students should summarize their findings in a written report. Remind them to proofread their work for spelling and grammar.

INDOOR AIR POLLUTION AND ASTHMA: WHAT YOU CAN DO

ACCESSING INFORMATION

NHES Standard 2 Students will demonstrate the ability to access valid health information and health-promoting products and services.

Objectives

- Develop strategies to evaluate information relating to environmental health issues.
- Identify measures that can improve indoor air quality.

Motivator

Ask students to name asthma triggers that are also indoor air pollutants.

Teaching Strategies

1. Review strategies on how to reduce exposure to allergens and asthma triggers from Chapter 26.
2. Advise students to access the state environmental agency or the U.S. EPA online.

✓Assessment

Using a rubric, student work should provide comprehensive evidence of the following criteria to achieve the highest score:

✔ citation of specific sources
✔ evaluation of the validity of the source
✔ rationale for the appropriateness of the source
✔ ability to access appropriate community resources to meet specific needs
✔ type of help available from the sources

Real-Life Application

Indoor Air Pollution and Asthma: What You Can Do

The incidence of asthma in people of all ages is increasing. Indoor air pollution has been identified as a major contributor to this increase. Study the graph, answer the questions on the right, and then complete the activity.

Estimated Number of Asthma Cases

All Ages   Under 18

Asthma cases per 100,000
80
70
60
50
40
30

82 83 84 85 86 87 88 89 90 91 92 93 94 95
Year

Source: National Center for Health Statistics, National Health Survey, 1982–1995

ACTIVITY

Work with a small group. Use reliable library and online sources to investigate additional measures that can improve indoor air quality. Cite your sources, and provide an explanation of why each source is reliable.

What can be done to reduce the levels of such triggers as dust and pet dander in the home?

In the 1960s children and teens were outside at least three hours each day. Today, they are outside less than two hours each day. How might these facts relate to the increase in asthma?

Today's homes allow less air to circulate. How might this contribute to the increase in asthma? What can be done to increase ventilation?

Tobacco smoke is one of the leading contributors to asthma attacks. How can exposure to tobacco smoke be limited or prevented?

Noise Pollution

Traffic, loud music, and power tools such as mowers and construction equipment are all sources of noise pollution. **Noise pollution** is *harmful and unwanted sound of sufficient intensity to damage hearing.* Hearing impairment caused by noise rarely leads to total deafness; however, the hearing loss is permanent, and hearing aids often do not compensate for the damage.

A **decibel** is *a unit used to express the relative intensity of loudness of sound.* Normal conversation is about 65 decibels. Exposure to noise levels of 85 decibels and above can result in temporary hearing loss, often accompanied by ringing in the ears. Normal hearing will usually return, but continued exposure can lead to permanent hearing loss. **Figure 29.3** shows the decibel levels of various sounds.

770 Chapter 29 Environmental Health

More About...

Poverty and Environmental Health

Residents of low-income communities are often exposed to more environmental toxins than residents of more affluent communities, and thus are more likely to suffer from health problems caused or aggravated by pollutants. Low-income neighborhoods are often located near highways and industrial areas that have high levels of air pollution; they are also common sites for hazardous waste production and disposal. Residents of substandard housing are more likely to come into contact with lead, asbestos, carbon monoxide, and other hazardous pollutants associated with peeling paint, old plumbing, and poorly maintained insulation and heating equipment.

FIGURE 29.3

DECIBEL LEVELS OF COMMON SOUNDS

Constant exposure at 85 decibels or greater may cause hearing loss.	Tractor, motorcycle, snowmobile		
Weakest sound heard by the average ear		Ambulance siren, amplified music	Rocket launch
	Normal conversation	Hair dryer, power lawn mower	Chain saw	Jet engine at takeoff

0   60   85   90   100   110   120   140   180

Reducing Noise Pollution

There are several ways to reduce noise pollution in your environment. Be sure to keep the volume down on stereos, radios, and television sets. Avoid unnecessary use of the car horn. When possible, use manual tools instead of power tools.

▶ Lesson 1 *Review*

Reviewing Facts and Vocabulary

1. Define *air pollution* and *noise pollution*.
2. Describe the EPA's role in monitoring air quality.
3. List two actions you can take to help reduce noise pollution.

Thinking Critically

4. **Evaluation.** Relate the nation's environmental health goals and objectives in *Healthy People 2010* to the health of individuals, families, and communities.
5. **Analyzing.** Imagine that the media has reported an AQI of 175. Paul, who has asthma, can't decide whether he wants to go in-line skating outdoors or play basketball in the air-conditioned gym. Determine which choice is healthier for Paul and explain your decision.

Applying Health Skills

Accessing Information. Think of a specific critical health issue related to air pollution. Find information on this topic, and develop strategies to evaluate the source of your information. Make a list of these strategies.

WORD PROCESSING   Use word processing to produce your list of strategies. See **health.glencoe.com** for help in using word-processing software.

Lesson 1 Air Quality   **771**

Figure 29.3 Give students a few minutes to study Figure 29.3. Have students discuss the decibel levels of some common sounds. Ask: What jobs might workers be exposed to the highest decibel levels? pilots, ambulance drivers, musicians, gardeners, etc.

3 ASSESS

EVALUATING THE LESSON

Assign and discuss the Lesson 1 Review; then administer, grade, and discuss Lesson Quiz 107 in the TCR. 🗀

RETEACHING

- Challenge the class to list as many strategies to reduce air pollution as they can without looking at their books.

- Ask students to complete Reteaching Activity 107 in the TCR. 🗀

ENRICHMENT

Have interested students investigate hybrid cars and present their findings to the class. 💊

4 CLOSE

Have students summarize the major causes of outdoor and indoor air pollution, their effects on health, and what they can do as individuals to reduce air pollution.

▶ Lesson 1 *Review*

Answers to Reviewing Facts and Vocabulary

1. See definitions on pages 766 and 770.
2. The EPA developed the AQI; it also informs the public about local air quality.
3. See actions on page 771.

Answers to Thinking Critically

4. One goal of *Healthy People 2010* is to reduce the number of persons exposed to air pollution. Improving air quality will result in fewer air pollution-related illnesses, positively affecting health.
5. An AQI of 175 indicates that all people may experience some minor negative effects. Paul has asthma, so he should play basketball in the gym.

Protecting Land and Water

Lesson 2

①FOCUS

QUICK START   Advise students to think of familiar water sources that supply drinking water or are used for fishing or other recreation. Have students work in pairs to create their PSAs. Encourage them to present their PSAs over the school's public address system.

TYING TO PRIOR KNOWLEDGE

Ask students to brainstorm wastes that end up in landfills or the water supply that might be particularly dangerous to health (e.g., batteries, cleaning products). Explain that this lesson discusses land and water pollution and ways to reduce it.

INTRODUCING VOCABULARY

- Have students give examples of *biodegradable* items and *hazardous waste*. Then ask them to define all the vocabulary terms in their own words.

- Ask students to complete the Chapter 29 Study Guide in the *Student Activity Workbook*. 📁

Protecting Land and Water

VOCABULARY
biodegradable
landfill
hazardous waste
deforestation
urban sprawl
wastewater

YOU'LL LEARN TO

- Identify sources of land and water pollution.

- Assess the impact of population on community and world health.

- Analyze the influence of laws on health-related environmental issues.

- Examine strategies for reducing land and water pollution.

QUICK START   Write a brief public service announcement encouraging people to help keep lakes, rivers, and streams free of pollution.

 Most wastes are disposed of in landfills and covered with soil to prevent the spread of disease by insects and rodents.

The wastes generated by human activity can pollute both land and water. However, there are many actions people can take to reduce pollution and help preserve land and water resources.

Waste Disposal

Many wastes are **biodegradable**, or *able to be broken down by microorganisms in the environment*. However, when biodegradable materials are discarded in quantities too large for nature to handle, or when materials are not biodegradable, other waste disposal solutions must be found.

Solid Waste

Much solid waste ends up in landfills. A **landfill** is *an area that has been safeguarded to prevent disposed wastes from contaminating groundwater*. Landfills must be located away from certain areas to protect groundwater (water that collects under the earth's surface) and must be lined with special materials to prevent leakage. Landfill operators must follow practices that reduce odor and control disease-carrying insects and rodents.

Lesson 2 *Resources*

Teacher Classroom Resources

📁 Concept Mapping Activity 108

📁 Current Health Issues 29

📁 Guided Reading Activities 108

📁 Lesson Plan 108

📁 Lesson Quiz 108

📁 Reteaching Activity 108

Student Activity Workbook

📁 Applying Health Skills 108

📁 Chapter 29 Study Guide

Multimedia

 Transparency 87

FIGURE 29.4

HAZARDOUS WASTES

Source/Activity That Generates Waste	Type of Waste Produced
Arts and crafts (e.g., painting, building models)	Solvents, paints, adhesives
Dry cleaning	Solvents
Construction	Oils, solvents, paints
Vehicle maintenance	Solvents, paints, ignitable wastes, used oil and batteries
Yardwork and gardening	Pesticides, herbicides, solvents
Household tasks	Solvents, oils, cleaning materials, paints, paint thinner

Hazardous Waste

A **hazardous waste** is *a substance that is explosive, corrosive, highly reactive, or toxic to humans or other life forms.* Industrial processes generate some hazardous wastes. Others are generated by common activities, including those described in **Figure 29.4.** Household products such as batteries are also considered hazardous wastes. Many of these wastes are banned from landfills and must be disposed of at special collection sites so that they don't contaminate the environment.

Nuclear wastes, a collection of radioactive materials that pose serious hazards to humans and other life forms, are a type of hazardous waste. Exposure to radiation can increase the risk of cancer. It can also alter a person's sex cells, causing genetic abnormalities to be passed on to offspring. Because of the long decay rates of some radioactive materials, these materials must be isolated in secure facilities for thousands of years.

Expansion and Development

Throughout history population growth has been accelerating. It took half a million years for humankind to reach a population size of 1 billion, but the next billion people were born in a span of only 80 years, and close to 1½ billion more have been born since 1975. In certain U.S. and world regions where population growth is rapid, there is a low quality of life and much human suffering. Rapid population growth also leads to swift deterioration of the land and to a severe drain on resources such as water.

Urban development can also have a dramatic impact on the land. As new cities are built, room for them must be cleared. This clearing has been at the expense of wilderness areas and rain forests.

Lesson 2 Protecting Land and Water **773**

2 TEACH

VISUAL LEARNING

Figure 29.4 Have volunteers read the information in Figure 29.4. Explain that solvents are liquids that can dissolve another substance, such as turpentine or paint thinner. Select one or two activities and ask students to identify wastes associated with the task. Have them identify which are hazardous and which are not.

Critical Thinking

What are some problems associated with landfill disposal? Answers will vary. Students may mention that acceptable landfill space is scarce, that some materials placed into landfills decompose slowly, and that some wastes can leak into surrounding soil and groundwater. **L2**

Explaining

Explain that each day's deposit in a landfill is covered with dirt. The dirt prevents the deposit from blowing away and reduces the odor produced by decaying waste. The landfill may be lined with plastic, concrete, or clay-rich soils that trap liquid waste. These measures reduce the chance that pollutants will leak into the surrounding soil and groundwater. However, some may still find their way into the environment. **L1**

Home and Community

Hazardous Waste Collection Ask students to find out whether your community designates certain days for the collection of hazardous household wastes. If so, have students obtain information about the dates, times, places, and types of wastes that the organization will take. Encourage students to post or distribute brochures with this information around the school and community. Alternatively, students may choose to create their own pamphlets for display or distribution.

Discussing

Ask: If you could pass one law to protect the global environment, what would it be? How would you enforce it? Have students explain their answers.

Activity

Ask students to write a story about the kind of world they might live in 20 years from now if the damage to the world's environment continues unchecked. Have as many students as possible read their stories to the class.

Activity

Explain to students that many of the world's medicines are derived from plants found within the rainforest. Have students use online and print sources to research medicines that come from the rainforest. Have students identify the specific illnesses that these medicines treat. 📖

Cooperative Learning

Discuss some of the problems associated with urban sprawl. Ask: What are some ways you can address the problems of urban sprawl? by riding a bike, walking, or taking public transit Divide students into groups. Invite each group to address the problem of urban sprawl by planning their own city or town. Encourage students to be creative with their projects. Students may wish to write reports, create models, or choose some other way to present their ideas. Have the groups share their ideas for their model cities or towns with the class. 📖

🔺 **Using public transportation instead of driving reduces pollution and helps conserve resources.** *How might an efficient public transportation system improve community health?*

Disappearing Forests

Developing nations in Central America, Africa, and Southeast Asia are rapidly expanding in agriculture and industry. These nations have been clearing tropical forests on a massive scale for fuel and to make way for farms and ranch land. This **deforestation**, or *destruction of forests,* has upset the fragile balance of nature.

Aside from providing a home to countless plant and animal species, the world's great forests play a vital part in controlling soil erosion, flooding, and sediment buildup in rivers, lakes, and reservoirs. Deforestation interferes with these processes. It can also change regional patterns of rainfall as a result of altered rates of evaporation, transpiration (vapor exhaled from the surface of green plants), and runoff. Without trees, precipitation declines and the region grows hotter and drier. Ultimately, desertlike conditions prevail where there were once rich, tropical grasslands.

Urban Sprawl

The spreading of city development (houses, shopping centers, businesses, and schools) onto undeveloped land is called **urban sprawl**. As the land surrounding cities becomes developed, environmental problems can occur. Runoff from parking lots and fertilized lawns may contaminate the drinking water supply. Air quality worsens as increased automobile and lawnmower usage adds more engine exhaust to the air.

To help address the problem of urban sprawl, city planners are rethinking the way suburbs are organized to help reduce consumption of natural resources and decrease the amount of pollution. In planned communities, schools and businesses are located within walking distance of homes, and sidewalks are required. Walking the short distances from home to work, school, or shopping provides physical activity for pedestrians, saves resources, and reduces pollution. The inclusion of efficient public transportation in these communities helps reduce the number of people driving to work. Consequently, fewer vehicles are on the highways, reducing both the level of pollution and the number of injuries and deaths caused by traffic accidents.

Water Supplies and Pollution

The EPA requires water suppliers to monitor and test water before sending it through municipal or community water systems. If the water is contaminated, the supplier must shut down the system and fix the problem. No agencies monitor the quality of water coming from private wells, however. Water treatment and purity depend on actions taken by those who use the well.

Curriculum Connections

Science Have students investigate why water is such a limited resource even though three-quarters of the earth's surface is covered with water, as well as technologies to obtain more fresh water supplies.

Art Ask students to create designs for T-shirts, bumper stickers, or baseball caps that promote a safe and clean water supply for the world.

Language Arts Direct students to investigate the major provisions of the 1987 Clean Water Act, how it encourages communities to reduce water pollution, and how effective the act has been.

All drinking water is susceptible to pollution. Because the water can come from large sources such as rivers, lakes, or aquifers (water-bearing layers of rock, sand, or gravel) that underlie several counties or states, the pollution source can be far away from where the water is used.

Polluted Runoff

About 40 percent of the nation's rivers, lakes, and coastal waters are not safe for swimming or other types of water recreation. Water pollution is sometimes caused by illegal dumping of industrial chemical wastes, but a greater contamination problem is created by pollution that comes from many sources throughout the environment. Most surface water contamination is caused by polluted runoff—rainwater or snowmelt that runs over the land, picking up such contaminants as pesticides, fertilizers, and wastes. Polluted runoff can also contaminate groundwater, the primary source of drinking water for millions of people in the United States.

Wastewater

Wastewater, *used water that comes from homes, communities, farms, and businesses,* is another source of water pollution. Along with sewage, wastewater includes water that is generated and discharged from industries, feedlots, and many other sources. Wastewater contains harmful substances such as human or animal wastes, metals, and pathogens. Some wastewater must be treated by cooling in order to prevent thermal pollution. Thermal pollution occurs when the temperature of discharged water is higher than the temperature of a body of water in the environment. Because this hot water can disrupt aquatic ecosystems, it must be cooled before it enters the environment. The EPA regulates the treatment and discharge of wastewater under the Clean Water Act. Treated water that is released back into the environment must be safe for humans and other living organisms.

Other Sources of Water Pollution

Other sources of water pollution include:

▶ **Sediment.** Sediment from land erosion can destroy aquatic ecosystems and clog lakes, stream channels, and harbors.

▶ **Oil.** Some oil contamination comes from the cleaning of oil tankers and the release of oil from offshore drilling rigs. Problems can also occur when people dump used motor oil or household chemicals down household and storm drains.

Health Minute

Strategies for Protecting Water Supplies

There are actions you can take to help prevent the contamination of drinking water.

To protect drinking water:

▶ **Recycle engine oil.** Just 1 quart of oil can contaminate up to 2 million gallons of drinking water.

▶ **Be careful about what you put down the drain.** In areas that use septic systems, harmful chemicals may end up in your drinking water.

▶ **Keep cars, boats, and watercraft maintained.** Prevent fuel and lubricant leaks by keeping engines well tuned.

Ⓨ **Polluted runoff is a major source of water pollution in the United States.**

Health Minute

Have volunteers read the strategies for protecting water supplies aloud. Ask interested students to research other ways to protect drinking water. Invite them to present their findings to the class in the form of a poster.

Community Involvement

Have students find out the source of their local water supply. Have them investigate who determines whether the supply is pure, how often the supply is tested, and how wastewater is treated. 🄻2 ⌷

Cross-Curriculum Connections

Social Studies Have students use library and online resources to research which illnesses related to water pollution are most common around the world. Have them write a report about these illnesses. Students may also want to include a map indicating regions where the illnesses are prevalent. Remind students to write several drafts, and proofread for errors. Have volunteers share their reports with the class.

Lesson 2 Protecting Land and Water **775**

More About...

Contaminated Shores Water at the shoreline can be contaminated by pathogens from sewage overflows, polluted storm water runoff, boating wastes, and malfunctioning septic systems. Bacteria, viruses, protozoa, and worms in sewage can cause gastrointestinal illness. State and local health and environmental protection officials are responsible for monitoring the water quality of the nation's beaches. When they determine that a beach is contaminated, they may post warnings or close the beach. Have students contact their local or state environmental office to find out more about monitoring beaches, rivers, or lakes in your area.

3 ASSESS

EVALUATING THE LESSON

Assign and discuss the Lesson 2 Review; then administer, grade, and discuss Lesson Quiz 108 in the TCR.

RETEACHING

- Divide the class into pairs. Provide each pair with poster board. Have them make posters depicting sources of water pollution and ways to reduce it.
- Ask students to complete Reteaching Activity 108 in the TCR.

ENRICHMENT

Ask interested students to research outbreaks caused by drinking municipal tap water contaminated with the parasite *Cryptosporidium*. They should report on why the organism was not killed by then-current wastewater treatments and on new federal requirements for wastewater treatment mandated as a result of these outbreaks.

4 CLOSE

Have students close their textbooks and write an outline of the lesson's major concepts. Then have them use their textbooks to check the accuracy of their outlines.

CHARACTER CHECK

Citizenship. When you dispose of hazardous household materials properly, you are demonstrating good citizenship and respect for the environment. **Make a pledge to always dispose of hazardous materials in a responsible manner. Share your knowledge about the dangers of hazardous materials with others, and encourage them to make responsible decisions.**

Reducing the Risks

You and your family can take steps to help keep our land and water clean.

▶ Recycle materials whenever possible to reduce the amount of waste going to landfills. You'll learn more about reducing solid wastes in Lesson 3.

▶ Dispose of all materials properly. Don't put oil paints, paint solvents, or batteries into the trash. Don't pour household chemicals or motor oil down the drain or onto the ground. Instead, take these and other hazardous materials to the appropriate collection sites.

▶ Follow directions when using chemicals such as cleaning products, fertilizers, and pesticides, and don't overuse them.

▶ Reduce water usage. Repair leaky faucets. Follow the recommendations for landscape watering that apply to your area. Reducing water usage decreases the amount of water that must be treated.

▶ Lesson 2 Review

Reviewing Facts and Vocabulary

1. What is a *landfill*?
2. Assess the impact of population on community and world health.
3. How can polluted runoff contaminate water supplies?

Thinking Critically

4. **Applying.** Analyze how laws like the Clean Water Act positively influence health and prevent disease.
5. **Analyzing.** You have probably heard the saying, "Water, water everywhere, but not a drop to drink." Explain this statement in terms of available drinking water.

Applying Health Skills

Advocacy. Create a comic book about a superhero named Captain Cleanup and his or her adventures cleaning up land and water pollution. The comic book should be targeted to elementary school students and contain a strong message about what young people can do to reduce land and water pollution.

WEB SITES Use your comic book as part of a Web page you develop on reducing pollution. See **health.glencoe.com** for help in planning and building your own Web site.

776 Chapter 29 Environmental Health

▶ Lesson 2 Review

Answers to Reviewing Facts and Vocabulary

1. See definition on page 772.
2. Rapid growth leads to deterioration of land and a severe drain on resources.
3. See page 775 for explanation.

Answers to Thinking Critically

4. Laws that enforce water quality make it less likely that people will drink contaminated water. This will prevent waterborne illness.
5. Possible answer: Not all water is safe for drinking because of contamination. Thus, one could be surrounded by water, yet not be able to drink it.

Advocating for a Healthy Environment

VOCABULARY
conservation
precycling
recycling

YOU'LL LEARN TO
- Identify strategies for conserving resources, precycling, and recycling.
- Develop strategies for protecting the environment.
- Describe a variety of community and world environmental protection programs.

QUICK START Make a list of the environmental benefits of participating in a recycling program.

M any of today's environmental problems result from the lifestyle and consumer choices we make. In this lesson you'll learn about what you can do to protect the health of the environment.

Conserving Resources

M ost natural resources don't exist in an endless supply. The coal, natural gas, and petroleum we use for fuel took millions of years to form. It takes about 20 years for a tree to become large enough to cut for use as paper. These examples illustrate the need to conserve our natural resources. **Conservation** is *the protection and preservation of the environment by managing natural resources to prevent abuse, destruction, and neglect.* The actions that you and your family take at home have an impact on the environment. Some actions you can take to conserve natural resources are featured on the next page.

Planting trees helps replenish this natural resource. *How do trees benefit the environment?*

Advocating for a Healthy Environment

1 FOCUS

QUICK START Suggest that students think of recyclable items they use every day and how recycling those items benefits the environment. Have volunteers share their responses with the class.

TYING TO PRIOR KNOWLEDGE

Ask if students are familiar with the recycling numbers imprinted on the bottom of plastic beverage bottles. Explain that this numbering system is helpful when the bottles are sorted for recycling. Tell students that this lesson will explain the importance of conservation in protecting the environment as well as ways to conserve resources.

INTRODUCING VOCABULARY

- Ask students to compare and contrast the terms *conservation*, *precycling*, and *recycling*.
- Ask students to complete the Chapter 29 Study Guide in the *Student Activity Workbook*. 📁

Lesson 3 Resources

Teacher Classroom Resources
- 📁 Concept Mapping Activity 109
- 📁 Cross-Curriculum Activity 29
- 📁 Enrichment Activity 29
- 📁 Guided Reading Activities 109
- 📁 Lesson Plan 109
- 📁 Lesson Quiz 109
- 📁 Reteaching Activity 109

Student Activity Workbook
- 📁 Applying Health Skills 109
- 📁 Chapter 29 Study Guide

Multimedia
- 🖨 Transparency 88

2 TEACH

Cross-Curriculum Activity

Language Arts Instruct students to access recent news articles about conservation issues on the local, national, and world level. Have students report on how and why the information in the articles is important to them. **L1**

ACTIVE READING

Cause-and-Effect Chart

In this strategy, students visually represent the causes and effects of an event or process. Have students list the environmental problems described in this chapter in one column. In a second column, have students list or illustrate the effects of each problem. They can then add a third column listing or illustrating solutions to each problem. For more strategies, see the *Guided Reading Activities* booklet in the TCR. 📁

Critical Thinking

Ask: **Why do you think more people do not recycle?** Possible answers: some people are not in the habit; many communities do not have recycling programs; recycling centers recycle only certain items **L2**

Activity

Have students research and prepare a list of natural resources that are renewable and those that are nonrenewable. **L2**

Putting on an extra layer of clothing instead of turning up the heat helps conserve natural resources. *Why is it important to conserve natural resources?*

Turning off lights saves electricity. *How else can you reduce electricity use in your home?*

Heating and Cooling

▶ Seal leaks around doors, windows, and electrical sockets to prevent heated or cooled air from escaping. Keep doors and windows shut and close fireplace vents when the fireplace is not in use to keep cooled or heated air inside the home.

▶ During heating season, wear an extra layer of clothing instead of turning up the thermostat. Keep the thermostat at about 68°F. For further conservation, turn the thermostat down at bedtime.

▶ Keep the thermostat at about 78°F during air-conditioning season. Use a fan to keep air circulating—this will make the area feel cooler.

Water Conservation

▶ Wash clothes in warm or cold, not hot, water. Accumulate a full load before washing laundry or running the dishwasher.

▶ Fix leaky faucets, and never let water run unnecessarily. Turning off the water while brushing your teeth or shaving can save 4.5 gallons of water per minute.

▶ If you have a large-capacity toilet tank, fill plastic bottles with water, seal them, and place them in the tank. The bottles will keep the tank from filling completely, which will save up to a gallon of water per flush.

Lighting and Appliances

▶ Replace traditional lightbulbs with compact fluorescent bulbs, which use less energy and last longer.

▶ Switch off lights when you leave a room.

▶ Turn off televisions, radios, computers, and other appliances when they are not in use.

▶ Use a microwave or toaster oven instead of a conventional oven when cooking a small amount of food.

▶ Don't preheat a conventional oven for longer than necessary. Avoid opening the oven door unnecessarily while the appliance is in use.

Home and Community

Environmental Threats Have students work in groups and imagine they have been assigned to a committee to identify conditions that are most likely to threaten the local environment in the near future. Suggest to groups that they first consider how the conditions are likely to affect them, their families, their community, and their region. What effects have they already observed?

Then have them identify possible threats generated locally. Individually, group members should write a brief description of a specific condition, such as improper waste disposal, including where it exists and how it threatens the local environment. Have each group rank the threats in order of importance.

Precycling and Recycling

The easiest, most cost-efficient way of conserving natural resources is reducing the quantity of waste. Precycling and recycling are two ways of accomplishing this goal.

Precycling

Precycling—*reducing waste before it is generated*—means purchasing and using products wisely. How can you precycle? Reduce your use of products that are used once and then discarded. For example, try using cloth napkins instead of paper ones. Purchase products in bulk or in the largest package appropriate for your use to reduce excess packaging. Buying products such as laundry detergent or fruit juice as concentrates also reduces packaging. Choose products designed to be recycled. For example, look for the code on plastic packages. Those that carry a 1, 2, or 3 are most easily recycled.

Precycling also involves reusing materials. Reusing paper or plastic shopping bags or carrying your own cloth bags is a form of precycling. So is donating unneeded household goods or clothing to charities instead of discarding them.

Recycling

Recycling is *the processing of waste materials so that they can be used again.* Recycling has several benefits:

▶ **Recycling conserves resources.** Both energy and raw materials are conserved by recycling. For example, making a can from recycled aluminum takes only 10 percent of the energy needed to make a new can from raw materials.

▶ **Recycling reduces reliance on landfills.** Landfill space is limited, and it cannot keep up with increasing demands. Because of this, it is important to reduce the amount of waste that gets deposited in landfills.

▶ **Recycling protects environmental health.** Recycling utilizes materials that might otherwise harm the environment if disposed of in landfills. Thus, recycling efforts lead to a cleaner and more healthful environment.

▼ Carrying your own cloth bags instead of using paper or plastic ones is one way to precycle. *What is another example of precycling?*

Discussing

Prepare by displaying ads for such items as paper plates and napkins, single-use plastic cups, and disposable razors. Ask: Why do consumers choose these products? What problems do these products create? What other choices can consumers make?

Explaining

If appropriate, help students recognize that the prefix *pre-* means "before" and *re-* means "again." Help students see the meanings of these prefixes when thinking about the terms *precycling* and *recycling*.

Activity

Have students generate a classroom list of everything that is commonly recycled. Possible answers: aluminum, batteries, cardboard, clothing and household items, glass, oil, paper, plastics, tin cans, tires, yard waste You may want to have students bring in common household items and create a classroom display about recycling. Have interested students decorate the display using paints and other supplies.

FYI

Buying recycled products reduces air and water pollution and mining wastes by 70 percent. Using recycled aluminum reduces pollution as much as 95 percent. Every ton of recycled paper bought in America saves 17 trees, 7,000 gallons of water, and enough energy to heat or air-condition a house for six months.

─⋀⋁⋀─ HEALTH LITERACY

Critical Thinker/Problem Solver Many environmental problems discussed in this chapter are the result of solutions to other problems. Lead was added to gasoline to prevent knocking. To reduce pollution from oil, coal, and gas, nuclear energy was harnessed, which led to nuclear wastes and accidents. Have students note or predict problems that might result from solutions to a current environmental problem. For example, they might want to predict what effect it would have on the economy if consumers suddenly stopped buying all disposable products. What strategies might solve the problem of waste and overconsumption without serious adverse economic effects?

Hands-On Health

ONE PLANET— YOUR ROLE

ADVOCACY

NHES Standard 7 Students will demonstrate the ability to advocate for personal, family, and community health.

Objectives

• Evaluate the effect of a variety of environmental factors on community health.

• Apply strategies for advocating for health issues.

Motivator

Tell students that each person in the United States uses about 2 pounds of paper per day. Ask: How many pounds would be saved if everyone in our school recycled paper?

Teaching Strategies

1. The day before doing this activity, ask students to keep a log of items they throw away.
2. Have students access reliable online resources that feature ideas for precycling and recycling.

✓Assessment

Using a rubric, student work should provide comprehensive evidence of the following criteria to achieve the highest score:

✔ clear, health-enhancing stand
✔ support for the position with relevant information
✔ awareness of the audience
✔ encouragement of others to make healthful choices
✔ passion/conviction

780

Hands-On Health ACTIVITY

One Planet—Your Role

In this activity you will create a chart that demonstrates the need to conserve resources.

What You'll Need

• pen or pencil and notebook paper
• poster board or construction paper
• markers

What You'll Do

1. Divide a sheet of paper into three columns. Label the columns "Items I Throw Away Every Week," "Ways of Precycling or Recycling," and "Why It Matters."
2. List at least five items in the first column, and complete the other two columns for those items

3. Work in a small group. Combine the best ideas and create a poster-sized chart, similar to the one on your sheet of paper, that includes several ways to precycle or recycle commonly used items. Use persuasive language, and illustrate your group's chart.

4. Present the chart to the class. Then display it in the classroom or in a school hallway.

Apply and Conclude

Find statistics on how precycling and recycling help reduce waste and pollution. Be sure to relate the data to the actions described in your poster.

Ⓥ Manufacturers put codes on plastic containers to give consumers information on how to recycle.

TIPS FOR RECYCLING AND REDUCING WASTE

More than 80 percent of household waste can be recycled. The following are some guidelines for specific recyclable materials.

▶ **Aluminum.** Rinse cans and other aluminum items such as pie pans and frozen food trays. Crush them to save space.

▶ **Cardboard.** Flatten cardboard boxes and tie them together.

▶ **Glass.** Rinse all glass containers. Recycle metal lids separately.

▶ **Plastics.** Look for the code on the container. Most recyclers take those marked with a 1, 2, or 3.

▶ **Newspaper.** Stack newspapers and tie the bundles with string or rope, or place the papers in paper shopping bags for easy handling.

▶ **Glossy Paper.** Contact services that help you remove your name from mailing lists. Find out whether a local retirement or community center can use discarded magazines. What you can't eliminate or redistribute, recycle.

780 **Chapter 29** Environmental Health

Myths & Reality

MYTH. Catalogs and other glossy paper cannot be recycled.

FACT. Almost any type of paper is recyclable. Check with recycling and paper companies to find out which ones take glossy paper.

MYTH. A person at the landfill sorts recyclable items from regular trash.

FACT. This practice is too labor-intensive to be practical. Anything you throw in the regular trash goes into the landfill.

Protecting the Environment

Here are some practical suggestions for becoming involved in protecting the environment:

▶ **Become an informed consumer.** Evaluate products with regard to their impact on natural resources. Give feedback to companies on ways they can help protect the environment.

▶ **Contact organizations that promote the conservation of resources and educate people on environmental issues.** Ask for ideas on how to conserve natural resources. Consider joining an environmental organization. Most of these organizations can give you information on current environmental issues. They can also suggest ways to promote the health of the environment.

▶ **Take action against local polluters.** The environmental problems in your community directly affect your health. Targeting local polluters is an effective way of protecting your health and that of your family and neighbors. Join with others to inform elected officials of your concerns.

 Much of the waste generated in a typical American home can be recycled. *What materials are recycled in your community?*

⚫3 ASSESS

EVALUATING THE LESSON

Assign and discuss the Lesson 3 Review; then administer, grade, and discuss Lesson Quiz 109 in the TCR. 📁

RETEACHING

- Have students list three actions presented in this lesson that they will try to take to conserve resources. Have students discuss why they made their choices and how they will implement them.

- Ask students to complete Reteaching Activity 109 in the TCR. 📁

ENRICHMENT

Ask students to write a one-page essay on whether they think recycling should be mandatory. Have them defend their point of view with data and other information, such as how mandatory recycling works in countries that have it. Remind students to proofread their writing for spelling and grammatical errors. They may need to write several drafts before handing in a final, error-free draft.

Lesson 3 *Review*

Reviewing Facts and Vocabulary

1. Define the term *conservation.*
2. What is the difference between *precycling* and *recycling*?
3. List three environmental benefits of recycling.

Thinking Critically

4. **Analyzing.** How does conserving resources protect the health of the environment?
5. **Applying.** Develop strategies to conserve natural resources in your home. List three strategies not included in this lesson that your family can undertake to conserve resources.

Applying Health Skills

Accessing Information. Research and describe a variety of environmental protection programs, both in your community and in countries throughout the world. Create a chart to display the information that you obtain. Include the name of the community or country, the name of the program, and a brief description of the program's mission.

SPREADSHEETS Use a spreadsheet to organize your information and create your chart. See **health.glencoe.com** for tips on how to create and use a spreadsheet.

Lesson 3 Advocating for a Healthy Environment **781**

⚫4 CLOSE

Discuss with students how they as individuals can make a difference in conserving resources and how this relates to human health.

Lesson 3 *Review*

Answers to Reviewing Facts and Vocabulary

1. See page 777 for definition.
2. Precycling is reducing waste before it is generated. Recycling is the processing of waste materials so that they can be used again in some form.
3. See page 779 for benefits.

Answers to Thinking Critically

4. Possible answer: Conserving resources reduces the need for more raw materials and reduces the need for energy to process those raw materials.
5. Answers will vary.

Eye ON THE Media

Environmental Health in the News

NHES Standard 4 Students will analyze the influence of culture, media, technology, and other factors on health.

Objective

Compare and contrast how different print media cover the same environmental health issue.

Motivator

Ask students if they listen to weather forecasts on local news programs. Do those forecasts include air quality alerts?

Teaching Strategies

Awareness Answers to the Motivator should increase students' awareness of where they hear about environmental health issues in their community.

Analysis Help students locate articles in different print media sources about the same topic.

Reflection Point out that national news magazines and larger city newspapers often relate the issue to the nation or the world. Local newspapers are more likely to focus on how the issue affects a particular community.

Take Action Encourage students to ask their parents about whether or not there is a carbon monoxide detector in their home or whether or not their home has been tested for radon or lead-based paints.

✓ Assessment

Analyses should describe the similarities and differences between the two articles. Position papers should link the issues in each article to *Healthy People 2010*.

Eye ON THE Media

Environmental Health in the News

In this activity, you will answer the following questions in order to compare and contrast how articles from two different print media cover the same environmental health issue.

Questions to Answer

1. What aspect of the environmental health issue does each article address?
2. How does each article convey the subject matter to the reader?
3. How does each article link the environmental issue to specific health problems?
4. Does each article include comments from environmental health experts, scientists, physicians, and/or politicians?
5. Can you detect any bias in either article?
6. Do the articles provide relevant information about how the issue affects a specific community?
7. Do the articles provide a regional or global perspective on the issue?
8. In your opinion, which source provides better coverage of the issue? Why?

ACTIVITY

Think of a specific environmental health issue. Then, locate articles in two different types of print media that pertain to this topic. You can choose from your local newspaper; a major city newspaper, such as the *New York Times* or the *Washington Post;* or a national news magazine, such as *Time* or *Newsweek.* Write an analysis of how these two different sources cover the same topic. Use the answers to the questions above to guide your analysis.

EXPRESS YOUR VIEWS

Healthy People 2010 has a number of goals that relate to environmental health issues that affect all Americans. Review these goals, and write a position paper that suggests how the media sources you analyzed have played or can play a role in helping reach the goals.

More About...

Pollution and Illness Occupational lung disease is the leading job-related illness in the United States. Per year, more than 17,000 lung cancer deaths result from inhalation of carcinogenic substances in the workplace. Long-term exposure to airborne contaminants can lead to chronic bronchitis, emphysema, asthma, and other respiratory diseases. Encourage interested students to investigate what can be done to address this problem.

CROSS-CURRICULUM CONNECTIONS

Compose a Haiku. Think about something in the natural environment that inspires you, such as a bird in flight, a shooting star, or the soothing sounds of a stream. Compose a haiku, a Japanese form of poetry that often focuses on nature, on the subject you've chosen. Use vivid language to describe a certain aspect of your subject, such as its shape, size, or color.

Conduct Team Research. The health of humans is undeniably linked to the health of the environment. Over the past 40 years, the environmental movement has worked to clean up the earth. Work with a team to research a specific environmental organization, such as the Sierra Club or the U.S. Fish & Wildlife Service. Report to the class on the history of the organization and its purpose and goals.

Compute the Cost. The health-related costs of outdoor air pollution range from $40 to $50 billion per year. Suppose that in a certain year, the health costs of air pollution were $45 billion. Given a U.S. population of 281.4 million people, how much does health care related to air pollution cost each person in this particular year?

Write a Report. Some people may think that air pollution is solely the result of human activity. However, there have always been natural sources of air pollution, such as dust storms. Use reliable online and print resources to find information on various natural sources of air pollution. Summarize your findings in a brief report.

CAREER Corner

Environmental Engineering Technician

Would you like to improve the quality of the environment? If so, you might enjoy a career as an environmental engineering technician.

Environmental engineering technicians work closely with environmental engineers and scientists in developing methods and devices used in the prevention, control, or correction of environmental hazards.

To become an environmental engineering technician, you will need a two-year associate's degree or extensive on-the-job training. Find out more about this and other health careers by clicking on Career Corner at **health.glencoe.com**.

Portfolio Assessment

Self-Evaluation Direct students to review the Health Skills Activities and other activities completed in the chapter. Encourage each student to select one finished product or activity that demonstrates his or her best work for the chapter and that represents the student's learning goals. Have students explain what they have learned and how the examples they have selected demonstrate their growth in health literacy, knowledge, and skills.

Teacher Classroom Resources Assign Performance Assessment 29, "Promoting Recycling," in the TCR. 📁

CROSS-CURRICULUM CONNECTIONS

Enrich student learning by connecting the topic of environmental health to one of the four subject areas presented on this page. The activity may be completed individually or with a partner.

Language Arts Through example, show students the format for a haiku. A haiku has three lines and seventeen syllables. The first and third lines have five syllables each; the middle line has seven.

Social Studies Help each team assign roles, such as researcher, fact checker, recorder, and presenter.

Math Answer:
$45,000,000,000/281,400,000 persons = $159.91 per person

Science Natural sources are of air pollution include forest, prairie, grass, and swamp fires; dust storms; volcanic eruptions; biological gas emissions from plants and trees; salt spray from oceans, wastes excreted by wild animals in their habitats; radon; fog and mist; and ozone.

CAREER Corner

Have students read and discuss the Career Corner information on becoming an environmental engineering technician. Ask interested students to explore the Glencoe Health Web site at **health.glencoe.com** for more information on this career.

CHECKING COMPREHENSION

- Assign and discuss the chapter review.
- Use the Chapter 29 MindJogger Videoquiz to review the chapter. ▷◁

CHAPTER 29 REVIEW ANSWERS

Exploring Health Terms

1. smog
2. Air Quality Index (AQI)
3. asbestos
4. radon
5. decibel
6. Biodegradable
7. hazardous waste
8. deforestation
9. urban sprawl
10. Wastewater
11. Conservation
12. Precycling
13. recycling

Recalling the Facts

1. Ozone, particulate matter, carbon monoxide, sulfur dioxide, and nitrogen oxides

2. Remove materials that are causing the problem, and increase exchange between indoor and outdoor air.

3. 85 decibels

4. Biodegradable materials are discarded in quantities too large to be handled by nature; many other materials are not biodegradable.

5. Nuclear waste is a collection of radioactive materials that pose serious hazards to humans and other life forms.

6. Sources: wastewater; runoff contaminated with fertilizer, sediments, oil, and other substances; illegal dumping. Possible solutions: reducing water usage; proper use and disposal

▶ **EXPLORING HEALTH TERMS** *Answer the following questions on a sheet of paper.*

Lesson 1 *Match each definition with the correct term.*

air pollution	noise pollution
asbestos	radon
decibel	smog
Air Quality Index (AQI)	

1. A yellow-brown haze that forms when sunlight reacts with air pollution.
2. An index for reporting daily air quality.
3. A fibrous mineral that has fireproof properties.
4. An odorless, radioactive gas that can cause cancer.
5. A unit used to express the relative intensity of loudness of sound.

Lesson 2 *Fill in the blanks with the correct term.*

landfill	biodegradable
deforestation	urban sprawl
hazardous waste	wastewater

6. _____ wastes can be broken down by microorganisms in the environment.
7. A substance that is explosive, corrosive, highly reactive, or toxic to humans or other life forms is known as _____ .
8. The destruction of forests is known as _____ .
9. The spreading of city development onto undeveloped land is called _____ .
10. _____ is used water that comes from homes, communities, farms, and businesses.

Lesson 3 *Replace the underlined words with the correct term.*

precycling	conservation
recycling	

11. <u>Recycling</u> is the protection and preservation of the environment by managing natural resources.
12. <u>Conservation</u> involves making decisions about products *before* you purchase them in order to reduce waste.
13. The processing of materials so that they can be used again in some form is <u>precycling</u>.

▶ **RECALLING THE FACTS** *Use complete sentences to answer the following questions.*

Lesson 1

1. Name five common air pollutants.
2. List two strategies for managing indoor air pollution.
3. Temporary hearing loss may occur when a person is exposed to noise levels at or above what decibel level?

Lesson 2

4. If many wastes are biodegradable, why are landfills necessary?
5. What is nuclear waste?
6. List three sources of water pollution and two ways of reducing this type of pollution.

Lesson 3

7. Name three ways to conserve natural resources.
8. List three precycling strategies.
9. What are three practical ways to become involved in protecting the environment?

of fertilizers, pesticides, and other chemicals; enforcing the laws and imposing fines.

7. Answers may vary, but will probably include some of the strategies listed on page 778.

8. Any three: Reduce use of disposable products, buy in bulk, choose products with less packaging, choose products designed to be recycled, reuse materials.

9. Become an informed consumer, contact organizations that promote the conservation of resources and educate people on environmental issues, take action against local polluters.

➤ **THINKING CRITICALLY**

1. **Evaluating.** Explain how keeping your automobile engine in good condition can reduce air pollution. *(LESSON 1)*

2. **Analyzing.** Before the development of modern landfills, trash was discarded in pits or open dumps. Explain how today's landfills are an improvement over this waste-disposal strategy. *(LESSON 2)*

3. **Applying.** List three grocery store items that create excessive waste. Suggest an alternative for each item. *(LESSON 3)*

➤ **HEALTH SKILLS APPLICATION**

1. **Accessing Information.** Choose one of the five air pollutants tracked by the EPA. Research whether that pollutant is present in the air in your community. Write a brief report summarizing your findings. *(LESSON 1)*

2. **Advocacy.** Polluted runoff may occur as a result of heavy rains that pick up fertilizers and pesticides from lawns. Write a public service announcement encouraging people to carefully follow application instructions for these products. *(LESSON 2)*

3. **Goal Setting.** Talk with your family about ways to conserve natural resources. Then use the goal-setting steps to choose and work toward a family conservation goal. As part of the goal-setting process, have each family member sign a pledge to do his or her part to conserve resources. *(LESSON 3)*

BEYOND *the* Classroom

Parent Involvement

Accessing Information. Find out what materials are recycled in your community. Work with a parent or other adult family member to interview managers of several recycling centers or hazardous waste collection sites. Put together an informative pamphlet that describes local waste management and recycling services. Make your pamphlet available to other families in your neighborhood.

School and Community

Volunteering Opportunities. Locate a recycling center or charitable organization in your community that collects donated items for resale. Contact the agency to find out what volunteer positions are available. Share what you have learned with your classmates.

Thinking Critically

1. An engine that is running efficiently will burn fuel cleanly and will not produce as much particulate matter.

2. Today, landfills are built and managed according to strict regulations. Landfills must be lined with special materials and wastes must be covered daily. These strategies help reduce the risk of groundwater contamination and spread of disease by animals and insects.

3. Answers will vary.

Health Skills Application

1.–3. Answers will vary.

EVALUATE

- Use the reproducible Chapter 29 Test in the TCR, or construct your own using the Testmaker software. 📁 💿

- Use Performance Assessment 29 in the TCR. 📁

ENRICHMENT

Ask students to complete Enrichment Activity 29 in the TCR. 📁

BEYOND *the* Classroom

Keep students involved in the community, and encourage parent participation by assigning the activities on this page for students to work on outside of class.

Appendix Table of Contents

	HEALTH SKILLS	NATIONAL HEALTH EDUCATION STANDARDS
	Comprehending Concepts	Students will comprehend concepts related to health promotion and disease prevention.
	Accessing Information	Students will demonstrate the ability to access valid health information and health-promoting products and services.
	Practicing Healthful Behaviors Stress Management	Students will demonstrate the ability to practice health-enhancing behaviors and reduce health risks.
	Analyzing Influences	Students will analyze the influence of culture, media, technology, and other factors on health.
	Communication Skills Conflict Resolution Refusal Skills	Students will demonstrate the ability to use interpersonal communication skills to enhance health.
	Decision Making Goal Setting	Students will demonstrate the ability to use goal-setting and decision-making skills to enhance health.
	Advocacy	Students will demonstrate the ability to advocate for personal, family, and community health.

Healthy People 2010

Healthy People 2010 is a set of 28 health objectives established for the nation to achieve over the first decade of the new century. The objectives, listed on these pages, were created after the Surgeon General's Report in 2000 identified specific National Health Promotion and Disease Prevention goals. The chapters and lessons in Glencoe Health provide strategies for addressing many of the objectives of *Healthy People 2010*.

1. Access to Quality Health Services Improve access to comprehensive, high-quality health care services.

2. Arthritis, Osteoporosis, and Chronic Back Conditions Prevent illness and disability related to arthritis and other rheumatic conditions, osteoporosis, and chronic back conditions.

3. Cancer Reduce the number of new cancer cases as well as the illness, disability, and death caused by cancer.

4. Chronic Kidney Disease Reduce new cases of chronic kidney disease and its complications, disability, death, and economic costs.

5. Diabetes Through prevention programs, reduce the disease and economic burden of diabetes, and improve the quality of life for all persons who have or are at risk for diabetes.

6. Disability and Secondary Conditions Promote the health of people with disabilities, prevent secondary conditions, and eliminate disparities between people with and without disabilities in the U.S. population.

7. Educational and Community-Based Programs Increase the quality, availability, and effectiveness of educational and community-based programs designed to prevent disease and improve health and quality of life.

8. Environmental Health Promote health for all through a healthy environment.

9. Family Planning Includes preventing unintended pregnancy.

10. Food Safety Reduce foodborne illnesses.

11. Health Communication Use communication strategically to improve health.

12. Heart Disease and Stroke Improve cardiovascular health and quality of life through the prevention, detection, and treatment of risk factors; early identification and treatment of heart attacks and strokes; and prevention of recurrent cardiovascular events.

13. HIV Prevent human immunodeficiency virus (HIV) infection and its related illness and death.

14. Immunization and Infectious Diseases Prevent disease, disability, and death from infectious diseases, including vaccine-preventable diseases.

15. Injury and Violence Prevention Reduce injuries, disabilities, and deaths due to unintentional injuries and violence.

16. Maternal, Infant, and Child Health Improve the health and well-being of women, infants, children, and families.

17. Medical Product Safety Ensure the safe and effective use of medical products.

18. Mental Health and Mental Disorders Improve mental health and ensure access to appropriate, quality mental health services.

19. Nutrition and Overweight Promote health and reduce chronic disease associated with diet and weight.

20. Occupational Safety and Health Promote the health and safety of people at work through prevention and early intervention.

21. Oral Health Prevent and control oral and craniofacial diseases, conditions, and injuries, and improve access to related services.

22. Physical Activity and Fitness Improve health, fitness, and quality of life through daily physical activity.

23. Public Health Infrastructure Ensure that Federal, Tribal, State, and local health agencies have the infrastructure to provide essential public health services effectively.

24. Respiratory Diseases Promote respiratory health through better prevention, detection, treatment, and education efforts.

25. Sexually Transmitted Diseases Promote responsible sexual behaviors, strengthen community capacity, and increase access to quality services to prevent sexually transmitted diseases (STDs) and their complications.

26. Substance Abuse Reduce substance abuse to protect the health, safety, and quality of life for all, especially children.

27. Tobacco Reduce illness, disability, and death related to tobacco use and exposure to secondhand smoke.

28. Vision and Hearing Improve the visual and hearing health of the Nation through prevention, early detection, treatment, and rehabilitation.

40 Developmental Assets

Search Institute has identified the following building blocks of healthy development that help young people grow up healthy, caring, and responsible.

External Assets

Support
1. **Family support**—Family life provides high levels of love and support.
2. **Positive Family Communication**—Young person and her or his parent(s) communicate positively, and young person is willing to seek advice and counsel from parents.
3. **Other Adult Relationships**—Young person receives support from three or more nonparent adults.
4. **Caring Neighborhood**—Young person experiences caring neighbors.
5. **Caring School Climate**—School provides a caring, encouraging environment.
6. **Parent Involvement in Schooling**—Parent(s) are actively involved in helping young person succeed in school.

Empowerment
7. **Community Values Youth**—Young person perceives that adults in the community value youth.
8. **Youth as Resources**—Young people are given useful roles in the community.
9. **Service to Others**—Young person serves in the community one hour or more per week.
10. **Safety**—Young person feels safe at home, school, and in the neighborhood.

Boundaries and Expectations
11. **Family Boundaries**—Family has clear rules and consequences and monitors the young person's whereabouts.
12. **School Boundaries**—School provides clear rules and consequences.
13. **Neighborhood Boundaries**—Neighbors take responsibility for monitoring young people's behavior.
14. **Adult Role Models**—Parent(s) and other adults model positive, responsible behavior.
15. **Positive Peer Influence**—Young person's best friends model responsible behavior.
16. **High Expectations**—Both parent(s) and teachers encourage the young person to do well.

Constructive Use of Time
17. **Creative Activities**—Young person spends three or more hours per week in lessons or practice in music, theater, or other arts.
18. **Youth Programs**—Young person spends three or more hours per week in sports, clubs, or organizations at school and/or in the community.
19. **Religious Community**—Young person spends one or more hours per week in activities in a religious institution.
20. **Time at Home**—Young person is out with friends "with nothing special to do" two or fewer nights per week.

Internal Assets

Commitment to Learning
21. **Achievement Motivation**—Young person is motivated to do well in school.
22. **School Engagement**—Young person is actively engaged in learning.
23. **Homework**—Young person reports doing at least one hour of homework every school day.
24. **Bonding to School**—Young person cares about her or his school.
25. **Reading for Pleasure**—Young person reads for pleasure three or more hours per week.

Positive Values
26. **Caring**—Young person places high value on helping other people.
27. **Equality and Social Justice**—Young person places high value on promoting equality and reducing hunger and poverty.
28. **Integrity**—Young person acts on convictions and stands up for her or his beliefs.
29. **Honesty**—Young person "tells the truth even when it is not easy."
30. **Responsibility**—Young person accepts and takes personal responsibility.
31. **Restraint**—Young person believes it is important not to be sexually active or to use alcohol or other drugs.

Social Competencies
32. **Planning and Decision Making**—Young person knows how to plan ahead and make choices.
33. **Interpersonal Competence**—Young person has empathy, sensitivity, and friendship skills.
34. **Cultural Competence**—Young person has knowledge of and comfort with people of different cultural/racial/ethnic backgrounds.
35. **Resistance Skills**—Young person can resist negative peer pressure and dangerous situations.
36. **Peaceful Conflict Resolution**—Young person seeks to resolve conflict nonviolently.

Positive Identity
37. **Personal Power**—Young person feels he or she has control over the "things that happen to me."
38. **Self-Esteem**—Young person reports having a high self-esteem.
39. **Sense of Purpose**—Young person reports that "my life has a purpose."
40. **Positive View of Personal Future**—Young person is optimistic about her or his personal future.

PHYSICAL ACTIVITY AND FITNESS GUIDELINES

The Surgeon General's Report on Physical Activity and Health, along with the President's Council on Physical Fitness and Sports, identified fitness as a major public health concern. The Physical Fitness Objectives from *Healthy People 2010* for children and adolescents appear below.

Physical Activity in Children and Adolescents

- Increase the proportion of adolescents who engage in moderate physical activity for at least 30 minutes on 5 or more of the previous 7 days.

- Increase the proportion of adolescents who engage in vigorous physical activity that promotes cardiorespiratory fitness 3 or more days per week for 20 or more minutes per occasion.

- Increase the proportion of the nation's public and private schools that require daily physical education for all students.

- Increase the proportion of adolescents who participate in daily school physical education.

- Increase the proportion of adolescents who spend at least 50 percent of school physical education class time being physically active.

- Increase the proportion of adolescents who view television 2 or fewer hours on a school day.

PHYSICAL FITNESS GUIDELINES

Regular physical activity performed on a daily basis reduces the risk of developing illness or disease. Moderate physical activity can be achieved in a variety of ways, and the Centers for Disease Control and Prevention have developed this list of examples showing moderate amounts of activity that can contribute to an individual's health.

Physical Activities Arranged by Energy Level and Time

- Washing and waxing a car for 45-60 minutes
- Washing windows or floors for 45-60 minutes
- Playing volleyball for 45 minutes
- Playing touch football for 30-45 minutes
- Gardening for 30-45 minutes
- Wheeling self in wheelchair for 30-40 minutes
- Walking 1 $\frac{3}{4}$ miles in 35 minutes (20 min/mile)
- Basketball (shooting baskets) for 30 minutes
- Bicycling 5 miles in 30 minutes
- Dancing fast (social) for 30 minutes
- Pushing a stroller 1 $\frac{1}{2}$ miles in 30 minutes

- Raking leaves for 30 minutes
- Walking 2 miles in 30 minutes (15 min/mile)
- Water aerobics for 30 minutes
- Swimming laps for 20 minutes
- Wheelchair basketball for 20 minutes
- Basketball (playing a game) for 15-20 minutes
- Bicycling 4 miles in 15 minutes
- Jumping rope for 15 minutes
- Running 1 $\frac{1}{2}$ miles in 15 minutes (10 min/mile)
- Shoveling snow for 15 minutes
- Stair walking for 15 minutes

Source: CDC, Physical Activity and Health, A Report of the Surgeon General

A

Absorption The passage of digested food from the digestive tract into the cardiovascular system (Ch. 17, 442)

Abstinence A deliberate decision to avoid harmful behaviors, including sexual activity before marriage and the use of tobacco, alcohol, and other drugs (Ch. 1, 20; Ch. 12, 318; Ch. 25, 649)

Abuse Physical, mental/emotional, or sexual mistreatment of one person by another (Ch. 13, 348)

Accident chain A sequence of events that leads to an unintentional injury (Ch. 27, 707)

Acquired immune deficiency syndrome (AIDS) A disease in which the immune system of the patient is weakened (Ch. 25, 658)

Action plan A multistep strategy to identify and achieve your goals (Ch. 2, 36)

Active immunity Immunity your body develops to protect you from disease (Ch. 24, 631)

Active listening Paying close attention to what someone is saying and communicating (Ch. 10, 256)

Addiction A physiological or psychological dependence on a drug (Ch. 23, 595)

Addictive drug A substance that causes physiological or psychological dependence (Ch. 21, 540)

Additive interaction Medicines working together in a positive way (Ch. 23, 589)

Adolescence The period from childhood to adulthood (Ch. 20, 514)

Adoption The legal process of taking a child of other parents as one's own. (Ch. 20, 527)

Adrenal glands Glands that help the body recover from stress and respond to emergencies (Ch. 18, 466)

Advertising A written or spoken media message designed to interest consumers in purchasing a product or service (Ch. 3, 49)

Advocacy Taking action to influence others to address a health-related concern or to support a health-related belief (Ch. 2, 32)

Aerobic exercise Any activity that uses large muscle groups, is rhythmic in nature, and can be maintained continuously for at least 10 minutes three times a day or for 20 to 30 minutes at one time (Ch. 4, 83)

Affection A feeling of fondness for someone (Ch. 12, 313)

Affirmation Positive feedback that helps others feel appreciated and supported (Ch. 11, 278)

Aggressive Overly forceful, pushy, hostile, or otherwise attacking in their approach (Ch. 12, 312)

Air pollution The contamination of the earth's atmosphere by substances that pose a health threat to living things (Ch. 29, 766)

Air Quality Index (AQI) An index for reporting daily air quality (Ch. 29, 768)

Alcohol abuse The excessive use of alcohol (Ch. 22, 565)

Alcohol poisoning A severe and potentially fatal physical reaction to an alcohol overdose (Ch. 22, 572)

Alcoholic An addict who is dependent on alcohol (Ch. 22, 576)

Alcoholism A disease in which a person has a physical or psychological dependence on drinks that contain alcohol (Ch. 22, 576)

Alienation Feeling isolated and separated from everyone else (Ch. 9, 230)

Allergy A specific reaction of the immune system to a foreign and frequently harmless substance (Ch. 26, 688)

Americans with Disabilities Act A law prohibiting discrimination against people with physical or mental disabilities in the workplace, transportation, public accommodations, and telecommunications (Ch. 26, 699)

Amniocentesis A procedure in which a syringe is inserted through a pregnant female's abdominal wall into the amniotic fluid surrounding the developing fetus (Ch. 19, 501)

Amniotic sac A thin, fluid-filled membrane that surrounds and protects the developing embryo (Ch. 19, 487)

Anabolic-androgenic steroids Synthetic substances similar to the male hormone testosterone (Ch. 4, 94; Ch. 23, 601)

Anaerobic exercise Intense short bursts of activity in which the muscles work so hard that they produce energy without using oxygen (Ch. 4, 84)

Analgesics Pain relievers (Ch. 23, 588)

Anemia A condition in which the ability of the blood to carry oxygen is reduced (Ch. 16, 426)

Angina pectoris Chest pain that results when the heart doesn't get enough oxygen (Ch. 26, 676)

Anorexia nervosa A disorder in which the irrational fear of becoming obese results in severe weight loss from self-imposed starvation (Ch. 6, 154)

Antagonistic interaction Occurs when the effect of one medicine is canceled or reduced when taken with another medicine (Ch. 23, 589)

Antibody A protein that acts against a specific antigen (Ch. 24, 631)

Antigen A substance that is capable of triggering an immune response (Ch. 24, 630)

Anxiety The condition of feeling uneasy or worried about what may happen (Ch. 8, 210)

Anxiety disorder A condition in which real or imagined fears are difficult to control (Ch. 9, 225)

Appendicitis Inflammation of the appendix (Ch. 17, 450)

Appendicular skeleton The 126 bones of the upper and lower limbs, shoulders, and hips (Ch. 15, 387)

Appetite A desire, rather than a need, to eat (Ch. 5, 111)

Arrhythmia Irregular heartbeats (Ch. 26, 676)

Arteries Blood vessels that carry blood away from the heart (Ch. 16, 419)

Arthritis A group of more than 100 different diseases that cause pain and loss of movement in the joints (Ch. 26, 693)

Asbestos A fibrous mineral that has fireproof properties, once widely used as an insulator. (Ch. 29, 769)

Assailant A person who commits a violent act against another (Ch. 13, 341)

Assault An unlawful attack on a person with the intent to harm or kill (Ch. 13, 344)

Assertive Standing up for your rights and beliefs in firm but positive ways (Ch. 12, 310; Ch. 13, 332)

Asthma An inflammatory condition in which the trachea, bronchi, and bronchioles become narrowed, causing difficulty in breathing (Ch. 16, 434; Ch. 26, 690)

Asymptomatic stage A period of time during which a person infected with HIV has no symptoms (Ch. 25, 662)

Atherosclerosis The process in which plaques accumulate on artery walls (Ch. 26, 675)

Auditory ossicles Three small bones linked together that connect the eardrum to the inner ear (Ch. 14, 377)

Autoimmune disease A condition in which the immune system mistakenly attacks itself, targeting the cells, tissues, and organs of a person's own body (Ch. 26, 691)

Autonomy The confidence that a person can control his or her own body, impulses, and environment (Ch. 19, 505)

Axial skeleton The 80 bones of the skull, spine, ribs, vertebrae, and sternum, or breastbone (Ch. 15, 387)

B

Bacteria Single-celled microorganisms (Ch. 24, 623)

Behavior therapy A treatment process that focuses on changing unwanted behaviors through rewards and reinforcements (Ch. 9, 237)

Benign Noncancerous (Ch. 26, 681)

Bile A yellow-green, bitter fluid important in the breakdown and absorption of fats (Ch. 17, 445)

Binge drinking Drinking five or more alcoholic drinks at one sitting (Ch. 22, 572)

Binge eating disorder A disorder characterized by compulsive overeating (Ch. 6, 155)

Biodegradable Able to be broken down by microorganisms in the environment (Ch. 29, 772)

Biomedical therapy The use of certain medications to treat or reduce the symptoms of a mental disorder (Ch. 9, 237)

Biopsy The removal of a small piece of tissue for examination (Ch. 26, 686)

Birthing center A facility in which females with low-risk pregnancies can deliver their babies in a homelike setting (Ch. 19, 492)

Bladder A hollow muscular organ that acts as a reservoir for urine (Ch. 17, 455)

Blizzard A snowstorm with winds of at least 35 miles per hour (Ch. 27, 728)

Blood alcohol concentration (BAC) The amount of alcohol in a person's blood expressed as a percentage (Ch. 22, 570)

Blood pressure A measure of the amount of force that the blood places on the walls of blood vessels, particularly large arteries, as it is pumped through the body (Ch. 16, 424)

Body composition The ratio of body fat to lean body tissue, including muscle, bone, water, and connective tissue such as ligaments, cartilage, and tendons (Ch. 4, 81)

Body image The way you see your body (Ch. 6, 144)

Body language Nonverbal communication through gestures, facial expressions, behaviors, and posture (Ch. 10, 258; Ch. 13, 332)

Body mass index (BMI) A ratio that allows you to assess your body size in relation to your height and weight (Ch. 6, 145)

Brain stem A three-inch-long stalk of nerve cells and fibers that connects the spinal cord to the rest of the brain (Ch. 15, 403)

Bronchi The airways that connect the trachea and the lungs (Ch. 16, 431)

Bronchitis An inflammation of the bronchi caused by infection or exposure to irritants such as tobacco smoke or air pollution (Ch. 16, 433)

Bulimia nervosa A disorder in which some form of purging or clearing of the digestive tract follows cycles of overeating (Ch. 6, 154)

Bullying The act of seeking power or attention through the psychological, emotional, or physical abuse of another person (Ch. 13, 336)

C

Calories Units of heat that measure the energy used by the body and the energy that foods supply to the body (Ch. 5, 110)

Cancer Uncontrollable growth of abnormal cells (Ch. 26, 681)

Capillaries Small vessels that carry blood between arterioles and small vessels called venules (Ch. 16, 419)

Carbohydrates The starches and sugars present in foods (Ch. 5, 114)

Carbon monoxide A colorless, odorless, and poisonous gas (Ch. 21, 541)

Carcinogen A cancer-causing substance (Ch. 21, 541; Ch. 26, 682)

Cardiac muscle A type of striated muscle that forms the wall of the heart (Ch. 15, 395)

Cardiopulmonary resuscitation (CPR) A life-saving first-aid procedure that combines rescue breaths with chest compressions, supplying oxygen to the body until normal body functions can resume (Ch. 28, 743)

Cardiorespiratory endurance The ability of the heart, lungs, and blood vessels to use and send fuel and oxygen to the body's tissues during long periods of moderate-to-vigorous activity (Ch. 4, 80)

Cardiovascular disease (CVD) A disease that affects the heart or blood vessels (Ch. 26, 674)

Cartilage A strong, flexible connective tissue (Ch. 15, 387)

Cerebellum The second largest part of the brain (Ch. 15, 403)

Cerebral palsy A group of nonprogressive neurological disorders that are the result of damage to the brain before, during, or just after birth or in early childhood (Ch. 15, 409)

Cerebrum The largest and most complex part of the brain (Ch. 15, 402)

Cervix The opening to the uterus (Ch. 18, 476)

Chain of survival A sequence of actions that maximize the victim's chances of survival (Ch. 28, 742)

Character Those distinctive qualities that describe how a person thinks, feels, and behaves (Ch. 2, 37)

Child abuse Domestic abuse directed at a child (Ch. 11, 288)

Chlamydia A bacterial infection that affects the reproductive organs of both males and females (Ch. 25, 654)

Chorionic villi sampling (CVS) A procedure in which a small piece of membrane is removed from the chorion, a layer of tissue that develops into the placenta (Ch. 19, 501)

Choroid A thin structure that lines the inside of the sclera (Ch. 14, 372)

Chromosomes Threadlike structures found within the nucleus of a cell that carry the codes for inherited traits (Ch. 19, 499)

Chronic stress Stress associated with long-term problems that are beyond a person's control (Ch. 8, 204)

Chyme A creamy, fluid mixture of food and gastric juices (Ch. 17, 444)

Citizenship The way you conduct yourself as a member of the community (Ch. 10, 249)

Clique A small circle of friends, usually with similar backgrounds or tastes, who exclude people viewed as outsiders (Ch. 12, 304)

Club drugs Drugs associated with concerts, dance clubs, and all-night parties called raves. (Ch. 23, 606)

Cluster suicides A series of suicides occurring within a short period of time and involving several people in the same school or community (Ch. 9, 233)

Cognition The ability to reason and think out abstract solutions (Ch. 20, 516)

Cognitive therapy A treatment method designed to identify and correct distorted thinking patterns that can lead to feelings and behaviors that may be troublesome, self-defeating, or self-destructive (Ch. 9, 237)

Commitment A promise or a pledge (Ch. 20, 524)

Communicable disease A disease that is spread from one living thing to another or through the environment (Ch. 24, 622)

Communication The ways in which you send messages to and receive messages from others (Ch. 10, 250)

Comparison shopping A method of judging the benefits of different products by comparing several factors, such as quality, features, and cost (Ch. 3, 50)

Compromise A problem-solving method that involves each participant's giving up something to reach a solution that satisfies everyone (Ch. 10, 251)

Concussion A jarring injury to the brain that affects normal brain function (Ch. 28, 752)

Conduct disorder A pattern of behavior in which the rights of others or basic social rules are violated (Ch. 9, 228)

Confidentiality Respecting the privacy of another and keeping details secret (Ch. 10, 267)

Conflict Any disagreement, struggle, or fight (Ch. 10, 262)

Conflict resolution The process of solving a disagreement through cooperation and problem solving (Ch. 2, 30; Ch. 10, 264)

Congenital A condition that is present at birth (Ch. 16, 425)

Conservation The protection and preservation of the environment by managing natural resources to prevent abuse, destruction, and neglect (Ch. 29, 777)

Constructive criticism Nonhostile comments that point out problems and encourage improvement (Ch. 7, 183; Ch. 10, 260)

Consumer advocate People or groups whose sole purpose is to take on regional, national, and even international consumer issues (Ch. 3, 63)

Cool-down An activity that prepares the muscles to return to a resting state (Ch. 4, 92)

Cooperation Working together for the good of all (Ch. 10, 250)

Coping Dealing successfully with difficult changes in your life (Ch. 9, 239)

Cornea A transparent tissue that bends and focuses light before it enters the lens (Ch. 14, 372)

Crisis center A facility that handles emergencies and provides referrals to an individual needing help (Ch. 11, 291)

Cross-contamination The spreading of bacteria or other pathogens from one food to another (Ch. 5, 136)

Culture The collective beliefs, customs, and behaviors of a group (Ch. 1, 14)

Cumulative risks Related risks that increase in effect with each added risk (Ch. 1, 19)

Curfew A set time at which you must be home at night (Ch. 12, 317)

Custody A legal decision about who has the right to make decisions affecting the children in a family and who has the responsibility of physically caring for them (Ch. 11, 281)

Cycle of violence Pattern of repeating violent or abusive behaviors from one generation to the next (Ch. 11, 289)

Cystitis An inflammation of the urinary bladder (Ch. 17, 456)

─────────── **D** ───────────

Dandruff A condition that can occur if the scalp becomes too dry and dead skin cells are shed as sticky, white flakes (Ch. 14, 365)

Date rape When one person in a dating relationship forces the other person to participate in sexual intercourse (Ch. 13, 350)

Decibel A unit used to express the relative intensity of loudness of sound (Ch. 29, 770)

Decision-making skills Steps that enable you to make a healthful decision (Ch. 2, 33)

Defense mechanisms Mental processes that protect individuals from strong or stressful emotions and situations (Ch. 7, 189)

Defensive driver A driver who is aware of potential hazards and reacts to avoid them (Ch. 27, 722)

Defibrillator A device that delivers an electric shock to the heart to restore its normal rhythm (Ch. 28, 742)

Deforestation Destruction of forests (Ch. 29, 774)

Depressants Drugs that tend to slow the central nervous system (Ch. 22, 563; Ch. 23, 606)

Depression A prolonged feeling of helplessness, hopelessness, and sadness (Ch. 8, 211)

Dermis The thicker layer of the skin beneath the epidermis that is made up of connective tissue and contains blood vessels and nerves (Ch. 14, 360)

Designer drugs Synthetic substances meant to imitate the effects of hallucinogens and other dangerous drugs (Ch. 23, 609)

Detoxification A process in which the body adjusts to functioning without alcohol (Ch. 22, 578)

Developmental assets Building blocks of development that help young people grow up as healthy, caring, and responsible individuals (Ch. 7, 179)

Developmental task An event that needs to happen in order for a person to continue growing toward becoming a healthy, mature adult (Ch. 19, 504)

Diabetes A chronic disease that affects the way body cells convert food into energy (Ch. 26, 691)

Diaphragm The muscle that separates the chest from the abdominal cavity (Ch. 16, 429)

Dietary Guidelines for Americans A set of recommendations for healthful eating and active living (Ch. 5, 122)

Dietary supplement Nonfood form of one or more nutrients (Ch. 6, 161)

Digestion The mechanical and chemical breakdown of foods for use by the body's cells (Ch. 17, 442)

Disability Any physical or mental impairment that limits normal activities, including seeing, hearing, walking, or speaking (Ch. 26, 695)

Divorce A legal end to a marriage contract (Ch. 11, 281)

DNA (deoxyribonucleic acid) The chemical unit that makes up chromosomes (Ch. 19, 499)

Domestic violence Any act of violence involving family members (Ch. 11, 286)

Drug watches Organized community efforts by neighborhood residents to patrol, monitor, report, and otherwise try to stop drug deals and drug abuse (Ch. 23, 612)

Drug-free school zone An area within 1,000 feet of a school and designated by signs, within which people caught selling drugs receive especially severe penalties (Ch. 23, 612)

Drugs Substances other than food that change the structure or function of the body or mind (Ch. 23, 586)

─────────── **E** ───────────

Earthquake A violent shaking movement of the earth's surface (Ch. 27, 729)

Eating disorder An extreme, harmful eating behavior that can cause serious illness or even death (Ch. 6, 153)

EIA A test that screens for the presence of HIV antibodies in the blood (Ch. 25, p. 663)

Electrolytes Minerals that help maintain the body's fluid balance (Ch. 6, 158)

Elimination The expulsion of undigested food or body wastes (Ch. 17, 442)

Embryo The developing child from the time of implantation until about the eighth week of development (Ch. 19, 486)

Emergency survival kit A group of items that can be used for a short time until an emergency situation has stabilized (Ch. 27, 726)

Emerging infection Communicable disease whose incidence in humans has increased within the past two decades or threatens to increase in the near future (Ch. 24, 641)

Emotional abuse A pattern of behavior that attacks the emotional development and sense of worth of an individual (Ch. 11, 287)

Emotional intimacy Ability to experience a caring, loving relationship with another person with whom you can share your innermost feelings (Ch. 20, 523)

Emotional maturity State at which the mental and emotional capabilities of an individual are fully developed (Ch. 20, 520)

Emotions Signals that tell your mind and body how to react (Ch. 7, 184)

Empathy The ability to imagine and understand how someone else feels (Ch. 7, 186)

Emphysema A disease that progressively destroys the walls of the alveoli (Ch. 16, 435)

Empty-nest syndrome Feelings of sadness or loneliness that accompany children's leaving home and entering adulthood (Ch. 20, 531)

Endocrine glands Ductless—or tubeless—organs or group of cells that secrete hormones directly into the bloodstream (Ch. 18, 464)

Environment The sum of your surroundings (Ch.1, 13)

Environmental tobacco smoke (ETS) Air that has been contaminated by tobacco smoke (Ch. 21, 551)

Epidemic Occurrences of diseases in which many people in the same place at the same time are affected (Ch. 25, 648)

Epidemiology The scientific study of patterns of disease in a population (Ch. 3, 65)

Epidermis The outer, thinner layer of the skin that is composed of living and dead cells (Ch. 14, 360)

Epilepsy A disorder of the nervous system that is characterized by recurrent seizures—sudden episodes of uncontrolled electrical activity in the brain (Ch. 15, 409)

Ethanol The type of alcohol in alcoholic beverages (Ch. 22, 562)

Euphoria A feeling of intense well-being or elation (Ch. 23, 605)

Exercise Purposeful physical activity that is planned, structured, and repetitive and that improves or maintains personal fitness (Ch. 4, 81)

Extended family Your immediate family and other relatives such as grandparents, aunts, uncles, and cousins (Ch. 11, 277)

Extensor The muscle that opens a joint (Ch. 15, 395)

External auditory canal A passageway about one inch long that leads to the remaining portion of the outer ear, the eardrum (Ch. 14, 376)

F

F.I.T.T. Frequency, intensity, time/duration, and type of activity (Ch. 4, 91)

Fad diets Weight-loss plans that are popular for only a short time (Ch. 6, 151)

Fallopian tubes A pair of tubes with fingerlike projections that draw in the ovum (Ch. 18, 475)

Family counseling Therapy to restore healthy relationships in a family (Ch. 11, 294)

Family The basic unit of society (Ch. 11, 274)

Fermentation The chemical action of yeast on sugars (Ch. 22, 563)

Fertilization Union of a male sperm cell and a female egg cell (Ch. 19, 486)

Fetal alcohol syndrome (FAS) A group of alcohol-related birth defects that includes both physical and mental problems (Ch. 19, 494; Ch. 22, 576)

Fetus Developing embryo in the uterus (Ch. 19, 486)

Fiber An indigestible complex carbohydrate (Ch. 5, 115)

Fire extinguisher A portable device that puts out small fires by ejecting fire-extinguishing chemicals (Ch. 27, 708)

First aid The immediate, temporary care given to an ill or injured person until professional medical care can be provided (Ch. 28, 736)

Flash flood A flood with great volume and short duration that is usually caused by heavy rainfall (Ch. 27, 728)

Flexibility The ability to move a body part through a full range of motion (Ch. 4, 81)

Flexor The muscle that closes a joint (Ch. 15, 395)

Food additives Substances intentionally added to food to produce a desired effect (Ch. 5, 131)

Food allergy A condition in which the body's immune system reacts to substances in some foods (Ch. 5, 133)

Food Guide Pyramid A guide for making healthful daily food choices (Ch. 5, 123)

Food intolerance A negative reaction to a food or part of food caused by a metabolic problem, such as the inability to digest parts of certain foods or food components (Ch. 5, 134)

Foodborne illness Food poisoning (Ch. 5, 134)

Foster care A temporary arrangement in which a child is placed under the guidance and supervision of a family or an adult who is not related to the child by birth (Ch. 11, 292)

Fracture A break in the bone (Ch. 28, 750)

Fraud Deliberate deceit or trickery (Ch. 3, 61)

Friendship A significant relationship between two people that is based on caring, trust, and consideration (Ch. 10, 249; Ch. 12, 303)

Frostbite A condition that results when body tissues become frozen (Ch. 4, 100)

G

Gametes Reproductive cells (Ch. 20, 515)

Gang A group of people who associate with one another to take part in criminal activity (Ch. 13, 337)

Gastric juices Secretions from the stomach lining that contain hydrochloric acid and pepsin, an enzyme that digests protein (Ch. 17, 444)

Gene therapy The process of inserting normal genes into human cells to correct genetic disorders (Ch. 19, 503)

Genes The basic units of heredity (Ch. 19, 499)

Genetic disorder A disorder caused partly or completely by a defect in genes (Ch. 19, 500)

Genital herpes An STD caused by the herpes simplex virus (HSV) (Ch. 25, 654)

Goal Something you aim for that takes planning and work (Ch. 2, 34)

Gonads The ovaries and testes (Ch. 18, 466)

Gonorrhea A bacterial STD that usually affects mucous membranes (Ch. 25, 655)

Graduated driver's license A licensing program that gradually increases a new driver's driving privileges over time as experience and skill are gained (Ch. 27, 720)

Grief The sorrow caused by the loss of a loved one (Ch. 11, 282)

Grief response An individual's total response to a major loss (Ch. 9, 239)

Group therapy Treating a group of people who have similar problems and who meet regularly with a trained counselor (Ch. 9, 237)

H

Hair follicle A structure that surrounds the root of a hair (Ch. 14, 365)

Hallucinogens Drugs that alter moods, thoughts, and sense perceptions including vision, hearing, smell, and touch (Ch. 23, 609)

Harassment Persistently annoying others (Ch. 12, 308)

Hazardous waste A substance that is explosive, corrosive, highly reactive, or toxic to humans or other life forms (Ch. 29, 773)

Health The combination of physical, mental/emotional, and social well being (Ch. 1, 4)

Health care system All the medical care available to a nation's people, the way they receive care, and the method of payment (Ch. 3, 54)

Health consumer Anyone who purchases or uses health products or services (Ch. 3, 48)

Health education The providing of accurate health information to help people make healthy choices (Ch. 1, 7)

Health fraud Sale of worthless products or services claimed to prevent diseases or cure other health problems (Ch. 3, 61)

Health insurance A plan in which private companies or government programs pay for part or all of a person's medical costs (Ch. 3, 57)

Health literacy A person's capacity to learn about and understand basic health information and services and use these resources to promote his or her health and wellness (Ch. 1, 8)

Health screening A search or check for diseases or disorders that an individual would otherwise not have knowledge of or seek help for (Ch. 4, 96)

Health skills Specific tools and strategies that help you maintain, protect, and improve all aspects of your health (Ch. 2, 28)

Healthy People 2010 A nationwide health promotion and disease prevention plan designed to serve as a guide for improving the health of all people in the United States (Ch. 1, 7)

Heartburn A burning sensation in the center of the chest that may rise from the bottom, or tip, of the breastbone up to the throat (Ch. 17, 448)

Heat cramps Muscle spasms that result from a loss of large amounts of salt and water through perspiration (Ch. 4, 99)

Heat exhaustion An overheating of the body that results in cold, clammy skin and symptoms of shock (Ch. 27, 715)

Heatstroke A condition in which the body loses the ability to rid itself of excessive heat through perspiration (Ch. 4, 99)

Hemodialysis A technique in which an artificial kidney machine removes waste products from the blood (Ch. 17, 457)

Hemoglobin The oxygen-carrying protein in blood (Ch. 16, 418)

Herbal supplement Chemical substance from plants that may be sold as a dietary supplement (Ch. 6, 161)

Heredity All the traits that are biologically passed from parents to their children (Ch. 1, 12; Ch. 19, 498)

Hernia When an organ or tissue protrudes through an area of weak muscle (Ch. 15, 398)

Hiatal hernia A condition in which part of the stomach pushes through an opening in the diaphragm (Ch. 17, 448)

Hierarchy of needs A ranked list of those needs essential to human growth and development, presented in ascending order starting with basic needs and building toward the need for reaching your highest potential (Ch. 7, 172)

Histamines Chemicals that can stimulate mucus and fluid production in an area (Ch. 26, 689)

Hodgkin's disease A type of cancer that affects the lymph tissue (Ch. 16, 427)

Homicide The willful killing of one human being by another (Ch. 13, 344)

Hormones Chemical substances that are produced in glands and help regulate many of your body's functions (Ch. 7, 185; Ch. 18, 464; Ch. 20, 514)

Hostility The intentional use of unfriendly or offensive behavior (Ch. 7, 187)

Human immunodeficiency virus (HIV) A virus that attacks the immune system (Ch. 25, 658)

Human papillomavirus (HPV) A virus that can cause genital warts or asymptomatic infection (Ch. 25, 652)

Hunger A natural physical drive that protects you from starvation (Ch. 5, 111)

Hurricane A powerful storm that originates at sea, characterized by winds of at least 74 miles per hour, heavy rains, flooding, and sometimes tornadoes (Ch. 27, 727)

Hydration Taking in fluids so that the body functions properly (Ch. 4, 94)

Hypertension High blood pressure (Ch. 26, 675)

Hypothermia A condition in which body temperature becomes dangerously low (Ch. 4, 101; Ch. 27, 715)

I

"I" message A statement in which a person describes how he or she feels by using the pronoun "I" (Ch.10, 256)

Illegal drugs Chemical substances that people of any age may not lawfully manufacture, possess, buy, or sell (Ch. 23, 592)

Illicit drug use The use or sale of any substance that is illegal or otherwise not permitted (Ch. 23, 592)

Immune system A network of cells, tissues, organs, and chemicals that fights pathogens (Ch. 24, 627)

Immunity The state of being protected against a particular disease (Ch. 24, 630)

Implantation The attachment of the zygote to the uterine wall (Ch. 19, 486)

Indigestion A feeling of discomfort in the upper abdomen (Ch. 17, 448)

Infatuation Exaggerated feelings of passion for another person (Ch. 12, 313)

Infection A condition that occurs when pathogens enter the body, multiply, and damage body cells (Ch. 24, 622)

Infertility The inability to conceive a child (Ch. 18, 478)

Inflammatory response A reaction to tissue damage caused by injury or infection (Ch. 24, 628)

Inhalants Substances whose fumes are sniffed or inhaled to achieve a mind-altering effect (Ch. 23, 600)

Integrity A firm adherence to a moral code (Ch. 20, 532)

Interpersonal communication The exchange of thoughts, feelings, and beliefs between two or more people (Ch. 2, 29)

Interpersonal conflict Disagreement between groups of any size, from two people to entire nations (Ch. 10, 262)

Intoxication The state in which the body is poisoned by alcohol or another substance and the person's physical and mental control is significantly reduced (Ch. 22, 563)

J

Jaundice Yellowing of the skin and eyes (Ch. 24, 637)

L

Labor The final stage of pregnancy in which the uterus contracts and pushes the baby out of the mother's body (Ch. 19, 490)

Labyrinth The inner ear (Ch. 14, 377)

Lacrimal gland The gland that secretes tears into ducts that empty into the eye (Ch. 14, 371)

Landfill An area that has been safeguarded to prevent disposed wastes from contaminating groundwater (Ch. 29, 772)

Larynx Voice box (Ch. 16, 431)

Leukemia A form of cancer in which any one of the different types of white blood cells is produced excessively and abnormally (Ch. 16, 426)

Leukoplakia Thickened, white, leathery-looking spots on the inside of the mouth that can develop into oral cancer (Ch. 21, 542)

Ligament A band of fibrous, slightly elastic connective tissue that attaches bone to bone (Ch. 15, 389)

Lipid A fatty substance that does not dissolve in water (Ch. 5, 117)

Long-term goal A goal that you plan to reach over an extended period of time (Ch. 2, 35)

Lymph The clear fluid that fills the spaces around body cells (Ch. 16, 421)

Lymphocytes Specialized white blood cells that provide the body with immunity (Ch. 16, 421; Ch. 24, 630)

M

Mainstream smoke The smoke exhaled from the lungs of a smoker (Ch. 21, 551)

Malignant Cancerous (Ch. 26, 681)

Malpractice Failure by a health professional to meet accepted standards (Ch. 3, 61)

Manipulation An indirect, dishonest way to control or influence others (Ch. 12, 308)

Marijuana Plant whose leaves, buds, and flowers are usually smoked for their intoxicating effects (Ch. 23, 598)

Marital adjustment How well a person adjusts to marriage and to his or her spouse (Ch. 20, 525)

Mastication The process of chewing (Ch. 17, 443)

Media The various methods of communicating information (Ch. 1, 15; Ch. 3, 49)

Mediation A process in which specially trained people help others resolve their conflicts peacefully (Ch. 10, 267)

Mediator A person who helps others resolve issues to the satisfaction of both parties (Ch. 11, 294)

Medical history Complete and comprehensive information about your immunizations and any health problems you have had to date (Ch. 3, 58)

Medicines Drugs that are used to treat or prevent diseases or other conditions (Ch. 23, 586)

Megadose Very large amount of a dietary supplement (Ch. 6, 161)

Melanin A pigment that gives the skin, hair, and iris of the eyes their color (Ch. 14, 361)

Melanoma The most serious form of skin cancer (Ch. 14, 364)

Menopause The end of the reproductive years for a female (Ch. 18, 476)

Menstruation Shedding of the uterine lining (Ch. 18, 476)

Mental disorder An illness of the mind that can affect the thoughts, feelings, and behaviors of a person, preventing him or her from leading a happy, healthful, and productive life (Ch. 9, 224)

Mental retardation The below-average intellectual ability present from birth or early childhood and associated with difficulties in learning and social adaptation (Ch. 26, 697)

Mental/emotional health The ability to accept yourself and others, adapt to and manage emotions, and deal with the demands and challenges you meet in life (Ch. 7, 170)

Metabolism The process by which the body breaks down substances and gets energy from food (Ch. 4, 78; Ch. 22, 569)

Metastasis Spread of cancer from the point where it originated to other parts of the body (Ch. 26, 681)

Minerals Substances that the body cannot manufacture but that are needed for forming healthy bones and teeth and for regulating many vital body processes (Ch. 5, 120)

Miscarriage The spontaneous expulsion of a fetus that occurs before the twentieth week of a pregnancy (Ch. 19, 496)

Modeling Observing and learning from the behaviors of those around you (Ch. 7, 175)

Mood disorder An illness, often with an organic cause, that involves mood extremes that interfere with everyday living (Ch. 9, 226)

Mourning The act of showing sorrow or grief (Ch. 9, 240)

Muscle cramp A spasm or sudden tightening of a muscle (Ch. 4, 102)

Muscle tone The natural tension in the fibers of a muscle (Ch. 15, 396)

Muscular endurance The ability of the muscles to perform physical tasks over a period of time without becoming fatigued (Ch. 4, 80)

Muscular strength The amount of force a muscle can exert (Ch. 4, 80)

--- **N** ---

Narcotics Specific drugs derived from the opium plant that are obtainable only by prescription and are used to relieve pain (Ch. 23, 608)

Neglect Failure to provide for a child's physical or emotional needs (Ch. 11, 288)

Negotiation The use of communication and often compromise to settle a disagreement (Ch. 10, 266)

Nephrons The functional units of the kidneys (Ch. 17, 454)

Neurons Nerve cells (Ch. 15, 400)

Nicotine substitute A product that delivers small amounts of nicotine into the user's system while he or she is trying to give up the tobacco habit (Ch. 21, 549)

Nicotine The addictive drug found in tobacco leaves (Ch. 21, 541)

Nicotine withdrawal The process that occurs in the body when nicotine, an addictive drug, is no longer used (Ch. 21, 548)

Noise pollution Harmful and unwanted sound of sufficient intensity to damage hearing (Ch. 29, 770)

Noncommunicable disease A disease that is not transmitted by another person or a vector nor from the environment (Ch. 26, 674)

Nutrient-dense foods Foods that are high in nutrients compared with their calorie content (Ch. 6, 148)

Nutrients Substances in food that your body needs to grow, to repair itself, and to supply you with energy (Ch. 5, 110)

Nutrition The process by which the body takes in and uses food (Ch. 5, 110)

--- **O** ---

Obesity Having an excess amount of body fat (Ch. 6, 146)

Occupational Safety and Health Administration (OSHA) The agency in the federal government that is responsible for promoting safe and healthful conditions in the workplace (Ch. 27, 713)

Online shopping Using the Internet to buy products and services (Ch. 3, 52)

Opportunistic infection An infection that occurs in an individual who does not have a healthy immune system (Ch. 25, 659)

Ossification The process by which bone is formed, renewed, and repaired (Ch. 15, 387)

Osteoarthritis A disease of the joints in which cartilage breaks down (Ch. 26, 693)

Osteoporosis A condition in which there is the progressive loss of bone tissue (Ch., 4, 78; Ch. 15, 391)

Ova Female reproductive cells (Ch. 18, 474)

Ovaries The female sex glands that store the ova and produce female sex hormones (Ch. 18, 474)

Over-the-counter (OTC) medicines Medicines that you can buy without a prescription (Ch. 23, 590)

Overdose A strong, sometimes fatal reaction to taking a large amount of a drug (Ch. 23, 594)

Overexertion Overworking the body (Ch. 4, 99)

Overload Working the body harder than it is normally worked (Ch. 4, 90)

Overweight A condition in which a person is heavier than the standard weight range for his or her height (Ch. 6, 146)

Ovulation The process of releasing a mature ovum into the uterine tube each month (Ch. 18, 474)

———————— **P** ————————

Pancreas Gland that serves two systems—the digestive and the endocrine systems (Ch. 18, 465)

Pandemic A global outbreak of infectious disease (Ch. 25, p. 665)

Paranoia Irrational suspiciousness or distrust of others (Ch. 23, 602)

Parathyroid glands Glands that produce a hormone that regulates the body's calcium and phosphorus balance (Ch. 18, 465)

Passive A tendency to give up, give in, or back down without standing up for rights and needs (Ch. 12, 312)

Passive immunity Temporary immunity received from another person or from antibodies (Ch. 24, 631)

Pasteurization The process of treating a substance with heat to destroy or slow the growth of pathogens (Ch. 5, 135)

Pathogen An organism that causes disease (Ch. 24, 622)

Peer mediation A process in which trained students help other students find fair ways to resolve conflict and settle their differences (Ch. 13, 339)

Peer mediators Students trained to help other students find fair resolutions to conflicts and disagreements (Ch. 10, 267)

Peer pressure The influence that people your age may have on you (Ch. 12, 307)

Peers People of similar age who share similar interests (Ch. 1, 13; Ch. 12, 302)

Penis A tube-shaped organ that extends from the trunk of the body just above the testes (Ch. 18, 469)

Peptic ulcer A sore in the lining of the digestive tract (Ch. 17, 451)

Perception The act of becoming aware through the senses (Ch. 8, 198)

Periodontal disease An inflammation of the periodontal structures (Ch. 14, 370)

Periodontium The area immediately around the teeth (Ch. 14, 367)

Peristalsis A series of involuntary muscle contractions that move food through the digestive tract (Ch. 17, 443)

Personal identity Your sense of yourself as a unique individual (Ch. 7, 178)

Personality A complex set of characteristics that makes you unique (Ch. 7, 175)

Phagocyte A white blood cell that attacks invading pathogens (Ch. 24, 629)

Pharynx Throat (Ch. 16, 431)

Physical abuse The intentional infliction of bodily harm or injury on another person (Ch. 11, 287; Ch. 13, 349)

Physical activity Any form of movement that causes your body to use energy (Ch. 4, 74)

Physical fitness The ability to carry out daily tasks easily and have enough reserve energy to respond to unexpected demands (Ch. 4, 74)

Physical maturity State at which the physical body and all its organs are fully developed (Ch. 20, 520)

Physiological dependence A condition in which a user has a chemical need for a drug (Ch. 23, 595)

Pituitary gland Regulates and controls the activities of all other endocrine glands (Ch. 18, 465)

Placenta A thick, blood-rich tissue that lines the walls of the uterus during pregnancy and nourishes the embryo (Ch. 19, 487)

Plaque A sticky, colorless film that acts on sugar to form acids that destroy tooth enamel and irritate gums (Ch. 14, 368)

Plasma The fluid in which other parts of the blood are suspended (Ch. 16, 418)

Platelets Cells that prevent the body's loss of blood (Ch. 16, 420)

Platonic friendship A friendship with a member of the opposite gender in which there is affection, but the two people are not considered a couple (Ch. 12, 303)

Pleurisy An inflammation of the lining of the lungs and chest cavity (Ch. 16, 433)

Pneumonia An inflammation of the lungs commonly caused by a bacterial or viral infection (Ch. 16, 433; Ch. 24, 636)

Poison Any substance—solid, liquid, or gas—that causes injury, illness, or death when introduced into the body (Ch. 28, 755)

Poison control center A 24-hour hot line that provides emergency medical advice on treating poisoning victims (Ch. 28, 755)

Post-traumatic stress disorder A condition that may develop after a person's exposure to a terrifying event that threatened or caused physical harm (Ch. 9, 226)

Precycling Reducing waste before it is generated (Ch. 29, 779)

Prejudice An unfair opinion or judgment of a particular group of people (Ch. 10, 260; Ch. 13, 342)

Prenatal care Steps that a pregnant female can take to provide for her own health and for the health of her baby (Ch. 19, 492)

Prescription medicine Medicines that cannot be used without the written approval of a licensed physician (Ch. 23, 590)

Prevention Practicing health and safety habits to remain free of disease and injury (Ch. 1, 6)

Preventive care Actions that prevent the onset of disease or injury (Ch. 3, 55)

Primary care physician Medical doctor who provides physical checkups and general care (Ch. 3, 54)

Priorities Those goals, tasks, and activities that you judge to be more important than others (Ch. 12, 319)

Profound deafness A hearing loss so severe that a person affected cannot benefit from mechanical amplification, such as a hearing aid (Ch. 26, 696)

Progression The gradual increase in overload necessary to achieve higher levels of fitness (Ch. 4, 90)

Protective factors Conditions that shield individuals from the negative consequences of exposure to risk (Ch. 8, 216)

Proteins Nutrients that help build and maintain body cells and tissues (Ch. 5, 116)

Psychoactive drugs Chemicals that affect the central nervous system and alter activity in the brain (Ch. 23, 604)

Psychological dependence Condition in which a person believes that a drug is needed in order to feel good or to function normally (Ch. 23, 595)

Psychosomatic response A physical reaction that results from stress rather than from an injury or illness (Ch. 8, 202)

Psychotherapy An ongoing dialogue between a patient and a mental health professional (Ch. 9, 237)

Puberty The time when a person begins to develop certain traits of adults of his or her own gender (Ch. 20, 514)

Public health A community-wide effort to monitor and promote the welfare of the population (Ch. 3, 64)

Pulp The tissue that contains the blood vessels and nerves of a tooth (Ch. 14, 368)

R

Radon An odorless, radioactive gas (Ch. 29, 769)

Random violence Violence committed for no particular reason (Ch. 13, 344)

Rape Any form of sexual intercourse that takes place against a person's will (Ch. 13, 346)

Recovery The process of learning to live an alcohol-free life (Ch. 22, 579)

Recycling The processing of waste materials so that they can be used again in some form (Ch. 29, 779)

Reflex A spontaneous response of the body to a stimulus (Ch. 15, 404)

Refusal skills Communication strategies that can help you say no when you are urged to take part in behaviors that are unsafe, unhealthful, or that go against your values (Ch. 2, 30; Ch. 12, 310)

Rehydration Restoring lost body fluids (Ch. 6, 158)

Relationship A bond or connection you have with other people (Ch. 10, 248)

Relaxation response A state of calm that can be reached if one or more relaxation techniques are practiced regularly (Ch. 8, 209)

Remission A period of time when symptoms disappear (Ch. 26, 686)

Repetitive motion injury Damage to tissues caused by prolonged, repeated movements (Ch. 15, 393)

Reproductive system The system of organs involved in producing offspring (Ch. 18, 468)

Resiliency The ability to adapt effectively and recover from disappointment, difficulty, or crisis (Ch. 8, 214; Ch. 11, 285)

Respiration The exchange of gases between the body and the environment (Ch. 16, 428)

Resting heart rate The number of times your heart beats in one minute when you are not active (Ch. 4, 92)

Retina The light-sensitive membrane on which images are cast by the cornea (Ch. 14, 372)

Rheumatoid arthritis A disease characterized by the debilitating destruction of the joints due to inflammation (Ch. 26, 694)

Risk behaviors Actions that can potentially threaten your health or the health of others (Ch. 1, 17)

Road rage A practice of endangering drivers by using your vehicle as a weapon (Ch. 27, 722)

Role A part you play in a relationship (Ch. 10, 250)

Role model Someone whose success or behavior serves as an example for others (Ch. 2, 40)

S

Sclera The white part of the eye (Ch. 14, 372)

Scoliosis A lateral, or side-to-side, curvature of the spine (Ch. 15, 391; Ch. 19, 507)

Scrotum An external skin sac that extends outside the body and contains the testes (Ch. 18, 469)

Sebaceous glands Structures within the skin that produce an oily secretion called sebum (Ch. 14, 361)

Sedentary lifestyle A way of life that involves little physical activity (Ch. 4, 77)

Self-actualization The striving to become the best you can be (Ch. 7, 174)

Self-control A person's ability to use responsibility to override emotions (Ch. 12, 319)

Self-defense Any strategy for protecting oneself from harm (Ch. 13, 332)

Self-directed Able to make correct decisions about behavior when adults are not present to enforce rules (Ch. 20, 528)

Semen A thick fluid containing sperm and other secretions from the male reproductive system (Ch. 18, 469)

Separation A decision between married individuals to live apart from each other (Ch. 11, 281)

Severe weather Harsh or dangerous weather conditions (Ch. 27, 725)

Sex characteristics The traits related to a person's gender (Ch. 20, 515)

Sexual abuse Any sexual contact that is forced upon a person against his or her will (Ch. 11, 287)

Sexual assault Any intentional sexual attack against another person (Ch. 13, 346)

Sexual harassment Uninvited and unwelcome sexual conduct directed at another person (Ch. 13, 336)

Sexual violence Any form of unwelcome sexual conduct directed at an individual, including sexual harassment, sexual assault, and rape (Ch. 13, 345)

Sexually transmitted diseases (STDs) Infections spread from person to person through sexual contact (Ch. 12, 318; Ch. 25, 648)

Sexually transmitted infections (STIs) Infections spread from person to person through sexual contact (Ch. 25, 648)

Shock A failure of the cardiovascular system to keep an adequate supply of blood circulating to the vital organs of the body (Ch. 28, 747)

Short-term goal A goal that you can reach in a short length of time (Ch. 2, 35)

Sibling A brother or sister (Ch. 11, 278)

Side effects Reactions to medicine other than the one intended (Ch. 23, 589)

Sidestream smoke The smoke from the burning end of a cigarette, pipe, or cigar (Ch. 21, 551)

Sinusitis Inflammation of the tissues that line the sinuses (Ch. 16, 435)

Skeletal muscles Muscles that are attached to bone and cause body movements (Ch. 15, 395)

Smog A yellow-brown haze that forms when sunlight reacts with air pollution (Ch. 29, 767)

Smoke alarm An alarm that is triggered by the presence of smoke (Ch. 27, 708)

Smokeless tobacco Tobacco that is sniffed through the nose, held in the mouth, or chewed (Ch. 21, 542)

Smooth muscles Muscles that act on the lining of passageways and internal organs (Ch. 15, 395)

Sobriety Living without alcohol (Ch. 22, 578)

Specialist Medical doctor trained to handle particular kinds of patients or medical conditions (Ch. 3, 54)

Specificity Particular exercises and activities that improve particular areas of health-related fitness (Ch. 4, 90)

Sperm Male reproductive cells (Ch. 18, 468)

Spousal abuse Domestic violence directed at a spouse (Ch. 11, 287)

Sprain An injury to the ligament surrounding a joint (Ch. 4, 102)

Stalking The repeated following, harassment, or threatening of an individual to frighten or cause him or her harm (Ch. 13, 349)

Stereotype An exaggerated and oversimplified belief about an entire group of people, such as an ethnic or religious group, or a gender (Ch. 12, 305)

Sterility The inability to reproduce (Ch. 18, 472)

Stillbirth A dead fetus expelled from the body after the twentieth week of pregnancy (Ch. 19, 496)

Stimulant A drug that increases the action of the central nervous system, the heart, and other organs (Ch. 21, 541; Ch. 23, 605)

Strain A condition resulting from damaging a muscle or tendon (Ch. 4, 102)

Stress The reaction of the body and mind to everyday challenges and demands (Ch. 8, 198)

Stress management Ways to deal with or overcome the negative effects of stress (Ch. 2, 31)

Stress-management skills Skills that help an individual handle stress in a healthful, effective way (Ch. 8, 208)

Stressor Anything that causes stress (Ch. 8, 199)

Stroke A condition where an arterial blockage interrupts the flow of blood to the brain (Ch. 26, 678)

Substance abuse Any unnecessary or improper use of chemical substances for nonmedical purposes (Ch. 23, 592)

Suicide The act of intentionally taking one's own life (Ch. 9, 230)

Suppression Holding back or restraining (Ch. 7, 189)

Sweat glands Structures within the dermis that secrete perspiration through ducts to pores on the skin's surface (Ch. 14, 361)

Symptomatic stage The stage in which a person infected with HIV has symptoms as a result of a severe drop in immune cells (Ch. 25, 663)

Synergistic effect Interaction of two or more medicines that results in a greater effect than when the medicines are taken alone (Ch. 23, 589)

Syphilis A bacterial STD that attacks many parts of the body and is caused by a small bacterium called a spirochete (Ch. 25, 655)

T

Tar A thick, sticky, dark fluid produced when tobacco burns (Ch. 21, 541)

Tartar The hard, crustlike substance formed when plaque hardens (Ch. 14, 370)

Tendon A fibrous cord that attaches muscle to the bone (Ch. 15, 389)

Tendonitis The inflammation of a tendon (Ch. 15, 398)

Testes Two small glands that produce sperm (Ch. 19, 469)

Testosterone Male sex hormone (Ch. 18, 469)

Thyroid gland Produces hormones that regulate metabolism, body heat, and bone growth (Ch. 18, 465)

Tinnitus A condition in which a ringing, buzzing, whistling, roaring, hissing, or other sound is heard in the ear in the absence of external sound (Ch. 14, 379)

Tolerance The ability to accept others' differences and allow them to be who they are without expressing disapproval (Ch. 10, 260)

Tolerance A condition in which the body becomes used to the effects of a medicine. (Ch. 23, 589)

Tornado A whirling, funnel-shaped windstorm that drops from the sky to the ground and produces a narrow path of destruction on land (Ch. 27, 728)

Toxin A substance that kills cells or interferes with their functions (Ch. 24, 623)

Trachea Windpipe (Ch. 16, 431)

Training program A program of formalized physical preparation for involvement in a sport or another physical activity (Ch. 4, 93)

Transitions Critical changes that occur at all stages of life (Ch. 20, 529)

Trichomoniasis An STD caused by a microscopic protozoan that results in infections of the vagina, urethra, and bladder (Ch. 25, 655)

Tuberculosis A contagious bacterial infection that usually affects the lungs (Ch. 16, 435)

Tumor An abnormal mass of tissue that has no natural role in the body (Ch. 26, 681)

U

Umbilical cord A ropelike structure that connects the embryo and the mother's placenta (Ch. 19, 487)

Unconditional love Love without limitation or qualification (Ch. 20, 528)

Unconsciousness A condition in which a person is not alert and aware of his or her surroundings (Ch. 28, 751)

Underweight A condition in which a person is less than the standard weight range for his or her height (Ch. 6, 147)

Unintentional injury An injury resulting from an unexpected event, or accident (Ch. 27, 706)

Universal precautions Actions taken to prevent the spread of disease by treating all blood and other body fluids as if they contained pathogens (Ch. 28, 737)

Urban sprawl The spreading of city development (houses, shopping centers, businesses, and schools) onto undeveloped land (Ch. 29, 774)

Ureters Tubes that connect the kidneys to the bladder (Ch. 17, 454)

Urethra The tube that leads from the bladder to the outside of the body (Ch. 17, 455)

Urethritis The inflammation of the urethra (Ch. 17, 456)

Urine Liquid waste material (Ch. 17, 453)

Uterus A hollow, muscular, pear-shaped organ inside a female's body (Ch. 18, 474)

V

Vaccine A preparation of dead or weakened pathogens, which are introduced into the body to stimulate an immune response (Ch. 23, 587; Ch. 24, 631)

Vagina A muscular, elastic passageway that extends from the uterus to the outside of the body (Ch. 18, 475)

Values The ideas, beliefs, and attitudes about what is important that help guide the way you live (Ch. 2, 34)

Vector An organism, such as a tick, that carries and transmits pathogens to humans or other animals (Ch. 24, 625)

Vegan Vegetarians who eat only foods of plant origin (Ch. 6, 160)

Vegetarian A person who eats mostly or only foods that come from plant sources (Ch. 6, 159)

Vehicular safety Obeying the rules of the road, as well as exercising common sense and good judgment (Ch. 27, 719)

Veins Blood vessels that return blood to the heart (Ch. 16, 419)

Venom A poisonous substance secreted by a snake, spider, or other creature (Ch. 28, 755)

Verbal abuse Using words to mistreat or injure another person (Ch. 13, 349)

Violence Threatened or actual use of physical force or power to harm another person or to damage property (Ch. 13, 335)

Virus A form of genetic material that invades living cells to reproduce (Ch. 24, 623)

Vitamins Compounds that help regulate many vital body processes, including the digestion, absorption, and metabolism of other nutrients (Ch. 5, 119)

W

Warm-up An activity that prepares the muscles for work (Ch. 4, 90)

Warranty A company's or a store's written agreement to repair a product or refund your money should the product not function properly (Ch. 3, 50)

Wastewater Used water that comes from homes, communities, farms, and businesses (Ch. 29, 775)

Weight cycling The repeated pattern of loss and regain of body weight (Ch. 6, 152)

Wellness An overall state of well-being, or total health (Ch. 1, 5)

Western blot (WB) The most common confirmation test for HIV in the United States (Ch. 25, 664)

Withdrawal A condition that occurs when a person stops using a medicine on which he or she has a chemical dependence (Ch 23. 589)

Workout The part of an exercise program when the activity is performed at its highest peak (Ch. 4, 90)

A

Absorption/absorción Proceso mediante el cual la comida digerida pasa desde el aparato digestivo al sistema cardiovascular.

Abstinence/abstinencia Una decisión deliberada de evitar una conducta considerada arriesgada o dañina como la actividad sexual prematrimonial, el consumo de tabaco, alcohol, y otras drogas.

Abuse/abuso El maltrato físico, mental/ emocional o sexual de una persona a otra.

Accident chain/cadena de accidentes Una serie de sucesos que generan situaciones o acciones peligrosas sin intención.

Acquired immune deficiency syndrome (AIDS)/síndrome de inmunodeficiencia adquirida (SIDA) Enfermedad en la cual el sistema inmunológico del paciente se encuentra debilitado.

Action plan/plan de acción Una estrategia que ayuda a identificar y lograr metas.

Active immunity/inmunidad activa La inmunidad que desarrolla el cuerpo para protegerse de enfermedades.

Active listening/ audición activa Escuchar atentamente lo que alguien dice o comunica.

Addiction/afición La dependencia psicológica o fisiológica a las drogas.

Addictive drug/droga adictiva Una substancia que causa la dependencia psicológica o fisiológica de una persona.

Additive interaction/interacción aditiva Medicinas que trabajan en conjunto de una manera positiva.

Adolescence/adolescencia La etapa entre la infancia y la edad adulta.

Adoption/adopción Proceso legal de elegir para tenerlo como hijo un niño de otros padres.

Adrenal glands/glándulas de adrenalina Glándulas que ayudan al cuerpo a recuperarse del estrés y a actuar ante emergencias.

Advertising/publicidad Un mensaje, oral o escrito, diseñado para incentivar a los consumidores a comprar un producto o servicio.

Advocacy/apoya Apoyar o defender acciones que tienen como objetivo influenciar a otras personas para que respalden situaciones o creencias relacionadas con la salud.

Aerobic exercise/ejercicio aeróbico Cualquier actividad física que sea rítmica, que implique el uso de los principales músculos del cuerpo humano y que pueda ser mantenida por al menos 10 minutos tres veces al día o por 20 a 30 minutos en una acción continua.

Affection/afección El sentimiento de cariño por otra persona.

Affirmation/afirmación Una reacción positiva que ayuda a que otras se sientan apreciadas y respaldadas.

Aggressive/agresivo Excesivamente fuerte, insistente, hostil, o de predisposición belicosa.

Air pollution/contaminación atmosférica La contaminación de la atmósfera de la tierra por sustancias que presentan peligro a la salud de los seres vivos.

Air quality index (AQI)/índice de calidad del aire Un indicador que reporta diariamente la calidad del aire.

Alcohol abuse/abuso de alcohol Uso excesivo de alcohol.

Alcohol poisoning/envenenamiento alcohólico Una reacción física severa y algunas veces fatal a una sobredosis de alcohol.

Alcoholic/alcoholico Una persona que es adicta al alcohol.

Alcoholism/alcoholismo Enfermedad en que la persona es adicta física y psicológicamente a bebidas alcohólicas.

Alienation/alienación Sentirse solo y separado de todo el mundo.

Allergy/alergia Una reacción específica del sistema inmunológico a una substancia extraña que es usualmente inofensiva.

Americans with Disabilities Act/ El Acta de Americanos Incapacidados Una ley que prohíbe la discriminación de personas discapacitadas por parte de los lugares de trabajo, transporte, lugares públicos y telecomunicaciones.

Amniocentesis/amniocentesis Un procedimiento en la cual se inserta una jeringa a través de la pared abdominal de una mujer embarazada al líquido amniótico alrededor del embrión en desarrollo.

Amniotic sac/sac amniótico Una membrana delgada lleno de líquido que envuelve y protege al embrión.

Anabolic-androgenic steroids/esteroides anabolizantes-androgénicos Substancias sintéticas semejante de testosterona, la hormona masculina.

Anaerobic exercise/ejercicio anaerobio Actividad física intensiva en la cual los músculos trabajan tan fuerte que producen energía sin usar oxígeno.

Analgesics/analgésico Medicamento que alivia el dolor.

Anemia/anemia Condición en la cual la habilidad de la sangre de transportar oxígeno se encuentra debilitada.

Angina pectoris/angina de pecho Un dolor en el pecho que es causado porque el corazón no está recibiendo suficiente oxígeno.

Anorexia nervosa/anorexia nerviosa Un desorden de alimentación en el cual el miedo irracional a convertirse obeso/a resulta en pierda extrema de peso por dieta de hambre autoimpuesta.

Antagonistic interaction/interacción antagónesco Situación en la cual el efecto de n medicamento se elimina o reduce por tomar otro medicamento.

Antibody/anticuerpo Una proteína que ataca antígenos específicos.

Antigen/antígeno Una substancia que es capaz de liberar un agente inmune.

Anxiety/ansiedad La condición de sentirse abrumado o preocupado acerca de lo que que pasará.

Anxiety disorder/trastorno de ansiedad Una condición en la cual el miedo, ya sea real o imaginado, es difícil de controlar.

Appendicitis/apendicitis La inflamación del apéndice.

Appendicular skeleton/esqueleto apendicular Los 126 huesos de las extremidades superiores y inferiores, los hombros, y los las caderas.

Appetite/apetito El deseo, mas que la necesidad, de comer.

Arrhythmia/arritmia Palpitaciones irregulares del corazón.

Arteries/arterias Vasos sanguíneos que llevan la sangre desde el corazón a otras partes del cuerpo humano.

Arthritis/artritis Un grupo de mas de 100 condiciones que causan dolor y la pérdida de movimiento en las articulaciones

Asbestos/asbesto Una fibra mineral que tiene propiedades contra combustión y que fue comúnmente usado como aislante.

Assailant/agresor Una persona que comete un acto violento contra otra persona.

Assault/asalto El ataque ilegal a una persona con la intención de dañarlo o matarlo.

Assertive/asertivo Tener una posición firme, pero a la vez positiva, de tus derechos y creencias.

Asthma/asma Una condición inflamatoria que se caracteriza porque la traquea, los bronquios y los bronquiolos se cierren provocando dificultad para respirar.

Asymptomatic stage/Etapa sin síntomas Un período de tiempo durante la cuál una persona infectada por VIH no tiene síntomas.

Atherosclerosis/artereosclorosis El proceso en el cual las plaquetas se acumulan en las paredes de las arterias.

Auditory ossicles/huesecillos auditorios Tres pequeños huesos que se encuentran unidos y conectan el tímpano con el oído interior.

Autoimmune disease/enfermedad autoinmunológica Una condición en la cuál el sistema inmune se ataca a sí mismo por error, afectando a las células, los tejidos, y los órganos de cuerpo de la misma persona.

Autonomy/autonomía La capacidad que una persona tiene para controlar su propio cuerpo, impulsos y medio ambiente.

Axial skeleton/esqueleto axial Los 80 huesos del cráneo, la columna vertebral, la caja

---

B

Bacteria/bacteria Microorganismos compuestos de una sola célula

Behavior therapy/terapia de comportamiento Un terapia cuyo objetivo es cambiar conductas indeseadas a través de recompensas y refuerzos.

Benign/benigno No canceroso.

Bile/bilis Un líquido amargo de color amarillo-verde que es importante para descomposición y absorción de las grasas.

Binge drinking/borrachera El consumo de cinco o más bebidas alcohólicas en un corto plazo.

Binge eating disorder/trastorno de la alimentación excesiva Un desorden de alimentación caracterizado por comer demasiado y de manera impulsiva

Biodegradable/biodegradable Algo que se descompone por los microorganismos del medioambiente.

Biomedical therapy/terapia biomédica El uso de ciertos medicamentos para tratar o reducir los síntomas de un desorden mental.

Biopsy/biopsia La extirpación de una pequeña muestra de tejido diagnóstica.

Birthing center/centro de partos Un lugar en el cual mujeres con un embarazo de bajo riesgo pueden dar a luz a sus hijos de una manera natural.

Bladder/vejiga Un órgano muscular hueco que actúa como recipiente para la orina.

Blizzard/ventisca Una tormenta de nieve con vientos que superan las 35 millas por hora.

Blood alcohol concentration (BAC)/concentración de alcohol en la sangre La cantidad de alcohol contenida en la sangre expresada como un porcentaje.

Blood pressure/tensión arterial Una medida de la presión que la sangre genera en las paredes de los vasos sanguíneos, especialmente en las arterias grandes, cuando la sangre es impulsada por el cuerpo.

Body composition/composición del cuerpo La proporción entre tejido grasa y tejido magro (incluyendo los músculos) los huesos, el agua, y los tejidos conjuntivos tales como ligamentos, cartílagos y tendones.

Body image/autoimagen La forma en que uno se ve a sí mismo.

Body language/lenguaje del cuerpo Comunicación no-verbal a través de gestos, expresiones faciales, comportamientos y postura.

Body mass index (BMI)/índice de masa corporal Una medida que permite la evaluación del tamaño de un cuerpo en relación con su peso y estatura.

Brain stem/vástago del cerebro Un ramificación de neuronas y fibras de tres pulgadas de largo que conecta la médula espinal al resto del cerebro.

Bronchi/bronquio Los pasajes que conectan la traquea con los pulmones.

Bronchitis/bronquitis Una inflamación de los bronquios causada por la infección o exposición a irritantes como el humo de tabaco o contaminación ambiental.

Bulimia nervosa/bulimia nerviosa Un trastorno de episodios de comer con exceso seguidos de alguna forma de auto-purgación o limpiar del aparato digestivo.

Bullying/intimidación Buscar poder o atraer atención por abuso psicológico, emocional o físico de otra persona.

— C —

Calories/calorías Unidades de calor que miden la energía que usa el cuerpo y la energía que la comida proporciona al cuerpo.

Cancer/cáncer El crecimiento incontrolable de células anormales.

Capillaries/capilares Vasos muy pequeños que transportan la sangre entre las arteriolas y las vénulas.

Carbohydrate/carbohidrato Las féculas y azúcares contenidos en los alimentos.

Carbon monoxide/monóxido de carbono Un gas sin color, inodoro, y venenoso.

Carcinogen/cancerígeno Un substancia que produce cáncer.

Cardiac muscle/músculo cardiaco Un tipo de músculo estriado que forma las paredes del corazón.

Cardiopulmonary resuscitation (CPR)/resucitación cardiopulmonar Un procedimiento de primeros auxilios que combina la respiración artificial con presiones en el pecho, proveyendo oxígeno hasta que las funciones vitales puedan resumir.

Cardiorespiratory endurance/resistencia cardiorespiratoria La habilidad que tiene el corazón, los pulmones y los vasos sanguíneos de utilizar y enviar energía y oxígeno a los tejidos del cuerpo durante largos períodos de tiempo con actividad moderada hasta enérgica.

Cardiovascular disease (CVD)/enfermedad cardiovascular Una enfermedad que afecta el corazón o los vasos sanguíneos.

Cartilage/cartílago Tejido conjuntivo que es fuerte y flexible.

Cerebellum/cerebelo La segunda parte más grande del cerebro.

Cerebral palsy/parálisis cerebral Un grupo de desordenes neurológicos no progresivos y que son el resultado de daños al cerebro antes, durante, e justo después del nacimiento o durante la niñez temprana.

Cerebrum/cerebro La parte más grande y compleja del cerebro.

Cervix/cuello del útero La entrada del útero.

Chain of survival/cadena de supervivencia Una secuencia de acciones que tiene como objetivo maximizar las posibilidades de supervivencia de una víctima.

Character/carácter Las características distintivas que describen como una persona piensa, siente y actúa.

Child abuse/maltrato infantil Abuso doméstico dirigido hacia los niños.

Chlamydia/chlamydia Una infección bacteriana que afecta los órganos reproductores de los hombres y mujeres.

Chorionic Villi Sampling (CVS)/muestreo de villi coriónico Un procedimiento mediante el cual se remueve una pequeña muestra de membrana de una capa de tejido a se desarrolla en a placenta llamada corión.

choroid/coroides Una estructura delgada que cubre la parte interna de la esclerótica.

chromosomes/cromosomas Estructuras parecidas a hilos encontradas dentro del núcleo de una célula y que cargan los códigos para rasgos heredados.

Chronic stress/estrés crónico El estrés relacionado con problemas de largo plazo y fuera del control de una persona.

Chyme/chyme Una mezcla cremosa y líquida de alimento y jugos gástricos.

Citizenship/ciudadanía La manera de comportarse como miembro de la comunidad.

Clique/pandilla Un grupo pequeño de amigos generalmente con gustos y experiencias similares que excluyen a otras personas vistas como ajenas a ellos.

Club drugs/drogas de club Drogas asociadas con conciertos, clubes de baile, y fiestas nocturnas conocidos como raves.

Cluster suicides/serie de suicidios Una serie de suicidios que ocurren en un período de tiempo corto que involucran varias personas de un mismo colegio o comunidad.

Cognition/cognición La habilidad de razonar y pensar con soluciones abstractas.

Cognitive therapy/terapia Cognoscitiva Una terapia diseñada para identificar y corregir modelos de pensamientos los cuales pueden generar comportamientos que sean problemáticos, contraproducentes, o destructivos a sí mismo.

Commitment/compromiso Una promesa u obligación.

Communicable disease/enfermedad contagiosa Una enfermedad que se puede transmitir desde un ser vivo a otro a través del medio ambiente.

Communication/comunicación Las maneras de enviar los mensajes a otros y de recibir mensajes enviados por otros.

Comparison shopping/compras comparadas
Evaluar los beneficios de diferentes productos comparando factores tales como calidad, características y precio.

Compromise/acuerdo Un método para resolver problemas en que cada participante debe sacrificar algo con el fin de solucionar el problema.

Concussion/conmoción cerebral Una situación que es el resultado de un golpe en el cerebro y que afecta su normal funcionamiento.

Conduct disorder/desorden de conducta Un diseño de comportamiento en la cual los derechos de otros o las reglas sociales básicas son violadas.

Confidentiality/confidencial Respetar la vida privada de otros y guardar detalles secretos.

Conflict/conflicto Cualquier desacuerdo, pelea o enojo.

Conflict resolution/resolución de conflicto Proceso de resolver un desacuerdo a través de la cooperación y solución de problemas.

Congenital/congénito Una condición que se presenta al nacimiento

Conservation/conservación La protección y preservación del medio ambiente a través de la prevención de abusos, destrucción e incorrecto uso de los recursos naturales.

Constructive criticism/crítica constructiva Comentarios no hostiles acerca del problema y tienen objetivo mejorar un comportamiento o situación.

Consumer advocate/defensor del consumidor Gente o grupos quienes único propósito es confrontar los problemas regionales, nacionales, y hasta internacionales del consumidor.

Cool-down/enfriamiento Una actividad que prepara los músculos para volver a un estado de relajación.

Cooperation/cooperación Trabajar juntos para el beneficio de todos.

Coping/hacer frente a Resolver exitosamente con cambios difíciles en la vida.

Cornea/córnea Un tejido transparente que refracta y hace foco a la luz antes de pasar al ojo.

Crisis center/centro para los crisis Una facilidad que maneja emergencias y le envía a un individuo que necesita ayuda a los recursos remedios.

Cross-contamination/contra-contaminación La dispersión de bacteria u otros microbios patogénicos desde una comida a otra.

Culture/cultura Las creencias, costumbres y comportamiento colectivos de un grupo de personas.

Cumulative risks/riesgos acumulados Riesgos relacionados que aumentan en efecto con cada riesgo más.

Curfew/toque de queda Un período de tiempo de restricción en casa al horario nocturno.

Custody/custodia Una decisión legal acerca de quién tiene el derecho de tomar las decisiones que afectarán a un niño, y quién tiene la responsabilidad de hacer cargo de él.

Cycle of violence/ ciclo de violencia Diseño de repetir comportamiento violento o abusivo desde una generación a la próxima.

Cystitis/cistitis La inflamación de la vejiga.

D

Dandruff/caspa Una condición que puede resultar si el cuero cabelludo se seca y las células muertas de la piel se desprenden como partículas blancas pegajosas.

Date rape/violación Cuando una persona que se encuentra en una cita obliga a la otra a participar en una actividad sexual.

Decibel/decibelios Una medida que se usa para expresar la intensidad relativa del volumen del sonido.

Decision-making skills/habilidades para tomar decisiones Los pasos necesarios para tomar una correcta decisión.

Defense mechanisms/mecanismos de defensa Procesos mentales que protegen a individuos de emociones y situaciones fuertes o estresantes.

Defensive driver/manejo defensivo Un conductor consciente de peligros posibles y reacciona para evitarlos.

Defibrillator/máqina de defibrilación Un aparato que proporciona choques eléctricos al corazón para restaurar su ritmo normal.

Deforestation/desforestación Destrucción de los bosques.

Depressants/sedantes Sustancias que tienden a disminuir la función del sistema nervioso central.

Depression/depresión Un sentimiento prolongado de soledad, desesperación y tristeza.

Dermis/dermis La capa más gruesa de la piel que se encuentra debajo de la epidermis que está compuesta de tejidos conectivos y contiene vaso sanguíneos y nervios.

Designer drugs/droga de diseño Sustancias sintéticas que tratan de imitar los efectos de los alucinógenos y otras drogas peligrosas.

Detoxification/desintoxicación Un proceso mediante el cual el cuerpo está ajustando para funcionar sin alcohol.

Developmental assets/activos para el desarrollo Construir un ambiente que ayudara a que los jóvenes crecen saludables, afectuosos, y responsables.

Developmental task/tareas requeridas para el desarrollo Sucesos necesarios para que una persona continúe creciendo y se convierta en un adulto saludable y maduro.

Diabetes/diabetes Una enfermedad crónica que impide que las células del cuerpo conviertan los alimentos en energía.

Diaphragm/diafragma El músculo que separa los pulmones de la cavidad abdominal.

Dietary Guidelines for Americans/Pautas alimenticias para los estadounidenses Una serie de recomendaciones para la alimentación saludable y la vida activa de los estadounidenses.

Dietary supplement/suplemento alimenticio Uno o más alimentos nutritivos que no son comida.

Digestion/digestión La descomposición mecánica y química de la comida para uso por las células corporales.

Disability/incapacidad Cualquier impedimento físico o mental que limita el desarrollo de actividades normales inclusive ver, oír, caminar o hablar.

Divorce/divorcio Un fin legal de un contrato de matrimonio.

DNA (deoxyribonucleic acid)/ ADN (acido desoxirribonucleico La unidad química que compone los cromosomas.

Domestic violence/violencia doméstica Cualquier acto de violencia que incluya a los miembros de una familia.

Drug watches/vigilantes de la droga Un grupo de personas de un vecindario organizadas para espiar, seguir, reportar o directamente frenar el abuso y venta de drogas.

Drug-free school zone/zona de escuela libre de drogas Una área que contempla 1,000 pies alrededor de una escuela y se encuentra señalizada, en la cual las personas que son atrapadas vendiendo drogas son severamente penalizadas o castigadas, más que lo usual.

Drugs/drogas Sustancias, excepto alimentos, que cambian la estructura o funcionamiento del cuerpo o mente de las personas.

━━━━━━━━ **E** ━━━━━━━━

Earthquake/terremoto Un temblor que mueve fuertemente la superficie de la tierra.

Eating disorder/desorden alimenticio Un comportamiento que se caracteriza por comer en forma extrema y dañina causando que la persona se pueda enfermar o morir.

EIA/ensayo inmunoenzimático de enzimas Un análisis que estudia la presencia de VIH en la sangre.

Electrolytes/electrolitos Minerales que ayudan a mantener el balance de los fluidos del cuerpo.

Elimination/eliminación La expulsión de comida no digerida o desechos del cuerpo.

Embryo/embrión El estado de desarrollo de un organismo que va desde la concepción hasta a las ocho semanas de desarrollo.

Emergency survival kit/botiquín de primeros auxilios Un grupo de artículos que pueden ser utilizados por un corto plazo hasta que la situación de emergencia se haya estabilizado.

Emerging infection/infección emergente Una enfermedad infecciosa cuya incidencia en humanos ha aumentado durante las últimas dos décadas o que amenaza con incrementar en el futuro cercano.

Emotional abuse/abuso emocional Un comportamiento que ataca el desarrollo emocional y la estima de un individuo.

Emotional intimacy/intimidad emocional La habilidad de experimentar una relación de amor y cuidado con otra persona con la cual también se pueden compartir los sentimientos más íntimos.

Emotional maturity/madurez emocional Un estado en el cual las capacidades mentales y emocionales de una persona se encuentran totalmente desarrolladas.

Emotions/emociones Señales que le comunican a la mente y el cuerpo como actuar.

Empathy/empatía La habilidad para imaginar y entender como otra persona siente.

Emphysema/enfisema Una enfermedad que destruye progresivamente las paredes de los alveolos.

Empty-nest syndrome/síndrome del nido vacío Sentimiento de tristeza y soledad que ocurre cuando los hijos, quienes ya se convirtieron en adultos, se van de la casa de sus padres.

Endocrine glands/glándulas endocrinas Sin conductos o tubos—órganos o grupos de células que secretan directamente en el flujo sanguíneo.

Environment/medio ambiente Todo lo que nos rodea.

Environmental tobacco smoke (ETS)/ambiente con humo de cigarro Aire que ha sido contaminado por el humo de cigarrillos.

Epidemic/epidemia Una situación en la cual mucha gente contrae una enfermedad al mismo tiempo y en el mismo lugar.

Epidemiology/epidemiología El estudio científico de las características de las enfermedades en una población.

Epidermis/epidermis La capa visible y más externa de la piel la cual se encuentra compuesta de células vivas y muertas.

Epilepsy/epilepsia Un desorden del sistema nervioso caracterizado por convulsiones continuas- repentinos episodios de incontrolable actividad eléctrica del cerebro.

Ethanol/etano El alcohol que se encuentra en las bebidas alcohólicas.

Euphoria/euforia El sentimiento de un intenso bienestar o alegría.

Exercise/ejercicio Actividad física que es planeada, estructurada y repetitiva, y que tiene como objetivo el mantenimiento o el mejoramiento del estado físico de una persona.

Extended family/familia extendida La familia inmediata (padres y hermanos) y otros parientes como por ejemplo tíos, tías, primos y abuelos.

Extensor/extensor Un músculo que abra una articulación.

External auditory canal/ canal auditivo externo Un pasaje de cerca de una pulgada de largo el cual conecta el oído externo con el tímpano.

F

F.I.T.T./F.I.T.A. Frecuencia, intensidad, tiempo/duración, y tipo de actividad.

Fad diets/dietas de moda Planes para perder peso que sirven solamente en el corto plazo.

Fallopian tubes/trompa de Falapio Un par de conductos con forma de dedos que ayudan al óvulo en su camino hacia el útero.

Family counseling/consejería familiar Terapia que ayuda a restaurar las relaciones entre los miembros de una familia.

Family/familia La unidad básica de una sociedad.

Fermentation/fermentación La reacción química de la levadura en el azúcar.

Fertilization/fertilización La unión del espermatozoide y el óvulo.

Fetal alcohol syndrome (FAS)/síndrome de alcoholismo fetal Un grupo de defectos de nacimiento causados por el alcohol y que incluyen problemas físicos y mentales.

Fetus/feto El Embrión en desarrollo que se encuentra dentro del útero.

Fiber/fibra Un carbohidrato que no es digerible.

Fire extinguisher/extintor de incendios Un aparato portátil que ayuda a apagar incendios a través de la aplicación de químicos extinguidores de fuego.

First aid/primeros auxilios La atención inmediata y temporal que se le proporciona a una persona enferma o herida hasta que una atención medica profesional pueda ser proporcionada.

Flash flood/inundación repentina Una inundación de gran volumen y corta duración que es comúnmente causada por fuertes lluvias.

Flexibility/flexibilidad La habilidad de mover una parte del cuerpo fácilmente y en muchas direcciones.

Flexor/músculo flexor Los músculos que cierren las articulaciones.

Food additives/aditivos alimentarios Substancias que son adicionadas a los alimentos en forma intencional para generar un efecto deseado.

Food allergy/alergia a comida Una condición en la cuál el sistema inmunológico del cuerpo reacciona a substancias contenidas en algunos alimentos.

Food Guide Pyramid/pirámide alimenticia Una guía para la elección diaria de alimentos saludables.

Food intolerance/intolerancia a la comida Una reacción negativa a los alimentos (o un elemento particular del alimento) causado por un problema metabólico como por ejemplo la inhabilidad de digerir ciertos alimentos o algunos de sus componentes.

Foodborne illness/enfermedad alimenticia Intoxicación alimenticia.

Foster care/custodia temporal Un acuerdo temporal en la cuál un niño es entregado a una familia o adulto, quienes no son sus familiares, para que lo guíen y supervisen.

Fracture/fractura La rotura de un hueso.

Fraud/fraude Engaño deliberado.

Friendship/amistad Una relación importante entre dos personas que esta basada en solidaridad, confianza y consideración.

Frostbite/congelación Una condición en la cual los tejidos del cuerpo se congelan.

G

Gametes/gametos Células reproductoras.

Gang/banda criminal Un grupo de personas quienes se encuentran vinculados por haber participado en una actividad criminal.

Gastric juices/jugos gástricos La secreciones que provienen de la capa estómago y que contienen ácido de clorhídrico y pepsina, una enzima digiere la proteína.

Gene therapy/terapia genética Un proceso que consiste en introducir genes normales en las células humanas de manera de corregir trastornos genéticos.

Genes/genes Las unidades básicas de la herencia

Genetic disorder/trastorno genético Un trastorno causado parcial o completamente por defectos en los genes.

Genital herpes/herpes genitales Infección de transmisión sexual causada por el virus herpes simple.

Goal/objetivo Algo que una persona desea y para lo cual hace planes y trabaja. Gonads/ gónadas Los ovarios y los testículos.

Gonorrhea/gonorrea Una infección bacteriana de transmisión sexual que comúnmente afecta a las membranas mucosas.

Graduated driver's license/ icencia de manejar graduada Un programa de licencias que incrementa los privilegios de los conductores nuevos en el tiempo como premio a la experiencia y habilidad.

Grief response/aflicción La respuesta de un individuo a una gran pérdida.

Grief/aflicción La pena causada por la pérdida de un ser querido.

Group therapy/terapia de grupo Consejería a un grupo de personas quienes tienen problemas similares.

H

Hair follicle/folículo de pelo Una estructura que rodea la raíz de un pelo. Hallucinogens/ alucinógenos Drogas que alteran el estado de ánimo, pensamientos, y los sentidos incluyendo la visión, audición, olfato y tacto.

Harassment/acoso Molestar persistentemente a otra persona.

Hazardous waste/desechos peligrosos Substancia que es explosiva, corrosiva, altamente reactiva, o tóxica para los seres humanos o otras formas de vida.

Health/salud La combinación de bienestar físico, mental/emocional y social.

Health care system/sistema de sanidad Toda la asistencia médica disponible para la población de una nación, la forma en que la atención es recibida y la forma en que se paga.

Health consumer/consumidor de salud Cualquier persona que consume o usa productos o servicios de salud.

Health education/educación de salud Proveer a las personas con información adecuada de tal manera que ellos puedan tomar decisiones que sean saludables.

Health fraud/engaño a la salud La venta de productos o servicios inútiles que supuestamente sirven para prevenir enfermedades o mejorar otros problemas de la salud. Health insurance/ seguro médico Un plan en el que una compañía o el gobierno paga una parte o la totalidad de los gastos médicos de una persona.

Health literacy/instrucción de salud La capacidad que tiene una persona para aprender y comprender información básica acerca de servicios relacionado, y usar esos conocimientos para mejorar su propia salud y bienestar.

Health screening/diagnóstico de la salud Estudiar o chequear de la salud de una persona con objetivo detectar anticipadamente enfermedades u otros problemas de salud.

Health skills/habilidade de la salud Herramientas y estrategias que ayudan a mantener, proteger, y mejorar todos los aspectos de la salud.

Healthy People 2010/Gente saludable 2010 Un plan nacional de salud y prevención de enfermedades que fue diseñado para promover el mejoramiento de la salud de todas las personas en los Estados Unidos.

Heartburn/acidez Una sensación de quemadura en el centro del pecho que puede subir desde la parte inferior del esternón hasta la garganta.

Heat cramps/calambre debido al calor Espasmos musculares que son el resultado de la pérdida de grandes cantidades de sal y agua a través de la respiración.

Heat exhaustion/agotamiento debido al calor Un sobrecalentamiento del cuerpo que produce síntomas de un estado de choque y que hace que la piel se ponga helada y húmeda.

Heatstroke/insolación Una condición en la cuál el cuerpo pierde la habilidad para deshacerse del calor excesivo a través de la respiración.

Hemodialysis/hemodiálisis Una técnica a través de la cual una máquina de diálisis limpia los desechos de la sangre.

Hemoglobin/hemoglobina La proteína que lleva el oxígeno en la sangre.

Herbal supplement/suplemento herbario Una substancia química de hierbas las cuales se pueden vender como suplemento nutritivo.

Heredity/herencia Todos los rasgos que biológicamente los cuales son transferidos desde los padres a los hijos.

Hernia/hernia Cuando un órgano o tejido sobresale en un área de músculos débiles.

Hiatal hernia/hernia de hiato Una condición en la cuál una parte del estómago abre paso al diafragma.

Hierarchy of needs/pirámides de las necesidades Una graduación de tales necesidades esenciales al crecimiento y desarrollo humano, presentadas en orden ascendiente desde las necesidades más bajos y básicas hasta alcanzar la potencial más alta.

Histamines/histaminas Químicas que pueden estimular la mucosa y la producción de fluidos en una área del cuerpo.

Hodgkin's disease/enfermedad de Hodgkin Un tipo de cáncer que afecta el tejido linfático.

Homicide/homicidio Cuando una persona mata a otra.

Hormones/hormonas Substancias químicas producidas por las glándulas y que ayudan a regular muchas funciones del cuerpo humano.

Hostility/hostilidad Un comportamiento intencional que es antipático, desagradable o ofensivo.

Human immunodeficiency virus (HIV)/virus de inmunodeficiencia humana (VIH) Un virus que ataca al sistema inmunológico.

Human papillomavirus (HPV)/virus del humano papiloma (VHP) Un virus que puede causar verrugas genitales o infecciones asintomáticas.

Hunger/hambre La necesidad física y natural de alimentos que nos protege de la inanición.

Hurricane/huracán Una tormenta muy fuerte que se origina en el mar, y que se caracteriza por vientos de al menos 74 millas por hora, fuertes lluvias, inundaciones, y algunas veces tornados.

Hydration/hidratación Tomar los líquidos necesarios para mantener las funciones corporales normales.

Hypertension/hipertensión Presión de la sangre alta.

Hypothermia/ hipotermia Una condición en la cual la temperatura del cuerpo baja demasiado.

— I —

"I" message/mensaje "YO" Una declaración en la

cual una persona describe como él o ella se siente por usar el pronombre "yo."

Illegal drugs/drogas ilegales Substancias químicas que ninguna persona, cualquiera sea su edad, puede legalmente producir, poseer, comprar o vender.

Illicit drug use/uso ilegal de drogas El uso o venta de cualquier substancia que es ilegal o no permitida.

Immune system/Sistema de defensas Una combinación de células, tejidos, órganos, y químicos que combaten agentes patógenos.

Immunity/inmunidad El estado de estar protegido contra una enfermedad en particular.

Implantation/implantación Cuando el zigoto es colocado en la pared del útero.

Indigestion/indigestión Un sentimiento de molestia en la parte superior del abdomen.

Infatuation/adoración Los sentimientos de pasión exagerados por otra persona.

Infection/infección Una condición que ocurre cuando agentes patógenos entran al cuerpo, se multiplican y dañan las células.

Infertility/infertilidad La incapacidad de poder concebir un hijo.

Inflammatory response/respuesta inflamatoria Una reacción que se caracteriza por el daño de los tejidos como causa de una lesión o infección.

Inhalants/inhalantes Substancias cuyos gases se aspiran o inhalan para alcanzar un estado alucinante.

Integrity/integridad Una adherencia firme al código moral.

Interpersonal communication/comunicación entre personas El intercambio de pensamientos, sentimientos y creencias entre dos o más personas.

Interpersonal conflict/conflicto entre personas Desacuerdo entre dos o más personas.

Intoxication/Intoxicación Un estado en el cual el cuerpo se encuentra embriagado por alcohol u otra substancia, y el control físico y mental de la persona se encuentra reducido significativamente.

J

Jaundice/ictericia Estado en el cual la piel y los ojos se ponen de color amarillo.

L

Labor/parto El estado final del embarazo en el cual el útero se contrae y empuja el bebé hacia afuera del cuerpo de la madre.

Labyrinth/laberinto Oído interno.

Lacrimal gland/glándula lagrimal La glándula que produce las lágrimas y que las libera por los canales que se vacían en el ojo

Landfill/terraplenes sanitarios Un área en donde se deposita la basura y que garantiza que no contaminará el medio ambiente.

Larynx/laringe Lugar donde se encuentran las cuerdas vocales.

Leukemia/leucemia Un tipo de cáncer en el cual los glóbulos blancos de la sangre se reproducen excesiva y anormalmente.

Leukoplakia/leukoplaquia Granos con apariencia de piel blanca dura y espesa que se encuentran dentro de la boca y que pueden llegar a producir un cáncer oral.

Ligament/ligamento Un tejido fuerte y elástico que une los huesos.

Lipid/lípido Una substancia que no se disuelve con el agua.

Long-term goal/objetivo de largo plazo Un objetivo que se planea alcanzar en un periodo largo de tiempo.

Lymph/linfático Un líquido claro que llena los espacios entre las células del cuerpo.

Lymphocytes/linfocitos Células blancas de sangre que son especialistas en proporcionar la inmunidad al cuerpo humano.

M

Mainstream smoke/humo directo El humo exhalado por los pulmones de un fumador. Malignant/maligno Canceroso.

Malpractice/mala práctica médica Condición en la que un profesional de la salud no cumple con los estándares aceptados.

Manipulation/manipulación Controlar o influenciar a otros de manera indirecta y desonesta.

Marijuana/marijuana Una planta cuyas hojas, brotes y flores son generalmente fumadas para su efecto embriagador.

Marital adjustment/adaptación matrimonial La manera como una persona se ajusta al matrimonio y a su esposo o esposa.

Mastication/Masticación El proceso de masticar.

Media/media Los métodos diferentes usados para comunicar información.

Mediation/mediación Proceso mediante el cual la gente especializada ayuda a resolver conflictos de manera pacífica.

Mediator/mediador Una persona quien ayuda a otros a resolver problemas al medio de la satisfacción de las dos partes.

Medical history/historia médica La información completa acerca de las vacunas y problemas de salud que una persona ha tenido a lo largo de su vida.

Medicines/medicamentos Drogas que son tomadas para terminar o prevenir una enfermedad u otra condición de la salud.

Megadose/megadosis Una cantidad grande de suplemento alimenticio.

Melanin/melanina El pigmento que da el color a la piel, cabello y el iris de los ojos. Melanoma/melanoma Un tipo de cáncer a la piel considerado el más serio.

Menopause/menopausia La época que marca el fin de la vida reproductora de una mujer.

Menstruation/menstruación La eliminación de materia celular procedente del útero.

Mental disorder/desorden mental Una enfermedad mental que afecta la manera de pensar, el comportamiento y los sentimientos de una persona, y que le impide tener una vida feliz, saludable y productiva.

Mental retardation/retardo mental La habilidad intelectual inferior al promedio que se presenta desde el nacimiento o niñez y que se relaciona con dificultades de aprendizaje y adaptación social.

Mental/emotional health/salud mental/emocional La habilidad de aceptarse a sí mismo y a otras personas, y de adaptarse y hacer frente a las emociones, cambios y nuevas demandas de la vida.

Metabolism/metabolismo Proceso mediante el cual el cuerpo procesa y obtiene energia de los alimentos.

Metastasis/metástasis La extensión del cáncer desde el punto de origen a otras partes del cuerpo.

Minerals/minerales Substancias no producidas por el cuerpo pero que son necesarios para la formación de huesos y dientes saludables, y para regular otros procesos vitales del cuerpo.

Miscarriage/aborto (natural) La expulsión espontánea del feto que ocurre antes de la semana número veinte del embarazo.

Modeling/modelando El proceso de observar y aprender del comportamiento de las personas de alrededor.

Mood disorder/desorden del carácter Una enfermedad, comúnmente de causa orgánica, que se caracteriza por cambios extremos del humor de una persona y que afecta la vida diaria.

Mourning/luto El acto de mostrar pena o dolor.

Muscle cramp/calambre muscular El espasmo o endurecimiento repentino de un músculo.

Muscle tone/tono muscular La tensión natural de los tejidos de los músculos. Muscular endurance/resistencia muscular La habilidad de los músculos para desarrollar actividad física sin fatigarse.

Muscular strength/fuerza muscular La fuerza que un músculo puede ejercer.

N

Narcotics/narcóticos Drogas específicas que se obtiene de una planta llamada opio, que se usan para aliviar el dolor y que sólo se pueden obtener con receta médica y.

Neglect/negligencia La no-satisfacción de las necesidades físicas y emocionales de un niño.

Negotiation/negociación El uso de comunicación y compromiso para resolver un desacuerdo

Nephrons/nefrona La unidad de funcionamiento de los riñones.

Neurons/neuronas Células nerviosas.

Nicotine substitute/substituto de nicotina Un producto que libera una pequeña cantidad de nicotina en el cuerpo de una persona que está tratando de dejar de fumar.

Nicotine withdrawal/retiro de nicotina El proceso que ocurre en el cuerpo cuando la nicotina, una droga adictiva, deja de ser consumida.

Nicotine/nicotina Una droga adictiva que se encuentra en las hojas del tabaco.

Noise pollution/contaminación auditiva Un nivel de ruido no deseado y que es lo suficientemente alto dañar en la audición de las personas.

Noncommunicable disease/enfermedad no contagiosa Una enfermedad que no se transmite entre las personas o una vector, y que tampoco proviene del medio ambiente.

Nutrient-dense foods/alimentos fuertes en elementos nutritivos Alimentos que proporcionan una alta cantidad de elementos nutritivos comparado a las calorías contenidas.

Nutrients/nutrientes Substancias contenidas en los alimentos y que el cuerpo necesita para crecer, mantener un buen estado de salud y generar energía.

Nutrition/nutrición Proceso mediante el cual el cuerpo lleva y usa los alimentos.

O

Obesity/obesidad El exceso de gordura en el cuerpo.

Occupational Safety and Health Administration (OSHA)/Agencia de Seguridad y la Salud Ocupacional Agencia del gobierno federal que es responsable de promover el uso de condiciones de trabajo seguras y saludables

Online shopping/compras en Internet Comprar bienes o servicios vía Internet.

Opportunistic infection/infección oportunista Una infección que ataca a un individuo con sistema inmunológico debilitado.

Ossification/osificación El proceso mediante el cual el hueso se forma, renueva y repara.

Osteoarthritis/osteoartritis Una enfermedad de las articulaciones en la cual el cartílago se deteriora.

Osteoporosis/osteoporosis Una condición que se caracteriza por la pérdida progresiva de los tejidos de los huesos.

Ova/óvulos Células reproductoras femeninas.

Ovaries/ovarios Las glándulas sexuales femeninas que contienen los óvulos y producen hormonas sexuales.

Over-the-counter (OTC) medicines/medicamento sin receta Medicamentos que pueden ser comprados sin una receta médica.

Overdose/sobredosis Una reacción fuerte, y algunas veces fatal, al consumo de una gran cantidad de drogas.

Overexertion/sobrefuerzo Cuando el cuerpo trabaja demasiado.

Overload/sobrecarga Hacer trabajar el cuerpo mas fuerte de lo normal.

Overweight/sobrepeso Una condición en la cual una persona pesa mas que de lo apropiado para su estatura.

Ovulation/ovulación Proceso mensual que se caracteriza por el desprendimiento de un óvulo maduro.

— P —

Pancreas/páncreas Una glándula que ayuda al funcionamiento de los sistemas digestivo y endocrino.

Pandemic/pandemia El comienzo global de una enfermedad infecciosa.

Paranoia/paranoia La sospecha o desconfianza irracional acerca de otras personas.

Parathyroid glands/glándulas paratiroides Glándulas que producen una hormona que regula el balance de calcio y fósforo en el cuerpo.

Passive/pasivo Una tendencia a entregarse, rendirse, o echarse atrás sin defender sus derechos y ni necesidades.

Passive immunity/inmunidad pasiva La inmunidad temporal recibida por medio de otra persona o anticuerpos.

Pasteurization/pasteurización Proceso mediante el cual una substancia es tratada con calor para destruir o reducir agentes patógenos.

Pathogen/patógeno Un organismo que causa enfermedades.

Peer mediation/mediación por pares Un proceso mediante el cual estudiantes entrenados ayudan a otros estudiantes a encontrar el camino para resolver un conflicto y a terminar con sus diferencias.

Peer mediators/mediadores pares Estudiantes entrenados que ayudan a otros estudiantes a encontrar una manera justa de resolver conflictos y desacuerdos.

peer pressure/presión de los pares La influencia que gente de tu misma edad puede tener en ti.

peers/pares Gente cuya edad e intereses son similares a los tuyos.

Penis/pene Un órgano con forma de tubo que se encuentra en el tronco del cuerpo y justo abajo de los testículos.

Peptic ulcer/ úlcera péptica Una llaga en el revestimiento del tracto digestivo.

Perception/percepción El acto de estar atento a través de los sentidos.

Periodontal disease/enfermedad periodontal La inflamación de la estructura de soporte dental.

Periodontium/periostio dental El área inmediatamente alrededor de los dientes.

Peristalsis/peristalsis Una serie de contracciones musculares involuntarias que mueven la comida a través del aparato digestivo.

Personal identity/identidad personal El sentirse como un individuo único. **Personality/ personalidad** Un grupo complejo de características que hacen a una persona ser única.

Phagocyte/fagocito Un célula blanco de la sangre que ataca la invasión de patógenos.

Pharynx/faringe Garganta.

Physical abuse/abuso físico El acto intencional de dañar o herir el cuerpo de otra persona.

Physical activity/actividad física Cualquier forma de movimiento que provoque que el cuerpo consuma energía.

Physical fitness/condición física La habilidad de responder fácilmente a tareas diarias y tener suficiente energía para responder a demandas inesperadas.

Physical maturity/madurez física Un estado en el cual el cuerpo físico y todos sus organismos se encuentran totalmente desarrollados.

Physiological dependence/dependencia fisiológico Cuando un drogadicto o consumidor de drogas tiene una necesidad química por éstas.

Pituitary gland/glándula pituitaria Glándula que regula o controla las actividades de todas las glándulas endocrinas.

Placenta/placenta El tejido espeso y rico en sangre que cubre las paredes del útero durante el periodo de embarazo y que alimenta al feto.

Plaque/placa Una película blanda e incolora que actúa a través del azúcar para formar los ácidos que destruyen el esmalte de los dientes e irritan la encías.

Plasma/plasma Un fluido en el cual los otros componentes de la sangre se encuentran suspendidos.

Platelets/plaquetas Células que previenen la pérdida de sangre del cuerpo.

Platonic friendship/amistad platónica Una amistad con una persona del sexo opuesto en la cual hay sentimientos mutuos de afecto, pero que no son considerados una pareja

Pleurisy/pleuritis Una inflamación de la pleura, la membrana que recubre los pulmones, y de la cavidad del pecho.

Pneumonia/pulmonía Una inflamación de los revestimientos de los pulmones y pecho.

Poison/veneno Cualquier substancia – sólido, líquido o gas—que al entrar el cuerpo causa una herida, una enfermedad o la muerte.

Poison control center/Centro para el control de envenenamientos Una línea telefónica que funciona las 24 horas del día para dar consejo sobre el tratamiento de envenenamiento para víctimas.

Post-traumatic stress disorder/Desorden de estrés post-traumático Una condición que se puede desarrollar después que una persona ha sido expuesta a un evento aterrador que le causo una amenaza o daño físico.

Precycling/prereciclage Reducir la basura antes de generarla.

Prejudice/prejuicio Una opinión o juicio injusto acerca de un grupo particular de personas.

Prenatal care/cuidado prenatal Todas las medidas que una mujer embarazada puede tomar para cuidar su propia salud y la de su bebé.

Prescription medicine/medicinas recetadas Medicinas que no pueden ser usadas sin la aprobación escrita de un médico.

Prevention/prevención La práctica de hábitos saludables y seguros que permiten evitar enfermedades y daños.

Preventive care/cuidado preventivo Las acciones que previenen el comienzo de una enfermedad o lesión.

Primary care physician/médico general Un médico que proporciona chequeos y el cuidado general de sus pacientes.

Priorities/prioridades Los objetivos, tareas y actividades que son consideradas más importantes que otras.

Profound deafness/sordera profunda Una pérdida severa de la audición y la cual no puede ser tratada con amplificación mecánica como por ejemplo un audífono.

Progression/progresión El aumento gradual en la sobrecarga necesaria lograr los niveles más altos de la salud.

Protective factors/ factores protectores Condiciones que protegen a una persona de las consecuencias negativas de una exposición a situaciones arriesgadas.

Proteins/proteínas Elementos nutritivos que ayudan a construir y mantener las células y tejidos.

Psychoactive drugs/drogas psico-activas Químicos que afectan el sistema central nervioso y alteran la actividad de la mente.

Psychological dependence/dependencia psicológica Una condición en la cual una persona cree que se necesita una droga para sentirse bien o funcionar normalmente.

Psychosomatic response/respuesta psicosomática Una reacción física que es resultado del estrés en vez de una enfermedad o herida.

Psychotherapy/psicoterapia Una terapia a través del diálogo entre el paciente y un médico de la salud mental.

Puberty/pubertad El periodo de tiempo en el cual una persona comienza a desarrollar ciertos rasgos que son característicos de su sexo.

Public health/salud pública Un esfuerzo comunitario para la protección y el fomento de la salud de la población.

Pulp/pulpa Un tejido que contiene los vasos sanguíneos y los nervios de un diente.

R

Radon/radón Un gas inodoro y radioactivo.

Random violence/violencia aleatoria Violencia cometida sin una razón en especial.

Rape/violación Cualquier tipo de acto sexual que es desarrollada contra la voluntad de una persona.

Recovery/recuperación El proceso de aprender a vivir una vida sin alcohol.

Recycling/reciclar El procesamiento de la basura de tal manera que pueda ser utilizada nuevamente en alguna forma.

Reflex/reflejo La respuesta espontánea del cuerpo a estímulos

Refusal skills/habilidad de negarse Estrategias de comunicación que ayudan a decir no cuando la persona esta a punto de participar en actividades arriesgadas, no saludables o que van en contra de sus valores.

Rehydration/rehidración La restauración de líquidos perdidos por el cuerpo.

Relationship/relaciones Las conexiones que una persona tiene con otros.

Relaxation response/ respuesta de relajamiento Un estado de calma que puede ser alcanzado cuando una o varias técnicas de relajación son practicadas regularmente.

Remission/remisión El periodo de tiempo cuando los síntomas desaparecen.

Repetitive motion injury/Daño por movimiento repetido El daño a los tejidos causado por movimientos prolongados y repetitivos.

Reproductive system/aparato reproductor El conjunto de órganos que permiten la reproducción.

Resiliency/fuerza moral La habilidad de adaptarse eficazmente y recuperarse después de una decepción, dificultad o crisis.

Respiration/respiración El intercambio de gases entre el cuerpo humano y el medio ambiente.

Resting heart rate/ritmo cardíaco en descanso El número de latidos del corazón que se producen cuando la persona se encuentra en estado pasivo.

Retina/retina Membrana sensitiva a la luz y en la cual las imágenes son proyectadas por la córnea.

Rheumatoid arthritis/reuma articular Una enfermedad caracterizada por la destrucción debilitadora de las articulaciones debido a la inflamación.

Risk behaviors/comportamiento arriesgado Acciones que pueden poner en peligro su salud o la de otras personas.

Road rage/violencia al conducir Acciones causadas cuando un conductor maneja en forma peligrosa usando su vehículo como un arma.

Role model/modelo a conducta Alguien cuyo éxito o compartimiento sirve de ejemplo para otros.

Role/función La participación de una persona en una relación.

Sclera/esclerótica La parte blanca del ojo.

Scoliosis/escoliosis Una desviación lateral, o de lado a lado, de la columna

Scrotum/escroto Un saco externo de piel que se extiende afuera del cuerpo y que contiene los testículos.

Sebaceous glands/glándulas sebáceas Estructuras dentro de la piel que producen una secreción aceitosa que llamado sebo.

Sedentary lifestyle/estilo de vida sedentario Un estilo de vida que incluye poca actividad física.

Self-actualization/realización personal El esfuerzo realizado para lograr lo mejor de uno mismo.

Self-control/dominio de sí mismo La habilidad de una persona para controlar sus emociones.

Self-defense/defensa propia Cualquier estrategia para protegerse a sí misma de un daño.

Self-directed/auto-dirigido La habilidad para tomar decisiones correctas acerca de su comportamiento en la ausencia de adultos para imponer las reglas.

Semen/semen Un líquido espeso que contiene los espermatozoides y otras secreciones del aparato reproductor masculino.

Separation/separación Cuando una pareja de personas casadas decide vivir aparte uno del otro.

Severe weather/clima severo Condiciones climáticas severas o peligrosas.

Sex characteristics/características sexuales Los rasgos relacionados con el sexo de una persona.

Sexual abuse/abuso sexual Cualquier contacto sexual que es realizado a la fuerza o contra el consentimiento de una persona.

Sexual assault/agresión sexual Cualquier ataque sexual intencional en contra de otra persona.

Sexual harassment/acoso sexual Cualquier conducta sexual no solicitada y desagradable que se dirige a otra persona.

Sexual violence/violencia sexual Cualquier acto sexual no solicitado que es dirigido a una persona y que incluye acoso sexual, agresión sexual y violación.

Sexually transmitted diseases (STDs)/enfermedades transmitidas sexualmente Enfermedades que se transmiten a través del contacto sexual entre dos personas.

Sexually transmitted infections (STIs)/infecciones transmitidas sexualmente Infecciones que se transmiten a través del contacto sexual entre dos personas.

Shock/choque Una falla en el sistema cardiovascular que no permite una circulación suficiente de sangre a los órganos vitales del cuerpo.

Short-term goal/Objetivo de corto plazo Un objetivo que se puede alcanzar en un corto periodo de tiempo.

Sibling/Un hermano o hermana.

Side effects/ efecto secundario Cualquier reacción inesperada a una medicina.

Sidestream smoke/humo indirecto El humo que proviene de una colilla de cigarrillo, pipa o cigarro.

Sinusitis/sinusitis La inflamación de los tejidos nasales.

Skeletal muscles/músculos del esqueleto Músculos unidos a los huesos y que producen el movimiento del cuerpo.

Smog/smog Una neblina de color amarillo-café que se produce cuando la luz solar reacciona con la contaminación ambiental.

Smoke alarm/alarma de humo Una alarma que se active por la presencia de humo.

Smokeless tobacco/tabaco sin humo Tabaco que es olfateado a través de la nariz, mantenido en la boca, y masticado.

Smooth muscles/músculo liso Músculos que actúan sobre el forro de los tubos y órganos internos.

Sobriety/sobriedad Vivir sin consumir alcohol.

Specialist/especialista Un médico entrenado para tratar una determinada clase de pacientes y condiciones médicas.

Specificity/especificidad Una clase especial de actividades y ejercicios para mejoran partes especiales del estado físico que están relacionados con la salud.

Sperm/espermatozoides Células reproductoras masculinas.

Spousal abuse/abuso al esposo Violencia doméstica dirigida hacia el esposo.

Sprain/torcedura El daño de los ligamentos que circundan una articulación.

Stalking/acecho El seguimiento, acoso, o amenaza repetido que un individuo hace a otro para atemorizarlo o dañarlo.

Stereotype/estereotipo Una creencia exagerada y sobresimplificada que se extiende a todo un grupo, como un grupo étnico o religioso o a un sexo.

Sterility/esterilidad La incapacidad de reproducirse.

Stillbirth/aborto La expulsión de un feto muerto desde el cuerpo de la madre después de la semana número veinte.

Stimulant/estimulante Una droga que acelera el funcionamiento del sistema central nervioso, el corazón y otros órganos.

Strain/tensión Una condición resultante del daño de un músculo o tendón.

Stress/estrés La reacción del cuerpo o la mente a los cambios y demandas de la vida diaria.

Stress management/manejo del estrés Los medios para hacer frente o superar los efectos negativos del estrés.

Stress-management skills/habilidades para superar el estrés Habilidades que ayudan a una persona a manejar el estrés de una manera saludable y efectiva.

Stressor/estresante Cualquier cosa que produce el estrés.

Stroke/accidente cerebrovascular Una condición en la cual un vaso sanguíneo se bloquea impidiendo el flujo de la sangre al cerebro.

Substance abuse/abuso de substancias Cualquier uso inapropiado o excesivo de substancias químicas con propósitos no médicos.

Suicide/suicidio El acto de restringir o retener.

Suppression/supresión El acto de restringirse o retenerse.

Sweat glands/glándulas sudoríferas Estructuras dentro de la dermis que secreta el sudor por conductos hasta los poros en la superficie de la piel.

Symptomatic stage/estado sintomático El estado en el cual una persona afectada por el VIH presenta síntomas resultantes de una reducción severa de las células inmunológicas.

Synergistic effect/efecto sinergénico El efecto de tomar dos medicinas al mismo tiempo es mayor que el efecto de tomarlas por separado. La interacción entre dos medicinas con resultado más fuerte que tomarlas por separado.

Syphilis/sífilis Una enfermedad de transmisión sexual bacteriana que ataca muchas partes del cuerpo y es causada por una bacteria llamado espiroqueta.

––––––––––– **T** –––––––––––

Tar/alquitrán Un líquido espeso, pegajoso y oscuro que se forma al quemarse el tabaco.

Tartar/sarro La substancia dura y con forma de corteza que se forma en los dientes cuando la placa se endurece.

Tendon/tendón Un tejido fuerte que une los músculos a los huesos

Tendonitis/tendinitis La inflamación de un tendón

Testes/testículos Dos glándulas pequeñas que producen la esperma.

Testosterone/testosterona Hormona sexual masculina.

Thyroid gland/glándula del tiroides Glándula que produce las hormonas que regulan el metabolismo, el calor del cuerpo, y el crecimiento de los huesos.

Tinnitus/zumbido Una condición en que se oye un timbre, un zumbido, un silbido, un bisbiseo, un rugido, u otro sonido se escucha en el oído en la ausencia de sonido externo.

Tolerance/tolerancia La habilidad de aceptar puntos de vista diferentes y permitir que otras personas se expresen sin mostrar desaprobación.

Tolerance/tolerancia Una condición en la que el cuerpo se acostumbra a los efectos de los medicamentos.

Tornado/tornado Una tormenta en forma de torbellino que cae desde el cielo a la tierra y que produce la destrucción al pasar.

Toxin/toxina Una substancia que mata células o que interviene con su funcionamiento.

Trachea/traquea Vía respiratoria.

Training program/programa de entrenamiento Un programa formal de preparación física para participación en un deporte o cualquier otra actividad física.

Transitions/transición Cambios críticos que ocurren en todas las etapas de la vida. trichomoniasis/trichomoniasis Una enfermedad de transmisión sexual causado por un protozoo microscópico que tiene como resultado las infecciones de la vagina, de la uretra, y de la vejiga.

Tuberculosis/tuberculosis Una infección bacteriana contagiosa que comúnmente afecta los pulmones.

Tumor/tumor Una masa de tejidos anormales que no tiene ningún papel natural en el cuerpo.

––––––––––– **U** –––––––––––

Umbilical cord/cordón umbilical Una estructura igual a una soga que conecta el embrión a la placenta de la madre

Unconditional love/amor incondicional Amor sin limitaciones ni exigencias.

Unconsciousness/inconsciencia Una condición en la cual una persona no esta consciente del ambiente que lo rodea.

Underweight/bajo peso Una condición en la que una persona pesa menos que lo que debería pesar de acuerdo a su estatura.

Unintentional injury/daños no intencionales Daños que resultan de situaciones inesperadas o accidentes

Universal precautions/precauciones universales Acciones tomadas para prevenir la expansión de enfermedades por tratar la sangre o cualquier otro líquido corporal como si estuviera contaminado.

Urban sprawl/expansión urbana La expansión de la ciudad (casas, centros comerciales, negocios, y escuelas) a tierras no urbanizadas.

Ureters/uréter Cada uno de los dos canales que conjuntan los riñones y la vejiga.

Urethra/uretra El canal que conduce desde la vejiga afuera del cuerpo.

Urethritis/uretritis La inflamación de la uretra.

Urine/orina Líquido compuesto de desechos.

Uterus/útero Un órgano muscular y con forma de pera dentro del cuerpo femenino.

––––––––––– **V** –––––––––––

Vaccine/vacuna Una preparación de agentes patógenos muertos o debilitados introducidos en el cuerpo para estimular el sistema de defensas.

Vagina/vagina Una cavidad muscular y elástica que

va desde el útero hasta la parte externa del cuerpo de una mujer.

Values/valores Las ideas, creencias y actitudes consideradas importantes y guían la vida de una persona.

Vector/vector Un organismo, como por ejemplo un insecto, que lleva y transmite agentes patógenos a personas y otros animales.

Vegan/vegetariano estricto Vegetariano quien come exclusivamente alimentos de origen natural.

Vegetarian/vegetariano Una persona que come principalmente o solamente alimentos que provienen de la naturaleza o plantas.

Vehicular safety/seguridad vehicular Usar el sentido común, un buen criterio y obedecer las reglas de la carretera.

Veins/venas Vasos sanguíneos que llevan la sangre al corazón.

Venom/veneno Una substancia venenosa secretada por serpientes, arañas o otra criatura viviente.

Verbal abuse/abuso verba Usar palabras para maltratar o dañar a otras personas.

Violence/violencia Cualquier amenaza o acto físico para dañar o maltratar a una persona o propiedad.

Virus/virus Material genético que invade las células vivas para reproducirse.

Vitamins/vitaminas Substancias que ayudan a regular las funciones vitales del cuerpo inclusive la digestión, la absorción de líquidos y el metabolismo de otros elementos nutritivos.

W

Warm-up/precalentamiento Una actividad que prepara los músculos para el ejercicio.

Warranty/garantía Una promesa escrita, en la cual una empresa o compañía se compromete a reparar un producto o devolver el dinero si éste no funciona bien

Wastewater/agua de desperdicio Agua sucia que proviene de casas, comunidades, granjas, e industrias.

Weight cycling/ciclo de peso La situación repetida de subir y bajar de peso corporal.

Wellness/bienestar El estado de buena salud.

Western blot (WB)/Western Blot La prueba para confirmar el SIDA mas usado en los Estados Unidos.

Withdrawal/síndrome de abstinencia Es una condición en alguien con farmacodependencia que se presenta al interrumpírselo un medicamento.

Workout/entrenamiento La parte de un programa de actividad física en la que los ejercicios se realizan al más alto nivel.

Index

Note: Page numbers in italic type refer to a picture or feature only.

of teens, 77–78
Ligaments, 102, 389, 392, 393, 455, 682, 749, 750
Lightning, 727
Lipid, 117, 361
Listening skills and techniques, 29, 256–57. *See also* Communication
Liver, *444,* 445, *See also* Hepatitis
    cancer of, 650
    effect of alcohol on, 569, 574, 575
    effects of drugs on, 605
    syphilis and, 655
Love
    as emotional need, 173
    family and, 274, 276, 278, 517
    parents and, 276
    unconditional, 528
Low birth weight, 494, 496, 497
LSD, *604,* 609
Lungs, 429, 430, 557
    cancer of, 682, 701, 769
    effect of alcohol on, 569, 573
    effect of drugs on, 599, *604, 608*
    effect of smoking on, 542–44
    effect of tobacco on, 541, *543*
    transplants of, 437
Lyme disease, 623, 625, *639,* 640, 693
Lymph, 421, 422
Lymphatic system, 421–24, 427, 631
Lymphocytes, 421, 630–31, *632,* 658
Lymphoma, 682

M

Macrophages, 630
Macular degeneration, 375, 696
Magnesium, 121
Magnetic resonance imaging (MRI), *403,* 676
Mainstream smoke, 551
Malaria, 623, 625, 639
Malignant tumor, 681. *See also* Cancer
Malnutrition, 154, 155, *604,* 605
Malocclusion, 370
Malpractice, 61
Mammography, 683
Managed care plan, 57
Manic-depressive disorder, 227
March of Dimes, 64
Marijuana, 424, 425, 598–600, 617
Marriage, 281, 524–26, 526
Maslow, Abraham, 172
Mastication, 443
Maturity, 519
MDMA. *See* Ecstasy
Measles, *623,* 633, 634, *640*
Media. *See also* Advertising
    body image and, 144, 151
    definition of, 15
    drug use and, 594
    exposure to alcohol, 563–65
    as information source, 9, 15–16, 32, 666
    techniques used, 49
    violence and, 343
    weather warnings, 725
Mediation, 265, 267, 294, 339–40
Medicaid, 65, 533
Medical checkups, 423, 424, 471, 479
Medical records, 58
Medicare, 65, 533

Medicines. *See also* Multiplier effect
    advertisements for, 700
    alcohol interactions with, 569–70
    for cardiovascular disease, *676*
    classification by use, 586–88
    for drug withdrawal, 614
    genetically engineered, 503
    information about, 59
    labeling of, *590*
    misuse of, 591
    poisoning and, 710
    pregnancy and, 487, 495
    prescription vs. over-the-counter, 590
    safe use of, 590–91
Melanin, 361, 362, 364
Melanoma, *364*–65
Melatonin, 465, 518
Memory
    effect of alcohol on, 569
    effect of drugs on, 600, *604, 606*
    endocrine system and, 481
    nervous system and, 402–03
Meningitis, *623, 640,* 697
Menopause, 476, 530
Menstrual cramps, 477
Menstruation, 154, 476, 515, 530
Mental challenges, 697–99, 701
Mental changes, 516. *See also* Transitions
Mental disorders, 225–29
    eating disorders, 153, 227
    suicide and, 230
Mental health
    abuse and, 287, 289, 349
    character and, 38
    characteristics of, 11, 170–71
    drug use and, 594
    emotions and, 185–86
    family relationships and, 275, 276
    marijuana and, 600
    physical activity and, 75–76
    professionals, 236
    self-esteem and, 170
    sexual activity and, 320
    signs of, 171
    sources of help, 236
    substance abuse and, 596
    tobacco-free lifestyle and, 547
Mental health professionals, 235, 236
Mental retardation, 494, 501, 576, 697
Metabolism, 78–79, 569
    anorexia nervosa and, 154
    caloric intake and, 165
    control of, 404, *465,* 466
Metastasis, 681. *See also* Cancer
Methamphetamine, *604,* 606
Minerals, 120, 121, 386, 387, 466. *See also specific mineral*
Miscarriage, 495, 496
Moles, 364
Mononucleosis, *623, 640*
Monosaturated fatty acids, 117
Mood disorders, 226–27, 588
Mood swings, 185, 203, 226, 602
Morphine, 604, 608
Mothers Against Drunk Driving (MADD), 570

Motorcycle safety, 406, 724
Motor impairment, 697
Movement
    muscles and, 395
    nervous system and, 403
    skeletal system and, 386, 389, 394
MRI. *See* Magnetic resonance imaging (MRI)
Multiple sclerosis (MS), 408
Multiplier effect, 569
Mumps, 472, 633, 634
Muscle endurance, 91
Muscles, 105, 395, 405
    cancer of, 682
    fitness and, 80
    healthful behaviors and, *530*
    increasing mass, 85, 94, 146, 150, 158, 531, 601
    injuries to, 102, 749–50
    strength of, 81–82
    stress response and, 200
    tone, 396
    warm-up/cool-down and, 92, 102
Muscular dystrophy, 398
Muscular endurance, 80, 81–82, 85
Muscular strength, 80, 81–82, 85
Muscular system, 394, 396, *397,* 398
    drug use and, 607, *610*
    excess weight and, 147
    injuries to, 102
Myocardium, 417

N

Nails, 366
Narcotics, 588, *604, 608,* 617
National Association of Children of Alcoholics, 579
National Cancer Institute (NCI), 65, 701
National Center for Statistics and Analysis, 720
National Clearinghouse for Alcohol and Drug Information, 579
National Dairy Council, 410
National Drug and Treatment Referral Routing Service, 579
National Household Survey on Drug Abuse (NHSDA), 593
National Institutes of Health (NIH), 65, 364, 532, *666,* 701
National Safety Council, 706, 709, 720
National Weather Service (NWS), 725, 727
Natural disasters, 241, 725–29
Natural resources, 777–79
Nausea, 450, 604
Nearsightedness, 373, 374
Needs, 172, 174
    family and, 275–76, 277
    Maslow's hierarchy of, 172–73
Neglect, 288, 349, 355, 565, 596
Negotiation, 266, 269
Neighborhood watch programs, 334, 357
Nephrons, 454, 456
Nerve cells, 362
Nerve impulse, 373, 377, 399
Nerves, 399
Nervous system, 399–405, 407

Uterus, 474, *475*, 486, *487*, 491
UV radiation, 361, 364, 365, 373, 715

V

Vaccination. *See* Immunizations
Vaccine
    action of, 587
    genetically engineered, 503
    for Hepatitis A and B, 637, 638
    HIV and, 661, *662*, 664, *665*, 666
    immunity and, 631
    against influenza, 636
    types of, 633
Vagina, 475, 476, 653, 655
Vaginal yeast infections, *475*, 623
Vaginitis, 655
Vaginosis, 479, *656*
Varicose veins, 425
Vas deferens, 470
Vectors, *624*, 625, 643
Vegetarianism, 159–60
Veins, 419, 420, 425
Vena cava, 417, 419, *454*
Ventricles, 417
Verbal abuse, 349
Victims
    of abuse, 291–94, 352
    preventive behavior, *344*, 350, 351
    of sexual violence, 346
Violence. *See also* Abuse; Rape
    alcohol-related, *344*, 565, 576, 578
    anabolic steroids and, 94
    causes of, 187, 341–42, 366–67
    cycle of, 289, 294, 353
    in dating relationships, 350–51
    drug-related, 344, 596, 597, *604*, 608, 610
    family and, 286–90
    gang-related, 347
    reducing risks of, 336–37, 338–40
    at school, 335–36, 335–40, 342
    strategies for avoiding/escape, 344, 346, 350, 351
    television and, 343
    weapons and, 337
Viruses. *See also* Human immunodeficiency virus (HIV)
    antiviral drugs and, 587
    diseases caused by, *622*, 636, 752
    reproduction of, 623
    STD causing, 650, 652–53
Vision, 371, 372, 373, 403, 507. *See also* Blindness; Eye; Sight impairment
Vitamins, 119–20, 160, 362, 458, 493
Vitiligo, 364
Volunteering, 39, 45, 67, 182, 315, 340, 381, 533
Vomiting, 403, 450, 571, 751, 756

W

Warm-up, 90, 91, 96, 102, *394*
Warranty, 50
Warts, 364
Waste disposal, 772–73
Waste elimination, 120, 416, 442, 446, 449, 450, 453, 487. *See also* Digestive system; Urinary system

Water
    conservation of, 778
    dehydration, 99–100, 135, 152, 155, 158
    digestion and, 448, 449, 459
    function in body, 94, 120
    as nutrient, 120
    pollution, 774–76
    recreational safety and, 714, 715
    safety in, 406, 716–18
    urinary system and, 456, 459
Weapons, 335–36, 337–38, 342, 710
Weather, 98–101, 725–29
Weight
    appropriate range, 145–46
    caloric/energy balance and, 144–45
    cancer and, 685
    cholesterol and, 118
    cycling, 152
    diabetes and, 691, 692
    diet and, 117, 118
    eating habits and, 113
    fitness and, 6, 123
    health risks of excess, 146–47, 683
    management of, 148, 151, 158
    osteoarthritis and, 693
    physical activity and, 77, 78–79
    pregnancy and, 493
    smoking and, 548–49
    strategies for gaining, 149
    strategies for losing, 148, 151–52
Western blot test (WB), 664
West Nile encephalitis, 640, *642*
White blood cells, 386, 387, 418, 426. *See also* Leukemia
Whooping cough, *633*
Withdrawal
    from alcohol, 578
    from drugs, 595, 607
    from medicines, 589
    from narcotics, 608, 614
    in newborns, 596
    from tobacco, 542, 548–49
World Health Organization (WHO), 66
Wounds, 738–40

X, Y, Z

X ray, 403, 472, 496, *683*, 686
Youth Risk Behavior Surveillance Survey, 18, 23, 335, 594
Zero-tolerance policy, 338, 566, 612
Zinc, 160
Zygote, 475, 486, 487, 499

PHOTOGRAPHS/ILLUSTRATIONS
Cover:
Joe Michl/Workbookstock.com (top)
Ed Bock/Corbis (bottom)

A.D.A.M., Inc. 741, Jack Affleck/Superstock 100, AFP/CORBIS 473, Bill Aron/PhotoEdit 173, 435, Bruce Ayres/Stone/Getty Images 294, Bill BSIP/ Photo Researchers 656, Bachmann/PhotoEdit 315, Jean Marc Barey/Vandystadt/Photo Researchers 147, Billy E. Barnes/PhotoEdit 380, Paul Barton/CORBIS 251, 512, 531, 537, Scott Bauer/ARS/USDA 624, Lester V. Bergman/CORBIS 741, Nathan Bilow/ All Sport/Getty Images 93, Biophoto Associates/ Photo Researchers 365, 500, 542, Ed Bock/CORBIS 295, Bohemian Nomad Picturemakers/CORBIS 5, John Boykin/PhotoEdit 305, Robert Brenner/ PhotoEdit 27, 175, Michelle D. Bridwell/PhotoEdit 59, 92, 145, 275, 385, 581, 633, Keith Brofsky/Getty Images 461, Keith Brofsky/PhotoDisc/Getty Images 617, Gareth Brown/CORBIS 248, Rolf Bruderer/ CORBIS 306, 521, China Tourism Press/The Image Bank/Getty Images 668, Cleve Bryant/PhotoEdit 136, David Buffington/Getty Images 237, Burke/Triolo/ Brand X Pictures/PictureQuest 598, Mark C. Burnett/ Photo Researchers 576, 667, Dan Bridy/Wilkinson Studios 125, 125, 125, 125, 125, 159, 159, 159, 159, 564, 571, 571, 707, 707, 707, 707, 707, 709, 709, 710, 710, 711, 711, 711, 711, 711, 711, 711, 711, 711, Brooks/Kraft/CORBIS 242, Jason Burns/Dr. Ryder/ Phototake 468, CC Studios/Science Photo Library/ Photo Researchers 152, Guy Call/Stock Connection/ PictureQuest 724, Jose Carillo/PhotoEdit 638, Carolina Biological Supply Company/PhotoTake 675, 675, Ken Cavanagh/Photo Researchers 162, Jonathan Cavendish/CORBIS 307, Ron Chapple/Taxi/Getty Images 399, Cleo Photography/PhotoEdit 629, Anna Clopet/CORBIS 346, Stewart Cohen/Index Stock Imagery 337, Dean Conger/CORBIS 766, Paul Conklin/PhotoEdit 183, Gary Conner/PhotoEdit 643, W. Perry Conway/Corbis 772, CORBIS/Royalty-free 158, 232, 255, 419, 717, Corbis Stock Market/ CORBIS 246, CORBIS/PictureQuest 590, Jim Cummins/ CORBIS 476, 628, Custom Medical Stock 55, 139, 414, 489, 677, 677, 690, 690, 747 , Bob Daemerich/ Stock, Boston/PictureQuest 319, 585, Renee Daily/ HK Portfolio 104, 200, 712, 717, 717, 737, 739, 740, 743, 743, 744, 744, 746, 746, 746, 746, 746, 748, 748, 751, 756, 756, 756, 756, Michael Kevin Daly/ CORBIS 467, Mary Kate Denny/PhotoEdit 8, 14, 40, 182, 193, 216, 281, 335, 381, 517, 563, 614, Digital Vision/Getty Images 144, DiMaggio/Kalish/CORBIS 103, George DiSario/CORBIS 371, Laura Dwight/ CORBIS 511, Laura Dwight/PhotoEdit 221, 505, Dennis Dzielak 743, Duomo/CORBIS 466, Rachel Epstein/PhotoEdit 568, Miles Ertman/MasterFile 328, Robert Essel NYC/CORBIS 783, Amy Etra/PhotoEdit 349, 527, EyeWire Collection/Getty Images 719, David Falconer/Superstock 551, Myrleen Ferguson Cate/Index Stock Imagery 195, Myrleen Ferguson Cate/PhotoEdit 30, 172, 179, 198, 333, 350, 390, 506, First Light/Image State 406, Tony Freeman/ PhotoEdit 17, 56, 151, 151, 275, 284, 328, 344, 347, 431, 440, 601, 602, 603, 605, 714, 718, 731, 753, Fotosearch.com 108, 233, 245, 669, GCA/Photo-Take 677, G.D.T./Stone/Getty Images 188, Rob Gage/Getty Images 404, Mark Garvin 408, Garry Gay/Image State 124, Keerle Georges De/CORBIS 332, 332, Lowell Georgia/CORBIS 727, Patrik Giardino/CORBIS 38, Mark Giolas/Index Stock Imagery 439, Pascal Goetgheluck/Science Photo Library/Photo Researchers 606, Rick Gomez/CORBIS 36, 521, Carla R. Gonzalez/The Mazer Corporation 755, Stevie Grand/Photo Researchers 494, Stevie Grand/Science Photo Library/Photo Researchers 741, Spencer Grant/PhotoEdit 48, 58, 133, 179, 308, 436, 597, 742, Spencer Grant/Stock Boston/PictureQuest 365, Jeff Greenberg/Index Stock Imagery 299, Jeff Greenberg/PhotoEdit 20, 45, 399, 464, 505, 703, Jeff Greenberg/Photo Researchers 172, 212, Jeff Greenberg/Visuals Unlimited 215, 566, Annie Griffiths Belt/CORBIS 496, David M. Grossman/ PhotoTake 426, Klaus Guldbrandsen/Science Photo Library/Photo Researchers 663, HIRB/Index Stock Imagery 129, 763, Bruce Hands/Stone/Getty Images 540, Will Hart/PhotoEdit 184, 342, 383, 652, Aaron Haupt/Stock, Boston/PictureQuest 576, Richard Heinzen/Superstock 360, John Henley/CORBIS 18, 656, Jack Holtel/Photographik Company 238, 254, 541, 572, 586, 681, Richard Hutchings/PhotoEdit 10, ISM/PhotoTake 134, Iconos Explorer/Photo Researchers 175, ImageState/FotoSearch.com 262, International Stock/Image State 74, 169, 275, 313, 411, 424, 484, 522, 547, 570, 577, 584, 592, 729, 736, R.W. Jones/CORBIS 530, Phil Jude/Science Photo Library/Photo Researchers 365, Bonnie Kamin/ PhotoEdit 25, 508, 706, 758, Catherine Karnow/ CORBIS 583, Michael Keller/CORBIS 54, 101, 535, 738, Michael Keller/Index Stock Imagery 689, David Kelly Crow/PhotoEdit 685, Dan Kenyon/Getty Images 230, Dennis Kunkel/PhotoTake 474, 690, John Lamb/Getty Images 654, Lee White Photography 764, Lisette Le Bon/SuperStock 137, 685, Rick Leckrone/Index Stock Imagery 781, Lester Lefkowitz/ CORBIS 677, Rob Lewine/CORBIS 552, Robert Llewellyn/CORBIS 351, Patti Longmire/WirePix/